1998
OUR SUNDAY VISITOR'S
CATHOLIC ALMANAC

The Most Complete One-Volume Source Of Facts And Information On The Catholic Church

Compiled and Edited By
Felician A. Foy, O.F.M.
and Rose M. Avato

Our Sunday Visitor Publishing Division
Our Sunday Visitor, Inc.
Huntington, Indiana 46750

ACKNOWLEDGMENTS: Catholic News Service, for coverage of news and documentary texts; *The Documents of Vatican II,* ed. W. M. Abbott (Herder and Herder, America Press: New York 1966), for quotations of Council documents; *Annuario Pontificio (1997); Statistical Year-book of the Church (1995); L'Osservatore Romano* (English editions); *The Official Catholic Directory* — Excerpts of statistical data and other material, reprinted with permission of *The Official Catholic Directory,* © 1997 by Reed Reference Publishing, a division of Reed Publishing (USA) Inc. Trademark used under license from Reed Publishing (Nederland) B.V.; *The Papal Encyclicals,* 5 vols., ed. C. Carlen (Pierian Press, Ann Arbor, Mich.); Newsletter of the U.S. Bishops' Committee on the Liturgy; The United States Catholic Mission Assoc. (3029 Fourth St. N.E., Washington, D.C. 20017), for U.S. overseas-mission compilations and statistics; *Catholic Press Directory (1997); Annuaire Directory 1996-1997,* Canadian Conference of Catholic Bishops, for latest available Canadian Catholic statistics; Rev. Thomas J. Reese, S.J., for names of dioceses for which U.S. bishops were ordained; other sources as credited in particular entries.

1998 Catholic Almanac

Published annually by Our Sunday Visitor Publishing Division,
Our Sunday Visitor, Inc.,
200 Noll Plaza, Huntington, IN 46750
Address queries to the Publisher.
ISBN 0-87973-900-2 (Kivar edition)
ISBN 0-87973-901-0 (cloth edition)
Library of Congress Catalog Card No. 73-641001
International Standard Serial Number (ISSN) 0069-1208

TABLE OF CONTENTS

INDEX

Pro-Cathedral, 323
Procyk, Judson M., Abp., 466
Pro Ecclesia et Pontifice Medal, 596
Pro Ecclesia Foundation, 580
Project Children, 580
Pro Maria Committee, 580
Promoter of the Faith, 323
Pro-Nuncio, 168
Propagation of the Faith, Cong. of
(Evangelization of Peoples), 146
Society of, 581
Proper of the Mass, 214
Prophecies of St. Malachy, 323
Prophecy, 324
Prophets, 189-90
Pro Sanctity Movement, 374, 580
Prost, Jude, O.F.M., Bp., 488
Protestant
Canon of the Bible, 186
Churches in the U.S., Major, 279-82
See also Ecumenism
Protestants and Intercommunion, 227
Protocanonical Books (Canons of Bible),
186
Proverbs, 189
Providence, Daughters of Divine, 521
Providence, Sisters of, 521
Providence, Sons of Divine, 503
Providence Association of Ukrainian
Catholics, 580
Province, 324
Provinces, Ecclesiastical, Canada, 375-
76
United States, 421-22
Provincial Councils, 305
Providentissimus Deus, 194
Prudence, 324
Psalms, 189
Pseudepigrapha, 187
Public Affairs of Church, Council for,
see Secretariat of State
Public Schools, U.S.
Meeting Place Use (Court Decisions),
417, 418
Released Time, 531
Religion in, 418-19
Publications, Vatican, 176-77
Puerto Rico, 358, 371
Dates in Catholic History, 414
Episcopal Conference, 371
Minor Basilica, 443
Statistics, 435, 535
Puerto Rican Catholics in U.S., see
Hispanics
Puljic, Vinko, Card., 160, 165, 166
Pulpit, 217
Punishment Due for Sin, 324
Purgatory, 324
Purification (Presentation of the Lord),
248-49
Purificator, 216
Purim, 291
Puritans, 279
Pursley, Leo A., Bp., 466
Puscas, Louis, Bp., 466
Pyx, 216

Q

Qatar, 358
Quakers, 279
Quam Singulari, see Communion, First
and First Confession
Quanta Cura (1864), 118
Quarracino, Antonio, Card., 160, 165,
166
Quartodecimans (Easter Controversy),
309
Queen of the Americas Guild, 580
Queenship of Mary, 249
Quinlan, Joseph (Death), 600
Quinn, Alexander James, Bp., 466
Quinn, Francis A., Bp., 466
Quinn, John R., Abp., 466
Quiroga, Vasco de, 392
Qumran Scrolls, see Dead Sea Scrolls

R

Racism, 324
Radio, Catholic, U.S., 594
Radio, Vatican, 175-76
Radio Maria, 595
Rafaela Maria Porras y Ayllon, St.,256
Ramadan Message, 295
Rambusch, Viggio (Death), 530
Ramirez, Ricardo, C.S.B., Bp., 73, 466
Raphael, Archangel, 248
Rash Judgment, 324
Raskob Foundation, 580
Rationalism, 324
Ratzinger, Joseph, Card., 70, 771, 160-
61, 165, 166
Ravalli, Antonio, 392
Raya, Joseph M., Abp., 466
Raymbaut, Charles, 392
Raymond Nonnatus, St., 256
Raymond of Penyafort, St., 256
Razafindratandra, Armand Gaetan,
Card., 161, 165, 166
RCIA (Rite of Christian Initiation of
Adults), 219-20, 224-25
Reader (Lector), 229
Readings, Mass, 213
Readings, Office of (Liturgy of Hours),
211
Reason, Age of, 298
Recollection, 324
Recollects, Augustinian, 496
Reconciliation, see Penance
Reconciliation Room (Confessional),217
Red Mass, 69
Redeemer, Oblates of Most Holy, 521
Order of Most Holy, 521
Sisters of Divine, 521
Sisters of Holy, 521
Redemptorists, 63, 503
Reformation (1517), 116
Men, Doctrines, Churches, 277-78
Reformed Churches-Roman Catholic
Conversations, 287
Refuge, Sisters of Our Lady of Charity,
520
Refugees, 68, 71, 80, 85, 91, 96,
Regina Caeli (Angelus), 299
Regina Medal, 598
Regular Clergy (Clergy), 304-05
Reichert, Stephen J., O.F.M., Bp., 466
Reilly, Daniel P., Bp., 65, 466-67
Reilly, Thomas F., C.SS.R., Bp., 489
Reiss, John C., Bp., 467
Relativism, 67, 324
Released Time, 531
See also Church-State Decisions
Relics, 324
Relief Services, Catholic, see Catholic
Relief Services
Religion, 324
Religion and Healing, 76-7
Religion News Service, 594
Religions, Traditional, 296
Religious, 496
Congregation for, 146
Latin American Confederation, 524
Retirement Fund Collection, 93, 101
Salaries, 88
Superiors, Internatl. Union, 523
Vicars for, Conference of, 524
Religious, Men, 496
Brothers National Association, 524
Brothers (World Statistics), 368
Conference of Major Superiors, U.S.,
523
in U.S. (List), 496-504
in U.S. (Statistics), 432-35
Priests (World Statistics), 368
World Membership, 505-06
Religious, Women, U.S., 506-23
Council of Major Superiors, 523
Leadership Conference, 523
Organizations, 523-24
Statistics, 432-35
Teachers, Catholic Schools, 536
Religious, Women (World Statistics), 368

Religious Education, U.S., Pupils
Receiving Instruction, 536
Religious Education Congress, 93
Religious Formation Conference, 524
Religious Freedom, 312
Religious Freedom Restoration Act
(RFRA), 48
Religious Life, Institute on, 524
Reliquary, 324
Remedial Education Classes see Aguilar
v. Felton, 417
Renew International, 565
Reparation, 324
Reparation of the Congregation of Mary,
Sisters of, 521
Reparation Society of the Immaculate
Heart of Mary, 581
Representatives, Vatican, 168-72
Requiem Mass (Mass of Christian
Burial), 214
Rerum Novarum Centenary, see
Centesimus Annus
Rescript, 325
Reserved Case, 325
Restitution, 325
Resurrection (Easter), 247
Resurrection, Congregation, 503
Resurrection, Sisters of, 521
Retired, Facilities for, 548-58
Retreat Houses, U.S., 565-70
Retreats International, 565
Retrouvaille, 236
Reunion, 358
Revelation (Dogmatic Constitution), 121,
182-85, 311
See also Bible
Revelation, Book of, 192
Revised Standard Version (Bible), 186
Revollo Bravo, Mario, Card.(Death),
600
Rheims, Synod (1148), 114
Rhode Island, 411, 434, 437, 439, 534,
542, 556, 570
Rhodes, 358
Rhodesia, see Zimbabwe
Riashi, Georges, B.C.O., Abp., 467
Ribeiro, Antonio, Card., 161, 165, 166
Ricard, John, S.S.J., Bp., 467
Ricci, Matteo (1610), 117
Richard, Andre, C.S.C., Bp., 387
Richard, Gabriel, 392
Rigali, Justin, Abp., 43-4 467
Righi-Lambertini, Egano, Card., 161,
165, 166
Right to Die and Constitution, 96
Right to Life Threat, see Abortion;
Suicide, Assisted
Riley, Lawrence J., Bp., 467
Ring, 325
Fisherman's, 311
See also Papal Election
Rio de Janeiro, University, 543
Rio Grande do Sul, University, 543
Rita, St., Sisters of, 521
Rita of Cascia, St., 256
Rites, 212
Rites, Eastern, 267-70
Ritter, Joseph (U.S. Cardinals), 167, 489,
504
Ritual, 325
Rivest, Andre, Bp., 387
Roach, John R., Abp., 467
Robert Bellarmine, St., 198
Robert Southwell, St., 256
Robert Wood Johnson University
Hospital, 101
Roch, St., 256
Roch Gonzalez, St., 391
Rochet, 216
Rodimer, Frank J., Bp., 467
Rodriguez, Alfonso, St., 392
Rodriguez, Miguel, C.SS.R., Bp., 467
Rodriguez, Placido, C.M.F., Bp., 468
Rodrigues Maradiago, Oscar Andres,
Abp., 93, 94,
Roe v. Wade, 42

Rose Avato, 1925-1997

Rose Avato, co-editor of the Catholic Almanac, had only recently completed her work on this 1998 edition when she died in her sleep on Oct. 20, 1997. Rose has been an integral part of the Catholic Almanac since 1952. Her dedication and hard work these past 45 years were indispensable in creating this valuable resource, and she will be sorely missed.

Our Sunday Visitor Publishing dedicates the 1998 Catholic Almanac to the memory of Rose Avato. Eternal rest grant unto her, O Lord, and let perpetual light shine upon her.

MOTHER TERESA OF CALCUTTA

Mother Teresa died of cardiac arrest in Calcutta Sept. 4, 1997, nearly 50 years after she founded the Missionaries of Charity and began caring for the poorest of the poor in one of the most remarkable social-service ministries in the history of the Church.

At the time of her death at age 87, some 4,500 professed Missionaries of Charity and about 500 Missionary Brothers of Charity along with a whole legion of dedicated volunteers were continuing her, and their own, mission of mercy among people who in virtually every case were so poor and helpless that they had no one else to turn to, especially the dying poor but also others in dire circumstances of want and need. Missionaries were working in 550 convents in more than 125 countries.

Mother Teresa was born of Albanian parents in 1910 in Skopje, Yugoslavia. Named Agnes Gonxha Bojaxhiu, she joined the Loreto Sisters in Ireland at the age of 18, taught school in India until 1948, and in 1950 founded the Missionaries of Charity devoted, eventually, to the care of hundreds of thousands of poor people in shelters and other places in scores of countries of the world.

She was a woman of mixed contemplative-active spirituality, single-minded and direct in pursuit of the goals of her order. She was a hands-on person of service to the poor, "one at a time," while also handling administrative duties of the order as its superior and best known member.

Love and caring are the most important things in the world, she said. Their lack is tragic: "The biggest disease today is not leprosy or tuberculosis, but rather the feeling of being unwanted, uncared for and deserted by everybody. The greatest evil is the lack of love and charity, the terrible indifference toward one's neighbor who lives at the roadside, assaulted by exploitation, corruption, poverty and disease."

Beloved by Many

She was beloved and honored by many people, most of all by those she and her Missionaries served. Tens of thousands of them flowed past her body as it lay in state in St. Thomas Church. They escorted her remains to the enclosed sports stadium where the Mass of Christian Burial was celebrated Sept. 13 and came back with her to the Missionaries' complex where she was buried.

Pope John Paul told several thousands of people at Castel Gandolfo not long after her death:

"This morning I celebrated, with intimate emotion, holy Mass for her, unforgettable witness to a love made up of concrete and ceaseless service to the poorest and most down-and-out brothers.

Traveling tirelessly the streets of the entire world, Mother Teresa marked the history of our century.

With courage, she defended life — she served every human being by always promoting dignity and respect."

Her pro-life stance was firm and often stated. "To me," she said, "the nations who have legalized abortion are the poorest nations. They are afraid of the unborn child, and the child must die."

The Holy Father sent a message to Sister Nimala Joshi, elected earlier in the year as Mother Teresa's successor, offering "fervent thanks" for Mother Teresa, whom he called "a gift to the Church and to the world."

The government of India, where Catholics are a small minority but Mother Teresa was a citizen and major public figure, granted her a state funeral.

"As a matter of respect and homage, the government decided to break out of protocol and observe state mourning all over the country and to accord her state-funeral status," said a spokesman for Prime Minister Inder Kumar Gujral."

India had given Mother Teresa its highest honor, Bharat Ratan in 1980, a year after she had been awarded the Nobel Peace Prize. Among other honors accorded her was the U.S. Congressional Gold Medal for her humanitarian activities around the world, presented June 5, 1997.

Even the government of Albania, where the Church had been persecuted for many years, formally sought to have Mother Teresa buried in her Balkan birthplace.

President Clinton said in a statement: "Mother Teresa is gone but, as the Gospels teach us, these things endure: faith, hope and love. She had them in abundance."

Bishop Anthony M. Pilla, head of the U.S. bishops' conferences, paid tribute in a statement, saying:

"Mother Teresa transcended cultures and politics as she spoke of God's call to love and assist the poor. She had a profound realization that everyone she was with — immigrant, alien, president or prime minister — was, first of all, a child of God and intrinsically worthy of respect. Her life will stand as a reminder to all of us that we are called to care for one another, and especially that we are called to respect and aid the poorest among us."

WORLD YOUTH DAY 1997

World Youth Day 1997 was an Aug. 19 to 24 celebration in Paris of thousands of Catholic young people from 140 or more countries of the world. It was the sixth such celebration, preceded by others convened in Buenos Aires in 1987, Santiago de Compostela in 1989, Czestochowa in 1991, Denver in 1993 and Manila in 1995. Pope John Paul announced the inauguration of these celebrations in 1986.

Youth Day observances bring together young people from different places and cultures to celebrate not only their youth but especially their faith and its meaning and relevance in their lives, to provide them with an experience of solidarity and unity in the faith, to deepen their appreciation of the doctrines and practices of the Church, and to inspire them to lead integral Christian lives in their particular vocations.

The Paris celebrations got under way Aug. 19 with a Mass celebrated by Cardinal Jean-Marie Lustiger in the Cathedral of Notre Dame and continued that day and the next with a variety of activities, including catechetical sessions, prayer and other types of meetings of young people with their peers, youth ministers, priests, religious and more than a few bishops. In addition, recreational times and events were on the agenda.

PAPAL ITINERARY

The following events were on the papal and youth itinerary.

Aug. 21: Welcome at Orly Airport by President Jacques Chirac and Cardinal Jean-Marie Lustiger; visit to Human Rights Square to pay tributte to deceased Father Joseph Wresinski, founder of an association that helps people of the Fourth World, the poor and destitute of France; afternoon meeting with youths; evening vigil and prayer service on vocational themes.

Aug. 22: Mass with bishops and beatification of Frederic Ozanam; visit to the tomb of Dr. Jerome Lejeune, a personal friend, geneticist, founder of the chromosome that causes Down's syndrome, vigorous pro-life advocate. Stations of the Cross, outdoors and in churches throughout Paris; eight-hour fast by many youths.

Aug. 23: Mass with 320 members (from 140 countries) of the Sixth International Youth Forum involved in organizing the celebration; vigil with baptism and confirmation of 10 young people at the Longchamps Racecourse, where thousands of youths spent the night. During the day, youths joined hands in a boulevard chain of fraternity 20 miles in circumference.

Aug. 24: Concluding Mass of the Youth Day celebration; announcement that St. Therese of the Child Jesus would be named a Doctor of the Church Oct. 19; meeting organizers of the celebration before departure for Rome.

EXCERPTS OF PAPAL ADDRESSES BLESSED FREDERIC OZANAM

At the Mass for the beatification of Frederic Ozanam Aug. 22.

"Frederic Ozanam loved everyone who was deprived. From his youth, he became aware that it was not enough to speak about charity and the mission of the Church in the world; rather, what was needed was an effective commitment of Christians in the service of the poor. In order to show this concretely, at age 20, with a group of friends, he created the Conferences of St. Vincent de Paul which aimed at helping the very poor, in a spirit of service and sharing. These conferences rapidly spread beyond France and to all the European countries and to the world."

"Blessed Frederic Ozanam, apostle of charity, exemplary spouse and father, grand figure of the Catholic laity of the 19th century, was a university student who played an important role in the intellectual movement of his time. A student, and then an eminent professor at Lyons and later at Paris, at the Sorbonne, he aimed above all at seeking and communicating the truth in serenity and respect for the convictions of those who did not share his own.... With the courage of a believer, denouncing all selfishness, he participated actively in the renewal of the presence and the action of the Church in the society of his time.

"Today the Church confirms the kind of Christian life which Ozanam chose, as well as the path which

he undertook. ...She tells him: Frederic, your path has truly been the path of holiness. ... It is necessary that all these young people ... should recognize that this path is also theirs. They must understand that, if they want to be authentic Christians, they must take the same road. May they open wider the eyes of the spirit to the needs of so many people today. May they see these needs as challenges. May Christ call them, each one by name, so that each one may say: This is my path!"

BAPTISMAL VIGIL

At Longchamps Race Track Aug. 23, with the baptism and confirmation of 10 young people.

"Dear young people, do you know what the sacrament of baptism does to you? God acknowledges you as his children and transforms your existence into a story of love with him. He conforms you to Christ so that you will be able to fulfill your personal vocation. He has come to make a pact with you, and he offers you his peace. Live from now on as children of the light who know that they are reconciled by the cross of the Savior.

"Baptism is the most beautiful of God's gifts, inviting us to become disciples of the Lord. It brings us into intimacy with God, into the life of the Trinity, from this day forward and on into eternity. It is a grace given to the sinner, a grace which purifies us from sin and opens to us a new future, It is a bath which washes and regenerates. It is an anointing which conforms us to Christ, priest, prophet and king. It is an enlightenment which illumines our path and gives it full meaning. It is a garment of strength and perfection."

The Church Is Counting on You

"Baptism and Confirmation, however, do not remove us from the world, for we share the joys and hopes of people today and we make our contribution to the human community, in the life of society and in every technical and scientific field. Thanks to Christ, we are close to all of our brothers and sisters, and we are called to show the profound joy which is found in living with him. The Lord calls us to undertake our mission right where we are.... Whatever we do, our existence is for the Lord; that is our hope and our title to glory. In the Church, the presence of young people, catechumens and newly baptized is a great treasure and a source of vitality for the whole Christian commmunity, called to account for its faith and to bear witness to that faith to the ends of the earth."

"Dear Young People, by your baptismal anointing you have become members of the holy people. By your anointing at confirmation you share fully in the Church's mission. The Church, of which you are a part, has confidence in you and is counting on you. May your Christian lives be a progressive 'getting used to life with God' ... so that you may be missionaries of the Gospel."

St. Bartholomew's Day Massacre

Early on in the homily, the Pope alluded to the Massacre of St. Bartholomew's Day in 1572 when 3,000 French Protestants, Huguenots, followers of John Calvin, were killed.

"On the eve of 24 August we cannot forget the sad Massacre of St. Bartholomew's Day, an event of very obscure causes in the political and religious history of France. Christians did things which the Gospel condemns. If I speak of the past, it is because acknowledging the weaknesses of the past is an act of honesty and courage which helps us to strenghen our faith, which alerts us to face today's temptations and challenges, and prepares us to meet them. Therefore, I willingly suppport the initiatives of the French bishops, for, with them, I am convinced that only forgiveness, offered and received, leads little by little to a fruitful dialogue, which will in turn ensure a fully Christian reconciliation. Belonging to different religious traditions must not constitute today a source of opposition and tension. Quite the contrary, our common love for Christ impels us to seek tirelessly the path of full unity."

CHRIST'S PRESENCE

At the Mass which ended celebrations of the Sixth World Youth Day Aug. 24 before a million people at the Longchamps Race Track, on the theme of Christ's presence in the Eucharist and people.

"Rabbi, where are you staying?" Each day the Church responds: Christ is present in the Eucharist, in the sacrament of his death and resurrection. In and through the Eucharist, you acknowledge the dwelling place of the living God in human history. For the Eucharist is the sacrament of the love which conquers death; it is the sacrament of the Covenant, pure gift of love for the reconciliation of all humanity. It is the gift of the real presence of Jesus the Redeemer, in the bread which is his body given up for us, in the wine which is his blood poured out for all. Thanks to the Eucharist, constantly renewed among all the peoples of the world, Christ continues to build his Church; he brings us together in praise and thanksgiving for salvation, in the communion which only infinite love can forge. Our worldwide gathering now takes on its fullest meaning, through the celebration of Mass. Dear young friends, may your presence here mean a true commitment in faith. For Christ is now answering your own question and the questions of all those who seek the living God. He answers by offering an invitation: This is my body, take it and eat. To the Father, he entrusts his supreme desire: that all those whom he loves may be one in the same communion."

The Holy Father also spoke about the presence of Christ in his people:

"All of you, assembled from many countries and continents, bear witness to the universal vocation of the people of God redeemed by Christ! The ultimate answer to the question, 'Teacher, where are you staying?' should then be understood as: I live in all the human beings who have been saved. Yes, Christ dwells in his people."

In conclusion, the Pope said:

"Dear Young People, your journey does not end here. Time does not come to a halt. Go forth now along the roads of the world, along the pathways of humanity, while remaining ever united in Christ's Church.

"Forgiven and reconciled, be faithful to the baptism which you have received! Be witnesses to the Gospel! As active and responsible members of the Church, be disciples and witnesses of Jesus Christ who reveals the Father! And abide always in the unity of the Spirit who is the giver of life.

St. Therese, Doctor To Be

After Mass Aug., 24 the Pope announced that St.Therese of Lisieux would be named a Doctor of the Church. He said:

"In response to many requests and after attentive study, I have the joy of announcing that on Mission Sunday, Oct. 19, 1997, in St.Peter's Basilica in Rome, I will proclaim St. Therese of the Child Jesus and the Holy Face, a Doctor of the Church."

"I have wished to solemnly announce this event here because the message of St. Therese, a young, holy woman so present to our times, is of particular interest to you, young people. At the school of the Gospel, she indicates to you the path of Christian maturity. She calls you to an infinite generosity; she invites you to remain in the heart of the Church as disciples and ardent witnesses of Christ's charity."

"Therese's teaching," the Holy Father said, "is a true science of love, is the luminous expression of her knowledge of the mystery of Christ and of her personal experience of grace; she helps the men and women of today, and she will help those of tomorrow, to be more aware of the gifts of God and to spread the Good News of his love."

STATEMENT OF YOUTH FORUM DELEGATES

Pope John Paul celebrated Mass Aug. 23 for 320 International Youth Forum delegates who were among organizers of the Youth Day celebrations. As representatives of their various regions, they issued the following statement.

"Each one of us is responsible for working to build up the Kingdom of God in every human situation. We all have our part to play in this construction, and no one can do it for us. We must all answer personally the call of Jesus who invites us to meet him. But where does he live?

"Christ is alive and present, especially in those who are poor or unhappy. They are the voiceless prophets of today. Through them Jesus keeps asking us, 'What have you done for me?' We ask ourselves the question, 'How do we respond to his call to be a witness of hope, love and solidarity in the world and in the Church.' "

"We want to show the world our commitment by meaningful, simple and visible acts. We propose to young people to become instruments of Christ's peace from now on and especially as the year 2000 approaches. We can all give signs of this peace through new initiatives, prayer vigils for peace, and every type of action which will inspire nations to adopt an attitude where there is no place for violence or conflict.

"During these three years before the third millennium, let us meditate on the unity of the Trinity as a sign of the unity which we desire between the churches of the world. We entrust ourselves to Mary, who is the living example of abandonment to God and of readiness to proclaim the Good News of Jesus Christ.

"We have come and we have seen; now it is time to go and proclaim!"

MILLENNIUM PREPARATION: Year of the Holy Spirit

Pope John Paul issued an apostolic letter Nov. 10, 1994, in which he called for an appropriate celebration of the beginning of the third millennium of Christianity in Jubilee Year 2000.

The letter, entitled *Tertio Millennnio Adveniente,* outlined several stages of preparation for the celebration, beginning with an antepreparatory phase from 1994 to 1996 and continuing with focus on Christ (1997), the Holy Spirit (1998) and the Father (1999).

The introductory phase of preparation, the Pope wrote, was meant to revive in Christians an awareness of the value and meaning of the Jubilee in human history. "The Jubilee of the Year 2000 is meant to be a great prayer of praise and thanksgiving, especially for the gift of the Incarnation of the Son of God and of the Redemption which he accomplished."

With reference to spiritual preparation for the Jubilee, the Pope wrote:

"The approaching end of the second millennium demands of everyone an examination of conscience. Christians need to place themselves humbly before the Lord and examine themselves on the responsibility which they have for the evils of our day," including:

"Religious indifference which causes many people to live as if God did not exist."

"Related to this is the loss of the transcendent sense of human life and confusion in the ethical sphere, even about the fundamental values of respect for life and the family and other moral obligations."

"Spiritual life, for many Christians, is passing through a time of uncertainty which affects not only their moral life but also their life of prayer and the theological correctness of their faith. Faith is sometimes disoriented by erroneous theological views, the spread of which is abetted by the crisis of obedience vis-a-vis the magisterium."

"Lack of discernment, which at times becomes even acquiescence, shown by many Christians concerning the fundamental human rights denied by totalitarian regimes."

"And in our own day, the responsibility shared by so many Christians for grave forms of injustice and exclusion."

"How many Christians really know and put into practice the principles of the Church's social doctrine?"

Year of the Holy Spirit

"1998, the second year of this preparatory phase, will be dedicated in a particular way to the Holy Spirit and to his sanctifying presence within the community of Christ's disciples."

"The Church cannot prepare for the new millennium in any other way than in the Holy Spirit. What was accomplished by the power of the Holy Spirit in the fullness of time can only through the Spirit's power now emerge from the memory of the Church."

"The Spirit, in fact, makes present in the Church of every time and place the unique revelation brought by Christ to humanity, making it alive and active in the soul of each individual."

"The primary tasks of the preparation for the Jubilee include a renewed appreciation of the presence and activity of the Spirit, who acts within the Church both in the sacraments, especially in confirmation, and in the variety of charisms, roles and ministries which he inspires for the good of the Church."

"In our own day, too, the Spirit is the principal agent of the new evangelization. Hence, it will be important to gain a renewed appreciation of the Spirit as the one who builds the kingdom of God within the course of history and prepares its full manifestation in Jesus Christ."

"Believers should be called to a renewed appreciation of the theological virtue of hope, which they have already heard proclaimed 'in the word of the truth, the Gospel.' The basic attitude of hope, on the one hand, encourages the Christian not to lose sight of the final goal which gives meaning and value to life, and, on the other, offers solid and profound reasons for a daily commitment to transform reality in order to make it correspond to God's plan."

"Christians are called to prepare for the Great Jubilee of the beginning of the third millennium by renewing their hope in the definitive coming of the kingdom of God, preparing for it daily in their hearts, in the Christian community to which they belong, in their particular social context and in world history itself."

"There is also need for a better appreciation and understanding of the signs of hope present in the last part of this century, even though they often remain hidden from our eyes."

"The reflection of the faithful in the second year of preparation ought to focus particularly on the value of unity within the Church, to which the various gifts and charisms bestowed upon her by the Spirit are directed."

"Mary, who conceived the incarnate Word by the power of the Holy Spirit and then in the whole of her life allowed herself to be guided by his interior activity, will be contemplated and imitated during this year, above all, as the woman who was docile to the voice of the Spirit, a woman of silence and attentiveness, a woman of hope."

SYNODAL ASSEMBLIES

In the apostolic letter entitled Tertio Millennio Adveniente, outlining preparations for the celebration of Jubilee Year 2000, Pope John Paul wrote that special assemblies of the Synod of Bishops would be held for America, Asia and Oceania.

The Pope wrote: "A need emphasized by the cardinals and bishops is that of continental synods, fol-

lowing the example of those already held for Europe and Africa.

"The last General Conference of the Latin American episcopate accepted, in agreement with the bishops of North America, the proposal for a synod for the Americas on the problems of the new evangelization in both parts of the same continent, so different in origin and history, and on issues of justice and of international, economic relations in view of the enormous gap between North and South.

"Another plan for a continent-wide synod will concern Asia where the issue of the encounter of Christianity with ancient local cultures and religions is a pressing one. This is a great challenge for evangelization, since religious systems such as Buddhism or Hinduism have a clearly soteriological character. There is also an urgent need for a synod on the occasion of the Great Jubilee in order to illustrate and explain more fully the truth that Christ is the one mediator between God and man, and the sole redeemer of the world, to be clearly distinguished from the founders of other great religions. With sincere esteem, the Church regards the elements of truth found in those religions as a reflection of the truth which enlightens all men and women.

" 'Ecce natus est Salvator mundi.' In the Year 2000 the proclamation of this truth should resound with renewed power.

"Also for Oceania a regional synod could be useful. In this region there arises the question, among others, of the aboriginal people, who in a unique way evoke aspects of human prehistory. In this synod a matter not to be overlooked, together with other problems of the region, would be the encounter of Christianity with the most ancient forms of religion, marked by a monotheistic orientation."

Questionnaires circulated by the Vatican in the three areas indicate the nature and scope of discussions expected to take place. Following are listings of key questions seeking answers in the context of the state of the Church in each of the three regions.

AMERICAN ASSEMBLY

Theme of the Special Assembly of the Synod of Bishops for America: "Encounter with the Living Jesus Christ: Way to Conversion, Communion and Solidarity." It was expected that the assembly would be convened in November, 1997.

Questions

1. How is the person of Jesus Christ, savior and evangelizer, proclaimed and presented to the men and women of the present era so that they might have a true encounter with him in the concrete circumstances of life ... (and in the) liturgy, systematic catechesis, formation in the faith, apostolic and charitable activities?

2. List and describe concrete signs of the religious awakening in the local church. On the other hand, what are the most urgent aspects needing conversion within the church?

3. What elements in contemporary society in your area can be considered positive with regard to the Gospel message? What elements of society call for conversion?

4. In your area, what are the factors causing significant divisions in the Church with regard to bishops, priests, men and women religious, ecclesial movements, the faithful in general? How can these elements which damage communion be overcome?

5. Evaluate to what measure the teachings of the Second Vatican Council, especially in relation to ecclesial communion, have been faithfully applied in your particular church....

6. What is being done concretely in the particular churches or at the interdiocesan level to promote ecumenical dialogue, prayer and cooperation in acts of solidarity with our Christian brethren...?

7. Evaluate the relations which your Christian community maintains with non-Christian religions.

8. Describe briefly the religious situation concerning sects, syncretistic religious movements and other spiritual currents. What are they? What types of activities are they developing? What can the Church do to confirm believers in their faith in light of this situation?

9. What is the Church doing to evangelize the world of culture (the arts, literature, science, etc.) ... through programs of evangelization in the various fields of education...?

10. What are the most significant elements in the cultures of indigenous groups, African-Americans or immigrants ... which deserve to be reconsidered or utilized as "seeds of evangelization?"

11. What are the more significant characteristics of popular piety...? What place does the Blessed Virgin Mary hold in popular devotion?

12. What is the Church in your area doing at present to promote the proper use of the means of social communication and to make them useful tools at the service of the new evangelization?

13. What activities are promoted by the Church in your area to offer assistance in solidarity to those most in need, and how do the faithful respond in general to these initiatives...?

14. What use is being made of the Church's social teaching in your area in the new evangelization in light of the diverse situations which demand social action...?

15. How does the Church promote respect for human life in all its phases, from conception ... to the point of natural death...?

Jesuit Father Avery Dulles commented on the American assembly in an address delivered at the annual convention of the Catholic Press Association in May, 1997:

"The general synod for the Americas, scheduled to be held in November, 1997, will open up broad areas for the participation of the laity on all levels, including the local, the national and the international. The synod is being convoked to deal with the problems of the new evangelization in the Northern and Southern hemispheres and with the relevant issues of justice and international relations."

ASIAN ASSEMBLY

Theme: "Jesus Christ the Savior: Mission of Love and Service in Asia." It was expected that the assembly would be convened in the spring of 1998.

Questions

1. Describe some of the positive aspects as well as the shortcomings of evangelization in your area in relation to Asian realities, i.e., religious, socioeconomic, political, etc....

2. Evaluate the state of the Church's missionary activity in Asia and in your area....

3. What is being done for the formation of the agents of missionary activity...?

4. What is being done in your area to help members of the Church become better acquainted with the tradi-

tions of other religions in Asia? What can the Church learn from her dialogue with other Asian religions and the knowledge obtained? To what extent can the specific aspects of Asian religions be used and developed in the fulfillment of the Church's mission of bringing salvation to all peoples in Asia?

5. How is the person of Christ viewed and proposed in the Church's mission of proclaiming him and his salvation to the Asian people? Describe ways in which the Church can maintain the centrality of the proclamation of Jesus Christ in very difficult political, social and cultural situations. In what ways can the Church present Jesus Christ as the one and only savior as well as the universality of salvation in him?

6. Evaluate in your area the Church's understanding of the need and responsibility of carrying on Christ's mission in the Spirit....

7. Give an assessment of how church communion is lived in the local Church in your area. Describe how various Christian churches give a common witness in their evangelizing activities.

8. What efforts are being made in your area toward fostering greater ecumenical understanding and unity among various churches and various ecclesial traditions?

9 What is being done by the Church in your area to engage in dialogue with other religions: Hindu-Christian, Buddhist-Christian, Islamic-Christian, traditional religion, etc...?

10. Describe the extent of inculturation in the various aspects of the Church's life in your area, (e.g, Christian theology, liturgy, spirituality, liturgical art, architecture, etc.) and its effects in relation to the Church's mission....

11. How is the social doctrine of the Church being utilized in the Church's evangelizing mission of love and service in Asia...?

12. What has the Church done in your area to use the means of social communications in the Church's evangelizing mission...?

13. How would you describe Marian spirituality and devotion in your area as a means of evangelization and catechesis...?

For several theoretical and historical reasons, an opinion has been expressed in some quarters in Asia during the last three decades that the age of mission is over. Now is the time for dialogue and inculturation. Radical pluralism of religion and salvation seems to become a dogma itself. At times one's culture is so absolutized that conversion is looked upon as violence done to the other. Others claim that the Church's mission is only the proclamation of the values of the kingdom, human promotion and liberation.

Referring to such tendencies, Paul VI already in 1975 reconfirmed the need and urgency for the proclamation of Christ: "We wish to point out, above all today, that neither respect and esteem for these religions nor the complexity of the questions raised is an invitation to the Church to withhold from these non-Christians the proclamation of Jesus Christ."

In the current theological, missiological and missionary situation of Asia, the proclamation of Jesus Christ is the central issue of the faith and life of the Church. It is incumbent on the pastors of the Church to give priority to proclamation in all their pastoral planning. They must be seen primarily as evangelizers.

OCEANIA ASSEMBLY

The assembly for Australia, New Zealand and the South Pacific was expected to convene in the fall of 1998.

Questions

1. What can be done in Oceania to ensure that the Gospel is proclaimed to groups and areas where it has not yet been heard, or needs to be heard anew?

2. What is the special contribution of Christians to a greater dialogue among (diverse) cultures?

3. To what extent is the inculturation of the Gospel taking place in your (local) church?

4. Describe the situation of ethnic minorities in your part of Oceania concerning human rights, education, economic development, health care, housing, etc. What pastoral measures is the Church taking to address these peoples' spiritual needs?

5. How is the phenomenon of migration affecting your part of Oceania? How is the Church responding to the pastoral needs of the people involved?

6. How is the Church responding to opportunities and challenges presented by the rise in urbanization in your part of Oceania?

7. In a program of new evangelization, how is the Church "telling the truth of Jesus Christ" within the church community through encouraging and providing opportunity for spiritual renewal of her members?

8. In your local church, what is the present state of catechetics?

9. What is the Church doing in her relations with other religions, e.g., Jews, Muslims, Hindus, traditional religions?

10. How can the Church better respond to the challenges posed by sects and (similar) religious movements?

11. How can the Church's social teaching be better made known, particularly in light of justice and peace issues?

12. How was the Second Vatican Council received in Oceania? How would you assess the changes it brought about?

13. As stewards of the gift of life, ... how are members of your church community — individually and collectively — raising the consciousness of others regarding the sacredness and dignity of every human life?

14. How can the Church contribute to strengthening the institution of marriage and thereby ensure for the family a stable and healthy environment which welcomes human life, nurtures children, guides youth, provides fulfillment and attention to all the personal needs of those in the family?

15. Describe any particular vocations, charisms or issues which are presently receiving attention in your church community, specifically in light of the focus of "living the life of Christ" in a new evangelization of Oceania.

16. How is the Church in your area responding, through her members and structures, to her vocation to be a builder of communion within the church community?. How is she fulfilling her mission to be the sacrament of unity in the world?

17. Evaluate the situation of the Church in Oceania in

relation to the universal Church. What specific contribution can the Church in Oceania make to the universal Church? How can the Church in Oceania benefit from the gift of communion with the worldwide Church?

YOUTH MINISTRY

(By Jerry Filteau, CNS)
Youth ministry is "a top priority for the entire church community," the bishops of the United States said June 20, 1997, in a statement adopted unanimously at their general meeting in Kansas City, Mo.
The 75-page statement lays out the essential goals and elements of Catholic ministry to and with young people.

Entitled "Renewing the Vision — A Framework for Catholic Youth Ministry,'" it was written by the Subcommittee on Youth of the bishops' Committee on the Laity.

The statement takes its direction from Pope John Paul, noting that he "has emphasized repeatedly the importance of young people and ministry with them."

The introduction describes the statement as "a blueprint for the continued development of effective ministry with young and older adolescents."

It says that statement "was the catalyst for a dramatic increase in new and innovative pastoral practice with adolescents." Since the late 1970s the Church has seen the growth of multidimensional parish youth ministries throughout the country.

It differs from the 1976 statement in two ways, according to Bishop G. Patrick Ziemann, head of the Laity Committee.

"It recognizes that youth need to be incorporated into the full life of the Church."

"The whole parish community needs to be responsive to the needs and concerns of youth."

Essential Goals

The new statement declares that there are "three essential goals for youth ministry:

"to empower young people to live as disciples of Jesus Christ in our world today;

"to draw young people to responsible participation in the life, mission and work of the Catholic faith community;

"To foster the total personal and spiritual growth of each young person."

It reaffirms the definition of youth ministry set out by the 1976 statement, which said: "Youth ministry is the response of the Christian community to the needs of young people and the sharing of the unique gifts of young people with the larger community."

It says that renewal in youth ministry since 1976, based on that vision, has been "one of the most hopeful signs" in the Church in this country.

The approach to youth ministry that has evolved and matured over the past two decades is ministerial, pastoral, relational and goal-centered.

Youth ministry has also become multidimensional, as "a needed response to social-only, athletics-only or religious-only programming" once found in many parishes.

"Since the late 1970s, the statement says, youth ministries have grown in quality and scope, with more parish resources and trained personnel devoted to the task."

But the document says new challenges and developments in the past 20 years call for an updating and expansion of the 1976 statement.

"The changes in our society present the Church with a new set of issues. We are deeply concerned by America's neglect of young people. The United States is losing its way as a society by not ensuring that all youth move safely and successfully into adulthood," it says.

It adds that "new research has provided insight into the factors that make for healthy adolescent development," paving the way for more refined models of effective, comprehensive youth ministry.

Fundamental Ways of Ministry

The growth in the Church's understanding and practice of all ministry since 1970 must also be incorporated into the total vision and strategy of youth ministry, it says. In addition to detailed discussion of the goals of youth ministry, the statement recounts and analyzes the "eight fundamental ways to minister effectively with adolescents," spelled out in the 1976 statement: advocacy, catechesis, community life, evangelization, justice and service, leadership development, pastoral care, prayer and worship.

Nearly half of the statement is devoted to detailed description and analysis of each of those components and their specific applications and implications in ministry among adolescents. It says that the idea of helping young people find and develop a personal relationship with Christ is at the heart of effective youth ministry.

That approach, developed in the 1976 statement out of the Gospel story of the disciples' meeting with Jesus on the road to Emmaus after the Resurrection, has become a "guiding image" for youth ministry.

"The Emmaus story will continue to guide the Church's ministry with adolescents," the statement says, "but a new image is emerging to guide such ministry — the image of young people with a mission. Just as Jesus sent out the 12 and the 72 to carry out his mission, today he sends out young people to proclaim the Good News and to build a better world."

AGE FOR RECEPTION OF CONFIRMATION

In the midst of differences of opinion regarding the appropriate age for reception of the sacrament of confirmation, Bishop Thomas J. Tobin of Youngstown addressed a letter to the people of the diocese Mar. 31, 1997. Following are excerpts.

A diocesan committee ... has conducted a very comprehensive and objective consultation about this matter (the question of the age for reception of confirmation) and related questions. This study has affirmed that in this diocese, as throughout the United

States, there is a great diversity of theological understanding, pastoral practice, opinion and emotion surrounding the issue.

This study was occasioned by the fact that under our current policy, in which students are presented for confirmation in the 11th or 12th grade of high school, approximately one-half of the young people of the diocese have not been receiving the sacrament in recent years. This despite the fact that many of our parishes have had very successful and inspiring confirmation programs for our young people.

Nevertheless, this serious problem, which together we must try to resolve, was first indicated by diocesan statistics and has been verified by the consultation which has taken place. Documents of the Church, including the Code of Canon Law and the Catechism of the Catholic Church, make it very clear that it is expected as a norm that every Catholic receive the sacrament of confirmation. And, more important perhaps, there are compelling practical and spiritual reasons emphasizing the importance of the sacrament of confirmation in the life of the Catholic today.

New Policy

As a result of the consultation which has taken place and after considerable prayer and reflection on my part, I wish to announce and hereby promulgate a new policy regarding the age for the reception of the sacrament of confirmation: In the Diocese of Youngstown the age at which young people will be presented for the sacrament of confirmation is during the eighth grade. This policy is to become effective Sept. 1, 1998. This choice will help us to achieve the following practical goals:

• Moving confirmation from its present position to the eighth grade will achieve the first and motivating goal of our study. It will encourage more students to be prepared for and presented for the sacrament.

• By receiving confirmation in the eighth grade, our young people will be strengthened by the Holy Spirit and the gifts of the Holy Spirit as they encounter what will be, perhaps, the most difficult and challenging years of their lives. The Holy Spirit will help them to make good decisions and to remain faithful to God and the Church despite the many pressures and temptations they face as teen-agers. It

will also allow us to work more closely with their parents and sponsors at this important time in their lives.

• This policy will motivate our people to remain in programs of religious education until at least the eighth grade and will allow them to be adequately prepared to receive the sacrament. Hopefully, it will also encourage them to continue their involvement in the Church through youth ministry programs during their high school years.

• The move into an eighth-grade program should prove to be less disruptive to the overall catechetical and liturgical life of the diocese than a move to an earlier age. It will, however, better position the diocese in the event that at some point in the future an earlier age is accepted nationwide or in this diocese.

Confirmation and Youth Ministry

As a transition into a program of eighth-grade confirmation, in the academic year 1997-1998 a student in the ninth grade or older who has fulfilled the basic requirements for the sacrament of confirmation should be presented for the sacrament. In the following year, 1998-1999, students in the eighth and ninth grades will be eligible for the sacrament, and in following years eighth grade will be the normal time for the reception of the sacrament. When the number of eighth-grade students in a parish is very small, confirmation may be delayed for one year. Consequently, confirmation would be offered for eighth-and ninth-grade students.

I wish to emphasize that the Diocese of Youngstown, along with dioceses throughout the nation, should remain open to future developments in confirmation practice in the years to come. This question will continue to be studied by the National Conference of Catholic Bishops and the Holy See.

One of the themes which has emerged during the discussion about confirmation is the importance of a vital youth ministry program in the diocese. With the implementation of an eighth-grade policy for confirmation, the need for high-school youth ministry in our parishes will become even more urgent. It is my firm intention to do everything possible to encourage Catholic youth ministry in every parish in our diocese.

HUMAN CLONING

(By John Thavis, CNS)
The Vatican issued a detailed condemnation of human cloning, saying the technique would violate a number of ethical norms and turn the human being into an "industrial product."

Human cloning would exploit women, bring suffering to the cloned person and lead humanity further down the road to eugenics, or selective breeding, said the Pontifical Academy for Life in a statement issued June 24, 1997.

The six-page statement was the most comprehensive Vatican critique of the process since the road to human cloning was opened earlier in the year, when scientists announced the first successful cloning of a mammal. That news was greeted with strong statements of alarm from many quarters, including the Church.

The Pontifical Academy said the initial outcry focused on worse-case and rather far-fetched cloning scenarios. It warned, however, that sentiment exists for accepting human cloning in some circumstances and urged strong action to make sure that does not happen.

"Stopping the human cloning project is a moral task that should be translated into cultural, social and legislative terms," the statement said.

The procedure, in which a genetic replica of a person would be reproduced in the laboratory in embryo form and then brought to term, represents an example of "scientific despotism," it said.

Ethical Objections

The statement listed several ethical objections to human cloning.

As an extreme form of manipulation, it would destroy the complementarity and personalistic nature of human reproduction, replacing it with "the logic of industrial production."

It would violate the basic human rights of equal dignity and nondiscrimination, by the very selectivity inherent in human cloning.

It would promote a "radical exploitation" of women, reducing their role to the strictly biological functions of provider of ovum and uterus.

It would destroy the natural family relationships that have always existed for human beings, such as parentage and blood relation. For example: "A woman could be the twin sister of her mother, lack a biological father and be the daughter of her grandfather."

It would create a context of psychological suffering for the cloned subject, who would come into the world as a biological "copy" of someone else, perhaps with a set of expectations to live up to.

"The 'human cloning' project represents the terrible aberration to which value-free science is driven and is a sign of the profound malaise of our civilization, which looks to science, technology and the 'quality of life' as surrogates for the meaning of life and its salvation."

The statement repeated the Church's condemnation of all in-vitro fertilization, including that involved in cloning, because it violates church teaching about responsible sexual procreation.

It said that, if experiments in human cloning were undertaken, it would also no doubt involve experiments on or destruction of human embryos. Such practises would always be immoral.

The statement underlined that the popular perception of human cloning — that a perfect double of the person cloned would be created — is misplaced. The spiritual soul, created by God and the essential source of personality, cannot be cloned. Neither can psychological development, which depends largely on experiences.

The statement said that, while human cloning should be condemned, cloning practices in animal or vegetable life can be beneficial, so long as respect for animals and individual species is maintained.

A Theologian's View

Vatican theologian Father Gino Concetti, O.F.M., commented on human cloning in the Mar. 5, 1997,

English-language edition of *L'Osservatore Romano.*

"Cloning was a topic of conversation before the recent experiment on sheep in a Scottish laboratory, and it will continue to be discussed in the future. The human desire to discover new scientific methods and the possibilities offered by technology, together with the benefits they are expected to bring, are the driving force behind these efforts.

"But scientific research and experiments also have inviolable limits based on the ethical order and that of nature itself. From time to time, the Church has clearly stated these limits, rejecting the utilitarian criteria and denying that everything technically possible is also morally permissible.

"As for the procedures successfully tried in plants and animals, the Church with John XXIII had already warned that they should not be transferred to man. In particular, the Congregation for the Doctrine of the Faith, in the 1987 document *Donum Vitae,* explicitly said of cloning: 'Attempts or hypotheses of obtaining a human being without any connection with sexuality ... are to be considered contrary to the moral law, since they are in opposition to the dignity of both human procreation and of the conjugal union.'"

"In the sacred book of origins (Genesis) the law for the transmission of human life is set down indubitably. This transmission must occur in marriage by a reasonable act of the couple.

"Any different way or method is unacceptable: first, because it would contradict the creative plan of God; secondly, because it would offend the dignity of the person and of marriage. The human person has the right to be born in a human way and not in a laboratory. The intransigence of these principles must be understood not as opposition to science or as a check on progress, but as a defense of the constitutive value of the human being and his existence.

"It is highly desirable that states — following the European Parliament (Resolution of 16 March 1989} — immediately pass legislation to forbid human cloning, and that they have the strength not to yield in any way to the pressure of those seeking compromise on the issue. This is a compelling demand of reason and humanity."

COMMITMENT AND CHALLENGE OF CATHOLIC HEALTH CARE

The commitment of Catholic health care ministry to the teachings of the Church and the welfare of patients is under increasing challenge in the milieu of unacceptable ethics, practices and bottom-line economics prevailing and gaining ground in the health care field in the United States and other countries of the world.

The Catholic tradition and mission that form the core of Catholic health care make it unique, said ethicist Charles Dougherty June 8, 1997, during the national meeting of the Catholic Health Association in Chicago.

Dougherty was vice president for academic affairs at Creighton University and an author of numerous books and articles on health care and ethics.

"The first thing to be said about Catholicism is

obvious: Catholic institutions bring normative assumptions into the health care arena," he said.

He said this has become critically important because most U.S. health care has gone through a great change in moral tone since the 1960s. It has fallen into "an ethical dead-end" in which the ethical norms of the healing profession that once held sway have been replaced by the notion of patient choice as the definitive standard.

A Countercultural Position

"Legally, a patient's informed consent — philosophically his or her autonomy, practically his or her choice — these now direct much of the decision making in American health care. Where they do not, economic forces prevail," he said.

"When the only moral standards are what individuals want or the market forces ... then there are no moral standards." And "this rejection of standards represents a profound breach with tradition — not only with our traditions, but with tradition as such."

The result, according to Dougherty, is that Catholic health care has been placed "in a countercultural position."

A wide range of concerns — from administrative to pastoral, from canonical to moral and ethical — formed the agenda of a health care workshop for bishops June 19 in Kansas City, Mo. Bishop Donald W. Wuerl of Pittsburgh organized and served as host of the meeting.

Its main purpose was to share information with the bishops and "give them an overview of the situation as it involves Catholic health care institutions and therefore themselves, as bishops who have a pastoral responsibility and pastoral role in this.

Systemic Changes

Health care is "a rapidly changing world," Bishop Wuerl said. "The whole face of health care in this country is changing so rapidly — mergers, partnerships, alliances — with almost dizzying speed."

Among issues discussed at the workshop were pressures on Catholic institutions to enter partnerships with non-Catholic institutions and the need to assure Catholic identity in such situations.

For reasons of Catholic identity and integrity, merger or partnership with other Catholic institutions is plainly preferred, and provisions to assure Catholic integrity are needed in relationships entered into with other non-profit institutions.

When the question of merger or partnership with the rapidly expanding for-profit systems arises, "it's very difficult to see a compatibility between ministry and stock-held, for-profit entities."

"We do health care in ministry out of a call to make Christ present, to heal. A stock-held entity has as its primary consideration a dividend to its stockholders. There's a basic incompatibility there," said Bishop Wuerl.

No to Pro-Profit Status

The U.S. bishops' Administrative Committee, in a mid-April, 1997, statement, reiterated its opposition to converting any Catholic health ministry to for-profit status. "We believe that ownership arrangements between Catholic health ministry organizations and publicly traded, investor-owned hospital chains compromise the Church's mission to an unacceptable degree."

The statement was originally approved early in 1996 by the National Coalition on Catholic Health Care Ministry.

The coalition included representatives of the Association of Catholic Health Science Centers, Catholic Charities USA, the Catholic Health Association, the Conference of Major Superiors of Men, the Council of Major Superiors of Women Religious and the Leadership Conference of Women Religious.

The statement called health care ministry "one of the most significant services which the Church offers to society," and said it is "fundamentally different from most goods and services and is, consequently, best delivered in a setting where human and community needs are the primary concerns."

It said "the primary motivation of publicly traded, investor-owned hospital chains is to provide a return to shareholders." But "the first commitment of our ministry is to render services in the name of Jesus.

"In that context, because health care is so integral to the Church's healing ministry, we strongly urge that, as partnership arrangements are being explored, priority be given to those involving Catholic health care providers."

Challenges

Managed care and "merger mania" were on the table at a meeting of Catholic doctors Nov. 9 and 10, 1996, in Scottsdale, Ariz.

The relationship between the Church and health care were the subjects of a talk by Bishop John J. Myers of Peoria who said:

"Our health care ministry it too precious to lose. In the words of the Holy Father, 'it remains one of our most vital apostolates.' "

"In these times, characterized by fundamental shifts both in the structure and cultural shifts in society, Catholic health care must remain the treasured ministry that it is by adapting prudently, bravely and confidently — and always in ways that are absolutely faithful to the teachings of Christ and his Church."

In addition to merger concerns, Bishop Myers addressed other problems, including lack of respect for human life, the impact of managed care on the doctor-patient relationship and treating the spiritual aspect of illness.

Arguing that there is a definite place for Catholic health care, he said: "I would emphatically say that wherever humanity is, there the Church belongs."

"My concern about the culture of death affecting esteem for life from the beginning and throughout the life cycle is a primary reason why we must remain firmly committed to the survival of the apostolate," he said. "We have a large stake in the provision of health care in the United States as the largest non-federal provider. We must use what clout we have to offer an alternative to the deathward trends in contemporary society and medicine."

A Warning

An alarm bell for Catholics in health care ministry was sounded at an international conference held July 28 to 31, 1997, at Queens' College of the University of Cambridge, England. "Issues for a Catholic Bioethic" was the theme of the conference.

"For the foreseeable future, Christian health care professionals responding to their vocation as they should will work as aliens in the world," said Germain Grisez, a professor of Christian ethics at St. Mary's College, Emmitsburg, Md. "They find it more and more difficult to maintain their standards in doing their work....

"Their consciences are increasingly disrespected. Some fields of activity are already closed to them, and others will be. They are being pressured to help manufacture babies, prevent them and kill them. They soon will be pressured to help people commit suicide and to kill people unwanted by those close to them or by society."

Grisez warned: "Some committed people will not

be able to keep their jobs, maintain their practices, continue to operate their facilities unless they betray their commitments."

Hope

On the final day of the Catholic Health Association convention, retiring president John E. Curley said in a farewell address:

"You (CHA members) and I continue the healing ministry of Jesus despite the trepidations of some doomsayers." Some others, however, "may see health care as a commodity to be bought and sold rather than as a service to fellow human beings."

"I believe we are equipped to face the challenges of the future. I have faith in our ability. And I believe we are equipped by the tradition of the Gospel values to maintain and offer quality health care to those who need it."

ASSISTED SUICIDE BAN

State laws in Washington and New York that would ban assisted suicide for mentally competent, terminally ill persons were upheld unanimously in twin rulings June 26, 1997, by the U.S. Supreme Court.

Chief Justice William Rehnquist delivered the opinion of the court in each decision, "Washington v. Glucksberg" and "Vacco v. Quill," the case from New York.

New York's prohibition of assisted suicide did not violate the Equal Protection Clause of the 14th Amendment to the U.S. Constitution, Rehnquist said. Also rejected was the claim that Washington's ban of assisted suicide violated the Due Process Clause of the 14th Amendment

"Attitudes toward suicide itself have changed ... but our laws have consistently condemned and continue to prohibit assisted suicide," he said. " Despite changes in medical technology and notwithstanding an increased emphasis on the importance of end-of-life decision making, we have not retreated from this prohibition."

Although all nine justices concurred in upholding the state bans, several wrote separate opinions leaving open the possibility that states might not always have an overriding interest in preventing all suicides. Rehnquist himself said at the conclusion of the opinion on Washington's law that the court's holding would permit the debate in the United States over the "morality, legality and practicality of physician-assisted suicide" to continue.

An Important Distinction

In the Washington case, the chief justice rejected the argument that there was no real distinction between assisted-suicide and a patient's refusal of unwanted medical treatment — the sort of withdrawal of care that arose as a question for the court in the 1990 case of Nancy Beth Cruzan.

In that decision, he said "we recognized that most states outlawed assisted suicide — and even more do today — and we certainly gave no intimation that the right to refuse medical treatment could somehow be transmuted into a right to assistance in committing suicide."

Rehnquist said that assisted suicide "could make it more difficult for the state to protect depressed or mentally ill persons, or those suffering from untreated pain, from suicidal impulses." He said the state has an interest "in protecting vulnerable groups — including the poor, the elderly and disabled persons — from abuse, neglect and mistakes," and that "the state may fear that permitting assisted suicide will start it down the path to voluntary and perhaps even involuntary euthanasia." Also, assisted suicide could prove extremely difficult to police and contain.

Euthanasia in the Netherlands

"This concern," the opinion said, "is ... supported by evidence about the practice of euthanasia in the Netherlands. The Dutch government's own study revealed that in 1990 there were 2,300 cases of voluntary euthanasia (defined as `the deliberate termination of another's life at his request'), 400 cases of assisted suicide and more than 1,000 cases of euthanasia without an explicit request. In addition to these latter 1,000 cases, the study found an additional 4,941 cases where physicians administered lethal morphine overdoses without the patients' explicit consent.

"This study suggests that, despite the existence of various reporting procedures, euthanasia in the Netherlands has not been limited to competent, terminally ill adults who are enduring physical suffering, and that regulation of the practice may not have prevented abuses in cases involving vulnerable persons, including severely disabled neonates and elderly persons suffering from dementia."

The opinion added: "The New York Task Force, in *Compassion in Dying,* citing the Dutch experience, observed that `assisted suicide and euthanasia are closely linked, and concluded that the risk of ... abuse is neither speculative nor distant.'"

Physician-assisted suicide could, it is argued, undermine the trust that is essential to the doctor-patient relationship by blurring the time-honored line between healing and harming."

Rulings Praised

The Supreme Court's ruling upholding states' rights to prohibit assisted suicide were praised for respecting moral wisdom and legal tradition.

Cardinal Bernard F. Law, chairman of the bishops' Committee for Pro-Life Activities, said the court "displayed wisdom and restraint" in upholding laws against assisted suicide: "The court's ruling is consonant with two centuries of legal tradition and over 20 centuries of moral wisdom recognizing that healers must not be agents of death."

Cardinal Anthony J. Bevilacqua, a civil lawyer and member of the Supreme Court Bar, called the decision "a monumental step toward the formation of a culture which values human life and the rejection of the current culture of death so prevalent in our society."

He called the ruling "a special triumph for the disabled, ill and elderly who would have been the most at risk of being legally killed by the same doctors from whom they once sought compassion and healing."

Franciscan Brother Daniel Sulmasy, a physician and director of Georgetown University's Center for Clinical Bioethics, said the court's opinion made important statements about the need for doctors to be trained in how to provide better palliative care and to address the loneliness and depression that lead people to want to commit suicide.

He said he was surprised that none of the Supreme Court justices seemed convinced by the arguments that there is a constitutional right to assisted suicide.

Avoidance of Roe Mistake

Brother Sulmasy also said the fact that their opinion — united as it was in upholding the state laws — left doors open, struck him as an interesting contrast to the Roe v. Wade opinion legalizing abortion.

Given how brief a time the national discussion on assisted suicide had been under way, the case went to the Supreme Court very quickly, he noted. The court seemed quite conscious of how little time the nation had to weigh the subject.

"We weren't even thinking about this six or seven years ago," he said. "What they're saying is, they don't want to close the debate and rule by judicial 'fiat' as they did with Roe."

ROE V. WADE; OTHER ABORTION DECISIONS

The key abortion-related decisions were handed down by the U.S. Supreme Court in the case of Roe v. Wade and the companion case of Dole v. Bolton. The court ruled 7-to-2 Jan. 22, 1973:

(1) During the first three months of pregnancy, a woman's right to privacy is paramount. Accordingly, she has an unrestricted right to abortion with the consent and cooperation of a physician.

(2) In the second trimester, the principle controlling legislation is the health or welfare of the mother.

(3) In the third trimester, the "state subsequent to viability," the controlling principles of legislation are the State's "interest in the potentiality of human life" and "the preservation of the life or health of the mother."

The decisions legalized abortion nationwide, practically on demand.

In the 24 years subsequent to the Roe v. Wade, Dole v. Bolton decisions, an estimated 40 million legal abortions have been performed in the United States.

Webster v. Reproductive Health Services

The court upheld, July 3, 1989, 5 to 4, provisions of the Missouri law:

(1) forbidding public employees to perform or assist in abortions

(2) barring the use of public facilities for abortion;

(3) requiring physicians to take steps to determine fetal viability when a woman 20 or more weeks pregnant seeks an abortion.

At issue was an appeal of a lower court ruling in Webster v. Reproductive Health Services, Inc., with respect to the statute, Missouri Senate Committee Substitute for House Bill No. 1596, which was signed into law in June, 1986.

Rust v. Sullivan

The U.S. Supreme Court ruled 5-to-4 May 23, 1991 that provisions of Title X (the National Family Planning Program) of the 1970 Public Health Service Act were in accord with the U.S. Constitution. Pertinent regulations forbade family planning clinics from counseling or advising abortion if they received federal funds disbursed under Title X.

The Court observed:

(1) Abortion cannot be equated with family plan-

ning. The family planning legislation of 1970 distinguished between abortion and family planning, and intended to restrict federal funding to planning human life, not destroying it.

(2) The admission of a legal right (in this case, abortion) does not necessarily imply a government duty to promote the right.

(3) The fact that abortion is a legal right does not mean the government and those who do not subscribe to this right have to pay for it.

The Court ruled that the government can establish rules for funding only family planning programs which do not "encourage, promote or advocate abortion."

Planned Parenthood v. Casey

On June 29, 1992, the court declared constitutional provisions of a 1989 Pennsylvania law regulating the practice of abortion.

Women seeking abortion must receive information about risks, fetal development and alternatives to abortion, and must wait at least 24 hours after receiving such information before having an abortion.

Medical offices must fie detailed, confidential reports about each abortion performed.

Minors must get permission from one parent or a judge before having an abortion.

Pro-Abortion Executive Orders

Abortion developments in 1993 included President Clinton's executive orders, effective as of Jan. 22, 1994, which reversed:

• regulations prohibiting abortion counseling in federally funded family planning clinics;

• a ban on fetal tissue research;

• restrictions on access to abortion in U.S. military hospitals overseas;

• the "Mexico City Policy" which denied U.S. foreign aid to programs overseas that promoted abortion.

U.S. Supreme Court Associate Justice Antonin Scalia refused Aug. 18, 1994, to set aside a lower court order permitting the federal government to cut off Medicaid funding to Louisiana because of its practice of paying only for abortions deemed necessary to save a mother's life.

Partial Birth Abortion: The Senate and House have voted to ban this barbaric procedure but President Clinton has adamantly refused to sign the appropriate measure.

STELLA MARIS: Apostleship of the Sea

Pope John Paul issued an apostolic letter Jan. 1, 1997, on the Apostleship of the Sea, "an organization concerned with the specific pastoral care of people of the sea."

People of the sea as defined in the document are:
•seafarers, those who are actually serving on merchant ships or fishing boats, and those who have undertaken a voyage by ship for any reason;
•"maritime personnel: 1. seafarers; 2. those who serve usually on shipboard because of work; 3. those who work on oil rigs; 4. pensioners retired from the aforesaid jobs; 5. students of maritime academies; 6. those who work in ports;
•"people of the sea: 1. seafarers and maritime personnel; 2. their spouses, minor children and all those who live in a maritime person's home even if he is not currently a seafarer (for example, pensioners); 3. those who work on a permanent basis with the Apostleship of the Sea."

The papal letter stated, with pastoral concern:
"Mindful of the unusual circumstances in which people of the sea live, and taking into account the privileges which for many years the Apostolic See has granted these faithful, the following is established:

"1. Maritime personnel can fulfill their Easter duty regarding Holy Communion throughout the year, after previously hearing an appropriate homily or catechesis about this precept.

"2. Seafarers are not bound by the law of fast and abstinence prescribed in Canon 1251; they are advised, however, when taking advantage of this dispensation, to undertake a comparable work of piety in place of the law of abstinence, and, as far as possible, to observe both laws on Good Friday in memory of the passion and death of Jesus Christ."

The letter also dealt with special conditions under which maritime personnel can gain specific indulgences.

Ministry Summary

The letter described in considerable detail the ministry of chaplains and authorities of the Apostleship of the Sea. Summarily, the document said:

"The chaplains and authorities of the Apostleship of the Sea will do their utmost to enable people of the sea to have easy recourse to the necessary means for living a holy life, and will recognize and promote the mission which all the faithful, and particularly lay people, exercise in the Church and in the maritime world according to their specific state."

"The Pontifical Council for the Pastoral Care of Migrants and Itinerant People is responsible for the overall direction of the Apostleship of the Sea."

Bishop promoters named by episcopal conferences in countries throughout the world and national directors are charged with responsibility for supporting and developing the ministry of priests, religious and lay persons who work among seafaring people in all kinds of maritime settings.

The Pontifical Council for the Pastoral Care of Migrants and Itinerant People reported in April, 1997, that "the ministry of the Apostleship of the Sea exists in some form or other in about 400 places in 91 countries.

(See separate entry.)

McVEIGH DEATH PENALTY

Archbishop Eusebius J. Beltran of Oklahoma City addressed the following letter to people of the archdiocese June 10, 1997, before Timothy McVeigh was sentenced to death for bombing the Murrah building in which 168 people were killed and many more were injured.

Two years ago, on Apr. 19, 1995, together with the entire nation but especially with our Oklahoma neighbors, we were jolted into a profound realization of the existence of evil. The bombing of the Murrah Building brought destruction, death, suffering, pain and sorrow. But, as a people of faith, we banded together to search the rubble, to provide whatever assistance we could to the rescuers and solace to the victims and their families. It was a terrible tragedy, yet the spirit of love, compassion and solidarity which emerged, while it could not restore the past, did positively affect us and indeed the future of our society. We have come to a greater appreciation of the gift of life as we witnessed the reality and uncertainty that surrounds us.

Following the recent guilty verdict handed down for Timothy McVeigh, many people have expressed their thoughts about the possibility that Mr. McVeigh might be sentenced to death. In the midst of these questions and with the memory of our loved ones still close to our hearts, I find myself compelled to proclaim my own convictions on this matter as well as my faith.

Against the Death Penalty

As a fellow citizen of Oklahoma City, I have shared in the anguish that touched each one of us a little more than two years ago. Throughout this incident, I have felt as though we stand much like those who stood at the foot of the cross and gazed upon profound suffering. From such a perspective, I believe there is much to be learned. Perhaps the most important lesson is found in recalling that our Lord suffered on the cross. He extended forgiveness to those who had harmed him. Indeed, his entire life was a message of healing and reconciliation. As men and women who place all our hope in that same compassionate mercy of God, we must never fail to acknowledge that we too are called to mercy and forgiveness.

In the past, the death penalty seemed to be a necessary protection for society. Therefore, in our Catholic tradition, capital punishment was allowed under certain strict circumstances. In more recent years, however, similar safeguards for society can be achieved in other ways. Actually, while the death penalty has not been excluded absolutely as a just punishment in Catholic theology, the teaching of the Church has gradually developed away from it. The Catholic bishops of the United States, in union with the teaching of Pope John Paul II, have come to see that the death penalty perpetuates a terrible cycle of violence, diminishes respect for human life and ultimately fails to ease the pain of those who grieve. I completely concur in this teaching, which repudiates the death penalty and acknowledges the dignity of human life and God's sole dominion over us.

Again, I extend my most sincere sympathy to those whose suffering has been intense and long-lasting. You are daily remembered in my prayers and Masses. May almighty God grant all of us healing and peace.

A Similar View

Archbishop Justin Rigali also commented on the unacceptability of the death penalty. In a column published in the *St. Louis Review* June 13, he said in part:

"While it is true that in the long history of the Catholic tradition the death penalty has not been excluded absolutely, it is likewise nevertheless true — especially since the encyclical *Evangelium Vitae* was given to the world by Pope John II in March of 1995 — that it is becoming ever more apparent that capital punishment is inconsistent with the Gospel of life that we profess. Our modern world has other ways to defend society and to promote justice.

"In his consideration of the punishment of those who have been found guilty of criminal actions, the Holy Father teaches this in the encyclical when he says that 'the nature and extent of the punishment must be carefully evaluated and decided upon, and ought not go to the extreme of executing the offender except in cases of absolute necessity; in other words, when it would not be possible otherwise to defend society. Today, however, as a result of steady improvements in the organization of the penal system, such cases are very rare if not practically nonexistent.' That teaching of the Pope is one which I have consistently made my own.

"This is, I realize, a difficult teaching for many. Nonetheless, it professes the truth about human life. As pastor of this local church, each time it has been opportune I have urged that the death penalty never be imposed. I do so now once again."

COR UNUM ACTIVITIES

"The activities of the Pontifical Council 'Cor Unum' for human and Christian advancement were continued throughout 1996," said a report in the Feb. 26, 1997, English-language edition of "L'Osservatore Romano."

Activities included: publication of a document on world hunger; efforts to cope with the serious situation in the Great Lakes region of Africa; humanitarian relief for disaster-stricken peoples; projects for integral development; circulation of the Pope's message for Lent; preparations for the 1999 Year of Charity; the work of papal foundations for the Sahel and for poor rural populations in Latin America.

Donations on behalf of the Pope for support of these activities included: 1.5 billion lire for aid to peoples affected by disasters and for community development projects; 4.3 billion lire allocated by the John Paul II Foundation for the Sahel to projects to fight drought and desertification; 22 billion lire earmarked by the Populorum Progressio Foundation for development projects for the communities of indigenous peoples, African-Americans, *mestizos* and *campesinos* in Latin America and the Caribbean.

World Hunger

"Cor Unum" made public Oct. 4, 1996, a document entitled "World Hunger. A Challenge to All: Development in Solidarity." The document, dealing with the plight of 800,000,000 people throughout the world and published just before the World Food Summit held in November in Rome, was widely circulated and elicited significant responses from the United Nations, governments of many nations, international and national relief agencies.

Pope John Paul, at a Christmas meeting with personnel of the Roman Curia, cited the "scandal" of hunger affecting one-fifth of the world's population. He commented: "It is necessary and urgent that states strive to pursue economic and food policies based not only on profit, but also on sharing and solidarity.

In this perspective, the Pontifical Council 'Cor Unum' recently published a document on world hunger, in which interesting proposals to encourage a more equitable distribution of food resources are made." The papal statement also committed the agency to continue efforts to make an even more effective contribution to ways and means of dealing with the unjust and reprehensible scourge of hunger.

Great Lakes Region

The report said: "The gaping wound afflicting the peoples of Rwanda since the tragic events of 1994 is still painful; new disturbances are occurring with worrying regularity in the other countries of the Great Lakes Region...

"The Holy Father has frequently appealed for reconciliation and solidarity, and 'Cor Unum' has relayed these appeals so that the attention of the Christian community and of funding organizations will remain focused on the problem. 'Cor Unum' has made donations for building houses for Rwandan refugees repatriated in their land of origin... The dicastery (agency) has actively participated in the various assemblies and meetings sponsored by the Committee of Coordination for Rwanda, which rapidly expanded its sphere of activity to include the whole Great Lakes Region. Aid was also sent in the Pope's name to refugees in Burundi, Tanzania and Zaire."

Natural Disasters

The report noted that "Cor Unum" had "a special interest in this area." Liaison was maintained with the U.N. Department for Humanitarian Affairs. The Pope made available at least a half-million dollars for the relief of victims of natural disasters in more than 30 countries.

Sahel Foundation

The John Paul II Foundation for the Sahel approved funding of more than four billion lire in support of a variety of development projects in the nine-country region. Funded projects included: 199 concerned with the environment, agriculture and renewable energy; 128 aimed at community guidance and management; 57 concerned with water supply and means of extraction; 18 focused on medical and health care; 20 in the technical and professional areas.

The foundation was established by Pope John Paul Feb. 22, 1994, to fight drought and desertification in the Sahel region, comprised of Burkino Faso, Cape Verde, Chad, The Gambia, Mali, Mauritania, Niger, Senegal and Guinea-Bissau.

Populorum Progressio

The Populorum Progressio Foundation, established by Pope John Paul Feb. 13, 1992, aims at promoting the integral development of the communities of the poorest *campesinos* in Latin America and the Caribbean.

In the four-year period of 1993 to 1996, the foundation funded 581 projects with a total sum of $4,628,449. One hundred and 59 projects were funded in 1996 with a total sum of $1,229,825.

In conclusion, the report said: "At the root of all these acts of solidarity and fraternal sharing there is a whole process of formation and education in love centered on the person and message of Christ. This occurs with ever-greater intensity wherever the Church is present, thanks to the tireless work of pastors, teachers and social and charitable organizations. The results of this work effectively show how the theological virtue of charity is the lifeblood of every initiative of solidarity by the people of God."

COMMON ECUMENICAL DECLARATIONS

POPE AND ANGLICAN ARCHBISHOP

This is the text of a common declaration signed by Pope John Paul and Anglican Archbishop George Carey Dec.5, 1996.

Once again in the city of Rome an Archbishop of Canterbury, His Grace George Carey representing the Anglican Communion, and the Bishop of Rome, His Holiness Pope John Paul II, have met together and joined in prayer.

Conscious that the second Christian millennium, now in its closing years, has seen division, even open hostility and strife between Christians, our fervent prayer has been for the grace of reconciliation. We have prayed earnestly for conversion — conversion to Christ and to one another in Christ. We have asked that Catholics and Anglicans may be granted the wisdom to know, and the strength to carry out, the Father's will. This will enable progress toward that full visible unity which is God's gift and our calling.

We have given thanks that in many parts of the world Anglicans and Catholics, joined in one baptism, recognize one another as brothers and sisters in Christ and give expression to this through joint prayer, common action and joint witness. This is a testimony to the communion we know we already share by God's mercy and demonstrates our intention that it should come to the fullness willed by Christ. We have given particular thanks for the spirit of faith in God's promises, persevering hope and mutual love which has inspired all who have worked for unity between the Anglican Communion and the Catholic Church since our predecessors, Archbishop Michael Ramsey and Pope Paul VI, met and prayed together. In the Church of St. Gregory on the Caelian Hill, we have remembered with gratitude the common heritage of Anglicans and Catholics rooted in the mission to the English people which Pope Gregory the Great entrusted to St. Augustine of Canterbury.

25 Years of Dialogue

For over 25 years a steady and painstaking international theological dialogue has been undertaken by the Anglican-Roman Catholic International Commission. We affirm the signs of progress provided in the statements of ARCIC II on the Eucharist and on the understanding of ministry and ordination, which have received an authoritative response from both partners of the dialogue. ARCIC II has produced further statements on salvation and the church, the understanding of the church as communion, and on the kind of life and fidelity to Christ we seek to share. These statements deserve to be more widely known. They require analysis, reflection and response.

At present, the international commission is seeking to further the convergence on authority in the church. Without agreement in this area, we shall not reach the full visible unity to which we are both committed. The obstacle to reconciliation caused by the ordination of women as priests and bishops in some provinces of the Anglican Communion has also become increasingly evident, creating a new situation. In view of this, it may be opportune at this stage in our journey to consult further about how the relationship between the Anglican Communion and the Catholic Church is to progress. At the same time, we encourage ARCIC to continue and deepen our theological dialogue, not only over issues connected with our present difficulties but also in all areas where full agreement has still to be reached.

Called To Preach and Witness

We are called to preach the Gospel "in season and out of season" (2 Tm. 4:2). In many parts of the world Anglicans and Catholics attempt to witness together in the face of growing secularism, religious apathy and moral confusion. Whenever they are able to give united witness to the Gospel, they must do so, for our divisions obscure the Gospel message of reconciliation and hope. We urge our people to make full use of the possibilities already available to them, for example, in the Catholic Church's "Directory for the Application of Principles and Norms of Ecumenism" (1993). We call on them to repent of the past, to pray for the grace of unity and to open themselves to God's transforming power, and to cooperate in all appropriate ways at local, national and provincial levels. We pray that the spirit of dialogue may prevail, which will contribute to reconciliation and prevent new difficulties from emerging. Whenever actions take place which show signs of an attitude of proselytism, they prevent our common witness and must be eliminated.

We look forward to the celebration of 2,000 years since the Word became flesh and dwelt among us (cf. Jn. 1:14). This is an opportunity to proclaim afresh our common faith in God who loved the world so much that he sent his Son, not to condemn the world, but so that the world might be saved through him (cf. Jn. 3:16-17). We encourage Anglicans and Catholics, with their Christian brothers and sisters, to pray, celebrate and witness together in the year 2000. We make this call with humility, recognizing that credible witness will only be fully given when Anglicans and Catholics, with their Christian brothers and sisters, have achieved that full, visible union that corresponds to Christ's prayer "that they may all be one ... so that the world may believe" (Jn. 17:21).

POPE AND CATHOLICOS

Pope John Paul and Aram I, Armenian Catholicos of Cilicia, signed a common declaration Jan. 25, 1997, saying in part:

The Bishop of Rome, successor of Peter, and the Catholicos of Cilicia pray that their communion of faith in Jesus Christ may progress because of the blood of the martyrs and the fidelity of the Fathers of the Gospel and the apostolic Tradition, manifesting itself in the rich diversity of their respective ecclesial traditions. Such a community of faith must be concretely expressed in the life of the faithful and must lead us toward full communion.

Thus, the two spiritual leaders stress the vital importance of sincere dialogue bearing on theological and pastoral areas, as well as on other dimensions of the life and witness of believers. The relations already existing are an experience that encourages direct and fruitful collaboration between them. Their Holinesses are firmly convinced that in this century, when Christian communities are more deeply engaged in ecumenical dialogue, a serious rapprochement supported by mutual respect and understanding is the only sound and reliable way to full communion.

The Catholic Church and the Catholicate of Cilicia also have an immense field of constructive cooperation before them. The contemporary world, because of ideologies expressed in materialistic values and by reason of the harm done by injustice and violence, represents a real risk to the integrity and identity of the Christian faith. Now more than ever, Christ's Church must, by her fidelity to the Gospel, bring the world a message of hope and charity and become the ardent herald of Gospel values.

Aram I's jurisdiction, headquartered in Antelias, Lebanon, extended to Syria, Iran, Cyprus and Greece.

CATECHETICAL TEXT DEFICIENCIES

Archbishop Daniel M. Buechlein of Indianapolis, at the June, 1997, meeting of the U.S. bishops, reported "rather consistent deficiencies" in catechetical texts in use in this country. Archbishop Buechlein, head of the bishops' Ad Hoc Committee to Oversee the Use of the Catechism, said that the more texts were reviewed, the more "that there seemed to be a number of doctrinal deficiencies common to many of them."

He listed the 10 most common weaknesses:

1. "Insufficient attention to the Trinity and the trinitarian structure of Catholic beliefs and teachings."

2. "Obscured presentation of the centrality of Christ in salvation history and insufficient emphasis on the divinity of Christ."

3. "Indistinct treatment of the ecclesial context of Catholic beliefs and magisterial (authoritative) teachings."

4. "Inadequate sense of a distinctively Christian anthropology."

5. "Insufficient emphasis on God's initiative in the world, with a corresponding overemphasis on human action."

6. "Insufficient recognition of the transforming effects of grace."

7. "Inadequate presentation of the sacraments."

8. "Deficient teaching on original sin and sin in general."

9. "Meager exposition of Christian moral life."

10. "Inadequate presentation of eschatology," the study of Christian beliefs about death, life after death and the end of the world."

Archbishop Buechlein said publishers had "been very cooperative in making changes" when notified about the deficiencies in their texts.

COMMUNION GUIDELINES

This is the text of "Guidelines for the Reception of Communion" approved by the U.S. bishops Nov. 14, 1996, for insertion in missalettes and related publications. The purpose of the guidelines is to prevent abuse in reception of the Eucharist.

For Catholics

As Catholics, we fully participate in the celebration of the Eucharist when we receive Holy Communion. We are encouraged to receive Communion devoutly and frequently. In order to be properly disposed to receive Communion, participants should not be conscious of grave sin and normally should have fasted for one hour. A person who is conscious of grave sin is not to receive the Body and Blood of the Lord without prior sacramental confession except for a grave reason where there is no opportunity for confession. In this case, the person is to be mindful of the obligation to make an act of perfect contrition, including the intention of confessing as soon as possible (Canon 916). A frequent reception of the sacrament of penance is encouraged for all.

For Our Fellow Christians

We welcome our fellow Christians to this celebration of the Eucharist as our brothers and sisters. We pray that our common baptism and the action of the Holy Spirit in this Eucharist will draw us closer to one another and begin to dispel the sad divisions which separate us. We pray that these will lessen and finally disappear, in keeping with Christ's prayer for us, "that they may all be one" (Jn 17:21).

Because Catholics believe that the celebration of the Eucharist is a sign of the reality of the oneness of faith and worship, members of those churches with whom we are not yet fully united are ordinarily not admitted to Holy Communion. Eucharistic sharing in exceptional circumstances by other Christians requires permission according to the directives of the diocesan bishop and the provisions of Canon Law (Canon 844, para 4). Members of the Orthodox churches, the Assyrian Church of the East and the Polish National Catholic Church are urged to re-spect the discipline of their own churches. According to Roman Catholic discipline, the Code of Canon Law does not object to the reception of Communion by Christians of these churches (Canon 844, para 3).

For Those Not Receiving Communion
All who are not receiving Holy Communion are encouraged to express in their hearts a prayerful desire for unity with the Lord Jesus and with one another.

For Non-Christians
We also welcome to this celebration those who do not share our faith in Jesus Christ. While we cannot admit them to Holy Communion, we ask them to offer their prayers for the peace and unity of the human family.

AGOSTINI V. FELTON

(By Patricia Zapor, CNS)
Church organizations, teachers' groups and government agencies across the country praised the Supreme Court's June 23 ruling that will allow public school teachers to conduct tax-funded remedial programs in religious schools.

The court ruled 5-to-4 in Agostini v. Felton to reverse its 1985 Aguilar v. Felton decision which found it unconstitutional for teachers employed by public schools to hold Title I remedial classes for low-income students on the property of religious schools.

Supporters of stronger church-state separation sounded the only negative notes in response to the ruling, although some who agreed with it voiced apprehension about how the decision might be applied to other types of public-parochial school collaboration.

Appropriate Decision
At a minimum, the decision means public school districts no longer have to pay out tens of thousands of dollars a year from their Title I grants to provide mobile classrooms or rented space in which to hold the remedial classes for students from Catholic, Lutheran, Hebrew or other religiously-affiliated schools.

President Clinton, Education Secretary Richard W. Riley, Catholic bishops and representatives of public and private teachers' groups were among those who said the ruling was appropriate and necessary.

"Because of today's ruling, all school children, whether in public or private schools, can benefit equally from the important supplemental remedial programs of Title I," said a statement from President Clinton. "No longer will children have to leave their school buildings in order to get the assistance they need."

Background
Title I was established in 1965 to pay for remedial education for low-income children no matter what type of school they attended. The 1985 ruling came out of a lawsuit by New York taxpayers who objected to public school teachers working in parochial schools.

An appeal was made to the Supreme Court to reconsider its 1985 ruling on the grounds that subsequent court decisions invalidated Aguilar. In the June 23 ruling, the court agreed.

U.S. Solicitor General Walter Dellinger had argued at the Supreme Court in favor of the finding the court made — that the separation of church and state is not endangered by having tax-paid teachers provide the remedial classes at parochial schools.

The president of the National Catholic Educational Association called the decision "a victory for the nation."

"Giving children improved educational opportunities results in better students, better citizens," said a statement from Leonard DeFiore, president of the group representing Catholic educators.

The National Education Association and the American Federation of Teachers, which represent public school teachers, agreed.

"Now, rather than millions of dollars being spent on the senseless purchase of vans, teachers will be able to go into classrooms to provide remedial services," said a statement from Sandra Feldman, president of the American Federation of Teachers. "It makes a lot more sense to teach in a classroom than in a truck."

Guidelines
The U.S. Education Department issued guidelines July 18 for bringing Title I educational programs into parochial schools. Following are some of the regulations.

• Only public employees may serve as Title I instructors and counselors.

• Assignment of public school personnel to parochial schools must be made without regard to religious affiliation of the employee.

• Religious symbols must be removed from classrooms used for Title I services.

• Title I employees are accountable only to public school supervisors and may not participate in team teaching or religious activities of a parochial school.

• No religious material may be used in Title I course work.

RELIGIOUS FREEDOM LAW OVERTURNED

(Patricia Zapor, CNS)
Congress had no constitutional right to try to get around the Supreme Court's religious rights rulings by passing the Religious Freedom Restoration Act, the high court ruled June 25, 1997, in the case of Boerne v. Flores.

In the 6-to-3 opinion in a case involving a Catholic parish in Boerne, Texas, in the Archdiocese of San Antonio, the court rebuked Congress for overstepping its constitutional authority with the 1993 law.

"Our national experience teaches that the Constitution is preserved best when each part of the government respects both the Constitution and the proper actions and determinations by the other branches," said the majority opinion, written by Justice Anthony Kennedy.

He was joined by Chief Justice William Rehnquist and Justices John Paul Stevens, Clarence Thomas, Ruth Bader Ginsburg and Antonin Scalia in the key points of the ruling.

Courts' Authority

The courts, not Congress, have the authority to decide what constitutional rights exist, Kennedy said.

"Congress does not enforce a constitutional right by changing what the right is," Kennedy wrote. "It has been given the power 'to enforce,' not the power to determine what constitutes a constitutional violation."

Kennedy said, against the background of judicial interpretation, it is up to the court to decide how to address legal precedents in later cases and controversies.

"RFRA was designed to control cases and controversies such as the one before us; but, as the provisions of the federal statute here invoked are beyond congressional authority, it is this court's precedent, not RFRA, which must control," Kennedy wrote.

The case arose when St. Peter the Apostle Parish in Boerne relied on the Religious Freedom Restoration Act to challenge a local law preventing it from tearing down and rebuilding its church.

RFRA was passed to reverse the effects of the Supreme Court's 1990 Smith v. Employment ruling.

In Smith, the court found that the religious rights of an employee to smoke peyote during a Native American ritual were superseded by an Oregon state law making the hallucinogenic substance illegal.

As lower courts interpreted the Smith ruling to shift the historic balance of First Amendment rights and government authority to give greater weight to state laws over religious rights, religious groups and politicians teamed up to create RFRA.

At Issue

Boerne v. Flores — Archbishop Patrick F. Flores — arose in 1993 as St. Peter's Parish sought the permits necessary to tear down its circa 1923 church building to replace it with one large enough for the growing parish. The permits were blocked because the building was within Boerne's historic preservation district. The parish offered to leave the church's mission-style front wall intact and build a larger sanctuary behind it, but the preservation group vetoed any such structural changes.

That led the archdiocese, acting on behalf of the parish, to sue on the grounds that the local regulations were infringing on the religious rights of parishioners.

In January, 1996, the 5th U.S. Circuit Court of Appeals overruled a Texas federal court and found RFRA met standards of constitutionality.

At subsequent oral arguments, many of the justices' questions and comments seemed to chastise Congress for trying to legislate around their interpretation of the Constitution.

In overturning RFRA the Supreme Court only addressed the constitutionality of the parish's claim that it should be exempt from the local ordinance under RFRA.

In the summer of 1997, the basic question of whether the parish's plans may be approved remains to be settled by lower courts against the backdrop of the court's rulings prior to RFRA.

Chopko Comment

Mark Chopko, general counsel to the U.S. Catholic Conference, said in comment the court's majority opinion made it clear that the justices were unhappy that Congress passed RFRA to get around their interpretation of the Constitution in Smith. Less clear was whether the court would accept any legislation to protect religious rights, whether from Congress or state legislatures.

POPE JOHN PAUL IN HUNGARY

Pope John Paul visited Hungary Sept. 6 and 7, 1996; it was his second visit there and the 73rd foreign trip of his pontificate.

"Christ Our Hope" was the theme of the visit, during which he celebrated Mass before thousands of people in Gyor and spoke about a variety of subjects, including Hungarian identity and Christian unity. Special events were celebrations of the 1100th anniversary of the Magyar Conquest of 896 and the millennium of the founding in 996 of an historic abbey.

Following are highlights of the visit.

Purpose of the Visit

On arrival Sept. 6 at Budapest's Ferihegy International Airport, Pope John Paul said the reasons for his pastoral visit were especially significant because "this year Hungary is celebrating its 1100th anniversary and, in particular, is commemorating the millennium of the foundation of the (Benedictine) Abbey of Pannonhalma."

He also said the celebration of Jubilee Year 2000 would be "a providential occasion for the generous Hungarian people to renew their faith in Christ, whose light has illuminated their path through the centuries. For believers, Christ is the Way, the Truth and the Life. Therefore, with ever greater ardor may the saving message of his word be heard on Hungarian soil and may Hungary's citizens feel its invigorating spiritual effect ...

"No other reason but that of renewing this proclamation of salvation has brought me among you once more. I have come to share the anxieties and the hopes of your people, convinced ... that the renewal of Hungary will take place."

Benedictine Influence

During Vespers Sept. 6 at the historic Benedictine Archabbey of Pannonhalma, the Pope recalled its foundation in 996 and its influence on Hungarian and European civilization.

"St. Benedict and his spiritual sons 'renewed the face of the earth' (Ps. 104:30) and Europe, especially in the first millennium, is indebted in great part to them for the overwhelming cultural and social renewal from which it benefitted. The simple phrase, *ora et labora,* laid the foundations for a vast program thanks to which the Continent, after the great migrations of peoples, began to take on the cultural patterns which have characterized even to our own day the European nation's and their particular role in the world....

"Celebrating the 1,000th anniversary of the foundation of Pannonhalma Abbey makes us recall, in a certain sense, a millennium of that Benedictine Europe upon whose foundations European civilization was built, and the civilization of your own country, Hungary."

Addressing the Benedictine monks regarding their role in the quest for unity among Christians, the Holy Father said: "In your daily ministry, work to foster Christian unity, engaging in dialogue with everyone. From your commitment to dialogue, to listening, to promoting common ground, the ecumenical movement can benefit greatly. May your abbey be a house which is always open to the needs of the brethren."

Look to the Future with Trust

Despite difficulties of the past and gloomy forecasts, "look to your future with trust," the Pope urged the thousands of people attending Mass Sept. 7 in Ipari Park, Gyor.

"Do not be discouraged by economic and social difficulties, by unemployment, by widespread poverty, by the decline of moral values in the generation which grew up without religion. The temptation of letting go, passively accepting the situation, is great indeed. St. Paul described the pagans as 'those who have no hope' (cf. 1 Thes. 4:13). We Christians, on the other hand, draw life from the presence of Christ. Christ is our hope! We are the sheep of Christ, the Good Shepherd, who is always with us."

"At the end of the 20th century, how great is the need to know Christ: his person, his life, his teaching! There are numerous ideologies and cultural trends which promote themselves; they promise happiness, success and freedom, but they cannot explain the real purpose of life. Christ alone is the Way, the Truth and the Life. He did not simply point the way to salvation, but said: 'He who be-

lieves has eternal life' (Jn. 6:47). In him is revealed the truth for which all people long in the depths of their heart."

"Dear Brothers and Sisters: Look to your future with trust. Do not be discouraged by the pessimistic predictions made by some people. Do not be slowed by the obstacles placed in your way by others. With God's help and your own commitment, the difficulties will be overcome and the objectives set for yourselves will be met. Yours is the task of 'putting off your old nature which belongs to your former way of life,' in order that you might 'put on the new nature, created after the likeness of God in true righteousness and holiness' (Eph. 4:22-24). This is Christianity's unending program: renewal in spirit and in mind, putting on the new nature which is alive in Christ, the risen Lord."

The Task of Bishops

This was the subject of the Holy Father's remarks at luncheon with the bishops Sept. 7.

"The vocation and task of each one of you is to lead the people entrusted to you toward 'the new heavens and the new earth,' of which the Scriptures speak (cf. Rv. 21:1; 2 Pt. 3:13). Remain firm in this vocation. For your fellow citizens, who for centuries have defended Christian Europe without ever losing hope, be courageous ministers of the Gospel of God, the vehicle of salvation for all men and women. God, in his mysterious Providence, has given you this task. Accept it with trust and ask him for the strength to persevere. Safeguard, above all, the integrity of the word of God and of Christian teaching."

He called on the bishops to be "defenders of the human person," "defenders of human life," defenders "of those who are weakest" and of the family.

Reorganization of Church Life

Addressing representatives of the Diocese of Gyor, the Pope spoke about the need for reorganization of church life in Hungary in the wake of "decades of great trials" under dictatorial governments and other influences. Accordingly, he said: "The commitment to a renewed proclamation of the Gospel in Hungarian society requires as its primary objective the rediscovery of Jesus Christ ... and full adherence to his truth."

"A renewed apostolic commitment cannot fail to lead Christians to question themselves about the reasons for religious indifference and moral relativism, about the failure to bear witness to one's faith, about inconsistency and unfaithfulness, about a permissive attitude toward abortion and other crimes directed against life in the womb."

"The many and varied tasks to be done makes the dedicated and responsible commitment of the laity altogether necessary. The Church asks them to assume the responsibilities of their state, keeping in mind that the proper sphere for their evangelizing activity is the vast and complicated world of politics, social concerns, the economy, the mass media, the sciences and arts, international life."

"The laity's task becomes ever more important in the face of the new opportunities for taking part in public life. In that sphere, the Christian lay faithful, driven by the conviction that the kingdom of

God is at one and the same time a gift and a commitment, will avoid every form of fundamentalism and will adopt an attitude of dialogue and service, with full respect for the dignity of every person, which always remains the true goal of all social action."

Challenge to Youths

At the airport before leaving for Rome, the Pope challenged youths "to seek an understanding of the events of this century which is now coming to an end. Learn about them and reflect on them so that the errors and suffering which preceded you will become useful lessons for you.

"The third millennium ... will begin with you. You are the hope of your nation. Yours, therefore, is the duty to put the stamp of new vitality on its history. Yours is not an easy inheritance! But, with God's help, you will be able to bear it.

"Do not be discouraged, and stay on the path of truth and faith.

"Accept the challenge which is set before you. Be the builders of a new world, a world firmly set on the foundations of those values which inspired the actions of St. Stephen the King.

"Know that God, the Lord of history, will help you bring this mission of yours to completion for the good of all."

POPE JOHN PAUL IN FRANCE

Pope John Paul, on the 74th foreign trip of his pontificate, made a pastoral visit to France Sept. 19 to 22, 1996.

During the four-day visit, his fifth to France, the Holy Father celebrated three outdoor Masses, made nearly 20 other public appearances and delivered about 12 speeches on timely and pastoral subjects.

Following are the itinerary of the visit and coverage of principal events and subjects of addresses.

Itinerary

Sept. 19: Arrival at Tours; private meetings with President Jacques Chirac and other civic officials; celebration of Evening Prayer with religious from the western region of France.

Sept. 20: Flight from Tours to Lorient; Mass at the shrine of Sainte-Anne-d'Auray and visit to the same-named basilica; meeting with young couples and their children; return to Tours.

Sept. 21: At Tours: Mass marking the 1,600th anniversary of the death of St. Martin; meeting with representatives of poor, sick and suffering people at the Basilica of St. Martin.

Sept. 22: Flight from Tours to Reims; Mass on the occasion of the 1,500th anniversary of the baptism of Clovis; meetings with members of the French bishops' conference, pastoral workers and representatives of lay persons; private meeting with Prime Minister Alain Juppe before departure for Rome.

Pilgrim Visitor

On arrival at the Tours airport, Pope John Paul said: "I come as a pilgrim to meet the Catholics of France and to join with them in prayer in those places that are important to the religious history of their country and of Europe, in order to strengthen and deepen their Christian life and faith." He praised the French people "who continue a long tradition of solidarity and brotherhood."

With controversy over commemoration of the baptism of Clovis in mind, the Pope said: "It is to France's credit that it is rising above legitimate differences of opinion in remembering that the baptism of Clovis is one of the events that brought it (the nation) into being. It is good for the citizens of a country to turn back to their history in celebrating the values that motivated their forebears and that remain

both a foundation of their present life and an orientation for their future."

Vendee Martyrs

At Saint-Laurent-sur-Sevre in the afternoon of Sept.19, The Pope praised the martyrs of the Vendee who gave their lives during the French Revolution rather than renounce the freedom and independence of the Church. "In the numerous acts of witness which have come down to us, it is moving to see that the people of the Vendee remained attached to their parishes and their priests despite the cruelty of the persecution."

"You are the heirs of the men and women who were courageous enough to remain faithful to the Church of Jesus Christ at a time when its freedom and independence were threatened. They were not detached from the movements of the time and they sincerely desired the necessary renewal of a society, but they could not accept the imposition of a break with the universal Church and, in particular, with the Successor of Peter."

The Pope urged young people: "Be brave. Do not let yourselves be overcome by the indifference so widespread around you. Do not let yourselves be impressed by those who reject the demands of our Christian faith or who scorn it.... I pray that the martyrs of times past will guide you on your way ... and communicate to you their joy in believing and their courage in serving, after the example of Christ."

Faithful Witness of Religious

At Vespers with religious of western France, the Holy Father said their "practice of the evangelical counsels has no other meaning than to witness with an undivided heart to the infinite love of God, man's greatest good.... Your life also witnesses to the freedom which results from filial, not servile, dependence on God."

He called on religious to "enthusiastically put into practice today the charisms of your founders. Continue to write the loving history of your congregations!"

Message of Hope

The Holy Father spoke about the missionary tradition of the Church as he celebrated Mass in the morning of Sept. 20 near the Shrine of Sainte-Anne-d'Auray in Brittany. He said in his homily: "Today, I have come to invite you to deepen the hope that is in you and around you. Like your fathers in the faith, be builders of the Church in the new generations!"

"The Church is sent to all peoples in their different societies, to proclaim to them the salvation God offers them all. All Christians are responsible for this mission. Together, they must work so as to establish the kingdom of God.... Each member of the lay faithful should always be fully aware of being a member of the Church, yet entrusted with a unique task which cannot be done by another and which is to be fulfilled for the good of all."

"We hope that the Church in France, continuing her journey in the footsteps of her fathers in faith, proud of her centuries-old tradition, will continue to shine with a salutary radiance in the history of peoples and nations."

Light and Salt

The Pope told young parents and their children that they are "the salt of the earth" and "the light of the world," during a Liturgy of the Word in the afternoon of Sept. 20 at the Shrine of Sainte-Anne-d'Auray. "The Church counts on you parents ... so that the young may get to know Christ and follow him with generosity.... You are invited to show the world the beauty of parenthood and to promote the culture of life, which consists in accepting the children given to you and helping them grow. Every human being conceived has the right to life."

The Holy Father also said the Church is "concerned for those who are separated, divorced or divorced and remarried; they remain members of the Christian community. In fact, as baptized persons they can, and indeed must, share in the Church's life, while accepting in faith the truth of which the Church is bearer in its discipline regarding marriage."

An Exceptional Witness

The Holy Father commemorated the 16th centenary of the death of St. Martin during a morning Mass Sept. 21 at the Tours airport. He called Martin "a remarkable witness of evangelical love," "a man of prayer," "one of the founders of monasticism in the West," an outstanding bishop in the history of the Church in France.

"St. Martin," the Pope said, "leaves you an exceptional witness of belonging to Christ. His total availability is a model and encouragement for you. Continue to announce the Gospel as he did himself.... Offer your life to Christ with trust and serenity; he will take it and make it the very best possible."

Concern for Poor and Suffering

During a Liturgy of the Word with poor, sick and suffering people Sept. 21, Pope John Paul said that in St. Martin "the Church recognizes the example of a Christian totally concerned about his neighbor."

"Like St. Martin," he added, "we are invited to open our eyes and recognize in the poor man dying of cold at the city gates, in the stranger who knocks at our door, a brother to be welcomed and loved. A society is judged by how it treats life's wounded and the attitude it adopts toward them."

"Every human person, however destitute he may be, is created in the image and likeness of God, and nothing can deprive him of that dignity. Whatever his origin, whatever the weight of his problems, to refuse to see him is to condemn oneself to understanding nothing about life."

"Concern for the poor is one of the major criteria of belonging to Christ. It should mark the Christian's temporal commitment." We are called to "serve everyone, those we love and those we do not love enough.:... The Church would be seriously lacking in her mission if she did not remind everyone of this urgent duty to do everything possible, in the rich societies of the West and in every society, to root out the scourges which continue to rage across our planet. Christ came 'to preach the Good News to the poor.' None of his disciples, none of his brethren, is dispensed from taking part in this exacting, salutary and gratifying work."

Baptism of Clovis

The Pope celebrated Mass Sept. 22 at the Reims airport before a throng of more than 200,000 people, marking the 15th centenary of the baptism of Clovis, King of the Franks. He said in his homily: "By accepting the Catholic faith Clovis, in his own way and according to the ideas of his time, was able to lead different peoples toward the founding of a single nation.

"It is thus fitting that, in keeping with its deepest feelings and beliefs, and within the limits of its competence and its particular goals, France should wish to honor the memory of one of the significant moments of its origins with civic initiatives, cultural events and religious celebrations. It is to France's credit that it is rising above legitimate differences of opinion in remembering that the baptism of Clovis is one of the events that brought it into being. It is good for the citizens of a country to turn back to their history in celebrating the values that motivated their forebears and that remain both a foundation of their present life and an orientation for their future."

The Pope also said: The Church "does not see her heritage as a treasure of the past, but as a powerful inspiration to advance on the pilgrimage of faith, following ever-new paths.... The Church is always a Church of the present age."

Youth and Jubilee 2000

These were two of the many topics mentioned by the Pope in an address to members of the French bishops' conference Sept. 22.

"Do not slacken in your efforts to reach out to the young," he said, "in spite of the aging of many leaders in your dioceses. The young want to be listened to, to be guided and to have their efforts recognized in church life. Large numbers of youths are preparing for the World (Youth) Day in Paris (in 1997). Tell them that the Pope counts on them to welcome their comrades from the whole world and to share the best of their experiences."

Of the great Jubilee celebration in the year 2000, the Pope said: "We must look clearly at past ages, as we do today in commemorating the baptism of Clovis, from which starting point the nation, established little by little, developed strong ties with the Church of Christ. But the Jubilee invites us to be open to new perspectives. Without doubt, it is a question of appreciating what is most noble in the tradition of your nation, whose influence has been so great; but we do so in order to learn from that experience how better to respond to the challenges of our time.

Words before Departure

The Pope delivered two addresses before taking off from the Reims airport for the flight to Rome.

He urged pastoral workers of the Archdiocese of Reims to give true witness to the faith in fidelity to the commitment of their baptism and in participation in various forms of pastoral service.

At the airport with Prime Minister Alain Juppe, Cardinal Jean-Marie Lustiger and other dignitaries, the Pope reviewed highlights of his visit and added: "I offer all the French people my heartfelt good wishes for prosperity in fraternal understanding. May your nation remain welcoming. May it continue to share its culture. May it contribute to continually advancing the ideals of liberty, equality and fraternity which it has presented to the world."

POPE JOHN PAUL IN SARAJEVO

Pope John Paul, "pilgrim of peace," spent 25 hours of Apr. 12-13, 1997, in Sarajevo, for meetings with bishops, priests and religious, lay persons, community leaders of Bosnia-Herzegovina and representatives of other churches.

Peace and reconciliation were key themes of several addresses.

Pilgrim of Peace

On arrival at the Sarajevo airport, Pope John Paul called himself "a pilgrim of peace and friendship desirous of serving as best I can the cause of peace in justice and of reconciliation."

Addressing government leaders and others who greeted him, the Pope said in part: "I gladly take the opportunity of this direct contact with the leaders of Bosnia-Herzegovina to extend to each of them my cordial encouragement to continue along the path of peace and the rebuilding of the country and its institutions. It is not a matter of material reconstruction alone; what is needed above all is to provide for the spiritual rebuilding of minds and hearts, which the devastating fury of war has often shaken and perhaps even compromised the values which are the foundation of all civil coexistence. It is here, from the spiritual foundations of human coexistence, that a new beginning must be made.

Never again war! Never again hatred and intolerance! This is the lesson taught by this century and this millennium which are drawing to a close. This is the message with which I begin my pastoral visit. The inhuman logic of violence must be replaced by the constructive logic of peace."

Commitment to Reconciliation

This was the theme of the Pope's remarks in an address to priests, men and women religious, and seminarians at Sarajevo's Sacred Heart Cathedral early in the evening of Apr. 12.

"The time has come for a profound examination of conscience. The time has come for a decisive commitment to reconciliation and peace.

"As ministers of God's love, you have been sent to dry the tears of the many people who grieve for their murdered relatives, to hear the impotent cry of those who have seen their rights trampled and their families torn apart. As brothers and sisters to all, be near to the refugees and the evacuees, to those driven from their homes and deprived of the resources with which

they planned to build their future. Give support to the elderly, orphans and widows. Encourage the young, who often have been cheated of serene passage into adult life and forced by the harshness of conflict to grow up much too soon.

"We need to say loud and strong: Never again war! We need each day to make a renewed effort to encounter others and to make a personal examination of conscience, not only about one's failings, but also about the energy one is willing to invest in building peace. We need to acknowledge the primacy of ethical, moral and spiritual values, by defending the right of every individual to live in peace and harmony, and by condemning every form of intolerance and persecution rooted in ideologies which show contempt for persons in their inviolable dignity."

Give and Seek Forgiveness

"Let us forgive and let us ask for forgiveness," said the Holy Father at a Mass celebrated in wind- and snow-swept Kosevo Stadium Apr. 13 before a throng of 50,000 people.

"The hope of all people of good will is that what Sarajevo symbolizes will remain confined to the 20th century, and that its tragedies will not be repeated in the millennium about to begin."

"We ask the Prince of Peace, through the intercession of Mary his Mother ... that Sarajevo may become a model of coexistence and peaceful cooperation between peoples of different ethnic origins and religions for the whole of Europe."

"When in 1994 I wanted so intensely to come here among you, I referred to a thought that had come to be extraordinarily significant at a crucial moment of European history: 'Let us forgive and let us ask for forgiveness.' It was said then that the time was not right. Has not that time now come?

"I return today, therefore, to this thought and to the words which I wish to repeat, so that they can come into the minds of all those who are united in the painful experience of your city and land, of all the peoples and nations torn apart by war: 'Let us forgive and let us ask for forgiveness.'

" If Christ is to be our advocate with the Father, we cannot fail to utter these words. We cannot fail to undertake the difficult but necessary pilgrimage of forgiveness, which leads to a profound reconciliation."

Task of the Bishops

The Pope addressed the bishops' conference of Bosnia-Herzegovina after Mass Apr. 13.

"The conflict which took place in your region for five very long years puts before you problems which are certainly not easy. With the din of arms ended, the will to build peace must now become ever stronger. The first task which awaits you on this arduous path is to heal minds tried by suffering and, at times, hardened by feelings of hatred and revenge."

"You are called to be the bearers of a new culture which, flowing from the inexhaustible source of the Gospel, preaches respect for everyone; it calls for mutual forgiveness of faults as the presupposition of the renewal of civil life; it fights with the arms of love to ensure that the will to cooperate on the promotion of the one common good will be strengthened."

"After the recent violence, it is a question of re-building not only the Christian community but also civil society."

"The witness of charity favors greater understanding between the different cultures and religions which flourish in this region, since suffering and need have no frontiers."

"The method of dialogue, pursued with perseverance and in depth, must in the first place mark relations with your Orthodox brothers and sisters, and also the other Christian brethren with whom we are united by many bonds of faith. With cordial words and a sincere attitude, you should also look for opportunities for meeting and understanding the followers of Islam. This will favor the establishment of peaceful coexistence in mutual respect for the rights of every individual and with every people."

Meetings with Community Leaders

Reconciliation, mutual forgiveness and respect were themes of Pope John Paul's remarks to representatives of religious and political communities Apr. 13.

Serbian Orthodox: "Divine grace unites us in our faith in the one and triune God ... and makes us one in our esteem and love for the Sacred Scriptures, which constitute the common roots of the doctrine preached by the Fathers and enunciated ever since the first ecumenical councils. We are called to make ourselves proclaimers of this doctrine, in the footsteps of the apostles to whom the ministry of reconciliation was entrusted.

"This is a task which ... impels us to join forces in order to offer to our contemporaries ... the only word which truly heals and the grace which gives hope. After the years of the deplorable fratricidal war, at the approaching dawn of a new Christian millennium, we all feel the urgent need for a real reconciliation between Catholics and Orthodox.... Let us forgive and let us ask for forgiveness; this is the first step for creating new trust and new relationships between all those who recognize in the Son of God the sole Savior of humanity."

Political Leaders: "Building a true and lasting peace is a great task entrusted to everyone. Certainly, much depends on those who have public responsibilities. But the future of peace, while largely entrusted to institutional formulations ... depends no less decisively on a renewed solidarity of minds and hearts. It is this interior attitude which must be fostered, both within the frontiers of Bosnia-Herzegovina and also in relations with neighboring states and the community of nations. But an attitude of this kind can only be established on the foundation of forgiveness. For the edifice of peace to be solid, against the background of so much blood and hatred, it will have to be built on the courage of forgiveness. People must know how to ask for forgiveness and to forgive!"

Muslims: "The time has come to resume a sincere dialogue of brotherhood, accepting and offering forgiveness; the time has come to overcome the hatred and vengeance which still hinder the reestablishment of genuine peace in Bosnia-Herzegovina."

"It is my hope that the communities of Islam, a religion of prayer, can join in the prayer which all people of good will raise to almighty God, to implore, with unity of purpose, an active peace which enables people to live and work together effectively for the common good."

Jews: "The great spiritual patrimony which unites us in the divine word proclaimed in the Law and the Prophets is for all of us a constant and sure guide on the path of peace, harmony and mutual respect. In fact, it is God who proclaims peace to his people and who guarantees the good things which come from it. He evokes in us a powerful commitment to bring it about, for peace is his design for the People of the Covenant."

"Let us go forward courageously as true brothers and heirs of the promises, on the path of reconciliation and mutual forgiveness."

POPE JOHN PAUL IN THE CZECH REPUBLIC

Pope John Paul, on the 76th foreign trip of his pontificate, visited the region of the Czech Republic for the third time Apr. 25 to 27, 1997, to participate in celebrations marking the millennium of the martyrdom of St. Adalbert, the first Czech bishop of Prague.

Significant events of his visit were his meeting Apr. 25 with the bishops of the country in Prague; Mass for youths at Hradec Kralove and a meeting with sick persons and religious at the Brevnov Monastery, Apr. 26; a Mass commemorating the life and death of St. Adalbert, celebrated before 100,000 people, and an ecumenical prayer service in Prague, Apr. 27.

Following are excerpts from several of the addresses he delivered during his weekend in the Czech Republic.

To Honor St. Adalbert

On arrival at Prague-Ruzyne International Airport, Pope John Paul stated the reason for his visit:

"We wish to celebrate on Sunday the Solemnity of St. Adalbert and, on that occasion, to meditate on the message that emerges from the decade of spiritual renewal" that preceded the celebration.

"The Millennium and the Decade: It is precisely to experience with you these two great moments of the historical and spiritual life of your country that I have returned. And I have come all the more willingly because this year 1997 is also the first year of the three-year period of immediate preparation for the great Jubilee of the Year 2000."

St. Adalbert, the Pope observed, was "the first Czech to occupy the See of Prague, the first Czech of truly European importance.... St. Adalbert, along with the patrons of Europe, Benedict and Cyril and Methodius, belongs among the founders of Christian culture in Europe, especially in Central Europe."

Challenges

In an address to the Czech bishops, the Holy Father called attention to challenges facing them, saying they were "no less demanding than those" which confronted St. Adalbert.

"I think in the first place of religious indifference which ....leads many people to live as if God did not exist, or to be content with a vague religiosity incapable of adequately responding to the problem of truth and the duty of consistency."

He also said: "Forty years of systematic repression of the Church, the elimination of her pastors, bishops and priests, the intimidation of individuals and families, weigh heavily upon the present generation."

Specifically, the Pope cited problems related to family morality, the influence of pleasure-seeking, the need for vocations to the priesthood and religious life, the training of young people, the lack of clear guidelines for church-state relations, the question of restitution of church properties confiscated by the government and handed over to the Orthodox, and the teaching of religion in state schools.

The New Leaven of Youth

The Pope called on young people to be courageous witnesses to their faith and to spread the Gospel in their country.

"On the threshold of the third millennium, you are living in a situation that, under certain aspects, is like the situation of the first Christians. The world around them did not know the Gospel. But they did not lose their way. Once they received the gift of the Holy Spirit, they kept close to the apostles, with fraternal love for one another. They knew that they were the new leaven which the declining Roman world needed. United like this in love, they overcame all resistance.

"You too, be like them! Be Church, to bring today's world the joyful news of the Gospel. St. Adalbert was a wholehearted servant of the Church. You too, be the same! The Church needs you! After 40 years of attempts to silence her, she is experiencing here among you a wonderful revival, even in the midst of many difficulties. She is counting on your fresh energies, on the contribution of your intelligence and enthusiasm. Have confidence in the Church, just as she has confidence in you."

Bearers of the Cross

At the Archabbey of Brevnov, founded by St. Adalbert in 992, the Pope addressed the sick and members of religious communities.

To the sick, he said: "The Church is grateful to you

for the patience, the Christian resignation and indeed the generosity and dedication with which you carry ... the cross which Jesus has placed upon your shoulders....

"I entrust to you my intentions for the universal Church and for the Church in your country. Offer up your sufferings for the needs of the new evangelization of the Church in mission lands ... and for those who are distant or who have lost the faith. I also ask you to pray for the work being done in this country, for your bishops and priests, and for an increase of vocations to the priesthood and the religious life, and for the cause of ecumenism."

Pillars in the Lord's Temple

Speaking to men and women religious, the Holy Father said: "The Lord wants to place you too as pillars in his spiritual temple, the Church, for the new evangelization. In the new climate of freedom which you are now experiencing and among profound transformations in culture and mentality, you are realizing, perhaps more than in the past, how the consecrated life meets resistance and obstacles, and how it can appear difficult and lacking in purpose.

"Do not lose heart! Communicate lofty and demanding ideals to the young men and women who knock on the doors of your houses. Pass on to them the experience of the paschal mystery in daily religious life. Live intensely the splendor of love, from which springs the beauty of total consecration to God."

Saint for Christians Today

In a homily delivered during the solemn Mass which climaxed his visit to the Czech Republic, Pope John Paul said: "St. Adalbert is a saint for the Christians of today. He invites them not to be defensive, not to keep for themselves the treasury of truths in their possession, with an attitude of sterile self-defense against the world. On the contrary, he asks them to be open to present-day society, to seek out all that is good and valid in it, in order to raise it up and, if necessary, to purify it in the light of the Gospel."

In conclusion, the Pope prayed: "May the work of salvation first begun in this land by St. Adalbert remain steadfast and bear abundant fruit among you, his fellow-countrymen, as also among those to whom he was sent."

Ecumenical Opportunities

Not long after the Sunday Mass at Prague's Letna esplanade, the Pope took part in an ecumenical prayer service in St. Vitus Cathedral. Among representatives of other churches in attendance was Dr. Smetana, president of the National Council of Churches (of the Evangelical Church of the Bohemian Brethren).

The Pope called attention to the fact that "the search for the truth makes us aware of our sinfulness. We are divided from one another because of mutual misunderstandings, often due to mistrust, if not enmity. We have sinned. We have distanced ourselves from the spirit of Christ."

Nevertheless, "I am happy to acknowledge the efforts of reconciliation and dialogue which in this land the various churches and ecclesial communities are making in order to heal past wounds."

"Much work remains to be done; there are opportunities not to be lost, heavenly gifts not to be overlooked, in order (for us) to respond to what the Lord expects from each and every one of the baptized. It is important that all the churches concern themselves with the theological dimension of ecumenical dialogue and persevere in a frank and serious examination of the growing convergences. We must seek unity as the Lord wants it, and for this we must be ever more converted to the demands of his kingdom. We are called to be, following the example of Bishop Adalbert, fellow workers of truth, hope and love."

POPE JOHN PAUL IN LEBANON

The Pope, on the 77th foreign trip of his pontificate, paid a 31-hour visit to Lebanon May 10 and 11, 1997, as reported by CNS correspondent John Thavis.

From an altar built upon the rubble of war, Pope John Paul urged Lebanese to put aside their differences and make their country into a model of Christian-Muslim harmony.

The papal appeal capped a 31-hour visit that prompted an outpouring of good will by hundreds of thousands of Lebanese Christians and Muslims.

"Spirit of God, pour your light and your love into human hearts to achieve reconciliation between individuals, within families, between neighbors, in cities and villages, and within the institutions of civil society," the Pope said at a seaside Mass May 11 in downtown Beirut.

Enthusiastic Welcome

An estimated 500,000 people poured into the Mass site, a landfill created with the debris of buildings destroyed in the 1975-90 conflict; authorities said it was the largest crowd ever assembled in Lebanese history.

Unprecedented security was deployed, with some 20,000 soldiers and police placed along the Pope's route and at events. Despite apprehension, the entire visit occurred without incident.

To a country still bearing the inner and outer scars of factional fighting, the Pope brought a healing message and carefully avoided reopening old wounds between religious and political communities.

He met with government officials, Muslim leaders, bishops and Catholic youths, emphasizing to all groups a dominant theme: Lebanon's future depends on establishing forgiveness and dialogue as the guiding values in personal life and public policy.

At a brief ceremony following the Mass, the Pope presented his 194-page apostolic exhortation on Lebanon, a final synod document that sketched out pastoral reforms for the Church and pledged cooperation with Muslims.

Presence the Big Story

But more than the document and speeches, the Pope's presence was the big story for the massive crowds — Christians and Muslims — who lined the streets of Beirut to cheer him as he rode through their neighborhoods in his glass-walled popemobile.

Even the church organizers were not expecting such a warm welcome and this enormous number of people on the streets. "The Pope is tremendously happy," said papal spokesman Joaquin Navarro-Valls. He called it a "miracle" visit.

From the moment his plane touched down May 10 at Beirut's airport, the Pope appeared satisfied to have finally arrived in Lebanon and the Middle East. He told the country's leaders that he came as "a friend who wishes to visit a people and support them in their daily journey."

The Pope later held private talks with the president and other government officials. The politicians, in remarks to reporters, focused on the political aspects of the Pope's visit, in particular expressing satisfaction at earlier Vatican statements favoring Israeli withdrawal from southern Lebanon.

In a similar vein, some Christians used the papal visit as an occasion to urge withdrawal of Syria's 35,000 troops from Lebanon and an end to what they saw as Syrian interference in political life.

The Pope, however, steered clear of a detailed discussion of internal and international political issues, instead issuing a general call for Lebanese independence. He said Lebanon should become "ever more democratic, in the full independence of its institutions and in recognition of its borders, which are indispensable conditions to guarantee its integrity" as a nation. He was a little more specific in the post-synodal document, referring to the "threatening" occupation in the South and the continued presence of other non-Lebanese soldiers.

New Hope for Lebanon

"A New Hope for Lebanon" was the title of the Pope's apostolic exhortation, a reflection on the work of the 1995 Special Assembly of the Synod of Bishops for Lebanon.

In the document, he called for greater cooperation among Lebanese Catholic communities and "prophetic gestures" of reconciliation among Christians, Muslims and political leaders.

It said mutual respect and dialogue were the "primordial conditions for the construction and survival of a democratic Lebanon."

"In this way, a new era will open for the country and the region, thanks to ever-deeper acts of forgiveness and cooperation among all the components of society," the document said.

The Pope urged the government to protect human rights for all, including those of the beleaguered Christian community, and pledged more intense church help for the poor and needy.

Much of the papal document focused on internal church affairs, especially the need for better coordination of pastoral programs and structures among Lebanon's six Catholic rites, which frequently overlapped.

While calling for a wide variety of structural changes, the Pope said Lebanese Catholics needed something more basic: an "interior liberation" to help them overcome narrow allegiances and experience real church communion.

"Every person and every organization that does not try to cooperate is impoverished and becomes a dead branch" in the living Church, he said.

Recommendations

Among his recommendations were:
• making the recently reorganized Assembly of Patriarchs and Catholic Bishops in Lebanon the central point of reference for all church programs in the country;
• reorganization of the geographical division of eparchies or dioceses;
• creation of inter-parish associations, to facilitate parish cooperation and church-sharing among rites;
• a complete review of church-run health programs, aimed at making more services available to the poor;
• moratorium on establishing new Catholic universities and educational institutions, in favor of better coordination among existing ones.

POPE JOHN PAUL IN POLAND

Pope John Paul made an 11-day pilgrimage to Poland May 31 to June 10, 1997. It was the 78th foreign trip of his pontificate and one of the busiest, with visits to 12 cities, the celebration of seven solemn Masses, the delivery of more than 25 prepared addresses, and meetings with bishops, priests, religious, lay persons and seven heads of state.

Following are: (1) The Pontiff's own reflections on the visit, made during a general audience June 18, 1997, and reported in the June 25 English-language edition of *L'Osservatore Romano.*

(2) Events and excerpts from selected addresses.

Reasons for the Visit

I would like to begin today's meeting by telling you about the recent pilgrimage to Poland which divine Providence gave me the opportunity to make.

There were three principal reasons for this pastoral visit: the International Eucharistic Congress in Wroclaw, the 1,000th anniversary of St. Adalbert's martyrdom and the 600th anniversary of the foundation of the Jagiellonian University of Krakow.

These events were the nucleus of the whole itinerary, which from 31 May to 10 June included Wroclaw, Legnica, Gorzow, Wielkopolski, Gniezno, Poznan, Kalisz, Czestochowa, Zakopane, Ludzmierz, Krakow, Dukla and Krosno, concentrating on three great cities: Wroclaw, the site of the 46th International Eucharistic Congress , Gniezno, a city linked with the death of St. Adalbert, and Krakow, where the Jagiellonian University was founded.

Eucharistic Congress

The 46th International Eucharistic Congress in Wroclaw began on Trinity Sunday, 25 May, with the Eucharistic celebration presided over by my Legate, Cardinal Angelo Sodano, secretary of state. A rich spiritual and liturgical program filled the entire week, centering on the main theme: "For freedom Christ has set us free" (Gal. 5:1). The Lord enabled me to take part in the conclusion of the work and so, on the last day of May, I was able to venerate Christ in the Eucharist, adoring him in the cathedral of Wroclaw together with people who had come from all over the world. That same day I took part in an ecumenical prayer service with representatives of the churches and ecclesial communities. The next day, Sunday, ended with a solemn Mass — *statio orbis.*

An extraordinary ecclesial experience, the International Eucharistic Congress brought together many theologians, priests, religious and lay people. It was certainly a time of deep reflection on the mystery of the Eucharist and gave Christians from Poland, Europe and other parts of the world an opportunity to spend much time in prayer, led at times by the cardinals and bishops of different nations who had been invited for the occasion. The Congress held in Wroclaw was the 46th since the first, held in Lille, France in 1881.... The next one will be held in Rome, to mark the Great Jubilee of the Year 2000.

St. Adalbert

The millennium of St. Adalbert, martyred in the year 997, was the second reason for my visit.

He came from Bohemia and belonged to the princely Slavnik family. Born in Lidice in the territory of the present-day Diocese of Hradec Kralove, he became Bishop of Prague at a young age. At the end of last April, we solemnly celebrated Adalbert's millennium, with the participation of many bishops from countries linked with this saint's life and work.

St. Adalbert came to Poland toward the end of his life, invited by King Boleslaw the Brave. He accepted the invitation to evangelize the pagan peoples who lived in the regions of the Baltic Sea. There he met his death, and after martyrdom his body was ransomed by King Boleslaw the Brave and taken to Gniezno, which then became the center of devotion to St. Adalbert.

An important meeting, not only religious but also political, took place near the relics of the holy martyr in the year 1000. Emperor Otto III and the papal legate both went to Gniezno for the occasion. Their meeting with King Boleslaw the Brave is known as the Gniezno Meeting, and it was precisely then, in Gniezno, that the first metropolitan see was established in what was then Poland. From the political standpoint, the Gniezno Meeting was an important event because it marked Poland's entry, under the Piasts, into a united Europe.

At the recent commemoration of the millennium of St. Adalbert's death, we were once again linked with that historic event and with its particular importance for our continent. The presidents of the countries connected with the tradition of St. Adalbert came to Gniezno to remember him; from the Czech Republic, Lithuania, Germany, Poland, Slovakia, Ukraine and Hungary.

Jagiellonian University

The foundation of the Jagiellonian University in Krakow was the third reason for my visit. This first university in Poland was founded by King Casimir the Great in 1364. It was a *Studium Generale* but not yet a full university since it lacked a faculty of theology. In 1397, Queen Hedwig and her husband, Wladyslaw Jagiello, did all that was required to establish the theology faculty. Thanks to the initiative taken by the founders of the Jagiellonian dynasty, a university with full rights came into being in Krakow, which very soon became an important center of study, famous not only in Poland but throughout the Europe of that time.

Two Canonizations

For the city of Krakow and the university community, 8 June was a great celebration: Queen Hedwig was canonized at last, after 600 years. On that occasion, there was a meeting with representatives of the Polish universities, who not only took part in the solemn Eucharistic celebration but also in the academic convocation held at the tomb of St. John of Kety, in the academy's church of St. Anne. For those linked with the Alma Mater of Krakow, it was an unusually solemn moment

On my last day in Poland,, another canonization took place, that of John Dukla, a 15th century Franciscan who was also connected with academic life at the University of Krakow. Although he was born in Dukla, he lived his life and served as a Franciscan in Lviv. I thank the Lord for allowing me to honor his memory at his birthplace, although his canonization took place in Krosno, in the Archdiocese of Przemysl.

In addition to the two canonizations during my pilgrimage, I had the joy of proclaiming two blesseds on the Solemnity of the Sacred Heart of Jesus 6 June, in Zakopane: Maria Bernardina Jablonska, cofoundress of the Congregation of the Albertine Sisters, and Maria Karlowska, foundress of the Congregation of the Good Shepherd Sisters.

I would once again like to express my deep gratitude to everyone who in various ways contributed to preparing and conducting this pilgrimage to my homeland.

I express my deep joy at having been able, during my 11-day pilgrimage to my country, to join so many of my compatriots in singing the *Te Deum* to thank the Lord for the many blessings granted to Poland and the whole world over the last 1,000 years.

Events and Addresses

The Church Lives by the Eucharist. So stated the Pope June 1 at the Mass which concluded the week-long International Eucharistic Congress in Wroclaw:

"She draws from it the spiritual energy to carry out her mission. It is the Eucharist that gives her the strength to grow and to be united. The Eucharist is the heart of the Church."

"Christ came into the world to bestow upon man divine life. He not only proclaimed the Good News but also instituted the Eucharist, the sacrament of life in God, which is to make present until the end of time his redeeming mystery."

"During this Statio Orbis, we need to recall the whole 'geography of hunger,' which includes many areas of the world.... The tragedy of hunger is a great challenge and a great indictment! ... During this Eucharistic Congress there cannot fail to be a joint invocation for bread in the name of all who are suffering from hunger.... Let us learn to share our bread with those who have none, or who have less than we do."

Referring to the congress theme of freedom, the Pope said: "True freedom is measured by readiness to serve and by the gift of self.... Christ invites us to enter this Eucharistic school of freedom so that, gazing at the Eucharist with the eyes of faith, we will become builders of a new, evangelical order of freedom— deep within ourselves and within the societies in which we live and work."

We Cannot Remain Indifferent to Social Problems. This was the theme of the Pope's address during Mass June 2 at Legnica.

Today, in these times of the building of a democratic state, in these times of dynamic economic development, we see with particular clarity all the shortcomings in the social life of our country. Every day we become aware of how many families are suffering from poverty, especially large families. How many single mothers are struggling to take care of their children! How many old people there are who are abandoned and without means to live!! In institutions for orphans and abandoned children there is no lack of those without enough food and clothing. How can we fail to mention the sick who cannot be given proper care because of a lack of resources? On the streets and in the squares the number of homeless people is increasing. We cannot pass over in silence the presence in our midst of all these brothers and sisters who are also members of the same nation and of the Mystical Body of Christ. As we approach the Eucharistic table to be fed with his Body, we cannot remain indifferent to those who lack daily bread. We need to talk about them, but we must also meet their needs. This is an obligation that rests especially on those who exercise authority: those who are at the service of the common good have the obligation to establish appropriate laws and to guide the national economy in such a way that these painful phenomena of social life find a proper solution. But it is also a common duty for us all, a duty of love, to provide help according to our abilities to those who expect it."

European Unity. At a June 3 Mass in Gniezno marking the millennium of the martyrdom of St. Adalbert, the Pope said: "There will be no European unity until it is based on unity of the spirit. The foundations of the identity of Europe are built on Christianity. Its present lack of spiritual unity arises principally from the crisis of this Christian self-awareness."

Respect for Human Dignity. Afterwards, in the presence of heads of state from Poland, the Czech Republic, Lithuania, Germany, Slovakia, Ukraine and Hungary, the Pope said:

"The greatness of the role of political leaders is to act always with respect for the dignity of every human being, to create the conditions of a generous solidarity which never marginalizes any citizen, to permit each individual to have access to culture, to recognize and put into practice the loftiest human and spiritual values, to profess and to share one's religious beliefs. By advancing in this direction, the European continent will strengthen its cohesion, will prove faithful to those who have laid the foundations of its culture and will respond to its age-old vocation in the world."

"In recent years the distance which separates the churches and ecclesial communities from one another has diminished significantly. Even so, it is still too great! Too great! Christ did not will it so! ... With sincere prayer, let us support our ecumenical commitment. In this our second millennium, in which the unity of Christ's disciples has suffered tragic divisions in the East and in the West, prayer (with action) for the rediscovery of full unity is a special obligation of ours."

Jagiellonian University Anniversary. During ceremonies June 8 marking the 600th anniversary of the university, the Pope said:

"In the daily work of a scholar, a particular ethical sensitivity is needed. For it is not enough to be concerned about the logical, formal correctness of one's thinking. The workings of the mind must necessarily be nourished by the spiritual climate of indispensable moral virtues, like sincerity, courage, humility, honesty and an authentic concern for man. Moral sensitivity makes it possible to perceive a connection between truth and goodness which is very essential for science. These two problems cannot in fact be separated! The principle of scientific research cannot be separated from the ethical responsibility of every scholar. In the case of men and women of science, this ethical responsibility is particularly important. Ethical relativism and purely utilitarian attitudes represent a danger not only for science but directly for individuals and for society."

Health Care: This was the subject of papal remarks June 9 at the Heart Surgery Clinic of John Paul II Hospital in Krakow. Addressing health care workers, he said: "Accept today the expression of my appreciation for this generous work (of yours), undertaken with self-sacrifice. In a certain sense, you take on your own shoulders the weight of the suffering and pain of your brothers and sisters, by trying to give them relief and to restore the health for which they yearn. My appreciation goes in a special way to all who courageously remain on the side of the divine law which guides human life. I repeat once more what I wrote in my encyclical *Evangelium Vitae:*

'Your profession calls for you to be guardians and servants of human life. In today's cultural and social context, in which science and the practice of medicine risk losing sight of their inherent ethical dimension, you can be strongly tempted at times to become

manipulators of life, or even agents of death. In the face of this temptation, your responsibility today is greatly increased. Its deepest inspiration and strongest support lie in the intrinsic and undeniable dimension of the health-care profession, something already recognized by the ancient and still relevant Hippocratic Oath, which requires every doctor to commit himself to absolute respect for human life and its sacredness.'"

St. John Dukla. Speaking June 9, the day before the canonization, Pope John Paul said:

"The holiness of Blessed John sprang from his deep faith. His entire life and his apostolic zeal, his love of prayer and of the Church, all this was founded in faith. It was his source of strength, thanks to which he was able to refuse everything that was material and temporal, in order to devote himself to what was of God and the spirit ... Blessed John earned fame as a wise preacher and zealous confessor. There crowded around him people hungry for sound doctrine of God, to hear his preaching or, at the confessional grill, to seek comfort and counsel. He became famous as a guide of souls and prudent adviser of many."

Creative Fidelity to Roots. This was the theme of Pope John Paul's remarks on departing from Poland at the end of his sixth papal visit to the country of his birth.

"At each of the stages of this visit, we have sought to interpret together the place which Christ occupies in the life of the nation. This was brought home to us by the Eucharistic Congress in Wroclaw and the historic gathering in Gniezno, at the tomb of St. Adalbert, where we celebrated the millennium of his martyrdom. Adalbert has reminded us of our duty to build a Poland faithful to her roots."

"Fidelity to roots does not mean a mechanical copying of the patterns of the past. Fidelity to roots is always creative, alert to the 'signs of the times.' Fidelity to roots means, above all, the ability to create an organic synthesis of perennial values, confirmed so often in history, and the challenge of today's world, faith and culture, the Gospel and life. My wish for my countrymen and for Poland is that she will be faithful to herself and to the roots from which she has grown."

EVOLUTION

These are excerpts from an address delivered by Pope John Paul to members of the Pontifical Academy of Sciences Oct. 22, 1996.

I am pleased with the first theme you have chosen (for consideration), that of the origins of life and evolution, an essential subject which deeply interests the Church, since revelation, for its part, contains teaching concerning the nature and origins of man. How do the conclusions reached by the various scientific disciplines coincide with those contained in the message of revelation? And if, at first sight, there are apparent contradictions, in what direction do we look for their solution? We know, in fact, that truth cannot contradict truth. Moreover, to shed greater light on historical truth, your research on the Church's relations with science between the

16th and 18th centuries is of great importance.

During this plenary session, you are undertaking a "reflection on science at the dawn of the third millennium," starting with the identification of the principal problems created by the sciences and which affect humanity's future. With this step you point the way to solutions which will be beneficial to the whole human community. In the domain of inanimate and animate nature, the evolution of science and its applications give rise to new questions. The better the Church's knowledge of their essential aspects, the more she will understand their impact. Consequently, in accordance with her specific mission she will be able to offer criteria for discerning the moral conduct required of all human beings in view of their integral salvation.

No Real Opposition

Before offering you several reflections that more specifically concern the subject of the origin of life and its evolution, I would like to remind you that the *magisterium* of the Church has already made pronouncements on these matters within the framework of her own competence. I will cite here two interventions.

In his encyclical *Humani Generis* (1950), my predecessor Pius XII had already stated that there was no opposition between evolution and the doctrine of the faith about man and his vocation, on condition that one did not lose sight of several indisputable points.

For my part, when I received those taking part in your academy's plenary assembly on Oct. 31, 1992, I had the opportunity with regard to Galileo to draw attention to the need of a rigorous hermeneutic for the correct interpretation of the inspired word. It is necessary to determine the proper sense of Scripture, while avoiding any unwarranted interpretations that make it say what it does not intend to say. In order to delineate the field of their own study, the exegete and the theologian must keep informed about the results achieved by the natural sciences.

Methodologies

Taking into account the state of scientific research at the time as well as of the requirements of theology, the encyclical *Humani Generis* considered the doctrine of "evolutionism" a serious hypothesis, worthy of investigation and in-depth study equal to that of the opposing hypothesis. Pius XII added two methodological conditions: that this opinion should not be adopted as though it were a certain, proven doctrine and as though one could totally prescind from revelation with regard to the questions it raises. He also spelled out the condition on which this opinion would be compatible with the Christian faith.

Today, nearly half a century after the publication of the encyclical, new knowledge leads to recognition of the theory of evolution as more than a hypothesis. It is indeed remarkable that this theory has been progressively accepted by researchers, following a series of discoveries in various fields of knowledge. The convergence, neither sought nor provoked, of the results of work that was conducted independently is in itself a significant argument in favor of this theory.

What is the significance of such a theory? To address this question is to enter the field of epistemology. A theory is a metascientific elaboration, distinct from the results of observation but consistent with them. By means of it, a series of independent data and facts can be related and interpreted in a unified explanation. A theory's validity depends on whether or not it can be verified; it is constantly tested against the facts; wherever it can no longer explain the latter, it shows its limitations and unsuitability.

Furthermore, while the formulation of a theory like that of evolution complies with the need for consistency with the observed data, it borrows certain notions from natural philosophy.

Several Theories

And, to tell the truth, rather than the theory of evolution, we should speak of several theories of evolution. On the one hand, this plurality has to do with the different explanations advanced for the mechanism of evolution and, on the other, with the various philosophies on which it is based. Hence the existence of materialist, reductionist and spiritualist interpretations. What is to be decided here is the true role of philosophy and, beyond it, of theology.

The Church's *magisterium* is directly concerned with the question of evolution, for it involves the conception of man: Revelation teaches us that he was created in the image and likeness of God (cf. Gn. 1:27-29). The conciliar constitution *Gaudium et Spes* has magnificently explained this doctrine, which is pivotal to Christian thought. It recalled that man is "the only creature on earth that God willed for itself" (No.24). In other terms, the human individual cannot be subordinated as a pure means or a pure instrument, either to the species or to society; he has value per se. He is a person. With his intellect and will, he is capable of forming a relationship of communion, solidarity and self-giving with his peers.

St. Thomas observes that man's likeness to God resides especially in his speculative intellect, for his relationship with the object of his knowledge resembles God's relationship with what he has created. But even more, man is called to enter into a relationship of knowledge and love with God himself, a relationship which will find its complete fulfillment beyond time, in eternity. All the depth and grandeur of this vocation are revealed to us in the mystery of the risen Christ (cf. *Gaudium et Spes* 22). It is by virtue of his spiritual soul that the whole person possesses such a dignity even in his body. Pius XII stressed this essential point: If the human body takes its origin from pre-existent living matter, the spiritual soul is immediately created by God.

Consequently, theories of evolution which, in accordance with the philosophies inspiring them, consider the spirit as emerging from the forces of living matter or as a mere epiphenomenon of this matter, are incompatible with the truth about man. Nor are they able to ground the dignity of the human person.

Philosophy and Theology

With man, then, we find ourselves in the presence of an ontological difference, an ontological leap, one could say. However, does not the posing of such ontological discontinuity run counter to that physical continuity which seems to be the main thread of research into evolution in the fields of physics and chemistry? Consideration of the method used in the various branches of knowledge makes it possible to reconcile two points of view which would seem irreconcilable. The sciences of observation describe and measure the multiple manifestations of life with increasing precision and correlate them with the time line. The moment of transition to the spiritual is not the object of this kind of observation, which nevertheless can discover at the experimental level a series of very valuable signs indicating what is specific to the human being. But the experience of metaphysical knowledge, of self-awareness and self-reflection, of moral conscience, freedom, or again of aesthetic and religious experience, falls within the competence of philosophical analysis and reflection, while theology brings out its ultimate meaning according to the Creator's plans.

In conclusion, I would like to call to mind a Gospel truth which can shed a higher light on the horizon of your research into the origin and unfolding of living matter. The Bible, in fact, bears an extraordinary message of life inasmuch as it describes the loftiest forms of existence. This vision guided me in the encyclical which I dedicated to respect for human life, and which I called precisely *Evangelium Vitae*.

It is significant that in St. John's Gospel life refers to the divine life which Christ communicates to us. We are called to enter into eternal life, that is to say, into the eternity of divine beatitude.

"Life" is one of the most beautiful titles which the Bible attributes to God. He is the living God.

PAPAL ELECTION

Revised regulations for the government of the Church during a vacancy of the Holy See and for the election of a pope were published Feb. 22, 1996, in an apostolic constitution entitled "Universi Dominici Gregis" ("Of the Lord's Whole Flock"). Excerpts are as follows.

During the Vacancy

"The College of Cardinals has no power or jurisdiction in matters which pertain to the supreme pontiff during his lifetime or in the exercise of his office."

"The government of the Church is entrusted to the College of Cardinals solely for the dispatch of ordinary business and of matters which cannot be postponed, and for the preparation of everything necessary for the election of the new pope."

Business is handled by particular and general congregations.

Particular congregations, with a three-day mandate and consisting of the cardinal chamberlain of the Holy Roman Church and three elected cardinals, deal with matters of lesser importance.

General congregations, presided over by the dean or subdean of the College, handle details regarding funeral arrangements and rites for the deceased pope over a period of nine consecutive days, destruction of the Fisherman's Ring and the leaden seal with which apostolic letters are dispatched, and the day and hour of the beginning of the voting process.

"At the death of the pope, all the heads of the dicasteries of the Roman Curia — the cardinal secretary of state and the cardinal prefects, the archbishop presidents, together with the members of the dicasteries — cease to exercise their office." Exceptions are made for the chamberlain of the Holy Roman Church, the major penitentiary, the cardinal vicar for the Diocese of Rome, the cardinal archpriest of the Vatican basilica and the vicar general for Vatican City.

Two officials with key responsibilities are the chamberlain of the Holy Roman Church and the dean of the College.

Election of the Pope

Electors: "The right to elect the Roman Pontiff belongs exclusively to the cardinals of the holy Roman church, with the exception of those who have reached their 80th birthday before the day of the Roman pontiff's death or the day when the Apostolic See becomes vacant. The maximum number of cardinal electors must not exceed 120. The right of active election by any other ecclesiastical dignitary or the intervention of any lay power whatsoever is absolutely excluded."

If a vacancy of the Apostolic See should occur while an ecumenical council or an assembly of the Synod of Bishops is in progress, the council or assembly would be automatically suspended.

The electoral conclave must begin 15 to 20 days after the death of the pope. It takes place within the territory of Vatican City. Voting takes place in the Sistine Chapel in the Apostolic Palace. The cardinal electors reside at the Domus Sanctae Marthae; suitable accommodations are provided for necessary service personnel.

At the beginning of the conclave, the electors bind themselves by oath to observe strict secrecy and all other requirements related to the papal election as prescribed in the apostolic constitution of the Supreme Pontiff John Paul II, *Universi Dominici Gregis,* published on Feb. 22, 1996.

Procedure: "The forms of election" by acclamation and compromise "are abolished," and "the form of electing the Roman pontiff shall henceforth be by balloting alone."

"I therefore decree that for the valid election of the Roman pontiff two-thirds of the votes are required, calculated on the basis of the total number of electors present."

"Should it be impossible to divide the number of cardinals present into three equal parts, for the validity of the election of the supreme pontiff one additional vote is required."

"Should the election begin on the afternoon of the first day, only one ballot is to be held; then, on the following days, if no one is elected on the first ballot, two ballots shall be held in the morning and two in the afternoon."

"In the event that the cardinal electors find it difficult to agree on the person to be elected, after balloting has been carried out for three days — without result, voting is to be suspended for a maximum of one day in order to allow for prayer, informal discussion among the voters and a brief spiritual exhortation." Given the same circumstances, this procedure can be repeated three times.

"If the balloting does not result in an election, — the cardinal electors shall be invited — to express an opinion about the manner of proceeding. The election will then proceed in accordance with what the absolute majority of the electors decides.

"Nevertheless, there can be no waiving of the requirement that a valid election takes place only by an absolute majority of the votes or else by voting only on the two names which in the ballot immediately preceding have received the greatest number of votes; also in this second case, only an absolute majority is required."

The New Pope

After his acceptance (of the canonical election to

the papacy) and the designation of his name as pope, "the person elected, if he has already received episcopal ordination, is immediately bishop of the Church of Rome, true pope and head of the college of bishops. He thus acquires and can exercise full and supreme power over the universal Church.

"If the person elected is not already a bishop, he shall immediately be ordained bishop."

After the observance of required formalities, the cardinal electors make an act of homage and obedience to the new pope, who is then introduced to the people, to whom he imparts his blessing "To the City and the World," in accord with custom.

"The conclave ends immediately after the new supreme pontiff assents to his election, unless he should determine otherwise."

"After the solemn ceremony of the inauguration of the pontificate and within an appropriate time, the pope will take possession of the Patriarchal Archbasilica of the Lateran."

In accord with longstanding custom, the election of the pope is signalled to the outside world by the white smoke from the burning of the last ballots cast by the cardinals.

ECONOMIC PROGRESS: Looking Beyond the Numbers

This is the text of the 1997 Labor Day Statement signed by Bishop William S. Skylstad of Spokane, chairman of the U.S. Bishops' Committee on Domestic Policy, on behalf of the U.S. Catholic Conference.

Growing Together, Growing Apart

This Labor Day, many people in the United States are experiencing a time of economic stability, growth and confidence. Unemployment rates are the lowest in decades; families are leaving public assistance to participate in the job market; businesses are growing and reaping profits, and the stock market is setting new records. There are even major steps toward finally balancing the federal budget.

But there is uneasiness in the land. While more people have work, many workers feel insecure about their future. As welfare recipients try to join the work force, some find no jobs, while others struggle to raise their families with very low wages. Some business leaders are creating jobs, other corporations seek mergers, downsize work forces, and uproot local companies without apparent concern for the immediate community. A recent strike (Teamsters vs. United Parcel Service) focused on the growth of part-time jobs in the economy. The stock market reacts almost perversely to economic news. In some cases, stocks climb on reports of increased unemployment or a huge layoff of employees. And few in the federal government are talking about reducing the size of the accumulated debt that annually extracts nearly $300 billion in interest payments from the federal coffers. But, perhaps most disturbing of all is the widening gap between the rich and the poor in our land.

Survey of Work Force

Alan Greenspan, chairman of the Federal Reserve Board, in recent testimony before Congress, attributed the current economic condition in part to a heightened sense of job insecurity among workers and "the reduced market power of labor unions."

According to the American Management Association's 1996 survey of the U.S. work force, 49 percent of large and mid-sized firms reported job eliminations in the 12 months ending in June, 1996. Another 1996 poll, this one reported in *Business News* (Oct. '96), asked people how they felt about their own job security. Only 40 percent of the respondents described their jobs as "very secure"; 49 percent of the affluent report a high confidence in their job security vs. 33 percent of their poorest income counterparts (many of them part-time workers).

These developments come on the heels of a decade which saw a dramatic rise in the income gap between high- and low-income families, reversing uninterrupted progress in the postwar period toward lower inequality. The Bureau of the Census reported that upper-income groups experienced substantial income growth in the 1980s (the average income of the top one percent of American families grew 87.5 percent) while the bottom 40 percent of families experienced a decline.

Common sense tells us that some things should be different. Workers who add to the wealth of the company and the community should share in the prosperity they help create. A single parent, accepting responsibility for her life and that of her children, should be better off participating in the work force than receiving welfare. Businesses that create jobs and serve local needs should prosper. Corporations have an obligation to the people and communities they serve, as well as increasing their return on investment. The economy should be moving toward full employment with prosperity shared fairly and widely. We should be growing together, not pulling apart.

A Framework for Economic Life

Catholic social doctrine draws on the person of Jesus Christ, sacred Scripture and our rich tradition and experience to place in perspective the relationship of the economy to human life — to offer a moral framework for economic life. This teaching was summarized in 10 principles by the U.S. bishops on the 10th anniversary of their economic pastoral letter, "Economic Justice for All." (See separate entry.)

The bishops developed this summary because they recognize that it is easy to get distracted by our daily schedules, weekly budgets, and trying to stretch a paycheck to cover the bills. It is understandable that workers become preoccupied by the uncertainty of employment or the fear of job loss, the cost of health care, the kids' education, and the demands of a materialistic society. But our union with Jesus Christ and our faith in him reminds us that it is not enough to focus simply on how we personally are faring. We cannot neglect the common good nor the economic health of the large community we are part of. Despite the difficulties that we may face in life, we cannot become blind to the difficulties that are experienced by our neighbors.

The Meaning of Work

Workers need to see themselves and their workplace in the light of these principles. In our tradition, human work cannot be treated merely as a factor necessary for production — people are more than a "human resource." A person cannot be regarded as a tool of production. Work, at its best, helps people share in the creative activity of God. Work helps each of us to realize our God-given potential and is a vital part of the way in which we contribute to the community. Workplaces should be structured to advance these human and spiritual needs. Work schedules should permit workers time to rest and be with their families. Steps must be taken to ensure that work does not lose its proper focus — work is an expression of our dignity.

Workers, at the same time, need to assess whether their choices and behavior reflect principles of fairness and ethics — e.g., giving a fair day's work for a day's pay, unnecessarily accumulating overtime, the openness of apprentice programs and employment opportunities to women and minorities. Every economic decision must be judged by whether it helps or hurts people; whether it strengthens or weakens family life; whether it advances or diminishes the quality of justice in our land.

The new welfare law challenges our society to create jobs and open opportunities for people who now must accept their obligation to work in order to support themselves and their children. Those providing these new opportunities must not exploit the situation through inadequate wages, lack of health care insurance, or little or no legal worker protections. The moral obligation to insure these rights falls to employers with the appropriate oversight of public authorities.

Role of the Church

Our Church is one of the few institutions in American life crossing economic, racial, ethnic and class lines. We are in the middle and at the edges of society. We are CEOs and migrant farmworkers, union presidents and homeless children. We are called to be a bridge community to help overcome the social distance and isolation in our nation. We can help American society rediscover a sense of national community and restore our determination to pursue the common good rather than narrow economic interests.

We must resist those who would selectively use our Catholic tradition to advance their own particular political agendas or use our moral principles as sound bites for partisan purposes. Ours is a complex and balanced tradition, emphasizing both rights and responsibilities, solidarity and subsidiarity, private virtue and public responsibility, the limits and duties of the state, the advantages and limitations of the market, the vital role of voluntary groups and the legitimate obligations of government.

Real Jobs Needed

As Catholics, we believe that those who can work, should work. But we believe new rules and repeated lectures on responsibility are no substitute for real jobs with decent wages and a genuine national commitment to help families overcome poverty.

Catholic doctrine supports the right to join unions and bargain collectively, and the duty of both labor and management to seek the common good, not simply their own economic advantage.

In Catholic tradition, we believe workers should be paid a wage that can support a family and insist that workers owe an honest day's work for an honest day's pay. We believe in a real social contract between employer and employee, with a worker's labor and loyalty matched by just treatment and loyalty in return.

These principles are not new and they do not offer easy answers for business owners, workers, labor leaders or public officials. But they do offer a way of looking at the choices we face every day in this economy of growing wealth, growing insecurity and growing income gaps. The affirmation of these principles is a celebration of Labor Day!

CATHOLIC COMMON GROUND INITIATIVE

Cardinal Joseph L. Bernardin of Chicago launched a Catholic Common Ground Initiative Aug. 12, 1996, about three months after We-Are-Church people announced the previous May 22 circulation of a referendum for church reform.

The cardinal and others involved in the project urged Catholics divided over church-related issues to join in constructive dialogue and efforts to end "distrust, acrimony and deadlock," along with a "dynamic of fear and polarization" in the Church.

The foundational document of the project said Catholics, whatever their particular interests or agenda, "must be accountable to the Catholic tradition and to the Spirit-filled, living Church."

It said there can be "legitimate debate, discussion and diversity" about aspects of church teaching and tradition," but "accountability demands serious engagement with the tradition and its authoritative representatives. It rules out pop scholarship, sound-byte theology, unhistorical assertions and flippant dismissals that have become all too common on both the right and left of the Church."

Several millions of Austrian and German Catholics had already signed reform referenda; so had others in Italy, France, Belgium and Australia. We-Are-Church participants in the United States failed to reach their goal of a million signatures by Pentecost, 1997.

The first conference of the Catholic Common Ground Initiative was held Mar. 7 to 9, 1997, under the leadership of Archbishop Oscar H. Lipscomb of Mobile, who succeeded deceased Cardinal Bernardin as head of the project.

In remarks to the 40 participants in the conference, the archbishop examined the stages of reaction to the basic statement of the Initiative, use of the word "dialogue," and the type of common ground sought by the project.

For some critics, the word "dialogue" is a loaded term and "one might wonder whether it carries so much baggage that its use is counterproductive," But, it is imperative "that we continue to affirm ... that, in the dialogue of which we speak, Jesus Christ is central and all dialogue is accountable to Scripture and Catholic tradition."

SEPTEMBER 1996

VATICAN

Jerusalem Statement — "We encourage all leaders to carry out gestures that favor trust and to avoid acts that foment the desperation of Palestinians." So stated Christian, Muslim and Jewish representatives in a document adopted at a meeting Aug. 25 to 29 in Solanaceae, Greece. The meeting was co-sponsored by a commission of the Pontifical Council for Interreligious Dialogue, the World Council of Churches and the Lutheran World Federation. The statement:

• Denounced all violence by individuals and authorities, and called for educational efforts for peace.

• Criticized the "collective and indiscriminate closure of Jerusalem" to Palestinians, saying that other means existed to protect Israel and Palestinian security. The closure prevented people from reaching places of worship, employment, education and health care.

• Warned that violations of human rights and acts of humiliation were underlying the confidence needed for progress toward peace. "In this regard, we strongly urge the Israeli government not to confiscate land, build and expand settlements, demolish Palestinian homes or revoke Palestinian residency rights in Jerusalem."

• Said Palestinian institutions in Jerusalem were under threat, at a time when confidence-building required that the Palestinian infrastructure be maintained.

Malines Conversations Remembered — In a letter addressed to participants in a celebration marking the 75th anniversary of the Malines Conversations, Pope John Paul said in a message released Sept. 3: "Impelled by indomitable faith, these remarkable witnesses to the urgency of Christ's plea for unity hoped for the return to full communion within the Catholic Church of 'the Anglican Church united not absorbed.'" The "indomitable witnesses" were Anglican Lord Halifax and Cardinal Desire Mercier of Belgium who organized a five-year series of discussions on possible conditions for Catholic-Anglican union. "The dialogue," said the Pope, "was marked by a sincere desire for reconciliation and was conducted in a spirit of genuine humility, shared conversion to the Gospel, love for truth and fraternal charity." The informal conversations "made an enduring contribution to a fundamental principle of ecumenism, namely, that legitimate diversity is not an obstacle to church unity.

Aid to Migrants — Church aid to refugees and other migrant peoples must involve evangelization efforts, the Pope said in a message prepared for World Migration Day 1997. The text, released Sept. 3, cited the growing number of people fleeing conditions of war, ethnic conflict and hunger, noting that their plight clearly challenges Christians to work for social justice on their behalf. But the situation also highlights a special responsibility to "transmit the faith…. The Church's commitment to migrants and refugees cannot be reduced to simply organizing structures of welcome and solidarity but, above all, to unveil the mystery of Christ."

Eastern Spirituality — "Among the signs of hope in our times, so rich with lights and shadows, there is a renewed need for spirituality" the Pope told visitors at Castel Gandolfo Sept. 8. Speaking in the same vein Sept. 29, he said Western culture, increasingly dominated by scientific and technological knowledge, could learn much from Eastern spirituality with its deep "awareness of the heart." In a message to Benedictine abbots late in the month, the Holy Father said the long tradition of monastic life offers valuable gifts of prayer and contemplation to modern society.

Illiteracy a Form of Poverty — "Illiteracy is a form of poverty that keeps people from reaching their full potential and participation in the life of society," the Pope said in a message to UNESCO on the occasion of its celebration Sept. 9 of World Literacy Day. He offered special thanks to people "who work so that children can benefit from an education that gives them a real chance to have a worthy existence and to be active participants in community life." He added: "I encourage all people who participate in the formation of young people and adults to struggle against illiteracy, a form of poverty, and to allow everyone to take part in the life of their country."

Nuclear Safety — The Vatican believes safety must be given "'absolute priority" in the use of nuclear energy and wants to see the evolution of a "global nuclear safety culture" that relies on treaties, safety codes and information-sharing to prevent accidents. So stated Msgr. Mario Zenari, Vatican delegate to the Vienna meeting of the International Atomic Energy Agency Sept. 16 to 20. With the 1986 Chernobyl nuclear disaster in mind, he said people were increasingly aware that nuclear technology can serve people or turn against them, endangering the environment and threatening all forms life. "The more power is placed in human hands, the more its individual and collective responsibility must grow," he said.

In a related development, another Vatican official said a proposed Comprehensive Nuclear Test Ban Treaty was the best agreement possible under existing international conditions. "This treaty responds largely to the expectations of world public opinion" with respect to the enforcement and monitoring of secret nuclear testing, declared Archbishop Giuseppe Bertello in a Vatican Radio broadcast Sept. 9.

Solidarity for Peace — "Security cannot consist in a permanent and ever-evolving armed peace; it must be the result of a certain way of living together in society," the Pope told participants in a course sponsored by the Center for Higher Studies of Defense and the Western European Union. The key, he told the group Sept. 17, is solidarity, "a firm and persevering determination to commit oneself to the common good." It "must be open to everyone, for it is not possible to live in safety or with peace of mind when our brothers or sisters are beset by fear and anguish."

Redemptorists and the Poor — The Pope encouraged Redemptorists to renew their efforts to help poor and abandoned persons, and to take inspiration from the life of their founder, St. Alphonsus Liguori. In an address marking the 300th anniversary of his birth, Pope John Paul said Sept. 27: "The world of the abandoned became the world of St. Alphonsus. It should remain the world of every Redemptorist.

General Audience Topics:
• On declaring herself the "handmaid of the Lord," Mary showed total obedience to God's will and made it her own with all her personal resources (Sept. 4).
• Reflections on his visit to Hungary (Sept. 11).
• "Mary, associated with Christ's victory over the sin of our first parents, appears as the true 'mother of the living.'" (Sept. 18).
• Reflections on his visit to France (Sept. 25).

Briefs:
• Government-rebel violence at the end of August and the beginning of September prompted the Pope to plead with Mexicans for peaceful resolution of their continuing conflict.
• As Northern Ireland peace talks resumed, the Pope urged both sides Sept. 8 to intensify efforts to end sectarian violence.
• People who call themselves atheists usually do not deny the existence of God so much as a false idea of God, the Pope said Sept.15. He also noted that, while it is possible with the use of one's intelligence to conclude that God exists, the fullness of faith comes through love.
• After a week of renewed bloodshed in which more than 70 people were killed and hundreds injured, the Pope urged Israelis and Palestinians Sept. 29 to "make a courageous effort to not suffocate the hope of peace," and to "avoid further provocations and injustices and their consequent violent reactions." The appeal came after Israelis opened a tourist tunnel near a place sacred to the Palestinians.

Visits to Hungary and France

"Christ Our Hope" was the theme of Pope John Paul's second visit to Hungary Sept. 6 to 9. One of the principal events of the trip was the commemoration of the millennium of the founding of the Benedictine Abbey of Pannonhalma.

In France Sept. 19 to 22 for the fifth time in his pontificate, the Holy Father commemorated the 16th centenary of the death of St. Martin of Tours and the 15th centenary of the baptism of Clovis. He praised the spiritual heritage of the French and emphasized the missionary mandate of the Church.
(See separate entries.)

NATIONAL

First Amendment Suit — A priest, a rabbi and the Muslim Military Association filed suit Sept.. 10 in the U.S. District Court in Washington, charging the secretaries of the Department of Defense — the Navy, the Air Force and the Army — with violations of the constitutional rights to free speech and free exercise of religion, and a violation of the Religious Freedom Restoration Act. At issue was a June 7 Air Force memorandum forbidding chaplains from participating in the Project Life Campaign of the U.S.. Bishops for congressional override of President Clinton's veto of the Partial Birth Abortion Act.

Anencephalic Children — The bishops' Committee on Doctrine issued a statement Sept. 20 saying that, when an anencephalic child is born, he or she should be baptized and be given "the comfort and palliative care appropriate to all the dying." The statement ruled out abortion of the child as well as the removal of organs for transplant "before the donor child is certainly dead." The statement, entitled "Moral Principles concerning Infants with Anencephaly," noted that "most infants who have anencephaly do not survive for more than a few days after birth." Christian burial is in order, in witness to the Church's respect for human life.

Civility in Public Life — "An Interfaith Call for Civility in Public Life" was issued Sept. 20 over the signatures of more than 40 Catholic, Jewish, Protestant and Orthodox representatives. It said in part: "We call on those running for office in 1996 to campaign positively on the issues and, once and for all, to leave personal attacks behind. We call on all political commentators to foster debate that elevates public discourse rather than resorts to shrill attacks that demean it. We urge our congregants and all Americans to remember, even as they argue and debate with neighbors, co-workers and friends, that we are all created in the image of God and that the dignity of every person ought to be protected and not assaulted by how we act in this election year."

Social Service Concerns — The U.S. government has an essential role in promoting the common good, especially for those most in need, said speakers during the annual meeting of Catholic Charities USA Sept. 20 to 23 in Cleveland. "We know that the measure of a nation's greatness is its commitment to its most vulnerable members," said Bishop Anthony M. Pilla in a keynote address. "The pursuit of progress without a concern for those left behind cannot succeed. Securing a future without safeguarding the dignity of every person will fail."

Too much of current American politics appeals to selfishness, pitting one group against another by generation, race, state, gender or community, said Jesuit Father Fred Kammer, president of Catholic Charities USA. Addressing Cleveland's City Club, he told members that "the fundamental appeal to the 'common good' which is deep in Catholic teaching and in our national history" would be heard infrequently in this election year. Also missing from campaign rhetoric would be an acknowledgment that the federal government and most of its social programs work well, despite Americans' "visceral bias against government." He observed that many programs in need of change had their most serious problems at the state level, but that was not taken into adequate account in the latest welfare reform bill. "For those of us up close," he said, "federal social programs consistently have proven to be better designed, better financed and, frankly, better administered than state social welfare programs."

Greek Orthodox Archbishop — Archbishop Spyridon was enthroned Sept. 21 in New York as head of the Greek Orthodox Archdiocese of America. The Ohio-born prelate succeeded Archbishop Iakovos, former head of the see for 37 years.

Housing Units — Catholic institutions were sponsors of nearly 50,000 housing units with almost 70,000 residents in the country, according to a survey sponsored by Catholic Charities USA and released Sept. 22. "The Catholic Church is committed to providing decent housing for people who need it, particularly the most vulnerable," said Jesuit Father Fred Kammer. He also called attention to the fact that, "while Catholic organizations should be commended for spearheading the development of housing," it should remembered that partnerships with the private sector and government at all levels make most of these projects possible."

Taped Confession Case — The U.S. Catholic Conference and other religious organizations filed a joint friend-of-the-court brief urging the destruction of a secretly taped recording and transcript of an Oregon prisoner's sacramental confession. The brief was filed in an appeal of a lower court ruling brought to the 9th U.S. District Court of Appeals by Archbishop Francis E. George of Portland, Ore., and Father Timothy Mockaitis, who heard the confession. Their appeal, filed Aug. 23, followed a ruling Aug. 12 by a federal district court judge that the tape's role in a murder case outweighed the Catholic Church's religious liberty-interest in having it destroyed. The friend-of-the-court brief, filed Sept. 23 and released Sept. 27, said it was "difficult to imagine any more blatant and bald-faced an affront to the basic tenets of a religion, short of intentionally committing acts of sacrilege as a matter of state policy." Preservation of the tape and its transcript, the brief said, compounded the wrong, and maintenance of the tape and subsequent uses of it perpetuated the violation. The only appropriate remedy was to destroy the "ill-gotten gain," as the brief called the tape and transcript. The recording was made secretly in jail by the Lane County sheriff's department in April in Eugene, Ore., when Conan Wayne Hale, then a murder suspect, confessed his sins to Father Mockaitis.

Self-Help Grants — The bishops' Campaign for Human Development announced Sept. 23 the distribution of $7.3 million in grants for 235 projects in 44 states, the District of Columbia and Puerto Rico. The average grant was $3,000. Funds were raised in a nationwide collection in the fall of 1995.

Nuclear Test Ban — President Clinton's decision to sign the Comprehensive Nuclear Test Ban Treaty Sept. 24 was praised by Bishop Daniel P. Reilly, chairman of the bishops' International Policy Committee. He said the decision and U.S. leadership securing an almost unanimous vote of approval of the ban in the U.N. General Assembly was "an encouraging demonstration of our commitment to halt the spread of nuclear weapons."

Euthanasia Report — A congressional report on abuses of physician-assisted suicide in The Netherlands was hailed in various quarters. Richard M. Doerflinger, an official of the bishops' Secretariat for Pro-Life Activities, said: "By issuing its report on euthanasia in The Netherlands, the House Judiciary Constitution Subcommittee persuasively demonstrates how a practice advanced in the name of 'freedom of choice'" becomes a way to dispose of inconvenient people." Rep.. Charles T. Canady, chairman of the subcommittee, said Sept. 27 at a press conference: "Simply put, an individual's so-called 'right to die,' over time, can be transformed into a demand by society that certain individuals have a duty to die.' ... Particularly, as the United States Supreme Court decides whether to strike down state statutes prohibiting physician-assisted suicide, the development of Dutch law and the current practice of euthanasia in The Netherlands should be closely examined." The subcommittee's report was based on the 1991 Kemmelink Report which revealed that in 1990 there were more than 1,000 cases in which physicians in The Netherlands terminated the lives of patients without their consent.

Briefs:
• The second meeting of the reconstituted Southern Baptist Convention-National Conference of Catholic Bishops' Conversation was held Sept. 12-14 in Washington.. The Bible and faith were the central subjects of discussion.

• Cardinal Edward I. Cassidy, president of the Pontifical Council for Promoting Christian Unity, said in a New York lecture Sept. 16 that Catholics and Evangelicals were "beginning to recognize each other as sharing in common faith and hence being, in fact, brothers and sisters in the Lord.... The work being done by the informal dialogue in the United States is, to my mind, of great importance in this context."

• Archbishop Harry J. Flynn of St. Paul-Minneapolis and Episcopal Bishop James L. Jelinek of the Diocese of Minnesota signed a covenant encouraging common prayer, dialogue and cooperation on matters of ethical and social concern, Sept. 29.

Veto Upheld

President Clinton's veto of the Partial-Birth Abortion Ban Act was upheld by the Senate with a less-than-two-thirds majority vote of 57 to 41 Sept. 26. Seven days earlier, the House had voted to override the veto with a vote of 285-137. Public opinion polls had reported 60 to 70 percent of voters in favor of an override.

Massive efforts by the Church and pro-life people of all classes failed to end legal sanction of the barbaric virtual infanticide of partial-birth abortion — in which, in the very act of delivery, the head of a baby is pierced and the brain extracted in order to ease removal of the body.

The presidential veto and its support in the Senate represented a glaring aspect of a culture of death in contemporary society.

INTERNATIONAL

Missionaries Freed — Five missionaries, released after nearly two weeks in detention by rebels in Mapourdit, Sudan, were reported to be in good health Sept. 3. They said they had been physically mistreated but not tortured by their captors.. A sixth priest, also freed, chose to stay in Mapourdit to keep the mission open.

Abortion in Poland — "Parliamentarians elected to defend society and safeguard human life have declared themselves in favor of the death of innocent, helpless people," said Bishop Tadeusz Pieronek, secretary general of the bishops' conference. He spoke in the wake of an Aug. 30 vote in the Sejm, the lower house of Parliament, to allow abortions up to 12 weeks of pregnancy for women facing "burdensome living conditions or a difficult personal situation.... It is horrifying that someone can coldbloodedly calculate the death of another." Pope John Paul also commented Sept. 1: "I am filled with sadness by the fact that in our homeland, which suffered so much during the Second World War, the drama of the death of innocent human beings continues."

Prison Chaplains' Conference — In a statement

issued Sept. 13 in Warsaw, the Ninth World Congress of Catholic Prison Chaplains called on bishops' conferences throughout the world to upgrade pastoral ministry among inmates. The 140 chaplains — from 46 countries in Europe, the Americas and the Third World — spoke also of other concerns: "We observe with anxiety the prevalence of torture, violence and other forms of brutality toward prisoners, and the alarming disregard for prisoners' civil rights through police arrests and other preventive actions....We support all efforts aimed at the death penalty's total abolition, and we particularly condemn the practices of many countries that still retain this barbaric way of dealing with people."

Archbishop, Thousands Killed in Burundi — Stop the massacres and the mourning of an entire nation, Cardinal Jozef Tomko said Sept. 17 at a Mass for Archbishop Joachim Ruhuna of Giteg, who was killed in an ambush eight days earlier. "In the name of God, let me say: 'Thou shalt not kill.'" The Pope condemned the attacks as "new set of cruelty which has been added to a chain of unheard-of violence" in Burundi. It was estimated that more than 150,000 people had been killed in three years of Hutu-Tutsi warfare in the country.

Reconciliation in Chile — Cardinal Carlos Oviedo Cavada of Santiago called Sept. 18 for "unity and reconciliation" in the wake of violent protests in the capital during activities marking the anniversary of the 1973 Pinchot-led military coup that overthrew the civilian government of President Salvador Allende. "A divided society cannot progress," he said. "Reconciliation will always be a process which will never be totally attained, due to our human weakness." Part of the process of reconciliation should be "the awareness that we are all responsible for the present and the future of our country, showing solidarity and brotherhood to one another."

Disaster in Somalia — People in the Jubba Valley were experiencing disasters of biblical proportions, according to Msgr. George Bertin, apostolic administrator of Mogadishu, following two years of drought, then flooding and the destruction of crops. Adding to deteriorating conditions were renewed fighting among warlords, killing and looting, starvation and the misery of refugees.

Step toward Peace in Guatemala — Church authorities commended government and rebel representatives for signing Seppt. 19 an agreement meant to bring the nation closer to ending the last and longest war in Central America. "This accord is extremely important, possibly the most important that has yet been signed, because it represents moving from a structured, military vision to a civilian one. (It) will act as a lever to enable civil society to govern without military interference." So stated Carlos Aldana, director of the information office of the Archdiocese of Guatemala.

Proposed Belarus Law Worse — The head of the Church in Belarus warned that a proposed law on religion would impose "even worse restrictions" on Catholic activities than those experienced during communist rule. "When I worked here by myself, my parish stretched from the Baltic to the Pacific Ocean, since I was told I had a right to travel around the whole Soviet Union, visiting the sick and conduct-

ing funerals," said Cardinal Kazimierz Swiatek of Minsk-Mogilev in a Polish newspaper interview. "But under the new law, I must obtain the authorities' consent to assign a priest to a parish and must consult with them again if I wish to move him.. It is proposed that parish priests will not even be able to celebrate Mass elsewhere in their diocese." Priests already faced "permanent personal difficulties," especially about 100 on loan from Poland, many of whom had no work permits." The situation of more than 50 nuns refused legal status was critical. "Even those who at one stage had registration documents have since had them withdrawn," said the cardinal.

The Jerusalem Question — The only way to defuse growing tensions between Israelis and Palestinians was to bring the question of Jerusalem to the bargaining table, said Latin-rite Patriarch Michel Sabbah. "First, the question of Jerusalem" must be resolved, he said Sept.29 at a special prayer service called by the heads of Christian churches in the city. "They must meet to talk and to resolve the question of Jerusalem, to deal with this question despite all its difficulties." Both sides had to face the reality that Jerusalem would never be exclusively theirs, that it would always be a city belonging to two peoples and three religions.

Briefs:

• Palestinian leader Yasser Arafat met Sept.. 5 with Cardinal Angelo Sodano, papal secretary of state, for discussion of peace prospects in the Middle East.

• The appointment of Msgr. Roger C. Roensch as director of the U.S. bishops' Rome office for visitors to the Vatican was announced Sept.10. About 15,000 pilgrims from the United States visit the Vatican every year..

• Mother Teresa was released Sept. 25 from Woodlands Nursing Home, Calcutta, where she had been hospitalized for 10 days after suffering a head injury.

• Father Franco Decaminid was honored by the Albanian government for his role in rebuilding the nation's post-communist health system.

• Korean Father John Oh Woong-jin was one of five recipients of the 1996 Magsaysay Award for his work on behalf of beggars, mentally retarded persons, tuberculosis patients, homeless and elderly persons, and alcoholics at a social service complex which he founded in 1983.

First Legal-Assisted Suicide

The first legalized killing of a terminally ill person in Australia's Northern Territory Sept. 22 triggered instant condemnation. Cardinal Edward B. Clancy of Sydney attacked the killing as "an act of reckless disregard for the convictions of people around the world." Auxiliary Bishop Patrick Power of Canberra said the killing had become "a day of shame for Australia." Bishop Elio Sgreccia, a member of the Pontifical Council for the Family, called the killing a "despicable crime against life and an abandonment of the medical duty to assist the dying." These comments and others in the same vein came following news that Robert Dent, a 66-year-old resident of Darwin suffering from terminal prostate cancer, died at his home after a doctor administered a computer-delivered lethal injection.

OCTOBER 1996

VATICAN

Liberation Theology and Relativism — These were topics discussed by Cardinal Joseph Ratzinger at meetings with bishops in recent months. The head of the Congregation for the Doctrine of the Faith said that in the 1980s liberation theology in its more radical forms was a serious challenge to the faith, but that its appeal collapsed along with Marxist regimes when people realized that redemption is not a political process. Relativism, however, may ultimately be more dangerous because it is popularized in efforts to "democratize" the Church, to arbitrarily modify the liturgy and to blur and erase differences with other religions. With developments in India and other places apparently in mind, the cardinal said "relativism has become the central problem for the faith at the present time." Among some theologians, Jesus is regarded as "one religious leader among others" and not as the unique Redeemer. Likewise, some concepts like the Church, dogma and the sacraments are viewed as too "unconditional" or absolute, and the Church is accused of being intransigent and fundamentalist.

In a related development, Dominican Father Georges Cottier, theologian of the Papal Household and secretary of the International Theological Commission, told Catholic News Service Oct. 7 that a small but vocal group of contemporary theologians had expressed the opinion that other religions may "mediate salvation" in a way similar to the Christian Church. He called this a "very serious problem." He also cited another problem, searching for religious experiences while ignoring the reality of one true God.

Papal Surgery — Pope John Paul underwent a 50-minute surgical procedure of an appendectomy Oct. 8 after suffering from "recurring episodes of inflammation of the appendix." The chief surgeon ruled out any more serious intestinal disease. After normal recovery, the Pope left Gemelli Hospital Oct. 15 — with thanks to hospital personnel and thousands of well-wishers — and made his first public appearance Oct. 20.

Year of Charity — The Pontifical Council "Cor Unum" held a day-long brainstorming session Oct. 19 to generate suggestions on how to explain and promote charity, with an eye toward 1999, already designated by the Pope as a Year of Charity in preparation for the Jubilee Year 2000. In an Oct. 20 interview with Vatican Radio, council secretary Msgr. Ivan Marin-Lopez, said that, although charity is a timeless concept, it needs special, renewed attention in the contemporary world. "People yesterday and today have always understood the language of love when it is authentic. Conscious of the necessity to regain the profound meaning of charity, the Pope affirms that we must now place emphasis on the virtue of charity." The council was encouraging dioceses and bishops' councils to develop educational and other programs about the two aspects of charity: love toward God and love toward people.

Catholic-Orthodox Relations — Cardinal Achille Silvestrini, head of the Congregation for Eastern Churches, said that Catholic-Orthodox relations in Ukraine had recently improved, and that the government was seriously considering a visit by Pope John Paul. "I would say that the previous (ecumenical) tensions are now disappearing. At least, they're being reduced," the cardinal noted in an interview with Vatican Radio Oct. 21. "There is calm and there is good will." Also, "there is much interest in a visit (by the Pope). Both the Eastern and Latin bishops have invited the Holy Father, and the government is studying the possibility." The cardinal noted that ecumenical relations in Ukraine were complicated by the existence of three local Orthodox groups, the problem of restitution to the Catholic Church of properties expropriated and turned over to the Orthodox by the former communist government, and Orthodox allegations of aggressive proselytism by Catholics.

Christ Is the Unique and Universal Savior — Indian bishops and Vatican personnel met Oct. 21 to 24 to discuss a current in Indian theology that refrains from proclaiming Christ as the Savior of all mankind out of respect for members of other religions. It is the responsibility of bishops to ensure that Catholic theologians acknowledge "the uniqueness and universality" of Christ's role as Savior "as well as the salvific role of the Church as sacrament and instrument of salvation," Pope John Paul said in a message: "Your meeting has underlined the absolute character of Christian revelation, always with the proper respect for the values present in other religions."

According to a Vatican announcement, the meeting "was intended to coordinate a common approach to the authentic and correct development of theology in India, taking particular account of the context of religious pluralism and interreligious dialogue which characterizes the present ecclesial situation in that country. "The announcement said the bishops emphasized the importance of preaching salvation in Christ, an effort "which at times has been hampered by incorrect theological perspectives."

World Hunger Problem — The problem of world hunger cannot be solved without major ethical changes in the ways food is bought, sold and consumed." So stated a document entitled "World Hunger," released by the Pontifical Council "Cor Unum" Oct. 24 in advance of a November summit meeting to be held in Rome under the auspices of the U.N. Food and Agriculture Organization. "It is generally acknowledged that the resources of the planet, taken as a whole, are sufficient to feed everyone on it," said the document. "It is the selfishness of the well-off that makes it impossible that these food resources are shared," said Archbishop Paul J. Cordes, president of "Cor Unum."

Pope John Paul, in a message marking the observance of World Food Day Oct. 16, deplored the tragedy of world hunger and said the right to nutrition must be guaranteed. He called it a striking paradox that, in an age of global cooperation, "the world remains divided between those who live in abundance and those who lack necessary daily bread."

Vocations Crisis — Dwindling numbers of priests and religious, coupled with growth in the Catholic population, were a cause of crisis for the Church in many parts of Europe, said a report released by the Vatican Oct. 29. "Statistics on priesthood and religious congregations confirm an obvious process of aging, not balanced out by new vocations," according to information supplied by 28 bishops' conferences. The document said that in the previous two decades Europe had witnessed a steady increase in Catholic population — 4.3 percent between 1978 and 1994 — while the number of priests dropped 13 percent and their age increased. At the same time, the number of male and female religious in Europe declined from 37,104 in 1978 to 26,141 in 1994, a drop of 30 percent.

General Audience Topics:
• The Church rejoices that Mary, Mother of the Lord, constantly cooperates in his saving mission (Oct.. 2).
[There were no general audiences Oct. 9 and 16 because of the Holy Father's surgery and hospitalization.]
• The missionary commitment of the Church (Oct.23).
• "The Eucharist is the pivot and heart of every priestly life" (Oct. 30).

Briefs:
• The Pope called on Cistercian monks and nuns to dedicate themselves completely to Christ after the example of their seven brothers who were slain in Algeria in May.
• The Holy Father observed World Mission Day Oct. 20 with prayers for missionaries.
• In a message circulating among bishops throughout the world, the Vatican stressed the need for vigilance and caution with respect to admission into their seminaries of candidates who had left or been dismissed from other seminaries.

Evolution

The Church's acceptance of evolution was the subject of a papal message to members of the Pontifical Academy of Sciences Oct. 22. Pope John Paul noted that the matter had already been the subject of papal reflection: "In his encyclical *Humani Generis* (1950), my predecessor Pius XII stated that there was no opposition between evolution and the doctrine of the faith about man and his vocation, on condition that one did not lose sight of several indisputable points."

Among such points are:
• "Revelation ... contains teaching concerning the nature and origins of man."
• "It is necessary to determine the proper sense of Scripture, while avoiding any unwarranted interpretations that make it say what it does not intend to say."
• "Theories of evolution which ... consider the spirit as emerging from the forces of living matter or as a mere epiphenomenon of this matter are incompatible with the truth about man. Nor are they able to ground the dignity of the human person."
(See separate entry for text of the message.)

NATIONAL

Welfare Reform — Implementation of new federal welfare reform legislation Oct. 1 was called an urgent issue by officials of state Catholic conferences. Provisions of the law included a lifetime limitation on benefits, work requirements, cuts in food stamp, child care and other programs, as well as denial of many benefits to legal immigrants. The law replaced federally run welfare funding with block grants to states for state-run programs. Jane Chiles, executive director of the Catholic Conference of Kentucky, voiced the sentiments of many social workers, saying the new law's "impact on the poor is horrific."

Fund for Women Refugees — The National Council of Catholic Women and Catholic Relief Services launched a joint program of aid for refugee and displaced women victims of disasters. The plan was unveiled Oct. 5 during the NCCW's general assembly by NCCW executive director Annette Kane and CRS head Kenneth Hackett. Hackett told the assembly there were "more than 57 million refugees and displaced people throughout the world, and 60 percent of them were women." The new Refugee Women Emergency Fund aimed to provide women and children with enough food to meet their basic nutritional needs, and would also provide psychological trauma counseling for victims of genocide and ethnic cleansing. For the long term, Kane said the program would seek to educate women about empowerment, literacy and running small businesses.

Morally Flawed Managed Care — Managed care is a "morally flawed system" that interferes with the integrity of the relationship between physician and patient, according to a Franciscan brother who is also a physician. It is flawed at its core because it pits the physician's income against the patient's need through a system of "restrictive gatekeeping" and capitation, Dr. Daniel P. Salmasy said at a conference of health care personnel at Sacred Heart University in Fairfield, Conn. He was the director of clinical bioethics at Georgetown University School of Medicine and a visiting assistant professor of medicine at Johns Hopkins University.

Social Health Index — In 1994, the nation's social health reached its lowest level in 25 years, according to the Index of Social Health released Oct. 14 by Fordham University's Institute for Innovation in Social Policy. In 1970, the first year the index was compiled, the figure stood at 74, on a scale of 100. It peaked at 77.5 in 1973, and dropped thereafter, reaching in 1994 a low of 51 percent of its 1970 value. The index examined 16 social areas, ranging from infant mortality and child abuse to housing and the gap between rich and poor.

Stewardship — Empowering Catholics to become better disciples of Jesus should be the goal of any parish or diocesan stewardship program, not just raising money to meet specific needs. So stated Archbishop Thomas J. Murphy of Seattle at a meeting of the National Catholic Stewardship Conference Oct.15 in New Orleans. He told 1,000 conference delegates that it would be a mistake to "compartmentalize stewardship and only use its challenges when we need resources, time and talent…. The issue is not fund-raising, development or capital campaigns. The issue is a far more radical call to put ourselves in the position of those first disciples who began to walk after Jesus."

Hunger — Despite a worldwide reduction over the previous 20 years, hunger increased dramatically in Africa and the United States, according to the annual World Food Day report issued by Bread for the World Oct.16. Africa's hungry population more than doubled, from 103 million in 1969-1971 to 215 million in 1990-1992, according to statistics for Sub-Saharan Africa. In the United States, hunger increased 50 percent between 1985 and 1995, going from 20 million to 30 million; about 12 million of those were children under 18 years of age. It was estimated that 880 million people worldwide suffered from hunger. The Rev. David Beckmann, a Lutheran minister and president of Bread for the World, called U.S. child hunger and child poverty rates "scandalous."

Catholic Charities —*Money* magazine, in its November edition, ranked Catholic Charities USA second among 25 major U.S. charities "on the basis of how they spend your dollars." Catholic Charities spent 87.7 percent of its 1995 income on programs, second only to 91.5 percent by the American Red Cross. *The Chronicle of Philanthropy* reported Oct. 31 that only the Salvation Army and the American Red Cross received more contributions in 1995 than the approximately $419 million given to the nation's Catholic Charities agencies.

Challenge of Poverty — Poverty is "a challenge we cannot refuse to take up," and the Church has a unique role in meeting it, Archbishop Rembert G. Weakland said at the sixth annual urban ministry conference sponsored by the National Pastoral Life Center. "With the presence we have in those neighborhoods suffering from urban poverty and with our connectedness to the whole society, we should be able to make a difference." He noted that "many urban sectors of our northern cities have already begun to resemble Third World cities."

Catholic Common Ground Project — Cardinal Joseph L. Bernardin told members of its steering committee Oct. 24 that the aim of the project was to help U.S. Catholics rise above hardened party lines and find "renewal in the splendor of the truth revealed in the Person of Jesus who is our Lord and Savior," by promoting dialogue and mutual understanding on divisive issues. Because of his failing health, he named Archbishop Oscar H. Lipscomb of Mobile to succeed him as chairman of the steering committee.

Campaign Banned — Criticizing its "questionable goals, " Archbishop J. Francis Stafford of Denver banned organizers of the "We Are Church" campaign from using Catholic institutions or buildings to gather signatures or hold meetings. In an Oct. 23 column in the archdiocesan newspaper, he said he was taking the action "to safeguard the Catholic faith of the people of God in northern Colorado and the unity of the local church with the Catholic Church throughout the world." "We Are Church," a coalition of groups seeking radical changes in the Church, announced in May plans to gather at least a million signatures to a referendum before Pentecost 1997.

Aguilar v. Felton — The U. S. Education Department urged the Supreme Court to reconsider and overturn its 11-year-old decision on remedial educational services for students in church-run schools. A brief filed late in the month on behalf of Secretary of Education Richard Riley said the decision "has had a significant, adverse impact on the provision of secular educational and counseling services to low-income students in need of remedial aid in both public and private schools." The brief said the requirement that such services take place outside religious schools in order to avoid "excessive entanglement" of church and state wastes federal tax money, provides an inferior education and does not conform with other Supreme Court decisions since 1985.

Briefs:

• President Clinton signed a resolution Oct. 1 conferring honorary citizenship on Mother Teresa.

• True freedom can come only through seeking and living the truth, Cardinal William H. Keeler said Oct. 6 in a homily at the Red Mass in Washington, before the start of the 1996-97 judicial year.

• Bishop James C. Timlin announced Oct. 9 that St. Ann's Monastery Shrine in Scranton, Pa., had been designated a minor basilica.

• The Archdiocese of Chicago participated in a local interfaith coalition that contributed more than $112,000 to the Burned Churches Fund established by the National Council of Churches for the rebuilding of two churches destroyed by arson.

• World Mission Sunday, Oct. 20, was called "critical to the daily work of the Church in close to 1,000 mission dioceses" throughout the world,, said Auxiliary Bishop William J. McCormack of New York, head of the U.S. Society for the Propagation of the Faith.

Media and the Bible

New Testament scholar Father Raymond E. Brown said that public understanding of the Bible is hampered by a tendency of the media to convey fundamentalist teachings, headline-grabbing opinions or skeptical views like those of the Jesus Seminar rather than the solid views of competent scholars at institutions such as the interdenominational Union Seminary in New York. The power of the media in American life makes that a problem in getting a balanced view of the Bible across to Catholic lay persons and the general public, said Father Brown, a member of the Pontifical Biblical Commission, during the annual Merton Lecture at Columbia University Oct.10. He found the media "entranced" by the Jesus Seminar, a group of scholars who had gained publicity by announcing their views that many incidents reported in the Gospels did not happen and that Jesus did not make many of the statements attributed to him. Their pronouncements were often presented as what "scholars" say, as though seminar members constituted the total scholarly community — and the only alternative people heard was fundamentalist teaching.

INTERNATIONAL

Ukrainian Church Council — KAI, Poland's Catholic Information Agency, reported that Cardinal Myroslav Lubachivsky had summoned the first general council of the Ukrainian Catholic Church to "reflect on the church's present situation and point the way for its development in the contemporary world." Among actions taken during the Oct. 6-to-11 meeting in Lviv was the formation of five commissions to monitor the training of priests, family affairs, religious education, youth activities and religious orders. The cardinal turned administrative authority over to Bishop Lubomyr Husar.

West Bank Aid Needed — The Commission for Justice and Peace of the Latin Patriarchate of Jerusalem issued an urgent appeal for assistance and action by bishops worldwide on behalf of Palestinians in areas closed by Israeli troops. "Amid largely false reports to the world media that the closure of the territories and Gaza has been eased, the Israeli government has strictly enforced a policy that the West Bank and Gaza is a closed military zone. That means Palestinians are being denied the freedom to travel," said the Oct. 11 statement. "We ask that you take concrete steps to assist in alleviating the situation.... The anxiety, distress and discouragement of the Palestinian people is growing daily. The closure of the West Bank and Gaza must be lifted immediately."

Christian Brother Robert J. Daszkiewicz, living in Bethlehem, said Israeli military forces had turned the town into a "a virtual prison" and that Bethlehem University had been forced to cancel classes.

Religion Classes Devalued — Hope for the restoration of religion classes to their former status in Spain's public schools faded six months after a new government took office, said the nation's bishops. In a widely perceived slap in the face to the Church in 1995, then-Prime Minister Felipe Gonzalez reduced the academic value of classes in religion. It had been hoped that the new administration would repeal government regulations that stripped religion courses of academic value in time for the start of the 1996-97 school year. In June, however, the new head of government told Congress that there would be no repeal of the anti-religion-class regulation.

Canadian Complaints — In a pastoral letter issued in the middle of the month, the nation's bishops criticized the federal government for its failure to do something about poverty, especially among children and native people. Government was pursuing three objectives, they said: "to cut social spending, to reduce deficits and to pay back our debts. But who raises their voice on behalf of the 4.8 million people living in poverty? Do Canadians realize the human cost of sustaining an overall national poverty level of 16.6 percent?" The statement said "the existence of poverty in Canada seems contradictory to the fact that the country appears at the top of the United Nations Human Development Index" in 1995 and 1996.

At the same time, the Catholic Health Association of Canada said in a statement that massive cuts in federal transfers to the provinces were creating a two-tiered health care system, one for the affluent and one for the poor."

Different Wavelengths — A Vatican envoy cited some progress in recent talks with Vietnamese officials, but said the two sides were still on "different wavelengths" when it came to religious freedom. While churches were open and seminaries were full, the government continued to limit the scope of the Church's religious life and its action in society, Archbishop Claudio Celli said on Vatican Radio Oct. 25 after returning from a visit to the country. One small but gratifying point of agreement connected with "intense and not easy"' talks was Vietnam's consent to the appointment of two coadjutor bishops for the Diocese of Ho Chi Minh City.

Common Church Problem in Europe — "How can we as Christians have the courage to enliven the faith in a pluralistic society with determination and with full trust in the love of God?" was the question framed by Cardinal Miloslav Vlk for discussion at the meeting of the Council of European Bishops' Conferences Oct. 23 to 27 in Rome. Delegates considered problems related to secular influence in society and on the Church, cultural pluralism and "a decrease (among Catholics) in adherence to and participation in the church community." The meeting was attended by 150 delegates; 100 of them were bishops.

Freedom To Broadcast — Cardinal Nasrallah P. Sfeir, Maronite patriarch, emphasized the importance of freedom of religion and expression after an agreement was reached with the Lebanese government to allow Catholic-run radio and television stations to continue broadcasting. "Freedom belongs to everybody; it is a natural right and is not a gift from anybody," he said. "And when (the authorities) in a democratic society take from the opposition their instruments of expression, it signals that there is a defect which must be corrected before it is too late. It is known that there is no respect and no peace without freedom." The patriarch's remarks were prompted by a controversial restructuring of the broadcast system in Lebanon.

Briefs:

• Mehmet Ali Agca, the man who shot Pope John Paul in 1981, said the alleged "Bulgarian Connection" to the assassination attempt was a fabrication of Italian intelligence personnel.

• The much-discussed Third Secret of Fatima is neither sensational nor apocalyptic, said Cardinal Joseph Ratzinger, one of the few people who had actually read it. He made the remark during a visit to the Marian shrine on the 79th anniversary of the last apparition of Mary to three Portuguese children.

• A Catholic priest from Georgia said the Church there enjoyed better relations with local Muslims than with Orthodox Christians. "We have nothing against contacts with the Orthodox," he said; "but the Orthodox Church, including its most senior hierarchs, treats Catholicism as a sect, making any kind of links very difficult."

New Repression in China

"Since the start of this year, some very serious efforts have been made by the Chinese state to gain control of and resolve the problem of the underground Church," an unnamed cleric from China told the congress of Aid to the Church in Need which met in Konigstein, Germany, Sept. 26 to 29. He said centers of the underground Church in Hebei Province had been crushed and a number of bishops forced to flee from their dioceses. "The churches have been shut again, and in some villages there are said to have been collective forswearings of the faith," he added.

In another development, Harry Wu, a Catholic dissident who spent two months in a Chinese prison in 1995, said in several U.S. lectures during the month that at least six million people were in custody in China's estimated 1,100 forced labor camps, farms, wineries, mines and factories. At the same time, "the United States and other industrialized countries (were) more concerned about economics than human rights, freedom and democracy for China."

NOVEMBER 1996

VATICAN

Golden Anniversary — The Holy Father celebrated the actual day of the 50th anniversary of his ordination to the priesthood at a Mass concelebrated Nov. 1 with bishops and priests of the Diocese of Rome. Celebrations on a grander scale began Nov. 7, reaching a climax Nov. 10 with a Mass concelebrated by the Pope with more than 1,500 priests from about 85 countries together with 100 cardinals and 100 bishops — all golden jubilarians. The focus of events was on gratitude for the gift and ministry of the priesthood and the central significance of the Eucharist in the lives of priests.

Predecessors Remembered — Pope John Paul marked All Souls Day Nov. 2 with private prayer at their tombs in the grotto of St. Peter's Basilica.

Contraception Condemned — The Pope condemned contraceptive birth control and said family planning methods deserved better support in demographic campaigns.... In a message to bioethics experts Nov. 8, he criticized the "harmful campaigns of certain demographic policies that try to present contraception as permissible and proper, spreading and imposing an exploitative and utilitarian vision of the life of individuals and peoples.... We need to respond with every initiative that can scientifically support, with correct information, the validity of natural methods." Such an effort is needed to combat a false sense of sexual freedom, "for which contraception provides both the incentive and the instrument, weakening consciences and eclipsing values."

New Approach to Theologians — The Congregation for the Doctrine of the Faith was going to take a more circumspect approach to its monitoring of theologians, said Cardinal Joseph Ratzinger and Archbishop Tarcisio Berone at a Nov. 8 workshop on the roles of the theologian and the teaching authority of the Church. They said a recent plenary assembly of the congregation acknowledged that its review process for theological writings could be improved to "protect even more the author's right to a precise understanding of his thought and respect for his person." In general, said Archbishop Bertone, the congregation was trying to assume an attitude of "listening and consultation," without trying to mortify new theological theories, even if they present problems, until their elements can be fully studied by a wide range of experts. The idea was to "leave as much creative space as possible" to theologians and to avoid boxing them into "pre-fixed "categories."

U.N. Contraception Plan — Vatican officials criticized United Nations' plans to include contraceptives and "morning after" pills in aid packages for Rwandan refugees. The criticism came in the wake of a Nov. 15 U.N. press release saying a six-month pilot project would make a "package of reproductive health services" available to hundreds of thousands of refugees in flight along the Zairean-Rwandan border.

Refugee Hunger — Moments after inaugurating a World Food Summit in Rome, the Pope urged international leaders to turn their words into action for an estimated million hungry refugees in eastern Zaire. Echoing widespread frustration among church and other relief personnel, he criticized as inexcusable delays in sending food and medical supplies to isolated camps, many of which had been overrun in ethnic fighting... The world must send relief "without delay," he told a general audience Nov. 13. "How can one remain indifferent toward people who have been pushed to the limit, while they could be receiving urgently needed food and medicine stocked up in great qualities not far away? ... No uncertainty, no pretext, no calculation can ever justify additional delays in humanitarian assistance!"

Later in the month the Pope said Nov. 22 that, to resolve the refugee crisis in Zaire, it was essential to promote dialogue and solidarity among different religious and ethnic groups there.

"Let all the parties responsible for the drama have the courage for dialogue, for a sincere search in the hope of real reconciliation, with justice and respect for the human person.... I exhort also the international community to redouble efforts to create a real solidarity after bringing aid to the populations of this region."

Gorbachev, Castro and Pope John Paul — The Holy Father had private audiences Nov. 18 and 19, respectively, with former Soviet President Mikhail Gorbachev and Fidel Castro. Vatican spokesman Joaquin Navarro-Valls said the Cuban leader renewed his invitation to the Pope to visit his island nation in the course of discussion of church-state relations.

Cardinal Ratzinger Reappointed — Cardinal Joseph Ratzinger agreed, with some reluctance, to stay on as head of the Congregation for the Doctrine of the Faith for a fourth five-year term, effective Nov. 25. He said: "For now, I have to continue to carry out my job, because the Holy Father wants it. But I hope this doesn't continue for too much longer."

Jubilee Conferences — Anti-Semitism, the Inquisitions and other delicate subjects pertaining to church history would be examined at length in Vatican-sponsored initiatives leading up to the Great Jubilee of the Year 2000, papal theologian Father Georges Cottier told Catholic News Service Nov. 27. He said the Vatican would release a study on anti-Semitism in 1997 and would hold a seminar on the Inquisitions sometime in 1998. Archbishop Sergio Sebastiani, secretary-general of the Vatican Jubilee Committee, provided a general idea of the initiatives, saying: "Two international congresses of high scholarly value are being considered, to take place in Rome before the celebration of the Great Jubilee. This ... could improve comprehension of what has happened, and will help in the discovery of historical truth without subjective and polemical distortion."

Mental Illness — Pope John Paul joined church and medical personnel in calling for respect and legal protection for the mentally ill, at a Nov. 28-to-30 international conference sponsored by the Pontifical Council for Pastoral Assistance to Health Care Workers. "The person who suffers from mental illness ... always has the inalienable right not only to be considered an image of God and therefore a person, but also to be treated as such," the Pope said. Cardinal Fiorenzo Angelini, outgoing president of the council, said that, when mental illness limits the exercise of one's intellect or free will, the Christian community must remind people that "the divine image" continues to be present, that the person must be cared for, and that his or her human dignity must be defended.

Catholic-Orthodox Unity — The faith that Catholics and Orthodox already share calls them to work even harder to become one, the Pope said in a traditional message delivered to Orthodox Patriarch Bartholomew I on the feast of St. Andrew, patron of the Orthodox, Nov. 30.

General Audience Topics:

• In the Magnificat, the Blessed Virgin proclaims the greatness of God who called her to be the Mother of his incarnate Son (Nov. 6).

• "Let us pray that the suffering of so many innocent people and the blood shed by faithful servants of the Church and of the human cause may serve to defeat hatred ... in the beloved African continent" (Nov. 13).

• St. Luke's description of the birth of Jesus invites us to consider that in every age those who wish to encounter him must find him with his Mother (Nov. 20).

• The Council of Ephesus (431) taught that Mary is truly the Mother of God, since she gave birth to the Second Person of the Trinity who became man for our sake (Nov. 27).

Briefs:

• Addressing members of the Pontifical Council for Justice and Peace Nov. 8, the Pope said: "In many countries, democracy could be put in peril by points of view ... of indifference or relativism in the moral domain."

• At a press conference Nov. 9, Cardinal Edmund C. Szoka, head of the Prefecture for the Economic Affairs of the Holy See, predicted a 1997 Vatican budget surplus of $642,000.

• The Pope sent a message to Catholics in southern Sudan, encouraging them to give witness to their faith "in the midst of adversity and even of persecution."

• "Insofar as it is formed by beings created equal by God, society has the obligation to promote solidarity at its heart and to establish structures to make it operative," said the Pope Nov. 23 at a meeting on social justice.

Jubilee 2000 Preparation

The Holy Father celebrated a "Liturgy of Light" and special evening prayer service Nov. 30, the eve of the first Sunday of Advent, to mark the beginning of three years of prayer, study and works of charity in preparation for Holy Year 2000. He urged Catholics to focus attention in 1997 on efforts "to discover the glory of God revealed in Christ."

The preparatory itinerary "will lead us to the threshold of the Holy Door which I will open, if it pleases God, on the night of Christmas 1999," the Pope said in reference to the practice of opening a bricked-up door in St. Peter's Basilica at the beginning of a holy year.

NATIONAL

No School Prayer — The U. S. Supreme Court let stand Nov. 4 a ruling that overturned a Mississippi law which would have allowed student-led prayer in the state's public schools. Without comment, the court left intact a ruling by the 5th U.S. Circuit Court of Appeals that found unconstitutional the 1994 statute which would have required public schools to permit invocations, benedictions and "nonsectarian, nonproselytizinng, student-initiated prayer" at all stu-

dent activities including assemblies and sports events.Teacher-led prayer in public schools was declared unconstitutional by the Supreme Court in 1992.

Election Results — It was estimated that 53 percent of the Catholic vote Nov. 5 went to President Bill Clinton. On state ballot initiatives followed by Catholic officials, voters eliminated affirmative action in California, rejected gambling in Ohio and Arkansas, upheld a property tax exemption for nonprofit bodies, including churches, in Colorado, and passed wage increases in California and Oregon. Catholic officials took positions on only a fraction of the 90 initiatives put on ballots by citizen petitions in the 24 states allowing such procedure.

Black-Hispanic Dialogue — Participants in the third national dialogue of African-Americans with Hispanics and other Latinos agreed to share some religious and civic observances as a way of building bridges between their communities. A resolution signed by representatives from Texas, New York, Nicaragua and California called for a joint worship service on the Nov. 3 feast of St. Martin de Porres, son of a Spanish father and a black mother. Also, African Americans made a commitment to go to Hispanic and Latino communities to celebrate the feast of Our Lady of Guadalupe Dec. 12, while Hispanics agreed to join African-Americans for the national holiday commemorating the birthday of the Rev. Martin Luther King, Jr., Jan.15. The dialogue, held Nov. 7 to 9 in Rochester, N.Y., was attended by 200 representatives from 14 states and five colleges and universities.

Crisis in Zaire — While the humanitarian crisis in eastern Zaire demanded swift international response, responsibility for establishing peace rested mainly with leaders in Africa's Great Lakes region, according to Bishop Daniel P. Reilly, chairman of the International Policy Committee, U.S. Catholic Conference. He said in a statement Nov. 8: "The greatest responsibility rests with the leadership of the region who, through their actions, will determine the effectiveness of any future peace." He urged U.S. action "to take the lead" in the international community in using diplomatic pressure on regional governments in order to: end the conflict between Zairean, Hutu and Tutsi forces; develop safe corridors and roads to allow people to move to safety; prepare air lifts of supplies to refugee and local populations; reimpose an arms embargo on Rwanda; impose an embargo on countries contributing to conflict by arms dealing and shipment.

Managed Health Care — Managed care and "merger mania" in the hospital industry were priority topics at the 65th annual meeting of the Catholic Medical Association Nov. 9 and 10 in Scottsdale, Ariz. Bishop John J. Myers of Peoria discussed the relationship between the Church and health care, particularly with respect to mergers involving Catholic providers and other entities. "Our health care ministry is too precious to lose," he said. "It remains one of our most vital apostolates. In these times ... (it) must remain the treasured ministry that it is by adapting prudently, bravely and confidently — and always in ways that are absolutely faithful to the teachings of Christ and his Church.... We have a large stake in the provision of health care in the United States as the largest nonfederal provider. We must use what clout we have to offer an alternative to the downward trends in contemporary science and medicine."

Different Concepts of Faith — A study on the concept of faith held by Catholics in different age groups indicated that those who grew up in the 1970s and 1980s followed a "societal shift" of recent decades "from an institutional-collective world view to a personal-individual emphasis." The study, entitled "Catholic Conceptions of Faith: A Generational Analysis," was written by Andrea S. Williams and James D. Davidson of Purdue University. Their study concluded that "the post-Vatican II generation maintains the most individualistic views of faith. Concern with whether an individual is a 'good person' dominates their discussions," adding that members of this group "do not describe the Church as an essential component of their faith." The study used focus groups made up of 135 Indiana residents from diverse ethnic and racial backgrounds.

Budgeting on Backs of the Poor — A Catholic Charities official said Nov. 26 that the poor had already paid a disproportionate price in efforts to balance the federal budget, and must not suffer more. "In the name of the 30 million Americans living in poverty, we must insist: Enough is enough! There cannot and must not be more budget cuts to programs that serve poor people," said Father John White of Rockville Center, N.Y., "We have no quarrel with the effort to cut the deficit and reduce the debt. We support that effort.But, we cannot remain silent as poor families become the soft underbelly of deficit reduction."

Briefs:

• U.S. Catholics do less volunteer work for their church than members of several other religious groups, according to the findings of a research group headed by Dean Hoge of The Catholic University of America.

•Two bishops — Archbishop Theodore E. McCarrick of Newark and Bishop Ricardo Ramirez of Las Cruces — were among 20 religious leaders and academics named to a new U.S. State Department Advisory Committee on Religious Freedom Abroad.

• Cardinal William H. Keeler of Baltimore told an anti-porn summit meeting Nov. 22 that more Jewish and Muslim representation was needed in the anti-pornography movement.

Cardinal Joseph L. Bernardin

Cardinal Joseph L. Bernardin, one of the most notable leaders of the Church in the United States, died of pancreatic cancer Nov. 14 and, widely mourned, was buried Nov. 20. He was born in 1928, ordained to the priesthood in 1952, became a bishop in 1966, was named archbishop of Chicago in 1982 and became a cardinal in 1983. He served in several Vatican congregations, attended six assemblies of the Synod of Bishops and was a member of its ordinary council for several terms. He also served as general secretary and president of the National Conference of Catholic Bishops and the U. S. Catholic Conference, the only one to hold both offices, and was active in conference activities and the writing of significant documents since 1968. In the 1980s he delivered a series of lectures outlining the "consistent ethic of life" ("seamless garment") theme as a framework for applying Catholic social and moral teachings to is-

sues related to the fundamental human rights of life and dignity. In 1983, he headed the conference committee which wrote the pastoral letter entitled "The Challenge of Peace: God's Promise and Our Response," Three months before his death, Cardinal Bernardin initiated the Catholic Common Ground Project to promote dialogue among Catholics with differing views on church-related issues.

INTERNATIONAL

UNICEF Donation Suspended — Vatican concern about recent trends of UNICEF climaxed Nov. 4 with the suspension of its annual gifts that are symbolic in amount but significant as moral endorsements. "The Holy See regrets to inform that it has decided it cannot offer any symbolic contribution to UNICEF this year," said Vatican Nuncio Archbishop Renato R. Martino. The Holy See's U.N. Mission said in a statement that UNICEF had been involved in distributing contraceptives, advocating abortion-related legislation and preparing an official U.N. manual advocating "post-coital contraceptives" for refugee women in emergency situations. Archbishop Martino told Catholic News Service in a later interview that the Vatican had decided it had to act when UNICEF failed to provide any means of assuring that funds designated for specific activities in harmony with Catholic principles would be used only in that way.

Vatican Representations to the United Nations — In addresses before U.N. agencies during the month, Archbishop Renato R. Martino called for:

• more investment and aid to African nations by the international community, Nov. 5;

• easing of sanctions imposed on Burundi, Nov. 20;

• Israeli-Palestinian negotiations to address the issue of Israeli settlement in the West Bank and Gaza, Nov. 22.

He also cited the taping of a prisoner's sacramental confession the previous April in Oregon as an example of improper "intrusion of the state into the practice of religion."

Syro-Malabar Synod and Problem — A synod of the Syro-Malabar Church ended Nov. 15 without resolving differences between one group seeking to revive ancient tradition and another group wanting revision along modern lines. Also involved in the dispute were allegations of Vatican "domination" of the church that traces its origin to St. Thomas the Apostle.

Not Obliged to Catholics of Vision — Members of an Ottawa-based group calling for radical changes in the Church should not count on circulating their petitions in parishes of the Archdiocese of Toronto. So stated Father John Murphy, chancellor of spiritual affairs. "The church is not obliged to cooperate with these individuals in a manner they'd like," he said regarding a petition of Catholics of Vision: Canada, a network of Catholics seeking a church that would be "inclusive, egalitarian, affirming and democratic." They would be calling for married priests, lay involvement in the choice of bishops, more ecumenical action on social justice and ecological issues, readmission of divorced and remarried Catholics to full sacramental communion, lay participation in the development of teaching on sexuality, and freedom for theologians to do research, publish and teach without censure.

In another development, protest groups from 10 countries met in Rome late in the month to present a united front to the Vatican in an effort to bring about changes in the Church. Assembled under the name We Are Church, they established a coordinating body, agreed to organize a pilgrimage, and produced a declaration in "response to the suffering of many in the Church due to lack of freedom, justice and compassion."

Moonies in Uruguay — The Uruguayan bishops' conference warned Catholics not to become involved in the Unification Church of the Rev. Sun Myung Moon. "New situations of confusion and deceitful campaigning have affected the good faith of Christians both in Uruguay and in other Latin American countries," they said in a statement issued Nov. 14. "The ideas of Mr. Moon are a denial of our Christian faith. The Unification Church cannot be presented as a Christian church, forming part of the ecumenical movement," the declaration added. The warning was issued in the wake of an announcement that 4,200 female Unification "missionaries," the majority from Japan, were coming to the country for 10 days of training led by Moon and would then be sent to the United States and Canada as well as to parts of Latin America and the Caribbean.

Criticism of Neocatechumenal Way — The Neocatechumenal Way was criticized in a report produced for Bishop Mervyn Alexander of Clifton in southwestern England. He established a panel of enquiry after receiving complaints from parishioners of three churches that their parishes had been harmed by the presence of Way members. The Neocatechumenal Way was founded in Spain in 1964. Its members describe themselves as "a group of people who wish to rediscover and to live Christian life to the full; to live the essential consequences of their baptism by means of a Neocatechumenal Way divided into different stages, like that of the early Church." The report concluded that the Way had not brought new vitality to the three parishes concerned. "Regrettably, the opposite is the case. These parishes lack unity and have declined pastorally as a parish community within the Clifton diocese since the introduction of the NC Way," it said. The report, published Nov. 7, recommended that all parishes in the diocese should receive pastoral guidance from the bishop and those appointed by him. It also said that parish activities should never be "exclusively Neocatechumenate" but "should be representative of the parish as a whole."

Resignation of Seminary Staff — Five staff members of Corpus Christi College seminary in Melbourne, Australia, resigned rather than help institute reforms designed to support the spiritual development of students for the priesthood. Archbishop George Pell, who asked the staff to put the changes into effect, said the reforms were in line with Vatican recommendations and concerned practices Catholics would expect to find in a seminary: "daily Mass, morning meditation, morning prayer of the Church, evening prayer of the Church, a Holy Hour once a week in front of the Blessed Sacrament, private recitation of the Rosary and devotions to Our Lady in May." The archbishop called the program "very non-controversial. The five staff members, including the rector, thought otherwise.

Report on Aboriginals — The release of a long-awaited report of the Royal Commission on Aboriginal Peoples marked a "prophetic moment" in Canada's history, said Father Doug Crosby, general secretary of the Canadian Conference of Catholic Bishops.. "It really does call us into a new relationship with native people," he said Nov. 21. "We are committed to working in solidarity with aboriginal peoples. That commitment is grounded in the Gospel's demand for justice and action." But he and representatives of other churches echoed concerns of aboriginal leaders that the federal government might shelve the report, five years in the making at a cost of $58 million. The Rev. Marion Best, moderator of the United Church of Canada, said: "The question for the government and for all of us is whether we will, in fact, move on some of the things in this report as a nation to put in place a more just society. We believe there is a tremendous amount of healing that needs to go on."

Briefs:
• The Archdiocese of San Salvador ended Nov. 1 the first phase of the cause for the canonization of Archbishop Oscar A. Romero with completion of a review of his life.

A revised report by the General House of the Marist Brothers said that four of their members serving refugees in Zaire had been killed by Hutu militia men Oct. 31.

• Father Bill Anderson of Aberdeen, Scotland, was named Great Britain's "Preacher of the Year" by the College of Preachers, an ecumenical in-service resource center for preachers.

• Father Luke Tsui Kam-yiu, a diocesan priest, and Teresa Yiu Shau-hing were chosen as members of the Selection Committee to elect Hong Kong's post-1997 chief executive and provisional legislature.

World Food Summit

The Vatican and 14 countries that signed the final document of the World Food Summit expressed their reservations about it in separate amendments. On the last day of the conference, the Vatican listed its concerns about population control, reproduction and gender issues, and said its consent to the document did not imply change in church teaching.

Pope John Paul, in an address at the opening of the Nov. 13-to-17 summit in Rome, said it was intolerable that 800 million people worldwide did not have enough food while so many others had so much. Contrasts "between poverty and wealth are intolerable for humanity," he said. "It is up to nations, to their leaders, to their economic authorities and to all people of good will to research how to share resources most equitably in every way possible."

The final document set the following nonbinding commitments for the 186 governments that took part in the conference, under the sponsorship of the Food and Agriculture Organization of the United Nations:
• find ways to ensure a social and economic environment that allows for land reform;
• implement policies to eradicate poverty and inequality;
• pursue sustainable agricultural development;
• foster a fair and market-oriented world trade system;
• encourage public and private investment so that food security might be guaranteed.

DECEMBER 1996

VATICAN

Defining Papal Primacy — Because the bishop of Rome is meant to serve and guarantee the unity of the Church, any progress in defining the essential elements of papal primacy will help the ecumenical movement, Pope John Paul said. A Catholic exploration of primacy, "far from constituting a difficulty for ecumenical dialogue, represents a necessary condition for it," because the dialogue must be based on truth. The Pope made his comments in a message to a symposium on "The Primacy of the Successor of Peter," sponsored by the Congregation for the Doctrine of the Faith and held Dec.2 to 4. The bishop of Rome — his role, power and authority in the Church — is one of the key questions dividing Christians. The subject under discussion, said the Pope, is the way in which the primacy of the bishop of Rome is exercised, not its very existence. Comments on the matter were solicited by the Pope in his 1995 encyclical letter *Ut Unum Sent.*

Unity among Chinese Catholics — In a strongly worded message, the Pope urged the restoration of unity among Chinese Catholics and their full communion with Rome. Such communion means "visible unity among all, pastors and the faithful, around the Pope," said the message, read at a Mass for China broadcast Dec. 3 on Vatican Radio. "I know the Church in the People's Republic of China wants to be truly Catholic, even in suffering and in its particular historic condition.... Therefore, it should remain united with Christ, with the successor of Peter and with the entire universal Church, above all through the ministry of bishops in communion with the Apostolic See. This is a truth of faith," he said. The Holy Father's words had special significance in China, where the government-approved and -controlled Chinese Catholic Patriotic Association rejects papal authority and elects bishops without Vatican authorization. An underground Church, however, estimated to number in the millions, professes loyalty to the Pope — under repressive conditions.

Natural Family Planning — The Pope defended natural family planning as an effective method of spacing births and said it frees women from "unjust" programs of birth control. He called on parishes and other organizations involved in counseling married couples to make sure experts on natural family planning are available. "The scientific validity of these methods and their educational value make them increasingly appreciated," he said Dec. 7. Unlike contraceptive methods, which are morally wrong, natural family planning methods promote a type of "human ecology," a balance between respect for nature and human behavior. "On a worldwide level, this choice supports the process of freedom and emancipation of women and of populations from unjust programs of family planning."

Traditional Visit — Pope John Paul made a traditional visit to Rome's Spanish Steps, the site of a statue of Mary erected to commemorate the proclamation of the dogma of the Immaculate Conception Dec. 8, 1854.

Grandmother-Surrogate — *L'Osservatore Romano* said the case of a British grandmother who carried her daughter's baby to term was a "reprehensible" act that harms human dignity. Human procreation cannot be handed over to "artificial techniques" but "must take place according to the plan established by God," said an editorial in the Dec.10 edition of the Vatican newspaper. The 52-year-old woman gave birth to a girl Dec. 6. She had been implanted with an embryo created from her daughter's egg and the sperm of her daughter's husband. The daughter had been born without a womb. The editorial said the case was against medical ethics for two reasons: the use of in vitro fertilization to create the embryo and the use of a surrogate mother.

Idolatry of Homosexuality — In a Dec. 18 editorial by staff theologian Father Gino Concetti, the Vatican newspaper warned that a public campaign for greater acceptance of homosexual lifestyles was leading to an "idolatry of homosexuality," and that "the leaders of homosexuality want to win at any cost." The editorial said that well-known homosexuals had adopted a "strategy of attack" in order to push their agenda in general society," and that "the siege has become more aggressive and bold."

Poor People Can't Wait — In a pre-Christmas address to Vatican personnel, the Pope denounced widespread poverty around the world and said the poor could not wait for long-term solutions. "Unfortunately, while the international community reflects on the problems of humanity, often taking a long time to deal with them, men, women and children are experiencing unspeakable suffering," he said Dec.21. "Every day we witness a frightful spectacle of individuals and populations pushed to the limit by situations of poverty." Their plight clashes with "the consumerism of well-off regions." He added: "It is urgently necessary for states to commit themselves to economic and food policies based not only on profit but also on sharing."

Christmas Message — The Holy Father prayed that the peace and joy invoked in Christmas carols of every language would inspire true harmony in Africa, the Middle East and other places of strife. "To resign ourselves to such violence and injustice would be too grave a rejection of the joy and hope which Christmas brings," he said in his annual message to the city of Rome and the world. "I pray that the source of joy issuing forth in human history with the birth of the Son of God will be plentiful for all, so that each person may draw from it and quench his thirst." In the message broadcast by television stations in about 70 countries, the Pope extended Christmas greetings in 55 languages.

With a reduced Christmas schedule of events which, for the first time did not include a public Mass Christmas morning, the Pope appeared in good condition.

Cemetery Desecration Condemned — The Vatican condemned "the profanation of the Jewish tombs in the Roman cemetery at Prima Porta" said spokesman Joaquin Navarro-Valls. This offense against the memory of the dead is also an offense against history," he said in a statement Dec. 30. The profanation took place during the night of Dec. 28-29 when 14 tombstones marked with the Star of David were torn from graves, broken apart and thrown into a trash container; also, Nazi swastikas mounted on long sticks were planted into the ground among the desecrated graves.

End-of-Year Prayer Service — Pope John Paul rang out 1996 with a *Te Deum* of thanksgiving and an appeal to Catholics in Rome to make moral preparations for Jubilee Year 2000. "I truly hope for everyone's commitment in giving this city an image more in keeping with the values of faith, culture and civility that stem from its vocation and its ancient history, especially in view of the Great Jubilee of the Year 2000," he said Dec. 31. He noted that he had visited 10 Roman parishes during the year, and a total of 251 since he became Pope.

Briefs:

• The Pope told a group of Italian legal experts Dec. 7 that protecting the legal rights of minors is a "fundamental duty of justice."

• At a special Mass Dec. 2, the Pope told 10,000 students along with their chaplains that they could profoundly influence the spiritual development of people.

• Tensions in the Middle East were the subject of conversation at a Dec. 19 meeting of the Pope and Palestinian leader Yasser Arafat.

• The Pope encouraged Bishop Carlos Felipe Ximenes Belo of East Timor to continue working for peace and reconciliation in his homeland. The bishop was a co-winner of the 1996 Nobel Peace Prize.

• The Pope said Dec. 22 that the taking and holding of hundreds of hostages by Peruvian rebels was a "cruel and immoral" action. The hostages were seized Dec. 17 by partisans of the Tupac Amaru Revolutionary Movement and detained in the Japanese embassy in Lima.

Meetings of Pope with Archbishop and Catholicos

Pope John Paul met during the month with Archbishop George L. Carey of Canterbury, head of the Anglican Communion, and Catholicos Karekin I of Etchmiadzin, supreme patriarch of the Armenian Apostolic Church. Both meetings produced common declarations of commitment to continuing efforts to achieve Christian unity.

The Pope welcomed Archbishop Carey Dec. 3 on his arrival for a three-day visit of the Vatican during which the two prelates met privately, delivered matching public addresses, took part in an evening prayer service Dec. 5 and afterwards signed a Common Declaration. They called it "a testimony to the communion we know we already share by God's mercy and demonstrates our intention that it should come to the fullness willed by Christ." The declaration cited positive interrelations over the previous 25 years or more while acknowledging the existence of serious disagreements needing further consultation "about how the relationship between the Anglican Communion and the Catholic Church is to progress."

Two days before the end of his five-day visit, the Catholicos and the Pope signed Dec. 13 a Common Declaration which marked the completion of a series of agreements with independent Oriental Orthodox churches, expressing a common understanding of the humanity and divinity of Christ. Such understanding had been clouded since the fifth century because of East-West differences in terminology and culture, not in a different understanding of Christ. The declaration said of Christ: "Perfect God as to his divinity, perfect man as to his humanity, his divinity is united to his humanity in the Person of the only-begotten Son of God, in a union which is real, perfect, without confusion, without alteration, without division, without any form of separation."

In a formal address to the Catholicos and his entourage, the Pope said their two churches "mutually recognize the validity of the priestly ministry and the episcopy, and celebrate the same sacraments, particularly baptism and the Eucharist."

(See separate coverage of the declarations.)

NATIONAL

Same-Sex Marriage — The Hawaii Catholic Conference labeled as "a terrible mistake" a judge's ruling that a ban on same-sex marriages was unconstitutional and said it would participate in an appeal of the decision.. Hawaii Circuit Court Judge Kevin Chang ruled Dec. 3 in Baehr v Miiki that the state, during a non-jury trial the previous September, failed to find a "compelling state interest" to ban same-sex marriages. In 1993, the Hawaii Supreme Court ruled that the state could not deny marriage licenses to couples on the basis of their sex unless there was "compelling state interest" to do so. The day after Chang handed down his ruling, he issued an order to put it on hold while the state appealed.

African-Americans and Hispanics — Hispanic Catholics and African-American Catholics must learn to recognize their similarities and respect their differences, according to a joint statement issued by two committees of U.S. bishops. They said they wrote the statement, "Reconciled through Christ," to "help pastoral leaders and church personnel to gain a deeper understanding about the two diverse groups which find themselves in close proximity in neighborhoods and parishes." The statement was approved the previous month during the annual meeting of the bishops. They said the approximately 20 million Hispanic Catholics and three million African-American Catholics have much in common.

Business Should Do More — The president of Covenant House called for more businesses to get involved in programs of direct assistance to youth. "At Covenant House, we have worked closely with companies and individuals to provide mentorships and job opporunities for our kids," said Sister Mary Rose McGeady. "One thousand corporations have assisted us by providing entry-level jobs for kids. My challenge is for every company in America to provide similar opportunities for youth." Sister McGeady issued her appeal Dec. 4 during the sixth annual Covenant House "Candlelight Vigil for Homeless Kids."

Religion Helps To Heal — Ninety-nine percent of 269 members of the American Academy of Family Physicians agreed that religious belief can contribute to the healing of a patient, according to a survey conducted by Yankelovich Partners the previous October. Results of the survey were announced Dec. 16 during a three-day Harvard Medical School continuing education course on "Spirituality and Healing in

Medicine." "Through the ages physicians have witnessed recoveries they can't attribute solely to medical procedures," said Dr. Herbert Benson, president of the Mind/Body Medical Institute at Beth Israel Deaconess Medical Center in Boston. "Now, many physicians are beginning to hold that religious belief can have a profound influence on health and well-being, and they see it as an integral part of their traditional treatment plan," he added.

Christian Officers for Bible Club — The U.S. Supreme Court let stand a ruling that allowed a Bible club at Roslyn High School, Long Island, to require its officers to be Christians. Without comment Dec. 16, the court let stand an earlier ruling by the 2nd U.S. Circuit Court of Appeals. The law suit at issue was brought by Emil and Timothy Hsu against the Roslyn Union Free School District in 1993. They contended that a district regulation interfered with their religious freedom and with federal law requiring equal access to school facilities to all religious groups. The case involved the 1984 Equal Access Act which ensures non-discriminatory access to public high schools acceptng federal funding.

Millions Left Out — Despite the three-year economic upturn, "milllions of families are being left out of the economic good times," the president of Catholic Charities USA said Dec. 17. "The demand for emergency food and shelter rose steadily during the last recession, but it has not gone down after three years of recovery," said Jesuit Father Fred Kammer at a Washington press conference as he released statistics on the organization's work in 1995, when Catholic Charities agencies nationwide served nearly 10.8 million people. "Bread lines and homelessness — hallmarks of the Depression — now have become permanent fixtures in communities across the United States," he said. And, "this is happening at a time when the federal government is ending its 60-year welfare commitment to poor people and taking away food stamps from hungry families."

Venerable Pierre Toussaint — Pierre Toussaint (1766-1853), the Haitian slave who was brought to and freed in the United States where he became known in New York for works of charity and the practice of "heroic virtue," was declared venerable by Pope John Paul Dec. 17, in an early step toward possible canonization as a saint.

Leading 1996 News Stories — Thirty-eight editors of Catholic News Service client newspapers listed the following stories as tops in 1996: (1) abortion, especially regarding partial-birth abortion; (2) the death of Cardinal Bernardin of Chicago; (3) elections; (4) assisted suicide; (5) papal health and succession; (6) Common Ground project; (7) Africa; (8) welfare reform; (9) Mother Teresa's health; (10) burning of black churches. Newmakers were rated: (1) Cardinal Bernardin; (2) Pope John Paul; (3) Mother Teresa; (4) President Clinton; (5) Sister Helen Prejean.

Briefs:
• Father Robert J. Vitillo, Caritas Internationalis' delegate to the United Nations and the World Bank, was named executive director of the bishops' Campaign for Human Development, effective Jan. 6, 1997.
• The Diocese of St. Petersburg advised Catholics to be skeptical about what some people believed was an apparition of Mary in the glass panels of a finance company's office building in Clearwater, Fla.

Role of Ambassador to the Vatican

Three former U.S. ambassadors to the Holy See wrote to President Clinton, urging him to return the Vatican ambassadorship to a more traditional role, avoiding "the appearance that the post is a political toy." They said that, although Clinton's expansion of the role was unusal but "evidently well intended," it caused a "series of controversies which have clouded the integrity of the U.S. diplomatic mission." Among controversies cited were a proposed fund-raiser that never materialized and "enormous correspondence" with Americans. The letter, dated Nov. 25 and obtained by Catholic News Service Dec. 19, was timed to coincide with the Clinton team's transition after his reelection, said a source familiar with the letter. It was signed by William A. Wilson, Frank Shakespeare and Thomas P. Melady.

INTERNATIONAL

Racial Intolerance — In the midst of continuing public debate on migration and aboriginal policy, the bishops of Australia issued a pastoral letter at the end of their November meeting condemning racial intolerance and declaring any form of it incompatible with Catholic faith. In the letter entitled "A Rich and Diverse Australia," they urged all Australians to respect the equal dignity and rights of all citizens, regardless of culture and ethnic origin. They said: "It is right for the people of Australia to conduct a rational and ongoing discussion concerning the number of migrants who should be allowed to enter the country." However, "It is not right to link this discussion to racist attitudes toward Asians or any other people. It is never right to say or do anything that arouses racism."

Forced Sterilization in Peru — The secretary-general of the Peruvian bishops' conference denounced a forced sterilization campaign among Quechua-speaking Andean women peasants by heath authorities. In a letter to regional health director Dr. Ulises Jorge Aguilar, Bishop Luis Armando Bambaren Gastelumendi claimed to have "consistent proof confirming that peasant women are forced to go through 'family planning' before getting any health treatment at local hospitals.... Even women who arrive at hospitals in emergency situations are first forced to go to the family planning department" as a precondition to receiving medical assistance. The campaign, mentioned in the bishop's late November letter, was under way despite President Alberto Fujimori's commitment to limit birth control programs to providing information.

Pope Rebuked by Chinese — Chinese officials rebuked Pope John Paul for remarks he made on religious freedom in the country, and demanded that the Vatican stop "interfering" in their domestic affairs. News agencies in China reported that a spokesman for the administration said the Vatican "must cease its interference in China's internal affairs, including ... making use of religion." The "interference" was a statement made by the Pope Dec. 3 during a Vatican-Radio broadcast of a Mass for the people of China. He urged China to let its Catholics have official links to the Vatican: "Let the civil authorities of the People's Republic of China be reassured: A disciple of Christ can live his faith in any kind of political order so long as there is respect for his right to act according to the dictates of his conscience and faith." The government-controlled Chinese Catholic Patriotic Association claimed three million members. An additional 3 to 10 million Catholics loyal to the Holy See were thought to belong to the "underground" Church.

Jubilee People Declaration — The Jubilee People organization in England issued Dec. 7 a declaration calling for church reforms ranging from democratic decision-making, optional celibacy for priests, ordination of women to the priesthood, sexual morality, a new attitude toward women and the primacy of individual conscience. The "We-Are-Church" declaration had the support of a variety of groups including the Catholic Caucus of the Lesbian and Gay Christian Movement; Advent, a group of priests who had left the ministry and married; the Catholic Women's Network, and Catholic Women's Ordination. The concerns of the alliance of Jubilee People were essentially the same as those of their counterparts in Austria and Germany who gathered a reported 2.5 million reform-seeking signatures.

Nobel Peace Prize for Bishop — Bishop Carlos Filipe Ximenes Belo of Dili, East Timor, and human rights activist Jose Ramos-Horta were awarded the 1996 Nobel Peace Prize Dec. 10 in Oslo. The laureates received gold medals, diplomas and their $1.2 million prize from Nobel committee chairman Francis Sejersted during a ceremony attended by hundreds of dignitaries, including King Harald V of Norway. The two men were honored "for their long-lasting efforts to achieve a just and peaceful solution to the 20-year-old conflict in East Timor." At issue in the conflict involving Portugal and Indonesia was the future of East Timor. Bishop Belo, apostolic administrator of Dili since 1983, was a champion of human rights for the East Timorese. He was instrumental in attracting international attention to the situation in East Timor following a 1991 massacre in which troops shot and killed up to 200 marchers at a funeral procession in Dili, and again in 1994 after hundreds of mainly Catholic protestors were beaten by police. "It is high time that the guns of war are silenced in East Timor, once and forever," the bishop said in his acceptance speech. It is high time that tranquility is returned to the lives of the people of my homeland. It is high time that there be authentic dialogue.... It is my fervent hope that the 1996 Nobel Prize for Peace will advance these goals."

Need To Unite against Sects — Catholics and Orthodox in the former Soviet Union must put aside their differences and present a united front against the growing inroads of sects, said leaders of the two churches at a meeting Dec. 17 and 18 in Moscow. They focused discussions on "the serious danger for the internal life of the Christian communities" posed by the influx and growing activities of "the numerous so-called new religious movements and sects." They proposed holding a high-level conference of theologians, church historians and missionary experts to seek ways and means of dealing with the problem.

Peace Appeal — Latin-rite Patriarch Michel Sabbah called on Israelis and Palestinians to continue working toward peace and said that, despite current difficulties, he still had hope. "We call upon Israelis and Palestinians, religious leaders and also upon our fellow Christians and Muslim brothers, to work together to build peace," he said at his annual Christmas press conference. "We ask them to take up a common initiative to build trust between Palestinians and Israelis. We call upon (Jewish, Christian and Muslim) religious leaders to assume this responsibility."

Briefs:

• The first campus of the first Catholic university in Haiti, inaugurated in the fall, was open and running with sessions of its medical and nursing schools.

• The Holy See demonstrated its continuing support of the U.N. Relief and Works Agency for Palestine Refugees in the Near East by making another symbolic contribution of $20,000, the Holy See's nuncio to the United Nations announced Dec. 5.

• About 100 female and male theologians from around the world took part in the assembly of the Ecumenical Association of Third World Theologians early in the month in Manila. The theme of the meeting was "The Quest for a New Just World Order: Challenges to Theology."

• Peruvian Archbishop Juan Luis Cipriani Thorne celebrated Christmas Mass in the presence of more than 100 hostages detained in the Japanese Embassy in Lima by members of the Tupac Amaru Revolutionary Movement.

• Thirty-one missionaries, men and women members of Comboni and Dominican communities, were awaiting an airlift to safety Dec. 31 after fleeing from marauding Zairean troops that looted and sacked their stations in the town of Isiro.

Factors of Ethnicity and Arms

Power struggles fueled by ethnic differences and easy access to weapons on the global arms market had mired the Great Lakes region of Africa in blood, bishops of the region said at a meeting Dec. 18 to 21 in Nairobi, Kenya. They also said "even members of our own churches have succumbed to the contamination" of ethnic hatred. The bishops met with Cardinal Roger Etchegaray, president of the Pontifical Council for Justice and Peace, to discuss the Church's role in ending conflict in the region and caring for the hundreds of thousands of people displaced by the fighting. The prelates said, among other things:

• Ethnicity becomes the worst of threats when private or political interests transform it into an ideology, an instrument of conquest and of power."

• Combined with "the sordid trafficking of arms, politics based on ethnic identity "breeds conflict and increases the spiral of discrimination, exclusion and violence to the point of massacres and even genocide.... Ethnocentric ideology is contrary to the Gospel."

• The bishops called on Catholics in the region to repent of their prejudices while praising those who had made heroic sacrifices on behalf of others. "The Church has a pressing need for artisans of reconciliation."

JANUARY 1997

VATICAN

Day of Peace — "Offer forgiveness and receive peace" was the theme of Pope John Paul's message for the World Day of Peace 1997. At Mass in St. Peter's Basilica, he said: "How necessary forgiveness is if peace is to spring forth in the heart of every believer and every person of good will.... The Church prays and strives for peace in every dimension: for the peace of consciences, for the peace of families, for peace among the nations. She is concerned for peace in the world since she is aware that only through peace can the great community of men develop authentically."

Ordination of 12 Bishops — On the feast of the Epiphany, Jan. 6, the Holy Father ordained 12 bishops from seven countries. He charged them: "Strengthened by (the help of Christ), go forth without hesitating; be faithful and courageous apostles of Christ, proclaiming and witnessing to the Gospel, the light that illumines all peoples. Do not be afraid! Christ is with us every day."

He spoke in a like vein at a meeting with French bishops five days later: "Is it necessary to repeat that episcopal responsibility belongs first and foremost to the spiritual order? Watchful and vigilant, the pastor looks on his faithful and on the whole of society in the light of the Gospel and of his occlusal experience. I wish to strengthen you in your task of proclaiming the Gospel."

International Role of the Holy See — The Pope spoke about the role of the Holy See in international affairs as he welcomed nine new ambassadors to the Vatican Jan. 11. He said: "Within the international community, the Holy See supports every effort to establish effective juridical structures for safeguarding the dignity and fundamental rights of individuals and communities. Such structures, however, can never be sufficient in themselves; they are only mechanisms which need to be inspired by a firm and persevering moral commitment to the good of the human family as a whole. For communities no less than for individuals, commitment to solidarity, reconciliation and peace demands a genuine conversion of heart and an openness to the transcendent truth which is the ultimate guarantee of human freedom and dignity."

Science and Conscience — In an address Jan 11 to participants in the International Conference on Space Research, the Pope said: "I address an appeal to all your colleagues in the various fields of scientific investigation: Make every effort to respect the primacy of ethics in your work; always be concerned with the moral implications of your methods and your discoveries. It is my prayer that scientists will never forget that the cause of humanity is authentically served only if knowledge is joined to conscience."

Celebration of Baptism — "We should celebrate the day of our baptism as we do our birthday," the Pope said on the feast of the Baptism of the Lord, Jan. 12: "Today's feast sheds light on one of the spiritual priorities of our journey toward the Holy Year (2000): the need to have an ever deeper awareness of baptism as the 'basis of Christian living.'

Those who receive this sacrament are baptized in the Spirit of God, to become members of Christ and, with him and with our brothers and sisters, to form 'one body' (1 Cor. 12:13). An immense gift! We should celebrate the day of our baptism as we do our birthday! But, how many of the baptized are fully aware of what they have received? We must give a new impetus to catechesis, to rediscover this gift."

Hopes for Peace — The Pope, in a Jan.13 address to the diplomatic corps accredited to the Holy See, said he wished his reflections on a wide range of international developments would "inspire your own reflection and activity in the service of justice, solidarity and peace between the nations which you represent." Despite many troubles in the world, "hope is not absent from the horizon of humanity. Disarmament has taken important steps forward with the signing of the treaty completely banning nuclear testing, a treaty which the Holy See also signed in the hope that it will be accepted by everyone." He said the "panorama of the international situation suffices to show that between the progress already made and the problems still unresolved, political leaders have a broad field of action. And what the international community perhaps lacks most of all today is not written conventions or forums for self-expression ... but a moral law and the courage to abide by it....There is an urgent need to organize the post-Cold War peace and the post-1989 freedom on the foundation of moral values which are diametrically opposed to that law which would see the stronger, the richer or the bigger imposing on others their cultural models, economic dictates or ideological models."

Priests' Consecration, Mission, Prayer — These are key factors in the lives of priests confronted with contemporary challenges to their identity and ministry, said the Pope Jan. 18 at a meeting with a second group of French bishops. St. Paul's "exhortation to Timothy reminds us of the close link that exists between consecration and mission. Without this unity, the ministry would be merely a social function. Called and chosen by the Lord, priests share in his mission of building up the Church, the body of Christ and the temple of the Spirit. In the Church and on behalf of the Church, priests are a sacramental representation of Jesus Christ, the head and shepherd. Taken from among their brethren, they are first of all men of God; it is important that they do not neglect their spiritual life, for all pastoral and theological activity must in fact begin with prayer.

Legalized Drugs No Answer — Drug abuse is a symptom of deep social and psychological problems that cannot be addressed by the legalization of so-called "soft" drugs, said the Pontifical Council for the Family in a statement issued Jan. 21. Instead of making drug use easier to control, as some proponents of liberalization argue, it would make drug use more acceptable. It makes no sense to distinguish between "soft" and "hard" drugs when both are used as a means of escape from reality and impede a person's maturation and acceptance of responsibility. "The consumption of such substances favors isolation, above all, and then dependence with the passing on to ever-stronger products."

Meeting with Catholicos of Cilicia — On Jan. 25, the last day of the Week of Prayer for Christian Unity, Pope John Paul and the Catholicos of Cilicia met and signed a Common Declaration of faith and of their intention to continue the quest for unity of their churches. His Holiness Aram I Keshishian said he was convinced that their "meeting will be an important factor in reinforcing the fraternal ties that bind us as well as in deepening and expanding the relations and ecumenical collaboration between the Church of Rome and the Catholicate of Cilicia," The Pope told the Catholicos: "Your visit, Holiness, is in keeping with our common will to advance on the way to perfect communion between the Armenian Apostolic Church and the Catholic Church." (See separate entry regarding the Common Declaration.)

General Audience Topics:
• Simeon's words and Anna's example at the presentation of Jesus in the temple shed light on the role of women in Jesus' work of redemption (Jan. 8).
• The episode of the finding of the young Jesus in the temple sheds light on Mary's growing participation in the life and work of her divine Son (Jan. 15).
• During the Week of Prayer for Christian Unity, all followers of Christ are invited to implore the grace of reconciliation and to bear witness to the Gospel (Jan. 22).
• As Jesus grew in wisdom, age and grace, Mary understood better the meaning of her own motherhood and her life with Christ (Jan. 29). This was the 43rd in a series of papal reflections on Mary.

Briefs:
• The Pope told members of the movement Jan. 24 that the history of the Neocatechumenal Way "belongs to that blossoming of movements and ecclesial groups which is one of the most beautiful fruits of the spiritual renewal begun by the Second Vatican Council."
• The pastoral care of divorced and remarried Catholics was the subject of papal remarks Jan.24 at a plenary session of the Pontifical Council for the Family.
• The personalist view of marriage does not exclude law but demands it, said the Pope Jan. 27 in an annual address to personnel of the Roman Rota.

Sri Lankan Theologian Excommunicated

The Congregation for the Doctrine of the Faith issued a notification Jan. 2 saying that Father Tissa Balasuriya "has deviated from the integrity of the truth of the Catholic faith and, therefore, cannot be considered a Catholic theologian; moreover, he has incurred (automatic) excommunication." Among issues involved in the case, according to a statement issued by the bishops of Sri Lanka in 1994, were four "glaring errors":
• downplaying the tradition of the Church;
• minimizing the validity of faith;
• presenting original sin in a way that casts doubt on the divinity of Jesus and his role as Savior, and Mary's role in salvation history;
• implying that the basic role of religion is to work for humanistic liberation.
Father Balasuriya appealed the decision, claiming he was unfairly targeted for censure.

NATIONAL

Care of the Dying — Principles aimed at improving the quality of care for dying persons were endorsed by 40 groups, including the Catholic Health Association, the National Council of Catholic Women and the American Medical Association. The principles addressed: physical and emotional symptoms; support of function and autonomy; advance care planning; aggressive care near death, site of death, CPR and hospitalization; patient and family satisfaction; global quality of life; family burden; survival time; provider continuity and skill; bereavement.

Assisted Suicide Arguments — As they heard arguments in cases that could result in a fundamental change in the American approach to dying, members of the U.S. Supreme Court Jan. 8 appeared concerned that legalizing physician assisted suicide might lead to acceptance of euthanasia for less critically ill persons. Although attorneys arguing in favor of legalizing physician assisted suicide insisted that such a right should be limited only to those in the final stage of terminal illness, most of the Justices questioned whether finding such a constitutional right would be necessary or wise. The questions arose as the court heard arguments in Vacco v. Quill and Washington v. Glucksberg. The cases challenged findings by the 2nd U.S. Circuit Court of Appeals and the 9th Circuit, respectively, that the New York and Washington state laws prohibiting assisted suicide were unconstitutional.

Two days before the Supreme Court hearing, the American Medical Association released the findings of a survey indicating that, when given all the facts about physician assisted suicide and such alternatives as hospice care and natural death, Americans by a 5-to-1 margin would choose an alternative if they were terminally ill. "This survey reinforces our belief that, once informed of their available options and rights at the end of life, most patients would opt for comfort care and natural death," said Dr. Nancy W. Dickey, chairwoman of the AMA board.

Married Melkite Man Ordained — Catholic News Service reported early in the month that Melkite Bishop John A. Elya of Newton, Mass., had ordained a married man to the priesthood the previous Dec. 21. Father St. Germain thus became the first married man to be ordained to the priesthood in the Melkite Catholic Church in the United States, and possibly in any Catholic Eastern rite in the U.S. since 1929. The bishop said he followed the advice of his canon lawyers who said that, since the 1990 Code of Canons of the Eastern Churches took effect, older Vatican prohibitions against the ordination of married men to the priesthood in Eastern Catholic Churches in the U.S. no longer applied. The ban he referred to was a 1929 decree forbidding the ordination of married men for service in Eastern churches in this country. A similar decree was issued for Canada in 1930.

Catholics in Congress — One hundred and 55 Catholics —24 Senators and 31 Representatives — were members of the 105th Congress.

Aguilar v. Felton — The U.S. Supreme Court agreed Jan. 17 to reconsider its 12-year-old decision barring children in church-related schools from receiving publicly funded remedial education in their schools. In the fall of 1996 the Clinton administration joined New York City school officials and parents of parochial school students in asking the court to reconsider its 1985 decision in Aguilar v. Felton. At stake were hundreds of millions of dollars being spent not for educational purposes but for the purpose of complying with that ruling. A new decision could set significant new guidelines for the manner in which public funds might be used to provide students in nonpublic schools with benefits available to their public school counterparts. Aguilar v. Felton arose when advocates of strict church-state separation challenged the constitutionality of New York City's practice of sending public school teachers into religious schools to provide special remedial programs for poor children that were mandated by Congress since the 1960s. The court ruled 5-to-4 that sending public school teachers into religiously-run schools involved the government in "excessive entanglement" with religion. In a friend-of-the-court brief submitted in October, 1996, the U.S. Department of Education urged the court to reverse the decision because the ruling, in addition to costing a great deal of money, "has had a significant adverse impact on the provision of secular educational and counseling services to low-income students in need of remedial aid in both public and private schools." The brief said the prohibition of on-site programs wasted federal tax money, provided inferior education and did not conform to other Supreme Court decisions since 1965.

March for Life — Tens of thousands of people from all parts of the country converged on Washington for the annual March for Life Jan. 22, the 24th anniversary of the Supreme Court's Roe v. Wade and Doe v. Bolton decisions which legalized abortion virtually on demand in the United States. Cardinal Bernard F. Law struck the keynote of the march during a pre-rally Mass, saying we must be "unconditionally pro-life." Participants in the march said the same thing with their presence, matched in greater or less degree by nearly a hundred demonstrations in 37 states against the practice of abortion. Members of Congress in the Washington demonstration included Republican Senator Mike DeWine of Ohio and Representatives Michael. P. Forbes of New York, Roscoe Bartlett of Maryland, Jim Ryun of Kansas, Steve Chabot of Ohio and Chris Smith of New Jersey, chairman of the House Pro-Life Caucus. Robert P. Casey, former governor of Pennsylvania, addressing nearly 1,000 people in Long Beach, Calif., said: "Legal abortion will never rest easy in America. This is why it's a bone in our throat. It won't go down."

Domestic Partner Benefits — Archbishop William J. Levada of San Francisco asked Mayor Willie L. Brown, Jr., to amend a domestic partners ordinance that would imperil $5.6 million worth of Catholic Charities services to the poor, sick and needy. The ordinance required all city contractors to guarantee domestic partners of city employees the same benefits they give to employees' spouses. In a letter to Brown, the archbishop said the ordinance would require a church or religiously affiliated organization "to adopt policies which would be contrary to the church or organization's religious and ethical tenets....It is an important role for the Catholic Church in particular, and religious organizations in general, to cooperate with public authorities in serving human needs and the common good," he said. But such organizations "must also be permitted to maintain their operations — including employee benefit plans — in a manner that is consistent with their religious principles."

Briefs:

• In its first year of independent operations, the Catholic Alliance reported a membership of 20,000. The alliance, formed as an offshoot of the Christian Alliance, became separately incorporated in mid-1996.

• Gerald M. Costello, founding editor of The Beacon, of Paterson, N.J., and Catholic New York, was awarded an honorary doctorate by St. John's University Jan. 25 in recognition of his career in the Catholic press.

• At a Mass for peace in St. Patrick's Cathedral Jan. 26, Cardinal John J. O'Connor assured Kofi Annan, the new secretary-general of the United Nations, of his "prayers and total support" for the work of the organization.

• Archbishop Theodore E. McCarrick, head of the bishops' International Policy Committee, urged the Clinton administration in a letter Jan. 27 to act more boldly to ban anti-personnel land mines around the world.

• The Knights of Columbus issued more than $4 billion in insurance during 1996, making it the largest sales total ever in one year.

• The Lilly Endowment announced a new matching grant program expected to provide $5 million to Catholic elementary and secondary schools in and around Indianapolis.

• Philanthropist George Soros gave $3 million to the Catholic Legal Immigration Network, to help legal immigrants become U.S. citizens.

Taping of Confession Illegal

A federal appeals court ruled Jan. 27 that Lane County, Ore., officials violated federal law when they secretly taped a prisoner's sacramental confession. In comment on the decision, Archbishop Francis E. George of Portland, who had filed suit against use of the tape, said: "The ruling affirms the position of the Church and strengthens the religious freedom of all Oregonians." Father Michael Maslowsky, an attorney who directed the appeal, said: "In every private religious exchange with a leader of their faith, all citizens can now feel confident of the privacy and inviolability of that encounter." The 9th U.S. Circuit Court of Appeals ruled that the jailhouse recording of the confession between murder suspect Conan Wayne Hale and a priest was illegal and violated their free exercise of religion. "For the first time since this affair began (Apr. 22, 1996), we have a court that has said categorically that this tape recording is illegal, unconstitutional and cannot happen again," said Father Maslowsky. "This issue has never before been addressed in this manner." The three-judge panel ruled that the secret taping violated the federal Religious Freedom Restoration Act and the Constitution's Fourth Amendment, and ordered an injunction against any such tapings in the future. The court stopped short of granting the Church's original request to have the tape destroyed, but asked the federal district court to determine its disposition in accord with appropriate laws and in light of the appellate ruling.

INTERNATIONAL

Resignation from UNICEF Committee — Cardinal Cahal B. Daly, former primate of Ireland, resigned as head of the Irish National Committee for UNICEF and Archbishop Sean Brady of Armagh said he would not take his place. The moves followed the Vatican's decision to end its annual "symbolic contribution" of $2,500 to the organization because of its involvement in unacceptable family planning activities.

Aid Anniversary — The Aid to the Church in Need organization observed its 50th anniversary Jan. 17. Founded to help Germans after World War II, the agency was reported to be raising funds in wealthier countries to be spent in poorer ones to build church communities, publish religious books, encourage vocations to the priesthood and religious life and support evangelization efforts.

Forgiveness Urged — Five years after the end of El Salvador's civil war, Archbishop Fernando Saenz Lacalle of San Salvador called on Salvadorans to seek reconciliation through forgiveness. "It's not a question of forgetting what happened, but of re-examining it with new thoughts," he said during a Mass Jan. 18. Eighty thousand people died, 9,000 more "disappeared" and tens of thousands of people fled their homes during the 12 years of civil war.

IRA Violence — Archbishop Sean Brady of Armagh, Northern Ireland, made a fresh plea to the Irish Republican Army to end its campaign of violence, but within hours of his appeal the IRA launched a mortar bomb attack on a Royal Ulster Constabulary Land Rover in Downpatrick Jan. 18, injuring two policemen and a woman civilian. "The use of violence or the threat of violence can never be acceptable in our community," the archbishop said. "An unequivocal restoration of the cease-fire by the IRA is therefore an indispensable precondition for the comprehensive negotiations which are now so urgently needed. I call for intense prayer on the part of all our people that the cease-fire may be restored."

Membership in Council of Churches —The Canadian Conference of Catholic Bishops announced Jan. 21 that it had formally applied for full membership status in the Canadian Council of Churches. The announcement signaled "the commitment of the Roman Catholic Church to ecumenism," said Sister of Charity Donna Geernaert, ecumenical officer of the bishops' conference.

Changes in Cuba — Some changes for the better in Cuba were noted during the month. In 1992, the constitution was changed with deletion of a line reading that Cuba was an "atheist" nation. More recently, the government approved the visas of perhaps more than 100 foreign missionaries; published a communique from Cardinal Jaime Ortega Alamino of Havana in the state-run daily newspaper, and gave private Catholic groups, particularly Caritas Cuba, more freedom for their activities. Most observers and members of the hierarchy said relations between the government and the bishops had improved gradually since the late 1980s, and that more recent events had moved things far beyond what was once considered unimaginable.

Eucharistic Congress in the Philippines — Cardinal Anthony J,. Bevilacqua was a featured speaker during ceremonies of the Fifth National Eucharistic Congress in Manila. In a homily at a Jan. 26 Mass attended by about a million people, he focused attention on the theme of freedom, saying: "In this mystery (of the Eucharist), the freedom of Jesus becomes our own.... In a way possible only to himself, he left to his followers as a free gift the gift he was about to make of himself to the Father for our sakes. This Eucharist, which is ours, is totally inseparable from freedom.... It is the memorial of a death freely accepted. It is a memorial freely possessed as (a) gift until the end of time." Two days earlier, in an address to the general assembly of the congress, he said: "The Eucharist, the sign and sacrament of our life, embodies for us the choice which leads to freedom. Participating in the eucharistic liturgy becomes the foundation and motivation for self-giving, the only path of true, personal freedom. Our coming together for this National Eucharistic Congress is to proclaim with all the intensity and sincerity at our disposal our faith that Jesus is really sacramentally present in the Eucharist."

Hostage Crisis in Peru — At the end of January, more than 40 days after they and more than 400 others were seized, 72 people remained hostages of members of the Tupac Amaru Revolutionary Movement in the Japanese ambassador's residence in Lima. The revolutionaries were holding the hostages as pawns in their efforts to secure the release of some of their fellow terrorists held in prison, but were being stonewalled by the Peruvian government. A cardinal and an archbishop had been permitted to enter the compound of the Japanese embassy but had not succeeded in inducing the revolutionaries to take part in a dialogue for resolution of the crisis.

Briefs:
• All six dioceses of the Anglican Church in Wales held ordinations of women to the priesthood on the same weekend during the month.
• Cardinal Jean-Marie Lustiger addressed thousands of young people in Paris and foreign cities via television Jan. 19 in preparation for the 1997 World Youth Day to be held in Paris in the summer.
• Maryknoll nuns expelled from Sudan in 1992 were back in the country and continuing their missionary work.
• Church authorities in Florence were formally investigating the possible cause for canonization of Dominican Father Girolamo Savonarola, a controversial preacher who was burned at the stake in 1498 after denouncing corruption in the Church.

Missionary Airlift

Eighty missionaries and a bishop were airlifted from a besieged town in Zaire after hiding in forests for more than 10 days. The Italian Foreign Ministry announced Jan. 5 that the Italian, Spanish and Portuguese embassies in Zaire, with assistance from the Canadian and German governments, had evacuated the missionaries from the northeastern town of Isiro. Most of the missionaries had to flee from their homes, convents, schools and churches as retreating government troops looted and pillaged them, taking everything of value and even setting fire to the provincial house of the Comboni Sisters.

FEBRUARY 1997

VATICAN

Consecrated Life Day — Pope John Paul marked the first Day of Consecrated Life Feb. 2 at Mass with several thousands of men and women belonging to religious orders and secular institutes. He told them the Church entrusts consecrated persons with "the task of proclaiming with word and example the primacy of the Absolute over every human reality. It is an urgent task in our times, which often seem to have lost an authentic sense of God. In our days, there is truly a great urgency for consecrated life to show itself ever more full of joy and the Holy Spirit, that it forge ahead dynamically in the paths of mission (and) that it be backed up by the strength of lived witness.... May your mission in the Church and in the world be a light and source of hope.."

Day of the Sick — Illness is an appeal to conversion, a call to place all of one's trust in God, the Pope said after Mass marking the feast of Our Lady of Lourdes Feb. 11. Greeting more than 10,000 persons, including many suffering from illness, he called on all Catholics to turn their sufferings into a new act of trust in Christ, "the unique source of salvation for every person and for the whole person." He also gave special praise to the pilgrimage office in Rome that organizes an annual pilgrimage of sick and seriously handicapped persons to St. Peter's Basilica for the feast of Our Lady of Lourdes.

Lenten Message — In a special message to Roman Catholics beginning the observance of Lent Feb. 12, Pope John Paul said, among other things:

• "Lent is a providential opportunity for fostering the spiritual detachment from riches necessary if we are to open ourselves to God."

• "The Gospel call to be close to Christ, who is 'homeless,' is an invitation to all the baptized to examine their own lives and to treat their brothers and sisters with practical solidarity by sharing their hardships. By openness and generosity, as a community and as individuals, Christians can serve Christ present in the poor, and bear witness to the Father's love.... Christ's presence is a source of strength and encouragement; he sets us free and makes us witnesses of love."

• "It is from the love of God that Christians learn to help the needy and to share with them their own material and spiritual goods. Such concern not only provides those experiencing hardship with material help but also represents an opportunity for the spiritual growth of the giver, who finds in it an incentive to become detached from worldly goods."

Among those in need of help, the Pope noted: refugees, victims of wars and natural disasters, persons forced to migrate for economic reasons, evicted families, persons unable to find housing, elderly people with inadequate pensions and insufficient housing, persons suffering from alcoholism, drug addiction, violence, prostitution.

Toward Jubilee Year 2000 — Church-government cooperation in preparing for events of Jubilee Year 2000 was the subject of the Pope's remarks Feb. 15 at a meeting with politicians and administrators responsible for the area around Rome. He told members of the Latium regional council: "A pilgrimage is, by its nature, a double experience: spiritual, with deep and strong religious motivations; and practical, insofar as it requires concrete realization such as the journey, the stops, the visits, transfers and meetings.... I deeply hope that the regional administration and the church community will work with respect for each other's competence and in a spirit of great collaboration to create a welcoming and efficient context around Rome." The day before the meeting, the Italian government released almost $2.2 billion for public works projects for facilities to accommodate the estimated 20 million pilgrims expected in the year 2000.

46 Missionaries Killed — The International Fides Service reported Feb. 20 that at least 46 missionaries were killed in 1996 — three bishops, 18 priests, eight men religious, 13 nuns and four other persons. Forty-one of the missionaries were killed in Africa; 19 of them were in Zaire.

The 1995 death toll by violence was 30.

Norms for Switched Priests — Late in the month, Catholic News Service in Rome obtained a copy of agreed-to guidelines for regulating cases in which priests change from the Roman Catholic Church to the Utrecht Union of Old Catholic Churches, and vice-versa. The norms provide for a waiting period of at least three months before a priest who has gone from one church to the other begins active ministry; they also stipulate that he not be appointed to a pastoral position in the territory of his previous ministry in the other church. The guidelines were signed by Cardinal Edward I. Cassidy, president of the Pontifical Council for Promoting Christian Unity, and Archbishop Antonius Jan Glazemaker, president of the International Old Catholic Bishops' Conference of the Utrecht Union.

Responsibility in Advertising — This is the theme of a 33-page booklet published Feb 25 by the Pontifical Council for Social Communications. It said advertising professionals must behave in an ethical manner, despite external pressures from clients and competition in their industry. It recommended the establishment of voluntary ethical codes and public involvement in their formulation and enforcement. It also said the news media and schools should do more to educate the public about the types of persuasion used in advertising in order to sensitize people to its use and abuse. The council said: "We call upon advertising professionals and upon all those involved in the process of commissioning and disseminating advertising to eliminate its socially harmful aspects and to observe high ethical standards in regard to truthfulness, human dignity and social responsibility."

Media and Jubilee 2000 — The Gospel message "must be broadcast with increasing effectiveness in order to help the people of our time to escape or shake off the spiritual emptiness which weighs heavily on the hearts of so many." So stated the Pope Feb. 28 at a meeting of the Pontifical Council for Social Communications. The focus of his remarks was the role of the media in preparations for the celebration of Jubilee Year 2000. The challenge for the Church in relation to the media "is to see to it that the world is properly informed of the true meaning of the year 2000, the anniversary of the birth of Jesus Christ....The Jubilee cannot be a mere remembrance of a past event, however extraordinary. It is to be the celebration of a living presence and an invitation to look toward the second coming of our Savior, when he will establish once and for all his kingdom of justice, love and peace."

General Audience Topics:
• The Holy Father, suffering a bout of flu, spoke very briefly Feb. 5 about the goodness of God.
• Lent is a time for growth in holiness through meditation on the word of God and the discipline of prayer, fasting and almsgiving (Feb. 12).
• Mary's faith, prayer and cooperation in the saving mission of Jesus invite Christians to complete trust in the Lord (Feb. 26).

Briefs:
• Marking Italy's Pro-Life Day Feb. 2, the Pope called abortion a symptom of selfishness in contemporary society.
• The Vatican reported that the Pope gave almost $600,000 for disaster relief in 1996.
• The Pope encouraged mutual trust between teachers and teen-agers, in a message to teachers Feb. 18.
• The Pope appointed Feb. 28 an Italian bishop to oversee the Society of St. Paul's media work, the focus of recent controversies, and to assume many of the duties of the order's superior general.

No Human Cloning

A Vatican official issued a warning against the cloning of humans after scientists in Scotland reported the first successful cloning of an adult mammal. Human cloning would violate human dignity, the dignity of marriage and the very principle of human equality, Bishop Elio Sgreccia, an expert on medical ethics, said in a written statement Feb. 26. Even animal cloning should be performed only under strict ethical guidelines, maintaining respect for the integrity of species. His comments came after researchers in Edinburgh produced a lamb using DNA from an adult sheep, creating, in effect, a cloned twin. The procedure involved fusing the DNA from one sheep into the egg of another, which then grew into an embryo genetically identical to the DNA donor. Bishop Sgreccia was one of many experts who raised ethical questions about the experiment. "If there is a tendency toward applying this procedure to humans, it needs to be immediately remembered that cloning of humans is prohibited by international documents and various national laws." He noted that the European Parliament banned human cloning in 1989, two years after the Vatican condemned the procedure in the document entitled *Donum Vitae*.

NATIONAL

"Schools You Can Believe In" — This was the theme of the annual Catholic Schools Week which ended Feb. 1. "In recent months, the media have put a spotlight on Catholic schools, highlighting our success in character development, academic achievement and graduation rates," said a statement issued by Leonard DeFiore, president of the National Catholic Educational Association. "These results underscore that Catholic educators are providing an exceptional service to our Church and the country.

Catholic Schools Week celebrates their courage and commitment."

Consecrated Life — Commenting on the observance of Consecrated Life Day Feb. 2, two bishops sent a memorandum to their fellow bishops saying: "Too often the witness of religious sisters, priests and brothers, as well as members of secular institutes, is taken for granted....It is our hope that this day enables us to come to a deeper appreciation for the gift of consecrated life and to encourage more of our young people to consider giving their lives to God in this radical way of living the Gospel."

Lawsuit over Ads — The City of Phoenix was being sued in federal court by civil liberties groups which said it had again restricted advertising on city buses in order to exclude religious and other messages considered controversial. After refusing to accept religious-themed advertisements from the St. Vincent de Paul Society and Children of the Rosary, which opposed abortion, the city was ordered by a federal court in June, 1996, to allow religious advertising. But the city revised its policy to get around the order, and the American Center for Law and Justice and the Arizona Civil Liberties Union were joining forces to challenge the advertising limitations again.

Welfare Policy — Catholics must put aside partisan agendas and work together in faith to serve the needs of the impoverished and vulnerable, according to speakers at a conference on welfare policy. The Feb. 6-to-8 conference on "The Welfare Revolution and Catholic Social Thought" brought together theologians, policy makers and political scientists to discuss various aspects of welfare reform, including the effect of recent legislative changes on children and the relationship between theological and public policy issues. Many of those attending the conference at the University of Notre Dame expressed concern about the Personal Responsibility and Work Opportunity Act of 1996. The law, signed by President Clinton in August, limits welfare assistance to five years and requires the head of every welfare family to find work within two years in order to remain eligible for benefits. Father J. Bryan Hehir of Harvard University said the new welfare legislation had done little to improve the effectiveness of welfare policy: "While no one wanted to support the old system, I think many of us are asking if the cure might be worse than the cause." John Carr, secretary for Social Development and World Peace, U.S. Catholic Conference, said families have less to fall back on following passage of the new legislation: "The bill served the interest of politicians, but not poor families. It failed to preserve the safety net."

Permissible Aid — Early in the month, Mark E. Chopko, general counsel of the U.S. Catholic Conference, praised the decision of a federal court in Louisiana that it is constitutional to use public funds for non-religious educational materials in church-related schools. U.S. District Court Judge Marcel Livaudais reversed Jan. 28 earlier decisions in which the court ruled that such aid was unconstitutional. Chopko called the decision "a common-sense approach to constitutional law" which "will assure that more students receive the assistance that Congress intended." At issue was the loan to private, mostly Catholic, schools of secular instructional aids — materials such as books, audiovisual equipment, computer hardware and software — purchased by Louisiana state educational authorities with federal funds disbursed under Title I , of the 1965 Elementary and Secondary Education Act. The law calls for use of such funds to provide instructional improvement assistance for students in public and private schools on an equitable basis. It specifies that the benefits provided for children in non-public schools must consist of "secular, neutral and non-ideological services, materials and equipment." Chopko said the program is "religion-neutral."

Population Control Protested — Third World bishops attending a medical-moral conference in Dallas issued a statement Feb. 7 opposing U.S. funding of population control measures, including abortion funding, in their respective countries. House and Senate action was expected on President Clinton's proposal to increase and release $123 million already appropriated for international family planning programs. Opponents of the measure feared indirect use of the funds by organizations such as the International Planned Parenthood Federation to cover their administrative costs, thus freeing other organization money for abortion services. Thirty-one bishops said in the statement: "This proposal is unjust, offensive and criminal.... We believe the people of the United States should not contribute to these contraceptive campaigns and must not include abortion as though it were a contraceptive method."

Bishop James T. McHugh, a member of the U.S. bishops' Committee for Pro-Life Activities, said that "funds for family planning have long been part of U.S. foreign aid." He noted that such funds cannot be used to pay directly for abortions, and that from 1984 to 1993 they could not be given to organizations providing or promoting abortion as well as contraception and sterilization. He also said: "As one of his first acts in office in 1993, President Clinton reversed this policy," thus making organizations with abortion activities eligible for U.S. family planning funds. "Money for abortion" is the agenda behind the Clinton administration's push to increase U.S. funding for family planning abroad."

Lenten Service for 11,000 — An Ash Wednesday prayer service in Phoenix was attended by more than 11,000 people, including 1,490 candidates for the Rite of Election. Bishop Thomas J. O'Brien accepted the candidates and catechumens, saying: "This is a spectacular night for you. I am very, very proud of you, and I welcome you.... My hope is that you have much enjoyment and fulfillment in your life. I greet you in the name of the Lord.... Let's continue our journey together to Easter and into the third millennium."

Ethical Concerns about Cloning — Reports about the successful cloning of mammals raised ethical concerns about cloning humans, said Richard Doerflinger, associate director of the bishops' Secretariat for Pro-Life Activities. His statement came Feb. 25 after news broke worldwide about the first-ever cloning of an adult animal at the Roslin Institute near Edinburgh, Scotland. Nine cloned lambs were produced; the first, named Dolly, was born in July, 1996. Genetic scientists generally agreed that the relatively simple cloning procedure raised questions about the cloning of humans. Doerflinger commented:

"Catholic teaching rejects the cloning of human beings because this is not a worthy way to bring a human being into the world. Children have a right to have real parents, and to be conceived as the fruit of marital love between husband and wife." Children "are not products we can manufacture to our specifications. Least of all should they be produced as deliberate 'copies' of other people to ensure that they have certain desired features."

Millions of Refugees — The official count of refugees, most recently tallied at 14 million, does not tell the entire story of the world's displaced people, agreed speakers at a panel discussion held Feb. 26 during the 1997 Catholic Social Ministry Gathering, co-sponsored by the U.S. Catholic Conference and 11 other Catholic organizations. The 14-million figure included only those not in their respective nations of origin; uncounted were Gypsies along with people displaced in their own countries. Under review at the gathering were plans and programs of church-related organizations, such as Catholic Relief Services and the National Council of Catholic Women, in the wide-ranging field of social ministry with displaced persons.

Briefs:
• "Catholic Schools — Schools You Can Believe In," was the theme of the 32nd annual Catholic Schools Week which ended Feb. 1.
• "Words To Live By" was the theme of the year's observance of Catholic Press Month.
• The Catholic Communications Committee announced approval of grants totaling $431,950 for communications projects in the U.S. and abroad.
• Marist Brother Cyprian L. Rowe announced he was leaving the Catholic Church to become a priest and bishop of the African-American Catholic Congregation, the Imani Temple community formed in 1989 by the former Catholic priest, now Archbishop George A. Stallings, Jr. Rowe was the former executive director of the National Office for Black Catholics (1978-80) and the National Black Catholic Clergy Caucus (1981-83).

Perilous Decision

The 9th U.S. Circuit Court of Appeals ruled Feb.27 that a lawsuit challenging a 1994 Oregon law allowing assisted suicide had to be dismissed because there was no proof that those trying to block the law faced immediate harm. Gaylee Atteberry, director of Oregon Right to Life, said that, according to the court's logic, only a dead person or someone within days of death, would have standing to challenge the law. In effect, she said, the ruling "puts elderly, weak, disabled, those without health care, in imminent danger of death." Bob Castagna, director of the Oregon Catholic Conference, agreed, saying the decision placed everyone in jeopardy. He called the ruling "unbelievable."

In other developments:
• Dr. Percy Wootton, president-elect of the American Medical Association, said opposition to physician-assisted suicide was a top priority for the 300,000-member organization because "it impinges on the patient-physician covenant."
• The Florida Catholic Conference denounced a Jan. 31 ruling by Judge S. Joseph Davis, Jr., of the Palm

Beach Circuit Court that Charles E. Hall had a constitutional right to have his physician help him die.

INTERNATIONAL

Japanese Martyrs' Anniversary — More than 6,000 people participated Feb. 5 in a Mass and related ceremonies marking the fourth centenary of the martyrdom of Japan's first martyrs. The congregation included pilgrims from Australia, France, South Korea and Spain, representatives of disabled peoples' organizations, and members of Protestant churches active in church unity movements.

Deportations on Hold — The head of the Church in Belarus said in a telephone interview Feb. 12 that a government threat to deport priests was suspended following talks with an official of a newly appointed state commission. However, Cardinal Kazimierz Swiatek warned that more priests could face eventual deportation and said the plight of nuns was very serious. "Both sides have now had a chance to present their worries and concerns openly and to discuss possible solutions," he said. "I am certain there will be no expulsions or major new restrictions while current negotiations and procedures are in progress," he added.

Papal Visits Not Advised — A visit by Pope John Paul to Jerusalem would not be opportune until Israelis and Palestinians have worked out the future status of the city. So stated Afif Safieh, head of the Palestinian delegation to the Holy See, in a Feb. 13 letter to Archbishop Jean-Louis Tauran, an assistant secretary of state. Russian Orthodox Patriarch Alexei II, citing persistent Catholic-Orthodox tensions, said Feb.15 in a newspaper interview it was still too soon for Pope John Paul to make a long-sought visit to Russia.

Croatian Ecumenical Committee — A Croatian church official said the formation of a new ecumenical committee marked an "important step" toward reconciling the region's bitterly divided religious communities. However, he cautioned that relations with the Serbian Orthodox Church remained uneasy, noting that it was not clear what might happen when Orthodox priests and bishops who fled during the 1991-92 Serb-Croat war would return to the country. Father Anton Skvorcevic, secretary of the Croatian bishops' Council for Ecumenism and Dialogue, said: "We have tried to formulate ecumenical priorities in the new democratic situation.... There are more possibilities now for all churches to foster ethical attitudes in society than there were in former Yugoslavia." A real issue, he said, "is whether Orthodox clergy accept our country's new political system. This is up to the Serbian church." Father Skvorcevic spoke in a telephone interview after representatives of Croatia's Catholic, Serbian Orthodox, Lutheran, Baptist, Pentecostal and Calvinist churches announced the formation of an ecumenical committee. A founding declaration of the committee said: "What we have in common is more significant than what divides us.... After so much division, misunderstanding and intolerance in these regions, caused especially by the war, the churches of Croatia wish to offer a sign of hope, peace and reconciliation, and thus make their contribution to the well-being of Croatian society."

China after Deng — China watchers in Rome thought the death of 92-year-old Deng Xiaoping Feb. 19 would have little immediate effect on government policies, including those affecting the Catholic Church. However, there were differences in long-term predictions. Jesuit Father Joseph Shih, director of the Chinese program at Vatican Radio, said: "I think there will be greater religious freedom in the future; that is how history is moving, but it is independent of his death." Father Giancarlo Politi, an Italian missionary based in Hong Kong for many years, said "the great unknown is, who will be able to take possession of the greatest slice of power." He added: "In fact, things could get worse," citing "a party decree aimed at suppressing what they call the clandestine movement of Catholics faithful to Rome."

WCC's Financial Problems — The financially troubled World Council of Churches reported that its financial picture had brightened in the last half-year, but that it still needed to cut staff and restructure because of diminished income. At the same time, the Rev. Konrad Raiser, general secretary, chided member churches (174 of 330) for failing to pay their dues.

Briefs:

• Nicaraguan government officials and Catholic leaders inaugurated a museum in Managua to commemorate Pope John Paul's 1996 visit to the country. The John Paul II Museum was officially opened Feb. 9 by President Arnoldo Aleman, together with Cardinal Miguel Obando Bravo and Managua Mayor Roberto Cedeno.

• "It is necessary to build a satisfactory international economic and political order that all nations will support and participate in that will ensure the well-being of migrants and refugees," stated Bishop James T. McHugh of Camden Feb. 24 in an address at the United Nations.

• The head of the Polish bishops' conference condemned the firebomb attack that damaged Warsaw's only functioning Jewish synagogue Feb. 26.

Catholic-Russian Orthodox Relations

Relations between the Russian Orthodox Church and the Catholic Church will not improve until the Vatican addresses issues of perennial concern to the Orthodox, said Metropolitan Filaret Bakhromeyev of Minsk Feb. 21 at the conclusion of the church's Episcopal Synod in Moscow. "Until today's problems of proselytizing and the Uniate (Eastern-rite Catholic) Church are solved, there will not be a dialogue," he said. A synodal pastoral letter said ongoing talks between the churches should continue, but there was great concern over the so-called expansion of Eastern-rite churches in Ukraine and proselytizing by Catholics in the "canonical territory" of the Russian Orthodox Church. A Catholic official criticized remarks by the metropolitan and defended the right of Catholics to set up parishes. Father Antoni Hej, chancellor of the Apostolic Administration of European Russia, said: "Whether people like it or not, we have a duty to provide for Catholic believers..... No priest or bishop has set up any Catholic parish by himself. It is the local people who have requested pastoral help and organized a church community, out of a natural desire to be cared for in their places of residence. Catholic parishes are established all over the world. It is only here in Russia that it is proving difficult." European Russia's Apostolic Administration had 300,000 members, 91 parishes and 49 functioning places of worship, 104 nuns and 102 priests.

MARCH 1997

VATICAN

Manipulation of Nature — Because all creation belongs to God, it must not be manipulated for business purposes, Pope John Paul declared Mar. 2: "Christ raises his voice against the 'temple merchants' of our time, against those who make the market their 'religion,' going so far as to trample — in the name of the 'power god' — the dignity of the human person with abuses of every type." He said respect for life is sacrificed to money or power in modern experiments, ecological pollution, the marketing of sex, drug-pushing and the exploitation of the poer and of children.

Christian Principles for European Union — The genesis of the European Union in 1957 was due partly to the application of Christian principles, which are important as well for its future, said the Pope Mar. 6 in commemorating the union's 50th anniversary. "Christians contributed greatly to forming the conscience and cultures of Europe, and Christian involvement remains important for the future of the continent, he told visiting legislators Mar. 6. On the other hand, "if Europe constructs itself separately from the transcendent dimension of the person," and "refuses to recognize the inspiring faith in Christ and the message of the Gospel, it loses a large part of its foundation." He said Christian legislators cannot separate their faith from their work, which requires "a profound vision of humanity and society, and a courage beyond the common." He did not address specific issues debated recently in the European Parliament, preferring instead to address in general the principles which define truly Christian politicians, who are called upon in particular to look after the needs of the poor, the downcast and the defenseless. "Through your debates and through your decisions, you are among the craftsmen of the European society of tomorrow," he said. "On giving faith back to those who have lost it, in favoring social integration for those who live on the continent and those who settle here, you respond to your calling as Christian politicians."

Divorced and Remarried Catholics — "Divorced and remarried faithful must be inclined toward a form of life which is not in contradiction with the evangelical norm of the indissolubility of marriage," said Msgr. Francesco Di Felice, undersecretary of the Pontifical Council for the Family. His remarks were published in the Mar. 4 edition of *L'Osservatore Romano*" in reference to a council document entitled "The Pastoral Care of the Divorced and Remarried," issued Feb. 25. He said the Church, "even when it cannot approve a practice in contrast with the Gospel, does not stop loving its children who are in irregular family situations," and continues to "accompany them in their difficult itinerary of faith."

Grave Decisions Threaten Peace — The Pope voiced rare public criticism of Israel Mar. 9, saying recent "grave decisions" by Israeli authorities could seriously undermine the peace process in the Middle East. While not specifying what the decisions were, his remarks seemed to reflect deep Vatican concern over Israel's decision to press ahead on a controversial Jewish housing project in the Arab sector of Jerusalem.

Diplomatic Relations with Libya — On Mar. 10, the Vatican explained its reasons for establishing diplomatic relations with Libya, governed by Moammar Gadhafi, saying the step was aimed in part at furthering international dialogue and helping Libya take its place in the "community of nations." The Vatican also said diplomatic relations would enable the Church in carrying out its pastoral ministry among the minority Catholic population in the predominantly Muslim nation. The Vatican move was opposed by the United States and in some other quarters which considered Gadhafi an international pariah because of alleged complicity in terrorist actions, including the bombing in 1988 of Pan Am Flight 103 in which 270 people died.

Pastoral Care of Seafarers — This is the subject of an apostolic letter issued Mar. 11 on the initiative (*motu proprio*) of Pope John Paul bearing the Marian title *Stella Maris* ("Star of the Sea"). Provisions of the document concern the whole range of maritime personnel, from seaman and their families to oil rig and port workers along with travelers by sea. The letter does not, however, include military personnel, whose pastoral care is handled by appropriate chaplains. Archbishop Giovanni Cheli, president of the Pontifical Council for Migrants and Travelers, said at a news conference that the Pope initiated the letter in order to encourage chaplains charged with pastoral ministry among maritime personnel. An estimated 400 priests, religious and lay workers in ports around the globe were engaged in part- or full-time maritime ministry. Among other things, the Pope requested national conferences of bishops to appoint bishops to oversee maritime ministry. (See separate entry.)

New Ways of Evangelizing — World changes demand that the Church explore the best possible — traditional to high-tech — ways and means of spreading the Gospel, said a statement issued by a three-day meeting of experts held in mid-month under the auspices of the Pontifical Council for Culture. Participants in the meeting said "the message of Christ remains a dead letter if it does not transform consciences, mentalities and customs." Hence, the need for effective ways of evangelization.

Peer Mentors — At an evening meeting with youths Mar. 20, the Holy Father said: One thing young people must learn from Christ "is to go out of ourselves, our groups, our parishes and our beautiful meetings to bring the Gospel to the many friends we know who await the salvation only he can give.... You yourselves must become points of reference for your peers. Become the friend of those who have no friends, the family of those who do not have a family, and the community of those who do not have a community."

Compassion for Albanians — The Pope called for prayers for Albanian shipwreck victims and refugees over the Easter weekend. He invited prayers "for those found dead in the Adriatic Sea," victims of the ramming of their boat by an Italian naval vessel Mar. 28, and encouraged aid workers struggling to help some 13,000 refugees who had reached Italy. Meanwhile, chaos reigned in Albania as frantic civilians who had lost their life savings rioted in protest against government failure to protect them from fraudulent pyramid schemes.

Holy Week Celebrations — The Holy Father celebrated the round of solemn ceremonies marking the deep mysteries of faith in Holy Week: the entrance of Jesus into Jerusalem on Palm Sunday, Masses of Chrism and the Last Supper on Holy Thursday, Liturgy of the Passion and Stations of the Cross on Good Friday, and the Easter Vigil.

On Easter Sunday morning, the Pope celebrated Mass on the steps of St. Peter's Basilica and delivered his message to the city of Rome and the world. He prayed that people afflicted by suffering, violence and war the world over might find hope in Christ's victory over sin and death. He extended Easter wishes worldwide in 57 languages.

General Audience Topics:
• Mary's cooperation in the messianic mission of Jesus (Mar. 5 and 12).
• Workers have primacy over money; work should be organized in ways that serve the well-being of workers (Mar. 19, the feast of St. Joseph, patron of workers).
• The sufferings of Christ continue in the sufferings of people today (Mar. 26).

Briefs:
• Preparation for Jubilee Year 2000 must involve reflection on the importance of Jesus in a person's own life, Cardinal Joseph Ratzinger told a gathering of Italian cultural leaders Mar. 5.
• Strong personal commitment must complement study and spiritual training in the course of becoming a priest, Pope John Paul told faculty, students and directors of North American College Mar. 13.
• The Pope's Holy Thursday letter to priests was a reflection on "the truth about Christ's very special friendship with his priests, to the point that he allows them to work in his name."

Guidelines for Confessors

Proclaiming "the mystery of mercy" along with moral obligations is the theme running through a 25-page "Vademecum for Confessors concerning Some Aspects of the Morality of Conjugal Life." The document, prepared at the request of the Pontifical Council for the Family, was published Mar.1. The guidelines emphasize four basic principles in dealing with penitents on matters related to responsible procreation:
• the example of the merciful Christ;
• a "prudent reserve" in inquiring about these sins;
• help and encouragement toward repentance;
• advice that leads penitents gradually to "embrace the path of holiness."

The vademecum states the Church condemns contraceptive birth control as "intrinsically evil" because it makes sexual acts in marriage intentionally unfruitful and harms the mutual self-giving of spouses. This teaching is to be held as "definitive and irreformable." Noting that doctrinal principles must confront "concrete human situations," the guidelines counsel a compassionate approach in the confessional. While confessors should admonish persons about grave transgressions, and make sure they really want absolution and are resolved to correct their behavior, they should also assume the good will of those coming to confession. This applies even to those who try but fail to keep to church teaching on birth control and other sexual matters: "Frequent relapse into sins of contraception does not in itself constitute a motive for denying absolution." Confessors should "avoid demonstrating lack of trust either in the grace of God or in the dispositions of the penitent" by demanding impossible, absolute guarantees of irreproachable future conduct."

NATIONAL

Lied about Partial-Birth Abortions — The executive director of the National Coalition of Abortion Providers admitted that he and other supporters of legalized abortion lied about partial-birth abortion during debate over legislation to ban the procedure. Ron Fitzsimmons said in an interview in the Mar. 3 edition of *American Medical News* that abortion supporters used "spins" and "half-truths" in the debate that ultimately led Congress to fail to override President Clinton's veto of the Partial-Birth Abortion Ban Act. He admitted lying in a Nov. 1995 interview on "Nightline" when he said that women had partial-birth abortions only in cases of danger to the mother's life or of severe fetal abnormalities. He said the vast majority of partial-birth abortions were performed in the second trimester on healthy fetuses and healthy mothers. "The abortion rights folks know it, the anti-abortion folks know it and so, probably, does everyone else." Kate Michelman, president of the National Abortion and Reproductive Rights Action League, denied Fitzsimmons' statements.

Pay of Religious Employees — The average stipend paid to members of religious orders working for 85 dioceses in 1997 was $15,977. Stipends were based on the amount a church entity felt it could afford, regardless of whether or not it met the financial needs of religious congregations. By comparison, 44 dioceses paid "market value"salaries, with pay and benefits equal to the earnings of a layperson doing comparable work. The figures were reported on the findings of an annual survey conducted under the auspices of the National Association of Treasurers of Religious Institutes.

Common Ground Conference — Forty persons took part Mar. 7 to 9 in the first meeting of the Catholic Common Ground Project initiated by Cardinal Joseph L. Bernardin the previous August. They explored a number of subjects of concern — the influence of contemporary culture, viewpoints of younger Catholics, roles and status of women, the nature and exercise of authority, and more — vis-a-vis the Church, without agreeing on ways and means of coping with them. Archbishop Oscar H. Lipscomb of Mobile, Cardinal Bernardin's successor as head of the project, spoke at the first session of the conference. Subsequent sessions were held behind closed doors.

Polish National Catholic Centenary — In a pastoral letter read Mar. 9 at a Mass marking the 100th anniversary of the Polish National Catholic Church, Bishop James C. Timlin of Scranton said: "I come to you with profound sorrow. I beg your forgiveness for every offense, misunderstanding, unkind act, mistaken judgment, or any thought, word or deed ever committed against you on the part of anyone in the Roman Catholic commuinity.... And I pledge on the occasion of this meaningful anniversary that my desire, as long as I live, will be to ever strive to restore the unity that once was ours." The establishment of the church Mar. 14, 1897, resulted from disputes over pastoral and administrative matters.

Refugees and Their Problems — The assistant high commissioner for the U.N. High Commissioner for Refugees told an audience of Catholic refugee and migration workers that more international support was needed to deal with refugee problems. Sergio Vieira de Mello spoke Mar. 14 at a conference of the U.S. Catholic Conference's Migration and Refugee Services and the Catholic Legal Immigration Network. Of the 26 million people he classified as being "of concern" to the agencies charged with helping refugees, 13.2 million had been pushed from their home countries by war, famine, political or economic conditions.. The others included people displaced within their own countries and those whose status was so unsettled that they could not be sure where to call home.

Signatures Wanting — The effort to gather a million signatures for the "We Are Church" Catholic reform referendum was extended to October, five months past its original deadline of the feast of Pentecost in May. Announcement of the extension was made by Sister Maureen Fiedler, national coordinator of the referendum. Signature seekers in 10 cities had little success in February. Sister Fiedler said in a mid-March interview with Catholic News Service: "We're not releasing any numbers until October. I'm not going to give you numbers.... I certainly don't have as many as I'd like, that I can tell you."

Farm Monopolies —There is ample evidence that large corporations are gradually taking control over the nation's food supply as the number of family-owned farms steadily shrinks, speakers told a three-day Ohio Rural Life Conference. "I sometimes find myself wondering whether there's going to be any farm land left in a decade or so," said Archbishop Daniel E. Pilarczyk of Cincinnati. "How long is it going to be before farmers can no longer make a living out of what we now consider a big family farm or even a family corporation of farms?"

Sect Suicide — Although not much was known about the Heaven's Gate group of 39 members whose bodies were discovered Mar. 26, cult experts said the apparent mass suicide bore the marks of cult activity. The male and female victims were found on cots and bunks in several rooms of a million-dollar mansion in the exclusive community of Rancho Santa Fe, Calif. Police believed the victims died in successive groups after taking a drug-alcohol cocktail. According to former members and videos sent out by the group just before the mass suicide, Heaven's Gate members thought it was time to shed their "containers" and rendezvous with a UFO they believed was traveling in the wake of the Hale-Bopp comet. They may have shared "some idea that the end of the world might be coming or the New Age concept that they could space-travel or do anything they wanted," said Father James J. LeBar, chaplain at the Hudson River

Psychiatric Center and consultant on cult phenomena to the Archdiocese of New York.

Briefs:
• The papacy, church authority and their respective understandings of the sacraments of baptism and confirmation were under dicussion at the Feb. 27-to-March 1 meeting of the U.S. United Methodist-Roman Catholic Dialogue in Washington.
• More than nine thousand Catholic men and boys took part in the annual Answer the Call conference in Cincinnati.
• Archbishop Francis T. Hurley of Anchorage was honored as the 1997 Alaskan of the Year Mar.29; he was the first religious leader to receive the award in its 30-year history.

Church-State Decision

According to a delayed report, the U.S. Supreme Court let stand lower court rulings affirming the right of the Diocese of Pittsburgh to reorganize its parishes. The court's Feb. 8 decision involved two parishes in Ambridge, Pa., and one in New Castle, Pa. Confirming the diocese's view that there is no role for civil courts in internal decisions of the Church about parish life and sacramental ministry, the court refused to hear an appeal filed on behalf of 17 people from the parishes concerned. At issue in the case was the right of the Church under both canon and civil law to own property and to manage property as it saw fit.

INTERNATIONAL

Caritas in Cuba — The social service agency reported that coordination of its relief efforts through governmental ministries was enhancing church-state relations. "We have good relations with the government," said Rolando Suarez Cobian, Caritas director. "We organize our programs jointly with the ministries inviolved.... The Health Ministry helps us to pinpoint the areas in need, and then we set out to work." This kind of coordination helped dispel the myth that government and church could not work together. Mutual mistrust between the government and the Church appeared to be diminishing.

Warning about Unification Church — It is not possible to belong to both the Catholic Church and the denomination founded by the Rev. Sun Myung Moon, declared a Latin American church official. Controversy about the Unification Church was sparked in Chile after spokesman Sergio Gonzalez announced that the Rev. Moon was planning to start a massive investment campaign in the country. Father Francisco Sampedro, head of the Department of Ecumenism and Interreligious Dialogue of the Latin American Bishops' Council, said: "After listening to Moon and his followers (at a 1996 meeting in Montevideo), we concluded that no Catholic can be simultaneously a member of his movement, and that there is no possible ecumenical dialogue."

Refusal to Perform Abortions — "From all over the country (SouthAfrica), reports are streaming in of nurses and doctors who are refusing to perform abortions," said a statement from Durban-based Doctors for Life, despite government implementation of the Choice on Termination of Pregnancy Act. Doctors for Life also said it hoped the government would "not resort to undemocratic tactics and discriminate against doctors and nurses who refuse to kill babies."

Forgiveness Sought — The bishops of Switzerland asked forgiveness from the heirs of Holocaust victims, saying that a history of anti-Semitism in the country and the Church made the Holocaust possible. They said in a statement issued Mar. 5: "Neither acts of injustice committed in the past nor suffering without bounds can be allowed to sink into forgetfulness.... One must take a lesson from them and engage in the future so that such atrocities may not be repeated." The statement came amid a barrage of international disputes over the involvement of countries in World War II that had declared themselves neutral. Switzerland in particular was being confronted, from abroad and from within, with long-suppressed or neglected evidence that it had facilitated the transfer of Nazi wealth, had failed to respond with adequate vigor to threats against Jews, and had hoarded hastily deposited assets of Holocaust victims in Swiss banks to prevent relatives from making successful claims to inheritances.

Renault Factory Closure — The bishops of France and Belgium protested the abrupt closing of an automobile factory in Belgium and the consequent loss of more than 4,000 jobs. "By its suddenness, this decision surprised everyone, starting with the workers in the factory," they said in a joint statement Mar. 7. "By its scope, it strikes forcefully men, women and a region of Europe." They also said that people, no matter where they live, cannot become disinterested in what happens to workers.

Help Offered — Cardinal Thomas Winning's offer of aid to women considering abortion prompted cash offers of help totaling more than $80,000. In an address Mar. 9 at the annual conference of the Society for the Protection of Unborn Children in Glasgow, he said: "Today I issue an open invitation to any woman, any family, any couple who may be facing the possibility of an unwanted pregnancy: If you want help to cope with raising the baby on your own, we will help you. If you want to discuss adoption of your unborn child, we will help you. If you need financial assistance or equipment, we will help you."

Successor to Mother Teresa — By unanimous vote Mar. 12, the Missionaries of Charity elected Sister Nirmala to succeed Mother Teresa as head of their order. Sister Nirmala, a 63-year-old Hindu convert, was the leader of the contemplative wing of the Missionaries of Charity at the time of her election. She had previously been a missionary in the United States.

Two Jesuits Falsely Accused — The beating, jailing and charging of two Jesuits with murder in the State of Chiapas were called part of a "low-intensity" war against the Church in southern Mexico, according to Coadjutor Bishop Raul Vera Lopez of San Cristobal de Las Casas. "We believe that we're dealing with a political question to drain confidence in ... the work of the diocese," he said after visiting the priests in custody Mar. 10. Their arrest and charges against them were called "arbitrary action" against the Church because of its support of farmers in their struggle against wealthy landowners. The priests were released by Mar. 13.

Social Justice in Germany — The Catholic bishops and Protestant leaders in Germany urged the government during Holy Week to reverse what they considered dangerous changes to the nation's social system. On Good Friday, the bishops' conference and the country's largest Protestant church organization issued a 100-page document on solidarity and social justice, in light of changes in Germany since the end of the Cold War. Bishop Karl Lehmann, conference chairman, said in a nationally broadcast Easter sermon that social reform must be guided not only by the head, but also by the heart. "We need fresh courage every day to end conflicts and to hold out our hands to one another," he said. "Reconciliation must be at the center of all politics." Bishop Klaus Engelhardt, chairman of the Protestant churches, said in an Easter statement that the holiday offered Christians an opportunity to reflect on "the way out" of social injustice.

No Peace in Israel — Latin-rite Patriarch Michel Sabbah decried conflict between Israelis and Palestinians during the Easter season and urged both communities to follow the way of peace. In a homily at Mass, he said this year's season was comprised of renewed violence, the shedding of innocent blood and a "governmental decision awakening more hatred, more insecurity for Israelis and more despair for Palestinians.... These present days are, humanly speaking, signed by death and destruction.... The paths of peace are not the paths followed in these days." Backgrounding the patriarch's remarks were the tensions surrounding the Israeli decision to build a new Jewish neighborhood on the hill called Har Homa in Jerusalem.

Briefs:
• The Catholic Health Association of Canada urged the government Mar. 4 to "clearly prohibit interventions (cloning, included) that may affect the integrity or dignity of unborn human life at any stage of its development.
• Cardinal Edward I. Cassidy of Sydney, Australia, was relieved at passage of a bill which overturned a Northern Territory law allowing voluntary euthanasia.
• A relatively smaller number of people than usual attended Easter Mass at the Church of the Holy Sepulchre in Jerusalem, as tensions increased between Israelis and Palestinians.

Plea for Peace in Albania

With the nation in the throes of anarchy, Pope John Paul said Mar. 16: Let us "implore the Lord for peace in Albania. The crisis shaking that nation ... has now extended to the whole territory, immersing those dear people in total insecurity. For the good of Albania, I ask all those who have taken up arms to lay them down. Destructive violence is certainly not a suitable way to resolve social problems. On the contrary, may each individual feel obliged to cooperate, with respect for persons and the law, in reestablishing trust between the citizens and their authorities. None of this can happen without public order. These tragic events call for a response from all of Europe. It must help the authorities and people of Albania to build their country on the basis of democracy and on political and social dialogue. May the Blessed Virgin Mary, Our Lady of Good Counsel, intercede for us so that the force of arms may not gain the advantage over peace, and indifference may not prevail over solidarity."

APRIL 1997

VATICAN

Danger of Demographic Winter — A Vatican official warned that the world was slowly drifting toward a catastrophic "demographic winter," resulting in part from sterilization campaigns in the Third World. Cardinal Alfonso Trujillo, president of the Pontifical Council for the Family, told a Rome conference Apr. 4 that fear of parenthood was greatly reducing population growth in a number of countries. "The world's populations, like the Titanic, are slowly navigating toward the iceberg of demographic winter out of fear of maternity and paternity," he said.

Child Soldiers — Pope John Paul asked the international community to help curb the deployment of children as armed combatants in wars around the world. "These inexperienced and fragile people are themselves the first victims of violence and warfare.... If we want peace, let's provide an education in peace to those who are preparing to build the society of the future," he said. He made the remarks a few days before the U.N. Human Rights Commission in Geneva was scheduled to hold a special session on juridical protection of children and minors in armed conflicts. He said he considered it an important issue and noted that he devoted much of his 1996 World Peace Day message to the theme. "Today, I want to reiterate how deeply the Church feels about respect for children and for their complete, harmonious development," he said.

To Know Christ — The full significance of Christ's Incarnation can be grasped only with knowledge of and respect for the Jewish scriptures, declared the Pope. Ignoring his Jewish roots and the whole history of God's relationship with the Israelites, "Christ would appear like a meteor which accidentally plunged to earth and lacks a connection with human history," he said Apr. 11. He spoke about the importance of the Old Testament for Christians during an audience with members of the Pontifical Biblical Commission. The commission met Apr. 7 to 11 for discussion on the relation between the Old and New Testaments and between Judaism and Christianity.

Charity without Ulterior Motives — Christian acts of charity must be carried out in a spirit of service without ulterior motives, not even of conversion, said the Pope during the Apr. 16 to 19 plenary meeting of the Pontifical Council "Cor Unum." "Charity leads us into the mystery of God, makes us open to the Holy Spirit, makes us rediscover the value of reconciliation with the Lord and with our brothers and sisters, and leads us to do good works." The council's task, he said, "is to revive without ceasing the desire of the faithful to show the love of the Lord." Charitable activity is an eloquent means of Catholic evangelization because it witnesses to a spirit of giving and of communion inspired by God. But the primary motivation for Catholic giving is to serve Christ in the poor and suffering, and to promote justice, peace and development worthy of the children of God. "Actions of aid, relief and assistance should be conducted in a spirit of service and free giving for the benefit of all persons, without the ulterior motive of eventual tutelage or proselytism."

Also during the meeting, council president Archbishop Paul J. Cordes said Catholic charitable agencies should be cautious about political involvement and the acceptance of government funding.

Appointees to Pontifical Academy of Sciences — The Vatican announced Apr. 18 the appointment of three new members to the Academy: Gary S. Becker, Nobel Prize professor of economics at the University of Chicago; Te-Tzu Chang of Taiwan, Shanghai-born director of an international center for genetic research on rice; Chen Ning Yang, Chinese-born Nobel Prize physicist teaching at the State University of New York at Stoney Brook.

Appeal for Bosnian Refugees — Cardinal Roger Etchegaray appealed for the safe return of an estimated 1.5 million refugees in Bosnia-Herzegovina, saying a lasting peace depends on the right to return to one's home. The president of the Pontifical Commission for Justice and Peace made the remark in mid-month during a meeting in Geneva with the U.N. High Commissioner for Refugees.

Trust Needed in Albania — A Vatican assistant secretary of state urged the international community to help restore a climate of trust in Albania, so the country would not repeat the mistakes of its violence-stricken Balkan neighbors. "We hope the Albanian people have the wisdom to draw some lessons from the recent past, which is still burning," Archbishop Jean-Louis Tauran told the Rome newspaper *La Repubblica* Apr. 19. He spoke as an Italian-led multinational humanitarian force was being deployed to protect relief operations. More than 400 Albanians were reported killed in recent weeks of political turmoil.

Ban Land Mines — Speaking Apr. 20 on behalf of land-mine victims around the world, Pope John Paul urged international leaders to ban the weapons as quickly as possible. In the presence of a number of victims of mine explosions, he prayed that "government leaders may have the courage to listen to the cries of these victims and to successfully conclude, as rapidly as possible, negotiations currently under way to reach the total elimination of these insidious weapons." It was estimated that 25,000 people, mostly civilians, were killed or wounded each year by some of the 100 million land mines scattered in 64 countries.

For Peace in Zaire — Pope John Paul launched an appeal for peace in Zaire amid news of more atrocities in the war-torn nation. "I ask insistently that all the parties involved in the conflict accept an honest dialogue and a true negotiation, cooperating with the forces of the international community, so that the cessation of hostilities can come about and the path toward an authentic democracy can be taken once more," he said Apr. 23. "In this way alone, many innocents will be spared further and more serious suffering."

General Audience Topics:

• By consenting to her Son's sacrifice, Mary had a part in his self-offering to the Father (Apr. 2).

• Mary's cooperation in the Redemption is totally unique (Apr. 9).

• The message of forgiveness, reconciliation and dialogue he presented on his visit to Sarajevo (Apr. 16).

• Mary's mission of love with all of Jesus' disciples (Apr. 23).

• The historical significance of the life of St. Adalbert, patron of Bohemia and Poland (Apr. 30).

Briefs:

• Pope John Paul received a donation of $1.7 million from the Philadelphia-based Papal Foundation, for humanitarian aid and evangelization projects.

• The Holy See's Internet web site was accessed more than 2.9 million times from the end of March to the beginning of April.

• Exaggerated emphasis on ethnic identity was the cause of enormous suffering to the people of Africa as well as a direct challenge to the social teaching of the Church. So stated Cardinal Jozef Tomko in an address at the Apr. 15-to-18 meeting of the presidents of African bishops' conferences.

• The Pope ordained 31 men to the priesthood Apr. 20.

• Pope John Paul sent birthday greetings Apr. 21 to the City of Rome as it celebrated the 2,750th anniversary of its founding by the legendary Romulus.

• In talks to new ambassadors accredited to the Holy See, the Pope said Apr. 24 that global peace depends ultimately on willingness to align social policies with moral truths.

No Capitulation

The Pope called on Scandinavian bishops to stand against trends in their societies which erode respect for human life. "Do not give people only what they want," he told the prelates from Sweden, Norway, Finland, Denmark and Iceland. "Give them what they need. To dedicate oneself to this task is the nature of apostolic work." The bishops, making their ad limina visits, reported that abortion and divorce had gained more acceptance in their countries since they visited the Vatican five years earlier. The Holy Father warned against giving the faithful the impression that the Church approves of these and similar developments. He exhorted them to speak out against such matters. "A society which lets its Christian foundation slowly erode is sawing off the branch on which it sits," he said.

NATIONAL

Gag Orders Struck Down — A federal judge struck down orders prohibiting military chaplains from preaching on or counseling people to participate in the bishops' campaign against partial-birth abortion. U.S. District Court Judge Stanley Sporkin rejected Apr. 7 what he called "the government's attempt to override the Constitution and the laws of the land by a directive that clearly interferes with military chaplains' free exercise and free speech rights." Concluding a 36-page opinion in which he dismissed as unfounded all the government's arguments for June, 1996, orders to chaplains in the Army, Navy and Air Force, he granted an injunction blocking enforcement of the orders. The case arose after the bishops asked priests to encourage participation by Catholics in a postcard campaign in support of a bill that would ban the partial-birth abortion procedure. The Air Force Judge Advocate General's Office responded with an opinion saying such lobbying would violate directives of the Department of Defense. A lawsuit filed on behalf of the chaplains said the orders infringed on their constitutional rights. Attorney Kevin J. Hasson commented: "The

Pentagon's gag order was the first time in U.S. history that the government dared to dictate the content of chaplains' sermons. I don't think the government will ever try something like this again."

Boycott vs. RU-486 — The bishops' pro-life spokeswoman praised the efforts of pro-life people which led to the decision by the European makers of RU-486 to stop manufacturing, marketing and distributing the abortion drug. "This is due to the efforts of so many pro-life groups which have ceaselessly spoken about the threat this drug poses to women and children," said Helen Alvare in a statement Apr. 9. Roussel Uclaf in France and its German parent, Hoechst AG, conceded that a U.S. boycott by pro-life groups contributed to the decision to transfer patent rights and to dissociate the companies from RU-486. "Roussel Uclaf no longer has the means to be able to withstand the boycott threats," said Hoechst spokeswoman Catherine Euvrard in Paris. "This product can no longer be part of the strategy of an international company." The European companies gave patent rights outside the United States to Dr. Edouard Sakis, one of the drug's creators. U.S. patent rights had already been transferred, in 1994, to The Population Council based in New York City.

Anti-Catholicism Stronger — Anti-Catholicism continues to plague U.S. society, said William Donohue Apr. 12 in an address at a dinner of the Catholic Defense League of Minnesota. The president of the Catholic League for Religious and Civil Rights said: "Catholics think that, when (John) Kennedy got elected president, anti-Catholicism went away." Since that time "we've made strides as individuals, but I think we're going backward when it comes to anti-Catholicism against the Church as an institution."

U.S. Christians — Christian churches in the U.S. registered a net increase of about a quarter of a million in 1996, according to the *1997 Yearbook of American and Canadian Churches*, published by the National Council of Churches of Christ. The number of Mormons increased by 98,400, of Catholics by 89,849 and of Southern Baptists by 49,236. Large mainline Protestant churches, which had lost members steadily for the last two decades or more, "continued to decline, but they lost fewer members this year (1996) than in previous years."

For-Profit Health Care Not Wanted — The Administrative Committee of the U.S. Catholic Conference reiterated its opposition to converting any Catholic health care ministry to for-profit status. "We believe that ownership arrangements between Catholic health care ministry organizations and publicly traded, investor-owned hospital chains compromise the Church's mission to an unacceptable degree," the bishops said in a statement made public in mid-April. They called health care ministry "one of the most significant services which the Church offers to society," saying it is "fundamentally different from most goods and services and is consequently best delivered in a setting where human and community needs are the primary concerns…. The primary motive of publicly traded, investor-owned hospital chains is to provide a return to shareholders." But "the first commitment of our ministry is to render service in the name of Jesus. In that context, because health care is so integral to the Church's healing ministry, we strongly urge that, as ownership arrangements are being explored, priority be given to those involving Catholic health care providers."

In a related development, the committee issued a 14-page document entitled "The Pastoral Role of the Diocesan Bishop in Catholic Health Care Ministry." The document said: "The leadership of the diocesan bishop is best exercized in collaboration with sponsors and other leaders who have devoted their energies to the health care ministry with exemplary consistency and vigor, and who, together with the bishop, seek to ensure the continuance of this vital ministry in a rapidly changing environment."

Differences in Hiring Catholic Theologians — Leading Catholic theology schools hired graduates of non-Catholic theology schools as faculty members at a higher rate than U.S. non-Catholic theology schools hired graduates of Catholic institutions. This was the finding of a study conducted by Father William Ribando, C.S.C., chairman of the theology department at King's College, Wilkes-Barre, Pa. Reasons for the hiring differences appeared to range from bigotry to perceptions that Catholic theology programs are not as rigorous as those at non-Catholic schools. Father Ribando said the discrepancy was "a matter of justice to those who have the right to fair consideration for positions in institutions which promote themselves as ecumenical and offer their programs as outstanding preparation for teaching and other positions in both Protestant and Catholic settings."

Cremation Indult — The Holy See authorized local bishops in the U.S. to decide whether or not to allow the presence of cremated remains at funeral Masses in their respective dioceses. Bishop Anthony M. Pilla, president of the National Conference of Catholic Bishops, notified bishops of the decision Apr. 18, and asked them not to implement it until the Holy See approves appropriate liturgical texts and rites.

Volunteerism Summit — The President's Summit for America's Future was a "call for persons to come forward and to change the world through the example of their lives," Cardinal Anthony J. Bevilacqua said in a prayer at ceremonies opening the event Apr. 27 in Philadelphia. He prayed that God would help people to share their "gifts and talents for the purpose of building a culture of love in all of our communities.... Help us to be more aware of our many needy sisters and brothers in our midst, to do all that we can to alleviate their suffering."

Generous Contribution — Catholics donated $26.4 million in the 1996 national collection for aging religious sisters, brothers and priests. Bishop Anthony M. Pilla said the collection, the second highest since the first collection in 1988, "reflects well on people's sense of regard for the religious who give their lives in service to the Church, and on the generous nature of our people themselves. I know of no other collection in our Church which has been supported as consistently and generously as this one."

Briefs:

• Bishop Thomas J. Tobin announced that, starting in 1998, the usual age for reception of the sacrament of confirmation in the Diocese of Youngstown would be lowered from 11th grade to eighth grade. (See separate entry.)

• Meetings during the month included those of: the National Association of Diaconate Directors, Apr. 9 to 11 in Atlanta; Network, the 25-year-old social justice lobby, Apr. 12 in Washington; the National Conference of Catechetical Leadership, Apr. 13 to 17 in Orlando; the 34th National Workshop on Christian Unity, Apr. 21 to 24 in Sacramento.

No Federal Funding for Suicide

President Clinton signed into law Apr. 30 a bill prohibiting federal funding for assisted suicide or euthanasia. The President said on signing the bill: "Over the years, I have clearly expressed my personal opposition to assisted suicide, and I continue to believe that assisted suicide is wrong." While feeling "deep sympathy for those who suffer greatly from incurable illness," he said he believed endorsement of "assisted suicide would set us on a disturbing and perhaps dangerous path." Wanda Franz, president of the National Right to Life Committee, called the bill a sign that "the American people, Congress and the President have resoundingly said no to funding assisted suicide. "The Senate and the House passed the bill on votes of 99-0 and 398-10, respectively. The Church's position on the matter was well known.

INTERNATIONAL

Latin American Problems — Archbishop Oscar Andres Rodriguez Maradiaga, president of the Latin American Bishops' Council, spoke about three of them during an Apr. 1 interview in New York.

"We now have democracy in all nations but one. But our democracies are weak because of social unrest and great poverty."

"People who advocated Marxism are disappointed. They, some of them people of good faith, were looking for social changes but the changes never came. A positive result of liberation theology, however, was 'the engagement with the poor' and the impulse for solidarity as an answer to poverty. The principal impediment to economic development was external debt."

The archbishop called for international action to alleviate the debt burden. There was need for a "strong war against corruption." A major weakness of Latin Anerican governments was their "internal corruption," said the archbishop.

Chapel and School Bulldozed — Sudanese police bulldozed a Catholic center housing a chapel and school on the outskirts of Khartoum late in March, but were prevented from destroying two other chapels when parishioners blocked their path, according to a delayed report released Apr. 4 by Comboni missionaries. A female parishioner, defying police orders, managed to enter the center and remove consecrated hosts from the tabernacle before destruction was completed Mar. 31.

Void Created by Globalization — Cardinal Joseph Ratzinger said in a newspaper interview that globalization of the international economy was creating a spiritual void and accentuating rich-poor divisions around the world. He also said: "The collapse of communism did not cofirm the goodness of capitalism in all its forms. On the contrary, today we see that even capitalism does not resolve the problems of humanity, and that we must find new forms in which the free market is combined with a sense of peoples' responsibility to each other." A new model is needed to transform the "pure, cruel law of the market into a structure of cooperation and sharing between rich and poor."

Debt Relief — The Bishops' Conference of England and Wales called for fresh measures to alleviate the debt problems of the world's poorest countries, in a statement of support for a campaign by CAFOD, the Church's official development agency. CAFOD director Julian Filochowski said in a statement Apr. 7: "The health, education and development of the poorest of the poor in Third World countries are suffering because their governments have had to cut public spending in order to pay massive debts to the financial institutions of the First World." CAFOD was campaigning for the cancellation of unpayable debts.

Unemployment and Work — The Council oif Churches for Britain and Ireland issued a report critical of Britain's political parties for failing to adequately address poverty and unemployment in their electoral campaigns. The report also denounced the parties' promise of tax cuts to the well-off when so many people were living in poverty and without jobs. Cardinal George Basil Hume of Westminster said in a statement Apr. 8: "This major report ... will demand careful study.... It deserves to be widely debated and discussed, as the issues it deals with are of profound moral, social and political importance. Inevitably, it will take time to digest a substantial document of this nature, and I caution against instant reactions."

Religious Tolerance in Libya — The Holy See's new nuncio to Libya praised the government of Moammar Gadhafi for showing religious tolerance and an openness to dialogue with the minority Catholic community. Archbishop Sebastian Laboa did so on presentation of his credentials in Tripoli, the Libyan capital. He thanked authorities "for the great esteem which they have for our religious sisters who work in hospitals and other health centers." He added: "I thank them also for their tolerance and readiness in granting necessary permits to our priests for the service of the Christian community." The nuncio also said the Holy See's decision to open diplomatic relations with Libya was based on a belief that dialogue is the only way to attain peace. The action was opposed by the United States, which argued that Libya should be isolated by the international community because of its alleged role in international terrorism.

Bridging Past and Present — The new Israeli ambassador to the Holy See, a descendant of Jews expelled from Spain by King Ferdinand during the Inquisition, said he regarded himself as a bridge between past and present. "I am some kind of bridge between a different period of relations between the Jewish people and the Catholic Church to the present time, when we've embarked on a field of cooperation and fruitful dialogue," he said after presenting his credentials at the Vatican. "It is very important to try and find common denominators and understand each other and close that gap on both sides." The best way of building mutual understanding is to "remove the white gloves of diplomats" and to talk openly, sincerely and honestly about the challenges facing both entities."

Hostages Rescued — Seventy-two hostages held by members of the Tupac Amaru Revolutionary Movement for 126 days in the Japanese embassy in Lima were rescued by Peruvian military troops Apr. 22. Fourteen rebels, two soldiers and a judge died in the raid. One of those rescued was Jesuit Father Juan Julio Wicht, who chose to remain with the other hostages throughout their ordeal. The military raid came after negotiations failed to resolve the four-month crisis. Archbishop Juan Luis Cipriani Thorn of Ayacucho took part in the fruitless effort to end the crisis by peaceful means.

Hong Kong Worries — With Hong Kong's reversion to China scheduled for July 1, Coadjutor Bishop Joseph Zeng of Hong Kong said many local people were worried about what might happen because of their memory of events in China, such as the religious persecution of the 1966-to-1976 Cultural Revolution and the Tiananmen Square incident in 1989 in which many people were believed to have been killed during pro-democracy demonstrations. The bishop said: "There are priests and faithful who even died or were imprisoned for 20 to 30 years in China in the past. Now the underground church is not accepted by the government, and there is control over the official (government-sanctioned) church."

Briefs:

• Father Okun Lagora Matthew, social development coordinator for the Diocese of Gulu, said peacemaking and peacekeeping work under existing circumstances must have priority over development projects in Uganda.

• Italian members of Rotary International hoped their associates worldwide would join their efforts to finance a church for the Pope for Jubilee Year 2000.

• Archbishop Fernando Saenz Lacalle of San Salvador expressed satisfaction Apr. 27 over the decision by the Salvadoran Congress to outlaw practically all forms of abortion in the Central American nation.

• Priests and laypersons need to know how to use the media and not be content simply to criticize their faults, said Archbishop Dario Castrillon Hoyos, pro-prefect of the Congrgeation for the Clergy, Apr. 28.

Don't Deport Central Americans

The head of the Latin American Bishops' Council called on the United States not to deport thousands of Central American immigrants under a new federal law. "These massive deportations sadden us, because the great nation of the North was built by immigrants. Immigration isn't something bad, it's not a damger," said Archbishop Oscar Rodriquez Maradiaga, president of CELAM. At a press conference Apr.11 in Tegucigalpa, he said the bishops were worried that Latin American immigrants were becoming scapegoats for economic hard times in the United States. "There's a simplistic ideology that maintains that, if there's an economic crisis in the United States, it's because we Hispanics are invading and taking away jobs, something that's completely absurd," he said. The numbers of Central American immigrants in the U.S. were hard to pinpoint, but Central American observers estimated that some 330,000 Hondurans, 336,000 Salvadorans, 185,000 Guatemalans and 60,000 Nicaraguans living in the U,.S. could be subject to immediate deportation.

MAY 1997

VATICAN

Seminarians Slain — Pope John Paul condemned the slaying of more than 30 students for the priesthood in Burundi as a "barbaric act" and urged the country's ethnic groups to curb another escalating round of bloodshed. Vatican Radio reported May 2 that armed Hutu rebels had attacked the minor seminary in Buta, leaving many dead and wounded. It quoted an unnamed missionary priest as saying about 46 people were killed, including seminarians and other students, and at least that many wounded. The attack took place Apr. 28 but was made known only several days later.

On May 30, at a meeting with members of the Congregation of Priests of the Sacred Heart of Jesus, the Pope praised the courage of missionaries who chose to remain in the former Zaire. "With great admiration," he said, " I have learned that you did not leave any of your missions in Congo-Zaire, accepting all the risks of the present moment. God surely will bless your courageous witness of love for Christ and for the local populations so sorely tried."

Religious Freedom in Iran — The Pope called for Vatican-Iranian cooperation on fundamental moral and human rights issues, with primary emphasis on religious freedom, at a meeting May 3 with the new Iranian ambassador to the Holy See. He said freedom of religion was especially important for the small Christian minority in the Islamic republic.

Gypsy Beatified — Gypsies from throughout Europe celebrated May 4 with the Holy Father as he beatified the first of their own, Ceferino Jimenez Malla, who "showed how Christ is present in different peoples and races, and how all are called to holiness." Blessed Jimenez Malla was arrested in Barbastro, Spain, during the civil war of the 1930s for coming to the aid of a young priest and was subsequently shot to death for failing to stop praying as ordered by his captors.

Chemical Weapons Accord — The Pope praised the new global Chemical Weapons Convention and urged its signatories to put it into effect as soon as possible. Noting that chemical weapons pose an "enormous danger," he said May 7 that all of humanity was awaiting completion of the ban "in order to look to the future with more serenity." The accord, which took effect and was ratified by the United States in April, ruled out the use, production, stockpiling and transfer of chemical weapons. Ratification by 20 other nations was pending.

Poverty and Health —Increasing poverty and government cuts in health care spending threaten to reverse progress made in improving health care throughout the world, said a Vatican official. Archbishop Javier Lozano Barragan, president of the Pontifical Council for Pastoral Assistance to Health Care Workers, told the World Health Organization that the "plague of poverty" is the biggest obstacle to its efforts to promote "health for all in the 21st century." The human person must be the measure of every policy decision, he told the organization's general assembly May 7. The archbishop also repeated Vatican concern that WHO's "reproductive health" recommendations had an almost exclusive emphasis on birth limitation. "My delegation would like to underline the fact that this program directly concerns human life and cannot be limited to one phase of human existence," he said. Narrowing the focus of "reproductive health" to sexually transmitted disease, contraception and abortion is "in contradiction with WHO's own definition of health, which is 'the state of physical, psychological and social well-being of an individual.'"

Vocations Congress —The Pope applauded the efforts of European church personnel to share insights and examine ways and means of promoting vocations to the priesthood and religious life. He urged those attending the May 5-to-10 European Vocations Congress to work for a new blossoming of interest in consecrated life and the priesthood, reminding them May 9 that "this blossoming is not the product of spontaneous generation, nor of an activism that rests only on human means. It is, therefore, urgent that a great movement of prayer sweep across the ecclesial community of the European continent, against the wind of secularism."

Fatima Anniversary — The enduring value of the apparitions of Mary at Fatima, which began May 13, 1917, was the subject of a commemorative message of Pope John Paul. He said: "The message which the Most Holy Virgin sent to all humanity on this occasion continues to resound with all its prophetic force, inviting everyone to insistent prayer, to interior conversion and to a generous commitment of expiation for one's own sins and for those of the world."

May 13 was also the 16th anniversary of Mehmet Ali Agca's attempt to kill the Pope.

Corpus Christi — Pope John Paul celebrated the feast of the Body and Blood of Christ May 29 with an evening Mass in the Lateran Basilica and a procession of the Blessed Sacrament from there to the Basilica of St. Mary Major. He said in a homily: "Today's solemnity helps us give Christ the centrality that is his in the divine plan for humanity and urges us to configure our lives to that of Christ, the supreme and eternal priest."

On May 25, the Pope said that, as the core of Christian life, the eucharistic mystery needed to be better understood by the faithful: "The Eucharist represents the summit and the synthesis of Christianity. Under the species of consecrated bread and wine, Christ continues to live among his people."

General Audience Topics:

• The words, "Behold your Mother," express the intention of Jesus to inspire in his followers an attitude of love for and trust in Mary (May 7).

• Reflections on his visit to Lebanon earlier in the month (May 14).

• While the Gospels do not mention Jesus appearing to Mary after the Resurrection, it was fitting that she should have been the first to experience his glory (May 21).

• Mary's powerful intercession obtains for the Church an ever-fresh outpouring of the enlightening and strengthening gifts of the Holy Spirit (May 28).

Briefs:

• In a message to delegates attending the general chapter of the Order of Friars Minor, the Pope praised the order for its focus on evangelization, "reemphasizing with vigor (its) commitment to follow the poor, chaste and obedient Christ in order to be able to better announce to all the sublime truths of the Good News."

• The Pope celebrated his 77th birthday May 18 while making his 259th visit to a Roman parish.

• In an address May 23 during a meeting with the James Madison Council of the U.S. Library of Congress, the Pope said the wisdom of the past as explained and celebrated in the holdings of the world's libraries should be made as accessible as possible. "The patrimony of human thought, cultural achievement and religious truth contained in the world's libraries is not only a monument to past human endeavor," but "the solid ground on which each new generation can strive to build a better future."

• Cardinal Roger M. Mahony of Los Angeles was appointed by the Pope to serve as one of the three presiding officers of the forthcoming special assembly of the Synod of Bishops for America..

Married Priests May Not Administer Sacraments

Priests who have civilly married (attempted marriage) may not administer the sacraments, except for granting absolution when there is a danger of death, according to a Vatican ruling approved by the Pope and made public May 20. The ruling was issued in response to Catholics who asked whether church law allows for married priests who have never been openly censured to administer the sacraments. The ruling came from the Pontifical Council for the Interpretation of Legislative Texts. It said that attempted marriage by a priest is such a serious violation of the obligation of clerical celibacy that it creates a condition of "objective unsuitability" for administration of the sacraments. Therefore, the priest cannot licitly exercise the sacramental ministry, nor can the faithful legitimately request it — except for the benefit of a penitent in danger of death who seeks absolution in the absence of another priest in good standing.

NATIONAL

Hoechst Boycott Still On — The National Right to Life Committee, saying the Hoechst Marion Roussel pharmaceutical company had failed to "wash its hands of the abortion pill" RU-486, announced May 8 it would continue to boycott the antihistamine Allegra and the firm's other products. The committee called on Hoechst to take four specific steps to end association with the drug:

• immediately cease production of the pill and destroy stockpiles;

• withdraw the granting of rights to the pill to Dr. Edouard Sakis, one of the drug's creators; and The Population Council;

• make public any relevant agreements made with Sakis, The Population Council, the French and/or U.S. government or anyone else about the drug;

• "make neither the drug, its rights nor its formula available to any other individuals or entities."

Fewer Refugees — A report released May 19 by the U.S. Committee for Refugees said the number of refugees and asylum seekers worldwide at the end of 1996 was about 14.5 million people, about five percent less than a year earlier and the lowest number since 1988. At least another 19 million people were considered "internally displaced." Also reported in countries was an increasingly unwelcoming climate for refugees.

Constitutional Rights, So-Called — Neither abortion nor the right to die is guaranteed by the U.S. Constitution, despite efforts by some jurists to create constitutional rights where none existed before, said Supreme Court Justice Antonin Scalia May 20 in an address to nearly 500 members and guests of the Justinian Law Society. He said he believed interpretation of the Constitution should be based on the text and the document's original purpose, not on some current extrapolation of the text. Some judges showed no qualms about creating rights that had no grounding in the original intent of the Constitution, "believing in the Constitution not for what it means, but for what (they think) it ought to mean." They believe that if "you want a right to an abortion, it's in there. If you want a right to die, it's in there."

Health Care Leadership — A principal challenge facing health care in the United States is finding a way to "pass the baton" from the declining number of nuns to lay leaders, according to a bishop specialist in the field. Auxiliary Bishop Joseph M. Sullivan of Brooklyn said more than 90 percent of Catholic health care in the country was sponsored by nuns. While some health care is conducted by dioceses and other sponsors, the health care ministry as a whole has come to the Church as "the gift of religious women." Finding their successors in the field is a critical matter.

CPA Awards — Recipients of awards at the annual convention of the Catholic Press Association May 21 to 23 in Denver included: Franciscan Father Norman Perry, editor of the *St. Anthony Messsenger* magazine, with the 1997 St. Francis de Sales Award; *Our Sunday Visitor,* first place for general excellence in the category of national newspapers; *Chicago Catolico,* first place for general excellence in the category of Spanish-language newspapers; the Jesuit weekly, *America,* first place for general excellence in the category of general-interest magazines.

Seminary and Ministry Enrollments — The number of post-college U.S. seminarians increased by 120 in 1996, the Center for Applied Research in the Apostolate reported May 23. The report indicated:

• There were 3,292 seminarians in theology or pretheology programs at the start of the 1996-97 school year, up from 3,172 the previous year.

• There were at least 2,183 men preparing to become permanent deacons.

• More than 20,000 Catholics were enrolled in lay ministry formation programs; nearly two-thirds of them were women.

Catholic Tradition and Global Economy — The Church must apply Catholic social tradition to the global economy, Archbishop Rembert G. Weakland told a conference on social responsibility in the age of globalization. "Globalization could be a good thing for all nations on this planet," he said May 27 in the opening address to a three-day conference in Milwaukee. "It would be wishful thinking to try to imagine a different kind of economy," he added. "The global village is here to stay. Let us make the most of it." The conference marked the 10th anniversary of the

U.S. bishops' pastoral letter "Economic Justice for All." The archbishop said globalization makes it harder to grapple with (economic) issues, since they are so vast. But ... we must be more courageous in confronting the issues and bolder in suggesting solutions." He reiterated the duty of the Church to speak on economic issues and said: "Perhaps the role of the Church — I imply here all the faithful — is to develop this perspective of a global world and to meditate on how to bring a new and positive vision of harmony and justice to it. It is only right that religion be concerned about ethical standards and how they can be brought to bear on our society today."

CHD Grants and Welfare Laws — The Campaign for Human Development announced distribution of $169,000 in matching grants among groups working to change federal and state welfare laws so they might better serve the poor. The grants, ranging from $5,000 to $20,000, were going to 14 organizations in 11 states. Father Robert Vitillo, CHD executive director, said in the announcement: "We are pleased that CHD is able to give suppor to groups and coalitions working to diminish the punitive effects of welfare reform laws on the nation's poor and needy citizens.... We must renew our efforts to defend the life and dignity of all persons in society, especially of those who are most vulnerable."

Norms on Higher Education — U.S. bishops were asked by the Congregation for Education to redraft a proposal they had sent the congregation on putting into effect Vatican norms for Catholic higher education. The National Conference of Catholic Bishops announced May 27 that Cardinal Pio Laghi, head of the congregation, had expressed "profound gratitude" for the work that went into the bishops' document, but asked for a second draft that would include:

• the addition of "essential elements" of a mission statement;

• juridical elements the congregation regarded as necessary for "an effective functioning institutionally of Catholic universities as Catholic in all aspects of their organization, life and activity;

• additional attention to Canon 812 of the Code of Canon Law, which states that teachers of the theological disciplines in Catholic higher education need "a mandate from the competent ecclesiastical authority" to teach.

Basic documents on the norms in question were the bishops' 1989 document, "Doctrinal Responsibilities: Approaches to Promoting Cooperation and Resolving Misunderstandings between Bishops and Theologians," and *Ex Corde Ecclesiae,* Pope John Paul's apostolic constitution on Catholic universities, issued in 1990.

Briefs:

• Jesuit Father Robert F. Drinan issued a statement May 12 in which he withdrew comments he made the previous year saying that, although he opposed abortion, he believed President Clinton was right in vetoing a bill that would have banned partial-birth abortions.

• Bishop Michael A. Saltarelli of Wilmington announced May 29 that, as of January, 1998, Catholic couples wanting to be married in the diocese would be required to take part in a three-stage preparation process that would take a year to complete.

• Two thousand Asians, mostly from New York, made the first Asian Marian Pilgrimage to the National Shrine of the Immaculate Conception in Washington May 31.

AMA for Ban

Pro-life supporters, including a spokeswoman for the U.S. bishops, praised the May 19 decision of the American Medical Association to back an amended version of a bill banning partial-birth abortions. "No longer are there any 'medical' pretenses left with which to defend this horrible procedure," said Helen Alvare. "We urge senators who have relied on these to abandon them and to cast a vote for ending partial-birth abortions in the nation." Gary Bauer, president of the Family Research Council, said the AMA decision "means the other shoe has dropped. First, we learned that the abortion industry lied about the number and nature of abortions when they lied about the healthy mothers and healthy, viable children subjected to this barbaric procedure. And now we learn that this inhumane way of ending life is never necessary." Senate voting on the bill was not expected until after the summer congressional recess.

INTERNATIONAL

Zimbabwe Atrocities — Massacres, rapes, forced cannibalism and live burials of infant children were among atrocities detailed in a report published May 2 by *The Mail and Guardian,* a South African weekly newspaper. The report listed more than 7,000 cases of killings, torture and human rights abuses which occurred in the western province of Matabeleland from 1981 to 1987. The report was compiled from witness accounts by the Catholic Commission for Justice and Peace in Zimbabwe and the Legal Resources Foundation, a group of human rights lawyers.

Not Much Done — A Jerusalem bishop and the mayor of Nazareth said not enough preparations had been made for Jubilee Year 2000. Auxiliary Bishop Kamal Hanna Bathish said activity of the Vatican-Israeli bilateral Jubilee Committee had "really slowed down to the point where it is not working now." Mayor Ramez Jarrisi said neither the Palestinians nor the Israelis were moving at the necessary pace to assure that sites throughout the Holy Land would be ready to provide necessary services for large numbers of pilgrims.

Fundamental Issues in Britain — Cardinal George Basil Hume of Westminster, writing in the London daily newspaper, *The Independent,* May 6, said the British people as well as the government had to address the nation's problems while working for the common good and the protection of human life. "We cannot expect any government alone to solve the most fundamental problems we face, for these are not only economic and social but also moral and spiritual. We have to recognize, first, that respect is due to every human being simply by virtue of our common humanity. Then, we must realize that we are interdependent." He cited a number of issues including abortion, euthanasia, family life, sexual responsibility and education.

Rehab for Ex-Soldiers —Salesians of St. John

Bosco, with the support of Catholic Relief Services, were running rehabilitation centers for young ex-combatants in Liberia. CRS spokesman Tom Price said the centers were providing "an alternative to violence" to former child fighters and street children by teaching courses in a variety of trades. The "vast majority" were boys from eight to 20 years of age.

Catholic Membership in Canadian Council — The Catholic Church in Canada was officially accepted as a full member of the Canadian Council of Churches, announced the Rev. Robert Mills, interim general secretary of the council, May 15. "The cause of ecumenism has been advanced in Canada today," he said. Approval of membership for the Canadian Catholic Bishops' Conference says clearly that the churches "are serious about their intention to work together and strive for the unity for which Christ prayed, 'that they all may be one.'"

Franciscan Mission — The mission of the Franciscans at the end of the 20th century is "to spread a message of reconciliation, communion and peace," declared Father Giacomo Bini at a press conference in Assisi May 15, the day after his election as minister general of the Order of Friars Minor. Their primary task is to help people find hope and to combat a growing sense of loneliness in the world, said the former missionary to Africa.

For Unity in Middle East — All Arab lands "must be liberated" and the Palestinians given the right to establish a state in their "own land" with Jerusalem as its capital, said the presidents of the Middle East Council of Churches. "We declare our commitment to those causes which all Arabs advocate in common. We affirm our dedication to the common conviction that all our Arabs' lands must be liberated," they said. "We censure all unilateral efforts which prejudice Jerusalem's future, imposing a *fait accompli* upon the Jewish, Christian and Muslim people of this holy city." The presidents also stressed greater unity among Middle East Christians and urged continuing Christian-Muslim dialogue, following an early May meeting in Damascus, Syria. Latin-rite Patriarch Michel Sabbah of Jerusalem was one of the four current presidents of the council who took part in the meeting, which was chaired by Coptic Pope Shenouda III.

Resignation Sought — Two auxiliary bishops appointed by Pope John Paul to help bring peace to a troubled Swiss diocese were reported to have asked their bishop to resign. Auxiliary bishops Peter Henrici and Paul Vollmar asked Bishop Wolfgang Haas of Chur to leave his post, according to the Newsletter of the Central Commission of the Zurich Canton. The Newsletter said Bishop Haas had volunteered this information to a national committee on the priesthood in a confidential meeting in mid-March. Bishop Haas was widely criticized for his authoritarian and unresponsive administration

Hope Encouraged — Although people in the Holy Land were experiencing "among the most difficult days," because of the Israeli-Palestinian conflict, many initiatives were keeping hope alive, said Latin-rite Patriarch Michel Sabbah. "Here ... many good wills are manifested and expressed," he said on Pentecost Sunday.. "However, the official positions of those who hold the power seem by themselves to bring an end to hope and to prompt death and violence. Their unique criteria and guidelines are, unfortunately, material strength." He called on Christians living in the Holy Land not to "fall prey to despair" despite the "stifling difficulties" in their daily lives, so that they can resume their position as builders and partners in society. We ask the spirit of God to support the good will of all our churches and to support our course toward communion. We pray that the spirit of God, which has hallowed this land, may enlighten those to whom it has been given to rule this land in these days."

Low Religious Interest in Rome — A poll on religious attitudes in Italy indicated that 40 percent of Rome residents had little or no interest in their faith. Poll results were greeted with skepticism by some experts. Newspapers announced the news with headlines proclaiming Rome the "capital of atheism." The poll, conducted in 1995, involved a nationwide sample of 4,500 people who responded to a detailed questionnaire. In Rome, the study found, 19.1 percent of respondents showed no interest in religion; another 21.4 percent showed little interest. Rome residents indicating a medium interest in religious faith made up 35 percent of the sample, while 13.9 percent fell into the "medium-high" range and 10.6 percent were in the "high" category. The results indicated that only one in four Romans followed religious affairs closely, particularly in regard to personal attitudes and behavior, according to Roberto Cipriani, a professor of sociology at Rome III University. Another sociologist, Sister Enrica Rosanna, challenged the interpretation. "To speak of Rome as an atheistic city is nonsense," she commented, saying that religious attitudes were too complex to be reduced to simple categories.

Briefs:
• The Israeli government posthumously honored two Salesian priests — Fathers Francesco Antonioli and Armando Alessandrini — who helped save 70 Jews of Rome from Nazi persecution.
• For want of personnel and funding, the Upper Canada Province of Jesuits announced plans to discontinue the work of its Center for Social Faith and Justice in Toronto.
• Synthesizing an Asian approach to the study of God was said to be the first major task of the newly formed Office of Theological Concerns, under the auspices of the Federation of Asian Bishops' Conferences.

Abortion Developments

Abortion was on the public agenda of several European countries in the spring. In Germany, bishops nationwide were considering whether to close pregnancy counseling centers rather than comply with unacceptable conditions required by law. In Poland, the constitutional high court struck down the nation's permissive new abortion law on the grounds that it did not protect the right to life. In Britain, Cardinal Hume called on the new government of Tony Blair to revise the nation's abortion law which placed no restrictions on the practice of abortion within the first 12 weeks of pregnancy.

JUNE 1997

VATICAN

Visit to Poland — Pope John Paul completed an 11-day pastoral pilgrimage to Poland June 10. On this 78th foreign trip of his pontificate, he visited more than 10 cities, celebrated Mass at special events, canonized two saints and delivered more than 25 addresses. (See separate articles.)

Christians Must Dialogue — Even in places where they are a tiny minority, Christians must be active in promoting dialogue and social commitment, Pope John Paul said in a mesage to the first Congress of Lay Catholics of the Middle East meeting June 10 to 14 in Beirut. Christians sharing in the "dialogue of daily life" in the same neighborhoods and exercizing "simple and sincere dialogue" with Muslims and Jews are the primary agents for fostering friendship, interreligious respect and religious freedom, he said. The meeting, attended by about 200 lay representatives from throughout the region, was organized by the Pontifical Council for the Laity.

Moral Criteria for Economics — Economic policies that do not provide for the welfare of the poor and do not offer incentives for solidarity jeopardize social peace, a Vatican official told participants in the Economic Forum of the Organization for Security and Cooperation in Europe. "It is crucial to maintain the basic moral criteria for evaluating economic systems; this consists of examining the standard of living of the poorest and the weakest." So stated Msgr. Ivan Jurkovic, a staff member of the Vatican Secretariat of State. He said June 11: "Economic laws risk becoming ineffective in a given society if there is no 'critical mass' of people willing to work for the segment of the population that has become impoverished and defenseless." Solidarity, care and concern for the poor are best fostered by families and regional and nongovernmental organizations. Governments should ensure that these three social structures have the support they need in order to survive.

Brain-Damaged Children — Working with medical experts, but insisting on personal, at-home care of children with serious brain damage, families can testify to "the miracle of love," the Pope said at a Vatican-sponsored conference of scientists, parents and pastoral workers. "The Lord of Life accompanies families who welcome and love their children with serious cerebral abnormalities and who know how great is their dignity," he commented during the June 12-to-14 meeting. He noted that the conference offered parents a model to follow by giving primary place to love, care and education within the family, but doing so with information and assistance from the medical community. The conference issued a final statement proclaiming the "absolute and inviolable dignity of persons with cerebral impairments" and warning against a dominant utilitarian mentality that views such persons as a burden. The statement recommended:

- opposition to pre-natal diagnosis whenever it is intended to seek out and eliminate those with impairments;
- rejection of sterilization of persons with cerebral impairments;
- emphasis on family care instead of that provided by state institutions;
- guaranteed health care options and appropriate tax breaks for families caring for a brain-damaged member.

Advertising Norms — The Vatican's increasing attention to ethics in advertising was not aimed at curbing publicity but at keeping it morally honest, according to Archbishop John P. Foley, president of the Pontifical Council for Social Communications. He told a symposium of Italian media experts June 16 that "advertising is becoming more and more our environment," and that the "Church wants to make sure it holds to some basic rules. Advertising should respect fundamental ethical principles: respect for the truth, the person and social life. In other words, it must always be honest and responsible."

Letters to Netanyahu and Arafat — Saying he was "deeply worried" about the stalled Middle East peace process, Pope John Paul urged Israeli Prime Minister Benjamin Netanyahu and Palestinian President Yasser Arafat to re-launch negotiations before uncontrollable violence could break out. The appeal came in separate, strongly worded letters dated June 16. To Netanyahu, he said he shared the sadness and frustration felt by ordinary people on both sides: "The Israeli and Palestinian people are already shouldering a burden of suffering which is too heavy; this burden must not be increased." To Arafat, he said repeated efforts to restart serious negotiations in recent months had been in vain. As a result, keeping the lid on violence might not be easy. "I am deeply worried, and I share the pain of those, especially Palestinians and Israelis, who feel let down and frustrated, and yet do not give in to the terrible temptation to re-kindle the conflict and carry it to greater levels of hatred and violence." To both men, he said: "In the name of God, I appeal to the Palestinian and Israeli leaders to consider, above all, the good of their peoples and the future of the younger generations."

Budget Surplus — Thanks to reduced spending and increased income, the Vatican turned its fourth straight budget surplus in 1996. Final figures showed that expenses at the Holy See totaled about $194.2 million in 1996 — about $5 million less than in 1995 — with income at $194.5 million. The resulting surplus of $258,000 was described by Vatican officials as modest but encouraging.

Family Values in Argentina — The Pope encouraged Argentina to defend its traditional family values against abortion, divorce, sexual immorality and an "anti-birth" mentality. "It must not be forgotten that, without the stability of the family, not only church life but also the common good of the nation is weakened," he said June 20 as he received the credentials of Esteban Juan Caselli, the nation's new ambassador to the Holy See.

Moral Truth in Research — The Pope urged doctors to follow fundamental moral and ethical truths in their research and practice, especially when it concerns the right to life. Addressing participants in an international conference on gynecology June 21, he said the dramatic facts of abortion and euthanasia called for a new synthesis between faith and culture.

He said it was an historical task of medical research to promote "whatever favors human dignity, and that such a responsibility goes beyond any specific legislation and is particularly applicable to the field of human sexuality." Unless scientists keep this perspective in mind, they can easily become immersed in commercial interests divorced from the larger good, he said.

Eastern-Rite Autonomy — The Pope encouraged Eastern-rite churches to maintain their distinctive liturgical and pastoral practices, saying such diversity enriches church unity. He made the comment June 23 at a meeting with Armenian-rite bishops. The prelates were meeting in Rome to devise a special set of canons to complement the universal Code of Canon Law of the Eastern Churches. The Pope said the development of church law specific to their rite was an expression of the "just autonomy and freedom" enjoyed by the Armenian Church and 20 other Eastern Catholic communities around the world.

Ecumenical Reconciliation — The Holy Father cited "a particular urgency" for reconciliation among Christians in a June 22 address in which he asked people to pray for participants in the Second European Ecumenical Assembly June 23 to 29 in Graz, Austria. The theme of the assembly was "Reconciliation — Gift of God and Source of New Life."

General Audience Topics
• Reflections on his 11-day visit to Poland (June 18). (See separate article.)
• "Mary's passage from this life to the next was the full development of grace in glory, so that no death can ever be so fittingly described as a 'dormition' as hers" (June 25).

Briefs:
• The Pope appealed June 15 for peace in Africa, saying he was worried about new outbreaks of civil unrest in the Republic of Congo and Sierra Leone.
• Vatican Radio reported June 19 that the Pope had accepted the resignation of Archbishop Fernando Saenz Lacalle as military bishop of El Salvador. The archbishop had been a target of controversy over his relationship with the nation's government.
• The Pope awarded the prestigious Paul VI Prize June 20 to Jean Vanier, founder of the International L'Arche Federation which operates homes where staff and persons with developmental disabilities live and work together.
• Relaxation of the celibacy rule for Latin-rite priests would not ease the vocations crisis, according to Archbishop Crescenzio Sepe, secretary of the Congregation for the Clergy. Such an approach would have "no theological, spiritual or pastoral foundation," he said June 24 on Vatican Radio.

No Pope-Patriarch Meeting

Orthodox Ecumenical Patriarch Bartholomew I of Constantinople issued a statement May 30 cancelling a planned meeting with Pope John Paul June 21 at an Austrian monastery, presumably because of differences regarding the wording of a proposed statement, allegations of Roman-rite proselytizing in Russia and, possibly, the timing and process of a papal meeting with Russian Orthodox Patriarch Alexei II scheduled for June 21. Bartholomew also notified the Vatican June 27 that he would not honor the custom, observed since 1977, of sending a delegation to the Vatican for the celebration of the feast of Sts. Peter and Paul June 29.

Bartholomew, as well as Alexei, declined attendance at the Second European Ecumenical Assembly June 23 to 29 in Graz.

NATIONAL

Sexual Morality the Same for All — Morality for homosexuals is no different than it is for single heterosexuals — which is to lead chaste lives — said Bishop William L. Higi of Lafayette, Ind. "Outside the sacred bond of matrimony — of its nature the union of male and female for life — all are called to lead celibate lives," he wrote in a pastoral letter in the June 1 edition of *The Catholic Moment*, the diocesan newspaper. "Genital sexuality outside of marriage ... is objectively sinful behavior. Be a person homosexual or heterosexual, this is not a popular message," he wrote.

1996 Statistics — The number of U.S. Catholics grew by nearly a million, to more than 61.2 million, in 1996, but there were 974 fewer priests and 1,481 fewer nuns, according to figures compiled and reported in the 1997 edition of the *Official Catholic Directory*. The number of students increased in Catholic elementary and high schools, and also in parish religious education programs. The number of Catholic educational institutions on all levels also increased, including 145 more diocesan or parish elementary schools. There were fewer Catholic health care facilities, but those in operation treated about five million more patients. The number of baptisms and confirmations increased but not the number of marriages, which declined slightly. Other slight decreases were reported in parishes, missions and pastoral centers. (See other entries for statistics in various categories.)

Ordination of Women Report — The Catholic Theological Society of America, meeting June 5 to 8 in Minneapolis, endorsed the conclusion of a task force report which said prayer and study were needed regarding the Church's stance against the ordination of women to the priesthood, because "serious doubts" remained about the claims of authority and grounding in tradition of the teaching of Pope John Paul and the Congregation for the Doctrine of the Faith. Church teaching against the ordination of women was the subject of a statement issued by the congregation in 1995. Before the society voted to accept the report, Archbishop Charles J. Chaput of Denver said in a column published in the June 4 edition of the *Denver Catholic Register:* "For members of the Catholic Theological Society of America to revisit this teaching at such a late date, when so many other urgent issues face the Church, is more than just disappointing. (The report) will not solve the vocations problem. It creates unnecessary and belated confusion. And it raises questions about the society's continuing usefulness for the life of the Church." He called for retirement of "this document as briskly as possible." The archbishop's criticism was echoed in remarks by Bishop James T. McHugh of Camden and Bishop John J. Myers of Peoria.

"Christ and the Eucharist" was the theme of society's meeting.

Safety Net Needed — Welfare and immigration policies that remove the safety net of basic food and financial assistance for the poor cannot be tolerated. Eliminating a safety net that "provides sustenance and shelter" to children, families, the elderly and disabled is a "matter of fundamental morality and justice in our society," said Archbishop William J. Levada. His remarks came during ceremonies for the blessing of a facility for homeless families in San Francisco. He said key targets for welfare and immigration legislation should include:

• assisting people to make the transition from welfare to employment by job training and other means;

• strengthening family life by helping parents "meet the social, economic, educational and moral needs of their children";

• providing a safety net by keeping in place Supplemental Security Income and food stamps for the elderly and disabled.

Catholic-Anglican Dialogue — The co-chairmen of the U.S - Anglican-Roman Catholic dialogue issued a joint statement June 13 saying that their dialogue would focus for the next several years on the manner in which authority is exercised in the church. They said the issue was "the heart of the matter that keeps us from full communion." Topics would include "how authority is exercised relative to teaching, governance, discipline, decision-making, conciliarity, reception, the fostering of unity, and recognition of apostolicity between our two churches."

Theology School Censured — The American Association of University Professors voted June 14 to censure the administration of St. Meinrad School of Theology for firing tenured professor Sister Carmel E. McEnroy without a due process hearing. She was fired because of what the school called "public dissent" against church teaching on the prohibition of priestly ordination for women.

Hospital Affiliation Rejected — The Congregation for the Clergy announced rejection June 16 of a proposed affiliation agreement between St. Peter's Medical Center and the Robert Wood Johnson University Hospital because of "a sense of risk … that the Catholic Christian perspective was not adequately addressed." Vatican approval of the agreement had been sought because St. Peter's was a diocesan-fcsponsored facility.

Partial-Birth Abortion — New Jersey Governor Christine Todd Whitman issued June 23 a "conditional veto" of a bill that would ban partial-birth abortions in the state. The condition for her signing was a "health" exception which would, in effect, nullify the ban.

In Washington, where the House of Representatives had already passed a ban against partial-birth abortions, Senate action was put off to the fall, when it was expected President Clinton and the Senate would not approve a bill against the procedure.

Trade Status of China — The House of Representatives defeated a bid June 24 to revoke China's Most Favored Nation trade status by a vote of 259 to 173. At issue in the debate was an effort to end that status because of China's record of violations of human rights and religious freedom.

Aid for Religious — The National Religious Retirement Office distributed $24.5 million from its 1996 national collection to 504 orders of women and men religious to help meet their retirement needs. It distributed or allocated another $2.25 million for special project grants or to meet critical needs in some orders.

Briefs:

• Christian-Muslim relations in the next century should be characterized by respect for religious differences and joint efforts toward peace, said Cardinal Francis Arinze, head of the Pontifical Council for Interreligious Dialogue, June 5 at Georgetown University.

• Archbishop Theodore E. McCarrick of Newark and Bishop John H. Ricard of Pensacola, in a letter dated June 6, urged President Clinton to authorize the resumption of direct flights to Cuba at least for delivery of critically needed humanitarian aid.

• Bishop Carlos Felipe Ximenes Belo, 1996 Nobel Peace Prize winner, asked U.S. church and government leaders to continue work and prayer for peace in his native land of East Timor, in control of Indonesia since 1976.

Supreme Court Decisions

In the last few days of its 1996-97 term, the U.S. Supreme Court ruled in major cases having to do with physician-assisted suicide, federally funded educational programs in religious schools, the Religious Freedom Reformation Act and censorship of the Internet. (See separate entries.)

INTERNATIONAL

Peace in Nicaragua? — An accord worked out with mediation by the Church and signed May 30, by the Nicaraguan government and armed former guerrillas was an important but small step toward lasting peace in the country, according to a number of churchmen. They welcomed the settlement but had some misgivings. "Let's hope (the agreement) lasts, because we must finally put an end to the violence in the countryside," said Msgr. Francisco Eddy Montenegro Avendano, vicar general of the Archdiocese of Managua.

Broadcasting Cuts — The Southern African Catholic Bishops' Conference criticized the South African Broadcasting Corporation's announcement that religious broadcasting time would be cut and staff reduced. They said in a letter June 3: "Our greatest fears are being realized; religion is being sidelined and practically the whole department is being closed down." They called on the corporation not to put the cuts into effect and asked for reconsideration of the matter.

Concordat Ratification Delayed — Polish parliamentarians voted again June 4 to delay ratification of a concordat with the Holy See, despite calls for an agreement during Pope John Paul's pilgrimage to Poland during the month. Ratification, pending since the accord was signed by both parties in July, 1993, would give international treaty status to Catholic Church rights in Poland. Members of Parliament from the Democratic Left Alliance demanded that ratification be postponed until after the adoption of a new, post-communist constitutuion.

No Aid To Guerrillas — The president of the

National Council of Christian Churches in Brazil denied any involvement by the World Council of Churches in financing guerrilla groups, as stated in a book published by the Vatican publishing house. The Rev. Glauco Soares de Lima called the accusations absurd, and added that "the Catholic Church, although not an actual member, participates at the meetings of the WCC and would have noticed any decision to finance guerrilla groups." The book, written by Father Nicola Bux, was entitled *The Fifth Seal: Christian Unity toward the Third Millennium.*

Compensation in Hungary — The Hungarian government became the first country in Eastern Europe to reach agreement with the Vatican on a program for funding Catholic activities. Under provisions of the agreement, most churches and sacred buildings confiscated by the communist regime in 1948 will be returned by the year 2011. "It signifies an interesting change in attitudes and, broadly speaking, church leaders are satisfied," said Piarist Father Laszlo Lukacs, spokesman for the bishops.

Council Vice President — Delegates to the triennial assembly of the Canadian Council of Churches elected Bishop Brendan O'Brien of Pembroke, Ontario, as a vice president, representing the Canadian Conference of Catholic Bishops. Nearly 20 Catholic officials from across Canada were among the 122 delegates to the June 12-to-15 assembly in Ottawa.

Albanian Agreement — Leaders of Albania's main political parties signed a peace accord brokered by a Rome-based lay organization six days before scheduled national elections. Presidents of the three leading parties subscribed to a commitment to free and fair elections and also agreed to create conditions for reconciliation and cooperation after the completion of balloting. The party leaders presented the document and their viewpoints to the media June 23 at the headquarters of the San Egidio Community, which had been active in Albanian affairs since the end of the Cold War.

Guatemalan War Victims — Catholics were taking part in the tortuous process of recovering the remains of some of the estimated 140,000 victims of Guatemala's 36-year civil war. Over the previous five years, forensic teams discovered the remains of about 1,000 victims. The search quickened with the end of the war in December, 1996. A peace accord was signed that month by President Alvaro Arzu Irigoyen and the leftist rebels of the National Guatemalan Revolutionary Unity, marking an end to the conflict. Among casualties of the war were more than 400 indigenous communities believesd destroyed in government anti-guerrilla sweeps in the early 1980s.

Threat of Muslim Fundamentalism — Although it may have appeared relatively quiet on Israel's northern border, the worldwide threat of Muslim fundamentalists was growing from there, said an officer of the Christian South Lebanese Army. "We are fighting against Hezbollah and other fundamentalists for the whole world, not just for us and the Israelis," said retired Col. Sharbel Barakat at a June 25 Jerusalem symposium on Christians in Lebanon. "We are fighting fundamentalists who want to show they have the strength to fight the whole world with their weapons and ideology. Lebanon is a showcase. If the fundamentalists succeed there, they will succeed elsewhere."

Earlier in the month, Vatican personnel and Muslim representatives discussed the problem of religious minorities at the third annual meeting of the Muslim-Catholic Liaison Committee, held June 18 and 19 in Rabat, Morocco. A statement issued after the meeting said: "The participants confirmed their sincere desire to understand problems which minorities face in many countries of the world, and to help overcome the difficulties which they suffer."

Briefs:

• Councilor Alban Maginness was elected June 2 the first Catholic Lord Mayor of Belfast, Northern Ireland.

• Ontario's top Mafia boss, John Papalia, was denied a Catholic burial by Bishop Anthony T. Tonnos of Hamilton because of the violent nature of his life and death.

• Two communist secret police generals were due to go on trial a second time in Poland on charges related to the 1984 kidnapping and murder of Father Jerzy Popieluszko, who was active in the Solidarity labor movement.

• Tribute was paid by Pope John Paul to Irish missionary saints for their role in evangelizing Europe, in a message commemorating the 1,400th anniversary of the death of St. Columcille.

Ecumenical Assembly

Seven hundred official delegates plus more than 9,000 other persons attended the Second European Ecumenical Assembly June 23 to 29 in Graz, Austria. "Reconciliation — Gift of God and Source of New Life" was the theme of the assembly. It was organized by the Council of European Bishops' Conferences and the Conference of European Churches; chairpersons were the presidents of both groups. Numerous participants told Catholic News Service that ecumenism had been advanced in large and small ways during the week of discussions and related events. The most tangible product was a three-page statement assesssing assemby aims and achievemens, and a longer text on reconciliation. The document dealt with ways to promote dialogue between religions and cultures, commitment to reconciliation and nonviolent conflict resolution between peoples and nations, and ways of overcoming social injustice and social exclusion. The Rev. John Arnold, an Anglican and head of the Conference of European Churches, reminded delegates that the document was "being sent to the churches, not for the episcopal wastebasket." Cardinal Miloslav Vlk, president of the Council of European Bishops' Conferences, said approval of the document was neither an end nor a beginning to the ecumenical movement. "We have come a long way to Graz," he said. "And the path stretches a long way from here. We must have patience."

Disappointing was the absence of Ecumenical Orthodox Patriarch Bartholomew I of Constantinople, who canceled his appearance May 30 after reports circulated that Pope John Paul would meet Russian Orthodox Patriarch Alexei II of Moscow in Vienna before the Graz assembly. That meeting did not take place.

JULY 1997

VATICAN

More Compassion in Medical Care — Medical care should reflect more compassion and less avarice, the Holy Father said in a message issued in advance of the the annual World Day of the Sick, Feb.11. "The Christian community strives to care for the sick and promote the quality of life, cooperating with all men of good will." In so doing the Church should encourage "support for equitable distribution of health resources and the promotion of greater solidarity between rich and poor peoples."

Eastern Churches — The Pope called on the 21 Eastern churches in union with Rome to seek greater agreement among themselves and to help reduce "misunderstandings and tensions" between Catholic and Orthodox churches. He made the appeal in a July 3 message to a meeting of Eastern-rite leaders held June 30 to July 6 in Niyregyhaza, Hungary. Praying together and discussing common interests and differences give leaders the opportunity to better define their churches, as well as their role in the universal Church, he said. "I trust a more clear consciousness of this identity would facilitate the precious placement of the Eastern-rite Catholics in the field of ecumenism, promoting the overcoming of misunderstandings and of tensions that have brought, and continue to bring, no small amount of suffering." Members of the group said in a final document that the reconstruction of Eastern-rite church identity is "a tremendous process that requires time, patience, respect for the feelings of the faithful, and great determination."

Evangelization in West Africa — The Pope urged the bishops of Burkina Faso and Niger July 4 to increase their efforts to reach the faithful and to create interreligious harmony. "In the midst of the difficulties and conflicts that the African continent has experienced, may your communities provide bold signs of hope," he said. Noting that Cathoics and other Christians are called upon to provide witness to the same Gospel teachings, he underscored the importance of ecumenical dialogue. He also stressed the value of interreligious cooperation and of finding solutions based on justice and solidarity" to problems and differences.

Diocesan Synod Guidelines — In a new set of guidelines for diocesan synods, the Vatican emphasized the leadership role of bishops and cautioned that such assemblies must not be used to challenge episcopal authority. The document, released July 8, offered instructions on the nature and purpose of local synods, on participants and on procedures to be observed. The synod is, above all, an instrument designed to aid the bishop in carrying out his ministry of guiding and teaching the people of his diocese. As the bishop, he has an authoritative role in all phases of such synods, reflecting his position at the head of the diocese. "Thus, any attempt to place the synod in opposition to the bishop on the grounds of 'representation of the people of God,' is contrary to the authentic order of ecclesial relations."

Ecumenism Moving — Improvements in Catholic-Lutheran relations were irreversible and the ecumenical movement unstoppable, Pope John Paul told attendants at a global Lutheran gathering. "The progress made in our relations over the years since the Second Vatican Council is a sign that the Lord is blessing our efforts," he said July 9 in a message addressed to the Rev. Gottfried Brakemeier, outgoing president of the Lutheran World Federation. He expressed hope that, whenever Lutherans and Catholics gather to pray and to work toward unity, they would receive "the support they need in the urgent task of bearing witness before the world to our common faith."

They're Not Sects — While the close-knit, committed, obedient life of new Catholic movements and communities may seem to go against modern notions of individual freedom, they cannot be called "sects,"an Austrian archbishop said. Such criticisms of church-approved movements are "indirectly a reproach against the Pope and the bishops" who have blessed and continue to oversee them," said Archbishop Christoph Schonborn of Vienna. His comments came in the July 17 edition of *L'Osservatore Romano* about three months after a Belgian parliamentary report listed several Catholic organizations — including Opus Dei and the charismatic renewal — among religious sects gaining influence in Belgium.

Support Urged for Developing Countries — The Vatican appealed for greater world support for developing countries in the process of economic globalization so they do not become further marginalized. "Very often, the losers of today's new order are those who were losers in the older one also," said Msgr. Diarmuid Martin, secretary of the Pontifical Council for Justice and Peace, at a meeting of the U.N. Economic and Social Council. "As fellow human beings, we have the responsibility to see that they are not the losers again tomorrow." Msgr. Martin represented the Holy See at the June 30-to-July 25 annual meeting in Geneva.

$1.4 Million for Development — The administrative council of the Populorum Progressio Foundation announced late in the month a commitment of $1.4 million to development programs in Latin America and the Caribbean. The money was to be divided among about 200 projects promoting health care, agriculture, education, means of communication and other programs and services for indigenous communities, minorities and poor people in rural areas.

NATIONAL

Black Priest Honored — Hundreds of people from midwestern and southern states gathered in Quincy, Ill., June 12 and 13 to pay tribute to the first U.S.-born African-American priest and founder of the first black Catholic church in Chicago. He was Father Augustus Tolton, ordained Apr. 25, 1886. "For black Catholics, he is the father of all," said Benedictine Father Cyprian Davis, author of *The History of Black Catholics in the United States.*

Aid for Bosnians — Catholic Relief Services received a $1.5 million grant to help members of the Croat Catholic, Serbian Orthodox and Muslim communities to return to the areas of Bosnia-Herzegovina from which they had been displaced during hostilities in the region. The grant was announced July 14 by the U.S. State Department's Bureau of Population Refugees and Migration.

Sprituality-Health Link — A yearlong review of research into the relationship between spirituality and medicine indicated that acceptance of the link was moving from the margins to the mainstream of medical practice. Dr. David B. Larson, president of the National Institute for Health Care Research, said at a Washington press conference July 18: "We have compiled enough evidence to suggest that the field of faith and medicine has matured and is now ready for growth. We are placing a wake-up call to the medical and scientific communities to stop, look and listen to the compelling collection of data on this forgotten factor in medicine.

K. of C. Records — Knights of Columbus contributed more than $105 million and well over 48 million hours of service to church, community and youth programs lin 1996. Contributions and services went to: parishes, schools and religious education programs; pro-life activities and health projects; institutions and programs for the elderly and disabled; disaster relief efforts, and various youth programs.

. **Religious Persecution** —The U.S. State Department issued an 86-page report on the status of religious rights in 78 countries. Highest on the list of persecutors was China, despite protestations to the contrary by Ye Xiao Wen, director of China's Religious Affairs Bureau.

Also released June 22 was another State Department report entitled "United States Policies in Support of Religious Freedom: Focus on Christians." Some commentators remarked that the Clinton administration's concern for trade with China was more important than its concern for religious freedom in the country.

Sex-Abuse Judgment — The Diocese of Dallas said it would appeal a judgment of $120 million ordered against it by a jury July 24 in a sex-abuse case involving a former priest of the diocese. It was the largest verdict of its kind in the country in a case involving a priest. Previously, one of the highest awards was a reported $5 million in a civil lawsuit against the Diocese of Fall River, Mass., in 1993, involving former priest James Porter.

In Dallas, the suit alleged sexual abuse by former priest Rudolph Kos while he served in the diocese from 1985 until his removal as a pastor in 1992 following a complaint of abuse. Plaintiffs in the case included 10 former altar boys and the parents of a young man who committed suicide in 1992. Their lawyers claimed the diocese had ignored evidence that Kos was molesting boys. The diocese did not dispute the molestation claims but denied it was engaged in any cover-up or was negligent in responding to accusations against the priest.

Meetings — Meetings during the month included the following: 10th annual National Catholic HIV/AIDS Ministry Conference, July 17 to 22 at Loyola University, Chicago, attended by more than 200; 26th Worldwide Marriage Encounter International Convention July 18 to 20, in San Antonio.

INTERNATIONAL

Hong Kong's Future? — Hong Kong Catholics, with mixed feelings about the return of the British colony to China July 1, gathered to pray for the future. Before and during the handover and in the days following, they met for Masses, prayer vigils and demonstrations to express concern for their freedom. Hong Kong's coadjutor and auxiliary bishops urged Catholics to have confidence in the future and to be united and committed to evangelizing and serving society.

Not a Catholic Organization — The Brazilian bishops' conference said in a statement July 4 that the Latin American branch of the pro-abortion, U.S.-based Catholics for a Free Choice could not be considered a Catholic organization. "We concur with the National Conference of Catholic Bishops from the United States that several people can be misled to believe that it is a Catholic organization, but it is not and it does not have any affiliation or relation with the Catholic Church."

South African Schools — After years of negotiations with the South African government, Catholic education officials reported that, in accord with a new agreement, the Church has the right to determine what is needed to preserve the distinctive religious character of its schools.

False Charges — In his first comprehensive comments on new accusations that he was involved in Argentina's "dirty war" of the 1970s, Cardinal Pio Laghi said he "certainly was not an accomplice." In a mid-month interview with a Catholic magazine published in Bologna, he said accusations against him seem to come up cyclically, and "every time their absurdity grows."

Unacceptable Definition of Spouse — The Archdiocese of Vancouver denounced British Columbia's decision to include lesbians and gays under the definition of spouse, with the same rights and responsibilities heterosexual couples have for child support, custody and access. Msgr. Gregory Smith, chancellor of the archdiocese, said he considered the change in the provincial government's definition of spouse as "part of a pattern of attack on the family as a foundation of society." The Anglican Church supported the new law.

Yeltsin Veto Applauded — Russian President Boris Yeltsin vetoed controversal legislation that Pope John Paul and others said would severely restrict religious bodies. The legislation, passed by the Parliament in June and vetoed July 22, would have designated only Orthodox Christianity, Islam, Buddhism and Judaism as "traditional" religions "worthy of respect." It would have imposed a number of harsh legal restrictions on all other religious bodies, including a 15-year waiting period between a group's application for and receipt of legal status. Archbishop Tadeusz Kondrusiewicz, apostolic administrator of European Russia, welcomed the veto, along with other religious leaders.

Bombing Condemned —Latin-rite Patriarch Michel Sabbah condemned July 30 the Jerusalem market bombing that killed 15 persons and injured more than 170 others. A Vatican statement said: "The Holy See deplores this blind violence which sows indiscriminate death. It is not with actions of this sort that peace is constructed.The Holy Father has mentioned many times that violence generates only violence. Peace, on trhe contrary, is constructed by persevering dialogue and respect for commitments already made."

AUGUST 1997

VATICAN

Nearly a Billion — According to figures in the just published *Statistical Yearbook of the Church,* there were 989.4 million Catholics in the world as of Dec. 31, 1995. The five countries with the most Catholics were Brazil with 134.8 million, Mexico with 86.3 million, The Philippines with 58.7 million, the United States with 57 million and Italy with 55.6 million. (See additional entries for statistics in various categories.)

Tribute to Paul VI — Pope John Paul paid tribute to Pope Paul VI Aug. 6, the 19th anniversary of his death. He said Paul "was totally dedicated to the Gospel cause. ... He loved Christ ... and lived for the Church." He quoted his predecessor: "'I can say that I have always loved the Church, and I believe I have lived for her and for nothing else. But I would like the Church to know it; and that I had the strength to tell her so, as a secret which only at the very end of life one has the courage to reveal.'"

Dialogue with Reformed Alliance — Pope John Paul sent a message of reconciliation to the global organization that oversees Reformed churches and applauded their ongoing dialogue with the Catholic Church. "Catholics and Reformed must continue to seek a healing of memories as part of their common pilgrimage toward unity," he said Aug. 11. "The Catholic Church is committed to continuing this theological dialogue.

New Rules for Deacons and Priests — The Congregation for Divine Worship and the Sacraments sent a circular letter to diocesan bishops and heads of religious orders with priests advising them of new rules relaxing some of the former provisions for releasing priests from the obligation of celibacy and for allowing widowed permanent deacons to marry again under certain conditions. The rules make it much easier for deacons to marry while continuing their ministry, They ease the process for the laicization of priests married in civil ceremonies who are in danger of death. The new rules also make it clear that, while the Vatican usually does not consider laicization requests from priests under age 40, it will do so "when grave scandal in present."

Role of Young People — Young people must be the ones to lay the foundations for a world marked by greater solidarity in the coming millennium. By building a closer relation with Christ, the source of true peace, and through living the Gospel, young Catholics can fulfill their potential as artisans of a better world, the Pope said Aug.10. With the later-in-the-month Youth Day celebration in mind, he noted: "The meeting in Paris— where young men and women from every continent, every race and culture will come together — will be like an image of the Church of the third millennium and of the future of humanity."

World Youth Day — Pope John Paul joined hundreds of thousands of young people from all over the world for the Aug. 19-to-24 celebration of World Youth Day in Paris. (See separate entry.)

St. Therese, Doctor — Pope John Paul announced Aug. 24 that he would proclaim St.Therese of Lisieux a Doctor of the Church on Oct. 19, World Mission Sunday. "Therese's teaching, a true science of love, is the luminous expression of her knowledge of the mystery of Christ and of her personal experience of grace," he said. "Humble and poor, Therese shows the 'little way' of children who confide in the Father with 'bold trust.' The heart of her message, her spiritual attitude, is for all the faithful." St. Therese was named co-patron of the missions, along with St. Francis Xavier, by Pope Pius XI in 1927. Known as the "Little Flower," she is the 33rd Doctor of the Church and the third woman — after St.Teresa of Avila and St. Catherine of Siena — with the title.

Princess Diana — Pope John Paul joined other world leaders in messages of sympathy and prayer at the death of Diana, Princess of Wales, in a car crash the night of Aug. 30-31 in Paris.

NATIONAL

No Same-Sex Marriage — In the wake of a lawsuit to force Vermont to recognize same-sex unions as marriages, Bishop Kenneth A. Angell of Burlington said "there can be no confusion" about the Church's opposition to the idea. "The Church's position on marriage is absolutely, clearly defined as a "faithful, exclusive and lifelong union between one man and one woman, established by God with its own proper laws," he said. "The Church's opposition to same-sex marriage has also been vocally and adamantly stated." He commented on the issue after three same-sex couples who were denied marriage licenses sued the state of Vermont and three of its towns for the right to marry. They said the state's refusal to let them marry denied them access to the rights of heterosexual couples such as spousal pension and medical benefits. None of the states recognized same-sex unions as marriages.

Mission Challenge — Native Americans must stop being "missioned to" and instead become missionaries, the Rev. Ben Bushyhead told Native American Catholics attending the 58th annual Tekakwitha Conference Aug. 6 to 10 in Milwaukee. The Rev. Bushyhead, pastor of the Native American Ministry United Methodist Church in Milwaukee, gave the opening keynote address of the conference. He urged Native Americans to "get our own house in order" as Christians engaged in mission.

New Books, New Collection — On the completion of mail balloting, the U.S. bishops announced Aug. 11 their approval of the first part of a new Lectionary, the book of readings at Mass, and a new Sacramentary, the book of Mass prayers. Ratification by the Vatican was required.

The bishops also approved a new national, annual Collection for Home Missions, scheduled for the last Sunday in April, bringing to 12 the number of designated national collections.

The other collections and their dates are: the Church in Latin America, fourth Sunday in January; Aid to the Church in Central and Eastern Europe, Ash Wednesday or a Sunday in Lent; Black and Indian Home Missions, first Sunday in Lent; American Bishops' Overseas Appeal, fourth Sunday in Lent; Holy Land, Good Friday; Catholic Communications Campaign, third Sunday in May; Peter's Pence, Sunday nearer June 29; Catholic University of America, first or second Sunday in September; World Mission Sunday, next-to-last Sunday in October; Campaign for Human Development, Sunday before Thanksgiving; Retirement Fund for Religious, second Sunday in December.

Assyrian-Chaldean Agreement — In a joint synodal decree, the Assyrian Church of the East and the Chaldean Catholic Church announced Aug. 15 a series of initiatives aimed at full restoration of unity. The decree commits the churches to collaborate in preparing and printing liturgical books, to work together in the development of catechetical and similar materials, and to establish a joint ecclesial education institute to train future priests, deacons and catechists of both churches.

Indian Oratory — About 4,000 Asian Indians celebrated Aug. 16 the dedication of an oratory honoring Our Lady of Vailankanni (Good Health) at the Basilica of the Immaculate Conception in Washington.

Spanish Radio Mass — Thanks to phone calls from interested listeners, a live Spanish-language Sunday Mass returned to the airwaves of Albuquerque's KALY after a four-week absence. No reason was given by the station for the temporary suspension of the broadcast.

Lutheran Assembly Actions — The churchwide assembly of the Evangelical Lutheran Church in America declared Aug. 19 that Lutherans and Catholics share a common understanding of justification, the central doctrinal issue over which they split in the 16th century. The declaration does not claim to cover "all that either church teaches about justification." But it says it "does encompass a consensus on basic truths of the doctrine of justification and shows that remaining differences in its explication are no longer the concern for doctrinal condemnations."

The assembly also approved a proposal declaring "full communion" of the Evangelical Lutheran Church in America with the Presbyterian Church (U.S.A.), the Reformed Church in America and the United Church of Christ. The assembly narrowly defeated a similar but separate proposal that would have established full communion with the U.S. Episcopal Church.

INTERNATIONAL

Famine in North Korea — U.S. Catholic Relief Services, the Canadian Catholic Organization for Development and Peace, and Caritas-Hong Kong were among relief agencies mobilizing food aid for North Koreans living in disastrous conditions of famine.

Siberian Cathedral — The first Catholic cathedral in Siberia, named Transfiguration, was dedicated with a solemn Mass and attendance by 11 bishops, 140 priests and many lay persons Aug.10 in Novosibirsk.

Documentation on Rights Violations — The Archdiocese of Guatemala announced Aug. 14 it would give documents relating to 22,000 violations of human rights to the country's Truth Commission which was investigating abuses committed during the nation's civil war. The casualty toll of the 36-year-long conflict was estimated to include 150,000 deaths and another 40,000 disappearances.

Against Corruption — Christians of all denominations, marking 50 years of independence, pledged to work toward the eradication of social evils in India. Government officials marked the anniversary in the Parliament House where the transfer of power from the British to Indian leaders took place Aug. 15, 1947.

Priests Elected — Four priests were elected to serve in Vietnam's National Assembly.

Peruvian Archbishop under Threat — Archbishop Juan Luis Cipriani, mediator in the hostage siege negotiations in April in Lima, was under armed guard against assassination attempts by the Tupac Amaru Revolutionary Movement.

Objection to Mother Teresa Film — The Missionaries of Charity said Aug. 20 they "strongly object" to an "unauthorized" movie on their founder by a U.S. entertainment company. Sister Nirmala Joshi, superior general, said the film by Hallmark Entertainment was "not authorized by Mother Teresa and does not carry her endorsement nor that of the Missionaries of Charity.

Bethlehem Still Closed — Bethlehem remained Aug. 20 the only Palestinian city still under closure imposed by Israel three weeks after two suicide bombers killed 14 people in a Jerusalem market. Palestinian residents of the city were enduring conditions nearing "crisis proportions," said Father Emil Salayta, general director of schools of the Jerusalem Latin-rite Patriarchate.

Polish Missionaries —More than 3,000 Polish priests, 12 percent of the national total, were working abroad in 92 countries, as of January, 1997, according to a report compiled by the Redemptorist-run Statistics Office in Warsaw.

No New Dogmas — Petitions circulating in the United States asking Pope John Paul to solemnly declare one or more titles for Mary were called, "theologically inadequate, historically a mistake, pastorally imprudent and ecumenically unacceptable," by Father Salvatore Perrella, a professor of dogmatics and Marian studies at the Marianum Theological Faculty in Rome.

Weapons Control — Archbishop Renato R. Martino, apostolic nuncio and permanent observer of the Holy See at the United Nations, delivered to the secretary general the Holy See's document of agreement to an international treaty banning the use of certain weapons. At the same time, the archbishop presented a statement in which the Holy See said: "The Holy See, as a signatory of the 'Convention on prohibitions or restrictions on the use of certain conventional weapons which may be deemed to be excessively injurious or to have indiscriminate effects,' adopted in Geneva on 10 October 1980, ... in keeping with its proper nature and with the particular condition of Vatican City State, intends to renew its encouragement to the international community to continue on the path it has taken for the reduction of human suffering caused by armed conflict. ... The Holy See ... reiterates the objective hoped for by many parties: an agreement that would totally ban anti-personnel mines, the effects of which are tragically well known." After noting the partial, positive step represented by the convention, the statement said it still fell short of the mark: The Holy See considered one of its protocols "insufficient and inadequate."

POPE JOHN PAUL II

(See many related entries under John Paul II in the Index.)

Cardinal Archbishop Karol Wojtyla of Krakow was elected Bishop of Rome Oct. 16, 1978, on the seventh or eighth ballot cast on the second day of voting at a conclave of 111 cardinals. He chose the name John Paul II and was invested with the pallium, the symbol of his papal office, Oct. 22 in ceremonies attended by more than 250,000 persons in St. Peter's Square.

The 263rd successor of St. Peter as Bishop of Rome and Supreme Pastor of the Universal Church, he is the first non-Italian Pope since Adrian VI (1522-23), the first Polish Pope in the history of the Church, and the youngest at the time of his election since Pius IX (1846-78).

Early Career

Karol Wojtyla was born May 18, 1920, in Wadowice, Poland.

He began higher studies at the age of 18, with major interests in poetry and theater arts. Forced to suspend university courses because of the outbreak of World War II, he went to work in a stone quarry and a chemical plant, thereby earning the later designation of himself as the "Worker Cardinal."

He started studies for the priesthood in 1942 in the underground seminary of Krakow, whose operations had been banned after the Nazi invasion of Poland.

Ordained to the priesthood Nov. 1, 1946, he was immediately sent to Rome for studies at the Angelicum University, where he earned a doctorate in ethics.

Back home in Poland, he worked as an assistant pastor in a village parish and as a chaplain to university students while continuing studies at the Catholic University of Lublin. He was awarded another doctorate there, in moral theology.

He began writing about this time, and eventually produced more than 100 articles and several books on ethical and other themes. Phenomenology was one of his fields of expertise.

University teaching came next, in 1953, with appointment in 1954 to the position of lecturer and later to the chair of ethics at the Catholic University of Lublin, the most prestigious institute of higher learning in Poland.

Bishop and Cardinal

He was ordained Auxiliary Bishop of Krakow Sept. 28, 1958, became Vicar Capitular in 1962 after the death of Apostolic Administrator Eugeniusz Baziak, and was appointed Archbishop Jan. 13, 1964. He was the first residential head of the see since the death of Cardinal Adam Sapieha in 1951. Between then and 1964 the archdiocese was run by administrators because the communist government refused to permit the appointment and ministry of a residential bishop.

Archbishop Wojtyla attended all sessions of the Second Vatican Council from 1962 to 1965, and was one of the writers of the Pastoral Constitution on the Church in the Modern World. He also contributed input to the Declaration on Religious Freedom and the Decree on the Instruments of Social Communication.

His efforts to put into effect the directives of the council induced him to write a book, Foundations of Renewal, in 1972 and to start that same year an archdiocesan synod he saw concluded as Pope during his visit to Poland in 1979.

He was inducted into the College of Cardinals June 26, 1967, as one of the younger members, and subsequently served actively in the Congregation for the Sacraments and Divine Worship, the Congregation for the Clergy, and the Congregation for Catholic Education.

He served as a theological consultant to Pope Paul VI, attended assemblies of the Synod of Bishops as a representative of the Polish Bishops' Conference, and was a member of the Synod's permanent council.

From the beginning of his priestly career, and especially during his episcopate, the Cardinal was vigorous in the defense of human and religious rights, the rights of workers, and rights to religious education.

Close to Cardinal Wyszynski and in company with his fellow bishops, he negotiated the tightrope of Catholic survival in a country under communist control. With them, and as their spokesman at times, he was stalwart in resisting efforts of the regime to impose atheism, materialism and secularism on the people and culture of Poland.

Active in Rome and Italy

Since the beginning of his pontificate, John Paul has been active as Bishop of Rome, with frequent visits to parishes and institutions of the diocese for the celebration of Mass and participation in other events. During these visits as well as others to places of pilgrimage and historic significance in Italy, he has had more personal contact with the faithful than any other pope. The number of attendants at weekly general audiences at the Vatican and Castel Gandolfo has been unprecedented.

79 Foreign Pastoral Trips

At the time of writing (Sept. 1, 1997) the Pope had traveled more than 550,000 miles in 79 pastoral trips and visits to more than 115 countries since the start of his pontificate. Homilies and addresses delivered by the Pope on these trips covered a wide variety of doctrinal, pastoral and social subjects.

• 1979, four trips: Dominican Republic and Mexico, Jan 5 to Feb. 1; Poland, June 2 to 10; Ireland and the United States, Sept. 29 to Oct. 7; Turkey, Nov. 28 to 30.

• 1980, four trips: Africa (Zaire, Congo Republic, Kenya, Ghana, Upper Volta, Ivory Coast), May 2 to 12; France, May 30 to June 2; Brazil (13 cities), June 30 to July 12; West Germany, Nov. 15 to 19.

• 1981, one trip: Philippines, Guam and Japan, with stopovers in Pakistan and Alaska, Feb. 16 to 27.

• 1982, seven trips: Africa (Nigeria, Benin, Gabon, Equatorial Guinea), Feb. 12 to 19; Portugal, May 12 to 15; Great Britain, May 28 to June 2; Argentina, June 11 and 12; Switzerland, June 15; San Marino, Aug. 29; Spain, Oct. 31 to Nov. 9.

• 1983, four trips: Central America (Costa Rica, Nicaragua, Panama, El Salvador, Guatemala, Belize, Honduras) and Haiti, Mar. 2 to 10; Poland, June 16 to 23; Lourdes, France, Aug. 14 and 15; Austria, Sept. 10 to 13.

• 1984, four trips: South Korea, Papua New Guinea, Solomon Islands, Thailand, May 2 to 12; Switzerland, June 12 to 17; Canada, Sept. 9 to 20; Spain, Dominican Republic and Puerto Rico, Oct. 10 to 12.

• 1985, four trips: Venezuela, Ecuador, Peru, Trinidad and Tobago, Jan. 26 to Feb. 6; Belgium, The Netherlands and Luxembourg, May 11 to 21; Africa (Togo, Ivory Coast, Cameroon, Central African Republic, Zaire, Kenya and Morocco), Aug. 8 to 19; Liechtenstein, Sept. 8.

• 1986, four trips: India, Feb. 1 to 10; Colombia and Saint Lucia, July 1 to 7; France, Oct. 4 to 7; Oceania (Australia, New Zealand, Bangladesh, Fiji, Singapore and Seychelles), Nov. 18 to Dec. 1.

• 1987, four trips: Uruguay, Chile and Argentina, Mar. 31 to Apr. 12; West Germany, Apr. 30 to May 4; Poland, June 8 to 14; the United States and Canada, Sept. 10 to 19.

• 1988, four trips: Uruguay, Bolivia, Peru and Paraguay, May 7 to 18; Austria, June 23 to 27; Africa (Zimbabwe, Botswana, Lesotho, Swaziland and Mozambique), Sept. 10 to 19; France, Oct. 8 to 11.

• 1989, four trips: Madagascar, Reunion, Zambia and Malawi, Apr. 28 to May 6; Norway, Iceland, Finland, Denmark and Sweden, June 1 to 10; Spain, Aug. 19 to 21; South Korea, Indonesia, East Timor and Mauritius, Oct. 6 to 16.

• 1990, five trips: Africa (Cape Verde, Guinea Bissau, Mali and Burkina Faso), Jan. 25 to Feb. 1; Czechoslovakia, Apr. 21 and 22; Mexico and Curacao, May 6 to 13; Malta, May 25 to 27; Africa (Tanzania, Burundi, Rwanda and Ivory Coast), Sept. 1 to 10.

• 1991, four trips: Portugal, May 10 to 13; Poland, June 1 to 9; Poland and Hungary, Aug. 13 to 20; Brazil, Oct. 12 to 21.

• 1992, three trips: Africa (Senegal, The Gambia, Guinea), Feb. 10 to 26; Africa (Angola, Sao Tome and Principe), June 4 to 10; Dominican Republic, Oct. 10 to 14.

• 1993, five trips: Africa (Benin, Uganda, Sudan), Feb. 2 to 10; Albania, April 25; Spain, June 12 to 17; Jamaica, Mexico, Denver (U.S.), Aug. 9 to 15; Lithuania, Latvia, Estonia, Sept. 4 to 10.

• 1994, one trip: Zagreb, Croatia, Sept. 10

• 1995, six trips: Philippines, Papua New Guinea, Australia, Sri Lanka, Jan. 12 to 21; Czech Republic and Poland, May 20 to 22; Belgium, June 3 and 4; Slovakia, June 30 to July 3; Africa (Cameroon, South Africa, Kenya), Sept. 14 to 20; United Nations and United States, Oct. 4 to 8.

• 1996, six trips: Central America (Guatemala, Nicaragua, El Salvador), Feb. 5 to 11; Tunisia, Apr. 17; Slovenia, May 17 to 19; Germany, June 21 to 23; Hungary, Sept. 6 to 7; France, Sept.. 19 to 22.

• 1997: five trips: Sarajevo, Apr. 12 to 13; Czech Republic, Apr. 25 to 27; Lebanon, May 10 to 11; Poland, May 31 to June 10; France, Aug. 21 to 24.

Encyclical Letters

Encyclical letters, as well as homilies and other addresses, have generally been related in greater or less degree to the key document issued in the first year of the Pope's pontificate. That was the encyclical letter, *Redemptor Hominis* ("Redeemer of Man"), a treatise on Christian anthropology dealing with the divine and human aspects of redemption and the mission of the Church to carry on a dialogue of sal-

vation with all peoples. His other encyclical letters are: *Dives in Misericordia* ("On the Mercy of God") in 1980 and *Laborem Exercens* ("On Human Work") in 1981; *Slavorum Apostoli* in 1985 honoring Sts. Cyril and Methodius, apostles of the Slavic peoples; *Dominum et Vivificantem* ("Lord and Giver of Life") in 1986; *Redemptoris Mater* ("Mother of the Redeemer") in 1987; *Sollicitudo Rei Socialis* ("On Social Concerns") in 1988; *Redemptoris Missio* ("Mission of the Redeemer") and *Centesimus Annus* ("The Hundredth Year") in 1991; *Veritatis Splendor* ("The Splendor of Truth") in 1993; *Evangelium Vitae* ("The Gospel of Life") and *Ut Unum Sint* ("That All May Be One") in 1995.

The Pope's most recent apostolic letters are *Tertio Millennio Adveniente*, Nov. 14, 1994, regarding the jubilee celebration of the third millennium of Christianity; and *Orientale Lumen*, May 2, 1995, on the need for greater understanding and appreciation of the traditions of the Eastern Churches.

The Pope also addressed a letter to women throughout the world July 10, 1995, in anticipation of the Fourth International Conference on Women scheduled to be held in September in Beijing, China.

Other Writings

The Pope published a lengthy exhortation on the family, Familiaris Consortio in 1981.

Writings published in 1984 included two apostolic letters — on suffering, *Salvifici Doloris*, and on Jerusalem; an apostolic exhortation, *Redemptionis Donum*, addressed to and about religious; a "Charter on the Rights of the Family," and an apostolic exhortation, "Reconciliation and Penance in the Ministry of the Church."

In 1986, the Pope issued an apostolic letter on the 1600th anniversary of the conversion of St. Augustine. Two apostolic letters were published in 1988, on the millennium of Christianity in the Ukraine and the present territory of the Soviet Union.

Writings issued in 1989 included *Christifideles Laici*, an apostolic exhortation on the theme of the 1987 assembly of the Synod of Bishops, and an apostolic letter commemorating the 25th anniversary of the Second Vatican Council's Constitution on the Liturgy.

In 1990, the Pope issued the first-ever papal statement exclusively on ecology, entitled "Peace with God and All of Creation." *Pastores Dabo Vobis* ("I Will Give You Pastors"), an apostolic exhortation on the formation of priests, was issued in 1992.

Ordinatio Sacerdotalis, on the ordination of men only to the priesthood, was issued May 30, 1994.

The most recent apostolic letters of Pope John Paul are *Tertio Millennio Adveniente*, on the coming of the third millennium of Christianity, Nov. 14, 1994; and Orientale Lumen, on the need for greater understanding and appreciation of the traditions of Eastern Churches, May 2, 1995.

Also in 1995, the Pope addressed a letter to women throughout the world on July 10 in anticipation of the Fourth International Conference on Women to be held in September, 1995, in Beijing, China.

In 1996 the Pope issued an apostolic exhortation entitled *Vita Consecrata* ("The Consecrated Life") and the apostolic constitution.

Universi Dominici Gregis ("Of the Lord's Whole Flock") on the election of a pope and the government of the Church during a vacancy of the Apostolic See.

Various Subjects

Doctrinal Concerns: The Holy Father regarded as extremely important a series of talks begun at general audiences in the summer of 1984 on marriage and sexual morality, explaining and firmly supporting traditional doctrine, with emphasis on teaching contained in the encyclical letter, Humanae Vitae, by Pope Paul VI.

Clarification of issues involved in liberation theology were published in 1984 and 1986.

Doctrine concerning the nature of the Church and the roles of its members in mission were running subjects of general audience talks in 1993-94. The mystery of the Church and the role of Mary were the principal themes of general audience talks in 1995.

Canon Law: The Pope was deeply involved in the work of completing the revision of the Code of Canon Law, which he ordered into effect as of Nov. 27, 1983. He called it, in effect, the final act of the Second Vatican Council. He emphasized its innovative force in an address Jan. 26, 1984, to personnel of the Roman Rota.

He promulgated the Code of Canon Law for the Eastern Churches Apr. 18, 1990.

Catechism of the Catholic Church: On publication of the new Catechism of the Catholic Church, first in French in 1992, the Pope called it, along with the new Code of Canon Law, one of the most significant events in the line of accomplishments since the Second Vatican Council.

Causes of Saints: Pope John Paul has canonized more than 270 saints. (See Canonizations.)

Synods: The Holy Father has convoked six general assemblies of the Synod of Bishops and two significant particular assemblies.

With the bishops of The Netherlands at the Vatican in January, 1980, he called for measures to cope with differences among the prelates and polarization among the people, along with action to remedy doctrinal and disciplinary irregularities; later reports indicated that results of the synod were less than satisfactory. Meeting in special assembly with Ukrainian bishops in March, also in 1980, he named a successor to Cardinal Josyf Slipyi as the ranking bishop and turned down demands of some Ukrainians for a patriarchate.

Holy Year: The Holy Father proclaimed a Jubilee celebration of the 1950th anniversary of the Redemption from the Solemnity of the Annunciation of the Lord, Mar. 25, 1983, to Easter Sunday, Apr. 22, 1984, and a Marian Year from Pentecost, 1987, to the Solemnity of the Ascension, 1988.

Cardinals: In June, 1979, the Pope inducted 14 new cardinals into the Sacred College, raising its membership to 135. A second group was inducted Feb. 3, 1983, at which time the total membership was 138. Twenty-eight new cardinals inducted May 25, 1985, brought membership to 152. Twenty-four were inducted in 1988. By late September, 1990, the total was 144. Twenty-two new cardinals were inducted in 1991, along with a cardinal whose name

had been held in secret since 1979. Thirty new cardinals were inducted into the college in 1995. As of Aug. 10, 1996, there were 154 cardinals; 112 of them were eligible to vote in a papal election; 42 others were over the electoral age limit of 80.

Ecumenism: Ecumenical and interfaith relations have been high on the list of the Pope's priorities since the beginning of his pontificate. He has had numerous meetings with representatives of other churches and ecclesial bodies; has repeatedly spoken about the quest for unity among Christians and called on Catholics and members of other churches to pray and work together for unity. Two significant events of 1995 were the publication of the encyclical letter, "That All May Be One," May 30 and the meeting of the Pope and Orthodox Patriarch Bartholomew I late in June.

While visiting the headquarters of the World Council of Churches in Geneva June 12, 1984, the Pope said the Church's engagement in the quest for religious unity is irreversible. At the same time, he mentioned two points of extreme significance in Catholic doctrine and practice.

The Church, he said, "entered on the hard ecumenical task, bringing with it a conviction" about the role of the bishop of Rome. "It is convinced that in the ministry of the bishop of Rome it has preserved the visible pole and guarantee of unity in full fidelity to the apostolic tradition and to the faith of the Fathers."

He also reiterated doctrinal opposition to sharing the Eucharist until full unity is achieved. "It is not yet possible for us to celebrate the Eucharist together and communicate at the same table," he said. Nevertheless, he placed emphasis on things Christians have in common.

World Affairs: In 1984, the Pope agreed to a new concordat with Italy, regulating church-state relations. He agreed also to the establishment of diplomatic relations with the United States. In July, 1989, following years of negotiations, diplomatic relations were re-established with Poland. Relations have also been established with other Eastern European countries, Mexico and a number of other nations.

One of the more significant diplomatic accomplishments was the 1993 agreement for the establishment of Vatican-Israeli relations at the ambassadorial level; the agreement was implemented in 1994.

For years, the Pope has repeatedly called for peace in the Middle East, the Balkans, beleaguered nations of Africa and other countries, and stressed the need for re-evangelization worldwide, but especially in Europe. Since 1993 he has pleaded constantly for the end of hostilities and mass murder in Bosnia-Herzegovina, Rwanda and other countries.

In 1994 Pope John Paul mounted a strong and sustained campaign against proposals on population control, abortion, contraception, adolescent sexuality and related subjects on the agenda of the third U.N.-sponsored International Conference on Population and Development be held Sept. 5 to 13, 1994, in Cairo. On his travels as well as at the Vatican the Pope has been an outstanding advocate for human rights and dignity, respect for life, peace, nuclear and conventional disarmament, reconciliation among nations, aid and relief for distressed peoples and nations; of people first and things second in all areas of life.

DATES AND EVENTS IN CHURCH HISTORY

FIRST CENTURY

c. 33: First Christian Pentecost; descent of the Holy Spirit upon the disciples; preaching of St. Peter in Jerusalem; conversion, baptism and aggregation of some 3,000 persons to the first Christian community.

St. Stephen, deacon, was stoned to death at Jerusalem; he is venerated as the first Christian martyr.

c. 34: St. Paul, formerly Saul the persecutor of Christians, was converted and baptized. After three years of solitude in the desert, he joined the college of the apostles; he made three major missionary journeys and became known as the Apostle to the Gentiles; he was imprisoned twice in Rome and was beheaded there between 64 and 67.

39: Cornelius (the Gentile) and his family were baptized by St. Peter; a significant event signalling the mission of the Church to all peoples.

42: Persecution of Christians in Palestine broke out during the rule of Herod Agrippa; St. James the Greater, the first apostle to die, was beheaded in 44; St. Peter was imprisoned for a short time; many Christians fled to Antioch, marking the beginning of the dispersion of Christians beyond the confines of Palestine. At Antioch, the followers of Christ were called Christians for the first time.

49: Christians at Rome, considered members of a Jewish sect, were adversely affected by a decree of Claudius which forbade Jewish worship there.

51: The Council of Jerusalem, in which all the apostles participated under the presidency of St. Peter, decreed that circumcision, dietary regulations, and various other prescriptions of Mosaic Law were not obligatory for Gentile converts to the Christian community. The crucial decree was issued in opposition to Judaizers who contended that observance of the Mosaic Law in its entirety was necessary for salvation.

64: Persecution broke out at Rome under Nero, the emperor said to have accused Christians of starting the fire which destroyed half of Rome.

64 or 67: Martyrdom of St. Peter at Rome during the Neronian persecution. He established his see and spent his last years there after preaching in and around Jerusalem, establishing a see at Antioch, and presiding at the Council of Jerusalem.

70: Destruction of Jerusalem by Titus.

88-97: Pontificate of St. Clement I, third successor of St. Peter as bishop of Rome, one of the Apostolic Fathers. The *First Epistle of Clement to the Corinthians,* with which he has been identified, was addressed by the Church of Rome to the Church at Corinth, the scene of irregularities and divisions in the Christian community.

95: Domitian persecuted Christians, principally at Rome.

c. 100: Death of St. John, apostle and evangelist, marking the end of the Age of the Apostles and the first generation of the Church.

By the end of the century, Antioch, Alexandria and Ephesus in the East and Rome in the West were established centers of Christian population and influence.

SECOND CENTURY

c. 107: St. Ignatius of Antioch was martyred at Rome. He was the first writer to use the expression, "the Catholic Church."

112: Emperor Trajan, in a rescript to Pliny the Younger, governor of Bithynia, instructed him not to search out Christians but to punish them if they were publicly denounced and refused to do homage to the Roman gods. This rescript set a pattern for Roman magistrates in dealing with Christians.

117-38: Persecution under Hadrian. Many *Acts of Martyrs* date from this period.

c. 125: Spread of Gnosticism, a combination of elements of Platonic philosophy and Eastern mystery religions. Its adherents claimed that its secret-knowledge principle provided a deeper insight into Christian doctrine than divine revelation and faith. One gnostic thesis denied the divinity of Christ; others denied the reality of his humanity, calling it mere appearance (Docetism, Phantasiasm).

c. 144: Excommunication of Marcion, bishop and heretic, who claimed that there was total opposition and no connection at all between the Old Testament and the New Testament, between the God of the Jews and the God of the Christians; and that the Canon (list of inspired writings) of the Bible consisted only of parts of St. Luke's Gospel and 10 letters of St. Paul. Marcionism was checked at Rome by 200 and was condemned by a council held there about 260, but the heresy persisted for several centuries in the East and had some adherents as late as the Middle Ages.

c. 155: St. Polycarp, bishop of Smyrna and disciple of St. John the Evangelist, was martyred.

c. 156: Beginning of Montanism, a form of religious extremism. Its principal tenets were the imminent second coming of Christ, denial of the divine nature of the Church and its power to forgive sin, and excessively rigorous morality. The heresy, preached by Montanus of Phrygia and others, was condemned by Pope St. Zephyrinus (199-217).

161-80: Reign of Marcus Aurelius. His persecution, launched in the wake of natural disasters, was more violent than those of his predecessors.

165: St. Justin, an important early Christian writer, was martyred at Rome.

c. 180: St. Irenaeus, bishop of Lyons and one of the great early theologians, wrote *Adversus Haereses.* He stated that the teaching and tradition of the Roman See was the standard for belief.

196: Easter Controversy, concerning the day of celebration — a Sunday, according to practice in the West, or the 14th of the month of Nisan (in the Hebrew calendar), no matter what day of the week, according to practice in the East. The controversy was not resolved at this time.

The *Didache,* whose extant form dates from the second century, is an important record of Christian belief, practice and governance in the first century. Latin was introduced as a liturgical language in the West. Other liturgical languages were Aramaic and Greek.

The Catechetical School of Alexandria, founded about the middle of the century, gained increasing influence on doctrinal study and instruction, and interpretation of the Bible.

THIRD CENTURY

202: Persecution under Septimius Severus, who wanted to establish a simple common religion in the Empire.

206: Tertullian, a convert since 197 and the first great ecclesiastical writer in Latin, joined the heretical Montanists; he died in 230.

215: Death of Clement of Alexandria, teacher of Origen and a founding father of the School of Alexandria.

217-35: St. Hippolytus, the first antipope; he was reconciled to the Church while in prison during persecution in 235.

232-54: Origen established the School of Caesarea after being deposed in 231 as head of the School of Alexandria; he died in 254. A scholar and voluminous writer, he was one of the founders of systematic theology and exerted wide influence for many years.

c. 242: Manichaeism originated in Persia: a combination of errors based on the assumption that two supreme principles (good and evil) are operative in creation and life, and that the supreme objective of human endeavor is liberation from evil (matter). The heresy denied the humanity of Christ, the sacramental system, the authority of the Church (and state), and endorsed a moral code which threatened the fabric of society. In the 12th and 13th centuries, it took on the features of Albigensianism and Catharism.

249-51: Persecution under Decius. Many of those who denied the faith *(lapsi)* sought readmission to the Church at the end of the persecution in 251. Pope St. Cornelius agreed with St. Cyprian that *lapsi* were to be readmitted to the Church after satisfying the requirements of appropriate penance. Antipope Novatian, on the other hand, contended that persons who fell away from the Church under persecution and/or those guilty of serious sin after baptism could not be absolved and readmitted to communion with the Church. The heresy was condemned by a Roman synod in 251.

250-300: Neo-Platonism of Plotinus and Porphyry gained followers.

251: Novatian, an antipope, was condemned at Rome.

256: Pope St. Stephen I upheld the validity of baptism properly administered by heretics, in the Rebaptism Controversy.

257: Persecution under Valerian, who attempted to destroy the Church as a social structure.

258: St. Cyprian, bishop of Carthage, was martyred.

c. 260: St. Lucian founded the School of Antioch, a center of influence on biblical studies.

Pope St. Dionysius condemned Sabellianism, a form of modalism (like Monarchianism and Patripassianism). The heresy contended that the Father, Son and Holy Spirit are not distinct divine persons but are only three different modes of being and self-manifestations of the one God.

St. Paul of Thebes became a hermit.

261: Gallienus issued an edict of toleration which ended general persecution for nearly 40 years.

c. 292: Diocletian divided the Roman Empire into East and West. The division emphasized political, cultural and other differences between the two parts of the Empire and influenced different developments in the Church in the East and West. The prestige of Rome began to decline.

FOURTH CENTURY

303: Persecution broke out under Diocletian; it was particularly violent in 304.

305: St. Anthony of Heracles established a foundation for hermits near the Red Sea in Egypt.

c. 306: The first local legislation on clerical celibacy was enacted by a council held at Elvira, Spain; bishops, priests, deacons and other ministers were forbidden to have wives.

311: An edict of toleration issued by Galerius at the urging of Constantine and Licinius officially ended persecution in the West; some persecution continued in the East.

313: The *Edict of Milan* issued by Constantine and Licinius recognized Christianity as a lawful religion in the Roman Empire.

314: A council of Arles condemned Donatism, declaring that baptism properly administered by heretics is valid, in view of the principle that sacraments have their efficacy from Christ, not from the spiritual condition of their human ministers. The heresy was condemned again by a council of Carthage in 411.

318: St. Pachomius established the first foundation of the cenobitic (common) life, as compared with the solitary life of hermits in Upper Egypt.

325: Ecumenical Council of Nicaea (I). Its principal action was the condemnation of Arianism, the most devastating of the early heresies, which denied the divinity of Christ. The heresy was authored by Arius of Alexandria, a priest. Arians and several kinds of Semi-Arians propagandized their tenets widely, established their own hierarchies and churches, and raised havoc in the Church for several centuries. The council contributed to formulation of the Nicene Creed (Creed of Nicaea-Constantinople); fixed the date for the observance of Easter; passed regulations concerning clerical discipline; adopted the civil divisions of the Empire as the model for the jurisdictional organization of the Church.

326: Discovery of the True Cross on which Christ was crucified.

337: Baptism and death of Constantine.

c. 342: Beginning of a 40-year persecution in Persia.

343-44: A council of Sardica reaffirmed doctrine formulated by Nicaea I and declared also that bishops had the right of appeal to the pope as the highest authority in the Church.

361-63: Emperor Julian the Apostate waged an unsuccessful campaign against the Church in an attempt to restore paganism as the religion of the Empire.

c. 365: Persecution under Valens in the East.

c. 376: Beginning of the barbarian invasion in the West.

379: Death of St. Basil, the Father of Monasticism in the East. His writings contributed greatly to the development of rules for the life of Religious.

381: Ecumenical Council of Constantinople (I). It condemned various brands of Arianism as well as Macedonianism, which denied the divinity of the Holy Spirit; contributed to formulation of the Nicene Creed; approved a canon acknowledging Constantinople as the second see after Rome in honor and dignity.

382: The Canon of Sacred Scripture, the official list of the inspired books of the Bible, was contained in the *Decree of Pope St. Damasus* and published by a regional council of Carthage in 397; the Canon was formally defined by the Council of Trent in the 16th century.

382-c. 406: St. Jerome translated the Old and New Testaments into Latin; his work is called the Vulgate version of the Bible.

396: St. Augustine became bishop of Hippo in North Africa.

FIFTH CENTURY

410: Visigoths sacked Rome.

430: St. Augustine, bishop of Hippo for 35 years, died. He was a strong defender of orthodox doctrine against Manichaeism, Donatism and Pelagianism. The depth and range of his writings made him a dominant influence in Christian thought for centuries.

431: Ecumenical Council of Ephesus. It condemned Nestorianism, which denied the unity of the divine and human natures in the Person of Christ; defined *Theotokos* (Bearer of God) as the title of Mary, Mother of the Son of God made Man; condemned Pelagianism. The heresy of Pelagianism, proceeding from the assumption that Adam had a natural right to supernatural life, held that man could attain salvation through the efforts of his natural powers and free will; it involved errors concerning the nature of original sin, the meaning of grace and other matters. Related Semi-Pelagianism was condemned by a council of Orange in 529.

432: St. Patrick arrived in Ireland. By the time of his death in 461 most of the country had been converted, monasteries founded and the hierarchy established.

438: The *Theodosian Code,* a compilation of decrees for the Empire, was issued by Theodosius II; it had great influence on subsequent civil and ecclesiastical law.

451: Ecumenical Council of Chalcedon. Its principal action was the condemnation of Monophysitism (also called Eutychianism), which denied the humanity of Christ by holding that he had only one, the divine, nature.

452: Pope St. Leo the Great persuaded Attila the Hun to spare Rome.

455: Vandals sacked Rome. The decline of imperial Rome dates approximately from this time.

484: Patriarch Acacius of Constantinople was excommunicated for signing the *Henoticon,* a document which capitulated to the Monophysite heresy. The excommunication triggered a schism which lasted for 35 years.

494: Pope St. Gelasius I declared in a letter to Emperor Anastasius that the pope had power and authority over the emperor in spiritual matters.

496: Clovis, King of the Franks, was converted and became the defender of Christianity in the West. The Franks became a Catholic people.

SIXTH CENTURY

520 on: Irish monasteries flourished as centers for spiritual life, missionary training and scholarly activity.

529: The Second Council of Orange condemned Semi-Pelagianism.

c. 529: St. Benedict founded the Monte Cassino Abbey. Some years before his death in 543 he wrote a monastic rule which exercised tremendous influence on the form and style of religious life. He is called the Father of Monasticism in the West.

533: John II became the first pope to change his name. The practice did not become general until the time of Sergius IV (1009).

533-34: Emperor Justinian promulgated the *Corpus Juris Civilis* for the Roman world; like the *Theodosian Code,* it influenced subsequent civil and ecclesiastical law.

c. 545:. Death of Dionysius Exiguus who was the first to date history from the birth of Christ, a practice which resulted in use of the B.C. and A.D. abbreviations. His calculations were at least four years late.

553: Ecumenical Council of Constantinople (II). It condemned the *Three Chapters,* Nestorian-tainted writings of Theodore of Mopsuestia, Theodoret of Cyrus and Ibas of Edessa.

585: St. Columban founded an influential monastic school at Luxeuil.

589: The most important of several councils of Toledo was held. The Visigoths renounced Arianism, and St. Leander began the organization of the Church in Spain.

590-604: Pontificate of Pope St. Gregory I the Great. He set the form and style of the papacy which prevailed throughout the Middle Ages; exerted great influence on doctrine and liturgy; was strong in support of monastic discipline and clerical celibacy; authored writings on many subjects. Gregorian Chant is named in his honor.

596: Pope St. Gregory I sent St. Augustine of Canterbury and 40 monks to do missionary work in England.

597: St. Columba died. He founded an important monastery at Iona, established schools and did notable missionary work in Scotland. By the end of the century, monasteries of nuns were common; Western monasticism was flourishing; monasticism in the East, under the influence of Monophysitism and other factors, was losing its vigor.

SEVENTH CENTURY

613: St. Columban established the influential monastery of Bobbio in northern Italy; he died there in 615.

622: The Hegira (flight) of Mohammed from Mecca to Medina signalled the beginning of Islam which, by the end of the century, claimed almost all of the southern Mediterranean area.

628: Heraclius, Eastern Emperor, recovered the True Cross from the Persians.

649: A Lateran council condemned two erroneous formulas (*Ecthesis* and *Type*) issued by emperors Heraclius and Constans II as means of reconciling Monophysites with the Church.

664: Actions of the Synod of Whitby advanced the adoption of Roman usages in England, especially regarding the date for the observance of Easter. (See Easter Controversy.)

680-81: Ecumenical Council of Constantinople (III). It condemned Monothelitism, which held that Christ had only one will, the divine; censured Pope Honorius I for a letter to Sergius, bishop of Constantinople, in which he made an ambiguous but not infallible statement about the unity of will and/or operation in Christ.

692: Trullan Synod. Eastern-Church discipline on clerical celibacy was settled, permitting marriage before ordination to the diaconate and continuation in marriage afterwards, but prohibiting marriage following the death of the wife thereafter. Anti-Roman canons contributed to East-West alienation.

During the century, the monastic influence of Ireland and England increased in Western Europe; schools and learning declined; regulations regarding clerical celibacy became more strict in the East.

EIGHTH CENTURY

711: Muslims began the conquest of Spain.

726: Emperor Leo III, the Isaurian, launched a campaign against the veneration of sacred images and relics; called Iconoclasm (image-breaking), it caused turmoil in the East until about 843.

731: Pope Gregory III and a synod at Rome condemned Iconoclasm, with a declaration that the veneration of sacred images was in accord with Catholic tradition.

Venerable Bede issued his *Ecclesiastical History of the English People.*

732: Charles Martel defeated the Muslims at Poitiers, halting their advance in the West.

744: The Monastery of Fulda was established by St. Sturmi, a disciple of St. Boniface; it was influential in the evangelization of Germany.

754: A council of more than 300 Byzantine bishops endorsed Iconoclast errors. This council and its actions were condemned by the Lateran synod of 769.

Stephen II (III) crowned Pepin ruler of the Franks. Pepin twice invaded Italy, in 754 and 756, to defend the pope against the Lombards. His land grants to the papacy, called the Donation of Pepin, were later extended by Charlemagne (773) and formed part of the States of the Church.

c. 755: St. Boniface (Winfrid) was martyred. He was called the Apostle of Germany for his missionary work and organization of the hierarchy there.

781: Alcuin was chosen by Charlemagne to organize a palace school, which became a center of intellectual leadership.

787: Ecumenical Council of Nicaea (II). It condemned Iconoclasm, which held that the use of images was idolatry, and Adoptionism, which claimed that Christ was not the Son of God by nature but only by adoption. This was the last council regarded as ecumenical by Orthodox Churches.

792: A council at Ratisbon condemned Adoptionism. The famous *Book of Kells* ("The Great Gospel of Columcille") dates from the early eighth or late seventh century.

NINTH CENTURY

800: Charlemagne was crowned Emperor by Pope Leo III on Christmas Day.

Egbert became king of West Saxons; he unified England and strengthened the See of Canterbury.

813: Emperor Leo V, the Armenian, revived Iconoclasm, which persisted until about 843.

814: Charlemagne died.

843: The Treaty of Verdun split the Frankish kingdom among Charlemagne's three grandsons.

844: A Eucharistic controversy involving the writings of St. Paschasius Radbertus, Ratramnus and Rabanus Maurus occasioned the development of terminology regarding the doctrine of the Real Presence.

846: Muslims invaded Italy and attacked Rome.

847-52: Period of composition of the *False Decretals,* a collection of forged documents attributed to popes from St. Clement (88-97) to Gregory II (714-731). The *Decretals,* which strongly supported the autonomy and rights of bishops, were suspect for a long time before being repudiated entirely about 1628.

848: The Council of Mainz condemned Gottschalk for heretical teaching regarding predestination. He was also condemned by the Council of Quierzy in 853.

857: Photius displaced Ignatius as patriarch of Constantinople. This marked the beginning of the Photian Schism, a confused state of East-West relations which has not yet been cleared up by historical research. Photius, a man of exceptional ability, died in 891.

865: St. Ansgar, apostle of Scandinavia, died.

869: St. Cyril died and his brother, St. Methodius (d. 885), was ordained a bishop. The Apostles of the Slavs devised an alphabet and translated the Gospels and liturgy into the Slavonic language.

869-70: Ecumenical Council of Constantinople (IV). It issued a second condemnation of Iconoclasm, condemned and deposed Photius as patriarch of Constantinople and restored Ignatius to the patriarchate. This was the last ecumenical council held in the East. It was first called ecumenical by canonists toward the end of the 11th century.

871-c. 900: Reign of Alfred the Great, the only English king ever anointed by a pope at Rome.

TENTH CENTURY

910: William, duke of Aquitaine, founded the Benedictine Abbey of Cluny, which became a center of monastic and ecclesiastical reform, especially in France.

915: Pope John X played a leading role in the expulsion of Saracens from central and southern Italy.

955: St. Olga, of the Russian royal family, was baptized.

962: Otto I, the Great, crowned by Pope John XII, revived Charlemagne's kingdom, which became the Holy Roman Empire.

966: Mieszko, first of a royal line in Poland, was baptized; he brought Latin Christianity to Poland.

988: Conversion and baptism of St. Vladimir and the people of Kiev which subsequently became part of Russia.

993: John XV was the first pope to decree the official canonization of a saint — Bishop Ulrich (Uldaric) of Augsburg — for the universal Church.

997: St. Stephen became ruler of Hungary. He assisted in organizing the hierarchy and establishing Latin Christianity in that country.

999-1003: Pontificate of Sylvester II (Gerbert of Aquitaine), a Benedictine monk and the first French pope.

ELEVENTH CENTURY

1009: Beginning of lasting East-West Schism in the Church, marked by dropping of the name of Pope Sergius IV from the Byzantine diptychs (the listing of persons prayed for during the liturgy). The deletion was made by Patriarch Sergius II of Constantinople.

1012: St. Romuald founded the Camaldolese Hermits.

1025: The Council of Arras, and other councils later, condemned the Cathari (Neo-Manichaeans, Albigenses).

1027: The Council of Elne proclaimed the Truce of God as a means of stemming violence; it involved armistice periods of varying length, which were later extended.

1038: St. John Gualbert founded the Vallombrosians.

1043-59: Constantinople patriarchate of Michael Cerularius, the key figure in a controversy concerning the primacy of the papacy. His and the Byzantine synod's refusal to acknowledge this primacy in 1054 widened and hardened the East-West Schism in the Church.

1047: Pope Clement II died; he was the only pope ever buried in Germany.

1049-54: Pontificate of St. Leo IX, who inaugurated a movement of papal, diocesan, monastic and clerical reform.

1054: Great East-West Schism, separation of Orthodox Churches from unity with the pope.

1055: Condemnation of the Eucharistic doctrine of Berengarius.

1059: A Lateran council issued new legislation regarding papal elections; voting power was entrusted to the Roman cardinals.

1066: Death of St. Edward the Confessor, king of England from 1042 and restorer of Westminster Abbey.

Defeat, at Hastings, of Harold by William, Duke of Normandy (later William I), who subsequently exerted strong influence on the life-style of the Church in England.

1073-85: Pontificate of St. Gregory VII (Hildebrand). A strong pope, he carried forward programs of clerical and general ecclesiastical reform and struggled against Henry IV and other rulers to end the evils of lay investiture. He introduced the Latin liturgy in Spain and set definite dates for the observance of ember days.

1077: Henry IV, excommunicated and suspended from the exercise of imperial powers by Gregory VII, sought absolution from the pope at Canossa. Henry later repudiated this action and in 1084 forced Gregory to leave Rome.

1079: The Council of Rome condemned Eucharistic errors (denial of the Real Presence of Christ under the appearances of bread and wine) of Berengarius, who retracted.

1084: St. Bruno founded the Carthusians.

1097-99: The first of several Crusades undertaken between this time and 1265. Recovery of the Holy Places and gaining free access to them for Christians were the original purposes, but these were diverted to less worthy objectives in various ways. Results included: a Latin Kingdom of Jerusalem, 1099-1187; a military and political misadventure in the form of a Latin Empire of Constantinople, 1204-1261; acquisition, by treaties, of visiting rights for Christians in the Holy Land. East-West economic and cultural relationships increased during the period. In the religious sphere, actions of the Crusaders had the effect of increasing the alienation of the East from the West.

1098: St. Robert founded the Cistercians.

TWELFTH CENTURY

1108: Beginnings of the influential Abbey and School of St. Victor in France.

1115: St. Bernard established the Abbey of Clairvaux and inaugurated the Cistercian Reform.

1118: Christian forces captured Saragossa, Spain; the beginning of the Muslim decline in that country.

1121: St. Norbert established the original monastery of the Praemonstratensians near Laon, France.

1122: The Concordat of Worms (*Pactum Callixtinum*) was formulated and approved by Pope Callistus II and Emperor Henry V to settle controversy concerning the investiture of prelates. The concordat provided that the emperor could invest prelates with symbols of temporal authority but had no right to invest them with spiritual authority, which came from the Church alone, and that the emperor was not to interfere in papal elections. This was the first concordat in history.

1123: Ecumenical Council of the Lateran (I), the first of its kind in the West. It endorsed provisions of the Concordat of Worms concerning the investiture of prelates and approved reform measures in 25 canons.

1139: Ecumenical Council of the Lateran (II). It adopted measures against a schism organized by antipope Anacletus and approved 30 canons related to discipline and other matters; one of the canons stated that holy orders is an invalidating impediment to marriage.

1140: St. Bernard met Abelard in debate at the Council of Sens. Abelard, whose rationalism in theology was condemned for the first time in 1121, died in 1142 at Cluny.

1148: The Synod of Rheims enacted strict disciplinary decrees for communities of women Religious.

1152: The Synod of Kells reorganized the Church in Ireland.

1160: Gratian, whose *Decretum* became a basic text of canon law, died.

Peter Lombard, compiler of the *Four Books of Sentences,* a standard theology text for nearly 200 years, died.

1170: St. Thomas Becket, archbishop of Canterbury, who clashed with Henry II over church-state relations, was murdered in his cathedral.

1171: Pope Alexander III reserved the process of canonization of saints to the Holy See.

1179: Ecumenical Council of the Lateran (III). It enacted measures against Waldensianism and Albigensianism (see year 242 regarding Manichaeism), approved reform decrees in 27 canons, provided that popes be elected by a two-thirds vote of the cardinals.

1184: Waldenses and other heretics were excommunicated by Pope Lucius III.

THIRTEENTH CENTURY

1198-1216: Pontificate of Innocent III, during which the papacy reached its medieval peak of authority, influence and prestige in the Church and in relations with civil rulers.

1208: Innocent III called for a crusade, the first in Christendom itself, against the Albigensians; their beliefs and practices threatened the fabric of society in southern France and northern Italy.

1209: Verbal approval was given by Innocent III to a rule of life for the Order of Friars Minor, started by St. Francis of Assisi.

1212: The Second Order of Franciscans, the Poor Clares, was founded.

1215: Ecumenical Council of the Lateran (IV). It ordered annual reception of the sacraments of penance and the Eucharist; defined and made the first official use of the term transubstantiation to explain the change of bread and wine into the body and blood of Christ; adopted additional measures to counteract teachings and practices of the Albigensians and Cathari; approved 70 canons.

1216: Formal papal approval was given to a rule of life for the Order of Preachers, started by St. Dominic.

The Portiuncula Indulgence was granted by the Holy See at the request of St. Francis of Assisi.

1221: Rule of the Third Order Secular of St. Francis (Secular Franciscan Order) approved verbally by Honorius III.

1226: Death of St. Francis of Assisi.

1231: Pope Gregory IX authorized establishment of the Papal Inquisition for dealing with heretics. It was a creature of its time, when crimes against faith and heretical doctrines of extremists like the Cathari and Albigenses threatened the good of the Christian community, the welfare of the state and the very fabric of society. The institution, which was responsible for excesses in punishment, was most active in the second half of the century in southern France, Italy and Germany.

1245: Ecumenical Council of Lyons (I). It confirmed the deposition of Emperor Frederick II and approved 22 canons.

1247: Preliminary approval was given by the Holy See to a Carmelite rule of life.

1270: St. Louis IX, king of France, died.

Beginning of papal decline.

1274: Ecumenical Council of Lyons (II). It accom-
plished a temporary reunion of separated Eastern Churches with the Roman Church; issued regulations concerning conclaves for papal elections; approved 31 canons.

Death of St. Thomas Aquinas, Doctor of the Church, of lasting influence.

1280: Pope Nicholas III, who made the Breviary the official prayer book for clergy of the Roman Church, died.

1281: The excommunication of Michael Palaeologus by Pope Martin IV ruptured the union effected with the Eastern Church in 1274.

FOURTEENTH CENTURY

1302: Pope Boniface VIII issued the bull *Unam Sanctam,* concerning the unity of the Church and the temporal power of princes, against the background of a struggle with Philip IV of France; it was the most famous medieval document on the subject.

1309-77: For a period of approximately 70 years, seven popes resided at Avignon because of unsettled conditions in Rome and other reasons; see separate entry.

1311-12: Ecumenical Council of Vienne. It suppressed the Knights Templar and enacted a number of reform decrees.

1321: Dante Alighieri died a year after completing the *Divine Comedy.*

1324: Marsilius of Padua completed *Defensor Pacis,* a work condemned by Pope John XXII as heretical because of its denial of papal primacy and the hierarchical structure of the Church, and for other reasons. It was a charter for conciliarism (an ecumenical council is superior to the pope in authority).

1337-1453: Period of the Hundred Years' War, a dynastic struggle between France and England.

1338: Four years after the death of Pope John XXII, who had opposed Louis IV of Bavaria in a years-long controversy, electoral princes declared at the Diet of Rhense that the emperor did not need papal confirmation of his title and right to rule. Charles IV later (1356) said the same thing in a *Golden Bull,* eliminating papal rights in the election of emperors.

1347-50: The Black Death swept across Europe, killing perhaps one-fourth to one-third of the total population; an estimated 40 per cent of the clergy succumbed.

1374: Petrarch, poet and humanist, died.

1377: Return of the papacy from Avignon to Rome.

Beginning of the Western Schism; see separate entry.

FIFTEENTH CENTURY

1409: The Council of Pisa, without canonical authority, tried to end the Western Schism but succeeded only in complicating it by electing a third claimant to the papacy; see Western Schism.

1414-18: Ecumenical Council of Constance. It took successful action to end the Western Schism involving rival claimants to the papacy; rejected the teachings of Wycliff; condemned Hus as a heretic. One decree — passed in the earlier stages of the council but later rejected — asserted the superiority of an ecumenical council over the pope (conciliarism).

1431: St. Joan of Arc was burned at the stake.

1431-45: Ecumenical Council of Florence (also called Basel-Ferrara-Florence). It affirmed the primacy of the pope against the claims of conciliarists that an ecumenical council is superior to the pope. It also formulated and approved decrees of union with several separated Eastern Churches — Greek, Armenian, Jacobite — which failed to gain general or lasting acceptance.

1438: The Pragmatic Sanction of Bourges was enacted by Charles VII and the French Parliament to curtail papal authority over the Church in France, in the spirit of conciliarism. It found expression in Gallicanism and had effects lasting at least until the French Revolution.

1453: The fall of Constantinople to the Turks.

c. 1456: Gutenberg issued the first edition of the Bible printed from movable type, at Mainz, Germany.

1476: Pope Sixtus IV approved observance of the feast of the Immaculate Conception on Dec. 8 throughout the Church.

1478: Pope Sixtus IV, at the urging of King Ferdinand of Spain, approved establishment of the Spanish Inquisition for dealing with Jewish and Moorish converts accused of heresy. The institution, which was peculiar to Spain and its colonies in America, acquired jurisdiction over other cases as well and fell into disrepute because of its procedures, cruelty and the manner in which it served the Spanish crown, rather than the accused and the good of the Church. Protests by the Holy See failed to curb excesses of the Inquisition, which lingered in Spanish history until early in the 19th century.

1492: Columbus discovered the Americas.

1493: Pope Alexander VI issued a *Bull of Demarcation* which determined spheres of influence for the Spanish and Portuguese in the Americas.

The Renaissance, a humanistic movement which originated in Italy in the 14th century, spread to France, Germany, the Low Countries and England. A transitional period between the medieval world and the modern secular world, it introduced profound changes which affected literature and the other arts, general culture, politics and religion.

SIXTEENTH CENTURY

1512-17: Ecumenical Council of the Lateran (V). It stated the relation and position of the pope with respect to an ecumenical council; acted to counteract the Pragmatic Sanction of Bourges and exaggerated claims of liberty by the Church in France; condemned erroneous teachings concerning the nature of the human soul; stated doctrine concerning indulgences. The council reflected concern for abuses in the Church and the need for reforms but failed to take decisive action in the years immediately preceding the Reformation.

1517: Martin Luther signalled the beginning of the Reformation by posting 95 theses at Wittenberg. Subsequently, he broke completely from doctrinal orthodoxy in discourses and three published works (1519 and 1520); was excommunicated on more than 40 charges of heresy (1521); remained

the dominant figure in the Reformation in Germany until his death in 1546.

1519: Zwingli triggered the Reformation in Zurich and became its leading proponent there until his death in combat in 1531.

1524: Luther's encouragement of German princes in putting down the two-year Peasants' Revolt gained political support for his cause.

1528: The Order of Friars Minor Capuchin was approved as an autonomous division of the Franciscan Order; like the Jesuits, the Capuchins became leaders in the Counter-Reformation.

1530: The *Augsburg Confession* of Lutheran faith was issued; it was later supplemented by the *Smalcald Articles*, approved in 1537.

1533: Henry VIII divorced Catherine of Aragon, married Anne Boleyn, was excommunicated. In 1534 he decreed the Act of Supremacy, making the sovereign the head of the Church in England, under which Sts. John Fisher and Thomas More were executed in 1535. Despite his rejection of papal primacy and actions against monastic life in England, he generally maintained doctrinal orthodoxy until his death in 1547.

1536: John Calvin, leader of the Reformation in Switzerland until his death in 1564, issued the first edition of *Institutes of the Christian Religion,* which became the classical text of Reformed (non-Lutheran) theology.

1540: The constitutions of the Society of Jesus (Jesuits), founded by St. Ignatius of Loyola, were approved.

1541: Start of the 11-year career of St. Francis Xavier as a missionary to the East Indies and Japan.

1545-63: Ecumenical Council of Trent. It issued a great number of decrees concerning doctrinal matters opposed by the Reformers, and mobilized the Counter-Reformation. Definitions covered the Canon of the Bible, the rule of faith, the nature of justification, grace, faith, original sin and its effects, the seven sacraments, the sacrificial nature of the Mass, the veneration of saints, use of sacred images, belief in purgatory, the doctrine of indulgences, the jurisdiction of the pope over the whole Church. It initiated many reforms for renewal in the liturgy and general discipline in the Church, the promotion of religious instruction, the education of the clergy through the foundation of seminaries, etc. Trent ranks with Vatican II as the greatest ecumenical council held in the West.

1549: The first Anglican *Book of Common Prayer* was issued by Edward VI. Revised editions were published in 1552, 1559 and 1662 and later.

1553: Start of the five-year reign of Mary Tudor who tried to counteract actions of Henry VIII against the Roman Church.

1555: Enactment of the Peace of Augsburg, an arrangement of religious territorialism rather than toleration, which recognized the existence of Catholicism and Lutheranism in the German Empire and provided that citizens should adopt the religion of their respective rulers.

1558: Beginning of the reign (to 1603) of Queen Elizabeth I of England and Ireland, during which the Church of England took on its definitive form.

1559: Establishment of the hierarchy of the Church

of England, with the consecration of Matthew Parker as archbishop of Canterbury.

1563: The first text of the *39 Articles* of the Church of England was issued. Also enacted were a new Act of Supremacy and Oath of Succession to the English throne.

1570: Elizabeth I was excommunicated. Penal measures against Catholics subsequently became more severe.

1571: Defeat of the Turkish armada at Lepanto staved off the invasion of Eastern Europe.

1577: The *Formula of Concord,* the classical statement of Lutheran faith, was issued; it was, generally, a Lutheran counterpart of the canons of the Council of Trent. In 1580, along with other formulas of doctrine, it was included in the Book of Concord.

1582: The Gregorian Calendar, named for Pope Gregory XIII, was put into effect and was eventually adopted in most countries: England delayed adoption until 1752.

SEVENTEENTH CENTURY

1605: The Gunpowder Plot, an attempt by Catholic fanatics to blow up James I of England and the houses of Parliament, resulted in an anti-Catholic Oath of Allegiance.

1610: Death of Matteo Ricci, outstanding Jesuit missionary to China, pioneer in cultural relations between China and Europe.

Founding of the first community of Visitation Nuns by Sts. Francis de Sales and Jane de Chantal.

1611: Founding of the Oratorians.

1613: Catholics were banned from Scandinavia.

1625: Founding of the Congregation of the Mission (Vincentians) by St. Vincent de Paul. He founded the Sisters of Charity in 1633.

1642: Death of Galileo, scientist, who was censured by the Congregation of the Holy Office for supporting the Copernican theory of the sun-centered planetary system. The case against him was closed in his favor in 1992.

Founding of the Sulpicians by Jacques Olier.

1643: Start of publication of the Bollandist *Acta Sanctorum,* a critical work on lives of the saints.

1648: Provisions in the Peace of Westphalia, ending the Thirty Years' War, extended terms of the Peace of Augsburg (1555) to Calvinists and gave equality to Catholics and Protestants in the 300 states of the Holy Roman Empire.

1649: Oliver Cromwell invaded Ireland and began a severe persecution of the Church there.

1653: Pope Innocent X condemned five propositions of Jansenism, a complex theory which distorted doctrine concerning the relations between divine grace and human freedom. Jansenism was also a rigoristic movement which seriously disturbed the Church in France, the Low Countries and Italy in this and the 18th century.

1673: The Test Act in England barred from public office Catholics who would not deny the doctrine of transubstantiation and receive Communion in the Church of England.

1678: Many English Catholics suffered death as a consequence of the Popish Plot, a false allegation by Titus Oates that Catholics planned to assassi-

nate Charles II, land a French army in the country, burn London, and turn over the government to the Jesuits.

1682: The four Gallican articles, drawn up by Bossuet, asserted political and ecclesiastical immunities of France from papal control. The articles, which rejected the primacy of the pope, were declared null and void by Pope Alexander VIII in 1690.

1689: The Toleration Act granted a measure of freedom of worship to other English dissenters but not to Catholics.

EIGHTEENTH CENTURY

1704: Chinese Rites — involving the Christian adaptation of elements of Confucianism, veneration of ancestors and Chinese terminology in religion — were condemned by Clement XI.

1720: The Passionists were founded by St. Paul of the Cross.

1724: Persecution in China.

1732: The Redemptorists were founded by St. Alphonsus Liguori.

1738: Freemasonry was condemned by Clement XII and Catholics were forbidden to join, under penalty of excommunication; the prohibition was repeated by Benedict XIV in 1751 and by later popes.

1760s: Josephinism, a theory and system of state control of the Church, was initiated in Austria; it remained in force until about 1850.

1764: Febronianism, an unorthodox theory and practice regarding the constitution of the Church and relations between Church and state, was condemned for the first of several times. Proposed by an auxiliary bishop of Trier using the pseudonym Justinus Febronius, it had the effects of minimizing the office of the pope and supporting national churches under state control.

1773: Clement XIV issued a brief of suppression against the Jesuits, following their expulsion from Portugal in 1759, from France in 1764 and from Spain in 1767. Political intrigue and unsubstantiated accusations were principal factors in these developments. The ban, which crippled the society, contained no condemnation of the Jesuit constitutions, particular Jesuits or Jesuit teaching. The society was restored in 1814.

1778: Catholics in England were relieved of some civil disabilities dating back to the time of Henry VIII, by an act which permitted them to acquire, own and inherit property. Additional liberties were restored by the Roman Catholic Relief Act of 1791 and subsequent enactments of Parliament.

1789: Religious freedom in the United States was guaranteed under the First Amendment to the Constitution.

Beginning of the French Revolution which resulted in: the secularization of church property and the Civil Constitution of the Clergy in 1790; the persecution of priests, religious and lay persons loyal to papal authority; invasion of the Papal States by Napoleon in 1796; renewal of persecution from 1797-1799; attempts to dechristianize France and establish a new religion; the occupation of Rome by French troops and the forced removal of Pius VI to France in 1798.

This century is called the age of Enlightenment or Reason because of the predominating rational and scientific approach of its leading philosophers, scientists and writers with respect to religion, ethics and natural law. This approach downgraded the fact and significance of revealed religion. Also characteristic of the Enlightenment were subjectivism, secularism and optimism regarding human perfectibility.

NINETEENTH CENTURY

1809: Pope Pius VII was made a captive by Napoleon and deported to France where he remained in exile until 1814. During this time he refused to cooperate with Napoleon who sought to bring the Church in France under his own control.

The turbulence in church-state relations in France at the beginning of the century recurred in connection with the Bourbon Restoration, the July Revolution, the second and third Republics, the Second Empire and the Dreyfus case.

1814: The Society of Jesus, suppressed since 1773, was restored.

1817: Reestablishment of the Congregation for the Propagation of the Faith (Propaganda) by Pius VII was an important factor in increasing missionary activity during the century.

1820: Years-long persecution, during which thousands died for the faith, ended in China. Thereafter, communication with the West remained cut off until about 1834. Vigorous missionary work got under way in 1842.

1822: The Pontifical Society for the Propagation of the Faith, inaugurated in France by Pauline Jaricot for the support of missionary activity, was established.

1829: The Catholic Emancipation Act relieved Catholics in England and Ireland of most of the civil disabilities to which they had been subject from the time of Henry VIII.

1832: Gregory XVI, in the encyclical *Mirari vos,* condemned indifferentism, one of the many ideologies at odds with Christian doctrine which were proposed during the century.

1833: Start of the Oxford Movement which affected the Church of England and resulted in some notable conversions, including that of John Henry Newman in 1845, to the Catholic Church.

Bl. Frederic Ozanam founded the Society of St. Vincent de Paul in France. The society's objectives are works of charity.

1848: The *Communist Manifesto,* a revolutionary document symptomatic of socio-economic crisis, was issued.

1850: The hierarchy was reestablished in England and Nicholas Wiseman made the first archbishop of Westminster. He was succeeded in 1865 by Henry Manning, an Oxford convert and proponent of the rights of labor.

1853: The Catholic hierarchy was reestablished in Holland.

1854: Pius IX proclaimed the dogma of the Immaculate Conception in the bull *Ineffabilis Deus.*

1858: The Blessed Virgin Mary appeared to St. Bernadette at Lourdes, France; see separate entry.

1864: Pius IX issued the encyclical *Quanta cura* and the *Syllabus of Errors* in condemnation of some 80 propositions derived from the scientific mentality and rationalism of the century. The subjects in question had deep ramifications in many areas of thought and human endeavor; in religion, they explicitly and/or implicitly rejected divine revelation and the supernatural order.

1867: The first volume of *Das Kapital* was published. Together with the Communist First International, formed in the same year, it had great influence on the subsequent development of communism and socialism.

1869: The Anglican Church was disestablished in Ireland.

1869-70: Ecumenical Council of the Vatican (I). It defined papal primacy and infallibility in a dogmatic constitution on the Church; covered natural religion, revelation, faith, and the relations between faith and reason in a dogmatic constitution on the Cathoic faith.

1870-71: Victor Emmanuel II of Sardinia, crowned king of Italy after defeating Austrian and papal forces, marched into Rome in 1870 and expropriated the Papal States after a plebiscite in which Catholics, at the order of Pius IX, did not vote. In 1871, Pius IX refused to accept a Law of Guarantees. Confiscation of church property and hindrance of ecclesiastical administration by the regime followed.

1871: The German Empire, a confederation of 26 states, was formed. Government policy launched a Kulturkampf whose May Laws of 1873 were designed to annul papal jurisdiction in Prussia and other states and to place the Church under imperial control. Resistance to the enactments and the persecution they legalized forced the government to modify its anti-Church policy by 1887.

1878: Beginning of the pontificate of Leo XIII, who was pope until his death in 1903. Leo is best known for the encyclical *Rerum novarum,* which greatly influenced the course of Christian social thought and the labor movement. His other accomplishments included promotion of Scholastic philosophy and the impetus he gave to scriptural studies.

1881: The first International Eucharistic Congress was held in Lille, France.

Alexander II of Russia died. His policies of Russification — as well as those of his two predecessors and a successor during the century — caused great suffering to Catholics, Jews and Protestants in Poland, Lithuania, the Ukraine and Bessarabia.

1882: Charles Darwin died. His theory of evolution by natural selection, one of several scientific highlights of the century, had extensive repercussions in the faith-and-science controversy.

1887: The Catholic University of America was founded in Washington, D.C.

1893: The U.S. apostolic delegation was set up in Washington, D.C.

TWENTIETH CENTURY

1901: Restrictive measures in France forced the Jesuits, Benedictines, Carmelites and other religious orders to leave the country. Subsequently, 14,000 schools were suppressed; religious orders and congregations were expelled; the concordat was renounced in 1905; church property was confiscated in 1906. For some years the Holy See, refusing to comply with government demands for the control of bishops' appointments, left some ecclesiastical offices vacant.

1903-14: Pontificate of St. Pius X. He initiated the codification of canon law, 1904; removed the ban against participation by Catholics in Italian national elections, 1905; issued decrees calling upon the faithful to receive Holy Communion frequently and daily, and stating that children should begin receiving the Eucharist at the age of seven, 1905 and 1910, respectively; ordered the establishment of the Confraternity of Christian Doctrine in all parishes throughout the world, 1905; condemned Modernism in the decree *Lamentabili* and the encyclical *Pascendi,* 1907.

1908: The United States and England, long under the jurisdiction of the Congregation for the Propagation of the Faith as mission territories, were removed from its control and placed under the common law of the Church.

1910: Laws of separation were enacted in Portugal, marking a point of departure in church-state relations.

1911: The Catholic Foreign Mission Society of America — Maryknoll, the first U.S.-founded society of its type — was established.

1914: Start of World War I, which lasted until 1918.

1914-22: Pontificate of Benedict XV. Much of his pontificate was devoted to seeking ways and means of minimizing the material and spiritual havoc of World War I. In 1917 he offered his services as a mediator to the belligerent nations, but his pleas for settlement of the conflict went unheeded.

1917: The Blessed Virgin Mary appeared to three children at Fatima, Portugal; see separate entry.

A new constitution, embodying repressive laws against the Church, was enacted in Mexico. Its implementation resulted in persecution in the 1920s and 1930s.

Bolsheviks seized power in Russia and set up a communist dictatorship. The event marked the rise of communism in Russian and world affairs. One of its immediate, and lasting, results was persecution of the Church, Jews and other segments of the population.

1918: The *Code of Canon Law,* in preparation for more than 10 years, went into effect in the Western Church.

1919: Benedict XV stimulated missionary work through the decree *Maximum Illud,* in which he urged the recruiting and training of native clergy in places where the Church was not firmly established.

1920-22: Ireland was partitioned by two enactments of the British government which (1) made the six counties of Northern Ireland part of the United Kingdom in 1920 and (2) gave dominion status to the Irish Free State in 1922. The Irish Free State became an independent republic in 1949.

1922-39: Pontificate of Pius XI. He subscribed to the Lateran Treaty, 1929, which settled the Roman Question created by the confiscation of the Papal States in 1871; issued the encyclical *Casti connubii,* 1930, an authoritative statement on Christian marriage; resisted the efforts of Benito Mussolini to control Catholic Action and the Church, in the encyclical *Non abbiamo bisogno,* 1931; opposed various fascist policies; issued the encyclicals *Quadragesimo anno,* 1931, developing the social doctrine of Leo XIII's *Rerum novarum,* and *Divini Redemptoris,* 1937, calling for social justice and condemning atheistic communism; condemned anti-Semitism, 1937.

1926: The Catholic Relief Act repealed virtually all legal disabilities of Catholics in England.

1931: Leftists proclaimed Spain a republic and proceeded to disestablish the Church, confiscate church property, deny salaries to the clergy, expel the Jesuits and ban teaching of the Catholic faith. These actions were preludes to the civil war of 1936-1939.

1933: Emergence of Adolf Hitler to power in Germany. By 1935 two of his aims were clear, the elimination of the Jews and control of a single national church. Six million Jews were killed in the Holocaust. The Church was subject to repressive measures, which Pius XI protested futilely in the encyclical *Mit brennender sorge* in 1937.

1936-39: Civil war in Spain between the leftist Loyalist and rightist Franco forces. The Loyalists were defeated and one-man, one-party rule was established. Priests, Religious and lay persons fell victims to Loyalist persecution.

1939-45: World War II.

1939-58: Pontificate of Pius XII. He condemned communism, proclaimed the dogma of the Assumption of Mary in 1950, in various documents and other enactments provided ideological background for many of the accomplishments of the Second Vatican Council. (See Twentieth Century Popes.)

1940: Start of a decade of communist conquest in more than 13 countries, resulting in conditions of persecution for a minimum of 60 million Catholics as well as members of other faiths.

Persecution diminished in Mexico because of nonenforcement of anti-religious laws still on record.

1950: Pius XII proclaimed the dogma of the Assumption of the Blessed Virgin Mary.

1957: The communist regime of China established the Patriotic Association of Chinese Catholics in opposition to the Church in union with the pope.

1958-63: Pontificate of John XXIII. His principal accomplishment was the convocation of the Second Vatican Council, the twenty-first ecumenical council in the history of the Church. (See Twentieth Century Popes.)

1962-65: Ecumenical Council of the Vatican (II). It formulated and promulgated 16 documents — two dogmatic and two pastoral constitutions, nine decrees and three declarations — reflecting pastoral orientation toward renewal and reform in the Church, and making explicit dimensions of doctrine and Christian life requiring emphasis for the full development of the Church and the better accomplishment of its mission in the contemporary world.

1963-78: Pontificate of Paul VI. His main purpose and effort was to give direction and provide guidance for the authentic trends of church renewal set in motion by the Second Vatican Council. (See Twentieth Century Popes.)

1978: The thirty-four-day pontificate of John Paul I. (See Twentieth Century Popes.)

Start of the pontificate of John Paul II; see Index.

1983: The revised *Code of Canon Law*, embodying reforms enacted by the Second Vatican Council, went into effect in the Church of Roman Rite.

1985: Formal ratification of a Vatican-Italy concordat replacing the Lateran Treaty of 1929.

1989-91: Decline and fall of communist influence and control in Middle and Eastern Europe and the Soviet Union.

1991: The *Code of Canon Law for Eastern Churches* went into effect.

1992: Approval of the new *Catechism of the Catholic Church.*

1994: Initiation of preparations for celebration of the start of the third Christian millennium in the year 2000.

ECUMENICAL COUNCILS

An ecumenical council is an assembly of the college of bishops, with and under the presidency of the pope, which has supreme authority over the Church in matters pertaining to faith, morals, worship and discipline.

The Second Vatican Council stated: "The supreme authority with which this college (of bishops) is empowered over the whole Church is exercised in a solemn way through an ecumenical council. A council is never ecumenical unless it is confirmed or at least accepted as such by the successor of Peter. It is the prerogative of the Roman Pontiff to convoke these councils, to preside over them, and to confirm them" (*Dogmatic Constitution on the Church,* No. 22).

Pope Presides

The pope is the head of an ecumenical council; he presides over it either personally or through legates. Conciliar decrees and other actions have binding force only when confirmed and promulgated by him. If a pope dies during a council, it is suspended until reconvened by another pope. An ecumenical council is not superior to a pope; hence, there is no appeal from a pope to a council.

Collectively, the bishops with the pope represent the whole Church. They do this not as democratic representatives of the faithful in a kind of church parliament, but as the successors of the Apostles with divinely given authority, care and responsibility over the whole Church.

All and only bishops are council participants with deliberative vote. The supreme authority of the Church can invite others and determine the manner of their participation.

Basic legislation concerning ecumenical councils is contained in Canons 337-41 of the Code of Canon Law. Basic doctrinal considerations were stated by the Second Vatican Council in the *Dogmatic Constitution on the Church.*

Background

Ecumenical councils had their prototype in the Council of Jerusalem in 51, at which the Apostles under the leadership of St. Peter decided that converts to the Christian faith were not obliged to observe all the prescriptions of Old Testament law (Acts 15). As early as the second century, bishops got together in regional meetings, synods or councils to take common action for the doctrinal and pastoral good of their communities of faithful. The expansion of such limited assemblies to ecumenical councils was a logical and historical evolution, given the nature and needs of the Church.

Emperors Involved

Emperors were active in summoning or convoking the first eight councils, especially the first five and the eighth. Among reasons for intervention of this kind were the facts that the emperors regarded themselves as guardians of the faith; that the settlement of religious controversies, which had repercussions in political and social turmoil, served the cause of peace in the state; and that the emperors had at their disposal ways and means of facilitating gatherings of bishops. Imperial actions, however, did not account for the formally ecumenical nature of the councils.

Some councils were attended by relatively few bishops, and the ecumenical character of several was open to question for a time. However, confirmation and de facto recognition of their actions by popes and subsequent councils established them as ecumenical.

Role in History

The councils have played a highly significant role in the history of the Church by witnessing to and defining truths of revelation, by shaping forms of worship and discipline, and by promoting measures for the ever-necessary reform and renewal of Catholic life. In general, they have represented attempts of the Church to mobilize itself in times of crisis for self-preservation, self-purification and growth.

The first eight ecumenical councils were held in the East; the other 13, in the West. The majority of separated Eastern Churches — e.g., the Orthodox — recognize the ecumenical character of the first seven councils, which formulated a great deal of basic doctrine. Other separated Eastern Churches acknowledge only the first two or first three ecumenical councils.

The 21 Councils

The 21 ecumenical councils in the history of the Church are listed below, with indication of their names or titles (taken from the names of the places where they were held); the dates; the reigning and/ or approving popes; the emperors who were instrumental in convoking the eight councils in the East; the number of bishops who attended, when available; the number of sessions. Significant actions of the first 20 councils are indicated under appropriate dates in Dates and Events in Church History.

1. Nicaea I, 325: St. Sylvester I (Emperor Constantine I); attended by approximately 300 bishops; sessions held between May 20 or June 19 to near the end of August.

2. Constantinople I, 381: St. Damasus I (Emperor Theodosius I); attended by approximately 150 bishops; sessions held from May to July.

3. Ephesus, 431: St. Celestine I (Emperor Theodosius II); attended by 150 to 200 bishops; five sessions held between June 22 and July 17.

4. Chalcedon, 451: St. Leo I (Emperor Marcian); attended by approximately 600 bishops; 17 sessions held between Oct. 8 and Nov. 1.

5. Constantinople II, 553: Vigilius (Emperor Justinian I); attended by 165 bishops; eight sessions held between May 5 and June 2.

6. Constantinople III, 680-681: St.Agatho, St. Leo II (Emperor Constantine IV); attended by approximately 170 bishops; 16 sessions held between Nov. 7, 680, and Sept. 6, 681.

7. Nicaea II, 787: Adrian I (Empress Irene); attended by approximately 300 bishops: eight sessions held between Sept. 24 and Oct. 23.

8. Constantinople IV, 869-870: Adrian II (Emperor Basil I); attended by 102 bishops; six sessions held between Oct. 5, 869, and Feb. 28, 870.

9. Lateran I, 1123: Callistus II; attended by approximately 300 bishops; sessions held between Mar. 8 and Apr. 6.

10. Lateran II, 1139: Innocent II; attended by 900 to 1,000 bishops and abbots; three sessions held in April.

11. Lateran III, 1179: Alexander III; attended by at least 300 bishops; three sessions held between Mar. 5 and 19.

12. Lateran IV, 1215: Innocent III; sessions held between Nov. 11 and 30.

13. Lyons I, 1245: Innocent IV; attended by approximately 150 bishops; three sessions held between June 28 and July 17.

14. Lyons II, 1274: Gregory X; attended by approximately 500 bishops; six sessions held between May 7 and July 17.

15. Vienne, 1311-1312: Clement V; attended by 132 bishops; three sessions held between Oct. 16, 1311, and May 6, 1312.

16. Constance, 1414-1418: Gregory XII, Martin V; attended by nearly 200 bishops, plus other prelates and many experts; 45 sessions held between Nov. 5, 1414, and Apr. 22, 1418.

17. Florence (also called Basel-Ferrara-Florence), 1431-1445(?): Eugene IV; attended by many Latin-Rite and Eastern-Rite bishops; preliminary sessions were held at Basel and Ferrara before definitive work was accomplished at Florence.

18. Lateran V, 1512-1517: Julius II, Leo X; 12 sessions held between May 3, 1512, and Mar. 6, 1517.

19. Trent, 1545-1563: Paul III, Julius III, Pius IV; 25 sessions held between Dec. 13, 1545, and Dec. 4, 1563.

20. Vatican I, 1869-1870: Pius IX; attended by approximately 800 bishops and other prelates; four public sessions and 89 general meetings held between Dec. 8, 1869, and Sept. 1, 1870.

VATICAN II

The Second Vatican Council, which was forecast by Pope John XXIII Jan. 25, 1959, was held in four sessions in St. Peter's Basilica.

Pope John convoked it and opened the first session, which ran from Oct. 11 to Dec. 8, 1962. Following John's death June 3, 1963, Pope Paul VI reconvened the council for the other three sessions which ran from Sept. 29 to Dec. 4, 1963; Sept. 14 to Nov. 21, 1964; Sept. 14 to Dec. 8, 1965.

A total of 2,860 Fathers participated in council proceedings, and attendance at meetings varied between 2,000 and 2,500. For various reasons, including the denial of exit from Communist-dominated countries, 274 Fathers could not attend.

The council formulated and promulgated 16 documents — two dogmatic and two pastoral constitutions, nine decrees and three declarations — all of which reflect its basic pastoral orientation toward renewal and reform in the Church. Given below are the Latin and English titles of the documents and their dates of promulgation.

• *Lumen Gentium* (Dogmatic Constitution on the Church), Nov. 21, 1964.

• *Dei Verbum* (Dogmatic Constitution on Divine Revelation), Nov. 18, 1965.

• *Sacrosanctum Concilium* (Constitution on the Sacred Liturgy), Dec. 4, 1963.

• *Gaudium et Spes* (Pastoral Constitution on the Church in the Modern World), Dec. 7, 1965.

• *Christus Dominus* (Decree on the Bishops' Pastoral Office in the Church), Oct. 28, 1965.

• *Ad Gentes* (Decree on the Church's Missionary Activity), Dec. 7, 1965.

• *Unitatis Redintegratio* (Decree on Ecumenism), Nov. 21, 1964.

• *Orientalium Ecclesiarum* (Decree on Eastern Catholic Churches), Nov. 21, 1964.

• *Presbyterorum Ordinis* (Decree on the Ministry and Life of Priests), Dec. 7, 1965.

• *Optatam Totius* (Decree on Priestly Formation), Oct. 28, 1965.

• *Perfectae Caritatis* (Decree on the Appropriate Renewal of the Religious Life), Oct. 28, 1965.

• *Apostolicam Actuositatem* (Decree on the Apostolate of the Laity), Nov. 18, 1965.

• *Inter Mirifica* (Decree on the Instruments of Social Communication), Dec. 4, 1963.

• *Dignitatis Humanae* (Declaration on Religious Freedom), Dec. 7, 1965.

• *Nostra Aetate* (Declaration on the Relationship of the Church to Non-Christian Religions), Oct. 28, 1965.

• *Gravissimum Educationis* (Declaration on Christian Education), Oct. 28, 1965.

The key documents were the four constitutions, which set the ideological basis for all the others. To date, the documents with the most visible effects are those on the liturgy, the Church, the Church in the world, ecumenism, the renewal of religious life, the life and ministry of priests, the lay apostolate.

The main business of the council was to explore and make explicit dimensions of doctrine and Christian life requiring emphasis for the full development of the Church and the better accomplishment of its mission in the contemporary world.

Enactments of the Second Vatican Council have been points of departure for a wide variety of developments in the internal life of the Church and its mission in the world at large.

THE CHURCH AS COMMUNION

Following are excerpts from a "Letter to the Bishops of the Catholic Church on Some Aspects of the Church Understood as Communion," issued by the Congregation for the Doctrine of the Faith June 15, 1992.

These excerpts are from the Vatican text circulated by the CNS Documentary Service, Origins, June 25, 1992 (Vol. 22, No. 7). Subheads have been added.

Some approaches to ecclesiology suffer from a clearly inadequate awareness of the Church as a mystery of communion, especially insofar as they have not sufficiently integrated the concept of communion with the concepts of the people of God and body of Christ, and have not given due importance to the relationship between the Church as communion and the Church as sacrament.

Invisible and Visible Communion

Ecclesial communion is at the same time both invisible and visible. As an invisible reality, it is the communion of each human being with the Father through Christ in the Holy Spirit, and with the others who are fellow sharers in the divine nature, in the passion of Christ, in the same faith, in the same spirit. In the Church on earth, there is an intimate relationship between this invisible communion and the visible communion in the teaching of the apostles, in the sacraments and in the hierarchical order. . . . (The) link between the invisible and the visible elements of ecclesial communion constitutes the Church as the sacrament of salvation.

Ecclesial communion, into which each individual is introduced by faith and by baptism, has its root and center in the holy Eucharist. Indeed, baptism is an incorporation into a body that the risen Lord builds up and keeps alive through the Eucharist, so that this body can truly be called the body of Christ. The Eucharist is the creative force and source of communion among the members of the Church, precisely because it unites each one of them with Christ himself.

Universal and Particular Churches

The Church of Christ, which we profess in the Creed to be one, holy, catholic and apostolic, is the universal Church, that is, the worldwide community of the disciples of the Lord, which is present and active . . . . (in) those entities which are in themselves churches because, although they are particular (churches), the universal Church becomes present in them with all her essential elements. They are therefore constituted after the model of the universal Church, and each of them is a portion of the people of God entrusted to a bishop to be guided by him with the assistance of his clergy.

The universal Church is therefore the body of the churches. . . . Sometimes the idea of a communion of particular churches is presented in such a way as to weaken the concept of the unity of the Church at the visible and institutional level. Thus it is asserted that every particular church is a subject complete in itself, and that the universal Church is the result of a reciprocal recognition on the part of the particular churches. (But) the universal Church cannot be conceived as the sum of the particular churches or as a federation of particular churches.

From the point of view of the Church understood as communion, the universal communion of the faithful and the communion of the churches are not consequences of one another but constitute the same reality from different viewpoints.

Eucharistic and Episcopal Roots

Unity, or communion between the particular churches in the universal Church, is rooted not only in the same faith and in the common baptism, but above all in the Eucharist and in the episcopate. It is rooted in the Eucharist because the Eucharistic Sacrifice, while always offered in a particular community, is never a celebration of that community alone.

Supreme Authority of the Church

For each particular church to be fully church, that is, the particular presence of the universal Church with all its essential elements, and hence constituted after the model of the universal Church, there must be present in it, as a proper element, the supreme authority of the Church: the episcopal college together with their head, the Supreme Pontiff, and never apart from him. The primacy of the bishop of Rome and the episcopal college are proper elements of the universal Church that are not derived from the particularity of the churches, but are nevertheless interior to each particular church. Consequently we must see the ministry of the successor of Peter not only as a global service reaching each particular church from outside, as it were, but as belonging already to the essence of each particular church from within. Indeed, the ministry of the primacy involves, in essence, a truly episcopal power which is not only supreme, full and universal but also immediate, over all, whether pastors or faithful. The ministry of the successor of Peter as something interior to each particular church is a necessary expression of that fundamental mutual interiority between universal Church and particular church.

The concept of the Church as communion is complementary to other concepts like those described in the "constitution on the Church" — the people of God, the universal sacrament, the body of Christ. All such concepts represent attempts to clarify and deepen understanding of the manifold mystery of the Church established by Christ for the salvation of all peoples.

The Apr. 11, 1997, edition of *Fides* noted that "the theme, 'The Church Understood as Communion,' is ever pertinent as presupposition for missionary impulse in a period in which the borders between pastoral care of the faithful, new evangelization and missionary activity are fading, becoming ever less marked."

The concept of communion is a unifying dynamic for all the being and action of the Church.

POPES

Information includes the name of the pope, in many cases his name before becoming pope, his birthplace or country of origin, the date of accession to the papacy, and the date of the end of reign which, in all but a few cases, was the date of death. Double dates indicate date of election and date of solemn beginning of ministry as Pastor of the universal Church. Source: "Annuario Pontificio."

St. Peter (Simon Bar-Jona): Bethsaida in Galilee; d. c. 64 or 67.

St. Linus: Tuscany; 67-76.

St. Anacletus (Cletus): Rome; 76-88.

St. Clement: Rome; 88-97.

St. Evaristus: Greece; 97-105.

St. Alexander I: Rome; 105-115.

St. Sixtus I: Rome; 115-125.

St. Telesphorus: Greece; 125-136.

St. Hyginus: Greece; 136-140.

St. Pius I: Aquileia; 140-155.

St. Anicetus: Syria; 155-166.

St. Soter: Campania; 166-175.

St. Eleutherius: Nicopolis in Epirus; 175-189.

Up to the time of St. Eleutherius, the years indicated for the beginning and end of pontificates are not absolutely certain. Also, up to the middle of the 11th century, there are some doubts about the exact days and months given in chronological tables.

St. Victor I: Africa; 189-199.

St. Zephyrinus: Rome; 199-217.

St. Callistus I: Rome; 217-222.

St. Urban I: Rome; 222-230.

St. Pontian: Rome; July 21, 230, to Sept. 28, 235.

St. Anterus: Greece; Nov. 21, 235, to Jan. 3, 236.

St. Fabian: Rome; Jan. 10, 236, to Jan. 20, 250.

St. Cornelius: Rome; Mar., 251, to June, 253.

St. Lucius I: Rome; June 25, 253, to Mar. 5, 254.

St. Stephen I: Rome; May 12, 254, to Aug. 2, 257.

St. Sixtus II: Greece; Aug. 30, 257, to Aug. 6, 258.

St. Dionysius: birthplace unknown; July 22, 259, to Dec. 26, 268.

St. Felix I: Rome; Jan. 5, 269, to Dec. 30, 274.

St. Eutychian: Luni; Jan. 4, 275, to Dec. 7, 283.

St. Caius: Dalmatia; Dec. 17, 283, to Apr. 22, 296.

St. Marcellinus: Rome; June 30, 296, to Oct. 25, 304.

St. Marcellus I: Rome; May 27, 308, or June 26, 308, to Jan. 16, 309.

St. Eusebius: Greece; Apr. 18, 309, to Aug. 17, 309 or 310.

St. Melchiades (Miltiades): Africa; July 2, 311, to Jan. 11, 314.

St. Sylvester I: Rome; Jan. 31, 314, to Dec. 31, 335. (Most of the popes before St. Sylvester I were martyrs.)

St. Marcus: Rome; Jan. 18, 336, to Oct. 7, 336.

St. Julius I: Rome; Feb. 6, 337, to Apr. 12, 352.

Liberius: Rome; May 17, 352, to Sept. 24, 366.

St. Damasus I: Spain; Oct. 1, 366, to Dec. 11, 384.

St. Siricius: Rome; Dec. 15, or 22 or 29, 384, to Nov. 26, 399.

St. Anastasius I: Rome; Nov. 27, 399, to Dec. 19, 401.

St. Innocent I: Albano; Dec. 22, 401, to Mar. 12, 417.

St. Zozimus: Greece; Mar. 18, 417, to Dec. 26, 418.

St. Boniface I: Rome; Dec. 28 or 29, 418, to Sept. 4, 422.

St. Celestine I: Campania; Sept. 10, 422, to July 27, 432.

St. Sixtus III: Rome; July 31, 432, to Aug. 19, 440.

St. Leo I (the Great): Tuscany; Sept. 29, 440, to Nov. 10, 461.

St. Hilary: Sardinia; Nov. 19, 461, to Feb. 29, 468.

St. Simplicius: Tivoli; Mar. 3, 468, to Mar. 10, 483.

St. Felix III (II): Rome; Mar. 13, 483, to Mar. 1, 492.

He should be called Felix II, and his successors of the same name should be numbered accordingly. The discrepancy in the numerical designation of popes named Felix was caused by the erroneous insertion in some lists of the name of St. Felix of Rome, a martyr.

St. Gelasius I: Africa; Mar. 1, 492, to Nov. 21, 496.

Anastasius II: Rome; Nov. 24, 496, to Nov. 19, 498.

St. Symmachus: Sardinia; Nov. 22, 498, to July 19, 514.

St. Hormisdas: Frosinone; July 20, 514, to Aug. 6, 523.

St. John I, Martyr: Tuscany; Aug. 13, 523, to May 18, 526.

St. Felix IV (III): Samnium; July 12, 526, to Sept. 22, 530.

Boniface II: Rome; Sept. 22, 530, to Oct. 17, 532.

John II: Rome; Jan. 2, 533, to May 8, 535.

John II was the first pope to change his name. His given name was Mercury.

St. Agapitus I: Rome; May 13, 535, to Apr. 22, 536.

St. Silverius, Martyr: Campania; June 1 or 8, 536, to Nov. 11, 537 (d. Dec. 2, 537).

St. Silverius was violently deposed in March, 537, and abdicated Nov. 11, 537. His successor, Vigilius, was not recognized as pope by all the Roman clergy until his abdication.

Vigilius: Rome; Mar. 29, 537, to June 7, 555.

Pelagius I: Rome; Apr. 16, 556, to Mar. 4, 561.

John III: Rome; July 17, 561, to July 13, 574.

Benedict I: Rome; June 2, 575, to July 30, 579.

Pelagius II: Rome; Nov. 26, 579, to Feb. 7, 590.

St. Gregory I (the Great): Rome; Sept. 3, 590, to Mar. 12, 604.

Sabinian: Blera in Tuscany; Sept. 13, 604, to Feb. 22, 606.

Boniface III: Rome; Feb. 19, 607, to Nov. 12, 607.

St. Boniface IV: Abruzzi; Aug. 25, 608, to May 8, 615.

St. Deusdedit (Adeodatus I): Rome; Oct. 19, 615, to Nov. 8, 618.

Boniface V: Naples; Dec. 23, 619, to Oct. 25, 625.

Honorius I: Campania; Oct. 27, 625, to Oct. 12, 638.

Severinus: Rome; May 28, 640, to Aug. 2, 640.

John IV: Dalmatia; Dec. 24, 640, to Oct. 12, 642.

Theodore I: Greece; Nov. 24, 642, to May 14, 649.

St. Martin I, Martyr: Todi; July, 649, to Sept. 16, 655 (in exile from June 17, 653).

St. Eugene I: Rome; Aug. 10, 654, to June 2, 657.

St. Eugene I was elected during the exile of St. Martin I, who is believed to have endorsed him as pope.

St. Vitalian: Segni; July 30, 657, to Jan. 27, 672.

Adeodatus II: Rome; Apr. 11, 672, to June 17, 676.

Donus: Rome; Nov. 2, 676, to Apr. 11, 678.

St. Agatho: Sicily; June 27, 678, to Jan. 10, 681.

St. Leo II: Sicily; Aug. 17, 682, to July 3, 683.

St. Benedict II: Rome; June 26, 684, to May 8, 685.

John V: Syria; July 23, 685, to Aug. 2, 686.

Conon: birthplace unknown; Oct. 21, 686, to Sept. 21, 687.

St. Sergius I: Syria; Dec. 15, 687, to Sept. 8, 701.

John VI: Greece; Oct. 30, 701, to Jan. 11, 705.

John VII: Greece; Mar. 1, 705, to Oct. 18, 707.

Sisinnius: Syria; Jan. 15, 708, to Feb. 4, 708.

Constantine: Syria; Mar. 25, 708, to Apr. 9, 715.

St. Gregory II: Rome; May 19, 715, to Feb. 11, 731.

St. Gregory III: Syria; Mar. 18, 731, to Nov., 741.

St. Zachary: Greece; Dec. 10, 741, to Mar. 22, 752.

Stephen II (III): Rome; Mar. 26, 752, to Apr. 26, 757.

After the death of St. Zachary, a Roman priest named Stephen was elected but died (four days later) before his consecration as bishop of Rome, which would have marked the beginning of his pontificate. Another Stephen was elected to succeed Zachary as Stephen II. (The first pope with this name was St. Stephen I, 254-57.) The ordinal III appears in parentheses after the name of Stephen II because the name of the earlier elected but deceased priest was included in some lists. Other Stephens have double numbers.

St. Paul I: Rome; Apr. (May 29), 757, to June 28, 767.

Stephen III (IV): Sicily; Aug. 1 (7), 768, to Jan. 24, 772.

Adrian I: Rome; Feb. 1 (9), 772, to Dec. 25, 795.

St. Leo III: Rome; Dec. 26 (27), 795, to June 12, 816.

Stephen IV (V): Rome; June 22, 816, to Jan. 24, 817.

St. Paschal I: Rome; Jan. 25, 817, to Feb. 11, 824.

Eugene II: Rome; Feb. (May), 824, to Aug., 827.

Valentine: Rome; Aug. 827, to Sept., 827.

Gregory IV: Rome; 827, to Jan., 844.

Sergius II: Rome; Jan., 844 to Jan. 27, 847.

St. Leo IV: Rome; Jan. (Apr. 10), 847, to July 17, 855.

Benedict III: Rome; July (Sept. 29), 855, to Apr. 17, 858.

St. Nicholas I (the Great): Rome; Apr. 24, 858, to Nov. 13, 867.

Adrian II: Rome; Dec. 14, 867, to Dec. 14, 872.

John VIII: Rome; Dec. 14, 872, to Dec. 16, 882.

Marinus I: Gallese; Dec. 16, 882, to May 15, 884.

St. Adrian III: Rome; May 17, 884, to Sept., 885. Cult confirmed June 2, 1891.

Stephen V (VI): Rome; Sept., 885, to Sept. 14, 891.

Formosus: Bishop of Porto; Oct. 6, 891, to Apr. 4, 896.

Boniface VI: Rome; Apr., 896, to Apr., 896.

Stephen VI (VII): Rome; May, 896, to Aug., 897.

Romanus: Gallese; Aug., 897, to Nov., 897.

Theodore II: Rome; Dec., 897, to Dec., 897.

John IX: Tivoli; Jan., 898, to Jan., 900.

Benedict IV: Rome; Jan. (Feb.), 900, to July, 903.

Leo V: Ardea; July, 903, to Sept., 903.

Sergius III: Rome; Jan. 29, 904, to Apr. 14, 911.

Anastasius III: Rome; Apr., 911, to June, 913.

Landus: Sabina; July, 913, to Feb., 914.

John X: Tossignano (Imola); Mar., 914, to May, 928.

Leo VI: Rome; May, 928, to Dec., 928.

Stephen VII (VIII): Rome; Dec., 928, to Feb., 931.

John XI: Rome; Feb. (Mar.), 931, to Dec., 935.

Leo VII: Rome; Jan. 3, 936, to July 13, 939.

Stephen VIII (IX): Rome; July 14, 939, to Oct., 942.

Marinus II: Rome; Oct. 30, 942, to May, 946.

Agapitus II: Rome; May 10, 946, to Dec., 955.

John XII (Octavius): Tusculum; Dec. 16, 955, to May 14, 964 (date of his death).

Leo VIII: Rome; Dec. 4 (6), 963, to Mar. 1, 965.

Benedict V: Rome; May 22, 964, to July 4, 966.

Confusion exists concerning the legitimacy of claims to the pontificate by Leo VIII and Benedict V. John XII was deposed Dec. 4, 963, by a Roman council. If this deposition was invalid, Leo was an antipope. If the deposition of John was valid, Leo was the legitimate pope and Benedict was an antipope.

John XIII: Rome; Oct. 1, 965, to Sept. 6, 972.

Benedict VI: Rome; Jan. 19, 973, to June, 974.

Benedict VII: Rome; Oct. 974, to July 10, 983.

John XIV (Peter Campenora): Pavia; Dec., 983, to Aug. 20, 984.

John XV: Rome; Aug., 985, to Mar. 996.

Gregory V (Bruno of Carinthia): Saxony; May 3, 996, to Feb. 18, 999.

Sylvester II (Gerbert): Auvergne; Apr. 2, 999, to May 12, 1003.

John XVII (Siccone): Rome; June 1003, to Dec., 1003.

John XVIII (Phasianus): Rome; Jan., 1004, to July, 1009.

Sergius IV (Peter): Rome; July 31, 1009, to May 12, 1012.

The custom of changing one's name on election to the papacy is generally considered to date from the time of Sergius IV. Before his time, several popes had changed their names. After his time, this became a regular practice, with few exceptions; e.g., Adrian VI and Marcellus II.

Benedict VIII (Theophylactus): Tusculum; May 18, 1012, to Apr. 9, 1024.

John XIX (Romanus): Tusculum; Apr. (May), 1024, to 1032.

Benedict IX (Theophylactus): Tusculum; 1032, to 1044.

Sylvester III (John): Rome; Jan. 20, 1045, to Feb. 10, 1045.

Sylvester III was an antipope if the forcible removal of Benedict IX in 1044 was not legitimate.

Benedict IX (second time): Apr. 10, 1045, to May 1, 1045.

Gregory VI (John Gratian): Rome; May 5, 1045, to Dec. 20, 1046.

Clement II (Suitger, Lord of Morsleben and Hornburg): Saxony; Dec. 24 (25), 1046, to Oct. 9, 1047.

If the resignation of Benedict IX in 1045 and his removal at the December, 1046, synod were not legitimate, Gregory VI and Clement II were antipopes.

Benedict IX (third time): Nov. 8, 1047, to July 17, 1048 (d. c. 1055).

Damasus II (Poppo): Bavaria; July 17, 1048, to Aug. 9, 1048.

St. Leo IX (Bruno): Alsace; Feb. 12, 1049, to Apr. 19, 1054.

Victor II (Gebhard): Swabia; Apr. 16, 1055, to July 28, 1057.

Stephen IX (X) (Frederick): Lorraine; Aug. 3, 1057, to Mar. 29, 1058.

Nicholas II (Gerard): Burgundy; Jan. 24, 1059, to July 27, 1061.

Alexander II (Anselmo da Baggio): Milan; Oct. 1, 1061, to Apr. 21, 1073.

St. Gregory VII (Hildebrand): Tuscany; Apr. 22 (June 30), 1073, to May 25, 1085.

Bl. Victor III (Dauferius; Desiderius): Benevento; May 24, 1086, to Sept. 16, 1087. Cult confirmed July 23, 1887.

Bl. Urban II (Otto di Lagery): France; Mar. 12, 1088, to July 29, 1099. Cult confirmed July 14, 1881.

Paschal II (Raniero): Ravenna; Aug. 13 (14), 1099, to Jan. 21, 1118.

Gelasius II (Giovanni Caetani): Gaeta; Jan. 24 (Mar. 10), 1118, to Jan. 28, 1119.

Callistus II (Guido of Burgundy): Burgundy; Feb. 2 (9), 1119, to Dec. 13, 1124.

Honorius II (Lamberto): Fiagnano (Imola); Dec. 15 (21), 1124, to Feb. 13, 1130.

Innocent II (Gregorio Papareschi): Rome; Feb. 14 (23), 1130, to Sept. 24, 1143.

Celestine II (Guido): Citta di Castello; Sept. 26 (Oct. 3), 1143, to Mar. 8, 1144.

Lucius II (Gerardo Caccianemici): Bologna: Mar. 12, 1144, to Feb. 15, 1145.

Bl. Eugene III (Bernardo Paganelli di Montemagno): Pisa; Feb. 15 (18), 1145, to July 8, 1153. Cult confirmed Oct. 3, 1872.

Anastasius IV (Corrado): Rome; July 12, 1153, to Dec, 3, 1154.

Adrian IV (Nicholas Breakspear): England; Dec. 4 (5), 1154, to Sept. 1, 1159.

Alexander III (Rolando Bandinelli): Siena; Sept. 7 (20), 1159, to Aug. 30, 1181.

Lucius III (Ubaldo Allucingoli): Lucca; Sept. 1 (6), 1181, to Sept. 25, 1185.

Urban III (Uberto Crivelli): Milan; Nov. 25 (Dec. 1), 1185, to Oct. 20, 1187.

Gregory VIII (Alberto de Morra): Benevento; Oct. 21 (25), 1187, to Dec. 17, 1187.

Clement III (Paolo Scolari): Rome; Dec. 19 (20), 1187, to Mar., 1191.

Celestine III (Giacinto Bobone): Rome; Mar. 30 (Apr. 14), 1191, to Jan. 8, 1198.

Innocent III (Lotario dei Conti di Segni); Anagni; Jan. 8 (Feb. 22), 1198, to July 16, 1216.

Honorius III (Cencio Savelli): Rome; July 18 (24), 1216, to Mar. 18, 1227.

Gregory IX (Ugolino, Count of Segni): Anagni; Mar. 19 (21), 1227, to Aug. 22, 1241.

Celestine IV (Goffredo Castiglioni): Milan; Oct. 25 (28), 1241, to Nov. 10, 1241.

Innocent IV (Sinibaldo Fieschi): Genoa; June 25 (28), 1243, to Dec. 7, 1254.

Alexander IV (Rinaldo, House of Ienne): Ienne (Rome); Dec. 12 (20), 1254, to May 25, 1261.

Urban IV (Jacques Pantaléon): Troyes; Aug. 29 (Sept. 4), 1261, to Oct. 2, 1264.

Clement IV (Guy Foulques or Guido le Gros): France; Feb. 5 (15), 1265, to Nov. 29, 1268.

Bl. Gregory X (Teobaldo Visconti): Piacenza; Sept. 1, 1271 (Mar. 27, 1272), to Jan. 10, 1276. Cult confirmed Sept. 12, 1713.

Bl. Innocent V (Peter of Tarentaise): Savoy; Jan. 21 (Feb. 22), 1276, to June 22, 1276. Cult confirmed Mar. 13, 1898.

Adrian V (Ottobono Fieschi): Genoa: July 11, 1276, to Aug. 18, 1276.

John XXI (Petrus Juliani or Petrus Hispanus): Portugal; Sept. 8 (20), 1276, to May 20, 1277.

There is confusion in the numerical designation of popes named John. The error dates back to the time of John XV.

Nicholas III (Giovanni Gaetano Orsini): Rome; Nov. 25 (Dec. 26), 1277, to Aug. 22, 1280.

Martin IV (Simon de Brie): France; Feb. 22 (Mar. 23), 1281, to Mar. 28, 1285.

The names of Marinus 1 (882-84) and Marinus II (942-46) were construed as Martin. In view of these two pontificates and the earlier reign of St. Martin I (649-55), this pope was called Martin IV.

Honorius IV (Giacomo Savelli): Rome; Apr. 2 (May 20), 1285, to Apr. 3, 1287.

Nicholas IV (Girolamo Masci): Ascoli; Feb. 22, 1288, to Apr. 4, 1292.

St. Celestine V (Pietro del Murrone): Isernia; July 5 (Aug. 29), 1294, to Dec. 13, 1294; d. May 19, 1296. Canonized May 5, 1313.

Boniface VIII (Benedetto Caetani): Anagni; Dec. 24, 1294 (Jan. 23, 1295), to Oct. 11, 1303.

Bl. Benedict XI (Niccolo Boccasini): Treviso; Oct. 22 (27), 1303, to July 7, 1304. Cult confirmed Apr. 24, 1736.

Clement V (Bertrand de Got): France; June 5 (Nov. 14), 1305, to Apr. 20, 1314. (First of Avignon popes.)

John XXII (Jacques d'Euse): Cahors; Aug. 7 (Sept. 5), 1316, to Dec. 4, 1334.

Benedict XII (Jacques Fournier): France; Dec. 20, 1334 (Jan. 8, 1335), to Apr. 25, 1342.

Clement VI (Pierre Roger): France; May 7 (19), 1342, to Dec. 6, 1352.

Innocent VI (Etienne Aubert): France; Dec. 18 (30), 1352, to Sept. 12, 1362.

Bl. Urban V (Guillaume de Grimoard): France; Sept. 28 (Nov. 6), 1362, to Dec. 19, 1370. Cult confirmed Mar. 10, 1870.

Gregory XI (Pierre Roger de Beaufort): France; Dec. 30, 1370 (Jan. 5, 1371), to Mar. 26, 1378. (Last of Avignon popes.)

Urban VI (Bartolomeo Prignano): Naples; Apr. 8 (18), 1378, to Oct. 15, 1389.

Boniface IX (Pietro Tomacelli): Naples; Nov. 2 (9), 1389, to Oct. 1, 1404.

Innocent VII (Cosma Migliorati): Sulmona; Oct. 17 (Nov. 11), 1404, to Nov. 6, 1406.

Gregory XII (Angelo Correr): Venice; Nov. 30 (Dec. 19), 1406, to July 4, 1415, when he voluntarily resigned from the papacy to permit the election of his successor. He died Oct. 18, 1417. (See The Western Schism.)

Martin V (Oddone Colonna): Rome; Nov. 11 (21), 1417, to Feb. 20, 1431.

Eugene IV (Gabriele Condulmer): Venice; Mar. 3 (11), 1431, to Feb. 23, 1447.

Nicholas V (Tommaso Parentucelli): Sarzana; Mar. 6 (19), 1447, to Mar. 24, 1455.

Callistus III (Alfonso Borgia): Jativa (Valencia); Apr. 8 (20), 1455, to Aug. 6, 1458.

Pius II (Enea Silvio Piccolomini): Siena; Aug. 19 (Sept. 3), 1458, to Aug. 14, 1464.

Paul II (Pietro Barbo): Venice; Aug. 30 (Sept. 16), 1464, to July 26, 1471.

Sixtus IV (Francesco della Rovere): Savona; Aug. 9 (25), 1471, to Aug. 12, 1484.

Innocent VIII (Giovanni Battista Cibo): Genoa; Aug. 29 (Sept. 12), 1484, to July 25, 1492.

Alexander VI (Rodrigo Borgia): Jativa (Valencia); Aug. 11 (26), 1492, to Aug. 18, 1503.

Pius III (Francesco Todeschini-Piccolomini): Siena; Sept. 22 (Oct. 1, 8), 1503, to Oct. 18, 1503.

Julius II (Giuliano della Rovere): Savona; Oct. 31 (Nov. 26), 1503, to Feb. 21, 1513.

Leo X (Giovanni de' Medici): Florence; Mar. 9 (19), 1513, to Dec. 1, 1521.

Adrian VI (Adrian Florensz): Utrecht; Jan. 9 (Aug. 31), 1522, to Sept. 14, 1523.

Clement VII (Giulio de' Medici): Florence; Nov. 19 (26), 1523, to Sept. 25, 1534.

Paul III (Alessandro Farnese): Rome; Oct. 13 (Nov. 3), 1534, to Nov. 10, 1549.

Julius III (Giovanni Maria Ciocchi del Monte): Rome; Feb. 7 (22), 1550, to Mar. 23, 1555.

Marcellus II (Marcello Cervini): Montepulciano; Apr. 9 (10), 1555, to May 1, 1555.

Paul IV (Gian Pietro Carafa): Naples; May 23 (26), 1555, to Aug. 18, 1559.

Pius IV (Giovan Angelo de' Medici): Milan; Dec. 25, 1559 (Jan. 6, 1560), to Dec. 9, 1565.

St. Pius V (Antonio-Michele Ghislieri): Bosco (Alexandria); Jan. 7 (17), 1566, to May 1, 1572. Canonized May 22, 1712.

Gregory XIII (Ugo Buoncompagni): Bologna; May 13 (25), 1572, to Apr. 10, 1585.

Sixtus V (Felice Peretti): Grottammare (Ripatransone); Apr. 24 (May 1), 1585, to Aug. 27, 1590.

Urban VII (Giambattista Castagna): Rome; Sept. 15, 1590, to Sept. 27, 1590.

Gregory XIV (Niccolo Sfondrati): Cremona; Dec. 5 (8), 1590, to Oct. 16, 1591.

Innocent IX (Giovanni Antonio Facchinetti): Bologna; Oct. 29 (Nov. 3), 1591, to Dec. 30, 1591.

Clement VIII (Ippolito Aldobrandini): Florence; Jan. 30 (Feb. 9), 1592, to Mar. 3, 1605.

Leo XI (Alessandro de' Medici): Florence; Apr. 1 (10), 1605, to Apr. 27, 1605.

Paul V (Camillo Borghese): Rome; May 16 (29), 1605, to Jan. 28, 1621.

Gregory XV (Alessandro Ludovisi): Bologna; Feb. 9 (14), 1621, to July 8, 1623.

Urban VIII (Maffeo Barberini): Florence; Aug. 6 (Sept. 29), 1623, to July 29, 1644.

Innocent X (Giovanni Battista Pamfili): Rome; Sept. 15 (Oct. 4), 1644, to Jan. 7, 1655.

Alexander VII (Fabio Chigi): Siena; Apr. 7 (18), 1655, to May 22, 1667.

Clement IX (Giulio Rospigliosi): Pistoia; June 20 (26), 1667, to Dec. 9, 1669.

Clement X (Emilio Altieri): Rome; Apr. 29 (May 11), 1670, to July 22, 1676.

Bl. Innocent XI (Benedetto Odescalchi): Como; Sept. 21 (Oct. 4), 1676, to Aug. 12, 1689. Beatified Oct. 7, 1956.

Alexander VIII (Pietro Ottoboni): Venice; Oct. 6 (16), 1689, to Feb. 1, 1691.

Innocent XII (Antonio Pignatelli): Spinazzola (Venosa); July 12 (15), 1691, to Sept. 27, 1700.

Clement XI (Giovanni Francesco Albani): Urbino; Nov. 23, 30 (Dec. 8), 1700, to Mar. 19, 1721.

Innocent XIII (Michelangelo dei Conti): Rome; May 8 (18), 1721, to Mar. 7, 1724.

Benedict XIII (Pietro Francesco — Vincenzo Maria — Orsini): Gravina (Bari); May 29 (June 4), 1724, to Feb. 21, 1730.

Clement XII (Lorenzo Corsini): Florence; July 12 (16), 1730, to Feb. 6, 1740.

Benedict XIV (Prospero Lambertini): Bologna; Aug. 17 (22), 1740, to May 3, 1758.

Clement XIII (Carlo Rezzonico): Venice; July 6 (16), 1758, to Feb. 2, 1769.

Clement XIV (Giovanni Vincenzo Antonio — Lorenzo — Ganganelli): Rimini; May 19, 28 (June 4), 1769, to Sept. 22, 1774.

Pius VI (Giovanni Angelo Braschi): Cesena; Feb. 15 (22), 1775, to Aug. 29, 1799.

Pius VII (Barnaba — Gregorio — Chiaramonti): Cesena; Mar. 14 (21), 1800, to Aug. 20, 1823.

Leo XII (Annibale della Genga): Genga (Fabriano); Sept. 28 (Oct. 5), 1823, to Feb. 10, 1829.

Pius VIII (Francesco Saverio Castiglioni): Cingoli; Mar. 31 (Apr. 5), 1829, to Nov. 30, 1830.

Gregory XVI (Bartolomeo Alberto — Mauro — Cappellari): Belluno; Feb. 2 (6), 1831, to June 1, 1846.

Pius IX (Giovanni M. Mastai-Ferretti): Senigallia; June 16 (21), 1846, to Feb. 7, 1878.

Leo XIII (Gioacchino Pecci): Carpineto (Anagni); Feb. 20 (Mar. 3), 1878, to July 20, 1903.

St. Pius X (Giuseppe Sarto): Riese (Treviso); Aug. 4 (9), 1903, to Aug. 20, 1914. Canonized May 29, 1954.

Benedit XV (Giacomo della Chiesa): Genoa; Sept. 3 (6), 1914, to Jan. 22, 1922.

Pius XI (Achille Ratti): Desio (Milan); Feb. 6 (12), 1922, to Feb. 10, 1939.

Pius XII (Eugenio Pacelli): Rome; Mar. 2 (12), 1939, to Oct. 9, 1958.

John XXIII (Angelo Giuseppe Roncalli): Sotto il Monte (Bergamo); Oct. 28 (Nov. 4), 1958, to June 3, 1963.

Paul VI (Giovanni Battista Montini): Concessio (Brescia); June 21 (30), 1963, to Aug. 6, 1978.

John Paul I (Albino Luciani): Forno di Canale (Belluno); Aug. 26 (Sept. 3), 1978, to Sept. 28, 1978.

John Paul II (Karol Wojtyla): Wadowice, Poland; Oct. 16 (22), 1978.

ANTIPOPES

This list of men who claimed or exercised the papal office in an uncanonical manner includes names, birthplaces and dates of alleged reigns.
Source: "Annuario Pontificio."

St. Hippolytus: Rome; 217-235; was reconciled before his death.

Novatian: Rome; 251.

Felix II: Rome; 355 to Nov. 22, 365.

Ursinus: 366-367.

Eulalius: Dec. 27 or 29, 418, to 419.

Lawrence: 498; 501-505.

Dioscorus: Alexandria; Sept. 22, 530, to Oct. 14, 530.

Theodore: ended alleged reign, 687.

Paschal: ended alleged reign, 687.

Constantine: Nepi; June 28 (July 5), 767, to 769.

Philip: July 31, 768; retired to his monastery on the same day.

John: ended alleged reign, Jan., 844.

Anastasius: Aug., 855, to Sept., 855; d. 880.

Christopher: Rome; July or Sept., 903, to Jan., 904.

Boniface VII: Rome; June, 974, to July, 974; Aug., 984, to July, 985.

John XVI: Rossano; Apr., 997, to Feb., 998.

Gregory: ended alleged reign, 1012.
Benedict X: Rome; Apr. 5, 1058, to Jan. 24, 1059.
Honorius II: Verona; Oct. 28, 1061, to 1072.
Clement III: Parma; June 25, 1080 (Mar. 24, 1084), to Sept. 8, 1100.
Theodoric: ended alleged reign, 1100; d. 1102.
Albert: ended alleged reign, 1102.
Sylvester IV: Rome; Nov. 18, 1105, to 1111.
Gregory VIII: France; Mar. 8, 1118, to 1121.
Celestine II: Rome; ended alleged reign, Dec., 1124.
Anacletus II: Rome; Feb. 14 (23), 1130, to Jan. 25, 1138.
Victor IV: Mar., 1138, to May 29, 1138; submitted to Pope Innocent II.
Victor IV: Montecelio; Sept. 7 (Oct. 4), 1159, to Apr. 20, 1164; he did not recognize his predecessor (Victor IV, above).
Paschal III: Apr. 22 (26), 1164, to Sept. 20, 1168.
Callistus III: Arezzo; Sept., 1168, to Aug. 29, 1178; submitted to Pope Alexander III.
Innocent III: Sezze; Sept. 29, 1179, to 1180.
Nicholas V: Corvaro (Rieti); May 12 (22), 1328, to Aug. 25, 1330; d. Oct. 16, 1333.
Four antipopes of the Western Schism:
Clement VII: Sept. 20 (Oct. 31), 1378, to Sept. 16, 1394.
Benedict XIII: Aragon; Sept. 28 (Oct. 11), 1394, to May 23, 1423.
Alexander V: Crete; June 26 (July 7), 1409, to May 3, 1410.
John XXIII: Naples; May 17 (25), 1410, to May 29, 1415. (Date of deposition by Council of Constance which ended the Western Schism; d. Nov. 22, 1419.)
Felix V: Savoy; Nov. 5, 1439 (July 24, 1440), to April 7, 1449; d. 1451.

AVIGNON PAPACY

Avignon was the residence (1309-77) of a series of French popes (Clement V, John XXII, Benedict XII, Clement VI, Innocent VI, Urban V and Gregory XI). Prominent in the period were power struggles over the mixed interests of Church and state with the rulers of France (Philip IV, John II), Bavaria (Lewis IV), England (Edward III); factionalism of French and Italian churchmen; political as well as ecclesiastical turmoil in Italy, a factor of significance in prolong-ing the stay of popes in Avignon. Despite some positive achievements, the Avignon papacy was a prologue to the Western Schism which began in 1378.

WESTERN SCHISM

The Western Schism was a confused state of affairs which divided Christendom into two and then three papal obediences from 1378 to 1417.

It occurred some 50 years after Marsilius theorized that a general (not ecumenical) council of bishops and other persons was superior to a pope and nearly 30 years before the Council of Florence stated definitively that no kind of council had such authority.

It was a period of disaster preceding the even more disastrous period of the Reformation.

Urban VI, following the return of the papal residence to Rome after approximately 70 years at Avignon, was elected pope Apr. 8, 1378, and reigned until his death in 1389. He was succeeded by Boniface IX (1389-1404), Innocent VII (1404-1406) and Gregory XII (1406-1415). These four are considered the legitimate popes of the period.

Some of the cardinals who chose Urban pope, dissatisfied with his conduct of the office, declared that his election was invalid. They proceeded to elect Clement VII, who claimed the papacy from 1378 to 1394. He was succeeded by Benedict XIII.

Prelates seeking to end the state of divided papal loyalties convoked the Council of Pisa (1409) which, without authority, found Gregory XII and Benedict XIII, in absentia, guilty on 30-odd charges of schism and heresy, deposed them, and elected a third claimant to the papacy, Alexander V (1409-1410). He was succeeded by John XXIII (1410-1415).

The schism was ended by the Council of Constance (1414-1418). This council, although originally called into session in an irregular manner, acquired authority after being convoked by Gregory XII in 1415. In its early irregular phase, it deposed John XXIII whose election to the papacy was uncanonical anyway. After being formally convoked, it accepted the abdication of Gregory in 1415 and dismissed the claims of Benedict XIII two years later, thus clearing the way for the election of Martin V on Nov. 11, 1417. The Council of Constance also rejected the theories of John Wycliff and condemned John Hus as a heretic.

TWENTIETH CENTURY POPES

LEO XIII

Leo XIII (Gioacchino Vincenzo Pecci) was born May 2, 1810, in Carpineto, Italy. Although all but three years of his life and pontificate were of the 19th century, his influence extended well into the 20th century.

He was educated at the Jesuit college in Viterbo, the Roman College, the Academy of Noble Ecclesiastics, and the University of the Sapienza. He was ordained to the priesthood in 1837.

He served as an apostolic delegate to two States of the Church, Benevento from 1838 to 1841 and Perugia in 1841 and 1842. Ordained titular archbishop of Damietta, he was papal nuncio to Belgium from January, 1843, until May, 1846; in the post, he had controversial relations with the government over education issues and acquired his first significant experience of industrialized society.

He was archbishop of Perugia from 1846 to 1878. He became a cardinal in 1853 and chamberlain of the Roman Curia in 1877. He was elected to the papacy Feb. 20, 1878. He died July 20, 1903.

Canonizations: He canonized 18 saints and beatified a group of English martyrs.

Church Administration: He established 300 new dioceses and vicariates; restored the hierarchy in Scotland, set up an English, as contrasted with the Portuguese, hierarchy in India; approved the action of the Congregation for the Propagation of the Faith in reorganizing missions in China.

Encyclicals: He issued 86 encyclicals, on subjects ranging from devotional to social. In the former category were *Annum Sacrum,* on the Sacred Heart, in 1899, and 11 letters on Mary and the Rosary.

Social Questions: Much of Leo's influence stemmed from social doctrine stated in numerous encyclicals, concerning liberalism, liberty, the divine origin of authority; socialism, in *Quod Apostolici Muneris,* 1878; the Christian concept of the family, in *Arcanum,* 1880; socialism and economic liberalism, relations between capital and labor, in *Rerum Novarum,* 1891. Two of his social encyclicals were against the African slave trade.

Interfaith Relations: He was unsuccessful in unity overtures made to Orthodox and Slavic Churches. He declared Anglican orders invalid in the apostolic bull *Apostolicae Curae* Sept. 13, 1896.

International Relations: Leo was frustrated in seeking solutions to the Roman Question arising from the seizure of church lands by the Kingdom of Italy in 1870. He also faced anticlerical situations in Belgium and France and in the Kulturkampf policies of Bismarck in Germany.

Studies: In the encyclical *Aeterni Patris* of Aug. 4, 1879, he ordered a renewal of philosophical and theological studies in seminaries along scholastic, and especially Thomistic, lines, to counteract influential trends of liberalism and Modernism. He issued guidelines for biblical exegesis in *Providentissimus Deus* Nov. 18, 1893, and established the Pontifical Biblical Commission in 1902.

In other actions affecting scholarship and study, he opened the Vatican Archives to scholars in 1883 and established the Vatican Observatory.

United States: He authorized establishment of the apostolic delegation in Washington, D.C., Jan. 24, 1893. He refused to issue a condemnation of the Knights of Labor. With a document entitled *Testem Benevolentiae,* he eased resolution of questions concerning what was called an American heresy in 1899.

ST. PIUS X

St. Pius X (Giuseppe Melchiorre Sarto) was born in 1835 in Riese, Italy. Educated at the college of Castelfranco and the seminary at Padua, he was ordained to the priesthood Sept. 18, 1858. He served as a curate in Trombolo for nine years before beginning an eight-year pastorate at Salzano. He was chancellor of the Treviso diocese from November, 1875, and bishop of Mantua from 1884 until 1893. He was cardinal-patriarch of Venice from that year until his election to the papacy by the conclave held from July 31 to Aug. 4, 1903.

Aims: Pius' principal objectives as pope were "to restore all things in Christ, in order that Christ may be all and in all," and "to teach (and defend) Christian truth and law."

Canonizations, Encyclicals: He canonized four saints and issued 16 encyclicals. One of the encyclicals was issued in commemoration of the 50th anniversary of the proclamation of the dogma of the Immaculate Conception of Mary.

Catechetics: He introduced a whole new era of religious instruction and formation with the encyclical *Acerbo Nimis* of Apr. 15, 1905, in which he called for vigor in establishing and conducting parochial programs of the Confraternity of Christian Doctrine.

Catholic Action: He outlined the role of official Catholic Action in two encyclicals in 1905 and 1906. Favoring organized action by Catholics themselves, he had serious reservations about interconfessional collaboration.

He stoutly maintained claims to papal rights in the anticlerical climate of Italy. He authorized bishops to relax prohibitions against participation by Catholics in some Italian elections.

Church Administration: With the motu proprio *Arduum Sane* of Mar. 19, 1904, he inaugurated the work which resulted in the Code of Canon Law; the code was completed in 1917 and went into effect in the following year. He reorganized and strengthened the Roman Curia with the apostolic constitution *Sapienti Consilio* of June 29, 1908.

While promoting the expansion of missionary work, he removed from the jurisdiction of the Congregation for the Propagation of the Faith the Church in the United States, Canada, Newfoundland, England, Ireland, Holland and Luxembourg.

International Relations: He ended traditional prerogatives of Catholic governments with respect to papal elections, in 1904. He opposed anti-Church and anticlerical actions in several countries: Bolivia in 1905, because of anti-religious legislation; France in 1906, for its 1901 action in annulling its concordat with the Holy See, and for the 1905 Law of Separation by which it decreed separation of Church and state, ordered the confiscation of church property, and blocked religious education and the activities of religious orders; Portugal in 1911, for the separation of Church and state and repressive measures which resulted in persecution later.

In 1912 he called on the bishops of Brazil to work for the improvement of conditions among Indians.

Liturgy: "The Pope of the Eucharist," he strongly recommended the frequent reception of Holy Communion in a decree dated Dec. 20, 1905; in another decree, *Quam Singulari,* of Aug. 8, 1910, he called for the early reception of the sacrament by children. He initiated measures for liturgical reform with new norms for sacred music and the start of work on revision of the Breviary for recitation of the Divine Office.

Modernism: Pius was a vigorous opponent of "the synthesis of all heresies," which threatened the integrity of doctrine through its influence in philosophy, theology and biblical exegesis. In opposition, he condemned 65 of its propositions as erroneous in the decree *Lamentabili* July 3, 1907; issued the encyclical *Pascendi* in the same vein Sept. 8, 1907; backed both of these with censures; and published the Oath against Modernism in September, 1910, to be taken by all the clergy. Ecclesiastical studies suffered to some extent from these actions, necessary as they were at the time.

Pius followed the lead of Leo XIII in promoting the study of scholastic philosophy. He established the Pontifical Biblical Institute May 7, 1909.

His death, Aug. 20, 1914, was hastened by the outbreak of World War I. He was beatified in 1951 and canonized May 29, 1954. His feast is observed Aug. 21.

BENEDICT XV

Benedict XV (Giacomo della Chiesa) was born Nov. 21, 1854, in Pegli, Italy.

He was educated at the Royal University of Genoa and Gregorian University in Rome. He was ordained to the priesthood Dec. 21, 1878.

He served in the papal diplomatic corps from 1882 to 1907; as secretary to the nuncio to Spain from 1882 to 1887, as secretary to the papal secretary of state from 1887, and as undersecretary from 1901.

He was ordained archbishop of Bologna Dec. 22, 1907, and spent four years completing a pastoral visitation there. He was made a cardinal just three months before being elected to the papacy Sept. 3, 1914. He died Jan. 22, 1922. Two key efforts of his pontificate were for peace and the relief of human suffering caused by World War I.

Canonizations: Benedict canonized three saints; one of them was Joan of Arc.

Canon Law: He published the Code of Canon Law, developed by the commission set up by St. Pius X, May 27, 1917; it went into effect the following year.

Curia: He made great changes in the personnel of the Curia. He established the Congregation for the Oriental Churches May 1, 1917, and founded the Pontifical Oriental Institute in Rome later in the year.

Encyclicals: He issued 12 encyclicals. Peace was the theme of three of them. In another, published two years after the cessation of hostilities, he wrote about child victims of the war. He followed the lead of Leo XIII in *Spiritus Paraclitus,* Sept. 15, 1920, on biblical studies.

International Relations: He was largely frustrated on the international level because of the events and attitudes of the war period, but the number of diplomats accredited to the Vatican nearly doubled, from 14 to 26, between the time of his accession to the papacy and his death.

Peace Efforts: Benedict's stance in the war was one of absolute impartiality but not of uninterested neutrality. Because he would not take sides, he was suspected by both sides and the seven-point peace plan he offered to all belligerents Aug. 1, 1917, was turned down. The points of the plan were: recognition of the moral force of right; disarmament; acceptance of arbitration in cases of dispute; guarantee of freedom of the seas; renunciation of war indemnities; evacuation and restoration of occupied territories; examination of territorial claims in dispute.

Relief Efforts: Benedict assumed personal charge of Vatican relief efforts during the war. He set up an international missing persons bureau for contacts between prisoners and their families, but was forced to close it because of the suspicion of warring nations that it was a front for espionage operations. He persuaded the Swiss government to admit into the country military victims of tuberculosis.

Roman Question: Benedict prepared the way for the meetings and negotiations which led to settlement of the question in 1929.

PIUS XI

Pius XI (Ambrogio Damiano Achille Ratti) was born May 31, 1857, in Desio, Italy.

Educated at seminaries in Seviso and Milan, and at the Lombard College, Gregorian University and Academy of St. Thomas in Rome, he was ordained to the priesthood in 1879.

He taught at the major seminary of Milan from 1882 to 1888. Appointed to the staff of the Ambrosian Library in 1888, he remained there until 1911, acquiring a reputation for publishing works on paleography and serving as director from 1907 to 1911. He then moved to the Vatican Library, of which he was prefect from 1914 to 1918. In 1919, he was named apostolic visitor to Poland in April, nuncio in June, and was made titular archbishop of Lepanto Oct. 28. He was made archbishop of Milan and cardinal June 13, 1921, before being elected to the papacy Feb. 6, 1922. He died Feb. 10, 1939.

Aim: The objective of his pontificate, as stated in the encyclical *Ubi Arcano,* Dec. 23, 1922, was to establish the reign and peace of Christ in society.

Canonizations: He canonized 34 saints, including the Jesuit Martyrs of North America, and conferred the title of Doctor of the Church on Sts. Peter Canisius, John of the Cross, Robert Bellarmine and Albertus Magnus.

Eastern Churches: He called for better understanding of the Eastern Churches in the encyclical *Rerum Orientalium* of Sept. 8, 1928, and developed facilities for the training of Eastern-Rite priests. He inaugurated steps for the codification of Eastern-Church law in 1929. In 1935 he made Syrian Patriarch Tappouni a cardinal.

Encyclicals: His first encyclical, *Ubi Arcano,* in addition to stating the aims of his pontificate, blueprinted Catholic Action and called for its development throughout the Church. In *Quas Primas,* Dec. 11, 1925, he established the feast of Christ the King for universal observance. Subjects of some of his other encyclicals were: Christian education, in *Rappresentanti in Terra,* Dec. 31, 1929; Christian marriage, in *Casti Connubii,* Dec. 31, 1930; social conditions and pressure for social change in line with the teaching in *Rerum Novarum,* in *Quadragesimo Anno,* May 15, 1931; atheistic Communism, in *Divini Redemptoris,* Mar. 19, 1937; the priesthood, in *Ad Catholici Sacerdotii,* Dec. 20, 1935.

Missions: Following the lead of Benedict XV, Pius called for the training of native clergy in the pattern of their own respective cultures, and promoted missionary developments in various ways. He ordained six native bishops for China in 1926, one for Japan in 1927, and others for regions of Asia, China and India in 1933. He placed the first 40 mission dioceses under native bishops, saw the number of native priests increase from about 2,600 to more than 7,000 and the number of Catholics in missionary areas more than double from nine million.

In the apostolic constitution *Deus Scientiarum Dominus* of May 24, 1931, he ordered the introduction of missiology into theology courses.

Interfaith Relations: Pius was negative to the ecumenical movement among Protestants but approved the Malines Conversations, 1921 to 1926, between Anglicans and Catholics.

International Relations: Relations with the Mussolini government deteriorated from 1931 on, as indicated in the encyclical *Non Abbiamo Bisogno,* when the regime took steps to curb liberties and activities of the Church; they turned critical in 1938 with the emergence of racist policies. Relations deteriorated also in Germany from 1933 on, resulting finally in condemnation of the Nazis in the encyclical *Mit Brennender Sorge*, March, 1937. Pius sparked a revival of the Church in France by encouraging Catholics to work within the democratic framework of the Republic rather than foment trouble over restoration of a monarchy. Pius was powerless to influence developments related to the civil war which erupted in Spain in July, 1936, sporadic persecution and repression by the Calles regime in Mexico, and systematic persecution of the Church in the Soviet Union. Many of the 10 concordats and two agreements reached with European countries after World War I became casualties of World War II.

Roman Question: Pius negotiated for two and one-half years with the Italian government to settle the Roman Question by means of the Lateran Agreement of 1929. The agreement provided independent status for the State of Vatican City; made Catholicism the official religion of Italy, with pastoral and educational freedom and state recognition of Catholic marriages, religious orders and societies; and provided a financial payment to the Vatican for expropriation of the former States of the Church.

PIUS XII

Pius XII (Eugenio Maria Giovanni Pacelli) was born Mar. 2, 1876, in Rome.

Educated at the Gregorian University and the Lateran University, in Rome, he was ordained to the priesthood Apr. 2, 1899.

He entered the Vatican diplomatic service in 1901, worked on the codification of canon law, and was appointed secretary of the Congregation for Ecclesiastical Affairs in 1914. Three years later he was ordained titular archbishop of Sardis and made apostolic nuncio to Bavaria. He was nuncio to Germany from 1920 to 1929, when he was made a cardinal, and took office as papal secretary of state in the following year. His diplomatic negotiations resulted in concordats between the Vatican and Bavaria (1924), Prussia (1929), Baden (1932), Austria and the German Republic (1933). He took part in negotiations which led to settlement of the Roman Question in 1929.

He was elected to the papacy Mar. 2, 1939. He died Oct. 9, 1958, at Castel Gandolfo after the 12th longest pontificate in history.

Canonizations: He canonized 34 saints, including Mother Frances X. Cabrini, the first U.S. citizen-Saint.

Cardinals: He raised 56 prelates to the rank of cardinal in two consistories held in 1946 and 1953. There were 57 cardinals at the time of his death.

Church Organization and Missions: He increased the number of dioceses from 1,696 to 2,048. He established native hierarchies in China (1946), Burma (1955) and parts of Africa, and extended the native structure of the Church in India. He ordained the first black bishop for Africa.

Communism: In addition to opposing and condemning Communism on numerous occasions, he decreed in 1949 the penalty of excommunication for all Catholics holding formal and willing allegiance to the Communist Party and its policies. During his reign the Church was persecuted in some 15 countries which fell under communist domination.

Doctrine and Liturgy: He proclaimed the dogma of the Assumption of the Blessed Virgin Mary Nov. 1, 1950 (apostolic constitution, *Munificentissimus Deus*).

In various encyclicals and other enactments, he provided background for the aggiornamento introduced by his successor, John XXIII: by his formulations of doctrine and practice regarding the Mystical Body of Christ, the liturgy, sacred music and biblical studies; by the revision of the Rites of Holy Week; by initiation of the work which led to the calendar-missal-breviary reform ordered into effect Jan. 1, 1961; by the first of several modifications of the Eucharistic fast; by extending the time of Mass to the evening. He instituted the feasts of Mary, Queen, and of St. Joseph the Worker, and clarified teaching concerning devotion to the Sacred Heart.

His 41 encyclicals and nearly 1,000 public addresses made Pius one of the greatest teaching popes. His concern in all his communications was to deal with specific points at issue and/or to bring Christian principles to bear on contemporary world problems.

Peace Efforts: Before the start of World War II, he tried unsuccessfully to get the contending nations—Germany and Poland, France and Italy — to settle their differences peaceably. During the war, he offered his services to mediate the widened conflict, spoke out against the horrors of war and the suffering it caused, mobilized relief work for its victims, proposed a five-point program for peace in Christmas messages from 1939 to 1942, and secured a generally open status for the city of Rome. After the war, he endorsed the principles and intent of the United Nations and continued efforts for peace.

United States: Pius appointed more than 200 of the 265 American bishops resident in the U.S. and abroad in 1958, erected 27 dioceses in this country, and raised seven dioceses to archiepiscopal rank.

JOHN XXIII

John XXIII (Angelo Roncalli) was born Nov. 25, 1881, at Sotte il Monte, Italy.

He was educated at the seminary of the Bergamo diocese and the Pontifical Seminary in Rome, where he was ordained to the priesthood Aug. 10, 1904.

He spent the first nine or 10 years of his priesthood as secretary to the bishop of Bergamo and as an instructor in the seminary there. He served as a medic and chaplain in the Italian army during World War I. Afterwards, he resumed duties in his own diocese until he was called to Rome in 1921 for work with the Society for the Propagation of the Faith.

He began diplomatic service in 1925 as titular archbishop of Areopolis and apostolic visitor to Bulgaria. A succession of offices followed: apostolic delegate to Bulgaria (1931-1935); titular archbishop of Mesembria, apostolic delegate to Turkey and Greece, administrator of the Latin vicariate apostolic of Istanbul (1935-1944); apostolic nuncio to France (1944-1953). On these missions, he was engaged in delicate negotiations involving Roman, Eastern-Rite and Orthodox relations; the needs of people suffering from the consequences of World War II; and unsettling suspicions arising from wartime conditions. He was made a cardinal Jan. 12, 1953, and three days later was appointed patriarch of Venice, the position he held until his election to the papacy Oct. 28, 1958. He died of stomach cancer June 3, 1963.

John was a strong and vigorous pope whose influence far out-measured both his age and the shortness of his time in the papacy.

Second Vatican Council: John announced Jan. 25, 1959, his intention of convoking the 21st ecumenical council in history to renew life in the Church, to reform its structures and institutions, and to explore ways and means of promoting unity among Christians. Through the council, which completed its work two and one-half years after his death, he ushered in a new era in the history of the Church.

Canon Law: He established a commission Mar. 28, 1963, for revision of the Code of Canon Law. The revised Code was promulgated in 1983.

Canonizations: He canonized 10 saints and beatified Mother Elizabeth Ann Seton, the first native of the U.S. ever so honored. He named St. Lawrence of Brindisi a Doctor of the Church.

Cardinals: He created 52 cardinals in five consistories, raising membership of the College of Cardinals above the traditional number of 70; at one time in 1962, the membership was 87. He made the college more international in representation than it had ever been, appointing the first cardinals from the Philippines, Japan and Africa. He ordered episcopal ordination for all cardinals. He relieved the suburban bishops of Rome of ordinary jurisdiction over their dioceses so they might devote all their time to business of the Roman Curia.

Eastern Rites: He made all Eastern-Rite patriarchs members of the Congregation for the Oriental Churches.

Ecumenism: He assigned to the Second Vatican Council the task of finding ways and means of promoting unity among Christians. He established the Vatican Secretariat for Promoting Christian Unity June 5, 1960. He showed his desire for more cordial relations with the Orthodox by sending personal representatives to visit Patriarch Athenagoras I June 27, 1961; approved a mission of five delegates to the General Assembly of the World Council of Churches which met in New Delhi, India, in November, 1961; removed a number of pejorative references to Jews in the Roman-Rite liturgy for Good Friday.

Encyclicals: Of the eight encyclicals he issued, the two outstanding ones were *Mater et Magistra* ("Christianity and Social Progress"), in which he recapitulated, updated and extended the social doctrine stated earlier by Leo XIII and Pius XI; and *Pacem in Terris* ("Peace on Earth"), the first encyclical ever addressed to all men of good will as well as to Catholics, on the natural-law principles of peace.

Liturgy: In forwarding liturgical reforms already begun by Pius XII, he ordered a calendar-missal-breviary reform into effect Jan. 1, 1961. He authorized the use of vernacular languages in the administration of the sacraments and approved giving Holy Communion to the sick in afternoon hours. He selected the liturgy as the first topic of major discussion by the Second Vatican Council.

Missions: He issued an encyclical on the missionary activity of the Church; established native hierarchies in Indonesia, Vietnam and Korea; and called on North American superiors of religious institutes to have one-tenth of their members assigned to work in Latin America by 1971.

Peace: John spoke and used his moral influence for peace in 1961 when tension developed over Berlin, in 1962 during the Algerian revolt from France, and later the same year in the Cuban missile crisis. His efforts were singled out for honor by the Balzan Peace Foundation. In 1963, he was posthumously awarded the U.S. Presidential Medal of Freedom.

PAUL VI

Paul VI (Giovanni Battista Montini) was born Sept. 26, 1897, at Concesio in northern Italy.

Educated at Brescia, he was ordained to the priesthood May 29, 1920. He pursued additional studies at the Pontifical Academy for Noble Ecclesiastics and the Pontifical Gregorian University. In 1924 he began 30 years of service in the Secretariat of State; as undersecretary from 1937 until 1954, he was closely associated with Pius XII and was heavily engaged in organizing informational and relief services during and after World War II.

He was ordained archbishop of Milan Dec. 12, 1954, and was inducted into the College of Cardinals Dec. 15, 1958. He was elected to the papacy June 21, 1963, two days after the conclave began. He died of a heart attack Aug. 6, 1978.

Second Vatican Council: He reconvened the Second Vatican Council after the death of John XXIII, presided over its second, third and fourth sessions, formally promulgated the 16 documents it produced, and devoted the whole of his pontificate to the task of putting them into effect throughout the Church. The main thrust of his pontificate — in a milieu of cultural and other changes in the Church and the world — was toward institutionalization and control of the authentic trends articulated and set in motion by the council.

Canonizations: He canonized 84 saints. They included groups of 22 Ugandan martyrs and 40 martyrs of England and Wales, as well as two Americans — Elizabeth Ann Bayley Seton and John Nepomucene Neumann.

Cardinals: He created 144 cardinals, and gave the Sacred College a more international complexion than it ever had before. He limited participation in papal elections to 120 cardinals under the age of 80.

Collegiality: He established the Synod of Bishops in 1965 and called it into session five times. He stimulated the formation and operation of regional conferences of bishops, and of consultative bodies on other levels.

Creed and Holy Year: On June 30, 1968, he issued a Creed of the People of God in conjunction with the celebration of a Year of Faith. He proclaimed and led the observance of a Holy Year from Christmas Eve of 1974 to Christmas Eve of 1975.

Diplomacy: He met with many world leaders, including Soviet President Nikolai Podgorny in 1967, Marshal Tito of Yugoslavia in 1971 and President Nicolas Ceausescu of Romania in 1973. He worked constantly to reduce tension between the Church and the intransigent regimes of Eastern European countries by means of a detente type of policy called Ostpolitik. He agreed to significant revisions of the Vatican's concordat with Spain and initiated efforts to revise the concordat with Italy. More than 40 countries established diplomatic relations with the Vatican during his pontificate.

Encyclicals: He issued seven encyclicals, three of which are the best known. In *Populorum Progressio* ("Development of Peoples") he appealed to wealthy countries to take "concrete action" to promote human development and to remedy imbalances between richer and poorer nations; this encyclical, coupled with other documents and related actions, launched the Church into a new depth of involvement as a public advocate for human rights and for humanizing social, political and economic policies. In *Sacerdotalis Caelibatus* ("Priestly Celibacy") he reaffirmed the strict observance of priestly celibacy throughout the Western Church. In *Humanae Vitae* ("Of Human Life") he condemned abortion, sterilization and artificial birth control, in line with traditional teaching and in "defense of life, the gift of God, the glory of the family, the strength of the people."

Interfaith Relations: He initiated formal consultation and informal dialogue on international and national levels between Catholics and non-Catholics — Orthodox, Anglicans, Protestants, Jews, Muslims, Buddhists, Hindus, and unbelievers. He and Greek Orthodox Patriarch Athenagoras I of Constantinople nullified in 1965 the mutual excommunications imposed by their respective churches in 1054.

Liturgy: He carried out the most extensive liturgical reform in history, involving a new Order of the Mass effective in 1969, a revised church calendar in 1970, revisions and translations into vernacular languages of all sacramental rites and other liturgical texts.

Ministries: He authorized the restoration of the permanent diaconate in the Roman Rite and the establishment of new ministries of lay persons.

Peace: In 1968, he instituted the annual observance of a World Day of Peace on New Year's Day as a means of addressing a message of peace to all the world's political leaders and the peoples of all nations. The most dramatic of his many appeals for peace and efforts to ease international tensions was his plea for "No more war!" before the United Nations Oct. 4, 1965.

Pilgrimages: A "Pilgrim Pope," he made pastoral visits to the Holy Land and India in 1964, the United Nations and New York City in 1965, Portugal and Turkey in 1967, Colombia in 1968, Switzerland and Uganda in 1969, and Asia, Pacific islands and Australia in 1970. While in Manila in 1970, he was stabbed by a Bolivian artist who made an attempt on his life.

Roman Curia: He reorganized the central administrative organs of the Church in line with provisions of the apostolic constitution, *Regimini Ecclesiae Universae,* streamlining procedures for more effective service and giving the agencies a more international perspective by drawing officials and consultors from all over the world. He also instituted a number of new commissions and other bodies. Coupled with curial reorganization was a simplification of papal ceremonies.

JOHN PAUL I

John Paul I (Albino Luciani) was born Oct. 17, 1912, in Forno di Canale (now Canale d'Agordo) in northern Italy.

Educated at the minor seminary in Feltre and the major seminary of the Diocese of Belluno, he was ordained to the priesthood July 7, 1935. He pursued further studies at the Pontifical Gregorian University in Rome and was awarded a doctorate in theology. From 1937 to 1947 he was vice rector of the Belluno seminary, where he taught dogmatic and moral theology, canon law and sacred art. He was appointed vicar general of his diocese in 1947 and served as director of catechetics.

Ordained bishop of Vittorio Veneto Dec. 27, 1958, he attended all sessions of the Second Vatican Council, participated in three assemblies of the Synod of Bishops (1971, 1974 and 1977), and was vice president of the Italian Bishops' Conference from 1972 to 1975.

He was appointed archbishop and patriarch of Venice Dec. 15, 1969, and was inducted into the College of Cardinals Mar. 5, 1973.

He was elected to the papacy Aug. 26, 1978, on the fourth ballot cast by the 111 cardinals participating in the largest and one of the shortest conclaves in history. The quickness of his election was matched by the brevity of his pontificate of 33 days, during which he delivered 19 addresses. He died of a heart attack Sept. 28, 1978.

JOHN PAUL II

See separate entry.

PAPAL ENCYCLICALS — BENEDICT XIV (1740) TO JOHN PAUL II

(Source: *The Papal Encyclicals* [5 vols.], Claudia Carlen, I.H.M.; Pieran Press, Ann Arbor, Mich. Used with permission.)

An encyclical letter is a pastoral letter addressed by a pope to the whole Church. In general, it concerns matters of doctrine, morals or discipline, or significant commemorations. Its formal title consists of the first few words of the official text. Some encyclicals, notably *Pacem in terris* by John XXIII, *Ecclesiam Suam* by Paul VI and several by John Paul II, have been addressed to people of good will in general as well as to bishops and the faithful in communion with the Church.

An encyclical epistle resembles an encyclical letter but is addressed only to part of the Church.

The authority of encyclicals was stated by Pius XII in the encyclical *Humani generis* Aug. 12, 1950: "Nor must it be thought that what is contained in encyclical letters does not of itself demand assent, on the pretext that the popes do not exercise in them the supreme power of their teaching authority. Rather, such teachings belong to the ordinary magisterium, of which it is true to say: 'He who hears you, hears me' (Lk. 10:16); for the most part, too, what is expounded and inculcated in encyclical letters already appertains to Catholic doctrine for other reasons."

The Second Vatican Council declared: "Religious submission of will and of mind must be shown in a special way to the authentic teaching authority of the Roman Pontiff, even when he is not speaking *ex cathedra*. That is, it must be shown in such a way that his supreme magisterium is acknowledged with reverence, the judgments made by him are sincerely adhered to, according to his manifest mind and will. His mind and will in the matter may be known chiefly either from the character of the documents (one of which could be an encyclical), from his frequent repetition of the same doctrine, or from his manner of speaking" (*Dogmatic Constitution on the Church*, No. 25).

The following list contains the titles and indicates the subject matter of encyclical letters and epistles. The latter are generally distinguishable by the limited scope of their titles or contents.

Benedict XIV
(1740-1758)

1740: *Ubi primum* (On the duties of bishops), Dec. 3.

1741: *Quanta cura* (Forbidding traffic in alms), June 30.

1743: *Nimiam licentiam* (To the bishops of Poland: on validity of marriages), May 18.

1745: *Vix pervenit* (To the bishops of Italy: on usury and other dishonest profit), Nov. 1.

1748: *Magnae Nobis* (To the bishops of Poland: on marriage impediments and dispensations), June 29.

1749: *Peregrinantes* (To all the faithful: proclaiming a Holy Year for 1750), May 5.

Apostolica Constitutio (On preparation for the Holy Year), June 26.

1751: *A quo primum* (To the bishops of Poland: on Jews and Christians living in the same place), June 14.

1754: *Cum Religiosi* (To the bishops of the States of the Church: on catechesis), June 26.

Quod Provinciale (To the bishops of Albania: on Christians using Mohammedan names), Aug. 1.

1755: *Allatae sunt* (To missionaries of the Orient: on the observance of Oriental rites), July 26.

1756: *Ex quo primum* (To bishops of the Greek rite: on the Euchologion), Mar. 1.

Ex omnibus (To the bishops of France: on the apostolic constitution, *Unigenitus*), Oct. 16.

Clement XIII
(1758-1769)

1758: *A quo die* (Unity among Christians), Sept. 13.

1759: *Cum primum* (On observing canonical sanctions), Sept. 17.

Appetente Sacro (On the spiritual advantages of fasting), Dec. 20.

1761: *In Dominico agro* (On instruction in the faith), June 14.

1766: *Christianae reipublicae* (On the dangers of anti-Christian writings), Nov. 25.

1768: *Summa quae* (To the bishops of Poland: on the Church in Poland), Jan. 6.

Clement XIV
(1769-1774)

1769: *Decet quam maxime* (To the bishops of Sardinia: on abuses in taxes and benefices), Sept. 21.

Inscrutabili divinae sapientiae (To all Christians: proclaiming a universal jubilee), Dec. 12.

Cum summi (Proclaiming a universal jubilee), Dec. 12.

1774: *Salutis nostra* (To all Christians: proclaiming a universal jubilee), Apr. 30.

Pius VI
(1775-1799)

1775: *Inscrutabile* (On the problems of the pontificate), Dec. 25.

1791: *Charitas* (To the bishops of France: on the civil oath in France), Apr. 13.

Pius VII
(1800-1823)

1800: *Diu satis* (To the bishops of France: on a return to Gospel principles), May 15.

Leo XII
(1823-1829)

1824: *Ubi primum* (To all bishops: on Leo XII's assuming the pontificate), May 5.

Quod hoc ineunte (Proclaiming a universal jubilee), May 24.

1825: *Charitate Christi* (Extending jubilee to the entire Church), Dec. 25.

Pius VIII
(1829-1830)

1829: *Traditi humilitati* (On Pius VIII's program for the pontificate), May 24.

Gregory XVI
(1831-1846)

1832: *Summo iugiter studio* (To the bishops of Bavaria: on mixed marriages), May 27.

Cum primum (To the bishops of Poland: on civil obedience), June 9.

Mirari vos (On liberalism and religious indifferentism), Aug. 15.

1833: *Quo graviora* (To the bishops of the Rhineland: on the "pragmatic Constitution"), Oct. 4.

1834: *Singulari Nos* (On the errors of Lammenais), June 25.

1835: *Commissum divinitus* (To clergy of Switzerland: on Church and State), May 17.

1840: *Probe nostis* (On the Propagation of the Faith), Sept. 18.

1841: *Quas vestro* (To the bishops of Hungary: on mixed marriages), Apr. 30.

1844: *Inter praecipuas* (On biblical societies), May 8.

Pius IX
(1846-1878)

1846: *Qui pluribus* (On faith and religion), Nov. 9.

1847: *Praedecessores Nostros* (On aid for Ireland), Mar. 25.

Ubi primum (To religious superiors: on discipline for religious), June 17.

1849: *Ubi primum* (On the Immaculate Conception), Feb. 2.

Nostis et Nobiscum (To the bishops of Italy: on the Church in the Pontifical States), Dec. 8.

1851: *Exultavit cor Nostrum* (On the effects of jubilee), Nov. 21.

1852: *Nemo certe ignorat* (To the bishops of Ireland: on the discipline for clergy), Mar. 25.

Probe noscitis Venerabiles (To the bishops of Spain: on the discipline for clergy), May 17.

1853: *Inter multiplices* (To the bishops of France: pleading for unity of spirit), Mar. 21.

1854: *Neminem vestrum* (To clergy and faithful of Constantinople: on the persecution of Armenians), Feb. 2.

Optime noscitis (To the bishops of Ireland: on the proposed Catholic university for Ireland), Mar. 20.

Apostolicae Nostrae caritatis (Urging prayers for peace), Aug. 1.

1855: *Optime noscitis* (To the bishops of Austria: on episcopal meetings), Nov. 5.

1856: *Singulari quidem* (To the bishops of Austria: on the Church in Austria), Mar. 17.

1858: *Cum nuper* (To the bishops of the Kingdom of the Two Sicilies: on care for clerics), Jan. 20.

Amantissimi Redemptoris (On priests and the care of souls), May 3.

1859: *Cum sancta mater Ecclesia* (Pleading for public prayer), Apr. 27.

Qui nuper (On Pontifical States), June 18.

1860: Nullis certe verbis (On the need for civil sovereignty), Jan. 19.

1862: *Amantissimus* (To bishops of the Oriental rite: on the care of the churches), Apr. 8.

1863: *Quanto conficiamur moerore* (To the bishops of Italy: on promotion of false doctrines), Aug. 10.

Incredibili (To the bishops of Bogota: on persecution in New Granada), Sept. 17.

1864: *Maximae quidem* (To the bishops of Bavaria: on the Church in Bavaria), Aug. 18.

Quanta cura (Condemning current errors), Dec. 8.

1865: *Meridionali Americae* (To the bishops of South America: on the seminary for native clergy), Sept. 30.

1867: *Levate* (On the afflictions of the Church), Oct. 27.

1870: *Respicientes* (Protesting the taking of the Pontifical States), Nov. 1.

1871: *Ubi Nos* (To all bishops: on Pontifical States), May 15.

Beneficia Dei (On the twenty-fifth anniversary of his pontificate), June 4.

Saepe Venerabiles Fratres (On thanksgiving for twenty-five years of pontificate), Aug. 5.

1872: *Quae in Patriarchatu* (To bishops and people of Chaldea: on the Church in Chaldea), Nov. 16.

1873: *Quartus supra* (To bishops and people of the Armenian rite: on the Church in Armenia), Jan. 6.

Etsi multa (On the Church in Italy, Germany and Switzerland), Nov. 21.

1874: *Vix dum a Nobis* (To the bishops of Austria: on the Church in Austria), Mar. 7.

Gravibus Ecclesiae (To all bishops and faithful: proclaiming a jubilee for 1875), Dec. 24.

1875: *Quod nunquam* (To the bishops of Prussia: on the Church in Prussia), Feb. 5.

Graves ac diuturnae (To the bishops of Switzerland: on the Church in Switzerland), Mar. 23.

Leo XIII
(1878-1903)

1878: *Inscrutabili Dei consilio* (On the evils of society), Apr. 21.

Quod Apostolici muneris (On socialism), Dec. 28.

1879: *Aeterni Patris* (On the restoration of Christian philosophy), Aug. 4.

1880: *Arcanum* (On Christian marriage), Feb. 10.

Grande munus (On Sts. Cyril and Methodius), Sept. 30.

Sancta Dei civitas (On mission societies), Dec. 3.

1881: *Diuturnum* (On the origin of civil power), June 29.

Licet multa (To the bishops of Belgium: on Catholics in Belgium), Aug. 3.

1882: *Etsi Nos* (To the bishops of Italy: on conditions in Italy), Feb. 15.

Auspicato concessum (On St. Francis of Assisi), Sept. 17.

Cum multa (To the bishops of Spain: on conditions in Spain), Dec. 8.

1883: *Supremi Apostolatus officio* (On devotion to the Rosary), Sept. 1.

1884: *Nobilissima Gallorum gens* (To the bishops of France: on the religious question), Feb. 8.

Humanum genus (On Freemasonry), Apr. 20.

Superiore anno (On the recitation of the Rosary), Aug. 30.

1885: *Immortale Dei* (On the Christian constitution of states), Nov. 1.

Spectata fides (To the bishops of England: on Christian education), Nov. 27.

Quod auctoritate (Proclamation of extraordinary Jubilee), Dec. 22.

1886: *Iampridem* (To the bishops of Prussia: on Catholicism in Germany), Jan. 6.

Quod multum (To the bishops of Hungary: on the liberty of the Church), Aug. 22.

Pergrata (To the bishops of Portugal: on the Church in Portugal), Sept. 14.

1887: *Vi e ben noto* (To the bishops of Italy: on the Rosary and public life), Sept. 20.

Officio sanctissimo (To the bishops of Bavaria: on the Church in Bavaria), Dec. 22.

1888: *Quod anniversarius* (On his sacerdotal jubilee), Apr. 1.

In plurimis (To the bishops of Brazil: on the abolition of slavery), May 5.

Libertas (On the nature of human liberty), June 20.

Saepe Nos (To the bishops of Ireland: on boycotting in Ireland), June 24.

Paterna caritas (To the Patriarch of Cilicia and the archbishops and bishops of the Armenian people: on reunion with Rome), July 25.

Quam aerumnosa (To the bishops of America: on Italian immigrants), Dec. 10.

Etsi cunctas (To the bishops of Ireland: on the Church in Ireland), Dec. 21.

Exeunte iam anno (On the right ordering of Christian life), Dec. 25.

1889: *Magni Nobis* (To the bishops of the United

States: on the Catholic University of America), Mar. 7.

Quamquam pluries (On devotion to St. Joseph),Aug. 15.

1890: *Sapientiae Christianae* (On Christians as citizens), Jan. 10.

Dall'alto Dell'Apostolico seggio (To the bishops and people of Italy: on Freemasonry in Italy), Oct. 15.

Catholicae Ecclesiae (On slavery in the missions), Nov. 20.

1891: *In ipso* (To the bishops of Austria: on episcopal reunions in Austria), Mar. 3.

Rerum novarum (On capital and labor), May 15.

Pastoralis (To the bishops of Portugal: on religious union), June 25.

Pastoralis officii (To the bishops of Germany and Austria: on the morality of dueling), Sept. 12.

Octobri mense (On the Rosary), Sept. 22.

1892: *Au milieu des sollicitudes* (To the bishops, clergy and faithful of France: on the Church and State in France), Feb. 16.

Quarto abeunte saeculo (To the bishops of Spain, Italy, and the two Americas: on the Columbus quadricentennial), July 16.

Magnae Dei Matris (On the Rosary), Sept. 8.

Inimica vis (To the bishops of Italy: on Freemasonry), Dec. 8.

Custodi di quella fede (To the Italian people: on Freemasonry), Dec. 8.

1893: *Ad extremas* (On seminaries for native clergy), June 24.

Constanti Hungarorum (To the bishops of Hungary: on the Church in Hungary), Sept. 2.

Laetitiae sanctae (Commending devotion to the Rosary), Sept. 8.

Non mediocri (To the bishops of Spain: on the Spanish College in Rome), Oct. 25.

Providentissimus Deus (On the study of Holy Scripture), Nov. 18.

1894: *Caritatis* (To the bishops of Poland: on the Church in Poland), Mar. 19.

Inter graves (To the bishops of Peru: on the Church in Peru), May 1.

Litteras a vobis (To the bishops of Brazil: on the clergy in Brazil), July 2.

Iucunda semper expectatione (On the Rosary), Sept. 8.

Christi nomen (On the propagation of the Faith and Eastern churches), Dec. 24.

1895: *Longinqua* (To the bishops of the United States: on Catholicism in the United States), Jan. 6.

Permoti Nos (To the bishops of Belgium: on social conditions in Belgium), July 10.

Adiutricem (On the Rosary), Sept. 5.

1896: *Insignes* (To the bishops of Hungary: on the Hungarian millennium), May 1.

Satis cognitum (On the unity of the Church), June 29.

Fidentem piumque animum (On the Rosary), Sept. 20.

1897: *Divinum illud munus* (On the Holy Spirit), May 9.

Militantis Ecclesiae (To the bishops of Austria, Germany, and Switzerland: on St. Peter Canisius), Aug. 1.

Augustissimae Virginis Mariae (On the Confraternity of the Holy Rosary), Sept. 12.

Affari vos (To the bishops of Canada: on the Manitoba school question), Dec. 8.

1898: *Caritatis studium* (To the bishops of Scotland: on the Church in Scotland), July 25.

Spesse volte (To the bishops, priests, and people of Italy: on the suppression of Catholic institutions), Aug. 5.

Quam religiosa (To the bishops of Peru: on civil marriage law), Aug. 16.

Diuturni temporis (On the Rosary), Sept. 5.

Quum diuturnum (To the bishops of Latin America: on Latin American bishops' plenary council), Dec. 25.

1899: *Annum Sacrum* (On consecration to the Sacred Heart), May 25.

Depuis le jour (To the archbishops, bishops, and clergy of France: on the education of the clergy), Sept. 8.

Paternae (To the bishops of Brazil: on the education of the clergy), Sept. 18.

1900: *Omnibus compertum* (To the Patriarch and bishops of the Greek-Melkite rite: on unity among the Greek Melkites), July 21.

Tametsi futura prospicientibus (On Jesus Christ the Redeemer), Nov. 1.

1901: *Graves de communi re* (On Christian democracy), Jan. 18.

Gravissimas (To the bishops of Portugal: on religious orders in Portugal), May 16.

Reputantibus (To the bishops of Bohemia and Moravia: on the language question in Bohemia), Aug. 20.

Urbanitatis Veteris (To the bishops of the Latin church in Greece: on the foundation of a seminary in Athens), Nov. 20.

1902: *In amplissimo* (To the bishops of the United States: on the Church in the United States), Apr. 15.

Quod votis (To the bishops of Austria: on the proposed Catholic University), Apr. 30.

Mirae caritatis (On the Holy Eucharist), May 28.

Quae ad Nos (To the bishops of Bohemia and Moravia: on the Church in Bohemia and Moravia), Nov. 22.

Fin dal principio (To the bishops of Italy: on the education of the clergy), Dec. 8.

Dum multa (To the bishops of Ecuador: on marriage legislation), Dec. 24.

Saint Pius X
(1903-1914)

1903: *E supremi* (On the restoration of all things in Christ), Oct. 4.

1904: *Ad diem illum laetissimum* (On the Immaculate Conception), Feb. 2.

Iucunda sane (On Pope Gregory the Great), Mar. 12.

1905: *Acerbo nimis* (On teaching Christian doctrine), Apr. 15.

Il fermo proposito (To the bishops of Italy: on Catholic Action in Italy), June 11.

1906: *Vehementer Nos* (To the bishops, clergy, and people of France: on the French Law of Separation), Feb. 11.

Tribus circiter (On the Mariavites or Mystic Priests of Poland), Apr. 5.

Pieni l'animo (To the bishops of Italy: on the clergy in Italy), July 28.

Gravissimo officio munere (To the bishops of France: on French associations of worship), Aug. 10.

1907: *Une fois encore* (To the bishops, clergy, and people of France: on the separation of Church and State), Jan. 6.

Pascendi dominici gregis (On the doctrines of the Modernists), Sept. 8.

1909: *Communium rerum* (On St. Anselm of Aosta), Apr. 21.

1910: *Editae saepe* (On St. Charles Borromeo), May 26.

1911: *Iamdudum* (On the Law of Separation in Portugal), May 24.

1912: *Lacrimabili statu* (To the bishops of Latin America: on the Indians of South America), June 7.

Singulari quadam (To the bishops of Germany: on labor organizations), Sept. 24.

Benedict XV
(1914-1922)

1914: *Ad beatissimi Apostolorum* (Appeal for peace), Nov. 1.

1917: *Humani generis Redemptionem* (On preaching the Word of God), June 15.

1918: *Quod iam diu* (On the future peace conference), Dec. 1.

1919: *In hac tanta* (To the bishops of Germany: on St. Boniface), May 14.

Paterno iam diu (On children of central Europe), Nov. 24.

1920: *Pacem, Dei munus pulcherrimum* (On peace and Christian reconciliation), May 23.

Spiritus Paraclitus (On St. Jerome), Sept. 15.

Principi Apostolorum Petro (On St. Ephrem the Syrian), Oct. 5.

Annus iam plenus (On children of central Europe), Dec. 1.

1921: *Sacra propediem* (On the Third Order of St. Francis), Jan. 6.

In praeclara summorum (To professors and students of fine arts in Catholic institutions of learning: on Dante), Apr. 30.

Fausto appetente die (On St. Dominic), June 29.

Pius XI
(1922-1939)

1922: *Ubi arcano Dei consilio* (On the peace of Christ in the Kingdom of Christ), Dec. 23.

1923: *Rerum omnium perturbationem* (On St. Francis de Sales), Jan. 26.

Studiorum Ducem (On St. Thomas Aquinas), June 29.

Ecclesiam Dei (On St. Josaphat), Nov. 12.

1924: *Maximam gravissimamque* (To the bishops, clergy, and people of France: on French diocesan associations), Jan. 18.

1925: *Quas primas* (On the feast of Christ the King), Dec. 11.

1926: *Rerum Ecclesiae* (On Catholic missions), Feb. 28.

Rite expiatis (On St. Francis of Assisi), Apr. 30.

Iniquis afflictisque (On the persecution of the Church in Mexico), Nov. 18.

1928: *Mortalium animos* (On religious unity), Jan. 6.

Miserentissimus Redemptor (On reparation to the Sacred Heart), May 8.

Rerum Orientalium (On the promotion of Oriental Studies), Sept. 8.

1929: *Mens Nostra* (On the promotion of Spiritual Exercises), Dec. 20.

Quinquagesimo ante (On his sacerdotal jubilee), Dec. 23.

Rappresentanti in terra (On Christian education), Dec. 31. [Latin text, *Divini illius magistri*, published several months later with minor changes.]

1930: *Ad salutem* (On St. Augustine), Apr. 20.

Casti connubii (On Christian Marriage), Dec. 31.

1931: *Quadragesimo anno* (Commemorating the fortieth anniversary of Leo XIII's *Rerum novarum*: on reconstruction of the soical order), May 15.

Non abbiamo bisogno (On Catholic Action in Italy), June 29.

Nova impendet (On the economic crisis), Oct. 2.

Lux veritatis (On the Council of Ephesus), Dec. 25.

1932: *Caritate Christi compulsi* (On the Sacred Heart), May 3.

Acerba animi (To the bishops of Mexico: on persecution of the Church in Mexico), Sept. 29.

1933: *Dilectissima Nobis* (To the bishops, clergy, and people of Spain: on oppression of the Church in Spain), June 3.

1935: *Ad Catholici sacerdotii* (On the Catholic priesthood), Dec. 20.

1936: *Vigilanti cura* (To the bishops of the United States: on motion pictures), June 29.

1937: *Mit brennender Sorge* (To the bishops of Germany: on the Church and the German Reich), Mar. 14.

Divini Redemptoris (On atheistic communism), Mar. 19.

Nos es muy conocida (To the bishops of Mexico: on the religious situation in Mexico), Mar. 28.

Ingravescentibus malis (On the Rosary) Sept. 29.

Pius XII
(1939-1958)

1939: *Summi Pontificatus* (On the unity of human society), Oct. 20.

Sertum laetitiae (To the bishops of the United States: on the 150th anniversary of the establishment of the hierarchy in the United States), Nov. 1.

1940: *Saeculo exeunte octavo* (To the bishops of Portugal and its colonies: on the eighth centenary of the independence of Portugal), June 13.

1943: *Mystici Corporis Christi* (On the Mystical Body of Christ), June 29.

Divino afflante Spiritu (On promoting biblical studies, commemorating the fiftieth anniversary of *Providentissimus Deus*), Sept. 30.

1944: *Orientalis Ecclesiae* (On St. Cyril, Patriarch of Alexandria), Apr. 9.

1945: *Communium interpretes dolorum* (To the bishops of the world: appealing for prayers for peace during May), Apr. 15.

Orientales omnes Ecclesias (On the 350th anniversary of the reunion of the Ruthenian Church with the Apostolic See), Dec. 23.

1946: *Quemadmodum* (Pleading for the care of the world's destitute children), Jan. 6.

Deiparae Virginis Mariae (To all bishops: on the possibility of defining the Assumption of the Blessed Virgin Mary as a dogma of faith), May 1.

1947: *Fulgens radiatur* (On St. Benedict), Mar. 21.

Mediator Dei (On the sacred liturgy), Nov. 20.

Optatissima pax (Prescribing public prayers for social and world peace), Dec. 18.

1948: *Auspicia quaedam* (On public prayers for world peace and solution of the problem of Palestine), May 1.

In multiplicibus curis (On prayers for peace in Palestine), Oct. 24.

1949: *Redemptoris nostri cruciatus* (On the holy places in Palestine), Apr. 15.

1950: *Anni Sacri* (On the program for combatting atheistic propaganda throughout the world), Mar. 12.

Summi maeroris (On public prayers for peace), July 19.

Humani generis (Concerning some false opinions threatening to undermine the foundations of Catholic doctrine), Aug. 12.

Mirabile illud (On the crusade of prayers for peace), Dec. 6.

1951: *Evangelii praecones* (On the promotion of Catholic missions), June 2.

Sempiternus Rex Christus (On the Council of Chalcedon), Sept. 8.

Ingruentium malorum (On reciting the Rosary), Sept. 15.

1952: *Orientales Ecclesias* (On the persecuted Eastern Church), Dec. 15.

1953: *Doctor Mellifluus* (On St. Bernard of Clairvaux, the last of the fathers), May 24.

Fulgens corona (Proclaiming a Marian Year to commemorate the centenary of the definition of the dogma of the Immaculate Conception), Sept. 8.

1954: *Sacra virginitas* (On consecrated virginity), Mar. 25.

Ecclesiae fastos (To the bishops of Great Britain, Germany, Austria, France, Belgium, and Holland: on St. Boniface), June 5.

Ad Sinarum gentem (To the bishops, clergy, and people of China: on the supranationality of the Church), Oct. 7.

Ad Caeli Reginam (Proclaiming the Queenship of Mary), Oct. 11.

1955: *Musicae sacrae* (On sacred music), Dec. 25.

1956: *Haurietis aquas* (On devotion to the Sacred Heart), May 15.

Luctuosissimi eventus (Urging public prayers for peace and freedom for the people of Hungary), Oct. 28.

Laetamur admodum (Renewing exhortation for prayers for peace for Poland, Hungary, and especially for the Middle East), Nov. 1.

Datis nuperrime (Lamenting the sorrowful events in Hungary and condemning the ruthless use of force), Nov. 5.

1957: *Fidei donum* (On the present condition of the Catholic missions, especially in Africa), Apr. 21.

Invicti athletae (On St. Andrew Bobola), May 16.

Le pelerinage de Lourdes (Warning against materialism on the centenary of the apparitions at Lourdes), July 2.

Miranda prorsus (On the communications field: motion picture, radio, television), Sept. 8.

1958: *Ad Apostolorum Principis* (To the bishops of China; on Communism and the Church in China), June 29.

Meminisse iuvat (On prayers for persecuted Church), July 14.

John XXIII
(1958-1963)

1959: *Ad Petri Cathedram* (On truth, unity, and peace, in a spirit of charity), June 29.

Sacerdotii Nostri primordia (On St. John Vianney), Aug. 1.

Grata recordatio (On the Rosary: prayer for the Church, missions, international and social problems), Sept. 26.

Princeps Pastorum (On the missions, native clergy, lay participation), Nov. 28.

1961: *Mater et Magistra* (On Christianity and social progress), May 15.

Aeterna Dei sapientia (On fifteenth centenary of the death of Pope St. Leo I: the see of Peter as the center of Christian unity), Nov. 11.

1962: *Paenitentiam agere* (On the need for the practice of interior and exterior penance), July 1.

1963: *Pacem in terris* (On establishing universal peace in truth, justice, charity, and liberty), Apr. 11.

Paul VI
(1963-1978)

1964: *Ecclesiam Suam* (On the Church), Aug. 6.

1965: *Mense maio* (On prayers during May for the preservation of peace), Apr. 29.

Mysterium Fidei (On the Holy Eucharist), Sept. 3.

1966: *Christi Matri* (On prayers for peace during October), Sept. 15.

1967: *Populorum progressio* (On the development of peoples), Mar. 26.

Sacerdotalis caelibatus (On the celibacy of the priest), June 24.

1968: *Humanae vitae* (On the regulation of birth), July 25.

John Paul II
(1978-)

1979: *Redemptor hominis* (On redemption and dignity of the human race), Mar. 4

1980: *Dives in misericordia* (On the mercy of God), Nov. 30.

1981: *Laborem exercens* (On human work), Sept. 14.

1985: *Slavorum Apostoli* (Commemorating Sts. Cyril and Methodius, on the eleventh centenary of the death of St. Methodius), June 2.

1986: *Dominum et Vivificantem* (On the Holy Spirit in the life of the Church and the world), May 18.

1987: *Redemptoris Mater* (On the role of Mary in the mystery of Christ and her active and exemplary presence in the life of the Church), Mar. 25.

Sollicitudo Rei Socialis (On social concerns, on the twentieth anniversary of *Populorum progressio*), Dec. 30.

1991: *Redemptoris missio* (On the permanent validity of the Church's missionary mandate), Jan. 22.

Centesimus annus (Commemorating the centenary of *Rerum novarum* and addressing the social question in a contemporary perspective), May 1.

1993: *Veritatis Splendor* (Regarding fundamental questions on the Church's moral teaching), Aug. 6.

1995: *Evangelium Vitae* (On the value and inviolability of human life), Mar. 25.

Ut Unum Sint (On commitment to ecumenism), May 25.

CANONIZATIONS BY LEO XIII AND HIS SUCCESSORS

Canonization (see entry in Glossary) is an infallible declaration by the pope that a person who suffered martyrdom and/or practiced Christian virtue to a heroic degree is in glory with God in heaven and is worthy of public honor by the universal Church and of imitation by the faithful.

Biographies of some of the saints listed below are given elsewhere in the Almanac. See Index.

Leo XIII
(1878-1903)

1881: Clare of Montefalco (d. 1308); John Baptist de Rossi (1698-1764); Lawrence of Brindisi (d. 1619).

1883: Benedict J. Labre (1748-1783).

1888: Seven Holy Founders of the Servite Order; Peter Claver (1581-1654); John Berchmans (1599-1621); Alphonsus Rodriguez (1531-1617).

1897: Anthony M. Zaccaria (1502-1539); Peter Fourier of Our Lady (1565-1640).

1900: John Baptist de La Salle (1651-1719); Rita of Cascia (1381-1457).

St. Pius X
(1903-1914)

1904: Alexander Sauli (1534-1593); Gerard Majella (1725-1755).

1909: Joseph Oriol (1650-1702); Clement M. Hofbauer (1751-1820).

Benedict XV
(1914-1922)

1920: Gabriel of the Sorrowful Mother (1838-1862); Margaret Mary Alacoque (1647-1690); Joan of Arc (1412-1431).

Pius XI
(1922-1939)

1925: Therese of Lisieux (1873-1897); Peter Canisius (1521-1597); Mary Magdalen Postel (1756-1846); Mary Magdalen Sophie Barat (1779-1865); John Eudes (1601-1680); John Baptist Vianney (Curé of Ars) (1786-1859).

1930: Lucy Filippini (1672-1732); Catherine Tomas (1533-1574); Jesuit North American Martyrs; Robert Bellarmine (1542-1621); Theophilus of Corte (1676-1740).

1931: Albert the Great (1206-1280) (equivalent canonization).

1933: Andrew Fournet (1752-1834); Bernadette Soubirous (1844-1879).

1934: Joan Antida Thouret (1765-1826); Mary Michaeli (1809-1865); Louise de Marillac (1591-1660); Joseph Benedict Cottolengo (1786-1842); Pompilius M. Pirotti, priest (1710-1756); Teresa Margaret Redi (1747-1770); John Bosco (1815-1888); Conrad of Parzham (1818-1894).

1935: John Fisher (1469-1535); Thomas More (1478-1535).

1938: Andrew Bobola (1592-1657); John Leonardi (c. 1550-1609); Salvatore of Horta (1520-1567).

Pius XII
(1939-1958)

1940: Gemma Galgani (1878-1903); Mary Euphrasia Pelletier (1796-1868).

1943: Margaret of Hungary (d. 1270) (equvalent canonization).

1946: Frances Xavier Cabrini (1850-1917).

1947: Nicholas of Flue (1417-1487); John of Britto (1647-1693); Bernard Realini (1530-1616); Joseph Cafasso (1811-1860); Michael Garicoits (1797-1863); Jeanne Elizabeth des Ages (1773-1838); Louis Marie Grignon de Montfort (1673-1716); Catherine Laboure (1806-1876).

1949: Jeanne de Lestonnac (1556-1640); Maria Josepha Rossello (1811-1880).

1950: Emily de Rodat (1787-1852); Anthony Mary Claret (1807-1870); Bartolomea Capitanio (1807-1833); Vincenza Gerosa (1784-1847) Jeanne de Valois (1461-1504); Vincenzo M. Strambi (1745-1824); Maria Goretti (1890-1902); Mariana Paredes of Jesus (1618-1645).

1951: Maria Domenica Mazzarello (1837-1881); Emilie de Vialar (1797-1856); Anthony M. Gianelli (1789-1846); Ignatius of Laconi (1701-1781); Francis Xavier Bianchi (1743-1815).

1954: Pope Pius X (1835-1914); Dominic Savio (1842-1857); Maria Crocifissa di Rosa (1813-1855); Peter Chanel (1803-1841); Gaspar del Bufalo (1786-1837); Joseph M. Pignatelli (1737-1811).

1958: Herman Joseph, O. Praem. (1150-1241) (equivalent canonization).

John XXIII
(1958-1963)

1959: Joaquina de Vedruna de Mas (1783-1854); Charles of Sezze (1613-1670).

1960: Gregory Barbarigo (1625-1697) (equivalent canonization); John de Ribera (1532-1611).

1961: Bertilla Boscardin (1888-1922).

1962: Martin de Porres (1579-1639); Peter Julian Eymard (1811-1868); Anthony Pucci, priest (1819-1892); Francis Mary of Camporosso (1804-1866).

1963: Vincent Pallotti (1795-1850).

Paul VI
(1963-1978)

1964: Charles Lwanga and Twenty-One Companions, Martyrs of Uganda (d. between 1885-1887).

1967: Benilde Romacon (1805-1862).

1969: Julia Billiart (1751-1816).

1970: Maria Della Dolorato Torres Acosta (1826-

1887); Leonard Murialdo (1828-1900); Therese Couderc (1805-1885); John of Avila (1499-1569); Nicholas Tavelic, Deodatus of Aquitaine, Peter of Narbonne and Stephen of Cuneo, martyrs (d. 1391); Forty English and Welsh Martyrs (d. 16th cent.).
1974: Teresa of Jesus Jornet Ibars (1843-1897).
1975: Vicenta Maria Lopez y Vicuna (1847-1890); Elizabeth Bayley Seton (1774-1821); John Masias (1585-1645); Oliver Plunket (1629-1681); Justin de Jacobis (1800-1860); John Baptist of the Conception (1561-1613).
1976: Beatrice da Silva (1424 or 1426-1490); John Ogilvie (1579-1615).
1977: Rafaela Maria Porras y Ayllon (1850-1925); John Nepomucene Neumann (1811-1860); Sharbel Makhlouf (1828-1898).

John Paul II
(1978-)
1982: Crispin of Viterbo (1668-1750); Maximilian Kolbe (1894-1941); Marguerite Bourgeoys (1620-1700); Jeanne Delanoue (1666-1736).
1983: Leopold Mandic (1866-1942).
1984: Paola Frassinetti (1809-1892); 103 Korean Martyrs (d. between 1839-1867); Miguel Febres Cordero (1854-1910).
1986: Francis Anthony Fasani (1681-1742); Giuseppe Maria Tomasi (1649-1713).
1987: Giuseppe Moscati (d. 1927); Lawrence (Lorenzo) Ruiz and Fifteen Companions, Martyrs of Japan (d. 1630s).
1988: Eustochia Calafato (1434-1485); 117 Mar-

tyrs of Vietnam (96 Vietnamese, 11 Spanish, 10 French; included 8 bishops, 50 priests, 1 seminarian, 58 lay persons); Roque Gonzalez (1576-1628), Alfonso Rodriguez (1598-1628) and Juan de Castillo (1596-1628), Jesuit martyrs of Paraguay; Rose Philippine Duchesne (1796-1852); Simon de Rojas (1552-1624); Magdalen of Canossa (1774-1835); Maria Rosa Molas y Vollve (d. 1876).
1989: Clelia Barbieri (1847-1870); Gaspar Bertoni (1777-1853); Richard Pampuri, religious (1897-1930); Agnes of Bohemia (1211-1282); Albert Chmielowski (1845-1916); Mutien-Marie Wiaux (1841-1917).
1990: Marguerite D'Youville (1701-1777).
1991: Raphael (Jozef) Kalinowski (1835-1907).
1992: Claude La Colombiere (1641-1682); Ezequiel Moreno y Diaz (1848-1905).
1993: Marie of St. Ignatius (Claudine Thevenet) (1774-1837); Teresa "de los Andes" (Juana Fernandez Solar) (1900-20); Enrique de Ossó y Cervelló (1840-96).
1995: Jan Sarkander (1576-1620), Zdislava of Lemberk (d. 1252); Marek Krizin (1588-1619), Stefan Pongracz (1582-1619), Melichar Grodziecky (1584-1619), martyrs of Kosice; Eugene de Mazenod (1782-1861).
1996: Jean-Gabriel Perboyre (1802-40), Juan Grande Roman (1546-1600) and Bro. Egidio Maria of St. Joseph (1729-1812).
1997 (as of Aug. 15, 1997): Hedwig (1371-1399), John Dukla, O.F.M. (d. 1484).

BEATIFICATIONS BY POPE JOHN PAUL II, 1979-1997

1979: Francis Coll, O.P., Jacques Laval, S.S.Sp. (Apr. 29); Enrique de Ossó y Cervelló (Oct. 14; canonized June 16, 1993).
1980: Jose de Anchieta, Peter of St. Joseph Betancur, Francois de Montmorency Laval, Kateri Tekakwitha, Marie Guyard of the Incarnation (June 22); Don Luigi Orione, Bartolomea Longo, Maria Anna Sala (Oct. 26).
1981: Sixteen Martyrs of Japan (Lorenzo Ruiz and Companions) (Feb 18; canonized Oct. 18, 1987); Maria Repetto, Alan de Solminihac, Richard Pampuri, Claudine Thevenet (canonized 1993), Aloysius (Luigi) Scrosoppi (Oct. 4).
1982: Peter Donders, C.SS.R., Marie Rose Durocher, Andre Bessette, C.S.C., Maria Angela Astorch, Marie Rivier (May 23); Jeanne Jugan, Salvatore Lilli and 7 Armenian Companions (Oct. 3); Sr. Angela of the Cross (Nov. 5).
1983: Maria Gabriella Sagheddu (Jan. 25); Luigi Versiglia, Callisto Caravario (May 15); Ursula Ledochowska (June 20); Raphael (Jozef) Kalinowski (canonized 1991), Bro. Albert (Adam Chmielowski), T.O.R. (June 22); Fra Angelico (equivalent beatification) (July); Giacomo Cusmano, Jeremiah of Valachia, Domingo Iturrate Zubero (Oct. 30); Marie of Jesus Crucified (Marie Baouardy) (Nov. 13).
1984: Fr. William Repin and 98 Companions (Martyrs of Angers during French Revolution), Giovanni Mazzucconi (Feb. 19); Marie Leonie Paradis (Sept. 11); Federico Albert, Clemente Marchisio, Isidore of St. Joseph (Isidore de Loor), Rafaela Ybarra de

Villalongo (Sept. 30); Jose Manyanet y Vives, Daniel Brottier, C.S.Sp., Sr. Elizabeth of the Trinity (Elizabeth Catez) (Nov. 25).
1985: Mercedes of Jesus (Feb. 1); Ana de los Angeles Monteagudo (Feb. 2); Pauline von Mallinckrodt, Catherine Troiano (Apr. 14); Benedict Menni, Peter Friedhofen (June 23); Anwarite Nangapeta (Aug. 15); Virginae Centurione Bracelli (Sept. 22); Diego Luis de San Vitores, S.J., Jose M. Rubio y Peralto, S.J., Francisco Garate, S.J. (Oct. 6); Titus Brandsma, O.Carm. (Nov. 3); Pio Campidelli, C.P., Marie Teresa of Jesus Gerhardinger, Rafqa Ar-Rayes (Nov. 17).
1986: Alphonsa Mattathupadathus of the Immaculate Conception, Kuriakose Elias Chavara (Feb. 8); Antoine Chevrier (Oct. 4); Teresa Maria of the Cross Manetti (Oct. 19).
1987: Maria Pilar of St. Francis Borgia, Teresa of the Infant Jesus, Maria Angeles of St. Joseph, Cardinal Marcellis Spinola y Maestre, Emmanuel Domingo y Sol (Mar. 29); Teresa of Jesus "de los Andes" (Apr. 3; canonized Mar. 21, 1993); Edith Stein (Teresa Benedicta of the Cross) (May 1); Rupert Meyer, S.J. (May 3); Pierre-Francois Jamet, Cardinal Andrea Carlo Ferrari, Benedetta Cambiogio Frasinello, Louis Moreau (May 10); Carolina Kozka, Michal Kozal (June 10); George Matulaitis (Matulewicz) (June 28); Marcel Callo, Pierino Morosoni, Antonia Mesina (Oct. 4); Blandina Marten, Ulricke Nische, Jules Reche (Bro. Arnold) (Nov. 1); 85 Martyrs (d. between 1584-1689) of England, Scotland and Wales (Nov. 22).

1988: John Calabria, Joseph Nascimbeni (Apr. 17); Pietro Bonilli, Kaspar Stanggassinger, Francisco Palau y Quer, Savina Petrilli (Apr. 24), Laura Vicuna (Sept. 3); Joseph Gerard (Sept. 11); Miguel Pro, Giuseppe Benedetto Dusmet, Francisco Faa di Bruno, Junipero Serra, Frederick Janssoone, Josefa Naval Girke (Sept. 25); Bernardo Maria Silvestrelli, Charles Houben, Honoratus Kozminski (Oct. 16); Niels Stensen (Nicolaus Steno) (Oct. 23); Katharine Drexel, 3 Missionary Martyrs of Ethiopia (Liberato Weiss, Samuel Marzorati, Michele Pio Fasoli) (Nov. 20).

1989: Martin of Saint Nicholas, Melchior of St. Augustine, Mary of Jesus of the Good Shepherd, Maria Margaret Caiana, Maria Catherine of St. Augustine (Apr. 23); Victoria Rasoamanarivo (Apr. 30); Bro. Scubilionis (John Bernard Rousseau) (May 2); Elizabeth Renzi, Antonio Lucci (June 17); Niceforo de Jesus y Maria (Vicente Diez Tejerina and 25 Companions (martyred in Spain), Lorenzo Salvia, Gertrude Caterina Comensoli, Francisca Ana Cirer Carbonell (Oct. 1); 7 Martyrs from Thailand (Philip Sipong, Sr. Agnes Phila, Sr. Lucia Khambang, Agatha Phutta, Cecilia Butsi, Bibiana Khampai, Maria Phon), Timothy Giaccardo, Mother Maria of Jesus Deluil-Martiny (Oct. 22); Giuseppe Baldo (Oct. 31).

1990: 9 Martyrs of Astoria during Spanish Civil War (De la Salle Brothers Cyrill Bertran, Marciano Jose, Julian Alfredo, Victoriano Pio, Benjamin Julian, Augusto Andres, Benito de Jesus, Aniceto Adolfo; and Passionist priest Innocencio Inmaculada), Mercedes Prat, Manuel Barbal Cosan (Brother Jaime), Philip Rinaldi (Apr. 29); Juan Diego (confirmation of Apr. 9 decree), 3 Child Martyrs (Cristobal, Antonio and Juan), Fr. Jose Maria de Yermo y Porres (May 6); Pierre Giorgio Frassati (May 20); Hanibal Maria Di Francia, Joseph Allamano (Oct. 7); Marthe Aimee LeBouteiller, Louise Therese de Montaignac de Chauvance, Maria Schinina, Elisabeth Vendramini (Nov. 4).

1991: Annunciata Cocchetti, Marie Therese Haze, Clara Bosatta (Apr. 21); Jozef Sebastian Pelczar (June 2); Boleslava Lament (June 5); Rafael Chylinski (June 9); Angela Salawa (Aug. 13); Edoardo Giuseppe Rosaz (July 14, Susa, Italy); Pauline of the Heart of Jesus in Agony Visintainer (Oct. 18, Brazil); Adolph Kolping (Oct. 27).

1992: Josephine Bakhita, Josemaria Escriva de Balaguer (May 17); Francesco Spinelli (June 21, Caravaggio, Italy); 17 Irish Martyrs, Rafael Arnáiz Barón, Nazaria Ignacia March Mesa, Léonie Françoise de Sales Aviat, and Maria Josefa Sancho de Guerra (Sept. 27); 122 Martyrs of Spanish Civil War, Narcisa Martillo Morán (Oct. 25); Cristóbal

Magellanes and 24 companions, Mexican martyrs, and Maria de Jesús Sacramentado Venegas (Nov. 22).

1993: Dina Belanger (Mar. 20); John Duns Scotus (Mar. 20, cult solemnly recognized); Mary Angela Truszkowska, Ludovico of Casoria, Faustina Kowalska, Paula Montal Fornés (Apr. 18); Stanislaus Kazimierczyk (April 18, cult solemnly recognized); Maurice Tornay, Marie-Louise Trichet, Columba Gabriel and Florida Cevoli (May 16); Giuseppe Marello (Sept. 26); Eleven martyrs of Almeria, Spain, during Spanish Civil War (2 bishops, 7 brothers, 1 priest, 1 lay person); Maria Francesca (Anna Maria) Rubatto; Maria Crucified (Elisabetta Maria) Satellico (Oct. 10).

1994: Isidore Bakanja, Elizabeth Canori Mora; Dr. Gianna Beretta Molla (Apr. 24); Nicolas Roland, Alberto Hurtado Cruchaga, Maria Rafols, Petra of St. Joseph Perez Florido, Josephine Vannini (Oct. 16); Maddalena Caterina Morano (Nov. 5); Hyacinthe Marie Cormier, Marie Poussepin, Agnes de Jesus Galand, Eugenia Joubert, Claudio Granzotto (Nov. 20).

1995: Peter To Rot (Jan. 17); Mother Mary of the Cross MacKillop (Jan. 19); Joseph Vaz (Jan. 21); Rafael Guizar Valencia, Modestino of Jesus and Mary, Genoveva Torres Morales, Grimoaldo of the Purification (Jan. 29); Johann Nepomuk von Tschiderer (Apr. 30); Maria Helena Stollenwerk, Maria Alvarado Cardoza, Giuseppina Bonino, Maria Domenica Brun Barbantini, Agostino Roscelli (May 7); Damien de Veuster (June 4); 109 Martyrs (64 from French Revolution and 45 from Spanish Civil War) and Pietro Casini (Oct. 1); Mary Theresa Scherer, Maria Bernarda Butler and Marguerite Bays (Oct. 29).

1996: Daniel Comboni and Guido Maria Conforti (Mar. 17); Cardinal Alfredo Ildefonso Schuster, O.S.B., Filippo Smaldone and Gennaro Sarnelli (priests) and Candida Maria de Jesus Cipitria y Barriola, Maria Raffaella Cimatti, Maria Antonia Bandres (religious) (May 12), Bernhard Lichtenberg and Karl Leisner (June 23), Wincenty Lewoniuk and 12 companions, Edmund Rice, Maria Ana Mogas Fontcuberta and Marcelina Darowski (Oct 6); Otto Neururer, Jakob Gapp and Catherine Jarrige (Nov. 24).

1997 (as of Aug. 30, 1997): Bishop Florentino Asensio Barroso, Sr. Maria Encarnacion Rosal of the Sacred Heart, Fr. Gaetano Catanoso, Fr. Enrico Rebuschini and Ceferino Gimenez Malla, first gypsy beatified (May 4); Bernardina Maria Jablonski, Maria Karlowska (June 6); Frederic Ozanam (Aug. 22). The beatification of John Baptist Scalabrini was scheduled for Nov. 9.

BEATIFICATION OF FREDERIC OZANAM

Pope John Paul beatified Frederic Ozanam during a solemn Mass concelebrated with the bishops of France in the Cathedral of Notre Dame, Paris, Aug. 22, in one of the principal events of the celebration of World Youth Day 1997.

Ozanam was born Aug. 23, 1813, in Milan and died in Marseilles Sept. 8, 1853. He is best known as one of the key founders in 1833 of the Conference of Charity, which came to be known as the St.

Vincent de Paul Society, "for charity for all." He was also an historian, a teacher of law in Lyons and a professor of literature at the Sorbonne in Paris. His writing on social theory antedated the communism of Karl Marx and the *Rerum Novarum* of Pope Leo XIII.

A deeply religious man, Ozanam was devoted to family life, the lay apostolate, intellectual endeavors and, above all, service to the poor.

HIERARCHY OF THE CATHOLIC CHURCH

ORGANIZATION AND GOVERNMENT

As a structured society, the Catholic Church is organized and governed along lines corresponding mainly to the jurisdictions of the pope and bishops.

The pope is the supreme head of the Church. He has primacy of jurisdiction as well as honor over the entire Church.

Bishops, in union with and in subordination to the pope, are the successors of the Apostles for care of the Church and for the continuation of Christ's mission in the world. They serve the people of their own dioceses, or particular churches, with ordinary authority and jurisdiction. They also share, with the pope and each other, in common concern and effort for the general welfare of the whole Church.

Bishops of exceptional status are patriarchs of Eastern Catholic Churches who, subject only to the pope, are heads of the faithful belonging to their rites throughout the world.

Subject to the Holy Father and directly responsible to him for the exercise of their ministry of service to people in various jurisdictions or divisions of the Church throughout the world are: resident archbishops and metropolitans (heads of archdioceses), diocesan bishops, vicars and prefects apostolic (heads of vicariates apostolic and prefectures apostolic), certain abbots and prelates, apostolic administrators. Each of these, within his respective territory and according to the provisions of canon law, has ordinary jurisdiction over pastors (who are responsible for the administration of parishes), priests, Religious and lay persons.

Also subject to the Holy Father are titular archbishops and bishops, religious orders and congregations of pontifical right, pontifical institutes and faculties, papal nuncios and apostolic delegates.

Assisting the pope and acting in his name in the central government and administration of the Church are cardinals and other officials of the Roman Curia.

THE HIERARCHY

The ministerial hierarchy is the orderly arrangement of the ranks and orders of the clergy to provide for the spiritual care of the faithful, the government of the Church, and the accomplishment of the Church's total mission in the world.

Persons belong to this hierarchy by virtue of ordination and canonical mission.

The term hierarchy is also used to designate an entire body or group of bishops; for example, the hierarchy of the Church, the hierarchy of the United States.

Hierarchy of Order: Consists of the pope, bishops, priests and deacons. Their purpose, for which they are ordained to holy orders, is to carry out the sacramental and pastoral ministry of the Church.

Hierarchy of Jurisdiction: Consists of the pope and bishops by divine institution, and other church officials by ecclesiastical institution and mandate, who have authority to govern and direct the faithful for spiritual ends.

The Pope

His Holiness the Pope is the Bishop of Rome, the Vicar of Jesus Christ, the successor of St. Peter, Prince of the Apostles, the Supreme Pontiff who has the primacy of jurisdiction and not merely of honor over the universal Church, the Patriarch of the West, the Primate of Italy, the Archbishop and Metropolitan of the Roman Province, the Sovereign of the State of Vatican City, Servant of the Servants of God.

Cardinals

(See Index)

Patriarchs

Patriarch, a term which had its origin in the Eastern Church, is the title of a bishop who, second only to the pope, has the highest rank in the hierarchy of jurisdiction. He is the incumbent of one of the sees listed below. Subject only to the pope, a patriarch of the Eastern Church is the head of the faithful belonging to his rite throughout the world. The patriar-chal sees are so called because of their special status and dignity in the history of the Church.

The Council of Nicaea (325) recognized three patriarchs — the bishops of Alexandria and Antioch in the East, and of Rome in the West. The First Council of Constantinople (381) added the bishop of Constantinople to the list of patriarchs and gave him rank second only to that of the pope, the bishop of Rome and patriarch of the West; this action was seconded by the Council of Chalcedon (451) and was given full recognition by the Fourth Lateran Council (1215). The Council of Chalcedon also acknowledged patriarchal rights of the bishop of Jerusalem.

Eastern patriarchs are as follows: one of Alexandria, for the Copts; three of Antioch, one each for the Syrians, Maronites and Greek Melkites (the latter also has the personal title of Greek Melkite patriarch of Alexandria and of Jerusalem). The patriarch of Babylonia, for the Chaldeans, and the patriarch of Sis, or Cilicia, for the Armenians, should be called, more properly, *Katholikos* — that is, a prelate delegated for a universality of causes. These patriarchs are elected by bishops of their churches: they receive approval and the pallium, symbolic of their office, from the pope.

Latin Rite patriarchates were established for Antioch, Jerusalem, Alexandria and Constantinople during the Crusades; afterwards, they became patriarchates in name only. Jerusalem, however, was reconstituted as a patriarchate by Pius IX, in virtue of the bull *Nulla Celebrior* of July 23, 1847. In 1964, the Latin titular patriarchates of Constantinople, Alexandria and Antioch, long a bone of contention in relations with Eastern Churches, were abolished.

As of Aug. 15, 1997, the patriarchs in the Church were:

The Pope, Bishop of Rome, Patriarch of the West; Stephanos II Ghattas, C.M., of Alexandria, for the Copts; Ignace Antoine II Hayek, of Antioch, for the Syrians; Maximos V Hakim, of Antioch, for the Greek Melkites (he also has personal titles of Alexandria and Jerusalem for the Greek Melkites); Cardinal Nasrallah Pierre Sfeir, of Antioch, for the Maronites; Michel Sabbah, of Jerusalem, for the Latin Rite; Raphael I Bidawid, of Babylon, for the Chaldeans; Jean Pierre XVIII Kasparian, of Cilicia, for the Armenians.

The titular patriarchs (in name only) of the Latin Rite were: Cardinal Antonio Ribeiro, of Lisbon; Cardinal Marco Cé of Venice and Archbishop Raul Nicolau Gonsalves of the East Indies (Archbishop of Goa and Damao, India). The patriarchate of the West Indies has been vacant since 1963.

Major Archbishops

An archbishop with the prerogatives but not the title of a patriarch. As of May 15, 1997, there was one major archbishop: Cardinal Myroslav Ivan Lubachivsky of the major archbishopric of Lviv of the Ukrainian Catholic Church (Ukraine). The major archbishopric of Ernakulam-Angomaly of the Syro-Malabar Church (India) was vacant with the resignation Nov. 11, 1996, of Cardinal Anthony Padiyara.

Archbishops, Metropolitans

Archbishop: A bishop with the title of an archdiocese.

Coadjutor Archbishop: An assistant archbishop with right of succession.

Metropolitan: Archbishop of the principal see, an archdiocese, in an ecclesiastical province consisting of several dioceses. He has the full powers of bishop in his own archdiocese and limited supervisory jurisdiction and influence over the other (suffragan) dioceses in the province. The pallium, conferred by the pope, is the symbol of his status as a metropolitan.

Titular Archbishop: Has the title of an archdiocese which formerly existed in fact but now exists in title only. He does not have ordinary jurisdiction over an archdiocese. Examples are archbishops in the Roman Curia, papal nuncios, apostolic delegates.

Archbishop ad personam: A title of personal honor and distinction granted to some bishops. They do not have ordinary jurisdiction over an archdiocese.

Primate: A title of honor given to the ranking prelate of some countries or regions.

Bishops

Diocesan Bishop: A bishop in charge of a diocese.

Coadjutor Bishop: An assistant (auxiliary) bishop to a diocesan bishop, with right of succession to the see.

Titular Bishops: A bishop with the title of a diocese which formerly existed in fact but now exists in title only; an assistant (auxiliary) bishop to a diocesan bishop.

Episcopal Vicar: An assistant, who may or may not be a bishop, appointed by a residential bishop as his deputy for a certain part of a diocese, a determined type of apostolic work, or the faithful of a certain rite.

Eparch, Exarch: Titles of bishops of Eastern churches.

Nomination of Bishops: Nominees for episcopal ordination are selected in several ways. Final appointment and/or approval in all cases is subject to decision by the pope.

In the U.S., bishops periodically submit the names of candidates to the archbishop of their province. The names are then considered at a meeting of the bishops of the province, and those receiving a favorable vote are forwarded to the pro-nuncio for transmission to the Holy See. Bishops are free to seek the counsel of priests, religious and lay persons with respect to nominees.

Eastern Catholic churches have their own procedures and synodal regulations for nominating and making final selection of candidates for episcopal ordination. Such selection is subject to approval by the pope.

The Code of Canon Law concedes no rights or privileges to civil authorities with respect to the election, nomination, presentation or designation of candidates for the episcopate.

Ad Limina Visit: Diocesan bishops and apostolic vicars are obliged to make an *ad limina* visit ("to the threshold" of the Apostles) every five years to the tombs of Sts. Peter and Paul, have audience with the Holy Father and consult with appropriate Vatican officials. They are required to send a report on conditions in their jurisdiction to the Congregation for Bishops approximately six — and not less than three — months in advance of the scheduled visit.

Others with Ordinary Jurisdiction

Ordinary: One who has the jurisdiction of an office: the pope, diocesan bishops, vicars general, prelates of missionary territories, vicars apostolic prefects apostolic, vicars capitular during the vacancy of a see, superiors general, abbots primate and other major superiors of men Religious.

Some prelates and abbots, with jurisdiction like that of diocesan bishops, are pastors of the people of God in territories (prelatures and abbacies) not under the jurisdiction of diocesan bishops.

Vicar Apostolic: Usually a titular bishop who has ordinary jurisdiction over a mission territory.

Prefect Apostolic: Has ordinary jurisdiction over a mission territory.

Apostolic Administrator: Usually a bishop appointed to administer an ecclesiastical jurisdiction temporarily. Administrators of lesser rank are also appointed for special and more restricted supervisory duties.

Vicar General: A bishop's deputy for the administration of a diocese. Such a vicar does not have to be a bishop.

Prelates Without Jurisdiction

The title of protonotary apostolic was originally given by the fourth century or earlier to clergy who collected accounts of martyrdom and other church documents, or who served the Church with distinction in other ways. Other titles — e.g., domestic prelate, papal chamberlain, prelate of honor — are titles of clergy in service to the pope and the papal household, or of clergy honored for particular reasons. All prelates without jurisdiction are appointed by the pope, have designated ceremonial privileges and the title of Rev. Monsignor.

SYNOD OF BISHOPS

The Synod of Bishops was chartered by Pope Paul VI Sept. 15, 1965, in a document he issued on his own initiative under the title, *Apostolica Sollicitudo*. Provisions of this motu proprio are contained in Canons 342 to 348 of the Code of Canon Law. According to major provisions of the Synod charter:

• The purposes of the Synod are: "to encourage close union and valued assistance between the Sovereign Pontiff and the bishops of the entire world; to insure that direct and real information is provided on questions and situations touching upon the internal action of the Church and its necessary activity in the world of today; to facilitate agreement on essential points of doctrine and on methods of procedure in the life of the Church."

• The Synod is a central ecclesiastical institution, permanent by nature.

• The Synod is directly and immediately subject to the Pope, who has authority to assign its agenda, to call it into session, and to give its members deliberative as well as advisory authority.

• In addition to a limited number of ex officio members and a few heads of male religious institutes, the majority of the members are elected by and representative of national or regional episcopal conferences. The Pope reserved the right to appoint the general secretary, special secretaries and no more than 15 per cent of the total membership.

The Pope is president of the Synod.

The secretary general is Cardinal Jan Schotte, C.I.C.M., of Belgium. Address: Palazzo del Bramante, Via della Conciliazione 34, 00193 Rome, Italy.

An advisory council of 15 members (12 elected, three appointed by the pope) provides the secretariat with adequate staff for carrying on liaison with episcopal conferences and for preparing the agenda of synodal assemblies. Cardinal William H, Keeler, archbishop of Baltimore, is a member of the secretariat.

Assemblies

1. First Assembly: The first assembly was held from Sept. 29 to Oct. 29, 1967. Its objectives, as stated by Pope Paul VI, were "the preservation and strengthening of the Catholic faith, its integrity, its force, its development, its doctrinal and historical coherence." One result was a recommendation for the establishment of an international commission of theologians to assist the Congregation for the Doctrine of the Faith and to broaden approaches to theological research. Pope Paul set up the commission in 1969.

2. Pope-Bishop Relations: The second assembly held Oct. 11 to 28, 1969, was extraordinary in character. It opened the way toward greater participation by bishops with the pope and each other in the governance of the Church. Proceedings were oriented to three main points: (1) the nature and implications of collegiality; (2) the relationship of bishops and their conferences to the pope; (3) the relationships of bishops and their conferences to each other.

3. Priesthood and Justice: The ministerial priesthood and justice in the world were the principal topics under discussion at the second ordinary assembly, Sept. 30 to Nov. 6, 1971. In one report, the Synod emphasized the primary and permanent dedication of priests in the Church to the ministry of word, sacrament and pastoral service as a full-time vocation. In another report, the assembly stated: "Action on behalf of justice and participation in the transformation of the world fully appear to us as a constitutive dimension of the preaching of the Gospel; or, in other words, of the Church's mission for the redemption of the human race and its liberation from every oppressive situation."

4. Evangelization: The assembly of Sept. 27 to Oct. 26, 1974, produced a general statement on evangelization of the modern world, covering the need for it and its relationship to efforts for total human liberation from personal and social evil. The assembly observed: "The Church does not remain within merely political, social and economic limits (elements which she must certainly take into account) but leads towards freedom under all its forms _ liberation from sin, from individual or collective selfishness _ and to full communion with God and with men who are like brothers. In this way the Church, in her evangelical way, promotes the true and complete liberation of all men, groups and peoples."

5. Catechetics: The fourth ordinary assembly, Sept. 30 to Oct. 29, 1977, focused attention on catechetics, with special reference to children and young people. The participants issued a "Message to the People of God," the first synodal statement issued since inception of the body, and also presented to Pope Paul VI a set of 34 related propositions and a number of suggestions.

6. Family: "A Message to Christian Families in the Modern World" and a proposal for a "Charter of Family Rights" were produced by the assembly held Sept. 26 to Oct. 25, 1980. The assembly reaffirmed the indissolubility of marriage and the contents of the encyclical letter *Humanae Vitae* (see separate entry), and urged married couples who find it hard to live up to "the difficult but loving demands" of Christ not to be discouraged but to avail themselves of the aid of divine grace. In response to synodal recommendation, Pope John Paul issued a charter of family rights late in 1983.

7. Reconciliation: Penance and reconciliation in the mission of the Church was the theme of the assembly held Sept. 29 to Oct. 29, 1983. Sixty-three propositions related to this theme were formulated on a wide variety of subjects, including: personal sin and so-called systemic or institutional sin; the nature of serious sin; the diminished sense of sin and of the need of redemption, related to decline in the administration and reception of the sacrament of penance; general absolution; individual and social reconciliation; violence and violations of human rights; reconciliation as the basis of peace and justice in society. In a statement issued Oct. 27, the Synod stressed the need of the world to become, increasingly, "a reconciled community of peoples," and said that "the Church, as sacrament of reconciliation to the world, has to be an effective sign of God's mercy."

8. Vatican II Review: The second extraordinary assembly was convened Nov. 24 to Dec. 8, 1985, for the purposes of: (1) recalling the Second Vatican Council; (2) evaluating the implementation of its enactments during the 20 years since its conclusion; (3) seeking ways and means of promoting renewal in the Church in accordance with the spirit and letter of the council. At the conclusion of the assembly the bishops issued two documents. (1) In A Message to the People of God, they noted the need for greater appreciation of the enactments of Vatican II and for greater efforts to put them into effect, so that all members of the Church might discharge their responsibility of proclaiming the good news of salvation. (2) In a Final Report, the first of its kind published by a synodal assembly, the bishops reflected on lights and shadows since Vatican II, stating that negative developments had come from partial and superficial interpretations of conciliar enactments and from incomplete or ineffective implementation thereof. The report also covered a considerable number of subjects discussed during the assembly, including the mystery of the Church, inculturation, the preferential (but not exclusive) option for the poor, and a suggestion for the development of a new universal catechism of the Catholic faith.

9. Vocation and Mission of the Laity in the Church and in the World 20 years after the Second Vatican Council: The seventh ordinary assembly, Oct. 1 to 30, 1987, said in a Message to the People of God: "The majority of the Christian laity live out their vocation as followers and disciples of Christ in all spheres of life which we call 'the world': the family, the field of work, the local community and the like. To permeate this day-to-day living with the spirit of Christ has always been the task of the lay faithful; and it should be with still greater force their challenge today. It is in this way that they sanctify the world and collaborate in the realization of the kingdom of God." The assembly produced a set of 54 propositions which were presented to the Pope for consideration in the preparation of a document of his own on the theme of the assembly. He responded

with the apostolic exhortation, *Christifideles Laici,* "The Christian Faithful Laity," released by the Vatican Jan. 30, 1989.

10. Formation of Priests in Circumstances of the Present Day: The eighth general assembly, Sept. 30 to Oct. 28, 1990, dealt principally with the nature and mission of the priesthood; the identity, multifaceted formation and spirituality of priests; and, in a Message to the People of God, the need on all levels of the Church for the promotion of vocations to the priesthood. Forty-one proposals were presented to the Pope for his consideration in preparing a document of his own on the theme of the assembly. Pope John Paul issued an apostolic exhortation entitled *Pastores Dabo Vobis* ("I Will Give You Shepherds") Apr. 7, 1992, in response to the Synods' recommendations.

11. The Consecrated Life and Its Role in the Church and in the World: The ninth general assembly was held Oct. 2 to 29, 1994. Pope John Paul's reflections on the proceedings of the assembly and the recommendations of the bishops were the subjects of his apostolic exhortation entitled *Vita Consecrata* ("Consecrated Life"), issued Mar. 25, 1996. The document dealt with various forms of consecrated life: contemplative institutes, apostolic religious life, secular institutes, societies of apostolic life, mixed institutes and new forms of evangelical life.

By the time of writing the theme, but not the date, of the 10th ordinary assembly had been announced: "The Bishop, Minister of the Gospel of Jesus Christ for the Hope of the World."

Recent special assemblies of the Synod of Bishops have been held for Europe (Nov. 28 to Dec. 14, 1991), for Africa (Apr. 10 to May 8, 1994), and for Lebanon (Nov. 27 to Dec. 14, 1995).

At the time of writing, a special assembly for the Americas was scheduled for Nov. 16 to Dec. 12, 1997, on the theme, "Encounter with the Living Jesus Christ: Way to Conversion, Community and Solidarity"; and preparations were under way for special assemblies for Asia and Oceania. (See separate entries.)

ROMAN CURIA

The Roman Curia is the Church's network of central administrative agencies (called dicasteries) serving the Vatican and the local churches, with authority granted by the Pope.

The Curia evolved gradually from advisory assemblies or synods of the Roman clergy with whose assistance the popes directed church affairs during the first 11 centuries. Its original office was the Apostolic Chancery, established in the fourth century to transmit documents. The antecedents of its permanently functioning agencies and offices were special commissions of cardinals and prelates. Its establishment in a form resembling what it is now dates from the second half of the 16th century.

Pope Paul VI initiated a four-year reorganization study in 1963 which resulted in the constitution *Regimini Ecclesiae Universae.* The document was published Aug. 18, 1967, and went into full effect in March, 1968.

Pope John Paul II, in the apostolic constitution *Pastor Bonus,* published June 28, 1988, and effective Mar. 1, 1989, ordered modifications of the Curia based on the broad outline of Paul VI's reorganization.

The Curia (in accordance with Pope John Paul II's reform effective Mar. 1, 1989, and later revisions), consists of the Secretariat of State, nine congregations (governing agencies), three tribunals (judicial agencies), 11 councils (promotional agencies) and three offices (specialized service agencies). All have equal juridical status with authority granted by the Pope.

SECRETARIAT OF STATE

The Secretariat of State, Palazzo Apostolico Vaticano, Vatican City. Cardinal Angelo Sodano, Secretary of State; Most Rev. Giovanni Battista Re, Deputy for General Affairs; Most Rev. Jean Louis Tauran, Secretary for Relations with States.

The Secretariat of State provides the pope with the closest possible assistance in the care of the universal Church. It consists of two sections:

• The Section for General Affairs assists the Pope in expediting daily business of the Holy See. It coordinates curial operations; prepares drafts of documents entrusted to it by the pope; has supervisory duties over the *Acta Apostolicae Sedis, Annuario Pontificio,* the Vatican Press Office and the Central Statistics Office.

• The Section for Relations with States (formerly the Council for Public Affairs of the Church, a separate body) handles diplomatic and other relations with civil governments. Attached to it is a Council of Cardinals and Bishops.

Background: Evolved gradually from secretarial offices (dating back to the 15th century) and the Congregation for Extraordinary Ecclesiastical Affairs (dating back to 1793; restructured as the Council for the Public Affairs of the Church by Paul VI in 1967). John Paul II gave it its present form in his June 28, 1988, reform of the Curia.

CONGREGATIONS

Congregation for the Doctrine of the Faith: Piazza del S. Uffizio 11, 00193 Rome, Italy. Cardinal Joseph Ratzinger, prefect; Most Rev. Tarcisio Bertone, S.D.B., secretary.

Has responsibility to safeguard the doctrine of faith and morals. Accordingly, it examines doctrinal questions; promotes studies thereon; evaluates theological opinions and, when necessary and after prior consultation with concerned bishops, reproves those regarded as opposed to principles of the faith; examines books on doctrinal matters and can reprove such works, if the contents so warrant, after giving authors the opportunity to defend themselves. It examines matters pertaining to the Privilege of Faith (Petrine Privilege) in marriage cases, and safeguards the dignity of the sacrament of penance. Attached to the congregation are the Pontifical Biblical Commission and the Theological Commission.

Background: At the beginning of the 13th century, legates of Innocent III were commissioned as the Holy Office of the Inquisition to combat heresy; the same task was entrusted to the Dominican Order by Gregory IX in 1231 and to the Friars Minor by Innocent IV from 1243 to 1254. On July 21, 1542 (apostolic constitution Licet), Paul III instituted a permanent congregation of cardinals with supreme and universal competence over matters concerning heretics and those suspected of heresy. Pius IV, St. Pius V and Sixtus V further defined the work of the congregation. St. Pius X changed its name to the Congregation of the Holy Office. Paul VI (motu proprio *Integrae Servandae,* Dec. 7, 1965), began reorganization of the Curia with this body, to which he gave the new title, Congregation for the Doctrine of the Faith. Its orientation is not merely negative, in the condemnation of error, but positive, in the promotion of orthodox doctrine.

Congregation for the Oriental Churches: Palazzo del Bramante, Via della Conciliazione 34, 00193 Rome, Italy. Cardinal Achille Silvestrini, prefect; Most Rev. Miroslav Stefan Marusyn, secretary. Members include all patriarchs of the Eastern Catholic Churches and major archbishops.

Has competence in matters concerning the persons and discipline of Eastern Catholic Churches. It has jurisdiction over territories in which the majority of Christians belong to Eastern Churches (i.e., Egypt, the Sinai Peninsula, Eritrea, Northern Ethiopia, Southern Albania, Bulgaria, Cyprus, Greece, Iran, Iraq, Lebanon, Palestine, Syria, Jordan, Turkey, Afghanistan); also, over minority communities of Eastern Church members no matter where they live.

Background: Established by Pius IX Jan. 6, 1862 (apostolic constitution *Romani Pontifices*), and united with the Congregation for the Propagation of the Faith. The congregation was made autonomous by Benedict XV May 1, 1917 (motu proprio *Dei Providentis*), and given wider authority by Pius XI Mar. 25, 1938 (motu proprio *Sancta Dei Ecclesia*).

Congregation for Bishops: Piazza Pio XII 10, 00193 Rome, Italy. Cardinal Bernardin Gantin, prefect; Most Rev. Jorge Maria Mejia, secretary.

Has functions related in one way or another to bishops and the jurisdictions in which they serve. It supervises the Pontifical Commission for Latin America. Attached to the congregation are a central coordinating office for Military Vicars (established Feb. 2, 1985) and an office for coordinating *ad limina* visits (established June 29, 1988).

Background: Established by Sixtus V Jan. 22, 1588 (apostolic constitution *Immensa*); given an extension of powers by St. Pius X June 20, 1908, and Pius XII Aug. 1, 1952 (apostolic constitution *Exsul Familia*); given present title (was known as Consistorial Congregation) by Paul VI (Aug. 1, 1967); competencies redefined by John Paul II, June 28, 1988.

Congregation for Divine Worship and the Discipline of the Sacraments: Piazza Pio XII 10, 00193 Rome, Italy. Most Rev. Jorge Arturo Medina Estevez, pro-prefect; Most Rev. Geraldo Majella Agnelo, secretary.

Supervises everything pertaining to the promotion and regulation of the liturgy, primarily the sacraments, without prejudice to the competencies of the Congregation for the Doctrine of the Faith. Attached to the congregation are special commissions treating causes of nullity of sacred ordinations and dispensations from obligations of sacred ordination of deacons and priests.

Background: Originally two separate congregations: the Congregation for Divine Worship (instituted by Paul VI, May 8, 1969) and the Congregation for the Discipline of the Sacraments (established by St. Pius X, June 29, 1908, to replace the Congregation of Rites instituted by Pope Sixtus V in 1588). They were united by Paul VI, July 11, 1975, as the Congregation for the Sacraments and Divine Worship; reestablished as separate congregations by John Paul II in an autograph letter of Apr. 5, 1984, and reunited anew by the same Pope, June 28, 1988 (apostolic constitution *Pastor Bonus*) as the Congregation for Divine Worship and the Discipline of the Sacraments.

Congregation for the Causes of Saints: Piazza Pio XII 10, 00193 Rome, Italy. Most Rev. Alberto Bovone, pro-prefect; Most Rev. Edward Nowak, secretary.

Handles matters connected with beatification and canonization causes (in accordance with revised procedures decreed in 1983), and the preservation of relics.

Background: Established by Sixtus V in 1588 as the Congregation of Rites; affected by legislation of Pius XI in 1930; title changed and functions defined by Paul VI, 1969 (apostolic constitution *Sacra Rituum Congregatio*). It was restructured and canonization procedures were revised by John Paul II in 1983 (apostolic constitution *Divinus Perfectionis Magister*).

Congregation for the Clergy: Piazza Pio XII 3, 00193 Rome, Italy. Most Rev. Dario Castrillon Hoyos, pro-prefect; Most Rev. Crescenzio Sepe, secretary.

Has three offices with competencies concerning the life, discipline, rights and duties of the clergy; the preaching of the Word, catechetics, norms for religious education of children and adults; preservation and administration of the temporal goods of the Church. Attached to it are the International Council for Catechetics (established in 1973 by Paul VI) and the Institute "Sacrum Ministerium" for the permanent formation of the clergy (established in line with John Paul II's 1992 apostolic exhortation *Pastores dabo Vobis*).

Background: Established by Pius IV Aug. 2, 1564 (apostolic constitution *Alias Nos*), under the title, Congregation of the Cardinals Interpreters of the Council of Trent; affected by legislation of Gregory XIII and Sixtus V; known as Congregation of the Council until Aug. 15, 1967, when Paul VI renamed it the Congregation for the Clergy and redefined its competency; John Paul II gave it added responsibilities June 28, 1988.

Congregation for Institutes of Consecrated Life and Societies of Apostolic Life: Piazza Pio XII 3, 00193 Rome, Italy. Cardinal Eduardo Martinez Somalo, prefect; Most. Rev. Piergiorgio Silvano Nesti, C.P., secretary.

Has competence over institutes of Religious, secular institutes, societies of the apostolic life and third (secular) orders. With two sections, the congregation has authority in matters related to the establishment, general direction and suppression of the various institutes; general discipline in line with their rules and constitutions; the movement toward renewal and adaptation of institutes in contemporary circumstances; the setting up and encouragement of councils and conferences of major religious superiors for intercommunication and other purposes.

Background: Founded by Sixtus V May 27, 1586, with the title, Congregation for Consultations of Regulars; confirmed by the apostolic constitution *Immensa* Jan. 22, 1588; made part of the Congregation for Consultations of Bishops and other Prelates in 1601; made autonomous by St. Pius X in 1908 as Congregation of Religious; title changed to Congregation for Religious and Secular Institutes by Paul VI in 1967; given present title by John Paul II, June 28, 1988.

Congregation for Catholic Education (for Seminaries and Institutes of Study): Piazza Pio XII 3, 00193 Rome, Italy. Cardinal Pio Laghi, prefect; Most Rev. Jose Saraiva Martins, C.M.F., secretary.

Has supervisory competence over institutions and works of Catholic education. It carries on its work through three offices. One office handles matters connected with the direction, discipline and temporal administration of seminaries, and with the education of diocesan clergy, religious and members of secular institutes. A second office oversees Catholic universities, faculties of study and other institutions of higher learning inasmuch as they depend on the authority of the Church; encourages cooperation and mutual assistance among Catholic institutions, and the establishment of Catholic hospices and centers on campuses of non-Catholic institutions. A third office is concerned in various ways with all Catholic schools below the college-university level, with general questions concerning education and studies, and with the cooperation of conferences of bishops and civil authorities in educational matters. The congregation supervises Pontifical Works for Priestly Vocations.

Background: The title (Congregation of Seminaries and Universities) and functions of the congregation were defined by Benedict XV Nov. 4, 1915; Pius XI, in 1931 and 1932, and Pius XII, in 1941 and 1949, extended its functions; Paul VI changed its title to Congregation for Catholic Education in 1967; given its present title by Pope John Paul II, June 28, 1988. Its work had previously been carried on by two other congregations erected by Sixtus V in 1588 and Leo XII in 1824.

Congregation for the Evangelization of Peoples: Piazza di Spagna 48, 00187 Rome, Italy. Cardinal Jozef Tomko, prefect; Most Rev. Giuseppe Uhac, secretary; Most Rev. Charles A. Schleck, C.S.C., adjunct secretary.

Directs and coordinates missionary work throughout the world. Accordingly, it has competence over those matters which concern all the missions established for the spread of Christ's kingdom without prejudice to the competence of other congregations. These include: fostering missionary vocations; assigning missionaries to fields of work; establishing ecclesiastical jurisdictions and proposing candidates to serve them as bishops and in other capacities; encouraging the recruitment and development of indigenous clergy; mobilizing spiritual and financial support for missionary activity.

To promote missionary cooperation, the congregation has a Supreme Council for the Direction of Pontifical Missionary Works composed of the Missionary Union of the Clergy and Religious, the Society for the Propagation of the Faith, the Society of St. Peter the Apostle for Native Clergy, the Society of the Holy Childhood, and the International Center of Missionary Animation.

Background: Originated as a commission of cardinals by St. Pius V and Gregory XII for missions in East and West Indies, Italo-Greeks and for ecclesiastical affairs in Protestant territories of Europe; Clement VIII instituted a Congregation of the Propagation of the Faith in 1599 which ceased to exist after several years. Erected as a stable congregation by Gregory XV June 22, 1622 (apostolic constitution *Inscrutabili Divinae*); its functions were redefined by John Paul II, June 28, 1988.

Inter-Agency Curia Commissions

In accordance with provisions of the apostolic constitution *Pastor Bonus,* John Paul II established the following interdepartmental permanent commissions to handle matters when more than one agency of the Curia is involved in activities:

• For matters concerning appointments to local Churches and the setting up and alteration of them and their constitution (Mar. 22, 1989). Members include officials of the Secretariat of State and Congregation for Bishops. President, Cardinal Angelo Sodano, Secretary of State.

• For matters concerning members, individually or as a community, of Institutes of Consecrated Life founded or working in mission territories (Mar. 22, 1989). Members include officials of the Congregations for the Evangelization of Peoples and for Institutes of Consecrated Life and Societies of Apostolic Life. President: Cardinal Jozef Tomko, prefect of the Congregation for the Evangelization of Peoples.

• For the formation of candidates for Sacred Orders (Mar. 22, 1989). Members include officials of the Congregations for Catholic Education, for Institutes of Consecrated Life and Societies of Apostolic Life, for Evangelization of Peoples, for Oriental Churches. President: Cardinal Pio Laghi, prefect of the Congregation for Catholic Education.

• For promoting a more equitable distribution of priests throughout the world (July 20, 1991). Members include secretaries of congregations for Evangelization of Peoples, for the Clergy, Catholic Education, for the Institutes of Consecrated Life and Societies of Apostolic Life; and vice-president of Commission for Latin America. President: Cardinal Pio Laghi, prefect of the Congregation for Catholic Education.

• For the Church in Eastern Europe (Jan. 15, 1993), replacing the Pontifical Commission for Russia which was terminated. The commission is concerned with both Latin and Eastern-rite churches in territories of the former Soviet Union and other nations affected by the historical circumstances resulting from atheistic communism. It is responsible for promoting the apostolic mission of the Church and fostering ecumenical dialogue with the Orthodox and other Churches of the Eastern tradition. Members, under presidency of Cardinal Secretary of State, include the secretary and undersecretary of the Section for Relations with States and secretaries of Congregations for the Oriental Churches, for the Clergy, for Institutes of Consecrated Life and Societies of Apostolic Life, secretary of the Pontifical Council for Promoting Christian Unity. President, Cardinal Angelo Sodano.

TRIBUNALS

Apostolic Penitentiary: Piazza della Cancelleria 1, 00186 Rome, Italy. Cardinal William Wakefield Baum, major penitentiary; Msgr. Luigi de Magistris, regent.

Has jurisdiction for the internal forum only (sacramental and non-sacramental). It issues decisions on questions of conscience; grants absolutions, dispensations, commutations, sanations and condonations; has charge of non-doctrinal matters pertaining to indulgences.

Background: Origin dates back to the 12th century; affected by the legislation of many popes; radically reorganized by St. Pius V in 1569; jurisdiction limited to the internal forum by St. Pius X; Benedict XV annexed the Office of Indulgences to it Mar. 25, 1917.

Apostolic Signatura: Piazza della Cancelleria 1, 00186 Rome, Italy. Cardinal Gilberto Agustoni, prefect; Most Rev. Zenon Grocholewski, secretary.

The principal concerns of this supreme court of the Church are to resolve questions concerning juridical procedure and to supervise the observance of laws and rights at the highest level. It decides the jurisdictional competence of lower courts and has jurisdiction in cases involving personnel and decisions of the Rota. It is the supreme court of the State of Vatican City.

Background: A permanent office of the Signatura has existed since the time of Eugene IV in the 15th century; affected by the legislation of many popes; reorganized by St. Pius X in 1908 and made the supreme tribunal of the Church.

Roman Rota: Piazza della Cancelleria 1, 00186 Rome, Italy. Msgr. Mario Francesco Pompedda, dean.

The ordinary court of appeal for cases appealed to the Holy See. It is best known for its competence and decisions in cases involving the validity of marriage.

Background: Originated in the Apostolic Chancery; affected by the legislation of many popes; reorganized by St. Pius X in 1908; further revised by Pius XI in 1934; new norms approved and promulgated by John Paul II in 1982 and 1987.

COUNCILS

Pontifical Council for the Laity: Piazza S. Calisto 16, 00153 Rome, Italy. Most Rev. James Francis Stafford, president; Most Rev. Stanislaw Rylko, secretary; Prof. Guzman Carriquiry, undersecretary.

Its competence covers the apostolate of the laity and their participation in the life and mission of the Church. Members are mostly lay people from different parts of the world and involved in different apostolates.

Background: Established on an experimental basis by Paul VI Jan. 6, 1967; given permanent status Dec. 10, 1976 (motu proprio *Apostolatus Peragendi*).

Pontifical Council for Promoting Christian Unity: Via dell' Erba 1, 00193 Rome, Italy. Cardinal Edward I. Cassidy, president; Cardinal Johannes Willebrands, president emeritus; Most Rev. Pierre Duprey, M. Afr., secretary; Most Rev. Jean Claude Perisset, adjunct secretary.

Handles relations with members of other Christian ecclesial communities; deals with the correct interpretation and execution of the principles of ecumenism; initiates or promotes Catholic ecumenical groups and coordinates on national and international levels the efforts of those promoting Christian unity; undertakes dialogue regarding ecumenical questions and activities with churches and ecclesial communities separated from the Apostolic See; sends Catholic observer-representatives to Christian gatherings, and invites to Catholic gatherings observers of other churches; orders into execution conciliar decrees dealing with ecumenical affairs. The Commission for Religious Relations with Jews is attached to the secretariat.

Background: Established by John XXIII June 5, 1960, as a preparatory secretariat of the Second Vatican Council; raised to commission status during the first session of the council in the fall of 1962; status as a secretariat confirmed and functions defined by Paul VI in 1966 and 1967; made a pontifical council by John Paul II, June 28, 1988.

Pontifical Council for the Family: Piazza S. Calisto 16, 00153 Rome, Italy. Cardinal Alfonso Lopez Trujillo, president; Most Rev. Francisco Gil Hellin, secretary.

Is concerned with promoting the pastoral care of families so they may carry out their educative, evangelizing and apostolic mission and make their influence felt in areas such as defense of human life and responsible procreation according to the teachings of the Church. Members, chosen by the Pope, are married couples and men and women from all parts of the world and representing different cultures. They meet in general assembly at least once a year.

Background: Instituted by John Paul II May 9, 1981, replacing the Committee for the Family established by Paul VI Jan. 11, 1973.

Pontifical Council for Justice and Peace: Piazza S. Calisto 16, 00153 Rome, Italy. Cardinal Roger Etchegaray, president; Msgr. Diarmuid Martin, secretary.

Its primary competence is to promote justice and peace in the world according to the Gospels and social teaching of the Church.

Background: Instituted by Paul VI Jan. 6, 1967, on an experimental basis; reconstituted and made a permanent commission Dec. 10, 1976; its competence was redefined and it was made a pontifical council June 28, 1988, by John Paul II.

Pontifical Council "Cor Unum": Piazza S. Calisto 16, 00153 Rome, Italy. Most Rev. Paul Josef Cordes, president; Rev. Ivan Marin Lopez, secretary.

Its principal aims are to provide informational and coordinating services for Catholic aid and human development organizations and projects on a worldwide scale. Attached to the council are the John Paul II Foundation for the Sahel and "Populorum Progressio."

Background: Instituted by Paul VI July 15, 1971.

Pontifical Council for Pastoral Care of Migrants and Itinerant Peoples: Piazza S. Calisto 16, 00153 Rome, Italy. Most Rev. Giovanni Cheli, president; Most Rev. Francesco Gioia, O.F.M. Cap., secretary.

Is concerned with pastoral assistance to migrants, nomads, tourists, sea and air travelers.

Background: Instituted by Paul VI and placed under general supervision of Congregation for Bishops, Mar. 19, 1970; made autonomous as a pontifical council and renamed by John Paul II, June 28, 1988.

Pontifical Council for Pastoral Assistance to Health Care Workers: Via della Conciliazione 3, 00193 Rome, Italy. Most Rev. Javier Lozano Barragan, president; Very Rev. Jose Luis Redrado Marchite, O.H., secretary.

Its functions are to stimulate and foster the work of formation, study and action carried out by various international Catholic organizations in the health care field.

Background: Established in 1985 as a commission by John Paul II; made a council June 28, 1988.

Pontifical Council for the Interpretation of Legislative Texts: Piazza Pio XII 10, 00193 Rome, Italy. Most Rev. Julian Herranz, president; Most Rev. Bruno Bertagna, secretary.

Primary function is the authentic interpretation of the universal laws of the Church.

Background: Established by John Paul II, Jan. 2, 1984, as the Pontifical Commission for the Authentic Interpretation of the Code of Canon Law; name changed and given additional functions June 28, 1988. Its competency was extended in 1991 to include interpretation of Code of Canon Law of Oriental Church which was promulgated in 1990.

Pontifical Council for Interreligious Dialogue: Via dell' Erba 1, 00193 Rome, Italy. Cardinal Francis Arinze, president; Most Rev. Michael Louis Fitzgerald, M. Afr., secretary.

Its function is to promote studies and dialogue for the purpose of increasing mutual understanding and respect between Christians and non-Christians. The Commission for Religious Relations with Muslims is attached to the council.

Background: Established by Paul VI May 19, 1964, as the Secretariat for Non-Christians; given present title and functions by John Paul II, June 28, 1988.

Pontifical Council for Culture: Piazza S. Calisto 16, 00153 Rome, Italy. Cardinal Paul Poupard, president; Rev. Bernard Ardura, O. Praem., secretary.

Its functions are to foster the Church's and the Holy See's relations with the world of culture and to establish dialogue with those who do not believe in God or who profess no religion provided these are open to sincere cooperation. It consists of two sections: (1) faith and culture; (2) dialogue with cultures. Attached to it is the Coordinating Council for Pontifical Academies.

Background: Present council with expanded functions was instituted by John Paul II (motu proprio of Mar. 25, 1993) through the merger of the Pontifical Council for Culture (established May 20, 1982, by John Paul II) and the Pontifical Council for Dialogue with Non-Believers (established by Paul VI Apr. 9, 1965, as the secretariat for Non-Believers).

Pontifical Council for Social Communications: Palazzo S. Carlo, 00120 Vatican City. Most Rev. John P. Foley, president; Most Rev. Pierfranco Pastore, secretary; Mr. Hans-Peter Rothlin, undersecretary; Cardinal Andrzej M. Deskur, president emeritus.

Engaged in matters pertaining to instruments of social communication so that through them the message of salvation and human progress is fostered and carried forward in civil culture and mores.

Background: Instituted on an experimental basis by Pius XII in 1948; reorganized three times in the 1950s; made permanent commission by John XXIII Feb. 22, 1959; established as council and functions restated by John Paul II June 28, 1988.

OFFICES

Apostolic Chamber: Palazzo Apostolico, 00120 Vatican City. Cardinal Eduardo Martinez Somalo, chamberlain of the Holy Roman Church; Most Rev. Ettore Cunial, vice-chamberlain.

Administers the temporal goods and rights of the Holy See between the death of one pope and the election of another, in accordance with special laws.

Background: Originated in the 11th century; reorganized by Pius XI in 1934; functions redefined (especially of camerlengo) by subsequent legislation in 1945, 1962 and 1975.

Prefecture for the Economic Affairs of the Holy See: Largo del Colonnato 3, 00193 Rome, Italy. Cardinal Edmund C. Szoka, president; Most Rev. Luigi Sposito, secretary.

A financial office which coordinates and supervises administration of the temporalities of the Holy See.

Background: Established by Paul VI Aug. 15, 1967; functions redefined by John Paul II, June 28, 1988.

Administration of the Patrimony of the Apostolic See: Palazzo Apostolico, 00120 Vatican City. Most Rev. Lorenzo Antonetti, pro-president; Most Rev. Claudio Maria Celli, secretary.

Handles the estate of the Apostolic See under the direction of papal delegates acting with ordinary or extraordinary authorization.

Background: Some of its functions date back to 1878; established by Paul VI Aug. 15, 1967.

Other Curia Agencies

Prefecture of the Papal Household: Most Rev. Dino Monduzzi, prefect.

Oversees the papal chapel — which is at the service of the pope in his capacity as spiritual head of the Church — and the pontifical family — which is at the service of the pope as a sovereign. It arranges papal audiences, has charge of preparing non-liturgical elements of papal ceremonies, makes all necessary arrangements for papal visits and trips outside the Vatican, and settles questions of protocol connected with papal audiences and other formalities.

Background: Established by Paul VI Aug. 15, 1967, under the title, Prefecture of the Apostolic Palace; it supplanted the Sacred Congregation for Ceremonies founded by Sixtus V Jan. 22, 1588. The office was updated and reorganized under the present title by Paul VI, Mar. 28, 1968.

Office for Liturgical Celebrations of the Supreme Pontiff: Palazzo Apostolico Vaticano, 00120 Vatican City. Msgr. Piero Marini, Master of Ceremonies.

Prepares everything necessary for liturgical and other sacred celebrations by the Pope or in his name; directs everything in accordance with prescriptions of liturgical law.

Background: Evolved gradually from the early office of Apostolic Master of Ceremonies; affected by legislation of Pope Paul IV in 1563 and Benedict XV in 1917; restructured by Paul VI in 1967; given its present title (formerly known as Prefecture of Pontifical Ceremonies) and constituted as an autonomous agency of the Roman Curia by John Paul II, June 28, 1988.

Vatican Press Office: Via della Conciliazione, 00120 Vatican City. Joaquin Navarro-Valls, director.

Established Feb. 29, 1968, to replace service agencies formerly operated by *L'Osservatore Romano* and an office created for press coverage of the Second Vatican Council. New directives were issued in 1986.

Vatican Information Service (VIS): Via della Conciliazione 54, 00120 Vatican City.

Established Mar. 28, 1990, within the framework but distinct from the Vatican Press Office. Furnishes information, in English, French and Spanish, on pastoral and magisterial activity of the Pope through use of electronic mail and fax.

Central Statistics Office: Palazzo Apostolico, 00120 Vatican City.

Established by Paul VI Aug. 15, 1967; attached to the Secretariat of State. Compiles, systematizes and analyzes information on the status and condition of the Church.

Internationalization

As of May 15, 1997, principal officials of the Roman Curia were from the following countries: Italy (Cards. Fagiolo, Felici, Laghi, Noè, Silvestrini, Sodano; Abps. Antonetti, Bertone, Bovone, Celli, Cheli, Cunial, Lajolo, Marchisano, Re, Sepe; Bps. Bertagna, Monduzzi, Pastore, Sposito); France (Cards. Etchegaray, Poupard, Abp. Tauran, Bp. Duprey); United States (Cards. Baum, Szoka, Abps. Foley, Schleck, Stafford); Spain (Card. Martinez Somalo; Abp. Herranz); Argentina (Card. Pironio, Abp. Mejia); Germany (Card. Ratzinger, Bp. Cordes); Poland (Abps. Grocholewski, Nowak); Australia (Card. Cassidy); Belgium (Card. Schotte); Benin (Card. Gantin); Brazil (Abp. Agnelo); Canada (Card. Gagnon); Chile (Bp. Medina Estevez); Colombia (Card. Lopez Trujillo; Abp. Castrillon Hoyos); Croatia (Abp. Uhac); England (Bp. Fitzgerald); Mexico (Abp. Lozano Barragan); Nigeria (Card. Arinze); Portugal (Abp. Saraiva Martins); Slovakia (Card. Tomko); Switzerland (Card. Agustoni); Ukraine (Abp. Marusyn).

COMMISSIONS AND COMMITTEES

Listed below are non-curial institutes which assist in the work of the Holy See. Some are attached to curial agencies, as indicated. Other institutes are listed elsewhere in the Almanac; see Index.

Pontifical Commission for the Cultural Heritage of the Church: Established by John Paul II, June 28, 1988, as Pontifical Commission for Preserving the Church's Patrimony of Art and History and attached to the Congregation for the Clergy; made autonomous and given present title Mar. 25, 1993. Most Rev. Francesco Marchisano, president.

Pontifical Commission for Sacred Archeology: Instituted by Pius IX Jan, 6, 1852. Most Rev. Francesco Marchisano, president.

Pontifical Biblical Commission: Instituted by Leo XIII Oct. 30, 1902; completely restructured by Paul VI June 27, 1971; attached to the Congregation for the Doctrine of the Faith. Cardinal Joseph Ratzinger, president.

Pontifical Commission for Latin America: Instituted by Pius XII Apr. 19, 1958; attached to the Congregation for Bishops July, 1969; restructured by John Paul II in 1988. Cardinal Bernardin Gantin, president.

Pontifical Commission for the Revision and Emendation of the Vulgate: Established in 1984 by

John Paul II to replace the Abbey of St. Jerome instituted by Pius XI in 1933. Rev. Jean Mallet, O.S.B., director.

Pontifical Commission "Ecclesia Dei": Established by John Paul II, July 2, 1988, to facilitate the return to full ecclesial communion of priests, seminarians and religious who belonged to the fraternity founded by Marcel Lefebvre. Cardinal Angelo Felici, president.

International Theological Commission: Instituted by Paul VI Apr. 11, 1969, as an advisory adjunct of no more than 30 theologians to the Congregation for the Doctrine of the Faith; definitive statutes promulgated by John Paul II, Aug. 6, 1982. Cardinal Joseph Ratzinger, president.

Commission for Religious Relations with Jews: Instituted by Paul VI, Oct. 22, 1974, to promote and foster relations of a religious nature between Jews and Christians; attached to the Council for Promoting Christian Unity. Cardinal Edward I. Cassidy, president.

Commission for Religious Relations with Muslims: Instituted by Paul VI, Oct. 22, 1974, to promote, regulate and interpret relations between Catholics and Muslims; attached to the Council for Interreligious Dialogue. Cardinal Francis Arinze, president.

Pontifical Committee for International Eucharistic Congresses: Instituted, 1879, by Pope Leo XIII; established as a pontifical committee with new statutes by John Paul II, Feb. 11, 1986. Cardinal Edouard Gagnon, president.

Pontifical Committee for Historical Sciences: Instituted by Pius XII Apr. 7, 1954, as a continuation of a commission dating from 1883. Msgr. Victor Saxer, president.

Committee for the Grand Jubilee of the Holy Year 2000: Instituted by John Paul II Nov. 15, 1994. Cardinal Roger Etchegaray, president.

Vatican II Archives: Preserves the acts and other documents of the Second Vatican Council.

Disciplinary Commission of the Roman Curia: Cardinal Vincenzo Fagiolo, president.

Fabric of St. Peter: Administration, care and preservation of Vatican Basilica. Cardinal Virgilio Noè, Archpriest of the Patriarchal Vatican Basilica, president.

Office of Papal Charities: Distributes alms and aid to those in need in the name of the Pope. Most Rev. Oscar Rizzato, almoner.

Council of Cardinals for Study of Organizational and Economic Problems of the Holy See: Council established in 1981 by Pope John Paul II; composed of approximately 15 cardinals from countries throughout the world (present membership includes U.S. Cardinals O'Connor and Mahony).

Commission for the Protection of the Historical and Artistic Monuments of the Holy See: Instituted by Pius XI in 1923, reorganized by Paul VI in 1963. Cardinal Virgilio Noè, president.

Institute for Works of Religion: Instituted by Pius XII June 27, 1942, to bank and administer funds for works of religion; replaced an earlier administration established by Leo XIII in 1887; reorganized by John Paul II (chirograph of Mar. 1, 1990).

Labor Office of the Apostolic See (ULSA - Ufficio del Lavoro della Sede Apostolica): Has competence in regard to those who work for the Apostolic See; charged with settling labor issues. Instituted by John Paul II (motu proprio of Jan. 1, 1989); functions reaffirmed and definitive text of statutes approved by John Paul II (motu proprio of Sept. 30, 1994). Cardinal Jan Schotte, president.

COLLEGE OF CARDINALS

Cardinals are chosen by the pope to serve as his principal assistants and advisers in the central administration of church affairs. Collectively, they form the College of Cardinals. Provisions regarding their selection, rank, roles and prerogatives are detailed in Canons 349 to 359 of the Code of Canon Law.

History of the College

The College of Cardinals was constituted in its present form and categories of membership in the 12th century. Before that time the pope had a body of advisers selected from among the bishops of dioceses neighboring Rome, priests and deacons of Rome. The college was given definite form in 1150, and in 1179 the selection of cardinals was reserved exclusively to the pope. Sixtus V fixed the number at 70, in 1586. John XXIII set aside this rule when he increased membership at the 1959 and subsequent consistories. The number was subsequently raised by Paul VI and by John Paul II. The number of cardinals entitled to participate in papal elections was limited to 120 by Paul VI in 1973. As of Aug. 30, 1997, 110 of the 148 cardinals were eligible to vote.

In 1567 the title of cardinal was reserved to members of the college; previously it had been used by priests attached to parish churches of Rome and by

the leading clergy of other notable churches. The Code of Canon Law promulgated in 1918 decreed that all cardinals must be priests. Previously there had been cardinals who were not priests (e.g., Cardinal Giacomo Antonelli, d. 1876, Secretary of State to Pius IX, was a deacon). John XXIII provided in the motu proprio *Cum Gravissima* Apr. 15, 1962, that cardinals would henceforth be bishops; this provision is included in the revised Code of Canon Law.

Age Limits

Pope Paul VI placed age limits on the functions of cardinals in the apostolic letter *Ingravescentem Aetatem,* dated Nov. 21, 1970, and effective as of Jan. 1, 1971. At 80, they cease to be members of curial departments and offices, and become ineligible to take part in papal elections. They retain membership in the College of Cardinals, however, with relevant rights and privileges.

Three Categories

All cardinals except Eastern patriarchs are aggregated to the clergy of Rome. This aggregation is signified by the assignment to each cardinal, except the patriarchs, of a titular church in Rome.

The three categories of members of the college are cardinal bishops, cardinal priests and cardinal deacons.

Cardinal bishops include the six titular bishops of the suburbicarian sees and Eastern patriarchs.

First in rank are the titular bishops of the suburbicarian sees, neighboring Rome: Ostia, Palestrina, Porto-Santa Rufina, Albano, Velletri-Segni, Frascati, Sabina-Poggio Mirteto. The dean of the college holds the title of the See of Ostia as well as his other suburbicarian see. These cardinal bishops are engaged in full-time service in the central administration of church affairs in departments of the Roman Curia.

Full recognition is given in the revised Code of Canon Law to the position of Eastern patriarchs as the heads of sees of apostolic origin with ancient liturgies. They are assigned rank among the cardinals in order of seniority, following the suburbicarian titleholders.

Cardinal priests, who were formerly in charge of leading churches in Rome, are bishops whose dioceses are outside Rome.

Cardinal deacons, who were formerly chosen according to regional divisions of Rome, are titular bishops assigned to full-time service in the Roman Curia.

The dean and sub-dean of the college are elected by the cardinal bishops — subject to approval by the pope — from among their number. The dean, or the sub-dean in his absence, presides over the college as the first among equals. Cardinals Bernardin Gantin and Agostino Casaroli were elected dean and sub-dean, respectively, June 4, 1993 (papal approval June 5, 1993).

Selection and Duties

Cardinals are selected by the pope and are inducted into the college in appropriate ceremonies.

Cardinals under the age of 80: elect the pope when the Holy See becomes vacant (see Index: Papal Election); and are major administrators of church affairs, serving in one or more departments of the Roman Curia. Cardinals in charge of agencies of the Roman Curia and Vatican City are asked to submit their resignation from office to the pope on reaching the age of 75. All cardinals enjoy a number of special rights and privileges. Their title, while symbolic of high honor, does not signify any extension of the powers of holy orders. They are called princes of the Church.

A cardinal *in pectore (petto)* is one whose selection has been made by the pope but whose name has not been disclosed; he has no title, rights or duties until such disclosure is made, at which time he takes precedence from the time of the secret selection.

BIOGRAPHIES OF CARDINALS

Biographies of the cardinals, as of Aug. 30, 1997, are given below in alphabetical order. For historical notes, order of seniority and geographical distribution of cardinals, see separate entries.

An asterisk indicates cardinals ineligible to take part in papal elections.

Agustoni, Gilberto: b. July 26, 1922, Schaffhausen, Switzerland; ord. priest Apr. 20, 1946; called to Rome in 1950 to work under Cardinal Ottaviani in the Congregation for the Holy Office; a Prelate Auditor of the Roman Rota, 1970-86; ord. titular archbishop of Caorle, Jan. 6, 1987; secretary of the Congregation for the Clergy, 1986-92; pro-prefect of the Apostolic Signatura, 1992-94; cardinal Nov. 26, 1994; deacon Sts. Urban and Laurence at Prima Porta. Prefect of Supreme Tribunal of Apostolic Signatora (Nov. 26, 1994). Curial membership:

Bishops, Catholic Education (congregations); Interpretation of Legislative Texts (council).

Angelini,* Fiorenzo: b. Aug. 1, 1916, Rome, Italy; ord. priest Feb. 3, 1940; master of pontifical ceremonies, 1947-54; ord. bishop (titular see of Messene) July 29, 1956, and head of Rome Vicariate's section for apostolate to health care workers; archbishop, 1985; president of newly established Curia agency for health care workers; cardinal June 28, 1991, deacon, Holy Spirit (in Sassio). President of Pontifical Council for Pastoral Assistance to Health Care Workers, 1989-96.

Aponte Martinez, Luis: b. Aug. 4, 1922, Lajas, Puerto Rico; ord. priest Apr. 10, 1950; parish priest at Ponce; ord. titular bishop of Lares and auxiliary of Ponce, Oct. 12, 1960; bishop of Ponce, 1963-64; archbishop of San Juan, Nov. 4, 1964; cardinal Mar. 5, 1973; titular church, St. Mary Mother of Providence (in Monte Verde). Archbishop of San Juan.

Aramburu,* Juan Carlos: b. Feb. 11, 1912, Reduccion, Argentina; ord. priest in Rome, Oct. 28, 1934; ord. titular bishop of Plataea and auxiliary of Tucuman, Argentina, Dec. 15, 1946; bishop, 1953, and first archbishop, 1957, of Tucuman; titular archbishop of Torri di Bizacena and coadjutor archbishop of Buenos Aires, June 14, 1967; archbishop of Buenos Aires, Apr. 22, 1975 (resigned July 10, 1990); cardinal May 24, 1976; titular church, St. John Baptist of the Florentines. Archbishop emeritus of Buenos Aires.

Arinze, Francis: b. Nov. 1, 1932, Eziowelle, Nigeria; ord. priest Nov. 23, 1958; ord. titular bishop of Fissiana and auxiliary of Onitsha, Aug. 29, 1965; archbishop of Onitsha, 1967-84; pro-president of Secretariat for Non-Christians (now the Council for Interreligious Dialogue), 1985; cardinal May 25, 1985; deacon, St. John (della Pigna); transferred to the order of cardinal priests Jan. 29, 1996. President of Council for Interreligious Dialogue, 1985. Curial membership:

Doctrine of the Faith, Oriental Churches, Evangelization of Peoples, Causes of Saints (congregations); Laity, Christian Unity, Culture (councils); International Eucharistic Congresses, Holy Year 2000 (committees).

Arns, Paulo Evaristo, O.F.M.: b. Sept. 14, 1921, Forquilhinha, Brazil; ord. priest Nov. 30, 1945; held various teaching posts; director of *Sponsa Christi*, monthly review for religious, and of the Franciscan publication center in Brazil; ord. titular bishop of Respetta and auxiliary of Sao Paulo, July 3, 1966; archbishop of Sao Paulo, Oct. 22, 1970; cardinal Mar. 5, 1973; titular church, St. Anthony of Padua (in Via Tuscolana). Archbishop of Sao Paulo.

Bafile,* Corrado: b. July 4, 1903, L'Aquila, Italy; practiced law in Rome for six years before beginning studies for priesthood; ord. priest Apr. 11, 1936; served in Vatican secretariat of state, 1939-59; ord. titular archbishop of Antiochia in Pisidia, Mar. 19, 1960; apostolic nuncio to Germany, 1960-75; pro-prefect of Congregation for Causes of Saints, July 18, 1975; cardinal May 24, 1976; deacon, S. Maria (in Portico); transferred to order of cardinal priests, June 22, 1987; prefect of Congregation for Causes of Saints, 1976-80.

Ballestrero,* Anastasio Alberto, O.C.D.: b. Oct. 3, 1913, Genoa, Italy; professed in Order of Discalced Carmelites, 1929; ord. priest June 6, 1936; provincial, 1942-48, and superior general, 1955-67, of Carmelites; author of many books on Christian life; ord. archbishop of Bari, Feb. 2, 1974; archbishop of Turin, Aug. 1, 1977 (resigned Jan. 31, 1989); cardinal June 30, 1979; titular church, S. Maria (sopra Minerva). Archbishop emeritus of Turin.

Baum, William Wakefield: b. Nov. 21, 1926, Dallas, Tex.; moved to Kansas City, Mo., at an early age; ord. priest (Kansas City-St. Joseph diocese) May 12, 1951; executive director of U.S. bishops commission for ecumenical and interreligious affairs, 1964-69; attended Second Vatican Council as *peritus* (expert adviser); ord. bishop of Springfield-Cape Girardeau, Mo., Apr. 6, 1970; archbishop of Washington, D.C., 1973-80; cardinal May 24, 1976; titular church, Holy Cross (on the Via Flaminia); prefect of Congregation for Catholic Education (Seminaries and Institutes of Study), 1980-90. Major Penitentiary, 1990. Curial membership:

Secretariat of State (second section); Doctrine of the Faith, Bishops, Oriental Churches, Causes of Saints, Institutes of Consecrated Life and Societies of Apostolic Life, Evangelization of Peoples (congregations); Interpretation of Legislative Texts (council); Patrimony of Holy See (office).

Bertoli,* Paolo: b. Feb.1, 1908, Poggio Garfagnana, Italy; ord. priest Aug. 15, 1930; entered diplomatic service of the Holy See, serving in nunciatures in Yugoslavia, France, Haiti and Switzerland; ord. titular archbishop of Nicomedia, May 11, 1952; apostolic delegate to Turkey (1952-53), nuncio to Colombia (1953-59), Lebanon (1959-60), France (1960-69); cardinal Apr. 28, 1969; prefect of Congregation for Causes of Saints, 1969-73; entered order of cardinal bishops as titular bishop of Frascati, June 30, 1979; Chamberlain (Camerlengo) of Holy Roman Church, 1979-85.

Bevilacqua, Anthony Joseph: b. June 17, 1923, Brooklyn N.Y.; educ. Cathedral College (Brooklyn, N.Y.), Immaculate Conception Seminary (Huntington, N.Y.), Gregorian Univ. (Rome), Columbia Univ. and St. John's Univ. (New York); ord. priest (Brooklyn diocese) June 11, 1949; ord. titular bishop of Aquae Albae in Byzacena and auxiliary bishop of Brooklyn, Nov. 24, 1980; bishop of Pittsburgh Oct. 7, 1983, installed Dec. 12, 1983; archbishop of Philadelphia, Feb. 11, 1988; cardinal June 28, 1991; titular church, Most Holy Redeemer and St. Alphonsus (on Via Merulana). Archbishop of Philadelphia. Curial membership:

Clergy, Causes of Saints (congregations); "Cor Unum," Migrants and Itinerant People (councils).

Biffi, Giacomo: b. June 13, 1928, Milan, Italy; ord. priest Dec. 23, 1950; ord. titular bishop of Fidene and auxiliary of Milan, Jan. 11, 1976; archbishop of Bologna, Apr. 19, 1984; cardinal May 25, 1985; titular church, Sts. John the Evangelist and Petronius. Archbishop of Bologna. Curial membership:

Doctrine of the Faith, Divine Worship and Sacraments, Clergy, Catholic Education (congregations).

Canestri, Giovanni: b. Sept. 30, 1918, Castelspina, Italy; ord. priest Apr. 12, 1941; spiritual director of Rome's seminary, 1959; ord. titular bishop of Tenedo and auxiliary to the cardinal vicar of Rome, July 30, 1961; bishop of Tortona, 1971-75; titular bishop of Monterano (personal title of archbishop) and vice regent of Rome, 1975-84; archbishop of Cagliari, 1984-87; archbishop of Genoa, July 6, 1987 (resigned Apr. 20, 1995); cardinal June 28, 1988; titular church, St. Andrew of the Valley. Archbishop emeritus of Genoa. Curial membership:

Divine Worship and Sacraments, Causes of Saints, Bishops, Clergy (congregations); Patrimony of the Holy See (office).

Caprio,* Giuseppe: b. Nov. 15, 1914, Lapio, Italy; ord. priest Dec. 17, 1938; served in diplomatic missions in China (1947-51, when Vatican diplomats were expelled by communists), Belgium (1951-54), and South Vietnam (1954-56); internuncio in China with residence at Taiwan, 1959-67; ord. titular archbishop of Apollonia, Dec. 17, 1961; pro-nuncio in India, 1967-69; secretary, 1969-77, and president, 1979-81, of Administration of Patrimony of Holy See; substitute secretary of state, 1977-79; cardinal deacon June 30, 1979; transferred to order of cardinal priests, November, 1990; titular church, St. Mary of Victory; president of Prefecture of Economic Affairs of the Holy See, 1981-90. Grand Master of Equestrian Order of the Holy Sepulchre, 1988-95.

Carberry,* John J.: b. July 31, 1904, Brooklyn, N.Y.; ord. priest (Brooklyn diocese) July 28, 1929; ord. titular bishop of Elis and coadjutor bishop of Lafayette, Ind., July 25, 1956; bishop of Lafayette, Nov. 20, 1957; bishop of Columbus, Ohio, Jan. 16, 1965; archbishop of St. Louis, Mo., 1968-79; cardinal Apr. 28, 1969; titular church, St. John Baptist de Rossi (Via Latina). Archbishop emeritus of St. Louis.

Carles Gordó, Ricardo Maria: b. Sept. 24, 1926, Valencia, Spain; ord. priest June 29, 1951; ord. bishop of Tortosa, Aug. 3, 1969; archbishop of Barcelona, Mar. 23, 1990; cardinal Nov. 26, 1994; titular church, St. Mary of Consolation in Tiburtino. Archbishop of Barcelona. Curial membership:

Catholic Education (congregation); Justice and Peace (council).

Carter,* Gerald Emmett: b. Mar. 1, 1912, Montreal, Canada; ord. priest May 22, 1937; founder and president of St. Joseph Teachers' College and co-founder and director of Thomas More Institute for adult education; ord. titular bishop of Altiburo and auxiliary bishop of London, Ont., Feb. 2, 1962; bishop of London, Ont., 1964-78; vice president, 1971-73, and president, 1975-77, of Canadian Conference of Catholic Bishops; archbishop of Toronto, 1978-90; cardinal June 30, 1979; titular church, St. Mary (in Traspontina). Archbishop emeritus of Toronto.

Casaroli,* Agostino: b. Nov. 24, 1914, Castel San

Giovanni, Italy; ord. priest May 27, 1937; entered service of Vatican secretariat of state, 1940; undersecretary, 1961-67, of the Congregation for Extraordinary Ecclesiastical Affairs, and secretary, 1967-79, of its successor the Council for Public Affairs of the Church; ord. titular archbishop of Cartagina, July 16, 1967; chief negotiator for the Vatican with East European communist governments; missions included visits to Hungary, Yugoslavia, Poland, Czechoslovakia, Bulgaria; headed Vatican delegations to several UN conferences and the Helsinki Conference (1975); Pro-Secretary of State and Pro-Prefect of Council for Public Affairs of the Church, Apr. 28, 1979; cardinal June 30, 1979; titular church, the Twelve Apostles; president, 1981-84, of Administration of Patrimony of Holy See and Pontifical Commission for Vatican City; entered order of cardinal bishops (retaining title to church of the Twelve Apostles) as titular bishop of Porto-Santa Rufina, May 25, 1985. Secretary of State, 1979-90. Sub-dean of the college of cardinals, 1993.

Casoria,* Giuseppe: b. Oct. 1, 1908, Acerra, Italy; ord. priest Dec. 21, 1930; jurist; Roman Curia official from 1937; under-secretary, 1959-69, and secretary, 1969-73, of Congregation for Divine Worship and Sacraments; secretary of Congregation for Causes of Saints, 1973-81; ord. titular bishop of Vescovia with personal title of archbishop, Feb. 13, 1972; pro-prefect of Congregation for Divine Worship and Sacraments, 1981-83; cardinal deacon Feb. 2, 1983; transferred to order of cardinal priests Apr. 5, 1993; titular church, St. Joseph on Via Trionfale. Prefect of Congregation for Divine Worship and Sacraments, 1983-84.

Cassidy, Edward Idris: b. July 5, 1924, Sydney, Australia; ord. priest July 23, 1949; entered Vatican diplomatic service in 1955; served in nunciatures in India, Ireland, El Salvador and Argentina; ord. titular bishop of Amantia with personal title of archbishop, Nov. 15, 1970; pro-nuncio to Republic of China (Taiwan), 1970-79 and pro-nuncio to Bangladesh and apostolic delegate in Burma, 1973-79; pro-nuncio to Lesotho and apostolic delegate to southern Africa, 1979-84; pro-nuncio to the Netherlands, 1984-88; substitute of the Secretary of State for General Affairs, 1988-89; president of Pontifical Council for Promoting Christian Unity, 1989; cardinal June 28, 1991; deacon, St. Mary (in via Lata). President of Pontifical Council for Promoting Christian Unity. Curial membership: Secretariat of State (second section); Doctrine of the Faith, Divine Worship and Sacraments, Bishops, Oriental Churches, Evangelization of Peoples (congregations); Interreligious Dialogue, "Cor Unum" (councils); Patrimony of the Holy See (office); Latin America, Holy Year 2000 (commission/committee).

Castillo Lara, Rosalio Jose, S.D.B.: b. Sept. 4, 1922, San Casimiro, Venezuela; ord. priest Sept. 4, 1949; ord. titular bishop of Precausa, May 24, 1973; coadjutor bishop of Trujillo, 1973-76; archbishop May 26, 1982; pro-president of Pontifical Commission for Revision of Code of Canon Law, 1982-84; pro-president of Commission for Authentic Interpretation of Code of Canon Law, 1984-85; cardinal May 25, 1985; deacon, Our Lady of Coromoto (in St. John of God); transferred to order of cardinal priests Jan.

29, 1996; president of Administration of Patrimony of the Holy See, 1989-95. President of the Pontifical Commission for the State of Vatican City, 1990. Curial membership: Secretariat of State (second section); Bishops, Institutes of Consecrated Life and Societies of Apostolic Life (congregations); Apostolic Signatura (tribunal); Institute for Works of Religion (commission).

Cé, Marco: b. July 8, 1925, Izano, Italy; ord. priest Mar. 27, 1948; taught sacred scripture and dogmatic theology at seminary in his home diocese of Crema; rector of seminary, 1957; presided over diocesan liturgical commission, preached youth retreats; ord. titular bishop of Vulturia, May 17, 1970; auxiliary bishop of Bologna, 1970-76; general ecclesiastical assistant of Italian Catholic Action, 1976-78; patriarch of Venice, Dec. 7, 1978; cardinal June 30, 1979; titular church, St. Mark. Patriarch of Venice. Curial membership: Divine Worship and Sacraments, Oriental Churches (congregations).

Clancy, Edward Bede: b. Dec. 13, 1923, Lithgow, New South Wales, Australia; ord. priest July 23, 1949; ord. titular bishop of Ard Carna and auxiliary of Sydney, Jan. 19, 1974; archbishop of Canberra, 1978-83; archbishop of Sydney, Feb. 12, 1983; cardinal June 28, 1988; titular church, Holy Mary of Vallicella. Archbishop of Sydney. Curial membership: Secretariat of State (second section); Economic Affairs of the Holy See (office).

Corripio Ahumada, Ernesto: b. June 29, 1919, Tampico, Mexico; ord. priest Oct. 25, 1942, in Rome, where he remained until almost the end of World War II; taught and held various positions in local seminary of Tampico, 1945-50; ord. titular bishop of Zapara and auxiliary bishop of Tampico, Mar. 19, 1953; bishop of Tampico, 1956-67; archbishop of Antequera, 1967-76; archbishop of Puebla de los Angeles, 1976-77; archbishop of Mexico City and primate of Mexico, July 19, 1977 (resigned Sept. 29, 1994); cardinal June 30, 1979; titular church, Mary Immaculate al Tiburtino. Archbishop emeritus of Mexico City. Curial membership: Clergy (congregation).

Daly, Cahal Brendan: b. Oct. 1, 1917, Loughguile, Northern Ireland; ord. priest June 22, 1941; earned advanced degrees in philosophy and theology; 30 years of priestly life dedicated to teaching; attended Second Vatican Council as a theological adviser to members of Irish hierarchy; outspoken critic of violence in Northern Ireland; ord. bishop of Ardagh, July 16, 1967; bishop of Down and Connor, 1982-90; archbishop of Armagh and primate of All Ireland, Nov. 6, 1990; cardinal June 28, 1991; titular church, St. Patrick. Archbishop emeritus of Armagh (resigned Oct. 1, 1996). Curial membership: Evangelization of Peoples, Clergy (congregations); Christian Unity (council).

Danneels, Godfried: b. June 4, 1933, Kanegem, Belgium; ord. priest Aug. 17, 1957; professor of liturgy and sacramental theology at Catholic University of Louvain, 1969-77; ord. bishop of Antwerp Dec. 18, 1977; app. archbishop of Mechelen-Brussel, Dec. 19, 1979; installed Jan. 4, 1980; cardinal Feb. 2, 1983; titular church, St. Anastasia. Archbishop of

Mechelen-Brussel, military ordinary of Belgium.
Curial membership:
Secretariat of State (second section); Oriental
Churches, Divine Worship and Sacraments, Evangelization of Peoples, Catholic Education (congregations).
Darmaatmadja, Julius Riyadi, S.J.: b. Dec. 20,
1934, Muntilan, Mageland, Central Java, Indonesia;
entered Society of Jesus in 1957; ord. priest Dec.
18, 1969; ord. archbishop of Semarang, June 29,
1983 (transferred to Jakarta Jan. 11, 1996); cardinal
Nov. 26, 1994; titular church, Sacred Heart of Mary.
Archbishop of Jakarta, military ordinary of Indonesia (1984). Curial membership:
Evangelization of Peoples (congregation); Interreligious Dialogue (council).
Deskur, Andrzej Maria: b. Feb. 29, 1924,
Sancygniow, Poland; ord. priest Aug. 20, 1950, in
France; assigned to Vatican secretariat of state, 1952;
undersecretary and later secretary of Pontifical Com-
mission for Film, Radio and TV (Social Communi-
cations), 1954-73; ord. titular bishop of Tene, June
30, 1974; archbishop, 1980; president of Pontifical
Commission for Social Communications, 1974-84;
cardinal May 25, 1985; deacon, St. Cesario (in
Palatio); transferred to order of cardinal priests Jan.
29, 1996. President emeritus of Council for Social
Communications. Curial membership:
Divine Worship and Sacraments, Causes of Saints
(congregations); Health Care Workers (council);
State of Vatican City (commission).
Dezza,* Paolo, S.J.: b. Dec. 13, 1901, Parma, Italy;
entered Society of Jesus in 1918; ord. priest, Mar.
25, 1928; made solemn profession as Jesuit, 1935;
served as rector of Pontifical Gregorian University;
delegated as head of Society of Jesus by John Paul
II October, 1981, until the election of the new superior general; cardinal June 28, 1991, with permission to decline episcopal ordination; deacon, St.
Ignatius of Loyola (a Campo Marzio).
do Nascimento, Alexandre: b. Mar. 1, 1925,
Malanje, Angola; ord. priest Dec. 20, 1952, in Rome;
professor of dogmatic theology in major seminary
of Luanda, Angola; editor of O Apostolada, Catholic newspaper; forced into exile in Lisbon, Portugal,
1961-71; returned to Angola, 1971; active with student and refugee groups; professor at Pius XII Institute of Social Sciences; ord. bishop of Malanje, Aug.
31, 1975; archbishop of Lubango and apostolic administrator of Onjiva, 1977-86; held hostage by
Angolan guerrillas, Oct. 15 to Nov. 16, 1982; cardinal Feb. 2, 1983; titular church, St. Mark in Agro
Laurentino. Archbishop of Luanda, 1986. Curial
membership:
Evangelization of Peoples, Catholic Education
(congregations).
Echeverria Ruiz,* Bernardino, O.F.M.: b. Nov.
12, 1912, Cotacachi, Ecuador; entered Franciscans
1928; ord. priest July 4, 1937; ord. bishop of Ambato
Dec. 4, 1949; archbishop of Guayaquil, 1969-89;
apostolic administrator of Ibarra, 1989-95; cardinal
Nov. 26, 1994; titular church, Sts. Nereus and
Achilleus. Archbishop emeritus of Guayaquil.
Etchegaray, Roger: b. Sept. 25, 1922, Espelette,
France; ord. priest July 13, 1947; deputy director,
1961-66, and secretary general, 1966-70, of French

Episcopal Conference; ord. titular bishop of Gemelle
di Numidia and auxiliary of Paris, May 27, 1969;
archbishop of Marseilles, 1970-84; prelate of Mission de France, 1975-82; president of French Episcopal Conference, 1979-81; cardinal June 30, 1979;
titular church, St. Leo I; president of Council *Cor
Unum,* 1984-95. President (1984) of Council for
Justice and Peace and (1994) of Central Committee
for the Jubilee of the Holy Year 2000. Curial membership:
Oriental Churches, Evangelization of Peoples,
Catholic Education (congregations); Apostolic
Signatura (tribunal); Laity, Christian Unity, Social
Communications, Interreligious Dialogue (councils).
Etsou-Nzabi-Bamungwabi, Frédéric, C.I.C.M.:
b. Dec. 3, 1930, Mazalonga, Zaire; ord. priest July
13, 1958; educ. Catholic Institute of Paris (degree in
sociology) and "Lumen Vitae" in Belgium (degree
in pastoral theology); ord. titular bishop of Menefessi
and coadjutor archbishop of Mbandaka-Bikora, Nov.
7, 1976; archbishop of Mbandaka-Bikora, 1977-
1990; archbishop of Kinshasa, July 7, 1990; cardinal June 28, 1991; titular church, St. Lucy (a Piazza
d'Armi). Archbishop of Kinshasa. Curial membership:
Evangelization of Peoples (congregation); Family
(council).
Eyt, Pierre: b. June 4, 1934, Laruns, France; ord.
priest June 29, 1961; chaplain of St. Louis of the
French in Rome, 1963; taught theology at Catholic
Institute in Toulouse, 1967-72; ord. coadjutor archbishop of Bordeaux, Sept. 28, 1986; archbishop of
Bordeaux, May 31, 1989; cardinal Nov. 26, 1994;
titular church, Most Holy Trinity on Monte Pincio.
Archbishop of Bordeaux. Curial membership:
Doctrine of the Faith, Catholic Education (congregations).
Fagiolo, Vincenzo: b. Feb. 5, 1918, Segni, Italy;
ord. priest Mar. 6, 1943; prelate auditor of Roman
Rota, 1967-71; ord. archbishop of Chieti-Vasto, Dec.
19, 1971; resigned see July 15, 1984; secretary of
Congregation for Institutes of Consecrated Life and
Societies of Apostolic Life, 1984-90; president of
the Pontifical Council for the Interpretation of Legislative Texts, 1991-94; cardinal Nov. 26, 1994; deacon, St. Theodore. President of Diciplinary Commission of the Roman Curia, Dec. 29, 1990. Curial membership:
Secretariat of State (second section); Bishops (congregation); Apostolic Signatura (tribunal).
Falcao, Jose Freire: b. Oct. 23, 1925, Erere, Brazil; ord. priest June 19, 1949; ord. titular bishop of
Vardimissa and coadjutor of Limoeiro do Norte, June
17, 1967; bishop of Limoeiro do Norte, Aug. 19,
1967; archbishop of Teresina, Nov. 25, 1971; archbishop of Brasilia, Feb. 15, 1984; cardinal June 28,
1988; titular church, St. Luke (Via Prenestina). Archbishop of Brasilia. Curial membership:
Health Care Workers (council); Latin America
(commission).
Felici, Angelo: b. July 26, 1919, Segni, Italy; ord.
priest Apr. 4, 1942; in Vatican diplomatic service
from 1945; ord. titular bishop of Cesariana, with
personal title of archbishop, Sept. 24, 1967; nuncio
to Netherlands, 1967-76, Portugal, 1976-79, France,
1979-88; cardinal June 28, 1988; deacon, Sts. Blaise

and Charles in Catinari. Prefect of Congregation for Causes of Saints, 1988-95. President of Pontifical Commission "Ecclesia Dei," 1995. Curial membership:

Secretariat of State (second section); Oriental Churches, Bishops, Evangelization of Peoples, Clergy (congregations); Christian Unity (council).

Fresno Larrain,* Juan Francisco: b. July 26, 1914, Santiago, Chile; ord. priest Dec. 18, 1937; ord. bishop of Copiapo, Aug. 15, 1958; archbishop of La Serena, 1967-83; archbishop of Santiago, May 3, 1983 (resigned Mar. 30, 1990); cardinal May 25, 1985; titular church, St. Mary Immaculate of Lourdes (a Boccea). Archbishop emeritus of Santiago.

Furno, Carlo: b. Dec. 2, 1921, Bairo Canavese, Italy; ord. priest June 25, 1944; entered diplomatic service of the Holy See in the 1950s; served in Colombia, Ecuador and Jerusalem; worked in Secretariat of State for 11 years and taught at Pontifical Ecclesiastical Academy, 1966-73; ord. titular bishop of Abari with personal title of archbishop, Sept. 16, 1973; nuncio in Peru, 1973-78, Lebanon, 1978-82, Brazil, 1982-92, Italy, 1992-94; cardinal Nov. 26, 1994; deacon, Sacred Heart of Christ the King. Grand Master of the Equestrian Order of the Holy Sepulchre, 1995; pontifical delegate for Patriarchal Basilica of St. Francis in Assisi, 1996. Curial membership:

Secretariat of State (second section); Oriental Churches, Bishops, Evangelization of Peoples (congregations); State of Vatican City, Institute for Works of Religion (commissions).

Gagnon, Edouard, P.S.S.: b. Jan. 15, 1918, Port Daniel, Que., Canada; ord. priest Aug. 15, 1940; ord. bishop of St. Paul in Alberta Mar. 25, 1969 (resigned May 3, 1972); rector of Canadian College in Rome, 1972-77; vice president-secretary of Vatican Committee for the Family, 1973-80; titular archbishop of Giustiniana Prima, July 7, 1983; pro-president of Pontifical Council for the Family, 1983; cardinal May 25, 1985; deacon, St. Elena (fuori Porta Prenestina); transferred to order of cardinal priests Jan. 29, 1996; titular church St. Marcellus; president of Pontifical Council for the Family, 1985-90. President of Pontifical Committee for International Eucharistic Congresses, 1991. Curial membership:

Divine Worship and Sacraments, Causes of Saints (congregations); Apostolic Signatura (tribunal).

Gantin, Bernardin: b. May 8, 1922, Toffo, Dahomey (now Benin); ord. priest Jan. 14, 1951; ord. titular bishop of Tipasa di Mauritania and auxiliary bishop of Cotonou, Feb. 3, 1957; archbishop of Cotonou, 1960-71; associate secretary (1971-73) and secretary (1973-75) of Congregation for Evangelization of Peoples; vice-president (1975) and president (1976-84) of Pontifical Commission for Justice and Peace; cardinal deacon June 27, 1977; transferred to order of priests June 25, 1984; titular church, Sacred Heart of Christ the King; titular bishop of suburbicarian see of Palestrina Sept 29, 1986, when he entered the order of cardinal bishops, and of Ostia June 5, 1993, when he became dean of the college of cardinals. Prefect of Congregation for Bishops, 1984; president of commission for Latin America, 1984; dean of college of cardinals, 1993. Curial membership:

Secretariat of State (second section); Divine Worship and Sacraments, Causes of Saints, Evangelization of Peoples, Oriental Churches, Institutes of Consecrated Life and Societies of Apostolic Life, Catholic Education (congregations); Apostolic Signatura (tribunal); Interpretation of Legislative Texts (council).

Giordano, Michele: b. Sept. 26, 1930, S. Arcangelo, Italy; ord. priest July 5, 1953; ord. titular bishop of Lari Castello and auxiliary of Matera, Feb. 5, 1972; archbishop of Matera and Irsina, 1974-87; archbishop of Naples, May 9, 1987; cardinal June 28, 1988; titular church, St. Joachim. Archbishop of Naples. Curial membership:

Secretariat of State (second section); Divine Worship and Sacraments, Clergy (congregations); Health Care Workers (council).

Glemp, Jozef: b. Dec. 18, 1929, Inowroclaw, Poland; assigned to forced labor on German farm in Rycerzow during Nazi occupation; ord. priest May 25, 1956; studied in Rome, 1958-64; received degree in Roman and canon law from Pontifical Lateran University; secretary of primatial major seminary at Gniezno on his return to Poland, 1964; spokesman for secretariat of primate of Poland and chaplain of primate for archdiocese of Gniezno, 1967; ord. bishop of Warmia, Apr. 21, 1979; archbishop of Gniezno, 1981-92, with title of archbishop of Warsaw and primate of Poland; cardinal Feb. 2, 1983; titular church, St. Mary in Trastevere. Archbishop of Warsaw (Mar. 25, 1992), primate of Poland, ordinary for Eastern-rite faithful in Poland who do not have ordinaries of their own rites. Curial membership:

Oriental Churches (congregation); Justice and Peace, Culture (councils).

Gong (Kung) Pin-mei,* Ignatius: b. Aug. 2, 1901, P'ou-tong, China; ord. priest May 28, 1930; worked in schools and as a missionary; ord. bishop of Soochow Oct. 7, 1949; bishop of Shanghai July 15, 1950; imprisoned by Chinese communists in 1955 and sentenced to life imprisonment in 1960; paroled in 1985 after 30 years; pardoned and political rights restored Jan. 5, 1988, but was not permitted to function as a bishop; came to the United States in 1988; cardinal June 30, 1979 "in pectore"; name revealed and formally invested at June 28, 1991, public consistory; titular church, St. Sixtus. Bishop of Shanghai and apostolic administrator of Soochow. (Resides in U.S.)

Gonzalez Martin, Marcelo: b. Jan. 16, 1918, Villanubla, Spain; ord. priest June 29, 1941; taught theology and sociology at Valladolid diocesan seminary; founded organization for construction of houses for poor; ord. bishop of Astorga, Mar. 5, 1961; titular archbishop of Case Mediane and coadjutor of Barcelona, Feb. 21, 1966; archbishop of Barcelona, 1967-71; archbishop of Toledo, 1971-95; cardinal Mar. 5, 1973; titular church, St. Augustine. Archbishop emeritus of Toledo. Curial membership:

Clergy (congregation).

Gouyon,* Paul: b. Oct. 24, 1910, Bordeaux, France; ord. priest Mar. 13, 1937; ord. bishop of Bayonne, Oct. 7, 1957; titular archbishop of Pessinonte and coadjutor archbishop of Rennes, Sept. 6, 1963; archbishop of Rennes, Sept. 4, 1964 (resigned Oct. 15, 1985); cardinal Apr. 28, 1969; titular church, Nativity of Our Lord Jesus Christ (Via Gallia). Archbishop emeritus of Rennes.

Grillmeier,*Alois, S.J.: b. Jan. 1, 1910, Pechbrunn, Germany; entered Society of Jesus, 1929; ord. priest June 24, 1937; taught fundamental and dogmatic theology and the history of theology at various ecclesiastical institutes; author of a number of books on dogmatic theology and the history of theology; member of the theological commission of the Second Vatican Council; cardinal Nov. 26, 1994; deacon, St. Nicholas in Prison.

Groër, Hans Hermann, O.S.B.: b. Oct. 13, 1919, Vienna, Austria; ord. priest Apr. 12, 1942; ord. archbishop of Vienna, Sept. 14, 1986; cardinal June 28, 1988; titular church, Sts. Joachim and Anne al Tuscolano. Archbishop emeritus of Vienna (resigned Sept. 14, 1995). Curial membership:
Oriental Churches, Divine Worship and Sacraments, Institutes of Consecrated Life and Societies of Apostolic Life, Catholic Education (congregations).

Gulbinowicz, Henryk Roman: b. Oct. 17, 1928, Szukiszki, Poland; ord. priest June 18, 1950; ord. titular bishop of Acci and apostolic administrator of Polish territory in Lithuanian archdiocese of Vilnius (Vilna), Feb. 8, 1970; archbishop of Wroclaw, Poland, Jan. 3, 1976; cardinal May 25, 1985; titular church, Immaculate Conception of Mary (a Grottarosa). Archbishop of Wroclaw. Curial membership:
Oriental Churches, Evangelization of Peoples, Clergy (congregations).

Hickey, James A.: b. Oct. 11, 1920, Midland, Mich.; ord. priest (Saginaw diocese) June 15, 1946; ord. titular bishop of Taraqua and auxiliary of Saginaw, Apr. 14, 1967; rector of North American College, Rome, 1969-74; bishop of Cleveland, 1974-80; app. archbishop of Washington, D.C., June 17, 1980, installed Aug. 5, 1980; cardinal June 28, 1988; titular church, St. Mary Mother of the Redeemer. Archbishop of Washington, D.C. Curial membership:
Causes of Saints, Institutes of Consecrated Life and Societies of Apostolic Life, Catholic Education, Clergy (congregations); Family (council).

Hume, George Basil, O.S.B.: b. Mar. 2, 1923, Newcastle-upon-Tyne, England; began monastic studies at Benedictine Abbey of St. Laurence at Ampleforth, 1941; made solemn perpetual vows as Benedictine, 1945; ord. priest July 23, 1950; abbot of Ampleforth, 1963-76; ord. archbishop of Westminster, Mar. 25, 1976; cardinal May 24, 1976; titular church, St. Silvestro (in Capite). Archbishop of Westminster. Curial membership:
Oriental Churches, Divine Worship and Sacraments, Institutes of Consecrated Life and Societies of Apostolic Life (congregations); Christian Unity, Health Care Workers (councils).

Innocenti,* Antonio: b. Aug. 23, 1915, Poppi, Italy; ord. priest July 17, 1938; held curial and diplomatic positions; ord. titular bishop of Eclano with personal title of archbishop, Feb. 18, 1968; nuncio to Paraguay, 1967-73; secretary of Congregation for Causes of Saints, 1973-75; secretary of Congregation for Sacraments and Divine Worship, 1975-80; nuncio to Spain, 1980-85; cardinal deacon May 25,

1985; transferred to order of cardinal priests Jan. 29, 1996; titular church, St. Marie (in Aquiro); prefect of Congregation for the Clergy, 1986-91; president of Pontifical Commission for Preservation of Artistic Patrimony of the Church, 1988-91; president of Pontifical Commission "Ecclesia Dei," 1991-95.

Javierre Ortas, Antonio Maria, S.D.B.: b. Feb. 21, 1921, Sietamo, Spain; ord. priest Apr. 24, 1949; leading European writer on ecumenism; ord. titular bishop of Meta with personal title of archbishop, June 29, 1976; Secretary of Congregation for Catholic Education, 1976-88; cardinal June 28, 1988; deacon, St. Mary Liberator (a Monte Testaccio). Librarian and Archivist of the Holy Roman Church, 1988-92. Prefect of Congregation for Divine Worship and the Sacraments, 1992-96. Curial membership:
Doctrine of the Faith, Bishops, Catholic Education, Clergy (congregations); Apostolic Signatura (tribunal); Laity, Christian Unity, Interpretation of Legislative Texts (councils).

Keeler, William Henry: b. Mar. 4, 1931, San Antonio, Tex.; ord. priest (Harrisburg diocese) July 17, 1955; secretary to Bishop Leech at Vatican II, named peritus by Pope John XXIII; ord. titular bishop of Ulcinium and auxiliary bishop of Harrisburg, Sept. 21, 1979; bishop of Harrisburg, Nov. 10, 1983, installed Jan. 4, 1984; archbishop of Baltimore, Apr. 6, 1989; cardinal Nov. 26, 1994; titular church, St. Mary of the Angels. Archbishop of Baltimore. Curial membership:
Oriental Churches (congregation); Christian Unity (council).

Kim Sou Hwan, Stephen: b. May 8, 1922, Tae Gu, Korea; ord. priest Sept. 15, 1951; ord. bishop of Masan, May 31, 1966; archbishop of Seoul, Apr. 9, 1968; cardinal Apr. 28, 1969; titular church, St. Felix of Cantalice (Centocelle). Archbishop of Seoul, apostolic administrator of Pyeong Yang. Curial membership:
Evangelization of Peoples (congregation).

Kitbunchu, Michael Michai: b. Jan. 25, 1929, Samphran, Thailand; ord. priest Dec. 20, 1959, in Rome; rector of metropolitan seminary in Bangkok, 1965-72; ord. archbishop of Bangkok, June 3, 1973; cardinal Feb. 2, 1983, the first from Thailand; titular church, St. Laurence in Panisperna. Archbishop of Bangkok. Curial membership:
Evangelization of Peoples (congregation); Economic Affairs of the Holy See (office).

Koenig,* Franz: b. Aug. 3, 1905, Rabenstein, Lower Austria; ord. priest Oct. 29, 1933; ord. titular bishop of Livias and coadjutor bishop of Sankt Poelten, Aug. 31, 1952; archbishop of Vienna, May 10, 1956 (resigned Sept. 16, 1985); cardinal Dec. 15, 1958; titular church, St. Eusebius; president of Secretariat (now Council) for Dialogue with Non-Believers, 1965-80. Archbishop emeritus of Vienna.

Korec, Jan Chryzostom, S.J.: b. Jan. 22, 1924, Bosany, Slovakia; entered Society of Jesus in 1939; ord. priest Oct. 1, 1950; ord. bishop secretly Aug. 24, 1951; sentenced to 12 years in prison in 1960 for helping seminarians with their study and ordaining priests; paroled in 1968; appointed bishop of Nitra Feb. 6, 1990; cardinal June 28, 1991; titular church, Sts. Fabian and Venantius (a Villa Forelli). Bishop of Nitra. Curial membership:

Institutes of Consecrated Life and Societies of Apostolic Life (congregation); Culture (council).

Kuharic, Franjo: b. Apr. 15, 1919, Pribic, Croatia; ord. priest July 15, 1945; ord. titular bishop of Meta and auxiliary bishop of Zagreb, May 3, 1964; apostolic administrator of archdiocese of Zagreb, 1968-70; archbishop of Zagreb, June 16, 1970; cardinal Feb. 2, 1983; titular church, St. Jerome of the Croats. Archbishop emeritus of Zagreb (resigned July 5, 1997). Curial membership: Divine Worship and Sacraments, Clergy (congregations).

Laghi, Pio: b. May 21, 1922, Castiglione, Italy; ord. priest Apr. 20, 1946; entered diplomatic service of the Holy See in 1952; served in Nicaragua, the U.S. (as secretary of the apostolic delegation, 1954-61) and India; recalled to Rome and served on Council for Public Affairs of the Church; ord. titular archbishop of Mauriana June 22, 1969; apostolic delegate to Jerusalem and Palestine, 1969-74; nuncio to Argentina, 1974-80; apostolic delegate, 1980-84, and first pro-nuncio, 1984-90 to the U.S.; pro-prefect of Congregation for Catholic Education, 1990-91; cardinal June 28, 1991; deacon, St. Mary Auxiliatrix (in Via Tuscolana). Prefect of Congregation for Catholic Education, 1991. Grand chancellor of Pontifical Gregorian University. Patron of Sovereign Military Order of Malta , 1993. Curial membership: Secretariat of State (second section); Bishops, Oriental Churches, Evangelization of Peoples, Causes of Saints, Institutes of Consecrated Life and Societies of Apostolic Life, Clergy (congregations); Interpretation of Legislative Texts (council).

Law, Bernard F.: b. Nov. 4, 1931,Torreon, Mexico, the son of U.S. Air Force colonel; ord. priest (Jackson diocese) May 21, 1961; editor of Natchez-Jackson, Miss., diocesan paper, 1963-68; director of NCCB Committee on Ecumenical and Interreligious Affairs, 1968-71; ord. bishop of Springfield-Cape Girardeau, Mo., Dec. 5, 1973; archbishop of Boston, Jan. 11, 1984; cardinal May 25, 1985; titular church, St. Susanna. Archbishop of Boston. Curial membership: Oriental Churches; Divine Worship and Sacraments, Institutes of Consecrated Life and Societies of Apostolic Life, Evangelization of Peoples, Catholic Education (congregations); Culture (council).

Lebrun Moratinos, Jose Ali: b. Mar. 19, 1919, Puerto Cabello, Venezuela; ord. priest Dec. 19, 1943; ord. titular bishop of Arado and auxiliary bishop of Maracaibo, Sept. 2, 1956; first bishop of Maracay, 1958-62; bishop of Valencia, 1962-72; titular bishop of Voncario (personal title of archbishop) and coadjutor archbishop of Caracas, Sept. 16, 1972; archbishop of Caracas, 1980-95; cardinal Feb. 2, 1983; titular church, St. Pancratius. Archbishop emeritus of Caracas. Curial membership: Secretariat of State (second section).

Lopez Rodriguez, Nicolas de Jesus: b. Oct. 31, 1936, Barranca, Dominican Republic; ord. priest Mar. 18, 1961; sent to Rome for advanced studies at the Angelicum and Gregorian Univ.; served in various diocesan offices after returning to his home diocese of La Vega; ord. first bishop of San Francisco de Macoris Feb. 25, 1978; archbishop of Santo Domingo, Nov. 15, 1981; cardinal June 28, 1991;

titular church, St. Pius X (alla Balduina).Archbishop of Santo Domingo and Military Ordinary for Dominican Republic. Curial membership: Divine Worship and Sacraments, Clergy, Institutes of Consecrated Life and Societies of Apostolic Life (congregations); Social Communications (council); Latin America (commission) .

Lopez Trujillo, Alfonso: b. Nov. 8, 1935, Villahermosa, Colombia; ord. priest Nov. 13, 1960, in Rome; returned to Colombia, 1963; taught at major seminary; was pastoral coordinator for 1968 International Eucharistic Congress in Bogota; vicar general of Bogota, 1970-72; ord. titular bishop of Boseta, Mar. 25, 1971; auxiliary bishop of Bogota, 1971-72; secretary-general of CELAM, 1972-78; helped organize 1979 Puebla Conference in which Pope John Paul II participated; app. coadjutor archbishop of Medellin, May 22, 1978; archbishop of Medellin, June 2, 1979 (resigned Jan 9, 1991); president of CELAM, 1979-83; cardinal Feb. 2, 1983; titular church, St. Prisca. Archbishop emeritus of Medellin. President of the Pontifical Council for the Family, 1990. Curial membership: Doctrine of the Faith, Causes of Saints, Bishops, Evangelization of Peoples (congregations); Latin America (commission).

Lorscheider, Aloisio, O.F.M.: b. Oct. 8, 1924, Estrela, Brazil; received in Franciscan Order, Feb. 1, 1942; ord. priest Aug. 22, 1948; professor of theology at the Antonianum, Rome, and director of Franciscan international house of studies; ord. bishop of Santo Angelo, Brazil, May 20, 1962; archbishop of Fortaleza, 1973-95; president of CELAM, 1975-79; cardinal May 24, 1976; titular church, S. Pietro (in Montorio). Archbishop of Aparecida, July 12, 1995. Curial membership: Institutes of Consecrated Life and Societies of Apostolic Life (congregation).

Lourdusamy, D. Simon: b. Feb. 5, 1924, Kalleri, India; ord. priest Dec. 21, 1951; ord. titular bishop of Sozusa and auxiliary of Bangalore,Aug. 22, 1962; titular archbishop of Filippi and coadjutor archbishop of Bangalore, Nov. 9, 1964; archbishop of Bangalore, 1968-71; associate secretary, 1971-73 and secretary, 1973-85, of Congregation for Evangelization of Peoples; cardinal May 25, 1985; deacon, St. Mary of Grace; transferred to the order of cardinal priests Jan. 29, 1996; prefect of Congregation for Oriental Churches, 1985-91. Curial membership: Evangelization of Peoples, Causes of Saints, (congregations); Apostolic Signatura (tribunal); Interreligious Dialogue, Family, Interpretation of Legislative Texts (councils); International Eucharistic Congresses (commission).

Lubachivsky,* Myroslav Ivan: b. June 24, 1914, Dolyna, Ukraine; ord. priest Sept. 21, 1938; began pastoral work in U.S., 1947; became U.S. citizen, 1952; ord. archbishop of Ukrainian-rite archeparchy of Philadelphia, Nov. 12, 1979; coadjutor archbishop of Lviv of the Ukrainians, Mar. 27, 1980; archbishop of Lviv and major archbishop of Ukrainians, Sept. 7, 1984; cardinal May 25, 1985; titular church, St. Sofia (a Via Boccea). Major Archbishop of Lviv of the Ukrainians.

Lustiger, Jean-Marie: b. Sept. 17, 1926, Paris, France, of Polish-Jewish parents who emigrated to

France after World War I; taken in by Catholic family in Orleans when his parents were deported during Nazi occupation (his mother died in 1943 at Auschwitz); convert to Catholicism, baptized Aug. 25, 1940; active in Young Christian Students during university days; ord. priest Apr. 17, 1954; ord. bishop of Orleans, Dec. 8, 1979; archbishop of Paris, Jan. 31, 1981; cardinal Feb. 2, 1983; titular church, St. Louis of France. Archbishop of Paris, ordinary for Eastern-Rite faithful in France without ordinaries of their own. Curial membership:
Secretariat of State (second section); Divine Worship and Sacraments, Bishops, Oriental Churches, Clergy, Institutes of Consecrated Life and Societies of Apostolic Life (congregations); Culture (council).

Macharski, Franciszek: b. May 20, 1927, Kracow, Poland; ord. priest Apr. 2, 1950; engaged in pastoral work, 1950-56; continued theological studies in Fribourg, Switzerland, 1956-60; taught pastoral theology at the Faculty of Theology in Kracow; app. rector of archdiocesan seminary at Kracow, 1970; ord. archbishop of Kracow, Jan. 6, 1979, by Pope John Paul II; cardinal June 30, 1979; titular church, St. John at the Latin Gate. Archbishop of Kracow. Curial membership:
Secretariat of State (second section); Bishops, Clergy, Institutes of Consecrated Life and Societies of Apostolic Life, Catholic Education (congregations).

Mahony, Roger M.: b. Feb. 27, 1936, Hollywood, Calif.; educ. St. John's Seminary (Camarillo, Calif.), National Catholic School of Social Service (Catholic Univ., Washington D.C.); ord. priest (Fresno diocese) May 1, 1962; ord. titular bishop of Tamascani and auxiliary bishop of Fresno, Mar. 19, 1975; bishop of Stockton, Feb. 15, 1980, installed Apr. 25, 1980; archbishop of Los Angeles, July 16, 1985, installed Sept. 5, 1985; cardinal June 28, 1991; titular church, Four Crowned Saints. Archbishop of Los Angeles. Curial membership:
Justice and Peace, Social Communications (councils).

Maida, Adam Joseph: b. Mar. 18, 1930, East Vandergrift, Pa.; ord. priest (Pittsburgh diocese) May 26, 1956; ord. bishop of Green Bay, Jan. 25, 1984; app. archbishop of Detroit, Apr. 28, 1990, installed June 12, 1990; cardinal Nov. 26, 1994; titular church, Sts. Vitalis, Valeria, Gervase and Protase. Archbishop of Detroit. Curial membership:
Clergy, Catholic Education (congregations); Migrants and Itinerant Peoples (Council).

Margeot,* Jean: b. Feb. 3, 1916, Quatre-Bornes, Mauritius; ord. priest Dec. 17, 1938; ord. bishop of Port Louis, May 4, 1969; cardinal June 28, 1988; titular church, St. Gabriel the Archangel all'Acqua Traversa. Bishop emeritus of Port Louis (resigned Feb. 15, 1993).

Martinez Somalo, Eduardo: b. Mar. 31, 1927, Baños de Rio Tobia, Spain; ord. priest Mar. 19, 1950; ord. titular bishop of Tagora with personal title of archbishop, Dec. 13, 1975; in secretariat of state from 1956; substitute (assistant) secretary of state, 1979-88; cardinal June 28, 1988; protodeacon, Most Holy Name of Jesus; prefect of Congregation for Divine Worship and Sacraments, 1988-92. Prefect of Congregation for Institutes of Consecrated Life and So-

cieties of Apostolic Life, Jan. 21, 1992; Chamberlain (Camerlengo) of the Holy Roman Church, Apr. 5, 1993; Protodeacon 1996. Curial membership:
Secretariat of State (second section); Divine Worship and Sacraments, Bishops, Causes of Saints, Evangelization of Peoples, Clergy, Catholic Education (congregations); Interpretation of Legislative Texts (council); Latin America, Institute for Works of Religion (commissions).

Martini, Carlo Maria, S.J.: b. Feb. 15, 1927, Turin, Italy; entered Jesuits Sept. 25, 1944; ord. priest July 13, 1952; biblical scholar; seminary professor, Chieri, Italy, 1958-61; professor and later rector, 1969-78, of Pontifical Biblical Institute; rector of Pontifical Gregorian University, 1978-79; author of theological, biblical and spiritual works; ord. archbishop of Milan, Jan. 6, 1980, by Pope John Paul II; cardinal Feb. 2, 1983; titular church, St. Cecilia. Archbishop of Milan. Curial membership:
Secretariat of State (second section); Oriental Churches, Divine Worship and Sacraments, Institutes of Consecrated Life and Societies of Apostolic Life, Catholic Education (congregations); Culture (council).

Mayer,* Paul Augustin, O.S.B.: b. May 23, 1911, Altötting, Germany; ord. priest Aug. 25, 1935; rector of St. Anselm's Univ., Rome, 1949-66; secretary of Congregation for Religious and Secular Institutes, 1972-84; ord. titular bishop of Satriano with personal title of archbishop, Feb. 13, 1972; pro-prefect of Congregations for Sacraments and Divine Worship, 1984; cardinal May 25, 1985; deacon, St. Anselm; transferred to order of cardinal priests Jan. 29, 1996. Prefect of Congregation for Divine Worship and Sacraments, 1985-88; president of Pontifical Commission "Ecclesia Dei," 1988-91.

Meisner, Joachim: b. Dec. 25, 1933, Breslau, Silesia, Germany (present-day Wroclaw, Poland); ord. priest Dec. 22, 1962; regional director of Caritas; ord. titular bishop of Vina and auxiliary of apostolic administration of Erfurt-Meiningen, E. Germany, May 17, 1975; bishop of Berlin, 1980-88; cardinal Feb. 2, 1983; titular church, St. Prudenziana. Archbishop of Cologne, Dec. 20, 1988. Curial membership:
Divine Worship and Sacraments, bishops, Clergy (congregations); Interreligious Dialogue, Culture (councils); Economic Affairs of Holy See (office).

Neves, Lucas Moreira, O.P.: b. Sept. 16, 1925, Sao Joao del Rei, Brazil; ord. priest July 9, 1950; ord. titular bishop of Feradi maggiore and auxiliary of Sao Paulo, Aug. 26, 1967; assigned to Vatican, 1974; vice president of Pontifical Commission for Laity, 1974-79; archbishop Oct. 15, 1979; secretary of Congregation for Bishops, 1979-87; assigned titular see of Vescovia, Jan. 3, 1987; archbishop of Sao Salvador da Bahia, July 9, 1987; cardinal June 28, 1988; titular church, Sts. Boniface and Alexius. Archbishop of Sao Salvador da Bahia. Curial membership:
Secretariat of State (second section); Doctrine of the Faith, Bishops, Institutes of Consecrated Life and Societies of Apostolic Life, Catholic Education (congregations); Family, Culture (councils); Latin America (commission).

Noè, Virgilio: b. Mar. 30, 1922, Zelata di

Bereguardo, Italy; ord. priest Oct. 1, 1944; master of pontifical ceremonies and undersecretary of Congregation for Sacraments and Divine Worship, 1970-82; ord. titular bishop of Voncario with personal title of archbishop, Mar. 6, 1982; coadjutor Archpriest of St. Peter's Basilica, 1989; vicar general of Vatican City State, Jan. 14, 1991; cardinal June 28, 1991; deacon, St. John Bosco (in Via Tuscolana). Archpriest of St. Peter's Basilica, Vicar General of Vatican City State and President of the Fabric of St. Peter, 1991. Curial membership:
Divine Worship and Sacraments, Causes of Saints (congregations); Holy Year 2000 (committee).

Obando Bravo, Miguel, S.D.B.: b. Feb. 2, 1926, La Libertad, Nicaragua; ord. priest Aug. 10, 1958; ord. titular bishop of Puzia di Bizacena and auxiliary of Matagalpa, Mar. 31, 1968; archbishop of Managua, Feb. 16, 1970; cardinal May 25, 1985; titular church, St. John the Evangelist (a Spinaceta). Archbishop of Managua. Curial membership:
Clergy, Institutes of Consecrated Life and Societies of Apostolic Life (congregations); Latin America (commission).

O'Connor, John J.: b. Jan. 15, 1920, Philadelphia, Pa.; ord. priest (Philadelphia archdiocese) Dec. 15, 1945; joined U.S. Navy and Marine Corps as a chaplain, 1952; overseas posts included service in South Korea and Vietnam; U.S. Navy chief of chaplains, 1975; retired from Navy June 1, 1979, with rank of rear admiral; ord. titular bishop of Curzola and auxiliary of military vicariate, May 27, 1979; bishop of Scranton, May 6, 1983; archbishop of New York, Jan. 26, 1984; cardinal May 25, 1985; titular church, Sts. John and Paul. Archbishop of New York. Curial membership:
Secretariat of State (second section); Bishops, Oriental Churches, Evangelization of Peoples (congregations); Family, Health Care Workers, Migrants and Itinerant People (councils); Institute for Works of Religion (commission).

Oddi,* Silvio: b. Nov. 14, 1910, Morfasso, Italy; ord. priest May 21, 1933; ord. titular archbishop of Mesembria, Sept. 27, 1953; served in Vatican diplomatic corps, 1953-69; apostolic delegate to Jerusalem, Palestine, Jordan and Cyprus, internuncio to the United Arab Republic, and nuncio to Belgium and Luxembourg; cardinal Apr. 28, 1969; titular church, St. Agatha of the Goths. Pontifical legate for Patriarchal Basilica of St. Francis in Assisi; prefect of Sacred Congregation for the Clergy, 1979-86.

Ortega y Alamino, Jaime Lucas: b. Oct. 18, 1936, Jagüey Grande, Cuba; ord. priest Aug. 2, 1964; detained in work camps (UMAP) 1966-67; parish priest; ord. bishop of Pinar del Rio, Jan. 14, 1979; app. archbishop of Havana, Nov. 20, 1981; cardinal Nov. 26, 1994; titular church, Sts. Aquila and Priscilla. Archbishop of Havana. Curial membership:
Clergy (congregation); Health Care Workers (council); Latin America (commission).

Otunga, Maurice Michael: b. January, 1923, Chebukwa, Kenya; son of pagan tribal chief; baptized 1935, at age of 12; ord. priest Oct. 3, 1950, at Rome; taught at Kisumu major seminary for three years; attaché in apostolic delegation at Mombasa, 1953-56; ord. titular bishop of Tacape and auxiliary of Kisumu, Feb. 25, 1957; bishop of Kisii, 1960-69;

titular archbishop of Bomarzo and coadjutor of Nairobi, Nov. 15, 1969; archbishop of Nairobi, Oct. 24, 1971; cardinal Mar. 5, 1973; titular church, St. Gregory Barbarigo. Archbishop emeritus of Nairobi (he resigned May 14, 1997), military ordinary of Kenya, 1981. Curial membership:
Institutes of Consecrated Life and Societies of Apostolic Life, Evangelization of Peoples (congregations).

Oviedo Cavado, Carlos, O. de M.: b. Jan. 19, 1927, Santiago, Chile; entered Mercedarian novitiate in 1944 and made solemn profession Mar. 19, 1948; ord. priest Sept. 24, 1949; ord. titular bishop of Benevento and auxiliary bishop of Concepcion, June 7, 1964; archbishop of Antofagasta, 1974-90; archbishop of Santiago, Mar. 30, 1990; cardinal Nov. 26, 1994; titular church, St. Mary della Scala. Archbishop of Santiago. Curial membership:
Catholic Education (congregation); Culture (council).

Padiyara, Antony: b. Feb. 11, 1921, Manimala, India; raised in Syro-Malabar rite family; ord. priest for Latin rite diocese of Coimbatore, Dec. 19, 1945; first bishop of Ootacamund (Latin rite), Oct. 16, 1955; app. archbishop of Changanacherry (Syro-Malabar rite), June 14, 1970, at which time he returned to the Syro-Malabar rite; archbishop of Ernakulam, Apr. 23, 1985; cardinal June 28, 1988; titular church, St. Mary Queen of Peace (Monte Verde). First Major Archbishop of Major Archbishopric of Ernakulam-Angamaly of Syro-Malabar Church (established Dec. 16, 1992); enthroned May 20, 1993; resigned Nov. 11,1996. Major archbishop emeritus of Ernakulam-Angomaly of Syro Malabars. Curial membership:
Oriental Churches (congregation).

Palazzini,* Pietro: b. May 19, 1912, Piobbico, Pesaro, Italy; ord. priest Dec. 6, 1934; assistant vice-rector of Pontifical Major Roman Seminary and vice-rector and bursar of Pontifical Roman Seminary for Juridical Studies; professor of moral theology at Lateran University; held various offices in Roman Curia; secretary of Congregation of Council (now Clergy), 1958-73; ord. titular archbishop of Caesarea in Cappadocia, Sept. 21, 1962; author of numerous works on moral theology and law; cardinal Mar. 5, 1973; titular church, St. Jerome. Prefect of Congregation for Causes of Saints, 1980-88.

Pappalardo, Salvatore: b. Sept. 23, 1918, Villafranca Sicula, Sicily; ord. priest Apr. 12, 1941; entered diplomatic service of secretariat of state, 1947; ord. titular archbishop of Miletus, Jan. 16, 1966; pro-nuncio in Indonesia, 1966-69; president of Pontifical Ecclesiastical Academy, 1969-70; archbishop of Palermo, Oct. 17, 1970; cardinal Mar. 5, 1973; titular church, St. Mary Odigitria of the Sicilians. Archbishop emeritus of Palermo (resigned Apr. 4, 1996). Curial membership:
Oriental Churches, Clergy (congregations).

Paskai, Laszlo, O.F.M.: b. May 8, 1927, Szeged, Hungary; ord. priest Mar. 3, 1951; ord. titular bishop of Bavagaliana and apostolic administrator of Veszprem, Apr. 5, 1978; bishop of Veszprem Mar. 31, 1979; coadjutor archbishop of Kalocsa, Apr. 5, 1982; archbishop of Esztergom (renamed Esztergom-Budapest, 1993), Mar. 3, 1987; cardinal June 28, 1988;

titular church, St. Theresa (al Corso d'Italia). Archbishop of Esztergom-Budapest. Curial membership: Oriental Churches, Institutes of Consecrated Life and Societies of Apostolic Life (congregations); Interpretation of Legislative Texts (council).

Pham Dinh Tung, Paul Joseph: b. June 15, 1919, Binh-Hoa, Vietnam; ord. priest June 6, 1949; ord. bishop of Bac Ninh, Aug. 15, 1963; apostolic administrator of Hanoi, June 18, 1990; archbishop of Hanoi, Mar. 23, 1994; cardinal Nov. 26, 1994; titular church, St. Mary Queen of Peace in Ostia mare. Archbishop of Hanoi. Curial membership: Evangelization of Peoples (congregation); "Cor Unum" (council).

Pimenta, Simon Ignatius: b. Mar. 1, 1920, Marol, India; ord. priest Dec. 21, 1949; ord. titular bishop of Bocconia and auxiliary of Bombay, June 29, 1971; coadjutor archbishop of Bombay, Feb. 26, 1977; archbishop of Bombay, Sept. 11, 1978; cardinal June 28, 1988; titular church, Mary, Queen of the World (a Torre Spaccata). Archbishop emeritus of Bombay (resigned Nov. 8, 1996). Curial membership: Evangelization of Peoples, Catholic Education (congregations); Economic Affairs of the Holy See (office).

Piovanelli, Silvano: b. Feb. 21, 1924, Ronta di Mugello, Italy; ord. priest July 13, 1947; ord. titular bishop of Tubune di Mauretania and auxiliary of Florence, June 24, 1982; archbishop of Florence, Mar. 18, 1983; cardinal May 25, 1985; titular church, St. Mary of Graces (Via Trionfale). Archbishop of Florence. Curial membership: Justice and Peace (council).

Pironio, Eduardo: b. Dec. 3, 1920, Nueve de Julio, Argentina; ord. priest Dec. 5, 1943; taught theology at Pius XII Seminary of Mercedes diocese, 1944-59; vicar general of diocese 1958-60; attended Second Vatican Council as peritus; ord. titular bishop of Ceciri, May 31, 1964; apostolic administrator of diocese of Avellaneda, 1967-72; secretary general, 1967-72, and president, 1973-75, of CELAM; bishop of Mar del Plata, 1972-75; titular archbishop of Thiges and pro-prefect of Congregation for Religious and Secular Institutes, Sept. 20, 1975; cardinal deacon May 24, 1976; titular church, Sts. Cosmas and Damian; transferred to order of cardinal priests, June 22, 1987; transferred to cardinal bishops July 11, 1995, suburbicarian see of Sabina-Poggia Mirteto. Prefect of the Congregation for Religious and Secular Institutes, 1976-84. President of Pontifical Council for the Laity, 1984-96. Curial membership: Secretariat of State (second section); Bishops, Causes of Saints, Catholic Education, Oriental Churches, Evangelization of Peoples (congregations); Latin America (commission).

Poggi, Luigi: b. Nov. 25, 1917, Piacenza, Italy; ord. priest July 28, 1940; studied diplomacy at the Pontifical Ecclesiastical Academy, 1944-46; started to work at Secretariat of State; ord. titular bishop of Forontoniana with personal title of archbishop, May 9, 1965; apostolic delegate for Central Africa, 1965; nuncio in Peru; recalled to Rome, 1973; negotiated with various Eastern bloc governments to improve situation of the Church; named head of Holy See's delegation for permanent contact with government of Poland, 1974; nuncio in Italy, 1986-92; pro-librar-

ian and pro-archivist of the Holy Roman Church, 1992-94; cardinal Nov. 26, 1994; deacon, St. Mary in Domnica. Archivist and librarian of the Holy Roman Church (Nov. 26, 1994). Curial membership: Secretariat of State (second section); Bishops, Evangelization of Peoples (congregations).

Poupard, Paul: b. Aug. 30, 1930, Bouzille, France; ord. priest Dec. 18, 1954; scholar; author of a number of works; ord. titular bishop of Usula and auxiliary of Paris, Apr. 6, 1979; title of archbishop and pro-president of the Secretariat for Non-Believers, 1980; cardinal deacon May 25, 1985; transferred to order of cardinal priests Jan. 29, 1996; titular church, St. Praxedes; president of Pontifical Council for Dialogue with Non-Believers, 1985-93. President of Pontifical Council for Culture, 1988. Curial membership: Divine Worship and Sacraments, Evangelization of Peoples, Catholic Education (congregations); Interreligious Dialogue (council).

Primatesta, Raul Francisco: b. Apr. 14, 1919, Capilla del Senor, Argentina; ord. priest Oct. 25, 1942, at Rome; taught at minor and major seminaries of La Plata; contributed to several theology reviews; ord. titular bishop of Tanais and auxiliary of La Plata, Aug. 15, 1957; bishop of San Rafael, 1961-65; archbishop of Cordoba, Feb. 16, 1965; cardinal Mar. 5, 1973; titular church, Blessed Mary Sorrowful Virgin. Archbishop of Cordoba, Argentina. Curial membership: Clergy (congregation).

Puljic, Vinko: b. Sept. 8, 1945, Prijecani, Bosnia-Herzegovina; ord. priest June 29, 1970; spiritual director of minor seminary of Zadar, 1978-87; parish priest; app. vice-rector of Sarajevo major seminary, 1990; ord. archbishop of Vrhbosna (Sarajevo), Jan. 6, 1991, in Rome; cardinal Nov. 26, 1994; titular church, St. Clare in Vigna Clara. Archbishop of Sarajevo. Curial membership: Evangelization of Peoples (congregation); Interreligious Dialogue (council).

Quarracino, Antonio: b. Aug. 8, 1923, Pollica, Italy; moved to Argentina when he was a child; ord. priest Dec. 22, 1945; ord. bishop of Nueve de Julio Apr. 8, 1962; bishop of Avellaneda, 1968-85; archbishop of La Plata, 1985-90; archbishop of Buenos Aires, July 10, 1990; cardinal June 28, 1991; titular church, St. Mary of Health (a Primavalle). Archbishop of Buenos Aires, ordinary for Eastern-rite faithful in Argentina without ordinaries of their proper rite. Curial membership: Christian Unity, Health Care Workers (councils); Latin America (commission).

Ratzinger, Joseph: b. Apr. 16, 1927, Marktl am Inn, Germany; ord. priest June 29, 1951; professor of dogmatic theology at University of Regensburg, 1969-77; member of International Theological Commission, 1969-80; ord. archbishop of Munich-Freising, May 28, 1977 (resigned Feb. 15, 1982); cardinal June 27, 1977; titular church, St. Mary of Consolation (in Tiburtina); transferred to order of cardinal bishops as titular bishop of suburbicarian see of Velletri-Segni, Apr. 5, 1993. Prefect of Congregation for Doctrine of the Faith, 1981; president of Biblical and Theological Commissions. Curial membership:

Secretariat of State (second section); Bishops, Divine Worship and Sacraments, Oriental Churches, Evangelization of Peoples, Catholic Education (congregations); Christian Unity, Culture (councils); Latin America (commission).

Razafindratandra, Armand Gaétan: b. Aug. 7, 1925, Ambohimalaza, Madagascar; ord. priest July 27, 1954; ord. bishop of Mahajanga, July 2, 1978; app. archbishop of Antananarivo, Feb. 3, 1994, installed May 15, 1994; cardinal Nov. 26, 1994; titular church, Sts. Sylvester and Martin ai Monti. Archbishop of Antananarivo and apostolic administrator of Miarinarivo. Curial membership:
Evangelization of Peoples (congregation); Laity (council).

Ribeiro, Antonio: b. May 21, 1928, Gandarela de Basto, Portugal; ord. priest July 5, 1953; professor of fundamental theology at major seminary at Braga; ord. titular bishop of Tigillava and auxiliary of Braga, Sept. 17, 1967; patriarch of Lisbon, May 10, 1971; cardinal Mar. 5, 1973; titular church, St. Anthony of Padua (in Via Merulana). Patriarch of Lisbon, military ordinary for Portugal. Curial membership:
Clergy, Catholic Education (congregations); Culture (council).

Righi-Lambertini,* Egano: b. Feb. 22, 1906, Casalecchio di Reno, Italy; ord. priest May 25, 1929; entered service of secretariat of state, 1939; served in diplomatic missions in France (1949-54), Costa Rica (1955), England (1955-57); first apostolic delegate to Korea, 1957-60; ord. titular archbishop of Doclea, Oct. 28, 1960; apostolic nuncio in Lebanon, 1960-63, Chile, 1963-67, Italy, 1967-69; France, 1969-79; while nuncio in France he also served as special envoy at the Council of Europe, 1974-79; cardinal deacon June 30, 1979; transferred to order of cardinal priests, Nov. 26, 1990; titular church, Saint Mary (in Via).

Rossi,* Opilio: b. May 14, 1910, New York, N.Y.; holds Italian citizenship; ord. priest for diocese of Piacenza (now Piacenza-Bobbio), Italy, Mar. 11, 1933; served in nunciatures in Belgium, The Netherlands, and Germany, 1938-53; ord. titular archbishop of Ancyra, Dec. 27, 1953; nuncio in Ecuador, 1953-59, Chile, 1959-61, Austria 1961-76; cardinal deacon May 24, 1976; transferred to order of cardinal priests, June 22, 1987; titular church, St. Lawrence (in Lucina); president of Pontifical Committee for International Eucharistic Congresses, 1983-90; president of Commission for the Sanctuaries of Pompeii, Loreto and Bari, 1984-93.

Rugambwa,* Laurean: b. July 12, 1912, Bukongo, Tanzania; ord. priest Dec. 12, 1943; ord. titular bishop of Febiano and vicar apostolic of Lower Kagera, Feb. 10, 1952; bishop of Rutabo, 1953-60 (diocese was restructured as Bukoba); cardinal Mar. 28, 1960; titular church, St. Francis of Assisi (a Ripa Grande); bishop of Bukoba, 1960-68. Archbishop of Dar-es-Salaam, 1968-92. Archbishop emeritus of Dar-es-Salaam.

Ruini, Camillo: b. Feb. 19, 1931, Sassuolo, Italy; ord. priest Dec. 8, 1954; taught at seminaries in central Italy; ord. titular bishop of Nepte and auxiliary bishop of Reggio Emilia and Guastella, June 29, 1983; secretary general of Italian Bishops' Conference, 1986-91; archbishop Jan. 17, 1991 and pro-vicar general of the Pope for the Rome diocese; pro-Archpriest of Patriarchal Lateran Archbasilica; cardinal June 28, 1991; titular church, St. Agnes outside the Wall. Vicar General of the Pope for the Diocese of Rome and Archpriest of Patriarchal Lateran Basilica, July 1, 1991; Grand Chancellor of Pontifical Lateran University; President of the Peregrinatio ad Petri Sedem, 1992-96. Curial membership:
Bishops (congregation); Holy Year 2000 (committee).

Sabattani,* Aurelio: b. Oct. 18, 1912, Casal Fiumanese, Italy; ord. priest July 26, 1935; jurist; served in various assignments in his native diocese of Imola and as judge and later an official of the regional ecclesiastical tribunal of Bologna; called to Rome in 1955 as prelate auditor of the Roman Rota; ord. titular archbishop of Justinian Prima, July 25, 1965; prelate of Loreto, 1965-71; secretary of Supreme Tribunal of Apostolic Signatura and consultor of Secretariat of State, 1971; pro-prefect of Apostolic Signatura, 1982-83; cardinal deacon Feb. 2, 1983; transferred to order of cardinal priests Apr. 5, 1993; titular church, St. Apollinaris; prefect of Apostolic Signatura, 1983-88; archpriest of Patriarchal Vatican Basilica and president of the Fabric of St. Peter, 1983-91; former vicar general of the Pope for Vatican City.

Saldarini, Giovanni: b. Dec. 11, 1924, Cantu, Italy; ord. priest May 31, 1947; respected scripture scholar; taught scripture at Milan archdiocesan seminary, 1952-67; ord. titular bishop of Guadiaba and auxiliary bishop of Milan, Dec. 7, 1984; archbishop of Turin Jan. 31, 1989; cardinal June 28, 1991; titular church, Sacred Heart of Jesus (a Castro Pretorio). Archbishop of Turin. Curial membership:
Divine Worship and Sacraments, Bishops, Evangelization of Peoples, Clergy (congregations).

Sales, Eugenio de Araujo: b. Nov. 8, 1920, Acari, Brazil; ord. priest Nov. 21, 1943; ord. titular bishop of Tibica and auxiliary bishop of Natal, Aug. 15, 1954; archbishop of Sao Salvador, 1968-71; cardinal Apr. 28, 1969; titular church, St. Gregory VII. Archbishop of Rio de Janeiro (1971), ordinary for Eastern Rite Catholics in Brazil without ordinaries of their own rites. Curial membership:
Secretariat of State (second section); Oriental Churches, Divine Worship and Sacraments, Clergy, Evangelization of Peoples (congregations); Social Communications (council).

Sanchez, Jose T.: b. Mar. 17, 1920, Pandan, Philippines; ord. priest May 12, 1946; ord. titular bishop of Lesvi and coadjutor bishop of Lucena, May 12, 1968; bishop of Lucena, 1976-82; archbishop of Nueva Segovia Jan. 12, 1982 (resigned Mar. 22, 1986); secretary of Congregation for Evangelization of Peoples, 1985-91; cardinal June 28, 1991; deacon, St. Pius V (a Villa Carpegna); president of Commission for Preservation of Artistic and Historic Patrimony of the Holy See, 1991-93. Prefect of Congregation for the Clergy, 1991-96. Curial membership:
Secretariat of State (second section); Interpretation of Legislative Texts (council); International Eucharistic Congresses (committee), Latin America (commission).

Sandoval Iñiguez, Juan: b. Mar. 28, 1933,

Yahualica, Mexico; ord. priest Oct. 27, 1957; ord. coadjutor bishop of Ciudad Juárez, Apr. 30, 1988; bishop of Ciudad Juarez, July 11, 1992; app. archbishop of Guadalajara, Apr. 21, 1994; cardinal Nov. 26, 1994; titular church, Our Lady of Guadalupe and St. Philip the Martyr on Via Aurelia. Archbishop of Guadalajara. Curial membership:
Institutes of Consecrated Life and Societies of Apostolic Life, Catholic Education (congregations); Latin America (commission).

Santos, Alexandre Jose Maria dos, O.F.M.: b. Mar. 18, 1924, Zavala, Mozambique; ord. priest July 25, 1953; first Mozambican black priest; ord. archbishop of Maputo, Mar. 9, 1975; cardinal June 28, 1988; titular church, St. Frumentius (ai Prati Fiscali). Archbishop of Maputo. Curial membership:
Evangelization of Peoples (congregation); Culture (council).

Schotte, Jan Pieter, C.I.C.M.: b. Apr. 29, 1928, Beveren-Leie, Belgium; entered Congregation of the Immaculate Heart of Mary (Scheut Missionaries) in 1946; ord. priest Aug. 3, 1952; taught canon law at Louvain and was rector of community's seminary in Washington, D.C.; general secretary of Congregation of the Immaculate Heart of Mary in Rome, 1967-72; secretary (1980) and vice-president (1983) of the Pontifical Commission of Justice and Peace; ord. titular bishop of Silli, Jan. 6, 1984; promoted to titular archbishop, Apr. 24, 1985; cardinal Nov. 26, 1994; deacon St. Julian of the Flemings. Secretary general of the Synod of Bishops since 1985; president of the Labor Office of the Holy See, 1989. Curial membership:
Bishops, Evangelization of Peoples (congregations); Latin America (commission).

Schwery, Henri: b. June 14, 1932, Saint-Leonard, Switzerland; ord. priest July 7, 1957; director of minor seminary and later rector of the College in Sion; ord. bishop of Sion, Sept. 17, 1977; cardinal June 28, 1991; titular church, Protomartyrs (a via Aurelia Antica). Bishop emeritus of Sion (retired Apr. 1, 1995). Curial membership:
Divine Worship and Sacraments, Causes of Saints, Clergy (congregations); Social Communications (council).

Sensi,* Giuseppe Maria: b. May 27, 1907, Cosenza, Italy; ord. priest Dec. 21, 1929; entered Vatican diplomatic service; served in nunciatures in Hungary, Switzerland, Belgium and Czechoslovakia, 1934-49; ord. titular archbishop of Sardes, July 24, 1955; apostolic nuncio to Costa Rica, 1955; apostolic delegate to Jerusalem, 1956-62; nuncio to Ireland, 1962-67, and Portugal, 1967-76; cardinal deacon May 24, 1976; transferred to order of cardinal priests, June 22, 1987; titular church, Queen of Apostles.

Sfeir, Nasrallah Pierre: b. May 15, 1920, Reyfoun, in Maronite diocese of Sarba, Lebanon; ord. priest May 7, 1950; secretary of Maronite patriarchate, 1956-61; taught Arabic literature and philosphy at Marist Fathers College, Jounieh, 1951-61; ord. titular bishop of Tarsus for the Maronites, July 16, 1961; elected Patriarch of Antioch for Maronites, Apr. 19, 1986, granted ecclesial communion by John Paul II May 7, 1986; cardinal Nov. 26, 1994. Patriarch of Antioch for Maronites. Curial membership:

Oriental Churches (congregation); Health Care Workers, Interpretation of Liturgical Texts (councils).

Shirayanagi, Peter Seiichi: b. June 17, 1928, Hachioji City, Japan; ord. priest Dec. 21, 1954; ord. titular bishop of Atenia and auxiliary bishop of Tokyo, May 8, 1966; titular archbishop of Castro and coadjutor archbishop of Tokyo, Nov. 15, 1969; succeeded to see, Feb. 21, 1970; cardinal Nov. 26, 1994; titular church, St. Emerentiana in Tor Fiorenza. Archbishop of Tokyo. Curial membership:
Family, Interreligious Dialogue (councils).

Silva Henriquez,* Raul, S.D.B.: b. Sept. 27, 1907, Talca, Chile; ord. priest July 3, 1938; ord. bishop of Valparaiso, Nov. 29, 1959; archbishop of Santiago de Chile, 1961-83; cardinal Mar. 19, 1962; titular church, St. Bernard (alle Terme). Archbishop emeritus of Santiago de Chile.

Silvestrini, Achille: b. Oct. 25, 1923, Brisighella, Italy; ord. priest July 13, 1946; official in Secretariat of State from 1953; ord. titular bishop of Novaliciana with personal title of archbishop, May 27, 1979; undersecretary, 1973-79, and secretary, 1979-88, of the Council for Public Affairs of the Church (now the second section of the Secretariat of State); cardinal June 28, 1988; deacon, St. Benedict Outside St. Paul's Gate; prefect of Apostolic Signatura, 1988-91. Prefect of Congregation for Oriental Churches, 1991; Grand Chancellor of Pontifical Oriental Institute. Curial membership:
Secretariat of State (second section); Doctrine of the Faith, Bishops, Causes of Saints, Evangelization of Peoples, Catholic Education (congregations); Christian Unity, Interpretation of Legislative Texts, Interreligious Dialogue (councils).

Simonis, Adrianus J.: b. Nov. 26, 1931, Lisse, Netherlands; ord. priest June 15, 1957; ord. bishop of Rotterdam, Mar. 20, 1971; coadjutor archbishop of Utrecht, June 27, 1983; archbishop of Utrecht, Dec. 3, 1983; cardinal May 25, 1985; titular church, St. Clement. Archbishop of Utrecht. Curial membership:
Institutes of Consecrated Life and Societies of Apostolic Life, Catholic Education (congregations); Christian Unity (council).

Sin, Jaime L.: b. Aug. 31, 1928, New Washington, Philippines; ord. priest Apr. 3, 1954; diocesan missionary in Capiz, 1954-57; app. first rector of the St. Pius X Seminary, Roxas City, 1957; ord. titular bishop of Obba and auxiliary bishop of Jaro, Mar. 18, 1967; apostolic administrator of archdiocese of Jaro, June 20, 1970; titular archbishop of Massa Lubrense and coadjutor archbishop of Jaro, Jan. 15, 1972; archbishop of Jaro, 1972-74; archbishop of Manila, Jan. 21, 1974; cardinal May 24, 1976; titular church, S. Maria (ai Monti). Archbishop of Manila. Curial membership:
Divine Worship and Sacraments, Clergy, Institutes of Consecrated Life and Societies of Apostolic Life (congregations); Social Communications (council).

Sladkevicius, Vincentas, M.I.C.: b. Aug. 20, 1920, Zasliai, Lithuania; ord. priest Mar. 25, 1944; ord. titular bishop of Abora and auxiliary of Kaisiadorys, Dec. 25, 1957, but was not permitted to exercise his office; under house arrest 1959-82; apostolic administrator of Kaisiadorys, 1982-89; cardinal June 28, 1988; titular church, Holy Spirit (alla Ferratella).

Archbishop of Kaunas (Mar. 10, 1989; resigned May 4, 1996). Curial membership:
Catholic Education (congregation).

Sodano, Angelo: b. Nov. 23, 1927, Isola d'Asti, Italy; ord. priest Sept. 23, 1950; entered diplomatic service of the Holy See in 1959; served in Ecuador and Uruguay; ord. titular archbishop of Nova di Cesare, Jan. 15, 1978; nuncio to Chile, 1978-88; secretary of the Council for Relations with States, 1988-90; pro-Secretary of State, 1990 (Dec. 1)-1991; cardinal June 28, 1991; titular church, S. Maria Nuova; transferred to order of cardinal bishops, Jan 10, 1994, as titular bishop of suburbicarian see of Albano (while retaining title to S. Maria Nuova). Secretary of State, June 29, 1991. Curial membership:
Doctrine of the Faith, Bishops, Oriental Churches (congregations); Institute for Works of Religion (commission).

Sterzinsky, Georg Maximilian: b. Feb. 9, 1936, Warlack, Germany; ord. priest June 29, 1960; vicar general to the apostolic administrator of Erfurt-Meiningen, 1981-89; ord. bishop of Berlin, Sept. 9, 1989; cardinal June 28, 1991; titular church, St. Joseph (all'Aurelio). Archbishop of Berlin (June 27, 1994). Curial membership:
Catholic Education (congregation); Migrants and Itinerant People (council).

Stickler,* Alfons, S.D.B.: b. Aug. 23, 1910, Neunkirchen, Austria; ord. priest Mar. 27, 1937; director of the Vatican Library, 1971; ord. titular bishop of Bolsena, Nov. 1, 1983, with personal title of archbishop; Pro-Librarian and Pro-Archivist, 1984; cardinal May 25, 1985; deacon, St. George (in Velabro); transferred to order of cardinal priests Jan. 29, 1996. Librarian and Archivist of the Holy Roman Church, 1985-88.

Suarez Rivera, Adolfo Antonio: b. Jan. 9, 1927, San Cristobal, Mexico; ord. priest Mar. 8, 1952; ord. bishop of Tepic, Aug. 15, 1971; bishop of Tlalnepantla, May 8, 1980; app. archbishop of Monterrey, Nov. 8, 1983; cardinal Nov. 26, 1994; titular church, Our Lady of Guadalupe on Monte Mario. Archbishop of Monterrey. Curial membership:
Clergy (congregation); Latin America (commission).

Suquia Goicoechea,* Angel: b. Oct. 2, 1916, Zaldivia, Spain; ord. priest July 7, 1940; ord. bishop of Almeria, July 16, 1966; bishop of Malaga, 1969-73; archbishop of Santiago de Compostela, 1973-83; archbishop of Madrid, Apr. 12, 1983; cardinal May 25, 1985; titular church, Great Mother of God. Archbishop emeritus of Madrid (retired July 28, 1994).

Swiatek,* Kazimierz: b. Oct. 21, 1914, Walga, in apostolic administration of Estonia; ord. priest (of Pinsk, Belarus, clergy) Apr. 8, 1939; arrested by KGB Apr. 21, 1941, and imprisoned on death row until June 22, when he escaped during confusion of German invasion and returned to his parish; arrested again by KGB and imprisoned in Minsk until 1945; sentenced to 10 years of hard labor in concentration camps; released June 16, 1954; resumed pastoral work in cathedral parish in Pinsk; ord. archbishop of Minsk-Mohilev, Belarus, May 21, 1991, and also

appointed apostolic administrator of Pinsk; cardinal Nov. 26, 1994; titular church, St. Gerard Majella. Archbishop of Minsk-Mohilev; apostolic administrator of Pinsk.

Szoka, Edmund C.: b. Sept. 14, 1927, Grand Rapids, Mich.; educ. Sacred Heart Seminary (Detroit, Mich.), St. John's Provincial Seminary (Plymouth, Mich.), Lateran Univ. (Rome); ord. priest (Marquette diocese), June 5, 1954; ord. first bishop of Gaylord, Mich., July 20, 1971; archbishop of Detroit, 1981-90; cardinal June 28, 1988; titular church, Sts. Andrew and Gregory (al Monte Celio). President of Prefecture for Economic Affairs of the Holy See, 1990. Curial membership:
Secretariat of State (second section); Causes of Saints, Bishops, Evangelization of Peoples, Clergy, Institutes of Consecrated Life and Societies of Apostolic Life (congregations).

Taofinu'u, Pio, S.M.: b. Dec. 9, 1923, Falealupo, W. Samoa; ord. priest Dec. 8, 1954; joined Society of Mary, 1955; ord. bishop of Apia (Samoa and Tokelau), May 29, 1968, the first Polynesian bishop; cardinal Mar. 5, 1973; titular church, St. Humphrey. Archbishop of Samoa-Apia and Tokelau, Sept. 10, 1982 (title of see changed to Samoa-Apia, June 26, 1992).

Thiandoum, Hyacinthe: b. Feb. 2, 1921, Popongaine, Senegal; ord. priest Apr. 18, 1949; studied at Gregorian University, Rome, 1951-53; returned to Senegal, 1953; ord. archbishop of Dakar, May 20, 1962; cardinal May 24, 1976; titular church, S. Maria (del Popolo). Archbishop of Dakar. Curial membership:
Clergy, Institutes of Consecrated Life and Societies of Apostolic Life, Evangelization of Peoples (congregations); Social Communications (council).

Todea,* Alexandru: b. June 5, 1912, Teleac, Romania; ord. priest in the Byzantine Romanian rite Mar. 25, 1939; ord. bishop secretly (titular see of Cesaropoli), Nov. 19, 1950, by Archbishop Gerald P. O'Hara, Vatican representative to Romania; arrested, 1951, and sentenced to life imprisonment; granted amnesty in 1964; archbishop of Fagaras and Alba Julia, 1990-94; cardinal June 28, 1991; titular church, St. Athanasius. Archbishop emeritus of Fagaras and Alba Julia of the Romanians.

Tomko, Jozef: b. Mar. 11, 1924, Udavske, Slovakia; ord. priest Mar. 12, 1949; ord. titular archbishop of Doclea, Sept, 15, 1979; secretary-general of the Synod of Bishops, 1979-85; cardinal deacon May 25, 1985; transferred to order of cardinal priests Jan. 29, 1996; titular church, St. Sabina. Prefect of the Congregation for the Evangelization of Peoples, 1985; Grand Chancellor of Pontifical Urban University. Curial membership:
Secretariat of State (second section); Doctrine of the Faith, Divine Worship and Sacraments, Bishops, Clergy, Institutes of Consecrated Life and Societies of Apostolic Life, Catholic Education (congregations); Christian Unity, Interreligious Dialogue, Culture, Interpretation of Legislative Texts (councils); Latin America, State of Vatican City (commissions).

Tonino,* Ersilio: b. July 20, 1914, Centovera di San Giorgio Piacentino, Italy; ord. priest Apr. 18, 1937; vice-rector and later rector of the Piacenza seminary; taught Italian, Latin and Greek; editor of diocesan weekly; ord. bishop of Macerata-Tolentino, June 2, 1969; archbishop of Ravenna-Cervia, Nov. 22, 1975 (retired Oct. 27, 1990); cardinal Nov. 26, 1994; titular church, Most Holy Redeemer in Val Melaina. Archbishop emeritus of Ravenna-Cervia.

Tumi, Christian Wiyghan: b. Oct. 15, 1930, Kikaikelaki, Cameroon; ord. priest Apr. 17, 1966; ord. bishop of Yagoua, Jan. 6, 1980; coadjutor archbishop of Garoua, Nov. 19, 1982; archbishop of Garoua, 1984-91; cardinal June 28, 1988; titular church, Martyrs of Uganda (a Poggio Ameno). Archbishop of Douala, Aug. 31, 1991. Curial membership:
Evangelization of Peoples, Catholic Education (congregations); Interreligious Dialogue, Culture (councils).

Turcotte, Jean-Claude: b. June 26, 1936, Montreal, Canada; ord. priest May 24, 1959; ord. titular bishop of Suas and auxiliary of Montreal, June 29, 1982; archbishop of Montreal, Mar. 17, 1990; cardinal Nov. 26, 1994; titular church, Our Lady of the Blessed Sacrament and the Holy Canadian Martyrs. Archbishop of Montreal. Curial membership:
Causes of Saints (congregation); Social Communications (council).

Tzadua, Paulos: b. Aug. 25, 1921, Addifini, Ethiopia; ord. priest Mar. 12, 1944; ord. titular bishop of Abila di Palestina and auxiliary of Addis Ababa, May 20, 1973; archbishop of Addis Ababa, Feb. 24, 1977; cardinal May 25, 1985; titular church, Most Holy Name of Mary (a Via Latina). Archbishop of Addis Ababa. Curial membership:
Oriental Churches (congregation).

Ursi,* Corrado: b. July 26, 1908, Andria, Italy; ord. priest July 25, 1931; vice-rector and later rector of the Pontifical Regional Seminary of Molfetta, 1931-51; ord. bishop of Nardo, Sept. 30, 1951; archbishop of Acerenza, Nov. 30, 1961; archbishop of Naples, May 23, 1966 (resigned May 9, 1987); cardinal June 26, 1967; titular church, St. Callistus. Archbishop emeritus of Naples.

Vachon,* Louis-Albert: b. Feb. 4, 1912, Saint-Frederic-de-Beauce, Que., Canada; ord. priest June 11, 1938; ord. titular bishop of Mesarfelta and auxiliary of Quebec, May 14, 1977; archbishop of Quebec, Mar. 20, 1981 (resigned Mar. 17, 1990); cardinal May 25, 1985; titular church, St. Paul of the Cross (a Corviale). Archbishop emeritus of Quebec.

Vargas Alzamora, Augusto, S.J.: b. Nov. 9, 1922, Lima, Peru; entered Society of Jesus Mar. 9, 1940; ord. priest July 15, 1955; ord. titular bishop of Cissi, Aug. 15, 1978; vicar apostolic of Jaen in Peru (or San Francisco Javier), 1978-85; archbishop of Lima, De. 30, 1989; made passionate appeals against violence of the Sendero Luminoso; cardinal Nov. 26, 1994; titular see, St. Robert Bellarmine. Archbishop of Lima. Curial membership:
Institutes of Consecrated Life and Societies of Apostolic Life (congregation); Latin America (commission).

Vidal, Ricardo J.: b. Feb. 6, 1931, Mogpoc, Philippines; ord. priest Mar. 17, 1956; ord. titular bishop of Claterna and coadjutor of Melalos, Nov. 30, 1971; archbishop of Lipa, 1973-81; coadjutor archbishop of Cebu, Apr. 13, 1981; archbishop of Cebu, Aug. 24, 1982; cardinal May 25, 1985; titular church, Sts.

Peter and Paul (in Via Ostiensi). Archbishop of Cebu. Curial membership:
Evangelizaton of Peoples, Catholic Education (congregations); Health Care Workers (council).

Vlk, Miloslav: b. May 17, 1932, Lisnice, Czech Republic; during communist persecution when theological studies were impossible he studied archival science at Charles University and worked in various archives in Bohemia; ord. priest June 23, 1968, during "Prague Spring"; sent to isolated parishes in Bohemian Forest by State authorities in 1971; state authorization to exercise his priestly ministry was cancelled in 1978; from then until 1986 he worked as a window-washer in Prague, carrying out his priestly ministry secretly among small groups. In 1989, he was permitted to exercise his priestly ministry for a "trial" year; the situation changed with the "velvet revolution"; ord. bishop of Ceske Budejovice, Mar. 31, 1990; archbishop of Prague, Mar. 27, 1991; cardinal Nov. 26, 1994; titular church, Holy Cross in Jerusalem. Archbishop of Prague, President of the Council of European Episcopal Conferences, 1993- . Curial membership:
Oriental Churches (congregation); Social Communications (council).

Wamala, Emmanuel: b. Dec. 15, 1926, Kamaggwa, Uganda; ord. priest Dec. 21, 1957; ord. bishop of Kiyinda-Mityana, Nov. 22, 1981; coadjutor archbishop of Kampala, June 21, 1988; archbishop of Kampala, Feb. 8, 1990; cardinal Nov. 26, 1994; titular church, St. Hugh. Archbishop of Kampala. Curial membership:
Evangelization of Peoples (congregation); "Cor Unum" (council).

Wetter, Friedrich: b. Feb. 20, 1928, Landau, Germany; ord. priest Oct. 10, 1953; ord. bishop of Speyer, June 29, 1968; archbishop of Munich and Freising, Oct. 28, 1982; cardinal May 25, 1985; titular church, St. Stephen (al Monte Celio). Archbishop of Munich and Freising. Curial membership:
Evangelization of Peoples, Catholic Education (congregations).

Willebrands,* Johannes: b. Sept. 4, 1909, Bovenkarspel, The Netherlands; ord. priest May 26, 1934; ord. titular bishop of Mauriana, June 28, 1964; secretary of Secretariat for Christian Unity, 1960-69; cardinal Apr. 28, 1969; titular church, St. Sebastian (alle Catacombe); archbishop of Utrecht, 1975-83; president of Council for Christian Unity, 1969-89. President emeritus of the Council for Promoting Christian Unity; Camerlengo of the College of Cardinals, 1988.

Williams, Thomas Stafford: b. Mar. 20, 1930, Wellington, New Zealand; ord. priest Dec. 20, 1959, in Rome; studied in Ireland after ordination, receiving degree in social sciences; served in various pastoral assignments on his return to New Zealand; missionary in Western Samoa to 1976; ord. archbishop of Wellington, New Zealand, Dec. 20, 1979; cardinal Feb. 2, 1983; titular church, Jesus the Divine Teacher (at Pineda Sacchetti). Archbishop of Wellington; Military Ordinary for New Zealand (1995). Curial membership:
Evangelization of Peoples (congregation).

Winning, Thomas Joseph: b. June 3, 1925, Wishaw, Scotland; ord. priest Dec. 18, 1948; spiritual director of the Pontifical Scots College in Rome, 1961-66; returned to Scotland, 1966; served as parish priest, episcopal vicar for marriage in Motherwell diocese and first president and officialis (1970-72) of the newly established Scottish National Tribunal, Glasgow; ord. titular bishop of Lugmad and auxiliary of Glasgow Nov. 30, 1971; archbishop of Glasgow, Apr. 23, 1974; cardinal Nov. 26, 1994; titular church, St. Andrew delle Fratte. Archbishop of Glasgow. Curial membership: Christian Unity, Family (councils).

Wu Cheng-Chung, John Baptist: b. Mar. 26, 1925, Shui-Tsai, mainland China; ord. priest (for Hsinchu, Taiwan, diocese) July 6, 1952; ord. bishop of Hong Kong, July 25, 1975; cardinal June 28, 1988; titular church, Blessed Virgin Mary of Mount Carmel (a Mostacciano). Bishop of Hong Kong. Curial membership: Evangelization of Peoples (congregation); Interreligious Dialogue, Culture, Social Communications (councils).

Yago,* Bernard: b. July, 1916, Pass, Ivory Coast (now Côte d'Ivoire); ord. priest May 1, 1947; ord. archbishop of Abidjan, May 8, 1960, by Pope John XXIII in St. Peter's Basilica, becoming the first native member of the hierarchy of Côte d'Ivoire; cardinal Feb. 2, 1983; titular church, St. Chrysogonus. Archbishop emeritus of Abidjan (resigned Dec. 19, 1994).

Zoungrana, Paul, M. Afr.: b. Sept 3, 1917, Ouagadougou, Upper Volta (now Burkina Faso); ord. priest May 2, 1942; ord. archbishop of Ouagadougou at St. Peter's Basilica by John XXIII, May 8, 1960; cardinal Feb. 22, 1965; titular church, St. Camillus de Lellis. Archbishop emeritus of Ouagadougou (resigned June 10, 1995). Curial membership: Institutes of Consecrated Life and Societies of Apostolic Life (congregation); Health Care Workers (council).

CATEGORIES OF CARDINALS
(As of Aug. 15, 1997.)

Information below includes categories of cardinals and dates of consistories at which they were created. Seniority or precedence usually depends on order of elevation. Three of these 148 cardinals were named by John XXIII (consistories of Dec. 15, 1958, Mar. 28, 1960, and Mar. 19, 1962); 30 by Paul VI (consistories of Feb. 22, 1965, June 26, 1967, Apr. 28, 1969, Mar. 5, 1973, May 24, 1976, and June 27, 1977); 115 by John Paul II (consistories of June 30, 1979, Feb. 2, 1983, May 25, 1985, June 28, 1988, June 28, 1991, Nov. 26, 1994).

Order of Bishops

Titular Bishops of Suburbicarian Sees: Bernardin Gantin, dean (June 27, 1977); Agostino Casaroli, sub-dean (June 30, 1979); Paolo Bertoli (Apr. 28, 1969); Joseph Ratzinger (June 27, 1977) Angelo Sodano (June 28, 1991), Eduardo Pironio (May 24, 1976).

Eastern Rite Patriarch: Nasrallah Pierre Sfeir (Nov. 26, 1994).

Order of Priests

1958 (Dec. 15): Franz Koenig.
1960 (Mar. 28): Laurean Rugambwa.

1962 (Mar. 19): Raul Silva Henriquez, S.D.B.
1965 (Feb. 22): Paul Zoungrana.
1967 (June 26): Corrado Ursi.
1969 (Apr. 28): Silvio Oddi, Paul Gouyon, John J. Carberry, Stephan Sou Hwan Kim, Eugenio de Araujo Sales, Johannes Willebrands.
1973 (Mar. 5): Antonio Ribeiro, Pietro Palazzini, Luis Aponte Martinez, Raul Francisco Primatesta, Salvatore Pappalardo, Marcelo Gonzalez Martin, Maurice Otunga, Paulo Evaristo Arns, Pio Taofinu'u.
1976 (May 24): Opilio Rossi, Giuseppe Maria Sensi, Juan Carlos Aramburu, Corrado Bafile, Hyacinthe Thiandoum, Jaime L. Sin, William W. Baum, Aloisio Lorscheider, George Basil Hume, O.S.B.
1979 (June 30): Giuseppe Caprio, Marco Cé, Egano Righi-Lambertini, Ernesto Corripio Ahumada, Roger Etchegaray, Anastasio Alberto Ballestrero, O.C.D., Gerald Emmett Carter, Franciszek Macharski, Ignatius Gong (Kung) Pin-mei.
1983 (Feb. 2): Bernard Yago, Aurelio Sabattani, Franjo Kuharic, Giuseppe Casoria, Jose Ali Lebrun Moratinos, Michael Michai Kitbunchu, Alexandre do Nascimento, Alfonso Lopez Trujillo, Godfried Danneels, Thomas Stafford Williams, Carlo Maria Martini, Jean-Marie Lustiger, Jozef Glemp, Joachim Meisner.
1985 (May 25): Juan Francisco Fresno Larrain, Miguel Obando Bravo, Angel Suquia Goicoechea, Ricardo Vidal, Henryk Roman Gulbinowicz, Paulus Tzadua, Myroslav Ivan Lubachivsky, Louis-Albert Vachon, Friedrich Wetter, Silvano Piovanelli, Adrianus J. Simonis, Bernard F. Law, John J. O'Connor, Giacomo Biffi, Simon D. Lourdusamy, Francis A. Arinze, Antonio Innocenti, Paul Augustin Mayer, Jozef Tomko, Andrzej Maria Deskur, Paul Poupard, Rosalio Jose Castillo Lara, Edouard Gagnon, Alfons Stickler, S.D.B.
1988 (June 28): Antony Padiyara, Jose Freire Falcao, Michele Giordano, Alexandre Jose Maria dos Santos, O.F.M., Giovanni Canestri, Simon Ignatius Pimenta, Edward Bede Clancy, Lucas Moreira Neves, O.P., James Aloysius Hickey, Edmund C. Szoka, Laszlo Paskai, O.F.M., Christian Wiyghan Tumi, Hans Hermann Groër, O.S.B, Vincentas Sladkevicius, Jean Margeot, John Baptist Wu Cheng-Chung.
1991 (June 28): Alexandru Todea, Frédéric Etsou-Nzabi-Bamungwabi, Nicolas de Jesus Lopez Rodriguez, Antonio Quarracino, Roger Mahony, Anthony J. Bevilacqua, Giovanni Saldarini, Cahal Brendan Daly, Camillo Ruini, Jan Chryzostom Korec, Henri Schwery, Georg Sterzinsky.
1994 (Nov. 26): Miloslav Vlk, Peter Seiichi Shirayanagi, Carlos Oviedo Cavada, Thomas Joseph Winning, Adolfo Antonio Suarez Rivera, Jaime Lucas Ortega y Alamino, Julius Riyadi Darmaatmadja, Pierre Eyt, Emmanuel Wamala, William Henry Keeler, Augusto Vargas Alzamora, Jean-Claude Turcotte, Ricardo Maria Carles Gordó, Adam Joseph Maida, Vinko Puljic, Armand Gaétan Razafindratandra, Paul Joseph Pham Dinh Tung, Juan Sandoval Iñiguez, Bernardino Echeverria Ruiz, Kazimierz Swiatek, Ersilio Tonino.

Order of Deacons

1988 (June 28): Eduardo Martinez Somalo, Achille Silvestrini, Angelo Felici, Antonio Maria Javierre Ortas, S.D.B.

1991 (June 28): Pio Laghi, Edward I. Cassidy, Jose T. Sanchez, Virgilio Noè, Fiorenzo Angelini, Paolo Dezza, S.J. **1994** (Nov. 26): Luigi Poggi, Vincenzo Fagiolo, Carlo Furno, Jan Pieter Schotte, Gilberto Agustoni, Alois Grillmeier.

DISTRIBUTION OF CARDINALS

As of Aug. 30, 1997, there were 148 cardinals from more than 50 countries or areas. Listed below are areas, countries, number and last names.

Europe — 77

Italy (34): Angelini, Bafile, Ballestrero, Bertoli, Biffi, Canestri, Caprio, Casaroli, Casoria, Cé, Dezza, Fagiolo, Felici, Forno, Giordano, Innocenti, Laghi, Martini, Noè, Oddi, Palazzini, Pappalardo, Piovanelli, Poggi, Righi-Lambertini, Rossi, Ruini, Sabattani, Saldarini, Silvestrini, Sensi, Sodano, Tonino, Ursi.

Germany (6): Grillmeier, Mayer, Meisner, Ratzinger, Sterzinsky, Wetter.

Spain (5): Carles Gordó, Gonzalez Martin, Javierre Ortas, Martinez Somalo, Suquia Goicoechea.

France (5): Etchegaray, Eyt, Gouyon, Lustiger, Poupard.

Poland (4): Deskur, Glemp, Gulbinowicz, Macharski.

Austria (3): Groer, Koenig, Stickler.

Belgium (2): Danneels, Schotte.

Netherlands (2): Simonis, Willebrands.

Slovakia (2): Korec, Tomko.

Switzerland (2): Agustoni, Schwery.

One from each of the following countries: Belarus, Swiatek; Bosnia-Herzegovina, Puljic; Croatia, Kuharic; Czech Republic, Vlk; England, Hume; Hungary, Paskai; Ireland, Daly; Lithuania, Sladkevicius; Portugal, Ribeiro; Romania, Todea; Scotland, Winning; Ukraine, Lubachivsky.

Asia — 14

India (3): Lourdusamy, Padiyara, Pimenta.

Philippines (3): Sanchez, Sin, Vidal.

One from each of the following countries: China, Gong (Kung) Pin-mei (exiled); Hong Kong Wu Cheng-Chung; Indonesia, Darmaatmadja; Japan, Shirayangi; Korea, Kim; Lebanon, Sfeir; Thailand, Kitbunchu; Vietnam, Pham Dinh Tung.

Oceania — 4

Australia (2): Cassidy, Clancy. One each from: New Zealand, Williams; Pacific Islands (Samoa), Taofinu'u.

Africa — 15

One from each of the following countries: Angola, do Nascimento; Benin, Gantin; Burkina Faso, Zoungrana; Cameroon, Tumi; Congo (formerly Zaire), Etsou-Nzabi-Bamungwabi; Ethiopia, Tzadua; Ivory Coast, Yago; Kenya, Otunga; Madagascar, Razafindratandra; Mauritius, Margeot; Mozambique, Santos; Nigeria, Arinze; Senegal, Thiandoum; Tanzania, Rugambwa; Uganda, Wamala.

North America — 18

United States (10): Baum, Bevilacqua, Carberry, Hickey, Keeler, Law, Mahony, Maida, O'Connor, Szoka.

Canada (4): Carter, Gagnon, Turcotte, Vachon.

Mexico (3): Corripio Ahumada, Sandoval Iñiguez, Suarez Rivera.

Puerto Rico (1): Aponte Martinez.

Central and South America — 20

Brazil (5): Arns, Falcao, Lorscheider, Neves, Sales.

Argentina (4): Aramburu, Pironio, Primatesta, Quarrachino.

Chile (3): Fresno Larrain, Oviedo Cavada, Silva Henriquez.

Venezuela (2): Castillo Lara, Lebrun Moratinos.

One from each of the following countries: Colombia, Lopez Trujillo; Cuba, Ortega y Alamino; Dominican Republic, Lopez Rodriquez; Ecuador, Echeverria Ruiz; Nicaragua, Obando Bravo; Peru, Vargas Alzamora.

INELIGIBLE TO VOTE

As of Aug. 30, 1997, 38 of the 148 cardinals were ineligible to take part in a papal election in line with the apostolic letter *Ingravescentem Aetatem* effective Jan. 1, 1971, which limited the functions of cardinals after completion of their 80th year.

Cardinals affected were: Angelini, Aramburu, Bafile, Ballestrero, Bertoli, Caprio, Carberry, Carter, Casaroli, Casoria, Dezza, Echeverria Ruiz, Fresno Larrain, Gong Pin-Mei, Gouyon, Grillmeier, Innocenti, Koenig, Lubachivsky, Margeot, Mayer, Oddi, Palazzini, Righi-Lambertini, Rossi, Rugambwa, Sabattani, Sensi, Silva Henriquez, S.D.B., Stickler, S.D.B., Suguia Goicoeches, Swiatek, Todea, Tonino, Ursi, Vachon, Yago, Willebrands.

Other cardinals who will become ineligible to vote in 1997: Paul Zoungrana (Sept 3); Cahal Brendan Daly (Oct. 1); Luigi Poggi (Nov. 25).

Cardinals completing their 80th year in 1998: Edouard Gagnon, P.S.S., Jan.15; Marcelo Gonzalez Martin, Jan. 16; Vincenzo Fagiolo, Feb. 5; Salvatore Pappalardo, Sept. 23; Giovanni Canestri, Sept. 30.

CARDINALS OF U.S.

As of Aug. 30, 1997, U.S. cardinals according to years of elevation (for biographies, see Index under individual name).

1969: John J. Carberry (archbishop emeritus of St. Louis); **1976:** William W. Baum (major penitentiary); **1985:** Bernard F. Law (archbishop of Boston), John J. O'Connor (archbishop of New York); **1988:** James A. Hickey (archbishop of Washington), Edmund C. Szoka (president of Prefecture for Economic Affairs of the Holy See); **1991:** Roger M. Mahony (archbishop of Los Angeles), Anthony J. Bevilacqua (archbishop of Philadelphia); **1994:** William H. Keeler (archbishop of Baltimore), Adam J. Maida (archbishop of Detroit).

[Myroslav Lubachivsky, major archbishop of Lviv of the Ukrainians (Ukraine), was made a cardinal in 1985. He is a U.S. citizen and was metropolitan of the Philadelphia Ukrainian Rite Archeparchy, 1979-81.]

U.S. cardinals of the past, according to year of

elevation. (For biographical data, see Index: Bishops, U.S., of the Past.)

1875: John McCloskey; 1886: James Gibbons; 1911: John Farley, William O'Connell; 1921: Dennis Dougherty; 1924: Patrick Hayes, George Mundelein; 1946: John Glennon, Edward Mooney, Francis Spellman, Samuel Stritch; 1953: James F. McIntyre; 1958: John O'Hara, C.S.C., Richard Cushing; 1959: Albert Meyer, Aloysius Muench; 1961: Joseph Ritter; 1965: Lawrence J. Shehan; 1967: Francis Brennan, John P. Cody, Patrick A. O'Boyle, John J. Krol; 1969: John J. Wright, Terence J. Cooke, John F. Dearden;

1973: Humbertus S. Medeiros, Timothy Manning; 1983: Joseph L. Bernadin.

Prelates who became cardinals after returning to their native countries: John Lefebvre de Chevrus, first bishop of Boston (1808-23) and apostolic administrator of New York (1810-15), elevated to cardinalate, 1836, in France. Ignatius Persico, O.F.M. Cap., bishop of Savannah (1870-72), elevated to cardinalate, 1893, in Italy. Diomede Falconio, O.F.M., ord. priest Buffalo, N.Y.; missionary in U.S.; apostolic delegate to the U.S. (1902-11), elevated to cardinalate, 1911, in Italy.

PAPAL ADDRESSES TO BISHOPS OF FRANCE

Pope John Paul addressed a number of special concerns at meetings with French bishops during their ad limina visits in 1997. Following are excerpts from his remarks on the responsibility of bishops to proclaim the Gospel, the spiritual formation of lay persons, and the significance of the 1997 World Youth Day as an event of preparation for the celebration of Jubilee Year 2000.

Responsibility to Teach

As apostles of Christ, (the Pope said Jan. 11), you are among the first to experience the cross of indifference, misunderstanding and sometimes even hostility. In a society that is often unsure of itself and is going through a prolonged economic and social crisis, you see too many people and too many of the baptized living outside the ecclesial community, rejecting in a way the institution and preferring to live in individualistic isolation; each feels he is the arbiter of his own rules of life and, even if he retains a religious sense and the Church remains a distant reference point for him, he does not live a personal faith in Jesus Christ and ignores the ecclesial dimension.

Is it necessary to repeat that episcopal responsibility belongs first and foremost to the spiritual order? Watchful and vigilant, the pastor looks on his faithful and on the whole of society in the light of the Gospel and of his ecclesial experience.

I would like to strengthen you fraternally in your task of teaching and proclaiming the Gospel of Christ to men and women. The bishop, a prophet who proclaims the Good News, tirelessly preaches it, seeking the language that is the key to the meaning of the Scriptures, as the Lord did with the disciples at Emmaus. The (Second Vatican) Council says in particular: 'Bishops should present the doctrine of Christ in a manner suited to the needs of the times, that is, so it may be relevant to those difficulties and questions which men find especially worrying and intimidating.' These words suffice to show that your apostolic ministry is addressed to people of the present time, according to the needs, expressed or concealed, of the faithful who are visibly present in the diocesan community as persons standing on the threshold and searching for meaning in life.

In particular, the bishop stands in the front line of commitment to society's poor and marginalized.

Formation of Lay Persons

The spiritual formation and development of lay persons were the subjects of papal remarks Feb. 12.

Every Christian is continually invited to deepen his faith; this will help him to come closer to the risen Christ and to be his witness in society. In fact, in a world where people do not cease to improve their scientific and technical knowledge, knowledge of the faith cannot remain merely the catechism learned in childhood. To grow humanly and spiritually, the Christian has an obvious need for ongoing formation. Without this, he risks no longer being enlightened in the sometimes difficult choices he must make in his life and in carrying out his specific Christian mission among his brothers and sisters.

Day by day it is necessary for Catholics to practice enlightened discernment regarding the opinions whose influence is spreading and of which they must remain free. Whether it is a question of personal or social morals, a disciple of Christ must be able to recognize where the right way, the truth about man and respect for life truly lie. What is known as the evolution of morality cannot in itself reform norms of life based on the natural law that every person of good will can learn with his own right reason, and the Gospel. What civil law authorizes does not necessarily correspond to the truth of the human vocation, nor to the good which every person must try to accomplish in his personal choices and in his conduct toward others.

All in all, in a cultural context that tends to relativize most convictions, the believer must be devoted to the search for and the love of the truth. This is a central principle. The Lord Jesus himself said: 'I am the Way, and the Truth, and the Life' (Jn. 14:6).... A formation which truly helps one live the Christian life implies intelligent and responsible acceptance of the truth received from God through the Gospel.

Mystery of Christ

During an April meeting, the Holy Father spoke about the importance of World Youth Day in August as a preparatory event to Jubilee Year 2000. He also spoke about the need to present the mystery of Christ in all its fullness.

Do not spare efforts to ensure that the reception of the word of God is constantly renewed; the faithful must be able better to penetrate Scripture, to become familiar with it and make its message their own through the sacred reading.

REPRESENTATIVES OF THE HOLY SEE

Representatives of the Holy See and their functions were the subject of a document entitled *Sollicitudo Omnium Ecclesiarum* which Pope Paul VI issued on his own initiative under the date of June 24, 1969.

Delegates and Nuncios

Papal representatives "receive from the Roman Pontiff the charge of representing him in a fixed way in the various nations or regions of the world.

"When their legation is only to local churches, they are known as apostolic delegates. When to this legation, of a religious and ecclesial nature, there is added diplomatic legation to states and governments, they receive the title of nuncio, pro-nuncio, and internuncio."

An apostolic nuncio has the diplomatic rank of ambassador extraordinary and plenipotentiary. Traditionally, because the diplomatic service of the Holy See has the longest uninterrupted history in the world, a nuncio has precedence among diplomats in the country to which he is accredited and serves as dean of the diplomatic corps on state occasions. Since 1965 pro-nuncios, also of ambassadorial rank, have been assigned to countries in which this prerogative is not recognized. In recent years, the Vatican started to phase out the title of pro-nuncio. The title of nuncio (with an asterisk denoting he is not dean of the diplomatic corps) has been given to the majority of appointments of ambassadorial rank. See also: Other Representatives.

Service and Liaison

Representatives, while carrying out their general and special duties, are bound to respect the autonomy of local churches and bishops. Their service and liaison responsibilities include the following:

• Nomination of Bishops: To play a key role in compiling, with the advice of ecclesiastics and lay persons, and submitting lists of names of likely candidates to the Holy See with their own recommendations.

• Bishops: To aid and counsel local bishops without interfering in the affairs of their jurisdictions.

• Episcopal Conferences: To maintain close relations with them and to assist them in every possible way. (Papal representatives do not belong to these conferences.)

• Religious Communities of Pontifical Rank: To advise and assist major superiors for the purpose of promoting and consolidating conferences of men and women religious and to coordinate their apostolic activities.

• Church-State Relations: The thrust in this area is toward the development of sound relations with civil governments and collaboration in work for peace and the total good of the whole human family.

The mission of a papal representative begins with appointment and assignment by the pope and continues until termination of his mandate. He acts "under the guidance and according to the instructions of the cardinal secretary of state to whom he is directly responsible for the execution of the mandate entrusted to him by the Supreme Pontiff." Normally representatives are required to retire at the age of 75.

NUNCIOS AND DELEGATES

(Sources: *Annuario Pontificio, L'Osservatore Romano, Acta Apostolicae Sedis,* Catholic News Service.)

Data, as of July 30, 1997: country, rank of legation (corresponding to rank of legate unless otherwise noted), name of legate (archbishop unless otherwise noted) as available. An asterisk indicates a nuncio who is not presently dean of the diplomatic corps.

Delegate for Papal Representatives: Archbishop Francesco Monterisi, titular Archbishop of Alba Marittima. The post was established in 1973 to coordinate papal diplomatic efforts throughout the world. The office entails responsibility for "following more closely through timely visits the activities of papal representatives . . . and encouraging their rapport with the central offices" of the Secretariat of State.

Albania: Tirana, Nunciature; Giovanni Bulaitis*.

Algeria: Algiers, Nunciature; Antonio Sozzo*. (He is also Nuncio* to Tunisia.)

Andorra: Nunciature; Lajos Kada (Also nuncio to Spain).

Angola: Luanda, Nunciature; Aldo Cavalli* (also Nuncio* to Sao Tome and Principe). Diplomatic relations established July, 1997.

Antigua and Barbuda: Nunciature; Eugenio Sbarbaro, Pro-Nuncio (resides in Port of Spain, Trinidad).

Antilles: Apostolic Delegation; Eugenio Sbarbaro (resides in Port of Spain, Trinidad).

Arabian Peninsula: Apostolic Delegation; vacant (also nuncio in Kuwait and Lebanon; resides in Lebanon).

Argentina: Buenos Aires, Nunciature; Ubaldo Calabresi.

Armenia: Nunciature; Jean-Paul Gobel* (resides in Tbilisi, Georgia). (Diplomatic relations established May 23, 1992.)

Australia: Canberra, Nunciature; Franco Brambilla, Pro-Nuncio.

Austria: Vienna, Nunciature; Donato Squicciarini.

Azerbaijan: Nunciature; Jean-Paul Gobel* (resides in Tbilisi, Georgia). (Diplomatic relations established May 23, 1992.)

Bahamas: Nunciature; Eugenio Sbarbaro, Pro-Nuncio (resides in Port of Spain, Trinidad).

Bangladesh: Dhaka, Nunciature; Edward Joseph Adams*.

Barbados: Nunciature; Eugenio Sbarbaro, Pro-Nuncio (resides in Port of Spain, Trinidad).

Belarus: Nunciature; Dominik Hrusovsky*.

Belgium: Brussels, Nunciature; Giovanni Moretti (also Nuncio to Luxembourg).

Belize: Nunciature; Eugenio Sbarbaro, Pro-Nuncio (resides in Port of Spain, Trinidad).

Benin (formerly Dahomey): Nunciature; Andre Dupuy* (resides in Accra, Ghana).

Bolivia: La Paz, Nunciature; Rino Passigato.

Bosnia and Herzegovina: Nunciature; Francesco Monterisi*. (He is also delegate for Papal Representatives; resides in Vatican City.)

Botswana: See South Africa.
Brazil: Brasilia, Nunciature; Alfio Rapisarda.
Brunei: See Malaysia and Brunei.
Bulgaria: Sofia, Nunciature (reestablished, 1990); Blasco Francisco Collaco*.
Burkina Faso: Ouagadougou, Nunciature; Luigi Ventura*(resides in Abidjan, Côte d'Ivoire).
Burma: See Myanmar.
Burundi: Bujumbura, Nunciature; Emil Paul Tscherrig*.
Cambodia: Nunciature; Luigi Bressan* (resides in Bangkok, Thailand). Diplomatic relations established March, 1994.
Cameroon: Yaounde, Nunciature; Felix del Blanco Prieto* (also Nuncio to Equatorial Guinea).
Canada: Ottawa, Nunciature; Carlo Curis*.
Cape Verde, Republic of: Nunciature; Antonio Maria Veglio* (resides in Dakar, Senegal).
Central African Republic: Bangui, Nunciature; Diego Causero* (also Nuncio* to Chad).
Chad: Nunciature; Diego Causero* (resides in Bangui, Central African Republic).
Chile: Santiago, Nunciature; Piero Biggio.
China: Taipei (Taiwan), Nunciature; vacant.
Colombia: Bogota, Nunciature; Paolo Romeo.
Comoros: See Madagascar.
Congo (formerly Zaire): Kinshasa-Gombe, Nunciature; Faustino Sainz Muñoz*.
Congo: Brazzaville, Nunciature; Luigi Pezzuto* (also pro-nuncio to Gabon).
Costa Rica: San Jose, Nunciature; Giacinto Berloco.
Côte d'Ivoire (Ivory Coast): Abidjan, Nunciature; Luigi Ventura (also nuncio* to Niger and Burkina Faso).
Croatia: Zagreb, Nunciature; Giulio Einaudi.
Cuba: Havana, Nunciature; Benjamin Stella*.
Cyprus: Nicosia, Nunciature; Andrea Cordero Lanza di Montezemolo, Pro-Nuncio.
Czech Republic: Prague, Nunciature; Giovanni Coppa.
Denmark: Copenhagen, Nunciature; Giovanni Ceirano* (also Nuncio* to Finland, Iceland, Norway and Sweden).
Djibouti: Apostolic Delegation; Silvano Tomasi, C.S. (resides in Addis Ababa, Ethiopia).
Dominica: Nunciature; Eugenio Sbarbaro, Pro-Nuncio (resides in Port-of-Spain, Trinidad).
Dominican Republic: Santo Domingo, Nunciature; Francois Bacque (also serves as Apostolic Delegate to Puerto Rico).
Ecuador: Quito, Nunciature; Francesco Canalini.
Egypt: Cairo, Nunciature; Paolo Giglio*.
El Salvador: San Salvador, Nunciature; Manuel Monteiro de Castro.
Equatorial Guinea: Santa Isabel, Nunciature; Felix del Blanco Prieto* (resides in Yaounde, Cameroon).
Eritrea: Nunciature; Silvano Tomasi, C.S.* (resides in Ethiopia). Diplomatic relations established July 15, 1995.
Estonia: Nunciature; Erwin Josef Ender* (resides in Vilna, Lithuania).
Ethiopia: Addis Ababa, Nunciature; Silvano Tomasi, C.S.* (also nuncio* to Eritrea and apostolic delegate to Djibouti).

Fiji: Nunciature; Patrick Coveney* (resides in New Zealand).
Finland: Helsinki, Nunciature; Giovanni Ceirano* (resides in Denmark).
France: Paris, Nunciature; Mario Tagliaferri..
Gabon: Libreville, Nunciature; Luigi Pezzuto* (resides in Congo).
Gambia: Nunciature; Antonio Lucibello* (resides in Freetown, Sierra Leone).
Georgia: Tbilisi, Nunciature; Jean-Paul Gobel* (also nuncio* to Armenia and Azerbaijan). (Diplomatic relations established May 23, 1992.)
Germany: Bonn, Nunciature; Giovanni Lajolo.
Ghana: Accra, Nunciature; Andre Dupuy* (also Nuncio to Benin and Togo).
Great Britain: London, Nunciature; Pablo Puente* (also papal representative to Gibraltar).
Greece: Athens, Nunciature; Paul Fouad Tabet*.
Grenada: Nunciature; Eugenio Sbarbaro, Pro-Nuncio (resides in Port of Spain, Trinidad).
Guatemala: Guatemala City, Nunciature; Ramiro Moliner Inglés.
Guinea: Conakry, Nunciature; Antonio Lucibello*(resides in Freetown, Sierra Leone).
Guinea-Bissau: Nunciature; Antonio Maria Veglio* (resides at Dakar, Senegal).
Haiti: Port-au-Prince, Nunciature; Christophe Pierre.
Honduras: Tegucigalpa, Nunciature; Luigi Conti.
Hungary: Budapest, Nunciature; Karl-Josef Rauber (also nuncio* to Moldova).
Iceland: Nunciature; Giovanni Ceirano* (resides in Denmark).
India: New Delhi, Nunciature; Giorgio Zur, Pro-Nuncio (also Pro-Nuncio to Nepal).
Indonesia: Jakarta, Nunciature; Pietro Sambi, Pro-Nuncio.
Iran: Teheran, Nunciature; Romeo Panciroli M.C.C.I.*
Iraq: Baghdad, Nunciature; Giuseppe Lazzarotto* (also nuncio to Jordan).
Ireland: Dublin, Nunciature; Luciano Storero.
Israel: Nunciature; Andrea Cordero Lanza de Montezemolo*. Diplomatic relations established June 15, 1994.
Italy: Rome, Nunciature; Francesco Colasuonno.
Ivory Coast: See Côte d'Ivoire.
Jamaica: Nunciature; Eugenio Sbarbaro, Pro-Nuncio (resides in Port of Spain, Trinidad).
Japan: Tokyo, Nunciature; William A. Carew, Pro-Nuncio.
Jerusalem and Palestine: Apostolic Delegation; Andrea Cordero Lanza di Montezemolo (also Nuncio to Israel).
Jordan: Nunciature; Giuseppe Lazzarotto* (also nuncio to Iraq).
Kazakhstan: Almaty, Nunciature; Marian Oles * (also nuncio* to Kyrgyzstan, Tajikistan and Uzbekistan).
Kenya: Nairobi, Nunciature; Giovanni Tonucci*.
Kiribati: Nunciature; Patrick Coveney* (resides in New Zealand).
Korea: Seoul, Nunciature; Giovanni Battista Morandini* (also nuncio* to Mongolia).
Kuwait: Al Kuwait, Nunciature; vacant* (resides in Lebanon).

Kyrgyzstan: Nunciature; Marian Oles* (resides in Kazakhstan).

Laos: Apostolic Delegation; Luigi Bressan, (resides in Bangkok, Thailand).

Latvia: Nunciature; Erwin Josef Ender* (resides in Vilna, Lithuania).

Lebanon: Beirut, Nunciature; (also nuncio* to Kuwait and apostolic delegate to Arabian Peninsula).

Lesotho: Maseru, Nunciature; Ambrose De Paoli, Pro-Nuncio (resides in Pretoria, S. Africa).

Liberia: Monrovia, Nunciature; Antonio Lucibello* (resides in Freetown, Sierra Leone).

Libya: Nunciature; Jose Sebastian Laboa* (resides in Malta). Diplomatic relations established in 1997.

Liechtenstein: Nunciature; vacant (resides in Bern, Switzerland).

Lithuania: Vilnius, Nunciature; Erwin Josef Ender (also nuncio* to Estonia and Latvia.).

Luxembourg: Nunciature; Giovanni Moretti (resides in Brussels, Belgium).

Macedonia: Nunciature; Edmond Farhat* (also nuncio to Slovenia). Diplomatic relations established Dec. 21, 1994.

Madagascar: Antananarivo, Nunciature; Adriano Bernardini* (also Nuncio* to Seychelles, and Mauritius and Apostolic Delegate to Comoros and Reunion).

Malawi: Lilongwe, Nunciature; Giuseppe Leanza, Pro-Nuncio (resides in Zambia).

Malaysia and Brunei: Apostolic Delegation; Luigi Bressan (resides in Bangkok, Thailand).

Mali: Nunciature; Antonio Maria Veglio* (resides in Dakar, Senegal).

Malta: La Valletta, Nunciature; Jose Sebastian Laboa (also nuncio* to Libya).

Marshall Islands: Nunciature; Patrick Coveney* (resides in New Zealand).

Mauritania: Nouakchott, Apostolic Delegation; Antonio Maria Veglio (resides in Dakar, Senegal).

Mauritius: Port Louis, Nunciature; Adriano Bernardini* (resides in Antananarivo, Madagascar).

Mexico: Mexico City, Nunciature; Justo Mullor Garcia* (diplomatic relations established 1992).

Micronesia, Federated States of: Nunciature; Patrick Coveney* (resides in New Zealand).

Moldova: Nunciature; Karl-Josef Rauber* (resides in Budapest, Hungary). (Diplomatic relations established May 23, 1992.)

Mongolia: Nunciature; Giovanni Battista Morandini* (resides in Seoul, Korea).

Morocco: Rabat, Nunciature; Domenico De Luca*.

Mozambique: Maputo, nunciature; Peter Stephan Zurbriggen.* Diplomatic relations established 1995.

Myanmar (formerly Burma): Apostolic Delegation; Luigi Bressan (resides in Bangkok, Thailand).

Namibia: Nunciature; Ambrose De Paoli*.

Nauru: Nunciature; Patrick Coveney*.

Nepal: Nunciature; Giorgio Zur, Pro-Nuncio (resides in New Delhi, India).

Netherlands: The Hague, Nunciature; Angelo Acerbi*.

New Zealand: Wellington, Nunciature; Patrick Coveney*. (He is also Nuncio* to Fiji, Kiribati, Marshall Islands, Federated States of Micronesia, Tonga, Vanuatu and Western Samoa; Apostolic Delegate to Pacific Islands).

Nicaragua: Managua, Nunciature; Luigi Travaglino.

Niger: Niamey, Nunciature; Luigi Ventura* (resides in Abidjan, Côte d'Ivoire.)

Nigeria: Lagos, Nunciature; Carlo M. Vigano, Pro-Nuncio.

Norway: Nunciature; Giovanni Ceirano* (resides in Denmark).

Pacific Islands: Apostolic Delegation; Patrick Coveney (resides in New Zealand).

Pakistan: Islamabad, Nunciature; Renzo Fratini*.

Panama: Panama, Nunciature; Bruno Musaro.

Papua New Guinea: Port Moresby; Nunciature; Hans Schwemmer (also Nuncio* to Solomon Islands).

Paraguay: Asuncion, Nunciature; Lorenzo Baldisseri.

Peru: Lima, Nunciature; Fortunato Baldelli.

Philippines: Manila, Nunciature; Gian Vincenzo Moreni.

Poland: Warsaw; Nunciature; Jozef Kowalczyk.

Portugal: Lisbon, Nunciature; Edoardo Rovida.

Puerto Rico: See Dominican Republic.

Reunion: See Madagascar.

Romania: Bucharest, Nunciature. Janusz Bolenek, S.V.D.*

Rwanda: Kigali, Nunciature. Juliusz Janusz.

Saint Lucia: Nunciature; Eugenio Sbarbaro, Pro-Nuncio (resides in Port of Spain, Trinidad).

Saint Vincent and the Grenadines: Nunciature; Eugenio Sbarbaro, Pro-Nuncio (resides in Port of Spain, Trinidad).

San Marino: Nunciature; Francesco Colasuonno.

Sao Tome and Principe: Nunciature; Aldo Cavalli* (also nuncio* to Angola, where he resides).

Senegal: Dakar, Nunciature; Antonio Maria Veglio* (also Pro-Nuncio to Cape Verde, Guinea-Bissau and Mali; Apostolic Delegate to Mauritania.)

Seychelles Islands: Nunciature; Adriano Bernardini* (resides in Antananrivo, Madagascar).

Sierra Leone: Freetown, Nunciature (1996); Antonio Lucibello* (also Nuncio* to Gambia, Guinea and Liberia).

Singapore: Nunciature; Luigi Bressan* (He is also nuncio* to Cambodia and Thailand and apostolic delegate to Laos, Malaysia and Brunei, and Myanmar.)

Slovakia: Nunciature; Luigi Dossena.

Slovenia: Ljubljana, Nunciature; Edmond Farhat (also nuncio to Macedonia).

Solomon Islands: Nunciature; Hans Schwemmer (resides in Port Moresby, Papua New Guinea).

Somalia: Apostolic Delegation (est. 1992); vacant (resides in Sudan).

South Africa: Pretoria, Nunciature; Ambrose De Paoli*. (He is also nuncio* to Namibia and apostolic delegate to Botswana.)

Spain: Madrid, Nunciature; Lajos Kada.

Sri Lanka: Colombo, Nunciature; Osvaldo Padilla*

Sudan: Khartoum, Nunciature; vacant, Pro-Nuncio (also Apostolic Delegate to Somalia).

Suriname: Nunciature; Eugenio Sbarbaro * (resides in Trinidad).

Swaziland: Nunciature; Ambrose De Paoli* (resides in Pretoria, South Africa).

Sweden: Nunciature; Giovanni Ceirano* (resides in Denmark).

Switzerland: Bern, Nunciature; Oriano Quilici (also nuncio to Liechtenstein).

Syria: (Syrian Arab Republic): Damascus, Nunciature; Pier Giacomo De Nicola*.

Tajikistan: Nunciature; Marian Oles* (resides in Kazakhstan). Diplomatic relations established June 15, 1996.

Tanzania: Dar-es-Salaam, Nunciature; Francisco-Javier Lozano*.

Thailand: Bangkok, Nunciature; Luigi Bressan* (also Nuncio* to Cambodia and Singapore and Apostolic Delegate to Laos, Malaysia, Brunei, Myanmar).

Togo: Lome, Nunciature; Andre Dupuy* (resides in Accra, Ghana).

Tonga: Nunciature; Patrick Coveney* (resides in New Zealand).

Trinidad and Tobago: Port of Spain, Trinidad, Nunciature; Eugenio Sbarbaro, Pro-Nuncio (also Pro-Nuncio to Antigua and Barbuda, Bahamas, Barbados, Belize, Dominica, Grenada, Jamaica, Saint Lucia, Saint Vincent and the Grenadines, Suriname and Apostolic Delegate to Antilles).

Tunisia: Tunis, Nunciature; Antonio Sozzo* (resides in Algiers, Algeria).

Turkey: Ankara, Nunciature; Pier Luigi Celata*.

Turkmenistan: Nunciature; Pier Luigi Celata*. Diplomatic relations established July 10, 1996.

Ukraine: Kiev, Nunciature; Antonio Franco*.

Uganda: Kampala, Nunciature; Luiz Robles Diaz, Pro-Nuncio.

United States of America: Washington, D.C., Nunciature; Agostino Cacciavillan, Pro-Nuncio.

Uruguay: Montevideo, Nunciature; Francesco De Nittis.

Uzbekistan: Nunciature. Marian Oles* (resides in Kazakhstan).

Vanuatu: Nunciature; Patrick Coveney* (resides in New Zealand).

Venezuela: Caracas, Nunciature; Leonardo Sandri.

Vietnam: Apostolic Delegation.

Western Samoa: Nunciature; Patrick Coveney* (resides in New Zealand).

Yugoslavia: Belgrade, Nunciature; Santos Abril y Castello.

Zaire: See Congo.

Zambia: Lusaka, Nunciature; Giuseppe Leanza, Pro-Nuncio (also Pro-Nuncio to Malawi).

Zimbabwe: Harare, Nunciature; Peter Paul Prabhu*.

Russia (Federation of): Moscow; John Bukovsky, S.V.D., Apostolic Nuncio; appointed Representative of the Holy See to Russian Federation, Dec, 20, 1994.

European Community: Brussels, Belgium, Nunciature; vacant.

Pro-Nuncio to U.S.

The representative of the Pope to the Church in the United States is Archbishop Agostino Cacciavillan. Archbishop Cacciavillan was born Aug. 14, 1926, in Novale, Italy. Ordained to the priesthood June 26, 1949, he entered the Vatican diplomatic service in 1959. He was ordained archbishop (titular see of Amiternum) Feb. 28, 1976, and served as pro-nuncio to Kenya and apostolic delegate to the Seychelles (1976-81) and pro-nuncio to India and Nepal (1981-90). He was appointed pro-nuncio to the United States and permanent observer to the Organization of American States, June 13, 1990. He succeeded Archbishop Pio Laghi who served as first pro-nuncio from 1984-90 (see Index, U.S.-Vatican Relations).

The U.S. Apostolic Nunciature is located at 3339 Massachusetts Ave. N.W., Washington, D.C. 20008.

From 1893 to 1984, papal representatives to the Church in the U.S. were apostolic delegates (all archbishops): Francesco Satolli (1893-96), Sebastiano Martinelli, O.S.A. (1896-1902), Diomede Falconio, O.F.M. (1902-11), Giovanni Bonzano (1911-22), Pietro Fumasoni-Biondi (1922-33), Amleto Cicognani (1933-58), Egidio Vagnozzi (1958-67), Luigi Raimondi (1967-73), Jean Jadot (1973-80), Pio Laghi (apostolic delegate, 1980-84; first pro-nuncio, 1984-90).

OTHER REPRESENTATIVES

(Sources: *Annuario Pontificio;* Catholic News Service.)

The Holy See has representatives to or is a regular member of a number of quasi-governmental and international organizations. Most Rev. Ernesto Gallina was appointed delegate to International Governmental Organizations Jan. 12, 1991.

Governmental Organizations: United Nations (Abp. Renato Raffaele Martino, permanent observer); UN Office in Geneva and Specialized Institutes (Abp. Giuseppe Bertello, permanent observer); International Atomic Energy Agency (Msgr. Mario Zenari, permanent representative); UN Office at Vienna and UN Organization for Industrial Development (Msgr. Mario Zenari, permanent observer); UN Food and Agriculture Organization (Abp. Alois Wagner, permanent observer); UN Educational, Scientific and Cultural Organization (Msgr. Lorenzo Frana, permanent observer);

Council of Europe (Msgr. Michael Courtney, special representative with function of permanent observer); Council for Cultural Cooperation of the Council of Europe (Msgr. Michael Courtney, delegate); Organization of American States (Abp. Agostino Cacciavillan, permanent observer, with personal title of Apostolic Nuncio); Organization for Security and Cooperation in Europe (Mario Zenari, permanent representative); International Institute for the Unification of Private Law (Prof. Tommaso Mauro, delegate); International Committee of Military Medicine (Adolphe Vander Perre, delegate), World Organization of Tourism (Msgr. Piero Monni, permanent observer).

Universal Postal Union; International Telecommunications Union; International Council on Grain; World Organization of Intellectual Property; International Organization of Telecommunication via Satellite (Intelsat); European Conference of Postal and Telecommunication Administration (CEPT); European Organization of Telecommunication via Satellite (EUTELSAT).

Non-Governmental Organizations: International Committee of Historical Sciences (Msgr. Victor Saxer); International Committee of Paleography; International Committee of the History of Art; International Committee of Anthropological and Ethnological Sciences;

International Committee for the Neutrality of Medicine; International Center of Study for the Preservation and Restoration of Cultural Goods; International Council of Monuments and Sites (Msgr. Lorenzo Frana, delegate); International Alliance on Tourism; World Association of Jurists (Abp. Agostino Cacciavillan, delegate); International Commission of the Civil State; International Astronomical Union; International Institute of Administrative Sciences; International Technical Committee for Prevention and Extinction of Fires; World Medical Association; International Archives Council.

DIPLOMATS TO THE HOLY SEE

(Sources: *Annuario Pontificio, L'Osservatore Romano*).

Listed below are countries maintaining diplomatic relations with the Holy See, dates of establishment (in some cases) and names of Ambassadors (as of Aug. 30, 1997). Leaders (. . . . .) indicate the post was vacant.

The senior member of the diplomatic corps at the Vatican is Jean Wagner of Luxembourg who was appointed in Nov. 7, 1981, and presented his credentials Jan. 18, 1982.

Albania (1991): Pjeter Pepa.
Algeria (1972): Mohamed-Salah Dembri..
Andorra: Diplomatic relations established in June, 1995.
Angola: Diplomatic relations established July 1997.
Antigua and Barbuda (1986): . . . . .
Argentina: Esteban Juan Caselli.
Armenia (1992): Armen Sarkissian.
Australia (1973): Edward John Stevens.
Austria: Gustav Ortner.
Azerbaijan (1992): . . . . .
Bahamas (1979): . . . . .
Bangladesh (1972): Iftekhar Ahmed Chowdhury..
Barbados (1979): . . . . .
Belarus (1992): . . . . .
Belgium (1835): Juan Cassiers.
Belize (1983): Mrs. Ursula Helen Barrow.
Benin (formerly Dahomey) (1971): . . . . .
Bolivia: Armando Loaiza Mariaca.
Bosnia and Herzegovina (1992): . . . . .
Brazil: Francisco Thompson-Flores.
Bulgaria (1990): Kiril Kirilov Maritchkov.
Burkina Faso (1973): Felipe Savadogo..
Burundi (1963): Albert Mbonerane.
Cambodia (1994): . . . . .
Cameroon (1966): Jean Melaga.
Canada (1969): Leonard H. Legault.
Cape Verde (1976): Teofilo de Figueiredo Almeida.
Central African Republic (1975): . . . . .
Chad (1988): . . . . .
Chile: Javier Luis Egaña Baraona.
China, Republic of (Taiwan) (1966): Raymond R.M. Tai.
Colombia: Julio César Turbay Ayala.
Congo (formerly Zaire) (1963): Atembina-te-Bombo.
Congo (1977): Pierre-Michel Nguimbi.
Costa Rica: Rosemary Karpinski Dodero.

Côte d'Ivoire (Ivory Coast) (1971): Simeon Aké
Croatia (1992): Ive Livljanic.
Cuba: Hermes Herrera Hernandez.
Cyprus (1973): Theophilos V. Theophilou.
Czech Republic (1929-50, reestablished, 1990, with Czech and Slovak Federative Republic; reaffirmed, 1993): Frantisek X. Halas.
Denmark (1982): Jan Marcussen.
Dominica (1981): . . . . .
Dominican Republic: Cesar Ivan Feris Iglesias.
Ecuador: Alfredo Luna Tobar
Egypt (1966): Mohamed Hussein Said El-Sadre.
El Salvador Roberto Jose Siman Jacir.
Equatorial Guinea (1981): . . . . .
Eritrea (1995): Wolde-Mariam Goytom.
Estonia (1991): Margus Laidre.
Ethiopia (1969): Mulugeta Eteffa.
Fiji (1978): Filimone Jitoko.
Finland (1966): Alli Mennander.
France: Jean-Louis Lucet.
Gabon (1967): Eugene Milingout Mangaka.
Gambia, The (1978): . . . . . .
Georgia (1992): . . . . .
Germany: Philipp Jenninger.
Ghana (1976): Agnes Yahan Aggrey-Orleans.
Great Britain (1982): Miss Maureen Elisabeth MacGlashan.
Greece (1980): Nikolaos Kalantzianos.
Grenada (1979): . . . . .
Guatemala: Jose Maurice Rodriguez Wever.
Guinea (1986): Lamine Bolivogui.
Guinea-Bissau (1986): . . . . .
Haiti: Marc A. Trouillot.
Honduras: Alejandro Emilio Valladares Lanza.
Hungary (1990): Jozef Bratinka.
Iceland (1976): Ólafur Egilsson.
India: Kizhakke Pisharath Balakrishnan.
Indonesia (1965): Irawan Abidin.
Iran (1966): Mohammad Hedi Abd Khoda'i.
Iraq (1966): Wissam Chawkat Al-Zahawi.
Ireland: Gearoid P. O'Broin.
Israel (1994): Aharon Lopez.
Italy: Bruno Bottai.
Ivory Coast: See Côte d'Ivoire.
Jamaica (1979): Peter Carlisle Black.
Japan (1966): Hisakazu Takase.
Jordan (1994): Al-Sharif Fawaz Sharaf..
Kazakhstan (1992): . . . . .
Kenya (1965) Steven Loyatum.
Kiribati: Diplomatic relations established April, 1995.
Korea (1966): Heungsoo Kim.
Kuwait (1969): Tarek Razzouqi.
Kyrgyzstan (1992): Omar A. Sultanov..
Latvia (1991): Mrs. Aija Odina.
Lebanon (1966): Youssef Arsanios.
Lesotho (1967): Miss Lebohang Nts'Inyi.
Liberia (1966): . . . . .
Libya: Diplomatic relations established March 10, 1997.
Liechtenstein (1985): Nikolaus de Liechtenstein.
Lithuania (1992): Kazys Lozoraitis.
Luxembourg (1955): Jean Wagner.
Macedonia (1994): Dimitar Mircev.
Madagascar (1967): . . . . .
Malawi (1966): Geoffrey Gachuku Chipungu.

Mali (1979): N'Tji Laico Traore.
Malta (1965): Dr. Daniel Micallef
Marshall Islands (1993): . . . . .
Mauritius: Setcam Boolell.
Mexico (personal representative, 1990; diplomatic relations, 1992): Guillermo Jimenez Morales.
Micronesia, Federated States (1994): . . . . .
Moldova (1992): . . . . .
Monaco: Cesar Charles Solamito.
Mongolia (1992): Shirchinjavya Yumjav.
Morocco: . . . . .
Mozambique: Diplomatic relations established December, 1995.
Namibia: Diplomatic relations established September, 1995.
Nauru (1992): . . . . .
Nepal (1983): Novel Kishore Rai.
Netherlands (1967): Gijsbert Nicolaus Westerouen.
New Zealand (1973): Wilbur Dovey.
Nicaragua: Jose Cuadro Chamorro..
Niger (1971): . . . . .
Nigeria (1976): Yaro Yusufu Mamman.
Norway (1982): Jan G. Jolle.
Order of Malta (see Index): Christophe de Kallay.
Pakistan (1965): S. M. Inamullah.
Panama: Maria Teresa Viggiano de De Obarrio.
Papua New Guinea (1977): . . . . .
Paraguay: Maria Ramirez Boettner.
Peru: Augusto Antonioli Vasquez.
Philippines (1951): Mrs. Henrietta Tambunting de Villa.
Poland (1989): Stefan Frankiewicz.
Portugal: Antonio d'Oliveira Pinto da Franco.
Romania (1920; broken off, 948; reestablished, 1990): Gheorghe Pancratu Juliu Gheorghiu.
Rwanda (1964): Manzi Bakuramutsa.
Saint Lucia (1984): Desmond Arthur McNamara.
Saint Vincent and the Grenadines (1990): . . . . .
San Marino (1986): Giovanni Galassi.
Sao Tome and Principe (1984): . . . . .
Senegal (1966): Henri Antoine Turpin.
Seychelles (1984): . . . . .
Sierra Leone: Diplomatic relations established July 1996.
Singapore (1981): Eng Fong Pang.
Slovakia (1993; when it became independent republic): Anton Neuwirth.
Slovenia (1992): Stefan Falez.

Solomon Islands (1984): . . . . .
South Africa (1994): Ruth Segomotsi Mompati..
Spain: Carlos Abella y Ramallo.
Sri Lanka (1975): Bernard A. B. Goonetilleke.
Sudan (1972): Eltigani Salih Fidail.
Suriname (1994): Evert G. Azimullah.
Swaziland (1992): Mpumelelo Joseph Ndumiso Hlophe.
Sweden (1982): Anders Thunborg.
Switzerland (1992): Francois Pictet, Ambassador with special mission to Holy See.
Syria (Arab Republic) (1966): Elias Najmeh.
Tajikstan: Diplomatic relations established June 15, 1996.
Tanzania (1968): Andrew Mbando Daraja.
Thailand (1969): Don Pramudwinai.
Togo (1981): . . . . . .
Tonga (1994): . . . . .
Trinidad and Tobago (1978): Lingsten Lloyd Cumberbatch.
Tunisia (1972): . . . . .
Turkey (1966): Semih Belen.
Turkmenistan: Diplomatic relations established July 10, 1996.
Uganda (1966): . . . . . .
Ukraine (1992): . . . . .
United States (1984): Raymond L. Flynn.
Uruguay: Felipe H. Paolillo.
Uzbekistan (1992): . . . . .
Vanuatu (1994): . . . . .
Venezuela: Alberto J. Vollmer Herrera.
Western Samoa (1994): . . . . .
Yugoslavia: Dojcilo Maslovaric.
Zaire: See Congo.
Zambia (1965): Love Mtesa.
Zimbabwe (1980): Joey Mazorodze Bimba.

Special Representatives
Russia (Federation of) (1989): Guennadi Uranav, Ambassador Extraordinary and Plenipotentiary.
United Nations (Center of Information of UN at the Holy See): Dr. Nadia Younes, director.
United Nations High Commission for Refugees: Fazlul Karim, delegate.
Organization for the Liberation of Palestine: Afif E. Safieh, director.

U.S. - HOLY SEE RELATIONS

The United States and the Holy See announced Jan. 10, 1984, the establishment of full diplomatic relations, thus ending a gap of 117 years in their relations. The announcement followed action by the Congress in November, 1983, to end a prohibition on diplomatic relations enacted in 1867.

William A. Wilson, President Reagan's personal representative to the Holy See from 1981, was confirmed as the U.S. ambassador by the Senate, Mar. 7, 1984. He presented his credentials to Pope John Paul II, Apr. 9, 1984, and served until May 1986, when he resigned.

He was succeeded by Frank Shakespeare, 1986-89, and Thomas P. Melady, 1989-93. Raymond L. Flynn, Mayor of Boston, was appointed by President Bill Clinton and confirmed by the Senate in July, 1993.

Archbishop (now Cardinal) Pio Laghi, apostolic delegate to the U.S. since 1980, was named first pronuncio by the Pope on Mar. 26, 1984. He served until 1990, when he was named prefect of the Congregation for Catholic Education. Archbishop Agostino Cacciavillan was appointed pro-nuncio June 13, 1990.

Nature of Relations
The nature of relations was described in nearly identical statements by John Hughes, a State Department spokesman, and the Holy See.

Hughes said: "The United States of America and the Holy See, in the desire to further promote the existing mutual friendly relations, have decided by common agreement to establish diplomatic relations between them at the level of embassy on the part of the United States of America, and nunciature on the part of the Holy See, as of today, Jan. 10, 1984."

The Holy See statement said: "The Holy See and the United States of America, desiring to develop the mutual friendly relations already existing, have decided by common accord to establish diplomatic relations at the level of apostolic nunciature on the side of the Holy See and of embassy on the side of the United States beginning today, Jan. 10, 1984."

The establishment of relations was criticized as a violation of the separation-of-church-and-state principle by spokesmen for the National Council of Churches, the National Association of Evangelicals, the Baptist Joint Committee on Public Affairs, Seventh Day Adventists, Americans United for Separation of Church and State, and the American Jewish Congress.

Legal Challenge Dismissed

U.S. District Judge John P. Fullam, ruling May 7, 1985, in Philadelphia, dismissed a legal challenge to U.S.-Holy See relations brought by Americans United for Separation of Church and State. He stated that Americans United and its allies in the challenge lacked legal standing to sue, and that the courts did not have jurisdiction to intervene in foreign policy decisions of the executive branch of the U.S. government. Parties to the suit brought by Americans United were the National Association of Laity, the National Coalition of American Nuns and several Protestant church organizations.

Bishop James W. Malone, president of the U.S. Catholic Conference, said in a statement: "This matter has been discussed at length for many years. It is not a religious issue but a public policy question which, happily, has now been settled in this context."

Russell Shaw, a conference spokesman, said the decision to send an ambassador to the Holy See was not a church-state issue and "confers no special privilege or status on the Church."

Earlier Relations

Official relations for trade and diplomatic purposes were maintained by the United States and the Papal States while the latter had the character of and acted like other sovereign powers in the international community.

Consular relations developed in the wake of an announcement, made by the papal nuncio in Paris to the American mission there Dec. 15, 1784, that the Papal States had agreed to open several Mediterranean ports to U.S. shipping.

U.S. consular representation in the Papal States began with the appointment of John B. Sartori, a native of Rome, in June, 1797. Sartori's successors as consuls were: Felix Cicognani, also a Roman, and Americans George W. Greene, Nicholas Browne, William C. Sanders, Daniel LeRoy, Horatio V. Glentworth, W.J. Stillman, Edwin C. Cushman, David M. Armstrong.

Consular officials of the Papal States who served in the U.S. were: Count Ferdinand Lucchesi, 1826 to 1829, who resided in Washington; John B. Sartori, 1829 to 1841, who resided in Trenton, N.J.; Daniel J. Desmond, 1841 to 1850, who resided in Philadelphia; Louis B. Binsse, 1850 to 1895, who resided in New York.

U.S. recognition of the consul of the Papal States did not cease when the states were absorbed into the Kingdom of Italy in 1871, despite pressure from Baron Blanc, the Italian minister. Binsse held the title until his death Mar. 28, 1895. No one was appointed to succeed him.

Diplomatic Relations

The U.S. Senate approved a recommendation, made by President James K. Polk in December, 1847, for the establishment of a diplomatic post in the Papal States. Jacob L. Martin, the first charge d'affaires, arrived in Rome Aug. 2, 1848, and presented his credentials to Pius IX Aug. 19. Martin, who died within a month, was succeeded by Lewis Cass, Jr. Cass became minister resident in 1854 and served in that capacity until his retirement in 1858.

John P. Stockton, who later became a U.S. Senator from New Jersey, was minister resident from 1858 to 1861. Rufus King was named to succeed him but, instead, accepted a commission as a brigadier general in the Army. Alexander W. Randall of Wisconsin took the appointment. He was succeeded in August, 1862, by Richard M. Blatchford who served until the following year. King was again nominated minister resident and served in that capacity until 1867 when the ministry was ended because of objections from some quarters in the U.S. and failure to appropriate funds for its continuation. J. C. Hooker, a secretary, remained in the Papal States until the end of March, 1868, closing the ministry and performing functions of courtesy.

Personal Envoys

Myron C. Taylor was appointed by President Franklin D. Roosevelt in 1939 to serve as his personal representative to Pope Pius XII and continued serving in that capacity during the presidency of Harry S. Truman until 1951. Henry Cabot Lodge was named to the post by President Richard M. Nixon in 1970, served also during the presidency of Gerald Ford, and represented President Carter at the canonization of St. John Neumann in 1977.

Miami attorney David Walters served as the personal envoy of President Jimmy Carter to the Pope from July, 1977, until his resignation Aug. 16, 1978. He was succeeded by Robert F. Wagner who served from October, 1978, to the end of the Carter presidency in January, 1981. William A. Wilson, appointed by President Ronald Reagan in February, 1981, served as his personal envoy until 1984 when he was named ambassador to the Holy See.

None of the personal envoys had diplomatic status.

President Harry S. Truman nominated Gen. Mark Clark to be ambassador to the Holy See in 1951, but withdrew the nomination at Clark's request because of controversy over the appointment.

None of Truman's three immediate successors — Dwight D. Eisenhower, John F. Kennedy and Lyndon B. Johnson— had a personal representative to the Pope.

VATICAN CITY

The State of Vatican City (Stato della Citta del Vaticano) is the territorial seat of the papacy. The smallest sovereign state in the world, it is situated within the city of Rome, embraces an area of 108.7 acres, and includes within its limits the Vatican Palace, museums, art galleries, gardens, libraries, radio station, post office, bank, astronomical observatory, offices, apartments, service facilities, St. Peter's Basilica, and neighboring buildings between the Basilica and Viale Vaticano. The extraterritorial rights of Vatican City extend to more than 10 buildings in Rome, including the major basilicas and office buildings of various congregations of the Roman Curia, and to the papal villas at **Castel Gandolfo** 15 miles southeast of the City of Rome. Castel Gandolfo is the summer residence of the Holy Father.

The government of Vatican City is in the hands of the reigning pope, who has full executive, legislative and judicial power. The administration of affairs, however, is handled by the Pontifical Commission for the State of Vatican City. The legal system is based on Canon Law; in cases where this code does not obtain, the laws of the City of Rome apply. The City is an absolutely neutral state and enjoys all the rights and privileges of a sovereign power. The citizens of Vatican City, and they alone, owe allegiance to the pope as a temporal head of state.

Cardinals of the Roman Curia residing outside Vatican City enjoy the privileges of extraterritoriality.

The normal population is approximately 1,000. While the greater percentage is made up of priests and religious, there are several hundred lay persons living in Vatican City. They are housed in their own apartments in the City and are engaged in secretarial, domestic, trade and service occupations. About 3,400 lay persons are employed by the Vatican.

Services of honor and order are performed by the Swiss Guards, who have been charged with responsibility for the personal safety of popes since 1506. Additional police and ceremonial functions are under the supervision of a special office. These functions were formerly handled by the Papal Gendarmes, the Palatine Guard of Honor, and the Guard of Honor of the Pope (Pontifical Noble Guard) which Pope Paul VI disbanded Sept. 14, 1970.

The **Basilica of St. Peter**, built between 1506 and 1626, is the largest church in Christendom (with the exception of the Basilica of Our Lady Queen of Peace in Ivory Coast) and the site of most papal ceremonies. The pope's own patriarchal basilica, however, is **St. John Lateran**, whose origins date back to 324.

St. Ann's, staffed by Augustinian Fathers, is the parish church of Vatican City. Its pastor is appointed by the pope following the recommendation of the prior general of the Augustinians and the archpriest of the Vatican Basilica.

Pastoral care in Vatican City State, which is separate from the diocese of Rome, is entrusted to the archpriest of St. Peter's Basilica, who is also vicar general for Vatican City and the papal villas at Castel Gandolfo (chirograph of Pope John Paul II, Jan. 14, 1991). Cardinal Virgilio Noè was appointed to the posts, July 1, 1991.

The **Vatican Library** (00120 Vatican City; Rev. Raffaele Farins, S.D.B., prefect) has among its holdings 150,000 manuscripts, about 1,000,000 printed books, and 7,500 incunabula. The **Vatican Secret Archives** (00120 Vatican City; Rev. Sergio B. Pagano, prefect), opened to scholars by Leo XIII in 1881, contain central church documents dating back to the time of Innocent III (1198-1216). Cardinal Luigi Poggi is librarian and archivist of the Holy Roman Church.

The independent temporal power of the pope, which is limited to the confines of Vatican City and small areas outside, was for many centuries more extensive than it is now. As late as the nineteenth century, the pope ruled 16,000 square miles of Papal States across the middle of Italy, with a population of over 3,000,000. In 1870 forces of the Kingdom of Italy occupied these lands which, with the exception of the small areas surrounding the Vatican and Lateran in Rome and the Villas of Castel Gandolfo, became part of the Kingdom by the Italian law of May 13, 1871.

The **Roman Question,** occasioned by this seizure and the voluntary confinement of the pope to the Vatican, was settled with ratification of the Lateran Agreement June 7, 1929, by the Italian government and Vatican City. The agreement recognized Catholicism as the religion of Italy and provided, among other things, a financial indemnity to the Vatican in return for the former Papal States; it became Article 7 of the Italian Constitution Mar. 26, 1947.

The Lateran Agreement was superseded by a new concordat given final approval by the Italian Chamber of Deputies Mar. 20 and formally ratified June 3, 1985.

Papal Flag

The papal flag consists of two equal vertical stripes of yellow and white, charged with the insignia of the papacy on the white stripe — triple crown or tiara over two crossed keys, one of gold and one of silver, tied with a red cord and two tassels. The divisions of the crown represent the teaching, sanctifying and ruling offices of the pope. The keys symbolize his jurisdictional authority.

The papal flag is a national flag inasmuch as it is the standard of the Supreme Pontiff as the sovereign of the state of Vatican City. It is also universally accepted by the faithful as a symbol of the supreme spiritual authority of the Holy Father.

Vatican Radio

The declared purpose of Vatican Radio Station HVJ is "that the voice of the Supreme Pastor may be heard throughout the world by means of the ether waves, for the glory of Christ and the salvation of souls." Designed by Guglielmo Marconi, the inventor of radio, and supervised by him until his death, the station was inaugurated by Pope Pius XI in 1931. The original purpose has been extended to a wide variety of programming.

Vatican Radio operates on international wave lengths, transmits programs in 37 languages, and serves as a channel of communication between the

Vatican, church officials and listeners in general in many parts of the world. The station broadcasts about 400 hours a week throughout the world.

The daily English-language program for North America is broadcast on 6095, 7305, 9600 kilohertz as well as via satellite INTELSAT 325,5° East (Atlantic) — 4097.75 Mhz — LHCP polarization.

Frequencies, background information and audio files can be obtained via the World Wide Web homepages www.wrn.org/vatican-radio and www.vatican.va.

The staff of 415 broadcasters and technicians includes 30 Jesuits. Studios and offices are at Palazzo Pio, Piazza Pia, 3, 00193 Rome. The transmitters are situated at Santa Maria di Galeria, a short distance north of Rome.

1997 Vatican Stamps and Coins

The Vatican Philatelic and Numismatic Office (00120 Vatican City) scheduled the following issues of stamps and coins for 1997. Issue dates are given where available.

Stamps: Papal carriages and automobiles; issued March 20, 1997; series of ten stamps. Reproductions of papal carriages and automobiles from the Vatican Museums collection.

• Europe 1997 - Subject: Histories and Legends; issued March 20, 1997; series of two stamps. Portray Swiss Guards and their flag.

• 1000th Anniversary of the Death of St. Adalbert of Prague; issued jointly by Vatican City, Czech Republic, Germany, Poland and Hungary April 23, 1997.

• 46th International Eucharistic Congress, Wroclaw (Poland); issued May 27, 1997.

• " Looking at the Classics," issued April 23, 1997; series of four and a small sheet (3 stamps).

• 1600th Anniversary of the Death of St. Ambrose;

• Towards the Holy Year 2000;

• The Travels of His Holiness John Paul II (1966);

• Christian Solemnity of Christmas.

Postal Stationery: Aerogramme — IV Centenary of the First Free Public School in Europe.

Postcards: Geographical Discoveries of the XV Century; issued May 27, 1997.

Coins: Series for eighteenth year (1996) of the Pontificate of John Paul II; issued Feb. 28, 1997, in seven values. Subject: Let us give our children a future of peace..

•Gold Coins — XVIII Year (1996); issued Feb. 28, 1997, in two values (50,000 and 100,000 Lira) Subject: Towards the Holy Year 2000 (Basilica of St. John Lateran).

• Celebrative 500 Lire Silver Coin. Subject: XII World Youth Meeting; issued June 16, 1997.

• Diptych of 10,000 Lire Silver Coins. Subject: Towards the Holy Year 2,000 (The Healing of a Paralyzed Man — The Calming of the Tempest).

Papal Audiences

General audiences are scheduled weekly, on Wednesday.

In Vatican City, they are held in the Audience Hall on the south side of St. Peter's Basilica or, weather permitting, in St. Peter's Square. The hall, which was opened in 1971, has a seating capacity of 6,800 and a total capacity of 12,000.

Audiences have been held during the summer at Castel Gandolfo when the pope is there on a working vacation.

General audiences last from about 60 to 90 minutes, during which the pope gives a talk and his blessing. A résumé of the talk, which is usually in Italian, is given in several languages.

Arrangements for papal audiences are handled by an office of the Prefecture of the Apostolic Household.

American visitors can obtain passes for general audiences by applying to the Bishops' Office for United States Visitors to the Vatican, Casa Santa Maria, Via dell'Umilita, 30, 00187 Rome. Private and group audiences are reserved for dignitaries of various categories and for special occasions.

Publications

Acta Apostolicae Sedis, 00120 Vatican City: The only "official commentary" of the Holy See, was established in 1908 for the publication of activities of the Holy See, laws, decrees and acts of congregations and tribunals of the Roman Curia. The first edition was published in January, 1909.

St. Pius X made AAS an official organ in 1908. Laws promulgated for the Church ordinarily take effect three months after the date of their publication in this commentary.

The publication, mostly in Latin, is printed by the Vatican Press.

The immediate predecessor of this organ was *Acta Sanctae Sedis,* founded in 1865 and given official status by the Congregation for the Propagation of the Faith in 1904.

Annuario Pontificio, 00120 Vatican City: The yearbook of the Holy See. It is edited by the Central Statistics Office of the Church and is printed in Italian, with some portions in other languages, by the Vatican Press. It covers the worldwide organization of the Church, lists members of the hierarchy, and includes a wide range of statistical information.

The publication of a statistical yearbook of the Holy See dates back to 1716, when a volume called *Notizie* appeared. Publication under the present title began in 1860, was suspended in 1870, and resumed again in 1872 under the title *Catholic Hierarchy.* This volume was printed privately at first, but has been issued by the Vatican Press since 1885. The title *Annuario Pontificio* was restored in 1912, and the yearbook was called an "official publication" until 1924.

L'Osservatore Romano, Via del Pellegrino, 00120 Vatican City: The daily newspaper of the Holy See. It began publication July 1, 1861, as an independent enterprise under the ownership and direction of four Catholic laymen headed by Marcantonio Pacelli, vice minister of the interior under Pope Pius IX and a grandfather of the late Pius XII. Leo XIII bought the publication in 1890, making it the "pope's" own newspaper.

The only official material in *L'Osservatore Romano* is that which appears under the heading, "Nostre Informazioni." This includes notices of appointments by the Holy See, the texts of papal encyclicals and addresses by the Holy Father and others, various types of documents, accounts of decisions and rulings of administrative bodies, and similar items. Additional material includes news and comment on developments in the Church and the world. Italian is the language most used.

The editorial board is directed by Prof. Mario Agnes. A staff of about 15 reporters covers Rome news sources. A corps of correspondents provides foreign coverage.

A weekly roundup edition in English was inaugurated in 1968 (Rev. Robert J. Dempsey, on leave from Chicago archdiocese, is editor). Other weekly editions are printed in French (1949), Italian (1950), Spanish (1969), Portuguese (1970) and German (1971). The Polish edition (1980) is published monthly. *L'Osservatore della Domenica* is published weekly as a supplement to the Sunday issue of the daily edition.

Vatican Television Center (Centro Televisivo Vaticano, CTV), Palazzo Belvedere, 00120 Vatican City: Instituted by John Paul II Oct. 23, 1983, with the rescript, *Ex Audentia*. Dr. Emilio Rossi is president of the administrative council.

Vatican Press, 00120 Vatican City: The official printing plant of the Vatican. The Vatican press was conceived by Marcellus II and Pius IV but was actually founded by Sixtus V on Apr. 27, 1587, to print the Vulgate and the writings of the Fathers of the Church and other authors. A Polyglot Press was established in 1626 by the Congregation for the Propagation of the Faith to serve the needs of the Oriental Church. St. Pius X merged both presses under the title Vatican Polyglot Press. It was renamed Vatican Press July 1, 1991, by John Paul II following restructuring. The plant has facilities for the printing of a wide variety of material in about 30 languages.

Vatican Publishing House (Libreria Editrice Vaticano), Piazza S. Pietro, 00120 Vatican City: Formerly an office of the Vatican Press to assist in the circulation of the liturgical and juridical publications of the Apostolic See, the congregations and later the *Acta Apostolicae Sedis*. In 1926, with the expansion of publishing activities and following the promulgation of the 1917 Code, the office was made an independent entity. An administrative council and editorial commission were instituted in 1983; in 1988 *Pastor Bonus* listed it among institutes joined to the Holy See; new statutes were approved by the Secretariat of State July 1, 1991.

Activities of the Holy See: An annual documentary volume covering the activities of the pope and of the congregations, commissions, tribunals and offices of the Roman Curia.

Statistical Yearbook of the Church: Issued by the Central Statistics Office of the Church, it contains principal data concerning the presence and work of the Church in the world. The first issue was published in 1972 under the title Collection of Statistical Tables, 1969. It is printed in corresponding columns of Italian and Latin. Some of the introductory material is printed in other languages.

AMERICAN CHURCH

The Church of Santa Susanna was designated as the national church for Americans in Rome by Pope Benedict XV Jan. 10, 1922, and entrusted to the Paulist Fathers, who have served there continuously since then except for several years during World War II.

CATHOLICS AND JEWS: Remarks by Rabbi James Rudin

Rabbi James Rudin, national interreligious affairs director for the American Jewish Committee, received Apr. 14, 1997, the first Joseph Award from the Villa Nazareth Academy of Rome and the Cardinal Tardini Charitable Trust of Pittsburgh. The award is dedicated to the honor the memory of the biblical Joseph, noted for his roles of reconciliation and leadership. *Following are excerpts from Rudin's address during the awards ceremony.*

Before 1965, the year of *Nostra Aetate* (the Second Vatican Council's Declaration on the Relationship of the Church to Non-Christian Religions), in many communities Jews and Catholics often lived in mutual suspicion and mistrust. Longstanding stereotypes and caricatures frequently shaped those relationships.

Even though a pragmatic coexistence existed in the United States, thanks in part to the unique American experiment in religious pluralism, it seemed as if our two ancient communities of faith, one over 3,600 years old and the other nearly 2,000 years old, had little to say to one another and even less to do with one another.

Catholics often saw Jews as a spiritually exhausted and sometimes physically surplus people, and Jews, always a minority in European Catholic lands, frequently perceived Catholics as the perpetual adversary, the eternal "other." But in 1948, only three years after the Holocaust ended in heart of what many called 'Christian Europe,' the surplus people had risen from the actual ashes of Auschwitz and had reentered history as a free and sovereign people in their own land, the State of Israel.

Changed Relationship

The Second Vatican Council ... addressed and permanently changed the Church's relationship with Jews and Judaism.

(After alluding to the efforts of Pope John XXIII (then apostolic delegate in Bulgaria and Turkey) to save the lives of Jews during World War II, Rabbi Rudin continued):

In 1959, John XXIII deleted the chilling phrase, *perfidia Judaica*, from the Good Friday text. A rabbinical student at the time, I was deeply moved by the Pope's action, but more, much more, was to come. In October, 1960, John XXIII met a group of American Jewish leaders in Rome, and he greeted his visitors with the words from Geneis 45:4: 'I am Joseph, your brother!' By using his baptismal name Joseph, instead of his official John, the Pope broke through the barriers that had kept Catholics and Jews apart for centuries. And in October, 1965, only five years after John XXIII greeted his Jewish brothers, the world's Catholic bishops issued the landmark *Nostra Aetate* declaration.

DOCTRINE OF THE CATHOLIC CHURCH

Following are excerpts from the first two chapters of the "Dogmatic Constitution on the Church" promulgated by the Second Vatican Council. They describe the relation of the Catholic Church to the Kingdom of God, the nature and foundation of the Church, the People of God, the necessity of membership and participation in the Church for salvation. Additional subjects in the constitution are treated in other Almanac entries.

I. MYSTERY OF THE CHURCH

By her relationship with Christ, the Church is a kind of sacrament or sign of intimate union with God, and of the unity of all mankind (No. 1).

He (the eternal Father) planned to assemble in the holy Church all those who would believe in Christ. Already from the beginning of the world the foreshadowing of the Church took place. She was prepared for in a remarkable way throughout the history of the people of Israel and by means of the Old Covenant. Established in the present era of time, the Church was made manifest by the outpouring of the Spirit. At the end of time she will achieve her glorious fulfillment. Then ... all just men from the time of Adam, "from Abel, the just one, to the last of the elect," will be gathered together with the Father in the universal Church (No. 2).

When the work which the Father had given the Son to do on earth (cf. Jn. 17:4) was accomplished, the Holy Spirit was sent on the day of Pentecost in order that he might forever sanctify the Church, and thus all believers would have access to the Father through Christ in the one Spirit (cf. Eph. 2:18).

The Spirit dwells in the Church and in the hearts of the faithful as in a temple (cf. 1 Cor. 3:16; 6:19)....The Spirit guides the Church into the fullness of truth (cf. Jn. 16:13) and gives her a unity of fellowship and service. He furnishes and directs her with various gifts, both hierarchical and charismatic, and adorns her with the fruits of His grace (cf. Eph. 4:11-12; 1 Cor. 12:4; Gal. 5:22). By the power of the Gospel he makes the Church grow, perpetually renews her, and leads her to perfect union with her Spouse (No. 4).

Foundation of the Church

The mystery of the holy Church is manifest in her very foundation, for the Lord Jesus inaugurated her by preaching the Good News, that is, the coming of God's Kingdom, which, for centuries, had been promised in the Scriptures.... In Christ's word, in his works, and in his presence this Kingdom reveals itself to men.

The miracles of Jesus also confirm that the Kingdom has already arrived on earth.

Before all things, however, the Kingdom is clearly visible in the very Person of Christ, Son of God and Son of Man.

When Jesus rose up again after suffering death on the cross for mankind, he manifested that he had been appointed Lord, Messiah, and Priest forever (cf. Acts 2:36; Heb. 5:6; 7:17-21), and he poured out on his disciples the Spirit promised by the Father (cf. Acts 2:33). The Church, consequently, equipped with the gifts of her Founder and faithfully guarding his precepts ... receives the mission to proclaim and to establish among all peoples the Kingdom of Christ and of God. She becomes on earth the initial budding forth of that Kingdom. While she slowly grows, the Church strains toward the consummation of the Kingdom and, with all her strength, hopes and desires to be united in glory with her King (No. 5).

Figures of the Church

In the Old Testament the revelation of the Kingdom had often been conveyed by figures of speech. In the same way the inner nature of the Church was now to be made known to us through various images.

The Church is a sheepfold ... a flock ... a tract of land to be cultivated, the field of God ... his choice vineyard ... the true vine is Christ ... the edifice of God ... the house of God ... the holy temple (whose members are) living stones ... this holy city ... a bride ... our Mother ... the spotless spouse of the spotless Lamb ... an exile (No. 6).

In the human nature which he united to himself, the Son of God redeemed man and transformed him into a new creation (cf Gal. 6:15; 2 Cor. 5:17) by overcoming death through his own death and resurrection. By communicating his Spirit to his brothers, called together from all peoples, Christ made them mystically into his own body.

In that body, the life of Christ is poured into the believers, who, through the sacraments, are united in a hidden and real way to Christ who suffered and was glorified. Through baptism we are formed in the likeness of Christ.

Truly partaking of the body of the Lord in the breaking of the eucharistic bread, we are taken up into communion with him and with one another (No. 7).

One Body in Christ

As all the members of the human body, though they are many, form one body, so also are the faithful in Christ (cf. 1 Cor. 12:12). Also, in the building up of Christ's body there is a flourishing variety of members and functions. There is only one Spirit who ... distributes his different gifts for the welfare of the Church (cf. 1 Cor. 12:1-11). Among these gifts stands out the grace given to the apostles. To their authority, the Spirit himself subjected even those who were endowed with charisms (cf. 1 Cor. 14).

The head of this body is Christ (No. 7).

Mystical Body of Christ

Christ, the one Mediator, established and ceaselessly sustains here on earth his holy Church, the community of faith, hope, and charity, as a visible structure. Through her he communicates truth and grace to all. But the society furnished with hierarchical agencies and the Mystical Body of Christ are not to be considered as two realities, nor are the visible assembly and the spiritual community, nor the earthly Church and the Church enriched with heavenly things. Rather they form one interlocked reality which is comprised of a divine and a human element. For this reason ... this reality is compared to the mystery of the incarnate Word. Just as the assumed nature inseparably united to the divine Word serves him as a living instrument of salvation, so, in a similar way, does the communal structure of the Church serve

Christ's Spirit, who vivifies it by way of building up the body (cf. Eph. 4:16).

This is the unique Church of Christ which in the Creed we avow as one, holy, catholic, and apostolic. After his Resurrection our Savior handed her over to Peter to be shepherded (Jn. 21:17), commissioning him and the other apostles to propagate and govern her (cf. Mt. 28:18, ff.). Her he erected for all ages as "the pillar and mainstay of the truth" (1 Tm. 3:15). This Church, constituted and organized in the world as a society, subsists in the Catholic Church, which is governed by the successor of Peter and by the bishops in union with that successor, although many elements of sanctification and of truth can be found outside of her visible structure. These elements, however, as gifts properly belonging to the Church of Christ, possess an inner dynamism toward Catholic unity.

The Church, embracing sinners in her bosom, is at the same time holy and always in need of being purified, and incessantly pursues the path of penance and renewal.

The Church, "like a pilgrim in a foreign land, presses forward... " announcing the cross and death of the Lord until he comes (cf. 1 Cor. 11:26) (No. 8).

II. THE PEOPLE OF GOD

At all times and among every people, God has given welcome to whosoever fears him and does what is right (cf. Acts 10:35). It has pleased God, however, to make men holy and save them not merely as individuals without any mutual bonds, but by making them into a single people, a people which acknowledges him in truth and serves him in holiness. He therefore chose the race of Israel as a people unto himself. With it he set up a covenant. Step by step he taught this people by manifesting in its history both himself and the decree of his will, and by making it holy unto himself. All these things, however, were done by way of preparation and as a figure of that new and perfect covenant which was to be ratified in Christ.

Christ instituted this New Covenant, that is to say, the New Testament, in his blood (cf. 1 Cor. 11:25), by calling together a people made up of Jew and Gentile, making them one, not according to the flesh but in the Spirit.

This was to be the new People of God ... reborn ... through the Word of the living God (cf. 1 Pt. 1:23) ... from water and the Holy Spirit (cf. Jn. 3:5-6) ... "a chosen race, a royal priesthood, a holy nation, a purchased people.... You who in times past were not a people, but are now the People of God" (1 Pt. 2:9-10).

That messianic people has for its head Christ.... Its law is the new commandment to love as Christ loved us (cf. Jn. 13:34). Its goal is the Kingdom of God, which has been begun by God himself on earth, and which is to be further extended until it is brought to perfection by him at the end of time.

This messianic people, although it does not actually include all men, and may more than once look like a small flock, is nonetheless a lasting and sure seed of unity, hope, and salvation for the whole human race. Established by Christ as a fellowship of life, charity, and truth, it is also used by him as an instrument for the redemption of all, and is sent forth into the whole world as the light of the world and the salt of the earth (cf. Mt. 5:13-16).

Israel according to the flesh ... was already called the Church of God (Neh. 13:1; cf. Nm. 20:4; Dt. 23:1, ff.). Likewise the new Israel ... is also called the Church of Christ (cf. Mt. 16:18). For he has bought it for himself with his blood (cf. Acts 20:28), has filled it with his Spirit, and provided it with those means which befit it as a visible and social unity. God has gathered together as one all those who in faith look upon Jesus as the author of salvation and the source of unity and peace, and has established them as the Church, that for each and all she may be the visible sacrament of this saving unity (No. 9).

Priesthood

The baptized, by regeneration and the anointing of the Holy Spirit, are consecrated into ... a holy priesthood.

[All members of the Church participate in the priesthood of Christ, through the common priesthood of the faithful. See Priesthood of the Laity.]

Though they differ from one another in essence and not only in degree, the common priesthood of the faithful and the ministerial or hierarchical priesthood are nonetheless interrelated. Each of them in its own special way is a participation in the one priesthood of Christ (No. 10).

It is through the sacraments and the exercise of the virtues that the sacred nature and organic structure of the priestly community is brought into operation (No. 11). (See Role of the Sacraments.)

Prophetic Office

The holy People of God shares also in Christ's prophetic office. It spreads abroad a living witness to him, especially by means of a life of faith and charity and by offering to God a sacrifice of praise.... The body of the faithful as a whole, anointed as they are by the Holy One (cf. Jn. 2:20, 27), cannot err in matters of belief. Thanks to a supernatural sense of faith which characterizes the People as a whole, it manifests this unerring quality when, "from the bishops down to the last member of the laity," it shows universal agreement in matters of faith and morals.

God's People accepts not the word of men but the very Word of God (cf. 1 Thes. 2:13). It clings without fail to the faith once delivered to the saints (cf. Jude 3), penetrates it more deeply by accurate insights, and applies it more thoroughly to life. All this it does under the lead of a sacred teaching authority to which it loyally defers.

It is not only through the sacraments and Church ministries that the same Holy Spirit sanctifies and leads the People of God.... He distributes special graces among the faithful of every rank. By these gifts he makes them fit and ready to undertake the various tasks or offices advantageous for the renewal and upbuilding of the Church.... These charismatic gifts ... are to be received with thanksgiving and consolation, for they are exceedingly suitable and useful for the needs of the Church.

Judgment as to their genuineness and proper use belongs to those who preside over the Church, and to whose special competence it belongs ... to test all things and hold fast to that which is good (cf. 1 Thes. 5:12; 19-21) (No. 12).

All Are Called

All men are called to belong to the new People of God. Wherefore this People, while remaining one and unique, is to be spread throughout the whole world and must exist in all ages, so that the purpose of God's will may be fulfilled. In the beginning God made human nature one. After his children were scattered, he decreed that they should at length be united again (cf. Jn. 11:52). It was for this reason that God sent his Son ... that he might be Teacher, King, and Priest of all, the Head of the new and universal People of the sons of God. For this God finally sent his Son's Spirit as Lord and Lifegiver. He it is who, on behalf of the whole Church and each and every one of those who believe, is the principle of their coming together and remaining together in the teaching of the apostles and in fellowship, in the breaking of bread and in prayers (cf. Acts 2:42) (No. 13).

One People of God

It follows that among all the nations of earth there is but one People of God, which takes its citizens from every race, making them citizens of a Kingdom which is of a heavenly and not an earthly nature. For all the faithful scattered throughout the world are in communion with each other in the Holy Spirit. ... the Church or People of God ... foster(s) and take(s) to herself, insofar as they are good, the ability, resources and customs of each people. Taking them to herself, she purifies, strengthens, and ennobles them.... This characteristic of universality which adorns the People of God is a gift from the Lord himself. By reason of it, the Catholic Church strives energetically and constantly to bring all humanity with all its riches back to Christ its Head in the unity of his Spirit.

In virtue of this catholicity each individual part of the Church contributes through its special gifts to the good of the other parts and of the whole Church. Thus through the common sharing of gifts ... the whole and each of the parts receive increase.

All men are called to be part of this catholic unity of the People of God.... And there belong to it or are related to it in various ways, the Catholic faithful as well as all who believe in Christ, and indeed the whole of mankind. For all men are called to salvation by the grace of God (No. 13).

The Catholic Church

This sacred Synod turns its attention first to the Catholic faithful. Basing itself upon sacred Scripture and tradition, it teaches that the Church is necessary for salvation. For Christ, made present to us in his Body, which is the Church, is the one Mediator and the unique Way of salvation. In explicit terms he himself affirmed the necessity of faith and baptism (cf. Mk. 16:16; Jn. 3:5) and thereby affirmed also the necessity of the Church, for through baptism as through a door men enter the Church. Whosoever, therefore, knowing that the Catholic Church was made necessary by God through Jesus Christ, would refuse to enter her or to remain in her could not be saved.

They are fully incorporated into the society of the Church who, possessing the Spirit of Christ, accept her entire system and all the means of salvation given to her, and through union with her visible structure are joined to Christ, who rules her through the Supreme Pontiff and the bishops. This joining is effected by the bonds of professed faith, of the sacraments, of ecclesiastical government, and of communion. He is not saved, however, who, though he is part of the body of the Church, does not persevere in charity. He remains indeed in the bosom of the Church, but ... only in a "bodily" manner and not "in his heart."

Catechumens who, moved by the Holy Spirit, seek with explicit intention to be incorporated into the Church, are by that very intention joined to her.... Mother Church already embraces them as her own (No. 14).

Other Christians, The Unbaptized

The Church recognizes that in many ways she is linked with those who, being baptized, are honored with the name of Christian, though they do not profess the faith in its entirety or do not preserve unity of communion with the successor of Peter.

We can say that in some real way they are joined with us in the Holy Spirit, for to them also he gives his gifts and graces, and is thereby operative among them with his sanctifying power (No. 15).

Finally, those who have not yet received the Gospel are related in various ways to the People of God. In the first place there is the people to whom the covenants and the promises were given and from whom Christ was born according to the flesh (cf. Rom. 9:4-5). On account of their fathers, this people remains most dear to God, for God does not repent of the gifts he makes nor of the calls he issues (cf. Rom. 11:28-29).

But the plan of salvation also includes those who acknowledge the Creator. In the first place among these are the Moslems.... Nor is God himself far distant from those who in shadows and images seek the unknown God.

Those also can attain to everlasting salvation who through no fault of their own do not know the Gospel of Christ or his Church, yet sincerely seek God and, moved by grace, strive by their deeds to do his will as it is known to them through the dictates of conscience. Nor does divine Providence deny the help necessary for salvation to those who, without blame on their part, have not yet arrived at an explicit knowledge of God, but who strive to live a good life, thanks to his grace. Whatever goodness or truth is found among them is looked upon by the Church as a preparation for the Gospel. She regards such qualities as given by him who enlightens all men so that they may finally have life. (No. 16).

Oratory of St. Joseph

This oratory in Montreal is the world's largest pilgrimage site devoted to St. Joseph. The main church, at the top of 300 steps, is visited by about two million people a year. Its 56-bell carillon was originally designed for the Eiffel Tower.

THE POPE, TEACHING AUTHORITY, COLLEGIALITY

The Roman Pontiff — the successor of St. Peter as the bishop of Rome and head of the Church on earth — has full and supreme authority over the universal Church in matters pertaining to faith and morals (teaching authority), discipline and government (jurisdictional authority).

The primacy of the pope is real and supreme power. It is not merely a prerogative of honor — that is, of his being regarded as the first among equals. Neither does primacy imply that the pope is just the presiding officer of the collective body of bishops. The pope is the head of the Church.

Catholic belief in the primacy of the pope was stated in detail in the dogmatic constitution on the Church, *Pastor Aeternus,* approved in 1870 by the fourth session of the First Vatican Council. Some elaboration of the doctrine was made in the *Dogmatic Constitution on the Church* which was approved and promulgated by the Second Vatican Council Nov. 21, 1964. The entire body of teaching on the subject is based on Scripture and tradition and the centuries-long experience of the Church.

Infallibility

The essential points of doctrine concerning infallibility in the Church and the infallibility of the pope were stated by the Second Vatican Council in the *Dogmatic Constitution on the Church,* as follows:

"This infallibility with which the divine Redeemer willed his Church to be endowed in defining a doctrine of faith and morals extends as far as extends the deposit of divine revelation, which must be religiously guarded and faithfully expounded. This is the infallibility which the Roman Pontiff, the head of the college of bishops, enjoys in virtue of his office, when, as the supreme shepherd and teacher of all the faithful who confirms his brethren in their faith (cf. Lk. 22:32), he proclaims by a definitive act some doctrine of faith or morals. Therefore his definitions, of themselves, and not from the consent of the Church, are justly styled irreformable, for they are pronounced with the assistance of the Holy Spirit, an assistance promised to him in blessed Peter. Therefore they need no approval of others, nor do they allow an appeal to any other judgment. For then the Roman Pontiff is not pronouncing judgment as a private person. Rather, as the supreme teacher of the universal Church, as one in whom the charism of the infallibility of the Church herself is individually present, he is expounding or defending a doctrine of Catholic faith.

"The infallibility promised to the Church resides also in the body of bishops when that body exercises supreme teaching authority with the successor of Peter. To the resultant definitions the assent of the Church can never be wanting, on account of the activity of that same Holy Spirit, whereby the whole flock of Christ is preserved and progresses in unity of faith.

"But when either the Roman Pontiff or the body of bishops together with him defines a judgment, they pronounce it in accord with revelation itself. All are obliged to maintain and be ruled by this revelation, which, as written or preserved by tradition, is transmitted in its entirety through the legitimate succession of bishops and especially through the care of the Roman Pontiff himself.

"Under the guiding light of the Spirit of truth, revelation is thus religiously preserved and faithfully expounded in the Church. The Roman Pontiff and the bishops, in view of their office and of the importance of the matter, strive painstakingly and by appropriate means to inquire properly into that revelation and to give apt expression to its contents. But they do not allow that there could be any new public revelation pertaining to the divine deposit of faith" (No. 25).

Authentic Teaching

The pope rarely speaks *ex cathedra* — that is, "from the chair" of St. Peter, for the purpose of making an infallible pronouncement. More often and in various ways he states authentic teaching in line with Scripture, tradition, the living experience of the Church, and the whole analogy of faith. Of such teaching, the Second Vatican Council said in its *Dogmatic Constitution on the Church* (No. 25):

"Religious submission of will and of mind must be shown in a special way to the authentic teaching authority of the Roman Pontiff, even when he is not speaking *ex cathedra.* That is, it must be shown in such a way that his supreme magisterium is acknowledged with reverence, the judgments made by him are sincerely adhered to, according to his manifest mind and will. His mind and will in the matter may be known chiefly either from the character of the documents, from his frequent repetition of the same doctrine, or from his manner of speaking."

With respect to bishops, the constitution states: "They are authentic teachers, that is, teachers endowed with the authority of Christ, who preach to the people committed to them the faith they must believe and put into practice. By the light of the Holy Spirit, they make that faith clear, bringing forth from the treasury of revelation new things and old (cf. Mt. 13:52), making faith bear fruit and vigilantly warding off any errors which threaten their flock (cf. 2 Tm. 4:1-4).

"Bishops, teaching in communion with the Roman Pontiff, are to be respected by all as witnesses to divine and Catholic truth. In matters of faith and morals, the bishops speak in the name of Christ and the faithful are to accept their teaching and adhere to it with a religious assent of soul."

Magisterium — Teaching Authority

Responsibility for teaching doctrine and judging orthodoxy belongs to the official teaching authority of the Church.

This authority is personalized in the pope, the successor of St. Peter as head of the Church, and in the bishops together and in union with the pope, as it was originally committed to Peter and to the whole college of apostles under his leadership. They are the official teachers of the Church.

Others have auxiliary relationships with the magisterium: theologians, in the study and clarification of doctrine; teachers — priests, religious, lay persons — who cooperate with the pope and bishops in spreading knowledge of religious truth; the faithful, who by their sense of faith and personal witness contribute to the development of doctrine and the establishment of its relevance to life in the Church and the world.

The magisterium, Pope Paul VI noted in an address at a general audience Jan. 11, 1967, "is a subordinate and faithful echo and secure interpreter of the divine word." It does not reveal new truths, "nor is it superior to sacred Scripture." Its competence extends to the limits of divine revelation manifested in Scripture and tradition and the living experience of the Church, with respect to matters of faith and morals and related subjects. Official teaching in these areas is infallible when it is formally defined, for belief and acceptance by all members of the Church, by the pope, acting in the capacity of supreme shepherd of the flock of Christ; also, when doctrine is proposed and taught with moral unanimity of bishops with the pope in a solemn collegial manner, as in an ecumenical council, and/or in the ordinary course of events. Even when not infallibly defined, official teaching in the areas of faith and morals is authoritative and requires religious assent.

The teachings of the magisterium have been documented in creeds, formulas of faith, decrees and enactments of ecumenical and particular councils, various kinds of doctrinal statements, encyclical letters and other teaching instruments. They have also been incorporated into the liturgy, with the result that the law of prayer is said to be a law of belief.

Collegiality

The bishops of the Church, in union with the pope, have supreme teaching and pastoral authority over the whole Church in addition to the authority of office they have for their own dioceses.

This collegial authority is exercised in a solemn manner in an ecumenical council and can be exercised in other ways as well, "provided that the head of the college calls them to collegiate action, or at least so approves or freely accepts the united action of the dispersed bishops that it is made a true collegiate act."

This doctrine is grounded on the fact that: "Just as, by the Lord's will, St. Peter and the other apostles constituted one apostolic college, so in a similar way the Roman Pontiff as the successor of Peter, and the bishops as the successors of the apostles are joined together."

Doctrine on collegiality was stated by the Second Vatican Council in the Dogmatic Constitution on the Church (Nos. 22 and 23).

REVELATION

Following are excerpts from the "Dogmatic Constitution on Divine Revelation" promulgated by the Second Vatican Council. They describe the nature and process of divine revelation, inspiration and interpretation of Scripture, the Old and New Testaments, and the role of Scripture in the life of the Church.

I. REVELATION ITSELF

God chose to reveal himself and to make known to us the hidden purpose of his will (cf. Eph. 1:9) by which through Christ, the Word made flesh, man has access to the Father in the Holy Spirit and comes to share in the divine nature (cf. Eph. 2:18; 2 Pt. 1:4). Through this revelation, therefore, the invisible God (cf. Col. 1:15; 1 Tm. 1:17)... speaks to men as friends (cf. Ex. 33:11; Jn. 15:14-15) and lives among them (cf. Bar. 3:38) so that he may invite and take them into fellowship with himself. This plan of revelation is realized by deeds and words having an inner unity: the deeds wrought by God in the history of salvation manifest and confirm the teaching and realities signified by the words, while the words proclaim the deeds and clarify the mystery contained in them. By this revelation then, the deepest truth about God and the salvation of man is made clear to us in Christ, who is the Mediator and at the same time the fullness of all revelation (No. 2).

God ... from the start manifested himself to our first parents. Then after their fall his promise of redemption aroused in them the hope of being saved (cf. Gn. 3:15), and from that time on he ceaselessly kept the human race in his care, in order to give eternal life to those who perseveringly do good in search of salvation (cf. Rom. 2:6-7).... He called Abraham in order to make of him a great nation (cf. Gn. 12:2). Through the patriarchs, and after them through Moses and the prophets, he taught this nation to acknowledge himself as the one living and true God ... and to wait for the Savior promised by him. In this manner he prepared the way for the Gospel down through the centuries (No. 3).

Revelation in Christ

Then, after speaking in many places and varied ways through the prophets, God "last of all in these days has spoken to us by his Son" (Heb. 1:1-2)....Jesus perfected revelation by fulfilling it through his whole work of making himself present and manifesting himself: through his words and deeds, his signs and wonders, but especially through his death and glorious resurrection from the dead and final sending of the Spirit of truth. Moreover, he confirmed with divine testimony what revelation proclaimed: that God is with us to free us from the darkness of sin and death, and to raise us up to life eternal.

The Christian dispensation, therefore, as the new and definitive covenant, will never pass away, and we now await no further new public revelation before the glorious manifestation of our Lord Jesus Christ (cf. 1 Tm. 6:14; Ti. 2:13) (No. 4).

II. TRANSMISSION OF REVELATION

God has seen to it that what he had revealed for the salvation of all nations would abide perpetually in its full integrity and be handed on to all generations. Therefore Christ the Lord, in whom the full revelation of the supreme God is brought to completion (cf. 2 Cor. 1:20; 3:16; 4:6), commissioned the apostles to preach to all men that Gospel which is the source of all saving truth and moral teaching, and thus to impart to them divine gifts. This Gospel had been promised in former times through the prophets, and Christ himself fulfilled it and promulgated it with his own lips. This commission was faithfully fulfilled by the apostles who, by their oral preaching, by example, and by ordinances, handed on what they had received from ... Christ ... or what they had learned through the prompting of the Holy Spirit. The commission was fulfilled, too, by those apostles and apostolic men who under the inspiration of the same Holy Spirit committed the message of salvation to writing (No. 7).

Tradition

But in order to keep the Gospel forever whole and alive within the Church, the apostles left bishops as their successors, "handing over their own teaching role" to them. This sacred tradition, therefore, and sacred Scripture of both the Old and the New Testament are like a mirror in which the pilgrim Church on earth looks at God (No. 7).

The apostolic preaching, which is expressed in a special way in the inspired books, was to be preserved by a continuous succession of preachers until the end of time. Therefore the apostles, handing on what they themselves had received, warn the faithful to hold fast to the traditions which they have learned.... Now what was handed on by the apostles includes everything which contributes to the holiness of life, and the increase in faith of the People of God; and so the Church, in her teaching, life, and worship, perpetuates and hands on to all generations all that she herself is, all that she believes (No. 8).

Development of Doctrine

This tradition which comes from the apostles develops in the Church with the help of the Holy Spirit. For there is a growth in the understanding of the realities and the words which have been handed down. This happens through the contemplation and study made by believers ... through the intimate understanding of spiritual things they experience, and through the preaching of those who have received through episcopal succession the sure gift of truth. For, as the centuries succeed one another, the Church constantly moves forward toward the fullness of divine truth until the words of God reach their complete fulfillment in her.

The words of the holy Fathers witness to the living presence of this tradition, whose wealth is poured into the practice and life of the believing and praying Church. Through the same tradition the Church's full canon of the sacred books is known, and the sacred writings themselves are more profoundly understood and unceasingly made active in her; ... and the Holy Spirit, through whom the living voice of the Gospel resounds in the Church, and through her, in the world, leads unto all truth those who believe and makes the word of Christ dwell abundantly in them (cf. Col. 3:16) (No. 8).

Tradition and Scripture

Hence there exist a close connection and communication between sacred tradition and sacred Scripture. For both of them, flowing from the same divine wellspring, in a certain way merge into a unity and tend toward the same end. For sacred Scripture is

the word of God inasmuch as it is consigned to writing under the inspiration of the divine Spirit. To the successors of the apostles, sacred tradition hands on in its full purity God's word, which was entrusted to the apostles by Christ the Lord and the Holy Spirit. Thus, led by the light of the Spirit of truth, these successors can in their preaching preserve this word of God faithfully, explain it, and make it more widely known. Consequently, it is not from sacred Scripture alone that the Church draws her certainty about every thing which has been revealed. Therefore both sacred tradition and sacred Scripture are to be accepted and venerated with the same sense of devotion and reverence (No. 9).

Sacred tradition and sacred Scripture form one sacred deposit of the word of God, which is committed to the Church (No. 10).

Teaching Authority of Church

The task of authentically interpreting the word of God, whether written or handed on, has been entrusted exclusively to the living teaching office of the Church, whose authority is exercised in the name of Jesus Christ. This teaching office is not above the word of God, but serves it, teaching only what has been handed on ... it draws from this one deposit of faith everything which it presents for belief as divinely revealed.

It is clear, therefore, that sacred tradition, sacred Scripture, and the teaching authority of the Church ... are so linked and joined together that one cannot stand without the others, and that all together and each in its own way under the action of the one Holy Spirit contribute effectively to the salvation of souls (No. 10).

III. INSPIRATION, INTERPRETATION

Those ... revealed realities ... contained and presented in sacred Scripture have been committed to writing under the inspiration of the Holy Spirit. Holy Mother Church, relying on the belief of the apostles, holds that the books of both the Old and New Testament in their entirety, with all their parts, are sacred and canonical because, having been written under the inspiration of the Holy Spirit (cf. Jn. 20:31; 2 Tm. 3:16; 2 Pt. 1:19-21; 3:15-16) they have God as their author and have been handed on as such to the Church herself. In composing the sacred books, God chose men and, while employed by him, they made use of their powers and abilities, so that, with him acting in them and through them, they, as true authors, consigned to writing everything and only those things which he wanted (No. 11).

Inerrancy

Therefore, since everything asserted by the inspired authors or sacred writers must be held to be asserted by the Holy Spirit, it follows that the books of Scripture must be acknowledged as teaching firmly, faithfully, and without error that truth which God wanted put into the sacred writings for the sake of our salvation. Therefore "all Scripture is inspired by God and useful for teaching, for reproving, for correcting, for instruction in justice; that the man of God may be perfect, equipped for every good work" (2 Tm. 3:16-17) (No. 11).

Literary Forms

However, since God speaks in sacred Scripture through men in human fashion, the interpreter of sacred Scripture, in order to see clearly what God wanted to communicate to us, should carefully investigate what meaning the sacred writers really intended, and what God wanted to manifest by means of their words.

The interpreter must investigate what meaning the sacred writer intended to express and actually expressed in particular circumstances as he used contemporary literary forms in accordance with the situation of his own time and culture. For the correct understanding of what the sacred author wanted to assert, due attention must be paid to the customary and characteristic styles of perceiving, speaking, and narrating which prevailed at the time of the sacred writer, and to the customs men normally followed at that period in their everyday dealings with one another (No. 12).

Analogy of Faith

No less serious attention must be given to the content and unity of the whole of Scripture, if the meaning of the sacred texts is to be correctly brought to light. The living tradition of the whole Church must be taken into account along with the harmony which exists between elements of the faith.... All of what has been said about the way of interpreting Scripture is subject finally to the judgment of the Church, which carries out the divine commission and ministry of guarding and interpreting the word of God (No. 12).

IV. THE OLD TESTAMENT

In carefully planning and preparing the salvation of the whole human race, the God of supreme love, by a special dispensation, chose for himself a people to whom he might entrust his promises. First he entered into a covenant with Abraham (cf. Gn. 15:18) and, through Moses, with the people of Israel (cf. Ex. 24:8). To this people which he had acquired for himself, he so manifested himself through words and deeds as the one true and living God that Israel came to know by experience the ways of God with men.... The plan of salvation, foretold by the sacred authors, recounted and explained by them, is found as the true word of God in the books of the Old Testament: these books, therefore, written under divine inspiration, remain permanently valuable (No. 14).

Principal Purpose

The principal purpose to which the plan of the Old Covenant was directed was to prepare for the coming both of Christ, the universal Redeemer, and of the messianic Kingdom.... Now the books of the Old Testament, in accordance with the state of mankind before the time of salvation established by Christ, reveal to all men the knowledge of God and of man and the ways in which God ... deals with men. These books ... show us true divine pedagogy (No. 15).

The books of the Old Testament with all their parts, caught up into the proclamation of the Gospel, acquire and show forth their full meaning in the New Testament (cf. Mt. 5:17; Lk. 24:27; Rom. 16:25-26; 2 Cor. 3:14-16) and in turn shed light on it and explain it (No. 16).

V. THE NEW TESTAMENT

The word of God ... is set forth and shows its power in a most excellent way in the writings of the New Testament. For when the fullness of time arrived (cf. Gal. 4:4), the Word was made flesh and dwelt among us in the fullness of grace and truth (cf. Jn. 12:32)....This mystery had not been manifested to other generations as it was now revealed to his holy apostles and prophets in the Holy Spirit (cf. Eph. 3:4-6), so that they might preach the Gospel, stir up faith in Jesus, Christ and Lord, and gather the Church together. To these realities, the writings of the New Testament stand as a perpetual and divine witness (No. 17).

The Gospels and Other Writings

The Gospels have a special preeminence for they are the principal witness of the life and teaching of the incarnate Word, our Savior.

The Church has always and everywhere held and continues to hold that the four Gospels are of apostolic origin. For what the apostles preached ... afterwards they themselves and apostolic men, under the inspiration of the divine Spirit, handed on to us in writing: the foundation of faith, namely, the fourfold Gospel, according to Matthew, Mark, Luke, and John (No. 18).

The four Gospels, ... whose historical character the Church unhesitatingly asserts, faithfully hand on what Jesus Christ, while living among men, really did and taught for their eternal salvation until the day he was taken up into heaven (see Acts 1:1-2). Indeed, after the ascension of the Lord the apostles handed on to their hearers what he had said and done.... The sacred authors wrote the four Gospels, selecting some things from the many which had been handed on by word of mouth or in writing, reducing some of them to a synthesis, explicating some things in view of the situation of their churches, and preserving the form of proclamation but always in such fashion that they told us the honest truth about Jesus. For their intention in writing was that ... we might know "the truth" concerning those matters about which we have been instructed (cf. Lk. 1:2-4) (No. 19).

Besides the four Gospels, the canon of the New Testament also contains the Epistles of St. Paul and other apostolic writings, composed under the inspiration of the Holy Spirit. In these writings ... those matters which concern Christ the Lord are confirmed, his true teaching is more and more fully stated, the saving power of the divine work of Christ is preached, the story is told of the beginnings of the Church and her marvelous growth, and her glorious fulfillment is foretold (No. 20).

VI. SCRIPTURE IN CHURCH LIFE

The Church has always venerated the divine Scriptures just as she venerates the body of the Lord.... She has always regarded the Scriptures together with sacred tradition as the supreme rule of faith, and will ever do so. For, inspired by God and committed once and for all to writing, they impart the word of God himself without change, and make the voice of the Holy Spirit resound in the words of the prophets and apostles. Therefore, like the Christian religion itself, all the preaching of the Church must be nourished and ruled by sacred Scripture (No. 21).

Easy access to sacred Scripture should be provided for all the Christian faithful. That is why the Church from the very beginning accepted as her own that very ancient Greek translation of the Old Testament which is named after seventy men (the Septuagint); and she has always given a place of honor to other translations, Eastern and Latin, especially the one known as the Vulgate. But since the word of God should be available at all times, the Church with maternal concern sees to it that suitable and correct translations are made into different languages, especially from the original texts of the sacred books. And if, given the opportunity and the approval of Church authority, these translations are produced in cooperation with the separated brethren as well, all Christians will be able to use them (No. 22).

Biblical Studies, Theology

The constitution encouraged the development and progress of biblical studies "under the watchful care of the sacred teaching office of the Church."

It noted also: "Sacred theology rests on the written word of God, together with sacred tradition, as its primary and perpetual foundation," and that "the study of the sacred page is, as it were, the soul of sacred theology" (Nos. 23, 24).

(See separate article, Interpretation of the Bible.)

THE BIBLE

The Canon of the Bible is the Church's official list of sacred writings. These works, written by men under the inspiration of the Holy Spirit, contain divine revelation and, in conjunction with the tradition and teaching authority of the Church, constitute the rule of Catholic faith. The Canon was fixed and determined by the tradition and teaching authority of the Church.

The Catholic Canon

The Old Testament Canon of 46 books is as follows.

• **The Pentateuch,** the first five books: Genesis (Gn.), Exodus (Ex.), Leviticus (Lv.), Numbers (Nm.), Deuteronomy (Dt.).

• **Historical Books:** Joshua (Jos.), Judges (Jgs.), Ruth (Ru.) 1 and 2 Samuel (Sm.), 1 and 2 Kings (Kgs.), 1 and 2 Chronicles (Chr.), Ezra (Ezr.), Nehemiah (Neh.), Tobit (Tb.), Judith (Jdt.), Esther (Est.), 1 and 2 Maccabees (Mc.).

• **Wisdom Books:** Job (Jb.), Psalms (Ps.), Proverbs (Prv.), Ecclesiastes (Eccl.), Song of Songs (Song), Wisdom (Wis.), Sirach (Sir.).

• **The Prophets:** Isaiah (Is.), Jeremiah (Jer.), Lamentations (Lam.), Baruch (Bar.), Ezechiel (Ez.), Daniel (Dn.), Hosea (Hos.), Joel (Jl.), Amos (Am.), Obadiah (Ob.), Jonah (Jon.), Micah (Mi.), Nahum (Na.), Habakkuk (Hb.), Zephaniah (Zep.), Haggai (Hg.), Zechariah (Zec.) Malachi (Mal.).

The New Testament Canon of 27 books is as follows.

• **The Gospels** of Matthew (Mt.), Mark (Mk.), Luke (Lk.), John (Jn.)

• **The Acts of the Apostles** (Acts).

• **The Pauline Letters** — Romans (Rom.), 1 and 2 Corinthians (Cor.), Galatians (Gal.), Ephesians (Eph.), Philippians (Phil.), Colossians (Col.), 1 and 2 Thessalonians (Thes.) 1 and 2 Timothy (Tm.), Titus (Ti.), Philemon (Phlm.), Hebrews (Heb.).

• **The Catholic Letters** — James (Jas.), 1 and 2 Peter (Pt.), 1, 2 and 3 John (Jn.), Jude (Jude).

• **Revelation** (Rv.).

Developments

The Canon of the Old Testament was firm by the fifth century despite some questioning by scholars. It was stated by a council held at Rome in 382, by African councils held in Hippo in 393 and in Carthage in 397 and 419, and by Innocent I in 405.

All of the New Testament books were generally known and most of them were acknowledged as inspired by the end of the second century. The Muratorian Fragment, dating from about 200, listed most of the books recognized as canonical in later decrees. Prior to the end of the fourth century, however, there was controversy over the inspired character of several works — the Letter to the Hebrews, James, Jude, 2 Peter, 2 and 3 John and Revelation. Controversy ended in the fourth century and these books, along with those about which there was no dispute, were enumerated in the canon stated by the councils of Hippo and Carthage and affirmed by Innocent I in 405.

The Canon of the Bible was solemnly defined by the Council of Trent in the dogmatic decree *De Canonicis Scripturis,* Apr. 8, 1546.

Hebrew and Other Canons

The Hebrew Canon of sacred writings was fixed by tradition and the consensus of rabbis, probably by about 100 A.D. by the Synod or Council of Jamnia and certainly by the end of the second or early in the third century. It consists of the following works in three categories.

• **The Law** (Torah), the five books of Moses: Genesis, Exodus, Leviticus, Numbers, Deuteronomy.

• **The Prophets:** former prophets — Joshua, Judges, 1 and 2 Samuel, 1 and 2 Kings; latter prophets — Isaiah, Jeremiah, Ezekiel, and 12 minor prophets (Hosea, Joel, Amos, Obadiah, Jonah, Micah, Nahum, Habakkuk, Zephaniah, Haggai, Zechariah, Malachi).

• **The Writings:** 1 and 2 Chronicles, Ezra, Nehemiah, Job, Psalms, Proverbs, Ecclesiastes, Song of Songs, Ruth, Esther, Daniel.

This Canon, embodying the tradition and practice of the Palestine community, did not include a number of works contained in the Alexandrian version of sacred writings translated into Greek between 250 and 100 B.C. and in use by Greek-speaking Jews of the Dispersion (outside Palestine). The rejected works, called apocrypha and not regarded as sacred, are: Tobit, Judith, Wisdom, Sirach, Baruch, 1 and 2 Maccabees, the last six chapters of Esther and three passages of Daniel (3:24-90; 13; 14). These books have also been rejected from the Protestant Canon, although they are included in bibles under the heading, Apocrypha.

The aforementioned books are held to be inspired

and sacred by the Catholic Church. In Catholic usage, they are called deuterocanonical because they were under discussion for some time before questions about their canonicity were settled. Books regarded as canonical with little or no debate were called protocanonical. The status of both categories of books is the same in the Catholic Bible.

The Protestant Canon of the Old Testament is the same as the Hebrew.

The Old Testament Canon of some separated Eastern churches differs from the Catholic Canon.

Christians are in agreement on the Canon of the New Testament.

Languages

Hebrew, Aramaic and Greek were the original languages of the Bible. Most of the Old Testament books were written in Hebrew. Portions of Daniel, Ezra, Jeremiah, Esther, and probably the books of Tobit and Judith were written in Aramaic. The Book of Wisdom, 2 Maccabees and all the books of the New Testament were written in Greek.

Manuscripts and Versions

The original writings of the inspired authors have been lost. The Bible has been transmitted through ancient copies called manuscripts and through translations or versions.

Authoritative Greek manuscripts include the Sinaitic and Vatican manuscripts of the fourth century and the Alexandrine of the fifth century A.D. The Septuagint and Vulgate translations are in a class by themselves.

The Septuagint version, a Greek translation of the Old Testament for Greek-speaking Jews, was begun about 250 and completed about 100 B.C. The work of several Jewish translators at Alexandria, it differed from the Hebrew Bible in the arrangement of books and included several, later called deuterocanonical, which were not acknowledged as sacred by the community in Palestine.

The Vulgate was a Latin version of the Old and New Testaments produced from the original languages by St. Jerome from about 383 to 404. It became the most widely used Latin text for centuries and was regarded as basic long before the Council of Trent designated it as authentic and suitable for use in public reading, controversy, preaching and teaching. Because of its authoritative character, it became the basis for many translations into other languages. A critical revision was completed by a pontifical commission in 1977.

Hebrew and Aramaic manuscripts of great antiquity and value have figured more significantly than before in recent scriptural work by Catholic scholars, especially since their use was strongly encouraged, if not mandated, in 1943 by Pius XII in the encyclical *Divino Afflante Spiritu.*

The English translation of the Bible in general use among Catholics until well into the 20th century was the *Douay-Rheims,* so called because of the places where it was prepared and published, the New Testament at Rheims in 1582 and the Old Testament at Douay in 1609. The translation was made from the Vulgate text. As revised and issued by Bishop Richard Challoner in 1749 and 1750, it became the standard Catholic English version for about 200 years.

A revision of the Challoner New Testament, made on the basis of the Vulgate text by scholars of the Catholic Biblical Association of America, was published in 1941 in the United States under the sponsorship of the Episcopal Committee of the Confraternity of Christian Doctrine.

New American Bible

A new translation of the entire Bible, the first ever made directly into English from the original languages under Catholic auspices, was projected in 1944 and completed in the fall of 1970 with publication of the *New American Bible.* The Episcopal Committee of the Confraternity of Christian Doctrine sponsored the NAB. The translators were members of the Catholic Biblical Association of America and scholars of other faiths. The typical edition was produced by St. Anthony Guild Press, Paterson, N.J.

The Jerusalem Bible, published by Doubleday & Co., Inc., is an English translation of a French version based on the original languages.

Biblical translations approved for liturgical use by the National Conference of Catholic Bishops and the Holy See are the *New American Bible* (1970 edition), the *Revised Standard Version-Catholic Edition,* and the *Jerusalem Bible* (1966).

The Protestant counterpart of the *Douay-Rheims Bible* was the *King James Bible,* called the *Authorized Version* in England. Originally published in 1611 and in general use for more than three centuries, its several revisions include the *Revised Standard Version* and the *New Revised Standard Version.*

Biblical Federation

In November, 1966, Pope Paul VI commissioned the Secretariat for Promoting Christian Unity to start work for the widest possible distribution of the Bible and to coordinate endeavors toward the production of Catholic-Protestant Bibles in all languages.

The World Catholic Federation for the Biblical Apostolate, established in 1969, sponsors a program designed to create greater awareness among Catholics of the Bible and its use in everyday life.

The U. S. Center for the Catholic Biblical Apostolate is related to the Secretariat for Pastoral Research and Practices, National Conference of Catholic Bishops, 3211 Fourth St. N.E., Washington, DC 20017.

APOCRYPHA

In Catholic usage, Apocrypha are books which have some resemblance to the canonical books in subject matter and title but which have not been recognized as canonical by the Church. They are characterized by a false claim to divine authority; extravagant accounts of events and miracles alleged to be supplemental revelation; material favoring heresy (especially in "New Testament" apocrypha); minimal, if any, historical value. Among examples of this type of literature itemized by J. McKenzie, S.J., in *Dictionary of the Bible* are: the Books of Adam and sEve, Martyrdom of Isaiah, Testament of the Patriarchs, Assumption of Moses, Sibylline Oracles; Gospel of James, Gospel of Thomas, Arabic Gospel of the Infancy, History of Joseph the Carpenter; Acts of John, Acts of Paul, Acts of Peter, Acts of Andrew, and numerous epistles.

Books of this type are called pseudepigrapha by Protestants.

In Protestant usage, some books of the Catholic Bible (deuterocanonical) are called apocrypha because their inspired character is rejected.

DEAD SEA SCROLLS

The Qumran Scrolls, popularly called the Dead Sea Scrolls, are a collection of manuscripts, all but one of them in Hebrew, found since 1947 in caves in the Desert of Juda west of the Dead Sea.

Among the findings were a complete text of Isaiah dating from the second century, B.C., more or less extensive fragments of other Old Testament texts (including the deuterocanonical Tobit), and a commentary on Habakkuk. Until the discovery of these materials, the oldest known Hebrew manuscripts were from the 10th century, A.D.

Also found were messianic and apocalyptic texts, and other writings describing the beliefs and practices of the Essenes, a rigoristic Jewish sect.

The scrolls, dating from about the first century before and after Christ, are important sources of information about Hebrew literature, Jewish history during the period between the Old and New Testaments, and the history of Old Testament texts. They established the fact that the Hebrew text of the Old Testament was fixed before the beginning of the Christian era and have had definite effects in recent critical studies and translations of the Old Testament. Together with other scrolls found at Masada, they are still the subject of intensive study.

BOOKS OF THE BIBLE

OLD TESTAMENT BOOKS

Pentateuch

The Pentateuch is the collective title of the first five books of the Bible. Substantially, they identify the Israelites as Yahweh's Chosen People, cover their history from Egypt to the threshold of the Promised Land, contain the Mosaic Law and Covenant, and disclose the promise of salvation to come. Principal themes concern the divine promise of salvation, Yahweh's fidelity and the Covenant. Work on the composition of the Pentateuch was completed in the sixth century.

Genesis: The book of origins, according to its title in the Septuagint. In two parts, covers: religious prehistory, including accounts of the origin of the world and man, the original state of innocence and the fall, the promise of salvation, patriarchs before and after the Deluge, the Tower of Babel narrative, genealogies (first 11 chapters); the Covenant with Abraham and patriarchal history from Abraham to Joseph (balance of the 50 chapters). Significant are the themes of Yahweh's universal sovereignty and mercy.

Exodus: Named with the Greek word for departure, is a religious epic which describes the oppression of the 12 tribes in Egypt and their departure, liberation or passover therefrom under the leadership of Moses; Yahweh's establishment of the Covenant with them, making them his Chosen People, through the mediation of Moses at Mt. Sinai; instructions concerning the tabernacle, the sanctuary and Ark of the Covenant; the institution of the priesthood. The book is significant because of its theology of liberation and redemption. In Christian interpretation, the Exodus is a figure of baptism.

Leviticus: Mainly legislative in theme and purpose, contains laws regarding sacrifices, ceremonies of ordination and the priesthood of Aaron, legal purity, the holiness code, atonement, the redemption of offerings and other subjects. Summarily, Levitical laws provided directives for all aspects of religious observance and for the manner in which the Israelites were to conduct themselves with respect to Yahweh and each other. Leviticus was the liturgical handbook of the priesthood.

Numbers: Taking its name from censuses recounted at the beginning and near the end, is a continuation of Exodus. It combines narrative of the Israelites' desert pilgrimage from Sinai to the border of Canaan with laws related to and expansive of those in Leviticus.

Deuteronomy: The concluding book of the Pentateuch, recapitulates, in the form of a testament of Moses, the Law and much of the desert history of the Israelites; enjoins fidelity to the Law as the key to good or bad fortune for the people; gives an account of the commissioning of Joshua as the successor of Moses. Notable themes concern the election of Israel by Yahweh, observance of the Law, prohibitions against the worship of foreign gods, worship of and confidence in Yahweh, the power of Yahweh in nature. The Deuteronomic Code or motif, embodying all of these elements, was the norm for interpreting Israelite history.

Joshua, Judges, Ruth

Joshua: Records the fulfillment of Yahweh's promise to the Israelites in their conquest, occupation and division of Canaan under the leadership of Joshua. It also contains an account of the return of Transjordanian Israelites and of a renewal of the Covenant. It was redacted in final form probably in the sixth century or later.

Judges: Records the actions of charismatic leaders, called judges, of the tribes of Israel between the death of Joshua and the time of Samuel, and a crisis of idolatry among the people. The basic themes are sin and punishment, repentance and deliverance; its purpose was in line with the Deuteronomic motif, that the fortunes of the Israelites were related to their observance or non-observance of the Law and the Covenant. It was redacted in final form probably in the sixth century.

Ruth: Named for the Gentile (Moabite) woman who, through marriage with Boaz, became an Israelite and an ancestress of David (her son, Obed, became his grandfather). Themes are filial piety, faith and trust in Yahweh, the universality of messianic salvation. Dates ranging from c. 950 to the seventh century have been assigned to the origin of the book, whose author is unknown.

Historical Books

These books, while they contain a great deal of factual material, are unique in their preoccupation with presenting and interpreting it, in the Deuteronomic manner, in primary relation to the Covenant on which the nation of Israel was founded and in accordance with which community and personal life were judged.

The books are: Samuel 1 and 2, from the end of Judges (c. 1020) to the end of David's reign (c. 961); Kings 1 and 2, from the last days of David to the start of the Babylonian Exile and the destruction of the Temple (587); Chronicles 1 and 2, from the reign of Saul (c. 1020-1000) to the return of the people from the Exile (538); Ezra and Nehemiah, covering the reorganization of the Jewish community after the Exile (458-397); Maccabees 1 and 2, recounting the struggle against attempted suppression of Judaism (168-142).

Three of the books listed below — Tobit, Judith and Esther — are categorized as religious novels.

Samuel 1 and 2: A single work in concept and contents, containing episodic history of the last two Judges, Eli and Samuel, the establishment and rule of the monarchy under Saul and David, and the political consequences of David's rule. The royal messianic dynasty of David was the subject of Nathan's oracle in 2 Sm. 7. The books were edited in final form probably late in the seventh century or during the Exile.

Kings 1 and 2: Cover the last days of David and the career of Solomon, including the building of the Temple and the history of the kingdom during his reign; stories of the prophets Elijah and Elisha; the history of the divided kingdom to the fall of Israel in the North (721) and the fall of Judah in the South (587), the destruction of Jerusalem and the Temple. They reflect the Deuteronomic motif in attributing the downfall of the people to corruption of belief and practice in public and private life. They were completed probably in the sixth century.

Chronicles 1 and 2: A collection of historical traditions interpreted in such a way as to present an ideal picture of one people governed by divine law and united in one Temple worship of the one true God. Contents include genealogical tables from Adam to David, the careers of David and Solomon, coverage of the kingdom of Judah to the Exile, and the decree of Cyrus permitting the return of the people and rebuilding of Jerusalem. Both are related to and were written about 400 by the same author, the Chronicler, who composed Ezra and Nehemiah.

Ezra and Nehemiah: A running account of the return of the people to their homeland after the Exile and of practical efforts, under the leadership of Ezra and Nehemiah, to restore and reorganize the religious and political community on the basis of Israelite traditions, divine worship and observance of the Law. Events of great significance were the building of the second Temple, the building of a wall around Jerusalem and the proclamation of the Law by Ezra. This restored community was the start of Judaism. Both are related to and were written about 400 by the same author, the Chronicler, who composed Chronicles 1 and 2.

Tobit: Written in the literary form of a novel and having greater resemblance to wisdom than to historical literature, narrates the personal history of Tobit, a devout and charitable Jew in exile, and persons connected with him, viz., his son Tobiah, his kinsman Raguel and Raguel's daughter Sarah. Its purpose was to teach people how to be good Jews. One of its principal themes is patience under trial, with trust in divine Providence which is symbolized by the presence and action of the angel Raphael. It was written about 200.

Judith: Recounts, in the literary form of a historical novel or romance, the preservation of the Israelites from conquest and ruin through the action of Judith. The essential themes are trust in God for deliverance from danger and emphasis on observance of the Law. It was written probably during the Maccabean period.

Esther: Relates, in the literary form of a historical novel or romance, the manner in which Jews in Persia were saved from annihilation through the central role played by Esther, the Jewish wife of Ahasuerus; a fact commemorated by the Jewish feast of Purim. Like Judith, it has trust in divine Providence as its theme and indicates that God's saving will is sometimes realized by persons acting in unlikely ways. It may have been written near the end of the fourth century.

Maccabees 1 and 2: While related to some extent because of common subject matter, are quite different from each other.

The first book recounts the background and events of the 40-year (175-135) struggle for religious and political freedom led by Judas Maccabeus and his brothers against the Hellenist Seleucid kings and some Hellenophiles among the Jews. Victory was symbolized by the rededication of the Temple. Against the background of opposition between Jews and Gentiles, the author equated the survival of belief in the one true God with survival of the Jewish people, thus identifying religion with patriotism. It was written probably near the year 100.

The second book supplements the first to some extent, covering and giving a theological interpretation to events from 180 to 162. It explains the feast of the Dedication of the Temple, a key event in the survival of Judaism which is commemorated in the feast of Hanukkah; stresses the primacy of God's action in the struggle for survival; and indicates belief in an afterlife and the resurrection of the body. It was completed probably about 124.

Wisdom Books

With the exceptions of Psalms and the Song of Songs, the titles listed under this heading are called wisdom books because their purpose was to formulate the fruits of human experience in the context of meditation on sacred Scripture and to present them as an aid toward understanding the problems of life. Hebrew wisdom literature was distinctive from pagan literature of the same type, but it had limitations; these were overcome in the New Testament, which added the dimensions of the New Covenant to those of the Old. Solomon was regarded as the archtype of the wise man.

Job: A dramatic, didactic poem consisting mainly of several dialogues between Job and his friends concerning the mystery involved in the coexistence of the just God, evil and the suffering of the just. It describes an innocent man's experience of suffering and conveys the truth that faith in and submission to God rather than complete understanding, which is impossible, make the experience bearable; also, that the justice of God cannot be defended by affirming that it is realized in this world. Of unknown authorship, it was composed between the seventh and fifth centuries.

Psalms: A collection of 150 religious songs or lyrics reflecting Israelite belief and piety dating from the time of the monarchy to the post-Exilic period, a span of well over 500 years. The psalms, which are a compendium of Old Testament theology, were used in the temple liturgy and for other occasions. They were of several types suitable for the king, hymns, lamentations, expressions of confidence and thanksgiving, prophecy, historical meditation and reflection, and the statement of wisdom. About one-half of them are attributed to David; many were composed by unknown authors.

Proverbs: The oldest book of the wisdom type in the Bible, consisting of collections of sayings attributed to Solomon and other persons regarding a wide variety of subjects including wisdom and its nature, rules of conduct, duties with respect to one's neighbor, the conduct of daily affairs. It reveals many details of Hebrew life. Its nucleus dates from the period before the Exile. The extant form of the book dates probably from the end of the fifth century.

Ecclesiastes: A treatise about many subjects whose unifying theme is the vanity of strictly human efforts and accomplishments with respect to the achievement of lasting happiness; the only things which are not vain are fear of the Lord and observance of his commandments. The pessimistic tone of the book is due to the absence of a concept of afterlife. It was written by an unknown author probably in the third century.

Song of Songs: A collection of love lyrics reflecting various themes, including the love of God for Israel and the celebration of ideal love and fidelity between man and woman. It was written by an unknown author after the Exile.

Wisdom: Deals with many subjects including the reward of justice; praise of wisdom, a gift of Yahweh proceeding from belief in him and the practice of his Law; the part played by him in the history of his people, especially in their liberation from Egypt; the folly and shame of idolatry. Its contents are taken from the whole sacred literature of the Jews and represent a distillation of its wisdom based on the law, beliefs and traditions of Israel. The last of the Old Testament books, it was written in the early part of the first century before Christ by a member of the Jewish community at Alexandria.

Sirach: Resembling Proverbs, is a collection of sayings handed on by a grandfather to his grandson. It contains a variety of moral instruction and eulogies of patriarchs and other figures in Israelite history. Its moral maxims apply to individuals, the family and community, relations with God, friendship, education, wealth, the Law, divine worship. Its theme is that true wisdom consists in the Law. (It was formerly called Ecclesiasticus, the Church Book, because of its extensive use by the Church for moral instruction.) It was written in Hebrew between 200 and 175, during a period of strong hellenistic influence, and was translated into Greek after 132.

The Prophets

These books and the prophecies they contain "express judgments of the people's moral conduct, on the basis of the Mosaic alliance between God and Israel. They teach sublime truths and lofty morals. They contain exhortations, threats, announcements of punishment, promises of deliverance. In the affairs of men, their prime concern is the interests of God, especially in what pertains to the Chosen People through whom the Messiah is to come; hence their denunciations of idolatry and of that externalism in worship which exclude the interior spirit of religion. They are concerned also with the universal nature of the moral law, with personal responsibility, with the person and office of the Messiah, and with the conduct of foreign nations" (*The Holy Bible,* Prophetic Books, CCD Edition, 1961; Preface). There are four major (Isaiah, Jeremiah, Ezekiel, Daniel) and 12 minor (distinguished by the length of books), Lamentations and Baruch. Earlier prophets, mentioned in historical books, include Samuel, Gad, Nathan, Elijah and Elisha.

Before the Exile, prophets were the intermediaries through whom God communicated revelation to the people. Afterwards, prophecy lapsed and the written word of the Law served this purpose.

Isaiah: Named for the greatest of the prophets whose career spanned the reigns of three Hebrew kings from 742 to the beginning of the seventh century, in a period of moral breakdown in Judah and threats of invasion by foreign enemies. It is an anthology of poems and oracles credited to him and a number of followers deeply influenced by him. Of special importance are the prophecies concerning Immanuel (6 to 12), including the prophecy of the virgin birth (7:14). Chapters 40 to 55, called Deutero-Isaiah, are attributed to an anonymous poet toward the end of the Exile; this portion contains the Songs of the Servant. The concluding part of the book (56-66) contains oracles by later disciples. One of many themes in Isaiah concerned the saving mission of the remnant of Israel in the divine plan of salvation.

Jeremiah: Combines history, biography and prophecy in a setting of crisis caused by internal and external factors, viz., idolatry and general infidelity to the Law among the Israelites and external threats from the Assyrians, Egyptians and Babylonians. Jeremiah prophesied the promise of a new covenant as well as the destruction of Jerusalem and the Temple. His career began in 626 and ended some years after the beginning of the Exile. The book, the longest in the Bible, was edited in final form after the Exile.

Lamentations: A collection of five laments or elegies over the fall of Jerusalem and the fate of the people in Exile, written by an unknown eyewitness. They convey the message that Yahweh struck the people because of their sins and reflect confidence in his love and power to restore his converted people.

Baruch: Against the background of the already begun Exile, it consists of an introduction and several parts: an exile's prayer of confession and petition for forgiveness and the restoration of Israel; a poem praising wisdom and the Law of Moses; a lament in which Jerusalem, personified, bewails the fate of her people and consoles them with the hope of blessings to come; and a polemic against idolatry. Although ascribed to Baruch, Jeremiah's secretary, it was written by several authors probably in the second century.

Ezekiel: Named for the priest-prophet who prophesied in Babylon from 593 to 571, during the first phase of the Exile. To prepare his fellow early exiles for the impending fall of Jerusalem, he reproached the Israelites for past sins and predicted woes to come upon them. After the destruction of the city, the burden of his message was hope and promise of restoration. Ezekiel had great influence on the religion of Israel after the Exile.

Daniel: The protagonist is a young Jew, taken early to Babylon where he lived until about 538, who figured in a series of edifying stories which originated in Israelite tradition. The stories, whose characters are not purely legendary but rest on historical tradition, recount the trials and triumphs of Daniel and his three companions, and other episodes including those concerning Susannah, Bel, and the Dragon. The book is more apocalyptic than prophetic: it envisions Israel in glory to come and conveys the message that men of faith can resist temptation and overcome adversity. It states the prophetic themes of right conduct, divine control of men and events, and the final triumph of the kingdom. It was written by an unknown author in the 160's to give moral support to Jews during the persecutions of the Maccabean period.

Hosea: Consists of a prophetic parallel between Hosea's marriage and Yahweh's relations with his people. As the prophet was married to a faithless wife whom he would not give up, Yahweh was bound in Covenant with an idolatrous and unjust Israel whom he would not desert but would chastise for purification. Hosea belonged to the Northern Kingdom of Israel and began his career about the middle of the eighth century. He inaugurated the tradition of describing Yahweh's relation to Israel in terms of marriage.

Joel: Is apocalyptic and eschatological regarding divine judgment, the Day of the Lord, which is symbolized by a ravaging invasion of locusts, the judgment of the nations in the Valley of Josaphat and the outpouring of the Spirit in the messianic era to come. Its message is that God will vindicate and save Israel, in view of the prayer and repentance of the people, and will punish their enemies. It was composed about 400.

Amos: Consists of an indictment against foreign enemies of Israel; a strong denunciation of the people of Israel, whose infidelity, idolatry and injustice made them subject to divine judgment and punishment; and a messianic oracle regarding Israel's restoration. Amos prophesied in the Northern Kingdom of Israel, at Bethel, in the first half of the eighth century; chronologically, he was the first of the canonical prophets.

Obadiah: A 21-verse prophecy, the shortest and one of the sternest in the Bible, against the Edomites, invaders of southern Judah and enemies of those returning from the Exile to their homeland. It was probably composed in the fifth century.

Jonah: A parable of divine mercy with the theme that Yahweh wills the salvation of all, not just a few, men who respond to his call. Its protagonist is a disobedient prophet; forced by circumstances beyond his control to preach penance among Gentiles, he is highly successful in his mission but baffled by the divine concern for those who do not belong to the Chosen People. It was written after the Exile, probably in the fifth century.

Micah: Attacks the injustice and corruption of priests, false prophets, officials and people; announces judgment and punishment to come; foretells the restoration of Israel; refers to the saving remnant of Israel. Micah was a contemporary of Isaiah.

Nahum: Concerns the destruction of Nineveh in 612 and the overthrow of the Assyrian Empire by the Babylonians.

Habakkuk: Dating from about 605-597, concerns sufferings to be inflicted by oppressors on the people of Judah because of their infidelity to the Lord. It also sounds a note of confidence in the Lord, the Savior, and declares that the just will not perish.

Zephaniah: Exercising his ministry in the second half of the seventh century, during a time of widespread idolatry, superstition and religious degradation, he prophesied impending judgment and punishment for Jerusalem and its people. He prophesied too that a holy remnant of the people (anawim, mentioned also by Amos) would be spared. Zephaniah was a forerunner of Jeremiah.

Haggai: One of the first prophets after the Exile, Haggai in 520 encouraged the returning exiles to reestablish their community and to complete the second Temple (dedicated in 515), for which he envisioned greater glory, in a messianic sense, than that enjoyed by the original Temple of Solomon.

Zechariah: A contemporary of Haggai, he prophesied in the same vein. A second part of the book, called Deutero-Zechariah and composed by one or more unknown authors, relates a vision of the coming of the Prince of Peace, the Messiah of the Poor.

Malachi: Written by an anonymous author, presents a picture of life in the post-Exilic community between 516 and the initiation of reforms by Ezra and Nehemiah about 432. Blame for the troubles of the community is placed mainly on priests for failure to carry out ritual worship and to instruct the people in the proper manner; other factors were religious indifference and the influence of doubters who were scandalized at the prosperity of the wicked. The vision of a universal sacrifice to be offered to Yahweh (1:11) is interpreted in Catholic theology as a prophecy of the sacrifice of the Mass. Malachi was the last of the minor prophets.

OLD TESTAMENT DATES

c. 1800 — c. 1600: Period of the patriarchs (Abraham, Isaac, Jacob).

c. 1600: Israelites in Egypt.

c. 1250: Exodus of Israelites from Egypt.

c. 1210: Entrance of Israelites into Canaan.

c. 1210 — c. 1020: Period of the Judges.

c. 1020 — c. 1000: Reign of Saul, first king.

c. 1000 — c. 961: Reign of David.

c. 961 — 922: Reign of Solomon. Temple built during his reign.

922: Division of the Kingdom into Israel (North) and Judah (South).

721: Conquest of Israel by Assyrians.

587-538: Conquest of Judah by Babylonians.

Babylonian Captivity and Exile. Destruction of Jerusalem and the Temple, 587. Captivity ended with the return of exiles, following the decree of Cyrus permitting the rebuilding of Jerusalem.

515: Dedication of the Second Temple.

458-397: Restoration and reform of the Jewish religious and political community; building of the Jerusalem wall, 439. Leaders in the movement were Ezra and Nehemiah.

168-142: Period of the Maccabees; war against Syrians.

142: Independence granted to Jews by Demetrius II of Syria.

135-37: Period of the Hasmonean dynasty.

63: Beginning of Roman rule.

37-4: Period of Herod the Great.

NEW TESTAMENT BOOKS

Gospels

The term Gospel is derived from the Anglo-Saxon *god-spell* and the Greek *euangelion,* meaning good news, good tidings. In Christian use, it means the good news of salvation proclaimed by Christ and the Church, and handed on in written form in the Gospels of Matthew, Mark, Luke and John.

The initial proclamation of the coming of the kingdom of God was made by Jesus in and through his Person, teachings and actions, and especially through his Passion, death and resurrection. This proclamation became the center of Christian faith and the core of the oral Gospel tradition with which the Church spread the good news by apostolic preaching for some 30 years before it was committed to writing by the Evangelists.

Nature of the Gospels

The historical truth of the Gospels was the subject of an instruction issued by the Pontifical Commission for Biblical Studies Apr. 21, 1964.

• The sacred writers selected from the material at their disposal (the oral Gospel tradition, some written collections of sayings and deeds of Jesus, eyewitness accounts) those things which were particularly suitable to the various conditions (liturgical, catechetical, missionary) of the faithful and the aims they had in mind, and they narrated these things in such a way as to correspond with those circumstances and their aims.

• The life and teaching of Jesus were not simply reported in a biographical manner for the purpose of preserving their memory but were "preached" so as to offer the Church the basis of doctrine concerning faith and morals.

• In their works, the Evangelists presented the true sayings of Jesus and the events of his life in the light of the better understanding they had following their enlightenment by the Holy Spirit. They did not transform Christ into a "mythical" Person, nor did they distort his teaching. Passion narratives are the core of all the Gospels, covering the suffering, death and resurrection of Jesus as central events in bringing

about and establishing the New Covenant. Leading up to them are accounts of the mission of John the Baptizer and the ministry of Jesus, especially in Galilee and finally in Jerusalem before the Passion. The infancy of Jesus is covered by Luke and Matthew with narratives inspired in part by appropriate Old Testament citations.

Matthew, Mark and Luke, while different in various respects, have so many similarities that they are called Synoptic; their relationships are the subject of the Synoptic Problem.

Matthew: Written probably between 80 and 100 for Jewish Christians with clear reference to Jewish background and identification of Jesus as the divine Messiah, the fulfillment of the Old Testament. Distinctive are the use of Old Testament citations regarding the Person, activity and teaching of Jesus, and the presentation of doctrine in sermons and discourses.

Mark: The first of the Gospels, dating from about 70. Written for Gentile Christians, it is noted for the realism and wealth of concrete details with which it reveals Jesus as Son of God and Savior more by his actions and miracles than by his discourses. Theologically, it is less refined than the other Gospels.

Luke: Written about 75 for Gentile Christians. It is noted for the universality of its address, the insight it provides into the Christian way of life, the place it gives to women, the manner in which it emphasizes Jesus' friendship with sinners and compassion for the suffering.

John: Edited and arranged in final form probably between 90 and 100, is the most sublime and theological of the Gospels, and is different from the Synoptics in plan and treatment. Combining accounts of signs with longer discourses and reflections, it progressively reveals the Person and mission of Jesus — as Word, Way, Truth, Life, Light — in line with the purpose, "to help you believe that Jesus is the Messiah, the Son of God, so that through this faith you may have life in his name" (Jn. 20:31). There are questions about the authorship but no doubt about the Johannine authority and tradition behind the Gospel.

Acts of the Apostles

Acts of the Apostles: Written by Luke about 75 as a supplement to his Gospel. It describes the origin and spread of Christian communities through the action of the Holy Spirit from the resurrection of Christ to the time when Paul was placed in custody in Rome in the early 60s.

Letters (Epistles)

These letters, many of which antedated the Gospels, were written in response to existential needs of the early Christian communities for doctrinal and moral instruction, disciplinary action, practical advice, and exhortation to true Christian living.

Pauline Letters

These letters, which comprise approximately one-fourth of the New Testament, are primary and monumental sources of the development of Christian theology. Several of them may not have had Paul as their actual author, but evidence of the Pauline tradition behind them is strong. The letters to the Colossians,

Philippians, Ephesians and Philemon have been called the "Captivity Letters" because of a tradition that they were written while Paul was under house arrest or another form of detention.

Romans: Written about 57 probably from Corinth on the central significance of Christ and faith in him for salvation, and the relationship of Christianity to Judaism; the condition of mankind without Christ; justification and the Christian life; duties of Christians.

Corinthians 1: Written near the beginning of 57 from Ephesus to counteract factionalism and disorders, it covers community dissensions, moral irregularities, marriage and celibacy, conduct at religious gatherings, the Eucharist, spiritual gifts (charisms) and their function in the Church, charity, the resurrection of the body.

Corinthians 2: Written later in the same year as 1 Cor., concerning Paul's defense of his apostolic ministry, and an appeal for a collection to aid poor Christians in Jerusalem.

Galatians: Written probably between 54 and 55 to counteract Judaizing opinions and efforts to undermine his authority, it asserts the divine origin of Paul's authority and doctrine, states that justification is not through Mosaic Law but through faith in Christ, insists on the practice of evangelical virtues, especially charity.

Ephesians: Written probably between 61 and 63, mainly on the Church as the Mystical Body of Christ.

Philippians: Written between 56 and 57 or 61 and 63 to warn the Philippians against enemies of their faith, to urge them to be faithful to their vocation and unity of belief, and to thank them for their kindness to him while he was being held in detention.

Colossians: Written probably while he was under house arrest in Rome from 61 to 63, to counteract the influence of self-appointed teachers who were watering down doctrine concerning Christ. It includes two highly important Christological passages, a warning against false teachers, and an instruction on the ideal Christian life.

Thessalonians 1 and 2: Written within a short time of each other probably in 51 from Corinth, mainly on doctrine concerning the Parousia, the second coming of Christ.

Timothy 1 and 2, Titus: Written between 65 and 67, or perhaps in the 70's, giving pastoral counsels to Timothy and Titus who were in charge of churches in Ephesus and Crete, respectively. 1 Tm. emphasizes pastoral responsibility for preserving

unity of doctrine; 2 Tm. describes Paul's imprisonment in Rome.

Philemon: A private letter written between 61 and 63 to a wealthy Colossian concerning a slave, Onesimus, who had escaped from him; Paul appealed for kind treatment of the man.

Hebrews: Dating from sometime between 70 and 96, a complex theological treatise on Christology, the priesthood and sacrifice of Christ, the New Covenant, and the pattern for Christian living. Critical opinion is divided as to whether it was addressed to Judaeo or Gentile Christians.

Catholic Letters, Revelation

These seven letters have been called "catholic" because it was thought for some time, not altogether correctly, that they were not addressed to particular communities.

James: Written sometime before 62 in the spirit of Hebrew wisdom literature and the moralism of Tobit. An exhortation to practical Christian living, it is also noteworthy for the doctrine it states on good works and its citation regarding anointing of the sick.

Peter 1 and 2: The first letter may have been written between 64 and 67 or between 90 and 95; the second may date from 100 to 125. Addressed to Christians in Asia Minor, both are exhortations to perseverance in the life of faith despite trials and difficulties arising from pagan influences, isolation from other Christians and false teaching.

John 1: Written sometime in the 90s and addressed to Asian churches, its message is that God is made known to us in the Son and that fellowship with the Father is attained by living in the light, justice and love of the Son.

John 2: Written sometime in the 90s and addressed to a church in Asia, it commends the people for standing firm in the faith and urges them to perseverance.

John 3: Written sometime in the 90s, it appears to represent an effort to settle a jurisdictional dispute in one of the churches.

Jude: Written probably about 80, it is a brief treatise against erroneous teachings and practices opposed to law, authority and true Christian freedom.

Revelation: Written in the 90s along the lines of Johannine thought, it is a symbolic and apocalyptic treatment of things to come and of the struggle between the Church and evil combined with warning but hope and assurance to the Church regarding the coming of the Lord in glory.

OLD AND NEW TESTAMENT RELATIONSHIP

This was the theme of Pope John Paul's remarks at a meeting Apr. 11, 1997, with members of the Pontifical Biblical Commission. He said in part, as follows.

"Since the second century A.D., the Church has been faced with the temptation to separate the New Testament completely from the Old, and to oppose one to the other, attributing to them two different origins. The Old Testament, according to Marcion, came from a god unworthy of the name because he was vindictive and bloodthirsty, while the New Testament revealed a God of reconciliation and generosity. The Church firmly rejected this error, remind-

ing all that God's tenderness was already revealed in the Old Testament."

There is, however, "an ignorance of the deep ties linking the New Testament to the Old, an ignorance that gives some people the impression that Christians have nothing in common with Jews."

"The Church has well understood that the Incarnation is rooted in history and, consequently, she has fully accepted Christ's insertion into the history of the People of Israel. She has regarded the Hebrew Scriptures as the perennially valid word of God addressed to her as well as to the children of Israel."

INTERPRETATION OF THE BIBLE

According to the "Constitution on Revelation" issued by the Second Vatican Council, "the interpreter of Sacred Scripture, in order to see clearly what God wanted to communicate to us, should carefully investigate what meaning the sacred writers really intended, and what God wanted to manifest by means of their words" (No. 12).

Hermeneutics, Exegesis

This careful investigation proceeds in accordance with the rules of hermeneutics, the normative science of biblical interpretation and explanation. Hermeneutics in practice is called exegesis.

The principles of hermeneutics are derived from various disciplines and many factors which have to be considered in explaining the Bible and its parts. These include: the original languages and languages of translation of the sacred texts, through philology and linguistics; the quality of texts, through textual criticism; literary forms and genres, through literary and form criticism; cultural, historical, geographical and other conditions which influenced the writers, through related studies; facts and truths of salvation history; the truths and analogy of faith.

Distinctive to biblical hermeneutics, which differs in important respects from literary interpretation in general, is the premise that the Bible, though written by human authors, is the work of divine inspiration in which God reveals his plan for the salvation of men through historical events and persons, and especially through the Person and mission of Christ.

Textual, Form Criticism

Textual criticism is the study of biblical texts, which have been transmitted in copies several times removed from the original manuscripts, for the purpose of establishing the real state of the original texts. This purpose is served by comparison of existing copies; by application to the texts of the disciplines of philology and linguistics; by examination of related works of antiquity; by study of biblical citations in works of the Fathers of the Church and other authors; and by other means of literary study.

Since about 1920, the sayings of Christ have been a particular object of New Testament study, the purpose being to analyze the forms of expression used by the Evangelists in order to ascertain the words actually spoken by him.

Literary Criticism

Literary criticism aims to determine the origin and kinds of literary composition, called forms or genres, employed by the inspired authors. Such determinations are necessary for decision regarding the nature and purpose and, consequently, the meaning of biblical passages. Underlying these studies is the principle that the manner of writing was conditioned by the intention of the authors, the meaning they wanted to convey, and the then-contemporary literary style, mode or medium best adapted to carry their message — e.g., true history, quasi-historical narrative, poems, prayers, hymns, psalms, aphorisms, allegories, discourses. Understanding these media is necessary for the valid interpretation of their message.

Literal Sense

The key to all valid interpretation is the literal sense of biblical passages. Regarding this matter and the relevance to it of the studies and procedures described above, Pius XII wrote the following in the encyclical *Divino Afflante Spiritu.*

"What the literal sense of a passage is, is not always as obvious in the speeches and writings of ancient authors of the East as it is in the works of our own time. For what they wished to express is not to be determined by the rules of grammar and philology alone nor solely by the context; the interpreter must, as it were, go back wholly in spirit to those remote centuries of the East and with the aid of history, archeology, ethnology, and other sciences accurately determine what modes of writing, so to speak, the authors of that ancient period would be likely to use and in fact did use. In explaining the Sacred Scripture and in demonstrating and proving its immunity from all error (the Catholic interpreter) should make a prudent use of this means, determine to what extent the manner of expression or literary mode adopted by the sacred writer may lead to a correct and genuine interpretation; and let him be convinced that this part of his office cannot be neglected without serious detriment to Catholic exegesis."

The literal sense of the Bible is the meaning in the mind of and intended by the inspired writer of a book or passage of the Bible. This is determined by the application to texts of the rules of hermeneutics. It is not to be confused with word-for-word literalism.

Typical Sense

The typical sense is the meaning which a passage has not only in itself but also in reference to something else of which it is a type or foreshadowing. A clear example is the account of the Exodus of the Israelites: in its literal sense, it narrates the liberation of the Israelites from death and oppression in Egypt; in its typical sense, it foreshadowed the liberation of men from sin through the redemptive death and resurrection of Christ. The typical sense of this and other passages emerged in the working out of God's plan of salvation history. It did not have to be in the mind of the author of the original passage.

Accommodated Senses

Accommodated, allegorical and consequent senses are figurative and adaptive meanings given to books and passages of the Bible for moral and other purposes. Such interpretations involve the danger of stretching the literal sense beyond proper proportions. Hermeneutical principles require that interpretations like these respect the integrity of the literal sense of the passages in question.

In the Catholic view, the final word on questions of biblical interpretation belongs to the teaching authority of the Church. In other views, generally derived from basic principles stated by Martin Luther, John Calvin and other reformers, the primacy belongs to individual judgment acting in response to the inner testimony of the Holy Spirit, the edifying nature of biblical subject matter, the sublimity and simplicity of the message of salvation, the intensity with which Christ is proclaimed.

Biblical Studies

The first center for biblical studies, in some strict sense of the term, was the School of Alexandria, founded in the latter half of the second century. It was noted for allegorical exegesis. Literal interpretation was a hallmark of the School of Antioch.

St. Jerome, who produced the Vulgate, and St. Augustine, author of numerous commentaries, were the most important figures in biblical studies during the patristic period. By the time of the latter's death, the Old and New Testament canons had been stabilized. For some centuries afterwards, there was little or no progress in scriptural studies, although commentaries were written, collections were made of scriptural excerpts from the writings of the Fathers of the Church, and the systematic reading of Scripture became established as a feature of monastic life.

Advances were made in the 12th and 13th centuries with the introduction of new principles and methods of scriptural analysis stemming from renewed interest in Hebraic studies and the application of dialectics.

By the time of the Reformation, the Bible had become the first book set in movable type, and more than 100 vernacular editions were in use throughout Europe.

The Council of Trent

In the wake of the Reformation, the Council of Trent formally defined the Canon of the Bible; it also reasserted the authoritative role of tradition and the teaching authority of the Church as well as Scripture with respect to the rule of faith. In the heated atmosphere of the 16th and 17th centuries, the Bible was turned into a polemical weapon; Protestants used it to defend their doctrines, and Catholics countered with citations in support of the dogmas of the Church. One result of this state of affairs was a lack of substantial progress in biblical studies during the period.

Rationalists from the 18th century on and later Modernists denied the reality of the supernatural and doctrine concerning inspiration of the Bible, which they generally regarded as a strictly human production expressive of the religious sense and experience

of mankind. In their hands, the tools of positive critical research became weapons for biblical subversion. The defensive Catholic reaction to their work had the temporary effect of alienating scholars of the Church from solid advances in archeology, philology, history, textual and literary criticism.

Catholic Developments

Major influences in bringing about a change in Catholic attitude toward use of these disciplines in biblical studies were two papal encyclicals and two institutes of special study, the Ecole Biblique, founded in Jerusalem in 1890, and the Pontifical Biblical Institute established in Rome in 1909. The encyclical *Providentissimus Deus,* issued by Leo XIII in 1893, marked an important breakthrough; in addition to defending the concept of divine inspiration and the formal inspiration of the Scriptures, it encouraged the study of allied and ancillary sciences and techniques for a more fruitful understanding of the sacred writings. The encyclical *Divino Afflante Spiritu,* 50 years later, gave encouragement for the use of various forms of criticism as tools of biblical research. A significant addition to documents on the subject is "The Interpretation of the Bible," published by the Pontifical Biblical Commission in November, 1993. It presents an overview of approaches to the Bible and probes the question: "Which hermeneutical theory best enables a proper grasp of the profound reality of which Scripture speaks and its meaningful expression for people today?"

The documents encouraged the work of scholars and stimulated wide communication of the fruits of their study.

Great changes in the climate and direction of biblical studies have occurred in recent years. One of them has been an increase in cooperative effort among Catholic, Protestant, Orthodox and Jewish scholars. Their common investigation of the Dead Sea Scrolls is well known. Also productive has been the collaboration of Catholics and Protestants in turning out various editions of the Bible.

The development and results of biblical studies in this century have directly and significantly affected all phases of the contemporary renewal movement in the Church. Their influence on theology, liturgy, catechetics, and preaching indicate the importance of their function in the life of the Church.

APOSTLES AND EVANGELISTS

The Apostles were the men selected, trained and commissioned by Christ to preach the Gospel, to baptize, to establish, direct and care for his Church as servants of God and stewards of his mysteries. They were the first bishops of the Church.

St. Matthew's Gospel lists the Apostles in this order: Peter, Andrew, James the Greater, John, Philip, Bartholomew, Thomas, Matthew, James the Less, Jude, Simon and Judas Iscariot. Matthias was elected to fill the place of Judas. Paul became an Apostle by a special call from Christ. Barnabas was called an Apostle.

Two of the Evangelists, John and Matthew, were Apostles. The other two, Luke and Mark, were closely associated with the apostolic college.

Andrew: Born in Bethsaida, brother of Peter, disciple of John the Baptist, a fisherman, the first Apostle called; according to legend, preached the Gospel in northern Greece, Epirus and Scythia, and was martyred at Patras about 70; in art, is represented with an x-shaped cross, called St. Andrew's Cross; is honored as the patron of Russia and Scotland; Nov. 30.

Barnabas: Originally called Joseph but named Barnabas by the Apostles, among whom he is ranked because of his collaboration with Paul; a Jew of the Diaspora, born in Cyprus; a cousin of Mark and member of the Christian community at Jerusalem, influenced the Apostles to accept Paul, with whom he became a pioneer missionary outside Palestine and Syria, to Antioch, Cyprus and southern Asia Minor; legend says he was martyred in Cyprus during the Neronian persecution; June 11.

Bartholomew (Nathaniel): A friend of Philip; according to various traditions, preached the Gospel in Ethiopia, India, Persia and Armenia, where he was martyred by being flayed and beheaded; in art, is depicted holding a knife, an instrument of his death; Aug. 24 (Roman Rite), Aug. 25 (Byzantine Rite).

James the Greater: A Galilean, son of Zebedee, brother of John (with whom he was called a "Son of Thunder"), a fisherman; with Peter and John, witnessed the raising of Jairus' daughter to life, the transfiguration, the agony of Jesus in the Garden of Gethsemani; first of the Apostles to die, by the sword in 44 during the rule of Herod Agrippa; there is doubt about a journey legend says he made to Spain and also about the authenticity of relics said to be his at Santiago de Compostela; in art, is depicted carrying a pilgrim's bell; July 25 (Roman Rite), Apr. 30 (Byzantine Rite).

James the Less: Son of Alphaeus, called "Less" because he was younger in age or shorter in stature than James the Greater; one of the Catholic Epistles bears his name; was stoned to death in 62 or thrown from the top of the temple in Jerusalem and clubbed to death in 66; in art, is depicted with a club or heavy staff; May 3 (Roman Rite), Oct. 9 (Byzantine Rite).

John: A Galilean, son of Zebedee, brother of James the Greater (with whom he was called a "Son of Thunder"), a fisherman, probably a disciple of John the Baptist, one of the Evangelists, called the "Beloved Disciple"; with Peter and James the Greater, witnessed the raising of Jairus' daughter to life, the transfiguration, the agony of Jesus in the Garden of Gethsemani; Mary was commended to his special care by Christ; the fourth Gospel, three Catholic Epistles and Revelation bear his name; according to various accounts, lived at Ephesus in Asia Minor for some time and died a natural death about 100; in art, is represented by an eagle, symbolic of the sublimity of the contents of his Gospel; Dec. 27 (Roman Rite), May 8 (Byzantine Rite).

Jude Thaddeus: One of the Catholic Epistles, the shortest, bears his name; various traditions say he preached the Gospel in Mesopotamia, Persia and elsewhere, and was martyred; in art, is depicted with a halberd, the instrument of his death; Oct. 28 (Roman Rite), June 19 (Byzantine Rite).

Luke: A Greek convert to the Christian community, called "our most dear physician" by Paul, of whom he was a missionary companion; author of the third Gospel and Acts of the Apostles; the place — Achaia, Bithynia, Egypt — and circumstances of his death are not certain; in art, is depicted as a man, a writer, or an ox (because his Gospel starts at the scene of temple sacrifice); Oct. 18.

Mark: A cousin of Barnabas and member of the first Christian community at Jerusalem; a missionary companion of Paul and Barnabas, then of Peter; author of the Gospel which bears his name; according to legend, founded the Church at Alexandria, was bishop there and was martyred in the streets of the city; in art, is depicted with his Gospel and a winged lion, symbolic of the voice of John the Baptist crying in the wilderness, at the beginning of his Gospel; Apr. 25.

Matthew: A Galilean, called Levi by Luke and John and the son of Alphaeus by Mark, a tax collector, one of the Evangelists; according to various accounts, preached the Gospel in Judea, Ethiopia, Persia and Parthia, and was martyred; in art, is depicted with a spear, the instrument of his death, and as a winged man in his role as Evangelist; Sept. 21 (Roman Rite), Nov. 16 (Byzantine Rite).

Matthias: A disciple of Jesus whom the faithful 11 Apostles chose to replace Judas before the Resurrection; uncertain traditions report that he preached the Gospel in Palestine, Cappadocia or Ethiopia; in art, is represented with a cross and a halberd, the instruments of his death as a martyr; May 14 (Roman Rite), Aug. 9 (Byzantine Rite).

Paul: Born at Tarsus, of the tribe of Benjamin, a Roman citizen; participated in the persecution of Christians until the time of his miraculous conversion on the way to Damascus; called by Christ, who revealed himself to him in a special way; became the Apostle of the Gentiles, among whom he did most of his preaching in the course of three major missionary journeys through areas north of Palestine, Cyprus, Asia Minor and Greece; 14 epistles bear his name; two years of imprisonment at Rome, following initial arrest in Jerusalem and confinement at Caesarea, ended with martyrdom, by beheading, outside the walls of the city in 64 or 67 during the Neronian persecution; in art, is depicted in various ways with St. Peter, with a sword, in the scene of his conversion; June 29 (with St. Peter), Jan. 25 (Conversion).

Peter: Simon, son of Jona, born in Bethsaida, brother of Andrew, a fisherman; called Cephas or Peter by Christ who made him the chief of the Apostles and head of the Church as his vicar; named first in the listings of Apostles in the Synoptic Gospels and the Acts of the Apostles; with James the Greater and John, witnessed the raising of Jairus' daughter to life, the transfiguration, the agony of Jesus in the Garden of Gethsemani; was the first to preach the Gospel in and around Jerusalem and was the leader of the first Christian community there; established a local church in Antioch; presided over the Council of Jerusalem in 51; wrote two Catholic Epistles to the Christians in Asia Minor; established his see in Rome where he spent his last years and was martyred by crucifixion in 64 or 65 during the Neronian persecution; in art, is depicted carrying two keys, symbolic of his primacy in the Church; June 29 (with St. Paul), Feb. 22 (Chair of Peter).

Philip: Born in Bethsaida; according to legend, preached the Gospel in Phrygia where he suffered martyrdom by crucifixion; May 3 (Roman Rite), Nov. 14 (Byzantine Rite).

Simon: Called the Cananean or the Zealot; according to legend, preached in various places in the Middle East and suffered martyrdom by being sawed in two; in art, is depicted with a saw, the instrument of his death, or a book, symbolic of his zeal for the Law; Oct. 28 (Roman Rite), May 10 (Byzantine Rite).

Thomas (Didymus): Notable for his initial incredulity regarding the Resurrection and his subsequent forthright confession of the divinity of Christ risen from the dead; according to legend, preached the

Gospel in places from the Caspian Sea to the Persian Gulf and eventually reached India where he was martyred near Madras; Thomas Christians trace their origin to him; in art, is depicted kneeling before the risen Christ, or with a carpenter's rule and square; feast, July 3 (Roman Rite), Oct. 6 (Byzantine Rite).

Judas

The Gospels record only a few facts about Judas, the Apostle who betrayed Christ.

The only non-Galilean among the Apostles, he was from Carioth, a town in southern Judah. He was keeper of the purse in the apostolic band. He was called a petty thief by John. He voiced dismay at the waste of money, which he said might have been spent for the poor, in connection with the anointing incident at Bethany. He took the initiative in arranging the betrayal of Christ. Afterwards, he confessed that he had betrayed an innocent man and cast into the Temple the money he had received for that action. Of his death, Matthew says that he hanged himself; the Acts of the Apostles states that he swelled up and burst open; both reports deal more with the meaning than the manner of his death — the misery of the death of a sinner.

The consensus of speculation over the reason why Judas acted as he did in betraying Christ focuses on disillusionment and unwillingness to accept the concept of a suffering Messiah and personal suffering of his own as an Apostle.

APOSTOLIC FATHERS, FATHERS, DOCTORS OF THE CHURCH

The writers listed below were outstanding and authoritative witnesses to authentic Christian belief and practice, and played significant roles in giving them expression.

Apostolic Fathers

The Apostolic Fathers were Christian writers of the first and second centuries whose writings echo genuine apostolic teaching. Chief in importance are: St. Clement (d.c. 97), bishop of Rome and third successor of St. Peter in the papacy; St. Ignatius (50-c. 107), bishop of Antioch and second successor of St. Peter in that see, reputed to be a disciple of St. John; St. Polycarp (69-155), bishop of Smyrna and a disciple of St. John. The authors of the Didache and the Epistle of Barnabas are also numbered among the Apostolic Fathers.

Other early ecclesiastical writers included: St. Justin, martyr (100-165), of Asia Minor and Rome, a layman and apologist; St. Irenaeus (130-202), bishop of Lyons, who opposed Gnosticism; and St. Cyprian (210-258), bishop of Carthage, who opposed Novatianism.

Fathers and Doctors

The Fathers of the Church were theologians and writers of the first eight centuries who were outstanding for sanctity and learning. They were such authoritative witnesses to the belief and teaching of the Church that their unanimous acceptance of doctrines as divinely revealed has been regarded as evidence that such doctrines were so received by the Church in line with apostolic tradition and Sacred Scripture. Their unanimous rejection of doctrines branded them as heretical. Their writings, however, were not necessarily free of error in all respects.

The greatest of these Fathers were: Sts. Ambrose, Augustine, Jerome and Gregory the Great in the West; Sts. John Chrysostom, Basil the Great, Gregory of Nazianzen and Athanasius in the East.

The Doctors of the Church were ecclesiastical writers of eminent learning and sanctity who have been given this title because of the great advantage the Church has derived from their work. Their writings, however, were not necessarily free of error in all respects.

Albert the Great, St. (c. 1200-1280): Born in Swabia, Germany; Dominican; bishop of Regensburg (1260-1262); wrote extensively on logic, natural sciences, ethics, metaphysics, Scripture, systematic theology; contributed to development of Scholasticism; teacher of St. Thomas Aquinas; canonized and proclaimed doctor, 1931; named patron of natural scientists, 1941; called Doctor Universalis, Doctor Expertus; Nov. 15.

Alphonsus Liguori, St. (1696-1787): Born near Naples, Italy; bishop of Saint Agatha of the Goths (1762-1775); founder of the Redemptorists; in addition to his principal work, *Theologiae Moralis*, wrote on prayer, the spiritual life and doctrinal subjects in response to controversy; canonized, 1839; proclaimed doctor, 1871; named patron of confessors and moralists, 1950; Aug. 1.

Ambrose, St. (c. 340-397): Born in Trier, Germany; bishop of Milan (374-397); one of the strongest opponents of Arianism in the West; his homilies and other writings — on faith, the Holy Spirit, the Incarnation, the sacraments and other subjects — were pastoral and practical; influenced the development of a liturgy at Milan which was named for him; Father and Doctor of the Church; Dec. 7.

Anselm, St. (1033-1109): Born in Aosta, Piedmont, Italy; Benedictine; archbishop of Canterbury (1093-1109); in addition to his principal work, Cur Deus Homo, on the atonement and reconciliation of man with God through Christ, wrote about the existence and attributes of God and defended the Filioque explanation of the procession of the Holy Spirit from the Father and the Son; proclaimed doctor, 1720; called Father of Scholasticism; Apr. 21.

Anthony of Padua, St. (1195-1231): Born in Lisbon, Portugal; first theologian of the Franciscan Order; preacher; canonized, 1232; proclaimed doctor, 1946; called Evangelical Doctor; June 13.

Athanasius, St. (c. 297-373): Born in Alexandria, Egypt; bishop of Alexandria (328-373); participant in the Council of Nicaea I while still a deacon; dominant opponent of Arians whose errors regarding Christ he refuted in *Apology against the Arians, Discourses against the Arians* and other works; Father and Doctor of the Church; called Father of Orthodoxy; May 2.

Augustine, St. (354-430): Born in Tagaste, North Africa; bishop of Hippo (395-430) after conversion from Manichaeism; works include the autobiographical and mystical *Confessions, City of God*, treatises on the Trinity, grace, passages of the Bible and doctrines called into question and denied by Manichaeans, Pelagians and Donatists; had strong and lasting influence on Christian theology and philosophy; Father and Doctor of the Church; called Doctor of Grace; Aug. 28.

Basil the Great, St. (c. 329-379): Born in Caesarea, Cappadocia, Asia Minor; bishop of Caesarea (370-379); wrote three books *Contra Eunomium* in refutation of Arian errors, a treatise on the Holy Spirit, many homilies and several rules for monastic life, on which he had lasting influence; Father and Doctor of the Church; called Father of Monasticism in the East; Jan. 2.

Bede the Venerable, St. (c. 673-735): Born in Northumberland, England; Benedictine; in addition to his principal work, *Ecclesiastical History of the English Nation* (covering the period 597-731), wrote scriptural commentaries; regarded as probably the most learned man in Western Europe of his time; called Father of English History; May 25.

Bernard of Clairvaux, St. (c. 1090-1153): Born near Dijon, France; abbot; monastic reformer, called the second founder of the Cistercian Order; mystical theologian with great influence on devotional life; opponent of the rationalism brought forward by Abelard and others; canonized, 1174; proclaimed doctor, 1830; called Mellifluous Doctor because of his eloquence; Aug. 20.

Bonaventure, St. (c. 1217-1274): Born near Viterbo, Italy; Franciscan; bishop of Albano (1273-1274); cardinal; wrote *Itinerarium Mentis in Deum, De ReductioneArtium adTheologiam, Breviloquium,* scriptural commentaries, additional mystical works affecting devotional life and a life of St. Francis of Assisi; canonized, 1482; proclaimed doctor, 1588; called Seraphic Doctor; July 15.

Catherine of Siena, St. (c. 1347-1380): Born in Siena, Italy; member of the Third Order of St. Dominic; mystic; authored a long series of letters, mainly concerning spiritual instruction and encouragement, to associates, and *Dialogue*, a spiritual testament in four treatises; was active in support of a crusade against the Turks and efforts to end war between papal forces and the Florentine allies; had great influence in inducing Gregory XI to return himself and the Curia to Rome in 1377, to end the Avignon period of the papacy; canonized, 1461; proclaimed the second woman doctor, Oct. 4, l970; Apr. 29.

Cyril of Alexandria, St. (c. 376-444): Born in Egypt; bishop of Alexandria (412-444); wrote treatises on the Trinity, the Incarnation and other subjects, mostly in refutation of Nestorian errors; made key contributions to the development of Christology; presided at the Council of Ephesus, 431; proclaimed doctor, 1882; June 27.

Cyril of Jerusalem, St. (c. 315-386): Bishop of Jerusalem from 350; vigorous opponent of Arianism; principal work, *Catecheses,* a pre-baptismal explanation of the creed of Jerusalem; proclaimed doctor, 1882; Mar. 18.

Ephraem, St. (c. 306-373): Born in Nisibis, Mesopotamia; counteracted the spread of Gnostic and Arian errors with poems and hymns of his own composition; wrote also on the Eucharist and Mary; proclaimed doctor, 1920; called Deacon of Edessa and Harp of the Holy Spirit; June 9.

Francis de Sales, St. (1567-1622): Born in Savoy; bishop of Geneva (1602-1622); spiritual writer with strong influence on devotional life through treatises such as Introduction to a Devout Life, and The Love of God; canonized, 1665; proclaimed doctor, 1877; patron of Catholic writers and the Catholic press; Jan. 24.

Gregory Nazianzen, St. (c. 330-c. 390): Born in Arianzus, Cappadocia, Asia Minor; bishop of Constantinople (381-390); vigorous opponent of Arianism; in addition to five theological discourses on the Nicene Creed and the Trinity for which he is best known, wrote letters and poetry; Father and Doctor of the Church; called the Christian Demosthenes because of his eloquence and, in the Eastern Church, The Theologian; Jan. 2.

Gregory I, the Geat, St.. (c. 540-604): Born in Rome; pope (590-604): wrote many scriptural commentaries, a compendium of theology in the *Book of Morals* based on Job, Dialogues concerning the lives of saints, the immortality of the soul, death, purgatory, heaven and hell, and 14 books of letters; enforced papal supremacy and established the position of the pope vis-a-vis the emperor; worked for clerical and monastic reform and the observance of clerical celibacy; Father and Doctor of the Church; Sept. 3.

Hilary of Poitiers, St. (c. 315-368): Born in Poitiers, France; bishop of Poitiers (c. 353-368); wrote *De Synodis,* with the Arian controversy in mind, and *De Trinitate,* the first lengthy study of the doctrine in Latin; introduced Eastern theology to the West; contributed to the development of hymnology; proclaimed doctor, 1851; called the Athanasius of the West because of his vigorous defense of the divinity of Christ against Arians; Jan. 13.

Isidore of Seville, St. (c. 560-636): Born in Cartagena, Spain; bishop of Seville (c. 600-636); in addition to his principal work, *Etymologiae,* an encyclopedia of the knowledge of his day, wrote on theological and historical subjects; regarded as the most learned man of his time; proclaimed doctor, 1722; Apr. 4.

Jerome, St. (c. 343-420): Born in Stridon, Dalmatia; translated the OldTestament from Hebrew into Latin and revised the existing Latin translation of the New Testament to produce the Vulgate version of the Bible; wrote scriptural commentaries and treatises on matters of controversy; regarded as Father and Doctor of the Church from the eighth century; called Father of Biblical Science; Sept. 30.

John Chrysostom, St. (c. 347-407): Born in Antioch, Asia Minor; archbishop of Constantinople (398-407); wrote homilies, scriptural commentaries and letters of wide influence in addition to a classical treatise on the priesthood; proclaimed doctor by the Council of Chalcedon, 451; called the greatest of the Greek Fathers; named patron of preachers, 1909; called Golden-Mouthed because of his eloquence; Sept. 13.

John Damascene, St. (c. 675-c. 749): Born in Damascus, Syria; monk; wrote *Fountain of Wisdom,* a three-part work including a history of heresies and an exposition of the Christian faith, three Discourses against the Iconoclasts, homilies on Mary, biblical commentaries and treatises on moral subjects; proclaimed doctor, 1890; called Golden Speaker because of his eloquence; Dec. 4.

John of the Cross, St. (1542-1591): Born in Old Castile, Spain; Carmelite; founder of Discalced Carmelites; one of the greatest mystical theologians, wrote *The Ascent of Mt. Carmel — The Dark Night, The Spiritual Canticle, The Living Flame of Love;* canonized, 1726; proclaimed doctor, 1926; called Doctor of Mystical Theology; Dec. 14.

Lawrence of Brindisi, St. (1559-1619): Born in Brindisi, Italy; Franciscan (Capuchin); vigorous preacher of strong influence in the post-Reformation period; 15 tomes of collected works include scriptural commentaries, sermons, homilies and doctrinal writings; canonized, 1881; proclaimed doctor, 1959; July 21.

Leo I, the Great, St. (c. 400-461): Born in Tuscany, Italy; pope (440-461); wrote the *Tome of Leo,* to explain doctrine concerning the two natures and one Person of Christ, against the background of the Nestorian and Monophysite heresies; other works included sermons, letters and writings against the errors of Manichaeism and Pelagianism; was instrumental in dissuading Attila from sacking Rome in 452; proclaimed doctor, 1574; Nov. 10.

Peter Canisius, St. (1521-1597): Born in Nijmegen, Holland; Jesuit; wrote popular expositions of the Catholic faith in several catechisms which were widely circulated in 20 editions in his lifetime alone; was one of the moving figures in the Counter-Reformation period, especially in southern and western Germany; canonized and proclaimed doctor, 1925; Dec. 21.

Peter Chrysologus, St. (c. 400-450): Born in Imola, Italy; served as archbishop of Ravenna (c. 433-450); his sermons and writings, many of which were designed to counteract Monophysitism, were pastoral and practical; proclaimed doctor, 1729; July 30.

Peter Damian, St. (1007-1072): Born in Ravenna, Italy; Benedictine; cardinal; his writings and sermons, many of which concerned ecclesiastical and clerical reform, were pastoral and practical; proclaimed doctor, 1828; Feb. 21.

Robert Bellarmine, St. (1542-1621): Born in Tuscany, Italy; Jesuit; archbishop of Capua (1602-1605); wrote Controversies, a three-volume exposition of doctrine under attack during and after the Reformation, two catechisms and the spiritual work, *The Art of Dying Well;* was an authority on ecclesiology and Church-state relations; canonized, 1930; proclaimed doctor, 1931; Sept. 17.

Teresa of Jesus (Avila), St. (1515-1582): Born in Avila, Spain; entered the Carmelite Order, 1535; in the early 1560s, initiated a primitive Carmelite, discalced-Alcantarine reform which greatly influenced men and women religious, especially in Spain; wrote extensively on spiritual and mystical subjects; principal works included her *Autobiography, Way of Perfection, The Interior Castle, Meditations on the Canticle, The Foundations, Visitation of the Discalced Nuns;* canonized, 1622; proclaimed first woman doctor, Sept. 27, 1970; Oct. 15.

Thomas Aquinas, St. (1225-1274): Born near Naples, Italy; Dominican; teacher and writer on virtually the whole range of philosophy and theology; principal works were Summa contra Gentiles, a manual and systematic defense of Christian doctrine, and *Summa Theologiae,* a new (at that time) exposition of theology on philosophical principles; canonized, 1323; proclaimed doctor, 1567; called Doctor Communis, Doctor Angelicus, the Great Synthesizer because of the way in which he related faith and reason, theology and philosophy (especially that of Aristotle), and systematized the presentation of Christian doctrine; named patron of Catholic schools and education, 1880; Jan. 28.

CREEDS

Creeds are formal and official statements of Christian doctrine. As summaries of the principal truths of faith, they are standards of orthodoxy and are useful for instructional purposes, for actual profession of the faith and for expression of the faith in the liturgy.

The classical creeds are the Apostles' Creed and the Creed of Nicaea-Constantinople. Two others are the Athanasian Creed and the Creed of Pius IV.

Apostles' Creed

Text: I believe in God, the Father almighty, Creator of heaven and earth.

And in Jesus Christ, his only Son, our Lord; who was conceived by the Holy Spirit, born of the Virgin Mary, suffered under Pontius Pilate, was crucified, died, and was buried. He descended into hell; the third day he arose again from the dead; he ascended into heaven, sits at the right hand of God, the Father almighty; from thence he shall come to judge the living and the dead.

I believe in the Holy Spirit, the holy Catholic Church, the communion of saints, the forgiveness of sins, the resurrection of the body, and life everlasting. Amen.

Background: The Apostles' Creed reflects the teaching of the Apostles but is not of apostolic origin. It probably originated in the second century as a rudimentary formula of faith professed by catechumens before the reception of baptism. Baptismal creeds in fourth-century use at Rome and elsewhere in the West closely resembled the present text, which was quoted in a handbook of Christian doctrine written between 710 and 724. This text was in wide use throughout the West by the ninth century. The Apostles' Creed is common to all Christian confessional churches in the West, but is not used in Eastern Churches.

Nicene Creed

The following translation of the Latin text of the creed was prepared by the International Committee on English in the Liturgy.

Text: We believe in one God, the Father, the Almighty, maker of heaven and earth, of all that is seen and unseen.

We believe in one Lord, Jesus Christ, the only Son of God, eternally begotten of the Father, God from God, Light from Light, true God from true God, begotten, not made, one in Being with the Father. Through him all things were made. For us men and for our salvation he came down from heaven: by the power of the Holy Spirit he was born of the Virgin Mary, and became man. For our sake he was crucified under Pontius Pilate; he suffered, died, and was buried. On the third day he rose again in fulfillment of the Scriptures; he ascended into heaven and is seated at the right hand of the Father. He will come again in glory to judge the living and the dead, and his kingdom will have no end.

We believe in the Holy Spirit, the Lord, the giver of life, who proceeds from the Father and the Son. With the Father and the Son he is worshiped and glorified. He has spoken through the prophets.

We believe in one holy catholic and apostolic Church. We acknowledge one baptism for the forgiveness of sins. We look for the resurrection of the dead, and the life of the world to come. Amen.

Background: The Nicene Creed (Creed of Nicaea-Constantinople) consists of elements of doctrine contained in an early baptismal creed of Jerusalem and enactments of the Council of Nicaea (325) and the Council of Constantinople (381). Its strong trinitarian content reflects the doctrinal errors, especially of Arianism, it served to counteract. Theologically, it is much more sophisticated than the Apostles' Creed. Since late in the fifth century the Nicene Creed has been the only creed in liturgical use in the Eastern Churches. The Western Church adopted it for liturgical use by the end of the eighth century.

The Athanasian Creed

The Athanasian Creed, which has a unique structure, is a two-part summary of doctrine concerning the Trinity and the Incarnation-Redemption bracketed at the beginning and end with the statement that belief in the cited truths is necessary for salvation; it also contains a number of anathemas or condemnatory clauses regarding doctrinal errors. Although attributed to St. Athanasius, it was probably written after his death, between 381 and 428, and may have been authored by St. Ambrose. It is not accepted in the East; in the West, it formerly had place in the Roman-Rite Liturgy of the Hours and in the liturgy for the Solemnity of the Holy Trinity.

Creed of Pius IV

The Creed of Pius IV, also called the Profession of Faith of the Council of Trent, was promulgated in the bull *Injunctum Nobis,* Nov. 13, 1564. It is a summary of doctrine defined by the council concerning: Scripture and tradition, original sin and justification, the Mass and sacraments, veneration of the saints, indulgences, the primacy of the See of Rome. It was slightly modified in 1887 to include doctrinal formulations of the First Vatican Council.

MORAL OBLIGATIONS

The basic norm of Christian morality is life in Christ. This involves, among other things, the observance of the Ten Commandments, their fulfillment in the twofold law of love of God and neighbor, the implications of the Sermon on the Mount and the whole New Testament, and membership in the Church established by Christ.

THE TEN COMMANDMENTS

The Ten Commandments, the Decalogue, were given by God through Moses to his Chosen People for the guidance of their moral conduct in accord with the demands of the Covenant he established with them as a divine gift.

In the traditional Catholic enumeration and according to Dt. 5:6-21, the Commandments are:

1. "I, the Lord, am your God You shall not have other gods besides me. You shall not carve idols."

2. "You shall not take the name of the Lord, your God, in vain."

3. "Take care to keep holy the Sabbath day."

4. "Honor your father and your mother."

5. "You shall not kill."

6. "You shall not commit adultery."

7. "You shall not steal."

8. "You shall not bear dishonest witness against your neighbor."

9. "You shall not covet your neighbor's wife."

10. "You shall not desire your neighbor's house or field, nor his male or female slave, nor his ox or ass, nor anything that belongs to him (summarily, his goods).

Another version of the Commandments, substantially the same, is given in Ex. 20:1-17.

The traditional enumeration of the Commandments in Protestant usage differs from the above. Thus: two commandments are made of the first, as above; the third and fourth are equivalent to the second and third, as above, and so on; and the 10th includes the ninth and 10th, as above.

Love of God and Neighbor

The first three of the commandments deal directly with man's relations with God, viz.: acknowledgment of one true God and the rejection of false gods and idols; honor due to God and his name; observance of the Sabbath as the Lord's day.

The rest cover interpersonal relationships, viz.: the obedience due to parents and, logically, to other persons in authority, and the obligations of parents to children and of persons in authority to those under their care; respect for life and physical integrity; fidelity in marriage, and chastity; justice and rights; truth; internal respect for faithfulness in marriage, chastity, and the goods of others.

Perfection in Christian Life

The moral obligations of the Ten Commandments are complemented by others flowing from the twofold law of love, the whole substance and pattern of Christ's teaching, and everything implied in full and active membership and participation in the community of salvation formed by Christ in his Church. Some of these matters are covered in other sections of the Almanac under appropriate headings.

Precepts of the Church

The purpose of the precepts of the Church, according to the *Catechism of the Catholic Church*, is "to guarantee to the faithful the indispensable minimum in the spirit of prayer and moral effort, in the growth and love of God and neighbor" (No. 2041).

1. Attendance at Mass on Sundays and holy days of obligation. (Observance of Sundays and holy days of obligation involves refraining from work that hinders the worship due to God.)

2. Confession of sins at least once a year. (Not required by the precept in the absence of serious sin.)

3. Reception of the Eucharist at least during the Easter season (in the U.S., from the first Sunday of Lent to Trinity Sunday).

4. Keep holy the holy days of obligation.

5. Observance of specified days of fasting and abstinence.

There is also an obligation to provide for the material needs of the Church.

SOCIAL DOCTRINE

Since the end of the last century, Catholic social doctrine has been formulated in a progressive manner in a number of authoritative documents.

Outstanding examples are the encyclicals: *Rerum Novarum* ("On Capital and Labor") issued by Leo XIII in 1891; *Quadragesimo Anno* ("On Reconstruction of the Social Order") by Pius XI in 1931; *Mater et Magistra* ("Christianity and Social Progress") and *Pacem in Terris* ("Peace on Earth"), by John XXIII in 1961 and 1963, respectively; *Populorum Progressio* ("Development of Peoples"), by Paul VI in 1967; *Laborem Exercens* ("On Human Work"), *Sollicitudo Rei Socialis* ("On Social Concerns") and *Centesimus Annus* ("The 100th Year") by John Paul II in 1981, 1987 and 1991, respectively. Pius XII, among other accomplishments of ideological importance in the social field, made a distinctive contribution with his formulation of a plan for world peace and order in Christmas messages from 1939 to 1941, and in other documents.

Of particular significance are the "Pastoral Constitution on the Church in the Modern World" *(Gaudium et Spes)* issued by the Second Vatican Council and Pope John Paul's encyclical letter, *Centesimus Annus* ("The 100thYear").

These documents represent the most serious attempts in modern times to systematize the social implications of divine revelation as well as the socially relevant writings of the Fathers and Doctors of the Church. Their contents are theological penetrations into social life, with particular reference to human rights, the needs of the poor and those in underdeveloped countries, and humane conditions of life, freedom, justice and peace. In some respects, they read like juridical documents; essentially, however, they are Gospel-oriented and pastoral in intention.

Following are brief descriptions of the nature of social teaching, the contents of the pastoral constitution, and extensive excerpts from Centesimus Annus.

Nature of the Doctrine

Pope John XXIII, writing in *Christianity and Social Progress,* made the following statement about the nature and scope of the doctrine stated in the encyclicals in particular and related writings in general.

"What the Catholic Church teaches and declares regarding the social life and relationships of men is beyond question for all time valid.

"The cardinal point of this teaching is that individual men are necessarily the foundation, cause, and end of all social institutions insofar as they are social by nature, and raised to an order of existence that transcends and subdues nature.

"Beginning with this very basic principle whereby the dignity of the human person is affirmed and defended, Holy Church — especially during the last century and with the assistance of learned priests and laymen, specialists in the field — has arrived at clear social teachings whereby the mutual relationships of men are ordered. Taking general norms into account, these principles are in accord with the nature of things and the changed conditions of man's social life, or with the special genius of our day. Moreover, these norms can be approved by all."

THE CHURCH IN THE WORLD

Even more Gospel-oriented and pastoral in a distinctive way is the *Pastoral Constitution on the Church in the Modern World* promulgated by the Second Vatican Council in 1965.

Its purpose is to search out the signs of God's presence and meaning in and through the events of this time in human history. Accordingly, it deals with the situation of men in present circumstances of profound change, challenge and crisis on all levels of life.

The first part of the constitution develops the theme of the Church and man's calling, and focuses attention on the dignity of the human person, the problem of atheism, the community of mankind, man's activity throughout the world, and the serving and saving role of the Church in the world. This portion of the document, it has been said, represents the first presentation by the Church in an official text of an organized Christian view of man and society.

The second part of the document considers several problems of special urgency: fostering the nobility of marriage and the family (see Marriage Doctrine), the proper development of culture, socio-economic life, the life of the political community, the fostering of peace, and the promotion of a community of nations.

In conclusion, the constitution calls for action to implement doctrine regarding the role and work of the Church for the total good of mankind.

"Economic Progress: Looking Beyond the Numbers," is the title of the 1997 Labor Day Statement of the bishops of the United States. It represents a recent articulation of salient aspects of socio-economic concerns in the light of church teaching. (See separate article.)

CENTESIMUS ANNUS: ENCYCLICAL LETTER

Centesimus Annus ("The 100th Year"), the title of Pope John Paul's ninth encyclical letter, commemorated the 100th anniversary of Pope Leo XIII's encyclical *Rerum Novarum* ("On Capital and Labor"). Dated May 1, 1991, it was made public the following day. Its publication was one of the principal events of the year dedicated to commemoration and study of the social teaching of the Church.

Following are excerpts (in quotations) from the text circulated by the CNS Documentary Service, Origins, May 16, 1991 (Vol. 21,No. 1). Subheads have been added. Quotations indicated by single quotation marks are from other encyclicals, documents of the Second Vatican Council and other authoritative sources.

INTRODUCTION

3. "The present encyclical seeks to show the fruitfulness of the principles enunciated by Leo XIII, which belong to the Church's doctrinal patrimony and as such involve the exercise of her teaching authority. But pastoral solicitude also prompts me to propose an analysis of some events of recent history. Such an analysis is not meant to pass definitive judgments, since this does not fall per se within the magisterium's specific domain."

CHAPTER 1

Characteristics of Rerum Novarum

5. "The 'new things' to which the Pope devoted his attention were anything but positive. The first paragraph of the encyclical describes in strong terms the 'new things' (*rerum novarum*) which gave it its name: 'That the spirit of revolutionary change which has long been disturbing the nations of the world should have passed beyond the sphere of politics and made its influence felt in the related sphere of practical economics is not surprising. Progress in industry, the development of new trades, the changing relationship between employers and workers, the enormous wealth of a few as opposed to the poverty of the many, the increasing self-reliance of the workers and their closer association with each other, as well as a notable decline in morality: All these elements have led to the conflict now taking place.'"

"The Pope and the Church with him were confronted, as was the civil community, by a society which was torn by a conflict all the more harsh and inhumane because it knew no rule or regulation. It was the conflict between capital and labor or — as the encyclical puts it — the worker question."

Conditions for Justice

"What was essential to the encyclical was precisely its proclamation of the fundamental conditions for justice in the economic and social situation of the time."

"To teach and to spread her social doctrine pertains to the Church's evangelizing mission and is an essential part of the Christian message, since this doctrine points out the direct consequences of that message in the life of society and situates daily work and struggles for justice in the context of bearing witness to Christ the Savior. This doctrine is likewise a source of unity and peace in dealing with the conflicts which inevitably arise in social and economic life."

"We need to repeat that there can be no genuine solution of the 'social question' apart from the Gospel, and that the 'new things' can find in the Gospel the context for their correct understanding and the proper moral perspective for judgment on them."

Fundamental Rights

6. "Pope Leo XIII affirmed the fundamental rights of workers. Indeed, the key to reading the encyclical is the dignity of the worker as such and, for the same reason, the dignity of work."

7. to 9. The encyclical stated the important principle of the right to "private property," duly qualified by the "complementary" principle of "the universal destination of the earth's goods" for the good of all.

Also affirmed were the natural right to form private associations, the right to the limitation of working hours, the right to legitimate rest, and the right of children and women to be treated differently with regard to the type and duration of work, the right to a just wage (which should be sufficient to enable a worker to support himself, his wife and his children), and the right to religious freedom.

11. "Pope Leo's encyclical is an encyclical on the poor and on the terrible conditions to which the new and often violent process of industrialization had reduced great multitudes of people."

The Guiding Principle

"The main thread and in a certain sense the guiding principle of Pope Leo's encyclical and of all of the Church's social doctrine is a correct view of the human person and of his unique value, inasmuch as 'man is the only creature on earth which God willed for itself.' God has imprinted his own image and likeness on man, conferring upon him an incomparable dignity, as the encyclical frequently insists. In effect, beyond the rights which man acquires by his own work, there exist rights which do not correspond to any work he performs but which flow from his essential dignity as a person."

CHAPTER 2

Toward the 'New Things' of Today

12. "Pope Leo foresaw the negative consequences — political, social and economic — of the social order proposed by 'socialism.' "

13. He defined the nature of the socialism of his day as "the suppression of private property," and said "its fundamental error is anthropological in nature." It "considers the individual person simply as an element, a molecule within the social organism, so that the good of the individual is completely subordinated to the functioning of the socio-economic organism. Man is thus reduced to a series of social relationships."

However, "according to *Rerum Novarum* and the whole social doctrine of the Church, the social nature of man is not completely fulfilled in the state, but is realized in various intermediary groups, beginning with the family and including economic, social, political and cultural groups which stem from human nature itself and have their own autonomy, always with a view to the common good."

Atheism's Mistaken Concept

"The first cause of the mistaken concept of the nature of the person is atheism. The denial of God deprives the person of his foundation and consequently leads to a reorganization of the social order without reference to the person's dignity and responsibility."

14. Consequences of socialism, atheism and related errors are class struggle, militarism, war, subjection of people to the state, and a whole range of political, social and economic evils.

CHAPTER 3

The Year 1989

22. Centesimus Annus notes that "unexpected and promising" events of recent years have produced notable changes in countries in Eastern and Central Europe, as also in nations of Latin America, Asia and Africa. Contributing to these developments was the Church's commitment to human rights. Coupled with the developments was hope for progressive change and for the solution of problems through the exercise of dialogue and negotiation.

23. Among factors involved in the fall of oppressive regimes were the violation of workers' rights (called decisive), peaceful protest through dialogue and negotiation as opposed to Marxist violence, and witness to the truth about conditions, etc.

24. Another factor was the inefficiency of the (Marxist) economic system. The inefficiency was not so much technological as a consequence of violations of human rights to private initiative, ownership of property and economic freedom. A related factor was the failure of oppressive regimes to realize the importance of culture for the understanding of people.

Spiritual Void

The true cause of the fall of oppressive regimes was the spiritual void brought about by atheism; because of this void, people were cast adrift without any sense of direction. Another cause was the witness of the faithful to truth.

25. to 27. Events of 1989, which had effects not only in Eastern and Central Europe but also in Third World and other countries, were an example of the success achievable by a willingness to negotiate and of the success of the Gospel spirit to stand for moral principles, come what may.

Need for Reconciliation and Rebuilding

28. "The radical reordering of economic systems, hitherto collectivized, entails problems and sacrifices. It is right that in the present difficulties the formerly communist countries should be aided by the united effort of other nations. Obviously they themselves must be the primary agents of their own development, but they must also be given a reasonable opportunity to accomplish this goal, something

that cannot happen without the help of other countries." Such help, however, should not lead to neglect of the Third World or abandonment of the poor. Special effort must be made to mobilize resources necessary for development in the Third World.

29. "Development must not be understood solely in economic terms, but in a way that is fully human. The apex of development is the exercise of the right and duty to seek God, to know him and to live in accordance with that knowledge."

CHAPTER 4

Private Property and the Universal Destination of Material Goods

30. "In Rerum Novarum, Leo XIII strongly affirmed the natural character of the right to private property. This right, which is fundamental for the autonomy and development of the person, has always been defended by the Church up to our own day. At the same time, the Church teaches that the possession of material goods is not an absolute right and that its limits are inscribed in its very nature as a human right.

"While the Pope proclaimed the right to private ownership, he affirmed with equal clarity that the 'use' of goods, while marked by freedom, is subordinated to their original common destination" for the common good.

"Of its nature, private property has a social function which is based on the law of the common purpose of goods."

Origin of Material Goods

31. "The question can be raised concerning the origin of the material goods which sustain human life, satisfy people's needs and are an object of their rights.

"The original source of all that is good is the very act of God, who created both the earth and man, and who gave the earth to man so that he might have dominion over it by his work and enjoy its fruits (Gn. 1:28). God gave the earth to the whole human race for the sustenance of all its members, without excluding or favoring anyone. This is the foundation of the universal destination of the earth's goods. The earth, by reason of its fruitfulness and its capacity to satisfy human needs, is God's first gift for the sustenance of human life. But the earth does not yield its fruits without a particular human response to God's gift, that is to say, without work. It is through work that man, using his intelligence and exercising his freedom, succeeds in dominating the earth and making it a fitting home. In this way, he makes part of the earth his own, precisely the part which he has acquired through work; this is the origin of individual property. Obviously, he also has the responsibility not to hinder others from having their own part of God's gift; indeed, he must cooperate with others so that together all can dominate the earth."

Work and the Land

"In history, these two factors — work and the land — are to be found at the beginning of every human society. However, they do not always stand in the same relationship to each other. At one time the natural fruitfulness of the earth appeared to be, and was in fact, the primary factor of wealth, while work was, as it were, the help and support for this fruitfulness. In our time, the role of human work is becoming increasingly important as the productive factor both of non-material and of material wealth. Moreover, it is becoming clearer how a person's work is naturally interrelated with the work of others. More than ever, work is work with others and work for others: it is a matter of doing something for someone else. Work becomes ever more fruitful and productive to the extent that people become more knowledgeable of the productive potentialities of the earth and more profoundly cognizant of the needs of those for whom their work is done."

Ownership of Know-How

32. "In our time, in particular, there exists another form of ownership which is becoming no less important than land: the possession of know-how, technology and skill. The wealth of the industrialized nations is based much more on this kind of ownership than on natural resources."

"Today the decisive factor (in production) is increasingly man himself, that is, his knowledge, especially his scientific knowledge, his capacity for interrelated and compact organization, as well as his ability to perceive the needs of others and to satisfy them."

The Free Market

34. "It would appear that, on the level of individual nations and of international relations, the free market is the most efficient instrument for utilizing resources and effectively responding to needs." But this is true only for those needs which are "solvent," insofar as they are endowed with purchasing power, and for those resources which are "marketable," insofar as they are capable of obtaining a satisfactory price. But there are many human needs which find no place on the market. It is a strict duty of justice and truth not to allow fundamental human needs to remain unsatisfied, and not allow those burdened by such needs to perish. It is also necessary to help these needy people to acquire expertise, to enter the circle of exchange, and to develop their skills in order to make the best use of their capacities and resources. Even prior to the logic of a fair exchange of goods and the forms of justice appropriate to it, there exists something which is due to man because he is man, by reason of his lofty dignity. Inseparable from that required "something" is the possibility to survive and, at the same time, to make "an active contribution to the common good of humanity."

35. "Trade unions and other workers' organizations defend workers' rights and protect their interests as persons, while fulfilling a vital cultural role, so as to enable workers to participate more fully and honorably in the life of their nation and to assist them along the path of development."

A Society of Free Work

"In this sense, it is right to speak of a struggle against an economic system, if the latter is understood as a method of upholding the absolute predominance of capital, the possession of the means of production and of the land, in contrast to the free and personal nature of human work. In the struggle against such a system, what is being proposed as an alternative is not the socialist system, which in fact turns out to be state capitalism, but rather a society of free work, of enterprise and of participation. Such a society is not directed against the market, but demands that the market be appropriately controlled by the forces of society and by the state, so as to guarantee that the basic needs of the whole of society are satisfied."

Legitimacy of Profit

"The church acknowledges the legitimate role of profit as an indication that a business is functioning well. When a firm makes a profit, this means that productive factors have been properly employed and corresponding human needs have been duly satisfied. But profitability is not the only indicator of a firm's condition. It is possible for the financial accounts to be in order, and yet for the people — who make up the firm's most valuable asset — to be humiliated and their dignity offended. Besides being morally inadmissible, this will eventually have negative repercussions on the firm's economic efficiency. In fact, the purpose of a business firm is not simply to make a profit, but is to be found in its very existence as a community of persons who in various ways are endeavoring to satisfy their basic needs, and who form a particular group at the service of the whole of society. Profit is a regulator of the life of a business, but it is not the only one; other human and moral factors must also be considered which, in the long term, are at least equally important for the life of a business."

Stronger Nations Must Help

"It is unacceptable to say that the defeat of so-called 'real socialism' leaves capitalism as the only model of economic organization. It is necessary to break down the barriers and monopolies which leave so many countries on the margins of development, and to provide all individuals and nations with the basic conditions which will enable them to share in development. This goal calls for programmed and responsible efforts on the part of the entire international community. Stronger nations must offer weaker ones opportunities for taking their place in international life, and the latter must learn how to use these opportunities by making the necessary efforts and sacrifices, and by ensuring political and economic stability, the certainty of better prospects for the future, the improvement of workers' skills, and the training of competent business leaders who are conscious of their responsibilities."

Third World Debt

"At present, the positive efforts which have been made along these lines are being affected by the still largely unsolved problem of the foreign debt of the poorer countries. The principle that debts must be paid is certainly just. However, it is not right to demand or expect payment when the effect would be the imposition of political choices leading to hunger and despair for entire peoples. It cannot be expected that the debts which have been contracted should be paid at the price of unbearable sacrifices. In such cases it is necessary to find — as in fact is partly happening — ways to lighten, defer or even cancel the debt, compatible with the fundamental right of peoples to subsistence and progress."

Consumerism

36. "A given culture reveals its overall understanding of life through the choices it makes in production and consumption. It is here that the phenomenon of consumerism arises. In singling out new needs and new means to meet them, one must be guided by a comprehensive picture of man which respects all the dimensions of his being and which subordinates his material and instinctive dimensions to his interior and spiritual ones. If, on the contrary, a direct appeal is made to his instincts — while ignoring in various ways the reality of the person as intelligent and free — then consumer attitudes and lifestyles can be created which are objectively improper and often damaging to his physical and spiritual health. Of itself, an economic system does not possess criteria for correctly distinguishing new and higher forms of satisfying human needs from artificial new needs which hinder the formation of a mature personality. Thus, a great deal of educational and cultural work is urgently needed, including the education of consumers in the responsible use of their power of choice, the formation of a strong sense of responsibility among producers and among people in the mass media in particular, as well as the necessary intervention by public authorities."

"It is not wrong to want to live better; what is wrong is a style of life which is presumed to be better when it is directed toward 'having' rather than 'being,' and which wants to have more, not in order to be more but in order to spend life in enjoyment as an end in itself."

Ecological Considerations

37. "Equally worrying is the ecological question which accompanies the problem of consumerism and which is closely connected to it."

38. "In addition to the irrational destruction of the natural environment, we must also mention the more serious destruction of the human environment. Not only has God given the earth to man, who must use it with respect for the original good purpose for which it was given to him, but man too is God's gift to man. He must therefore respect the natural and moral structure with which he has been endowed. In this context, mention should be made of the serious problems of modern urbanization, of the need for urban planning which is concerned with how people are to live, and of the attention which should be given to a 'social ecology' of work.

"Man receives from God his essential dignity and with it the capacity to transcend every social order so as to move toward truth and goodness. But he is also conditioned by the social structure in which he lives, by the education he has received and by his environment. These elements can either help or hinder his living in accordance with the truth. The decisions which create a human environment can give rise to specific structures of sin which impede the full realization of those who are in any way oppressed by them. To destroy such structures and replace them with more au-

thentic forms of living in community is a task which demands courage and patience."

The Family and Human Ecology

39. "The first and fundamental structure for 'human ecology' is the family, in which man receives his first formative ideas about truth and goodness, and learns what it means to love and to be loved, and thus what it actually means to be a person. Here we mean the family founded on marriage, in which the mutual gift of self by husband and wife creates an environment in which children can be born and develop their potentialities, become aware of their dignity and prepare to face their unique and individual destiny." "It is necessary to go back to seeing the family as the sanctuary of life. The family is indeed sacred: it is the place in which life — the gift of God — can be properly welcomed and protected against the many attacks to which it is exposed, and can develop in accordance with what constitutes authentic human growth. In the face of the so-called culture of death, the family is the heart of the culture of life."

Abortion

"Human ingenuity seems to be directed more toward limiting, suppressing or destroying the sources of life — including recourse to abortion, which unfortunately is so widespread in the world — than toward defending and opening up the possibilities of life. The encyclical *Sollicitudo Rei Socialis* denounced systematic anti-childbearing campaigns which, on the basis of a distorted view of the demographic problem and in a climate of 'absolute lack of respect for the freedom of choice of the parties involved,' often subject them 'to intolerable pressures in order to force them to submit to this new form of oppression.' These policies are extending their field of action by the use of new techniques, to the point of poisoning the lives of millions of defenseless human beings, as if in a form of 'chemical warfare.' "

Economic Freedom Not Autonomous

"These criticisms are directed not so much against an economic system as against an ethical and cultural system. The economy in fact is only one aspect and one dimension of the whole of human activity. If economic life is absolutized, if the production and consumption of goods become the center of social life and society's only value, not subject to any other value, the reason is to be found not so much in the economic system itself as in the fact that the entire socio-cultural system, by ignoring the ethical and religious dimension, has been weakened, and ends by limiting itself to the production of goods and services alone.

"All of this can be summed up by repeating once more that economic freedom is only one element of human freedom. When it becomes autonomous, when man is seen more as a producer or consumer of goods than as a subject who produces and consumes in order to live, then economic freedom loses its necessary relationship to the human person and ends up by alienating and oppressing him."

41. "Obedience to the truth about God and man is the first condition of freedom, making it possible for a person to order his needs and desires and to choose the means of satisfying them according to a correct

scale of values, so that the ownership of things may become an occasion of growth for him."

Capitalism

42. "Can it perhaps be said that, after the failure of communism, capitalism is the victorious social system, and that capitalism should be the goal of the countries now making efforts to rebuild their economy and society? Is this the model which ought to be proposed to the countries of the Third World which are searching for the path to true economic and civil progress?

"The answer is obviously complex. If by capitalism is meant an economic system which recognizes the fundamental and positive role of business, the market, private property and the resulting responsibility for the means of production, as well as free human creativity in the economic sector, then the answer is certainly in the affirmative, even though it would perhaps be more appropriate to speak of a *business economy, market economy* or simply *free economy*. But if by capitalism is meant a system in which freedom in the economic sector is not circumscribed within a strong juridical framework which places it at the service of human freedom in its totality, and which sees it as a particular aspect of that freedom, the core of which is ethical and religious, then the reply is certainly negative."

Marginalization Remains

"The Marxist solution has failed, but the realities of marginalization and exploitation remain in the world, especially the Third World, as does the reality of human alienation, especially in the more advanced countries. Against these phenomena the Church strongly raises her voice. Vast multitudes are still living in conditions of great material and moral poverty. The collapse of the communist system in so many countries certainly removes an obstacle to facing these problems in an appropriate and realistic way, but it is not enough to bring about their solution. Indeed, there is a risk that a radical capitalistic ideology could spread which refuses even to consider these problems, in the a priori belief that any attempt to solve them is doomed to failure, and which blindly entrusts their solution to the free development of market forces."

Orientation of Church Teaching

43. "The Church has no models to present; models that are real and truly effective can only arise within the framework of different historical situations, through the efforts of all those who responsibly confront concrete problems in all their social, economic, political and cultural aspects, as these interact with one another. For such a task the church offers her social teaching as an indispensable and ideal orientation, a teaching which, as already mentioned, recognizes the positive value of the market and of enterprise, but which at the same time points out that these need to be oriented toward the common good. This teaching also recognizes the legitimacy of workers' efforts to obtain full respect for their dignity and to gain broader areas of participation in the life of industrial enterprises so that, while cooperating with others and under the direction of others, they can in a certain sense 'work for themselves' through the exercise of their intelligence and freedom.

"The integral development of the human person through work does not impede but rather promotes the greater productivity and efficiency of work itself, even though it may weaken consolidated power structures. A business cannot be considered only as a 'society of capital goods'; it is also a 'society of persons' in which people participate in different ways and with specific responsibilities, whether they supply the necessary capital for the company's activities or take part in such activities through their labor. To achieve these goals there is still need for a broad associated workers' movement, directed toward the liberation and promotion of the whole person."

Private Property and Work

"In the light of today's 'new things,' we have reread the relationship between individual or private property and the universal destination of material wealth. Man fulfills himself by using his intelligence and freedom. In so doing he utilizes the things of this world as objects and instruments and makes them his own. The foundation of the right to private initiative and ownership is to be found in this activity. By means of his work man commits himself, not only for his own sake but also for others and with others. Each person collaborates in the work of others and for their good. Man works in order to provide for the needs of his family, his community, his nation and ultimately all humanity. Moreover, he collaborates in the work of his fellow employees, as well as in the work of suppliers and in the customers' use of goods, in a progressively expanding chain of solidarity. Ownership of the means of production, whether in industry or agriculture, is just and legitimate if it serves useful work. It becomes illegitimate, however, when it is not utilized or when it serves to impede the work of others, in an effort to gain a profit which is not the result of the overall expansion of work and the wealth of society, but rather is the result of curbing them or of illicit exploitation, speculation or the breaking of solidarity among working people. Ownership of this kind has no justification, and represents an abuse in the sight of God and man.

"The obligation to earn one's bread by the sweat of one's brow also presumes the right to do so. A society in which this right is systematically denied, in which economic policies do not allow workers to reach satisfactory levels of employment, cannot be justified from an ethical point of view, nor can that society attain social peace. Just as the person fully realizes himself in the free gift of self, so too ownership morally justifies itself in the creation, at the proper time and in the proper way, of opportunities for work and human growth for all."

CHAPTER 5

State and Culture

44. "Pope Leo XIII was aware of the need for a sound theory of the state in order to ensure the normal development of man's spiritual and temporal activities, both of which are indispensable. For this reason, in one passage of *Rerum Novarum* he presents the organization of society according to the three powers —

legislative, executive and judicial — something which at the time represented a novelty in church teaching. Such an ordering reflects a realistic vision of man's social nature, which calls for legislation capable of protecting the freedom of all. To that end, it is preferable that each power be balanced by other powers and by other spheres of responsibility which keep it within proper bounds. This is the principle of the 'rule of law,' in which the law is sovereign, and not the arbitrary will of individuals."

46. "The Church values the democratic system inasmuch as it ensures the participation of citizens in making political choices, guarantees to the governed the possibility both of electing and holding accountable those who govern them, and of replacing them through peaceful means when appropriate. Thus, she cannot encourage the formation of narrow ruling groups which usurp the power of the state for individual interests or for ideological ends."

Authentic Democracy

"Authentic democracy is possible only in a state ruled by law, and on the basis of a correct conception of the human person. It requires that the necessary conditions be present for the advancement both of the individual through education and formation in true ideals, and of the 'subjectivity' of society through the creation of structures of participation and shared responsibility. Nowadays there is a tendency to claim that agnosticism and skeptical relativism are the philosophy and the basic attitude which correspond to democratic forms of political life. Those who are convinced that they know the truth and firmly adhere to it are considered unreliable from a democratic point of view, since they do not accept that truth is determined by the majority, or that it is subject to variation according to different political trends. It must be observed in this regard that if there is no ultimate truth to guide and direct political activity, then ideas and convictions can easily be manipulated for reasons of power. As history demonstrates, a democracy without values easily turns into open or thinly disguised totalitarianism.

"Nor does the Church close her eyes to the danger of fanaticism or fundamentalism among those who, in the name of an ideology which purports to be scientific or religious, claim the right to impose on others their own concept of what is true and good. Christian truth is not of this kind. Since it is not an ideology, the Christian faith does not presume to imprison changing socio-political realities in a rigid schema, and it recognizes that human life is realized in history in conditions that are diverse and imperfect. Furthermore, in constantly reaffirming the transcendent dignity of the person, the Church's method is always that of respect for freedom.

"But freedom attains its full development only by accepting the truth. In a world without truth, freedom loses its foundation and man is exposed to the violence of passion and to manipulation, both open and hidden. The Christian upholds freedom and serves it."

Rights To Be Recognized

47. "Following the collapse of communist totalitarianism and of many other totalitarian and 'national security' regimes, today we are witnessing a predominance, not without signs of opposition, of the democratic ideal, together with lively attention to and concern for human rights. But for this very reason it is necessary for peoples in the process of reforming their systems to give democracy an authentic and solid foundation through the explicit recognition of those rights. Among the most important of these rights, mention must be made of the right to life, an integral part of which is the right of the child to develop in the mother's womb from the moment of conception; the right to live in a united family and in a moral environment conducive to the growth of the child's personality; the right to develop one's intelligence and freedom in seeking and knowing the truth; the right to share in the work which makes wise use of the earth's material resources, and to derive from that work the means to support oneself and one's dependents; and the right freely to establish a family, to have and to rear children through the responsible exercise of one's sexuality. In a certain sense, the source and synthesis of these rights is religious freedom, understood as the right to live in the truth of one's faith and in conformity with one's transcendent dignity as a person."

Violations of Rights

"Even in countries with democratic forms of government, these rights are not always fully respected. Here we are referring not only to the scandal of abortion, but also to different aspects of a crisis within democracies themselves, which seem at times to have lost the ability to make decisions aimed at the common good. Certain demands which arise within society are sometimes not examined in accordance with criteria of justice and morality, but rather on the basis of the electoral or financial power of the groups promoting them. With time, such distortions of political conduct create distrust and apathy, with a subsequent decline in the political participation and civic spirit of the general population, which feels abused and disillusioned. As a result, there is a growing inability to situate particular interests within the framework of a coherent vision of the common good. The latter is not simply the sum total of particular interests; rather, it involves an assessment and integration of those interests on the basis of a balanced hierarchy of values; ultimately, it demands a correct understanding of the dignity and the rights of the person.

"The Church respects the legitimate autonomy of the democratic order and is not entitled to express preferences for this or that institutional or constitutional solution. Her contribution to the political order is precisely her vision of the dignity of the person revealed in all its fullness in the mystery of the Incarnate Word."

The State and the Economic Sector

48. "These general observations also apply to the role of the state in the economic sector. Economic activity, especially the activity of a market economy, cannot be conducted in an institutional, juridical or political vacuum. On the contrary, it presupposes sure guarantees of individual freedom and private property, as well as a stable currency and efficient public services. Hence the principal task of the state

is to guarantee this security, so that those who work and produce can enjoy the fruits of their labors and thus feel encouraged to work efficiently and honestly. The absence of stability, together with the corruption of public officials and the spread of improper sources of growing rich and of easy profits deriving from illegal or purely speculative activities, constitutes one of the chief obstacles to development and to the economic order."

State Oversight

"Another task of the state is that of overseeing and directing the exercise of human rights in the economic sector. However, primary responsibility in this area belongs not to the state but to individuals and to the various groups and associations which make up society. The state could not directly ensure the right to work for all its citizens unless it controlled every aspect of economic life and restricted the free initiative of individuals. This does not mean, however, that the state has no competence in this domain, as was claimed by those who argued against any rules in the economic sphere. Rather, the state has a duty to sustain business activities by creating conditions which will ensure job opportunities, by stimulating those activities where they are lacking or by supporting them in moments of crisis.

"The state has the further right to intervene when particular monopolies create delays or obstacles to development. In addition to the tasks of harmonizing and guiding development, in exceptional circumstances the state can also exercise a substitute function, when social sectors or business systems are too weak or are just getting under way, and are not equal to the task at hand. Such supplementary interventions, which are justified by urgent reasons touching the common good, must be as brief as possible, so as to avoid removing permanently from society and business systems the functions which are properly theirs, and so as to avoid enlarging excessively the sphere of state intervention to the detriment of both economic and civil freedom."

The Welfare State

"In recent years the range of such intervention has vastly expanded, to the point of creating a new type of state, the so-called 'welfare state.' This has happened in some countries in order to respond better to many needs and demands, by remedying forms of poverty and deprivation unworthy of the human person."

However, excesses and abuses, especially in recent years, have provoked very harsh criticisms of the welfare state, dubbed the 'social assistance state.' Malfunctions and defects in the social assistance state are the result of an inadequate understanding of the tasks proper to the state. Here again the principle of subsidiarity must be respected; a community of a higher order should not interfere in the internal life of a community of a lower order, depriving the latter of its functions, but rather should support it in case of need and help to coordinate its activity with the activities of the rest of society, always with a view to the common good.

"By intervening directly and depriving society of its responsibility, the social assistance state leads to a loss of human energies and an inordinate increase of public agencies, which are dominated more by bureaucratic ways of thinking than by concern for serving their clients, and which are accompanied by an enormous increase in spending. In fact, it would appear that needs are best understood and satisfied by people who are closest to them and who act as neighbors to those in need."

Church Concern for the Needy

49. "Faithful to the mission received from Christ her founder, the Church has always been present and active among the needy, offering them material assistance in ways that neither humiliate nor reduce them to mere objects of assistance, but which help them to escape their precarious situation by promoting their dignity as persons. With heartfelt gratitude to God, it must be pointed out that active charity has never ceased to be practiced in the Church; indeed, today it is showing a manifold and gratifying increase. In this regard, special mention must be made of volunteer work, which the Church favors and promotes by urging everyone to cooperate in supporting and encouraging its undertakings.

"In order to overcome today's widespread individualistic mentality, what is required is a concrete commitment to solidarity and charity, beginning in the family with the mutual support of husband and wife and the care which the different generations give to one another. It is urgent to promote not only family policies, but also those social policies which have the family as their principal object."

52. "Another name for peace is development. Just as there is a collective responsibility for avoiding war, so too there is a collective responsibility for promoting development. Just as within individual societies it is possible and right to organize a solid economy which will direct the functioning of the market to the common good, so too there is a similar need for adequate interventions on the international level."

CHAPTER 6

Man Is the Way of the Church

54. "Today, the Church's social doctrine focuses especially on man as he is involved in a complex network of relationships within modern societies. The human sciences and philosophy are helpful for interpreting man's central place within society and for enabling him to understand himself better as a 'social being.' However, man's true identity is only fully revealed to him through faith, and it is precisely from faith that the Church's social teaching begins. While drawing upon all the contributions made by the sciences and philosophy, her social teaching is aimed at helping man on the path of salvation."

"Given in Rome, at St. Peter's, on May 1, the memorial of St. Joseph the Worker, in the year 1991, the 13th of my pontificate."

UPS Strike: Msgr. George G. Higgins, on the Teamsters, said: "The downsizing and part-time work is a big issue. The Teamster situation is the first time it's been presented in a way the public can understand."

SOCIO-ECONOMIC STATEMENTS BY U.S. BISHOPS

Over a period of nearly 80 years, the bishops of the United States have issued a great number of socioeconomic statements reflecting papal documents in a U.S. context.

One such statement, entitled "Economic Justice for All: Social Teaching and the U.S. Economy," was issued in November, 1986. Its contents are related in various ways with the subsequently issued encyclical letter, *Centesimus Annus*. Principles drawn from the bishops'document are given in the following excerpt entitled "A Catholic Framework for Economic Life."

Another significant statement, entitled "The Harvest of Justice Is Sown in Peace," follows.

A CATHOLIC FRAMEWORK FOR ECONOMIC LIFE

As followers of Jesus Christ and participants in a powerful economy, Catholics in the United States, are called to work for greater economic justice in the face of persistent poverty, growing income gaps and increasing discussion of economic issues in the United States and around the world. We urge Catholics to use the following ethical framework for economic life as principles for reflection, criteria for judgment and directions for action.These principles are drawn directly from Catholic teaching on economic life.

1. The economy exists for the person, not the person for the economy.

2. All economic life should be shaped by moral principles.. Economic choices and institutions must be judged by how they protect or undermine the life and dignity of the human person, support the family and serve the common good.

3. A fundamental moral measure of an economy is how the poor and vulnerable are faring.

4. All people have a right to life and to secure the basic necessities of life (e.g., food, clothing, shelter, education, health care, safe environment, economic security)..

5. All people have the right to economic initiative, to productive work, to just wages and benefits, to decent working conditions as well as to organize and join unions or other associations.

6. All people, to the extent they are able, have a corresponding duty to work, a responsibility to provide for the needs of their families and an obligation to contribute to the broader society.

7. In economic life, free markets have both clear advantages and limits; government has essential responsibiities and limitations; voluntary groups have irreplaceable roles, but cannot substitute for the proper working of the market and the just policies of the state.

8. Society has a moral obligation, including governmental action where necessary, to assure opportunity, meet basic human needs and pursue justice in economic life.

9. Workers, owners, managers, stockholders and consumers are moral agents in economic life. By our choices, initiative, creativity and investment, we enhance or diminish economic opportunity, community life and social justice.

10. The global economy has moral dimensions and human consequences. Decisions on investment, trade, aid and development should protect human life and promote human rights, especially for those most in need wherever they might live on this globe.

The Harvest of Justice Is Sown in Peace

The National Conference of Catholic Bishops, at a meeting Nov. 17, 1993, issued a statement entitled "The Harvest of Justice Is Sown in Peace," marking the 10th anniversary of their earlier pastoral letter, "The Challenge of Peace: God's Promise and Our Response."

The Challenge

"The challenge of peace today is different, but no less urgent" than in 1983, and the threat of global nuclear war "may seem more remote than at any time in the nuclear age." Questions of peace and war, however, cannot be addressed "without acknowledging that the nuclear question remains of vital political and moral significance."

The statement outlines an agenda for action to guide future advocacy efforts of the bishops' national conference. It also urges that the cause of peace be reflected constantly in liturgical prayers of petition, preaching and Catholic education at all levels.

Confronting the temptation to isolationism in U.S. foreign policy is among "the major challenges peacemakers face in this new era."

Factors in a vision for peace include a commitment to the universal common good and recognition of the imperative of human solidarity.

Nonviolent revolutions in some countries "challenge us to find ways to take into full account the power of organized, active nonviolence."

With respect to just war criteria, the statement says that "important work needs to be done in refining, clarifying and applying the just war tradition to the choices facing our decision-makers in this still violent and dangerous world."

Subjects of concern include humanitarian intervention, deterrence, conscientious objection and the development of peoples.

Presumption against Force

"Our conference's approach, as outlined in 'The Challenge of Peace,' can be summarized in this way:

"1) In situations of conflict our constant commitment ought to be, as far as possible, to strive for justice through nonviolent means.

"2) But when sustained attempts at nonviolent action fail to protect the innocent against fundamental injustice, then legitimate political authorities are permitted as a last resort to employ limited force to rescue the innocent and establish justice."

Lethal Force

"Whether lethal force may be used is governed by the following criteria:

• "Just cause: Force may be used only to correct a grave, public evil, i.e., aggression or massive violation of the basic rights of whole populations.

• "Comparative justice: While there may be rights

and wrongs on all sides of a conflict, to override the presumption against the use of force, the injustice suffered by one party must significantly outweigh that suffered by the other.

• "Legitimate authority: Only duly constituted public authorities may use deadly force or wage war.

• "Right intention: Force may be used only in a truly just cause and solely for that purpose.

• "Probability of Success: Arms may not be used in a futile cause or in a case where disproportionate measures are required to achieve success.

• "Proportionality: The overall destruction expected from the use of force must be outweighed by the good to be achieved.

• "Last Resort: Force may be used only after all peaceful alternatives have been seriously tried and exhausted.

"These criteria (of just war), taken as a whole, must be satisfied in order to override the strong presumption against the use of force."

Just War

"The just war tradition seeks also to curb the violence of war through restraint on armed combat between the contending parties by imposing the following moral standards for the conduct of armed conflict:

• "Noncombatant Immunity: Civilians may not be the object of direct attack, and military personnel must take due care to avoid and minimize indirect harm to civilians.

• "Proportionality: In the conduct of hostilities, efforts must be made to attain military objectives with no more force than is militarily necessary and to avoid disproportionate collateral damage to civilian life and property.

• "Right Intention: Even in the midst of conflict, the aim of political and military leaders must be peace with justice so that acts of vengeance and indiscriminate violence, whether by individuals, military units or governments, are forbidden."

Structures for Justice and Peace

Quoting an address given by Pope John Paul in August, 1993, in Denver, the statement said:

" 'The international community ought to establish more effective structures for maintaining and promoting justice and peace. This implies that a concept of strategic interest should evolve which is based on the full development of peoples — out of poverty and toward a more dignified existence, out of injustice and exploitation toward fuller respect for the human person and the defense of universal rights.'

"As we consider a new vision of the international community, five areas deserve special attention: (1) strengthening global institutions; (2) securing human rights; (3) promoting human development; (4) restraining nationalism and eliminating religious violence; and (5) building cooperative security."

Humanitarian Intervention

"Pope John Paul, citing the 'conscience of humanity and international humanitarian law,' has been outspoken in urging that 'humanitarian intervention be obligatory where the survival of populations and entire ethnic groups is seriously compromised. This is a duty for nations and the international community.' He elaborated on this right and duty of humanitarian intervention in his 1993 annual address to the diplomatic corps (accredited to the Holy See):

" 'Once the possibilities afforded by diplomatic negotiations and the procedures provided for by international agreements and organizations have been put into effect, and that (sic), nevertheless, populations are succumbing to the attacks of an unjust aggressor, states no longer have a 'right to indifference.' It seems clear that their duty is to disarm this aggressor if all other means have proved ineffective. The principles of the sovereignty of states and of noninterference in their internal affairs — which retain all their value — cannot constitute a screen behind which torture and murder may be carried out.'"

INGREDIENTS OF CATECHESIS FOR THE 21ST CENTURY

Ingredients of a catechesis for the 21st century were presented Apr. 17, 1997, by Bishop Sylvester Ryan of Monterey in an address to the annual meeting of the National Conference of Catechetical Leadership in Orlando. He said in part, as follows.

First Ingredient, The Word of God: The stories of the Gospel are stories of encounters with the Lord Jesus Christ. ... The task of catechetics always remains to foster a living, conscious and real relationship with Jesus Christ, the risen Christ in our midst.

Second, The Mystery of Christ and the Church as Sacrament: The model of the Church as expounded in the documents of the Second Vatican Council is a dynamic one in which the essentials of faith remain solidly the same, while the forms of practice, tradition and institution undergo continuous renewal. Only in this way can the Church be an effective sign and sacrament of the kingdom of God in the world.

Third, A Baptismal Spirituality: Our baptism,

confirmation and Eucharist make us members of the Church. Baptism consecrates us for witness and service. It also sets us apart where, as the assembly, we are the body of Christ worshipping the Father and the anointed priests, prophets and servants to build the kingdom of God.

Fourth, Liturgy's Four Tasks: The first task is to lead people to understand fully that the assembly is truly the body of Christ, God's people at worship together.

A second task concerns making better connections between liturgy and life by greater attention to hearing the word of God proclaimed in the Liturgy of the Word.

A third task is a stronger understanding of one of our earliest liturgical principles, that the Eucharist makes the Church and the Church makes the Eucharist.

A fourth area is ritual and symbol; indeed, all the sacraments are ritual and symbolic actions ... in which Christ acts and we in faith respond.

The nature and purpose of the liturgy, along with norms for its revision, were the subject matter of the *Constitution on the Sacred Liturgy* promulgated by the Second Vatican Council. The principles and guidelines stated in this document, the first issued by the Council, are summarized here and/or are incorporated in other Almanac entries on liturgical subjects.

Nature and Purpose of Liturgy

The paragraphs under this and the following subhead are quoted directly from the "Constitution on the Sacred Liturgy."

"It is through the liturgy, especially the divine Eucharistic Sacrifice, that 'the work of our redemption is exercised.' The liturgy is thus the outstanding means by which the faithful can express in their lives, and manifest to others, the mystery of Christ and the real nature of the true Church " (No. 2).

"The liturgy is considered as an exercise of the priestly office of Jesus Christ. In the liturgy the sanctification of man is manifested by signs perceptible to the senses, and is effected in a way which is proper to each of these signs; in the liturgy full public worship is performed by the Mystical Body of Jesus Christ, that is, by the Head and his members.

"From this it follows that every liturgical celebration, because it is an action of Christ the priest and of his Body the Church, is a sacred action surpassing all others. No other action of the Church can match its claim to efficacy, nor equal the degree of it" (No. 7).

"The liturgy is the summit toward which the activity of the Church is directed; at the same time it is the fountain from which all her power flows. For the goal of apostolic works is that all who are made sons of God by faith and baptism should come together to praise God in the midst of his Church, to take part in her sacrifice, and to eat the Lord's Supper.

" From the liturgy, therefore, and especially from the Eucharist, as from a fountain, grace is channeled into us; and the sanctification of men in Christ and the glorification of God, to which all other activities of the Church are directed as toward their goal, are most powerfully achieved" (No. 10).

Full Participation

"Mother Church earnestly desires that all the faithful be led to that full, conscious, and active participation in liturgical celebrations which is demanded by the very nature of the liturgy. Such participation by the Christian people as 'a chosen race, a royal priesthood, a holy nation, a purchased people' (1 Pt. 2:9; cf. 2:4-5), is their right and duty by reason of their baptism.

"In the restoration and promotion of the sacred liturgy, this full and active participation by all the people is the aim to be considered before all else; for it is the primary and indispensable source from which the faithful are to derive the true Christian spirit " (No. 14).

"In order that the Christian people may more securely derive an abundance of graces from the sacred liturgy, holy Mother Church desires to undertake with great care a general restoration of the liturgy itself. For the liturgy is made up of unchangeable elements divinely instituted, and elements subject to change.

The latter not only may but ought to be changed with the passing of time if features have by chance crept in which are less harmonious with the intimate nature of the liturgy, or if existing elements have grown less functional.

"In this restoration, both texts and rites should be drawn up so that they express more clearly the holy things which they signify. Christian people, as far as possible, should be able to understand them with ease and to take part in them fully, actively, and as befits a community " (No. 21).

Norms

Norms regarding the reforms concern the greater use of Scripture; emphasis on the importance of the sermon or homily on biblical and liturgical subjects; use of vernacular languages for prayers of the Mass and for administration of the sacraments; provision for adaptation of rites to cultural patterns.

Approval for reforms of various kinds — in liturgical texts, rites, etc. — depends on the Holy See, regional conferences of bishops and individual bishops, according to provisions of law. No priest has authority to initiate reforms on his own. Reforms may not be introduced just for the sake of innovation, and any that are introduced in the light of present-day circumstances should embody sound tradition.

To assure the desired effect of liturgical reforms, training and instruction are necessary for the clergy, religious and the laity. The functions of diocesan and regional commissions for liturgy, music and art are to set standards and provide leadership for instruction and practical programs in their respective fields.

Most of the constitution's provisions regarding liturgical reforms have to do with the Roman Rite. The document clearly respects the equal dignity of all rites, leaving to the Eastern Churches control over their ancient liturgies.

(For coverage of the Mystery of the Eucharist, see The Mass; Other Sacraments, see separate entries.)

Sacramentals

Sacramentals, instituted by the Church, "are sacred signs which bear a resemblance to the sacraments: they signify effects, particularly of a spiritual kind, which are obtained through the Church's intercession. By them men are disposed to receive the chief effect of the sacraments, and various occasions in life are rendered holy" (No. 60).

"Thus, for well-disposed members of the faithful, the liturgy of the sacraments and sacramentals sanctifies almost every event in their lives; they are given access to the stream of divine grace which flows from the paschal mystery of the passion, death, and resurrection of Christ, the fountain from which all sacraments and sacramentals draw their power. There is hardly any proper use of material things which cannot thus be directed toward the sanctification of men and the praise of God" (No. 61).

Some common sacramentals are priestly blessings, blessed palm, candles, holy water, medals, scapulars, prayers and ceremonies of the Roman Ritual.

Liturgy of the Hours

The Liturgy of the Hours (Divine Office) is the public prayer of the Church for praising God and sanctifying the day. Its daily celebration is required as a sacred obligation by men in holy orders and by men and women religious who have professed solemn vows. Its celebration by others is highly commended and is to be encouraged in the community of the faithful.

"By tradition going back to early Christian times, the Divine Office is arranged so that the whole course of the day and night is made holy by the praises of God. Therefore, when this wonderful song of praise is worthily rendered by priests and others who are deputed for this purpose by Church ordinance, or by the faithful praying together with the priest in an approved form, then it is truly the voice of the bride addressing her bridegroom; it is the very prayer which Christ himself, together with his Body, addresses to the Father" (No. 84).

"Hence all who perform this service are not only fulfilling a duty of the Church, but also are sharing in the greatest honor accorded to Christ's spouse, for by offering these praises to God they are standing before God's throne in the name of the Church their Mother" (No. 85).

The Liturgy of the Hours, revised since 1965, was the subject of Pope Paul VI's apostolic constitution *Laudis Canticum,* dated Nov. 1, 1970. The master Latin text was published in 1971; its four volumes have been published in authorized English translation since May, 1975.

One-volume, partial editions of the Liturgy of the Hours containing Morning and Evening Prayer and other elements, have been published in approved English translation.

The revised Liturgy of the Hours consists of:

• Office of Readings, for reflection on the word of God. The principal parts are three psalms, biblical and non-biblical readings.

• Morning and Evening Prayer, called the "hinges" of the Liturgy of the Hours. The principal parts are a hymn, two psalms, an Old or New Testament canticle, a brief biblical reading, Zechariah's canticle (the *Benedictus,* morning) or Mary's canticle (the *Magnificat,* evening), responsories, intercessions and a concluding prayer.

• Daytime Prayer. The principal parts are a hymn, three psalms, a brief biblical reading and one of three concluding prayers corresponding to the time at which the prayer is offered (midmorning, midday, midafternoon).

• Night Prayer: The principal parts are one or two psalms, a brief biblical reading, Simeon's canticle (*Nunc Dimittis*), a concluding prayer and an antiphon in honor of Mary.

In the revised Liturgy of the Hours, the hours are shorter than they had been, with greater textual variety, meditation aids, and provision for intervals of silence and meditation. The psalms are distributed over a four-week period instead of a week; some psalms, entirely or in part, are not included. Additional canticles from the Old and New Testaments are assigned for Morning and Evening Prayer. Additional scriptural texts have been added and variously arranged for greater internal unity, correspondence to readings at Mass, and relevance to events and themes of salvation history. Readings include some of the best material from the Fathers of the Church and other

authors, and improved selections on the lives of the saints.

The book used for recitation of the Office is the **Breviary.**

For coverage of the Liturgical Year, see Church Calendar.

Sacred Music

"The musical tradition of the universal Church is a treasure of immeasurable value, greater even than that of any other art. The main reason for this pre-eminence is that, as sacred melody united to words, it forms a necessary or integral part of the solemn liturgy.

" Sacred music increases in holiness to the degree that it is intimately linked with liturgical action, winningly expresses prayerfulness, promotes solidarity, and enriches sacred rites with heightened solemnity. The Church indeed approves of all forms of true art, and admits them into divine worship when they show appropriate qualities" (No. 112).

The constitution decreed:

• Vernacular languages for the people's parts of the liturgy, as well as Latin, may be used.

• Participation in sacred song by the whole body of the faithful, and not just by choirs, is to be encouraged and brought about.

• Provisions should be made for proper musical training for clergy, religious and lay persons.

• While Gregorian Chant has a unique dignity and relationship to the Latin liturgy, other kinds of music are acceptable.

• Native musical traditions should be used, especially in mission areas.

• Various instruments compatible with the dignity of worship may be used.

Gregorian Chant: A form and style of chant called Gregorian was the basis and most highly regarded standard of liturgical music for centuries. It originated probably during the formative period of the Roman liturgy and developed in conjunction with Gallican and other forms of chant. Gregory the Great's connection with it is not clear, although it is known that he had great concern for and interest in church music. The earliest extant written versions of Gregorian Chant date from the ninth century. A thousand years later, the Benedictines of Solesmes, France, initiated a revival of chant which gave impetus to the modern liturgical movement.

Sacred Art and Furnishings

"Very rightly the fine arts are considered to rank among the noblest expressions of human genius. This judgment applies especially to religious art and to its highest achievement, which is sacred art. By their very nature both of the latter are related to God's boundless beauty, for this is the reality which these human efforts are trying to express in some way. To the extent that these works aim exclusively at turning men's thoughts to God persuasively and devoutly, they are dedicated to God and to the cause of his greater honor and glory" (No. 122).

The objective of sacred art is "that all things set apart for use in divine worship should be truly worthy, becoming, and beautiful, signs and symbols of heavenly realities. The Church has always reserved to herself the right to pass judgment upon the arts, deciding which of the works of artists are in accordance with faith, piety, and cherished traditional laws, and thereby suited to sacred purposes.

" Sacred furnishings should worthily and beautifully serve the dignity of worship " (No. 122).

According to the constitution:

• Contemporary art, as well as that of the past, shall "be given free scope in the Church, provided that it adorns the sacred buildings and holy rites with due honor and reverence " (No. 123).

• Noble beauty, not sumptuous display, should be sought in art, sacred vestments and ornaments.

• "Let bishops carefully exclude from the house of God and from other sacred places those works of artists which are repugnant to faith, morals, and Christian piety, and which offend true religious sense either by their distortion of forms or by lack of artistic worth, by mediocrity or by pretense.

• "When churches are to be built, let great care be taken that they be suitable for the celebration of liturgical services and for the active participation of the faithful" (No. 124).

• "The practice of placing sacred images in churches so that they may be venerated by the faithful is to be firmly maintained. Nevertheless, their number should be moderate and their relative location should reflect right order. Otherwise they may create confusion among the Christian people and promote a faulty sense of devotion" (No. 125).

• Artists should be trained and inspired in the spirit and for the purposes of the liturgy.

• The norms of sacred art should be revised. "These laws refer especially to the worthy and well-planned construction of sacred buildings, the shape and construction of altars, the nobility, location, and security of the Eucharistic tabernacle, the suitability and dignity of the baptistery, the proper use of sacred images, embellishments, and vestments " (No. 128).

RITES

Rites are the forms and ceremonial observances of liturgical worship coupled with the total expression of the theological, spiritual and disciplinary heritages of particular churches of the East and the West.

Different rites have evolved in the course of church history, giving to liturgical worship and church life in general forms and usages peculiar and proper to the nature of worship and the culture of the faithful in various circumstances of time and place. Thus, there has been development since apostolic times in the prayers and ceremonies of the Mass, in the celebration of the sacraments, sacramentals and the Liturgy of the Hours, and in observances of the liturgical calendar. The principal sources of rites in present use were practices within the patriarchates of Rome (for the West) and Antioch, Alexandria and Constantinople (for the East). Rites are identified as Eastern or Western on the basis of their geographical area of origin in the Roman Empire.

Eastern and Roman

Eastern rites are proper to Eastern Catholic Churches (see separate entry). The principal rites are Byzantine, Alexandrian, Antiochene, Armenian and Chaldean.

The Latin or Roman rite prevails in the Western Church. It was derived from Roman practices and the use of Latin from the third century onward, and has been the rite in general use in the West since the eighth century. Other rites in limited use in the Western Church have been the Ambrosian (in the Archdiocese of Milan), the Mozarabic (in the Archdiocese of Toledo), the Lyonnais, the Braga, and rites peculiar to some religious orders like the Dominicans, Carmelites and Carthusians.

The purpose of the revision of rites in progress since the Second Vatican Council is to renew them, not to eliminate the rites of particular churches or to reduce all rites to uniformity. The Council reaffirmed the equal dignity and preservation of rites as follows.

"It is the mind of the Catholic Church that each individual church or rite retain its traditions whole and entire, while adjusting its way of life to various needs of time and place. Such individual churches, whether of the East or the West, although they differ somewhat among themselves in what are called rites (that is, in liturgy, ecclesiastical discipline and spiritual heritage), are, nevertheless, equally entrusted to the pastoral guidance of the Roman Pontiff, the divinely appointed successor of St. Peter in supreme government over the universal Church. They are, consequently, of equal dignity, so that none of them is superior to the others by reason of rite."

Determination of Rite

Determination of a person's rite is regulated by church law. Through baptism, a child becomes a member of the rite of his or her parents. If the parents are of different rites, the child's rite is decided by mutual consent of the parents; if there is lack of mutual consent, the child is baptized in the rite of the father. A candidate for baptism over the age of 14 can choose to be baptized in any approved rite. Catholics baptized in one rite may receive the sacraments in any of the approved ritual churches; they may transfer to another rite only with the permission of the Holy See and in accordance with other provisions of the Code of Canon Law.

MASS, EUCHARISTIC SACRIFICE AND BANQUET

Declarations of Vatican II

The Second Vatican Council made the following declarations among others with respect to the Mass.

"At the Last Supper, on the night when he was betrayed, our Savior instituted the Eucharistic Sacrifice of his Body and Blood. He did this in order to perpetuate the Sacrifice of the Cross throughout the centuries until he should come again, and so to entrust to his beloved spouse, the Church, a memorial of his death and resurrection: a sacrament of love, a sign of unity, a bond of charity, a paschal banquet in which Christ is consumed, the mind is filled with grace, and a pledge of future glory is given to us" (*Constitution on the Sacred Liturgy*, No. 47).

"... As often as the Sacrifice of the Cross in which 'Christ, our Passover, has been sacrificed' (1 Cor.

5:7) is celebrated on an altar, the work of our redemption is carried on. At the same time, in the sacrament of the Eucharistic bread the unity of all believers who form one body in Christ (cf. 1 Cor. 10:17) is both expressed and brought about. All men are called to this union with Christ ..." (*Dogmatic Constitution on the Church,* No. 3).

"... The ministerial priest, by the sacred power he enjoys, molds and rules the priestly people. Acting in the person of Christ, he brings about the Eucharistic Sacrifice, and offers it to God in the name of all the people. For their part, the faithful join in the offering of the Eucharist by virtue of their royal priesthood ..." (*Ibid.,* No. 10).

Declarations of Trent

Among its decrees on the Holy Eucharist, the Council of Trent stated the following points of doctrine on the Mass.

1. There is in the Catholic Church a true sacrifice, the Mass instituted by Jesus Christ. It is the sacrifice of his Body and Blood, Soul and Divinity, himself, under the appearances of bread and wine.

2. This Sacrifice is identical with the Sacrifice of the Cross, inasmuch as Christ is the Priest and Victim in both. A difference lies in the manner of offering, which was bloody upon the Cross and is bloodless on the altar.

3. The Mass is a propitiatory Sacrifice, atoning for the sins of the living and dead for whom it is offered.

4. The efficacy of the Mass is derived from the Sacrifice of the Cross, whose superabundant merits it applies to men.

5. Although the Mass is offered to God alone, it may be celebrated in honor and memory of the saints.

6. Christ instituted the Mass at the Last Supper.

7. Christ ordained the Apostles priests, giving them power and the command to consecrate his Body and Blood to perpetuate and renew the Sacrifice.

ORDER OF MASS

The Mass consists of two principal divisions called the **Liturgy of the Word,** which features the proclamation of the Word of God, and the **Eucharistic Liturgy,** which focuses on the central act of sacrifice in the Consecration and on the Eucharistic Banquet in Holy Communion. (Formerly, these divisions were called, respectively, the **Mass of the Catechumens** and the **Mass of the Faithful.**) In addition to these principal divisions, there are ancillary introductory and concluding rites.

The following description covers the Mass as celebrated with participation by the people. This Order of the Mass was approved by Pope Paul VI in the apostolic constitution *Missale Romanum* dated Apr. 3, 1969, and promulgated in a decree issued Apr. 6, 1969, by the Congregation for Divine Worship. The assigned effective date was Nov. 30, 1969.

Introductory Rites

Entrance: The introductory rites begin with the singing or recitation of an entrance song consisting of one or more scriptural verses stating the theme of the mystery, season or feast commemorated in the Mass.

Greeting: The priest and people make the Sign of the Cross together. The priest then greets them in one of several alternative ways and they reply in a corresponding manner.

Introductory Remarks: At this point, the priest or another of the ministers may introduce the theme of the Mass.

Penitential Rite: The priest and people together acknowledge their sins as a preliminary step toward worthy celebration of the sacred mysteries.

This rite includes a brief examination of conscience, a general confession of sin and plea for divine mercy in one of several ways, and a prayer for forgiveness by the priest.

Glory to God: A doxology, a hymn of praise to God, sung or said on festive occasions.

Opening Prayer: A prayer of petition offered by the priest on behalf of the worshipping community.

I. Liturgy of the Word

Readings: The featured elements of this liturgy are readings of passages from the Bible. If three readings are in order, the first is usually from the Old Testament, the second from the New Testament (Letters, Acts, Revelation), and the third from one of the Gospels; the final reading is always a selection from a Gospel. The first reading(s) is (are) concluded with the formula, "The Word of the Lord" (effective Feb. 28, 1993; optional before that date), to which the people respond, "Thanks be to God." The Gospel reading is concluded with the formula, "The Gospel of the Lord," (effective as above), to which the people respond, "Praise to you, Lord Jesus Christ." Between the readings, psalm verses are sung or recited. A Gospel acclamation is either sung or omitted.

Homily: An explanation, pertinent to the mystery being celebrated and the special needs of the listeners, of some point in either the readings from sacred Scripture or in another text from the Ordinary or Proper parts of the Mass; it is a proclamation of the Good News for a response of faith.

Creed: The Nicene profession of faith, by priest and people, on certain occasions.

Prayer of the Faithful: Litany-type prayers of petition, with participation by the people. Called general intercessions, they concern needs of the Church, the salvation of the world, public authorities, persons in need, the local community.

II. Eucharistic Liturgy

Presentation and Preparation of Gifts: Presentation to the priest of the gifts of bread and wine, principally, by participating members of the congregation. Preparation of the gifts consists of the prayers and ceremonies with which the priest offers bread and wine as the elements of the sacrifice to take place during the Eucharistic Prayer and of the Lord's Supper to be shared in Holy Communion.

Washing of Hands: After offering the bread and wine, the priest cleanses his fingers with water in a brief ceremony of purification.

Pray, Brothers and Sisters: Prayer that the sacrifice to take place will be acceptable to God. The first part of the prayer is said by the priest; the second, by the people.

Prayer over the Gifts: A prayer of petition offered

by the priest on behalf of the worshipping community.

Eucharistic Prayer

Preface: A hymn of praise, introducing the Eucharistic Prayer or Canon, sung or said by the priest following responses by the people. The Order of the Mass contains a variety of prefaces, for use on different occasions.

Holy, Holy, Holy; Blessed is He: Divine praises sung or said by the priest and people.

Eucharistic Prayer (Canon): Its central portion is the Consecration, when the essential act of sacrificial offering takes place with the changing of bread and wine into the Body and Blood of Christ. The various parts of the prayer, which are said by the celebrant only, commemorate principal mysteries of salvation history and include petitions for the Church, the living and dead, and remembrances of saints.

Doxology: A formula of divine praise sung or said by the priest while he holds aloft the chalice containing the consecrated wine in one hand and the paten containing the consecrated host in the other.

Communion Rite

Lord's Prayer: Sung or said by the priest and people.

Prayer for Deliverance from evil: Called an **embolism** because it is a development of the final petition of the Lord's Prayer; said by the priest. It concludes with a memorial of the return of the Lord to which the people respond, "For the kingdom, the power, and the glory are yours, now and forever."

Prayer for Peace: Said by the priest, with corresponding responses by the people. The priest can, in accord with local custom, bid the people to exchange a greeting of peace with each other.

Lamb of God (*Agnus Dei*): A prayer for divine mercy sung or said while the priest breaks the consecrated host and places a piece of it into the consecrated wine in the chalice.

Communion: The priest, after saying a preparatory prayer, administers Holy Communion to himself and then to the people, thus completing the sacrifice-banquet of the Mass. (This completion is realized even if the celebrant alone receives the Eucharist.) On giving the Eucharist to each person under both species separately, the priest or eucharistic minister says, "The Body of Christ," "The Blood of Christ." The customary response is "Amen." If the Eucharist is given by intinction (in which the host is dipped into the consecrated wine), the priest says, "The Body and Blood of Christ."

Communion Song: Scriptural verses or a suitable hymn sung or said during the distribution of Holy Communion. After Holy Communion is received, some moments may be spent in silent meditation or in the chanting of a psalm or hymn of praise.

Prayer after Communion: A prayer of petition offered by the priest on behalf of the worshipping community.

Concluding Rite

Announcements: Brief announcements to the people are in order at this time.

Dismissal: Consists of a final greeting by the priest, a blessing, and a formula of dismissal. This rite is omitted if another liturgical action immediately follows the Mass; e.g., a procession, the blessing of the body during a funeral rite.

Some parts of the Mass are changeable with the liturgical season or feast, and are called the **proper** of the Mass. Other parts are said to be **common** because they always remain the same.

Additional Mass Notes

Catholics are seriously obliged to attend Mass in a worthy manner on Sundays and holy days of obligation. Failure to do so without a proportionately serious reason is gravely wrong.

It is the custom for priests to celebrate Mass daily whenever possible. To satisfy the needs of the faithful on Sundays and holy days of obligation, they are authorized to say Mass twice **(bination)** or even three times **(trination)**. Bination is also permissible on weekdays to satisfy the needs of the faithful. On Christmas every priest may say three Masses.

The **fruits of the Mass**, which in itself is of infinite value, are: **general,** for all the faithful; **special (ministerial),** for the intentions or persons specifically intended by the celebrant; **most special (personal),** for the celebrant himself. On Sundays and certain other days pastors are obliged to offer Mass for their parishioners, or to have another priest do so. If a priest accepts a stipend or offering for a Mass, he is obliged in justice to apply the Mass for the intention of the donor. Mass may be applied for the living and the dead, or for any good intention.

Mass can be celebrated in several ways: e.g., with people present, without their presence (privately), with two or more priests as co-celebrants (concelebration), with greater or less solemnity.

Some of the various types of Masses are: **for the dead** (Funeral Mass or Mass of Christian Burial, Mass for the Dead — formerly called Requiem Mass); **ritual,** in connection with celebration of the sacraments, religious profession, etc.; **nuptial,** for married couples, with or after the wedding ceremony; votive, to honor a Person of the Trinity, a saint, or for some special intention.

Places, Altars for Mass

The ordinary place for celebrating the Eucharist is a church or other sacred place, at a fixed or movable altar.

The altar is a table at which the Eucharistic Sacrifice is celebrated.

A fixed altar is attached to the floor of the church. It should be of stone, preferably, and should be consecrated. The Code of Canon Law orders observance of the custom of placing under a fixed altar relics of martyrs or other saints.

A movable altar can be made of any solid and suitable material, and should be blessed or consecrated.

Outside of a sacred place, Mass may be celebrated in an appropriate place at a suitable table covered with a linen cloth and corporal. An altar stone containing the relics of saints, which was formerly prescribed, is not required by regulations in effect since the promulgation Apr. 6, 1969, of *Institutio Generalis Missalis Romani.*

LITURGICAL VESTMENTS

In the early years of the Church, vestments worn by the ministers at liturgical functions were the same as the garments in ordinary popular use. They became distinctive when their form was not altered to correspond with later variations in popular style. Liturgical vestments are symbolic of the sacred ministry and add appropriate decorum to divine worship.

Mass Vestments

Alb: A body-length tunic of white fabric; a vestment common to all ministers of divine worship.

Amice: A rectangular piece of white cloth worn about the neck, tucked into the collar and falling over the shoulders; prescribed for use when the alb does not completely cover the ordinary clothing at the neck.

Chasuble: Originally, a large mantle or cloak covering the body, it is the outer vestment of a priest celebrating Mass or carrying out other sacred actions connected with the Mass.

Cincture: A cord which serves the purpose of a belt, holding the alb close to the body.

Dalmatic: The outer vestment worn by a deacon in place of a chasuble.

Stole: A long, band-like vestment worn by a priest about the neck and falling to about the knees. A deacon wears a stole over the left shoulder, crossed and fastened at his right side.

The material, form and ornamentation of the aforementioned and other vestments are subject to variation and adaptation, according to norms and decisions of the Holy See and concerned conferences of bishops. The overriding norm is that they should be appropriate for use in divine worship. The customary ornamented vestments are the chasuble, dalmatic and stole.

The minimal vestments required for a priest celebrating Mass are the alb, stole and chasuble.

Chasuble-Alb: A vestment combining the features of the chasuble and alb; for use with a stole by concelebrants and, by way of exception, by celebrants in certain circumstances.

Liturgical Colors

The colors of outer vestments vary with liturgical seasons, feasts and other circumstances. The colors and their use are:

Green: For the season of Ordinary Time; symbolic of hope and the vitality of the life of faith.

Violet (Purple): For Advent and Lent; may also be used in Masses for the dead; symbolic of penance. (See below, Violet for Advent.)

Red: For the Sunday of the Passion, Good Friday, Pentecost; feasts of the Passion of Our Lord, the Apostles and Evangelists, martyrs; symbolic of the supreme sacrifice of life for the love of God.

Rose: May be used in place of purple on the Third Sunday of Advent (formerly called Gaudete Sunday) and the Fourth Sunday of Lent (formerly called Laetare Sunday); symbolic of anticipatory joy during a time of penance.

White: For the seasons of Christmas and Easter; feasts and commemorations of Our Lord, except those of the Passion; feasts and commemorations of the Blessed Virgin Mary, angels, saints who are not martyrs, All Saints (Nov. 1), St. John the Baptist (June 24), St. John the Evangelist (Dec. 27), the Chair of St. Peter (Feb. 22), the Conversion of St. Paul (Jan. 25). White, symbolic of purity and integrity of the life of faith, may generally be substituted for other colors, and can be used for funeral and other Masses for the dead.

Options are provided regarding the color of vestments used in offices and Masses for the dead. The newsletter of the U.S. Bishops' Committee on the Liturgy, in line with No. 308 of the General Instruction of the Roman Missal, announced in July, 1970: "In the dioceses of the United States, white vestments may be used, in addition to violet (purple) and black, in offices and Masses for the dead."

On more solemn occasions, better than ordinary vestments may be used, even though their color (e.g., gold) does not match the requirements of the day.

Violet for Advent: Violet is the official liturgical color for the season of Advent, according to the September, 1988, edition of the newsletter of the U.S. Bishops' Committee on the Liturgy. Blue was being proposed in order to distinguish between the Advent season and the specifically penitential season of Lent. The newsletter said, however, that "the same effect can be achieved by following the official color sequence of the Church, which requires the use of violet for Advent and Lent, while taking advantage of the varying shades which exist for violet. Light blue vestments are not authorized for use in the United States."

Considerable freedom is permitted in the choice of colors of vestments worn for votive Masses.

Other Vestments

Cappa Magna: Flowing vestment with a train, worn by bishops and cardinals.

Cassock: A non-liturgical, full-length, close-fitting robe for use by priests and other clerics under liturgical vestments and in ordinary use; usually black for priests, purple for bishops and other prelates, red for cardinals, white for the pope. In place of a cassock, priests belonging to religious institutes wear the habit proper to their institute.

Cope: A mantle-like vestment open in front and fastened across the chest; worn by sacred ministers in processions and other ceremonies, as prescribed by appropriate directives.

Habit: The ordinary (non-liturgical) garb of members of religious institutes, analogous to the cassock of diocesan priests; the form of habits varies from institute to institute.

Humeral Veil: A rectangular vestment worn about the shoulders by a deacon or priest in Eucharistic processions and for other prescribed liturgical ceremonies.

Mitre: A headdress worn at some liturgical functions by bishops, abbots and, in certain cases, other ecclesiastics.

Pallium: A circular band of white wool about two inches wide, with front and back pendants, marked with six crosses, worn about the neck. It is a symbol of the fullness of the episcopal office. Pope Paul VI, in a document issued July 20, 1978, on his own initiative and entitled *Inter Eximia Episcopalis*, restricted its use to the pope and archbishops of metropolitan sees. In 1984, Pope John Paul II decreed that the pallium would ordinarily be conferred by the pope on the solemnity of Sts. Peter and Paul, June 29. The pallium is made from the wool of lambs blessed by the pope on the feast of St. Agnes (Jan. 21).

Rochet: A knee-length, white linen-lace garment of prelates worn under outer vestments.

Surplice: a loose, flowing vestment of white fabric with wide sleeves. For some functions, it is interchangeable with an alb.

Zucchetto: A skullcap worn by bishops and other prelates.

SACRED VESSELS, LINENS

Vessels

Paten and Chalice: The principal sacred vessels required for the celebration of Mass are the paten (plate) and chalice (cup) in which bread and wine, respectively, are offered, consecrated and consumed. Both should be made of solid and noble material which is not easily breakable or corruptible. Gold coating is required of the interior parts of sacred vessels subject to rust. The cup of a chalice should be made of non-absorbent material.

Vessels for containing consecrated hosts (see below) can be made of material other than solid and noble metal — e.g., ivory, more durable woods — provided the substitute material is locally regarded as noble or rather precious and is suitable for sacred use.

Sacred vessels should be blessed, according to prescribed requirements.

Vessels, in addition to the paten, for containing consecrated hosts are:

Ciborium: Used to hold hosts for distribution to the faithful and for reservation in the tabernacle.

Luna, Lunula, Lunette: A small receptacle which holds the sacred host in an upright position in the monstrance.

Monstrance, Ostensorium: A portable receptacle so made that the sacred host, when enclosed therein, may be clearly seen, as at Benediction or during extended exposition of the Blessed Sacrament.

Pyx: A watch-shaped vessel used in carrying the Eucharist to the sick.

Linens

Altar Cloth: A white cloth, usually of linen, covering the table of an altar. One cloth is sufficient. Three were used according to former requirements.

Burse: A square, stiff flat case, open at one end, in which the folded corporal can be placed; the outside is covered with material of the same kind and color as the outer vestments of the celebrant.

Corporal: A square piece of white linen spread on the altar cloth, on which rest the vessels holding the Sacred Species — the consecrated host(s) and wine — during the Eucharistic Liturgy. The corporal is similarly used whenever the Blessed Sacrament is removed from the tabernacle; e.g., during Benediction the vessel containing the Blessed Sacrament rests on a corporal.

Finger Towel: A white rectangular napkin used by the priest to dry his fingers after cleansing them following the offering of gifts at Mass.

Pall: A square piece of stiff material, usually covered with linen, which can be used to cover the chalice at Mass.

Purificator: A white rectangular napkin used for cleansing sacred vessels after the reception of Communion at Mass.

Veil: The chalice intended for use at Mass can be covered with a veil made of the same material as the outer vestments of the celebrant.

THE CHURCH BUILDING

A church is a building set aside and dedicated for purposes of divine worship, the place of assembly for a worshipping community.

A Catholic church is the ordinary place in which the faithful assemble for participation in the Eucharistic Liturgy and other forms of divine worship.

In the early years of Christianity, the first places of assembly for the Eucharistic Liturgy were private homes (Acts 2:46; Rom. 16:5; 1 Cor. 16:5; Col. 4:15) and, sometimes, catacombs. Church building began in the latter half of the second century during lulls in persecution and became widespread after enactment of the Edict of Milan in 313, when it finally became possible for the Church to emerge completely from the underground. The oldest and basic norms regarding church buildings date from about that time.

The essential principle underlying all norms for church building was reformulated by the Second Vatican Council, as follows: "When churches are to be built, let great care be taken that they be suitable for the celebration of liturgical services and for the active participation of the faithful" (*Constitution on the Sacred Liturgy,* No. 124).

This principle was subsequently elaborated in detail by the Congregation for Divine Worship in a document entitled *Institutio Generalis Missalis Romani,* which was approved by Paul VI Apr. 3 and promulgated by a decree of the congregation dated Apr. 6, 1969. Coverage of the following items reflects the norms stated in Chapter V of this document.

Main Features

Sanctuary: The part of the church where the altar of sacrifice is located, the place where the ministers of the liturgy lead the people in prayer, proclaim the word of God and celebrate the Eucharist. It is set off from the body of the church by a distinctive structural feature — e.g., elevation above the main floor — or by ornamentation. (The traditional communion rail, removed in recent years in many churches, served this purpose of demarcation.) The customary location of the sanctuary is at the front of the church; it may, however, be centrally located.

Altar: The main altar of sacrifice and table of the Lord is the focal feature of the sanctuary and entire church. It stands by itself, so that the ministers can move about it freely, and is so situated that they face the people during the liturgical action. In addition to this main altar, there may also be others; in new churches, these are ideally situated in side chapels or alcoves removed to some degree from the body of the church.

Adornment of the Altar: The altar table is covered with a suitable linen cloth. Required candelabra and a cross are placed upon or near the altar in plain sight of the people and are so arranged that they do not obscure their view of the liturgical action.

Seats of the Ministers: The seats of the ministers should be so arranged that they are part of the seating arrangement of the worshiping congregation and suitably placed for the performance of ministerial functions. The seat of the celebrant or chief concelebrant should be in a presiding position.

Ambo, Pulpit, Lectern: The stand at which scriptural lessons and psalm responses are read, the word of God preached, and the prayer of the faithful offered. It is so placed that the ministers can be easily seen and heard by the people.

Places for the People: Seats and kneeling benches (pews) and other accommodations for the people are so arranged that they can participate in the most appropriate way in the liturgical action and have freedom of movement for the reception of Holy Communion. Reserved seats are out of order.

Place for the Choir: Where it is located depends on the most suitable arrangement for maintaining the unity of the choir with the congregation and for providing its members maximum opportunity for carrying out their proper function and participating fully in the Mass.

Tabernacle: The best place for reserving the Blessed Sacrament is in a chapel suitable for the private devotion of the people. If this is not possible, reservation should be at a side altar or other appropriately adorned place. In either case, the Blessed Sacrament should be kept in a tabernacle, i.e., a safelike, secure receptacle.

Statues: Images of the Lord, the Blessed Virgin Mary and the saints are legitimately proposed for the veneration of the faithful in churches. Their number and arrangement, however, should be ordered in such a way that they do not distract the people from the central celebration of the Eucharistic Liturgy. There should be only one statue of one and the same saint in a church.

General Adornment and Arrangement of Churches: Churches should be so adorned and fitted out that they serve the direct requirements of divine worship and the needs and reasonable convenience of the people.

Other Items

Ambry: A box containing the holy oils, attached to the wall of the sanctuary in some churches.

Baptistery: The place for administering baptism. Some churches have baptisteries adjoining or near the entrance, a position symbolizing the fact that persons are initiated in the Church and incorporated in Christ through this sacrament. Contemporary liturgical practice favors placement of the baptistery near the sanctuary and altar, or the use of a portable font in the same position, to emphasize the relationship of baptism to the Eucharist, the celebration in sacrifice and banquet of the death and resurrection of Christ.

Candles: Used more for symbolical than illuminative purposes, they represent Christ, the light and life of grace, at liturgical functions. They are made of beeswax. (See Index: Paschal Candle.)

Confessional, Reconciliation Room: A booth-like structure for the hearing of confessions, with separate compartments for the priest and penitents and a grating or screen between them. The use of confessionals became general in the Roman Rite after the Council of Trent. Since the Second Vatican Council, there has been a trend in the U.S. to replace or supplement confessionals with small reconciliation rooms so arranged that priest and penitent can converse face-to-face.

Crucifix: A cross bearing the figure of the body of Christ, representative of the Sacrifice of the Cross.

Cruets: Vessels containing the wine and water used at Mass. They are placed on a credence table in the sanctuary.

Holy Water Fonts: Receptacles containing holy water, usually at church entrances, for the use of the faithful.

Sanctuary Lamp: A lamp which is kept burning continuously before a tabernacle in which the Blessed Sacrament is reserved, as a sign of the Real Presence of Christ.

LITURGICAL DEVELOPMENTS

The principal developments covered in this article are enactments of the Holy See and actions related to their implementation in the United States.

Modern Movement

Origins of the modern movement for renewal in the liturgy date back to the 19th century. The key contributing factor was a revival of liturgical and scriptural studies. Of special significance was the work of the Benedictine monks of Solesmes, France, who aroused great interest in the liturgy through the restoration of Gregorian Chant. St. Pius X approved their work in a motu proprio of 1903 and gave additional encouragement to liturgical study and development.

St. Pius X did more than any other single pope to promote early first Communion and the practice of frequent Communion, started the research behind a revised breviary, and appointed a group to investigate possible revisions in the Mass.

The movement attracted some attention in the 1920s and 30s but made little progress.

Significant pioneering developments in the U.S. during the 20s, however, were the establishment of the Liturgical Press, the beginning of publication of *Orate Fratres* (now *Worship*), and the inauguration of the League of the Divine Office by the Benedictines at St. John's Abbey, Collegeville, Minn. Later events of influence were the establishment of the Pius X School of Liturgical Music at Manhattanville College of the Sacred Heart and the organization of a summer school of liturgical music at Mary Manse College by the Gregorian Institute of America. The turning point toward real renewal was reached during and after World War II.

Pius XII gave it impetus and direction, principally through the background teaching in his encyclicals on the *Mystical Body* (1943), *Sacred Liturgy* (1947), and *On Sacred Music* (1955), and by means of specific measures affecting the liturgy itself. His work was continued during the pontificates of his successors. The Second Vatican Council, in virtue of its *Constitution on the Sacred Liturgy,* inaugurated changes of the greatest significance.

Before and After Vatican II

The most significant liturgical changes made in the years immediately preceding the Second Vatican Council were the following:

(1) Revision of the Rites of Holy Week, for universal observance from 1956.

(2) Modification of the Eucharistic fast and permission for afternoon and evening Mass, in effect from 1953 and extended in 1957.

(3) The Dialogue Mass, introduced in 1958.

(4) Use of popular languages in administration of the sacraments.

(5) Calendar-missal-breviary reform, in effect from Jan. 1, 1961.

(6) Seven-step administration of baptism for adults, approved in 1962.

The *Constitution on the Sacred Liturgy* approved (2,174 to 4) and promulgated by the Second Vatican Council Dec. 4, 1963, marked the beginning of a profound renewal in the Church's corporate worship. Implementation of some of its measures was ordered by Paul VI Jan. 25, 1964, in the motu proprio *Sacram Liturgiam.* On Feb. 29, a special commission, the Consilium for Implementing the Constitution on the Sacred Liturgy, was formed to supervise the execution of the entire program of liturgical reform. Implementation of the program on local and regional levels was left to bishops acting through their own liturgical commissions and in concert with their fellow bishops in national conferences.

Liturgical reform in the United States has been carried out under the direction of the Liturgy Committee, National Conference of Catholic Bishops. Its secretariat, established early in 1965, is located at 3211 Fourth St. N.E., Washington, D.C. 20017.

Stages of Development

Liturgical development after the Second Vatican Council proceeded in several stages. It started with the formulation of guidelines and directives, and with the translation into vernacular languages of virtually unchanged Latin ritual texts. Then came structural changes in the Mass, the sacraments, the calendar, the Divine Office and other phases of the liturgy. These revisions were just about completed with the publication of a new order for the sacrament of penance in February, 1974. A continuing phase of development, in progress from the beginning, involves efforts to deepen the liturgical sense of the faithful, to increase their participation in worship and to relate it to full Christian life.

Texts and Translations

The master texts of all documents on liturgical reform are in Latin. Effective dates of their implementation have depended on the completion and approval of appropriate translations into vernacular languages. English translations were made by the International Committee for English in the Liturgy.

The principal features of liturgical changes and the effective dates of their introduction in the United States are covered below under topical headings. (For expanded coverage of various items, especially the sacraments, see additional entries.)

The Mass

A new Order of the Mass, supplanting the one authorized by the Council of Trent in the 16th century, was introduced in the U.S. Mar. 22, 1970. It had been approved by Paul VI in the apostolic constitution *Missale Romanum,* dated Apr. 3, 1969.

Preliminary and related to it were the following developments.

Mass in English: Introduced Nov. 29, 1964. In the same year, Psalm 42 was eliminated from the prayers at the foot of the altar.

Incidental Changes: The last Gospel (prologue of John) and vernacular prayers following Mass were eliminated Mar. 7, 1965. At the same time, provision was made for the celebrant to say aloud some prayers formerly said silently.

Rubrics: An instruction entitled *Tres Abhinc Annos,* dated May 4 and effective June 29, 1967, simplified directives for the celebration of Mass, approved the practice of saying the canon aloud, altered the Communion and dismissal rites, permitted purple instead of black vestments in Masses for the dead, discontinued wearing of the maniple, and approved in principle the use of vernacular languages for the canon, ordination rites, and lessons of the Divine Office when read in choir.

Eucharistic Prayers (Canons): The traditional Roman Canon in English was introduced Oct. 22, 1967. Three additional Eucharistic prayers, authorized May 23, 1968, were approved for use in English the following Aug. 15.

The customary Roman Canon, which dates at least from the beginning of the fifth century and has remained substantially unchanged since the seventh century, is the first in the order of listing of the Eucharistic prayers. It can be used at any time, but is the one of choice for most Sundays, some special feasts like Easter and Pentecost, and for feasts of the Apostles and other saints who are commemorated in the canon. Any preface can be used with it.

The second Eucharistic prayer, the shortest and simplest of all, is best suited for use on weekdays and various special circumstances. It has a preface of its own, but others may be used with it. This canon bears a close resemblance to the one framed by St. Hippolytus about 215.

The third Eucharistic prayer is suitable for use on Sundays and feasts as an alternative to the Roman Canon. It can be used with any preface and has a special formula for remembrance of the dead.

The fourth Eucharistic prayer, the most sophisticated of them all, presents a broad synthesis of salvation history. Based on the Eastern tradition of Antioch, it is best suited for use at Masses attended by persons versed in Sacred Scripture. It has an unchangeable preface.

Five additional Eucharistic prayers — three for Masses with children and two for Masses of reconciliation — were approved in 1974 and 1975, respectively, by the Congregation for the Sacraments and Divine Worship.

Use of the Eucharistic Prayers for Various Needs and Occasions, was approved by the U.S. bishops in 1994, confirmed by the appropriate Vatican congregations May 9, 1995, and ratified for use beginning Oct. 1, 1995.

Lectionary: A new compilation of scriptural readings and psalm responsories for Mass was published in 1969. The Lectionary contains a three-year cycle of readings for Sundays and solemn feasts, a two-year weekday cycle, and a one-year cycle for the feasts of saints, in addition to readings for a variety of votive Masses, ritual Masses and Masses for various needs. There are also responsorial psalms to follow the first readings and gospel or alleluia versicles.

A second edition of the Lectionary, substantially the same as the first, was published in 1981. New features included an expanded introduction, extensive scriptural references and additional readings for a number of solemnities and feasts.

Sacramentary (Missal): The Vatican Polyglot Press began distribution in June, 1970, of the Latin text of a new **Roman Missal,** the first revision published in 400 years. The English translation was authorized for optional use beginning July 1, 1974; the mandatory date for use was Dec. 1, 1974.

The Sacramentary is the celebrant's Mass book of entrance songs, prayers, prefaces and Eucharistic prayers, including special common sets of texts for various commemorations and intentions — dedication of churches, Mary, the apostles, martyrs, doctors of the Church, virgins, holy men and women, the dead, other categories of holy persons, administration of certain sacraments, special intentions.

Study of the Mass: The Bishops' Committee on the Liturgy, following approval by the National Conference of Catholic Bishops in May, 1979, began a study of the function and position of elements of the Mass, including the Gloria, the sign of peace, the penitential rite and the readings. Major phases of the study have been completed, and work is still under way toward completion of the project.

Mass for Special Groups: Reasons and norms for the celebration of Mass at special gatherings of the faithful were the subject of an instruction issued May 15, 1969. Two years earlier, the U.S. Bishops' Liturgy Committee went on record in support of the celebration of Mass in private homes under appropriate conditions.

Sunday Mass on Saturday: The Congregation for the Clergy, under date of Jan. 10, 1970, granted the request that the faithful, where bishops consider it pastorally necessary or useful, may satisfy the precept of participating in Mass in the late afternoon or evening hours of Saturdays and the days before holy days of obligation. This provision is stated in Canon 1248 of the Code of Canon Law.

Bination and Trination: Canon 905 of the Code of Canon Law provides that local ordinaries may permit priests to celebrate Mass twice a day (bination), for a just cause; in cases of pastoral need, they may permit priests to celebrate Mass three times a day (trination) on Sundays and holy days of obligation.

Mass in Latin: According to notices issued by the Congregation for Divine Worship June 1, 1971, and Oct. 28, 1974: (1) Bishops may permit the celebration of Mass in Latin for mixed-language groups. (2) Bishops may permit the celebration of one or two Masses in Latin on weekdays or Sundays in any church, irrespective of mixed-language groups involved (1971). (3) Priests may celebrate Mass in Latin when people are not present. (4) The approved revised Order of the Mass is to be used in Latin as well as vernacular languages. (5) By way of exception, bishops may permit older and handicapped priests to use the Council of Trent's Order of the Mass in private celebration of the holy Sacrifice. (See Permission for Tridentine Mass.)

Mass Obligation Waived: The Congregation for Bishops approved July 4, 1992, a resolution of the U.S. bishops to waive the Mass attendance obligation for the holy days of Mary, the Mother of God (Jan. 1), the Assumption of Mary (Aug. 15) and All Saints (Nov. 1) when these solemnities fall on Saturday or Monday.

Inter-Ritual Concelebration: The Apostolic Delegation (now Nunciature) in Washington, D.C., announced in June, 1971, that it had received authorization to permit priests of Roman and Eastern rites to celebrate Mass together in the rite of the host church. It was understood that the inter-ritual concelebrations would always be "a manifestation of the unity of the Church and of communion among particular churches."

Ordo of the Sung Mass: In a decree dated June 24 and made public Aug. 24, 1972, the Congregation for Divine Worship issued a new *Ordo of the Sung Mass* — containing Gregorian chants in Latin — to replace the *Graduale Romanum.*

Mass for Children: Late in 1973, the Congregation for Divine Worship issued special guidelines for children's Masses, providing accommodations to the mentality and spiritual growth of pre-adolescents while retaining the principal parts and structures of the Mass. The *Directory for Masses with Children* was approved by Paul VI Oct. 22 and was dated Nov. 1, 1973. Three Eucharistic prayers for Masses with children were approved by the congregation in 1974; English versions were approved June 5, 1975. Their use, authorized originally for a limited period of experimentation, was extended indefinitely Dec. 15, 1980.

Lectionary for Children: A lectionary for Masses with children, with an announced publication date of Sept., 1993, was authorized for use by choice beginning Nov. 28, 1993.

Sacraments

The general use of English in administration of the sacraments was approved for the U.S. Sept. 14, 1964. Structural changes of the rites were subsequently made and introduced in the U.S. as follows.

Pastoral Care of the Sick: Revised rites, covering also administration of the Eucharist to sick persons, were approved Nov. 30, 1972, and published Jan. 18, 1973. The effective date for use of the provisional English prayer formula was Dec. 1, 1974. The mandatory effective date for use of the ritual, *Pastoral Care of the Sick in English,* was Nov. 27, 1983.

Baptism: New rites for the baptism of infants, approved Mar. 19, 1969, were introduced June 1, 1970.

Rite of Christian Initiation of Adults: Revised

rites were issued Jan. 6, 1972, for the Christian initiation of adults — affecting preparation for and reception of baptism, the Eucharist and confirmation; also, for the reception of already baptized adults into full communion with the Church. These rites, which were introduced in the U.S. on the completion of English translation, nullified a seven-step baptismal process approved in 1962. On Mar. 8, 1988, the National Conference of Catholic Bishops was notified that the Congregation for Divine Worship had approved the final English translation of the Rite of Christian Initiation of Adults. The mandatory date for putting the rite into effect was Sept. 1, 1988.

Confirmation: Revised rites, issued Aug. 15, 1971, became mandatory in the U.S. Jan. 1, 1973. The use of a stole by persons being confirmed should be avoided, according to an item in the December, 1984, edition of the Newsletter of the Bishops' Committee on the Liturgy. The item said: "The distinction between the universal priesthood of all the baptized and the ministerial priesthood of the ordained is blurred when the distinctive garb (the stole) of ordained ministers is used in this manner."

A decree regarding the proper age for confirmation, approved by the U.S. bishops in June, 1993, was ratified by the Congregation for Bishops Feb. 8, 1994. The decree reads: "In accord with prescriptions of canon 891, the National Conference of Catholic Bishops hereby decrees that the sacrament of confirmation in the Latin rite shall be conferred between the age of discretion, which is about the age of seven, and 18 years of age, within the limits determined by the diocesan bishop and with regard for the legitimate exceptions given in canon 891, namely, when there is danger of death or where, in the judgment of the minister, grave cause urges otherwise." The decree became effective July 1, 1994, and continues in effect until July 1, 1999.

Special Ministers of the Eucharist: The designation of lay men and women to serve as special ministers of the Eucharist was authorized by Paul VI in an "Instruction on Facilitating Communion in Particular Circumstances" (*Immensae Caritatis*), dated Jan. 29 and published by the Congregation for Divine Worship Mar. 29, 1973. Provisions concerning them are contained in Canons 230 and 910 of the Code of Canon Law.

Qualified lay persons may serve as special ministers for specific occasions or for extended periods in the absence of a sufficient number of priests and deacons to provide reasonable and appropriate service in the distribution of Holy Communion, during Mass and outside of Mass (to the sick and shut-ins). Appointments of ministers are made by priests with the approval of the appropriate bishop.

The Newsletter of the U.S. Bishops' Committee on the Liturgy stated in its February, 1988, edition: "When ordinary ministers (bishops, priests, deacons) are present during a Eucharistic celebration, whether they are participating in it or not, and are not prevented from doing so, they are to assist in the distribution of Communion. Accordingly, if the ordinary ministers are in sufficient number, special ministers of the Eucharist are not allowed to distribute Communion at that Eucharistic celebration." Pope John

Paul approved this decision and ordered it published June 15, 1987.

Holy Orders: Revised ordination rites for deacons, priests and bishops, validated by prior experimental use, were approved in 1970. The sacrament of holy orders underwent further revision in 1972 with the elimination of the Church-instituted orders of porter, reader, exorcist, acolyte and subdeacon, and of the tonsure ceremony symbolic of entrance into the clerical state. The former minor orders of reader and acolyte were changed from orders to ministries.

Matrimony: A revised rite for the celebration of marriage was promulgated by the Congregation for Divine Worship and the Discipline of the Sacraments Mar. 19, 1969, and went into effect June 1, 1970. A second typical edition of the order of celebration, with revisions in accord with provisions of the Code of Canon Law promulgated in 1983, was approved and published in 1990 (*Notitiae*, Vol. 26, No.6). The date for implementation was reported to be dependent on the completion of required translations and appropriate formalities.

Penance: Ritual revision of the sacraments was completed with the approval by Paul VI Dec. 2, 1973, of new directives for the sacrament of penance or reconciliation. The U.S. Bishops' Committee on the Liturgy set Feb. 27, 1977, as the mandatory date for use of the new rite. The committee also declared that it could be used from Mar. 7, 1976, after adequate preparation of priests and people. Earlier, authorization was given by the Holy See in 1968 for the omission of any reference to excommunication or other censures in the formula of absolution unless there was some indication that a censure had actually been incurred by a penitent.

Additional Developments

Music: An instruction on Music in the Liturgy, dated Mar. 5 and effective May 14, 1967, encouraged congregational singing during liturgical celebrations and attempted to clarify the role of choirs and trained singers. More significantly, the instruction indicated that a major development under way in the liturgy was a gradual erasure of the distinctive lines traditionally drawn between the sung liturgy and the spoken liturgy, between what had been called the high Mass and the low Mass.

In the same year, the U.S. Bishops' Liturgy Committee approved the use of contemporary music, as well as guitars and other suitable instruments, in the liturgy. The Holy See authorized in 1968 the use of musical instruments other than the organ in liturgical services, "provided they are played in a manner suitable to worship."

Calendar: A revised liturgical calendar approved by Paul VI Feb. 14 and made public May 9, 1969, went into effect in the U.S. in 1972. Since that time, memorials and feasts of beatified persons and saints have been added.

Communion in Hand: Since 1969, the Holy See has approved the practice of in-hand reception of the Eucharist in regions and countries where it had the approval of the appropriate episcopal conferences. The first grant of approval was to Belgium, in May, 1969. Approval was granted the United States in June, 1977.

Liturgy of the Hours: The background, contents, scope and purposes of the revised Divine Office, called the Liturgy of the Hours, were described by Paul VI in the apostolic constitution *Laudis Canticum*, dated Nov. 1, 1970. A provisional English version, incorporating basic features of the master Latin text, was published in 1971. The four complete volumes of the Hours in English have been published since May, 1975. One-volume, partial editions have also been published in approved form. Nov. 27, 1977, was set by the Congregation for Divine Worship and the National Conference of Catholic Bishops as the effective date for exclusive use in liturgical worship of the translation of the Latin text of the Liturgy of the Hours approved by the International Committee on English in the Liturgy.

Holy Week: The English version of revised Holy Week rites went into effect in 1971. They introduced concelebration of Mass, placed new emphasis on commemorating the institution of the priesthood on Holy Thursday and modified Good Friday prayers for other Christians, Jews and other non-Christians.

In another action, the Congregation for Divine Worship released Feb. 20, 1988, a "Circular Letter concerning the Preparation and Celebration of the Easter Feasts." It called the feasts the "summit of the whole liturgical year," and criticized practices which dilute or change appropriate norms for their celebration. Singled out for blame for the abuse or ignorance of norms was the "inadequate formation given to the clergy and the faithful regarding the paschal mystery as the center of the liturgical year and of Christian life." The document set out the appropriate norms for the Lenten season, Holy Week, the Easter Triduum, Easter and the weeks following. It was particularly insistent on the proper celebration of the Easter Vigil, to take place after nightfall on Saturday and before dawn on Sunday.

Oils: The Congregation for Divine Worship issued a directive in 1971 permitting the use of other oils — from plants, seeds or coconuts — instead of the traditional olive oil in administering some of the sacraments. The directive also provided that oils could be blessed at other times than at the usual Mass of Chrism on Holy Thursday, and authorized bishops' conferences to permit priests to bless oils in cases of necessity.

Dancing and Worship: Dancing and worship was the subject of an essay which appeared in a 1975 edition of Notitiae (11, pp. 202-205), the official journal of the Congregation for the Sacraments and Divine Worship. The article was called a "qualified and authoritative sketch," and should be considered "an authoritative point of reference for every discussion of the matter."

The principal points of the essay were:

• "The dance has never been made an integral part of the official worship of the Latin Church."

• "If the proposal of the religious dance in the West is really to be made welcome, care will have to be taken that in its regard a place be found outside of the liturgy, in assembly areas which are not strictly liturgical. Moreover, the priests must always be excluded from the dance."

Mass for Deceased Non-Catholic Christians: The Congregation for the Doctrine of the Faith released a decree June 11, 1976, authorizing the celebration of public Mass for deceased non-Catholic Christians under certain conditions: "(1) The public celebration of the Masses must be explicitly requested by the relatives, friends, or subjects of the deceased person for a genuine religious motive. (2) In the Ordinary's judgment, there must be no scandal for the faithful."

Environment and Art in Catholic Worship: A booklet with this title was issued by the U.S. Bishops' Committee on the Liturgy in March, 1978. Work is under way on a new edition.

Doxology: The bishops' committee called attention in August, 1978, to the directive that the Doxology concluding the Eucharistic Prayer is said or sung by the celebrant (concelebrants) alone, to which the people respond, "Amen."

Churches, Altars, Chalices: The Newsletter of the U.S. Bishops' Committee on the Liturgy reported in November, 1978, that the Congregation for Divine Worship had given provisional approval of a new English translation for the rite of dedicating churches and altars, and of a new form for the blessing of chalices.

Eucharistic Worship: This was the subject of two documents issued in 1980. *Dominicae Coenae* was a letter addressed by Pope John Paul to bishops throughout the world in connection with the celebration of Holy Thursday; it was dated Feb. 24 and released Mar.18. It was more doctrinal in content than the "Instruction on Certain Norms concerning Worship of the Eucharistic Mystery" (*Inaestimabile Donum*, "The Priceless Gift"), which was approved by the Pope Apr. 17 and published by the Congregation for the Sacraments and Divine Worship May 23. Its stated purpose was to reaffirm and clarify teaching on liturgical renewal contained in enactments of the Second Vatican Council and in several related implementing documents.

Tridentine Mass: The celebration of Mass according to the 1962 typical (master) edition of the Roman Missal — the so-called Tridentine Mass — was authorized by Pope John Paul under certain conditions. So stated a letter from the Congregation for Divine Worship, dated Oct. 3, 1984. The letter said the Pope wished to be responsive to priests and faithful who remained attached to the so-called Tridentine rite. The principal condition for the celebration was: "There must be unequivocal, even public, evidence that the priest and people petitioning have no ties with those who impugn the lawfulness and doctrinal soundness of the Roman Missal promulgated in 1970 by Pope Paul VI." (This, in particular, with reference to the followers of dissident Archbishop Marcel Lefebvre.)

Six guidelines for celebration of the Tridentine Mass were contained in the letter regarding its "wide and generous" use, for two purposes: to win back Lefebvre followers and to clear up misunderstandings about liberal permission for use of the Tridentine rite. The letter, from the Pontifical Commission Ecclesia Dei, said in part:

• The Tridentine Mass can be celebrated in a parish church, so long as it provides a pastoral service and is harmoniously integrated into the parish liturgical schedule.

• When requested, the Mass should be offered on a

regular Sunday and holyday basis, "at a central location, at a convenient time" for a trial period of several months, with "adjustment" later if needed.

• Celebrants of the Mass should make it clear that they acknowledge the validity of the postconciliar liturgy.

• Although the commission has the authority to grant use of the Tridentine rite to all groups that request it, the commission "would much prefer that such faculties be granted by the Ordinary himself so that ecclesial communion can be strengthened."

• While the new Lectionary in the vernacular can be used in the Tridentine Mass, as suggested by the Second Vatican Council, it should not be "imposed on congregations that decidedly wish to maintain the former liturgical tradition in its integrity."

• Older and retired priests who have asked permission to celebrate Mass according to the Tridentine rite should be given the chance to do so for groups that request it.

Spanish: In accord with decrees of the Congregation for Divine Worship, Spanish was approved as a liturgical language in the U.S. (Jan. 19, 1985). The *texto unico* of the Ordinary of the Mass became mandatory in the U.S. Dec. 3, 1989. Spanish translations of Proper-of-the-Mass texts proper to U.S. dioceses were approved Mar. 12, 1990. An approved Spanish version of the Rite for the Christian Initiation of Adults was published in 1991.

The Institute of Hispanic Liturgy opened its national office June 1, 1995, on the campus of the Catholic University of America in Washington.

Funeral Rites: A revised Order of Christian Funerals became mandatory in the U.S. Nov. 2, 1989.

Permission for the presence of cremated human remains in the funeral liturgy, including the Eucharist, was granted in 1997 to local bishops in the U.S. by the Congregation for Divine Worship and the Discipline of the Sacraments. Adaptations to existing rites are under study.

Popular Piety and Liturgy: The relation of popular piety to the liturgy was the subject of remarks by Pope John Paul at a meeting with a group of Italian bishops Apr. 24, 1986. He said, in part:

"An authentic liturgical ministry will never be able to neglect the riches of popular piety, the values proper to the culture of a people, so that such riches might be illuminated, purified and introduced into the liturgy as an offering of the people."

Extended Eucharistic Exposition: In response to queries, the Secretariat of the U.S. Bishops' Committee on the Liturgy issued an advisory stating that liturgical law permits and encourages in parish churches:

• a. exposition of the Blessed Sacrament for an extended period of time once a year, with consent of the local Ordinary and only if suitable numbers of the faithful are expected to be present;

• b. exposition ordered by the local Ordinary, for a grave and general necessity, for a more extended period of supplication when the faithful assemble in large numbers.

With regard to perpetual exposition, this form is generally permitted only in the case of those religious communities of men or women who have the general practice of perpetual Eucharistic adoration or adoration over extended periods of time.

The Secretariat's advisory appeared in the June-July, 1986, edition of the Newsletter of the Bishops' Committee on the Liturgy.

Native American Languages: The Newsletter of the U.S. Bishops' Committee on the Liturgy reported in December, 1986, and May, 1987, respectively, that the Congregation for Divine Worship had authorized Mass translations in Navajo and Choctaw. Lakota was approved as a liturgical language in 1989.

Communion Guidelines: In 1986 and again in 1996, the U.S. bishops' approved the insertion of advisories in missalettes and similar publications, stating that: (1) The Eucharist is to be received by Catholics only, except in certain specific cases. (2) To receive Communion worthily, a person must be in the state of grace (i.e., free of serious sin) and observe the eucharistic fast (See separate entry).

Unauthorized Eucharistic Prayers: The May, 1987, Newsletter of the U.S. Bishops' Committee on the Liturgy restated the standing prohibition against the use of any Eucharistic Prayers other than those contained in the Sacramentary. Specifically, the article referred to the 25 unauthorized prayers in a volume entitled *Spoken Visions.*

Homilist: According to the Pontifical Commission for the Authentic Interpretation of Canon Law, the diocesan bishop cannot dispense from the requirement of Canon 767, par. 1, that the homily in the liturgy be reserved to a priest or deacon. Pope John Paul approved this decision June 20, 1987.

Concerts in Churches: In a letter released Dec. 5, 1987, the Congregation for Divine Worship declared that churches might be used on a limited basis for concerts of sacred or religious music but not for concerts featuring secular music.

Blessings: A revised *Book of Blessings* was ordered into use beginning Dec. 3, 1989.

Litany of the Blessed Virgin Mary: "Queen of Families," a new invocation was reported by the U.S .bishops in 1996, for insertion between "Queen of the Rosary" and "Queen of Peace."

Inclusive Language: "Criteria for the Evaluation of Inclusive Language Translations of Scriptural Texts Proposed for Liturgical Use" was issued by the U.S. bishops in November, 1990. The criteria distinguish between non-use of vertical inclusiveness in references to God and use of horizontal, gender-inclusive terms (he/she, man/woman and the like) where appropriate in references to persons.

The Legacy of Liturgical Reforms

In an address in Houston early in 1997, Bishop Donald W. Trautman of Erie, a Scripture scholar and liturgical specialist, described the massive liturgical reforms since the Second Vatican Council as a lasting legacy for the Church in the coming century. He following were among the major achievements he listed.

• translation of the liturgy into vernacular languages, making it accessible to all the people;

• restoration of the full, conscious, active participation of the whole assembly in the liturgy;

• recovery of an understanding of the Church as the people of God;

• renewal of biblical preaching.

THE SACRAMENTS

The sacraments are actions of Christ and his Church (itself a kind of sacrament) which signify grace, cause it in the act of signifying it, and confer it upon persons properly disposed to receive it. They perpetuate the redemptive activity of Christ, making it present and effective. They infallibly communicate the fruit of that activity — namely grace — to responsive persons with faith. Sacramental actions consist of the union of sensible signs (matter of the sacraments) with the words of the minister (form of the sacraments).

Christ himself instituted the seven sacraments of the New Law by determining their essence and the efficacy of their signs to produce the grace they signify.

Christ is the principal priest or minister of every sacrament; human agents — an ordained priest, baptized persons contracting marriage with each other, any person conferring emergency baptism in a proper manner — are secondary ministers. Sacraments have efficacy from Christ, not from the personal dispositions of their human ministers.

Each sacrament confers sanctifying grace for the special purpose of the sacrament; this is, accordingly, called sacramental grace. It involves a right to actual graces corresponding to the purposes of the respective sacraments.

Baptism, confirmation and the Eucharist are sacraments of initiation; penance (reconciliation) and anointing of the sick, sacraments of healing; order and matrimony, sacraments for service.

While sacraments infallibly produce the grace they signify, recipients benefit from them in proportion to their personal dispositions. One of these is the intention to receive sacraments as sacred signs of God's saving and grace-giving action. The state of grace is also necessary for fruitful reception of the Holy Eucharist, confirmation, matrimony, holy orders and anointing of the sick. Baptism is the sacrament in which grace is given in the first instance and original sin is remitted. Penance is the secondary sacrament of reconciliation, in which persons guilty of serious sin after baptism are reconciled with God and the Chuch, and in which persons already in the state of grace are strengthened in that state.

Role of Sacraments

The Second Vatican Council prefaced a description of the role of the sacraments with the following statement concerning participation by all the faithful in the priesthood of Christ and the exercise of that priesthood by receiving the sacraments (*Dogmatic Constitution on the Church*, Nos. 10 and 11).

"The baptized by regeneration and the anointing of the Holy Spirit are consecrated into a spiritual house and a holy priesthood. Thus through all those works befitting Christian men they can offer spiritual sacrifice and proclaim the power of him who has called them out of darkness into his marvelous light (cf. 1 Pt. 2:4-10)."

"Though they differ from one another in essence and not only in degree, the common priesthood of the faithful and the ministerial or hierarchical priesthood (of those ordained to holy orders) are nonetheless interrelated. Each of them in its own special way is a participation in the one priesthood of Christ. The

ministerial priest, by the sacred power he enjoys, molds and rules the priestly people. Acting in the Person of Christ, he brings about the Eucharistic Sacrifice, and offers it to God in the name of all the people. For their part, the faithful join in the offering of the Eucharist by virtue of their royal priesthood. They likewise exercise that priesthood by receiving the sacraments, by prayer and thanksgiving, by the witness of a holy life, and by self-denial and active charity."

"It is through the sacraments and the exercise of the virtues that the sacred nature and organic structure of the priestly community is brought into operation."

Baptism: "Incorporated into the Church through baptism, the faithful are consecrated by the baptismal character to the exercise of the cult of the Christian religion. Reborn as sons of God, they must confess before men the faith which they have received from God through the Church."

Confirmation: "Bound more intimately to the Church by the sacrament of confirmation, they are endowed by the Holy Spirit with special strength. Hence they are more strictly obliged to spread and defend the faith both by word and by deed as true witnesses of Christ.

Eucharist: "Taking part in the Eucharistic Sacrifice, which is the fount and apex of the whole Christian life, they offer the divine Victim to God, and offer themselves along with It. Thus, both by the act of oblation and through holy Communion, all perform their proper part in this liturgical service, not, indeed. all in the same way but each in that way which is appropriate to himself. Strengthened anew at the holy table by the Body of Christ, they manifest in a practical way that unity of God's People which is suitably signified and wondrously brought about by this most awesome sacrament."

Penance: "Those who approach the sacrament of penance obtain pardon from the mercy of God for offenses committed against him. They are at the same time reconciled with the Church, which they have wounded by their sins, and which by charity, example, and prayer seeks their conversion."

Anointing of the Sick: "By the sacred anointing of the sick and the prayer of her priests, the whole Church commends those who are ill to the suffering and glorified Lord, asking that he may lighten their suffering and save them (cf. Jas. 5:14-16). She exhorts them, moreover, to contribute to the welfare of the whole People of God by associating themselves freely with the passion and death of Christ (cf. Rom. 8:17; Col. 1:24; 2 Tm. 2:11-12; 1 Pt. 4:13)."

Order: "Those of the faithful who are consecrated by holy orders are appointed to feed the Church in Christ's name with the Word and the grace of God."

Matrimony: "Christian spouses, in virtue of the sacrament of matrimony, signify and partake of the mystery of that unity and fruitful love which exists between Christ and his Church (cf. Eph. 5:32). The spouses thereby help each other to attain to holiness in their married life and by the rearing and education of their children. And so, in their state and way of life, they have their own special gift among the People of God (cf. 1 Cor. 7:7).

"For from the wedlock of Christians there comes

the family, in which new citizens of human society are born. By the grace of the Holy Spirit received in baptism these are made children of God, thus perpetuating the People of God through the centuries. The family is, so to speak, the domestic Church. In it parents should, by their word and example, be the first preachers of the faith to their children. They should encourage them in the vocation which is proper to each of them, fostering with special care any religious vocation."

"Fortified by so many and such powerful means of salvation, all the faithful, whatever their condition or state, are called by the Lord, each in his own way, to that perfect holiness whereby the Father himself is perfect."

Baptism

Baptism is the sacrament of spiritual regeneration by which a person is incorporated in Christ and made a member of his Mystical Body, given grace, and cleansed of original sin. Actual sins and the punishment due for them are remitted also if the person baptized was guilty of such sins (e.g., in the case of a person baptized after reaching the age of reason). The theological virtues of faith, hope and charity are given with grace. The sacrament confers a character on the soul and can be received only once.

The matter is the pouring of water. The form is: "I baptize you in the name of the Father and of the Son and of the Holy Spirit."

The minister of solemn baptism is a bishop, priest or deacon, but in case of emergency anyone, including a non-Catholic, can validly baptize. The minister pours water on the forehead of the person being baptized and says the words of the form while the water is flowing. The water used in solemn baptism is blessed during the rite.

Baptism is conferred in the Roman Rite by immersion or infusion (pouring of water), depending on the directive of the appropriate conference of bishops, according to the Code of Canon Law. The Church recognizes as valid baptisms properly performed by non-Catholic ministers. The baptism of infants has always been considered valid and the general practice of infant baptism was well established by the fifth century. Baptism is conferred conditionally when there is doubt about the validity of a previous baptism.

Baptism is necessary for salvation. If a person cannot receive the baptism of water described above, this can be supplied by baptism of blood (martyrdom suffered for the Catholic faith or some Christian virtue) or by baptism of desire (perfect contrition joined with at least the implicit intention of doing whatever God wills that people should do for salvation).

A sponsor is required for the person being baptized. (See Godparents, below).

A person must be validly baptized before he or she can receive any of the other sacraments.

Christian Initiation of Infants: Infants should be solemnly baptized as soon after birth as conveniently possible. In danger of death, anyone may baptize an infant. If the child survives, the ceremonies of solemn baptism should be supplied.

The sacrament is ordinarily conferred by a priest or deacon of the parents' parish.

Catholics 16 years of age and over who have received the sacraments of confirmation and the Eucharist and are practicing their faith are eligible to be sponsors or godparents. Only one is required. Two, one of each sex, are permitted. A non-Catholic Christian cannot be a godparent for a Catholic child, but may serve as a witness to the baptism. A Catholic may not be a godparent for a child baptized in a non-Catholic religion, but may be a witness.

"Because of the close communion between the Catholic Church and the Eastern Orthodox churches," states the *1993 Directory on Ecumenism,* "it is permissible for a just cause for an Eastern faithful to act as godparent together with a Catholic godparent at the baptism of a Catholic infant or adult, so long as there is provision for the Catholic education of the person being baptized and it is clear that the godparent is a suitable one.

"A Catholic is not forbidden to stand as godparent in an Eastern Orthodox Church if he/she is so invited. In this case, the duty of providing for the Christian education binds in the first place the godparent who belongs to the church in which the child is baptized."

The role of godparents in baptismal ceremonies is secondary to the role of the parents. They serve as representatives of the community of faith and with the parents request baptism for the child and perform other ritual functions. Their function after baptism is to serve as proxies for the parents if the parents should be unable or fail to provide for the religious training of the child.

At baptism every child should be given a name with Christian significance, usually the name of a saint, to symbolize newness of life in Christ.

Christian Initiation of Adults: According to the *Ordo Initiationis Christianae Adultorum* ("Rite of the Christian Initiation of Adults") issued by the Congregation for Divine Worship under date of Jan. 6, 1972, and put into effect in revised form Sept. 1, 1988, adults are prepared for baptism and reception into the Church in several stages:

• An initial period of inquiry, instruction and evangelization.

• The catechumenate, a period of at least a year of formal instruction and progressive formation in and familiarity with Christian life. It starts with a statement of purpose and includes a rite of election.

• Immediate preparation, called a period of purification and enlightenment, from the beginning of Lent to reception of the sacraments of initiation — baptism, confirmation, Holy Eucharist — during ceremonies of the Easter Vigil. The period is marked by scrutinies, formal giving of the creed and the Lord's Prayer, the choice of a Christian name, and a final statement of intention.

• A mystagogic phase whose objective is greater familiarity with Christian life in the Church through observances of the Easter season and association with the community of the faithful, and through extended formation for about a year.

National Statutes for the Catechumenate were approved by the National Conference of Catholic Bishops Nov. 11, 1986, and were subsequently ratified by the Vatican.

The priest who baptizes a catechumen can also administer the sacrament of confirmation.

A sponsor is required for the person being baptized.

The *Ordo* also provides a simple rite of initiation for adults in danger of death and for cases in which all stages of the initiation process are not necessary, and guidelines for: (1) the preparation of adults for the sacraments of confirmation and Holy Eucharist in cases where they have been baptized but have not received further formation in the Christian life; (2) for the formation and initiation of children of catechetical age.

The Church recognizes the right of anyone over the age of seven to request baptism and to receive the sacrament after completing a course of instruction and giving evidence of good will. Practically, in the case of minors in a non-Catholic family or environment, the Church accepts them when other circumstances favor their ability to practice the faith — e.g., well-disposed family situation, the presence of another or several Catholics in the family. Those who are not in such favorable circumstances are prudently advised to defer reception of the sacrament until they attain the maturity necessary for independent practice of the faith.

Reception of Baptized Christians: Procedure for the reception of already baptized Christians into full communion with the Catholic Church is distinguished from the catechumenate, since they have received some Christian formation. Instruction and formation are provided as necessary, however; and conditional baptism is administered if there is reasonable doubt about the validity of the person's previous baptism.

In the rite of reception, the person is invited to join the community of the Church in professing the Nicene Creed and is asked to state: "I believe and profess all that the holy Catholic Church believes, teaches, and proclaims as revealed by God." The priest places his hand on the head of the person, states the formula of admission to full communion, confirms (in the absence of a bishop), gives a sign of peace, and administers Holy Communion during a Eucharistic Liturgy.

Confirmation

Confirmation is the sacrament by which a baptized person, through anointing with chrism and the imposition of hands, is endowed with the fullness of baptismal grace; is united more intimately to the Church; is enriched with the special power of the Holy Spirit; is committed to be an authentic witness to Christ in word and action. The sacrament confers a character on the soul and can be received only once.

According to the apostolic constitution *Divinae Consortium Naturae* dated Aug. 15, 1971, in conjunction with the *Ordo Confirmationis* ("Rite of Confirmation"): "The sacrament of confirmation is conferred through the anointing with chrism on the forehead, which is done by the imposition of the hand (matter of the sacrament), and through the words: 'N , receive the seal of the Holy Spirit, the Gift of the Father' " (form of the sacrament). On May 5, 1975, bishops' conferences in English-speaking countries were informed by the Congregation for Divine Worship that Pope Paul had approved this English version of the form of the sacrament: "Be sealed with the gift of the Holy Spirit."

The ordinary minister of confirmation in the Roman Rite is a bishop. Priests may be delegated for the purpose. A pastor can confirm a parishioner in danger of death, and a priest can confirm in ceremonies of Christian initiation and at the reception of a baptized Christian into union with the Church.

Ideally, the sacrament is conferred during the Eucharistic Liturgy. Elements of the rite include renewal of the promises of baptism, which confirmation ratifies and completes, and the laying on of hands by the confirming bishop and priests participating in the ceremony.

"The entire rite," according to the Ordo; "has a twofold meaning. The laying of hands upon the candidates, done by the bishop and the concelebrating priests, expresses the biblical gesture by which the gift of the Holy Spirit is invoked. The anointing with chrism and the accompanying words clearly signify the effect of the Holy Spirit. Signed with the perfumed oil by the bishop's hand, the baptized person receives the indelible character, the seal of the Lord, together with the Spirit who is given and who conforms the person more perfectly to Christ and gives him the grace of spreading the Lord's presence among men."

A sponsor is required for the person being confirmed. Eligible is any Catholic 16 years of age or older who has received the sacraments of confirmation and the Eucharist and is practicing the faith. The baptismal sponsor, preferably, can also be the sponsor for confirmation. Parents may present their children for confirmation but cannot be sponsors.

In the Roman Rite, it has been customary for children to receive confirmation within a reasonable time after first Communion and confession. There is a trend, however, to defer confirmation until later when its significance for mature Christian living becomes more evident. In the Eastern Rites, confirmation is administered at the same time as baptism.

Eucharist

The Holy Eucharist is a sacrifice (see The Mass) and the sacrament in which Christ is present and is received under the appearances of bread and wine.

The matter is bread of wheat, unleavened in the Roman Rite and leavened in the Eastern Rites, and wine of grape. The form consists of the words of consecration said by the priest at Mass: "This is my body . This is the cup of my blood" (according to the traditional usage of the Roman Rite).

Only a priest can consecrate bread and wine so they become the body and blood of Christ. After consecration, however, the Eucharist can be administered by deacons and, for various reasons, by religious and lay persons.

Priests celebrating Mass receive the Eucharist under the species of bread and wine. In the Roman Rite, others receive under the species of bread only, i.e., the consecrated host, or in some circumstances they may receive under the species of both bread and wine. In Eastern-Rite practice, the faithful generally receive a piece of consecrated leavened bread which has been dipped into consecrated wine (i.e., by intinction).

Conditions for receiving the Eucharist, commonly called Holy Communion, are the state of grace, the right intention and observance of the Eucharistic fast.

The faithful of Roman Rite are required by a precept of the Church to receive the Eucharist at least once a year, ordinarily during the Easter time.

(See Eucharistic Fast, Mass, Transubstantiation, Viaticum.)

First Communion and Confession: Children are to be prepared for and given opportunity for receiving both sacraments (Eucharist and reconciliation, or penance) on reaching the age of discretion, at which time they become subject to general norms concerning confession and Communion. This, together with a stated preference for first confession before first Communion, was the central theme of a document entitled *Sanctus Pontifex* and published May 24, 1973, by the Congregation for the Discipline of the Sacraments and the Congregation for the Clergy, with the approval of Pope Paul VI.

What the document prescribed was the observance of practices ordered by St. Pius X in the decree *Quam Singulari* of Aug. 8, 1910. Its purpose was to counteract pastoral and catechetical experiments virtually denying children the opportunity of receiving both sacraments at the same time. Termination of such experiments was ordered by the end of the 1972-73 school year.

At the time the document was issued, two- or three-year experiments of this kind — routinely deferring reception of the sacrament of penance until after the first reception of Holy Communion — were in effect in more than half of the dioceses of the U.S. They have remained in effect in many places, despite the advisory from the Vatican.

One reason stated in support of such experiments is the view that children are not capable of serious sin at the age of seven or eight, when Communion is generally received for the first time, and therefore prior reception of the sacrament of penance is not necessary. Another reason is the purpose of making the distinctive nature of the two sacraments clearer to children.

The Vatican view reflected convictions that the principle and practice of devotional reception of penance are as valid for children as they are for adults, and that sound catechetical programs can avoid misconceptions about the two sacraments.

A second letter on the same subject and in the same vein was released May 19, 1977, by the aforementioned congregations. It was issued in response to the question:

" 'Whether it is allowed after the declaration of May 24, 1973, to continue to have, as a general rule, the reception of first Communion precede the reception of the sacrament of penance in those parishes in which this practice developed in the past few years.'

"The Sacred Congregations for the Sacraments and Divine Worship and for the Clergy, with the approval of the Supreme Pontiff, reply: Negative, and according to the mind of the declaration.

"The mind of the declaration is that one year after the promulgation of the same declaration, all experiments of receiving first Communion without the sacrament of penance should cease so that the discipline of the Church might be restored, in the spirit of the decree, *Quam Singulari*."

The two letters from the Vatican congregations have not produced uniformity of practice in this country. Simultaneous preparation for both sacraments is provided in some dioceses where a child has the option of receiving either sacrament first, with the counsel of parents, priests and teachers. Programs in other dioceses are geared first to reception of Communion and later to reception of the sacrament of reconciliation.

Commentators on the letters note that: they are disciplinary rather than doctrinal in content; they are subject to pastoral interpretation by bishops; they cannot be interpreted to mean that a person who is not guilty of serious sin must be required to receive the sacrament of penance before (even first) Communion.

Canon 914 of the Code of Canon Law states that sacramental confession should precede first Communion.

Holy Communion under the Forms of Bread and Wine (by separate taking of the consecrated bread and wine or by intinction, the reception of the host dipped in the wine): Such reception is permitted under conditions stated in instructions issued by the Congregation for Divine Worship (May 25, 1967; June 29, 1970), the *General Instruction on the Roman Missal* (No. 242), and directives of bishops' conferences and individual bishops.

Accordingly, Communion can be administered in this way to: persons being baptized, received into communion with the Church, confirmed, receiving anointing of the sick; couples at their wedding or jubilee; religious at profession or renewal of profession; lay persons receiving an ecclesiastical assignment (e.g., lay missionaries); participants at concelebrated Masses, retreats, pastoral commission meetings, daily Masses and, in the U.S., Masses on Sundays and holy days of obligation.

A communicant has the option of receiving the Eucharist under the form of bread alone or under the forms of bread and wine.

Holy Communion More Than Once a Day: A person who has already received the Eucharist may receive it (only) once again on the same day only during a Eucharistic celebration in which the person participates. A person in danger of death who has already received the Eucharist once or twice is urged to receive Communion again as Viaticum. Pope John Paul approved this decision, in accord with Canon 917, and ordered it published July 11, 1984.

Holy Communion and Eucharistic Devotion outside of Mass: These were the subjects of an instruction (*De Sacra Communione et de Cultu Mysterii Eucharistici extra Missam*) dated June 21 and made public Oct. 18, 1973, by the Congregation for Divine Worship.

Holy Communion can be given outside of Mass to persons unable for a reasonable cause to receive it during Mass on a given day. The ceremonial rite is modeled on the structure of the Mass, consisting of a penitential act, a scriptural reading, the Lord's Prayer, a sign or gesture of peace, giving of the Eucharist, prayer and final blessing. Viaticum and Communion to the sick can be given by extraordinary ministers (authorized lay persons) with appropriate rites.

Forms of devotion outside of Mass are exposition of the Blessed Sacrament (by men or women religious, especially, or lay persons in the absence of a priest; but only a priest can give the blessing), processions and congresses with appropriate rites.

Intercommunion: Church policy on intercommunion was stated in an "Instruction on the Admission of Other Christians to the Eucharist," dated June 1 and made public July 8, 1972, against the background of the Decree on Ecumenism approved by the Second Vatican Council, and the Directory on Ecumenism issued by the Secretariat for Promoting Christian Unity in 1967, 1970 and 1993.

Basic principles related to intercommunion are:

• "There is an indissoluble link between the mystery of the Church and the mystery of the Eucharist, or between ecclesial and Eucharistic communion; the celebration of the Eucharist of itself signifies the fullness of profession of faith and ecclesial communion" (1972 Instruction).

• "Eucharistic communion practiced by those who are not in full ecclesial communion with each other cannot be the expression of that full unity which the Eucharist of its nature signifies and which in this case does not exist; for this reason such communion cannot be regarded as a means to be used to lead to full ecclesial communion" (1972 Instruction).

• The question of reciprocity "arises only with those churches which have preserved the substance of the Eucharist, the sacrament of orders and apostolic succession" (1967 Directory).

• "A Catholic cannot ask for the Eucharist except from a minister who has been validly ordained" (1967 Directory).

The policy distinguishes between separated Eastern Christians and other Christians.

With Separated Eastern Christians (e.g., Orthodox): These may be given the Eucharist (as well as penance and anointing of the sick) at their request. Catholics may receive these same sacraments from priests of separated Eastern churches if they experience genuine spiritual necessity, seek spiritual benefit, and access to a Catholic priest is morally or physically impossible. This policy (of reciprocity) derives from the facts that the separated Eastern churches have apostolic succession through their bishops, valid priests, and sacramental beliefs and practices in accord with those of the Catholic Church.

With Other Christians (e.g., members of Reformation-related churches, others): Admission to the Eucharist in the Catholic Church, according to the *Directory on Ecumenism,* "is confined to particular cases of those Christians who have a faith in the sacrament in conformity with that of the Church, who experience a serious spiritual need for the Eucharistic sustenance, who for a prolonged period are unable to have recourse to a minister of their own community and who ask for the sacrament of their own accord; all this provided that they have proper dispositions and lead lives worthy of a Christian." The spiritual need is defined as "a need for an increase in spiritual life and a need for a deeper involvement in the mystery of the Church and its unity."

Circumstances under which Communion may be given to other properly disposed Christians are danger of death, imprisonment, persecution, grave spiritual necessity coupled with no chance of recourse to a minister of their own community.

Catholics cannot ask for the Eucharist from ministers of other Christian churches who have not been validly ordained to the priesthood.

Penance

Penance is the sacrament by which sins committed after baptism are forgiven and a person is reconciled with God and the Church.

Individual and integral confession and absolution are the only ordinary means for the forgiveness of serious sin and for reconciliation with God and the Church.

(Other than ordinary means are perfect contrition and general absolution without prior confession, both of which require the intention of subsequent confession and absolution.)

A revised ritual for the sacrament — *Ordo Paenitentiae,* published by the Congregation of Divine Worship Feb. 7, 1974, and made mandatory in the U.S. from the first Sunday of Lent, 1977— reiterates standard doctrine concerning the sacrament; emphasizes the social (communal and ecclesial) aspects of sin and conversion, with due regard for personal aspects and individual reception of the sacrament; prescribes three forms for celebration of the sacrament; and presents models for community penitential services.

The basic elements of the sacrament are sorrow for sin because of a supernatural motive, confession (of previously unconfessed mortal or grave sins, required; of venial sins also, but not of necessity), and reparation (by means of prayer or other act enjoined by the confessor), all of which comprise the matter of the sacrament; and absolution, which is the form of the sacrament.

The traditional words of absolution — "I absolve you from your sins in the name of the Father, and of the Son, and of the Holy Spirit"— remain unchanged at the conclusion of a petition in the new rite that God may grant pardon and peace through the ministry of the Church.

The minister of the sacrament is an authorized priest — i.e., one who, besides having the power of orders to forgive sins, also has faculties of jurisdiction granted by an ecclesiastical superior and/or by canon law.

The sacrament can be celebrated in three ways.

• For individuals: The traditional manner remains acceptable but is enriched with additional elements including: reception of the penitent and making of the Sign of the Cross; an exhortation by the confessor to trust in God; a reading from Scripture; confession of sins; manifestation of repentance; petition for God's forgiveness through the ministry of the Church and the absolution of the priest; praise of God's mercy, and dismissal in peace. Some of these elements are optional.

• For several penitents, in the course of a community celebration including a Liturgy of the Word of God and prayers, individual confession and absolution, and an act of thanksgiving.

• For several penitents, in the course of a community celebration, with general confession and general absolution. In extraordinary cases, reconciliation may be attained by general absolution without prior individual confession as, for example, under these circumstances: (1) danger of death, when there is neither time nor priests available for hearing confessions; (2) grave necessity of a number of penitents who, because of a shortage of confessors, would be deprived of sacramental grace or Communion for a lengthy period of time through no fault of their own. Persons receiving general absolution are obliged to be properly disposed and resolved to make an individual confession of the grave sins from which they have been absolved; this confession should be made as soon as the opportunity to confess presents itself and before any second reception of general absolution.

Norms regarding general absolution, issued by the Congregation for the Doctrine of the Faith in 1972, are not intended to provide a basis for convoking large gatherings of the faithful for the purpose of imparting general absolution, in the absence of extraordinary circumstances. Judgment about circumstances that warrant general absolution belongs principally to the bishop of the place, with due regard for related decisions of appropriate episcopal conferences.

Communal celebrations of the sacrament are not held in connection with Mass.

The place of individual confession, as determined by episcopal conferences in accordance with given norms, can be the traditional confessional or another appropriate setting.

A precept of the Church obliges the faithful guilty of grave sin to confess at least once a year.

The Church favors more frequent reception of the sacrament not only for the reconciliation of persons guilty of serious sins but also for reasons of devotion. Devotional confession — in which venial sins or previously forgiven sins are confessed — serves the purpose of confirming persons in penance and conversion.

Penitential Celebrations: Communal penitential celebrations are designed to emphasize the social dimensions of Christian life — the community aspects and significance of penance and reconciliation.

Elements of such celebrations are community prayer, hymns and songs, scriptural and other readings, examination of conscience, general confession and expression of sorrow for sin, acts of penance and reconciliation, and a form of non-sacramental absolution resembling the one in the penitential rite of the Mass.

If the sacrament is celebrated during the service, there must be individual confession and absolution of sin.

(See Absolution, Confession, Confessional, Confessor, Contrition, Faculties, Forgiveness of Sin, Power of the Keys, Seal of Confession, Sin.)

Anointing of the Sick

This sacrament, promulgated by St. James the Apostle (Jas. 5:13-15), can be administered to the faithful after reaching the age of reason who begin to be in danger because of illness or old age. By the anointing with blessed oil and the prayer of a priest, the sacrament confers on the person comforting grace; the remission of venial sins and inculpably unconfessed mortal sins, together with at least some of the temporal punishment due for sins; and, sometimes, results in an improved state of health.

The matter of this sacrament is the anointing with blessed oil (of the sick — olive oil, or vegetable oil if necessary) of the forehead and hands; in cases of necessity, a single anointing of another portion of the body suffices. The form is: "Through this holy anointing and his most loving mercy, may the Lord assist you by the grace of the Holy Spirit so that, when you have been freed from your sins, he may save you and in his goodness raise you up."

Anointing of the sick, formerly called extreme unction, may be received more than once, e.g., in new or continuing stages of serious illness. Ideally, the sacrament should be administered while the recipient is conscious and in conjunction with the sacraments of penance and the Eucharist. It should be administered in cases of doubt as to whether the person has reached the age of reason, is dangerously ill or dead.

The sacrament can be administered during a communal celebration in some circumstances, as in a home for the aged.

Matrimony

Coverage of the sacrament of matrimony is given in the articles: Marriage Doctrine, *Humanae Vitae,* Marriage Laws, Pastoral Ministry for Divorced and Remarried.

Order

Order is the sacrament by which the mission given by Christ to the Apostles continues to be exercised in the Church until the end of time; it is the sacrament of apostolic mission. It has three grades: episcopacy, priesthood and diaconate. The sacrament confers a character on the soul and can be received only once. The minister of the sacrament is a bishop.

Order, like matrimony but in a different way, is a social sacrament. As the Second Vatican Council declared in the *Dogmatic Constitution on the Church:*

"For the nurturing and constant growth of the People of God, Christ the Lord instituted in his Church a variety of ministries, which work for the good of the whole body. For those ministers who are endowed with sacred power are servants of their brethren, so that all who are of the People of God, and therefore enjoy a true Christian dignity, can work toward a common goal freely and in an orderly way, and arrive at salvation" (No. 18).

Bishop: The fullness of the priesthood belongs to those who have received the order of bishop. Bishops, in hierarchical union with the pope and their fellow bishops, are the successors of the Apostles as pastors of the Church: they have individual responsibility for the care of the local churches they serve and collegial responsibility for the care of the universal Church (see Collegiality). In the ordination or consecration of bishops, the essential form is the imposition of hands by the consecrator(s) and the assigned prayer in the preface of the rite of ordination.

"With their helpers, the priests and deacons, bishops have taken up the service of the community presiding in place of God over the flock whose shepherds they are, as teachers of doctrine, priests of sacred worship, and officers of good order" (No. 20).

Priests: A priest is an ordained minister with the power to celebrate Mass, administer the sacraments, preach and teach the word of God, impart blessings, and perform additional pastoral functions, according to the mandate of his ecclesiastical superior.

Concerning priests, the Second Vatican Council stated in the *Dogmatic Constitution on the Church* (No. 28):

"The divinely established ecclesiastical ministry is exercised on different levels by those who from antiquity have been called bishops, priests, and deacons. Although priests do not possess the highest degree of the priesthood, and although they are dependent on the bishops in the exercise of their power, they are nevertheless united with the bishops in sacerdotal dignity. By the power of the sacrament of orders, and in the image of Christ the eternal High Priest (Hb. 5:1-10; 7:24; 9:11-28), they are consecrated to preach the Gospel, shepherd the faithful, and celebrate divine worship as true priests of the New Testament.

"Priests, prudent cooperators with the episcopal order as well as its aides and instruments, are called to serve the People of God. They constitute one priesthood with their bishop, although that priesthood is comprised of different functions."

In the ordination of a priest of Roman Rite, the essential matter is the imposition of hands on the heads of those being ordained by the ordaining bishop. The essential form is the accompanying prayer in the preface of the ordination ceremony. Other elements in the rite are the presentation of the implements of sacrifice — the chalice containing the wine and the paten containing a host — with accompanying prayers.

Deacon: There are two kinds of deacons: those who receive the order and remain in it permanently, and those who receive the order while advancing to priesthood. The following quotation — from Vatican II's *Dogmatic Constitution on the Church* (No. 29) — describes the nature and role of the diaconate, with emphasis on the permanent diaconate.

"At a lower level of the hierarchy are deacons, upon whom hands are imposed 'not unto the priesthood, but unto a ministry of service.' For strengthened by sacramental grace, in communion with the bishop and his group of priests, they serve the People of God in the ministry of the liturgy, of the word, and of charity. It is the duty of the deacon, to the extent that he has been authorized by competent authority, to administer baptism solemnly, to be custodian and dispenser of the Eucharist, to assist at and bless marriages in the name of the Church, to bring Viaticum to the dying, to read the sacred Scripture to the faithful, to instruct and exhort the people, to preside at the worship and prayer of the faithful, to administer sacramentals, and to officiate at funeral and burial services. (Deacons are) dedicated to duties of charity and administration."

"The diaconate can in the future be restored as a proper and permanent rank of the hierarchy. It pertains to the competent territorial bodies of bishops, of one kind or another, to decide, with the approval of the Supreme Pontiff, whether and where it is opportune for such deacons to be appointed for the care of souls. With the consent of the Roman Pontiff, this diaconate will be able to be conferred upon men of more mature age, even upon those living in the married state. It may also be conferred upon suitable young men. For them, however, the law of celibacy must remain intact" (No. 29).

The Apostles ordained the first seven deacons (Acts 6:1-6): Stephen, Philip, Prochorus, Nicanor, Timon, Parmenas, Nicholas.

Former Orders, Ministries: With the revision of the sacrament of order which began in 1971, the orders of subdeacon, acolyte, exorcist, lector and porter were abolished because they and their respective functions had fallen into disuse or did not require ordination. The Holy See started revision of the sacrament of order in 1971. In virtue of an indult of Oct. 5 of that year, the bishops of the United States were permitted to discontinue ordaining porters and exorcists. Another indult, dated three days later, permitted the use of revised rites for ordaining acolytes and lectors.

To complete the revision, Pope Paul VI abolished Sept. 14, 1972, the orders of porter, exorcist and subdeacon; decreed that laymen, as well as candidates for the diaconate and priesthood, can be installed (rather than ordained) in the ministries (rather than orders) of acolyte and lector; reconfirmed the suppression of tonsure and its replacement with a service of dedication to God and the Church; and stated that a man enters the clerical state on ordination to the diaconate.

The abolished orders were:

• Subdeacon, with specific duties in liturgical worship, especially at Mass. The order, whose first extant mention dates from about the middle of the third century, was regarded as minor until the 13th century; afterwards, it was called a major order in the West but not in the East.

• Acolyte, to serve in minor capacities in liturgical worship; a function now performed by Mass servers.

• Exorcist, to perform services of exorcism for expelling evil spirits; a function which came to be reserved to specially delegated priests.

• Lector, to read scriptural and other passages during liturgical worship; a function now generally performed by lay persons.

• Porter, to guard the entrance to an assembly of Christians and to ward off undesirables who tried to gain admittance; an order of early origin and utility but of present insignificance.

PERMANENT DIACONATE

Restoration of the permanent diaconate in the Roman rite — making it possible for men to become deacons permanently, without going on to the priesthood — was promulgated by Pope Paul VI June 18, 1967, in a document entitled *Sacrum Diaconatus Ordinem* ("Sacred Order of the Diaconate").

The Pope's action implemented the desire expressed by the Second Vatican Council for reestablishment of the diaconate as an independent order in its own right not only to supply ministers for carrying on the work of the Church but also to complete the hierarchical structure of the Church of Roman rite.

Permanent deacons have been traditional in the Eastern Church. The Western Church, however, since the fourth or fifth century, generally followed the practice of conferring the diaconate only as a sacred order preliminary to the priesthood, and of restricting the ministry of deacons to liturgical functions.

The Pope's document, issued on his own initiative, provided:

• Qualified unmarried men 25 years of age or older may be ordained deacons. They cannot marry after ordination.

• Qualified married men 35 years of age or older may be ordained deacons. The consent of the wife of a prospective deacon is required. A married deacon cannot remarry after the death of his wife.

• Preparation for the diaconate includes a course of study and formation over a period of at least three years.

• Candidates who are not members of religious institutes must be affiliated with a diocese. Reestablishment of the diaconate among religious is reserved to the Holy See.

• Deacons will practice their ministry under the direction of a bishop and with the priests with whom they will be associated. (For functions, see also the description of deacon, under Holy Orders.)

Restoration of the permanent diaconate in the United States was approved by the Holy See in October, 1968. Shortly afterwards the U.S. bishops established a committee for the permanent diaconate, which was chaired by Bishop Edward U. Kmiec of Nashville in 1997. The committee operates through a secretariat, with offices at 3211 Fourth St. N. E., Washington, D.C. 20017. Deacon John Pistone is executive director.

Status and Functions

According to a study conducted under the auspices of the National Conference of Catholic Bishops and released in summary form in December, 1995, there were more than 11,000 permanent deacons in the United States, the highest total for any single country. Their ages ranged from the 30s to 86; the median age was almost 60. Sixty percent reported professional or managerial careers. Four percent were never married. Thirteen of the 18 percent with minority backgrounds were Hispanic Latino; four percent were African American.

Training programs of spiritual, theological and pastoral formation are based on guidelines emanating from the National Conference of Catholic Bishops.

Deacons have various functions, depending on the nature of their assignments. Liturgically, they can officiate at baptisms, weddings, wake services and funerals, can preach and distribute Holy Communion. Some are engaged in religious education work. All are intended to carry out works of charity and pastoral service of one kind or another.

The majority of deacons, 92 percent of whom are married, continue in their secular work. Their ministry of service is developing in three dimensions: of liturgy, of the word, and of charity. Depending on the individual deacon's abilities and preference, he is assigned by his bishop to either a parochial ministry or to another field of service. Deacons are active in a variety of ministries including those to prison inmates and their families, the sick in hospitals, nursing homes and homes for the aged, alienated youth, the elderly and the poor, and in various areas of legal service to the indigent, of education and campus ministry.

National Association of Diaconate Directors: Membership organization of directors, vicars and other staff personnel of diaconate programs. Established in 1977 to promote effective communication and facilitate the exchange of information and resources of members; to develop professional expertise and promote research, training and self evaluation; to foster accountability and seek ways to promote means of implementing solutions to problems. The association is governed by an executive board of elected officers. Officers include Deacons: Maurice Reed of Green Bay, president, 1997-98; Peter D'Heilly of St.Paul-Minneapolis, president-elect; Thomas Welch, executive director. Office: 1337 W. Ohio St., Chicago, Il 60622.

MARRIAGE DOCTRINE

The following excerpts, stating key points of doctrine on marriage, are from the *Pastoral Constitution on the Church in the Modern World* (Nos. 48 to 51) promulgated by the Second Vatican Council.

Conjugal Covenant

The intimate partnership of married life and love has been established by the Creator and qualified by his laws. It is rooted in the conjugal covenant of irrevocable personal consent.

God himself is the author of matrimony, endowed as it is with various benefits and purposes. All of these have a very decisive bearing on the continuation of the human race, on the personal development and eternal destiny of the individual members of a family, and on the dignity, stability, peace, and prosperity of the family itself and of human society as a whole. By their very nature, the institution of matrimony itself and conjugal love are ordained for the procreation and education of children, and find in them their ultimate crown.

Thus a man and a woman render mutual help and service to each other through an intimate union of their persons and of their actions. Through this union they experience the meaning of their oneness and attain to it with growing perfection day by day. As a mutual gift of two persons, this intimate union, as well as the good of the children, imposes total fidelity on the spouses and argues for an unbreakable oneness between them (No. 48).

Sacrament of Matrimony

Christ the Lord abundantly blessed this many-faceted love. The Savior of men and the Spouse of the Church comes into the lives of married Christians through the sacrament of matrimony. He abides with them thereafter so that, just as he loved the Church and handed himself over on her behalf, the spouses may love each other with perpetual fidelity through mutual self-bestowal.

Graced with the dignity and office of fatherhood and motherhood, parents will energetically acquit themselves of a duty which devolves primarily on them; namely, education, and especially religious education.

The Christian family, which springs from marriage as a reflection of the loving covenant uniting Christ with the Church, and as a participation in that covenant, will manifest to all men the Savior's living presence in the world, and the genuine nature of the Church (No. 48).

Conjugal Love

The biblical Word of God several times urges the betrothed and the married to nourish and develop their wedlock by pure conjugal love and undivided affection.

This love is an eminently human one since it is directed from one person to another through an affection of the will. It involves the good of the whole person. Therefore it can enrich the expressions of body and mind with a unique dignity, ennobling these expressions as special ingredients and signs of the friendship distinctive of marriage. This love the Lord has judged worthy of special gifts, healing, perfecting, and exalting gifts of grace and of charity.

Such love, merging the human with the divine, leads the spouses to a free and mutual gift of themselves, a gift proving itself by gentle affection and by deed. Such love pervades the whole of their lives. Indeed, by its generous activity it grows better and grows greater. Therefore it far excels mere erotic inclination, which, selfishly pursued, soon enough fades wretchedly away.

This love is uniquely expressed and perfected through the marital act. The actions within marriage by which the couple are united intimately and chastely are noble and worthy ones. Expressed in a manner which is truly human, these actions signify and promote that mutual self-giving by which spouses enrich each other with a joyful and a thankful will.

Sealed by mutual faithfulness and hallowed above all by Christ's sacrament, this love remains steadfastly true in body and in mind, in bright days or dark. It will never be profaned by adultery or divorce. Firmly established by the Lord, the unity of marriage will radiate from the equal personal dignity of wife and husband, a dignity acknowledged by mutual and total love.

The steady fulfillment of the duties of this Christian vocation demands notable virtue. For this reason, strengthened by grace for holiness of life, the couple will painstakingly cultivate and pray for constancy of love, largeheartedness, and the spirit of sacrifice (No. 49).

Fruitfulness of Marriage

Marriage and conjugal love are by their nature ordained toward the begetting and educating of children. Chilren are really the supreme gift of marriage and contribute very substantially to the welfare of their parents. God himself wished to share with man a certain special participation in his own creative work. Thus he blessed male and female, saying: "Increase and multiply" (Gn. 1:28).

Hence, while not making the other purposes of matrimony of less account, the true practice of conjugal love, and the whole meaning of the family life which results from it, have this aim: that the couple be ready with stout hearts to cooperate with the love of the Creator and the Savior, who through them will enlarge and enrich his own family day by day.

Parents should regard as their proper mission the task of transmitting human life and educating those to whom it has been transmitted. They should realize that they are thereby cooperators with the love of God the Creator, and are, so to speak, the interpreters of that love. Thus they will fulfill their task with human and Christian responsibility (No. 50).

Norms of Judgment

They will thoughtfully take into account both their own welfare and that of their children, those already born and those who may be foreseen. For this accounting they will reckon with both the material and the spiritual conditions of the times as well as of their state in life. Finally, they will consult the interests of the family group, of temporal society, and of the Church herself.

The parents themselves should ultimately make this judgment in the sight of God. But in their manner of acting, spouses should be aware that they cannot proceed arbitrarily. They must always be governed according to a conscience dutifully conformed to the divine law itself, and should be submissive toward the Church's teaching office, which authentically interprets that law in the light of the Gospel. That divine law reveals and protects the integral meaning of conjugal love, and impels it toward a truly human fulfillment.

Marriage, to be sure, is not instituted solely for procreation. Rather, its very nature as an unbreakable compact between persons, and the welfare of the children, both demand that the mutual love of the spouses, too, be embodied in a rightly ordered manner, that it grow and ripen. Therefore, marriage persists as a whole manner and communion of life, and maintains its value and indissolubility, even when offspring are lacking — despite, rather often, the very intense desire of the couple (No. 50).

Love and Life

This Council realizes that certain modern conditions often keep couples from arranging their married lives harmoniously, and that they find themselves in circumstances where at least temporarily the size of their families should not be increased. As a result, the faithful exercise of love and the full intimacy of their lives are hard to maintain. But where the intimacy of married life is broken off, it is not rare for its faithfuness to be imperiled and its quality of fruitfulness ruined. For then the upbringing of the children and the courage to accept new ones are both endangered.

To these problems there are those who presume to offer dishonorable solutions. Indeed, they do not recoil from the taking of life. But the Church issues the reminder that a true contradiction cannot exist between the divine laws pertaining to the transmission of life and those pertaining to the fostering of authentic conjugal love.

Church Teaching

For God, the Lord of Life, has conferred on men the surpassing ministry of safeguarding life — a ministry which must be fulfilled in a manner which is worthy of men. Therefore from the moment of its conception life must be guarded with the greatest care, while abortion and infanticide are unspeakable crimes. The sexual characteristics of man and the human faculty of reproduction wonderfully exceed the dispositions of lower forms of life. Hence the acts themselves which are proper to conjugal love and which are exercised in accord with genuine human dignity must be honored with great reverence (No. 51).

Therefore when there is question of harmonizing conjugal love with the responsible transmission of life, the moral aspect of any procedure does not depend solely on the sincere intentions or on an evaluation of motives. It must be determined by objective standards. These, based on the nature of the human person and his acts, preserve the full sense of mutual self-giving and human procreation in the context of true love. Such a goal cannot be achieved unless the virtue of conjugal chastity is sincerely practiced. Relying on these principles, sons of the Church may not undertake methods of regulating procreation which are found blameworthy by the teaching authority of the Church in its unfolding of the divine law.

Everyone should be persuaded that human life and the task of transmitting it are not realities bound up with this world alone. Hence they cannot be measured or perceived only in terms of it, but always have a bearing on the eternal destiny of men (No. 51).

HUMANAE VITAE

Marriage doctrine and morality were the subjects of the enyclical letter "Of Human Life," issued by Pope Paul VI, July 29, 1968. Following are a number of key excerpts from the document which was framed in the pattern of traditional teaching and statements by the Second Vatican Council.

Each and every marriage act ("quilibet matrimonii usus") must remain open to the transmission of life (No. 11).

Indeed, by its intimate structure, the conjugal act, while most closely uniting husband and wife, capacitates them for the generation of new lives according to laws inscribed in the very being of man and of woman. By safeguarding both these essential aspects, the unitive and the procreative, the conjugal act preserves in its fullness the sense of true mutual love and its ordination toward man's most high calling to parenthood (No. 12).

It is, in fact, justly observed that a conjugal act imposed upon one's partner without regard for his or her condition and lawful desires is not a true act of love, and therefore denies an exigency of right moral order in the relationships between husband and wife. Hence, one who reflects well must also recognize that a reciprocal act of love which jeopardizes the responsibility to transmit life — which God the Creator, according to particular laws, inserted therein — is in contradiction with the design constitutive of marriage and with the will of the Author of life. To use this divine gift, destroying, even if only partially, its meaning and its purpose, is to contradict the nature both of man and of woman and of their most intimate relationship, and therefore it is to contradict also the plan of God and his will (No. 13).

Forbidden Actions

The direct interruption of the generative process already begun, and, above all, directly willed and procured abortion, even if for therapeutic reasons, are to be absolutely excluded as licit means of regulating birth.

Equally to be excluded is direct sterilization, whether perpetual or temporary, whether of the man or of the woman. Similarly excluded is every action which, either in anticipation of the conjugal act, or in its accomplishment, or in the development of its natural consequences, proposes, whether as an end or as a means, to render procreation impossible.

To justify conjugal acts made intentionally infecund, one cannot invoke as valid reasons the lesser evil, or the fact that such acts would constitute a whole together with the fecund acts already performed or to follow later and hence would share in one and the same moral goodness. In truth, if it is sometimes licit to tolerate a lesser evil in order to avoid a greater evil or to promote a greater good, it is not licit, even for the gravest reasons, to do evil so that good may follow therefrom; that is, to make into the object of a positive act of the will something which is intrinsically disorder, and hence unworthy of the human person, even when the intention is to safeguard or promote individual, family or social well-being.

Consequently, it is an error to think that a conjugal act which is deliberately made infecund, and so is intrinsically dishonest, could be made honest and right by the ensemble of a fecund conjugal life (No. 14).

If, then, there are serious motives to space out births, which derive from the physical or psychological conditions of husband and wife, or from external conditions, the Church teaches that it is then licit to take into account the natural rhythms immanent in the generative functions, for the use of marriage in the infecund periods only, and in this way to regulate birth without offending earlier stated principles (No. 16).

Pastoral Concerns

We do not at all intend to hide the sometimes serious difficulties inherent in the life of Christian married persons; for them, as for everyone else, "the gate is narrow and the way is hard that leads to life." But the hope of that life must illuminate their way, as with courage they strive to live with wisdom, justice and piety in this present time, knowing that the figure of this world passes away.

Let married couples then, face up to the efforts needed, supported by the faith and hope which "do not disappoint because God's love has been poured into our hearts through the Holy Spirit, who has been given to us." Let them implore divine assistance by persevering prayer; above all, let them draw from the source of grace and charity in the Eucharist. And, if sin should still keep its hold over them, let them not be discouraged but rather have recourse with humble perseverance to the mercy of God, which is poured forth in the sacrament of penance (No. 25).

MARRIAGE LAWS

The Catholic Church claims jurisdiction over its members in matters pertaining to marriage. which is a sacrament. Church legislation on the subject is stated principally in 111 canons of the Code of Canon Law.

Marriage laws of the Church provide juridical norms in support of the marriage covenant. In 10 chapters, the revised Code covers: pastoral directives for preparing men and women for marriage; impediments in general and in particular; matrimonial consent; form for the celebration of marriage; mixed marriages; secret celebration of marriage; effects of marriage; separation of spouses, and convalidation of marriage.

Catholics are bound by all marriage laws of the Church. Non-Catholics, whether baptized or not, are not considered bound by these ecclesiastical laws except in cases of marriage with a Catholic. Certain natural laws, in the Catholic view, bind all men and women, irrespective of their religious beliefs; accordingly, marriage is prohibited before the time of puberty, without knowledge and free mutual consent, in the case of an already existing valid marriage bond, in the case of antecedent and perpetual impotence.

Formalities

These include, in addition to arrangements for the time and place of the marriage ceremony, doctrinal and moral instruction concerning marriage and the recording of data which verifies in documentary form the eligibility and freedom of the persons to marry. Records of this kind, which are confidential, are preserved in the archives of the church where the marriage takes place.

Premarital instructions are the subject matter of Pre-Cana Conferences.

Marital Consent

Matrimonial consent can be invalidated by an essential defect, substantial error, the strong influence of force and fear, the presence of a condition or intention against the nature of marriage.

Form of Marriage

A Catholic is required, for validity and lawfulness, to contract marriage — with another Catholic or with a non-Catholic — in the presence of a competent priest or deacon and two witnesses.

There are two exceptions to this law. A Roman Rite Catholic (since Mar. 25, 1967) or an Eastern Rite Catholic (since Nov. 21, 1964) can contract marriage validly in the presence of a priest of a separated Eastern Rite Church, provided other requirements of law are complied with. With permission of the competent Roman-Rite or Eastern-Rite bishop, this form of marriage is lawful, as well as valid. (See Eastern Rite Laws, below.)

With these two exceptions, and aside from cases covered by special permission, the Church does not regard as valid any marriages involving Catholics which take place before non-Catholic ministers of religion or civil officials.

(An excommunication formerly in force against Catholics who celebrated marriage before a non-Catholic minister was abrogated in a decree issued by the Sacred Congregation for the Doctrine of the Faith on Mar. 18, 1966.)

The ordinary place of marriage is the parish of either Catholic party or of the Catholic party in case of a mixed marriage.

Church law regarding the form of marriage does not affect non-Catholics in marriages among themselves. The Church recognizes as valid the marriages of non-Catholics before ministers of religion and civil officials, unless they are rendered null and void on other grounds.

The canonical form is not to be observed in the case of a marriage between a non-Catholic and a baptized Catholic who has left the Church by a formal act.

Impediments

Diriment Impediments to marriage are factors which render a marriage invalid.

• age, which obtains before completion of the 14th year for a woman and the 16th year for a man;

• impotency, if it is antecent to the marriage and permanent (this differs from sterility, which is not an impediment);

• the bond of an existing valid marriage;

• disparity of worship, which obtains when one party is a Catholic and the other party is unbaptized;

• sacred orders;

• religious profession of the perpetual vow of chastity;

• abduction, which impedes the freedom of the person abducted;

• crime, variously involving elements of adultery, promise or attempt to marry, conspiracy to murder a husband or wife;

• blood relationship in the direct line (father-daughter, mother-son, etc.) and to the fourth degree inclusive of the collateral line (brother-sister, first cousins);

• affinity, or relationship resulting from a valid marriage, in any degree of the direct line;

• public honesty, arising from an invalid marriage or from public or notorious concubinage; it renders either party incapable of marrying blood relatives of the other in the first degree of the direct line.

• legal relationship arising from adoption; it renders either party incapable of marrying relatives of the other in the direct line or in the second degree of the collateral line.

Dispensations from Impediments: Persons hindered by impediments cannot marry unless they are dispensed therefrom in view of reasons recognized in canon law. Local bishops can dispense from the impediments most often encountered (e.g., disparity of worship) as well as others.

Decision regarding some dispensations is reserved to the Holy See.

Separation

A valid and consummated marriage of baptized persons cannot be dissolved by any human authority or any cause other than the death of one of the persons. In other circumstances:

• 1. A valid but unconsummated marriage of baptized persons, or of a baptized and an unbaptized person, can be dissolved:

a. by the solemn religious profession of one of the persons, made with permission of the pope. In such a case, the bond is dissolved at the time of profession, and the other person is free to marry again.

b. by dispensation from the pope, requested for a grave reason by one or both of the persons. If the dispensation is granted, both persons are free to marry again.

Dispensations in these cases are granted for reasons connected with the spiritual welfare of the concerned persons.

• 2. A legitimate marriage, even consummated, of unbaptized persons can be dissolved in favor of one of them who subsequently receives the sacrament of baptism. This is the Pauline Privilege, so called because it was promulgated by St. Paul (1 Cor. 7:12-15) as a means of protecting the faith of converts. Requisites for granting the privilege are:

a. marriage prior to the baptism of either person;

b. reception of baptism by one person;

c. refusal of the unbaptized person to live in peace with the baptized person and without interfering with his or her freedom to practice the Christian faith. The privilege does not apply if the unbaptized person agrees to these conditions.

• 3. A legitimate and consummated marriage of a baptized and an unbaptized person can be dissolved by the pope in virtue of the Privilege of Faith, also called the Petrine Privilege.

Civil Divorce

Because of the unity and the indissolubility of marriage, the Church denies that civil divorce can break the bond of a valid marriage, whether the marriage involves two Catholics, a Catholic and a non-Catholic, or non-Catholics with each other.

In view of serious circumstances of marital distress, the Church permits an innocent and aggrieved party, whether wife or husband, to seek and obtain a civil divorce for the purpose of acquiring title and right to the civil effects of divorce, such as separate habitation and maintenance, and the custody of children. Permission for this kind of action should be obtained from proper church authority. The divorce, if obtained, does not break the bond of a valid marriage.

Under other circumstances — as would obtain if a marriage was invalid (see Annulment, below) — civil divorce is permitted for civil effects and as a civil ratification of the fact that the marriage bond really does not exist.

Annulment

This is a decision by a competent church authority — e.g., a bishop, a diocesan marriage tribunal, the Roman Rota — that an apparently valid marriage was actually invalid from the beginning because of the unknown or concealed existence, from the beginning, of a diriment impediment, an essential defect in consent, radical incapability for marriage, or a condition placed by one or both of the parties against the very nature of marriage.

Eastern Rite Laws

Marriage laws of the Eastern Church differ in several respects from the legislation of the Roman Rite. The regulations in effect since May 2, 1949, were contained in the motu proprio *Crebre Allatae* issued by Pius XII the previous February.

According to both the Roman Code of Canon Law and the Oriental Code, marriages between Roman Rite Catholics and Eastern Rite Catholics ordinarily take place in the rite of the groom and have canonical effects in that rite.

Regarding the form for the celebration of marriages between Eastern Catholics and baptized Eastern non-Catholics, the Second Vatican Council declared:

"By way of preventing invalid marriages between Eastern Catholics and baptized Eastern non-Catholics, and in the interests of the permanence and sanctity of marriage and of domestic harmony, this sacred Synod decrees that the canonical 'form' for the celebration of such marriages obliges only for lawfulness. For their validity, the presence of a sacred minister suffices, as long as the other requirements of law are honored" (*Decree on Eastern Catholic Churches,* No. 18).

Marriages taking place in this manner are lawful, as well as valid, with permission of a competent Eastern Rite bishop.

The Rota

The Roman Rota is the ordinary court of appeal for marriage, and some other cases, which are appealed to the Holy See from lower church courts. Appeals are made to the Rota if decisions by diocesan and archdiocesan courts fail to settle the matter in dispute. Pope John Paul, at annual meetings with Rota personnel, speaks about the importance of the court's actions in providing norms of practice for other tribunals.

MIXED MARRIAGES

"Mixed Marriages" (*Matrimonia Mixta*) was the subject of: (1) a letter issued under this title by Pope Paul VI Mar. 31, 1970, and (2) a statement, *Implementation of the Apostolic Letter on Mixed Marriages,* approved by the National Conference of Catholic Bishops Nov. 16, 1970.

One of the key points in the bishops' statement referred to the need for mutual pastoral care by ministers of different faiths for the sacredness of marriage and for appropriate preparation and continuing support of parties to a mixed marriage.

Pastoral experience, which the Catholic Church shares with other religious bodies, confirms the fact that marriages of persons of different beliefs involve special problems related to the continuing religious practice of the concerned persons and to the religious education and formation of their children.

Pastoral measures to minimize these problems include instruction of a non-Catholic party in essentials of the Catholic faith for purposes of understanding. Desirably, some instruction should also be given the Catholic party regarding his or her partner's beliefs.

Requirements

The Catholic party to a mixed marriage is required to declare his (her) intention of continuing practice of the Catholic faith and to promise to do all in his (her) power to share his (her) faith with children born of the marriage by having them baptized and raised as Catholics. No declarations or promises are required of the non-Catholic party, but he (she) must be informed of the declaration and promise made by the Catholic.

Notice of the Catholic's declaration and promise is an essential part of the application made to a bishop for (1) permission to marry a baptized non-Catholic, or (2) a dispensation to marry an unbaptized non-Catholic.

A mixed marriage can take place with a Nuptial Mass. (The bishops' statement added this caution: "To the extent that Eucharistic sharing is not permitted by the general discipline of the Church, this is to be considered when plans are being made to have the mixed marriage at Mass or not.")

The ordinary minister at a mixed marriage is an authorized priest or deacon, and the ordinary place is the parish church of the Catholic party. A non-Catholic minister may not only attend the marriage ceremony but may also address, pray with and bless the couple.

For appropriate pastoral reasons, a bishop can grant a dispensation from the Catholic form of marriage and can permit the marriage to take place in a non-Catholic church with a non-Catholic minister as the officiating minister. A priest may not only attend such a ceremony but may also address, pray with and bless the couple.

"It is not permitted," however, the bishops' statement declared, "to have two religious services or to have a single service in which both the Catholic marriage ritual and a non-Catholic marriage ritual are celebrated jointly or successively."

PASTORAL MINISTRY FOR DIVORCED AND REMARRIED

Ministry to divorced and remarried Catholics is a difficult field of pastoral endeavor, situated as it is in circumstances tantamount to the horns of a dilemma.

At Issue

On the one side is firm church teaching on the permanence of marriage and norms against reception of the Eucharist and full participation in the life of the Church by Catholics in irregular unions.

On the other side are men and women with broken unions followed by second and perhaps happier attempts at marriage which the Church does not recognize as valid and which may not be capable of being validated because of the existence of an earlier marriage bond.

Factors involved in these circumstances are those of the Church, upholding its doctrine and practice regarding the permanence of marriage, and those of many men and women in irregular second marriages who desire full participation in the life of the Church.

Sacramental participation is not possible for those whose first marriage was valid, although there is no bar to their attendance at Mass, or to sharing in other activities of the Church, or to their efforts to have children baptized and raised in the Catholic faith. An exception to this rule is the condition of a divorced and remarried couple living in a brother-sister relationship.

There is no ban against sacramental participation by separated or divorced persons who have not attempted a second marriage, provided the usual conditions for reception of the sacraments are in order.

Unverified estimates of the number of U.S. Catholics who are divorced and remarried vary between six and eight million.

Tribunal Action

What can the Church do for them and with them in pastoral ministry, is an old question charged with new urgency because of the rising number of divorced and remarried Catholics.

One way to help is through the agency of marriage tribunals charged with responsibility for investigating and settling questions concerning the validity or invalidity of a prior marriage. There are reasons in canon law justifying the Church in declaring a particular marriage null and void from the beginning, despite the short- or long-term existence of an apparently valid union.

Decrees of nullity (annulments) are not new in the history of the Church. If such a decree is issued, a man or woman is free to validate a second marriage and live in complete union with the Church.

The 1995 *Statistical Yearbook of the Church,* reported that in 1995 U.S. tribunals issued 54,013 annulments (in ordinary and documentary processes). The canonical reasons were: invalid consent (39,276), impotence (3), other impediments (2,731), defect of form (12,003). Worldwide, 73,108 decrees or declarations of nullity were issued in 1995.

Reasons behind Decrees

Pastoral experience reveals that some married persons, a short or long time after contracting an apparently valid marriage, exhibit signs that point back to the existence, at the time of marriage, of latent and serious personal deficiencies which made them incapable of valid consent and sacramental commitment.

Such deficiencies might include gross immaturity and those affecting in a serious way the capacity to love, to have a true interpersonal and conjugal relationship, to fulfill marital obligations, to accept the faith aspect of marriage.

Psychological and behavioral factors like these have been given greater attention by tribunals in recent years and have provided grounds for numerous decrees of nullity.

Decisions of this type do not indicate any softening of the Church's attitude regarding the permanence of marriage. They affirm, rather, that some persons who have married were really not capable of doing so.

Serious deficiencies in the capacity for real interpersonal relationship in marriage were the reasons behind a landmark decree of nullity issued in 1973 by the Roman Rota, the Vatican high court of appeals in marriage cases. Pope John Paul referred to such deficiencies — the "grave lack of discretionary judgment," incapability of assuming "essential matrimonial rights and obligations," for example — in an address Jan. 26, 1984, to personnel of the Rota.

The tribunal way to a decree of nullity regarding a previous marriage, however, is not open to many persons in second marriages — because grounds are either lacking or, if present, cannot be verified in tribunal process.

Unacceptable Solutions

One unacceptable solution of the problem, called "good conscience procedure," involves administration of the sacraments of penance and the Eucharist to divorced and remarried Catholics unable to obtain a decree of nullity for a first marriage who are living in a subsequent marriage "in good faith."

This procedure, despite the fact that it has no standing or recognition in church law, is being advocated and practiced by some priests and remarried Catholics.

This issue was addressed by the Congregation for the Doctrine of the Faith in a letter to bishops dated Oct. 14, 1994, and published with the approval of Pope John Paul. The letter said in part:

"Pastoral solutions in this area have been suggested according to which — divorced-and-remarried members of the faithful could approach holy Communion in specific cases when they considered themselves authorized according to a judgment of conscience to do so. This would be the case, for example, when they had been abandoned completely unjustly although they sincerely tried to save the previous marriage; or when they are convinced of the nullity of their previous marriage although (they are) unable to demonstrate it in the external forum; or when they have gone through a long period of reflection and

penance; or also when for morally valid reasons they cannot satisfy the obligation to separate.

"In some places it has also been proposed that, in order objectively to examine their actual situation, the divorced-and-remarried would have to consult a prudent and experienced priest. This priest, however, would have to respect their eventual decision in conscience to approach holy Communion, without this implying an official authorization.

"In these and similar cases, it would be a matter of a tolerant and benevolent pastoral solution in order to do justice to the different situations of the divorced-and-remarried.

"Even if analogous solutions have been proposed by a few fathers of the Church and in some measure were practiced, nevertheless these never attained the consensus of the fathers and in no way came to constitute the common doctrine of the Church nor to determine her discipline. It falls to the universal magisterium, in fidelity to sacred Scripture and tradition, to teach and to interpret authentically the deposit of faith."

Conditions for Receiving Communion

Practically speaking, "when for serious reasons — for example, for the children's upbringing — a man and a woman cannot satisfy the obligation to separate," they may be admitted to Communion if "they take on themselves the duty to live in complete continence, that is, by abstinence from the acts proper to married couples. In such a case they may receive holy Communion as long as they respect the obligation to avoid giving scandal."

The teaching of the Church on this subject "does not mean that the Church does not take to heart the situation of those faithful who, moreover, are not excluded from ecclesial communion. She is concerned to accompany them pastorally and invite them to share in the life of the Church in the measure that is compatible with the dispositions of divine law, from which the Church has no power to dispense. On the other hand, it is necessary to instruct these faithful so that they do not think their participation in the life of the Church is reduced exclusively to the question of the reception of the Eucharist. The faithful are to be helped to deepen their understanding of the value of sharing in the sacrifice of Christ in the Mass, or spiritual communion, of prayer, of meditation on the word of God, and of works of charity and justice."

RETROUVAILLE

Retrouvaille is a ministry to hurting marriages, consisting of a weekend experience with follow-up sessions designed to provide husbands and wives with ways and means of healing and reconciliation. Emphasis is on communication between husband and wife, enabling them to rediscover each other and to examine their lives in a new and positive way. Retrouvaille is not a retreat or a sensitivity group, does not include group dynamics or discussions. The program is conducted under the direction of trained couples and priests. Programs are usually offered under the auspices of diocesan family life agencies. International Coordinating Team: Bill and Peg Swaan, P.O.Box 25, Kelton, PA 19346.

MARRIAGE ENCOUNTER

Marriage Encounter brings couples together for a weekend program of events directed by a team of several couples and a priest, to develop their abilities to communicate with each other as husband and wife. This purpose is served by direction in techniques given by the team and by private dialogue of each couple. The address of National Marriage Encounter is 4704 Jamerson Pl., Orlando, FL 32807. The national office of Worldwide Marriage Encounter is located at 2210 East Highland Ave., #106, San Bernardino, CA 92404.

THE CHURCH CALENDAR

The calendar of the Roman Church consists of an arrangement throughout the year of a series of liturgical seasons, commemorations of divine mysteries and commemorations of saints for purposes of worship.

The key to the calendar is the central celebration of the Easter Triduum, commemorating the supreme saving act of Jesus in his death and resurrection to which all other observances and acts of worship are related.

The purposes of this calendar were outlined in the *Constitution on the Sacred Liturgy* (Nos. 102-105) promulgated by the Second Vatican Council.

Within the cycle of a year ... (the Church) unfolds the whole mystery of Christ, not only from his incarnation and birth until his ascension, but also as reflected in the day of Pentecost, and the expectation of a blessed, hoped-for return of the Lord.

Recalling thus the mysteries of redemption, the Church opens to the faithful the riches of her Lord's powers and merits, so that these are in some way made present at all times, and the faithful are enabled to lay hold of them and become filled with saving grace (No. 102).

In celebrating this annual cycle of Christ's mysteries, holy Church honors with special love the Blessed Mary, Mother of God (No. 103).

The Church has also included in the annual cycle days devoted to the memory of the martyrs and the other saints (who) sing God's perfect praise in heaven and offer prayers for us. By celebrating the passage of these saints from earth to heaven the Church proclaims the paschal mystery as achieved in the saints who have suffered and been glorified with Christ; she proposes them to the faithful as examples who draw all to the Father through Christ, and through their merits she pleads for God's favors (No. 104).

In the various seasons of the year and according to her traditional discipline, the Church completes the formation of the faithful by means of pious practices for soul and body, by instruction, prayer, and works of penance and mercy (No. 105).

THE ROMAN CALENDAR

Norms for a revised calendar for the Western Church as decreed by the Second Vatican Council were approved by Paul VI in the motu proprio *Mysterii Paschalis* dated Feb. 14, 1969. The revised calendar was promulgated a month later by a decree of the Congregation for Divine Worship and went into effect Jan. 1, 1970, with provisional modifications. Full implementation of all its parts was delayed in 1970 and 1971, pending the completion of work on related liturgical texts. The U.S. bishops ordered the calendar into effect for 1972.

The Seasons

Advent: The liturgical year begins with the first Sunday of Advent, which introduces a season of four weeks or slightly less duration with the theme of expectation of the coming of Christ. During the first two weeks, the final coming of Christ as Lord and Judge at the end of the world is the focus of attention. From Dec. 17 to 24, the emphasis shifts to anticipation of the celebration of his Nativity on the solemnity of Christmas.

Advent has four Sundays. Since the 10th century, the first Sunday has marked the beginning of the liturgical year in the Western Church. In the Middle Ages, a kind of pre-Christmas fast was in vogue during the season.

Christmas Season: The Christmas season begins with the vigil of Christmas and lasts until the Sunday after January 6, inclusive.

The period between the end of the Christmas season and the beginning of Lent belongs to the Ordinary Time of the year. Of variable length, the pre-Lenten phase of this season includes what were formerly called the Sundays after Epiphany and the suppressed Sundays of Septuagesima, Sexagesima and Quinquagesima.

Lent: The penitential season of Lent begins on Ash Wednesday, which occurs between Feb. 4 and Mar. 11, depending on the date of Easter, and lasts until the Mass of the Lord's Supper (Holy Thursday). It has six Sundays. The sixth Sunday marks the beginning of Holy Week and is known as Passion (formerly called Palm) Sunday.

The origin of Lenten observances dates back to the fourth century or earlier.

Easter Triduum: The Easter Triduum begins with evening Mass of the Lord's Supper and ends with Evening Prayer on Easter Sunday.

Easter Season: The Easter season whose theme is resurrection from sin to the life of grace, lasts for 50 days, from Easter to Pentecost. Easter, the first Sunday after the first full moon following the vernal equinox, occurs between Mar. 22 and Apr. 25. The terminal phase of the Easter season, between the solemnities of the Ascension of the Lord and Pentecost, stresses anticipation of the coming and action of the Holy Spirit.

Ordinary Time: The season of Ordinary Time begins on Monday (or Tuesday if the feast of the Baptism of the Lord is celebrated on that Monday) after the Sunday following January 6 and continues until the day before Ash Wednesday, inclusive. It begins again on Monday after Pentecost and ends on the Saturday before the first Sunday of Advent. It consists of 33 or 34 weeks. The last Sunday is celebrated as the Solemnity of Christ the King. The overall purpose of the season is to elaborate the themes of salvation history.

The various liturgical seasons are characterized in part by the scriptural readings and Mass prayers assigned to each of them. During Advent, for example, the readings are messianic; during the Easter season, from the Acts of the Apostles, chronicling the Resurrection and the original proclamation of Christ by the Apostles, and from the Gospel of John; during Lent, baptismal and penitential passages. Mass prayers reflect the meaning and purpose of the various seasons.

Commemorations of Saints

The commemorations of saints are celebrated concurrently with the liturgical seasons and feasts of our Lord. Their purpose is to illustrate the paschal mysteries as reflected in the lives of saints, to honor them as heroes of holiness, and to appeal for their intercession.

In line with revised regulations, some former feasts were either abolished or relegated to observance in particular places by local option for one of two reasons: (1) lack of sufficient historical evidence for observance of the feasts; (2) lack of universal significance.

The commemoration of a saint, as a general rule, is observed on the day of death (*dies natalis*, day of birth to glory with God in heaven). Exceptions to this rule include the feasts of St. John the Baptist, who is honored on the day of his birth; Sts. Basil the Great and Gregory Nazianzen, and the brother Saints, Cyril and Methodius, who are commemorated in joint feasts. Application of this general rule in the revised calendar resulted in date changes of some observances.

Sundays and Other Holy Days

Sunday is the original Christian feast day and holy day of obligation because of the unusually significant events of salvation history which took place and are commemorated on the first day of the week — viz., the Resurrection of Christ, the key event of his life and the fundamental fact of Christianity; and the descent of the Holy Spirit upon the Apostles on Pentecost, the birthday of the Church. The transfer of observance of the Lord's Day from the Sabbath to Sunday was made in apostolic times. The Mass and Liturgy of the Hours (Divine Office) of each Sunday reflect the themes and set the tones of the various liturgical seasons.

Holy days of obligation are special occasions on which Catholics who have reached the age of reason are seriously obliged, as on Sundays, to assist at Mass: they are also to refrain from work and involvement with business which impede participation in divine worship and the enjoyment of appropriate rest and relaxation.

The holy days of obligation observed in the United States are: Christmas, the Nativity of Jesus, Dec. 25; Solemnity of Mary the Mother of God, Jan. 1; Ascension of the Lord; Assumption of Blessed Mary the Virgin, Aug. 15; All Saints' Day, Nov. 1; Immaculate Conception of Blessed Mary the Virgin, Dec. 8.

The precept to attend Mass is abrogated in the U.S. whenever the Solemnity of Mary, the Assumption, or All Saints falls on a Saturday or Monday (1991 decree of U.S. bishops; approved by Holy See July 4, 1992, and effective Jan. 1, 1993).

In addition to these, there are four other holy days of obligation prescribed in the general law of the Church which are not so observed in the U.S.: Epiphany, Jan. 6; St. Joseph, Mar. 19; Corpus Christi; Sts. Peter and Paul, June 29. The solemnities of Epiphany and Corpus Christi are transferred to a Sunday in countries where they are not observed as holy days of obligation.

Solemnities, Feasts, Memorials

Categories of observances according to dignity and manner of observance are: solemnities, principal days in the calendar (observance begins with Evening Prayer I of the preceding day; some have their own vigil Mass); feasts (celebrated within the limits of the natural day); obligatory memorials (celebrated throughout the Church); optional memorials (observable by choice).

Fixed observances are those which are regularly celebrated on the same calendar day each year.

Movable observances are those which are not observed on the same calendar day each year. Examples of these are Easter (the first Sunday after the first full moon following the vernal equinox), Ascension (40 days after Easter), Pentecost (50 days after Easter), Trinity Sunday (first after Pentecost), Christ the King (last Sunday of the liturgical year).

Weekdays, Days of Prayer

Weekdays are those on which no proper feast or vigil is celebrated in the Mass or Liturgy of the Hours (Divine Office). On such days, the Mass may be that of the preceding Sunday, which expresses the liturgical spirit of the season, an optional memorial, a votive Mass, or a Mass for the dead. Weekdays of Advent and Lent are in a special category of their own.

Days of Prayer: Dioceses, at times to be designated by local bishops, should observe "days or periods of prayer for the fruits of the earth, prayer for human rights and equality, prayer for world justice and peace, and penitential observance outside of Lent." So stated the *Instruction on Particular Calendars* (No. 331) issued by the Congregation for the Sacraments and Divine Worship June 24, 1970.

These days are contemporary equivalents of what were formerly called ember and rogation days.

Ember days originated at Rome about the fifth century, probably as Christian replacements for seasonal festivals of agrarian cults. They were observances of penance, thanksgiving, and petition for divine blessing on the various seasons; they also were occasions of special prayer for clergy to be ordained. These days were observed four times a year.

Rogation days originated in France about the fifth century. They were penitential in character and also occasions of prayer for a bountiful harvest and protection against evil.

Days and Times of Penance

Fridays throughout the year and the season of Lent are penitential times.

• Abstinence: Catholics in the United States, from the age of 14 throughout life, are obliged to abstain from meat on Ash Wednesday, the Fridays of Lent and Good Friday. The law forbids the use of meat, but not of eggs, the products of milk or condiments made of animal fat. Permissible are soup flavored with meat, meat gravy and sauces. The obligation to abstain from meat is not in force on days celebrated as solemnities (e.g., Christmas, Sacred Heart).

• Fasting: Catholics in the United States, from the day after their 18th birthday to the day after their 59th birthday, are also obliged to fast on Ash Wednesday and Good Friday. The law allows only one full meal a day, but does not prohibit the taking of some food in the morning and evening, observing — as far as quantity and quality are concerned — approved local custom. The order of meals is optional; i.e., the full meal may be taken in the evening instead of at midday. Also: (1) The combined quantity of food taken at the two lighter meals should not exceed the quantity taken at the full meal. (2) The drinking of ordinary liquids does not break the fast.

• Obligation: There is a general obligation to do penance for sins committed and for the remission of punishment due because of sin. Substantial observance of fasting and abstinence, prescribed for the community of the Church, is a matter of serious obligation; it allows, however, for alternate ways of doing penance (e.g., works of charity, prayer and prayer-related practices, almsgiving).

Readings at Mass

The texts of scriptural readings for Mass on Sundays, holy days and some other days are indicated under the respective dates in the 1998 calendar pages which follow. The third (C) cycle is prescribed for Sunday Masses in the 1998 liturgical year (Nov. 30, 1997, to Nov. 28, 1998). The first (A) cycle is prescribed for the 1999 liturgical year which begins with the first Sunday of Advent, Nov. 29, 1998.

Weekday cycles of readings are the second and first, respectively, for liturgical years 1998 and 1999.

Monthly Prayer Intentions

Intentions chosen and recommended by Pope John Paul II to the prayers of the faithful and circulated by the Apostleship of Prayer are given for each month of the calendar. He has expressed his desire that all Catholics make these intentions their own "in the certainty of being united with the Holy Father and praying according to his intentions and desires."

Celebrations in U.S. Particular Calendar

The General Norms for the Liturgical Year and the Calendar, issued in 1969 and published along with the General Roman Calendar for the Universal Church, noted that the calendar consists of the General Roman Calendar used by the entire Church and of particular calendars used in particular churches (nations or dioceses) or in families of religious.

The particular calendar for the U.S. contains the following celebrations. **January:** 4, Elizabeth Ann Seton; 5, John Neumann; 6, Bl. Andre Bessette. **March:** 3, Bl. Katharine Drexel. **May:** 15, Isidore the Farmer. **July:** 1, Bl. Junipero Serra; 4, Independence Day; 14, Bl. Kateri Tekakwitha. **August:** 18, Jane Frances de Chantal. **September:** 9, Peter Claver. **October:** 6, Bl. Marie-Rose Durocher; 19, Isaac Jogues and John de Brebeuf and Companions; 20, Paul of the Cross. **November:** 13, Frances Xavier Cabrini; 18, Rose Philippine Duchesne; 23, Bl. Miguel Agustín Pro; Fourth Thursday, Thanksgiving Day. **December:** 9, Bl. Juan Diego; 12, Our Lady of Guadalupe.

TABLE OF MOVABLE FEASTS

Year	Ash Wednesday	Easter	Ascension	Pentecost	Weeks of Ordinary Time				First Sunday of Advent
					Before Lent		After Pent.		
					Wk.	Ends	Wk.	Begins	
1998	Feb. 25	Apr. 12	May 21	May 31	7	Feb. 24	9	June 1	Nov. 29
1999	Feb. 17	Apr. 4	May 13	May 23	6	Feb. 16	8	May 24	Nov. 28
2000	Mar. 8	Apr. 23	June 1	June 11	9	Mar. 7	10	June 12	Dec. 3
2001	Feb. 28	Apr. 15	May 24	June 3	8	Feb. 27	9	June 4	Dec. 2
2002	Feb. 13	Mar. 31	May 9	May 19	5	Feb. 12	7	May 20	Dec. 1
2003	Mar. 5	Apr. 20	May 29	June 8	8	Mar. 4	10	June 9	Nov. 30
2004	Feb. 25	Apr. 11	May 20	May 30	7	Feb. 24	9	May 31	Nov. 28
2005	Feb. 9	Mar. 27	May 5	May 15	5	Feb. 8	7	May 16	Nov. 27
2006	Mar. 1	Apr. 16	May 25	June 4	8	Feb. 28	9	June 5	Dec. 3
2007	Feb. 21	Apr. 8	May 17	May 27	7	Feb. 20	8	May 28	Dec. 2
2008	Feb. 6	Mar. 23	May 1	May 11	4	Feb. 5	6	May 12	Nov. 30
2009	Feb. 25	Apr. 12	May 21	May 31	7	Feb. 24	9	June 1	Nov. 29
2010	Feb. 17	Apr. 4	May 13	May 23	6	Feb. 16	8	May 24	Nov. 28
2011	Mar. 9	Apr. 24	June 2	June 12	9	Mar. 8	11	June 13	Nov. 27
2012	Feb. 22	Apr. 8	May 17	May 27	7	Feb. 21	8	May 28	Dec. 2
2013	Feb. 13	Mar. 31	May 9	May 19	5	Feb. 12	7	May 20	Dec. 1
2014	Mar. 5	Apr. 20	May 29	June 8	8	Mar. 4	10	June 9	Nov. 30
2015	Feb. 18	Apr. 5	May 14	May 24	6	Feb. 17	8	May 25	Nov. 29
2016	Feb. 10	Mar. 27	May 5	May 15	5	Feb. 9	7	May 16	Nov. 27
2017	Mar. 1	Apr. 16	May 25	June 4	8	Feb. 28	9	June 5	Dec. 3
2018	Feb. 14	Apr. 1	May 10	May 20	6	Feb. 13	7	May 21	Dec. 2
2019	Mar. 6	Apr. 21	May 30	June 9	8	Mar. 5	10	June 10	Dec. 1
2020	Feb. 26	Apr. 12	May 21	May 31	7	Feb. 25	9	June 1	Nov. 29
2021	Feb. 17	Apr. 4	May 13	May 23	6	Feb. 16	8	May 24	Nov. 28

JANUARY 1998

Prayer Intentions. That the Spirit of the Lord hasten reconciliation and unity among all the disciples of Christ(General). That the rise and development of the peoples of Africa may be accomplished in justice, brotherhood and peace (Mission).

1—Thurs. Solemnity of Mary, Mother of God. Holy day of obligation. (Nm. 6:22-27; Gal. 4:4-7; Lk. 2:16-21.)

2—Fri. Sts.Basil the Great and Gregory Nazianzen, bishops-doctors; memorial.

3—Sat. Weekday.

4—Sun. Epiphany of the Lord (U.S.); solemnity. (Is. 60:1-6; Eph. 3:2-3a, 5-6; Mt. 2:1-12.) [St, Elizabeth Ann Seton; memorial in U.S.]

5—Mon. St. John Neumann, bishop; memorial (in U.S.).

6—Tues. Weekday. Bl. André Bessette, religious; optional memorial (in U.S.).

7—Wed. Weekday. St. Raymond of Penyafort; optional memorial.

8—Thurs. Weekday.

9—Fri. Weekday.

10—Sat. Weekday.

11—Sun. The Baptism of the Lord; feast. (Is. 42:1-4, 6-7 or Is. 40:1-5, 9-11; Acts 10:34-38 or Ti 2:11-14 and 3: 4-7; Lk 3:15-16, 21-22.)

12—Mon. Weekday. (First Week in Ordinary Time.)

13—Tues. Weekday. St. Hilary, bishop-doctor; optional memorial.

14—Wed. Weekday.

15—Thurs. Weekday.

16—Fri. Weekday

17—Sat. St. Anthony, abbot; memorial.

18—Second Sunday in Ordinary Time. (Is 61:1-5; 1 Cor 12:4-11; Jn. 2:1-11.)

19—Mon. Weekday.

20—Tues. Weekday. St. Fabian, pope-martyr, or St. Sebastian, martyr; optional memorials.

21—Wed. St. Agnes, virgin-martyr; memorial.

22—Thurs. Weekday. St. Vincent, deacon-martyr; optional memorial.

23—Fri. Weekday.

24—Sat. St. Francis de Sales, bishop-doctor; memorial.

25—Third Sunday in Ordinary Time. (Neh 8:2-4a, 5-6, 8-10; 1 Cor 12:12-30 or 12:12-14, 27; Lk 1:1-4 and 4:14-21.) [Conversion of St. Paul; feast.]

26—Mon. Sts. Timothy and Titus, bishops; memorial.

27—Tues. Weekday. St. Angela Merici, virgin; optional memorial.

28—Wed. St. Thomas Aquinas, priest-doctor; memorial.

29—Thurs. Weekday.

30—Fri. Weekday.

31—Sat. St. John Bosco, priest; memorial.

Scheduled Events: World Day of Peace, Jan. 1; Catholic Campus Ministry Convention, Jan. 3 to 7; National Migration Week, Jan. 5 to 11; Martin Luther King Day observed, Jan. 19; Week of Prayer for Christian Unity, Jan. 18 to 25; National Prayer Vigil for Life, Jan. 21-22; March for Life, Jan. 22, anniversary of Roe v. Wade, the pro-abortion decision of the U.S. Supreme Court; Catholic Schools Week, Jan. 26 to Feb. 1.

FEBRUARY 1998

Prayer Intentions. That greater value be attributed to the sacrament of Confirmation in catechesis and in the life of the Church (General). That young Christian communities may find qualified and suitable educators for seminaries and higher education centers.)

1—Fourth Sunday in Ordinary Time. (Jer 1:4-5, 17-19; 1 Cor. 12:31 to 13:13 or 13:4-13; Lk 4:21-30.)

2—Mon. Presentation of the Lord; feast.

3—Tues. Weekday. St. Blase, bishop-martyr, or St. Ansgar, bishop; optional memorials.

4—Wed. Weekday.

5—Thurs. St. Agatha, virgin-martyr; memorial.

6—Fri. Sts. Paul Miki and Companions, martyrs; memorial.

7—Sat. Weekday. BVM on Saturday; optional memorial.

8—Fifth Sunday in Ordinary Time. (Is. 6:1-2a, 3-8; 1 Cor 15:1-11 or 15:3-8, 11; Lk 5:1-11.) [St. Jerome Emiliani; optional memorial].

9—Mon. Weekday.

10—Tues. St. Scholastica, virgin; memorial.

11—Wed. Weekday. Our Lady of Lourdes; optional memorial.

12—Thurs. Weekday.

13—Fri. Weekday.

14—Sat. Sts. Cyril, monk, and Methodius, bishop; memorial.

15—Sixth Sunday in Ordinary Time. (Jer 17:5-8; 1 Cor 15:12, 16-20; Lk 6:17, 20-26.)

16—Mon. Weekday.

17—Tues. Weekday. Seven Holy Founders of the Servite Order; optional memorial.

18—Wed. Weekday.

19—Thurs. Weekday.

20—Fri. Weekday.

21—Sat. Weekday. St. Peter Damien, bishop-doctor, or BVM on Saturday; optional memorials.

22—Seventh Sunday in Ordinary Time. (1 Sm 26:2, 7-9, 12-13, 22-23; 1 Cor 15:45-49; Lk 6:27-38.) [Chair of Peter, apostle; feast.]

23—Mon. St. Polycarp, bishop-martyr; memorial.

24—Tues. Weekday.

25—Ash Wednesday. Beginning of Lent. *Fast and abstinence.* Ashes are blessed on this day and imposed on the forehead of the faithful to remind them of their obligation to do penance for sin and to seek spiritual renewal by means of prayer, fasting, good works, and by bearing with patience and for God's purposes the trials and difficulties of everyday life.

26—Thurs. Weekday of Lent.

27—Fri. Weekday of Lent. *Abstinence.*

28—Sat. Weekday of Lent.

The blessing of candles for use during the year takes place on the feast of the Presentation, also called Candlemas Day, according to longstanding custom.

The blessing of throats takes place on the optional memorial of St. Blase Feb. 3,in accord with the legend that a boy in danger of choking to death was saved through his intercession.

Scheduled Events: Catholic Press Month; National Day of Prayer for the African-American Family, Feb. 1; World Day of the Sick, Feb. 11; Presidents Day, Feb. 16.

MARCH 1998

Prayer Intentions. That the fundamental rights of the human person may be recognized and respected in all the nations of the world (General). That the testimony of the martyrs of the 20th century may give young people a courageous faith and the joy of communicating it throughout the world (Mission).

1—First Sunday of Lent. (Dt. 26:4-10; Rom 10:8-13; Lk. 4:1-13.)

2—Mon. Weekday of Lent.

3—Tues. Weekday of Lent. [Bl. Katharine Drexel, virgin; optional memorial (in U.S.).]

4—Wed. Weekday of Lent. [St. Casimir; memorial.]

5—Thurs. Weekday of Lent.

6—Fri. Weekday of Lent. *Abstinence.*

7—Sat. Weekday of Lent. [Sts. Perpetua and Felicity, martyrs; memorial.]

8—Second Sunday of Lent. (Gn 15:5-12, 17-18; Phil 3:17 to 4:1 or 3:20 to 4:1; Lk 9:28b-36.) [St. John of God; optional memorial.]

9— Mon. Weekday of Lent. [St. Frances of Rome; optional memorial.]

10—Tues. Weekday of Lent.

11—Wed. Weekday of Lent.

12—Thurs. Weekday of Lent.

13—Fri. Weekday of Lent. *Abstinence.*

14—Sat. Weekday of Lent.

15—Third Sunday of Lent. (Ex.3:1-8a,13-15; 1 Cor 10:1-6, 10-12 Lk 13:1-9 . Or, Ex 17:3-7; Rom 5:1-2, 5-8; Jn 4:5-42 or 4:5-15, 19b-26, 39a, 40-42.)

16—Mon. Weekday of Lent.

17—Tues. Weekday of Lent. [St. Patrick, bishop; optional memorial.]

18—Wed. Weekday of Lent. [St. Cyril of Jerusalem, bishop-doctor; optional memorial.]

19—Thurs. St. Joseph, solemnity.

20—Fri. Weekday of Lent. *Abstinence.*

21—Sat. Weekday of Lent.

22—Fourth Sunday of Lent. (Jos 5:9a, 10-12; 2 Cor 5:17-21; Lk 15:1-3, 11-32. Or, 1 Sm 16:1b, 6-7, 10-13a; Eph 5:8-14; Jn 9:1-41 or 9:1, 6-9, 13-17, 34-38.)

23—Mon. Weekday of Lent. [St. Turibius de Mogrovejo, bishop; optional memorial.]

24—Tues. Weekday of Lent.

25—Wed. Annunciation of the Lord; solemnity.

26—Thurs. Weekday of Lent.

27—Fri. Weekday of Lent. *Abstinence.*

28—Sat. Weekday of Lent.

29—Fifth Sunday of Lent. (Is 43:16-21; Phil 3:8-14; Jn 8:1-11. Or, Ez 37:12-14; Rom 8:8-11; Jn 11:1-45 or 11:3-7, 17, 20-27, 33b-45.)

30—Mon. Weekday of Lent.

31—Tues. Weekday of Lent.

Support for the needy, care for others in straitened circumstances, is an expression of the virtue of charity or love of neighbor. Such witness is powerful, not only for the relief of the unfortunate but also as a convincing sign of faith in practice. The kind of sign that made people say, as noted in the Acts of the Apostles, "See how these Christians love one another."

Scheduled Events: Meetings of the U.S. bishops' National Advisory Committee and Administrative Board, Mar. 19 to 24 and 24 to 26.

APRIL 1998

Prayer Intentions. That, in the second year of preparation for the Great Jubilee, the faithful may foster with particular care the spirit of unity and community within the Church (General). That the international community may promote and protect the religious, ecological and social rights of the people of Oceania (Mission).

1—Wed. Weekday of Lent.

2—Thurs. Weekday of Lent. [St. Francis of Paola, hermit; optional memorial.]

3—Fri. Weekday of Lent. *Abstinence.*

4—Sat. Weekday of Lent. [St. Isidore of Seville, bishop-doctor; optional memorial.]

5—Passion (Palm) Sunday. (Procession—Lk 19:28-40. Mass—Is 50:4-7; Phil 2:6-11; Lk. 22:14 to 23:56, or 23:1-49.) [St. Vincent Ferrer, priest; optional memorial.]

6—Monday of Holy Week.

7—Tuesday of Holy Week. [St. John Baptist de la Salle, priest; memorial.]

8—Wednesday of Holy Week.

9—Holy Thursday. The Easter Triduum begins with evening Mass of the Supper of the Lord.

10—Good Friday. *Fast and Abstinence.*

11—Holy Saturday. [St. Stanislaus, bishop-martyr; memorial.]

12—Easter Sunday; solemnity. (Acts 10:34a, 37-43; Col. 3:1-4 or 1 Cor 5:6b-8; Jn 20:1-9 or Lk 24:1-12 or (evening Mass) Lk 24:13-35.)

13—Easter Monday; solemnity. [St. Martin I, pope-martyr; optional memorial.]

14—Easter Tuesday; solemnity.

15—Easter Wednesday; solemnity.

16—Easter Thursday; solemnity.

17—Easter Friday; solemnity.

18—Easter Saturday; solemnity.

19—Second Sunday of Easter; solemnity. (Acts 5:12-16; Rv 1:9-11a, 12-13, 17-19; Jn 20:19-31.)

20—Mon. Easter Weekday.

21—Tues. Easter Weekday. St. Anselm, bishop-doctor; optional memorial.

22—Wed. Easter Weekday.

23—Thurs. Easter Weekday. St. George, martyr or St. Adalbert, bishop-martyr; optional memorials.

24—Fri. Easter Weekday. St. Fidelis of Sigmaringen, priest-martyr; optional memoral.

25—Sat. St. Mark, evangelist; feast.

26—Third Sunday of Easter. (Acts 5:27b-32, 40b-41; Rv 5:11-14; Jn 21:1-19 or 21:1-14.)

27—Mon. Easter Weekday.

28—Tues. Easter Weekday. St. Peter Chanel, priest-martyr, or St.Louis de Montfort; optional memorials.

29—Wed. St. Catherine of Siena, virgin-doctor; memorial.

30—Thurs. Easter Weekday. St. Pius V, pope; optional memorial.

The Sacred Triduum, from Holy Thursday to the Vigil of Easter, and the week-long celebration of Easter comprise the most solemn and deeply mysterious period in the liturgical year.

Scheduled Events: Convention of the National Catholic Educational Association, Apr. 14 to 17; Beginning of Passover, Apr. 11.

MAY 1998

Prayer Intentions. That Mary's fidelity to the voice of the Spirit may be an example and a stimulus to a generous attentiveness to the will of God (General). That young people may be ready to accept a lifelong missionary vocation (Mission).

1—Fri. Easter Weekday. St. Joseph the Worker; optional memorial.
2—Sat. St. Athanasius, bishop-doctor; memorial.
3—**Fourth Sunday of Easter.** (Acts 13:14, 43-52; Rv 7:9, 14b-17; Jn 10:27-30.) [Sts. Philip and James, apostles; feast.]
4—Mon. Easter Weekday.
5—Tues. Easter Weekday.
6—Wed. Easter Weekday.
7—Thurs. Easter Weekday.
8—Fri. Easter Weekday.
9—Sat. Easter Weekday.
10—**Fifth Sunday of Easter.** (Acts 14:21b-27; Rv 21:1-5a; Jn 13:31-33a, 34-35.)
11—Mon. Easter Weekday.
12—Tues. Easter Weekday. Sts. Nereus and Achilleus, martyrs, or St. Pancras, martyr; optional memorials.
13—Wed. Easter Weekday.
14—Thurs. St. Matthias, apostle; feast.
15—Fri. Easter Weekday. St. Isidore the Farmer; optional memorial (in U.S.).
16—Sat. Easter Weekday.
17—**Sixth Sunday of Easter.** (Acts 15:1-2, 22-29; Rv 21:10-14, 22-23; Jn 14:23-29.)
18—Mon. Easter Weekday. St. John I, pope-martyr; optional memorial.
19—Tues. Easter Weekday.
20—Wed. Easter Weekday. St. Bernardine of Siena, priest; optional memorial.
21—**Thurs. The Ascension of the Lord; solemnity. Holy day of obligation.** (Acts 1:1-11 Eph 1:17-23 or Heb 9:24-28, 10:19-23; Lk 24:46-53.)
22—Fri. Easter Weekday.
23—Sat. Easter Weekday.
24—**Seventh Sunday of Easter.** (Acts 7:55-60; Rv 22:12-14, 16-17, 20; Jn 17:20-26.)
25—Mon. Easter Weekday. St. Bede the Venerable, priest-doctor, or St. Gregory VII, pope, or St. Mary Magdalene de Pazzi, virgin; optional memorials.
26—Tues. St. Philip Neri, priest; memorial.
27—Wed. Easter Weekday. St. Augustine of Canterbury, bishop; optional memorial.
28—Thurs. Easter Weekday.
29—Fri. Easter Weekday.
30—Sat. Easter Weekday.
31—**Pentecost Sunday; solemnity.** (Acts 2:1-11; 1 Cor 12:3b-7, 12-13; Jn 20:19-23. Or, Acts 2:1-11; Rom 8:8-17; Jn 14:15-16, 23b-26.) [Visitation of Blessed Mary the Virgin; feast.]

Solemnities of the Easter Season, Ascension of the Lord, May 21 and Pentecost, May 31. Visitation of the Blessed Virgin Mary, May 31, recalls Mary's readiness to help Elizabeth and the prophetic Magnificat canticle.

Scheduled Events: National Day of Prayer, May 1; Mother's Day, May 10; Memorial Day, May 25 (observed).

JUNE 1998

Prayer Intentions. That violence may never again be justified by appeals to religious motives (General). That the entire Church may recognize and invoke the Holy Spirit as "principal agent of the new evangelization (Mission).

1—Mon. St. Justin, martyr; memorial. (Ninth Week in Ordinary Time)
2—Tues. Weekday. Sts. Marcellinus and Peter, martyrs; optional memorial.
3—Wed. Sts. Charles Lwanga and Companions, martyrs; memorial.
4—Thurs. Weekday.
5—Fri. St. Boniface, bishop-martyr; memorial.
6—Sat. Weekday. St. Norbert, bishop; optional memorial.
7—**Sun. The Holy Trinity; solemnity.** (Prv 8:22-31; Rom 5:1-5; Jn 16:12-15.)
8—Mon. Weekday. (Tenth Week in Ordinary Time.)
9—Tues. Weekday. St. Ephraem, deacon-doctor, optional memorial.
10—Wed. Weekday.
11—Thurs. St. Barnabas, apostle; memorial.
12—Fri. Weekday.
13—Sat. St. Anthony of Padua, priest-doctor; memorial.
14—**Sun. The Body and Blood of Christ (Corpus Christi) (in U.S.); solemnity.** (Gn 14:18-20; 1 Cor 11:23-26; Lk 9:11b-17.)
15—Mon. Weekday. (Eleventh Week in Ordinary Time.)
16—Tues. Weekday.
17—Wed. Weekday.
18—Thurs. Weekday.
19—Fri. Sacred Heart of Jesus; solemnity. [St. Romuald, abbot; optional memorial.]
20—Sat. Immaculate Heart of Mary; memorial.
(This was raised from optional to obligatory memorial in 1996)
21—**Twelfth Sunday in Ordinary Time.** (Zec 12:10-11,13:1; Gal 3:26-29; Lk 9:18-24.) [St. Aloysius Gonzaga, religious; memorial.]
22—Mon. Weekday. St. Paulinus of Nola, bishop, or Sts. John Fisher, bishop-martyr, and Thomas More, martyr; optional memorials.
23—Tues. Weekday.
24—Wed. Birth of St. John the Baptist; solemnity.
25—Thurs. Weekday.
26—Fri. Weekday.
27—Sat. Weekday. St. Cyril of Alexandria, bishop-doctor, or BVM on Saturday; optional memorials.
28—**Thirteenth Sunday in Ordinary Time.** (1 Kgs 19:16b, 19-21; Gal 5:1, 13-18; Lk 9:51-62.) [St. Irenaeus, bishop-martyr; memorial.]
29—Mon. Sts. Peter and Paul, apostles; solemnity.
30—Tues. Weekday. First Martyrs of the Roman Church; optional memorial.

Feasts: Holy Trinity, June 7; St. Anthony of Padua, June 13; Corpus Christi, June 14 (in U.S.); Sacred Heart, June 19; Birth of St. John the Baptist, June 24; Sts. Peter and Paul, June 29.

Scheduled Events: General Meeting of the National Conference of Catholic Bishops; Father's Day, June 21.

JULY 1998

Prayer Intentions. That families may allow themselves to be guided by the Spirit of peace and faithfulness (General). That the Christian pastors and faithful in China may offer a testimony of faith and of ecclesial communion (Mission).

1—Wed. Weekday. Bl. Junipero Serra, priest; optional memorial (in U.S.).

2—Thurs. Weekday.

3—Fri. St. Thomas, apostle; feast.

4—Sat. Independence Day, proper Mass in U.S. Weekday. St. Elizabeth of Portugal or BVM on Saturday; optional memorials.

5—**Fourteenth Sunday in Ordinary Time.** (Is 66:10-14c; Gal 6:14-18; Lk 10:1-12, 17-20 or 10:1-9.)[St. Anthony Zaccaria, priest; optional memorial.]

6—Mon. Weekday. St. Maria Goretti, virgin-martyr; optional memorial.

7—Tues. Weekday.

8—Wed. Weekday.

9—Thurs. Weekday.

10—Fri. Weekday.

11—Sat. St. Benedict, abbot; memorial.

12—**Fifteenth Sunday in Ordinary Time.** (Dt 30:10-14; Col 1:15-20; Lk 10:25-37.)

13—Mon. Weekday. St Henry; optional memorial.

14—Tues. Bl. Kateri Tekakwitha, virgin; memorial (in U.S.). Weekday. St. Camillus de Lellis, priest; optional memorial.

15—Wed. St. Bonaventure, bishop-doctor; memorial.

16—Thurs. Weekday. Our Lady of Mt. Carmel; optional memorial.

17—Fri. Weekday.

18—Sat. Weekday. BVM on Saturday; optional memorial.

19—**Sixteenth Sunday in Ordinary Time.** (Gn 18:1-10a; Col 1:24-28; Lk 10:38-42.)

20—Mon. Weekday.

21—Tues. Weekday. St. Lawrence of Brindisi, priest-doctor; optional memorial.

22—Wed. St. Mary Magdalene; memorial.

23—Thurs. Weekday. St. Bridget of Sweden, religious; optional memorial.

24—Fri. Weekday.

25—Sat. St. James, apostle; feast.

26—**Seventeenth Sunday in Ordinary Time.** (Gn 18: 20-32; Col 2: 12-14; Lk 11:1-13.) [Sts. Joachim and Anne, parents of Blessed Mary the Virgin; memorial.]

27—Mon. Weekday.

28—Tues. Weekday.

29—Wed. St. Martha; memorial.

30—Thurs. Weekday. St. Peter Chrysologus, bishop-doctor; optional memorial.

31—Fri. St. Ignatius of Loyola, priest; memorial.

Feasts: Blessed Junipero Serra, whose optional memorial may be observed July 1, founder of California missions; St.Thomas, apostle, pioneer evangelizer of India, July 3; St. Benedict, July 11, founder of monasticism in Western Europe, patron saint of Europe; St. Bonaventure, July 15, called the second founder of the Franciscan Order; St. Ignatius of Loyola, July 31.

Scheduled Event: Independence Day, July 4.

AUGUST 1998

Prayer Intentions. That the Holy Spirit may raise up authentic and joyful witnesses of the living God (General). That the media may become everywhere platforms of evangelization (Mission).

1—Sat. St. Alphonsus Liguori, bishop-doctor; memorial.

2—**Eighteenth Sunday in Ordinary Time.** (Eccl 1:2, 2:21-23; Col 3:1-5, 9-11; Lk 12:13-21.) [St. Eusebius of Vercelli, bishop, or St. Peter Julian Eymard; optional memorials.]

3—Mon. Weekday.

4—Tues. St. John Vianney, priest; memorial.

5—Wed. Weekday. Dedication of St. Mary Major Basilica in Rome; optional memorial.

6—Thurs. Transfiguration of the Lord; feast.

7—Fri. Weekday. Sts. Sixtus II, pope, and Companions, martyrs, or St. Cajetan, priest; optional memorials.

8—Sat. St. Dominic, priest; memorial.

9—**Nineteenth Sunday in Ordinary Time.** (Wis 18:6-9; Heb 11:1-2, 8-19 or 11:1-2, 8-12; Lk 12:32-48 or 12:35-40.)

10—Mon. St. Lawrence, deacon-martyr; feast.

11—Tues. St. Clare, virgin; memorial.

12—Wed. Weekday.

13—Thurs. Weekday. Sts. Pontian, pope, and Hippolytus, priest, martyrs; optional memorial.

14—Fri. St. Maximilian Kolbe, priest-martyr; memorial.

15—**Sat. Assumption of Blessed Mary the Virgin; solemnity. Holy day.** Mass obligation abrogated in U.S. (Rv. 11:19a and 12:1-6a, 10ab; 1 Cor. 15:20-27; Lk. 1:39-56.)

16—**Twentieth Sunday in Ordinary Time.** (Jer 38:4-6, 8-10; Heb 12:1-4; Lk 12:49-53.) [St. Stephen of Hungary; optional memorial.]

17—Mon. Weekday.

18—Tues. St. Jane Frances de Chantal; optional memorial (in U.S.).

19—Wed. Weekday. St. John Eudes, priest; optional memorial.

20—Thurs. St. Bernard of Clairvaux, abbot-doctor; memorial.

21—Fri. St. Pius X, pope; memorial.

22—Sat. Queenship of Mary; memorial.

23—**Twenty-First Sunday in Ordinary Time.** (Is 66:18-21; Heb 12:5-7, 11-13; Lk 13:22-30.) [St. Rose of Lima, virgin; optional memoial.]

24—Mon.St. Bartholomew, apostle; feast.

25—Tues. Weekday. St. Louis, or St. Joseph Calasanz, priest; optional memorials.

26—Wed. Weekday.

27—Thurs. St. Monica, memorial.

28—Fri. St. Augustine, bishop-doctor; memorial.

29—Sat. Martyrdom of St. John the Baptist; memorial.

30—**Twenty-Second Sunday in Ordinary Time.** (Sir 3:17-18, 20, 28-29; Heb 12:18-19, 22-24a; Lk 14:1, 7-14.)

31—Mon. Weekday.

Feasts: Assumption of Mary, Aug. 15, St. Bernard of Clairvaux, Aug. 20, leader of monasticism; Aug. 22, Queenship of Mary, St. Augustine, Aug. 28, profoundly influential father and doctor of the Church.

SEPTEMBER 1998

Prayer Intentions. That all states may condemn the use of anti-personnel land mines and actively work toward having them banned (General). That the spirit of the new evangelization may spur the Church in Asia to announce Christ and to promote the inculturation of the Gospel and interreligious dialogue (Mission).

1—Tues. Weekday.
2—Wed. Weekday.
3—Thurs. St. Gregory the Great, pope-doctor; memorial.
4—Fri. Weekday.
5—Sat. Weekday. BVM on Saturday; optional memorial.
6—**Twenty-Third Sunday in Ordinary Time.** (Wis 9:13-18b Phlm 9b-10, 12-17; Lk 14:25-33.)
7—Mon. Labor Day, proper Mass in U.S. Weekday.
8—Tues. Birth of Mary; feast.
9—Wed. St. Peter Claver, priest; memorial (in U.S.). Weekday.
10—Thurs. Weekday.
11—Fri. Weekday.
12—Sat. Weekday. BVM on Saturday; optional memorial.
13—**Twenty-Fourth Sunday in Ordinary Time.** (Ex 32:7-11, 13-14; 1 Tm 1:12-17; Lk 15:1-32 or 15:1-10.) [St. John Chrysostom, bishop-doctor; memorial.]
14—Mon. The Holy Cross; feast.
15—Tues. Our Lady of Sorrows; memorial.
16—Wed. Sts. Cornelius, pope, and Cyprian, bishop, martyrs; memorial.
17—Thurs. Weekday. St. Robert Bellarmine, bishop-doctor; optional memorial.
18—Fri. Weekday.
19—Sat. Weekday. St. Januarius, bishop-martyr, or BVM on Saturday; optional memorials.
20—**Twemty-Fifth Sunday in Ordinary Time.** (Am 8:4-7; 1 Tm 2:1-8; Lk 16:1-13 or 16:10-13.) [Sts. Andrew Kim Taegon, priest, Paul Chong Hasang, lay apostle, and Companions, martyrs of Korea; memorial.]
21—Mon. St. Matthew, apostle-evangelist; feast.
22—Tues. Weekday.
23—Wed. Weekday.
24—Thurs. Weekday.
25—Fri. Weekday.
26—Sat. Weekday. Sts. Cosmas and Damian, martyrs, or BVM on Saturday; optional memorials.
27—**Twenty-Sixth Sunday in Ordinary Time.** (Am 6:1a, 4-7; 1 Tm 6:11-16; Lk 16:19-31.) [St. Vincent de Paul, priest; memorial.]
28—Mon. Weekday. St. Wenceslaus, martyr, or Sts. Lawrence Ruiz and Companions, martyrs; optional memorials.
29—Tues. Sts. Michael, Gabriel and Raphael, archangels; feast.
30—Wed. St. Jerome, priest-doctor; memorial.

The celebration of Labor Day pinpoints the dignity of work by Christians in collaborating with the Father in making good things, with the Son in sharing the mission of redemption, and with the Holy Spirit in sharing his gifts. The Labor Day theme, the dignity of work, was the subject of Pope John Paul's encyclical, "Laborem Exercens."

OCTOBER 1998

Prayer Intentions. That Christians may identify "the action of the Holy Spirit," as they discover "the seeds of the Word" wherever they are (General). That Mission Sunday may be promoted and lived as a moment of spiritual and effective solidarity with the mission of the Church in the whole world (Mission).

1—Thurs. St. Therese of the Child Jesus, virgin; memorial.
2—Fri. Guardian Angels; memorial.
3—Sat. Weekday. BVM on Saturday; optional memorial.
4—**Twenty-Seventh Sunday in Ordinary Time.** (Hb 1:2-3, 2:2-4; 2 Tm 1:6-8, 13-14; Lk 17:5-10.) [St. Francis of Assisi; memorial.]
5—Mon. Weekday.
6—Tues. Weekday. Bl. Marie-Rose Durocher, virgin; optional memorial (in U.S.). St. Bruno, priest; optional memorial.
7—Wed. Our Lady of the Rosary; memorial.
8—Thurs. Weekday.
9—Fri. Weekday. Sts. Denis, bishop, and Companions, martyrs, or St. John Leonardi, priest; optional memorials.
10—Sat. Weekday. BVM on Saturday; optional memorial.
11—**Twenty-Eighth Sunday in Ordinary Time.** (2 Kgs 5:14-17; 2 Tm 2:8-13; Lk 17:11-19.)
12—Mon. Weekday.
13—Tues. Weekday.
14—Wed. Weekday. St. Callistus I, pope-martyr optional memorial.
15—Thurs. Weekday. St. Teresa of Jesus (Avila), virgin-doctor; memorial.
16—Fri. Weekday. St. Hedwig, religious, or St. Margaret Mary Alacoque, virgin; optional memorials.
17—Sat. St. Ignatius of Antioch, bishop-martyr; memorial.
18—**Twenty-Ninth Sunday in Ordinary Time.** (Ex 17:8-13; 2 Tm 3:14 to 4:2; Lk 18: 1-8.) [St. Luke, evangelist; feast.]
19—Mon. Sts. Isaac Jogues, John de Brebeuf, priests, and Companions, martyrs; memorial in U.S.; St. Paul of the Cross (general calendar); optional memorial.]
20—Tues. St. Paul of the Cross (in U.S.); optional memorial.
21—Wed. Weekday.
22—Thurs. Weekday.
23—Fri. Weekday. St. John of Capistrano, priest; optional memorial.
24—Sat. Weekday. St. Anthony Mary Claret, bishop, or BVM on Saturday; optional memorials.
25—**Thirtieth Sunday in Ordinary Time.** (Sir 35:12-14, 16-18; 2 Tm 4:6-8, 16-18; Lk 18:9-14.)
26—Mon. Weekday.
27—Tues. Weekday.
28—Wed. Sts. Simon and Jude, apostles; feast.
29—Thurs. Weekday.
30—Fri. Weekday.
31—Sat. Weekday. BVM on Saturday; optional memorial.

Feasts: St. Therese of the Child Jesus, Oct. 1; Guardian Angels, Oct. 2; St. Francis of Assisi, Oct. 4.

NOVEMBER 1998

Prayer Intentions. For the victims of drugs and for all those who work toward their human and social recovery (General). That the spreading of "sects" may stimulate the local Churches to appreciate with a renewed vitality the true gifts of the Spirit (Mission).

1—Sun. All Saints; solemnity. Holy day of obligation. (Rv. 7:2-4, 9-14; 1 Jn. 3:1-3; Mt. 5:1-12a.)

2—Mon. Commemoration of All the Faithful Departed (All Souls' Day). (Thirty-First Week in Ordinary Time.)

3—Tues. Weekday. St. Martin de Porres, religious, optional memorial.

4—Wed. St. Charles Borromeo, bishop; memorial.

5—Thurs. Weekday.

6—Fri. Weekday.

7—Sat. Weekday. BVM on Saturday; optional memorial.

8—Thirty-Second Sunday in Ordinary Time. (2 Mc 7:1-2, 9-14; 2 Thes 2:16 to 3:5; Lk 20:27-38 or 20:27, 34-38.)

9—Mon. Dedication of St. John Lateran Basilica in Rome (Archbasilica of Most Holy Savior); feast.

10—Tues. St. Leo the Great, pope-doctor; memorial.

11—Wed. St. Martin of Tours, bishop; memorial.

12—Thurs. St. Josaphat, bishop-martyr; memorial.

13—Fri. St. Frances Xavier Cabrini, virgin; memorial (in U.S.).

14—Sat. Weekday. BVM on Saturday; optional memorial.

15—Thirty-Third Sunday in Ordinary Time. (Mal 3:19-20a; 2 Thes 3:7-12; Lk 21:5-19.) [St. Albert the Great, bishop-doctor; optional memorial.]

16—Mon. Weekday. St. Margaret of Scotland, or St. Gertrude, virgin; optional memorials.

17—Tues. St. Elizabeth of Hungary, religious; memorial.

18—Wed. Weekday. Dedication of Basilica of Sts. Peter and Paul or (in U.S.) St. Rose Philippine Duchesne, virgin; optional memorials.

19—Thurs. Weekday.

20—Fri. Weekday.

21—Sat. Presentation of Blessed Mary the Virgin; memorial.

22—Sun. Christ the King; solemnity. (2 Sm 5:1-3; Col 1:12-20; Lk 23:35-43.) [St. Cecilia, virgin-martyr; memorial.]

23—Mon. Weekday. Bl. Miguel Agustin Pro, priest-martyr, optional memorial in U.S.; St. Clement I, pope-martyr, or St. Columban, abbot; optional memorials. (Thirty-Fourth [Last] Week in Ordinary Time.)

24—Tues. St. Andrew Dung-Lac, priest, and Companions, martyrs; memorial.

25—Wed. Weekday.

26—Thurs. Thanksgiving Day (in U.S.); proper Mass. Weekday.

27—Fri. Weekday.

28—Sat. Weekday. BVM on Saturday; optional memorial. [Last day of 1998 liturgical year.]

29—First Sunday of Advent. [Start of 1999 liturgical year.] (Is 2:1-5; Rom 13:11-14a; Mt. 24: 37-44.)

30—Mon. St. Andrew, apostle; feast.

Feasts: All Saints, Nov. 1, and All Souls, Nov. 2.

DECEMBER 1998

Prayer Intentions. That the Spirit of Christ, who was poor and humble, may bring about in the Church more effective solidarity with the distressed and the underprivileged (General). That governments and international organizations may protect human life and may act with geater decisiveness against violence against children (Mission).

1—Tues. Advent Weekday.

2—Wed. Advent Weekday.

3—Thurs. St. Francis Xavier, priest; memorial.

4—Fri. Advent Weekday. St. John Damascene, priest-doctor; optional memorial.

5—Sat. Advent Weekday.

6—Second Sunday of Advent. (Is 11:1-10; Rom 15:4-9; Mt 3:1-12.) [St. Nicholas, bishop; optional memorial.]

7—Mon. St. Ambrose, bishop-doctor; memorial.

8—Tues. Immaculate Conception of Blessed Mary the Virgin; solemnity; Holy Day of Obligation. (Gn. 3:9-15, 20; Eph. 1:3-6, 11-12; Lk. 1:26-38.)

9—Wed. Advent Weekday. Bl. Juan Diego; optional memorial (in U.S.).

10—Thurs. Advent Weekday.

11—Fri. Advent Weekday. St. Damasus I, pope; optional memorial.

12—Sat. Our Lady of Guadalupe; feast (in U.S.).

13—Third Sunday of Advent. (Is 35:1-6a, 10; Jas 5:7-10; Mt 11:2-11.) [St. Lucy, virgin-martyr; memorial.]

14—Mon. St. John of the Cross, priest-doctor; memorial.

15—Tues. Advent Weekday.

16—Wed. Advent Weekday.

17—Thurs. Advent Weekday.

18—Fri. Advent Weekday.

19—Sat. Advent Weekday.

20—Fourth Sunday of Advent. (Is 7:10-14; Rom 1:1-7; Mt 1:18-24.)

21—Mon. Advent Weekday. St. Peter Canisius, priest-doctor; optional memorial.

22—Tues. Advent Weekday.

23—Wed. Advent Weekday. [St. John of Kanty, priest; optional memorial.]

24—Thurs. Advent Weekday.

25—Fri. Christmas. Birth of the Lord; solemnity. Holy day of obligation. (Vigil — Is. 62:1-5; Acts 13:16-17, 22-25; Mt. 1:1-25, or 1:18-25. Midnight — Is. 9:1-6; Ti. 2:11-14; Lk. 2:1-14. At Dawn — Is. 62:11-12; Ti. 3:4-7; Lk. 2:15-20. During the Day — Is. 52:7-10; Heb. 1:1-6; Jn. 1:1-18, or 1:1-5, 9-14.)

26—Sat. St. Stephen, first martyr; feast.

27—Sun. The Holy Family; feast. (Sir. 3:2-6, 12-14; Col. 3:12-17 or Col 3:12-21; Mt 2:13-15, 19-23.) [St. John, apostle-evangelist; feast.]

28—Mon. Holy Innocents, martyrs; feast.

29—Tues. Fifth Day in the Octave of Christmas. St. Thomas Becket, bishop-martyr; optional memorial.

30—Wed. Sixth Day in the Octave of Christmas.

31—Thurs. Seventh Day in the Octave of Christmas. St. Sylvester I, pope; optional memorial.

Feasts: St. Francis Xavier, Dec. 3, patron of missions and missionaries; Immaculate Conception, Dec. 8; Our Lady of Guadalupe, Dec. 12, patroness of the Americas; Birth of the Lord, Dec. 25.

HOLY DAYS AND OTHER OBSERVANCES

The following list includes the six holy days of obligation observed in the United States and additional observances of devotional and historical significance. The dignity or rank of observances is indicated by the terms: **solemnity** (highest in rank); **feast;** memorial (for universal observance); **optional memorial** (for celebration by choice).

All Saints, Nov. 1, holy day of obligation, solemnity. Commemorates all the blessed in heaven, and is intended particularly to honor the blessed who have no special feasts. The background of the feast dates to the fourth century when groups of martyrs, and later other saints, were honored on a common day in various places. In 609 or 610, the Pantheon, a pagan temple at Rome, was consecrated as a Christian church for the honor of Our Lady and the martyrs (later all saints). In 835, Gregory IV fixed Nov. 1 as the date of observance.

All Souls, Commemoration of the Faithful Departed, Nov. 2. The dead were prayed for from the earliest days of Christianity. By the sixth century it was customary in Benedictine monasteries to hold a commemoration of deceased members of the order at Pentecost. A common commemoration of all the faithful departed on the day after All Saints was instituted in 998 by St. Odilo, of the Abbey of Cluny, and an observance of this kind was accepted in Rome in the 14th century.

Annunciation of the Lord (formerly, Annunciation of the Blessed Virgin Mary), Mar. 25, solemnity. A feast of the Incarnation which commemorates the announcement by the Archangel Gabriel to the Virgin Mary that she was to become the Mother of Christ (Lk. 1:26-38), and the miraculous conception of Christ by her. The feast was instituted about 430 in the East. The Roman observance dates from the seventh century, when celebration was said to be universal.

Ascension of the Lord, movable observance held 40 days after Easter, holy day of obligation, solemnity. Commemorates the Ascension of Christ into heaven 40 days after his Resurrection from the dead (Mk. 16:19; Lk. 24:51; Acts 1:2). The feast recalls the completion of Christ's mission on earth for the salvation of all people and his entry into heaven with glorified human nature. The Ascension is a pledge of the final glorification of all who achieve salvation. Documentary evidence of the feast dates from early in the fifth century, but it was observed long before that time in connection with Pentecost and Easter.

Ash Wednesday, movable observance, six and one-half weeks before Easter. It was set as the first day of Lent by Pope St. Gregory the Great (590-604) with the extension of an earlier and shorter penitential season to a total period including 40 weekdays of fasting before Easter. It is a day of fast and abstinence. Ashes, symbolic of penance, are blessed and distributed among the faithful during the day. They are used to mark the forehead with the Sign of the Cross, with the reminder: "Remember you are dust, and to dust you will return," or: "Turn away from sin and be faithful to the Gospel."

Assumption, Aug. 15, holy day of obligation, solemnity. Commemorates the taking into heaven of Mary, soul and body, at the end of her life on earth, a truth of faith that was proclaimed a dogma by Pius XII on Nov. 1, 1950. One of the oldest and most solemn feasts of Mary, it has a history dating back to at least the seventh century when its celebration was already established at Jerusalem and Rome.

Baptism of the Lord, movable, usually celebrated on the Sunday after January 6, feast. Recalls the baptism of Christ by John the Baptist (Mk. 1:9-11), an event associated with the liturgy of the Epiphany. This baptism was the occasion for Christ's manifestation of himself at the beginning of his public life.

Birth of Mary, Sept. 8, feast. This is a very old feast which originated in the East and found place in the Roman liturgy in the seventh century.

Candlemas Day, Feb. 2. See Presentation of the Lord.

Chair of Peter, Feb. 22, feast. The feast, which has been in the Roman calendar since 336, is a liturgical expression of belief in the episcopacy and hierarchy of the Church.

Christmas, Birth of Our Lord Jesus Christ, Dec. 25, holy day of obligation, solemnity. Commemorates the birth of Christ (Lk. 2:1-20). This event was originally commemorated in the East on the feast of Epiphany or Theophany. The Christmas feast itself originated in the West; by 354 it was certainly kept on Dec. 25. This date may have been set for the observance to offset pagan ceremonies held at about the same time to commemorate the birth of the sun at the winter solstice. There are texts for three Christmas Masses — at midnight, dawn and during the day.

Christ the King, movable, celebrated on the last Sunday of the liturgical year, solemnity. Commemorates the royal prerogatives of Christ and is equivalent to a declaration of his rights to the homage, service and fidelity of all people in all phases of individual and social life. Pius XI instituted the feast Dec. 11, 1925.

Conversion of St. Paul, Jan. 25, feast. An observance mentioned in some calendars from the 8th and 9th centuries. Pope Innocent III (1198-1216) ordered its observance with great solemnity.

Corpus Christi (The Body and Blood of Christ), movable, celebrated on the Thursday (or Sunday, as in the U.S.) following Trinity Sunday, solemnity. Commemorates the institution of the Holy Eucharist (Mt. 26:26-28). The feast originated at Liege in 1246 and was extended throughout the Church in the West by Urban IV in 1264. St. Thomas Aquinas composed the Liturgy of the Hours for the feast.

Cross, The Holy, Sept. 14, feast. Commemorates the finding of the cross on which Christ was crucified, in 326 through the efforts of St. Helena, mother of Constantine; the consecration of the Basilica of the Holy Sepulchre nearly 10 years later: and the recovery in 628 or 629 by Emperor Heraclius of a major portion of the cross which had been removed by the Persians from its place of veneration at Jerusalem. The feast originated in Jerusalem and spread through the East before being adopted in the West. General adoption followed the building at Rome of the Basilica of the Holy Cross "in Jerusalem," so called because it was the place of enshrinement of a major portion of the cross of crucifixion.

Dedication of St. John Lateran, Nov. 9, feast. Commemorates the first public consecration of a church, that of the Basilica of the Most Holy Savior by Pope St. Sylvester about 324. The church, as well as the Lateran Palace, was the gift of Emperor Constantine. Since the 12th century it has been known as St. John Lateran, in honor of John the Baptist after whom the adjoining baptistery was named. It was rebuilt by Innocent X (1644-55), reconsecrated by Benedict XIII in 1726, and enlarged by Leo XIII (1878-1903). This basilica is regarded as the church of highest dignity in Rome and throughout the Roman Rite.

Dedication of St. Mary Major, Aug. 5, optional memorial. Commemorates the rebuilding and dedication by Pope Sixtus III (432-40) of a church in honor of Blessed Mary the Virgin. This is the Basilica of St. Mary Major on the Esquiline Hill in Rome. An earlier building was erected during the pontificate of Liberius (352-66); according to legend, it was located on a site covered by a miraculous fall of snow seen by a nobleman favored with a vision of Mary.

Easter, movable celebration held on the first Sunday after the full moon following the vernal equinox (between Mar. 22 and Apr. 25), solemnity with an octave. Commemorates the Resurrection of Christ from the dead (Mk. 16:1-7). The observance of this mystery, kept since the first days of the Church, extends throughout the Easter season which lasts until the feast of Pentecost, a period of 50 days. Every Sunday in the year is regarded as a "little" Easter. The date of Easter determines the dates of movable feasts, such as Ascension and Pentecost, and the number of weeks before Lent and after Pentecost.

Easter Vigil, called by St. Augustine the "Mother of All Vigils," the night before Easter. Ceremonies are all related to the Resurrection and renewal-in-grace theme of Easter: blessing of the new fire, procession with the Easter Candle, singing of the Easter Proclamation (Exsultet), Liturgy of the Word with at least three Old Testament readings, the Litany of Saints, blessing of water, baptism of converts and infants, renewal of baptismal promises, Liturgy of the Eucharist. The vigil ceremonies are held after nightfall on Saturday.

Epiphany of the Lord, Jan. 6 or (in the U.S.) a Sunday between Jan. 2 and 8, solemnity. Commemorates the manifestations of the divinity of Christ. It is one of the oldest Christian feasts, with an Eastern origin traceable to the beginning of the third century and antedating the Western feast of Christmas. Originally, it commemorated the manifestations of Christ's divinity — or Theophany — in his birth, the homage of the Magi, and baptism by John the Baptist. Later, the first two of these commemorations were transferred to Christmas when the Eastern Church adopted that feast between 380 and 430. The central feature of the Eastern observance now is the manifestation or declaration of Christ's divinity in his baptism and at the beginning of his public life. The Epiphany was adopted by the Western Church during the same period in which the Eastern Church accepted Christmas. In the Roman Rite, commemoration is made in the Mass of the homage of the wise men from the East (Mt. 2:1-12).

Good Friday, the Friday before Easter, the second day of the Easter Triduum. Liturgical elements of the observance are commemoration of the Passion and Death of Christ in the reading of the Passion (according to John), special prayers for the Church and people of all ranks, the veneration of the Cross, and a Communion service. The celebration takes place in the afternoon, preferably at 3:00 p.m.

Guardian Angels, Oct. 2, memorial. Commemorates the angels who protect people from spiritual and physical dangers and assist them in doing good. A feast in their honor celebrated in Spain in the 16th century was placed in the Roman calendar in 1615 and Oct. 2 was set as the date of observance. Earlier, guardian angels were honored liturgically in conjunction with the feast of St. Michael.

Holy Family, movable observance on the Sunday after Christmas, feast. Commemorates the Holy Family of Jesus, Mary and Joseph as the model of domestic society, holiness and virtue. The devotional background of the feast was very strong in the 17th century. In the 18th century, in prayers composed for a special Mass, a Canadian bishop likened the Christian family to the Holy Family. Leo XIII consecrated families to the Holy Family. In 1921, Benedict XV extended the Divine Office and Mass of the feast to the whole Church.

Holy Innocents, Dec. 28, feast. Commemorates the infants who suffered death at the hands of Herod's soldiers seeking to kill the child Jesus (Mt. 2:13-18). A feast in their honor has been observed since the fifth century.

Holy Saturday, the day before Easter. The Sacrifice of the Mass is not celebrated, and Holy Communion may be given only as Viaticum. If possible the Easter fast should be observed until the Easter Vigil.

Holy Thursday, the Thursday before Easter. Commemorates the institution of the sacraments of the Eucharist and holy orders, and the washing of the feet of the Apostles by Jesus at the Last Supper. The Mass of the Lord's Supper in the evening marks the beginning of the Easter Triduum. Following the Mass, there is a procession of the Blessed Sacrament to a place of reposition for adoration by the faithful. Usually at an earlier Mass of Chrism, bishops bless oils (of catechumens, chrism, the sick) for use during the year. (For pastoral reasons, diocesan bishops may permit additional Masses, but these should not overshadow the principal Mass of the Lord's Supper.)

Immaculate Conception, Dec. 8, holy day of obligation, solemnity. Commemorates the fact that Mary, in view of her calling to be the Mother of Christ and in virtue of his merits, was preserved from the first moment of her conception from original sin and was filled with grace from the very beginning of her life. She was the only person so preserved from original sin. The present form of the feast dates from Dec. 8, 1854, when Pius IX defined the dogma of the Immaculate Conception An earlier feast of the Conception, which testified to long-existing belief in this truth, was observed in the East by the eighth century, in Ireland in the ninth, and subsequently in European countries. In 1846, Mary was proclaimed patroness of the U.S. under this title.

Immaculate Heart of Mary, Saturday following the second Sunday after Pentecost, memorial. On May 4, 1944, Pius XII ordered this feast observed throughout the Church in order to obtain Mary's intercession for "peace among nations, freedom for the Church, the conversion of sinners, the love of purity and the practice of virtue." Two years earlier, he consecrated the entire human race to Mary under this title. Devotion to Mary under the title of her Most Pure Heart originated during the Middle Ages. It was given great impetus in the 17th century by the preaching of St. John Eudes, who was the first to celebrate a Mass and Divine Office of Mary under this title. A feast, celebrated in various places and on different dates, was authorized in 1799.

Joachim and Ann, July 26, memorial. Commemorates the parents of Mary. A joint feast, celebrated Sept. 9, originated in the East near the end of the sixth century. Devotion to Ann, introduced in the eighth century at Rome, became widespread in Europe in the 14th century; her feast was extended throughout the Latin Church in 1584. A feast of Joachim was introduced in the West in the 15th century.

John the Baptist, Birth, June 24, solemnity. The precursor of Christ, whose cousin he was, was commemorated universally in the liturgy by the fourth century. He is the only saint, except the Blessed Virgin Mary, whose birthday is observed as a feast. Another feast, on Aug. 29, commemorates his passion and death at the order of Herod (Mk. 6:14-29).

Joseph, Mar. 19, solemnity. Joseph is honored as the husband of the Blessed Virgin Mary, the patron and protector of the universal Church and workman. Devotion to him already existed in the eighth century in the East, and in the 11th in the West. Various feasts were celebrated before the 15th century when Mar. 19 was fixed for his commemoration; this feast was extended to the whole Church in 1621 by Gregory XV. In 1955, Pius XII instituted the feast of St. Joseph the Workman for observance May 1; this feast, which may be celebrated by local option, supplanted the Solemnity or Patronage of St. Joseph formerly observed on the third Wednesday after Easter. St. Joseph was proclaimed protector and patron of the universal Church in 1870 by Pius IX.

Michael, Gabriel and Raphael, Archangels, Sept. 29, feast. A feast bearing the title of Dedication of St. Michael the Archangel formerly commemorated on this date the consecration in 530 of a church near Rome in honor of Michael, the first angel given a liturgical feast. For a while, this feast was combined with a commemoration of the Guardian Angels. The separate feasts of Gabriel (Mar. 24) and Raphael (Oct. 24) were suppressed by the calendar in effect since 1970 and this joint feast of the three archangels was instituted.

Octave of Christmas, Jan. 1. See Solemnity of Mary, Mother of God.

Our Lady of Guadalupe, Dec. 12, feast (in the U.S.). Commemorates under this title the appearances of the Blessed Virgin Mary in 1531 to an Indian, Juan Diego, on Tepeyac hill outside Mexico City (see Apparitions of the Blessed Virgin Mary). The celebration, observed as a memorial in the U.S., was raised to the rank of feast at the request of the National Conference of Catholic Bishops. Approval was granted in a decree dated Jan. 8, 1988.

Our Lady of Sorrows, Sept. 15, memorial. Recalls the sorrows experienced by Mary in her association with Christ: the prophecy of Simeon (Lk. 2:34-35), the flight into Egypt (Mt. 2:13-21), the three-day separation from Jesus (Lk. 2:41-50), and four incidents connected with the Passion: her meeting with Christ on the way to Calvary, the crucifixion, the removal of Christ's body from the cross, and his burial (Mt. 27:31-61; Mk. 15:20-47; Lk. 23:26-56; Jn. 19:17-42). A Mass and Divine Office of the feast were celebrated by the Servites, especially, in the 17th century, and in 1814 Pius VII extended the observance to the whole Church.

Our Lady of the Rosary, Oct. 7, memorial. Commemorates the Virgin Mary through recall of the mysteries of the Rosary which recapitulate events in her life and the life of Christ. The feast was instituted in 1573 to commemorate a Christian victory over invading Mohammedan forces at Lepanto in 1571, and was extended throughout the Church by Clement XI in 1716.

Passion Sunday (formerly called **Palm Sunday**), the Sunday before Easter. Marks the start of Holy Week by recalling the triumphal entry of Christ into Jerusalem at the beginning of the last week of his life (Mt. 21:1-9). A procession and other ceremonies commemorating this event were held in Jerusalem from very early Christian times and were adopted in Rome by the ninth century, when the blessing of palm for the occasion was introduced. Full liturgical observance includes the blessing of palm and a procession before the principal Mass of the day. The Passion, by Matthew, Mark or Luke, is read during the Mass.

Pentecost, also called **Whitsunday,** movable celebration held 50 days after Easter, solemnity. Commemorates the descent of the Holy Spirit upon the Apostles, the preaching of Peter and the other Apostles to Jews in Jerusalem, the baptism and aggregation of some 3,000 persons to the Christian community (Acts 2:1-41). It is regarded as the birthday of the Catholic Church. The original observance of the feast antedated the earliest extant documentary evidence from the third century.

Peter and Paul, June 29, solemnity. Commemorates the martyrdoms of Peter by crucifixion and Paul by beheading during the Neronian persecution. This joint commemoration of the chief Apostles dates at least from 258 at Rome.

Presentation of the Lord (formerly called Purification of the Blessed Virgin Mary, also Candlemas), Feb. 2, feast. Commemorates the presentation of Jesus in the Temple — according to prescriptions of Mosaic Law (Lv. 12:2-8; Ex. 13:2; Lk. 2:22-32) — and the purification of Mary 40 days after his birth. In the East, where the feast antedated fourth century testimony regarding its existence, it was observed primarily as a feast of Our Lord; in the West, where it was adopted later, it was regarded more as a feast of Mary until the calendar in effect since 1970. Its date was set for Feb. 2 after the celebration of Christmas was fixed for Dec. 25, late in the fourth century. The blessing of candles, probably in commemoration of Christ who was the Light to enlighten the

Gentiles, became common about the 11th century and gave the feast the secondary name of Candlemas.

Queenship of Mary, Aug. 22, memorial. Commemorates the high dignity of Mary as Queen of heaven, angels and men. Universal observance of the memorial was ordered by Pius XII in the encyclical *Ad Caeli Reginam*, Oct. 11, 1954, near the close of a Marian Year observed in connection with the centenary of the proclamation of the dogma of the Immaculate Conception and four years after the proclamation of the dogma of the Assumption. The original date of the memorial was May 31.

Resurrection. See Easter.

Sacred Heart of Jesus, movable observance held on the Friday after the second Sunday after Pentecost (Corpus Christi, in the U.S.), solemnity. The object of the devotion is the divine Person of Christ, whose heart is the symbol of his love for all people — for whom he accomplished the work of Redemption. The Mass and Office now used on the feast were prescribed by Pius XI in 1929. Devotion to the Sacred Heart was introduced into the liturgy in the 17th century through the efforts of St. John Eudes who composed an Office and Mass for the feast. It was furthered as the result of the revelations of St. Margaret Mary Alacoque after 1675 and by the work of St. Claude La Colombiere, S.J. In 1765, Clement XIII approved a Mass and Office for the feast, and in 1856 Pius IX extended the observance throughout the Roman Rite.

Solemnity of Mary, Mother of God, Jan. 1, holy day of obligation, solemnity. The calendar in effect since 1970, in accord with Eastern tradition, reinstated the Marian character of this commemoration on the octave day of Christmas. The former feast of the Circumcision, dating at least from the first half of the sixth century, marked the initiation of Jesus (Lk. 2:21) in Judaism and by analogy focused attention on the initiation of persons in the Christian religion and their incorporation in Christ through baptism. The feast of the Solemnity supplants the former feast of the Maternity of Mary observed on Oct. 11.

Transfiguration of the Lord, Aug. 6, feast. Commemorates the revelation of his divinity by Christ to Peter, James and John on Mt. Tabor (Mt. 17:1-9). The feast, which is very old, was extended throughout the universal Church in 1457 by Callistus III.

Trinity, The Holy, movable observance held on the Sunday after Pentecost, solemnity. Commemorates the most sublime mystery of the Christian faith, i.e., that there are Three Divine Persons — Father, Son and Holy Spirit — in one God (Mt. 28:18-20). A votive Mass of the Most Holy Trinity dates from the seventh century; an Office was composed in the 10th century; in 1334, John XXII extended the feast to the universal Church.

Visitation, May 31, feast. Commemorates Mary's visit to her cousin Elizabeth after the Annunciation and before the birth of John the Baptist, the precursor of Christ (Lk. 1:39-47). The feast had a medieval origin and was observed in the Franciscan Order before being extended throughout the Church by Urban VI in 1389. It is one of the feasts of the Incarnation and is notable for its recall of the Magnificat, one of the few New Testament canticles, which acknowledges the unique gifts of God to Mary because of her role in the redemptive work of Christ. The canticle is recited at Evening Prayer in the Liturgy of the Hours.

SAINTS

Biographical sketches of additional saints and blessed are under other Almanac titles. See Index, under name of saint. For Beatification and Canonization procedures, see those entries in the Glossary.

An asterisk with a feast date indicates that the saint is listed in the General Roman Calendar or the proper calendar for U.S. dioceses. For rank of observances, see listing in calendar for current year on preceding pages.

Adalbert (956-997): Born in Bohemia; bishop of Prague; Benedictine; missionary in Poland, Prussia and Hungary; martyred by Prussians near Danzig; Apr. 23*.

Adjutor (d. 1131): Norman knight; fought in First Crusade; monk-recluse after his return; Apr. 30.

Agatha (d. c. 250): Sicilian virgin-martyr; her intercession credited in Sicily with stilling eruptions of Mt. Etna; patron of nurses; Feb. 5*.

Agnes (d. c. 304): Roman virgin-martyr; martyred at age of 10 or 12; patron of young girls; Jan. 21*.

Aloysius Gonzaga (1568-1591): Italian Jesuit; died while nursing plague-stricken; canonized 1726; patron of youth; June 21*.

Amand (d. c. 676): Apostle of Belgium; b. France; established monasteries throughout Belgium; Feb. 6.

Andre Bessette, Bl. (Bro. Andre) (1845-1937): Canadian Holy Cross Brother; prime mover in building of St. Joseph's Oratory, Montreal; beatified May 23, 1982; Jan. 6* (U.S.).

Andre Grasset de Saint Sauveur, Bl. (1758-1792): Canadian priest; martyred in France, Sept. 2, 1792, during the Revolution; one of a group called the Martyrs of Paris who were beatified in 1926; Sept. 2.

Andrew Bobola (1592-1657): Polish Jesuit; joined Jesuits at Vilna; worked for return of Orthodox to union with Rome; martyred; canonized 1938; May 16.

Andrew Corsini (1302-1373): Italian Carmelite; bishop of Fiesoli; mediator between quarrelsome Italian states; canonized 1629; Feb. 4.

Andrew Dung-Lac and Companions (d. 18th-19th c.): Martyrs of Vietnam. Total of 117 included 96 Vietnamese, 11 Spanish and 10 French missionaries (8 bishops; 50 priests, including Andrew Dung-Lac; 1 seminarian, 58 lay persons). Canonized June 19, 1988; inscribed in General Roman Calendar, 1989, as a memorial. Nov. 24*.

Andrew Fournet (1752-1834): French priest; co-founder with St. Jeanne Elizabeth Bichier des Anges of the Daughters of the Holy Cross of St. Andrew; canonized 1933; May 13.

Andrew Kim, Paul Chong and Companions (d. between 1839-1867): Korean martyrs (103) killed in persecutions of 1839, 1846, 1866, and 1867;

among them were Andrew Kim, the first Korean priest, and Paul Chong, lay apostle; canonized May 6, 1984, during Pope John Paul II's visit to Korea; entered into General Roman Calendar, 1985, as a memorial. Sept. 20*.

Angela Merici (1474-1540): Italian secular Franciscan; foundress of Company of St. Ursula, 1535, the first teaching order of women Religious in the Church; canonized 1807; Jan. 27*.

Angelico, Bl. (Fra Angelico; John of Faesulis) (1387-1455): Dominican; Florentine painter of early Renaissance; proclaimed blessed by John Paul II, Feb. 3, 1982; patron of artists; Feb. 18.

Anne Mary Javouhey, Bl. (1779-1851): French virgin; foundress of Institute of St. Joseph of Cluny, 1812; beatified 1950; July 15.

Ansgar (801-865): Benedictine monk; b. near Amiens; archbishop of Hamburg; missionary in Denmark, Sweden, Norway and northern Germany; apostle of Scandinavia; Feb. 3.*

Anthony (c. 251-c. 354): Abbot; Egyptian hermit; patriarch of all monks; established communities for hermits which became models for monastic life, especially in the East; friend and supporter of St. Athanasius in the latter's struggle with the Arias; Jan. 17*.

Anthony Claret (1807-1870): Spanish bishop; founder of Missionary Sons of the Immaculate Heart of Mary (Claretians), 1849; archbishop of Santiago, Cuba, 1851-57; canonized 1950; Oct. 24*.

Anthony Gianelli (1789-1846): Italian bishop; founded the Daughters of Our Lady of the Garden, 1829; bishop of Bobbio, 1838; canonized 1951; June 7.

Anthony Zaccaria (1502-1539): Italian priest; founder of Barnabites (Clerks Regular of St. Paul), 1530; canonized 1897; July 5*.

Apollonia (d. 249): Deaconess of Alexandria; martyred during persecution of Decius; her patronage of dentists and those suffering from toothaches probably rests on tradition that her teeth were broken by her persecutors; Feb. 9.

Augustine of Canterbury (d. 604 or 605): Italian missionary; apostle of the English; sent by Pope Gregory I with 40 monks to evangelize England; arrived there 597; first archbishop of Canterbury; May 27*.

Bartolomea Capitania (1807-1833): Italian foundress with Vincenza Gerosa of the Sisters of Charity of Lovere; canonized 1950; July 26.

Beatrice da Silva Meneses (1424-1490): Foundress, b. Portugal; founded Congregation of the Immaculate Conception, 1484, in Spain; canonized 1976; Sept. 1.

Benedict Joseph Labre (1748-1783): French layman; pilgrim-beggar; noted for his piety and love of prayer before the Blessed Sacrament; canonized 1883; Apr. 16.

Benedict of Nursia (c. 480-547): Abbot; founder of monasticism in Western Europe; established monastery at Monte Cassino; proclaimed patron of Europe by Paul VI in 1964; July 11*.

Benedict the Black (il Moro) (1526-1589): Sicilian Franciscan; born a slave; joined Franciscans as lay brother; appointed guardian and novice master; canonized 1807; Apr. 3.

Bernadette Soubirous (1844-1879): French peasant girl favored with series of visions of Blessed Virgin Mary at Lourdes (see Lourdes Apparitions); joined Institute of Sisters of Notre Dame at Nevers, 1866; canonized 1933; Apr. 16.

Bernard of Montjoux (or Menthon) (d. 1081): Augustinian canon; probably born in Italy; founded Alpine hospices near the two passes named for him; patron of mountaineers; May 28.

Bernardine of Feltre, Bl. (1439-1494): Italian Franciscan preacher; a founder of montes pietatis; Sept. 28.

Bernardine of Siena (1380-1444): Italian Franciscan; noted preacher and missioner; spread of devotion to Holy Name is attributed to him; represented in art holding to his breast the monogram IHS; canonized 1450; May 20*.

Blase (d. c. 316): Armenian bishop; martyr; the blessing of throats on his feast day derives from tradition that he miraculously saved the life of a boy who had half-swallowed a fish bone; Feb. 3*.

Boniface (Winfrid) (d. 754): English Benedictine; bishop; martyr; apostle of Germany; established monastery at Fulda which became center of missionary work in Germany; archbishop of Mainz; martyred near Dukkum in Holland; June 5*.

Brendan (c. 489-583): Irish abbot; founded monasteries; his patronage of sailors probably rests on a legend that he made a seven-year voyage in search of a fabled paradise; called Brendan the Navigator; May 16.

Bridget (Brigid) (c. 450-525): Irish nun; founded religious community at Kildare, the first in Ireland; patron, with Sts. Patrick and Columba, of Ireland; Feb. 1.

Bridget (Birgitta) (c. 1303-1373): Swedish mystic; widow; foundress of Order of Our Savior (Brigittines); canonized 1391; patroness of Sweden; July 23*.

Bruno (1030-1101): German monk; founded Carthusians, 1084, in France; Oct. 6*.

Cabrini, Mother: See Frances Xavier Cabrini.

Cajetan (Gaetano) of Thiene (1480-1547): Italian lawyer; religious reformer; a founder of Oratory of Divine Love, forerunner of the Theatines; canonized 1671; Aug. 7*.

Callistus I (d. 222): Pope, 217-222; martyr; condemned Sabellianism and other heresies; advocated a policy of mercy toward repentant sinners; Oct. 14*.

Camillus de Lellis (1550-1614): Italian priest; founder of Camillians (Ministers of the Sick); canonized 1746; patron of the sick and of nurses; July 14*.

Casimir (1458-1484): Polish prince; grand duke of Lithuania; noted for his piety; buried at cathedral in Vilna, Lithuania; canonized 1521; patron of Poland and Lithuania; Mar. 4*.

Cassian of Tangier (d. 298): Roman martyr; an official court stenographer who declared himself a Christian; patron of stenographers; Dec. 3.

Catherine Laboure (1806-1876): French Religious; favored with series of visions soon after she joined Sisters of Charity of St. Vincent de Paul in Paris in 1830; first Miraculous Medal (see Index) struck in 1832 in accord with one of the visions; canonized 1947; Nov. 28.

Catherine of Bologna (1413-1463): Italian Poor

Clare; mystic, writer, artist canonized 1712; patron of artists; May 9.

Cecilia (2nd-3rd century): Roman virgin-martyr; traditional patroness of musicians; Nov. 22.*

Charles Borromeo (1538-1584): Italian cardinal; nephew of Pope Pius IV; cardinal bishop of Milan; influential figure in Church reform in Italy; promoted education of clergy; canonized 1610; Nov. 4*.

Charles Lwanga and Companions (d. between 1885 and 1887): Twenty-two Martyrs of Uganda, many of them pages of King Mwanga of Uganda, who were put to death because they denounced his corrupt lifestyle; canonized 1964; first martyrs of black Africa; June 3.*

Charles of Sezze (1616-1670): Italian Franciscan lay brother who served in humble capacities; canonized 1959; Jan. 6.

Christopher (3rd cent.): Early Christian martyr inscribed in Roman calendar about 1550; feast relegated to particular calendars because of legendary nature of accounts of his life; traditional patron of travelers; July 25.

Clare (1194-1253): Foundress of Poor Clares; b. at Assisi; was joined in religious life by her sisters, Agnes and Beatrice, and eventually her widowed mother Ortolana; canonized 1255; patroness of television; Aug. 11.*

Claude La Colombiere (1641-1682): French Jesuit; spiritual director of St. Margaret Mary Alacoque; instrumental in spreading devotion to the Sacred Heart; beatified, 1929; canonized May 31, 1992; Feb. 15.

Clement Hofbauer (1751-1820): Redemptorist priest, missionary; born in Moravia; helped spread Redemptorists north of the Alps; canonized 1909; Mar. 15.

Clement I (d. c. 100): Pope, 88-97; third successor of St. Peter; wrote important letter to Church in Corinth settling disputes there; venerated as a martyr; Nov. 23*.

Columba (521-597): Irish monk; founded monasteries in Ireland; missionary in Scotland; established monastery at Iona which became the center for conversion of Picts, Scots, and Northern English; Scotland's most famous saint; patron saint of Ireland (with Sts. Patrick and Brigid); June 9.

Columban (545-615): Irish monk; scholar; founded monasteries in England and Brittany (famous abbey of Luxeuil), forced into exile because of his criticism of Frankish court; spent last years in northern Italy where he founded abbey at Bobbio; Nov. 23*.

Conrad of Parzham (1818-1894): Bavarian Capuchin lay brother; served as porter at the Marian shrine of Altotting in Upper Bavaria for 40 years; canonized 1934; Apr. 21.

Contardo Ferrini, Bl. (1859-1902): Italian secular Franciscan; model of the Catholic professor; beatified 1947; patron of universities; Oct. 20.

Cornelius (d. 253): Pope, 251-253; promoted a policy of mercy with respect to readmission of repentant Christians who had fallen away during the persecution of Decius (lapsi); banished from Rome during persecution of Gallus; regarded as a martyr; Sept. 16 (with Cyprian)*.

Cosmas and Damian (d. c. 303): Arabian twin brothers, physicians; martyred during Diocletian persecution; patrons of physicians; Sept. 26*.

Crispin and Crispinian (3rd cent.): Early Christian martyrs; said to have met their deaths in Gaul; patrons of shoemakers, a trade they pursued; Oct. 25.

Crispin of Viterbo (1668-1750): Capuchin brother; canonized June 20, 1982; May 21.

Cyprian (d. 258): Early ecclesiastical writer; b. Africa; bishop of Carthage, 249-258; supported Pope St. Cornelius concerning the readmission of Christians who had apostatized in time of persecution; erred in his teaching that baptism administered by heretics and schismatics was invalid; wrote De Unitate; Sept. 16 (with St. Cornelius)*.

Cyril and Methodius (9th century): Greek missionaries, bothers; venerated as apostles of the Slavs; Cyril (d. 869) and Methodius (d. 885) began their missionary work in Moravia in 863; developed a Slavonic alphabet; used the vernacular in the liturgy, a practice that was eventually approved; declared patrons of Europe with St. Benedict, Dec. 31, 1980; Feb. 14*.

Damasus I (d. 384): Pope, 366-384; opposed Arians and Apollinarians; commissioned St. Jerome to work on Bible translation; developed Roman liturgy; Dec. 11*.

Damian: See Cosmas and Damian.

David (5th or 6th cent.): Nothing for certain known of his life; said to have founded monastery at Menevia; patron saint of Wales; Mar. 1.

Denis and Companions (d. 3rd cent.): Denis, bishop of Paris, and two companions identified by early writers as Rusticus, a priest, and Eleutherius, a deacon; martyred near Paris; Denis is popularly regarded as the apostle and a patron saint of France; Oct. 9*.

Dismas (1st cent.): Name given to repentant thief (Good Thief) to whom Jesus promised salvation (Lk. 23:40-43); regarded as patron of prisoners; Mar. 25 (observed on second Sunday of October in U.S. prison chapels).

Dominic (Dominic de Guzman) (1170-1221): Spanish priest; founded the Order of Preachers (Dominicans), 1215, in France; preached against the Albigensian heresy; a contemporary of St. Francis of Assisi; canonized 1234; Aug. 8*.

Dominic Savio (1842-1857): Italian youth; pupil of St. John Bosco; died before his 15th birthday; canonized 1954; patron of choir boys; May 6.

Duns Scotus, John (d. 1308): Scottish Franciscan; theologian; advanced theological arguments for doctrine of the Immaculate Conception; proclaimed blessed; cult solemnly confirmed by John Paul II, Mar. 20, 1993; Nov. 8.

Dunstan (c. 910-988): English monk; archbishop of Canterbury; initiated reforms in religious life; counselor to several kings; considered one of greatest Anglo-Saxon saints; patron of goldsmiths, locksmiths, jewelers (trades in which he is said to have excelled); May 19.

Dymphna (dates unknown): Nothing certain known of her life; according to legend, she was an Irish maiden murdered by her heathen father at Gheel near Antwerp, Belgium, where she had fled to escape his advances; her relics were discovered there in the 13th century; since that time cures of mental illness and epilepsy have been attributed to her intercession; patron of those suffering from mental illness; May 15.

Edith Stein, Bl. (1891-1942): German Carmelite (Teresa Benedicta of the Cross); born of Jewish parents; author and lecturer; baptized in Catholic Church, 1922; arrested with her sister Rosa in 1942 and put to death at Auschwitz; beatified 1987, by Pope John Paul II during his visit to West Germany, Aug. 10. Her canonization was announced by John Paul II in 1997, but no date scheduled at the time of writing (June 11, 1997).

Edmund Campion (1540-1581): English Jesuit; convert 1573; martyred at Tyburn; canonized 1970, one of the Forty English and Welsh Martyrs; Dec. 1.

Edward the Confessor (d. 1066): King of England, 1042-66; canonized 1161; Oct. 13.

Eligius (c. 590-660): Bishop; born in Gaul; founded monasteries and convents; bishop of Noyon and Tournai; famous worker in gold and silver; Dec. 1.

Elizabeth Ann Seton (1774-1821): American foundress; convert, 1805; founded Sisters of Charity in the U.S.; beatified 1963; canonized Sept. 14, 1975; the first American-born saint; Jan. 4 (U.S.)*.

Elizabeth of Hungary (1207-1231): Became secular Franciscan after death of her husband in 1227; devoted life to poor and destitute; a patron of the Secular Franciscan Order; canonized 1235; Nov. 17*.

Elizabeth of Portugal (1271-1336): Queen of Portugal; b. Spain; retired to Poor Clare convent as a secular Franciscan after the death of her husband; canonized 1626; July 4*.

Emily de Rodat (1787-1852): French foundress of the Congregation of the Holy Family of Villefranche; canonized 1950; Sept. 19.

Emily de Vialar (1797-1856): French foundress of the Sisters of St. Joseph of the Apparition; canonized 1951; June 17.

Erasmus (Elmo) (d. 303): Life surrounded by legend; martyred during Diocletian persecution; patron of sailors; June 2.

Ethelbert (552-616): King of Kent, England; baptized by St. Augustine of Canterbury, 597; issued legal code; furthered spread of Christianity; Feb. 26.

Euphrasia Pelletier (1796-1868): French Religious; founded Sisters of the Good Shepherd at Angers, 1829; canonized 1940; Apr. 24.

Eusebius of Vercelli (283-370): Italian bishop; exiled from his see (Vercelli) for a time because of his opposition to Arianism; considered a martyr because of sufferings he endured; Aug. 2*.

Fabian (d. 250): Pope, 236-250; martyred under Decius; Jan. 20*.

Felicity: See Perpetua and Felicity.

Ferdinand III (1198-1252): King of Castile and Leon; waged successful crusade against Muhammadans in Spain; founded university at Salamanca; canonized 1671; May 30.

Fiacre (Fiachra) (d. c. 670): Irish hermit; patron of gardeners; Aug. 30.

Fidelis of Sigmaringen (Mark Rey) (1577-1622): German Capuchin; lawyer before he joined the Capuchins; missionary to Swiss Protestants; stabbed to death by peasants who were told he was agent of Austrian emperor; Apr. 24*.

Frances of Rome (1384-1440): Italian model for housewives and widows; happily married for 40 years; after death of her husband in 1436 joined community of Benedictine Oblates she had founded; canonized 1608; patron of motorists; Mar. 9*.

Frances Xavier Cabrini (Mother Cabrini) (1850-1917): American foundress; b. Italy; founded the Missionary Sisters of the Sacred Heart, 1877; settled in the U.S. 1889; became an American citizen at Seattle 1909; worked among Italian immigrants; canonized 1946, the first American citizen so honored; Nov. 13 (U.S.)*.

Francis Borgia (1510-1572): Spanish Jesuit; joined Jesuits after death of his wife in 1546; became general of the Order, 1565; Oct. 10.

Francis Caracciolo (1563-1608): Italian priest; founder with Father Augustine Adorno of the Clerics Regular Minor (Adorno Fathers); canonized 1807; declared patron of Italian chefs, 1996; June 4.

Francis Fasani (1681-1742); Italian Conventual Franciscan; model of priestly ministry, especially in service to poor and imprisoned; canonized 1986; Nov. 27.

Francis of Assisi (Giovanni di Bernardone) (1181/82-1226): Founder of the Franciscans, 1209; received stigmata 1224; canonized 1228; one of best known and best loved saints; patron of Italy, Catholic Action and ecologists; Oct. 4*.

Francis of Paola (1416-1507): Italian hermit: founder of Minim Friars; Apr. 2*.

Francis Xavier (1506-1552): Spanish Jesuit; missionary to Far East; canonized 1602; patron of foreign missions; considered one of greatest Christian missionaries; Dec. 3*.

Francis Xavier Bianchi (1743-1815): Italian Barnabite; acclaimed apostle of Naples because of his work there among the poor and abandoned; canonized 1951; Jan. 31.

Gabriel of the Sorrowful Mother (Francis Possenti) (1838-1862): Italian Passionist; died while a scholastic; canonized 1920; Feb. 27.

Gaspar (Caspar) del Bufalo (1786-1836): Italian priest; founded Missionaries of the Precious Blood, 1815; canonized 1954; Jan. 2.

Gemma Galgani (1878-1903): Italian laywoman; visionary; subject of extraordinary religious experiences; canonized 1940; Apr. 11.

Genesius (d. c. 300): Roman actor; according to legend, was converted while performing a burlesque of Christian baptism and was subsequently martyred; patron of actors; Aug. 25.

Genevieve (422-500): French nun; a patroness and protectress of Paris; events of her life not authenticated; Jan. 3.

George (d. c. 300): Martyr, probably during Diocletian persecution in Palestine; all other incidents of his life, including story of the dragon, are legendary; patron of England; Apr. 23*.

Gerard Majella (1725-1755): Italian Redemptorist lay brother; noted for supernatural occurrences in his life including bilocation and reading of consciences; canonized 1904; patron of mothers; Oct. 16.

Gertrude (1256-1302): German mystic; writer; helped spread devotion to the Sacred Heart; Nov. 16*.

Gregory VII (Hildebrand) (1020?-1085): Pope,

1075-1085; Benedictine monk; adviser to several popes; as pope, strengthened interior life of Church and fought against lay investiture; driven from Rome by Henry IV; died in exile; canonized 1584; May 25.*

Gregory Barbarigo (1626-1697): Italian cardinal; noted for his efforts to bring about reunion of separated Christians; canonized 1960; June 18.

Gregory of Nyssa (c. 335-395): Bishop; theologian; younger brother of St. Basil the Great; Mar. 9.

Gregory Thaumaturgus (c. 213-268): Bishop of Neocaesarea; missionary, famed as wonder worker; Nov. 17.

Gregory the Illuminator (257-332): Martyr; bishop; apostle and patron saint of Armenia; helped free Armenia from the Persians; Sept. 30.

Hedwig (1174-1243): Moravian noblewoman; married duke of Silesia, head of Polish royal family; fostered religious life in country; canonized 1266; Oct. 16*.

Helena (250-330): Empress; mother of Constantine the Great; associated with discovery of the True Cross; Aug. 18.

Henry (972-1024): Bavarian emperor; cooperated with Benedictine abbeys in restoration of ecclesiastical and social discipline; canonized 1146; July 13*.

Herman Joseph (1150-1241): German Premonstratensian; his visions were the subjects of artists; writer; cult approved, 1958; Apr. 7.

Hippolytus (d. c. 236): Roman priest; opposed Pope St. Callistus I in his teaching about the readmission to the Church of repentant Christians who had apostatized during time of persecution; elected antipope; exiled to Sardinia; reconciled before his martyrdom; important ecclesiastical writer; Aug. 13* (with Pontian).

Hubert (d. 727): Bishop; his patronage of hunters is based on legend that he was converted while hunting; Nov. 3.

Hugh of Cluny (the Great) (1024-1109): Abbot of Benedictine foundation at Cluny; supported popes in efforts to reform ecclesiastical abuses; canonized 1120; Apr. 29.

Ignatius of Antioch (d. c. 107): Early ecclesiastical writer; martyr; bishop of Antioch in Syria for 40 years; Oct. 17*.

Ignatius of Laconi (1701-1781): Italian Capuchin lay brother whose 60 years of religious life were spent in Franciscan simplicity; canonized 1951; May 11.

Ignatius of Loyola (1491-1556): Spanish soldier; renounced military career after recovering from wounds received at siege of Pampeluna (Pamplona) in 1521; founded Society of Jesus (Jesuits), 1534, at Paris; wrote *The Book of Spiritual Exercises*; canonized 1622; July 31*.

Irenaeus of Lyons (130-202): Early ecclesiastical writer; opposed Gnosticism; bishop of Lyons; traditionally regarded as a martyr; June 28*.

Isidore the Farmer (d. 1170): Spanish layman; farmer; canonized 1622; patron of farmers; May 15 (U.S.)*.

Jane Frances de Chantal (1572-1641): French widow; foundress, under guidance of St. Francis de Sales, of Order of the Visitation; canonized 1767; Dec. 12* (General Roman Calendar); Aug. 18* (U.S.).

Januarius (Gennaro) (d. 304): Bishop of Benevento; martyred during Diocletian persecution; fame rests on liquefaction of some of his blood preserved in a phial at Naples, an unexplained phenomenon which has occurred regularly several times each year for over 400 years; Sept. 19*.

Jeanne Delanoue (1666-1736): French foundress of Sisters of St. Anne of Providence, 1704; canonized 1982; Aug. 16.

Jeanne (Joan) de Lestonnac (1556-1640): French foundress; widowed in 1597; founded the Religious of Notre Dame 1607; canonized 1947; Feb. 2.

Jeanne de Valois (Jeanne of France) (1464-1505): French foundress; deformed daughter of King Louis XI; was married in 1476 to Duke Louis of Orleans who had the marriage annulled when he ascended the throne as Louis XII; Jeanne retired to life of prayer; founded contemplative Annonciades of Bourges, 1504; canonized 1950; Feb. 5.

Jeanne Elizabeth Bichier des Anges (1773-1838): French Religious; co-founder with St. Andrew Fournet of Daughters of the Cross of St. Andrew, 1807; canonized 1947; Aug. 26.

Jeanne Jugan, Bl. (1792-1879): French Religious; foundress of Little Sisters of the Poor; beatified Oct. 3, 1982; Aug. 30.

Jerome Emiliani (1481-1537): Venetian priest; founded Somascan Fathers, 1532, for care of orphans; canonized 1767; patron of orphans and abandoned children; Feb. 8*.

Joan Antida Thouret (1765-1826): French Religious; founded, 1799, congregation now known as Sisters of Charity of St. Joan Antida; canonized 1934; Aug. 24.

Joan of Arc (1412-1431): French heroine, called The Maid of Orleans, La Pucelle; led French army in 1429 against English invaders besieging Orleans; captured by Burgundians the following year; turned over to ecclesiastical court on charge of heresy, found guilty and burned at the stake; her innocence was declared in 1456; canonized 1920; patroness of France; May 30.

Joaquina de Vedruna de Mas (1783-1854): Spanish foundress; widowed in 1816; after providing for her children, founded the Carmelite Sisters of Charity; canonized 1959; Aug. 28.

John I (d. 526): Pope, 523-526; martyr; May 18*.

John Baptist de la Salle (1651-1719): French priest; founder of Brothers of the Christian Schools, 1680; canonized 1900; patron of teachers; Apr. 7*.

John Berchmans (1599-1621): Belgian Jesuit scholastic; patron of Mass servers; canonized 1888; Aug. 13.

John (Don) Bosco (1815-1888): Italian priest; founded Salesians, 1859, for education of boys; co-founder of Daughters of Mary Help of Christians for education of girls; canonized 1934; Jan. 31*.

John Capistran (1386-1456): Italian Franciscan; preacher; papal diplomat; canonized 1690; declared patron of military chaplains, Feb. 10, 1984. Oct. 23*.

John de Ribera (1532-1611): Spanish bishop and statesman; archbishop of Valencia, 1568-1611, and viceroy of that province; canonized 1960; Jan. 6.

John Eudes (1601-1680): French priest; founder of Sisters of Our Lady of Charity of Refuge, 1642, and Congregation of Jesus-Mary (Eudists), 1643; canonized 1925; Aug. 19*.

John Fisher (1469-1535): English prelate; theologian; martyr; bishop of Rochester, cardinal; refused to recognize validity of Henry VIII's marriage to Anne Boleyn; upheld supremacy of the pope; beheaded for refusing to acknowledge Henry as head of the Church; canonized 1935; June 22 (with St. Thomas More)*.

John Francis Regis (1597-1640): French Jesuit priest; preached missions among poor and unlettered; canonized 1737; patron of social workers, particularly medical social workers, because of his concern for poor and needy and sick in hospitals; July 2.

John Gualbert (d. 1073): Italian priest; founder of Benedictine congregation of Vallombrosians, 1039; canonized 1193; July 12.

John Kanty (Cantius) (1395-1473): Polish theologian; canonized 1767; Dec. 23*.

John Leonardi (1550-1609): Italian priest; worked among prisoners and the sick; founded Clerics Regular of the Mother of God; canonized 1938; Oct. 9*.

John Nepomucene (1345-1393): Bohemian priest; regarded as a martyr; canonized 1729; patron of Czechoslovakia; May 16.

John Nepomucene Neumann (1811-1860): American prelate; b. Bohemia; ordained in New York 1836; missionary among Germans near Niagara Falls before joining Redemptorists, 1840; bishop of Philadelphia, 1852; first bishop in U.S. to prescribe Forty Hours devotion in his diocese; beatified 1963; canonized June 19, 1977; Jan. 5 (U.S.)*.

John of Avila (1499-1569): Spanish priest; preacher; ascetical writer; spiritual adviser of St. Teresa of Jesus (Avila); canonized 1970; May 10.

John of Britto (1647-1693): Portuguese Jesuit; missionary in India where he was martyred; canonized 1947; Feb. 4.

John of God (1495-1550): Portuguese founder; his work among the sick poor led to foundation of Brothers Hospitallers of St. John of God, 1540, in Spain; canonized 1690; patron of sick, nurses, hospitals; Mar. 8*.

John of Matha (1160-1213): French priest; founder of the Order of Most Holy Trinity, whose original purpose was the ransom of prisoners from the Muslems; Feb. 8.

John Ogilvie (1579-1615): Scottish Jesuit; martyr; canonized 1976, the first canonized Scottish saint since 1250 (Margaret of Scotland); Mar. 10.

John Vianney (Cure of Ars) (1786-1859): French parish priest; noted confessor, spent 16 to 18 hours a day in confessional; canonized 1925; patron of parish priests; Aug. 4*.

Josaphat Kuncevyc (1584-1623): Basilian monk; b. Poland; archbishop of Polotsk, Lithuania; worked for reunion of separated Eastern Christians with Rome; martyred by mob of schismatics; canonized 1867; Nov. 12*.

Joseph Benedict Cottolengo (1786-1842): Italian priest; established Little Houses of Divine Providence (Piccolo Casa) for care of orphans and the sick; canonized 1934; Apr. 30.

Joseph Cafasso (1811-1860): Italian priest; renowned confessor; promoted devotion to Blessed Sacrament; canonized 1947; June 23.

Joseph Calasanz (1556-1648): Spanish priest; founder of Piarists (Order of Pious Schools); canonized 1767; Aug. 25*.

Joseph of Cupertino (1603-1663): Italian Franciscan; noted for remarkable incidents of levitation; canonized 1767; Sept. 18.

Joseph Pignatelli (1737-1811): Spanish Jesuit; left Spain when Jesuits were banished in 1767; worked for revival of the Order; named first superior when Jesuits were reestablished in Kingdom of Naples, 1804; canonized 1954; Nov. 28.

Juan Diego, Bl. (16th cent.): Mexican Indian, convert; indigenous name according to tradition Cuauhtlatohuac ("The eagle who speaks"); favored with apparitions of Our Lady (see Index: Our Lady of Guadalupe) on Tepeyac hill; beatified, 1990; Dec. 9* (U.S.).

Julia Billiart (1751-1816): French foundress; founded Sisters of Notre Dame de Namur, 1804; canonized 1969; Apr. 8.

Justin de Jacobis (1800-1860): Italian Vincentian; bishop; missionary in Ethiopia; canonized 1975; July 31.

Justin Martyr (100-165): Early ecclesiastical writer; Apologies for the Christian Religion, Dialog with the Jew Tryphon; martyred at Rome; June 1*.

Kateri Tekakwitha, Bl. (1656-1680): "Lily of the Mohawks." Indian maiden born at Ossernenon (Auriesville), N.Y.; baptized Christian, Easter, 1676, by Jesuit missionary Father Jacques de Lambertville; lived life devoted to prayer, penitential practices and care of sick and aged in Christian village of Caughnawaga near Montreal where her relics are now enshrined; beatified June 22, 1980; July 14* (in U.S.).

Katharine Drexel, Bl. (1858-1955): Philadelphia-born heiress; devoted wealth to founding schools and missions for Indians and Blacks; foundress of Sisters of Blessed Sacrament for Indians and Colored People, 1891; beatified 1988; Mar. 3* (U.S.).

Ladislaus (1040-1095): King of Hungary; supported Pope Gregory VII against Henry IV; canonized 1192; June 27.

Lawrence (d. 258): Widely venerated martyr who suffered death, according to a long-standing but unverifiable legend, by fire on a gridiron; Aug. 10*.

Lawrence (Lorenzo) Ruiz and Companions (d. 1630s): Martyred in or near the city of Nagasaki, Japan; Lawrence Ruiz, first Filipino saint, and 15 companions (nine Japanese, four Spaniards, one Italian and one Frenchman); canonized 1987; Sept. 28*.

Leonard Murialdo (1828-1900): Italian priest; educator; founder of Pious Society of St. Joseph of Turin, 1873; canonized 1970; Mar. 30.

Leonard of Port Maurice (1676-1751): Italian Franciscan; ascetical writer; preached missions throughout Italy; canonized 1867; patron of parish missions; Nov. 26.

Leopold Mandic (1866-1942): Croatian-born Franciscan priest, noted confessor; spent most of his priestly life in Padua, Italy; canonized, 1983, July 30.

Louis IX (1215-1270): King of France, 1226-1270; participated in Sixth Crusade; patron of Secular Franciscan Order; canonized 1297; Aug. 25*.

Louis de Montfort (1673-1716): French priest; founder of Sisters of Divine Wisdom, 1703, and Missionaries of Company of Mary, 1715; wrote *True Devotion to the Blessed Virgin;* canonized 1947; Apr. 28*.

Louis Zepherin Moreau, Bl. (d. 1901): Canadian bishop; headed St. Hyacinthe, Que., diocese, 1876-1901; beatified 1987; May 24.

Louise de Marillac (1591-1660): French foundress, with St. Vincent de Paul, of the Sisters of Charity; canonized 1934; Mar. 15.

Lucy (d. 304): Sicilian maiden; martyred during Diocletian persecution; one of most widely venerated early virgin-martyrs; patron of Syracuse, Sicily; invoked by those suffering from eye diseases; Dec. 13*.

Lucy Filippini (1672-1732): Italian educator, helped improve status of women through education; considered a founder of the Religious Teachers Filippini, 1692; canonized 1930; Mar. 25.

Madeleine Sophie Barat (1779-1865): French foundress of the Society of the Sacred Heart of Jesus; canonized 1925; May 25.

Malachy (1095-1148): Irish bishop; instrumental in establishing first Cistercian house in Ireland, 1142; canonized 1190; Nov. 3 (See Index: Prophecies of St. Malachy).

Marcellinus and Peter (d.c. 304): Early Roman martyrs; June 2*.

Margaret Clitherow (1556-1586): English martyr; convert shortly after her marriage; one of Forty Martyrs of England and Wales; canonized 1970; Mar. 25.

Margaret Mary Alacoque (1647-1690): French Religious; spread devotion to Sacred Heart in accordance with revelations made to her in 1675 (see Sacred Heart); canonized 1920; Oct. 16*.

Margaret of Cortona (1247-1297): Secular Franciscan; reformed her life in 1273 following the violent death of her lover; canonized 1728; May 16.

Margaret of Hungary (1242-1270): Contemplative; daughter of King Bela IV of Hungary; lived a life of self-imposed penances; canonized 1943; Jan. 18.

Margaret of Scotland (1050-1093): Queen of Scotland; noted for solicitude for the poor and promotion of justice; canonized 1250; Nov. 16*.

Maria Goretti (1890-1902): Italian virgin-martyr; a model of purity; canonized 1950; July 6*.

Mariana Paredes of Jesus (1618-1645): South American recluse; Lily of Quito; canonized, 1950; May 28.

Marie-Leonie Paradis, Bl. (1840-1912): Canadian Religious; founded Little Sisters of the Holy Family, 1880; beatified 1984; May 4.

Marie-Rose Durocher, Bl. (1811-1849): Canadian Religious; foundress of Sisters of Holy Names of Jesus and Mary; beatified 1982; Oct. 6* (in U.S.).

Martha (1st cent.): Sister of Lazarus and Mary of Bethany; Gospel accounts record her concern for homely details; patron of cooks; July 29*.

Martin I (d. 655): Pope, 649-55; banished from Rome by emperor in 653 because of his condemnation of Monothelites; considered a martyr; Apr. 13*.

Martin of Tours (316-397): Bishop of Tours; opposed Arianism and Priscillianism; pioneer of Western monasticism, before St. Benedict; Nov. 11*.

Mary Domenica Mazzarello (1837-1881): Italian foundress, with St. John Bosco, of the Daughters of Mary Help of Christians, 1872; canonized 1951; May 14.

Mary Josepha Rossello (1811-1881): Italian-born foundress of the Daughters of Our Lady of Mercy; canonized 1949; Dec. 7.

Mary Magdalen Postel (1756-1846): French foundress of the Sisters of Christian Schools of Mercy, 1807; canonized 1925; July 16.

Mary Magdalene (1st cent.): Gospels record her as devoted follower of Christ to whom he appeared after the Resurrection; her identification with Mary of Bethany (sister of Martha and Lazarus) and the woman sinner (Lk 7:36-50) has been questioned; July 22*.

Mary Magdalene dei Pazzi (1566-1607): Italian Carmelite nun; recipient of mystical experiences; canonized 1669; May 25*.

Mary Michaela Desmaisières (1809-1865): Spanish-born foundress of the Institute of the Handmaids of the Blessed Sacrament, 1848; canonized 1934; Aug. 24.

Maximilian Kolbe (1894-1941): Polish Conventual Franciscan; prisoner at Auschwitz who heroically offered his life in place of a fellow prisoner; beatified 1971, canonized 1982; Aug. 14*.

Methodius: See Index.

Miguel Febres Cordero (1854-1910): Ecuadorean Christian Brother; educator; canonized 1984; Feb. 9.

Miguel Pro, Bl. (1891-1927): Mexican Jesuit; joined Jesuits, 1911; forced to flee because of religious persecution; ordained in Belgium, 1925; returned to Mexico, 1926, to minister to people despite government prohibition; unjustly accused of assassination plot against president; arrested and executed; beatified 1988. Nov. 23* (U.S.).

Monica (332-387): Mother of St. Augustine; model of a patient mother; her feast is observed in the Roman calendar the day before her son's; Aug. 27*.

Nereus and Achilleus (d. c. 100): Early Christian martyrs; soldiers who, according to legend, were baptized by St. Peter; May 12*.

Nicholas of Flue (1417-1487): Swiss layman; at the age of 50, with the consent of his wife and 10 children, he retreated from the world to live as a hermit; called Brother Claus by the Swiss; canonized 1947; Mar. 21.

Nicholas of Myra (4th cent.): Bishop of Myra in Asia Minor; one of most popular saints in both East and West; most of the incidents of his life are based on legend; patron of Russia; Dec. 6*.

Nicholas of Tolentino (1245-1305): Italian hermit; famed preacher; canonized 1446; Sept. 10.

Nicholas Tavelic and Companions (Deodatus of Aquitaine, Peter of Narbonne, Stephen of Cuneo) (d. 1391): Franciscan missionaries; martyred by Muslems in the Holy Land: canonized 1970; Nov. 14.

Norbert (1080-1134): German bishop; founded Canons Regular of Premontre (Premonstratensians, Norbertines), 1120; promoted reform of the clergy, devotion to Blessed Sacrament; canonized 1582; June 6*.

Odilia (d. c. 720): Benedictine abbess; according to legend she was born blind, abandoned by her family and adopted by a convent of nuns where her sight was miraculously restored; patroness of blind; Dec. 13.

Oliver Plunket (1629-1681): Irish martyr; theologian; archbishop of Armagh and primate of Ireland; beatified 1920; canonized, 1975; July 1.

Pancras (d. c. 304): Roman martyr; May 12*.

Paola Frassinetti (1809-1882): Italian Religious; foundress, 1834, of Sisters of St. Dorothy; canonized 1984; June 11.

Paschal Baylon (1540-1592): Spanish Franciscan lay brother; spent life as door-keeper in various Franciscan friaries; defended doctrine of Real Presence in Blessed Sacrament; canonized 1690; patron of all Eucharistic confraternities and congresses, 1897; May 17.

Patrick (389-461): Famous missionary of Ireland; began missionary work in Ireland about 432; organized the Church there and established it on a lasting foundation; patron of Ireland, with Sts. Bridget and Columba; Mar. 17*.

Paul Miki and Companions (d. 1597): Martyrs of Japan; Paul Miki, Jesuit, and twenty-five other priests and laymen were martyred at Nagasaki; canonized 1862, the first canonized martyrs of the Far East; Feb. 6*.

Paul of the Cross (1694-1775): Italian Religious; founder of the Passionists; canonized 1867; Oct 19* (Oct. 20, U.S.*).

Paulinus of Nola (d. 451): Bishop of Nola (Spain); writer; June 22*.

Peregrine (1260-1347): Italian Servite; invoked against cancer (he was miraculously cured of cancer of the foot after a vision); canonized 1726; May 1.

Perpetua and Felicity (d. 203): Martyrs; Perpetua was a young married woman; Felicity was a slave girl; Mar. 7*.

Peter Chanel (1803-1841): French Marist; missionary to Oceania, where he was martyred; canonized 1954; Apr. 28*.

Peter Fourier (1565-1640): French priest; co-founder with Alice LeClercq (Mother Teresa of Jesus) of the Augustinian Canonesses of Our Lady, 1598; canonized 1897; Dec. 9.

Peter Gonzalez (1190-1246): Spanish Dominican; worked among sailors; court chaplain and confessor of King St. Ferdinand of Castile; patron of sailors; Apr. 14.

Peter Julian Eymard (1811-1868): French priest; founder of the Congregation of the Blessed Sacrament (men), 1856, and Servants of the Blessed Sacrament (women), 1864; dedicated to Eucharistic apostolate; canonized 1962; Aug. 2*.

Peter Nolasco (c. 1189-1258): Born in Langueduc area of present-day France; founded the Mercedarians (Order of Our Lady of Mercy), 1218, in Spain; canonized 1628; Jan. 31.

Peter of Alcantara (1499-1562): Spanish Franciscan; mystic; initiated Franciscan reform; confessor of St. Teresa of Jesus (Avila); canonized 1669; Oct. 22 (in U.S.).

Philip Benizi (1233-1285): Italian Servite; noted preacher, peacemaker; canonized 1671; Aug. 23.

Philip Neri (1515-1595): Italian Religious; founded Congregation of the Oratory; considered a second apostle of Rome because of his mission activity there; canonized 1622; May 26*.

Philip of Jesus (1517-157): Mexican Franciscan; martyred at Nagasaki, Japan; canonized 1862; patron of Mexico City; Feb. 6*.

Pius V (1504-1572): Pope, 1566-1572; enforced decrees of Council of Trent; organized expedition against Turks resulting in victory at Lepanto; canonized 1712; Apr. 30*.

Polycarp (2nd cent.): Bishop of Smyrna; ecclesiastical writer; martyr; Feb. 23*.

Pontian (d. c. 235): Pope, 230-235; exiled to Sardinia by the emperor; regarded as a martyr; Aug. 13 (with Hippolytus)*.

Rafaela Maria Porras y Ayllon (1850-1925): Spanish Religious; founded the Handmaids of the Sacred Heart, 1877; canonized 1977; Jan. 6.

Raymond Nonnatus (d. 1240): Spanish Mercedarian; cardinal; devoted his life to ransoming captives from the Moors; Aug. 31.

Raymond of Penyafort (1175-1275): Spanish Dominican; confessor of Gregory IX; systematized and codified canon law, in effect until 1917; master general of Dominicans, 1238; canonized 1601; Jan. 7*.

Rita of Cascia (1381-1457): Widow; cloistered Augustinian Religious of Umbria; invoked in impossible and desperate cases; May 22.

Robert Southwell (1561-1595): English Jesuit; poet; martyred at Tyburn; canonized 1970, one of the Forty English and Welsh Martyrs; Feb. 21.

Roch (1350-1379): French layman; pilgrim; devoted life to care of plague-stricken; widely venerated; invoked against pestilence; Aug. 17.

Romuald (951-1027): Italian monk; founded Camaldolese Benedictines; June 19*.

Rose of Lima (1586-1617): Peruvian Dominican tertiary; first native-born saint of the New World; canonized 1671; Aug. 23*.

Scholastica (d. c. 559): Sister of St. Benedict; regarded as first nun of the Benedictine Order; Feb. 10*.

Sebastian (3rd cent.): Roman martyr; traditionally pictured as a handsome youth with arrows; martyred; patron of athletes, archers; Jan. 20*.

Seven Holy Founders of the Servants of Mary (Buonfiglio Monaldo, Alexis Falconieri, Benedict dell'Antello, Bartholomew Amidei, Ricovero Uguccione, Gerardino Sostegni, John Buonagiunta Monetti): Florentine youths who founded Servites, 1233, in obedience to a vision; canonized 1888; Feb. 17*.

Sharbel Makhlouf (1828-1898): Lebanese Maronite monk-hermit; canonized 1977; Dec. 24.

Sixtus II and Companions (d. 258): Sixtus, pope 257-258, and four deacons, martyrs; Aug. 7*.

Stanislaus (1030-1079): Polish bishop; martyr; canonized 1253; Apr. 11*.

Stephen (d. c. 33): First Christian martyr; chosen by the Apostles as the first of the seven deacons; stoned to death; Dec. 26*.

Stephen (975-1038): King; apostle of Hungary; welded Magyars into national unity; canonized 1083; Aug. 16*.

Sylvester I (d. 335): Pope 314-335; first ecumenical council held at Nicaea during his pontificate; Dec. 31*.

Tarcisius (d. 3rd cent.): Early martyr; according to tradition, was martyred while carrying the Blessed Sacrament to some Christians in prison; patron of first communicants; Aug. 15.

Teresa Margaret Redi (1747-1770): Italian Carmelite; lived life of prayer and austere penance; canonized 1934; Mar. 11.

Teresa of Jesus Jornet Ibars (1843-1897): Spanish Religious; founded the Little Sisters of the Abandoned Aged, 1873; canonized 1974; Aug. 26.

Therese Couderc (1805-1885): French Religious; foundress of the Religious of Our Lady of the Retreat in the Cenacle, 1827; canonized 1970; Sept. 26.

Therese of Lisieux (1873-1897): French Carmelite nun; b. Therese Martin; allowed to enter Carmel at 15, died nine years later of tuberculosis; her "little way" of spiritual perfection became widely known through her spiritual autobiography; despite her obscure life, became one of the most popular saints; canonized 1925; patron of foreign missions; Oct. 1*.

Thomas Becket (1118-1170): English martyr; archbishop of Canterbury; chancellor under Henry II; murdered for upholding rights of the Church; canonized 1173; Dec. 29*.

Thomas More (1478-1535): English martyr; statesman, chancellor under Henry VIII; author of Utopia; opposed Henry's divorce, refused to renounce authority of the papacy; beheaded; canonized 1935; June 22 (with St. John Fisher)*.

Thorlac (1133-1193): Icelandic bishop; instituted reforms; although his cult was never officially approved, he was declared patron of Iceland, Jan. 14, 1984; Dec. 23.

Timothy (d. c. 97): Bishop of Ephesus; disciple and companion of St. Paul; martyr; Jan. 26*.

Titus (d. c. 96): Bishop; companion of St. Paul; recipient of one of Paul's epistles; Jan. 26*.

Titus Brandsma, Bl. (1881-1942): Dutch Carmelite priest; professor, scholar, journalist; denounced Nazi persecution of Jews; arrested by Na-zis, Jan. 19, 1942; executed by lethal injection at Dachau, July 26, 1942; beatified 1985; July 26.

Valentine (d. 269): Priest, physician; martyred at Rome; legendary patron of lovers; Feb. 14.

Vicenta Maria Lopez y Vicuna (1847-1896): Spanish foundress of the Daughters of Mary Immaculate for domestic service; canonized 1975; Dec. 26.

Vincent (d. 304): Spanish deacon; martyr; Jan. 22.*

Vincent de Paul (1581?-1660): French priest; founder of Congregation of the Mission (Vincentians, Lazarists) and co-founder of Sisters of Charity; declared patron of all charitable organizations and works by Leo XIII; canonized 1737; Sept. 27*.

Vincent Ferrer (1350-1418): Spanish Dominican; famed preacher; Apr. 5*.

Vincent Pallotti (1795-1850): Italian priest; founded Society of the Catholic Apostolate (Pallottines), 1835; Jan. 22.

Vincent Strambi (1745-1824): Italian Passionist; bishop; reformer; canonized 1950; Sept. 25.

Vincenza Gerosa (1784-1847): Italian co-foundress of the Sisters of Charity of Lovere; canonized 1950; June 28.

Vitus (d.c. 300): Martyr; died in Lucania, southern Italy; regarded as protector of epileptics and those suffering from St. Vitus Dance (chorea); June 15.

Walburga (d. 779): English-born Benedictine Religious; belonged to group of nuns who established convents in Germany at the invitation of St. Boniface; abbess of Heidenheim; Feb. 25.

Wenceslaus (d. 935): Duke of Bohemia; martyr; patron of Bohemia; Sept. 28*.

Zita (1218-1278): Italian maid; noted for charity to poor; patron of domestics; Apr. 27.

SAINTS—PATRONS AND INTERCESSORS

A patron is a saint who is venerated as a special intercessor before God. Most patrons have been so designated as the result of popular devotion and long-standing custom. In many cases, the fact of existing patronal devotion is clear despite historical obscurity regarding its origin. The Church has made official designation of relatively few patrons; in such cases, the dates of designation are given in parentheses in the list below. The theological background of the patronage of saints includes the dogmas of the Mystical Body of Christ and the Communion of Saints.

Listed below are patron saints of occupations and professions, and saints whose intercession is sought for special needs.

Accountants: Matthew.

Actors: Genesius.

Advertisers: Bernardine of Siena (May 20, 1960).

Alpinists: Bernard of Montjoux (or Menthon) (Aug. 20, 1923).

Altar servers: John Berchmans.

Anesthetists: Rene Goupil.

Animals: Francis of Assisi.

Archers: Sebastian.

Architects: Thomas, Apostle.

Art: Catherine of Bologna.

Artists: Luke, Catherine of Bologna, Bl. Angelico (Feb. 21, 1984).

Astronomers: Dominic.

Athletes: Sebastian.

Authors: Francis de Sales.

Aviators: Our Lady of Loreto (1920), Therese of Lisieux, Joseph of Cupertino.

Bakers: Elizabeth of Hungary, Nicholas.

Bankers: Matthew.

Barbers: Cosmas and Damian, Louis.

Barren women: Anthony of Padua, Felicity.

Basket-makers: Anthony, Abbot.

Beggars: Martin of Tours.

Blacksmiths: Dunstan.

Blind: Odilia, Raphael.

Blood banks: Januarius.

Bodily ills: Our Lady of Lourdes.

Bookbinders: Peter Celestine.

Bookkeepers: Matthew.

Booksellers: John of God.

Boy Scouts: George.

Brewers: Augustine of Hippo, Luke, Nicholas of Myra.

Bricklayers: Stephen.

Brides: Nicholas of Myra.

Brushmakers: Anthony, Abbot.

Builders: Vincent Ferrer.

Butchers: Anthony (Abbot), Luke.

Cabdrivers: Fiacre.

Cabinetmakers: Anne.

Cancer patients: Peregrine.
Canonists: Raymond of Peñafort.
Carpenters: Joseph.
Catechists: Viator, Charles Borromeo, Robert Bellarmine.
Catholic Action: Francis of Assisi (1916).
Chandlers: Ambrose, Bernard of Clairvaux.
Charitable societies: Vincent de Paul (May 12, 1885).
Children: Nicholas of Myra.
Children of Mary: Agnes, Maria Goretti.
Choirboys: Dominic Savio (June 8, 1956), Holy Innocents.
Church: Joseph (Dec. 8, 1870).
Clerics: Gabriel of the Sorrowful Mother.
Communications personnel: Bernardine.
Confessors: Alphonsus Liguori (Apr. 26, 1950), John Nepomucene.
Convulsive children: Scholastica.
Cooks: Lawrence, Martha.
Coopers: Nicholas of Myra.
Coppersmiths: Maurus.
Dairy workers: Brigid.
Deaf: Francis de Sales.
Dentists: Apollonia.
Desperate situations: Gregory of Neocaesarea, Jude Thaddeus, Rita of Cascia.
Dietitians (in hospitals): Martha.
Dyers: Maurice, Lydia.
Dying: Joseph.
Ecologists: Francis of Assisi (Nov. 29, 1979).
Editors: John Bosco.
Emigrants: Frances Xavier Cabrini (Sept. 8, 1950).
Engineers: Ferdinand III.
Epilepsy, Motor Diseases: Vitus, Willibrord.
Eucharistic congresses and societies: Paschal Baylon (Nov. 28, 1897).
Expectant mothers: Raymond Nonnatus, Gerard Majella.
Eye diseases: Lucy.
Falsely accused: Raymond Nonnatus.
Farmers: George, Isidore.
Farriers: John the Baptist.
Firemen: Florian.
Fire prevention: Catherine of Siena.
First communicants: Tarcisius.
Fishermen: Andrew.
Florists: Therese of Lisieux.
Forest workers: John Gualbert.
Foundlings: Holy Innocents.
Fullers: Anastasius the Fuller, James the Less.
Funeral directors: Joseph of Arimathea, Dismas.

Gardeners: Adelard, Tryphon, Fiacre, Phocas.
Glassworkers: Luke.
Goldsmiths: Dunstan, Anastasius.
Gravediggers: Anthony, Abbot.
Greetings: Valentine.
Grocers: Michael.
Hairdressers: Martin de Porres.
Happy meetings: Raphael.
Hatters: Severus of Ravenna, James the Less.
Headache sufferers: Teresa of Jesus (Avila).
Heart patients: John of God.
Hospital administrators: Basil the Great, Frances X. Cabrini.
Hospitals: Camillus de Lellis and John of God (June 22, 1886), Jude Thaddeus.
Housewives: Anne.
Hunters: Hubert, Eustachius.
Infantrymen: Maurice.
Innkeepers: Amand, Martha.
Invalids: Roch.
Jewelers: Eligius, Dunstan.
Journalists: Francis de Sales (Apr. 26, 1923).
Jurists: John Capistran.
Laborers: Isidore, James, John Bosco.
Lawyers: Ivo (Yves Helory), Genesius, Thomas More.
Learning: Ambrose.
Librarians: Jerome.
Lighthouse keepers: Venerius (Mar. 10, 1961).
Locksmiths: Dunstan.
Maids: Zita.
Marble workers: Clement I.
Mariners: Michael, Nicholas of Tolentino.
Medical record librarians: Raymond of Peñafort.
Medical social workers: John Regis.
Medical technicians: Albert the Great.
Mentally ill: Dymphna.
Merchants: Francis of Assisi, Nicholas of Myra.
Messengers: Gabriel.
Metal workers: Eligius.
Military chaplains: John Capistran (Feb. 10, 1984).
Millers: Arnulph, Victor.
Missions, Foreign: Francis Xavier (Mar. 25, 1904), Therese of Lisieux (Dec. 14, 1927).
Missions, Black: Peter Claver (1896, Leo XIII), Benedict the Black.
Missions, Parish: Leonard of Port Maurice (Mar. 17, 1923).
Mothers: Monica.
Motorcyclists: Our Lady of Grace.

Motorists: Christopher, Frances of Rome.
Mountaineers: Bernard of Montjoux (or Menthon).
Musicians: Gregory the Great, Cecilia, Dunstan.
Notaries: Luke, Mark.
Nurses: Camillus de Lellis and John of God (1930, Pius XI), Agatha, Raphael.
Nursing and nursing service: Elizabeth of Hungary, Catherine of Siena.
Orators: John Chrysostom (July 8, 1908).
Organ builders: Cecilia.
Orphans: Jerome Emiliani.
Painters: Luke.
Paratroopers: Michael.
Pawnbrokers: Nicholas.
Pharmacists: Cosmas and Damian, James the Greater.
Pharmacists (in hospitals): Gemma Galgani.
Philosophers: Justin.
Physicians: Pantaleon, Cosmas and Damian, Luke, Raphael.
Pilgrims: James the Greater.
Plasterers: Bartholomew.
Poets: David, Cecilia.
Poison sufferers: Benedict.
Policemen: Michael.
Poor: Lawrence, Anthony of Padua.
Poor souls: Nicholas of Tolentino.
Porters: Christopher.
Possessed: Bruno, Denis.
Postal employees: Gabriel.
Priests: Jean-Baptiste Vianney (Apr. 23, 1929).
Printers: John of God, Augustine of Hippo, Genesius.
Prisoners: Dismas, Joseph Cafasso.
Protector of crops: Ansovinus.
Public relations: Bernardine of Siena (May 20, 1960).
Public relations (of hospitals): Paul, Apostle.
Radiologists: Michael (Jan. 15, 1941).
Radio workers: Gabriel.
Retreats: Ignatius Loyola (July 25, 1922).
Rheumatism: James the Greater.
Saddlers: Crispin and Crispinian.
Sailors: Cuthbert, Brendan, Eulalia, Christopher, Peter Gonzalez, Erasmus, Nicholas.
Scholars: Brigid.
Schools, Catholic: Thomas Aquinas (Aug. 4, 1880), Joseph Calasanz (Aug. 13, 1948).
Scientists: Albert (Aug. 13, 1948).
Sculptors: Four Crowned Martyrs.
Seamen: Francis of Paola.

Searchers of lost articles: Anthony of Padua.

Secretaries: Genesius.

Secular Franciscans: Louis of France, Elizabeth of Hungary.

Seminarians: Charles Borromeo.

Servants: Martha, Zita.

Shoemakers: Crispin and Crispinian.

Sick: Michael, John of God and Camillus de Lellis (June 22, 1886).

Silversmiths: Andronicus.

Singers: Gregory, Cecilia.

Skaters: Lidwina.

Skiers: Bernard of Montjoux (or Menthon).

Social workers: Louise de Marillac (Feb. 12, 1960).

Soldiers: Hadrian, George, Ignatius, Sebastian, Martin of Tours, Joan of Arc.

Speleologists: Benedict.

Stenographers: Genesius, Cassian.

Stonecutters: Clement.

Stonemasons: Stephen.

Students: Thomas Aquinas.

Surgeons: Cosmas and Damian, Luke.

Swordsmiths: Maurice.

Tailors: Homobonus.

Tanners: Crispin and Crispinian, Simon.

Tax collectors: Matthew.

Teachers: Gregory the Great, John Baptist de la Salle (May 15, 1950).

Telecommunications workers: Gabriel (Jan. 12, 1951).

Television: Clare of Assisi (Feb. 14, 1958).

Television workers: Gabriel.

Theologians: Augustine, Alphonsus Liguori.

Throat ailments: Blase.

Travelers: Anthony of Padua, Nicholas of Myra, Christopher, Raphael.

Travel hostesses: Bona (Mar. 2, 1962).

Universities: Blessed Contardo Ferrini.

Vocations: Alphonsus.

Watchmen: Peter of Alcantara.

Weavers: Paul the Hermit, Anastasius the Fuller, Anastasia.

Wine merchants: Amand.

Women in labor: Anne.

Workingmen: Joseph.

Writers: Francis de Sales (Apr. 26, 1923), Lucy.

Yachtsmen: Adjutor.

Young girls: Agnes.

Youth: Aloysius Gonzaga (1729, Benedict XIII; 1926, Pius XI),

John Berchmans, Gabriel of the Sorrowful Mother.

Patron Saints of Places

Albania: Our Lady of Good Counsel.

Alsace: Odilia.

Americas: Our Lady of Guadalupe, Rose of Lima.

Angola: Immaculate Heart of Mary (Nov. 21, 1984).

Argentina: Our Lady of Lujan.

Armenia: Gregory Illuminator.

Asia Minor: John, Evangelist.

Australia: Our Lady Help of Christians.

Belgium: Joseph.

Bohemia: Wenceslaus, Ludmilla.

Bolivia: Our Lady of Copacabana "Virgen de la Candelaria."

Borneo: Francis Xavier.

Brazil: Nossa Senhora de Aparecida, Immaculate Conception, Peter of Alcantara.

Canada: Joseph, Anne.

Chile: James the Greater, Our Lady of Mt. Carmel.

China: Joseph.

Colombia: Peter Claver, Louis Bertran.

Corsica: Immaculate Conception.

Cuba: Our Lady of Charity.

Czechoslovakia: Wenceslaus, John Nepomucene, Procopius.

Denmark: Ansgar, Canute.

Dominican Republic: Our Lady of High Grace, Dominic.

East Indies: Thomas, Apostle.

Ecuador: Sacred Heart.

El Salvador: Our Lady of Peace (Oct. 10, 1966).

England: George.

Equatorial Guinea: Immaculate Conception (May 25, 1986).

Europe: Benedict (1964), Cyril and Methodius, co-patrons (Dec. 31, 1980).

Finland: Henry.

France: Our Lady of the Assumption, Joan of Arc, Therese (May 3, 1944).

Germany: Boniface, Michael.

Gibraltar: Blessed Virgin Mary under title, "Our Lady of Europe" (May 31, 1979).

Greece: Nicholas, Andrew.

Holland: Willibrord.

Hungary: Blessed Virgin, "Great Lady of Hungary," Stephen, King.

Iceland: Thorlac (Jan. 14, 1984).

India: Our Lady of Assumption.

Ireland: Patrick, Brigid and Columba.

Italy: Francis of Assisi, Catherine of Siena.

Japan: Peter Baptist.

Korea: Joseph and Mary, Mother of the Church.

Lesotho: Immaculate Heart of Mary.

Lithuania: Casimir, Bl. Cunegunda.

Luxembourg: Willibrord.

Malta: Paul, Our Lady of the Assumption.

Mexico: Our Lady of Guadalupe.

Monaco: Devota.

Moravia: Cyril and Methodius.

New Zealand: Our Lady Help of Christians.

Norway: Olaf.

Papua New Guinea (including northern Solomon Islands): Michael the Archangel (May 31, 1979).

Paraguay: Our Lady of Assumption (July 13, 1951).

Peru: Joseph (Mar. 19, 1957).

Philippines: Sacred Heart of Mary.

Poland: Casimir, Bl. Cunegunda, Stanislaus of Cracow, Our Lady of Czestochowa.

Portugal: Immaculate Conception, Francis Borgia, Anthony of Padua, Vincent of Saragossa, George.

Russia: Andrew, Nicholas of Myra, Therese of Lisieux.

Scandinavia: Ansgar.

Scotland: Andrew, Columba.

Silesia: Hedwig.

Slovakia: Our Lady of Sorrows.

South Africa: Our Lady of Assumption (Mar. 15, 1952).

South America: Rose of Lima.

Solomon Islands: BVM, under title Most Holy Name of Mary (Sept. 4, 1991).

Spain: James the Greater, Teresa.

Sri Lanka (Ceylon): Lawrence.

Sweden: Bridget, Eric.

Tanzania: Immaculate Conception (Dec. 8, 1964).

United States: Immaculate Conception (1846).

Uruguay: Blessed Virgin Mary under title "La Virgen de los Treinte y Tres" (Nov. 21, 1963).

Venezuela: Our Lady of Coromoto.

Wales: David.

West Indies: Gertrude.

Emblems, Portrayals of Saints

Agatha: Tongs, veil.

Agnes: Lamb.

Ambrose: Bees, dove, ox, pen.

Andrew: Transverse cross.

Anne, Mother of the Blessed Virgin: Door.

Anthony, Abbot: Bell, hog.

Anthony of Padua: Infant Jesus, bread, book, lily.

Augustine of Hippo: Dove, child, shell, pen.

Barnabas: Stones, ax, lance.

Bartholomew: Knife, flayed and holding his skin.

Benedict: Broken cup, raven, bell, crosier, bush.

Bernard of Clairvaux: Pen, bees, instruments of the Passion.

Bernardine of Siena: Tablet or sun inscribed with IHS.

Blase: Wax, taper, iron comb.

Bonaventure: Communion, ciborium, cardinal's hat.

Boniface: Oak, ax, book, fox, scourge, fountain, raven, sword.

Bridget of Sweden: Book, pilgrim's staff.

Bridget of Kildare: Cross, flame over her head, candle.

Catherine of Ricci: Ring, crown, crucifix.

Catherine of Siena: Stigmata, cross, ring, lily.

Cecilia: Organ.

Charles Borromeo: Communion, coat of arms with word Humilitas.

Christopher: Giant, torrent, tree, Child Jesus on his shoulders.

Clare of Assisi: Monstrance.

Cosmas and Damian: A phial, box of ointment.

Cyril of Alexandria: Blessed Virgin holding the Child Jesus, pen.

Cyril of Jerusalem: Purse, book.

Dominic: Rosary, star.

Edmund the Martyr: Arrow, sword.

Elizabeth of Hungary: Alms, flowers, bread, the poor, a pitcher.

Francis of Assisi: Wolf, birds, fish, skull, the Stigmata.

Francis Xavier: Crucifix, bell, vessel.

Genevieve: Bread, keys, herd, candle.

George: Dragon.

Gertrude: Crown, taper, lily.

Gervase and Protase: Scourge, club, sword.

Gregory I (the Great): Tiara, crosier, dove.

Helena: Cross.

Hilary: Stick, pen, child.

Ignatius of Loyola: Communion, chasuble, book, apparition of Our Lord.

Isidore: Bees, pen.

James the Greater: Pilgrim's staff, shell, key, sword.

James the Less: Square rule, halberd, club.

Jerome: Lion.

John Berchmans: Rule of St. Ignatius, cross, rosary.

John Chrysostom: Bees, dove, pen.

John of God: Alms, a heart, crown of thorns.

John the Baptist: Lamb, head on platter, skin of an animal.

John the Evangelist: Eagle, chalice, kettle, armor.

Josaphat Kuncevyc: Chalice, crown, winged deacon.

Joseph, Spouse of the Blessed Virgin: Infant Jesus, lily, rod, plane, carpenter's square.

Jude: Sword, square rule, club.

Justin Martyr: Ax, sword.

Lawrence: Cross, book of the Gospels, gridiron.

Leander of Seville: A pen.

Liborius: Pebbles, peacock.

Longinus: In arms at foot of the cross.

Louis IX of France: Crown of thorns, nails.

Lucy: Cord, eyes on a dish.

Luke: Ox, book, brush, palette.

Mark: Lion, book.

Martha: Holy water sprinkler, dragon.

Mary Magdalene: Alabaster box of ointment.

Matilda: Purse, alms.

Matthew: Winged man, purse, lance.

Matthias: Lance.

Maurus: Scales, spade, crutch.

Meinrad: Two ravens.

Michael: Scales, banner, sword, dragon.

Monica: Girdle, tears.

Nicholas: Three purses or balls, anchor or boat, child.

Patrick: Cross, harp, serpent, baptismal font, demons, shamrock.

Paul: Sword, book or scroll.

Peter: Keys, boat, cock.

Philip, Apostle: Column.

Philip Neri: Altar, chasuble, vial.

Rita of Cascia: Rose, crucifix, thorn.

Roch: Angel, dog, bread.

Rose of Lima: Crown of thorns, anchor, city.

Sebastian: Arrows, crown.

Simon Stock: Scapular.

Teresa of Jesus (Avila): Heart, arrow, book.

Therese of Lisieux: Roses entwining a crucifix.

Thomas, Apostle: Lance, ax.

Thomas Aquinas: Chalice, monstrance, dove, ox, person trampled under foot.

Vincent (Deacon): Gridiron, boat.

Vincent de Paul: Children.

Vincent Ferrer: Pulpit, cardinal's hat, trumpet, captives.

ROLE OF MARY IN THE MYSTERY OF CHRIST AND THE CHURCH

The following excerpts are from Chapter VIII of the Second Vatican Council's Constitution on the Church.

I. Preface

Wishing in his supreme goodness and wisdom to effect the redemption of the world, "when the fullness of time came, God sent his Son, born of a woman, ... that we might receive the adoption of sons" (Gal. 4:4-5). "He for us men, and for our salvation, came down from heaven, and was incarnate by the Holy Spirit from the Virgin Mary." This divine mystery of salvation is revealed to us and continued in the Church, which the Lord established as his own body. In this Church, adhering to Christ the head and having communion with all his saints, the faithful must also venerate the memory "above all of the glorious and perpetual Virgin Mary. Mother of our God and Lord Jesus Christ." (52)

At the message of the angel, the Virgin Mary received the Word of God in her heart and in her body, and gave Life to the world. Hence, she is acknowledged and honored as being truly the Mother of God and Mother of the Redeemer. Redeemed in an especially sublime manner by reason of the merits of her Son, and united to him by a close and indissoluble tie, she is endowed with the supreme office and dignity of being the Mother of the Son of God. As a result, she is also the favorite daughter of the Father and the temple of the Holy Spirit. Because of this gift of sublime grace, she far surpasses all other creatures, both in heaven and on earth.

At the same time, however, because she belongs to the offspring of Adam, she is one with all human beings in their need for salvation. Indeed, she is "clearly the Mother of the members of Christ ... since she cooperated out of love so that there might be born in the Church the faithful, who are members of

Christ their head. Therefore, she is also hailed as a pre-eminent and altogether singular member of the Church, and as the Church's model and excellent exemplar in faith and charity. Taught by the Holy Spirit, the Catholic Church honors her with filial affection and piety as a most beloved Mother. (53)

This sacred synod intends to describe with diligence the role of the Blessed Virgin in the mystery of the Incarnate Word and the Mystical Body. It also wishes to describe the duties of redeemed mankind toward the Mother of God, who is the Mother of Christ and Mother of men, particularly of the faithful.

The synod does not, however, have it in mind to give a complete doctrine on Mary, nor does it wish to decide those questions which have not yet been fully illuminated by the work of theologians. (54)

II. The Role of the Blessed Virgin in the Economy of Salvation

The Father of mercies willed that the consent of the predestined Mother should precede the Incarnation so that, just as a woman contributed to death, so also a woman should contribute to life. This contrast was verified in outstanding fashion by the Mother of Jesus. She gave to the world that very Life which renews all things, and she was enriched by God with gifts befitting such a role.

It is no wonder, then, that the usage prevailed among the holy Fathers whereby they called the Mother of God entirely holy and free from all stain of sin, fashioned by the Holy Spirit into a kind of new substance and new creature. Adorned from the first instant of her conception with the splendors of an entirely unique holiness, the Virgin of Nazareth is, on God's command, greeted by an angel messenger as "full of grace" (cf. Lk. 1:28). To the heavenly messenger she replies: "Behold the handmaid of the Lord; be it done to me according to thy word" (Lk. 1:38).

By thus consenting to the divine utterance, Mary, a daughter of Adam, became the Mother of Jesus. Embracing God's saving will with a full heart and impeded by no sin, she devoted herself totally as a handmaid of the Lord to the person and work of her Son. In subordination to him and along with him, by the grace of almighty God she served the mystery of redemption.

Rightly, therefore, the holy Fathers see her as used by God not merely in a passive way but as cooperating in the work of human salvation through free faith and obedience. (56)

This union of the Mother with the Son in the work of salvation was manifested from the time of Christ's virginal conception up to his death. It is shown first of all when Mary, arising in haste to go to visit Elizabeth, was greeted by her as blessed because of her belief in the promise of salvation, while the precursor leaped for joy in the womb of his mother (cf. Lk. 1:41-45). This association was shown also at the birth of our Lord, who did not diminish his Mother's virginal integrity but sanctified it, when the Mother of God joyfully showed her first-born Son to the shepherds and the Magi.

When she presented him to the Lord in the temple, making the offering of the poor, she heard Simeon foretelling at the same time that her Son would be a sign of contradiction and that a sword would pierce the Mother's soul, that out of many hearts thoughts might be revealed (cf. Lk. 2:34-35). When the Child Jesus was lost and they had sought him sorrowing, his parents found him in the temple, taken up with things which were his Father's business. They did not understand the reply of the Son. But his Mother, to be sure, kept all these things to be pondered over in her heart (cf. Lk. 2:41-51). (57)

In the public life of Jesus, Mary made significant appearances. This was so even at the very beginning, when she was moved with pity at the marriage feast of Cana, and her intercession brought about the beginning of the miracles by Jesus the Messiah (Cf. Jn. 2:1-11). In the course of her Son's preaching, she received his praise when, in extolling a kingdom beyond the calculations and bonds of flesh and blood, he declared blessed (cf. Mk. 3:35 par.; Lk. 11:27-28) those who heard and kept the word of the Lord as she was faithfully doing (cf. Lk. 2:19, 51).

Thus, the Blessed Virgin advanced in her pilgrimage of faith and loyally persevered in her union with her Son unto the cross. There she stood, in keeping with the divine plan (cf. Jn. 19:25), suffering grievously with her only-begotten Son. There she united herself with a maternal heart to his sacrifice, and lovingly consented to the immolation of this Victim whom she herself had brought forth. Finally, the same Christ Jesus dying on the cross gave her as a mother to his disciple. This he did when he said: "Woman, behold your son" (Jn. 19:26-27). (58)

But since it pleased God not to manifest solemnly the mystery of the salvation of the human race until he poured forth the Spirit promised by Christ, we see the apostles before the day of Pentecost "continuing with one mind in prayer with the women and Mary, the Mother of Jesus, and with his brethren" (Acts 1:14). We see Mary prayerfully imploring the gift of the Spirit, who had already overshadowed her in the Annunciation.

Finally, preserved free from all guilt of original sin, the Immaculate Virgin was taken up body and soul into heavenly glory upon the completion of her earthly sojourn. She was exalted by the Lord as Queen of all, in order that she might be the more thoroughly conformed to her Son, the Lord of lords (cf. Rev. 19:16) and the conqueror of sin and death. (59)

III. The Blessed Virgin and the Church

We have but one Mediator, as we know from the words of the apostle: "For there is one God, and one Mediator between God and men, himself man, Christ Jesus, who gave himself as a ransom for all" (1 Tim. 2:5-6). The maternal duty of Mary toward men in no way obscures or diminishes this unique mediation of Christ, but rather shows its power. For all the saving influences of the Blessed Virgin on men originate, not from some inner necessity, but from the divine pleasure. They flow forth from the superabundance of the merits of Christ, rest on his mediation, depend entirely on it, and draw all their power from it. In no way do they impede the immediate union of the faithful with Christ. Rather, they foster this union. (60)

In an utterly singular way, she (Mary) cooperated by her obedience, faith, hope and burning charity in the Savior's work of restoring supernatural life to souls. For this reason she is a mother to us in the order of grace. (61)

This maternity of Mary in the order of grace began with the consent which she gave in faith at the Annunciation and which she sustained without wavering beneath the cross. This maternity will last without interruption until the eternal fulfillment of all the elect. For, taken up to heaven, she did not lay aside this saving role, but by her manifold acts of intercession continues to win for us gifts of eternal salvation.

By her maternal charity, Mary cares for the brethren of her Son who still journey on earth surrounded by dangers and difficulties until they are led to their happy fatherland. Therefore, the Blessed Virgin is invoked by the Church under the titles of Advocate, Auxiliatrix, Adjutrix and Mediatrix. These, however, are to be so understood that they neither take away nor add anything to the dignity and efficacy of Christ the one Mediator.

For no creature could ever be classed with the Incarnate Word and Redeemer. But, just as the priesthood of Christ is shared in various ways both by sacred ministers and by the faithful; and as the one goodness of God is in reality communicated diversely to his creatures: so also the unique mediation of the Redeemer does not exclude but rather gives rise among creatures to a manifold cooperation which is but a sharing in this unique source.

The Church does not hesitate to profess this subordinate role of Mary. She experiences it continuously and commends it to the hearts of the faithful so that, encouraged by this maternal help, they may more closely adhere to the Mediator and Redeemer. (62)

Through the gift and role of divine maternity, Mary is united with her Son, the Redeemer, and with his singular graces and offices. By these, the Blessed Virgin is also intimately united with the Church. As St. Ambrose taught, the Mother of God is a model of the Church in the matter of faith, hope and charity, and perfect union with Christ. For in the mystery of the Church, herself rightly called Mother and Virgin, the Blessed Virgin stands out in eminent and singular fashion as exemplar of both virginity and motherhood. (63)

In the most holy Virgin, the Church has already reached that perfection whereby she exists without spot or wrinkle (cf. Eph. 5:27). Yet, the followers of Christ still strive to increase in holiness by conquering sin. And so they raise their eyes to Mary who shines forth to the whole community of the elect as a model of the virtues. Devotedly meditating on her and contemplating her in the light of the Word made man, the Church with reverence enters more intimately into the supreme mystery of the Incarnation and becomes ever increasingly like her Spouse.

The Church in her apostolic work looks to her who brought forth Christ, conceived by the Holy Spirit and born of the Virgin, so that through the Church Christ may be born and grow in the hearts of the faithful also. The Virgin Mary in her own life lived as an example of that maternal love by which all should be fittingly animated who cooperate in the apostolic mission of the Church on behalf of the rebirth of men. (65)

IV. Devotion to the Blessed Virgin in the Church

Mary was involved in the mystery of Christ. As the most holy Mother of God she was, after her Son, exalted by divine grace above all angels and men. Hence, the Church appropriately honors her with special reverence. Indeed, from most ancient times the Blessed Virgin has been venerated under the title of "God-bearer." In all perils and needs, the faithful; have fled prayerfully to her protection. Especially after the Council of Ephesus the cult of the people of God toward Mary wonderfully increased in veneration and love, in invocation and imitation, according to her own prophetic words: "All generations shall call me blessed; because he who is mighty has done great things for me" (Lk. 1:48).

As it has always existed in the Church, this cult (of Mary) is altogether special, Still, it differs essentially from the cult of adoration which is offered to the Incarnate Word, as well as to the Father and the Holy Spirit. Yet, devotion to Mary is most favorable to this supreme cult. The Church has endorsed many forms of piety toward the Mother of God, provided that they were within the limits of sound and orthodox doctrine. These forms have varied according to the circumstances of time and place, and have reflected the diversity of native characteristics and temperament among the faithful. While honoring Christ's Mother, these devotions cause her Son to be rightly known, loved and glorified, and all his commands observed. Through him all things have their beginning (cf. Col. 1: 15-16) and in him "it has pleased (the eternal Father) that ... all his fullness should dwell" (Col. 1:19). (66)

This most holy synod deliberately teaches this Catholic doctrine. At the same time, it admonishes all the sons of the Church that the cult, especially the liturgical cult, of the Blessed Virgin, be generously fostered. It charges that practices and exercises of devotion toward her be treasured as recommended by the teaching authority of the Church in the course of centuries.

This synod earnestly exhorts theologians and preachers of the divine word that, in treating of the unique dignity of the Mother of God, they carefully and equally avoid the falsity of exaggeration on the one hand and the excess of narrow-mindedness on the other.

Let the faithful remember, moreover, that true devotion consists neither in fruitless and passing emotion, nor in a certain vain credulity. Rather, it proceeds from the true faith, by which we are led to know the excellence of the Mother of God, and are moved to a filial love toward our Mother and to the imitation of her virtues. (67)

NO NEW MARIAN DOGMA

"It is not opportune to abandon the path marked out by the Second Vatican Council and proceed to the definition of a new dogma of faith ... regarding Mary as 'Coredemptrix,' 'Mediatrix' and 'Advocate.'" So stated the Theological Commission of the Pontifical International Marian Academy, established in 1996 to study the matter. In a declaration published in the June 4, 1997, English-language edition of *L'Osservatore Romano,* the commission said:

"The titles, as proposed, are ambiguous, as they can be understood in very different ways. Furthermore, the theological direction taken by the Second Vatican Council, which did not wish to define any of these titles, should not be abandoned. The Second Vatican Council did not use the title 'Coredemptrix,' and uses 'Mediatrix' and 'Advocate' in a very moderate way. In fact, from the time of Pope Pius XII, the term 'Coredemptrix' has not been used by the papal magisterium in its significant documents. There is evidence that Pope Pius XII himself

intentionally avoided using it. With respect to the title 'Mediatrix,' the history of the question should not be forgotten; in the first decades of this century the Holy See entrusted the study of the possibility of its definition to three different commissions, the result of which was that the Holy See decided to set the question aside.

"Even if the titles were assigned a content which could be accepted as belonging to the deposit of the faith, the definition of these titles, in the present situation, would be lacking in theological clarity, as such titles and the doctrines inherent in them still require further study in a renewed trinitarian, ecclesiological and anthropological perspective. Finally, the theologians, especially the non-Catholics (on the commission) were sensitive to the ecumenical difficulties which would be involved in such a definition."

MOTHER OF THE REDEEMER

Mater Redemptoris, Pope John Paul's sixth encyclical letter, is a "reflection on the role of Mary in the mystery of Christ and on her active and exemplary presence in the life of the Church." The letter was published Mar. 25, 1987.

Central to consideration of Mary is the fact that she is the Mother of God (*Theotokos*), since by the power of the Holy Spirit she conceived in her virginal womb and brought into the world Jesus Christ, the Son of God, who is of one being with the Father and the Holy Spirit.

Mary was preserved from original sin in view of her calling to be the Mother of Jesus. She was gifted in grace beyond measure. She fulfilled her role in a unique pilgrimage of faith. She is the Mother of the Church and the spiritual mother of all people.

The following excerpts from the encyclical are from the English text provided by the Vatican and circulated by the CNS Documentary Service, Origins, Apr. 9, 1987 (Vol. 16, No. 43). Subheads have been added. Quotations are from pertinent documents of the Second Vatican Council.

MARY'S PRESENCE IN THE CHURCH

Mary, through the same faith which made her blessed, especially from the moment of the Annunciation, is present in the Church's mission, present in the Church's work of introducing into the world the kingdom of her Son.

This presence of Mary finds as many different expressions in our day just as it did throughout the Church's history. It also has a wide field of action: through the faith and piety of individual believers; through the traditions of Christian families or "domestic churches," of parish and missionary communities, religious institutes and dioceses; through the radiance and attraction of the great shrines where not only individuals or local groups, but sometimes whole nations and societies, even whole continents, seek to meet the Mother of the Lord, the one who is blessed because she believed, is the first among believers, and therefore became the Mother of Emmanuel.

This is the message of the land of Palestine, the spiritual homeland of all Christians, because it was the homeland of the Savior of the world and of his Mother.

This is the message of the many churches in Rome and throughout the world which have been raised up in the course of the centuries by the faith of Christians. This is the message of centers like Guadalupe, Lourdes, Fatima and others situated in the various countries. Among them, how could I fail to mention the one in my own native land, Jasna Gora? One could perhaps speak of a specific "geography" of faith and Marian devotion which includes all of these special places of pilgrimage where the people of God seek to meet the Mother of God in order to find, within the radius of the maternal presence of her "who believed," a strengthening of their own faith.

MARY AND ECUMENISM

"In all of Christ's disciples the Spirit arouses the desire to be peacefully united, in the manner determined by Christ, as one flock under one shepherd." The journey of the Church, especially in our own time, is marked by the sign of ecumenism: Christians are seeking ways to restore that unity which Christ implored from the Father for his disciples on the day before his passion.

Christians must deepen in themselves and each of their communities that "obedience of faith" of which Mary is the first and brightest example.

Christians know that their unity will be truly rediscovered only if it is based on the unity of their faith. They must resolve considerable discrepancies of doctrine concerning the mystery and ministry of the Church, and sometimes also concerning the role of Mary in the work of salvation.

Mary, who is still the model of this pilgrimage, is to lead them to the unity which is willed by their one Lord, and which is so much desired by those who are attentively listening to what "the Spirit is saying to the churches" today.

A Hopeful Sign

Meanwhile, it is a hopeful sign that these churches and ecclesial communities are finding agreement with the Catholic Church on fundamental points of Christian belief, including matters relating to the Virgin Mary. For they recognize her as the Mother of the Lord and hold that this forms part of our faith in Christ, true God and true man. They look to her who at the foot of the cross accepted as her son the Beloved Disciple (John), the one who in his turn accepted her as his Mother.

On the other hand, I wish to emphasize how profoundly the Catholic Church, the Orthodox Church and the ancient churches of the East feel united by love and praise of the *Theotokos*. Not only "basic dogmas of the Christian faith concerning the Trinity and God's Word made flesh of the Virgin Mary were defined in ecumenical councils held in the East," but also in their liturgical worship "the Eastern Christians pay high tribute, in very beautiful hymns, to Mary ever-Virgin ... God's most holy Mother."

The churches which profess the doctrine of Ephesus proclaim the Virgin as "true Mother of God" since "our Lord Jesus Christ, born of the Father before time began according to his divinity, in the last days he himself, for our sake and for our salvation, was begotten of Mary the Virgin Mother of God according to his humanity." The Greek Fathers and the Byzantine tradition, contemplating the Virgin in the light of the Word made flesh, have sought to penetrate the depth of that bond which unites Mary, as the Mother of God, to Christ and the Church. The Virgin is a permanent presence in the whole reality of the salvific mystery.

MARIAN MEDIATION

The Church knows and teaches with St. Paul that there is only one mediator: "For there is one God, and there is one mediator between God and men, the man Christ Jesus, who gave himself as a ransom for all" (1 Tm. 2:5-6). "The maternal role of Mary toward people in no way obscures or diminishes the unique mediation of Christ, but rather shows its power." It is mediation in Christ.

The Church knows and teaches that "all the saving influences of the Blessed Virgin on mankind originate ... from the divine pleasure. They flow forth from the superabundance of the merits of Christ, rest on his mediation, depend entirely on it and draw all their power from it. In no way do they impede the immediate union of the faithful with Christ. Rather, they foster this union." This saving influence is sustained by the Holy Spirit, who, just as he overshadowed the Virgin Mary when he began in her the divine motherhood, in a similar way constantly sustains her solicitude for the brothers and sisters of her Son.

Mediation and Motherhood

In effect, Mary's mediation is intimately linked with her motherhood. It possesses a specifically maternal character, which distinguishes it from the mediation of the other creatures who in various and always subordinate ways share in the one mediation of Christ, although her own mediation is also a shared mediation. In fact, while it is true that "no creature could ever be classed with the Incarnate Word and Redeemer," at the same time "the unique mediation of the Redeemer does not exclude but rather gives rise among creatures a manifold cooperation which is but a sharing in this unique source." And thus "the

one goodness of God is in reality communicated diversely to his creatures."

Subordinate Mediation

The teaching of the Second Vatican Council presents the truth of Mary's mediation as "a sharing in the one unique source that is the mediation of Christ himself." Thus we read: "The Church does not hesitate to profess this subordinate role of Mary. She experiences it continuously and commends it to the hearts of the faithful so that, encouraged by this maternal help, they may more closely adhere to the Mediator and Redeemer."

This role is at the same time special and extraordinary. It flows from her divine motherhood and can be understood and lived in faith only on the basis of the full truth of this motherhood. Since by virtue of divine election Mary is the earthly Mother of the Father's consubstantial Son and his "generous companion" in the work of redemption, "she is a Mother to us in the order of grace." This role constitutes a real dimension of her presence in the saving mystery of Christ and the Church.

Mary is honored in the Church "with special reverence. Indeed, from most ancient times the Blessed Virgin Mary has been venerated under the title of 'God-bearer.' In all perils and needs, the faithful have fled prayerfully to her protection." This cult is altogether special; it bears in itself and expresses the profound link which exists between the Mother of Christ and the Church. As Virgin and Mother, Mary remains for the Church a "permanent model." It can therefore be said that, especially under this aspect, namely, as a model or rather as a "figure," Mary, present in the mystery of Christ, remains constantly present also in the mystery of the Church. For the Church too is "called mother and virgin," and these names have a profound biblical and theological justification.

MARY AND WOMEN

This Marian dimension of Christian life takes on special importance in relation to women and their status. In fact, femininity has a unique relationship with the Mother of the Redeemer, a subject which can be studied in greater depth elsewhere. Here I simply wish to note that the figure of Mary of Nazareth sheds light on womanhood as such by the very fact that God, in the sublime event of the incarnation of his Son, entrusted himself to the ministry, the free and active ministry, of a woman.

It can thus be said that women, by looking to Mary, find in her the secret of living their femininity with dignity and of achieving their own true advancement. In the light of Mary, the Church sees in the face of women the reflection of a beauty which mirrors the loftiest sentiments of which the human heart is capable: the self-offering totality of love; the strength that is capable of bearing the greatest sorrows; limitless fidelity and tireless devotion to work; the ability to combine penetrating intuition with words of support and encouragement.

APPARITIONS OF THE BLESSED VIRGIN MARY

Only seven of the best known apparitions of the Blessed Virgin Mary are described briefly below.

The sites of the following apparitions have become shrines and centers of pilgrimage. Miracles of the moral and physical orders have been reported as occurring at these places and/or in connection with related practices of prayer and penance.

Banneux, near Liege, Belgium: Mary appeared eight times between Jan. 15 and Mar. 2, 1933, to an 11-year-old peasant girl, Mariette Beco, in a garden behind the family cottage in Banneux, near Liege. She called herself the Virgin of the Poor, and has since been venerated as Our Lady of the Poor, the Sick, and the Indifferent. A small chapel was built by a spring near the site of the apparitions and was blessed Aug. 15, 1933. Approval of devotion to Our Lady of Banneux was given in 1949 by Bishop Louis J. Kerkhofs of Liege, and a statue of that title was solemnly crowned in 1956.

Beauraing, Belgium: Mary appeared 33 times between Nov. 29, 1932, and Jan. 3, 1933, to five children in the garden of a convent school in Beauraing. A chapel, which became a pilgrimage center, was erected on the spot. Reserved approval of devotion to Our Lady of Beauraing was given Feb. 2, 1943, and final approbation July 2, 1949, by Bishop Charue of Namur (d. 1977).

Fatima, Portugal: Mary appeared six times between May 13 and Oct. 13, 1917, to three children (Lucia dos Santos, 10, who is now a Carmelite nun; Francisco Marto, 9, who died in 1919; and his sister Jacinta, 7, who died in 1920) in a field called Cova da Iria near Fatima, north of Lisbon. She recommended frequent recitation of the Rosary; urged works of mortification for the conversion of sinners; called for devotion to herself under the title of her Immaculate Heart; asked that the people of Russia be consecrated to her under this title, and that the faithful make a Communion of reparation on the first Saturday of each month.

The apparitions were declared worthy of belief in October, 1930, after a seven-year canonical investigation, and devotion to Our Lady of Fatima was authorized under the title of Our Lady of the Rosary. In October, 1942, Pius XII consecrated the world to Mary under the title of her Immaculate Heart. Ten years later, in the first apostolic letter addressed directly to the peoples of Russia, he consecrated them in a special manner to Mary.

Fatima, with its sanctuary and basilica, ranks with Lourdes as the greatest of modern Marian shrines. (See First Saturday Devotion.)

Guadalupe, Mexico: Mary appeared four times in 1531 to an Indian, Juan Diego (declared Blessed in 1990), on Tepeyac hill outside of Mexico City, and instructed him to tell Bishop Zumarraga of her wish that a church be built there. The bishop complied with the request about two years later after being convinced of the genuineness of the apparition by the evidence of a miraculously painted life-size figure of the Virgin on the mantle of the Indian. The mantle bearing the picture has been preserved and is enshrined in the Basilica of Our Lady of Guadalupe, which has a long history as a center of devotion and pilgrimage in Mexico. The shrine church, originally dedicated in 1709 and subsequently enlarged, has the title of basilica.

Benedict XIV, in a decree issued in 1754, authorized a Mass and Office under the title of Our Lady of Guadalupe for celebration on Dec. 12, and named Mary the patroness of New Spain. Our Lady of Guadalupe was designated patroness of Latin America by St. Pius X in 1910 and patroness of the Americas by Pius XII in 1945.

La Salette, France: Mary appeared as a sorrowing and weeping figure Sept. 19, 1846, to two peasant children, Melanie Matthieu, 15, and Maximin Giraud, 11, at La Salette in southern France. The message she confided to them, regarding the necessity of penance, was communicated to Pius IX in 1851 and has since been known as the "secret" of La Salette. Bishop de Bruillard of Grenoble declared in 1851 that the apparition was credible, and devotion to Mary under the title of Our Lady of La Salette was authorized. The devotion has been confirmed by popes since the time of Pius IX, and a Mass and office with this title were authorized in 1942. The shrine church was given the title of minor basilica in 1879.

Lourdes, France: Mary, identifying herself as the Immaculate Conception, appeared 18 times between Feb. 11 and July 16, 1858, to 14-year-old Bernadette Soubirous (canonized in 1933) at the grotto of Massabielle near Lourdes in southern France. Her message concerned the necessity of prayer and penance for the conversion of peoples. Mary's request that a chapel be built at the grotto and spring was fulfilled in 1862 after four years of rigid examination established the credibility of the apparitions. Devotion under the title of Our Lady of Lourdes was authorized later, and a Feb. 11 feast commemorating the apparitions was instituted by Leo XIII. St. Pius X extended this feast throughout the Church in 1907.

The Church of Notre Dame was made a basilica in 1870, and the Church of the Rosary was built later. The underground Church of St. Pius X, with a capacity of 20,000 persons, was consecrated Mar. 25, 1958. Plans were announced in 1994 for renovation and reconstruction of the Lourdes sanctuary.

Our Lady of the Miraculous Medal, France: Mary appeared three times in 1830 to Catherine Laboure (canonized in 1947) in the chapel of the motherhouse of the Daughters of Charity of St. Vincent de Paul, Rue de Bac, Paris. She commissioned Catherine to have made the medal of the Immaculate Conception, now known as the Miraculous Medal, and to spread devotion to her under this title. In 1832, the medal was struck according to the model revealed to Catherine.

CRITERIA OF APPARITIONS

These were the subject of articles by Jesuit Father Giandomenico published early in 1990 in *La Civilta Cattolica*. Criteria of the authenticity of apparitions include the following.

• God can choose anyone to be a visionary; a visionary should show spiritual progress afterwards.

• To aid in discernment, visionaries need spiritual directors.

• Spiritual directors should never push seers to ask questions about people during apparitions.

• Apparitions should never produce any sentiment of contempt toward anyone.

EASTERN CATHOLIC CHURCHES

The Second Vatican Council, in its *Decree on Eastern Catholic Churches,* stated the following points regarding Eastern heritage, patriarchs, sacraments and worship.

Venerable Churches: The Catholic Church holds in high esteem the institutions of the Eastern Churches, their liturgical rites, ecclesiastical traditions, and Christian way of life. For, distinguished as they are by their venerable antiquity, they are bright with that tradition which was handed down from the Apostles through the Fathers, and which forms part of the divinely revealed and undivided heritage of the universal Church (No. 1).

That Church, Holy and Catholic, which is the Mystical Body of Christ, is made up of the faithful who are organically united in the Holy Spirit through the same faith, the same sacraments, and the same government and who, combining into various groups held together by a hierarchy, form separate Churches or rites. It is the mind of the Catholic Church that each individual Church or rite retain its traditions whole and entire, while adjusting its way of life to the various needs of time and place (No. 2).

Such individual Churches, whether of the East or of the West, although they differ somewhat among themselves in what are called rites (that is, in liturgy, ecclesiastical discipline, and spiritual heritage) are, nevertheless, equally entrusted to the pastoral guidance of the Roman Pontiff, the divinely appointed successor of St. Peter in supreme government over the universal Church. They are consequently of equal dignity, so that none of them is superior to the others by reason of rite (No. 3).

Eastern Heritage: Each and every Catholic, as also the baptized of every non-Catholic Church or community who enters into the fullness of Catholic communion, should everywhere retain his proper rite, cherish it, and observe it to the best of his ability (No. 4).

The Churches of the East, as much as those of the West, fully enjoy the right, and are in duty bound, to rule themselves. Each should do so according to its proper and individual procedures (No. 5).

All Eastern rite members should know and be convinced that they can and should always preserve their lawful liturgical rites and their established way of life, and that these should not be altered except by way of an appropriate and organic development (No. 6)

Patriarchs: The institution of the patriarchate has existed in the Church from the earliest times and was recognized by the first ecumenical Synods.

By the name Eastern Patriarch is meant the bishop who has jurisdiction over all bishops (including metropolitans), clergy, and people of his own territory or rite, in accordance with the norms of law and without prejudice to the primacy of the Roman Pontiff (No. 7).

Though some of the patriarchates of the Eastern Churches are of later origin than others, all are equal in patriarchal dignity. Still the honorary and lawfully established order of precedence among them is to be preserved (No. 8).

In keeping with the most ancient tradition of the Church, the Patriarchs of the Eastern Churches are to be accorded exceptional respect, since each presides over his patriarchate as father and head.

This sacred Synod, therefore, decrees that their rights and privileges should be re-established in accord with the ancient traditions of each Church and the decrees of the ecumenical Synods.

The rights and privileges in question are those which flourished when East and West were in union, though they should be somewhat adapted to modern conditions.

The Patriarchs with their synods constitute the superior authority for all affairs of the patriarchate, including the right to establish new eparchies and to nominate bishops of their rite within the territorial bounds of the patriarchate, without prejudice to the inalienable right of the Roman Pontiff to intervene in individual cases (No. 9).

What has been said of Patriarchs applies as well, under the norm of law, to major archbishops, who preside over the whole of some individual Church or rite (No. 10).

Sacraments: This sacred Ecumenical Synod endorses and lauds the ancient discipline of the sacraments existing in the Eastern Churches, as also the practices connected with their celebration and administration (No. 12).

With respect to the minister of holy chrism (confirmation), let that practice be fully restored which existed among Easterners in most ancient times. Priests, therefore, can validly confer this sacrament, provided they use chrism blessed by a Patriarch or bishop (No. 13).

In conjunction with baptism or otherwise, all Eastern-Rite priests can confer this sacrament validly on all the faithful of any rite, including the Latin; licitly, however, only if the regulations of both common and particular law are observed. Priests of the Latin rite, to the extent of the faculties they enjoy for administering this sacrament, can confer it also on the faithful of Eastern Churches, without prejudice to rite. They do so licitly if the regulations of both common and particular law are observed (No. 14).

The faithful are bound on Sundays and feast days to attend the divine liturgy or, according to the regulations or custom of their own rite, the celebration of the Divine Praises. That the faithful may be able to satisfy their obligation more easily, it is decreed that this obligation can be fulfilled from the Vespers of the vigil to the end of the Sunday or the feast day (No. 15).

Because of the everyday intermingling of the communicants of diverse Eastern Churches in the same Eastern region or territory, the faculty for hearing confession, duly and unrestrictedly granted by his proper bishop to a priest of any rite, is applicable to the entire territory of the grantor, also to the places and the faithful belonging to any other rite in the same territory, unless an Ordinary of the place explicitly decides otherwise with respect to the places pertaining to his rite (No. 16).

This sacred Synod ardently desires that where it has fallen into disuse the office of the permanent diaconate be restored. The legislative authority of each individual church should decide about the subdiaconate and the minor orders (No. 17).

By way of preventing invalid marriages between Eastern Catholics and baptized Eastern non-Catholics, and in the interests of the permanence and sanctity of marriage and of domestic harmony, this sacred Synod decrees that the canonical 'form' for the celebration of such marriages obliges only for lawfulness. For their validity, the presence of a sacred minister suffices, as long as the other requirements of law are honored (No. 18).

Worship: Henceforth, it will be the exclusive right of an ecumenical Synod or the Apostolic See to establish, transfer, or suppress feast days common to all the Eastern Churches. To establish, transfer, or suppress feast days for any of the individual Churches is within the competence not only of the Apostolic See but also of a patriarchal or archiepiscopal synod, provided due consideration is given to the entire region and to other individual Churches (No. 19).

Until such time as all Christians desirably concur on a fixed day for the celebration of Easter, and with a view meantime to promoting unity among the Christians of a given area or nation, it is left to the Patriarchs or supreme authorities of a place to reach a unanimous agreement, after ascertaining the views of all concerned, on a single Sunday for the observance of Easter (No. 20).

With respect to rules concerning sacred seasons, individual faithful dwelling outside the area or territory of their own rite may conform completely to the established custom of the place where they live. When members of a family belong to different rites, they are all permitted to observe sacred seasons according to the rules of any one of these rites (No. 21).

From ancient times the Divine Praises have been held in high esteem among all Eastern Churches. Eastern clerics and religious should celebrate these Praises as the laws and customs of their own traditions require. To the extent they can, the faithful too should follow the example of their forebears by assisting devoutly at the Divine Praises (No. 22).

Restoration of Ancient Practices

An "Instruction for the Application of the Liturgical Prescriptions of the Code of Canons of the Eastern Churches" was published in Italian by the Congregation for Eastern-Rite Churches in January, 1996. Msgr. Alan Detscher, executive director of the U.S. bishops' Secretariat for the Liturgy, said it was the first instruction on liturgical renewal of the Eastern Catholic Churches since the Second Vatican Council (1962-65).

RITES, JURISDICTIONS AND FAITHFUL OF EASTERN CHURCHES

Introduction

The Catholic Church originated in Palestine, whence it spread to other regions of the world where certain places became key centers of Christian life with great influence on the local churches in their respective areas. Such centers were Jerusalem, Alexandria, Antioch and Constantinople in the East, and Rome in the West. The eastern Mother Churches, with rites bearing their names, were Alexandrian, Antiochene, Armenian, Byzantine and Chaldean. The usages of these churches expressed the one faith in different ways in theology, liturgy, hierarchy and governance, tradition and culture. Hence, the different rites.

The main lines of Eastern Church patriarchal organization and usages were drawn before the Roman Empire became two empires, East (Byzantine) and West (Roman), in 292. Eastern Church members, originally within the boundaries of the Eastern Empire, eventually spread to other parts of the world where they have continued to maintain their distinctive religious identity and heritage on a par with the faithful of Roman (Latin) rite.

Most of the Eastern Churches now in communion with the Holy See were at some time in the past separated from it because of developments and events connected with the Schism of 1054.

Statistics

(Principal source: *Annuario Pontificio, 1997.*)

These statistics are for Eastern-rite jurisdictions only, and do not include Eastern-rite Catholics under the jurisdiction of Roman-rite bishops. Some of the figures reported are only approximate. Some of the jurisdictions listed were long inactive because of government suppression.

Alexandrian

Called the Liturgy of St. Mark, the Alexandrian Rite was modified by the Copts and Melkites, and contains elements of the Byzantine Rite of St. Basil and the liturgies of Sts. Mark, Cyril and Gregory of Nazianzen. The liturgy is substantially that of the Coptic Church, which is divided into two branches — the Coptic or Egyptian, and the Ethiopian or Abyssinian. The churches of this rite are:

COPTIC: Jurisdictions (located in Egypt): patriarchate of Alexandria, five dioceses; 192,955. Copts resumed communion with Rome about 1741; situated in Egypt, the Near East; liturgical languages are Coptic, Arabic.

ETHIOPIAN: Jurisdictions (located in Ethiopia and Eritrea): one metropolitan, four dioceses; 192,110. Ethiopians resumed communion with Rome in 1846: situated in Ethiopia, Eritrea, Jerusalem, Somalia; liturgical language is Geez.

Antiochene

This is the source of more derived rites than any of the other parent rites. Its origin can be traced to the Eighth Book of the Apostolic Constitutions and to the Liturgy of St. James of Jerusalem, which ultimately spread throughout the whole patriarchate and displaced older forms based on the Apostolic Constitutions. The churches of this rite are:

MALANKAR: Jurisdictions (located in India): one metropolitan, three dioceses; 322,988. Malankarese resumed communion with Rome in 1930; situated in India, North America; liturgical languages are Syriac, Malayalam.

MARONITE: Jurisdictions (located in Lebanon, Cyprus, Egypt, Syria, Israel, U.S., Argentina, Brazil, Australia, Canada, Mexico): patriarchate of Antioch, 23 archdioceses and dioceses; 2,948,949. Where no special jurisdictions exist, they are under jurisdiction of local Roman-rite bishops. United to the Holy See since the time of their founder, St. Maron; have no counterparts among the separated Eastern Christians: situated throughout the world: liturgical languages are Syriac, Arabic.

SYRIAN: Jurisdictions (located in Lebanon, Iraq, Egypt, Syria and the United States (for Canada and the U.S.): patriarchate of Antioch, two metropolitans, eight archdioceses and dioceses, three patriarchal vicariates; 109,547. Syrians resumed communion with Rome in 1781; situated in Asia, Africa, the Americas, Australia; liturgical languages are Syriac, Arabic.

Armenian

Substantially, although using a different language, this is the Greek Liturgy of St. Basil; it is considered an older form of the Byzantine Rite, and incorporates some modifications from the Antiochene Rite. The church of this rite is:

ARMENIAN, exclusively: Jurisdictions (located in Lebanon, Iran, Iraq, Egypt, Syria, Turkey, Ukraine, France, Greece, Romania, Armenia (for Eastern Europe), Argentina (eparchy and exarchate for Latin America, including Mexico), and the United States (for Canada and the U.S.): patriarchate of Cilicia, 10 archdioceses and dioceses, two patriarchal exarchates, two apostolic exarchates, three ordinariates; 334,860. Armenians resumed communion with Rome during the time of the Crusades; situated in the Near East, Europe, Africa, the Americas, Australasia: liturgical language is Classical Armenian.

Byzantine

Based on the Rite of St. James of Jerusalem and the churches of Antioch, and reformed by Sts. Basil and John Chrysostom, the Byzantine Rite is proper to the Church of Constantinople. (The city was called Byzantium before Constantine changed its name; the modern name is Istanbul.) It is now used by the majority of Eastern Catholics and by the Eastern Orthodox Church (which is not in union with Rome). It is, after the Roman, the most widely used rite. The churches of this rite are:

ALBANIAN: Jurisdiction (located in Albania): one apostolic administration ; 1,405. Albanians resumed communion with Rome about 1628; situated in Albania; liturgical language is Albanian.

BELARUSSIAN (formerly Byelorussian, also known as White Russian): Belarussians resumed communion with Rome in the 17th century; situated in Europe, the Americas, Australia; liturgical language is Old Slavonic.

BULGARIAN: Jurisdiction (located in Bulgaria): one apostolic exarchate; 20,000. Bulgarians resumed communion with Rome about 1861; situated in Bulgaria; liturgical language is Old Slavonic.

CZECH REPUBLIC: Jurisdiction: one apostolic exarchate established in 1996.

EPARCHY OF KRIZEVCI: Jurisdiction (located in Croatia): one diocese; 48,932. Resumed communion with Rome in 1611; situated in Croatia, the Americas; liturgical language is Old Slavonic.

GREEK: Jurisdictions (located in Greece and Turkey): two exarchates; 2,350. Greeks resumed communion with Rome in 1829; situated in Greece, Asia Minor, Europe; liturgical language is Greek.

HUNGARIAN: Jurisdictions (located in Hungary): one diocese and one exarchate: 280,750. Descendants of Ruthenians who resumed communion with Rome in 1646; situated in Hungary, the rest of Europe, the Americas; liturgical languages are Greek, Hungarian, English.

ITALO-ALBANIAN: Jurisdictions (located in Italy): two dioceses, one abbacy; 61,597. Italo-Albanians were never separated from Rome; situated in Italy, Sicily, the Americas; liturgical languages are Greek, Italo-Albanian.

MELKITE (GREEK MELKITE): Jurisdictions (located in Syria, Lebanon, Jordan, Israel, U.S., Brazil, Venezuela, Canada, Australia, Mexico): patriarchate of Antioch (with patriarchal vicariates in Egypt, Sudan, Jerusalem, Iraq and Kuwait), 19 archdioceses and dioceses, one exarchate; 1,073 340. Melkites resumed communion with Rome during the time of the Crusades, but definitive reunion did not take place until early in the 18th century; situated in the Middle East, Asia, Africa, Europe, the Americas, Australia; liturgical languages are Greek, Arabic, English, Portuguese, Spanish.

ROMANIAN: Jurisdictions (located in Romania and U.S.): one metropolitan, five dioceses; 1,423,800. Romanians resumed communion with Rome in 1697; situated in Romania, the rest of Europe, the Americas; liturgical language is Modern Romanian.

RUSSIAN: Jurisdictions (located in Russia and China): two exarchates. Russians resumed communion with Rome about 1905; situated in Europe, the Americas, Australia, China; liturgical language is Old Slavonic.

RUTHENIAN, or CARPATHO-RUSSIAN (Rusin): Jurisdictions (located in Ukraine and the U.S.): one metropolitan, four dioceses; 495,888. Ruthenians resumed communion with Rome in the Union of Brest-Litovsk, 1596, and the Union of Uzhorod, Apr. 24, 1646; situated in Europe, the Americas, Australia; liturgical languages are Old Slavonic, English.

SLOVAK: Jurisdictions (located in Slovakia and Canada): two dioceses; 229,190.

UKRAINIAN, or GALICIAN RUTHENIAN: Jurisdictions (located in Ukraine, Poland, the U.S., Canada, England, Australia, Germany, France, Brazil, Argentina): major archbishopric of Lviv, three metropolitans, 16 dioceses, three apostolic exarchates; 5,323,841. Ukrainians resumed communion with Rome about 1595; situated in Europe, the Americas, Australasia; liturgical languages are Old Slavonic and Ukrainian.

Chaldean

This rite, listed as separate and distinct by the Congregation for the Oriental Churches, was derived from the Antiochene Rite. The churches of this rite are:

CHALDEAN: Jurisdictions (located in Iraq, Iran, Lebanon, Egypt, Syria, Turkey, U.S.): patriarchate of Babylonia, 19 archdioceses and dioceses; 308,409. There is a patriarchal exarch for Jerusalem. Chaldeans, descendants of the Nestorians, resumed communion with Rome in 1692; situated throughout the Middle East, in Europe, Africa, the Americas; liturgical languages are Syriac, Arabic.

SYRO-MALABAR: Jurisdictions (located in India): major archbishopric of Ernakulam-Angamaly (1993), three metropolitans, 18 dioceses; 3,280,586. Descended from the St. Thomas Christians of India; liturgical languages are Syriac and Malayalam.

EASTERN JURISDICTIONS

For centuries Eastern Churches were identifiable with a limited number of nationality and language groups in certain countries of the Middle East, Eastern Europe, Asia and Africa. The persecution of religion in the former Soviet Union since 1917 and in communist-controlled countries for more than 40 years following World War II — in addition to decimating and destroying the Church in those places — resulted in the emigration of many Eastern-Rite Catholics from their homelands. This forced emigration, together with voluntary emigration, has led to the spread of Eastern Churches to many other countries.

Europe

(Bishop Krikor Ghabroyan, of the Armenian Eparchy of Sainte-Croix-de-Paris, France, is apostolic visitor for Armenian Catholics in Western Europe who do not have their own bishop. Bishop Youssef Ibrahim Sarraf of Cairo of the Chaldeans is apostolic visitor for Chaldeans in Europe. Bishop Samis Mazloum is apostolic visitor for Maronites in Western and Northern Europe.)

ALBANIA: Byzantine Rite, apostolic administration.

AUSTRIA: Byzantine Rite, ordinariate.

BULGARIA: Byzantine Rite (Bulgarians), apostolic exarchate.

CROATIA: Byzantine Rite, eparchy.

CZECH REPUBLIC: Byzantine Rite, apostolic exarchate.

FRANCE: Byzantine Rite (Ukrainians), apostolic exarchate.

Armenian Rite, eparchy (1986).

Ordinariate for all other Eastern-Rite Catholics.

GERMANY: Byzantine Rite (Ukrainians), apostolic exarchate.

GREAT BRITAIN: Byzantine Rite (Ukrainians), apostolic exarchate.

GREECE: Byzantine Rite, apostolic exarchate.

Armenian Rite, ordinariate.

HUNGARY: Byzantine Rite (Hungarians), eparchy, apostolic exarchate.

ITALY: Byzantine Rite (Italo-Albanians), two eparchies, one abbacy.

POLAND: Byzantine Rite (Ukrainian), metropolitan see (1996), one eparchy.

Ordinariate for all other Eastern-Rite Catholics.

ROMANIA: Byzantine Rite (Romanians), metropolitan, four eparchies.

Armenian Rite, ordinariate.

RUSSIA: Byzantine Rite (Russians), apostolic exarchate (for Byzantine-rite Catholics in Moscow).

SLOVAKIA: Byzantine Rite (Slovakians and other Byzantine-Rite Catholics), eparchy.

UKRAINE: Armenian Rite, archeparchy.

Byzantine Rite (Ruthenians), eparchy; (Ukrainians), major archbishopric, five eparchies.

Asia

ARMENIA: Armenian Rite, ordinariate (for Armenians of Eastern Europe).

CHINA: Byzantine Rite (Russians), apostolic exarchate.

CYPRUS: Antiochene Rite (Maronites), archeparchy.

INDIA: Antiochene Rite (Malankarese), metropolitan see, three eparchies.

Chaldean Rite (Syro-Malabarese), major archbishopric (1993), three metropolitan sees (1995), 18 eparchies.

IRAN: Chaldean Rite (Chaldeans), two metropolitan sees, one archeparchy, one eparchy.

Armenian Rite, eparchy.

IRAQ Antiochene Rite (Syrians), two archeparchies.

Byzantine Rite (Greek-Melkites), patriarchal exarchate.

Chaldean Rite (Chaldeans), patriarchate, two metropolitan sees, eight archeparchies and eparchies.

Armenian Rite, archeparchy.

ISRAEL (includes Jerusalem): Antiochene Rite (Syrians), patriarchal exarchate; (Maronites), archeparchy.

Byzantine Rite (Greek-Melkites), archeparchy, patriarchal exarchate.

Chaldean Rite (Chaldeans), patriarchal exarchate.

Armenian Rite, patriarchal exarchate.

JORDAN: Byzantine Rite (Greek-Melkites), archeparchy.

KUWAIT: Byzantine Rite (Greek-Melkites), patriarchal exarchate.

LEBANON: Antiochene Rite (Maronites), patriarchate, ten archeparchies and eparchies; (Syrians), patriarchate, patriarchal exarchate.

Byzantine Rite (Greek-Melkites), two metropolitan and five archeparchal sees.

Chaldean Rite (Chaldeans), eparchy.

Armenian Rite, patriarchate, metropolitan.

SYRIA: Antiochene Rite (Maronites), two archeparchies, one eparchy; (Syrians), two metropolitan and two archeparchal sees.

Byzantine Rite (Greek-Melkites), patriarchate, four metropolitan sees, one archeparchy.

Chaldean Rite (Chaldeans), eparchy.

Armenian Rite, archeparchy, eparchy, patriarchal exarchate.

TURKEY (Europe and Asia): Antiochene Rite (Syrians), patriarchal exarchate.

Byzantine Rite (Greeks), apostolic exarchate.

Chaldean Rite (Chaldeans), one archeparchy.

Armenian Rite, archeparchy.

Oceania

AUSTRALIA: Byzantine Rite (Ukrainians), eparchy; (Greek-Melkites), eparchy (1987).

Antiochene Rite (Maronites), eparchy.

Africa

EGYPT: Alexandrian Rite (Copts), patriarchate, five eparchies.

Antiochene Rite (Maronites), eparchy; (Syrians), eparchy.

Byzantine Rite (Greek-Melkites), patriarchal exarchate.

Chaldean Rite (Chaldeans), eparchy.
Armenian Rite, eparchy.
ERITREA: Alexandrian Rite (Ethiopians), three eparchies.
ETHIOPIA: Alexandrian Rite (Ethiopians), metropolitan see, one eparchy.
SUDAN: Byzantine Rite (Greek-Melkites), patriarchal vicariate.

North America

CANADA: Byzantine Rite (Ukrainians), one metropolitan, four eparchies; (Slovaks), eparchy; (Greek-Melkites), eparchy.
Armenian Rite, apostolic exarchate for Canada and the U.S. (New York is see city).
Antiochene Rite (Maronites), eparchy.
UNITED STATES: Antiochene Rite (Maronites), two eparchies; (Syrians), eparchy (1995).
Byzantine Rite (Ukrainians), one metropolitan see, three eparchies; (Ruthenians), one metropolitan see, three eparchies; (Greek-Melkites), eparchy; (Romanians), eparchy; (Belarussians), apostolic visitator.
Armenian Rite, apostolic exarchate for Canada and U.S. (New York is see city).
Chaldean Rite, eparchy.
Other Eastern-Rite Catholics are under the jurisdiction of local Roman-Rite bishops. (See Eastern-Rite Catholics in the United States.)
MEXICO: Byzantine Rite (Greek-Melkites), eparchy.
Antiochene Rite (Maronites), eparchy (1995).

South America

Armenian-Rite Catholics in Latin America (including Mexico and excluding Argentina) are under the jurisdiction of an apostolic exarchate (see city, Buenos Aires, Argentina).
ARGENTINA: Byzantine Rite (Ukrainians), eparchy.
Antiochene Rite (Maronites), eparchy.
Armenian Rite, eparchy.
Ordinariate for all other Eastern-Rite Catholics.
BRAZIL: Antiochene Rite (Maronites), eparchy.
Byzantine Rite (Greek-Melkites), eparchy; (Ukrainians), eparchy.
Ordinariate for all other Eastern-Rite Catholics.
VENEZUELA: Byzantine Rite (Greek-Melkites) apostolic exarchate.

SYNODS, ASSEMBLIES

These assemblies are collegial bodies which have pastoral authority over members of the Eastern Catholic Churches. (Canons 102-113, 152-153, 322 of Oriental Code of Canon Law.)
Patriarchal Synods: Synod of the Catholic Coptic Church: Stephanos II Ghattas, C.M., patriarch of Alexandria of the Copts.
Synod of the Greek-Melkite Catholic Church: Maximos V Hakim, patriarch of Antioch of the Greek Catholics-Melkites.
Synod of the Syrian Catholic Church: Ignace Antoine II Hayek, patriarch of Antioch of the Syrians.
Synod of the Maronite Church: Cardinal Nasrallah Pierre Sfeir, patriarch of Antioch of the Maronites.
Synod of the Chaldean Church: Raphael I Bidawid, patriarch of Babylonia of the Chaldeans.

Synod of the Armenian Catholic Church: Jean Pierre XVIII Kasparian, patriarch of Cilicia of the Armenians.
Major Archiepiscopal Synods: The Synod of the Ukrainian Catholic Church (raised to major archiepiscopal status Dec. 23, 1963): Cardinal Myroslav Ivan Lubachivsky, major archbishop of Lviv of the Ukrainians, president.
The Synod of the Syro-Malabar Church (raised to major archiepiscopal status, Jan. 29, 1993):Most Rev. Varkey Vithayathil, C.SS.R., apostolic administrator of Ernakulam-Angamaly of the Syro-Malabars, president.
Councils, Assemblies, Conferences: Council of Ethiopian Churches: Cardinal Paul Tzadua, president.
Council of Romanian Churches: Abp. Lucian Muresan of Fagaras and Alba Julia, president.
Council of Ruthenian Churches, U.S.A.: Abp. Judson Michael Procyk of Pittsburgh of the Byzantines, president.
Council of Syro-Malankarese Churches: Abp. Cyril Baselios Malaucharuvil, O.I.C., of Trivandrum of the Syro-Malankarese, president.
Assembly of the Catholic Hierarchy of Egypt (Dec. 5, 1983): Stephanos II Ghattas, C.M., patriarch of Alexandria of the Copts, president.
Assembly of Catholic Patriarchs and Bishops of Lebanon: Cardinal Nasrallah Pierre Sfeir, patriarch of Antioch of the Maronites, president.
Assembly of Ordinaries of the Syrian Arab Republic: Maximos V Hakim, patriarch of Antioch of the Greek Catholics-Melkites, president.
Assembly of Catholic Ordinaries of the Holy Land (Jan. 27, 1992): Michel Sabbah, patriarch of Jerusalem of the Latins, president.
Interritual Union of the Bishops of Iraq: Raphael I Bidawid, patriarch of Babylonia of the Chaldeans, president.
Iranian Episcopal Conference (Aug. 11, 1977): Most Rev. Vartan Tekeyan, bishop of Ispahan of the Armenians, president.
Episcopal Conference of Turkey (Nov. 30, 1987): Most Rev. Louis A. Pelatre, A.A., vicar apostolic of Istanbul, president.

EASTERN CATHOLIC CHURCHES IN U.S.

(Statistics, from the *1997 Annuario Pontificio* unless noted otherwise, are membership figures reported by Eastern-Rite jurisdictions. Additional Eastern-Rite Catholics are included in statistics for Roman-Rite dioceses.)

Byzantine Tradition

Ukrainians: There were 120,844 reported in four jurisdictions in the U.S.: the metropolitan see of Philadelphia (1924, metropolitan 1958) and the suffragan sees of Stamford, Conn. (1956), St. Nicholas of Chicago (1961) and St. Josaphat in Parma (1983).
Ruthenians: There were 175,880 reported in four jurisdictions in the U.S.: the metropolitan see of Pittsburgh (est. 1924 at Pittsburgh; metropolitan and transferred to Munhall, 1969; transferred to Pittsburgh, 1977) and the suffragan sees of Passaic, N.J. (1963), Parma, Ohio (1969) and Van Nuys, Calif. (1981). Hungarian and Croatian Byzantine Catho-

lics in the U.S. are also under the jurisdiction of Ruthenian-Rite bishops.

Melkites (Greek Catholics-Melkites): There were 27,000 reported under the jurisdiction of the Melkite eparchy of Newton, Mass. (established as an exarchate, 1965; eparchy, 1976).

Romanians: There were 5,300 reported in 15 Romanian Catholic Byzantine Rite parishes in the U.S., under the jurisdiction of the Romanian eparchy of St. George Martyr, Canton, Ohio (established as an exarchate, 1982; eparchy, 1987).

Belarussians: Have one parish in the U.S. — Christ the Redeemer, Chicago, Ill.

Russians: Have parishes in California (St. Andrew, El Segundo, and Our Lady of Fatima Center, San Francisco); New York (St. Michael's Chapel of St. Patrick's Old Cathedral). They are under the jurisdiction of local Roman-Rite bishops.

Alexandrian Tradition

Copts: Have a Catholic Chapel — Resurrection, in Brooklyn, N.Y.

Antiochene Tradition

Maronites: There were 51,860 reported in two jurisdictions in the U.S.: the eparchy of St. Maron, Brooklyn (established at Detroit as an exarchate, 1966; eparchy, 1972; transferred to Brooklyn, 1977) and the eparchy of Our Lady of Lebanon of Los Angeles (established Mar. 1, 1994).

Syrians: The eparchy of Our Lady of the Deliver-ance of Newark (see city, Newark, N.J.) was established in 1995 for Syrian-rite Catholics of the U.S. and Canada.

Malankarese: Have a mission in Chicago.

Armenian Tradition

An apostolic exarchate for Canada and the United States (see city, New York) was established July 3, 1981; 26,000 in both countries.

Chaldean Tradition

Chaldeans: There were 60,000 reported under the jurisdiction of the eparchy of St. Thomas Apostle of Detroit (established as an exarchate, 1982; eparchy, 1986).

Syro-Malabarese (Malabar): Have mission churches in Chicago and several other cities. Estimated 200,000 faithful with 50 priests.

Eastern Catholic Associates

Eastern Catholic Associates is the association of all Eastern Catholic bishops and their equivalents in law in the United States, representing the Armenian, Chaldean, Maronite, Melkite, Syriac, Romanian, Ruthenian and Ukrainian churches. The Syro-Malabar and Russian churches are also represented even though they do not have bishops in the U.S. President: Melkite Auxiliary Bishop Nicholas J. Samra of Newton, Mass. Address: 8525 Cole St., Warren, MI 48093.

The association meets at the same time as the National Conference of Catholic Bishops in the fall of each year.

BYZANTINE DIVINE LITURGY

The Divine Liturgy in all rites is based on the consecration of bread and wine by the narration-reactualization of the actions of Christ at the Last Supper. Aside from this fundamental usage, there are differences between the Roman (Latin) Rite ad Eastern Rites, and among the Eastern Rites themselves. Following is a general description of the Byzantine Divine Liturgy which is in widest use in the Eastern-Rite Churches.

In the Byzantine, as in all Eastern Rites, the bread and wine are prepared at the start of the Liturgy. The priest does this in a little niche or at a table in the sanctuary. Taking a round loaf of leavened bread stamped with religious symbols, he cuts out a square host and other particles while reciting verses expressing the symbolism of the action. When the bread and wine are ready, he says a prayer of offering and incenses the oblations, the altar, the icons and the people.

Liturgy of the Catechumens: At the altar a litany for all classes of people is sung by the priest. The congregation answers, "Lord, have mercy."

The Little Entrance comes next. In procession, the priest leaves the sanctuary carrying the Book of the Gospels, and then returns. He sings prayers especially selected for the day and the feast. These are followed by the solemn singing of the prayer, "Holy God, Holy Mighty One, Holy Immortal One."

The Epistle follows. The Gospel is sung or read by the priest facing the people at the middle door of the sanctuary.

An interruption after the Liturgy of the Catechumens, formerly an instructional period for those learning the faith, is clearly marked. Catechumens, if present, are dismissed with a prayer. Following this are a prayer and litany for the faithful.

Great Entrance: The Great Entrance or solemn Offertory Procession then takes place. The priest first says a long silent prayer for himself, in preparation for the great act to come. Again he incenses the oblations, the altar, the icons and people. He goes to the table on the gospel side for the veil-covered paten and chalice. When he arrives back at the sanctuary door, he announces the intention of the Mass in the prayer: "May the Lord God remember all of you in his kingdom, now and forever."

After another litany, the congregation recites the Nicene Creed.

Consecration: The most solemn portion of the sacrifice is introduced by the preface, which is very much like the preface of the Roman Rite. At the beginning of the last phrase, the priest raises his voice to introduce the singing of the Sanctus. During the singing he reads the introduction to the words of consecration.

The words of consecration are sung aloud, and the people sing "Amen" to both consecrations. As the priest raises the Sacred Species in solemn offering, he sings: "Thine of Thine Own we offer unto Thee in behalf of all and for all."

A prayer to the Holy Spirit is followed by the commemorations, in which special mention is made of the all-holy, most blessed and glorious Lady, the Mother of God and ever-Virgin Mary. The dead are remembered and then the living.

Holy Communion: A final litany for spiritual gifts precedes the Our Father. The Sacred Body and Blood are elevated with the words, "Holy Things for the Holy." The Host is then broken and commingled with the Precious Blood. The priest recites preparatory prayers for Holy Communion, consumes the Sacred Species, and distributes Holy Communion to the people under the forms of both bread and wine. During this time a communion verse is sung by the choir or congregation.

The Liturgy closes quickly after this. The consecrated Species of bread and wine are removed to the side table to be consumed later by the priest. A prayer of thanksgiving is recited, a prayer for all the people is said in front of the icon of Christ, a blessing is invoked upon all, and the people are dismissed.

BYZANTINE CALENDAR

The Byzantine-Rite calendar has many distinctive features of its own, although it shares common elements with the Roman-Rite calendar — e.g., general purpose, commemoration of the mysteries of faith and of the saints, identical dates for some feasts. Among the distinctive things are the following.

The liturgical year begins on Sept. 1, the **Day of Indiction,** in contrast with the Latin or Roman start on the First Sunday of Advent late in November or early in December. The Advent season begins on Dec. 10.

Cycles of the Year

As in the Roman usage, the dating of feasts follows the Gregorian Calendar. Formerly, until well into this century, the Julian Calendar was used. (The Julian Calendar, which is now about 13 days late, is still used by some Eastern-Rite Churches.)

The year has several cycles, which include proper seasons, the feasts of saints, and series of New Testament readings. All of these elements of worship are contained in liturgical books of the rite.

The ecclesiastical calendar, called the **Menologion,** explains the nature of feasts, other observances and matters pertaining to the liturgy for each day of the year. In some cases, its contents include the lives of saints and the history and meaning of feasts.

The Divine Liturgy (Mass) and Divine Office for the proper of the saints, fixed feasts, and the Christmas season are contained in the **Menaion.** The **Triodion** covers the pre-Lenten season of preparation for Easter; Lent begins two days before the Ash Wednesday observance of the Roman Rite. The **Pentecostarion** contains the liturgical services from Easter to the Sunday of All Saints, the first after Pentecost. The **Evangelion** and **Apostolos** are books in which the Gospels, and Acts of the Apostles and the Epistles, respectively, are arranged according to the order of their reading in the Divine Liturgy and Divine Office throughout the year.

The cyclic progression of liturgical music throughout the year, in successive and repetitive periods of eight weeks, is governed by the **Oktoechos,** the Book of Eight Tones.

Sunday Names

Many Sundays are named after the subject of the Gospel read in the Mass of the day or after the name of a feast falling on the day — e.g., Sunday of the Publican and Pharisee, of the Prodigal Son, of the Samaritan Woman, of St. Thomas the Apostle, of the Fore-Fathers (Old Testament Patriarchs). Other Sundays are named in the same manner as in the Roman calendar e.g., numbered Sundays of Lent and after Pentecost.

Holy Days

The calendar lists about 28 holy days. Many of the major holy days coincide with those of the Roman calendar, but the feast of the Immaculate Conception is observed on Dec. 9 instead of Dec. 8, and the feast of All Saints falls on the Sunday after Pentecost rather than on Nov. 1. Instead of a single All Souls' Day, there are five All Souls' Saturdays.

According to regulations in effect in the Byzantine-Rite (Ruthenian) Archeparchy of Pittsburgh and its suffragan sees of Passaic, Parma and Van Nuys, holy days are obligatory, solemn and simple, and attendance at the Divine Liturgy is required on five obligatory days — the feasts of the Epiphany, the Ascension, Sts. Peter and Paul, the Assumption of the Blessed Virgin Mary, and Christmas. Although attendance at the liturgy is not obligatory on 15 solemn and seven simple holy days, it is recommended.

In the Byzantine-Rite (Ukrainian) Archeparchy of Philadelphia and its suffragan sees of St. Josaphat in Parma, St. Nicholas (Chicago) and Stamford, the obligatory feasts are the Circumcision, Epiphany, Annunciation, Easter, Ascension, Pentecost, Dormition (Assumption of Mary), Immaculate Conception and Christmas.

Lent

The first day of Lent — the Monday before Ash Wednesday of the Roman Rite — and Good Friday are days of strict abstinence for persons in the age bracket of obligation. No meat, eggs, or dairy products may be eaten on these days.

All persons over the age of 14 must abstain from meat on Fridays during Lent, Holy Saturday, and the vigils of the feasts of Christmas and Epiphany; abstinence is urged, but is not obligatory, on Wednesdays of Lent. The abstinence obligation is not in force on certain "free" or "privileged" Fridays.

Synaxis

An observance without a counterpart in the Roman calendar is the synaxis. This is a commemoration, on the day following a feast, of persons involved with the occasion for the feast — e.g., Sept. 9, the day following the feast of the Nativity of the Blessed Virgin Mary, is the Synaxis of Joachim and Anna, her parents.

Holy Week

In the Byzantine Rite, Lent is liturgically concluded with the Saturday of Lazarus, the day before Palm Sunday, which commemorates the raising of Lazarus from the dead.

On the following Monday, Tuesday and Wednesday, the Liturgy of the Presanctified is prescribed.

On Holy Thursday, the Liturgy of St. Basil the Great is celebrated together with Vespers.

The Divine Liturgy is not celebrated on Good Friday.

On Holy Saturday, the Liturgy of St. Basil the Great is celebrated along with Vespers.

BYZANTINE FEATURES

Art: Named for the empire in which it developed, Byzantine art is a unique blend of imperial Roman and classic Hellenic culture with Christian inspiration. The art of the Greek Middle Ages, it reached a peak of development in the 10th or 11th century. Characteristic of its products, particularly in mosaic and painting, are majesty, dignity, refinement and grace. Its sacred paintings, called icons, are reverenced highly in all Eastern Rites.

Church Building: The classical model of Byzantine church architecture is the Church of the Holy Wisdom (Hagia Sophia), built in Constantinople in the first half of the sixth century and still standing. The square structure, extended in some cases in the form of a cross, is topped by a distinctive onion-shaped dome and surmounted by a triple-bar cross. The altar is at the eastern end of building, where the wall bellies out to form an apse. The altar and sanctuary are separated from the body of the church by a fixed or movable screen, the iconostas, to which icons or sacred pictures are attached (see below).

Clergy: The Byzantine Rite has married as well as celibate priests. In places other than the U.S., where married candidates have not been accepted for ordination since about 1929, men already married can be ordained to the diaconate and priesthood and can continue in marriage after ordination. Celibate deacons and priests cannot marry after ordination; neither can a married priest remarry after the death of his wife. Bishops must be unmarried.

Iconostas: A large screen decorated with sacred pictures or icons which separates the sanctuary from the nave of a church; its equivalent in the Roman Rite, for thus separating the sanctuary from the nave, is an altar rail.

An iconostas has three doors through which the sacred ministers enter the sanctuary during the Divine Liturgy: smaller (north and south) Deacons' Doors and a large central Royal Door.

The Deacons' Doors usually feature the icons of Sts. Gabriel and Michael; the Royal Door, the icons of the Evangelists — Matthew, Mark, Luke and John. To the right and left of the Royal Door are the icons of Christ the Teacher and of the Blessed Virgin Mary with the Infant Jesus. To the extreme right and left are the icons of the patron of the church and St. John the Baptist (or St. Nicholas of Myra).

Immediately above the Royal Door is a picture of the Last Supper. To the right are six icons depicting the major feasts of Christ, and to the left are six icons portraying the major feasts of the Blessed Virgin Mary. Above the picture of the Last Supper is a large icon of Christ the King.

Some icon screens also have pictures of the 12 Apostles and the major Old Testament prophets surmounted by a crucifixion scene.

Liturgical Language: In line with Eastern tradition, Byzantine practice has favored the use of the language of the people in the liturgy. Two great advocates of the practice were Sts. Cyril and Methodius, apostles of the Slavs, who devised the Cyrillic alphabet and pioneered the adoption of Slavonic in the liturgy.

Sacraments: Baptism is administered by immersion, and confirmation (Chrismation) is conferred at the same time. The Eucharist is administered by intinction, i.e., by giving the communicant a piece of consecrated leavened bread which has been dipped into the consecrated wine. When giving absolution in the sacrament of penance, the priest holds his stole over the head of the penitent. Distinctive marriage ceremonies include the crowning of the bride and groom. Ceremonies for anointing the sick closely resemble those of the Roman Rite. Holy orders are conferred by a bishop.

Sign of the Cross: The sign of the cross in conjunction with a deep bow expresses reverence for the presence of Christ in the Blessed Sacrament. (See also entry in Glossary.)

VESTMENTS, APPURTENANCES

Sticharion: A long white garment of linen or silk with wide sleeves and decorated with embroidery; formerly the vestment for clerics in minor orders, acolytes, lectors, chanters, and subdeacons; symbolic of purity.

Epitrachelion: A stole with ends sewn together, having a loop through which the head is passed; its several crosses symbolize priestly duties.

Zone: A narrow clasped belt made of the same material as the epitrachelion; symbolic of the wisdom of the priest, his strength against enemies of the Church and his willingness to perform holy duties.

Epimanikia: Ornamental cuffs; the right cuff symbolizing strength, the left, patience and good will.

Phelonion: An ample cape, long in the back and sides and cut away in front; symbolic of the higher gifts of the Holy Spirit.

Antimension: A silk or linen cloth laid on the altar for the Liturgy; it may be decorated with a picture of the burial of Christ and the instruments of his passion; the relics of martyrs are sewn into the front border.

Eileton: A linen cloth which corresponds to the Roman-Rite corporal.

Poterion: A chalice or cup which holds the wine and Precious Blood.

Diskos: A shallow plate, which may be elevated on a small stand, corresponding to the Roman-Rite paten.

Asteriskos: Made of two curved bands of gold or silver which cross each other to form a double arch; a star depends from the junction, which forms a cross; it is placed over the diskos holding the consecrated bread and is covered with a veil.

Veils: Three are used, one to cover the poterion, the second to cover the diskos, and the third to cover both.

Spoon: Used in administering Holy Communion by intinction; consecrated leavened bread is dipped into consecrated wine and spooned onto the tongue of the communicant.

Lance: A metal knife used for cutting up the bread to be consecrated during the Liturgy.

SEPARATED EASTERN CHURCHES

ORTHODOX

Orthodox Churches are churches of Eastern rites which were in communion with the Holy See until the Schism of 1054. Although they withdrew from communion at that time, they retained, and still retain, essential features of the Mother Churches from which they derived: matters of faith and morals, valid orders and sacraments, liturgy, patriarchal jurisdiction and general discipline. Along with the lack of communion with the Holy See, the Orthodox Churches recognize only the first seven ecumenical councils.

Like their Catholic counterparts, Orthodox Churches are organized in jurisdictions under patriarchs. The patriarchs are the heads of approximately 15 autocephalic and several other autonomous jurisdictions organized along lines of nationality and/ or language.

The Ecumenical Patriarch of Constantinople (Istanbul) has the primacy of honor among his equal patriarchs but his actual jurisdiction is limited to his own patriarchate. As the spiritual head of worldwide Orthodoxy, he keeps the book of the Holy Canons of the Autocephalous Churches, in which recognized Orthodox Churches are registered, and has the right to call Pan-Orthodox assemblies.

Top-level relations between the Churches have improved in recent years through the efforts of Ecumenical Patriarch Athenagoras I, John XXIII, Paul VI and Patriarch Dimitrios I. Pope Paul met with Athenagoras three times before the latter's death in 1972. The most significant action of both spiritual leaders was their mutual nullification of excommunications imposed by the two Churches on each other in 1054. Development of better relations with the Orthodox has been a priority of John Paul II since the beginning of his pontificate. Both he and Orthodox Ecumenical Patriarch Bartholomew have made known their commitment to better relations, despite contentions between Eastern Catholic and Orthodox Churches over charges of proselytism and rival property claims in places liberated from anti-religious communist control in the recent past.

The largest Orthodox body in the western hemisphere is the Greek Orthodox Archdiocese of North and South America consisting of the Archdiocese of New York, nine dioceses in the U.S., and one diocese each in Canada and South America; it has an estimated membership of 1.9 million. The second largest is the Orthodox Church in America, with more than one million members; it was given independent status by the Patriarchate of Moscow May 18, 1970, against the will of Athenagoras I who refused to register it in the book of the Holy Canons of Autocephalous Churches. An additional 650,000 or more Orthodox belong to smaller national and language jurisdictions.

Heads of orthodox jurisdictions in this hemisphere hold membership in the Standing Conference of Canonical Orthodox Bishops in the Americas.

Jurisdictions

The principal jurisdictions of the Greek, Russian and other Orthodox Churches are as follows.

Greek: Patriarchate of Constantinople, with jurisdiction in Turkey, Crete, the Dodecanese, Western Europe, the Americas, Australia.

Patriarchate of Alexandria, with jurisdiction in Egypt and the rest of Africa; there is also a native African Orthodox Church in Kenya and Uganda.

Patriarchate of Antioch (Melkites or Syrian Orthodox), with jurisdiction in Syria, Lebanon, Iraq, Australasia, the Americas; Syrian or Arabic, in place of Greek, is the liturgical language.

Patriarchate of Jerusalem, with jurisdiction in Israel and Jordan.

Churches of Greece, Cyprus and Sinai are autocephalic but maintain relations with their fellow Orthodox.

Russian: Patriarchate of Moscow with jurisdiction centered in the former Soviet Union.

Other: Patriarchate of Serbia, with jurisdiction in Yugoslavia, Western Europe, the Americas, Australasia.

Patriarchates of Romania and Bulgaria.

Katholikate of Georgia, the Soviet Union.

Belarussians and Ukrainian Byzantines.

Churches of Albania, China, Czechoslovakia, Estonia, Finland, Hungary, Japan, Latvia, Lithuania, Poland.

Other minor communities in various places; e.g., Korea, the U.S., Carpatho-Russia.

The Division of Archives and Statistics of the Eastern Orthodox World Foundation reported a 1970 estimate of more than 200 million Orthodox Church members throughout the world. A contemporary estimate put the number close to 220 million.

Conference of Orthodox Bishops

The Standing Conference of Canonical Orthodox Bishops in the Americas was established in 1960 to achieve cooperation among the various Orthodox jurisdictions in the Americas. Ecumenical office: 8-10 East 79th St., New York, N.Y. 10021.

Member churches of the conference are the: Albanian Orthodox Diocese of America (Ecumenical Patriarchate), American Carpatho-Russian Orthodox Greek Catholic Diocese in the U.S.A. (Ecumenical Patriarchate), Antiochian Orthodox Christian Archdiocese of North America, Bulgarian Eastern Orthodox Church, Greek Orthodox Archdiocese of North and South America (Ecumenical Patriarchate), Orthodox Church in America, Romanian Orthodox Archdiocese in America and Canada, Serbian Orthodox Church in the United States of America and Canada, Ukrainian Orthodox Church in the United States (Ecumenical Patriarchate), Ukrainian Orthodox Church of Canada (Ecumenical Patriarchate).

ANCIENT CHURCHES OF THE EAST

Ancient Churches of the East, which are distinct from Orthodox Churches, were the subject of an article by Gerard Daucourt published in the Feb. 16, 1987, English edition of *L'Osservatore Romano.* Following is an excerpt.

By Ancient Churches of the East one means: the Assyrian Oriental Church (formerly called

Nestorian), the Armenian Church, the Coptic Church, the Ethiopian Church, the Syrian Church (sometimes called Syro-Jacobite) and the Syrian Church of India.

After the Council of Ephesus (431), the Assyrian Oriental Church did not maintain communion with the rest of the Christian world. For reasons as much and perhaps more political than doctrinal, it did not accept the Council's teaching (that Mary is the Mother of God, in opposition to the opinion of Nestorius; see Nestorianism. For this reason, the Assyrian Oriental Church came to be called Nestorian.) It is well known that in the 16th century a great segment of the faithful of this Church entered into communion with the See of Rome and constitutes today, among the Oriental Catholic Churches, the Chaldean Patriarchate.

The Patriarch of the Assyrian Oriental Church, His Holiness Mar Denkha IV, in the course of his visit to the Holy Father and to the Church of Rome of 7 to 9 November, 1984, requested that people stop using the term "Nestorian" to designate his Church and expressed the desire that a declaration made jointly by the Pope of Rome and himself may one day serve to express the common faith of the two Churches in Jesus Christ, Son of God incarnate, born of the Virgin Mary. The labours of Catholic historians and theologians have, moreover, already contributed to showing that such a declaration would be possible.

The other Ancient Churches of the East for a long time have been designated by the term "Monophysite Churches" (see Monophysitism). It is regrettable to find this name still employed sometimes in certain publications, since already in 1951, in the encyclical *Sempiternus Rex*, on the occasion of the 15th centenary of the Council of Chalcedon, Pius XII declared with regard to the Christians of these Churches: "They depart from the right way only in terminology, when they expound the doctrine of the Incarnation of the Lord. This may be deduced from their liturgical and theological books."

In this same encyclical, Pius XII expressed the view that the separation at the doctrinal level came about "above all, through a certain ambiguity of terminology that occurred at the beginning."

Since then, two important declarations have been arrived at in line with the ecumenical stance taken by the Church at the Second Vatican Council and the labors of the theologians (particularly in the framework of the Foundation "Pro Oriente" of Vienna). One was signed by Pope Paul VI and Coptic Patriarch Shenouda III on 10 May, 1973, and the other by Pope John Paul II and the Syrian Patriarch Ignace Zakka I Iwas, on 23 June, 1984. In both of these texts, the hierarchies of the respective Churches confess one and the same faith in the mystery of the Word Incarnate. After such declarations, it is no longer possible to speak in general terms of the "Monophysite" Churches.

The Armenian Church has communicants in the Soviet Union, the Middle and Far East, the Americas. The Coptic Church has communicants in the Middle East, the Americas, India.

Members of the Assyrian Oriental Church are scattered throughout the world.

It is estimated that there are approximately 10 million or more members of these other Eastern Churches throughout the world. For various reasons, a more accurate determination is not possible.

EASTERN ECUMENISM

The Second Vatican Council, in the *Decree on Eastern Catholic Churches,* pointed out the special role they have to play "in promoting the unity of all Christians. " The document also stated in part as follows.

The Eastern Churches in communion with the Apostolic See of Rome have a special role to play in promoting the unity of all Christians, particularly Easterners, according to the principles of this sacred Synod's *Decree on Ecumenism* first of all by prayer, then by the example of their lives, by religious fidelity to ancient Eastern traditions, by greater mutual knowledge, by collaboration, and by a brotherly regard for objects and attitudes (No. 24).

If any separated Eastern Christian should, under the guidance of grace of the Holy Spirit, join himself to Catholic unity, no more should be required of him than what a simple profession of the Catholic faith demands. A valid priesthood is preserved among Eastern clerics. Hence, upon joining themselves to the unity of the Catholic Church, Eastern clerics are permitted to exercise the orders they possess, in accordance with the regulations established by the competent authority (No. 25).

Divine Law forbids any common worship (*communicatio in sacris*) which would damage the unity of the Church, or involve formal acceptance of falsehood or the danger of deviation in the faith, of scandal, or of indifferentism. At the same time, pastoral experience clearly shows that with respect to our Eastern brethren there should and can be taken into consideration various circumstances affecting individuals, wherein the unity of the Church is not jeopardized nor are intolerable risks involved, but in which salvation itself and the spiritual profit of souls are urgently at issue.

Hence, in view of special circumstances of time, place, and personage, the Catholic Church has often adopted and now adopts a milder policy, offering to all the means of salvation and an example of charity among Christians through participation in the sacraments and in other sacred functions and objects. With these considerations in mind, and "lest because of the harshness of our judgment we prove an obstacle to those seeking salvation," and in order to promote closer union with the Eastern Churches separated from us, this sacred Synod lays down the following policy:

In view of the principles recalled above, Eastern Christians who are separated in good faith from the Catholic Church, if they ask of their own accord and have the right dispositions, may be granted the sacraments of penance, the Eucharist, and the anointing of the sick. Furthermore, Catholics may ask for these same sacraments from those non-Catholic ministers whose Churches possess valid sacraments, as often as necessity or a genuine spiritual benefit recommends such a course of action, and when access to a Catholic priest is physically or morally impossible (Nos. 26, 27).

Again, in view of these very same principles, Catholics may for a just cause join with their separated Eastern brethren in sacred functions, things, and places (No. 28). Bishops decide when and if to follow this lenient policy.

Recent Documents

Three recent documents of importance with respect to relations between Catholic and separated Eastern Churches are the apostolic letter, *Orientale Lumen,* issued May 5, 1995; the encyclical letter, *Ut Unum Sint,* issued May 30, 1995; and the Christological Declaration signed Nov. 11, 1994, by Pope John Paul and His Holiness Mar Dinkha IV, Catholicos-Patriarch of the Assyrian Church of the East.

Excerpts from the first two documents were given under their proper titles in the 1996 edition of the Almanac. The text of the Christological Document follows.

CHRISTOLOGICAL DECLARATION

Following is the text of the "Common Christological Declaration" between the Catholic Church and the Assyrian Church of the East, signed Nov. 11, 1994, by Pope John Paul II and His Holiness Mar Dinkha IV, Catholicos-Patriarch of the Assyrian Church of the East.

The declaration acknowledges that, despite past differences, both churches profess the same faith in the real union of divine and human natures in the divine Person of Christ. Backgrounding the declaration was the Assyrian Church's adherence to the teaching of Nestorius who, in the fifth century, denied the real unity of divine and human natures in the single divine Person of Christ.

The text was published in the Nov. 16, 1994, English edition of "L'Osservatore Romano."

As heirs and guardians of the faith received from the Apostles as formulated by our common Fathers in the Nicene Creed, we confess one Lord Jesus Christ, the only Son of God, begotten of the Father from all eternity who, in the fullness of time, came down from heaven and became man for our salvation. The Word of God, second Person of the Holy Trinity, became incarnate by the power of the Holy Spirit in assuming from the Virgin Mary a body animated by a rational soul, with which he was indissolubly united from the moment of conception.

Unity of Two Natures in One Person

Therefore our Lord Jesus Christ is true God and true man, perfect in his divinity and perfect in his humanity, consubstantial with the Father and consubstantial with us in all things but sin. His divinity and his humanity are united in one person, without confusion or change, without division or separation. In him has been preserved the difference of the natures of divinity and humanity, with all their properties, faculties and operations. But far from constituting "one and another," the dignity and humanity are united in the person of the same and unique Son of God and Lord Jesus Christ, who is the object of a single adoration.

Christ therefore is not an "ordinary man" whom God adopted in order to reside in him and inspire him, as in the righteous ones and the prophets. But the same God the Word, begotten of his Father before all worlds without beginning according to his divinity, was born of a mother without a father in the last times according to his humanity. The humanity to which the Blessed Virgin Mary gave birth always was that of the Son of God himself. That is the reason the Assyrian Church of the East is praying the Virgin Mary as "the Mother of Christ our God and Savior." In the light of this same faith the Catholic tradition addresses the Virgin Mary as "the Mother of God" and also as "the Mother of Christ." We both recognize the legitimacy and rightness of these expressions of the same faith and we both respect the preference of each Church in her liturgical life and piety.

Confession of the Same Faith

This is the unique faith that we profess in the mystery of Christ. The controversies of the past led to anathemas, bearing on persons and on formulas. The Lord's Spirit permits us to understand better today that the divisions brought about in this way were due in large part to misunderstandings.

Whatever our Christological divergences have been, we experience ourselves united today in the confession of the same faith in the Son of God who became man so that we might become children of God by his grace. We wish from now on to witness together to this faith in the One who is the Way, the Truth and the Life, proclaiming it in appropriate ways to our contemporaries, so that the world may believe in the Gospel of salvation.

The mystery of the Incarnation which we profess in common is not an abstract and isolated truth. It refers to the Son of God sent to save us. The economy of salvation, which has its origin in the mystery of communion of the Holy Trinity — Father, Son and Holy Spirit — is brought to its fulfillment through the sharing in this communion, by grace, within the one, holy, catholic and apostolic Church, which is the People of God, the Body of Christ and the Temple of the Spirit.

The Sacraments

Believers become members of this Body through the sacrament of Baptism, through which, by water and the working of the Holy Spirit, they are born again as new creatures. They are confirmed by the seal of the Holy Spirit who bestows the sacrament of anointing. Their communion with God and among themselves is brought to full realization by the celebration of the unique offering of Christ in the sacrament of the Eucharist. This communion is restored for the sinful members of the Church when they are reconciled with God and with one another through the sacrament of Forgiveness. The sacrament of Ordination to the ministerial priesthood in the apostolic succession assures the authenticity of the faith, the sacraments and the communion in each local Church.

Sister Churches but not Full Communion

Living by this faith and these sacraments, it follows as a consequence that the particular Catholic Churches and the particular Assyrian Churches can recognize each other as sister Churches. To be full and entire, communion presupposes the unanimity concerning the content of the faith, the sacraments and the constitution of the Church. Since this unanimity for which we aim has not yet been attained, we cannot unfortunately celebrate together the Eucharist which is the sign of the ecclesial communion already fully restored.

Nevertheless, the deep spiritual communion in the faith and the mutual trust already existing between our Churches entitles us from now on to consider witnessing together to the gospel message and cooperating in particular pastoral situations, including especially the areas of catechesis and the formation of future priests.

Commitment to Unity Efforts

In thanking God for having made us rediscover what already unites us in the faith and the sacraments, we pledge ourselves to do everything possible to dispel the obstacles of the past which still prevent the attainment of full communion between our Churches, so that we can better respond to the Lord's call for the unity of his own, a unity which has of course to be expressed visibly. To overcome these obstacles, we now establish a Mixed Committee for theological dialogue between the Catholic Church and the Assyrian Church of the East.

Given at Saint Peter's on 11 November 1994.

COMMON DECLARATIONS

John Paul II and Bartholomew I

Pope John Paul and Ecumenical Orthodox Patriarch Bartholomew I, after several days of meetings, signed a common declaration June 29, 1995, declaring:

"Our meeting has followed other important events which have seen our Churches declare their desire to relegate the excommunications of the past to oblivion and to set out on the way to establishing full communion.

"Our new-found brotherhood in the name of the Lord has led us to frank discussion, a dialogue that seeks understanding and unity. This dialogue — through the Joint International (Catholic-Orthodox) Commiission — has proved fruitful and has made substantial progress.

"A common sacramental conception of the Church has emerged, sustained and passed on in time by the apostolic succession. In our Churches, the apostolic succession is fundamental to the sanctification and unity of the People of God. Considering that in every local church the mystery of divine love is realized and that this is how the Church of Christ shows forth its active presence in each one of them, the Joint Commission has been able to declare that our Churches recognize one another as Sister Churches, responsible together for safeguarding the one Church of God, in fidelity to the divine plan, and in an altogether special way with regard to unity."

John Paul II and Karekin I

Pope John Paul and His Holiness Karekin I, Supreme Patriarch and Catholicos of All Armenians, signed Dec. 13, 1996, a common declaration in which they said in part:

"Pope John Paul II and Catholicos Karekin I recognize the deep spiritual communion which already unites them and the bishops and clergy and lay faithful of their churches. It is a communion which finds its roots in the common faith in the holy and life-giving Trinity proclaimed by the Apostles and transmitted down the centuries.... They rejoice in the fact that recent developments of ecumenical relations and theological discussions ... have dispelled many misunderstandings inherited from the controversies and dissensions of the past. Such dialogues and encounters have prepared a healthy situation of mutual understanding and recovery of the deeper spiritual communion based on the common faith in the holy Trinity that they have been given through the Gospel of Christ and in the holy tradition of the Church.

"They particularly welcome the great advance that their churches have registered in their common search for unity in Christ, the Word of God made flesh. Perfect God as to his divinity, perfect man as to his humanity, his divinity is united to his humanity in the Person of the only-begotten Son of God, in a union which is real, perfect, without confusion, without alteration, without division, without any form of separation.

"The reality of this common faith in Jesus Christ and in the same succession of apostolic ministry has at times been obscured or ignored. Linguistic, cultural and political factors have immensely contributed toward the theological divergences that have found expression in their terminology of formulating their doctrines. His Holiness John Paul II and His Holiness Karekin I have expressed their determined conviction that because of the fundamental common faith in God and in Jesus Christ, the controversies and unhappy divisions which sometimes have followed upon the divergent ways in expressing it, as a result of the present declaration, should not continue to influence the life and witness of the Church today. They humbly declare before God their sorrow for these controversies and dissensions and their determination to remove from the mind and memory of their churches the bitterness, mutual recriminations and even hatred which have sometimes manifested themselves in the past, and may even today cast a shadow over the truly fraternal and genuinely Christian relations between leaders and the faithful of both churches, especially as these have developed in recent times.

"The communion already existing between the two churches and the hope for and commitment to recovery of full communion between them should become factors of motivation for further contact, more regular and substantial dialogue, leading to a greater degree of mutual understanding and recovery of the community of their faith and service."

PROTESTANT CHURCHES

MEN, DOCTRINES, CHURCHES OF THE REFORMATION

Some of the leading figures, doctrines and churches of the Reformation are covered below. A companion article covers Major Protestant Churches in the United States.

John Wycliff (c. 1320-1384): English priest and scholar who advanced one of the leading Reformation ideas nearly 200 years before Martin Luther — that the Bible alone is the sufficient rule of faith — but had only an indirect influence on the 16th century Reformers. Supporting belief in an inward and practical religion, he denied the divinely commissioned authority of the pope and bishops of the Church; he also denied the Real Presence of Christ in the Holy Eucharist, and wrote against the sacrament of penance and the doctrine of indulgences. Nearly 20 of his propositions were condemned by Gregory XI in 1377; his writings were proscribed more extensively by the Council of Constance in 1415. His influence was strongest in Bohemia and Central Europe.

John Hus (c. 1369-1415): A Bohemian priest and preacher of reform who authored 30 propositions condemned by the Council of Constance. Excommunicated in 1411 or 1412, he was burned at the stake in 1415. His principal errors concerned the nature of the Church and the origin of papal authority. He spread some of the ideas of Wycliff but did not subscribe to his views regarding faith alone as the condition for justification and salvation, the sole sufficiency of Scripture as the rule of faith, the Real Presence of Christ in the Eucharist, and the sacramental system. In 1457 some of his followers founded the Church of the Brotherhood which later became known as the United Brethren or Moravian Church and is considered the earliest independent Protestant body.

Martin Luther (1483-1546): An Augustinian friar, priest and doctor of theology, the key figure in the Reformation. In 1517, as a special indulgence was being preached in Germany, and in view of needed reforms within the Church, he published at Wittenberg 95 theses concerning matters of Catholic belief and practice. Leo X condemned 41 statements from Luther's writings in 1520. Luther, refusing to recant, was excommunicated the following year. His teachings strongly influenced subsequent Lutheran theology; its statements of faith are found in the Book of Concord (1580).

Luther's doctrine included the following: The sin of Adam, which corrupted human nature radically (but not substantially), has affected every aspect of man's being. Justification, understood as the forgiveness of sins and the state of righteousness, is by grace for Christ's sake through faith. Faith involves not merely intellectual assent but an act of confidence by the will. Good works are indispensably necessary concomitants of faith, but do not merit salvation. Of the sacraments, Luther retained baptism, penance and the Holy Communion as effective vehicles of the grace of the Holy Spirit; he held that in the Holy Communion the consecrated bread and wine are the Body and Blood of Christ. The rule of faith is the divine revelation in the Sacred Scriptures. He rejected purgatory, indulgences and the invocation of the saints, and held that prayers for the dead have no efficacy. Lutheran tenets not in agreement with Catholic doctrine were condemned by the Council of Trent.

Anabaptism: Originated in Saxony in the first quarter of the 16th century and spread rapidly through southern Germany. Its doctrine included several key Lutheran tenets but was not regarded with favor by Luther, Calvin or Zwingli. Anabaptists believed that baptism is for adults only and that infant baptism is invalid. Their doctrine of the Inner Light, concerning the direct influence of the Holy Spirit on the believer, implied rejection of Catholic doctrine concerning the sacraments and the nature of the Church. Eighteen articles of faith were formulated in 1632 in Holland. Mennonites are Anabaptists.

Ulrich Zwingli (1484-1531): A priest who triggered the Reformation in Switzerland with a series of New Testament lectures in 1519, later disputations and by other actions. He held the Gospel to be the only basis of truth; rejected the Mass (which he suppressed in 1525 at Zurich), penance and other sacraments; denied papal primacy and doctrine concerning purgatory and the invocation of saints; rejected celibacy, monasticism and many traditional practices of piety. His symbolic view of the Eucharist, which was at odds with Catholic doctrine, caused an irreconcilable controversy with Luther and his followers. Zwingli was killed in a battle between the forces of Protestant and Catholic cantons in Switzerland.

John Calvin (1509-1564): French leader of the Reformation in Switzerland, whose key tenet was absolute predestination of some persons to heaven and others to hell. He rejected Catholic doctrine in 1533 after becoming convinced of a personal mission to reform the Church. In 1536 he published the first edition of Institutes of the Christian Religion, a systematic exposition of his doctrine which became the classic textbook of Reformed — as distinguished from Lutheran — theology. To Luther's principal theses — regarding Scripture as the sole rule of faith, the radical corruption of human nature, and justification by faith alone — he added absolute predestination, certitude of salvation for the elect, and the incapability of the elect to lose grace. His Eucharistic theory, which failed to mediate the Zwingli-Luther controversy, was at odds with Catholic doctrine. From 1555 until his death Calvin was the virtual dictator of Geneva, the capital of the non-Lutheran Reformation in Europe.

Arminianism: A modification of the rigid predestinationism of Calvin, set forth by Jacob Arminius (1560-1609) and formally stated in the Remonstrance of 1610. Arminianism influenced some Calvinist bodies.

Unitarianism: A 16th century doctrine which rejected the Trinity and the divinity of Christ in favor of a uni-personal God. It claimed scriptural support for a long time but became generally rationalistic with respect to "revealed" doctrine as well as in ethics and its world-view. One of its principal early proponents was Faustus Socinus (1539-1604), a leader of the Polish Brethren.

A variety of communions developed in England in the Reformation and post-Reformation periods.

Puritans: Extremists who sought church reform along Calvinist lines in severe simplicity. (Use of the term was generally discontinued after 1660.)

Presbyterians: Basically Calvinistic, called Presbyterian because church polity centers around assemblies of presbyters or elders. John Knox (c. 1513-1572) established the church in Scotland.

Congregationalists: Evangelical in spirit and seeking a return to forms of the primitive church, they uphold individual freedom in religious matters, do not require the acceptance of a creed as a condition for communion, and regard each congregation as autonomous. Robert Browne influenced the beginnings of Congregationalism.

Quakers: Their key belief is in internal divine illumination, the inner light of the living Christ, as the only source of truth and inspiration. George Fox (1624-1691) was one of their leaders in England. Called the Society of Friends, the Quakers are noted for their pacificism.

Baptists: So called because of their doctrine concerning baptism. They reject infant baptism and consider only baptism by immersion as valid. Leaders in the formation of the church were John Smyth (d. 1612) in England and Roger Williams (d. 1683) in America.

Methodists: A group who broke away from the Anglican Communion under the leadership of John Wesley (1703-1791), although some Anglican beliefs were retained. Doctrines include the witness of the Spirit to the individual and personal assurance of salvation. Wesleyan Methodists do not subscribe to some of the more rigid Calvinistic tenets held by other Methodists.

Univesalism: A product of 18th-century liberal Protestantism in England. The doctrine is not Trinitarian and includes a tenet that all men will ultimately be saved.

ANGLICAN COMMUNION

This communion, which regards itself as the same apostolic Church as that which was established by early Christians in England, derived not from Reformation influences but from the renunciation of papal jurisdiction by Henry VIII (1491-1547). His Act of Supremacy in 1534 called Christ's Church an assembly of local churches subject to the prince, who was vested with fullness of authority and jurisdiction. In spite of Henry's denial of papal authority, this Act did not reject substantially other principal articles of faith. Notable changes, proposed and adopted for the reformation of the church, took place in the subsequent reigns of James VI and Elizabeth, with respect to such matters as Scripture as the rule of faith, the sacraments, the nature of the Mass, and the constitution of the hierarchy. There are 27 provinces in the Anglican Communion. (See Episcopal Church, Anglican Orders, Anglican-Catholic Final Report.)

MAJOR PROTESTANT CHURCHES IN THE UNITED STATES

There are more than 250 Protestant church bodies in the United States.

The majority of U.S. Protestants belong to the following denominations: Baptist, Methodist, Lutheran, Presbyterian, Protestant Episcopal, the United Church of Christ, the Christian Church (Disciples of Christ), Evangelicals.

See Ecumenical Dialogues, Reports and related entries for coverage of relations between the Catholic Church and other Christian churches.

Baptist Churches

Baptist churches, comprising the largest of all American Protestant denominations, were first established by John Smyth near the beginning of the 17th century in England. The first Baptist church in America was founded at Providence by Roger Williams in 1639.

Largest of the nearly 30 Baptist bodies in the U.S. are:

The Southern Baptist Convention, 901 Commerce St., Suite 750, Nashville, Tenn. 37203, with 15.7 million members.

The National Baptist Convention, U.S.A., Inc., 915 Spain St., Baton Rouge, La. 70802, with 8 million members;

The National Baptist Convention of America, Inc., 1320 Pierre Ave., Shreveport, La. 71103, with 4.5 million members.

The American Baptist Churches in the U.S.A., P.O. Box 851, Valley Forge, Pa. 19482, with 1.5 million members.

The total number of U.S. Baptists is more than 29 million. The world total is 33 million.

Proper to Baptists is their doctrine on baptism. Called an "ordinance" rather than a sacrament, baptism by immersion is a sign that one has experienced and decided in favor of the salvation offered by Christ. It is administered only to persons who are able to make a responsible decision. Baptism is not administered to infants.

Baptists do not have a formal creed but generally subscribe to two professions of faith formulated in 1689 and 1832 and are in general agreement with classical Protestant theology regarding Scripture as the sole rule of faith, original sin, justification through faith in Christ, and the nature of the Church. Their local churches are autonomous.

Worship services differ in form from one congregation to another. Usual elements are the reading of Scripture, a sermon, hymns, vocal and silent prayer. The Lord's Supper, called an "ordinance," is celebrated at various times.

Christian Church (Disciples of Christ)

The Christian Church (Disciples of Christ) originated early in the 1800's from two movements against rigid denominationalism led by Presbyterians Thomas and Alexander Campbell in western Pennsylvania and Barton W. Stone in Kentucky. The two movements developed separately for about 25 years before being merged in 1832.

The church, which identifies itself with the Protestant mainstream, has nearly one million members in almost 4,000 congregations in the U.S. and Canada. The greatest concentration of members in the U.S. is located roughly along the old frontier line, in an arc sweeping from Ohio and Kentucky through the Midwest and down into Oklahoma and Texas.

The general offices of the church are located at 130 E. Washington St., Indianapolis, Ind. 46204.

The church's persistent concern for Christian unity is based on a conviction expressed in a basic document, *Declaration and Address,* dating from its founding. The document states: "The church of Christ upon earth is essentially, intentionally and constitutionally one."

The Disciples have no official doctrine or dogma. Their worship practices vary widely from more common informal services to what could almost be described as "high church" services. Membership is granted after a simple statement of belief in Jesus Christ and baptism by immersion; most congregations admit un-immersed transfers from other denominations. The Lord's Supper or Eucharist, generally called Communion, is always open to Christians of all persuasions. Lay men and women routinely preside over the Lord's Supper, which is celebrated each Sunday; they often preach and perform other pastoral functions as well. Distinction between ordained and non-ordained members is blurred somewhat because of the Disciples' emphasis on all members of the church as ministers.

The Christian Church is oriented to congregational government, and has a unique structure in which three sections of polity (general, regional and congregational) operate as equals rather than in a pyramid of authority. At the national or international level, it is governed by a general assembly which has voting representation direct from congregations and regions as well as all ordained and licensed clergy.

Episcopal Church

The Episcopal Church, which includes 113 dioceses in the United States, Central and South America, and elsewhere overseas, regards itself as part of the same apostolic church which was established by early Christians in England. Established in this country during the colonial period, it became independent of the jurisdiction of the Church of England when a new constitution and Prayer Book were adopted at a general convention held in 1789. It has approximately 2.5 million members worldwide.

Offices of the presiding bishop and the executive council are located at 815 Second Ave., New York, N.Y. 10017.

The presiding bishop is chief pastor and primate; he is elected by the House of Bishops and confirmed by the House of Deputies for a term of nine years.

The Episcopal Church, which is a part of the Anglican Communion, regards the Archbishop of Canterbury as the "First among Equals," though not under his authority.

The Anglican Communion, worldwide, has 70 million members in 36 self-governing churches.

Official statements of belief and practice are found in the Book of Common Prayer. Scripture has primary importance with respect to the rule of faith, and authority is also attached to tradition.

An episcopal system of church government prevails, but presbyters, deacons and lay persons also have an active voice in church affairs. The levels of government are the general convention, and executive council, dioceses, and local parishes. At the parish level, the congregation has the right to select its own rector, with the consent of the bishop.

Liturgical worship is according to the Book of Common Prayer as adopted in 1979, but details of ceremonial practice vary from one congregation to another.

Lutheran Churches

The origin of Lutheranism is generally traced to Oct. 31, 1517, when Martin Luther — Augustinian friar, priest, doctor of theology — tacked "95 Theses" to the door of the castle church in Wittenberg, Germany. This call to debate on the subject of indulgences and related concerns has come to symbolize the beginning of the Reformation. Luther and his supporters intended to reform the Church they knew. Though Lutheranism has come to be visible in separate denominations and national churches, at its heart it professes itself to be a confessional movement within the one, holy, catholic and apostolic Church.

The world's 61 million Lutherans form the third largest grouping of Christians, after Roman Catholics and Orthodox. About 57 million of them belong to church bodies which make up the Lutheran World Federation, headquartered in Geneva.

There are about 8.5 million Lutherans in the United States, making them the fourth largest Christian grouping, after Roman Catholics, Baptists and Methodists. Although there are nearly 20 U.S. Lutheran church bodies, all but 100,000 Lutherans belong to either the Evangelical Lutheran Church in America (with 5.2 million members and headquarters at 8765 W. Higgins Rd., Chicago, Ill. 60631), The Lutheran Church-Missouri Synod (with 2.61 million members and headquarters at 1333 S. Kirkwood Rd., St. Louis, Mo. 63122), or the Wisconsin Evangelical Lutheran Synod (with 420,000 members and headquarters at 2929 N. Mayfair Rd., Milwaukee, Wis. 53222).

The Evangelical Lutheran Church in America and the Lutheran Church-Missouri Synod carry out some work together through inter-Lutheran agencies such as Lutheran World Relief and Lutheran Immigration and Refugee Services; both agencies have offices at 390 Park Ave. South, New York, N.Y. 10010.

The statements of faith which have shaped the confessional life of Lutheranism are found in the *Book of Concord.* This 1580 collection includes the three ancient ecumenical creeds (Apostles', Nicene and Athanasian), Luther's *Large and Small Catechisms* (1529), the *Augsburg Confession* (1530) and the *Apology* in defense of it (1531), the *Smalcald Articles* (including the "Treatise on the Power and Primacy of the Pope") (1537), and the *Formula of Concord* (1577).

The central Lutheran doctrinal proposition is that Christians "receive forgiveness of sins and become righteous before God by grace, for Christ's sake." Baptism and the Lord's Supper (Holy Communion, the Eucharist) are universally celebrated among Lutherans as sacramental means of grace. Lutherans also treasure the Word proclaimed in the reading of the Scriptures, preaching and absolution.

Generally in Lutheranism, the bishop, or a pastor (presbyter/priest) authorized by the bishop, is the minister of ordination. Much of Lutheranism continues what it understands as the historic succession of bishops (though without considering the historic episcopate essential for the church). All of Lutheranism is concerned to preserve apostolic succession in life and doctrine.

Lutheran jurisdictions corresponding to dioceses are called districts or synods in North America. There are more than 100 of them; each of them is headed by a bishop or president.

Methodist Churches

John Wesley (1703-1791), an Anglican clergyman, was the founder of Methodism. In 1738, following a period of missionary work in America and strongly influenced by the Moravians, he experienced a new conversion to Christ and shortly thereafter became a leader in a religious awakening in England. By the end of the 18th century, Methodism was strongly rooted also in America.

The United Methodist Church, formed in 1968 by a merger of the Methodist Church and the Evangelical United Brethren Church, is the second largest Protestant denomination in the U.S., with more than nine million members; its principal agencies are located in New York, Evanston, Ill., Nashville, Tenn., Washington, D.C., Dayton, O., and Lake Junaluska, N.C. (World Methodist Council, P.O. Box 518. 28745). The second largest body, with just under two million communicants, is the African Methodist Episcopal Church. Four other major churches in the U.S. are the African Methodist Episcopal Zion, Christian Methodist Episcopal, Free Methodist Church and the Wesleyan Church. The total Methodist membership in the U.S. is about 15.5 million.

Worldwide, there are more than 73 autonomous Methodist/Wesleyan churches in 107 countries, with a membership of more than 33 million. All of them participate in the World Methodist Council, which gives global unity to the witness of Methodist communicants.

Methodism, although it has a base in Calvinistic theology, rejects absolute predestination and maintains that Christ offers grace freely to all men, not just to a select elite. Wesley's distinctive doctrine was the "witness of the Spirit" to the individual soul and personal assurance of salvation. He also emphasized the central themes of conversion and holiness. Methodists are in general agreement with classical Protestant theology regarding Scripture as the sole rule of faith, original sin, justification through faith in Christ, the nature of the Church, and the sacraments of baptism and the Lord's Supper. Church polity is structured along episcopal lines in America, with ministers being appointed to local churches by a bishop; churches stemming from British Methodism do not have bishops but vest appointive powers within an appropriate conference. Congregations are free to choose various forms of worship services; typical elements are readings from Scripture, sermons, hymns and prayers.

Presbyterian Churches

Presbyterians are so called because of their tradition of governing the church through a system of representative bodies composed of elders (presbyters).

Presbyterianism is a part of the Reformed Family of Churches that grew out of the theological work of John Calvin following the Lutheran Reformation, to which it is heavily indebted. Countries in which it acquired early strength and influence were Switzerland, France, Holland, Scotland and England.

Presbyterianism spread widely in this country in the latter part of the 18th century and afterwards. Presently, it has approximately 4.5 million communicants in nine bodies.

The two largest Presbyterian bodies in the country — the United Presbyterian Church in the U.S.A. and the Presbyterian Church in the United States — were reunited in June, 1983, to form the Presbyterian Church (U.S.A.), with a membership of 2.7 million. Its national offices are located at 100 Witherspoon St., Louisville, Ky. 40202.

These churches, now merged, are closely allied with the Reformed Church in America, the United Church of Christ, the Cumberland Presbyterian Churches, the Korean Presbyterian Church in America and the Associate Reformed Presbyterian Church.

In Presbyterian doctrine, baptism and the Lord's Supper, viewed as seals of the covenant of grace, are regarded as sacraments. Baptism, which is not necessary for salvation, is conferred on infants and adults The Lord's Supper is celebrated as a covenant of the Sacrifice of Christ. In both sacraments, a doctrine of the real presence of Christ is considered the central theological principle.

The Church is twofold, being invisible and also visible; it consists of all of the elect and all those Christians who are united in Christ as their immediate head.

Presbyterians are in general agreement with classical Protestant theology regarding Scripture as the sole rule of faith and practice, salvation by grace, and justification through faith in Christ.

Presbyterian congregations are governed by a session composed of elders elected by the communicant membership. On higher levels there are presbyteries, synods and a general assembly with various degrees of authority over local bodies; all such representative bodies are composed of elected elders and ministers in approximately equal numbers. The church annually elects a moderator who presides at the General Assembly and travels throughout the church to speak to and hear from the members.

Worship services, simple and dignified, include sermons, prayer, reading of the Scriptures and hymns. The Lord's Supper is celebrated at intervals.

Doctrinal developments of the past several years included approval in May, 1967, by the General Assembly of the United Presbyterian Church of a contemporary confession of faith to supplement the historic Westminster Confession. A statement entitled "The Declaration of Faith" was approved in 1977 by the Presbyterian Church in the U.S. for teaching and liturgical use.

The reunited church adopted "A Brief Statement of Reformed Faith" in 1991 regarding urgent concerns of the church.

United Church of Christ

The 1,501,310-member (in 1994) United Church of Christ was formed in 1957 by a union of the Congregational Christian and the Evangelical and Reformed Churches. The former was originally established by the Pilgrims and the Puritans of the Massachusetts Bay Colony, while the latter was founded in Pennsylvania in the early 1700s by settlers from Central Europe. The denomination had 6,362 congregations throughout the United States in 1988.

It considers itself "a united and uniting church" and keeps itself open to all ecumenical options.

Its headquarters are located at 700 Prospect, Cleveland, Ohio 44115.

Its statement of faith recognizes Jesus Christ as "our crucified and risen Lord (who) shared our common lot, conquering sin and death and reconciling the world to himself." It believes in the life after death, and the fact that God "judges men and nations by his righteous will declared through prophets and apostles."

The United Church further believes that Christ calls its members to share in his baptism "and eat at his table, to join him in his passion and victory." Each local church is free to adopt its own methods of worship and to formulate its own covenants and confessions of faith. Some celebrate communion weekly; others, monthly or on another periodical basis. Like other Calvinistic bodies, it believes that Christ is spiritually present in the sacrament.

The United Church is governed along congregational lines, and each local church is autonomous. However, the actions of its biennial General Synod are taken with great seriousness by congregations. Between synods, a 44-member executive council oversees the work of the church.

Evangelicalism

Evangelicalism, dating from 1735 in England (the Evangelical Revival) and after 1740 in the United States (the Great Awakening), has had and continues to have widespread influence in Protestant churches. It has been estimated that about 45 millon American Protestants — communicants of both large denominations and small bodies — are evangelicals.

The Bible is their rule of faith and religious practice. Being born again in a life-changing experience through faith in Christ is the promise of salvation. Missionary work for the spread of the Gospel is a normal and necessary activity.

Additional matters of belief and practice are generally of a conservative character. Fundamentalists, numbering perhaps 4.5 million, comprise an extreme right-wing subculture of evangelicalism. They are distinguished mainly by militant biblicism, belief in the absolute inerrancy of the Bible and emphasis on the Second Coming of Christ. Fundamentalism developed early in the 20th century in reaction against liberal theology and secularizing trends in mainstream and other Protestant denominations.

The Holiness or Perfectionist wing of evangelicalism evolved from Methodist efforts to preserve, against a contrary trend, the personal-piety and inner-religion concepts of John Wesley. There are at least 30 Holiness bodies in the U.S.

Pentecostals, probably the most demonstrative of evangelicals, are noted for speaking in tongues and the stress they place on healing, prophecy and personal testimony to the practice and power of evangelical faith.

Assemblies of God

Assemblies (Churches) of God form the largest body (more than 2 million members) in the Pentecostal Movement which developed from (1) the Holiness Revival in the Methodist Church after the Civil War and (2) the Apostolic Faith Movement at the beginning of the 20th century. Members share with other Pentecostals belief in the religious experience of conversion and in the baptism by the Holy Spirit that sanctifies. Distinctive to them is the emphasis they place on the charismatic gifts of the apostolic church, healing and speaking in tongues, which are signs of the "second blessing" of the Holy Spirit.

The Assemblies are strongly fundamentalist in theology; are loosely organized in various districts, with democratic procedures; are vigorously evangelistic. There is considerable freedom in expressions of the Spirit, sermons and hymns. The moral code is rigid.

EVENTS OF MEDJUGORJE

Alleged apparitions of Mary to six young people of Medjugorje, Bosnia-Herzegovina, have been the center of interest and controversy since they were first reported in June, 1981, initially in a neighboring hillside field, subsequently in the village church of St. James and even in places far removed from Medjugorje.

Reports say the alleged visionaries have seen, heard and touched Mary during visions, and that they have variously received several or all of 10 secret messages related to world events and urging a quest for peace through prayer, penance and personal conversion. An investigative commission appointed by former local Bishop Pavao Zanic of Mostar-Duvno reported in March, 1984, that the authenticity of the apparitions had not been established and that cases of reported healings had not been verified. He called the apparitions a case of "collective hallucination" exploited by local Franciscan priests at odds with him over control of a parish.

Former Archbishop Frane Franic of Split-Makarska, on the other hand, said in December, 1985: "Speaking as a believer and not as a bishop, my personal conviction is that the events at Medjugorje are of supernatural inspiration." He based his conviction on the observation of spiritual benefits related to the reported events, such as the spiritual development of the six young people, the increases in Mass attendance and sacramental practice at the scene of the apparitions, and the incidence of reconciliation among people.

"Further exploration" of the events at Medjugorje on the national level, as distinguished from the earlier diocesan investigation, was announced in a communique published in the Archdiocese of Zagreb, dated Jan. 29, 1987. It said: "On the basis of research conducted so far, one cannot affirm that supernatural apparitions are involved" at Medjugorje, declared the bishops of Yugoslavia (19 to 1).

ECUMENISM

The modern ecumenical movement, which started about 1910 among Protestants and led to formation of the World Council of Churches in 1948, developed outside the mainstream of Catholic interest for many years. It has now become for Catholics as well one of the great religious facts of our time.

The magna charta of ecumenism for Catholics is a complex of several documents which include, in the first place, the *Decree on Ecumenism* promulgated by the Second Vatican Council Nov. 21, 1964. Other enactments underlying and expanding this decree are the *Dogmatic Constitution on the Church,* the *Decree on Eastern Catholic Churches,* the *Pastoral Constitution on the Church in the Modern World* and the encyclical letter *Ut Unum Sint.*

VATICAN II DECREE

The following excerpts from the "Decree on Ecumenism" cover the broad theological background and principles and indicate the thrust of the Church's commitment to ecumenism, under the subheads: Elements Common to Christians, Unity Lacking, What the Movement Involves, Primary Duty of Catholics.

Men who believe in Christ and have been properly baptized are brought into a certain, though imperfect, communion with the Catholic Church. Undoubtedly, the differences that exist in varying degrees between them and the Catholic Church — whether in doctrine and sometimes in discipline, or concerning the structure of the Church — do indeed create many and sometimes serious obstacles to full ecclesiastical communion. These the ecumenical movement is striving to overcome (No. 3).

Elements Common to Christians

Moreover some, even very many, of the most significant elements or endowments which together go to build up and give life to the Church herself can exist outside the visible boundaries of the Catholic Church: the written word of God; the life of grace; faith, hope, and charity, along with other interior gifts of the Holy Spirit and visible elements. All of these, which come from Christ and lead back to Him, belong by right to the one Church of Christ (No. 3).

[In a later passage, the decree singled out a number of elements which the Catholic Church and other churches have in common but not in complete agreement: confession of Christ as Lord and God and as mediator between God and man; belief in the Trinity; reverence for Scripture as the revealed word of God; baptism and the Lord's Supper; Christian life and worship; faith in action; concern with moral questions.]

The brethren divided from us also carry out many of the sacred actions of the Christian religion. Undoubtedly, in ways that vary according to the condition of each church or community, these actions can truly engender a life of grace, and can be rightly described as capable of providing access to the community of salvation.

It follows that these separated Churches and Communities, though we believe they suffer from defects already mentioned, have by no means been deprived of significance and importance in the mystery of salvation. For the Spirit of Christ has not refrained from using them as means of salvation which derive their efficacy from the very fullness of grace and truth entrusted to the Catholic Church (No. 3).

Unity Lacking

Nevertheless, our separated brethren, whether considered as individuals or as Communities and Churches, are not blessed with that unity which Jesus Christ wished to bestow on all those whom he has regenerated and vivified into one body and newness of life — that unity which the holy Scriptures and the revered tradition of the Church proclaim. For it is through Christ's Catholic Church alone, which is the all-embracing means of salvation, that the fullness of the means of salvation can be obtained. It was to the apostolic college alone, of which Peter is the head, that we believe our Lord entrusted all the blessings of the New Covenant, in order to establish on earth the one Body of Christ into which all those should be fully incorporated who already belong in any way to God's People (No. 3).

What the Movement Involves

Today, in many parts of the world, under the inspiring grace of the Holy Spirit, multiple efforts are being expended through prayer, word, and action to attain that fullness of unity which Jesus Christ desires. This sacred Synod, therefore, exhorts all the Catholic faithful to recognize the signs of the times and to participate skillfully in the work of ecumenism.

The "ecumenical movement" means those activities and enterprises which, according to various needs of the Church and opportune occasions, are started and organized for the fostering of unity among Christians. These are:

• First, every effort to eliminate words, judgments, and actions which do not respond to the condition of separated brethren with truth and fairness and so make mutual relations between them more difficult.

• Then, "dialogue" between competent experts from different Churches and Communities [scholarly ecumenism].

• In addition, these Communions cooperate more closely in whatever projects a Christian conscience demands for the common good [social ecumenism].

• They also come together for common prayer, where this is permitted [spiritual ecumenism].

• Finally, all are led to examine their own faithfulness to Christ's will for the Church and, wherever necessary, undertake with vigor the task of renewal and reform.

It is evident that the work of preparing and reconciling those individuals who wish for full Catholic communion is of its nature distinct from ecumenical action. But there is no opposition between the two, since both proceed from the wondrous providence of God (No. 4).

Primary Duty of Catholics

In ecumenical work, Catholics must assuredly be concerned for their separated brethren, praying for them, keeping them informed about the Church, making the first approaches toward them. But their primary duty is to make an honest and careful appraisal of whatever needs to be renewed and achieved in the Catholic household itself, in order that its life may bear witness more loyally and luminously to the teachings and ordinances which have been handed down from Christ through the Apostles.

Every Catholic must aim at Christian perfection (cf. Jas. 1:4; Rom. 12:1-2) and, each according to his station, play his part so that the Church may daily be more purified and renewed, against the day when Christ will present her to himself in all her glory, without spot or wrinkle (cf. Eph. 5:27).

Catholics must joyfully acknowledge and esteem the truly Christian endowments from our common heritage which are to be found among our separated brethren.

Nor should we forget that whatever is wrought by the grace of the Holy Spirit in the hearts of our separated brethren can contribute to our own edification. Whatever is truly Christian never conflicts with the genuine interests of the faith; indeed, it can always result in a more ample realization of the very mystery of Christ and the Church (No. 4).

Participation in Worship

Norms concerning participation by Catholics in the worship of other Christian Churches were sketched in this conciliar decree and elaborated in a number of other documents such as: the *Decree on Eastern Catholic Churches,* promulgated by the Second Vatican Council in 1964; *Interim Guidelines for Prayer in Common,* issued June 18, 1965, by the U.S. Bishops' Committee for Ecumenical and Interreligious Affairs; a *Directory on Ecumenism,* published in 1967, 1970 and 1993 by the Pontifical Council for Promoting Christian Unity; additional communications from the U.S. Bishops' Committee, and numerous sets of guidelines issued locally by and for dioceses throughout the U.S.

The norms encourage common prayer services for Christian unity and other intentions. Beyond that, they draw a distinction between separated churches of the Reformation tradition and of the Anglican Communion, and separated Eastern churches, in view of doctrine and practice the Catholic Church has in common with the separated Eastern churches concerning the apostolic succession of bishops, holy orders, liturgy and other credal matters.

Full participation by Catholics in official Protestant liturgies is prohibited, because it implies profession of the faith expressed in the liturgy. Intercommunion by Catholics at Protestant liturgies is prohibited. Under certain conditions, Protestants may be given Holy Communion in the Catholic Church (see Intercommunion). A Catholic may stand as a witness, but not as a sponsor, in baptism, and as a witness in the marriage of separated Christians. Similarly, a Protestant may stand as a witness, but not as a sponsor, in a Catholic baptism, and as a witness in the marriage of Catholics.

Separated Eastern Churches

The principal norms regarding liturgical participation with separated Eastern Christians are included under Eastern Ecumenism.

DIRECTORY ON ECUMENISM

A new *Directory for the Application of the Principles and Norms of Ecumenism* was approved by Pope John Paul Mar. 25, 1993, and published early in June. The Pontifical Council for Promoting Christian Unity said on release of the document that revision of Directories issued in 1967 and 1970 was necessary in view of subsequent developments. These included promulgation of the *Code of Canon Law* for the Latin Church in 1983 and of the *Code of Canons of the Eastern Churches* in 1990; publication of the Catechism of the Catholic Church in 1992; additional documents and the results of theological dialogues.

The following excerpts are from the text published in the June 16, 1993, English edition of L'Osservatore Romano.

Address and Purpose

"The Directory is addressed to the pastors of the Catholic Church, but it also concerns all the faithful, who are called to pray and work for the unity of Christians, under the direction of their bishops."

"At the same time, it is hoped that the Directory will also be useful to members of churches and ecclesial communities that are not in full communion with the Catholic Church."

"The new edition of the Directory is meant to be an instrument at the service of the whole Church, and especially of those who are directly engaged in ecumenical activity in the Catholic Church. The Directory intends to motivate, enlighten and guide this activity, and in some particular cases also to give binding directives in accordance with the proper competence of the Pontifical Council for Promoting Christian Unity."

Outline

Principles and norms of the document are covered in five chapters.

"**I. The Search for Christian Unity.** The ecumenical commitment of the Catholic Church based on the doctrinal principles of the Second Vatican Council.

"**II. Organization in the Catholic Church at the Service of Christian Unity.** Persons and structures involved in promoting ecumenism at all levels, and the norms that direct their activity.

"**III. Ecumenical Formation in the Catholic Church.** Categories of people to be formed, those responsible for formation; the aims and methods of formation; its doctrinal and practical aspects.

"**IV. Communion in Life and Spiritual Activity among the Baptized.** The communion that exists with other Christians on the basis of the sacramental bond of baptism, and the norms for sharing in prayer and other spiritual activities, including, in particular cases, sacramental sharing.

"**V. Ecumenical Cooperation, Dialogue and Common Witness.** Principles, different forms and norms for cooperation between Christians with a view to dialogue and common witness in the world."

ECUMENICAL AGENCIES

Pontifical Council

The top-level agency for Catholic ecumenical efforts is the Pontifical Council for Promoting Christian Unity (formerly the Secretariat for Promoting Christian Unity), which originated in 1960 as a preparatory commission for the Second Vatican Council. Its purposes are to provide guidance and, where necessary, coordination for ecumenical endeavor by Catholics, and to establish and maintain relations with representatives of other Christian Churches for ecumenical dialogue and action.

The council, under the direction of Cardinal Edward I. Cassidy (successor to Cardinal Johannes Willebrands), has established firm working relations with representative agencies of other churches and the World Council of Churches. It has joined in dialogue with Orthodox Churches, the Anglican Communion, the Lutheran World Federation, the World Alliance of Reformed Churches, the World Methodist Council and other religious bodies. In the past several years, staff members and representatives of the council have been involved in one way or another in nearly every significant ecumenical enterprise and meeting held throughout the world.

While the council and its counterparts in other churches have focused primary attention on theological and other related problems of Christian unity, they have also begun, and in increasing measure, to emphasize the responsibilities of the churches for greater unity of witness and effort in areas of humanitarian need.

Bishops' Committee

The U.S. Bishops' Committee for Ecumenical and Interreligious Affairs was established by the American hierarchy in 1964. Its purposes are to maintain relationships with other Christian churches and other religious communities at the national level, to advise and assist dioceses in developing and applying ecumenical policies, and to maintain liaison with corresponding Vatican offices — the Councils for Christian Unity and for Interreligious Dialogue.

This standing committee of the National Conference of Catholic Bishops is chaired by Bishop Alexander J. Brunett of Helena. Operationally, the committee is assisted by a secretariat with the Rev. John F. Hotchkin, director; Dr. Eugene J. Fisher, executive secretary for Catholic-Jewish Relations; Dr. John Borelli, Jr., executive secretary for Interreligious Relations, the Rev. Ronald Roberson, C.S.P., and Brother Jeffrey Gros, associate directors.

The committee co-sponsors several national consultations with other churches and confessional families. These bring together Catholic representatives and their counterparts from the Episcopal Church, the Lutheran Church, the Polish National Catholic Church, the United Methodist Church, the Orthodox Churches, the Oriental Orthodox Churches, the Alliance of Reformed Churches (North American area), the Interfaith Witness Department of the Home Mission Board of the Southern Baptist Convention. (See Ecumenical Dialogues.)

The committee relates with the National Council of Churches of Christ, through membership in the Faith and Order Commission and through observer relationship with the Commission on Regional and Local Ecumenism, and has sponsored a joint study committee investigating the possibility of Roman Catholic membership in that body.

Advisory and other services are provided by the committee to ecumenical commissions and agencies in dioceses throughout the country.

Through its Section for Catholic-Jewish Relations, the committee is in contact with several national Jewish agencies and bodies. Issues of mutual interest and shared concern are reviewed for the purpose of furthering deeper understanding between the Catholic and Jewish communities.

Through its Section for Interreligious Relations, the committee promotes activity in wider areas of dialogue with other religions, notably, with Muslims, Buddhists and Hindus.

Offices of the committee are located at 3211 Fourth St. N.E., Washington, D.C. 20017.

World Council

The World Council of Churches is a fellowship of churches which acknowledge "Jesus Christ as Lord and Savior." It is a permanent organization providing constituent members — 330 churches with some 450 million communicants in 100 countries — with opportunities for meeting, consultation and cooperative action with respect to doctrine, worship, practice, social mission, evangelism and missionary work, and other matters of mutual concern.

The WCC was formally established Aug. 23, 1948, in Amsterdam with ratification of a constitution by 147 communions. This action merged two previously existing movements — Life and Work (social mission), Faith and Order (doctrine) — which had initiated practical steps toward founding a fellowship of Christian churches at meetings held in Oxford, Edinburgh and Utrecht in 1937 and 1938. A third movement for cooperative missionary work, which originated about 1910 and, remotely, led to formation of the WCC, was incorporated into the council in 1971 under the title of the International Missionary Council (now the Commission for World Mission and Evangelism).

Additional general assemblies of the council have been held since the charter meeting of 1948: in Evanston, Ill. (1954), New Delhi, India (1961), Uppsala, Sweden (1968), Nairobi, Kenya (1975), Vancouver, British Columbia, Canada (1983) and Canberra, Australia (1991). The 1998 general assembly is scheduled to be held in Harare, Zimbabwe.

The council continues the work of the International Missionary Council, the Commission on Faith and Order, and the Commission on Church and Society. The work of the council is carried out through four program units: unity and renewal; mission, education and witness; justice, peace and creation; sharing and service.

Liaison between the council and the Vatican has been maintained since 1966 through a joint working group. Roman Catholic membership in the WCC is a question officially on the agenda of this body. The Joint Commission on Society, Development and

Peace (SODEPAX) was an agency of the council and the Pontifical Commission for Justice and Peace from 1968 to Dec. 31, 1980, after which another working group was formed. Roman Catholics serve individually as full members of the Commission on Faith and Order and in various capacities on other program committees of the council.

WCC headquarters are located in Geneva, Switzerland. The United States Conference for the World Council of Churches at 475 Riverside Drive, Room 915, New York, N.Y. 10115, provides liaison between the U.S. churches and Geneva, a communications office for secular and church media relations, and a publications office. The WCC also maintains fraternal relations with regional, national and local councils of churches throughout the world.

The Rev. Konrad Raiser, a Lutheran from Germany, was elected general secretary, Aug. 24, 1992.

National Council of Churches

The National Council of the Churches of Christ in the U.S.A., the largest ecumenical body in the United States, is an organization of 33 Protestant, Orthodox and Anglican church bodies with an aggregate membership of about 50 million.

The NCC, established by the churches in 1950, was structured through the merger of 12 separate cooperative agencies. Presently, the NCC carries on work in behalf of member churches in overseas ministries, Christian education, domestic social action, communications, disaster relief, refugee assistance, rehabilitation and development, biblical translation, international affairs, theological dialogue, interfaith activities, worship and evangelism, and other areas.

Policies of the NCC are determined by a general board of approximately 270 members appointed by the constituent churches. The board meets once a year.

NCC presidents: Bishop Melvin Talbert (1996-97), Bishop Craig B. Anderson (1998-99). General secretary: The Rev. Joan Brown Campbell.

NCC headquarters are located at 475 Riverside Drive, New York, N.Y. 10115.

Consultation on Church Union

(Courtesy of Rev. David W.A. Taylor, General Secretary.)

The Consultation on Church Union, officially begun in 1962, is a venture of American churches seeking a united church "truly catholic, truly evangelical, and truly reformed." The churches engaged in this process, representing 25 million Christians, are the African Methodist Episcopal Church, the African Methodist Episcopal Zion Church, the Christian Church (Disciples of Christ), the Christian Methodist Episcopal Church, the Episcopal Church, the Presbyterian Church (U.S.A); the United Church of Christ, the United Methodist Church and the International Council of Community Churches.

At a plenary assembly of COCU in December, 1988, a plan of church unity was unanimously approved for submission to member churches for their action. The plan is contained in a 102-page document entitled "Churches in Covenant Communion: The Church of Christ Uniting." It proposes the formation of a covenant communion of the churches which, while remaining institutionally autonomous, would embrace together eight elements of ecclesial communion: claiming unity in faith, commitment to seek unity with wholeness, mutual recognition of members in one baptism, mutual recognition of each other as churches, mutual recognition and reconciliation of ordained ministries, celebrating the Eucharist together, engaging together in Christ's mission, and the formation together of covenanting councils at each level (national, regional, and local).

Vivian U. Robinson, Ph.D., a lay member of the Christian Methodist Episcopal Church, was elected president in 1988. The Rev. Daniell C. Hamby is general secretary. Offices are located at 258 Wall St., Princeton. N.J. 08540.

Graymoor Institute

The Graymoor Ecumenical and Interreligious Institute is a forum where issues that confront the Christian Churches are addressed, the spiritual dimensions of ecumenism are fostered, and information, documentation and developments within the ecumenical movement are published through *Ecumenical Trends*, a monthly journal. Director: The Rev. Elias D. Mallon, S.A. Address: 475 Riverside Dr., Rm. 1960, New York, N.Y. 10115.

INTERNATIONAL BILATERAL COMMISSIONS

Anglican-Roman Catholic International Commission, sponsored by the Pontifical Council for Promoting Christian Unity and the Lambeth Conference, from 1970 to 1981; succeeded by a **Second Anglican-Roman Catholic International Commission,** called into being by the Common Declaration of Pope John Paul and the Archbishop of Canterbury in 1982.

The International Theological Colloquium between Baptists and Catholics, established in 1984 by the Pontifical Council for Promoting Christian Unity and the Commission for Faith and Interchurch Cooperation of the Baptist World Alliance.

The Disciples of Christ-Roman Catholic Dialogue, organized by the Council of Christian Unity of the Christian Church (Disciples of Christ) and the

U.S. Bishops' Committee for Ecumenical and Interreligious Affairs, along with participation by the Disciples' Ecumenical Consultative Council and the Unity Council; since 1977.

The Evangelical-Roman Catholic Dialogue on Mission, organized by Evangelicals and the Pontifical Council for Promoting Christian Unity; from 1977.

The Joint Lutheran-Roman Catholic Study Commission, established by the Pontifical Council for Promoting Christian Unity and the Lutheran World Federation; from 1967.

The International Catholic-Orthodox Theological Commission, established by the Holy See and 14 autocephalous Orthodox Churches, began its work at a first session held at Patmos/Rhodes in 1980. Subsequent sessions have been held at Munich (1982), Crete (1984), Bari (1987), Valamo (1988) and Freising (1990).

Pentecostal-Roman Catholic Conversations, since 1966.

The Reformed-Roman Catholic Conversations, inaugurated in 1970 by the Pontifical Council for Promoting Christian Unity and the World Alliance of Reformed Churches.

U.S. ECUMENICAL DIALOGUES

Representatives of the Bishops' Committee for Ecumenical and Interreligious Affairs, National Conference of Catholic Bishops, have met in dialogue with representatives of other churches since the 1960s, for discussion of a wide variety of subjects related to the quest for unity among Christians. Following is a list of dialogue groups and the years in which dialogue began.

Anglican-Roman Catholic Consultation, 1965; Eastern Orthodox Consultation (Theologians), 1965; Eastern Orthodox and Roman Catholic Bishops, Joint Committee, 1981; Lutheran Consultation, 1965; Oriental Orthodox Consultation (with Armenian, Coptic, Ethiopian, Indian Malabar and Syrian Orthodox Churches), 1978; Polish National-Catholic Consultation, 1984; Presbyterian/Reformed Consultation, 1965; Southern Baptist Conversations, 1969; United Methodist Consultation, 1966.

ECUMENICAL REPORTS

(Source: Rev. John F. Hotchkin, Secretariat of the Bishops' Committee for Ecumenical and Interreligious Affairs, National Conference of Catholic Bishops.)

Common Declarations of Popes, Other Prelates

The following ecumenical statements, issued by several popes and prelates of other Christian churches, carry the authority given them by their signators.

Paul VI and Orthodox Ecumenical Patriarch Athenagoras I, First Common Declaration, Dec. 7, 1965: They hoped the differences between the churches would be overcome with the help of the Holy Spirit, and that their "full communion of faith, brotherly concord and sacramental life" would be restored.

Paul VI and Anglican Archbishop Michael Ramsey of Canterbury, Mar. 24, 1966: They stated their intention "to inaugurate between the Roman Catholic Church and the Anglican Communion a serious dialogue which, founded on the Gospels and on the ancient common traditions, may lead to that unity in truth for which Christ prayed."

Paul VI and Patriarch Athenagoras I, Second Common Declaration, Oct. 27, 1967: They wished "to emphasize their conviction that the restoration of full communion (between the churches) is to be found within the framework of the renewal of the Church and of Christians in fidelity to the traditions of the Fathers and to the inspirations of the Holy Spirit who remains always with the Church."

Paul VI and Vasken I, Orthodox Catholicos-Patriarch of All Armenians, May 12, 1970: They called for closer collaboration "in all domains of Christian life. .. . This collaboration must be based on the mutual recognition of the common Christian faith and the sacramental life, on the mutual respect of persons and their churches."

Paul VI and Mar Ignatius Jacob III, Syrian Orthodox Patriarch of Antioch, Oct. 27, 1971: They declared themselves to be "in agreement that there is no difference in the faith they profess concerning the mystery of the Word of God made flesh and be-

come really man, even if over the centuries difficulties have arisen out of the different theological expressions by which this faith was expressed."

Paul VI and Shenouda III, Coptic Orthodox Pope of Alexandria, May 10, 1973: Their common declaration recalls the common elements of the Catholic and Coptic Orthodox faith in the Trinity, the divinity and humanity of Christ, the seven sacraments, the Virgin Mary, the Church founded upon the Apostles, and the Second Coming of Christ. It recognizes that the two churches "are not able to give more perfect witness to this new life in Christ because of existing divisions which have behind them centuries of difficult history" dating back to the year 451 A.D. In spite of these difficulties, they expressed "determination and confidence in the Lord to achieve the fullness and perfection of that unity which is his gift."

Paul VI and Anglican Archbishop Donald Coggan of Canterbury, Apr. 29, 1977: They stated many points on which Anglicans and Roman Catholics hold the faith in common and called for greater cooperation between Anglicans and Roman Catholics.

John Paul II and Orthodox Ecumenical Patriarch Dimitrios I, First Common Declaration, Nov. 30, 1979: "Purification of the collective memory of our churches is an important fruit of the dialogue of charity and an indispensable condition of future progress." They announced the establishment of the Catholic-Orthodox Theological Commission.

John Paul II and Anglican Archbishop Robert Runcie of Canterbury, May 29, 1982: They agreed to establish a new Anglican-Roman Catholic commission with the task of continuing work already begun toward the eventual resolution of doctrinal differences.

John Paul II and Ignatius Zakka I, Syrian Orthodox Patriarch of Antioch, June 23, 1984: They recalled and solemnly reaffirmed the common profession of faith made by their predecessors, Paul VI and Mar Ignatius Jacob III, in 1971. They said: "The confusions and the schisms that occurred between the churches, they realize today, in no way affect or touch the substance of their faith, since these arose only because of differences in terminology and culture, and in the various formulae adopted by different theological schools to express the same matter. Accordingly, we find today no real basis for the sad divisions which arose between us concerning the doctrine of the Incarnation." On the pastoral level, they declared: "It is not rare for our faithful to find access to a priest of their own church materially or morally impossible. Anxious to meet their needs and with their spiritual benefit in mind, we authorize them in such cases to ask for the sacraments of penance, Eucharist and anointing of the sick from lawful priests of either of our two sister churches, when they need them."

John Paul II and Orthodox Ecumenical Patriarch Dimitrios I, Second Common Declaration, Dec. 7, 1987: Dialogue conducted since 1979 indicated that the churches can already profess together as common faith about the mystery of the Church and the connection between faith and the sacraments. They also stated that, "when unity of faith is assured,

a certain diversity of expressions does not create obstacles to unity, but enriches the life of the Church and the understanding, always imperfect, of the revealed mystery.

John Paul II and Anglican Archbishop Robert Runcie of Canterbury, Oct. 2, 1989: They said: "We solemnly re-commit ourselves and those we represent to the restoration of visible unity and full ecclesial communion in the confidence that to seek anything less would be to betray our Lord's intention for the unity of his people."

John Paul II and His Holiness Mar Dinkha IV, Catholicos-Patriarch of the Assyrian Church of the East, Nov. 11, 1994: They acknowledged that, despite past differences, both churches profess the same faith in the real union of divine and human natures in the divine Person of Christ.

(See Common Declarations of Pope John Paul with Ecumenical Orthdox Patriarch Bartholomew I (1995), Anglican Archbishop George Carey and Karekin I, Catholicos of All Armenians (1997).

INTERFAITH STATEMENTS

The ecumenical statements listed below, and others like them, reflect the views of participants in the dialogues which produced them. They have not been formally accepted by the respective churches as formulations of doctrine or points of departure for practical changes in discipline. (For other titles, see U.S. Ecumenical Dialogues, Ecumenical Reports.)

• The "Windsor Statement" on Eucharistic doctrine, published Dec. 31, 1971, by the Anglican-Roman Catholic International Commission of theologians. (For text, see pages 132-33 of the 1973 Catholic Almanac.)

• The "Canterbury Statement" on ministry and ordination, published Dec. 13, 1973, by the same commission. (For excerpts, see pages 127-30 of the 1975 Catholic Almanac.)

• "Papal Primacy / Converging Viewpoints," published Mar. 4, 1974, by the dialogue group sanctioned by the U.S.A. National Convention of the World Lutheran Federation and the U.S. Bishops' Committee for Ecumenical and Interreligious Affairs. (For excerpts, see pages 130-31 of the 1975 Catholic Almanac.)

• An "Agreed Statement on the Purpose of the Church," published Oct. 31, 1975, by the Anglican-Roman Catholic Consultation in the U.S.

• "Christian Unity and Women's Ordination," published Nov. 7, 1975, by the same consultation, in which it was said that the ordination of women (approved in principle by the Anglican Communion but not by the Catholic Church) would "introduce a new element" in dialogue but would not mean the end of consultation nor the abandonment of its declared goal of full communion and organic unity.

• "Holiness and Spirituality of the Ordained Ministry," issued early in 1976 by theologians of the Catholic Church and the United Methodist Church; the first statement resulting from dialogue begun in 1966.

• "Mixed Marriages," published in the spring of

1976 by the Anglican-Roman Catholic Consultation in the U.S.

• "Bishops and Presbyters," published in July, 1976, by the Orthodox-Roman Catholic Consultation in the U.S. on the following points of common understanding: (1) Ordination in apostolic succession is required for pastoral office in the Church. (2) Presiding at the Eucharistic Celebration is a task belonging to those ordained to pastoral service. (3) The offices of bishop and presbyter are different realizations of the sacrament of order. (4) Those ordained are claimed permanently for the service of the Church.

• "The Principle of Economy," published by the body named above at the same time, concerning God's plan and activities in human history for salvation.

• "Venice Statement" on authority in the Church, published Jan. 20, 1977, by the Anglican-Roman Catholic International Commission of theologians. (For text, see pages 145-50 of the 1978 Catholic Almanac.)

• "Response to the Venice Statement," issued Jan. 4, 1978, by the Anglican-Roman Catholic Consultation in the U.S.A., citing additional questions.

• "An Ecumenical Approach to Marriage," published in January, 1978, by representatives of the Catholic Church, the Lutheran World Federation and the World Alliance of Reformed Churches.

• "Teaching Authority and Infallibility in the Church," released in October, 1978, by the Catholic-Lutheran dialogue group in the U.S.

• "The Eucharist," reported early in 1979, in which the Roman Catholic-Lutheran Commission indicated developing convergence of views.

• "The Holy Spirit," issued Feb. 12, 1979, by the International Catholic-Methodist Commission.

• A statement on "Ministry in the Church," published in March, 1981, by the International Roman Catholic-Lutheran Joint Commission, regarding possible mutual recognition of ministries.

• The Final Report of the Anglican-Roman Catho-

lic International Commission, 1982, on the results of 12 years of dialogue. (See separate entry.)
• "Justification by Faith," issued Sept. 30, 1983, by the U.S. Lutheran-Roman Catholic dialogue group, claiming a "fundamental consensus on the Gospel."
• "Images of God: Reflections on Christian Anthropology," released Dec. 22, 1983, by the Anglican-Roman Catholic Dialogue in the United States.
• "The Journeying Together in Christ — The Report of the Polish National Catholic-Roman Catholic Dialogue (1984-89)."
• "Salvation and the Church," issued Jan. 22, 1987,

by the Second Anglican-Roman Catholic International Commission.
• "Faith, Sacraments and the Unity of the Church," issued by the Mixed International Commission for Theological Dialogue between the Catholic Church and the Orthodox Churches in June, 1987.
• "The Presence of Christ in Church and World" and "Toward a Common Understanding of the Church" (developed between 1984 and 1990), by the Reformed-Roman Catholic Conversations, under the auspices of the Pontifical Council for Promoting Christian Unity and the World Alliance of Reformed Churches.

ANGLICAN-ROMAN CATHOLIC FINAL REPORT

The Anglican-Roman Catholic International Commission issued a Final Report in 1982 on 12 years of dialogue on major issues of concern, especially the Eucharist and ordained ministry.

In 1988 the Lambeth Conference called parts of the report on these two subjects "consonant in substance with the faith of Anglicans." In 1991 the Congregation for the Doctrine of the Faith and the Pontifical Council for Promoting Christian Unity called the Report a significant milestone not only in relations between the Catholic Church and the Anglican Communion but in the ecumenical movement as a whole. They said, however, that it was not yet possible to state that substantial agreement had been reached on all the questions studied by the commission, and that important differences still remained with respect to essential matters of Catholic doctrine regarding the Eucharist, ordination and other subjects. Clarifications were asked for.

The Anglican-Roman Catholic Commission II responded in 1994, saying that its members were in agreement regarding:
• the substantial and sacramental presence of Christ in the Eucharist;
• the propitiatory nature of the Eucharistic Sacrifice, which can also be applied to the deceased;
• institution of the sacrament of order from Christ;
• the character of priestly ordination, implying configuration to the priesthood of Christ.

The clarifications have been under study at the Vatican since the summer of 1994, according to a letter addressed to the Catholic and Anglican co-chairmen of the commission by Cardinal Edward I. Cassidy, president of the Pontifical Council for Interreligious Dialogue. Questions still remained to be answered about a number of subjects, including the Eucharist, authority in the Church, infallibility and Marian doctrine.

THE QUESTION OF AUTHORITY

Authority is a key subject of interest and concern in the quest for unity among churches. Cases in point are the official Catholic-Orthodox and Catholic-Anglican dialogues.

On the eve of the annual Week of Prayer for Christian Unity in January, 1996, Pope John Paul told a general audience that there is substantial agreement between Catholics and Orthodox on most of the essential matters of faith and church life, including the sacraments. But, the key historical obstacle is the primacy of the bishop of Rome. That is why, in his 1995 encyclical letter *Ut Unum Sint* he "encouraged everyone to research, obviously together, the forms under which this ministry — that is, the bishop of Rome's ministry of unity — could perform a service of love recognized by both" Catholics and Orthodox.

Since 1994, the Anglican-Roman Catholic International Commission has been examining:
• the relationship of "the exercise of authority in the church to Scripture and tradition";
• ways in which the exercise of authority serves members' commitment to Christ;
• how authority promotes "the communion in faithfulness of all the churches."

Authority and unity within the Anglican Communion have been compromised by the ordination of women to the priesthood, according to an article written by an official of the Pontifical Council for Promoting Christian Unity.

Father Timothy Galligan said in an article published in January, 1996: "The question of the interrelationship of communion, authority and disagreement in the (Anglican) church has become a matter of considerable controversy among some Anglicans as the ordination of women becomes part of the life of Anglican communities in many parts of the world."

Not only are some Anglicans arguing about the authority the church has to ordain women, but also about the relationship among Anglican bishops who disagree on the issue and between bishops and Anglicans who disagree.

Women have been ordained priests in at least 15 Anglican provinces, about half of the world total.

In an effort to cope with the situation, the Church of England has appointed special bishops for parishes and clergy who do not accept women priests nor the bishops who ordained them.

"Such solutions," said Father Galligan, highlight the reality of diminished communion, with some clergy and lay people no longer prepared to accept the sacramental ministry of their diocesan bishop and some of his clergy.... That one fundamental expression of full ecclesial communion, namely a universally accepted ministry, is absent."

ECUMENICAL SETBACKS

(By John Thavis, CNS correspondent, June 27, 1997.)

Three years ago, Pope John Paul set the year 2000 as a target date for Christian cooperation, urging churches to put aside historic divisions and take some giant steps toward unity.

But in mid-1997, the Pope and other leaders were mulling over a series of new setbacks, and the hands of the ecumenical clock suddenly seemed stuck.

One of the biggest disappointments was the refusal — for the second time in a year — by Russian Orthodox Patriarch Alexei II to meet the Pontiff, in what would have been an unprecedented gesture of reconciliation. The Orthodox cited continuing difficulties over "proselytism" and the role of Eastern Catholics in their territrory.

The Patriarch's rebuff left Vatican officials shaking their heads in discouragement, and wondering what further assurances they could offer the Orthodox that the Church has no designs on their faithful.

One side effect of the effort to bring the Pope and Russian Patriarch together was that it upset another Orthodox leader, Ecumenical Patriarch Bartholomew I of Constantinople, who abruptly decided to boycott the Second European Ecumenical Assembly in Graz, Austria.

This was seen by several Rome observers as proof that worsening inter-Orthodox struggles —particularly between Moscow and Constantinople — would inevitably make Catholic-Orthodox dialogue more problematic.

A Second Cancelation

The situation took another bad turn in late June when the Ecumenical Patriarchate canceled its participation in the Vatican celebration of the feast of Sts. Peter and Paul, for the first time since the two churches began exchanging annual delegations in 1977.

An added blast came from the East when the Russian lower house of Parliament advanced a law that would, in effect, make Catholicism a second-class religion. It named Orthodox Christianity, Islam, Buddhism and Judaism as native Russian faiths, grouping Catholics with other outside sects.

Catholic officials voiced alarm at the legislation, and Vatican Secretary of State Cardinal Angelo Sodano said June 24 he hoped Russian President Boris Yeltsin would refuse to sign the bill, which was supported by the Orthodox Church.

The new sense of ecumenical frustration was evident in the words of Pope John Paul, who, although encouraging progress at the Graz assembly, said bluntly that "unexpected new disturbances are arising, new apprehensions are being born and unconscious fears are spreading."

To many, that seemed to sum up the current ecumenical atmosphere.

The problems with Orthodox were not just limited to Russia and Eastern Europe. In meetings in June with Egypt's bishops, the Pope got an earful about worsening tensions in that country with the Orthodox, who greatly outnumber Catholics and who resent the Church's pastoral expansion.

"They see us as rivals. They see a Catholic priest or parish established in an area that has few Catholics and they immediately mistrust us," said one prelate.

"This has to change. We Christians are experiencing scandalous divisions, and this is creating a very bad impression among the Muslim majority," he said.

On other fronts, too, ecumenical dialogue had visibly slowed.

Anglican, Lutheran Angles

A recent article in an authoritative Jesuit journal (*La Civilta Cattolica,* early April), for example, said the era of hope for Catholic recognition of Anglican priesthood and eventual shared communion, had now passed. It cited a number of new obstacles, including Anglican ordination of women to the priesthood.

In the Catholic dialogue with Lutherans, meanwhile, a long-sought agreed statement on justification planned for this year had been delayed at least until the end of 1998.

In this context, the recent publication of a contentious book on ecumenism may have been a sign of the times. The volume, *The Fifth Seal: Christian Unity toward the Third Millennium,* by Father Nicola Bux, was critical of many of the basic ecumenical approaches used by Catholic and other church leaders over the last 30 years.

Such criticism was not unusual in various corners of the Church. But this book was published by the Vatican's own publishing house, and was presented at a press conference by Cardinal Joseph Ratzinger, the Vatican's chief doctrinal official and a man with the Pope's ear.

Vatican ecumenical officials have always said that progress toward Christian unity may suffer slowdowns and obstacles, but that the overall direction remains unchanged. And beyond the recent headline-grabbing disappointments, the dialogues with all the churches have continued — an important fact that risks being overshadowed.

But, for Pope John Paul, who feels a special end-of-millennium urgency, the ecumenical picture is unsettling. Just last year, speaking at the June 29 Mass for Sts. Peter and Paul, he told the Orthodox delegation that he felt a "personal call from the Lord" to work for the unity of their churches.

This year, the Orthodox chairs will be empty.

JUDAISM

Judaism is the religion of the Hebrew Bible and of contemporary Jews. Divinely revealed and with a patriarchal background (Abraham, Isaac, Jacob), it originated with the Mosaic Covenant, was identified with the Israelites, and achieved distinctive form and character as the religion of the Torah (Law, "The Teaching") from this Covenant and reforms initiated by Ezra and Nehemiah after the Babylonian Exile.

Judaism does not have a formal creed but its principal points of belief are clear. Basic is belief in one transcendent God who reveals himself through the Torah, the prophets, the life of his people and events of history. The fatherhood of God involves the brotherhood of all humanity. Religious faith and practice are equated with just living according to God's Law. Moral conviction and practice are regarded as more important than precise doctrinal formulation and profession. Formal worship, whose principal act was sacrifice from the Exodus times to 70 A.D., is by prayer, reading and meditating upon the sacred writings, and observance of the Sabbath and festivals.

Judaism has messianic expectations of the complete fulfillment of the Covenant, the coming of God's kingdom, the ingathering of his people, and final judgment and retribution for all. Views differ regarding the manner in which these expectations will be realized — through a person, the community of God's people, an evolution of historical events, an eschatological act of God himself. Individual salvation expectations also differ, depending on views about the nature of immortality, punishment and reward, and related matters.

Sacred Books

The sacred books are the 24 books of the Masoretic Hebrew Text of The Law, the Prophets and the Writings (see The Bible). Together, they contain the basic instruction or norms for just living. In some contexts, the term Law or Torah refers only to the Pentateuch (Genesis, Exodus, Leviticus, Numbers, Deuteronomy); in others, it denotes all the sacred books and/or the whole complex of written and oral tradition.

Also of great authority are two Talmuds which were composed in Palestine and Babylon in the fourth and fifth centuries A.D., respectively. They consist of the Mishna, a compilation of oral laws, and the Gemara, a collection of rabbinical commentary on the Mishna. Midrash are collections of scriptural comments and moral counsels.

Priests were the principal religious leaders during the period of sacrificial and temple worship. Rabbis were originally teachers; today they share with cantors the function of leaders of prayer. The synagogue is the place of community worship. The family and home are focal points of many aspects of Jewish worship and practice.

Of the various categories of Jews, Orthodox are the most conservative in adherence to strict religious traditions. Others — Reformed, Conservative, Reconstructionist — are liberal in comparison with the Orthodox. They favor greater or less modification of religious practices in accommodation to contemporary culture and living conditions.

Principal events in Jewish life include the circumcision of males, according to prescriptions of the Covenant; the bar and bat mitzvah which marks the coming-of-age of boys and girls in Judaism at the age of 13; marriage; and observance of the Sabbath and festivals.

Observances of the Sabbath and festivals begin at sundown of the previous calendar day and continue until the following sundown.

Sabbath: Saturday, the weekly day of rest prescribed in the Decalogue.

Sukkoth (Tabernacles): A seven-to-nine-day festival in the month of Tishri (Sept.-Oct.), marked by some Jews with Covenant-renewal and reading of The Law. It originated as an agricultural feast at the end of the harvest and got its name from the temporary shelters used by workers in the fields.

Hanukkah (The Festival of Lights, the Feast of Consecration and of the Maccabees): Commemorates the dedication of the new altar in the Temple at Jerusalem by Judas Maccabeus in 165 B.C. The eight-day festival, during which candles in an eight-branch candelabra are lighted in succession, one each day, occurs near the winter solstice, close to Christmas time.

Pesach (Passover): A seven-day festival commemorating the liberation of the Israelites from Egypt. The narrative of the Exodus, the Haggadah, is read at ceremonial Seder meals on the first and second days of the festival, which begins on the 14th day of Nisan (Mar.-Apr.).

Shavuoth, Pentecost (Feast of Weeks): Observed 50 days after Passover, commemorating the anniversary of the revelation of the Law to Moses.

Purim: A joyous festival observed on the 14th day of Adar (Feb.-Mar.), commemorating the rescue of the Israelites from massacre by the Persians through the intervention of Esther. The festival is preceded by a day of fasting. A gift- and alms-giving custom became associated with it in medieval times.

Rosh Hashana (Feast of Trumpets, New Year): Observed on the first day of Tishri (Sept.-Oct.), the festival focuses attention on the ways of life and the ways of death. It is second in importance only to the most solemn observance of Yom Kippur, which is celebrated 10 days later.

Yom Kippur (Day of Atonement): The highest holy day, observed with strict fasting. It occurs 10 days after Rosh Hashana.

Yom HaShoah (Holocaust Memorial Day): Observed in the week after Passover; increasingly observed with joint Christian-Jewish services of remembrance.

CATHOLIC-JEWISH RELATIONS

The Second Vatican Council, in addition to the *Decree on Ecumenism* concerning the movement for unity among Christians, stated the mind of the Church on a similar matter in a Declaration on the Relationship of the Church to Non-Christian Religions. This document, as the following excerpts indicate, backgrounds the reasons and directions of the Church's regard for the Jews. (Other portions of

the document refer to Hindus, Buddhists and Muslims.)

Spiritual Bond

As this sacred Synod searches into the mystery of the Church, it recalls the spiritual bond linking the people of the New Covenant with Abraham's stock. For the Church of Christ acknowledges that, according to the mystery of God's saving design, the beginnings of her faith and her election are already found among the patriarchs, Moses, and the prophets. She professes that all who believe in Christ, Abraham's sons according to faith (cf. Gal. 3:7), are included in the same patriarch's call, and likewise that the salvation of the Church was mystically foreshadowed by the Chosen People's exodus from the land of bondage.

The Church, therefore, cannot forget that she received the revelation of the Old Testament through the people with whom God in his inexpressible mercy deigned to establish the Ancient Covenant. Nor can she forget that she draws sustenance from the root of that good olive tree onto which have been grafted the wild olive branches of the Gentiles (cf. Rom. 11:17-24). Indeed, the Church believes that by his cross Christ, our Peace, reconciled Jew and Gentile, making them both one in himself (cf. Eph. 2:14-16).

The Jews still remain most dear to God because of their fathers, for he does not repent of the gifts he makes nor of the calls he issues (cf. Rom. 11:28-29). In company with the prophets and the same Apostle (Paul), the Church awaits that day, known to God alone, on which all peoples will address the Lord in a single voice and "serve him with one accord" (Zeph. 3:9; cf. Is. 66:23; Ps. 65:4; Rom. 11:11-32). Since the spiritual patrimony common to Christians and Jews is thus so great, this sacred Synod wishes to foster and recommend that mutual understanding and respect which is the fruit above all of biblical and theological studies, and of brotherly dialogues.

No Anti-Semitism

True, authorities of the Jews and those who followed their lead pressed for the death of Christ (cf. Jn. 19:6); still, what happened in his passion cannot be blamed upon all the Jews then living, without distinction, nor upon the Jews of today. Although the Church is the new People of God, the Jews should not be presented as repudiated or cursed by God, as if such views followed from the holy Scriptures. All should take pains, then, lest in catechetical instruction and in the preaching of God's Word they teach anything out of harmony with the truth of the Gospel and the spirit of Christ.

The Church repudiates all persecutions against any person. Moreover, mindful of her common patrimony with the Jews, and motivated by the Gospel's spiritual love and by no political considerations, she deplores the hatred, persecutions, and displays of anti-Semitism directed against the Jews at any time and from any source (No. 4).

The Church rejects, as foreign to the mind of Christ, any discrimination against men or harassment of them because of their race, color, condition of life, or religion (No. 5).

Bishops' Secretariat

The American hierarchy's first move toward implementation of the Vatican II *Declaration on the Relationship of the Church to Non-Christian Religions (Nostra Aetate)* was to establish, in 1965, a Subcommission for Catholic-Jewish Relations in the framework of its Commission for Ecumenical and Inter-religious Affairs. Its moderator is Cardinal William H. Keeler of Baltimore. The Secretariat for Ecumenical and Interreligious Relations is located at 3211 Fourth St. N.E., Washington, D.C. 20017. Its Catholic-Jewish efforts are directed by Dr. Eugene J. Fisher.

According to the key norm of a set of guidelines issued by the secretariat Mar. 16, 1967, and updated Apr. 9, 1985: "The general aim of all Catholic-Jewish meetings (and relations) is to increase our understanding both of Judaism and the Catholic faith, to eliminate sources of tension and misunderstanding, to initiate dialogue or conversations on different levels, to multiply intergroup meetings between Catholics and Jews, and to promote cooperative social action."

Vatican Guidelines

In a document issued Jan. 3, 1975, the Vatican Commission for Religious Relations with the Jews offered a number of suggestions and guidelines for implementing the Christian-Jewish portion of the Second Vatican Council's *Declaration on Relations with Non-Christian Religions*.

Among "suggestions from experience" were those concerning dialogue, liturgical links between Christian and Jewish worship, the interpretation of biblical texts, teaching and education for the purpose of increasing mutual understanding, and joint social action.

Notes on Preaching and Catechesis

On June 24, 1985, the Vatican Commission for Religious Relations with the Jews promulgated its "Notes on the Correct Way to Present Jews and Judaism in Preaching and Catechesis in the Roman Catholic Church," with the intent of providing "a helpful frame of reference for those who are called upon in the course of their teaching assignments to speak about Jews and Judaism and who wish to do so in keeping with the current teaching of the Church in this area."

The document states emphatically that, since the relationship between the Church and the Jewish people is one "founded on the design of the God of the Covenant," Judaism does not occupy "an occasional and marginal place in catechesis," but an "essential" one that "should be organically integrated" throughout the curriculum on all levels of Catholic education.

The Notes discuss the relationship between the Hebrew Scriptures and the New Testament, focusing especially on typology, which is called "the sign of a problem unresolved." Underlined is the "eschatological dimension," that "the people of God of the Old and the New Testament are tending toward a like end in the future: the coming or return of the Messiah." Jewish witness to God's Kingdom, the Notes declare, challenges Christians to "accept our responsibility to prepare the world for the coming of the Messiah by working together for social justice and reconciliation."

The Notes emphasize the Jewishness of Jesus' teaching, correct misunderstandings concerning the portrayal of Jews in the New Testament and describe the Jewish origins of Christian liturgy. One section addresses the "spiritual fecundity" of Judaism to the present, its continuing "witness — often heroic — of its fidelity to the one God," and mandates the development of Holocaust curricula and a positive approach in Catholic education to the "religious attachment which finds its roots in biblical tradition" between the Jewish people and the Land of Israel, affirming the "existence of the State of Israel" on the basis of "the common principles of international law."

Papal Statements

(Courtesy of Dr. Eugene Fisher, associate director of the Bishops' Committee for Ecumenical and Interreligious Affairs.)

Pope John Paul, in a remarkable series of addresses beginning in 1979, has sought to promote and give shape to the development of dialogue between Catholics and Jews.

In a homily delivered June 7, 1979, at Auschwitz, which he called the "Golgotha of the Modern World," he prayed movingly for "the memory of the people whose sons and daughters were intended for total extermination."

In a key address delivered Nov. 17, 1980, to the Jewish community in Mainz, the Pope articulated his vision of the three "dimensions" of the dialogue: (1) "the meeting between the people of God of the Old Covenant and the people of the New Covenant"; (2) the encounter of "mutual esteem between today's Christian churches and today's people of the Covenant concluded with Moses"; (3) the "holy duty" of witnessing to the one God in the world and "jointly to work for peace and justice."

On Mar. 22, 1984, at an audience with members of the Anti-Defamation League of B'nai B'rith, the Pope commented on "the mysterious spiritual link which brings us close together, in Abraham and through Abraham, in God who chose Israel and brought forth the Church from Israel." He urged joint social action on "the great task of promoting justice and peace."

In receiving a delegation of the American Jewish Committee Feb. 14, 1985, the Holy Father confirmed that *Nostra Aetate* "remains always for us a teaching which is necessary to accept not merely as something fitting, but much more as an expression of the faith, as an inspiration of the Holy Spirit, as a word of the divine wisdom."

During his historic visit to the Great Synagogue in Rome Apr. 13, 1986, the Holy Father affirmed that God's covenant with the Jewish people is "irrevocable," and stated: "The Jewish religion is not 'extrinsic' to us, but in a certain way is 'intrinsic' to our own religion. With Judaism, therefore, we have a relationship which we do not have with any other religion."

Meeting with the Jewish community in Sydney, Australia, Nov. 26, 1986, the Holy Father termed the 20th century "the century of the Shoah" (Holocaust) and called "sinful" any "acts of discrimination or persecution against Jews."

On June 14, 1987, meeting with the Jewish community of Warsaw, the Pope called the Jewish witness to the Shoah (Holocaust) a "saving warning before all of humanity" which reveals "your particular vocation, showing you (Jews) to be still the heirs of that election to which God is faithful."

A collection of Pope John Paul's addresses, *On Jews and Judaism* 1979-1986, prepared by the NCCB Secretariat was sent to the Pope Aug. 12, 1987. In a response of Aug. 17, the Pope reiterated his Warsaw statement and added: "Before the vivid memory of the extermination (Shoah), it is not permissible for anyone to pass by with indifference. The sufferings endured by the Jews are also for the Catholic Church a motive of sincere sorrow, especially when one thinks of the indifference and sometimes resentment which have divided Jews and Christians."

In 1995, an updated edition of the collection of papal texts entitled *Spiritual Pilgrimage* won the National Jewish Book Award and became the third best-selling "Jewish" book, according to the Jewish Book News.

Meeting with Jewish leaders Sept. 11, 1987, in Miami, the Pope praised the efforts in theological dialogue and educational reform implemented in the U.S. since the Second Vatican Council; affirmed the existence of the State of Israel "according to international law," and urged "common educational programs on the Holocaust so that never again will such a horror be possible. Never again!"

In an apostolic letter on the 50th anniversary of World War II (Aug. 27, 1989), the Pope stressed the uniqueness of the Jewish sufferings of the Shoah, "which will forever remain a shame for humanity."

On Aug. 14, 1991, during a visit to his home town of Wadowice, Poland, the Pope recalled with sadness the deaths of his Jewish classmates at the hands of the Nazis during World War II: "In the school of Wadowice there were Jewish believers who are no longer with us. There is no longer a synagogue near the school. It is true that your people (the Jews) were on the front lines. The Polish Pope has a special relationship to that period because, together with you, we lived through all that in our Fatherland."

On Apr. 7, 1994, the eve of *Yom HaShoah,* the Jewish day of prayer commemorating the victims of the Holocaust, Pope John Paul II hosted a memorial concert at the Vatican. It was, he noted, a moment of "common meditation and shared prayer," as the *Kaddish,* the prayer for the dead, and the *Kol Nidre,* the prayer for forgiveness and atonement, were recited.

Speaking Apr. 10, 1997, to Aharon Lopez, Israel's second ambassador to the Holy See, the Pope said: "The Catholic Church as a whole is committed to cooperating with the State of Israel in combatting all forms of anti-Semitism, racism and religious intolerance, and in promoting mutual understanding and respect for human life and dignity. There can be no question that in these areas more can and must be done. It is precisely such renewed efforts that will give to the Great Jubilee of the Year 2000 a truly universal significance, not limited to Catholics or Christians but embracing every prt of the world."

The Pope addressed members of the Pontifical Biblical Commission Apr. 11, 1997, saying: "Jesus' human identity is determined on the basis of his bond with the people of Israel, with the dynasty of David and his descent from Abraham. This does not mean only a physical belonging. By taking part in the synagogue celebrations where the Old Testament texts were read and commented on, Jesus nourished his mind and heart with them. .... From her origins, the Church has well understood that the Incarnation is rooted in history and, consequently, she has fully accepted Christ's insertion into the history of the people of Israel. She has regarded the Hebrew Scriptures as the perennially valid word of God addressed to her as well as to the children of Israel. It is of primary importance to preserve and renew this ecclesial awareness."

To the Jewish people of Sarajevo on Apr. 13, 1997, the Pope declared: "The great spiritual patrimony which unites us in the divine word proclaimed in the Law and the Prophets is for all of us a constant and sure guide. ... We (together are) the witnesses of the Ten Commandments. ... Let us therefore go forward courageously as true brothers and heirs of the promises on the path of reconciliation and mutual forgiveness. This is the will of God."

International Liaison Committee

The International Catholic-Jewish Liaison Committee was formed in 1971 and is the official link between the Commission for Religious Relations with the Jewish People and the International Jewish Committee for Interreligious Consultations. The committee meets every 18 months to examine matters of common interest.

Topics under discussion have included: mission and witness (Venice, 1977), religious education (Madrid, 1978), religious liberty and pluralism (Regensburg, 1979), religious commitment (London, 1981), the sanctity of human life in an age of violence (Milan, 1982), youth and faith (Amsterdam, 1984), the Vatican Notes on Preaching and Catechesis (Rome, 1985), the Holocaust (Prague, 1990), education and social action (Baltimore, Md., 1992), family and ecology (Jerusalem, 1994).

Pope John Paul, addressing in Rome a celebration of *Nostra Aetate* (the Second Vatican Council's "Declaration on the Relationship of the Church to Non-Christian Religions") by the Liaison Committee, stated: "What you are celebrating is nothing other than the divine mercy which is guiding Christians and Jews to mutual awareness, respect, cooperation and solidarity. The universal openness of *Nostra Aetate* is anchored in and takes its orientation from a high sense of the absolute singularity of God's choice of a particular people. The Church is fully aware that Sacred Scripture bears witness that the Jewish people, this community of faith and custodian of a tradition thousands of years old, is an intimate part of the mystery of revelation and of salvation."

Family Rights and Obligations

The Liaison Committee, at its May, 1994, meeting in Jerusalem, issued its first joint statement, on the family — in anticipation of the UN Cairo Conference subsequently held in September.

The statement affirmed that "the rights and obligations of the family do not come from the State but exist prior to the State and ultimately have their source in God the Creator. The family is far more than a legal, social or economic unit. For both Jews and Christians, it is a stable community of love and solidarity based on God's covenant."

Vatican-Israel Accord

On Dec. 30, 1993, a year of dramatic developments in the Middle East was capped by the signing in Jerusalem of a "Fundamental Agreement" between representatives of the Holy See and the State of Israel. The agreement acknowledged in its preamble that the signers were "aware of the unique nature of the relationship between the Catholic Church and the Jewish people, and of the historic process of reconciliation and growth in mutual understanding and friendship between Catholics and Jews." Archbishop William H. Keeler, president of the National Conference of Catholic Bishops, welcomed the accord together with the Israeli Ambassador to the United States at a ceremony at the NCCB headquarters in Washington.

In 1996, the Anti-Defamation League published a set of documents related to the accord, entitled *A Challenge Long Delayed,* edited by Eugene Fisher and Rabbi Klenicki.

U.S. Dialogue

The National Workshop on Christian-Jewish Relations, begun in 1973 by the NCCB Secretariat, draws more than 1,000 participants from around the world. Recent workshops have been held in Baltimore (1986), Minneapolis (1987), Charleston, S.C (1989), Chicago (1990), Pittsburgh (1992), Tulsa (1994) and Stamford (1996).

In October, 1987, the Bishops' Committee for Ecumenical and Interreligious Affairs began a series of twice-yearly consultations with representatives of the Synagogue Council of America. Topics of discussion have included education, human rights, respect for life, the Middle East. The consultation has issued three joint statements: "On Moral Values in Public Education" (1990), "On Stemming the Proliferation of Pornography" (1993) and "On Dealing with Holocaust Revisionism" (1994).

Ongoing relationships are maintained by the NCCB Secretariat with such Jewish agencies as the American Jewish Committee, the Anti-Defamation League of B'nai B'rith, the Union of American Hebrew Congregations, the American Jewish Congress and the National Jewish Community Relations Council.

In June, 1988, the Bishops' Committee for Ecumenical and Interreligious Affairs published in Spanish and English Criteria for the Evaluation of Dramatizations of the Passion, providing for the first time Catholic guidelines for passion plays.

In January, 1989, the Bishops' Committee for the Liturgy issued guidelines for the homiletic presentation of Judaism under the title, "God's Mercy Endures Forever."

When the Synagogue Council of America dissolved in 1995, the Bishops' Committee for Ecumenical and Interreligious Affairs initiated separate consultations with the new National Council of Synagogues (Reform and Conservative), chaired by Cardinal William H. Keeler, and the Orthodox Union/Rabbinical Council, chaired by Cardinal John J. O'Connor. The former consultation was occupied with issues of how the two communities might jointly celebrate the Millennium/Jubilee Year 2000; the latter was working on issues relating to aid for private education.

ISLAM

(Courtesy of Dr. John Borelli, executive secretary for Interreligious Relations, NCCB.)

Islam, meaning grateful surrender (to God), originated with Muhammad and the revelation he is believed to have received. Muslims acknowledge that this revelation, recorded in the Quran, is from the one God and do not view Islam as a new religion. They profess that Muhammad was the last in a long series of prophets, most of whom are named in the Hebrew Bible and the New Testament, beginning with Adam and continuing through Noah, Abraham, Moses, Jesus and down to Muhammad.

Muslims believe in the one God, Allah in Arabic, and cognate with the Hebrew Elohim and the ancient Aramaic Elah. According to the Quran, God is one and transcendent, Creator and Sustainer of the universe, all-merciful and all-compassionate Ruler and Judge. God possesses numerous other titles, known collectively as the 99 names of God. The profession of faith states: "There is no god but the God and Muhammad is the messenger of God."

The essential duties of Muslims are to: witness the faith by daily recitation of the profession of faith; worship five times a day facing in the direction of the holy city of Mecca; give alms; fast daily from dawn to dusk during the month of Ramadan; make a pilgrimage to Mecca once if possible.

Muslims believe in final judgment, heaven and hell. Morality and following divinely revealed moral norms are extremely important to Muslims. Some dietary regulations are in effect. On Fridays, the noon prayer is a congregational (juma) prayer which should be said in a mosque. The general themes of prayer are adoration and thanksgiving. Muslims do not have an ordained ministry.

The basis of Islamic belief is the Quran, the created word of God revealed to Muhammad through the angel Gabriel over a period of 23 years. The contents of this sacred book are complemented by the Sunna, a collection of sacred traditions from the life of the prophet Muhammad, and reinforced by Ijma, the consensus of Islamic scholars of Islamic Law (Shariah) which guarantees them against errors in matters of belief and practice.

Conciliar Statement

The attitude of the Church toward Islam was stated as follows in the Second Vatican Council's *Declaration on the Relation of the Church to Non-Christian Religions* (No. 3).

"The Church has a high regard for the Muslims. They worship God, who is one, living and subsistent, merciful and almighty, the Creator of heaven and earth, who has also spoken to men. They strive to submit themselves without reserve to the hidden decrees of God, just as Abraham submitted himself to God's plan, to whose faith Muslims eagerly link their own. Although not acknowledging him as God, they venerate Jesus as a prophet, his virgin Mother they also honor, and even at times devoutly invoke. Further, they await the day of judgment and the reward of God following the resurrection of the dead, For this reason, they highly esteem an upright life and worship God, especially by way of prayer, alms-deeds and fasting.

"Over the centuries many quarrels and dissensions have arisen between Christians and Muslims. The sacred Council now pleads with all to forget the past, and urges that a sincere effort be made to achieve mutual understanding; for the benefit of all men, let them together preserve and promote peace, liberty, social justice and moral values."

Dialogue

Pope John Paul has met with Muslim leaders and delegations both in Rome and during his trips abroad. He has addressed large gatherings of Muslims in Morocco, Indonesia, Mali and elsewhere. The Pontifical Council for Interreligious Dialogue has held formal dialogues with Islamic organizations from time to time. In the U.S., the bishops' Secretariat for Ecumenical and Interreligious Affairs has held consultations on relations with Muslims and several special dialogues with Muslims related to international issues. Dialogue with participation of Catholics and Muslims from several U.S. cities was initiated in October, 1991. These continue, and in 1996 a dialogue between representatives of the ministry of W.D. Mohammed and the National Conference of Catholic Bishops began.

In 1995, the American Muslim Council presented its Mahmoud Abu-Saud Award for Excellence to Cardinal William H. Keeler for his leadership in promoting Christian-Muslim relations during his term as president of the National Conference of Catholic Bishops/United States Catholic Conference.

Id al-Fitr Message

"Christians and Muslims: Believers in God, Faithful to Humanity," was the title of a message addressed to the Muslim community by Cardinal Francis Arinze, president of the Pontifical Council for Interreligious Dialogue, on the occasion of the observance of the Muslim feast of Id al-Fitr at the end of Ramadan, the month of fasting. The following major portion of the message is from the text in the Feb. 5, 1997, English-language edition of *L'Osservatore Romano.*

This period offers an opportunity for Christians to visit their Muslim friends to exchange greetings, and this helps to strengthen bonds of friendship that already exist and to create new ones. This annual meassage thus becomes like a bridge between Christians and Muslims which is constantly being built and consolidated. We thank God for this and we pray that the relations between Christians and Muslims may continue to grow stronger.

It is faith, that trusting and obedient submission to God which has motivated your fast during the month of Ramadan. Muslims and Christians, we define ourselves as "believers" and, together with Jews, we see in Abraham a model for our faith.

It was through faith that Abraham put his entire trust in God and obeyed his every command; he left his native land, his tribe, his father's family, to journey toward an unknown country. It was through faith that, without hesitating, he was ready to offer his son, when God put him to the test. This is why Abraham is such an outstanding model of complete dedication to God.

Following the example of Abraham, Jews, Christians and Muslims strive to give to God the place in their lives which is his due as Fount and Origin, Master and Guide, and Ultimate Destiny of all beings. Yet, they are aware too that there are also other believers, men and women with religious sentiments, who are worthy of respect. It is, in fact, in the name of God that every authentic believer shows respect for each human person. Religion cannot be thought to authorize us, on the basis of our differences, to adopt negative attitudes toward one another.

This is not to say that we should overlook differences. But, do we not have common concerns? How are we to transmit religious values to the next generation? How are we to educate young people to respect the faith of others when it differs from their own? How can we give common witness, in a way which is credible, to those who do not believe in God? How can we commit ourselves to the service of humanity, to every person and to the whole person, on the basis of our faith in God? Such are the questions and challenges that face us, Muslims and Christians, as humanity prepares to enter a new millennium. It may be necessary for Christians and Muslims to meet more often in order to search together, before God, for answers to these questions.

HINDUISM AND BUDDHISM

(Courtesy of Dr. John Borelli.)

Hinduism and Buddhism — along with Confucianism, Taoism, Shinto, Native American Traditions and other religions — unlike Judaism, Christianity and Islam, are called non-Abrahamic because in them Abraham is not shared as a father in faith.

Common elements among Judaism, Christianity and Islam are more extensive than each has with any other religion. All three are scriptural religions, with Christian scripture making reference to Jewish scripture and Islamic scripture making references to the earlier two. The life of the religious community of each religion is defined through the content and use of its scripture. More common elements among the three religions can be discovered through the study of religious law, liturgy, spirituality and theology.

Two of the principal non-Abrahamic religions are Hinduism and Buddhism.

In its *Declaration on the Relation of the Church to Non-Christian Religions,* the Second Vatican Council stated: "In Hinduism men explore the divine mystery and express it both in the limitless riches of myth and the accurately defined insights of philosophy. They seek release from the trials of the present life by ascetical practices, profound meditation and recourse to God in confidence and love." (2)

Catholics, especially in India, have sought good relations with Hindus and have engaged in numerous dialogues and conferences. In papal visits to India, Paul VI in 1964 and John Paul II in 1986 addressed words of respect for Indian, particularly Hindu, religious leaders. Pope John Paul said to Hindus in 1986: "Your overwhelming sense of the primacy of religion and of the greatness of the Supreme Being has been a powerful witness against a materialistic and atheistic view of life."

In 1995, the Pontifical Council for Interreligious Dialogue began sending a general message to Hindus on the occasion of Diwali, a feast commemorating the victory of light over darkness.

"Buddhism in its multiple forms acknowledges the radical insufficiency of this shifting world. It teaches a path by which men, in a devout and confident spirit, can either reach a state of absolute freedom or attain supreme enlightenment by their own efforts or by higher assistance." So stated the Second Vatican Council in its Declaration on the Relation of the Church to Non-Christian Religions.

Numerous delegations of Buddhists and leading monks have been received by the popes. At the 1986 World Day of Prayer for Peace at Assisi, the Dalai Lama, principal teacher of the Gelugpa lineage, was placed immediately to the Holy Father's left. Numerous dialogues and good relations between Catholics and Buddhists exist in many countries.

In 1995, the Pontifical Council for Interreligious Dialogue organized a Buddhist-Christian colloquium hosted by the Fo Kuang Shan Buddhist order in Taiwan. Also in 1995, the council began sending a message to Buddhists on the feast of Vesakh, the celebration of Gautama Buddha's life.

In 1996, Cardinal Arinze, in a letter to "Dear Buddhist Friends," wrote: "The pluralistic society in which we live demands more than mere tolerance. Tolerance is usually thought of as putting up with the other or, at best, as a code of public conduct. Yet, this resigned, lukewarm attitude does not create the right atmosphere for true harmonious coexistence. The spirit of our religions challenges us to go beyond this. We are commanded, in fact, to love our neighbors as ourselves." The cardinal wrote in the same vein to Muslims on the occasion of their 1996 celebration of Id al-Fitr.

Formal dialogues in the Archdioceses of Los Angeles, San Francisco, Chicago and the Diocese of Honolulu are held from time to time. The Monastic Interreligious Dialogue, a consortium of Catholic monastics, has enjoyed rich exchanges with Buddhist monastics since 1981. In 1989, the bishops' Secretariat for Ecumenical and Interreligious Affairs convened its first national consultation on relations with Buddhists; a second consultation was held in 1990.

TRADITIONAL RELIGIONS

Traditional religions are those which have remained in their original socio-cultural environments. Such religions in general have a strong sense of the sacred and a moral code handed down by past generations. It was expected that such religions would be subject to discussion and pastoral consideration during the forthcoming special assemblies of the Synod of Bishops for Asia and Oceania.

GLOSSARY

A

Abbacy: A non-diocesan territory whose people are under the pastoral care of an abbot acting in general in the manner of a bishop.

Abbess: The female superior of a monastic community of nuns; e.g., Benedictines, Poor Clares, some others. Elected by members of the community, an abbess has general authority over her community but no sacramental jurisdiction.

Abbey: See Monastery.

Abbot: The male superior of a monastic community of men religious; e.g., Benedictines, Cistercians, some others. Elected by members of the community, an abbot has ordinary jurisdiction and general authority over his community. Eastern-Rite equivalents of an abbot are a *hegumen* and an *archimandrite.* A regular abbot is the head of an abbey or monastery. An abbot general or archabbot is the head of a congregation consisting of several monasteries. An abbot primate is the head of the modern Benedictine Confederation.

Ablution: A term derived from Latin, meaning washing or cleansing, and referring to the cleansing of the hands of a priest celebrating Mass, after the offering of gifts; and to the cleansing of the chalice with water and wine after Communion.

Abortion: Abortion is not only "the ejection of an immature fetus" from the womb, but is "also the killing of the same fetus in whatever way at whatever time from the moment of conception it may be procured." (This clarification of Canon 1398, reported in the Dec. 5, 1988, edition of *L'Osservatore Romano,* was issued by the Pontifical Council for the Interpretation of Legislative Texts — in view of scientific developments regarding ways and means of procuring abortion.) Accidental expulsion, as in cases of miscarriage, is without moral fault. Direct abortion, in which a fetus is intentionally removed from the womb, constitutes a direct attack on an innocent human being, a violation of the Fifth Commandment. A person who procures a completed abortion is automatically excommunicated (Canon 1398 of the Code of Canon Law); also excommunicated are all persons involved in a deliberate and successful effort to bring about an abortion. Direct abortion is not justifiable for any reason, e.g.: therapeutic, for the physical and/or psychological welfare of the mother; preventive, to avoid the birth of a defective or unwanted child; social, in the interests of family and/or community. Indirect abortion, which occurs when a fetus is expelled during medical or other treatment of the mother for a reason other than procuring expulsion, is permissible under the principle of double effect for a proportionately serious reason; e.g., when a medical or surgical procedure is necessary to save the life of the mother.

Absolution, Sacramental: The act by which bishops and priests, acting as agents of Christ and ministers of the Church, grant forgiveness of sins in the sacrament of penance. The essential formula of absolution is: "I absolve you from your sins; in the name of the Father, and of the Son, and of the Holy Spirit. Amen." The power to absolve is given with ordination to the priesthood and episcopate. Priests exercise this power in virtue of authorization (faculties) granted by a bishop, a religious superior or canon law. Authorization can be limited or restricted regarding certain sins and penalties or censures. In cases of necessity, and also in cases of the absence of their own confessors, Eastern- and Latin-rite Catholics may ask for and receive sacramental absolution from an Eastern- or Latin-rite priest; so may Polish National Catholics, according to a Vatican decision issued in May, 1993. Any priest can absolve a person in danger of death; in the absence of a priest with the usual faculties, this includes a laicized priest or a priest under censure. (See additional entry under Sacraments.)

Adoration: The highest act and purpose of religious worship, which is directed in love and reverence to God alone in acknowledgment of his infinite perfection and goodness, and of his total dominion over creatures. Adoration, which is also called *latria,* consists of internal and external elements, private and social prayer, liturgical acts and ceremonies, and especially sacrifice.

Adultery: Marital infidelity. Sexual intercourse between a married person and another to whom one is not married, a violation of the obligations of the marital covenant, chastity and justice; any sin of impurity (thought, desire, word, action) involving a married person who is not one's husband or wife has the nature of adultery.

Adventists: Members of several Christian sects whose doctrines are dominated by belief in a more or less imminent second advent or coming of Christ upon earth for a glorious 1,000-year reign of righteousness. This reign, following victory by the forces of good over evil in a final Battle of Armageddon, will begin with the resurrection of the chosen and will end with the resurrection of all others and the annihilation of the wicked. Thereafter, the just will live forever in a renewed heaven and earth. A sleep of the soul takes place between the time of death and the day of judgment. There is no hell. The Bible, in fundamentalist interpretation, is regarded as the only rule of faith and practice. About six sects have developed in the course of the Adventist movement which originated with William Miller (1782-1849) in the United States. Miller, on the basis of calculations made from the Book of Daniel, predicted that the second advent of Christ would occur between 1843 and 1844. After the prophecy went unfulfilled, divisions occurred in the movement and the Seventh Day Adventists, whose actual formation dates from 1860, emerged as the largest single body. The observance of Saturday instead of Sunday as the Lord's Day dates from 1844.

Advent Wreath: A wreath of laurel, spruce, or similar foliage with four candles which are lighted successively in the weeks of Advent to symbolize the approaching celebration of the birth of Christ, the Light of the World, at Christmas. The wreath originated among German Protestants.

Agape: A Greek word, meaning love, love feast, designating the meal of fellowship eaten at some gatherings of early Christians. Although held in some places in connection with the Mass, the agape was not part of the Mass, nor was it of universal institution and observance. It was infrequently observed by the fifth century and disappeared altogether between the sixth and eighth centuries.

Age of Reason: (1) The time of life when one begins to distinguish between right and wrong, to understand an obligation and take on moral responsibility; seven years of age is the presumption in church law. (2) Historically, the 18th century period of Enlightenment in England and France, the age of the Encyclopedists and Deists. According to a basic thesis of the Enlightenment, human experience and reason are the only sources of certain knowledge of truth; consequently, faith and revelation are discounted as valid sources of knowledge, and the reality of supernatural truth is called into doubt and/or denied.

Aggiornamento: An Italian word having the general meaning of bringing up to date, renewal, revitalization, descriptive of the processes of spiritual renewal and institutional reform and change in the Church; fostered by the Second Vatican Council.

Agnosticism: A theory which holds that a person cannot have certain knowledge of immaterial reality, especially the existence of God and things pertaining to him. Immanuel Kant, one of the philosophical fathers of agnosticism, stood for the position that God, as well as the human soul, is unknowable on speculative grounds; nevertheless, he found practical imperatives for acknowledging God's existence, a view shared by many agnostics. The First Vatican Council declared that the existence of God and some of his attributes can be known with certainty by human reason, even without divine revelation. The word agnosticism was first used, in the sense given here, by T. H. Huxley in 1869.

Agnus Dei: A Latin phrase, meaning Lamb of God. (1) A title given to Christ, the Lamb (victim) of the Sacrifice of the New Law (on Calvary and in Mass). (2) A prayer said at Mass before the reception of Holy Communion. (3) A sacramental. It is a round paschal-candle fragment blessed by the pope. On one side it bears the impression of a lamb, symbolic of Christ. On the reverse side, there may be any one of a number of impressions; e.g., the figure of a saint, the name and coat of arms of the reigning pope. The *agnus dei* may have originated at Rome in the fifth century. The first definite mention of it dates from about 820.

Akathist Hymn: The most profound and famous expression of Marian devotion in churches of the Byzantine rite. It consists of 24 sections, 12 of which relate to the Gospel of the Infancy and 12 to the mysteries of the Incarnation and the virginal motherhood of Mary. In liturgical usage, it is sung in part in Byzantine churches on the first four Saturdays of Lent and in toto on the fifth Saturday; it is also recited in private devotion. It is of unknown origin prior to 626, when its popularity increased as a hymn of thanksgiving after the successful defense and liberation of Constantinople, which had been under siege by Persians and Avars. Akathist means "without sitting," indicating that the hymn is recited or sung while standing. Pope John Paul, in a decree dated May 25, 1991, granted a plenary indulgence to the faithful of any rite who recite the hymn in a church or oratory, as a family, in a religious community or in a pious association — in conjunction with the usual conditions of freedom from attachment to sin, reception of the sacraments of penance and the Eucharist, and prayers for the intention of the Pope (e.g., an Our

Father, the Apostles' Creed and an aspiration). A partial indulgence can be gained for recitation of the hymn in other circumstances.

Alleluia: An exclamation of joy derived from Hebrew, "All hail to him who is, praise God," with various use in the liturgy and other expressions of worship.

Allocution: A formal type of papal address, as distinguished from an ordinary sermon or statement of views.

Alms: An act, gift or service of compassion, motivated by love of God and neighbor, for the help of persons in need; an obligation of charity, which is measurable by the ability of one person to give assistance and by the degree of another's need. Almsgiving, along with prayer and fasting, is regarded as a work of penance as well as an exercise of charity. (See Mercy, Works of.)

Alpha and Omega: The first and last letters of the Greek alphabet, used to symbolize the eternity of God (Rv. 1:8) and the divinity and eternity of Christ, the beginning and end of all things (Rv. 21:6; 22:13). Use of the letters as a monogram of Christ originated in the fourth century or earlier.

Amen: A Hebrew word meaning truly, it is true. In the Gospels, Christ used the word to add a note of authority to his statements. In other New Testament writings, as in Hebrew usage, it was the concluding word to doxologies. As the concluding word of prayers, it expresses assent to and acceptance of God's will.

Anamnesis: A prayer recalling the saving mysteries of the death and resurrection of Jesus, following the consecration at Mass in the Latin rite.

Anaphora: A Greek term for the Canon or Eucharistic Prayer of the Mass.

Anathema: A Greek word with the root meaning of cursed or separated and the adapted meaning of excommunication, used in church documents, especially the canons of ecumenical councils, for the condemnation of heretical doctrines and of practices opposed to proper discipline.

Anchorite: A kind of hermit living in complete isolation and devoting himself exclusively to exercises of religion and severe penance according to a rule and way of life of his own devising. In early Christian times, anchorites were the forerunners of the monastic life. The closest contemporary approach to the life of an anchorite is that of Carthusian and Camaldolese hermits.

Angels: Purely spiritual beings with intelligence and free will whose name indicates their mission as servants and messengers of God. They were created before the creation of the visible universe. Good angels enjoy the perfect good of the beatific vision. They can intercede for persons. The doctrine of guardian angels, although not explicitly defined as a matter of faith, is rooted in long-standing tradition. No authoritative declaration has ever been issued regarding choirs or various categories of angels: seraphim, cherubim, thrones, dominations, principalities, powers, virtues, archangels and angels. Archangels commemorated in the liturgy are: Michael, leader of the angelic host and protector of the synagogue; Raphael, guide of Tobiah and healer of his father; Gabriel, angel of the Incarnation. Fallen angels, the chief of whom is called the Devil or Satan, rejected the love of God and were therefore banished from heaven to hell. They can tempt persons to commit sin.

Angelus: A devotion which commemorates the Incarnation of Christ. It consists of three versicles, three Hail Marys and a special prayer, and recalls the announcement to Mary by the Archangel Gabriel that she was chosen to be the Mother of Christ, her acceptance of the divine will, and the Incarnation (Lk. 1:26-38). The Angelus is recited in the morning, at noon and in the evening. The practice of reciting the Hail Mary in honor of the Incarnation was introduced by the Franciscans in 1263. The *Regina Caeli,* commemorating the joy of Mary at Christ's Resurrection, replaces the Angelus during the Easter season.

Anger (Wrath): Passionate displeasure arising from some kind of offense suffered at the hands of another person, frustration or other cause, combined with a tendency to strike back at the cause of the displeasure; a violation of the Fifth Commandment and one of the capital sins if the displeasure is out of proportion to the cause and/ or if the retaliation is unjust.

Anglican Orders: Holy orders conferred according to the rite of the Anglican Church, which Leo XIII declared null and void in the bull *Apostolicae Curae,* Sept. 13, 1896. The orders were declared null because they were conferred according to a rite that was substantially defective in form and intent, and because of a break in apostolic succession that occurred when Matthew Parker became head of the Anglican hierarchy in 1559. In making his declaration, Pope Leo cited earlier arguments against validity made by Julius III in 1553 and 1554 and by Paul IV in 1555. He also noted related directives requiring absolute ordination, according to the Catholic ritual, of convert ministers who had been ordained according to the Anglican Ordinal.

Anglican Use Parishes: In line with Vatican-approved developments since 1980, several Anglican use parishes have been established in the United States with the right to continue using some elements of Anglican usage in their liturgical celebrations. A Vatican document dated Mar. 31, 1981, said: "In June, 1980, the Holy See, through the Congregation for the Doctrine of the Faith, agreed to the request presented by the bishops of the United States of America in behalf of some clergy and laity formerly or actually belonging to the Episcopal (Anglican) Church for full communion with the Catholic Church. The Holy See's response to the initiative of these Episcopalians includes the possibility of a 'pastoral provision' which will provide, for those who desire it, a common identity reflecting certain elements of their own heritage."

Animals: Creatures of God, they are entrusted to human stewardship for appropriate care, use for human needs, as pets, for reasonable experimentation for the good of people. They should not be subject to cruel treatment.

Antichrist: The "deceitful one," the "antichrist" (2 Jn. 7), adversary of Christ and the kingdom of God, especially in the end time before the Second Coming of Christ. The term is also used in reference to anti-Christian persons and forces in the world.

Antiphon: (1) A short verse or text, generally from Scripture, recited in the Liturgy of the Hours before and after psalms and canticles. (2) Any verse sung or recited by one part of a choir or congregation in response to the other part, as in antiphonal or alternate chanting.

Apologetics: The science and art of developing and presenting the case for the reasonableness of the Christian faith, by a wide variety of means including facts of experience, history, science, philosophy. The constant objective of apologetics, as well as of the total process of pre-evangelization, is preparation for response to God in faith; its ways and means, however, are subject to change in accordance with the various needs of people and different sets of circumstances.

Apostasy: (1) The total and obstinate repudiation of the Christian faith. An apostate automatically incurs a penalty of excommunication. (2) Apostasy from orders is the unlawful withdrawal from or rejection of the obligations of the clerical state by a man who has received major orders. An apostate from orders is subject to a canonical penalty. (3) Apostasy from the religious life occurs when a Religious with perpetual vows unlawfully leaves the community with the intention of not returning, or actually remains outside the community without permission. An apostate from religious life is subject to a canonical penalty.

Apostolate: The ministry or work of an apostle. In Catholic usage, the word is an umbrella-like term covering all kinds and areas of work and endeavor for the service of God and the Church and the good of people. Thus, the apostolate of bishops is to carry on the mission of the Apostles as pastors of the People of God: of priests, to preach the word of God and to carry out the sacramental and pastoral ministry for which they are ordained; of religious, to follow and do the work of Christ in conformity with the evangelical counsels and their rule of life; of lay persons, as individuals and/or in groups, to give witness to Christ and build up the kingdom of God through practice of their faith, professional competence and the performance of good works in the concrete circumstances of daily life. Apostolic works are not limited to those done within the Church or by specifically Catholic groups, although some apostolates are officially assigned to certain persons or groups and are under the direction of church authorities. Apostolate derives from the commitment and obligation of baptism, confirmation, holy orders, matrimony, the duties of one's state in life, etc.

Apostolic Succession: Bishops of the Church, who form a collective body or college, are successors to the Apostles by ordination and divine right; as such they carry on the mission entrusted by Christ to the Apostles as guardians and teachers of the deposit of faith, principal pastors and spiritual authorities of the faithful. The doctrine of apostolic succession is based on New Testament evidence and the constant teaching of the Church, reflected as early as the end of the first century in a letter of Pope St. Clement to the Corinthians. A significant facet of the doctrine is the role of the pope as the successor of St. Peter, the vicar of Christ and head of the college of bishops. The doctrine of apostolic succession means more than continuity of apostolic faith and doctrine; its basic requisite is ordination by the laying on of hands in apostolic succession.

Archdiocese: An ecclesiastical jurisdiction headed

by an archbishop. An archdiocese is usually a metropolitan see, i.e., the principal one of a group of dioceses comprising a province; the other dioceses in the province are suffragan sees.

Archives: Documentary records, and the place where they are kept, of the spiritual and temporal government and affairs of the Church, a diocese, church agencies like the departments of the Roman Curia, bodies like religious institutes, and individual parishes. The collection, cataloguing, preserving, and use of these records are governed by norms stated in canon law and particular regulations. The strictest secrecy is always in effect for confidential records concerning matters of conscience, and documents of this kind are destroyed as soon as circumstances permit.

Ark of the Covenant: The sacred chest of the Israelites in which were placed and carried the tablets of stone inscribed with the Ten Commandments, the basic moral precepts of the Old Covenant (Ex. 25: 10-22; 37:1-9). The Ark was also a symbol of God's presence. The Ark was probably destroyed with the Temple in 586 B.C.

Asceticism: The practice of self-discipline. In the spiritual life, asceticism — by personal prayer, meditation, self-denial, works of mortification, and outgoing interpersonal works — is motivated by love of God and contributes to growth in holiness.

Ashes: Religious significance has been associated with their use as symbolic of penance since Old Testament times. Thus, ashes of palm blessed on the previous Sunday of the faithful on Ash Wednesday to remind them to do works of penance, especially during the season of Lent, and that they are dust and unto dust will return. Ashes are a sacramental.

Aspergillum: A vessel or device used for sprinkling holy water. The ordinary type is a metallic rod with a bulbous tip which absorbs the water and discharges it at the motion of the user's hand.

Aspersory: A portable metallic vessel, similar to a pail, for carrying holy water.

Aspiration (Ejaculation): Short exclamatory prayer; e.g., My Jesus, mercy.

Atheism: Denial of the existence of God, finding expression in a system of thought (speculative atheism) or a manner of acting (practical atheism) as though there were no God. The Second Vatican Council, in its *Pastoral Constitution on the Church in the Modern World* (Nos. 19 to 21), noted that a profession of atheism may represent an explicit denial of God, the rejection of a wrong notion of God, an affirmation of man rather than of God, an extreme protest against evil. It said that such a profession might result from acceptance of such propositions as: there is no absolute truth; man can assert nothing, absolutely nothing, about God; everything can be explained by scientific reasoning alone; the whole question of God is devoid of meaning. The constitution also cited two opinions of influence in atheistic thought. One of them regards recognition of dependence on God as incompatible with human freedom and independence. The other views belief in God and religion as a kind of opiate which sedates man on earth, reconciling him to the acceptance of suffering, injustice, shortcomings, etc., because of hope for greater things after death, and thereby hindering him from seeking and working for improvement and change for the better here and now. All of these views, in one way or another, have been involved in the No-God and Death-of-God schools of thought in recent and remote history.

Atonement: The redemptive activity of Christ, who reconciled man with God through his Incarnation and entire life, and especially by his suffering and Resurrection. The word also applies to prayer and good works by which persons join themselves with and take part in Christ's work of reconciliation and reparation for sin.

Attributes of God: Perfections of God. God possesses — and is — all the perfections of being, without limitation. Because he is infinite, all of these perfections are one, perfectly united in him. Because of the limited power of human intelligence, divine perfections — such as omnipotence, truth, love, etc. — are viewed separately, as distinct characteristics, even though they are not actually distinct in God.

Avarice (Covetousness): A disorderly and unreasonable attachment to and desire for material things; called a capital sin because it involves preoccupation with material things to the neglect of spiritual goods and obligations of justice and charity.

Ave Maria: See Hail Mary.

B

Baldachino: A canopy over an altar.

Base Ecclesial Communities: The concept and operational model of basic Christian communities — *comunidades de base* — envision relatively small communities of the faithful integrated for religious and secular life, with maximum potential for liturgical and sacramental participation, pastoral ministry, apostolic activity, and for personal and social development. Communities of this type originated mainly in Latin America; thousands of them are now contributing to the vitality of parishes and dioceses in many countries throughout the world.

Pope Paul VI, in *Evangelii Nuntiandi,* stated: The name "Ecclesial Communities" can be given only to those "that appear and develop within the Church, having solidarity with her life, being nourished by her teaching and united with her pastors." The name should not be attributed to those "that come together in a spirit of bitter criticism of the Church" and radically oppose the Church. Only the genuine base ecclesial communities "will be a place of evangelization for the benefit of the bigger communities, especially the individual churches and will be a hope for the universal Church to the extent that they constantly grow in missionary consciousness, fervor, commitment and zeal."

Beatification: A preliminary step toward canonization of a saint. It begins with an investigation of the candidate's life, writings and heroic practice of virtue, and, except in the case of martyrs, the certification of one miracle worked by God through his or her intercession. If the findings of the investigation so indicate, the pope decrees that the Servant of God may be called Blessed and may be honored locally or in a limited way in the liturgy. Additional procedures lead to canonization. (See separate entry).

Beatific Vision: The intuitive, immediate and direct vision and experience of God enjoyed in the light of glory by all the blessed in heaven. The vision is a supernatural mystery.

Beatitude: A literary form of the Old and New Testaments in which blessings are promised to persons for various reasons. Beatitudes are mentioned 26 times in the Psalms, and in other books of the Old Testament. The best known Beatitudes — identifying blessedness with participation in the kingdom of God and his righteousness, and descriptive of the qualities of Christian perfection — are those recounted in Mt. 5:3-12 and Lk. 6:20-23. The Beatitudes are of central importance in the teaching of Jesus.

Benedictus: The canticle or hymn of Zechariah at the circumcision of St. John the Baptist (Lk. 1:68-79). It is an expression of praise and thanks to God for sending John as a precursor of the Messiah. The *Benedictus* is recited in the Liturgy of the Hours as part of the Morning Prayer.

Biglietto: A papal document of notification of appointment to the cardinalate.

Biretta: A stiff, square hat with three ridges on top worn by clerics in church and on other occasions.

Blasphemy: Any internal or external expression of hatred, reproach, insult, defiance or contempt with respect to God and the use of his name, principally, and to the Church, saints and sacred things, secondarily; a serious sin, directly opposed to the second commandment.

Blasphemy against the Spirit: Deliberate refusal to accept divine mercy, rejection of forgiveness of sins and of the promise of salvation. The sin that is unforgivable because a person refuses to seek or accept forgiveness.

Blessing: Invocation of God's favor, by official ministers of the Church or by private individuals. Blessings are recounted in the Old and New Testaments, and are common in the Christian tradition. Many types of blessings are listed in the *Book of Blessings of the Roman Ritual.* Private blessings, as well as those of an official kind, are efficacious. Blessings are imparted with the Sign of the Cross and appropriate prayer.

Boat: A small vessel used to hold incense which is to be placed in the censer.

Brief, Apostolic: A papal letter, less formal than a bull, signed for the pope by a secretary and impressed with the seal of the Fisherman's Ring. Simple apostolic letters of this kind are issued for beatifications and with respect to other matters.

Bull, Apostolic: Apostolic letter, a solemn form of papal document, beginning with the name and title of the pope (e.g., John Paul II, Servant of the Servants of God), dealing with an important subject, sealed with a bulla or red-ink imprint of the device on the bulla. Bulls are issued to confer the titles of bishops and cardinals, to promulgate canonizations, to proclaim Holy Years and for other purposes. A collection of bulls is called a bullarium.

Burial, Ecclesiastical: Interment with ecclesiastical rites, a right of the Christian faithful. The Church recommends burial of the bodies of the dead, but cremation is permissible if it does not involve reasons against church teaching. Ecclesiastical burial is in order for catechumens; for unbaptized children whose parents intended to have them baptized before death; and even, in the absence of their own ministers, for baptized non-Catholics unless it would be considered against their will.

C

Calumny (Slander): Harming the name and good reputation of a person by lies; a violation of obligations of justice and truth. Restitution is due for calumny.

Calvary: A knoll about 15 feet high just outside the western wall of Jerusalem where Christ was crucified, so called from the Latin *calvaria* (skull) which described its shape.

Canon: A Greek word meaning rule, norm, standard, measure. (1) The word designates the Canon of Sacred Scripture, which is the list of books recognized by the Church as inspired by the Holy Spirit. (2) The term also designates the canons (Eucharistic Prayers, anaphoras) of the Mass, the core of the eucharistic liturgy. (3) Certain dignitaries of the Church have the title of Canon, and some religious are known as Canons.

Canonization: An infallible declaration by the pope that a person, who died as a martyr and/or practiced Christian virtue to a heroic degree, is now in heaven and is worthy of honor and imitation by all the faithful. Such a declaration is preceded by the process of beatification and another detailed investigation concerning the person's reputation for holiness, writings, and (except in the case of martyrs) a miracle ascribed to his or her intercession after death. The pope can dispense from some of the formalities ordinarily required in canonization procedures (equivalent canonization), as Pope John XXIII did in the canonization of St. Gregory Barbarigo on May 26, 1960. A saint is worthy of honor in liturgical worship throughout the universal Church. From its earliest years the Church has venerated saints. Public official honor always required the approval of the bishop of the place. Martyrs were the first to be honored. St. Martin of Tours, who died in 397, was an early non-martyr venerated as a saint. The earliest canonization by a pope with positive documentation was that of St. Ulrich (Uldaric) of Augsburg by John XV in 993. Alexander III reserved the process of canonization to the Holy See in 1171. In 1588 Sixtus V established the Sacred Congregation of Rites for the principal purpose of handling causes for beatification and canonization: this function is now the work of the Congregation for the Causes of Saints. The official listing of saints and blessed is contained in the *Roman Martyrology* (being revised and updated) and related decrees issued after its last publication. Butler's unofficial *Lives of the Saints* (1956) contains 2,565 entries. The Church regards all persons in heaven as saints, not just those who have been officially canonized. (See Beatification, Saints, Canonizations by Leo XIII and His Successors.)

Canon Law: The Code of Canon Law enacted and promulgated by ecclesiastical authority for the orderly and pastoral administration and government of the Church. A revised Code for the Latin rite, effective Nov. 27, 1983, consists of 1,752 canons in seven books under the titles of general norms, the people of God, the teaching mission of the Church, the sanctifying mission of the Church, temporal goods of the Church, penal law and procedural law. The antecedent of this Code was promulgated in 1917 and became effective in 1918; it consisted of 2,414 canons in five books covering general rules, ecclesiastical persons, sacred things, trials, crimes and punishments. There is a separate Code of the Canons of Eastern Churches, in effect since Oct. 1, 1991.

Canticle: A scriptural chant or prayer differing from the psalms. Three of the canticles prescribed for use in the Liturgy of the Hours are: the *Magnificat*, the Canticle of Mary (Lk. 1:46-55); the *Benedictus*, the Canticle of Zechariah (Lk. 1:68-79); and the *Nunc Dimittis*, the Canticle of Simeon (Lk. 2:29-32).

Capital Punishment: Punishment for crime by means of the death penalty. The political community, which has authority to provide for the common good, has the right to defend itself and its members against unjust aggression and may in extreme cases punish with the death penalty persons found guilty before the law of serious crimes against individuals and a just social order. Such punishment is essentially vindictive. Its value as a crime deterrent is a matter of perennial debate. The prudential judgment as to whether or not there should be capital punishment belongs to the civic community. The U.S. Supreme Court, in a series of decisions dating from June 29, 1972, ruled against the constitutionality of statutes on capital punishment except in specific cases and with appropriate consideration, with respect to sentence, of mitigating circumstances of the crime. Capital punishment was the subject of a statement issued Mar. 1, 1978, by the Committee on Social Development and World Peace, U.S. Catholic Conference. The statement said, in part: "The use of the death penalty involves deep moral and religious questions as well as political and legal issues. In 1974, out of a commitment to the value and dignity of human life, the Catholic bishops of the United States declared their opposition to capital punishment. We continue to support this position, in the belief that a return to the use of the death penalty can only lead to the further erosion of respect for life in our society." Additional statements against capital punishment have been issued by Pope John Paul II, numerous bishops and other sources. Pope John Paul, in his encyclical letter "The Gospel of Life," wrote: "There is a growing tendency, both in the Church and in civil society, to demand that it (capital punishment) be applied in a very limited way or even that it be abolished completely. The nature and extent of the punishment must be carefully evaluated and decided upon, and ought not go to the extreme of executing the offender except in cases of absolute necessity; in other words, when it would not be possible otherwise to defend society. Today such cases are rare if not practically nonexistent." Quoting the Catechism of the Catholic Church, the Pope wrote: " 'If bloodless means are sufficient to defend human lives against an aggressor and to protect public order and the safety of persons, public authority must limit itself to such means, because they better correspond to the concrete conditions of the common good and are more in conformity to the dignity of the human person.' "

Capital Sins: Sins which give rise to other sins: pride, avarice, lust, wrath (anger), gluttony, envy, sloth.

Cardinal Virtues: The four principal moral virtues are prudence, justice, temperance and fortitude.

Catacombs: Underground Christian cemeteries in various cities of the Roman Empire and Italy, especially in the vicinity of Rome; the burial sites of many martyrs and other Christians.

Catechesis: The whole complex of church efforts to make disciples of Christ, involving doctrinal instruction and spiritual formation through practice of the faith.

Catechism: A systematic presentation of the fundamentals of Catholic doctrine regarding faith and morals. Sources are Sacred Scripture, tradition, the magisterium (teaching authority of the Church), the writings of Fathers and Doctors of the Church, liturgy. The new Catechism of the Catholic Church, published Oct. 11, 1992, consists of four principal sections: the profession of faith, (the Creed), the sacraments of faith, the life of faith (the Commandments) and the prayer of the believer (the Lord's Prayer). The 16th century Council of Trent mandated publication of the Roman Catechism. Catechisms such as these two are useful sources for other catechisms serving particular needs of the faithful and persons seeking admission to the Catholic Church.

Catechumen: A person preparing in a program (catechumenate) of instruction and spiritual formation for baptism and reception into the Church. The Church has a special relationship with catechumens. It invites them to lead the life of the Gospel, introduces them to the celebration of the sacred rites, and grants them various prerogatives that are proper to the faithful (one of which is the right to ecclesiastical burial). (See Rite of Christian Initiation of Adults, under Baptism.)

Cathedra: A Greek word for chair, designating the chair or seat of a bishop in the principal church of his diocese, which is therefore called a cathedral (see separate entry).

Cathedraticum: The tax paid to a bishop by all churches and benefices subject to him for the support of episcopal administration and for works of charity.

Catholic: A Greek word, meaning universal, first used in the title Catholic Church in a letter written by St. Ignatius of Antioch about 107 to the Christians of Smyrna.

Celebret: A Latin word, meaning Let him celebrate, the name of a letter of recommendation issued by a bishop or other superior stating that a priest is in good standing and therefore eligible to celebrate Mass or perform other priestly functions.

Celibacy: The unmarried state of life, required in the Roman Church of candidates for holy orders and of men already ordained to holy orders, for the practice of perfect chastity and total dedication to the service of people in the ministry of the Church. Celibacy is enjoined as a condition for ordination by church discipline and law, not by dogmatic necessity. In the Roman Church, a consensus in favor of celibacy developed in the early centuries while the clergy included both celibates and men who had been married once. The first local legislation on the subject was enacted by a local council held in Elvira, Spain, about 306; it forbade bishops, priests, deacons and other ministers to have wives. Similar enactments were passed by other local councils from that time on, and by the 12th century particular laws regarded marriage by clerics in major orders to be not only unlawful but also null and void. The latter view was translated by the Second Lateran Council in 1139 into what seems to be the first written universal law making holy orders an invalidating impediment to marriage. In 1563 the Council of Trent ruled definitely on the matter and established the discipline in force in the Roman Church. Some exceptions to this discipline have been made in recent years. A number of married Protestant and Episcopalian (Anglican) clergymen who became converts and were subsequently ordained to the priesthood have been permitted to continue in marriage. Married men over the age of 35 can be ordained to the permanent diaconate. Eastern Church discipline on celibacy differs from that of the Roman Church. In line with legislation enacted by the Synod of Trullo in 692 and still in force, candidates for holy orders may marry before becoming deacons and may continue in marriage thereafter, but marriage after ordination is forbidden. Bishops of Eastern Catholic Churches in the U.S., however, do not ordain married candidates for the priesthood. Bishops of Eastern Catholic Churches are unmarried.

Cenacle: The upper room in Jerusalem where Christ ate the Las Supper with his Apostles.

Censer: A metal vessel with a perforated cover and suspended by chains, in which incense is burned. It is used at some Masses, Benediction of the Blessed Sacrament and other liturgical functions.

Censorship of Books: An exercise of vigilance by the Church for safeguarding authentic religious teaching. Pertinent legislation in a decree issued by the Congregation for the Doctrine of the Faith Apr. 9, 1975, is embodied in the Code of Canon Law (Book III, Title IV). The legislation deals with requirements for pre-publication review and clearance of various types of writings on religious subjects. Permission to publish works of a religious character, together with the apparatus of reviewing them beforehand, falls under the authority of the bishop of the place where the writer lives or where the works are published. Clearance for publication is usually indicated by the terms *Nihil obstat* (Nothing stands in the way) issued by the censor and *Imprimatur* (Let it be printed) authorized by the bishop. The clearing of works for publication does not necessarily imply approval of an author's viewpoint or his manner of handling a subject.

Censures: Sanctions imposed by the Church on baptized Roman Catholics 18 years of age or older for committing certain serious offenses and for being or remaining obstinate therein: (1) excommunication (exclusion from the community of the faithful, barring a person from sacramental and other participation in the goods and offices of the community of the Church), (2) suspension (prohibition of a cleric to exercise orders) and (3) interdict (deprivation of the sacraments and liturgical activities). The intended purposes of censures are to correct and punish offenders; to deter persons from committing sins which, more seriously and openly than others, threaten the common good of the Church and its members; and to provide for the making of reparation for harm done to the community of the Church. Censures may be incurred automatically (*ipso facto*) on the commission of certain offenses for which fixed penalties have been laid down in church law (*latae sententiae*); or they may be inflicted by sentence of a judge (*ferendae sententiae*). Automatic excommunication is incurred for the offenses of abortion, apostasy, heresy and schism. Obstinacy in crime — also called contumacy, disregard of a penalty, defiance of church authority — is presumed by law in the commission of offenses for which automatic censures are decreed. The presence and degree of contumacy in other cases, for which judicial sentence is required, is subject to determination by a judge. Absolution can be obtained from any censure, provided the person repents and desists from obstinacy. Absolution may be reserved to the pope, the bishop of a place, or the major superior of an exempt clerical religious institute. In danger of death, any priest can absolve from all censures; in other cases, faculties to absolve from reserved censures can be exercised by competent authorities or given to other priests. The penal law of the Church is contained in Book VI of the Code of Canon Law.

Ceremonies, Master of: One who directs the proceedings of a rite or ceremony during the function.

Chamberlain (Camerlengo): (1) the Chamberlain of the Holy Roman Church is a cardinal with special responsibilities, especially during the time between the death of one pope and the election of his successor; among other things, he safeguards and administers the goods and revenues of the Holy See and heads particular congregations of cardinals for special purposes. (See also Papal Election.) (2) the Chamberlain of the College of Cardinals has charge of the property and revenues of the College and keeps the record of business transacted in consistories. (3) the Chamberlain of the Roman Clergy is the president of the secular clergy of Rome.

Chancellor: Notary of a diocese, who draws up written documents in the government of the diocese; takes care of, arranges and indexes diocesan archives, records of dispensations and ecclesiastical trials.

Chancery: (1) A branch of church administration that handles written documents used in the government of a diocese. (2) The administrative office of a diocese, a bishop's office.

Chapel: A building or part of another building used for divine worship; a portion of a church set aside for the celebration of Mass or for some special devotion.

Chaplain: A priest — or, in some instances, a properly qualified religious or lay person — serving the pastoral needs of particular groups of people and institutions, such as hospitals, schools, correctional facilities, religious communities, the armed forces, etc.

Chaplet: A term, meaning little crown, applied to a rosary or, more commonly, to a small string of beads used for devotional purposes; e.g., the Infant of Prague chaplet.

Chapter: A general meeting of delegates of religious orders for elections and the handling of other important affairs of their communities.

Charismatic Renewal: A movement which originated with a handful of Duquesne University students and faculty members in the 1966-67 academic year and spread from there to Notre Dame, Michigan State University, the University of Michigan, other campuses and cities throughout the U.S., and to well over 100 other countries. Scriptural keys to the renewal are: Christ's promise to send the Holy Spirit upon the Apostles; the description, in the Acts of the Apostles, of the effects of the coming of the Holy Spirit upon the Apostles on Pentecost; St. Paul's explanation, in the Letter to the Romans and 1 Corinthians, of the charismatic gifts (for the good of the Church and persons) the Holy Spirit would bestow on Christians; New Testament evidence concerning the effects of charismatic gifts in and through the early Church. The personal key to the renewal is baptism in the Holy Spirit. This is not a new sacrament but the personally experienced actualization of grace already sacramentally received, principally in baptism and confirmation. The experience of baptism in the Holy Spirit is often accompanied by the reception of one or more charismatic gifts. A characteristic form of the renewal is the weekly prayer meeting, a gathering which includes periods of spontaneous prayer, singing, sharing of experience and testimony, fellowship and teaching. The office of the International Catholic Charismatic Renewal Services is located at Palazzo della Cancelleria, 00120 Vatican City. The mailing address of the U.S. National Service Committee is P.O. Box 628, Locust Grove, VA 22508.

Charisms: Gifts or graces given by God to persons for the good of others and the Church. Examples are special gifts for apostolic work, prophecy, healing, discernment of spirits, the life of evangelical poverty, here-and-now witness to faith in various circumstances of life. The Second Vatican Council made the following statement about charisms in the *Dogmatic Constitution on the Church* (No. 12): "It is not only through the sacraments and Church ministries that the same Holy Spirit sanctifies and leads the People of God and enriches it with virtues. Allotting his gifts 'to everyone according as he will' (1 Cor. 12:11), he distributes special graces among the faithful of every rank. By these gifts he makes them fit and ready to undertake the various tasks or offices advantageous for the renewal and upbuilding of the Church, according to the words of the Apostle: 'The manifestation of the Spirit is given to everyone for profit' (1 Cor. 12:7). These charismatic gifts, whether they be the most outstanding or the more simple and widely diffused, are to be received with thanksgiving and consolation, for they are exceedingly suitable and useful for the needs of the Church. Still, extraordinary gifts are not to be rashly sought after, nor are the fruits of apostolic labor to be presumptuously expected from them. In any case, judgment as to their genuineness and proper use belongs to those who preside over the Church, and to whose special competence it belongs, not indeed to extinguish the Spirit, but to test all things and hold fast to that which is good" (cf. 1 Thes. 5:12; 19-21).

Charity: Love of God above all things for his own sake, and love of one's neighbor as oneself because and as an expression of one's love for God; the greatest of the three theological virtues. The term is sometimes also used to designate sanctifying grace.

Chastity: Properly ordered behavior with respect to sex. In marriage, the exercise of the procreative power is integrated with the norms and purposes of marriage. Outside of marriage, the rule is self-denial of the voluntary exercise and enjoyment of the procreative faculty in thought, word or action. The vow of chastity, which reinforces the virtue of chastity with the virtue of religion, is one of the three vows professed publicly by members of institutes of consecrated life.

Chirograph or Autograph Letter: A letter written by a pope himself, in his own handwriting.

Christ: The title of Jesus, derived from the Greek translation *Christos* of the Hebrew term *Messiah,* meaning the Anointed of God, the Savior and Deliverer of his people. Christian use of the title is a confession of belief that Jesus is the Savior.

Christianity: The sum total of things related to belief in Christ — the Christian religion, Christian churches, Christians themselves, society based on and expressive of Christian beliefs, culture reflecting Christian values.

Christians: The name first applied about the year 43 to followers of Christ at Antioch, the capital of Syria. It was used by the pagans as a contemptuous term. The word applies to persons who profess belief in the divinity and teachings of Christ and who give witness to him in life.

Christian Science: A religious doctrine consisting of Mary Baker Eddy's interpretation and formulation of the actions and teachings of Christ. Its basic tenets reflect Mrs. Eddy's ideas regarding the reality of spirit and its control and domination of what is not spirit. The basic statement of the doctrine is contained in *Science and Health, with Key to the Scriptures,* which she first published in 1875, nine years after being saved from death and healed on reading the New Testament. Mary Baker Eddy (1821-1910) established the church in 1879, and in 1892 founded at Boston the First Church of Christ, Scientist, of which all other Christian Science churches are branches. The individual churches are self-governing and self-supporting under the general supervision of a board of directors. Services consist of readings of portions of Scripture and *Science and Health.* One of the church's publications, *The Christian Science Monitor,* has a worldwide reputation as a journal of news and opinion.

Church: (1) See several entries under Church, Catholic. The universal Church is the Church spread throughout the world. The particular Church is the Church in a particular locality; e.g., a diocese. The Church embraces all of its members — on earth, in heaven, in purgatory. (2) In general, any religious body. (3) A building set aside and dedicated for divine worship.

Circumcision: A ceremonial practice symbolic of initiation and participation in the covenant between God and Abraham.

Circumincession: The indwelling of each divine Person of the Holy Trinity in the others.

Clergy: Men ordained to holy orders and commissioned for sacred ministries and assigned to pastoral and other duties for the service of the people and the Church. (1) Diocesan or secular clergy are committed to pastoral ministry in parishes and in other capacities in a particular church (diocese) under the direction of their bishop, to whom they are bound by a promise of obedience. (2) Regular clergy belong to religious institutes (orders, congregations, societies — institutes of consecrated life) and are so called because they observe the rule (*regula,* in Latin) of their respective institutes. They are committed to the ways of life and apostolates of their institutes. In ordinary pastoral ministry, they are under the direction of local bishops as well as their own superiors.

Clericalism: A term generally used in a derogatory sense to mean action, influence and interference by the Church and the clergy in matters with which they allegedly should not be concerned. Anticlericalism is a reaction of antipathy, hostility, distrust and opposition to the Church and clergy arising from real and/or alleged faults of the clergy, overextension of the role of the laity, or for other reasons.

Cloister: Part of a monastery, convent or other house of religious reserved for use by members of the institute. Houses of contemplative Religious have a strict enclosure.

Code: A digest of rules or regulations, such as the Code of Canon Law.

Collegiality: A term in use especially since the Second Vatican Council to describe the authority exercised by the College of Bishops. The bishops of the Church, in union with and subordinate to the pope — who has full, supreme and universal power over the Church which he can always exercise independently — have supreme teaching and pastoral authority over the whole Church. In addition to their proper authority of office for the good of the faithful in their respective dioceses or other jurisdictions, the bishops have authority to act for the good of the universal Church. This collegial authority is exercised in a solemn manner in an ecumenical council and can also be exercised in other ways sanctioned by the pope. Doctrine on collegiality was set forth by the Second Vatican Council in the *Dogmatic Constitution on the Church.* (See separate entry.) By extension, the concept of collegiality is applied to other forms of participation and co-responsibility by members of a community.

Commissariat of the Holy Land: A special jurisdiction within the Order of Friars Minor, whose main purposes are the collecting of alms for support of the Holy Places in Palestine and staffing of the Holy Places and missions in the Middle East with priests and brothers. There are about 70 such commissariats in more than 30 countries. One of them has headquarters at Mt. St. Sepulchre, Washington, D.C. Franciscans have had custody of the Holy Places since 1342.

Communion of Saints: "The communion of all the faithful of Christ, those who are pilgrims on earth, the dead who are being purified, and the blessed in heaven, all together forming one Church; in this communion, the merciful love of God and his saints is always (attentive) to our prayers" (Paul VI, Creed of the People of God).

Communism: The substantive principles of modern communism, a theory and system of economics and social organization, were stated about the middle of the 19th century by Karl Marx, author of *The Communist Manifesto* and, with Friedrich Engels, *Das Kapital.* The elements of communist ideology include: radical materialism; dialectical determinism; the inevitability of class struggle and conflict, which is to be furthered for the ultimate establishment of a worldwide, classless society; common ownership of productive and other goods; the subordination of all persons and institutions to the dictatorship of the collectivity; denial of the rights, dignity and liberty of persons; militant atheism and hostility to religion, utilitarian morality. Communism in theory and practice has been the subject of many papal documents and statements. Pius IX condemned it in 1846. Leo XIII dealt with it at length in the encyclical letters *Quod Apostolici Muneris* in 1878 and *Rerum Novarum* in 1891. Pius XI wrote on the same subject in the encyclicals *Quadragesimo Anno* in 1931 and *Divini Redemptoris* in 1937. These writings have been updated and developed in new directions by Pius XII, John XXIII, Paul VI and John Paul II.

Concelebration: The liturgical act in which several priests, led by one member of the group, offer Mass together, all consecrating the bread and wine. Concelebration has always been common in churches of Eastern Rite. In the Roman Rite, it was long restricted, taking place only at the ordination of bishops and the ordination of priests. The *Constitution on the Sacred Liturgy* issued by the Second Vatican Council set new norms for concelebration, which is now relatively common in the Roman Rite.

Concordance, Biblical: An alphabetical verbal index enabling a user knowing one or more words of a scriptural passage to locate the entire text.

Concordat: A church-state treaty with the force of law concerning matters of mutual concern — e.g., rights of the Church, arrangement of ecclesiastical jurisdictions, marriage laws, education. Approximately 150 agreements of this kind have been negotiated since the Concordat of Worms in 1122.

Concupiscence: Any tendency of the sensitive appetite. The term is most frequently used in reference to desires and tendencies for sinful sense pleasure.

Confession: Sacramental confession is the act by which a person tells or confesses his sins to a priest who is authorized to give absolution in the sacrament of penance.

Confessor: A priest who administers the sacrament of penance. The title of confessor, formerly given to a category of male saints, was suppressed with publication of the calendar reform of 1969.

Confraternity: An association whose members practice a particular form of religious devotion and/or are engaged in some kind of apostolic work.

Conscience: Practical judgment concerning the moral goodness or sinfulness of an action (thought, word, desire). In the Catholic view, this judgment is made by reference of the action, its attendant circumstances and the intentions of the person to the requirements of moral law as expressed in the Ten Commandments, the summary law of love for God and neighbor, the life and teaching of Christ, and the authoritative teaching and practice of the Church with respect to the total demands of divine Revelation. A person is obliged: (1) to obey a certain and correct conscience; (2) to obey a certain conscience even if it is inculpably erroneous; (3) not to obey, but to correct, a conscience known to be erroneous or lax; (4) to rectify a scrupulous conscience by following the advice of a confessor and by other measures; (5) to resolve doubts of conscience before acting. It is legitimate to act for solid and probable reasons when a question of moral responsibility admits of argument (see Probabilism).

Conscience, Examination of: Self-examination to determine one's spiritual state before God, regarding one's sins and faults. It is recommended as a regular practice and is practically necessary in preparing for the sacrament of penance. The *particular examen* is a regular examination to assist in overcoming specific faults and imperfections.

Consistory: An assembly of cardinals presided over by the pope.

Constitution: (1) An apostolic or papal constitution is a document in which a pope enacts and promulgates law. (2) A formal and solemn document issued by an ecumenical council on a doctrinal or pastoral subject, with binding force in the whole Church; e.g., the four constitutions issued by the Second Vatican Council on the Church, liturgy, Revelation, and the Church in the modern world. (3) The constitutions of institutes of consecrated life and societies of apostolic life spell out details of and norms drawn from the various rules for the guidance and direction of the life and work of their members.

Consubstantiation: A theory which holds that the Body and Blood of Christ coexist with the substance of bread and wine in the Holy Eucharist. This theory, also called *impanation,* is incompatible with the doctrine of transubstantiation.

Contraception: Anything done by positive interference to prevent sexual intercourse from resulting in conception. Direct contraception is against the order of nature. Indirect contraception — as a secondary effect of medical treatment or other action having a necessary, good, non-contraceptive purpose — is permissible under the principle of the double effect. The practice of periodic continence is not contraception because it does not involve positive interference with the order of nature. (See *Humanae Vitae,* other entries.)

Contrition: Sorrow for sin coupled with a purpose of amendment. Contrition arising from a supernatural motive is necessary for the forgiveness of sin. (1) Perfect contrition is total sorrow for and renunciation of attachment to sin, arising from the motive of pure love of God. Perfect contrition, which implies the intention of doing all God wants done for the forgiveness of sin (including confession in a reasonable period of time), is sufficient for the forgiveness of serious sin and the remission of all temporal punishment due for sin. (The intention to receive the sacrament of penance is implicit — even if unrealized, as in the case of some persons — in perfect contrition.) (2) Imperfect contrition or attrition is sorrow arising from a quasi-selfish supernatural motive; e.g., the fear of losing heaven, suffering the pains of hell, etc. Imperfect contrition is sufficient for the forgiveness of serious sin when joined with absolution in confession, and sufficient for the forgiveness of venial sin even outside of confession.

Contumely: Personal insult, reviling a person in his presence by accusation of moral faults, by refusal of recognition or due respect; a violation of obligations of justice and charity.

Council, Plenary: A council held for the particular churches belonging to the same episcopal conference. Such a council can be convoked to take action related to the pastoral activity and mission of the Church in the territory. The membership of such councils is fixed by canon law; their decrees, when approved by the Holy See, are binding in the territory (see Index, Plenary Councils of Baltimore).

Councils, Provincial: Meetings of the bishops of a province. The metropolitan, or ranking archbishop, of an ecclesiastical province convenes and presides over such councils in a manner prescribed by canon law to take action related to the life and mission of the Church in the province. Acts and decrees must be approved by the Holy See before being promulgated.

Counsels, Evangelical: Gospel counsels of perfection, especially voluntary poverty, perfect chastity and obedience, which were recommended by Christ to those who would devote themselves exclusively and completely to the immediate service of God. Religious (members of institutes of consecrated life) bind themselves by public vows to observe these counsels in a life of total consecration to God and service to people through various kinds of apostolic works.

Counter-Reformation: The period of approximately 100 years following the Council of Trent, which witnessed a reform within the Church to stimulate genuine Catholic life and to counteract effects of the Reformation.

Covenant: A bond of relationship between parties pledged to each other. God-initiated covenants in the Old Testament included those with Noah, Abraham, Moses, Levi, David. The Mosaic (Sinai) covenant made Israel God's Chosen People on terms of fidelity to true faith, true worship, and righteous conduct according to the Decalogue. The New Testament covenant, prefigured in the Old Testament, is the bond people have with God through Christ. All people are called to be parties to this perfect and everlasting covenant, which was mediated and ratified by Christ. The marriage covenant seals the closest possible relationship between a man and a woman.

Creation: The production by God of something out of nothing. The biblical account of creation is contained in the first two chapters of Genesis.

Creator: God, the supreme, self-existing Being, the absolute and infinite First Cause of all things.

Creature: Everything in the realm of being is a creature, except God.

Cremation: The reduction of a human corpse to ashes by means of fire. Cremation is not in line with Catholic tradition and practice, even though it is not opposed to any article of faith. The Congregation for the Doctrine of the Faith, under date of May 8, 1963, circulated among bishops an instruction which upheld the traditional practices of Christian burial but modified anti-cremation legislation. Cremation may be permitted for serious reasons, of a private as well as public nature, provided it does not involve any contempt of the Church or of religion, or any attempt to deny, question, or belittle the doctrine of the resurrection of the body. In a letter dated Mar. 21, 1997, and addressed to Bishop Anthony M. Pilla, president of the National Conference of Catholic Bishops, the Congregation for Divine Worship and the Discipline of the Sacraments granted "a particular permission to the diocesan bishops of the United States of America. By this, local Ordinaries (heads of dioceses) are authorized ... to permit that the funeral liturgy, including where appropriate the celebration of the Eucharist, be celebrated in the presence of the cremated remains instead of the natural body." Bishop Pilla asked bishops not to use this indult until appropriate texts and ritual directives are approved by the Vatican. (See Burial, Ecclesiastical).

Crib: A devotional representation of the birth of Jesus. The custom of erecting cribs is generally attributed to St. Francis of Assisi who in 1223 obtained from Pope Honorius III permission to use a crib and figures of the Christ Child, Mary, St. Joseph, and others, to represent the mystery of the Nativity.

Crosier: The bishop's staff, symbolic of his pastoral office, responsibility and authority; used at liturgical functions.

Crypt: An underground or partly underground chamber; e.g., the lower part of a church used for worship and/or burial.

Cura Animarum: A Latin phrase, meaning care of souls, designating the pastoral ministry and responsibility of bishops and priests.

Curia: The personnel and offices through which (1) the pope administers the affairs of the universal Church, the Roman Curia (see separate entry), or (2) a bishop the affairs of a diocese, diocesan curia. The principal officials of a diocesan curia are the vicar general of the diocese, the chancellor, officials of the diocesan tribunal or court, examiners, consultors, auditors, notaries.

Custos: A religious superior who presides over a number of convents collectively called a custody. In some institutes of consecrated life a custos may be the deputy of a higher superior.

D

Deaconess: A woman officially appointed and charged by the Church to carry out service-like functions. Phoebe apparently was one (Rom. 16:1-2); a second probable reference to the office is in 1 Tm. 3:11. The office — for assistance at the baptism of women, for pastoral service to women and for works of charity — had considerable development in the third and also in the fourth century when the actual term came into use (in place of such designations as diacona, vidua, virgo canonica). Its importance declined subsequently with the substitution of infusion in place of immersion as the common method of baptism in the West, and with the increase of the practice of infant baptism. There is no record of the ministry of deaconess in the West after the beginning of the 11th century. The office continued, however, for a longer time in the East. The Vatican's Theological Commission, in a paper prepared in 1971, noted that there had been in the past a form of diaconal ordination for women. With a rite and purpose distinctive to women, it differed essentially from the ordination of deacons, which had sacramental effects. Several Christian churches have had revivals of the office of deaconess since the 1830s. There is a contemporary movement in support of such a revival among some Catholics.

Dean: (1) A priest with supervisory responsibility over a section of a diocese known as a deanery. The post-Vatican II counterpart of a dean is an episcopal vicar. (2) The senior or ranking member of a group.

Dean of the College of Cardinals: See Index.

Decision: A judgment or pronouncement on a cause or suit, given by a church tribunal or official with judicial authority. A decision has the force of law for concerned parties.

Declaration: (1) An ecclesiastical document which presents an interpretation of an existing law. (2) A position paper on a specific subject; e.g., the three declarations issued by the Second Vatican Council on religious freedom, non-Christian religions, and Christian education.

Decree: An edict or ordinance issued by a pope and/or by an ecumenical council, with binding force in the whole Church; by a department of the Roman Curia, with binding force for concerned parties; by a territorial body of bishops, with binding force for persons in the area; by individual bishops, with binding force for concerned parties until revocation or the death of the bishop. The nine decrees issued by the Second Vatican Council were combinations of doctrinal and pastoral statements with executive orders for action and movement toward renewal and reform in the Church.

Dedication of a Church: The ceremony whereby a church is solemnly set apart for the worship of God. The custom of dedicating churches had an antecedent in Old Testament ceremonies for the dedication of the Temple, as in the times of Solomon and the Maccabees. The earliest extant record of the dedication of a Christian church dates from early in the fourth century, when it was done simply by the celebration of Mass. Other ceremonies developed later. A church can be dedicated by a simple blessing or a solemn consecration. The rite of consecration is generally performed by a bishop.

Deism: A system of natural religion which acknowledges the existence of God but regards him as so transcendent and remote from man and the universe that divine revelation and the supernatural order of things are irrelevant and unacceptable. It developed from rationalistic principles in England in the 17th and 18th centuries, and had Voltaire, Rousseau and the Encyclopedists among its advocates in France.

Despair: Abandonment of hope for salvation arising from the conviction that God will not provide the necessary means for attaining it, that following God's way of life for salvation is impossible, or that one's sins are unforgivable; a serious sin against the Holy Spirit and the theological virtues of hope and faith, involving distrust in the mercy and goodness of God and a denial of the truths that God wills the salvation of all persons and provides sufficient grace for it. Real despair is distinguished from unreasonable fear with respect to the difficulties of attaining salvation, from morbid anxiety over the demands of divine justice, and from feelings of despair.

Detraction: Revelation of true but hidden faults of a person without sufficient and justifying reason; a violation of requirements of justice and charity, involving the obligation to make restitution when this is possible without doing more harm to the good name of the offended party. In some cases, e.g., to prevent evil, secret faults may and should be disclosed.

Devil: (1) Lucifer, Satan, chief of the fallen angels who sinned and were banished from heaven. Still possessing angelic powers, he can cause such diabolical phenomena as possession and obsession, and can tempt men to sin. (2) Any fallen angel.

Devotion: (1) Religious fervor, piety; dedication. (2) The consolation experienced at times during prayer; a reverent manner of praying.

Devotions: Pious practices of members of the Church include not only participation in various acts of the liturgy but also in other acts of worship generally called popular or private devotions. Concerning these, the Second Vatican Council said in the *Constitution on the Sacred Liturgy* (No. 13): "Popular devotions of the Christian people are warmly commended, provided they accord with the laws and norms of the Church. Such is especially the case with devotions called for by the Apostolic See. Devotions proper to the individual churches also have a special dignity. These devotions should be so drawn up that they harmonize with the liturgical seasons, accord with the sacred liturgy, are in some fashion derived from it, and lead the people to it, since the liturgy by its very nature far surpasses any of them." Devotions of a liturgical type are Exposition of the Blessed Sacrament, recitation of Evening Prayer and Night Prayer of the Liturgy of the Hours. Examples of paraliturgical devotion are a Bible Service or Vigil, and the Angelus, Rosary and Stations of the Cross, which have a strong scriptural basis.

Diocese: A particular church, a fully organized ecclesiastical jurisdiction under the pastoral direction of a bishop as local Ordinary.

Discalced: Of Latin derivation and meaning without shoes, the word is applied to religious orders or congregations whose members go barefoot or wear sandals.

Disciple: A term used sometimes in reference to the Apostles but more often to a larger number of followers (70 or 72) of Christ mentioned in Lk. 10:1.

Disciplina Arcani: A Latin phrase, meaning discipline of the secret and referring to a practice of the early Church, especially during the Roman persecutions, to: (1) conceal Christian truths from those who, it was feared, would misinterpret, ridicule and profane the teachings, and persecute Christians for believing them; (2) instruct catechumens in a gradual manner, withholding the teaching of certain doctrines until the catechumens proved themselves of good faith and sufficient understanding.

Dispensation: The relaxation of a law in a particular case. Laws made for the common good sometimes work undue hardship in particular cases. In such cases, where sufficient reasons are present, dispensations may be granted by proper authorities. Bishops, religious superiors and others may dispense from certain laws; the pope can dispense from all ecclesiastical laws. No one has authority to dispense from obligations of the divine law.

Divination: Attempting to foretell future or hidden things by means of things like dreams, necromancy, spiritism, examination of entrails, astrology, augury, omens, palmistry, drawing straws, dice, cards, etc. Practices like these attribute to creatural things a power which belongs to God alone and are violations of the First Commandment.

Divine Praises: Fourteen praises recited or sung at Benediction of the Blessed Sacrament in reparation for sins of sacrilege, blasphemy and profanity. Some of these praises date from the end of the 18th century: Blessed be God. / Blessed be his holy Name. / Blessed be Jesus Christ, true God and true Man. / Blessed be the Name of Jesus. / Blessed be his most Sacred Heart. / Blessed be his most Precious Blood. / Blessed be Jesus in the most holy Sacrament of the Altar. / Blessed be the Holy Spirit, the Paraclete. / Blessed be the great Mother of God, Mary most holy. / Blessed be her holy and Immaculate Conception. / Blessed be her glorious Assumption. / Blessed be the name of Mary, Virgin and Mother. / Blessed be St. Joseph, her most chaste Spouse. / Blessed be God in his Angels and in his Saints.

Double Effect Principle: Actions sometimes have two effects closely related to each other, one good and the other bad, and a difficult moral question can arise: Is it permissible to place an action from which two such results follow? It is permissible to place the action, if: the action is good in itself and is directly productive of the good effect; the circumstances are good; the intention of the person is good; the reason for placing the action is proportionately serious to the seriousness of the indirect bad effect. For example: Is it morally permissible for a pregnant woman to undergo medical or surgical treatment for a pathological condition if the indirect and secondary effect of the treatment will be the loss of the child? The reply is affirmative, for these reasons: The action, i.e., the treatment, is good in itself, cannot be deferred until a later time without very serious consequences, and is ordered directly to the cure of critically grave pathology. By means of the treatment, the woman intends to save her life, which she has a right to do. The loss of the child is not directly sought as a means for the cure of the mother but results indirectly and in a secondary manner from the placing of the action, i.e., the treatment, which is good in itself. The double effect principle does not support the principle that the end justifies the means.

Doxology: (1) The lesser doxology, or ascription of glory to the Trinity, is the Glory be to the Father. The first part dates back to the third or fourth century, and came from the form of baptism. The concluding words, As it was in the beginning, etc., are of later origin. (2) The greater doxology, Glory to God in the highest, begins with the words of angelic praise at the birth of Christ recounted in the Infancy Narrative (Lk. 2:14). It is often recited at Mass. Of early Eastern origin, it is found in the *Apostolic Constitutions* in a form much like the present. (3) The formula of praise at the end of the Eucharistic Prayer at Mass, sung or said by the celebrant while he holds aloft the paten containing the consecrated host in one hand and the chalice containing the consecrated wine in the other.

Dulia: A Greek term meaning the veneration or homage, different in nature and degree from that given to God, paid to the saints. It includes honoring the saints and seeking their intercession with God.

Duty: A moral obligation deriving from the binding force of law, the exigencies of one's state in life, and other sources.

E

Easter Controversy: A three-phase controversy over the time for the celebration of Easter. Some early Christians in the Near East, called Quartodecimans, favored the observance of Easter on the 14th day of Nisan, the spring month of the Hebrew calendar, whenever it occurred. Against this practice, Pope St. Victor I, about 190, ordered a Sunday observance of the feast. The Council of Nicaea, in line with usages of the Church at Rome and Alexandria, decreed in 325 that Easter should be observed on the Sunday following the first full moon of spring. Uniformity of practice in the West was not achieved until several centuries later, when the British Isles, in delayed compliance with measures enacted by the Synod of Whitby in 664, accepted the Roman date of observance. Unrelated to the controversy is the fact that some Eastern Christians, in accordance with traditional calendar practices, celebrate Easter at a different time than the Roman and Eastern Churches.

Easter Duty, Season: The serious obligation binding Catholics of Roman Rite, to receive the Eucharist during the Easter season (in the U.S., from the first Sunday of Lent to and including Trinity Sunday).

Easter Water: Holy water blessed with special ceremonies and distributed on the Easter Vigil; used during Easter Week for blessing the faithful and homes.

Ecclesiology: Study of the nature, constitution, members, mission, functions, etc., of the Church.

Ecology: The natural environment of the total range of creation — mineral, vegetable, animal, human — entrusted to people for respect, care and appropriate use as well as conservation and development for the good of present and future generations.

Ecstasy: An extraordinary state of mystical experience in which a person is so absorbed in God that the activity of the exterior senses is suspended.

Ecumenism: The movement of Christians and their churches toward the unity willed by Christ. The Second Vatican Council called the movement "those activities and enterprises which, according to various needs of the Church and opportune occasions, are started and organized for the fostering of unity among Christians" (Decree on Ecumenism, No. 4). Spiritual ecumenism, i.e., mutual prayer for unity, is the heart of the movement. The movement also involves scholarly and pew-level efforts for the development of mutual understanding and better interfaith relations in general, and collaboration by the churches and their members in the social area. (See Index for other entries.)

Elevation: The raising of the host after consecration at Mass for adoration by the faithful. The custom was introduced in the Diocese of Paris about the close of the 12th century to offset an erroneous teaching of the time which held that transubstantiation of the bread did not take place until after the consecration of the wine in the chalice. The elevation of the chalice following the consecration of the wine was introduced in the 15th century.

End Justifies the Means: An unacceptable ethical principle which states that evil means may be used to produce good effects.

Envy: Sadness over another's good fortune because it is considered a loss to oneself or a detraction from one's own excellence; one of the seven capital sins, a violation of the obligations of charity.

Epiclesis: An invocation of the Holy Spirit, to bless the offerings consecrated at Mass; before the consecration in the Latin rite, after the consecration in Eastern usage.

Epikeia: A Greek word meaning reasonableness and designating a moral theory and practice, a mild interpretation of the mind of a legislator who is prudently considered not to wish positive law to bind in certain circumstances. Use of the principle is justified in practice when the lawgiver himself cannot be appealed to and when it can be prudently assumed that in particular cases, e.g., because of special hardship, he would not wish the law to be applied in a strict manner. Epikeia may not be applied with respect to acts that are intrinsically wrong or those covered by laws which automatically make them invalid.

Episcopate: (1) The office, dignity and sacramental powers bestowed upon a bishop at his ordination. (2) The body of bishops collectively.

Equivocation: (1) The use of words, phrases, or gestures having more than one meaning in order to conceal information which a questioner has no strict right to know. It is permissible to equivocate (have a broad mental reservation) in some circumstances. (2) A lie, i.e., a statement of untruth. Lying is intrinsically wrong. A lie told in joking, evident as such, is not wrong.

Eschatology: Doctrine concerning the last things: death, judgment, heaven and hell, and the final state of perfection of the people and kingdom of God at the end of time.

Eternity: The interminable, perfect possession of life in its totality without beginning or end; an attribute of God, who has no past or future but always is. Man's existence has a beginning but no end and is, accordingly, called immortal.

Ethics: Moral philosophy, the science of the morality of human acts deriving from natural law, the natural end of man, and the powers of human reason. It includes all the spheres of human activity — personal, social, economic, political, etc. Ethics is distinct from but can be related to moral theology, whose primary principles are drawn from divine revelation.

Eucharistic Congresses: Public demonstrations of faith in the Holy Eucharist. Combining liturgical services, other public ceremonies, subsidiary meetings, different kinds of instructional and inspirational elements, they are unified by central themes and serve to increase understanding of and devotion to Christ in the Eucharist, and to relate this liturgy of worship and witness to life. The first international congress developed from a proposal by Marie Marthe Tamisier of Touraine, organizing efforts of Msgr. Louis Gaston de Segur, and backing by industrialist Philibert Vrau. It was held with the approval of Pope Leo XIII at the University of Lille, France, and was attended by some 800 persons from France, Belgium, Holland, England, Spain and Switzerland. International congresses are organized by the Pontifical Committee for International Eucharistic Congresses. Participants include clergy, religious and lay persons from many countries, and representatives of national and international Catholic organizations. Forty-five international congresses were held from 1881 to 1993: Lille (1881), Avignon (1882), Liege (1883), Freiburg (1885), Toulouse (1886), Paris (1888), Antwerp (1890), Jerusalem (1893), Rheims (1894), Paray-le-Monial (1897), Brussels (1898), Lourdes (1899), Angers (1901), Namur (1902), Angouleme (1904), Rome (1905), Tournai (1906), Metz (1907), London (1908), Cologne (1909), Montreal (1910), Madrid (1911), Vienna (1912), Malta (1913), Lourdes (1914), Rome (1922), Amsterdam (1924), Chicago (1926), Sydney (1928), Carthage (1930), Dublin (1932), Buenos Aires (1934), Manila (1937), Budapest (1938), Barcelona (1952), Rio de Janeiro (1955), Munich, Germany (1960), Bombay, India (1964), Bogota, Colombia (1968), Melbourne, Australia (1973), Philadelphia (1976), Lourdes (1981), Nairobi, Kenya (1985), Seoul, South Korea (1989), Seville, Spain (1993). The 46th Congress was held May 25-June 1, 1997, in Wroclaw, Poland. The 47th Congress will be held in Rome in conjunction with the celebration of Jubilee Year 2000.

Eugenics: The science of heredity and environment for the physical and mental improvement of offspring. Extreme eugenics is untenable in practice because it advocates immoral means, such as compulsory breeding of the select, sterilization of persons said to be unfit, abortion, and unacceptable methods of birth regulation.

Euthanasia: Mercy killing, the direct causing of death for the purpose of ending human suffering. Euthanasia is murder and is totally illicit, for the natural law forbids the direct taking of one's own life or that of an innocent person. The use of drugs to relieve suffering in serious cases, even when this results in a shortening of life as an indirect and secondary effect, is permissible under conditions of the double effect principle. It is also permissible for a seriously ill person to refuse to follow — or for other responsible persons to refuse to permit — extraordinary medical procedures even though the refusal might entail shortening of life.

Evangelization: Proclamation of the Gospel, the Good News of salvation in and through Christ, among those who have not yet known or received it; and efforts for the progressive development of the life of faith among those who have already received the Gospel and all that it entails. Evangelization is the primary mission of the Church, in which all members of the Church are called to participate.

Evolution: Scientific theory concerning the development of the physical universe from unorganized matter (inorganic evolution) and, especially, the development of existing forms of vegetable, animal and human life from earlier and more primitive organisms (organic evolution). Various ideas about evolution were advanced for some centuries before scientific evidence in support of the main-line theory of organic evolution, which has several formulations, was discovered and verified in the second half of the 19th century and afterwards. This evidence — from the findings of comparative anatomy and other sciences — confirmed evolution of species and cleared the way to further investigation of questions regarding the processes of its accomplishment. While a number of such questions remain open with respect to human evolution, a point of doctrine not open to

question is the immediate creation of the human soul by God. For some time, theologians regarded the theory with hostility, considering it to be in opposition to the account of creation in the early chapters of Genesis and subversive of belief in such doctrines as creation, the early state of man in grace, and the fall of man from grace. This state of affairs and the tension it generated led to considerable controversy regarding an alleged conflict between religion and science. Gradually, however, the tension was diminished with the development of biblical studies from the latter part of the 19th century onwards, with clarification of the distinctive features of religious truth and scientific truth, and with the refinement of evolutionary concepts. So far as the Genesis account of creation is concerned, the Catholic view is that the writer(s) did not write as a scientist but as the communicator of religious truth in a manner adapted to the understanding of the people of his time. He used anthropomorphic language, the figure of days and other literary devices to state the salvation truths of creation, the fall of man from grace, and the promise of redemption. It was beyond the competency and purpose of the writer(s) to describe creation and related events in a scientific manner. (See additional article.)

Excommunication: A penalty or censure by which a baptized Roman Catholic is excluded from the communion of the faithful, for committing and remaining obstinate in certain serious offenses specified in canon law; e.g. heresy, schism, apostasy, abortion. As by baptism a person is made a member of the Church in which there is a communication of spiritual goods, so by excommunication he is deprived of the same spiritual goods until he repents and receives absolution. Even though excommunicated, a person is still responsible for fulfillment of the normal obligations of a Catholic. (See Censures).

Existentialism: A philosophy with radical concern for the problems of individual existence and identity viewed in particular here-and-now patterns of thought which presuppose irrationality and absurdity in human life and the whole universe. It is preoccupied with questions about freedom, moral decision and responsibility against a background of denial of objective truth and universal norms of conduct; is characterized by prevailing anguish, dread, fear, pessimism, despair; is generally atheistic, although its modern originator, Soren Kierkegaard (d. 1855), and Gabriel Marcel (d. 1973) attempted to give it a Christian orientation. Pius XII called it "the new erroneous philosophy which, opposing itself to idealism, immanentism and pragmatism, has assumed the name of existentialism, since it concerns itself only with the existence of individual things and neglects all consideration of their immutable essences" (Encyclical *Humani Generis*, Aug. 12, 1950).

Exorcism: (1) Driving out evil spirits; a rite in which evil spirits are charged and commanded on the authority of God and with the prayer of the Church to depart from a person or to cease causing harm to a person suffering from diabolical possession or obsession. The sacramental is officially administered by a priest delegated for the purpose by the bishop of the place. Elements of the rite include the Litany of Saints; recitation of the Our Father, one or more creeds, and other prayers; specific prayers of exorcism; the reading of Gospel passages and use of the Sign of the Cross. (2) Exorcisms which do not imply the conditions of either diabolical possession or obsession form part of the ceremony of baptism and are also included in formulas for various blessings; e.g., of water.

Exposition of the Blessed Sacrament: "In churches where the Eucharist is regularly reserved, it is recommended that solemn exposition of the Blessed Sacrament for an extended period of time should take place once a year, even though the period is not strictly continuous. Shorter expositions of the Eucharist (Benediction) are to be arranged in such a way that the blessing with the Eucharist is preceded by a reasonable time for readings of the word of God, songs, prayers and a period for silent prayer." So stated Vatican directives issued in 1973.

F

Faculties: Grants of jurisdiction or authority by the law of the Church or superiors (pope, bishop, religious superior) for exercise of the powers of holy orders; e.g., priests are given faculties to hear confessions, officiate at weddings; bishops are given faculties to grant dispensations, etc.

Faith: In religion, faith has several aspects. Catholic doctrine calls faith the assent of the mind to truths revealed by God, the assent being made with the help of grace and by command of the will on account of the authority and trustworthiness of God revealing. The term faith also refers to the truths that are believed (content of faith) and to the way in which a person, in response to Christ, gives witness to and expresses belief in daily life (living faith). All of these elements, and more, are included in the following statement: " 'The obedience of faith' (Rom. 16:26; 1:5; 2 Cor. 10:5-6) must be given to God who reveals, an obedience by which man entrusts his whole self freely to God, offering 'the full submission of intellect and will to God who reveals' (First Vatican Council, *Dogmatic Constitution on the Catholic Faith,* Chap. 3), and freely assenting to the truth revealed by him. If this faith is to be shown, the grace of God and the interior help of the Holy Spirit must precede and assist, moving the heart and turning it to God, opening the eyes of the mind, and giving 'joy and ease to everyone in assenting to the truth and believing it' " (Second Council of Orange, Canon 7) (Second Vatican Council, *Constitution on Revelation,* No. 5). Faith is necessary for salvation.

Faith, Rule of: The norm or standard of religious belief. The Catholic doctrine is that belief must be professed in the divinely revealed truths in the Bible and tradition as interpreted and proposed by the infallible teaching authority of the Church.

Fast, Eucharistic: Abstinence from food and drink, except water and medicine, is required for one hour before the reception of the Eucharist. Persons who are advanced in age or suffer from infirmity or illness, together with those who care for them, can receive Holy Communion even if they have not abstained from food and drink for an hour. A priest celebrating two or three Masses on the same day can eat and drink something before the second or third Mass without regard for the hour limit.

Father: A title of priests, who are regarded as spiritual fathers because they are the ordinary ministers of baptism, by which persons are born to supernatural life, and because of their pastoral service to people.

Fear: A mental state caused by the apprehension of present or future danger. Grave fear does not necessarily remove moral responsibility for an act, but may lessen it.

First Friday: A devotion consisting of the reception of Holy Communion on the first Friday of nine consecutive months in honor of the Sacred Heart of Jesus and in reparation for sin. (See Sacred Heart, Promises.)

First Saturday: A devotion tracing its origin to the apparitions of the Blessed Virgin Mary at Fatima in 1917. Those practicing the devotion go to confession and, on the first Saturday of five consecutive months, receive Holy Communion, recite five decades of the Rosary, and meditate on the mysteries for 15 minutes.

Fisherman's Ring: A signet ring engraved with the image of St. Peter fishing from a boat, and encircled with the name of the reigning pope. It is not worn by the pope. It is used to seal briefs, and is destroyed after each pope's death.

Forgiveness of Sin: Catholics believe that sins are forgiven by God through the mediation of Christ in view of the repentance of the sinner and by means of the sacrament of penance. (See Penance, Contrition).

Fortitude: Courage to face dangers or hardships for the sake of what is good; one of the four cardinal virtues and one of the seven gifts of the Holy Spirit.

Fortune Telling: Attempting to predict the future or the occult by means of cards, palm reading, etc.; a form of divination, prohibited by the First Commandment.

Forty Hours Devotion: A Eucharistic observance consisting of solemn exposition of the Blessed Sacrament coupled with special Masses and forms of prayer, for the purposes of making reparation for sin and praying for God's blessings of grace and peace. The devotion was instituted in 1534 in Milan. St. John Neumann of Philadelphia was the first bishop in the U.S. to prescribe its observance in his diocese. For many years in this country, the observance was held annually on a rotating basis in all parishes of a diocese. Simplified and abbreviated Eucharistic observances have taken the place of the devotion in some places.

Forum: The sphere in which ecclesiastical authority or jurisdiction is exercised. (1) External: Authority is exercised in the external forum to deal with matters affecting the public welfare of the Church and its members. Those who have such authority because of their office (e.g., diocesan bishops) are called ordinaries. (2) Internal: Authority is exercised in the internal forum to deal with matters affecting the private spiritual good of individuals. The sacramental forum is the sphere in which the sacrament of penance is administered; other exercises of jurisdiction in the internal forum take place in the non-sacramental forum.

Franciscan Crown: A seven-decade rosary used to commemorate the seven Joys of the Blessed Virgin: the Annunciation, the Visitation, the Nativity of Our Lord, the Adoration of the Magi, the Finding of the

Child Jesus in the Temple, the Apparition of the Risen Christ to his Mother, the Assumption and Coronation of the Blessed Virgin. Introduced in 1422, the Crown originally consisted only of seven Our Fathers and 70 Hail Marys. Two Hail Marys were added to complete the number 72 (thought to be the number of years of Mary's life), and one Our Father, Hail Mary and Glory be to the Father are said for the intention of the pope.

Freedom, Religious: The Second Vatican Council declared that the right to religious freedom in civil society "means that all men are to be immune from coercion on the part of individuals or of social groups and of any human power, in such wise that in matters religious no one is to be forced to act in a manner contrary to his own beliefs. Nor is anyone to be restrained from acting in accordance with his own beliefs, whether privately or publicly, whether alone or in association with others, within due limits" of requirements for the common good. The foundation of this right in civil society is the "very dignity of the human person" (*Declaration on Religious Freedom,* No. 2). The conciliar statement did not deal with the subject of freedom within the Church. It noted the responsibility of the faithful "carefully to attend to the sacred and certain doctrine of the Church" (No. 14).

Freemasons: A fraternal order which originated in London in 1717 with the formation of the first Grand Lodge of Freemasons. From England, the order spread to Europe and elsewhere. Its principles and basic rituals embody a naturalistic religion, active participation in which is incompatible with Christian faith and practice. Grand Orient Freemasonry, developed in Latin countries, is atheistic, irreligious and anti-clerical. In some places, Freemasonry has been regarded as subversive of the state; in Catholic quarters, it has been considered hostile to the Church and its doctrine. In the United States, Freemasonry has been widely regarded as a fraternal and philanthropic order. For serious doctrinal and pastoral reasons, Catholics were forbidden to join the Freemasons under penalty of excommunication, according to church law before 1983. Eight different popes in 17 different pronouncements, and at least six different local councils, condemned Freemasonry. The first condemnation was made by Clement XII in 1738. Eastern Orthodox and many Protestant bodies have also opposed the order. In the U.S., there was some easing of the ban against Masonic membership by Catholics in view of a letter written in 1974 by Cardinal Franjo Seper, prefect of the Congregation for the Doctrine of the Faith. The letter was interpreted to mean that Catholics might join Masonic lodges which were not anti-Catholic. This was called erroneous in a declaration issued by the Doctrinal Congregation Feb. 17, 1981. The prohibition against Masonic membership was restated in a declaration issued by the Doctrinal Congregation Nov. 26, 1983, with the approval of Pope John Paul II, as follows. "The Church's negative position on Masonic associations remains unaltered, since their principles have always been regarded as irreconcilable with the Church's doctrine. Hence, joining them remains prohibited by the Church. Catholics enrolled in Masonic associations are involved in serious sin and may not approach Holy Communion. Local ecclesiastical authorities do not have the faculty to pronounce a judgment on the nature of Masonic associations which might include a diminution of the above-mentioned judgment." This latest declaration, like the revised Code of Canon Law, does not include a penalty of excommunication for Catholics who join the Masons. Local bishops are not authorized to grant dispensations from the prohibition. The foregoing strictures against Masonic membership by Catholics were reiterated in a report by the Committee for Pastoral Research and Practice, National Conference of Catholic Bishops, released through Catholic News Service June 7, 1985.

Free Will: The faculty or capability of making a reasonable choice among several alternatives. Freedom of will underlies the possibility and fact of moral responsibility.

Friar: Term applied to members of mendicant orders to distinguish them from members of monastic orders. (See Mendicants.)

Fruits of the Holy Spirit: Charity, joy, peace, patience, kindness, goodness, generosity, gentleness, faithfulness, modesty, self-control, chastity.

G

Gambling: The backing of an issue with a sum of money or other valuables, which is permissible if the object is honest, if the two parties have the free disposal of their stakes without prejudice to the rights of others, if the terms are thoroughly understood by both parties, and if the outcome is not known beforehand. Gambling often falls into disrepute and may be forbidden by civil law, as well as by divine law, because of cheating, fraud and other accompanying evils.

Gehenna: Greek form of a Jewish name, Gehinnom, for a valley near Jerusalem, the site of Moloch worship; used as a synonym for hell.

Genuflection: Bending of the knee, a natural sign of adoration or reverence, as when persons genuflect with the right knee in passing before the tabernacle to acknowledge the Eucharistic presence of Christ.

Gethsemani: A Hebrew word meaning oil press, designating the place on the Mount of Olives where Christ prayed and suffered in agony the night before he died.

Gifts of the Holy Spirit: Supernatural habits disposing a person to respond promptly to the inspiration of grace; promised by Christ and communicated through the Holy Spirit, especially in the sacrament of confirmation. They are: wisdom, understanding, counsel, fortitude, knowledge, piety, fear of the Lord.

Gluttony: An unreasonable appetite for food and drink; one of the seven capital sins.

God: The infinitely perfect Supreme Being, uncaused and absolutely self-sufficient, eternal, the Creator and final end of all things. The one God subsists in three equal Persons, the Father and the Son and the Holy Spirit. God, although transcendent and distinct from the universe, is present and active in the world in realization of his plan for the salvation of human beings, principally through Revelation, the operations of the Holy Spirit, the life and ministry of Christ, and the continuation of Christ's ministry in the Church. The existence of God is an article of faith, clearly communicated in divine Revelation. Even without this Revelation, however, the Church teaches, in a declaration by the First Vatican Council, that human beings can acquire certain knowledge of the existence of God and some of his attributes. This can be done on the bases of principles of reason and reflection on human experience. Non-revealed arguments or demonstrations for the existence of God have been developed from the principle of causality; the contingency of human beings and the universe; the existence of design, change and movement in the universe; human awareness of moral responsibility; widespread human testimony to the existence of God.

Grace: A free gift of God to persons (and angels), grace is a created sharing or participation in the life of God. It is given to persons through the merits of Christ and is communicated by the Holy Spirit. It is necessary for salvation. The principal means of grace are the sacraments (especially the Eucharist), prayer and good works. (1) Sanctifying or habitual grace makes persons holy and pleasing to God, adopted children of God, members of Christ, temples of the Holy Spirit, heirs of heaven capable of supernaturally meritorious acts. With grace, God gives persons the supernatural virtues and gifts of the Holy Spirit. The sacraments of baptism and penance were instituted to give grace to those who do not have it; the other sacraments, to increase it in those already in the state of grace. The means for growth in holiness, or the increase of grace, are prayer, the sacraments, and good works. Sanctifying grace is lost by the commission of serious sin. Each sacrament confers sanctifying grace for the special purpose of the sacrament; in this context, grace is called sacramental grace. (2) Actual grace is a supernatural help of God which enlightens and strengthens a person to do good and to avoid evil. It is not a permanent quality, like sanctifying grace. It is necessary for the performance of supernatural acts. It can be resisted and refused. Persons in the state of serious sin are given actual grace to lead them to repentance.

Grace at Meals: Prayers said before meals, asking a blessing of God, and after meals, giving thanks to God. In addition to traditional prayers for these purposes, many variations suitable for different occasions are possible, at personal option.

H

Habit: (1) A disposition to do things easily, given with grace (and therefore supernatural) and/or acquired by repetition of similar acts. (2) The garb worn by Religious.

Hagiography: Writings or documents about saints and other holy persons.

Hail Mary: A prayer addressed to the Blessed Virgin Mary; also called the Ave Maria (Latin equivalent of Hail Mary) and the Angelic Salutation. In three parts, it consists of the words addressed to Mary by the Archangel Gabriel on the occasion of the Annunciation, in the Infancy Narrative (Hail full of grace, the Lord is with you, blessed are you among women.); the words addressed to Mary by her cousin Elizabeth on the occasion of the Visitation (Blessed is the fruit of your womb.); a concluding petition (Holy Mary, Mother of God, pray for us sinners now and at the hour of our death. Amen.). The first two salutations

were joined in Eastern Rite formulas by the sixth century, and were similarly used at Rome in the seventh century. Insertion of the name of Jesus at the conclusion of the salutations was probably made by Urban IV about 1262. The present form of the petition was incorporated into the breviary in 1514.

Heaven: The state of those who, having achieved salvation, are in glory with God and enjoy the beatific vision. The phrase, kingdom of heaven, refers to the order or kingdom of God, grace, salvation.

Hell: The state of persons who die in mortal sin, in a condition of self-alienation from God which will last forever.

Heresy: The obstinate post-baptismal denial or doubt by a Catholic of any truth which must be believed as a matter of divine and Catholic faith (Canon 751, of the Code of Canon Law). Formal heresy involves deliberate resistance to the authority of God who communicates revelation through Scripture and tradition and the teaching authority of the Church. Heretics automatically incur the penalty of excommunication (Canon 1364 of the Code of Canon Law). Heresies have been significant not only as disruptions of unity of faith but also as occasions for the clarification and development of doctrine. Heresies from the beginning of the Church to the 13th century are described in Dates and Events in Church History.

Hermit: See Anchorite.

Heroic Act of Charity: The completely unselfish offering to God of one's good works and merits for the benefit of the souls in purgatory rather than for oneself. Thus a person may offer to God for the souls in purgatory all the good works he performs during life, all the indulgences he gains, and all the prayers and indulgences that will be offered for him after his death. The act is revocable at will, and is not a vow. Its actual ratification depends on the will of God.

Heterodoxy: False doctrine teaching or belief; a departure from truth.

Holy See: (1) The diocese of the pope, Rome. (2) The pope himself and/or the various officials and bodies of the Church's central administration at Vatican City — the Roman Curia — which act in the name and by authority of the pope.

Holy Spirit: God the Holy Spirit, third Person of the Holy Trinity, who proceeds from the Father and the Son and with whom he is equal in every respect; inspirer of the prophets and writers of sacred Scripture; promised by Christ to the Apostles as their advocate and strengthener; appeared in the form of a dove at the baptism of Christ and as tongues of fire at his descent upon the Apostles; soul of the Church and guarantor, by his abiding presence and action, of truth in doctrine; communicator of grace to human beings, for which reason he is called the sanctifier.

Holy Water: Water blessed by the Church and used as a sacramental, a practice which originated in apostolic times.

Holy Year: A year during which the pope grants the plenary Jubilee Indulgence to the faithful who fulfill certain conditions. For those who make a pilgrimage to Rome during the year, the conditions are reception of the sacraments of penance and the Eucharist, visits and prayer for the intention of the pope in the basilicas of St. Peter, St. John Lateran, St. Paul and St.

Mary Major. For those who do not make a pilgrimage to Rome, the conditions are reception of the sacraments and prayer for the pope during a visit or community celebration in a church designated by the bishop of the locality. Holy Year observances have biblical counterparts in the Years of Jubilee observed at 50-year intervals by the pre-exilic Israelites — when debts were pardoned and slaves freed (Lv. 25:25-54) — and in sabbatical years observed from the end of the Exile to 70 A.D. — in which debts to fellow Jews were remitted. The practice of Christians from early times to go on pilgrimage to the Holy Land, the shrines of martyrs and the tombs of the Apostles in Rome influenced the institution of Holy Years. There was also a prevailing belief among the people that every 100th year was a year of "Great Pardon." Accordingly, even before Boniface VIII formally proclaimed the first Holy Year Feb. 22, 1300, scores of thousands of pilgrims were already on the way to or in Rome. Medieval popes embodied in the observance of Holy Years the practice of good works (reception of the sacraments of penance and the Eucharist, pilgrimages and/or visits to the tombs of the Apostles, and related actions) and spiritual benefits (particularly, special indulgences for the souls in purgatory). These and related practices, with suitable changes for celebrations in local churches, remain staple features of Holy Year observances. The first three Holy Years were observed in 1300, 1350 and 1390. Subsequent ones were celebrated at 25-year intervals except in 1800 and 1850 when, respectively, the French invasion of Italy and political turmoil made observance impossible. Pope Paul II (1464-1471) set the 25-year timetable. In 1500, Pope Alexander VI prescribed the start and finish ceremonies — the opening and closing of the Holy Doors in the major basilicas on successive Christmas Eves. All but a few of the earlier Holy Years were classified as ordinary. Several — like those of 1933 and 1983-84 to commemorate the 1900th and 1950th anniversaries of the death and resurrection of Christ — were in the extraordinary category. Pope John Paul has designated Jubilee Year 2000 to be a Holy Year ending the second and beginning the third millennium of Christianity. (See Jubilee Year 2000.)

Homosexuality: The condition of a person whose sexual orientation is toward persons of the same rather than the opposite sex. The condition, is not sinful in itself. Homosexual acts are seriously sinful in themselves; subjective responsibility for such acts, however, may be conditioned and diminished by compulsion and related factors.

Hope: The theological virtue by which a person firmly trusts in God for the means and attainment salvation.

Hosanna: A Hebrew word, meaning O Lord, save, we pray.

Host, The Sacred: The bread under whose appearances Christ is and remains present in a unique manner after the consecration which takes place during Mass. (See Transubstantiation.)

Humanism: A world view centered on man. Types of humanism which exclude the supernatural are related to secularism.

Humility: A virtue which induces a person to evaluate himself or herself at his or her true worth, to

recognize his or her dependence on God, and to give glory to God for the good he or she has and can do.

Hyperdulia: The special veneration accorded the Blessed Virgin Mary because of her unique role in the mystery of Redemption, her exceptional gifts of grace from God, and her pre-eminence among the saints. Hyperdulia is not adoration; only God is adored.

Hypnosis: A mental state resembling sleep, induced by suggestion, in which the subject does the bidding of the hypnotist. Hypnotism is permissible under certain conditions: the existence of a serious reason, e.g., for anesthetic or therapeutic purposes, and the competence and integrity of the hypnotist. Hypnotism may not be practiced for the sake of amusement. Experiments indicate that, contrary to popular opinion, hypnotized subjects may be induced to perform immoral acts which, normally, they would not do.

Hypostatic Union: The union of the human and divine natures in the one divine Person of Christ.

I

Icons: Byzantine-style paintings or representations of Christ, the Blessed Virgin and other saints, venerated in the Eastern Churches where they take the place of statues.

Idolatry: Worship of any but the true God; a violation of the First Commandment.

IHS: In Greek, the first three letters of the name of Jesus — Iota, Eta, Sigma.

Immortality: The survival and continuing existence of the human soul after death.

Impurity: Unlawful indulgence in sexual pleasure. (See Chastity.)

Incardination: The affiliation of a priest to his diocese. Every secular priest must belong to a certain diocese. Similarly, every priest of a religious community must belong to some jurisdiction of his community; this affiliation, however, is not called incardination.

Incarnation: (1) The coming-into-flesh or taking of human nature by the Second Person of the Trinity. He became human as the Son of Mary, being miraculously conceived by the power of the Holy Spirit, without ceasing to be divine. His divine Person hypostatically unites his divine and human natures. (2) The supernatural mystery coextensive with Christ from the moment of his human conception and continuing through his life on earth; his sufferings and death; his resurrection from the dead and ascension to glory with the Father; his sending, with the Father, of the Holy Spirit upon the Apostles and the Church; and his unending mediation with the Father for the salvation of human beings.

Incense: A granulated substance which, when burnt, emits an aromatic smoke. It symbolizes the zeal with which the faithful should be consumed, the good odor of Christian virtue, the ascent of prayer to God.

Incest: Sexual intercourse with relatives by blood or marriage; a sin of impurity and also a grave violation of the natural reverence due to relatives. Other sins of impurity desire, etc.) concerning relatives have the nature of incest.

Inculturation: This was one of the subjects of an address delivered by Pope John Paul II Feb. 15,

1982, at a meeting in Lagos with the bishops of Nigeria. "An important aspect of your own evangelizing role is the whole dimension of the inculturation of the Gospel into the lives of your people. The Church truly respects the culture of each people. In offering the Gospel message, the Church does not intend to destroy or to abolish what is good and beautiful. In fact, she recognizes many cultural values and, through the power of the Gospel, purifies and takes into Christian worship certain elements of a people's customs. The Church comes to bring Christ; she does not come to bring the culture of another race. Evangelization aims at penetrating and elevating culture by the power of the Gospel.— It is through the Providence of God that the divine message is made incarnate and is communicated through the culture of each people. It is forever true that the path of culture is the path of man, and it is on this path that man encounters the one who embodies the values of all cultures and fully reveals the man of each culture to himself. The Gospel of Christ, the Incarnate Word, finds its home along the path of culture, and from this path it continues to offer its message of salvation and eternal life."

Index of Prohibited Books: A list of books which Catholics were formerly forbidden to read, possess or sell, under penalty of excommunication. The books were banned by the Holy See after publication because their treatment of matters of faith and morals and related subjects were judged to be erroneous or serious occasions of doctrinal error. Some books were listed in the Index by name; others were covered under general norms. The Congregation for the Doctrine of the Faith declared June 14, 1966, that the Index and its related penalties of excommunication no longer had the force of law in the Church. Persons are still obliged, however, to take normal precautions against occasions of doctrinal error.

Indifferentism: A theory that any one religion is as true and good — or false — as any other religion, and that it makes no difference, objectively, what religion one professes, if any. The theory is completely subjective, finding its justification entirely in personal choice without reference to or respect for objective validity. It is also self-contradictory, since it regards as equally acceptable — or unacceptable — the beliefs of all religions, which in fact are not only not all the same but are in some cases opposed to each other.

Indulgence: According to *The Doctrine and Practice of Indulgences,* an apostolic constitution issued by Paul VI Jan. 1, 1967, an indulgence is the remission before God of the temporal punishment due for sins already forgiven as far as their guilt is concerned, which a follower of Christ — with the proper dispositions and under certain determined conditions — acquires through the intervention of the Church. The Church grants indulgences in accordance with doctrine concerning the superabundant merits of Christ and the saints, the Power of the Keys, and the sharing of spiritual goods in the communion of saints. An indulgence is partial or plenary, depending on whether it does away with either part or all of the temporal punishment due for sin. Both types of indulgences can always be applied to the dead by way of suffrage; the actual disposition of indulgences applied to the dead rests with God. (1) Partial indulgence: Properly disposed faithful who perform an action to which a partial indulgence is attached obtain, in addition to the remission of temporal punishment acquired by the action itself, an equal remission of punishment through the intervention of the Church. (This grant was formerly designated in terms of days and years.) The proper dispositions for gaining a partial indulgence are sorrow for sin and freedom from serious sin, performance of the required good work, and the intention (which can be general or immediate) to gain the indulgence. In addition to customary prayer and other good works to which partial indulgences are attached, there are general grants of partial indulgences to the faithful who: (a) with some kind of prayer, raise their minds to God with humble confidence while carrying out their duties and bearing the difficulties of everyday life; (b) motivated by the spirit of faith and compassion, give of themselves or their goods for the service of persons in need; (c) in a spirit of penance, spontaneously refrain from the enjoyment of things which are lawful and pleasing to them. (2) Plenary indulgence: To gain a plenary indulgence, it is necessary for a person to be free of all attachment to sin, to perform the work to which the indulgence is attached, and to fulfill the three conditions of sacramental confession, Eucharistic Communion, and prayer for the intention of the pope. The three conditions may be fulfilled several days before or after the performance of the prescribed work, but it is fitting that Communion be received and prayers for the intentions of the pope be offered on the same day the work is performed. The condition of praying for the pope's intention is fully satisfied by praying one Our Father and one Hail Mary, and sometimes the Creed, but persons are free to choose other prayers. Four of the several devotional practices for which a plenary indulgence is granted are: (a) adoration of the Blessed Sacrament for at least one-half hour; (b) devout reading of sacred Scripture for at least one-half hour; (c) the Way of the Cross; (d) recitation of the Rosary in a church, public oratory or private chapel, or in a family group, a religious community or pious association. Only one plenary indulgence can be gained in a single day. The Apostolic Penitentiary issued a decree Dec. 14, 1985, granting diocesan bishops the right to impart — three times a year on solemn feasts of their choice — the papal blessing with a plenary indulgence to those who cannot be physically present but who follow the sacred rites at which the blessing is imparted by radio or television transmission. In July, 1986, publication was announced of a new and simplified *Enchiridion Indulgentiarum,* in accord with provisions of the revised Code of Canon Law.

Indult: A favor or privilege granted by competent ecclesiastical authority, giving permission to do something not allowed by the common law of the Church.

Infant Jesus of Prague: An 18-inch-high wooden statue of the Child Jesus which has figured in a form of devotion to the Holy Childhood and Kingship of Christ since the 17th century. Of uncertain origin, the statue was presented by Princess Polixena to the Carmelites of Our Lady of Victory Church, Prague, in 1628.

Infused Virtues: The theological virtues of faith, hope, and charity; principles or capabilities of supernatural action, they are given with sanctifying grace by God rather than acquired by repeated acts of a person. They can be increased by practice; they are lost by contrary acts. Natural-acquired moral virtues, like the cardinal virtues of prudence, justice, temperance, and fortitude, can be considered infused in a person whose state of grace gives them supernatural orientation.

Inquisition: A tribunal for dealing with heretics, authorized by Gregory IX in 1231 to search them out, hear and judge them, sentence them to various forms of punishment, and in some cases to hand them over to civil authorities for punishment. The Inquisition was a creature of its time when crimes against faith, which threatened the good of the Christian community, were regarded also as crimes against the state, and when heretical doctrines of such extremists as the Cathari and Albigensians threatened the very fabric of society. The institution, which was responsible for many excesses, was most active in the second half of the 13th century.

Inquisition, Spanish: An institution peculiar to Spain and the colonies in Spanish America. In 1478, at the urging of King Ferdinand, Pope Sixtus IV approved the establishment of the Inquisition for trying charges of heresy brought against Jewish (Marranos) and Moorish (Moriscos) converts It acquired jurisdiction over other cases as well, however, and fell into disrepute because of irregularities in its functions, cruelty in its sentences, and the manner in which it served the interests of the Spanish crown more than the accused persons and the good of the Church. Protests by the Holy See failed to curb excesses of the Inquisition, which lingered in Spanish history until early in the 19th century.

I N R I: The first letters of words in the Latin inscription atop the cross on which Christ was crucified: (I)esus (N)azaraenus, (R)ex (I)udaeorum — Jesus of Nazareth, King of the Jews.

Insemination, Artificial: The implanting of human semen by some means other than consummation of natural marital intercourse. In view of the principle that procreation should result only from marital intercourse, donor insemination is not permissible.

In Sin: The condition of a person called spiritually dead because he or she does not possess sanctifying grace, the principle of supernatural life, action and merit. Such grace can be regained through repentance.

Instruction: A document containing doctrinal explanations, directive norms, rules, recommendations, admonitions, issued by the pope, a department of the Roman Curia or other competent authority in the Church. To the extent that they so prescribe, instructions have the force of law.

Intercommunion, Eucharistic Sharing: The common celebration and reception of the Eucharist by members of different Christian churches; a pivotal issue in ecumenical theory and practice. Catholic participation and intercommunion in the Eucharistic liturgy of another church without a valid priesthood and with a variant Eucharistic belief is out of order. Under certain conditions, other Christians may receive the Eucharist in the Catholic Church. (See additional Intercommunion entry). Intercommunion is acceptable to some Protestant churches and unacceptable to others.

Interdict: A censure imposed on persons for certain violations of church law. Interdicted persons may not take part in certain liturgical services, administer or receive certain sacraments.

Intinction: A method of administering Holy Communion under the dual appearances of bread and wine, in which the consecrated host is dipped in the consecrated wine before being given to the communicant. The administering of Holy Communion in this manner, which has been traditional in Eastern-Rite liturgies, was authorized in the Roman Rite for various occasions by the *Constitution on the Sacred Liturgy* promulgated by the Second Vatican Council.

Irenicism: Peace-seeking, conciliation, as opposed to polemics; an important element in ecumenism, provided it furthers pursuit of the Christian unity willed by Christ without degenerating into a peace-at-any-price disregard for religious truth.

Irregularity: A permanent impediment to the lawful reception or exercise of holy orders. The Church instituted irregularities — which include apostasy, heresy, homicide, attempted suicide — out of reverence for the dignity of the sacraments.

Itinerarium: Prayers for a spiritually profitable journey.

J

Jansenism: Opinions developed and proposed by Cornelius Jansenius (1585-1638). He held that: human nature was radically and intrinsically corrupted by original sin; some men are predestined to heaven and others to hell; Christ died only for those predestined to heaven; for those who are predestined, the operations of grace are irresistible. Jansenism also advocated an extremely rigorous code of morals and asceticism. The errors were proscribed by Urban VIII in 1642, by Innocent X in 1653, by Clement XI in 1713, and by other popes. Despite these condemnations, the rigoristic spirit of Jansenism lingered for a long time afterwards, particularly in France.

Jehovah's Witnesses: The Witnesses, together with the Watchtower and Bible Tract Society, trace their beginnings to a Bible class organized by Charles Taze Russell in 1872 at Allegheny, Pa. They take their name from a passage in Isaiah (43:12): " 'You are my witnesses,' says Jehovah." They are generally fundamentalist and revivalist with respect to the Bible, and believe that Christ is God's Son but is inferior to God. They place great emphasis on the Battle of Armageddon (as a decisive confrontation of good and evil) that is depicted vividly in Revelation, believing that God will then destroy the existing system of things and that, with the establishment of Jehovah's Kingdom, a small band of 144,000 spiritual sons of God will go to heaven, rule with Christ, and share in some way their happiness with some others. Each Witness is considered by the society to be an ordained minister charged with the duty of spreading the message of Jehovah, which is accomplished through publications, house-to-house visitations, and other methods. The Witnesses refuse to salute the flag of any nation, regarding this as a form of idolatry, or to sanction blood transfusions even for the saving of life. There are approximately one million Witnesses in more than 22,000 congregations in some 80 countries. The freedom and activities of Witnesses are restricted in some places.

Jesus: The name of Jesus, meaning "God saves," expressing the identity and mission of the second Person of the Trinity become man; derived from the Aramaic and Hebrew *Yeshua* and *Joshua,* meaning *Yahweh* is salvation.

Jesus Prayer: A prayer of Eastern origin, dating back to the fifth century: "Lord Jesus Christ, Son of God, have mercy on me (a sinner)."

Judgment: (1) Last or final judgment: Final judgment by Christ, at the end of the world and the general resurrection. (2) Particular judgment: The judgment that takes place immediately after a person's death, followed by entrance into heaven, hell or purgatory.

Jurisdiction: Right, power, authority to rule. Jurisdiction in the Church is of divine institution; has pastoral service for its purpose; includes legislative, judicial and executive authority; can be exercised only by persons with the power of orders. (1) Ordinary jurisdiction is attached to ecclesiastical offices by law; the officeholders, called Ordinaries, have authority over those who are subject to them. (2) Delegated jurisdiction is that which is granted to persons rather than attached to offices. Its extent depends on the terms of the delegation.

Justice: One of the four cardinal virtues by which a person gives to others what is due to them as a matter of right. (See Cardinal Virtues.)

Justification: The act by which God makes a person just, and the consequent change in the spiritual status of a person, from sin to grace; the remission of sin and the infusion of sanctifying grace through the merits of Christ and the action of the Holy Spirit.

K

Kerygma: Proclaiming the word of God, in the manner of the Apostles, as here and now effective for salvation. This method of preaching or instruction, centered on Christ and geared to the facts and themes of salvation history, is designed to dispose people to faith in Christ and or to intensify the experience and practice of that faith in those who have it.

Keys, Power of the: Spiritual authority and jurisdiction in the Church, symbolized by the keys of the kingdom of heaven. Christ promised the keys to St. Peter, as head-to-be of the Church (Mt. 16:19), and commissioned him with full pastoral responsibility to feed his lambs and sheep (Jn. 21:15-17), The pope, as the successor of St. Peter, has this power in a primary and supreme manner. The bishops of the Church also have the power, in union with and subordinate to the pope. Priests share in it through holy orders and the delegation of authority. Examples of the application of the Power of the Keys are the exercise of teaching and pastoral authority by the pope and bishops, the absolving of sins in the sacrament of penance, the granting of indulgences, the imposing of spiritual penalties on persons who commit certain serious sins.

L

Laicization: The process by which a man ordained to holy orders is relieved of the obligations of orders and the ministry and is returned to the status of a lay person.

Languages of the Church: The first language in church use, for divine worship and the conduct of ecclesiastical affairs, was Aramaic, the language of the first Christians in and around Jerusalem. As the Church spread westward, Greek was adopted and prevailed until the third century when it was supplanted by Latin for official use in the West. According to traditions established very early in churches of the Eastern Rites, many different languages were adopted for use in divine worship and for the conduct of ecclesiastical affairs. The practice was, and still is, to use the vernacular or a language closely related to the common tongue of the people. In the Western Church, Latin prevailed as the general official language until the promulgation on Dec. 4, 1963, of the *Constitution on the Sacred Liturgy* by the second session of the Second Vatican Council. Since that time, vernacular languages have come into use in the Mass, administration of the sacraments, and the Liturgy of the Hours. The change was introduced in order to make the prayers and ceremonies of divine worship more informative and meaningful to all. Latin, however, remains the official language for documents of the Holy See, administrative and procedural matters.

Law: An ordinance or rule governing the activity of things. (1) Natural law: Moral norms corresponding to man's nature by which he orders his conduct toward God, neighbor, society and himself. This law, which is rooted in human nature, is of divine origin, can be known by the use of reason, and binds all persons having the use of reason. The Ten Commandments are declarations and amplifications of natural law. The primary precepts of natural law, to do good and to avoid evil, are universally recognized, despite differences with respect to understanding and application resulting from different philosophies of good and evil. (2) Divine positive law: That which has been revealed by God. Among its essentials are the twin precepts of love of God and love of neighbor, and the Ten Commandments. (3) Ecclesiastical law: That which is established by the Church for the spiritual welfare of the faithful and the orderly conduct of ecclesiastical affairs. (See Canon Law.) (4) Civil law: That which is established by a socio-political community for the common good.

Liberalism: A multiphased trend of thought and movement favoring liberty, independence and progress in moral, intellectual, religious, social, economic and political life. Traceable to the Renaissance, it developed through the Enlightenment, the rationalism of the 19th century, and modernist- and existentialist-related theories of the 20th century. Evaluations of various kinds of liberalism depend on the validity of their underlying principles. Extremist positions — regarding subjectivism, libertarianism, naturalist denials of the supernatural, and the alienation of individuals and society from God and the Church — were condemned by Gregory XVI in the 1830s, Pius IX in 1864, Leo XIII in 1899, and St. Pius X in 1907. There is, however, nothing objectionable about forms of liberalism patterned according to sound principles of Christian doctrine.

Liberation Theology: Deals with the relevance of Christian faith and salvation — and, therefore, of the mission of the Church — to efforts for the promotion of human rights, social justice and human development. It originated in the religious, social, political and economic environment of Latin America, with its contemporary need for a theory and corresponding action by the Church, in the pattern of its overall mission, for human rights and integral personal and social development. Some versions of liberation theology are at variance with the body of church teaching because of their ideological concept of Christ as liberator, and also because they play down the primary spiritual nature and mission of the Church. Instructions from the Congregation for the Doctrine of the Faith — "On Certain Aspects of the Theology of Liberation" (Sept. 3, 1984) and "On Christian Freedom and Liberation" (Apr. 5, 1986) — contain warnings against translating sociology into theology and advocating violence in social activism.

Life in Outer Space: Whether rational life exists on other bodies in the universe besides earth, is a question for scientific investigation to settle. The possibility can be granted, without prejudice to the body of revealed truth.

Limbo: The limbo of the fathers was the state of rest and natural happiness after death enjoyed by the just of pre-Christian times until they were admitted to heaven following the Ascension of Christ.

Litany: A prayer in the form of responsive petition; e.g., St. Joseph, pray for us, etc. Examples are the litanies of Loreto (Litany of the Blessed Mother), the Holy Name, All Saints, the Sacred Heart, the Precious Blood, St. Joseph, Litany for the Dying.

Loreto, House of: A Marian shrine in Loreto, Italy, consisting of the home of the Holy Family which, according to an old tradition, was transported in a miraculous manner from Nazareth to Dalmatia and finally to Loreto between 1291 and 1294. Investigations conducted shortly after the appearance of the structure in Loreto revealed that its dimensions matched those of the house of the Holy Family missing from its place of enshrinement in a basilica at Nazareth. Among the many popes who regarded it with high honor was John XXIII, who went there on pilgrimage Oct. 4, 1962. The house of the Holy Family is enshrined in the Basilica of Our Lady.

Lust: A disorderly desire for sexual pleasure; one of the seven capital sins.

M

Magi: In the Infancy Narrative of St. Matthew's Gospel (2:1-12), three wise men from the East whose visit and homage to the Child Jesus at Bethlehem indicated Christ's manifestation of himself to non-Jewish people. The narrative teaches the universality of salvation. The traditional names of the Magi are Caspar, Melchior and Balthasar.

Magnificat: The canticle or hymn of the Virgin Mary on the occasion of her visitation to her cousin Elizabeth (Lk. 1:46-55). It is an expression of praise, thanksgiving and acknowledgment of the great blessings given by God to Mary, the Mother of the Second Person of the Blessed Trinity made Man. The Magnificat is recited in the Liturgy of the Hours as part of the Evening Prayer.

Martyr: A Greek word, meaning witness, denoting one who voluntarily suffered death for the faith or some Christian virtue.

Martyrology: A catalogue of martyrs and other saints, arranged according to the calendar. The *Roman Martyrology* contains the official list of saints venerated by the Church. Additions to the list are made in beatification and canonization decrees of the Congregation for the Causes of Saints.

Mass for the People: On Sundays and certain feasts throughout the year pastors are required to offer Mass for the faithful entrusted to their care. If they cannot offer the Mass on these days, they must do so at a later date or provide that another priest offer the Mass.

Materialism: Theory which holds that matter is the only reality, and everything in existence is merely a manifestation of matter; there is no such thing as spirit, and the supernatural does not exist. Materialism is incompatible with Christian doctrine.

Meditation: Mental, as distinguished from vocal, prayer, in which thought, affections, and resolutions of the will predominate. There is a meditative element to all forms of prayer, which always involves the raising of the heart and mind to God.

Mendicants: A term derived from Latin and meaning beggars, applied to members of religious orders without property rights; the members, accordingly, worked or begged for their support. The original mendicants were Franciscans and Dominicans in the early 13th century; later, the Carmelites, Augustinians, Servites and others were given the mendicant title and privileges, with respect to exemption from episcopal jurisdiction and wide faculties for preaching and administering the sacrament of penance. The practice of begging is limited at the present time, although it is still allowed with the permission of competent superiors and bishops. Mendicants are supported by free will offerings and income received for spiritual services and other work.

Mercy, Divine: The love and goodness of God, manifested particularly in a time of need.

Mercy, Works of : Works of corporal or spiritual assistance, motivated by love of God and neighbor, to persons in need. (1) Corporal works: feeding the hungry, giving drink to the thirsty, clothing the naked, visiting the imprisoned, sheltering the homeless, visiting the sick, burying the dead. (2) Spiritual works: counseling the doubtful, instructing the ignorant, admonishing sinners, comforting the afflicted, forgiving offenses, bearing wrongs patiently, praying for the living and the dead.

Merit: In religion, the right to a supernatural reward for good works freely done for a supernatural motive by a person in the state of and with the assistance of grace. The right to such reward is from God, who binds himself to give it. Accordingly, good works, as described above, are meritorious for salvation.

Metempsychosis: Theory of the passage or migration of the human soul after death from one body to another for the purpose of purification from guilt. The theory denies the unity of the soul and human personality, and the doctrine of individual moral responsibility.

Millennium: A thousand-year reign of Christ and the just upon earth before the end of the world. This belief of the Millenarians, Chiliasts, and some sects of modern times is based on an erroneous interpretation of Rv. 20.

Miracles: Observable events or effects in the physical or moral order of things, with reference to salvation, which cannot be explained by the ordinary operation of laws of nature and which, therefore, are attributed to the direct action of God. They make known, in an unusual way, the concern and intervention of God in human affairs for the salvation of men. The most striking examples are the miracles worked by Christ. Numbering about 35, they included his own Resurrection; the raising of three persons to life (Lazarus, the daughter of Jairus, the son of the widow of Naim); the healing of blind, leprous and other persons; nature miracles; and prophecies, or miracles of the intellectual order. The foregoing notion of miracles, which is based on the concept of a fixed order of nature, was not known by the writers of Sacred Scripture. In the Old Testament, particularly, they called some things miraculous which, according to the definition in contemporary use, may or may not have been miracles. Essentially, however, the occurrences so designated were regarded as exceptional manifestations of God's care and concern for the salvation of his people. The miracles of Christ were miracles in the full sense of the term. The Church believes it is reasonable to accept miracles as manifestations of divine power for purposes of salvation. God, who created the laws of nature, is their master; hence, without disturbing the ordinary course of things, he can — and has in the course of history before and after Christ — occasionally set aside these laws and has also produced effects beyond their power of operation. The Church does not regard as miraculous just anything which does not admit of easy explanation; on the contrary, miracles are acknowledged only when the events have a bearing on the order of grace and every possible natural explanation has been tried and found wanting. (The transubstantiation — i.e., the conversion of the whole substance of bread and wine, their sensible appearances alone remaining, into the Body and Blood of Christ in the act of Consecration at Mass — is not an observable event. Traditionally, however, it has been called a miracle.)

Missiology: Study of the missionary nature, constitution and activity of the Church in all aspects: theological reasons for missionary activity, laws and instructions of the Holy See, history of the missions, social and cultural background, methods, norms for carrying on missionary work.

Mission: (1) Strictly, it means being sent to perform a certain work, such as the mission of Christ to redeem mankind, the mission of the Apostles and the Church and its members to perpetuate the prophetic, priestly and royal mission of Christ. (2) A place where: the Gospel has not been proclaimed; the Church has not been firmly established; the Church, although established, is weak. (3) An ecclesiastical territory with the simplest kind of canonical organization, under the jurisdiction of the Congregation for the Evangelization of Peoples. (4) A church or chapel without a resident priest. (5) A special course of sermons and spiritual exercises conducted in parishes for the purpose of renewing and deepening the spiritual life of the faithful and for the conversion of lapsed Catholics.

Modernism: The "synthesis of all heresies," which appeared near the beginning of the 20th century. It undermines the objective validity of religious beliefs and practices which, it contends, are products of the subconscious developed by mankind under the stimulus of a religious sense. It holds that the existence of a personal God cannot be demonstrated, the Bible is not inspired, Christ is not divine, nor did he establish the Church or institute the sacraments. A special danger lies in modernism, which is still influential, because it uses Catholic terms with perverted meanings. St. Pius X condemned 65 propositions of modernism in 1907 in the decree *Lamentabili* and issued the encyclical *Pascendi* to explain and analyze its errors.

Monastery: The dwelling place, as well as the community thereof, of monks belonging to the Benedictine and Benedictine-related orders like the Cistercians and Carthusians; also, the Augustinians and Canons Regular. Distinctive of monasteries are: their separation from the world; the enclosure or cloister; the permanence or stability of attachment characteristic of their members; autonomous government in accordance with a monastic rule, like that of St. Benedict in the West or of St. Basil in the East; the special dedication of its members to the community celebration of the liturgy as well as to work that is suitable to the surrounding area and the needs of its people. Monastic superiors of men have such titles as abbot and prior; of women, abbess and prioress. In most essentials, an abbey is the same as a monastery.

Monk: A member of a monastic order — e.g., the Benedictines, the Benedictine-related Cistercians and Carthusians, and the Basilians, who bind themselves by religious profession to stable attachment to a monastery, the contemplative life and the work of their community. In popular use, the title is wrongly applied to many men religious who really are not monks.

Monotheism: Belief in and worship of one God.

Morality: Conformity or difformity of behavior to standards of right conduct. (See Moral Obligations, Commandments of God, Precepts of the Church, Conscience, Law.)

Mormons: Members of the Church of Jesus Christ of Latter-Day Saints. The church was established by Joseph Smith (1805-1844) at Fayette, N.Y., three years after he said he had received from an angel golden tablets containing the *Book of the Prophet Mormon.* This book, the Bible, *Doctrine and Covenants,* and *The Pearl of Great Price,* are the basic doctrinal texts of the church. Characteristic of the Mormons are strong belief in the revelations of their leaders, among whom was Brigham Young; a strong community of religious-secular concern; a dual secular and spiritual priesthood, and vigorous missionary activity. The headquarters of the church are located at Salt Lake City, Utah, where the Mormons first settled in 1847.

Mortification: Acts of self-discipline, including prayer, hardship, austerities and penances undertaken for the sake of progress in virtue.

Motu Proprio: A Latin phrase designating a document issued by a pope on his own initiative. Documents of this kind often concern administrative matters.

Mystagogy: Experience of the mystery of Christ, especially through participation in the liturgy and the sacraments.

Mysteries of Faith: Supernatural truths whose existence cannot be known without revelation by God and whose intrinsic truth, while not contrary to reason, can never be wholly understood even after revelation. These mysteries are above reason, not against reason. Among them are the divine mysteries of the Trinity, Incarnation and Eucharist. Some mysteries — e.g., concerning God's attributes — can be known by reason without revelation, although they cannot be fully understood.

N

Necromancy: Supposed communication with the dead; a form of divination.

Non-Expedit: A Latin expression. It is not expedient (fitting, proper), used to state a prohibition or refusal of permission.

Novena: A term designating public or private devotional practices over a period of nine consecutive days; or, by extension, over a period of nine weeks, in which one day a week is set aside for the devotions.

Novice: A man or woman preparing, in a formal period of trial and formation called a novitiate, for membership in an institute of consecrated life. The novitiate lasts a minimum of 12 and a maximum of 24 months; at its conclusion, the novice professes temporary promises or vows of poverty, chastity and obedience. Norms require that certain periods of time be spent in the house of novitiate; periods of apostolic work are also required, to acquaint the novice with the apostolate(s) of the institute. A novice is not bound by the obligations of the professed members of the institute, is free to leave at any time, and may be discharged at the discretion of competent superiors. The superior of a novice is a master of novices or director of formation.

Nun: (1) Strictly, a member of a religious order of women with solemn vows (moniales). (2) In general, all women religious, even those in simple vows who are more properly called sisters.

Nunc Dimittis: The canticle or hymn of Simeon at the sight of Jesus at the Temple on the occasion of his presentation (Lk. 2:29-32). It is an expression of joy and thanksgiving for the blessing of having lived to see the Messiah. It is prescribed for use in the Night Prayer of the Liturgy of the Hours.

O

Oath: Calling upon God to witness the truth of a statement. Violating an oath, e.g., by perjury in court, or taking an oath without sufficient reason, is a violation of the honor due to God.

Obedience: Submission to one in authority. General obligations of obedience fall under the Fourth Commandment. The vow of obedience professed by religious is one of the evangelical counsels.

Obsession, Diabolical: The extraordinary state of one who is seriously molested by evil spirits in an external manner. Obsession is more than just temptation.

Occultism: Practices involving ceremonies, rituals, chants, incantations, other cult-related activities intended to affect the course of nature, the lives of practitioners and others, through esoteric powers of magic, diabolical or other forces; one of many forms of superstition.

Octave: A period of eight days given over to the celebration of a major feast such as Easter.

Oils, Holy: The oils blessed by a bishop at the Chrism Mass on Holy Thursday or another suitable day, or by a priest under certain conditions. (1) The oil of catechumens (olive or vegetable oil), used at baptism; also, poured with chrism into the baptismal water blessed in Easter Vigil ceremonies. (2) Oil of the sick (olive or vegetable oil) used in anointing the sick. (3) Chrism (olive or vegetable oil mixed with balm), which is ordinarily consecrated by a bishop, for use at baptism, in confirmation, at the ordination of a priest and bishop, in the dedication of churches and altars.

Old Catholics: Several churches, including: (1) The Church of Utrecht, which severed relations with Rome in 1724; (2) The Polish National Catholic Church in the U.S., which had its origin near the end of the 19th century; (3) German, Austrian and Swiss Old Catholics, who broke away from union with Rome following the First Vatican Council in 1870 because they objected to the dogma of papal infallibility. The formation of the Old Catholic communion of Germans, Austrians and Swiss began in 1870 at a public meeting held in Nuremberg under the leadership of A. Dollinger. Four years later episcopal succession was established with the ordination o an Old Catholic German bishop by a prelate of the Church of Utrecht. In line with the "Declaration of Utrecht" of 1889, they accept the first seven ecumenical councils and doctrine formulated before 1054, but reject communion with the pope and a number of other Catholic doctrines and practices. They have a valid priesthood and valid sacraments. The Oxford Dictionary of the Christian Church notes that they have recognized Anglican ordinations since 1925, that they have had full communion with the Church of England since 1932, and that their bishops, using their own formula, have taken part in the ordination of Anglican bishops. This communion does not recognize the "Old Catholic" status of several smaller ecclesial bodies calling themselves such. In turn, connection with it is disavowed by the Old Roman Catholic Church headquartered in Chicago, which contends that it has abandoned the traditions of the Church of Utrecht. The United States is the only English-speaking country with Old Catholic communities.

Opus Dei: Opus Dei was founded in 1928 in Madrid by Msgr. Josemaria Escriva (beatified in 1992) with the aim of spreading throughout all sectors of society a profound awareness of the universal call to holiness and apostolate (of Christian witness and action) in the ordinary circumstances of life, and, more specifically, through one's professional work. On Nov. 28, 1982, Pope John Paul II established Opus Dei as a personal prelature with the full title, Prelature of the Holy Cross and Opus Dei. The 1997 edition of *Annuario Pontificio* reported that the prelature had 1,611 priests (54 newly ordained) and 372 major seminarians. Also, there were 79,027 lay persons — men and women, married and single, of every class and social condition — of about 80 nationalities. In the United States, members of Opus Dei, along with cooperators and friends, conduct apostolic works corporately in major cities in the East and Midwest,

Texas and on the West Coast. Elsewhere, corporate works include universities, vocational institutes, training schools for farmers and numerous other apostolic initiatives. An information office is located at 524 North Ave., Suite 200, New Rochelle, NY 10801.

Oratory: A chapel.

Ordinariate: An ecclesiastical jurisdiction for special purposes and people. Examples are military ordinariates for armed services personnel (in accord with provisions of the apostolic constitution Spirituali militum curae, Apr. 21, 1986) and Eastern-Rite ordinariates in places where Eastern-Rite dioceses do not exist.

Ordination: The consecration of sacred ministers for divine worship and the service of people in things pertaining to God. The power of ordination comes from Christ and the Church, and must be conferred by a minister capable of communicating it.

Organ Transplants: The transplanting of organs from one person to another is permissible provided it is done with the consent of the concerned parties and does not result in the death or essential mutilation of the donor. Advances in methods and technology have increased the range of transplant possibilities in recent years.

Original Sin: The sin of Adam (Gn. 2:8—3:24), personal to him and passed on to all persons as a state of privation of grace. Despite this privation and the related wounding of human nature and weakening of natural powers, original sin leaves unchanged all that man himself is by nature. The scriptural basis of the doctrine was stated especially by St. Paul in 1 Cor. 15:21ff., and Romans 5:12-21. Original sin is remitted by baptism and incorporation in Christ, through whom grace is given to persons. Pope John Paul, while describing original sin during a general audience Oct. 1, 1986, called it "the absence of sanctifying grace in nature which has been diverted from its supernatural end."

O Salutaris Hostia: The first three Latin words, O Saving Victim, of a Benediction hymn.

Ostpolitik: Policy adopted by Pope Paul VI in an attempt to improve the situation of Eastern European Catholics through diplomatic negotiations with their governments.

Oxford Movement: A movement in the Church of England from 1833 to about 1845 which had for its objective a threefold defense of the church as a divine institution, the apostolic succession of its bishops, and the Book of Common Prayer as the rule of faith. The movement took its name from Oxford University and involved a number of intellectuals who authored a series of influential Tracts for Our Times. Some of its leading figures — e.g., F. W. Faber, John Henry Newman and Henry Edward Manning — became converts to the Catholic Church. In the Church of England, the movement affected the liturgy, historical and theological scholarship, the status of the ministry, and other areas of ecclesiastical life.

P

Paganism: A term referring to non-revealed religions, i.e., religions other than Christianity, Judaism and Mohammedanism.

Palms: Blessed palms are a sacramental. They are blessed and distributed on the Sunday of the Passion in commemoration of the triumphant entrance of Christ into Jerusalem. Ashes of the burnt palms are used on Ash Wednesday.

Pange Lingua: First Latin words, Sing, my tongue, of a hymn in honor of the Holy Eucharist, used particularly on Holy Thursday and in Eucharistic processions.

Pantheism: Theory that all things are part of God, divine, in the sense that God realizes himself as the ultimate reality of matter or spirit through being and/or becoming all things that have been, are, and will be. The theory leads to hopeless confusion of the Creator and the created realm of being, identifies evil with good, and involves many inherent contradictions.

Papal Election: The Pope is elected by the College of Cardinals during a secret conclave which begins no sooner than 15 days and no later than 20 days after the death of his predecessor. Cardinals under the age of 80, totaling no more than 120, are eligible to take part in the election by secret ballot. Election is by a two-thirds vote of participating cardinals. If the number voting cannot be divided by three, one additional vote is required. New legislation regarding papal elections and church government during a vacancy of the Holy See was promulgated by Pope John Paul Feb. 23, 1996, in the apostolic constitution *Universi Dominici Gregis* ("Shepherd of the Lord's Whole Flock"). (For excerpts, see separate article.)

Paraclete: A title of the Holy Spirit meaning, in Greek, Advocate, Consoler.

Parental Duties: All duties related to the obligation of parents to provide for the welfare of their children. These obligations fall under the Fourth Commandment.

Parish: A community of the faithful served by a pastor charged with responsibility for providing them with full pastoral service. Most parishes are territorial, embracing all of the faithful in a certain area of a diocese: some are personal or national, for certain classes of people, without strict regard for their places of residence.

Parousia: The coming, or saving presence, of Christ which will mark the completion of salvation history and the coming to perfection of God's kingdom at the end of the world.

Paschal Candle: A large candle, symbolic of the risen Christ, blessed and lighted on the Easter Vigil and placed at the altar until Pentecost. It is ornamented with five large grains of incense, representing the wounds of Christ, inserted in the form of a cross; the Greek letters Alpha and Omega, symbolizing Christ the beginning and end of all things, at the top and bottom of the shaft of the cross; and the figures of the current year of salvation in the quadrants formed by the cross.

Paschal Precept: Church law requiring reception of the Eucharist in the Easter season (see separate entry) unless, for a just cause, once-a-year reception takes place at another time.

Passion of Christ: Sufferings of Christ, recorded in the four Gospels.

Pastor: An ordained minister charged with responsibility for the doctrinal, sacramental and related service of people committed to his care; e.g., a bishop for the people in his diocese, a priest for the people of his parish.

Pater Noster: The initial Latin words, Our Father, of the Lord's Prayer.

Peace, Sign of: A gesture of greeting — e.g., a handshake — exchanged by the ministers and participants at Mass.

Pectoral Cross: A cross worn on a chain about the neck and over the breast by bishops and abbots as a mark of their office.

Penance or Penitence: (1) The spiritual change or conversion of mind and heart by which a person turns away from sin, and all that it implies, toward God, through a personal renewal under the influence of the Holy Spirit. In the apostolic constitution *Paenitemini,* Pope Paul VI called it "a religious, personal act which has as its aim love and surrender to God." Penance involves sorrow and contrition for sin, together with other internal and external acts of atonement. It serves the purposes of reestablishing in one's life the order of God's love and commandments, and of making satisfaction to God for sin. A divine precept states the necessity of penance for salvation: "Unless you do penance, you shall all likewise perish" (Lk. 13:3) "Be converted and believe in the Gospel" (Mk. 1:15). In the penitential discipline of the Church, the various works of penance have been classified under the headings of prayer (interior), fasting and almsgiving (exterior). The Church has established minimum requirements for the common and social observance of the divine precept by Catholics — e.g., by requiring them to fast and/or abstain on certain days of the year. These observances, however, do not exhaust all the demands of the divine precept, whose fulfillment is a matter of personal responsibility; nor do they have any real value unless they proceed from the internal spirit and purpose of penance. Related to works of penance for sins actually committed are works of mortification. The purpose of the latter is to develop — through prayer, fasting, renunciations and similar actions —self-control and detachment from things which could otherwise become occasions of sin. (2) Penance is a virtue disposing a person to turn to God in sorrow for sin and to carry out works of amendment and atonement. (3) The sacrament of penance and sacramental penance.

Perjury: Taking a false oath, lying under oath, a violation of the honor due to God.

Persecution, Religious: A campaign waged against a church or other religious body by persons and governments intent on its destruction. The best known campaigns of this type against the Christian Church were the Roman persecutions which occurred intermittently from about 54 to the promulgation of the Edict of Milan in 313; the most extensive persecutions took place during the reigns of Nero, the first major Roman persecutor, Domitian, Trajan, Marcus Aurelius, and Diocletian. More Catholics have been persecuted in the 20th century than in any other period in history.

Personal Prelature: A special-purpose jurisdiction — for particular pastoral and missionary work, etc. — consisting of secular priests and deacons and open to lay persons willing to dedicate themselves to its apostolic works. The prelate in charge is an Ordinary,

with the authority of office; he can establish a national or international seminary, incardinate its students and promote them to holy orders under the title of service to the prelature. The prelature is constituted and governed according to statutes laid down by the Holy See. Statutes define its relationship and mode of operation with the bishops of territories in which members live and work. Opus Dei is a personal prelature.

Peter's Pence: A collection made each year among Catholics for the maintenance of the pope and his works of charity. It was originally a tax of a penny on each house, and was collected on St. Peter's day, whence the name. It originated in England in the eighth century.

Petition: One of the four purposes of prayer. In prayers of petition, persons ask of God the blessings they and others need.

Pharisees: Influential class among the Jews, referred to in the Gospels, noted for their self-righteousness, legalism, strict interpretation of the Law, acceptance of the traditions of the elders as well as the Law of Moses, and beliefs regarding angels and spirits, the resurrection of the dead and judgment. Most of them were laymen, and they were closely allied with the Scribes; their opposite numbers were the Sadducees. The Pharisaic and rabbinical traditions had a lasting influence on Judaism following the destruction of Jerusalem in 70 A.D.

Pious Fund: Property and money originally accumulated by the Jesuits to finance their missionary work in Lower California. When the Jesuits were expelled from the territory in 1767, the fund was appropriated by the Spanish Crown and used to support Dominican and Franciscan missionary work in Upper and Lower California. In 1842 the Mexican government took over administration of the fund, incorporated most of the revenue into the national treasury, and agreed to pay the Church interest of six per cent a year on the capital so incorporated. From 1848 to 1967 the fund was the subject of lengthy negotiations between the U.S. and Mexican governments because of the latter's failure to make payments as agreed. A lump-sum settlement was made in 1967 with payment by Mexico to the U.S. government of more than $700,000, to be turned over to the Archdiocese of San Francisco.

Polytheism: Belief in and worship of many gods or divinities, especially prevalent in pre-Christian religions.

Poor Box: Alms-box; found in churches from the earliest days of Christianity.

Pope Joan: Alleged name of a woman falsely said to have been pope from 855-858, the years of the reign of Benedict III. The myth was not heard of before the 13th century.

Portiuncula: (1) Meaning little portion (of land), the Portiuncula was the chapel of Our Lady of the Angels near Assisi, Italy, which the Benedictines gave to St. Francis early in the 13th century. He repaired the chapel and made it the first church of the Franciscan Order. It is now enshrined in the Basilica of St. Mary of the Angels in Assisi. (2) The plenary Portiuncula Indulgence, or Pardon of Assisi, was authorized by Honorius III. Originally, it could be gained for the souls in purgatory only in the chapel of

Our Lady of the Angels; by later concessions, it could be gained also in other Franciscan and parish churches. The Portiuncula Indulgence (applicable also to the souls in purgatory) can ordinarily be gained from noon of Aug. 1 to midnight of Aug. 2. The conditions are, in addition to freedom from attachment to sin: reception of the sacraments of penance and the Eucharist on or near the day and a half; a visit to a parish church within the day and a half, during which the Our Father, the Creed and another prayer are offered for the intentions of the pope.

Possession, Diabolical: The extraordinary state of a person who is tormented from within by evil spirits who exercise strong influence over his powers of mind and body.

Postulant: One of several names used to designate a candidate for membership in a religious institute during the period before novitiate.

Poverty: (1) The quality or state of being poor, in actual destitution and need, or being poor in spirit. In the latter sense, poverty means the state of mind and disposition of persons who regard material things in proper perspective as gifts of God for the support of life and its reasonable enrichment, and for the service of others in need. It means freedom from unreasonable attachment to material things as ends in themselves, even though they may be possessed in small or large measure. (2) One of the evangelical counsels professed as a public vow by members of an institute of consecrated life. It involves the voluntary renunciation of rights of ownership and of independent use and disposal of material goods; or, the right of independent use and disposal, but not of the radical right of ownership. Religious institutes provide their members with necessary and useful goods and services from common resources. The manner in which goods are received and/or handled by religious is determined by poverty of spirit and the rule and constitutions of their institute.

Pragmatism: Theory that the truth of ideas, concepts and values depends on their utility or capacity to serve a useful purpose rather than on their conformity with objective standards; also called utilitarianism.

Prayer: The raising of the mind and heart to God in adoration, thanksgiving, reparation and petition. Prayer, which is always mental because it involves thought and love of God, may be vocal, meditative, private and personal, social, and official. The official prayer of the Church as a worshiping community is called the liturgy.

Precepts: Commands or orders given to individuals or communities in particular cases; they establish law for concerned parties. Preceptive documents are issued by the pope, departments of the Roman Curia and other competent authority in the Church.

Presence of God: A devotional practice of increasing one's awareness of the presence and action of God in daily life.

Presumption: A sin against hope, by which a person striving for salvation (1) either relies too much on his own capabilities or (2) expects God to do things which he cannot do, in keeping with his divine attributes, or does not will to do, according to his divine plan. Presumption is the opposite of despair.

Preternatural Gifts: Exceptional gifts, beyond the exigencies and powers of human nature, enjoyed by Adam in the state of original justice: immunity from suffering and death, superior knowledge, integrity or perfect control of the passions. These gifts were lost as the result of original sin; their loss, however, implied no impairment of the integrity of human nature.

Pride: Unreasonable self-esteem; one of the seven capital sins.

Prie-Dieu: A French phrase, meaning pray God, designating a kneeler or bench suitable for kneeling while at prayer.

Priesthood: (1) The common priesthood of the non-ordained faithful. In virtue of baptism and confirmation, the faithful are a priestly people who participate in the priesthood of Christ through acts of worship, witness to the faith in daily life, and efforts to foster the growth of God's kingdom. (2) The ordained priesthood, in virtue of the sacrament of order, of bishops, priests and deacons, for service to the common priesthood.

Primary Option: The life-choice of a person for or against God which shapes the basic orientation of moral conduct. A primary option for God does not preclude the possibility of serious sin.

Prior: A superior or an assistant to an abbot in a monastery.

Privilege: A favor, an exemption from the obligation of a law. Privileges of various kinds, with respect to ecclesiastical laws, are granted by the pope, departments of the Roman Curia and other competent authority in the Church.

Probabilism: A moral system for use in cases of conscience which involve the obligation of doubtful laws. There is a general principle that a doubtful law does not bind. Probabilism, therefore, teaches that it is permissible to follow an opinion favoring liberty, provided the opinion is certainly and solidly probable. Probabilism may not be invoked when there is question of: a certain law or the certain obligation of a law; the certain right of another party; the validity of an action; something which is necessary for salvation.

Pro-Cathedral: A church used as a cathedral.

Promoter of the Faith: An official of the Congregation for the Causes of Saints, whose role in beatification and canonization procedures is to establish beyond reasonable doubt the validity of evidence regarding the holiness of prospective saints and miracles attributed to their intercession.

Prophecies of St. Malachy: These so-called prophecies, listing the designations of 102 popes and 10 antipopes, bear the name they have because they have been falsely attributed to St. Malachy, bishop of Armagh, who died in 1148. Actually, they are forgeries by an unknown author and came to light only in the last decade of the 16th century. The first 75 prophecies cover the 65 popes and 10 antipopes from Celestine II (1143-1144) to Gregory XIV (1590-91), and are exact with respect to names, coats of arms, birthplaces, and other identifying characteristics. This portion of the work, far from being prophetic, is the result of historical knowledge or hindsight. The 37 designations following that of Gregory are vague, fanciful, and subject to wide interpretation. According to the prophecies, John Paul II, from the Labor of the Sun, will have only two successors before the end of the world.

Prophecy: (1) The communication of divine revelation by inspired intermediaries, called prophets, between God and his people. Old Testament prophecy was unique in its origin and because of its ethical and religious content, which included disclosure of the saving will of Yahweh for the people, moral censures and warnings of divine punishment because of sin and violations of the Law and Covenant, in the form of promises, admonitions, reproaches and threats. Although Moses and other earlier figures are called prophets, the period of prophecy is generally dated from the early years of the monarchy to about 100 years after the Babylonian Exile. From that time on the written Law and its interpreters supplanted the prophets as guides of the people. Old Testament prophets are cited in the New Testament, with awareness that God spoke through them and that some of their oracles were fulfilled in Christ. John the Baptist is the outstanding prophetic figure in the New Testament. Christ never claimed the title of prophet for himself, although some people thought he was one. There were prophets in the early Church, and St. Paul mentioned the charism of prophecy in 1 Cor. 14:1-5. Prophecy disappeared after New Testament times. Revelation is classified as the prophetic book of the New Testament. (2) In contemporary non-scriptural usage, the term is applied to the witness given by persons to the relevance of their beliefs in everyday life and action.

Province: (1) A territory comprising one archdiocese called the metropolitan see and one or more dioceses called suffragan sees. The head of the archdiocese, an archbishop, has metropolitan rights and responsibilities over the province. (2) A division of a religious order under the jurisdiction of a provincial superior.

Prudence: Practical wisdom and judgment regarding the choice and use of the best ways and means of doing good; one of the four cardinal virtues.

Punishment Due for Sin: The punishment which is a consequence of sin. It is of two kinds: (1) Eternal punishment is the punishment of hell, to which one becomes subject by the commission of mortal sin. Such punishment is remitted when mortal sin is forgiven. (2) Temporal punishment is a consequence of venial sin and/or forgiven mortal sin; it is not everlasting and may be remitted in this life by means of penance. Temporal punishment unremitted during this life is remitted by suffering in purgatory.

Purgatory: The state or condition of those who have died in the state of grace but with some attachment to sin, and are purified for a time before they are admitted to the glory and happiness of heaven. In this state and period of passive suffering, they are purified of unrepented venial sins, satisfy the demands of divine justice for temporal punishment due for sins, and are thus converted to a state of worthiness of the beatific vision.

R

Racism: A theory which holds that any one or several of the different races of the human family are inherently superior or inferior to any one or several of the others. The teaching denies the essential unity of the human race, the equality and dignity of all persons because of their common possession of the same human nature, and the participation of all in the divine plan of redemption. It is radically opposed to the virtue of justice and the precept of love of neighbor. Differences of superiority and inferiority which do exist are the result of accidental factors operating in a wide variety of circumstances, and are in no way due to essential defects in any one or several of the branches of the one human race. The theory of racism, together with practices related to it, is incompatible with Christian doctrine.

Rash Judgment: Attributing faults to another without sufficient reason; a violation of the obligations of justice and charity.

Rationalism: A theory which makes the mind the measure and arbiter of all things, including religious truth. A product of the Enlightenment, it rejects the supernatural, divine revelation, and authoritative teaching by any church.

Recollection: Meditation, attitude of concentration or awareness of spiritual matters and things pertaining to salvation and the accomplishment of God's will.

Relativism: Theory which holds that all truth, including religious truth, is relative, i.e., not absolute, certain or unchanging; a product of agnosticism, indifferentism, and an unwarranted extension of the notion of truth in positive science. Relativism is based on the tenet that certain knowledge of any and all truth is impossible. Therefore, no religion, philosophy or science can be said to possess the real truth; consequently, all religions, philosophies and sciences may be considered to have as much or as little of truth as any of the others.

Relics: The physical remains and effects of saints, which are considered worthy of veneration inasmuch as they are representative of persons in glory with God. Catholic doctrine proscribes the view that relics are not worthy of veneration. In line with norms laid down by the Council of Trent and subsequent enactments, discipline concerning relics is subject to control by the Congregations for the Causes of Saints and for Divine Worship and the Discipline of the Sacraments.

Religion: The adoration and service of God as expressed in divine worship and in daily life. Religion is concerned with all of the relations existing between God and human beings, and between humans themselves because of the central significance of God. Objectively considered, religion consists of a body of truth which is believed, a code of morality for the guidance of conduct, and a form of divine worship. Subjectively, it is a person's total response, theoretically and practically, to the demands of faith; it is living faith, personal engagement, self-commitment to God. Thus, by creed, code and cult, a person orders and directs his or her life in reference to God and, through what the love and service of God implies, to all people and all things.

Reliquary: A vessel for the preservation and exposition of a relic; sometimes made like a small monstrance.

Reparation: The making of amends to God for sin committed; one of the four ends of prayer and the purpose of penance.

Rescript: A written reply by an ecclesiastical superior regarding a question or request; its provisions bind concerned parties only. Papal dispensations are issued in the form of rescripts.

Reserved Case: A sin or censure, absolution from which is reserved to religious superiors, bishops, the pope, or confessors having special faculties. Reservations are made because of the serious nature and social effects of certain sins and censures.

Restitution: An act of reparation for an injury done to another. The injury may be caused by taking and/or retaining what belongs to another or by damaging either the property or reputation of another. The intention of making restitution, usually in kind, is required as a condition for the forgiveness of sins of injustice, even though actual restitution is not possible.

Ring: In the Church a ring is worn as part of the insignia of bishops, abbots, et al.; by sisters to denote their consecration to God and the Church. The wedding ring symbolizes the love and union of husband and wife.

Ritual: A book of prayers and ceremonies used in the administration of the sacraments and other ceremonial functions. In the Roman Rite, the standard book of this kind is the Roman Ritual.

Rogito: The official notarial act or document testifying to the burial of a pope.

Rosary: A form of mental and vocal prayer centered on mysteries or events in the lives of Jesus and Mary. Its essential elements are meditation on the mysteries and the recitation of a number of decades of Hail Marys, each beginning with the Lord's Prayer. Introductory prayers may include the Apostles' Creed, an initial Our Father, three Hail Marys and a Glory be to the Father; each decade is customarily concluded with a Glory be to the Father; at the end, it is customary to say the Hail, Holy Queen and a prayer from the liturgy for the feast of the Blessed Virgin Mary of the Rosary. The Mysteries of the Rosary, which are the subject of meditation, are: (1) Joyful — the Annunciation to Mary that she was to be the Mother of Christ, her visit to Elizabeth, the birth of Jesus, the presentation of Jesus in the Temple, the finding of Jesus in the Temple. (2) Sorrowful — Christ's agony in the Garden of Gethsemani, scourging at the pillar, crowning with thorns, carrying of the Cross to Calvary, and crucifixion. (3) Glorious — the Resurrection and Ascension of Christ, the descent of the Holy Spirit upon the Apostles, Mary's Assumption into heaven and her crowning as Queen of angels and men. The complete Rosary, called the Dominican Rosary, consists of 15 decades. In customary practice, only five decades are usually said at one time. Rosary beads are used to aid in counting the prayers without distraction. The Rosary originated through the coalescence of popular devotions to Jesus and Mary from the 12th century onward. Its present form dates from about the 15th century. Carthusians contributed greatly toward its development; Dominicans have been its greatest promoters.

S

Sabbath: The seventh day of the week, observed by Jews and Sabbatarians as the day for rest and religious observance.

Sacrarium: A basin with a drain leading directly into the ground; standard equipment of a sacristy.

Sacred Heart, Enthronement: An acknowledgment of the sovereignty of Jesus Christ over the Christian family, expressed by the installation of an image or picture of the Sacred Heart in a place of honor in the home, accompanied by an act of consecration.

Sacred Heart, Promises: Twelve promises to persons having devotion to the Sacred Heart of Jesus, which were communicated by Christ to St. Margaret Mary Alacoque in a private revelation in 1675: (1) I will give them all the graces necessary in their state in life. (2) I will establish peace in their homes. (3) I will comfort them in all their afflictions. (4) I will be their secure refuge during life and, above all, in death. (5) I will bestow abundant blessing upon all their undertakings. (6) Sinners shall find in my Heart the source and the infinite ocean of mercy. (7) By devotion to my Heart tepid souls shall grow fervent. (8) Fervent souls shall quickly mount to high perfection. (9) I will bless every place where a picture of my Heart shall be set up and honored. (10) I will give to priests the gift of touching the most hardened hearts. (11) Those who promote this devotion shall have their names written in my Heart, never to be blotted out. (12) I will grant the grace of final penitence to those who communicate (receive Holy Communion) on the first Friday of nine consecutive months.

Sacrilege: Violation of and irreverence toward a person, place or thing that is sacred because of public dedication to God; a sin against the virtue of religion. Personal sacrilege is violence of some kind against a cleric or religious, or a violation of chastity with a cleric or religious. Local sacrilege is the desecration of sacred places. Real sacrilege is irreverence with respect to sacred things, such as the sacraments and sacred vessels.

Sacristy: A utility room where vestments, church furnishings and sacred vessels are kept and where the clergy vest for sacred functions.

Sadducees: The predominantly priestly party among the Jews in the time of Christ, noted for extreme conservatism, acceptance only of the Law of Moses, and rejection of the traditions of the elders. Their opposite numbers were the Pharisees.

Saints, Cult of: The veneration, called dulia, of holy persons who have died and are in glory with God in heaven; it includes honoring them and petitioning them for their intercession with God. Liturgical veneration is given only to saints officially recognized by the Church; private veneration may be given to anyone thought to be in heaven. The veneration of saints is essentially different from the adoration given to God alone; by its very nature, however, it terminates in the worship of God. According to the Second Vatican Council's *Dogmatic Constitution on the Church* (No. 50): "It is supremely fitting that we love those friends and fellow heirs of Jesus Christ, who are also our brothers and extraordinary benefactors, that we render due thanks to God for them and 'suppliantly invoke them and have recourse to their prayers, their power and help in obtaining benefits from God through his Son, Jesus Christ, our Lord, who is our sole Redeemer and Savior.' For by its very nature every genuine testimony of love which we show to those in heaven tends toward and terminates in Christ, who is the 'crown of all saints.' Through him it tends toward and terminates in God, who is wonderful in his saints and is magnified in them."

Salvation: The liberation of persons from sin and its effects, reconciliation with God in and through Christ, the attainment of union with God forever in the glory of heaven as the supreme purpose of life and as the God-given reward for fulfillment of his will on earth. Salvation-in-process begins and continues in this life through union with Christ in faith professed and in action; its final term is union with God and the whole community of the saved in the ultimate perfection of God's kingdom. The Church teaches that: God wills the salvation of all men; men are saved in and through Christ; membership in the Church established by Christ, known and understood as the community of salvation, is necessary for salvation; men with this knowledge and understanding who deliberately reject this Church, cannot be saved. The Catholic Church is the Church founded by Christ. (See below, Salvation outside the Church.)

Salvation History: The facts and the record of God's relations with human beings, in the past, present and future, for the purpose of leading them to live in accordance with his will for the eventual attainment after death of salvation, or everlasting happiness with him in heaven. The essentials of salvation history are: God's love for all human beings and will for their salvation; his intervention and action in the world to express this love and bring about their salvation; the revelation he made of himself and the covenant he established with the Israelites in the Old Testament; the perfecting of this revelation and the new covenant of grace through Christ in the New Testament; the continuing action-for-salvation carried on in and through the Church; the communication of saving grace to people through the merits of Christ and the operations of the Holy Spirit in the here-and-now circumstances of daily life and with the cooperation of people themselves.

Salvation outside the Church: The Second Vatican Council covered this subject summarily in the following manner: "Those also can attain to everlasting salvation who through no fault of their own do not know the Gospel of Christ or his Church, yet sincerely seek God and, moved by grace, strive by their deeds to do his will as it is known to them through the dictates of conscience. Nor does divine Providence deny the help necessary for salvation to those who, without blame on their part, have not yet arrived at an explicit knowledge of God, but who strive to live a good life, thanks to his grace. Whatever good or truth is found among them is looked upon by the Church as a preparation for the Gospel. She regards such qualities as given by him who enlightens all men so that they may finally have life" (*Dogmatic Constitution on the Church,* No. 16).

Satanism: Worship of the devil, a blasphemous inversion of the order of worship which is due to God alone.

Scandal: Conduct which is the occasion of sin to another person.

Scapular: (1) A part of the habit of some religious orders like the Benedictines and Dominicans; a nearly shoulder-wide strip of cloth worn over the tunic and reaching almost to the feet in front and behind. Originally a kind of apron, it came to symbolize the cross and yoke of Christ. (2) Scapulars worn by lay persons as a sign of association with religious orders and for devotional purposes are an adaptation of monastic scapulars. Approved by the Church as sacramentals, they consist of two small squares of woolen cloth joined by strings and are worn about the neck. They are given for wearing in a ceremony of investiture or enrollment. There are nearly 20 scapulars for devotional use: the five principal ones are generally understood to include those of Our Lady of Mt. Carmel (the brown Carmelite Scapular), the Holy Trinity, Our Lady of the Seven Dolors, the Passion, the Immaculate Conception.

Scapular Medal: A medallion with a representation of the Sacred Heart on one side and of the Blessed Virgin Mary on the other. Authorized by St. Pius X in 1910, it may be worn or carried in place of a scapular by persons already invested with a scapular.

Scapular Promise: According to a legend of the Carmelite Order, the Blessed Virgin Mary appeared to St. Simon Stock in 1251 at Cambridge, England, and declared that wearers of the brown Carmelite Scapular would be the beneficiaries of her special intercession. The scapular tradition has never been the subject of official decision by the Church. Essentially, it expresses belief in the intercession of Mary and the efficacy of sacramentals in the context of truly Christian life.

Schism: Derived from a Greek word meaning separation, the term designates formal and obstinate refusal by a baptized Catholic, called a schismatic, to be in communion with the pope and the Church. The canonical penalty is excommunication. One of the most disastrous schisms in history resulted in the definitive separation of the Church in the East from union with Rome about 1054.

Scholasticism: The term usually applied to the Catholic theology and philosophy which developed in the Middle Ages.

Scribes: Hebrew intellectuals noted for their knowledge of the Law of Moses, influential from the time of the Exile to about 70 A.D. Many of them were Pharisees. They were the antecedents of rabbis and their traditions, as well as those o the Pharisees, had a lasting influence on Judaism following the destruction of Jerusalem in 70 A.D.

Scruple: A morbid, unreasonable fear and anxiety that one's actions are sinful when they are not, or more seriously sinful than they actually are. Compulsive scrupulosity is quite different from the transient scrupulosity of persons of tender or highly sensitive conscience, or of persons with faulty moral judgment.

Seal of Confession: The obligation of secrecy which must be observed regarding knowledge of things learned in connection with the confession of sin in the sacrament of penance. The seal covers matters whose revelation would make the sacrament burdensome. Confessors are prohibited, under penalty of excommunication, from making any direct revelation of confessional matter; this prohibition holds, outside of confession, even with respect to the person who made the confession unless the person releases the priest from the obligation. Persons other than confessors are obliged to maintain secrecy, but not under penalty of excommunication. General, non-specific discussion of confessional matter does not violate the seal.

Secularism: A school of thought, a spirit and manner of action which ignores and/or repudiates the validity or influence of supernatural religion with respect to individual and social life. In describing secularism in their annual statement in 1947, the bishops of the United States said in part: " There are many men — and their number is daily increasing — who in practice live their lives without recognizing that this is God's world. For the most part they do not deny God. On formal occasions they may even mention his name. Not all of them would subscribe to the statement that all moral values derive from merely human conventions. But they fail to bring an awareness of their responsibility to God into their thought and action as individuals and members of society. This, in essence, is what we mean by secularism."

See: Another name for diocese or archdiocese.

Seminary: A house of study and formation for men, called seminarians, preparing for the priesthood. Traditional seminaries date from the Council of Trent in the middle of the 16th century; before that time, candidates for the priesthood were variously trained in monastic schools, universities under church auspices, and in less formal ways. At the present time, seminaries are undergoing considerable change for the improvement of academic and formation programs and procedures.

Sermon on the Mount: A compilation of sayings of Our Lord in the form of an extended discourse in Matthew's Gospel (5:1 to 7:27) and, in a shorter discourse, in Luke (6:17-49). The passage in Matthew, called the "Constitution of the New Law," summarizes the living spirit of believers in Christ and members of the kingdom of God. Beginning with the Beatitudes and including the Lord's Prayer, it covers the perfect justice of the New Law, the fulfillment of the Old Law in the New Law of Christ, and the integrity of internal attitude and external conduct with respect to love of God and neighbor, justice, chastity, truth, trust and confidence in God.

Seven Last Words of Christ: Words of Christ on the Cross. (1) "Father, forgive them; for they do not know what they are doing." (2) To the penitent thief: "I assure you: today you will be with me in Paradise." (3) To Mary and his Apostle John: "Woman, there is your son There is your mother." (4) "My God, my God, why have you forsaken me?" (5) "I am thirsty." (6) "Now it is finished." (7) "Father, into your hands I commend my spirit."

Shrine, Crowned: A shrine approved by the Holy See as a place of pilgrimage. The approval permits public devotion at the shrine and implies that at least one miracle has resulted from devotion at the shrine. Among the best known crowned shrines are those of the Virgin Mary at Lourdes and Fatima. Shrines with statues crowned by Pope John Paul in 1985 in South America were those of Our Lady of Coromoto, patroness of Venezuela, in Caracas, and Our Lady of Carmen of Paucartambo in Cuzco, Peru.

Shroud of Turin: A strip of brownish linen cloth, 14 feet, three inches in length and three feet, seven inches in width, bearing the front and back imprint of a human body. A tradition dating from the seventh century, which has not been verified beyond doubt, claims that the shroud is the fine linen in which the body of Christ was wrapped for burial. The early history of the shroud is obscure. It was enshrined at Lirey, France, in 1354 and was transferred in 1578 to Turin, Italy, where it has been kept in the cathedral down to the present time. Scientific investigation, which began in 1898, seems to indicate that the markings on the shroud are those of a human body. The shroud, for the first time since 1933, was placed on public view from Aug. 27 to Oct. 8, 1978, and was seen by an estimated 3.3 million people. Scientists conducted intensive studies of it thereafter, finally determining that the material of the shroud dated from between 1260 and 1390. The shroud, which had been the possession of the House of Savoy, was willed to Pope John Paul II in 1983.

Sick Calls: When a person is confined at home by illness or other cause and is unable to go to church for reception of the sacraments, a parish priest should be informed and arrangements made for him to visit the person at home. Such visitations are common in pastoral practice, both for special needs and for providing persons with regular opportunities for receiving the sacraments. If a priest cannot make the visitation, arrangements can be made for a deacon or Eucharistic minister to bring Holy Communion to the homebound or bedridden person.

Sign of the Cross: A sign, ceremonial gesture or movement in the form of a cross by which a person confesses faith in the Holy Trinity and Christ, and intercedes for the blessing of himself or herself, other persons and things. In Roman-Rite practice, a person making the sign touches the fingers of the right hand to forehead, below the breast, left shoulder and right shoulder while saying: "In the name of the Father, and of the Son, and of the Holy Spirit." The sign is also made with the thumb on the forehead, the lips, and the breast. For the blessing of persons and objects, a large sign of the cross is made by movement of the right hand. In Eastern-Rite practice, the sign is made with the thumb and first two fingers of the right hand joined together and touching the forehead, below the breast, the right shoulder and the left shoulder; the formula generally used is the doxology, "O Holy God, O Holy Strong One, O Immortal One." The Eastern manner of making the sign was general until the first half of the 13th century; by the 17th century, Western practice involved the whole right hand and the reversal of direction from shoulder to shoulder.

Signs of the Times: Contemporary events, trends and features in culture and society, the needs and aspirations of people, all the factors that form the context in and through which the Church is to carry on its saving mission. The Second Vatican Council spoke on numerous occasions about these signs and the relationship between them and a kind of manifestation of God's will, positive or negative, and about subjecting them to judgment and action corresponding to the demands of divine revelation through Scripture, Christ, and the experience, tradition and teaching authority of the Church.

Simony: The deliberate intention and act of selling

and/or buying spiritual goods or material things so connected with the spiritual that they cannot be separated therefrom; a violation of the virtue of religion, and a sacrilege, because it wrongfully puts a material price on spiritual things, which cannot be either sold or bought. In church law, actual sale or purchase is subject to censure in some cases. The term is derived from the name of Simon Magus, who attempted to buy from Sts. Peter and John the power to confirm people in the Holy Spirit (Acts 8:4-24).

Sin: (1) Actual sin is the free and deliberate violation of God's law by thought, word or action. (a) Mortal sin — involving serious matter, sufficient reflection and full consent — results in the loss of sanctifying grace and alienation from God, and renders a person incapable of performing meritorious supernatural acts and subject to everlasting punishment. (b) Venial sin — involving less serious matter, reflection and consent — does not have such serious consequences. (2) Original sin is the sin of Adam, with consequences for all human beings. (See separate entry.)

Sins against the Holy Spirit: Despair of salvation, presumption of God's mercy, impugning the known truths of faith, envy at another's spiritual good, obstinacy in sin, final impenitence. Those guilty of such sins stubbornly resist the influence of grace and, as long as they do so, cannot be forgiven.

Sins, Occasions of: Circumstances (persons, places, things, etc.) which easily lead to sin. There is an obligation to avoid voluntary proximate occasions of sin, and to take precautions against the dangers of unavoidable occasions.

Sins That Cry to Heaven for Vengeance: Willful murder, sins against nature, oppression of the poor, widows and orphans, defrauding laborers of their wages.

Sister: Any woman religious, in popular speech; strictly, the title applies only to women religious belonging to institutes whose members never professed solemn vows. Most of the institutes whose members are properly called Sisters were established during and since the 19th century. Women religious with solemn vows, or belonging to institutes whose members formerly professed solemn vows, are properly called nuns.

Sisterhood: A generic term referring to the whole institution of the life of women religious in the Church, or to a particular institute of women religious.

Situation Ethics: A subjective, individualistic ethical theory which denies the binding force of ethical principles as universal laws and preceptive norms of moral conduct, and proposes that morality is determined only by situational conditions and considerations and the intention of the person. In an instruction issued on the subject in May, 1956, the Congregation for the Holy Office (now the Congregation for the Doctrine of the Faith) said: "It ignores the principles of objective ethics. This 'New Morality,' it is claimed, is not only the equal of objective morality, but is superior to it. The authors who follow this system state that the ultimate determining norm for activity is not the objective order as determined by the natural law and known with certainty from this law. It is instead some internal judgment and illumi-

nation of the mind of every individual by which the mind comes to know what is to be done in a concrete situation. This ultimate decision of man is, therefore, not the application of the objective law to a particular case after the particular circumstances of a 'situation' have been considered and weighed according to the rules of prudence, as the more important authors of objective ethics teach; but it is, according to them, immediate, internal illumination and judgment. With regard to its objective truth and correctness, this judgment, at least in many things, is not ultimately measured, is not to be measured or is not measurable by any objective norm found outside man and independent of his subjective persuasion, but it is fully sufficient in itself. Much that is stated in this system of 'Situation Ethics' is contrary to the truth of reality and to the dictate of sound reason. It gives evidence of relativism and modernism, and deviates far from the Catholic teaching handed down through the ages."

Slander: Attributing to a person faults which he or she does not have; a violation of the obligations of justice and charity, for which restitution is due.

Sloth (Acedia): One of the seven capital sins; spiritual laziness, involving distaste and disgust for spiritual things; spiritual boredom, which saps the vigor of spiritual life. Physical laziness is a counterpart of spiritual sloth.

Sorcery: A kind of black magic in which evil is invoked by means of diabolical intervention; a violation of the virtue of religion.

Soteriology: The division of theology which treats of the mission and work of Christ as Redeemer.

Species, Sacred: The appearances of bread and wine (color, taste, smell, etc.) which remain after the substance has been changed at the Consecration of the Mass into the Body and Blood of Christ. (See Transubstantiation.)

Spiritism: Attempts to communicate with spirits and departed souls by means of seances, table tapping, ouija boards, and other methods; a violation of the virtue of religion. Spiritualistic practices are noted for fakery.

Stational Churches, Days: Churches, especially in Rome, where the clergy and lay people were accustomed to gather with their bishop on certain days for the celebration of the liturgy. The 25 early titular or parish churches of Rome, plus other churches, each had their turn as the site of divine worship in practices which may have started in the third century. The observances were rather well developed toward the latter part of the fourth century, and by the fifth they included a Mass concelebrated by the pope and attendant priests. On some occasions, the stational liturgy was preceded by a procession from another church called a collecta. There were 42 Roman stational churches in the eighth century, and 89 stational services were scheduled annually in connection with the liturgical seasons. Stational observances fell into disuse toward the end of the Middle Ages. Some revival was begun by John XXIII in 1959 and continued by Paul VI and John Paul II.

Stations (Way) of the Cross: A form of devotion commemorating the Passion and death of Christ, consisting of a series of meditations (stations): (1) his condemnation to death, (2) taking up of the cross, (3) the first fall on the way to Calvary, (4) meeting his Mother, (5) being assisted by Simon of Cyrene and (6) by the woman Veronica who wiped his face, (7) the second fall, (8) meeting the women of Jerusalem, (9) the third fall, (10) being stripped and (11) nailed to the cross, (12) his death, (13) the removal of his body from the cross and (14) his burial. Depictions of these scenes are mounted in most churches, chapels and in some other places, beneath small crosses. A person making the Way of the Cross passes before these stations, or stopping points, pausing at each for meditation. If the stations are made by a group of people, only the leader has to pass from station to station. A plenary indulgence is granted to the faithful who make the stations, under the usual conditions: freedom from all attachment to sin, reception of the sacraments of penance and the Eucharist, and prayers for the intentions of the pope. Those who are impeded from making the stations in the usual manner can gain the same indulgence if, along with the aforementioned conditions, they spend at least a half hour in spiritual reading and meditation on the passion and death of Christ. The stations originated remotely from the practice of Holy Land pilgrims who visited the actual scenes of incidents in the Passion of Christ. Representations elsewhere of at least some of these scenes were known as early as the fifth century. Later, the stations evolved in connection with and as a consequence of strong devotion to the Passion in the 12th and 13th centuries. Franciscans, who were given custody of the Holy Places in 1342, promoted the devotion widely; one of them, St. Leonard of Port Maurice, became known as the greatest preacher of the Way of the Cross in the 18th century. The general features of the devotion were fixed by Clement XII in 1731. On Good Friday, 1991, Pope John Paul made the stations in a manner different from the usual way, using stations based entirely on Gospel texts: (1) Jesus in the Garden of Olives, (2) Jesus is betrayed by Judas and arrested, (3) Jesus is condemned by the Sanhedrin, (4) Jesus is denied by Peter, (5) Jesus is condemned by Pilate, (6) Jesus is scourged and crowned with thorns, (7) Jesus is made to carry his cross, (8) Simon of Cyrene helps Jesus carry his cross, (9) Jesus meets the women of Jerusalem, (10) Jesus is crucified, (11) Jesus promises the Kingdom to the repentant thief, (12) On the cross Jesus speaks to his mother and his beloved disciple John, (13) Jesus dies on the cross, (14) Jesus is laid in the tomb.

Statutes: Virtually the same as decrees (see separate entry), they almost always designate laws of a particular council or synod rather than pontifical laws.

Stigmata: Marks of the wounds suffered by Christ in his crucifixion, in hands and feet by nails, and side by the piercing of a lance. Some persons, called stigmatists, have been reported as recipients or sufferers of marks like these. The Church, however, has never issued any infallible declaration about their possession by anyone, even in the case of St. Francis of Assisi whose stigmata seem to be the best substantiated and may be commemorated in the Roman-Rite liturgy. Ninety percent of some 300 reputed stigmatists have been women. Judgment regarding the presence, significance, and manner of causation of stigmata would depend, among other things, on irrefutable experimental evidence.

Stipend, Mass: An offering given to a priest for applying the fruits of the Mass according to the intention of the donor. The offering is a contribution to the support of the priest. The disposition of the fruits of the sacrifice, in line with doctrine concerning the Mass in particular and prayer in general, is subject to the will of God. In the early Christian centuries, when Mass was not offered for the intentions of particular persons, the participants made offerings of bread and wine for the sacrifice and their own Holy Communion, and of other things useful for the support of the clergy and the poor. Some offerings may have been made as early as the fourth century for the celebration of Mass for particular intentions, and there are indications of the existence of this practice from the sixth century when private Masses began to be offered. The earliest certain proof of stipend practice, however, dates from the eighth century. By the 11th century, along with private Mass, it was established custom. Mass offerings and intentions were the subjects of a decree approved by John Paul II and made public Mar. 22, 1991. (1) Normally, no more than one offering should be accepted for a Mass; the Mass should be offered in accord with the donor's intention; the priest who accepts the offering should celebrate the Mass himself or have another priest do so. (2) Several Mass intentions, for which offerings have been made, can be combined for a "collective" application of a single Mass only if the previous and explicit consent of the donors is obtained. Such Masses are an exception to the general rule.

Stole Fee: An offering given on certain occasions; e.g., at a baptism, wedding, funeral, for the support of the clergy who administer the sacraments and perform other sacred rites.

Stoup: A vessel used to contain holy water.

Suffragan See: Any diocese, except the archdiocese, within a province.

Suicide: The taking of one's own life; a violation of God's dominion over human life. Ecclesiastical burial is denied to persons while in full possession of their faculties; it is permitted in cases of doubt.

Supererogation: Actions which go beyond the obligations of duty and the requirements enjoined by God's law as necessary for salvation. Examples of these works are the profession and observance of the evangelical counsels of poverty, chastity, and obedience, and efforts to practice charity to the highest degree.

Supernatural: Above the natural; that which exceeds and is not due or owed to the essence, exigencies, requirements, powers and merits of created nature. While human beings have no claim on supernatural things and do not need them in order to exist and act on a natural level, they do need them in order to exist and act in the higher order or economy of grace established by God for their salvation. God has freely given them certain things which are beyond the powers and rights of their human nature. Examples of the supernatural are: grace, a kind of participation by human beings in the divine life, by which they become capable of performing acts meritorious for salvation; divine revelation by which God manifests himself to them and makes known truth that is inaccessible to human reason alone; faith, by which they believe divine truth because of the authority of God who reveals it through Sacred Scripture and tradition and the teaching of his Church.

Superstition: A violation of the virtue of religion, by which God is worshipped in an unworthy manner or creatures are given honor which belongs to God alone. False, vain, or futile worship involves elements which are incompatible with the honor and respect due to God, such as error, deception, and bizarre practices. Examples are: false and exaggerated devotions, chain prayers and allegedly unfailing prayers, the mixing of unbecoming practices in worship. The second kind of superstition attributes to persons and things powers and honor which belong to God alone. Examples are: idolatry, divination, magic, spiritism, necromancy.

Suspension: A censure by which a cleric is forbidden to exercise some or all of his powers of orders and jurisdiction, or to accept the financial support of his benefices.

Swearing: Taking an oath; calling upon God to witness the truth of a statement; a legitimate thing to do for serious reasons and under proper circumstances, as in a court of law. To swear without sufficient reason is to dishonor God's name; to swear falsely in a court of law is perjury.

Swedenborgianism: A doctrine developed in and from the writings of Emmanuel Swedenborg (1688-1772), who claimed that during a number of visions he had in 1745 Christ taught him the spiritual sense of Sacred Scripture and commissioned him to communicate it to others. He held that, just as Christianity succeeded Judaism, so his teaching supplemented Christianity. He rejected belief in the Trinity, original sin, the Resurrection, and all the sacraments except baptism and the Eucharist. His followers are members of the Church of the New Jerusalem or of the New Church.

Syllabus, The: (1) When not qualified, the term refers to the list of 80 errors accompanying Pope Pius IX's encyclical *Quanta Cura,* issued in 1864. (2) The *Syllabus* of St. Pius X in the decree *Lamentabili,* issued by the Holy Office July 4, 1907, condemning 65 heretical propositions of modernism. This schedule of errors was followed shortly by that pope's encyclical *Pascendi,* the principal ecclesiastical document against modernism, issued Sept. 8, 1907.

Synod, Diocesan: Meeting of representative persons of a diocese — priests, religious, lay persons — with the bishop, called by him for the purpose of considering and taking action on matters affecting the life and mission of the Church in the diocese. Persons taking part in a synod have consultative status; the bishop alone is the legislator, with power to authorize synodal decrees. According to canon law, every diocese should have a synod every 10 years.

T

Te Deum: The opening Latin words, Thee, God, of a hymn of praise and thanksgiving prescribed for use in the Office of Readings of the Liturgy of the Hours on many Sundays, solemnities and feasts.

Temperance: Moderation, one of the four cardinal virtues.

Temptation: Any enticement to sin, from any source: the strivings of one's own faculties, the action of the devil, other persons, circumstances of life, etc. Temptation itself is not sin. Temptation can be avoided and overcome with the use of prudence and the help of grace.

Thanksgiving: An expression of gratitude to God for his goodness and the blessings he grants; one of the four ends of prayer.

Theism: A philosophy which admits the existence of God and the possibility of divine revelation; it is generally monotheistic and acknowledges God as transcendent and also active in the world. Because it is a philosophy rather than a system of theology derived from revelation, it does not include specifically Christian doctrines, like those concerning the Trinity, the Incarnation and Redemption.

Theological Virtues: The virtues which have God for their direct object: faith, or belief in God's infallible teaching; hope, or confidence in divine assistance; charity, or love of God. They are given to a person with grace in the first instance, through baptism and incorporation in Christ.

Theology: Knowledge of God and religion, deriving from and based on the data of divine Revelation, organized and systematized according to some kind of scientific method. It involves systematic study and presentation of the truths of divine Revelation in Sacred Scripture, tradition, and the teaching of the Church. The Second Vatican Council made the following declaration about theology and its relation to divine Revelation: "Sacred theology rests on the written word of God, together with sacred tradition, as its primary and perpetual foundation. By scrutinizing in the light of faith all truth stored up in the mystery of Christ, theology is most powerfully strengthened and constantly rejuvenated by that word. For the sacred Scriptures contain the word of God and, since they are inspired, really are the word of God; and so the study of the sacred page is, as it were, the soul of sacred theology" (*Constitution on Revelation,* No. 24). Theology has been divided under various subject headings. Some of the major fields have been: dogma (systematic theology), moral, pastoral, ascetics (the practice of virtue and means of attaining holiness and perfection), mysticism (higher states of religious experience). Other subject headings include ecumenism (Christian unity, interfaith relations), ecclesiology (the nature and constitution of the Church), Mariology (doctrine concerning the Blessed Virgin Mary), the sacraments, etc.

Tithing: Contribution of a portion of one's income, originally one-tenth, for purposes of religion and charity. The practice is mentioned 46 times in the Bible. In early Christian times, tithing was adopted in continuance of Old Testament practices of the Jewish people, and the earliest positive church legislation on the subject was enacted in 567. Catholics are bound in conscience to contribute to the support of their church, but the manner in which they do so is not fixed by law. Tithing, which amounts to a pledged contribution of a portion of one's income, has aroused new attention in recent years in the United States.

Titular Sees: Dioceses where the Church once flourished but which now exist only in name or title. Bishops without a territorial or residential diocese of their own; e.g., auxiliary bishops, are given titular sees. There are more than 2,000 titular sees; 16 of them are in the United States.

Transfinalization, Transignification: Terms coined to express the sign value of consecrated bread and wine with respect to the presence and action of Christ in the Eucharistic sacrifice and the spiritually vivifying purpose of the Eucharistic banquet in Holy Communion. The theory behind the terms has strong undertones of existential and "sign" philosophy, and has been criticized for its openness to interpretation at variance with the doctrine of transubstantiation and the abiding presence of Christ under the appearances of bread and wine after the sacrifice of the Mass and Communion have been completed. The terms, if used as substitutes for transubstantiation, are unacceptable; if they presuppose transubstantiation, they are acceptable as clarifications of its meaning.

Transubstantiation: "The way Christ is made present in this sacrament (Holy Eucharist) is none other than by the change of the whole substance of the bread into his Body, and of the whole substance of the wine into his Blood (in the Consecration at Mass) this unique and wonderful change the Catholic Church rightly calls transubstantiation" (encyclical *Mysterium Fidei* of Paul VI, Sept. 3, 1965). The first official use of the term was made by the Fourth Council of the Lateran in 1215. Authoritative teaching on the subject was issued by the Council of Trent.

Treasury of Merit: The superabundant merits of Christ and the saints from which the Church draws to confer spiritual benefits, such as indulgences.

Triduum: A three-day series of public or private devotions.

U-Z

Usury: Excessive interest charged for the loan and use of money; a violation of justice.

Veronica: A word resulting from the combination of a Latin word for true, *vera,* and a Greek word for image, *eikon,* designating a likeness of the face of Christ or the name of a woman said to have given him a cloth on which he caused an imprint of his face to appear. The veneration at Rome of a likeness depicted on cloth dates from about the end of the 10th century; it figured in a popular devotion during the Middle Ages, and in the Holy Face devotion practiced since the 19th century. A faint, indiscernible likeness said to be of this kind is preserved in St. Peter's Basilica. The origin of the likeness is uncertain, and the identity of the woman is unknown. Before the 14th century, there were no known artistic representations of an incident concerning a woman who wiped the face of Christ with a piece of cloth while he was carrying the Cross to Calvary.

Viaticum: Holy Communion given to those in danger of death. The word, derived from Latin, means provision for a journey through death to life hereafter.

Vicar General: A priest or bishop appointed by the bishop of a diocese to serve as his deputy, with ordinary executive power, in the administration of the diocese.

Virginity: Observance of perpetual sexual abstinence. The state of virginity, which is embraced for the love of God by religious with a public vow or by others with a private vow, was singled out for high praise by Christ (Mt. 19:10-12) and has always been so regarded by the Church. In the encyclical *Sacra Virginitas,* Pius XII stated: "Holy virginity and that perfect chastity which is consecrated to the service of God is without doubt among the most perfect treasures which the founder of the Church has left in heritage to the society which he established." Paul VI approved in 1970 a rite in which women can consecrate their virginity "to Christ and their brethren" without becoming members of a religious institute. The *Ordo Consecrationis Virginum,* a revision of a rite promulgated by Clement VII in 1596, is traceable to the Roman liturgy of about 500.

Virtue: A habit or established capability for performing good actions. Virtues are natural (acquired and increased by repeating good acts) and/or supernatural (given with grace by God).

Vocation: A call to a way of life. Generally, the term applies to the common call of all persons, from God, to holiness and salvation. Specifically, it refers to particular states of life, each called a vocation, in which response is made to this universal call; viz., marriage, the religious life and/or priesthood, the single state freely chosen or accepted for the accomplishment of God's will. The term also applies to the various occupations in which persons make a living. The Church supports the freedom of each individual in choosing a particular vocation, and reserves the right to pass on the acceptability of candidates for the priesthood and religious life. Signs or indicators of particular vocations are many, including a person's talents and interests, circumstances and obligations, invitations of grace and willingness to respond thereto.

Vow: A promise made to God with sufficient knowledge and freedom, which has as its object a moral good that is possible and better than its voluntary omission. A person who professes a vow binds himself or herself by the virtue of religion to fulfill the promise. The best known examples of vows are those of poverty, chastity and obedience professed by religious (see Evangelical Counsels, individual entries). Public vows are made before a competent person, acting as an agent of the Church, who accepts the profession in the name of the Church, thereby giving public recognition to the person's dedication and consecration to God and divine worship. Vows of this kind are either solemn, rendering all contrary acts invalid as well as unlawful; or simple, rendering contrary acts unlawful. Solemn vows are for life; simple vows are for a definite period of time or for life. Vows professed without public recognition by the Church are called private vows. The Church, which has authority to accept and give public recognition to vows, also has authority to dispense persons from their obligations for serious reasons.

Week of Prayer for Christian Unity: Eight days of prayer, from Jan. 18 to 25, for the union of all persons in the Church established by Christ. On the initiative of Father Paul James Francis Wattson, S.A., of Graymoor, N.Y., it originated in 1908 as the Chair of Unity Octave. In recent years, its observance on an interfaith basis has increased greatly.

Witness, Christian: Practical testimony or evidence given by Christians of their faith in all circumstances of life — by prayer and general conduct, through good example and good works, etc.; being and acting in accordance with Christian belief; actual practice of the Christian faith.

1997 CPA AWARDS

Catholic Press Association Awards for material published in1996 were presented during the annual convention held May 21 to 24 in Denver, Colo. Some of the awards are listed below.

Newspapers — General Excellence
National Newspapers: *Our Sunday Visitor* (first place); *Catholic Twin Circle* (second place); *National Catholic Reporter* (third place).

Diocesan Newspapers, 40,001 and over circulation: *Catholic Standard and Times* (first place); *Catholic New York* (second); *The Saint Cloud Visitor* (third).

Diocesan Newspapers, 17,001 to 40,000 circulation: *The Catholic Spirit* (first place); *The New Catholic Explorer* (second); *The Pilot* (third).

Diocesan Newspapers, to 17,000 circulation: *The Compass* (first place); *The Catholic Northwest Progress* (second); *The Catholic Spirit* (third)

Spanish Language Periodicals: *Chicago Catolico* (first place); *Nosotros* (second); *El Centinela* (third).

Magazines — General Excellence
General Interest: *America* (first place); *Commonweal* (second).

Mission: *Maryknoll* (first place); *Mission* (second)

Religious Order: *SALT/Sisters of Charity, BVM* (first place); *The Anthonian* (second).

Professional/Special Interest: *Catholic Parent* (first place); *Health Progress* (second).

Magazines for Clergy and Religious: *Emmanuel* (first place); *Review for Religious* (second).

Scholarly: *Catholic Southwest* (first place). Only award given.

Prayer and Spirituality: *Forefront* (first place); *Spiritual Life* (second).

Newsletters
General Interest: *Catholic Update* (first place); *Scripture from Scratch* (second)

Special Interest: *Foundations* (first place); *Comboni Mission Newsletter* (second).

Books — First Place Awards
Popular Presentation of the Catholic Faith: The Liturgical Press, *Catholicism at the Dawn of the Third Millennium,* by Thomas P. Rausch.

Spirituality: Soft Cover — Crossroad Publishing Co., *Thomas Aquinas: Spiritual Master,* by Robert Barron. Hard Cover — Orbis Books, *A Passion for Life: Fragments of the Face of God,* Chittister/Lentz.

Theology: The Liturgical Press, *Collegeville Pastoral Dictionary of Biblical Theology,* Carroll Stuhlmueller, editor.

Scripture: HarperSan Francisco, *The Dead Sea Scrolls: A New Translation,* Wise/Abegg/Cook.

Liturgy: Trinity Press International, *The Landscape of Praise,* Blair Gilmer Meeks, editor.

Pastoral Ministry: Orbis Books, *Pastoral Theology from a Global Perspective,* Wilson/ Poerwowidagdo/Mofokeng/Evans/Evans.

Professional Books: Ave Maria Press, *Celibacy: Means of Control or Mandate of the Heart?* by Michael H. Crosby.

Educational Books: Liturgy Training Publications, *The Catechetical Documents: A Parish Resource,* Martin Connell, editor.

Design and Production: St. Anthony Messenger Press, *Can You Find Jesus?* Gallery/Harlow.

Children's Books: St. Anthony Messenger Press, *Can You Find Jesus?* Gallery/Harlow.

First Time Author of a Book: Gregory Mayers, *Listen to the Desert,* Triumph Books.

Family Life: The Liturgical Press, *Christian Marriage and Family,* Lawler/Roberts, editors.

History/Biography: Orbis Books, *History of Vatican II: Volume I,* Alberigo/Komonchak, editors.

Gender Issues: Fortress Press, *Casting Stones,* Nakashima Brock/Brooks Thistlethwaite

Hispanic Titles: OCP Publications, *Palabras y Cantos de Jesus,* Freeburg/Fuertes/Walker/Germano.

BAPTISM, EUCHARIST, MINISTRY

"Baptism, Eucharist and Ministry," produced under the auspices of the Faith and Order Commission of the World Council of Churches and approved by more than 100 Christian theologians at a meeting held in Lima, Peru, in January, 1982. The Lima Document (also referred to as BEM) is an attempt to state what divided Christians can say in common about baptism, the Eucharist and ministry. It was called a significant development in the ecumenical movement by the Secretariat for Promoting Christian Unity and the Congregation for the Doctrine of the Faith; their response was reported by the NC Documentary Service, Origins, Nov. 19, 1987 (Vol. 17, No. 23).

However, the Vatican agencies declared, it "does not offer a fully systematic treatment of baptism, Eucharist or ministry." Deficiencies have to do with, among other things, the notion of sacrament and the treatment of apostolic tradition and decisive authority in the church.

THE CHURCH IN COUNTRIES THROUGHOUT THE WORLD

(Principal sources for statistics: *Statistical Yearbook of the Church, 1995* (the most recent edition); *Annuario Pontificio, 1997*. Figures are as of Dec. 31, 1995, except for cardinals (as of August 30, 1997) and others which are indicated. For 1997 developments, see Index entries for individual countries.)

An asterisk indicates that the country has full diplomatic relations with the Holy See (see Index: Diplomats to the Holy See).

Abbreviations (in order in which they appear): archd. — archdiocese; dioc. — diocese; ap. ex. — apostolic exarchate; prel. — prelature; abb. — abbacy; v.a. — vicariate apostolic; p.a. — prefecture apostolic; a.a. — apostolic administration; mil. ord. — military ordinariate; card. — cardinal; abp. — archbishops; bp. — bishops (diocesan and titular); priests (dioc. — diocesan or secular priests; rel. — those belonging to religious orders); p.d. — permanent deacons; sem. — major seminarians, diocesan and religious; bros. — brothers; srs. — sisters; bap. — baptisms; Caths. — Catholic population; tot. pop. — total population; (AD), apostolic delegate (see Index: Papal Representatives).

Afghanistan

Republic in south-central Asia (in transition); capital, Kabul. Christianity antedated Muslim conquest in the seventh century but was overcome by it. All inhabitants are subject to the law of Islam. Christian missionaries are prohibited.

Population, 20,140,000.

Albania*

Archd., 2; dioc., 3; a.a. 1; abp., 2; bp., 2; parishes, 99; priests, 85 (29 dioc., 56 rel.); p.d.,1; sem., 23; bros., 17; srs., 217; bap., 3,226; Caths., 541,000 (15.7%); tot. pop., 3,440,000.

Republic in the Balkans, bordering the Adriatic Sea; capital, Tirana. Christianity was introduced in apostolic times. The northern part of the country remained faithful to Rome while the south broke from unity following the schism of 1054. A large percentage of the population was forcibly Islamized following the invasion (15th century) and long centuries of occupation by the Ottoman Turks. Many Catholics fled to southern Italy, Sicily and Greece. In 1945, at the time of the communist take-over, an estimated 68 per cent of the population was Muslim; 19 per cent, Orthodox and 13 per cent, Roman Catholic. The Catholic Church prevailed in the north. During 45 years of communist dictatorship, the Church fell victim, as did all religions, to systematic persecution: non-Albanian missionaries were expelled; death, prison sentences and other repressive measures were enacted against church personnel and laity; Catholic schools and churches were closed and used for other purposes, and lines of communication with the Holy See were cut off. In 1967, the government, declaring it had eliminated all religion in the country, proclaimed itself the first atheist state in the world. The right to practice religion was restored in late 1990. In March, 1991, a delegation from the Vatican was allowed to go to Albania; later in the year diplomatic relations were established with the Holy See at the request of the Albanian prime minister. Pope John Paul II made a historic one-day visit to the country April 25, 1993, during which he ordained four bishops appointed by him in December, 1992, to fill long-vacant sees. Restoration of the Church is a slow and difficult process. The first Albanian cardinal was named in November, 1994.

Algeria*

Archd., 1; dioc., 3; abp., 1; bp., 3; parishes, 40; priests, 105 (42 dioc., 63 rel.); sem., 2; bros., 16; srs., 186; bap., 12; Caths., 3,000 (.01%); tot. pop., 28,550,000.

Republic in northwest Africa: capital, Algiers. Christianity, introduced at an early date, succumbed to Vandal devastation in the fifth century and Muslim conquest in 709, but survived for centuries in small communities into the 12th century. Missionary work was unsuccessful except in service to traders, military personnel and captives along the coast. Church organization was established after the French gained control of the territory in the 1830s. A large number of Catholics were among the estimated million Europeans who left the country after it secured independence from France July 5, 1962. Sunni-Muslim is the state religion. Seven Trappist monks were among the victims of Muslim terrorist violence in May, 1996.

Andorra*

Parishes, 7; priests, 17 (12 dioc., 5 rel.); bros., 2; srs., 12; bap., 395; Caths., 59,000 (84.2%); tot. pop., 70,000.

Parliamentary state (1993) in the Pyrenees; capital, Andorra la Vella. From 1278-1993, it was a co-principality under the rule of the French head of state and the bishop of Urgel, Spain, who retain their titles. Christianity was introduced at an early date. Catholicism is the state religion. Ecclesiastical jurisdiction is under the Spanish Diocese of Urgel.

Angola*

Archd., 3; dioc., 12; card., 1; abp., 5; bp., 16; parishes, 255; priests, 419 (165 dioc., 254 rel.); p.d.,9; sem., 720; bros., 88; srs., 1,359; catechists, 22,165; bap., 117,861; Caths., 6,523,000 (58.9%); tot. pop., 11,070,000.

Republic in southwest Africa; capital, Luanda. Evangelization by Catholic missionaries, from Portugal, dating from 1491, reached high points in the 17th and 18th centuries. Independence from Portugal in 1975 and the long civil war which followed (peace accord signed in 1991) left the Church with a heavy loss of personnel through the departure of about half of the foreign missionaries and the persecution and martyrdom experienced by the Church during the war. Renewed fighting following elections in late 1992 brought repeated appeals for peace from the nation's bishops and religious in 1993 and 1994. Despite another peace accord signed by the rebels and the government in late 1994, conditions have remained unsettled. The first Angolan cardinal (Alexandre do Nascimento) was named in 1983.

Anguilla

Parish, 1; catechists, 4; bap., 10; Caths., 200; tot. pop., 7,000. (AD)

Self-governing British island territory in the Carib-

bean; capital, The Valley. Under ecclesiastical jurisdiction of St. John's-Basseterre diocese, Antigua.

Antigua and Barbuda*
*Dioc., 1; bp., 1; parishes, 2; priests, 8 (3 dioc., 5
rel.); sem., 1; bros., 5; srs., 11; catechists, 51; bap.,
85; Caths., 8,000 (12.5%); tot. pop., 64,000.*
Independent (1981) Caribbean island nation; capital, St. John's, Antigua.

Arabian Peninsula
Christianity, introduced in various parts of the peninsula in early Christian centuries, succumbed to
Islam in the seventh century. The native population
is entirely Muslim. The only Christians are foreign
workers mainly from the Philippines, India and Korea. Most of the peninsula is under the ecclesiastical
jurisdiction of the Vicariate Apostolic of Arabia with
its seat in Abu Dhabi, United Arab Emirates. See
individual countries: Bahrain, Oman, Qatar, Saudi
Arabia, United Arab Emirates and Yemen.

Argentina*
*Archd., 13; dioc. (1997), 50; prel., 3; ap. ex., 1
(for Armenians of Latin America); ord., 1; mil. ord.;
card., 4; abp., 19; bp., 83; parishes, 2,480; priests,
5,856 (3,439 dioc., 2,417 rel.); p.d., 354; sem.,
2,105; bros., 904; srs., 11,190; bap., 561,715;
Caths., 31,546,000 (90.7%); tot. pop., 34,770,000*
Republic in southeast South America, bordering on
the Atlantic; capital, Buenos Aires. Priests were with
the Magellan exploration party and the first Mass in
the country was celebrated Apr. 1, 1519. Missionary
work began in the 1530s, diocesan organization in
the late 1540s, and effective evangelization about
1570. Independence from Spain was proclaimed in
1816. Since its establishment in the country, the
Church has been influenced by Spanish cultural and
institutional forces, antagonistic liberalism, government interference and opposition; the latter reached a
climax during the last five years of the first presidency of Juan Peron (1946-1955). Widespread human rights violations including the disappearance of
thousands of people marked the period of military
rule from 1976 to December, 1983, when an elected
civilian government took over.

Armenia*
*Ord., 1 (for Catholic Armenians of Eastern Eu-
rope, with seat in Armenia); a.a., 1 (for Latin-rite
Catholics, with seat in Georgia); parishes, 18;
priests, 16 (rel.); sem., 5; srs., 15; bap., 1,111;
Caths., 141,000 (3.7%); tot. pop., 3,760,000.*
Republic in Asia Minor; capital Yerevan. Part of the
USSR from 1920 until it declared its sovereignty in
September, 1991. Ancient Armenia, which also in-
cluded territory annexed by Turkey in 1920, was
Christianized in the fourth century. Diplomatic rela-
tions were established with the Holy See May 23,
1992.

Aruba
*Parishes, 8; priests, 14 (8 dioc., 6 rel.); bros., 5;
srs., 6; catechists, 16; bap., 701; Caths., 56,000;
tot. pop., 70,000. (AD)*
Autonomous island member of The Netherlands in

West Indies. Under ecclesiastical jurisdiction of
Willemstad, Curacao, in Netherlands Antilles.

Australia*
*Archd., 7; dioc., 24; mil. ord., 1; card., 2; abp., 9;
bp., 49; parishes, 1,426; priests, 3,462 (2,098 dioc.,
1,364 rel.); p.d., 46; sem., 278; bros., 1,364; srs.,
8,868; bap., 75,174; Caths., 5,102,000 (28.2%);
tot. pop. 18,050,000.*
Commonwealth; island continent southeast of Asia;
capital, Canberra. The first Catholics in the country
were Irish under penal sentence, 1795-1804; the first
public Mass was celebrated May 15, 1803. Official
organization of the Church dates from 1820. The
country was officially removed from mission status
in March, 1976.

Austria*
*Archd., 2; dioc., 7; abb., 1; ord., 1; mil. ord.;
card., 3; abp., 3; bp., 15; parishes, 3,037; priests,
4,891 (2,976 dioc., 1,915 rel.); p.d., 350; sem., 470;
bros., 445; srs., 7,185; bap., 71,669; Caths.,
6,677,000 (78.2%); tot. pop., 8,530,000.*
Republic in central Europe; capital, Vienna. Christianity was introduced by the end of the third century,
strengthened considerably by conversion of the Ba-
varians from about 600, and firmly established in the
second half of the eighth century. Catholicism survived and grew stronger as the principal religion in
the country in the post-Reformation period, but suffered from Josephinism in the 18th century. Although
liberated from much government harassment in the
aftermath of the Revolution of 1848, the Church
came under pressure again some 20 years later in the
Kulturkampf. During this time the Church became
involved with a developing social movement. The
Church faced strong opposition from Socialists after
World War I and suffered persecution from 1938 to
1945 during the Nazi regime. Some Church-state
matters are regulated by a concordat originally concluded in 1934.

Azerbaijan*
Independent republic (1991) bordering Iran and
Turkey; formerly part of the USSR; capital, Baku.
Islam is the prevailing religion. There is a small
Catholic community of Polish and Armenian origin
near the capital. Latin-rite Catholics are under the
apostolic administration of the Caucasus (seat in
Georgia) established in December, 1993.
Tot. pop., 7,470,000.

Azores
North Atlantic island group 750 miles west of Portugal, of which it is part. Christianity was introduced
in the second quarter of the 15th century. The diocese
of Angra was established in 1534. Statistics are included in Portugal.

Bahamas*
*Dioc., 1; bp., 1; parishes, 29; priests, 30 (13 dioc.,
17 rel.); p.d., 9; sem., 4; bros., 2; srs., 30; catechists, 71; bap., 1,379; Caths., 47,000 (16.8%);
tot. pop., 280,000.*
Independent (July 10, 1973) island group consisting of some 700 (30 inhabited) small islands south-

east of Florida and north of Cuba; capital, Nassau. On Oct. 12, 1492, Columbus landed on one of these islands, where the first Mass was celebrated in the New World. Organization of the Catholic Church in the Bahamas dates from about the middle of the 19th century.

Bahrain

Parish, 1; priests, 3 (dioc.); srs., 7; bap., 250; Caths., 30,000; tot. pop., 590,000. (AD)

Island state in Persian Gulf; capital, Manama. Population is Muslim; Catholics are foreign workers. Under ecclesiastical jurisdiction of Arabia vicariate apostolic.

Balearic Islands

Spanish province consisting of an island group in the western Mediterranean. Statistics are included in those for Spain.

Bangladesh*

Archd., 1; dioc., 5; abp., 2; bp., 5; parishes, 73; priests, 275 (146 dioc., 129 rel.); sem., 99; bros., 62; srs., 919; catechists, 1,150; bap., 6,496; Caths., 231,000 (.19%); tot. pop. 120,430,000.

Formerly the eastern portion of Pakistan. Officially constituted as a separate nation Dec. 16, 1971; capital, Dhaka. Islam, the principal religion, was declared the state religion in 1988; freedom of religion is granted. There were Jesuit, Dominican and Augustinian missionaries in the area in the 16th century. A vicariate apostolic (of Bengali) was established in 1834; the hierarchy was erected in 1950.

Barbados*

Dioc., 1; bp., 2; parishes, 6; priests, 9 (3 dioc., 6 rel.); p.d., 1; srs., 11; bap., 175; Caths., 10,000 (3.8%); tot. pop., 260,000.

Parliamentary democracy (independent since 1966), easternmost of the Caribbean islands; capital, Bridgetown. About 70 per cent of the people are Anglicans.

Belarus*

Archd., 1; dioc., 2; card., 1; bp., 1; parishes, 338; priests, 227 (101 dioc., 126 rel.); sem., 197; bros., 9; srs., 272; bap., 8,607; Caths., 1,245,000 (12%); tot. pop., 10,140,000.

Independent republic (1991) in eastern Europe; former Soviet republic (Byelorussia); capital, Minsk. Slow but steady recovery of the Church was reported after years of repression in the Soviet Union.

Belgium*

Archd., 1; dioc., 7; mil ord.; card., 2; bp., 24; parishes, 3,962; priests, 9,158 (5,673 dioc., 3,485 rel.); p.d., 500; sem., 360; bros., 1,507; srs., 19,368; bap., 87,423; Caths., 8,462,000 (83.7%); tot. pop., 10,110,000.

Constitutional monarchy in northwestern Europe; capital, Brussels. Christianity was introduced about the first quarter of the fourth century and major evangelization was completed about 730. During the rest of the medieval period the Church had firm diocesan and parochial organization, generally vigorous monastic life, and influential monastic and cathedral schools. Lutherans and Calvinists made some gains during the Reformation period but there was a strong Catholic restoration in the first half of the 17th century, when the country was under Spanish rule. Jansenism disturbed the Church from about 1640 into the 18th century. Josephinism, imposed by an Austrian regime, hampered the Church late in the same century. Repressive and persecutory measures were enforced during the Napoleonic conquest. Freedom came with separation of Church and state in the wake of the Revolution of 1830, which ended the reign of William I. Thereafter, the Church encountered serious problems with philosophical liberalism and political socialism. Catholics have long been engaged in strong educational, social and political movements. Except for one five-year period (1880-84), Belgium has had diplomatic relations with the Holy See since 1835.

Belize*

Dioc., 1; bp., 1; parishes, 13; priests, 44 (15 dioc., 29 rel.); p.d., 1; sem., 4; bros., 8; srs., 74; bap., 3,308; Caths., 123,000 (58%); tot. pop., 211,000.

Formerly British Honduras. Independent (Sept. 21, 1981) republic on east coast of Central America; capital, Belmopan. Its history has points in common with Guatemala, where evangelization began in the 16th century.

Benin*

Archd., 1; dioc., 8; card., 1; abp., 2; bp., 8; parishes, 141; priests, 321 (204 dioc., 117 rel.); p.d., 1; sem., 277; bros., 49; srs., 590; catechists, 6,851; bap., 43,182; Caths., 1,198,000 (21.5%); tot. pop., 5,560,000.

Formerly Dahomey. Democratic republic in west Africa, bordering on the Atlantic; capital, Porto Novo. Missionary work was very limited from the 16th to the 18th centuries. Effective evangelization dates from 1861. The hierarchy was established in 1955. The majority of Christians are Catholics.

Bermuda

Dioc., 1; bp., 2; parishes, 6; priests, 7 (1 dioc., 6 rel.); srs., 4; catechists, 97; bap., 125; Caths., 10,000 (16%); tot. pop., 60,000. (AD)

British dependency, consisting of 360 islands (20 of them inhabited) nearly 600 miles east of Cape Hatteras; capital, Hamilton. Catholics were not permitted until about 1800. Occasional pastoral care was provided the few Catholics there by visiting priests during the 19th century. Early in the 1900s priests from Halifax began serving the area. A prefecture apostolic was set up in 1953. The first bishop assumed jurisdiction in 1956 when it was made a vicariate apostolic; diocese established, 1967.

Bhutan

Parish, 1; priest, 1 (rel.); srs., 5; catechist, 2; bap., 32; Caths., 1,000; tot. pop., 1,640,000.

Kingdom in the Himalayas, northeast of India; capital, Thimphu. Buddhist is the state religion. Jesuits (1963) and Salesians (1965) were invited to country to direct schools. Salesians were expelled in February, 1982, on disputed charges of proselytism. The only Catholic missionary allowed to stay in the country was Canadian Jesuit Father William Mackey who served Catholics there from 1963 until his death in 1995. Ecclesiastical jurisdiction is under the Darjeeling diocese, India.

Bolivia*

Archd., 4; dioc., 6; prel., 2; v.a., 5; mil. ord.; abp., 6; bp., 31; parishes, 520; priests, 1,083 (367 dioc., 716 rel.); p.d., 46; sem., 602; bros., 214; srs., 2,092; catechists, 779; bap., 202,722; Caths., 6,636,000 (89.5%); tot. pop., 7,410,000.

Republic in central South America; capital, Sucre; seat of government, La Paz. Catholicism, the official religion, was introduced in the 1530s and the first bishopric was established in 1552. Effective evangelization among the Indians, slow to start, reached high points in the middle of the 18th and the beginning of the 19th centuries and was resumed about 1840. Independence from Spain was proclaimed in 1825, at the end of a campaign that started in 1809. Church-state relations are regulated by a 1951 concordat with the Holy See. In recent years, human rights violations in conditions of political, economic and social turmoil have occasioned strong protests by members of the hierarchy and other people of the Church.

Bosnia and Herzegovina*

Archd., 1; dioc., 3; card., 1; bp., 3; parishes, 284; priests, 549 (249 dioc., 300 rel.); sem., 149; bros., 16; srs., 445; bap., 4,470; Caths., 769,000 (22.2%); tot. pop., 4,480,000.

Independent republic (1992) in southeastern Europe; formerly part of Yugoslavia; capital Sarajevo. (See Index for papal visit to Sarajevo.)

Botswana

Dioc., 1; bp., 1; parishes, 26; priests, 45 (6 dioc., 39 rel.); p.d., 1; sem., 9; bros., 5; srs., 54; catechists, 138; bap., 1,735; Caths., 55,000 (3.7%); tot. pop., 1,460,000. (AD)

Republic (independent since 1966) in southern Africa; capital, Gaborone. The first Catholic mission was opened in 1928 near Gaborone; earlier attempts at evangelization dating from 1879 were unsuccessful.

Brazil*

Archd., 38; dioc., 210; prel., 13; abb., 2; ord., 1; mil. ord.; card., 5; abp., 49; bp., 310; parishes, 7,997; priests, 15,482 (7,882 dioc., 7,600 rel.); p.d., 754; sem., 6,944; bros., 2,140; srs., 36,031; bap., 2,169,775; Caths., 134,818,000 (86.5%); tot. pop., 155,820,000.

Federal republic in northeast South America; capital, Brasilia. One of several priests with the discovery party celebrated the first Mass in the country Apr. 26, 1500. Evangelization began some years later and the first diocese was erected in 1551. During the colonial period, which lasted until 1822, evangelization made some notable progress — especially in the Amazon region between 1680 and 1750 — but was seriously hindered by government policy and the attitude of colonists regarding Amazon Indians the missionaries tried to protect from exploitation and slavery. The Jesuits were suppressed in 1782 and

other missionaries expelled as well. Liberal anti-Church influence grew in strength. The government gave minimal support but exercised maximum control over the Church. After the proclamation of independence from Portugal in 1822 and throughout the regency, government control was tightened and the Church suffered greatly from dissident actions of ecclesiastical brotherhoods, Masonic anticlericalism and general decline in religious life. Church and state were separated by the constitution of 1891, proclaimed two years after the end of the empire. The Church carried into the 20th century a load of inherited liabilities and problems amid increasingly difficult political, economic and social conditions affecting the majority of the population. A number of bishops, priests, religious and lay persons have been active in movements for social and religious reform.

Brunei Darussalam

Parishes, 3; priests, 2 (1 dioc., 1 rel); srs., 1; Caths., 8,000; tot. pop., 280,000.

Independent state (1984) on the northern coast of Borneo; capital, Bandar Seri Begawan. Islam is the official religion; other religions are allowed with some restrictions. Most of the Catholics are technicians and skilled workers from other countries who are not permanent residents; under ecclesiastical jurisdiction of Miri diocese, Malaysia.

Bulgaria*

Dioc., 2; ap. ex., 1; abp., 2; bp., 4; parishes, 45; priests, 40 (12 dioc., 28 rel.); sem., 12; srs., 65; bap., 655; Caths., 91,000 (1%), tot. pop., 8,400,000.

Republic in southeastern Europe on the eastern part of the Balkan peninsula; capital, Sofia. Most of the population is Orthodox. Christianity was introduced before 343 but disappeared with the migration of Slavs into the territory. The baptism of Boris I about 865 ushered in a new period of Christianity which soon became involved in switches of loyalty between Constantinople and Rome. Through it all the Byzantine, and later Orthodox, element remained stronger and survived under the rule of Ottoman Turks into the 19th century. The Byzantines are products of a reunion movement of the 19th century. In 1947 the constitution of the new republic decreed the separation of Church and state. Catholic schools and institutions were abolished and foreign religious banished in 1948. A year later the apostolic delegate was expelled. Ivan Romanoff, vicar general of Plovdiv, died in prison in 1952. Bishop Eugene Bossilkoff, imprisoned in 1948, was sentenced to death in 1952; his fate remained unknown until 1975 when the Bulgarian government informed the Vatican that he had died in prison shortly after being sentenced. Roman and Bulgarian Rite vicars apostolic were permitted to attend the Second Vatican Council from 1962 to 1965. All church activity was under surveillance and/or control by the government, which professed to be atheistic. Pastoral and related activities were strictly limited. There was some improvement in Bulgarian-Vatican relations in 1975, following a visit of Bulgarian President Todor Zhivkov to Pope Paul VI June 19 and talks between Vatican and Bulgarian representatives at the Helsinki Conference in late

July. In 1979, the Sofia-Plovdiv vicariate apostolic was raised to a diocese and a bishop was appointed for the vacant see of Nicopoli. Diplomatic relations with the Holy See were established in 1990.

Burkina Faso*

Archd., 1; dioc. (1997), 9; card., 1; bp., 10; parishes, 108; priests, 463 (320 dioc., 143 rel.); sem., 389; bros., 138; srs., 894; catechists, 8,346; bap., 54,606; Caths., 1,109,000 (10.8%); tot. pop., 10,200,000.

Republic inland in western Africa; capital, Ouagadougou; formerly, Upper Volta. White Fathers (now known as Missionaries of Africa) started the first missions in 1900 and 1901. White Sisters began work in 1911. A minor and a major seminary were established in 1926 and 1942, respectively. The first native bishop in modern times from West Africa was ordained in 1956 and the first cardinal created in 1965. The hierarchy was established in 1955.

Burma
(See Myanmar)

Burundi*

Archd., 1; dioc., 6; abp., 3; bp., 8; parishes, 118; priests, 317 (242 dioc., 75 rel.); sem., 278; bros., 139; srs., 872; catechists, 4,678; bap., 115,127; Caths., 3,594,000 (60%); tot. pop., 5,980,000.

Republic since 1966, near the equator in east-central Africa; capital, Bujumbura. The first permanent Catholic mission station was established late in the 19th century. Large numbers of persons were received into the Church following the ordination of the first Burundi priests in 1925. The first native bishop was appointed in 1959. In 1972-73, the country was torn by tribal warfare between the Tutsis, the ruling minority, and the Hutus. Since 1979, approximately 100 Catholic missionaries have been expelled. In 1986, seminaries were nationalized. A gradual resumption of church activity since 1987 has been hampered by continuing ethnic violence which exploded in 1996 and 1997. (See News Events.)

Cambodia*

V.a., 1; p.a., 2; bp., 1; parishes, none (there were 35 mission stations without resident priests) ; priests, 27 (10 dioc., 17 rel.); sem.,8; bros., 2; srs., 33; catechists, 26; baptisms, 50; Caths., 20,000 (.2%); tot. pop., 9,840,000.

Republic in southeast Asia, bordering on the Gulf of Siam, Thailand, Laos and Vietnam; capital Phnom Penh. Evangelization dating from the second half of the 16th century had limited results, more among Vietnamese than Khmers. Thousands of Catholics of Vietnamese origin were forced to flee in 1970 because of Khmer hostility. The status of the Church remained uncertain following the Khmer Rouge takeover in April, 1975, the Vietnamese invasion in 1979 and the long civil war which followed. Foreign missionaries were expelled, local clergy and religious were sent to work the land and a general persecution followed. Religious freedom was reestablished in 1990. Diplomatic relations with the Holy See were established in March, 1994. Buddhism is the state religion.

Cameroon*

Archd., 5; dioc., 17; card., 1; abp., 6; bp., 20; parishes, 554; priests, 1,059 (581 dioc., 478 rel.); p.d., 22; sem., 885; bros., 170; srs., 1,566; catechists, 13,516; bap., 85,130; Caths., 3,431,000 (25.8%); tot. pop., 13,280,000.

Republic in west Africa, bordering on the Gulf of Guinea; capital, Yaounde. Effective evangelization began in 1890, although Catholics had been in the country long before that time. In the 40-year period from 1920 to 1960, the number of Catholics increased from 60,000 to 700,000. The first native priests were ordained in 1935. Twenty years later the first native bishops were ordained and the hierarchy established. The first Cameroonian cardinal (Christian Wiyghan Tumi) was named in 1988.

Canada*

Archd., 19; dioc., 53; abb., 1; ap. ex., 1; mil. ord.; card., 4; abp., 26; bp., 94; abbots, 2; parishes, 5,706; priests, 10,676 (6,161 dioc., 4,515 rel.); p.d., 804; sem., 633; bros., 2,719; srs., 27,644; lay assistants, 1,784; bap., 174,128; Caths., 12,600,000 (44%); tot. pop., 28,435,000. (Principal sources: 1996-1997 Directory of the Canadian Conference of Catholic Bishops; StatisticalYearbook of the Church; 1997 Annuario Pontificio.)

Independent federation comprising the northern half of North America; capital, Ottawa. (See Index.)

Canary Islands

Two Spanish provinces, consisting of seven islands, off the northwest coast of Africa. Evangelization began about 1400. Almost all of the one million inhabitants are Catholic. Statistics are included in those for Spain.

Cape Verde*

Dioc., 1; bp., 1; parishes, 31; priests, 47 (13 dioc., 34 rel.); sem., 10; bros., 7; srs., 104; catechists, 3,080; bap. ,11,132; Caths., 390,000 (96%); tot. pop., 405,000.

Independent (July 5, 1975) island group in the Atlantic 300 miles west of Senegal; formerly a Portuguese overseas province; capital, Praia, San Tiago Island. Evangelization began some years before the establishment of a diocese in 1532.

Cayman Islands

Parish, 1; priests, 2 (dioc.); srs., 2; catechists, 11; bap., 46; Caths. 4,000; tot. pop., 29,000. (AD)

British dependency in Caribbean; capital, Georgetown on Grand Cayman. Under ecclesiastical jurisdiction of Kingston archdiocese, Jamaica.

Central African Republic*

Archd., 1; dioc. (1997), 7; abp., 2; bp., 10; parishes, 112; priests, 289 (103 dioc., 186 rel.); sem., 149; bros., 54; srs., 392; catechists, 3,962; bap., 27,321; Caths., 622,000 (18.8%); tot. pop., 3,310,000.

Former French colony (independent since 1960) in central Africa; capital, Bangui. Effective evangelization dates from 1894. The region was organized as a mission territory in 1909. The first native priest was ordained in 1938. The hierarchy was organized in 1955.

Ceuta

Spanish possession (city) on the northern tip of Africa, south of Gibraltar. Statistics are included in those for Spain.

Chad*

Archd., 1; dioc., 4; abp., 1; bp., 6; parishes, 98; priests, 191 (65 dioc., 126 rel.); sem., 86; bros., 48; srs., 285; catechists, 6,509; bap., 13,130; Caths., 433,000 (6.8%); tot. pop., 6,360,000.

Republic (independent since 1960) in north-central Africa; former French possession; capital, N'Djamena. Evangelization began in 1929, leading to firm organization in 1947 and establishment of the hierarchy in 1955.

Chile*

Archd., 5; dioc., 17; prel., 2; v.a., 2; mil. ord.; card., 3; abp., 10; bp., 35; parishes, 892; priests, 2,289 (1,068 dioc., 1,221 rel.); p.d., 363; sem., 796; bros., 428; srs., 6,916; catechists, 1,416; bap., 182,862; Caths., 11,330,000 (79.8%); tot. pop., 14,200,000.

Republic on the southwestern coast of South America; capital, Santiago. Priests were with the Spanish conquistadores on their entrance into the territory early in the 16th century. The first parish was established in 1547 and the first bishopric in 1561. Overall organization of the Church took place later in the century. By 1650 most of the peaceful Indians in the central and northern areas were evangelized. Missionary work was more difficult in the southern region. Church activity was hampered during the campaign for independence, 1810 to 1818, and through the first years of the new government, to 1830. Later gains were made, into this century, but hindering factors were shortages of native clergy and religious and attempts by the government to control church administration through the patronage system in force while the country was under Spanish control. Separation of Church and state was decreed in the constitution of 1925. Church-state relations were strained during the regime of Marxist president Salvator Allende Gossens (1970-73). Conditions remained unsettled under the military government which assumed control after the coup. The Chilean bishops issued numerous statements strongly critical of human rights abuses by the military dictatorship which remained in power until 1990 when an elected president took office.

China

Archd., 20; dioc., 92; p.a., 29. No Catholic statistics are available. In 1949 there were between 3,500,000-4,000,000 Catholics, about .7 per cent of the total population. Tot. pop. 1,199,074,000.

People's republic in eastern part of Asia (mainland China under communist control since 1949); capital, Peking (Beijing). Christianity was introduced by Nestorians who had some influence on part of the area from 635 to 845 and again from the 11th century until 1368. John of Monte Corvino started a Franciscan mission in 1294; he was ordained an archbishop about 1307. Missionary activity involving more priests increased for a while thereafter but the Franciscan mission ended in 1368. The Jesuit Matteo

Ricci initiated a remarkable period of activity in the 1580s. By 1700 the number of Catholics was reported to be 300,000. The Chinese Rites controversy, concerning the adaptation of rituals and other matters to Chinese traditions and practices, ran throughout the 17th century, ending in a negative decision by mission authorities in Rome. Bl. Francis de Capillas, the protomartyr of China, was killed in 1648. Persecution, a feature of Chinese history as recurrent as changes in dynasties, occurred several times in the 18th century and resulted in the departure of most missionaries from the country. The Chinese door swung open again in the 1840s and progress in evangelization increased with an extension of legal and social tolerance. At the turn of the 20th century, however, the Boxer Rebellion took one or the other kind of toll among an estimated 30,000 victims. Missionary work in the 1900s reached a new high in every respect. The hierarchy was instituted by Pope Pius XII, April 11, 1946 (Apostolic Constitution Quotidie Nos). Then followed the disaster of persecution initiated by communists, before and especially after they established the republic in 1949. The government began a savage persecution as soon as it came into power. Among its results were the expulsion of over 5,000 foreign missionaries, 510 of whom were American priests, brothers and nuns; the arrest, imprisonment and harassment of all members of the native religious, clergy and hierarchy; the forced closing of 3,932 schools, 216 hospitals, 781 dispensaries, 254 orphanages, 29 printing presses and 55 periodicals; denial of the free exercise of religion to all the faithful; the detention of hundreds of priests, religious and lay persons in jail and their employment in slave labor; the proscription of the Legion of Mary and other Catholic Action groups for "counter-revolutionary activities" and "crimes against the new China"; complete outlawing of missionary work and pastoral activity. The government formally established a Patriotic Association of Chinese Catholics, independent of the Holy See, in July, 1957. Relatively few priests and lay persons joined the organization, which was condemned by Pius XII in 1958. The government formed the nucleus of what it hoped might become the hierarchy of a schismatic Chinese church in 1958 by "electing" 26 bishops and having them consecrated validly but illicitly between Apr. 13, 1958, and Nov. 15, 1959, without the permission or approval of the Holy See. Additional bishops were subsequently ordained. Activity of the Patriotic Association and official policy of the government are in direct opposition to any connection between the (Underground) Church in China and the Vatican. Growth of the underground Church has been reported for several years despite government actions to the contrary. (See also Hong Kong.)

Colombia*

Archd., 12; dioc., 41; prel., 2; v.a., 8; p.a., 5; mil. ord., card., 1; abp., 16; bp., 71; parishes, 2,955; priests, 6,883 (4,823 dioc., 2,060 rel.); p.d., 120; sem., 4,298; bros., 811; srs., 17,723; catechists, 4,451; bap., 830,414; Caths., 32,260,000 (91.9%); tot. pop., 35,100,000.

Republic in northwest South America, with Atlantic and Pacific borders; capital, Bogota. Evangelization began in 1508. The first two dioceses were established in 1534. Vigorous development of the Church was reported by the middle of the 17th century despite obstacles posed by the multiplicity of Indian languages, government interference through patronage rights and otherwise, rivalry among religious orders and the small number of native priests among the predominantly Spanish clergy. Some persecution, including the confiscation of property, followed in the wake of the proclamation of independence from Spain in 1819. The Church was affected in many ways by the political and civil unrest of the nation through the 19th century and into the 20th. Various aspects of Church-state relations are regulated by a concordat with the Vatican signed July 12, 1973, and ratified July 2, 1975. Guerrilla warfare aimed at Marxist-oriented radical social reform and redistribution of land, along with violence related to drug traffic, has plagued the country since the 1960s, posing problems for the Church which backed reforms but rejected actions of radical groups.

Comoros

A.a., 1; parishes, 3; priests, 3 (rel.); sem., 1; bro., 1; srs., 11; catechists, 10; bap., 2,311; Caths..5,000; tot. pop., 650,000. (AD)

Consists of main islands of Grande Comore, Anjouan and Moheli in Indian Ocean off southeast coast of Africa; capital, Moroni, Grande Comore Island. Former French territory; independent (July 6, 1975). The majority of the population is Muslim. An apostolic administration was established in 1975.

Congo*

Archd., 1; dioc., 5; abp., 1; bp., 5; parishes, 102; priests, 257 (167 dioc., 90 rel.); sem., 180; bros., 73; srs.,314; catechists, 2,562; bap., 16,442; Caths., 1,259,000 (48%); tot. pop., 2,590,000.

Republic (independent since 1960) in west central Africa; former French possession; capital, Brazzaville. Small-scale missionary work with little effect preceded modern evangelization dating from the 1880s. The work of the Church has been affected by political instability, Communist influence, tribalism and hostility to foreigners. The hierarchy was established in 1955.

Democratic Republic of Congo*

Archd., 6; dioc., 41; card., 1; abp., 7; bp., 51; parishes, 1,191; priests, 3,580 (1,402 dioc., 2,178 rel.); p.d., 7; sem., 3,092; bros., 1,118; srs., 5,168; catechists, 60,243; bap., 544,091; Caths., 22,310,000 (50.8%); tot. pop., 43,900,000.

Republic in south central Africa (formerly Zaire 1971-97)); capital, Kinshasa. Christianity was introduced in 1484 and evangelization began about 1490. The first native bishop in black Africa was ordained in 1518. Subsequent missionary work was hindered by factors including 18th and 19th century anticlericalism. Modern evangelization started in the second half of the 19th century. The hierarchy was established in 1959. In the civil disorders which followed independence in 1960, some missions and other church installations were abandoned, thousands of people reverted to tribal religions and many priests and religious were killed. Church-state tensions have

developed in recent years because of the Church's criticism of the anti-Christian thrust of Pres. Mobutu's "Africanization" policies. Six missionary Sisters, who contracted the disease while ministering to patients, were among the victims of the Ebola outbreak in 1995. Rebel forces took over the country in 1997 following months of fierce fighting along tribal lines in Zaire and neighboring Rwanda and Burundi. (See News Events.)

Cook Islands

Dioc., 1; bp., 1; parishes, 15; priests, 9 (4 dioc., 5 rel.); bros., 5; srs., 8; bap., 139; Caths., 3,000; tot. pop., 20,000.

Self-governing territory of New Zealand, an archipelago of small islands in Oceania. Evangelization by Protestant missionaries started in 1821, resulting in a predominantly Protestant population. The first Catholic missionary work began in 1894. The hierarchy was established in 1966.

Costa Rica*

Archd., 1; dioc., 5; abp., 2; bp., 7; parishes, 249; priests, 699 (460 dioc., 239 rel.); sem., 267; bros., 42; srs., 906; bap., 82,362; Caths., 3,009,000 (93%); tot. pop., 3,330,000.

Republic in Central America; capital, San Jose. Evangelization began about 1520 and proceeded by degrees to real development and organization of the Church in the 17th and 18th centuries. The republic became independent in 1838. Twelve years later church jurisdiction also became independent with the establishment of a bishopric in the present capital.

Côte d'Ivoire (Ivory Coast)*

Archd., 4; dioc., 10; card., 1; abp., 5; bp., 10; parishes, 214; priests, 653 (429 dioc., 224 rel.); p.d., 2; sem., 467; bros., 222; srs., 869; catechists, 13,458; bap., 46,886; Caths., 1,989,000 (13.9%); tot. pop., 14,230,000.

Republic in western Africa; capital, Abidjan (de facto); Yamoussouka (official). The Holy Ghost Fathers began systematic evangelization in 1895. The first native priests from the area were ordained in 1934. The hierarchy was set up in 1955; the first native cardinal (Bernard Yago) was named in 1983. Three ecclesiastical provinces were established in 1995.

Croatia*

Archd., 4; dioc. (1997), 9; mil. ord. (1997); card., 1; abp., 7; bp., 15; parishes, 1,535; priests, 2,256 (1,432 dioc., 824 rel.); sem., 483; bros., 89; srs., 3,712; bap., 53,272; Caths., 3,726,000 (83%); tot. pop., 4,490,000.

Independent (1991) republic in southeastern Europe; capital Zagreb; formerly a constituent republic of Yugoslavia. (See Yugoslavia for earlier history and events following communist takeover.) Christianity was introduced in the seventh century. Activity of the Church since 1992 has been adversely affected by civil war. Pope John Paul II visited the country Sept. 10 to 11, 1994.

Cuba*

Archd., 2; dioc., 8; card., 1; abp., 2; bp., 10; parishes, 252; priests, 270 (138 dioc., 132 rel.);

p.d., 35; sem., 59; bros., 29; srs., 445; bap., 76,127; Caths. 4,701,000 (42.5%); tot. pop., 11,040,000.

Republic under Communist dictatorship, south of Florida; capital, Havana. Effective evangelization began about 1514, leading eventually to the predominance of Catholicism on the island. Native vocations to the priesthood and religious life were unusually numerous in the 18th century but declined in the 19th. The island became independent of Spain in 1902 following the Spanish-American War. Fidel Castro took control of the government Jan. 1, 1959. In 1961, after Cuba was officially declared a socialist state, the University of Villanueva was closed, 350 Catholic schools were nationalized and 136 priests expelled. A greater number of foreign priests and religious had already left the country. Freedom of worship and religious instruction are limited to church premises and no social action is permitted the Church, which survives under surveillance. A new constitution approved in 1976 guaranteed freedom of conscience but restricts its exercise. Appeals by the bishops for dialogue with the government to improve church-state relations have had little, if any, effect. Despite some recent surfacing and increase of church activity, the Church is still operating in a limited manner.

Cyprus*

Archd., 1 (Maronite); abp., 1; parishes, 13; priests, 17 (6 dioc., 11 rel.); bros., 7; srs., 44; bap., 87; Caths., 11,000 (1.5%); tot. pop., 740,000.

Republic in the eastern Mediterranean; capital, Nicosia. Christianity was preached on the island in apostolic times and has a continuous history from the fourth century. Latin and Eastern rites were established but the latter prevailed and became Orthodox after the schism of 1054. Roman and Orthodox Christians have suffered under many governments, particularly during the period of Turkish dominion from late in the 16th to late in the 19th centuries, and from differences between the 80 per cent Greek majority and the Turkish minority. About 80 per cent of the population are Orthodox. Catholics are under the jurisdiction of the archdiocese of Cyprus (of the Maronites).

Czech Republic*

Archd., 2; dioc., 6; ap. ex., 1; card., 1; abp., 2; bp., 9; parishes, 3,119; priests, 1,877 (1,294 dioc., 583 rel.); p.d., 129; sem., 418; bros., 143; srs., 2,545; bap., 32,378; Caths., 4,009,392 (39.3%); tot. pop., 10,409,000. (Population figures are from 1997 Annuario Pontificio.)

Independent state (Jan. 1, 1993); formerly part of Czechoslovakia; capital, Prague. The martyrdom of Prince Wenceslaus in 929 triggered the spread of Christianity. Prague has had a continuous history as a diocese since 973. A parish system was organized about the 13th century in Bohemia and Moravia, the land of the Czechs. Mendicant orders strengthened relations with the Latin rite in the 13th century. In the next century the teachings of John Hus in Bohemia brought trouble to the Church in the forms of schism and heresy, and initiated a series of religious wars which continued for decades following his death at the stake in 1415. Church property was confiscated, monastic communities were scattered and even murdered, ecclesiastical organization was shattered, and so many of the faithful joined the Bohemian Brethren that Catholics became a minority. The Reformation, with the way prepared by the Hussites and cleared by other factors, affected the Church seriously. A Counter Reformation got under way in the 1560s and led to a gradual restoration through the thickets of Josephinism, the Enlightenment, liberalism and troubled politics. In 1920, two years after the establishment of the Republic of Czechoslovakia, the schismatic Czechoslovak Church was proclaimed at Prague, resulting in numerous defections from the Catholic Church in the Czech region. In Ruthenia, 112,000 became Russian Orthodox between 1918 and 1930. (See Index for papal visit.) (For the situation of the Church during the long years of communist domination, see Czechoslovakia, below.)

Czechoslovakia

The Czech and Slovak Federal Republic, formed in 1918, was dissolved Jan. 1, 1993, and became two independent states. (See separate entries in this section for Czech Republic and Slovakia for early history of the Church and statistics.) Information below covers the situation of the Church during the long period of communist domination.

Vigorous persecution of the Church began in Slovakia before the end of World War II when Communists mounted a 1944 offensive against bishops, priests and religious. In 1945, church schools were nationalized, youth organizations were disbanded, the Catholic press was curtailed, the training of students for the priesthood was seriously impeded. Msgr. Josef Tiso, president of the Slovak Republic, was tried for "treason" in December, 1946, and was executed the following April. Between 1945 and 1949 approximately 10 percent of the Slovak population spent some time in jail or a concentration camp. Persecution began later in the Czech part of the country, following the accession of the Gottwald regime to power early in 1948. Hospitals, schools and property were nationalized and Catholic organizations were liquidated. A puppet organization was formed in 1949 to infiltrate the Church and implement an unsuccessful plan for establishing a schismatic church. In the same year Archbishop Josef Beran of Prague was placed under house arrest. (He left the country in 1965, was made a cardinal, and died in 1969 in Rome.) A number of theatrical trials of bishops and priests were staged in 1950. All houses of religious were taken over between March, 1950, and the end of 1951. Pressure was applied on the clergy and faithful of the Eastern Rite in Slovakia to join the Orthodox Church. Diplomatic relations with the Holy See were terminated in 1950. About 3,000 priests were deprived of liberty in 1951 and attempts were made to force "peace priests" on the people. In 1958 it was reported that 450 to 500 priests were in jail; an undisclosed number of religious and Byzantine-Rite priests had been deported; two bishops released from prison in 1956 were under house arrest; one bishop was imprisoned at Leopoldov and two at the Mirov reformatory. In Bohemia, Moravia and Silesia, five of six dioceses were without ruling bishops; one archbishop and two bishops were active but subject to "supervision"; most of the clergy refused to join the "peace priests." In 1962 only three bishops were permitted to attend the first session of the Second Vatican Council. From January to October, 1968, church-state relations improved to some extent under the Dubcek regime: a number of bishops were reinstated; some 3,000 priests were engaged in the pastoral ministry, although 1,500 were still barred from priestly work; the "peace priests" organization was disbanded; the Eastern-Rite Church, with 147 parishes, was reestablished. In 1969, an end was ordered to rehabilitation trials for priests and religious, but no wholesale restoration of priests and religious to their proper ways of life and work was in prospect. In 1972, the government ordered the removal of nuns from visible but limited apostolates to farms and mental hospitals where they would be out of sight. In 1973, the government allowed the ordination of four bishops — one in the Czech region and three in the Slovak region. Reports from Slovakia late in the same year stated that authorities there had placed severe restrictions on the education of seminarians and the functioning of priests. Government restrictions continued to hamper the work of priests and nuns. Signatories of the human rights declaration called Charter 77 were particular objects of government repression and retribution. In December, 1983, the Czechoslovakian foreign minister met with the Pope at Vatican City; it was the first meeting of a high Czech official with a pope since the country came under communist rule. In 1984, two Vatican officials visited Czechoslovakia. Despite the communication breakthrough, there was no indication of any change of policy toward the Church in the country. In 1988, three new bishops were ordained in Czechoslovakia, the first since 1973. Three more episcopal appointments were made in 1989. The communist government fell in late 1989. In 1990: bishops were appointed to fill vacant sees; announcement was made of the reestablishment of diplomatic relations between the Holy See and Czechoslovakia after 40 years, and Pope John Paul II paid a historic visit to the country. (See Czech Republic; Slovakia.)

Denmark*

Dioc., 1; bp., 2; parishes, 50; priests, 96 (38 dioc., 58 rel.); p.d., 1; sem., 4; bros., 4; srs., 272; bap., 623; Caths., 32,000 (.6%); tot. pop., 5,230,000.

Includes the Faroe Islands and Greenland. Constitutional monarchy in northwestern Europe, north of Germany; capital, Copenhagen. Christianity was introduced in the ninth century and the first diocese for the area was established in 831. Intensive evangelization and full-scale organization of the Church occurred from the second half of the 10th century and ushered in a period of great development and influence in the 12th and 13th centuries. Decline followed, resulting in almost total loss to the Church during the Reformation when Lutheranism became the national religion. Catholics were considered foreigners until religious freedom was legally assured in 1849. Modern development of the Church dates from the second half of the 19th century. About 95 per cent of the population are Evangelical Lutherans.

Djibouti

Dioc., 1; bp., 1; parishes, 5; priests, 6 (1 dioc., 5 rel.); bros., 6; srs., 25; bap., 13; Caths., 8,000 (1.4%); tot. pop., 580,000. (AD)

Formerly French Territory of Afars and Issas. Independent (1977) republic in east Africa, on the Gulf of Aden; capital, Djibouti. Christianity in the area, formerly part of Ethiopia, antedated but was overcome by the Arab invasion of 1200. Modern evangelization, begun in the latter part of the 19th century, had meager results. The hierarchy was established in 1955.

Dominica*

Dioc., 1; bp., 2; parishes, 17; priests, 35 (5 dioc., 30 rel.); sem., 2; bros., 7; srs., 28; catechists, 520; bap., 955; Caths., 57,000 (79%); tot. pop., 72,000.

Independent (Nov. 3, 1978) state in Caribbean; capital, Roseau. Evangelization began in 1642.

Dominican Republic*

Archd., 2; dioc. (1997), 9; mil. ord.; card., 1; abp., 3; bp., 11; parishes, 320; priests, 644 (256 dioc., 388 rel.); p.d., 172; sem., 550; bros.. 75; srs., 1,470; bap., 112,279; Caths., 7,162,000 (90.5%); tot. pop., 7,910,000.

Caribbean republic on the eastern two-thirds of the island of Hispaniola, bordering on Haiti; capital, Santo Domingo. Evangelization began shortly after discovery by Columbus in 1492 and church organization, the first in America, was established by 1510. Catholicism is the state religion.

Ecuador*

Archd., 4; dioc., 11; v.a., 7; p.a., 1; mil. ord.; card., 1; abp., 5; bp., 30; parishes, 1,123; priests, 1,764 (943 dioc., 821 rel.); p.d., 41; sem., 875; bros., 322; srs., 4,527; catechists, 2,966; bap., 242,094; Caths., 10,729,000 (93.6%); tot. pop., 11,460,000.

Republic on the west coast of South America, includes Gallapogos Islands; capital, Quito. Evangelization began in the 1530s. The first diocese was established in 1545. A synod, one of the first in the Americas, was held in 1570 or 1594. Multiphased missionary work, spreading from the coastal and mountain regions into the Amazon, made the Church highly influential during the colonial period. The Church was practically enslaved by the constitution enacted in 1824, two years after Ecuador, as part of Colombia, gained independence from Spain. Some change for the better took place later in the century, but from 1891 until the 1930s the Church labored under serious liabilities imposed by liberal governments. The concordat of 1866 was violated; foreign missionaries were barred from the country for some time; the property of religious orders was confiscated; education was taken over by the state; traditional state support was refused; legal standing was denied; attempts to control church offices were made through insistence on rights of patronage. A period of harmony and independence for the Church began after agreement was reached on Church-state relations in 1937.

Egypt*

Patriarchates, 2 (Alexandria for the Copts and for the Melkites); dioc., 9; v.a., 1; patriarch, 1; abp., 2; bp., 13; parishes, 221; priests, 394 (217 dioc., 177 rel.); p.d., 5; sem., 151; bros., 71; srs., 1,411; bap., 2,862; Caths., 213,000 (.35%); tot. pop., 59,230,000.

Arab Republic in northeastern Africa, bordering on the Mediterranean; capital, Cairo. Alexandria was the influential hub of a Christian community established by the end of the second century; it became a patriarchate and the center of the Coptic Church, and had great influence on the spread of Christianity in various parts of Africa. Monasticism developed from desert communities of hermits in the third and fourth centuries. Arianism was first preached in Egypt in the 320s. In the fifth century, the Coptic church went Monophysite through failure to accept doctrine formulated by the Council of Chalcedon in 451 with respect to the two natures of Christ. The country was thoroughly Arabized after 640 and was under the rule of Ottoman Turks from 1517 to 1798. English influence was strong during the 19th century. A monarchy established in 1922 lasted about 30 years, ending with the proclamation of a republic in 1953-54. By that time Egypt had become the leader of pan-Arabism against Israel. It waged two unsuccessful wars against Israel in 1948-49 and 1967. Between 1958 and 1961 it was allied with Syria and Yemen, in the United Arab Republic. In 1979, following negotiations initiated by Pres. Anwar el-Sadat in 1977, Egypt and Israel signed a peace agreement. Islam, the religion of some 90 percent of the population, is the state religion.

El Salvador*

Archd., 1; dioc., 7; mil. ord.; abp., 2; bp., 10; parishes, 292; priests, 525 (336 dioc., 189 rel.); p.d., 2; sem., 318; bros., 119; srs., 1,203; bap., 91,111; Cath., 5,399,000 (93.5%); tot. pop., 5,770,000.

Republic in Central America; capital, San Salvador. Evangelization affecting the whole territory followed Spanish occupation in the 1520s. The country was administered by the captaincy general of Guatemala until 1821 when independence from Spain was declared and it was annexed to Mexico. El Salvador joined the Central American Federation in 1825, decreed its own independence in 1841 and became a republic formally in 1856. Church efforts in recent years to achieve social justice have resulted in persecution of the Church. Archbishop Oscar Romero of San Salvador, peace advocate and outspoken champion of human rights, was murdered Mar. 24, 1980, while celebrating Mass. Six Jesuits were assassinated Nov. 16, 1989, at Central American University in El Salvador.

England*

Archd., 4; dioc., 15; ap. ex., 1; mil. ord. (Great Britain); card., 1; abp., 3; bp., 33; parishes, 2,593; priests, 5,381 (3,636 dioc., 1,745 rel.); newly ordained priests, 76; p.d., 339; sem., 326; bros., 660; srs., 8,341; bap., 72,887; Caths., 4,011,368 (8.2%); tot. pop., 48,854,000. (1997 Annuario Pontificio.)

Center of the United Kingdom of Great Britain (England, Scotland, Wales) and Northern Ireland, off the northwestern coast of Europe; capital, London. The arrival of St. Augustine of Canterbury and a band of monks in 597 marked the beginning of evangelization. Real organization of the Church took place some years after the Synod of Whitby, held in 663. Heavy losses were sustained in the wake of the Danish invasion in the 780s, but recovery starting from

the time of Alfred the Great and dating especially from the middle of the 10th century led to Christianization of the whole country and close Church-state relations. The Norman Conquest of 1066 opened the Church in England to European influence. The 13th century was climactic, but decline had already set in by 1300 when the country had an all-time high of 17,000 religious. In the 14th century, John Wycliff presaged the Protestant Reformation. Henry VIII, failing in 1529 to gain annulment of his marriage to Catherine of Aragon, refused to acknowledge papal authority over the Church in England, had himself proclaimed its head, suppressed all houses of religious, and persecuted persons _ Sts. Thomas More and John Fisher, among others _ for not subscribing to the Oath of Supremacy and Act of Succession. He held the line on other-than-papal doctrine, however, until his death in 1547. Doctrinal aberrations were introduced during the reign of Edward VI (1547-53), through the Order of Communion, two books of Common Prayer, and the Articles of the Established Church. Mary Tudor's attempted Catholic restoration (1553-58) was a disaster, resulting in the deaths of more than 300 Protestants. Elizabeth (1558-1603) firmed up the Established Church with formation of a hierarchy, legal enactments and multi-phased persecution. One hundred and 11 priests and 62 lay persons were among the casualties of persecution during the underground Catholic revival which followed the return to England of missionary priests from France and The Lowlands. Several periods of comparative toleration ensued after Elizabeth's death. The first of several apostolic vicariates was established in 1685; this form of church government was maintained until the restoration of the hierarchy and diocesan organization in 1850. The revolution of 1688 and subsequent developments to about 1781 subjected Catholics to a wide variety of penal laws and disabilities in religious, civic and social life. The situation began to improve in 1791, and from 1801 Parliament frequently considered proposals for the repeal of penal laws against Catholics. The Act of Emancipation restored citizenship rights to Catholics in 1829. Restrictions remained in force for some time afterwards, however, on public religious worship and activity. The hierarchy was restored in 1850. Since then the Catholic Church, existing side by side with the Established Churches of England and Scotland, has followed a general pattern of growth and development.

Equatorial Guinea*

Archd., 1; dioc., 2; abp., 1; bp., 2; parishes, 48; priests, 92 (40 dioc., 52 rel.); p.d. 1; sem., 52; bros., 31; srs., 208; catechists, 1,943; bap., 15,362; Caths., 364,000 (88%); tot. pop., 410,000.

Republic on the west coast of Africa, consisting of Rio Muni on the mainland and the islands of Bioko (formerly Fernando Po) and Annobon in the Gulf of Guinea: capital, Malabo (Santa Isabel). Evangelization began in 1841. The country became independent of Spain in 1968. The Church was severely repressed during the 11-year rule of Pres. Macias (Masie) Nguema. Developments since his overthrow (August, 1979) indicated some measure of improvement. An ecclesiastical province was established in October, 1982.

Eritrea*

Dioc., 3; bp., 2; parishes, 94; priests, 273 (65 dioc., 208 rel); p.d., 9; sem., 124; bros., 77; srs., 324; bap., 2,610; Caths., 126,000 (3%); tot. pop., 3,582,000.

Independent state (May 24, 1993) in northeast Africa; formerly a province of Ethiopia. Christianity was introduced in the fourth century. Population is evenly divided between Christians and Muslims. Catholics form a small minority; most of the population is Orthodox Christian or Muslim.

Estonia*

A.a., 1; abp., 1 (nuncio is apostolic administrator); parishes, 5; priests, 8 (2 dioc., 6 rel); sem., 4; bros., 5; srs., 14; bap.,135; Caths., 4,000; tot. pop., 1,530,000.

Independent (1991) Baltic republic; capital, Tallinn. (Forcibly absorbed by the U.S.S.R. in 1940; it regained independence in 1991.) Catholicism was introduced in the 11th and 12th centuries. Jurisdiction over the area was made directly subject to the Holy See in 1215. Lutheran penetration was general in the Reformation period and Russian Orthodox influence was strong from early in the 18th century until 1917 when independence was attained. The first of several apostolic administrators was appointed in 1924. The small Catholic community was hard hit during the 1940-91 Soviet occupation (not recognized by the Holy See or the United States).

Ethiopia*

Archd., 1; dioc., 1; v.a., 5; p.a., 1; card., 1; abp., 1; bp., 8; parishes, 171; priests, 390 (141 dioc., 249 rel.); p.d., 1; sem., 260; bros., 66; srs., 674; bap., 16,968; Caths., 346,000 (.65%); tot. pop., 53,098,000.

People's republic in northeast Africa; capital, Addis Ababa. The country was evangelized by missionaries from Egypt in the fourth century and had a bishop by about 340. Following the lead of its parent body, the Egyptian (Coptic) Church, the Church in the area succumbed to the Monophysite heresy in the sixth century. Catholic influence was negligible for centuries. An ordinariate for the Ethiopian Rite was established in Eritrea in 1930. An apostolic delegation was set up in Addis Ababa in 1937 and several jurisdictions were organized, some under the Congregation for the Oriental Churches and others under the Congregation for the Evangelization of Peoples. The first Ethiopian cardinal (Abp. Paulos Tzadua of Addis Ababa) was named in 1985.

Falkland Islands

P.a., 1; parish, 1; priests, 4 (rel.); srs., 2;bap., 5; Caths.,570; tot. pop., 4,200. (1997 Annuario Pontificio.)

British colony off the southern tip of South America; capital, Port Stanley. The islands are called Islas Malvinas by Argentina which also claims sovereignty.

Faroe Islands

Parish, 1; p.d., 1; srs., 8; Caths., 100; tot. pop., 47,000.

Self-governing island group in North Atlantic; Danish possession. Under ecclesiastical jurisdiction of Copenhagen diocese.

Fiji*

Archd., 1; abp., 1; parishes, 34; priests, 113 (28 dioc., 85 rel.); sem., 33; bros., 66; srs., 172; bap., 2,163; Caths., 79,000 (9.9%); tot. pop., 796,000.

Independent island group (100 inhabited) in the southwest Pacific; capital, Suva. Marist missionaries began work in 1844 after Methodism had been firmly established. A prefecture apostolic was organized in 1863. The hierarchy was established in 1966.

Finland*

Dioc., 1; bp., 1; parishes, 7; priests, 23 (7 dioc., 16 rel.); p.d., 2; sem., 1; srs., 38; bap., 160; Caths., 6,000 (.1%); tot. pop., 5,110,000.

Republic in northern Europe; capital, Helsinki. Swedes evangelized the country in the 12th century. The Reformation swept the country, resulting in the prohibition of Catholicism in 1595, general reorganization of ecclesiastical life and affairs, and dominance of the Evangelical Lutheran Church. Catholics were given religious liberty in 1781 but missionaries and conversions were forbidden by law. The first Finnish priest since the Reformation was ordained in 1903 in Paris. A vicariate apostolic for Finland was erected in 1920 (made a diocese in 1955). A law on religious liberty, enacted in 1923, banned the foundation of monasteries.

France*

Archd., 19; dioc., 75; prel., 1; ap. ex., 1; ord., 1; mil. ord.; card., 5; abp., 26; bp., 148; parishes, 32,086; priests, 28,685 (22,190 dioc., 6,495 rel.); p.d., 1,102; sem., 1,659; bros. 4,177; srs., 56,735; bap., 424,829; Caths., 47,773,000 (82.1%); tot. pop., 58,150,000.

Republic in western Europe; capital, Paris. Christianity was known around Lyons by the middle of the second century. By 250 there were 30 bishoprics. The hierarchy reached a fair degree of organization by the end of the fourth century. Vandals and Franks subsequently invaded the territory and caused barbarian turmoil and doctrinal problems because of their Arianism. The Frankish nation was converted following the baptism of Clovis about 496. Christianization was complete by some time in the seventh century. From then on the Church, its leaders and people, figured in virtually every important development — religious, cultural, political and social — through the periods of the Carolingians, feudalism, the Middle Ages and monarchies to the end of the 18th century. The great University of Paris became one of the intellectual centers of the 13th century. Churchmen and secular rulers were involved with developments surrounding the Avignon residence of the popes and curia from 1309 until near the end of the 14th century and with the disastrous Western Schism that followed. Strong currents of Gallicanism and conciliarism ran through ecclesiastical and secular circles in France; the former was an ideology and movement to restrict papal control of the Church in the country, the latter sought to make the pope subservient to a general council. Calvinism invaded the country about the middle of the 16th century and won a strong body of converts. Jansenism with its rigorous spirit and other aberrations appeared in the next century, to be followed by the highly influential Enlightenment. The Revolution which started in 1789 and was succeeded by the Napoleonic period completely changed the status of the Church, taking a toll of numbers by persecution and defection and disenfranchising the Church in practically every way. Throughout the 19th century the Church was caught up in the whirl of imperial and republican developments and made the victim of official hostility, popular indifference and liberal opposition. In this century, the Church has struggled with problems involving the heritage of the Revolution and its aftermath, the alienation of intellectuals, liberalism, the estrangement of the working classes because of the Church's former identification with the ruling class, and the massive needs of contemporary society. (See Index for World Youth Day; papal visits.)

French Guiana

Dioc., 1; bp., 1; parishes, 26; priests, 31 (6 dioc., 25 rel.); p.d., 5; b sem., 1; ros., 2; srs., 85; bap., 1,913; Caths., 120,000 (80%); tot. pop., 150,000. (AD)

French overseas department on the northeast coast of South America; capital, Cayenne. Catholicism was introduced in the 17th century. The Cayenne diocese was established in 1956.

French Polynesia

Archd., 1; dioc., 1; abp., 1; bp., 2; parishes, 85; priests, 34 (15 dioc., 19 rel.); p.d., 17; sem., 14; bros., 47; srs., 69; bap., 1,559; Caths., 89,000 (40%); tot. pop., 220,000. (AD)

French overseas territory in the southern Pacific, including Tahiti and the Marquesas Islands; capital, Papeete. The first phase of evangelization in the Marquesas Islands, begun in 1838, resulted in 216 baptisms in 10 years. A vicariate was organized in 1848 but real progress was not made until after the baptism of native rulers in 1853. Persecution caused missionaries to leave the islands several times. By the 1960s, more than 95 per cent of the population was Catholic. Isolated attempts to evangelize Tahiti were made in the 17th and 18th centuries. Two Picpus Fathers began missionary work in 1831. A vicariate was organized in 1848. By 1908, despite the hindrances of Protestant opposition, disease and other factors, the Church had firm roots.

Gabon*

Archd., 1; dioc., 3; abp., 1; bp., 3; parishes, 65; priests, 107 (36 dioc., 71 rel.); p.d., 1; sem., 66; bros., 19; srs., 154; catechists, 800; bap., 10,101; Caths., 655,000 (49.6%); tot. pop., 1,320,000.

Republic on the west coast of central Africa; capital Libreville. Sporadic missionary effort took place before 1881 when effective evangelization began. The hierarchy was established in 1955.

The Gambia*

Dioc., 1; bp., 1; parishes, 14; priests, 25 (7 dioc., 18 rel.); sem., 27; bros., 13; srs., 62; bap., 1,465; Caths., 27,000 (2%); tot. pop., 1,320,000.

Republic (1970) on the northwestern coast of Af-

rica, capital, Banjui. Christianity was introduced by Portuguese explorers in the 15th century; effective evangelization began in 1822. The country was under the jurisdiction of a vicariate apostolic until 1931. The hierarchy was established in 1957.

Georgia*

A.a., 1; parishes, 28; priests, 10 (2 dioc., 8 rel); sem., 2; srs., 14; bap, 740; Caths., 100,000 (1.8%); tot. pop., 5,460,000

Independent (1991) state in the Caucasus; former Soviet republic; capital, Tbilisi. Christianity came to the area under Roman influence and, according to tradition, was spread through the efforts of St. Nino (or Christiana), a maiden who was brought as a captive to the country and is venerated as its apostle. The apostolic administration of the Caucasus (with seat in Georgia) was established in December, 1993, for Latin-rite Catholics of Armenia, Azerbaijan and Georgia.

Germany*

Archd., 7; dioc., 20; ap. ex., 1; mil. ord.; card., 6; abp., 9; bp., 91; parishes, 12,507; priests, 20,896 (16,022 dioc., 4,874 rel.); p.d., 1,803; sem., 1,757; bros., 2,160; srs., 45,361; bap., 253,418; Caths., 28,403,000 (34.8%); tot. pop., 81,640,000.

Country in northern Europe; capital, Berlin; seat of government, Bonn. From 1949-90 it was partitioned into the Communist German Democratic Republic in the East (capital, East Berlin) and the German Federal Republic in the West (capital, Bonn). Christianity was introduced in the third century, if not earlier. Trier, which became a center for missionary activity, had a bishop by 400. Visigoth invaders introduced Arianism in the fifth century but were converted in the seventh century by the East Franks, Celtic and other missionaries. St. Boniface, the apostle of Germany, established real ecclesiastical organization in the eighth century. The Church had great influence during the Carolingian period. Bishops from that time onward began to act in dual roles as pastors and rulers, a state of affairs which led inevitably to confusion and conflict in Church-state relations and perplexing problems of investiture. The Church developed strength and vitality through the Middle Ages but succumbed to abuses which antedated and prepared the ground for the Reformation. Luther's actions from 1517 made Germany a confessional battleground. Religious strife continued until conclusion of the Peace of Westphalia at the end of the Thirty Years' War in 1648. Nearly a century earlier the Peace of Augsburg (1555) had been designed, without success, to assure a degree of tranquillity by recognizing the legitimacy of different religious confessions in different states, depending on the decisions of princes. The implicit principle that princes should control the churches emerged in practice into the absolutism and Josephinism of subsequent years. St. Peter Canisius and his fellow Jesuits spearheaded a Counter Reformation in the second half of the 16th century. Before the end of the century, however, 70 per cent of the population of north and central Germany were Lutheran. Calvinism also had established a strong presence. The Church gained internal strength in a defensive position. Through much of the 19th century, however, its influence was eclipsed by Protestant intellectuals and other influences. It suffered some impoverishment also as a result of shifting boundaries and the secularization of property shortly after 1800. It came under direct attack in the Kulturkampf of the 1870s but helped to generate the opposition which resulted in a dampening of the campaign of Bismarck against it. Despite action by Catholics on the social front and other developments, discrimination against the Church spilled over into the 20th century and lasted beyond World War I. Catholics in politics struggled with others to pull the country through numerous postwar crises. The dissolution of the Center Party, agreed to by the bishops in 1933 without awareness of the ultimate consequences, contributed negatively to the rise of Hitler to supreme power. Church officials protested the Nazi anti-Church and anti-Semitic actions, but to no avail. After World War II Christian leadership had much to do with the recovery of Western Germany. East Germany, gone Communist under Russian auspices, initiated a program of control and repression of the Church in 1948 and 1949. With no prospect of success for measures designed to split bishops, priests, religious and lay persons, the regime concentrated most of its attention on mind control, especially of the younger generation, by the elimination of religious schools, curtailment of freedom for religious instruction and formation, severe restriction of the religious press, and the substitution from the mid-50s of youth initiation and Communist ceremonies for the rites of baptism, confirmation, marriage, and funerals. Bishops were generally forbidden to travel outside the Republic. The number of priests decreased, partly because of reduced seminary enrollments ordered by the East German government. In 1973, the Vatican appointed three apostolic administrators and one auxiliary (all titular bishops) for the areas of three West German dioceses located in East Germany. The official reunification of Germany took place Oct. 3, 1990. The separate episcopal conferences for East and West Germany were merged to form one conference in November, 1990. In July, 1994, ecclesiastical jurisdictions in eastern Germany were reorganized.

Ghana*

Archd., 3; dioc., 12; abp., 5; bp., 13; parishes, 244; priests, 793 (612 dioc., 181 rel.); p.d., 1; sem., 395; bros., 193; srs., 776; catechists, 3,929; bap., 35,972; Caths., 2,109,000 (12%); tot. pop., 17,450,000.

Republic on the western coast of Africa, bordering on the Gulf of Guinea; capital, Accra. Priests visited the country in 1482, 11 years after discovery by the Portuguese, but missionary effort _ hindered by the slave trade and other factors _ was slight until 1880 when systematic evangelization began. A prefecture apostolic was set up in 1879. The hierarchy was established in 1950. Five new dioceses were established in 1995.

Gibraltar

Dioc., 1; bp., 1; parishes, 5; priests, 12 (dioc.); sem., 2; srs., 6; bap., 218; Caths., 23,000; tot. pop., 27,000.

British dependency on the tip of the Spanish Peninsula on the Mediterranean. Evangelization took place after the Moors were driven out near the end of the 15th century. The Church was hindered by the British who acquired the colony in 1713. Most of the Catholics were, and are, Spanish and Italian immigrants and their descendants. A vicariate apostolic was organized in 1817. The diocese was erected in 1910.

Greece*

Archd., 4; dioc., 4; v.a., 1; ap. ex., 1; ord., 1; abp., 6; bp., 3; parishes, 65; priests, 95 (51 dioc., 44 rel.); p.d., 1; sem., 5; bros., 39; srs., 126; bap., 616; Caths., 61,000 (.6%); tot. pop., 10,460,000.

Republic in southeastern Europe on the Balkan Peninsula; capital, Athens. St. Paul preached the Gospel at Athens and Corinth on his second missionary journey and visited the country again on his third tour. Other Apostles may have passed through also. Two bishops from Greece attended the First Council of Nicaea. After the division of the Roman Empire, the Church remained Eastern in rite and later broke ties with Rome as a result of the schism of 1054. A Latin-Rite jurisdiction was set up during the period of the Latin Empire of Constantinople, 1204-1261, but crumbled afterwards. Unity efforts of the Council of Florence had poor results. The country now has Greek Catholic and Latin jurisdictions. The Greek Orthodox Church is predominant.

Greenland (Kalaallit Nunaat)

Parish, 1; priest, 1 (rel.); Caths., 100; tot. pop., 56,000.

Danish island province northeast of North America; granted self rule in 1979; capital, Nuuk (Godthaab). Catholicism was introduced about 1000. The first diocese was established in 1124 and a line of bishops dated from then until 1537. The first known churches in the western hemisphere, dating from about the 11th century, were on Greenland; the remains of 19 have been unearthed. The departure of Scandinavians and spread of the Reformation reduced the Church to nothing. The Moravian Brethren evangelized the Eskimos from the 1720s to 1901. By 1930 the Danish Church — Evangelical Lutheran — was in full possession. Since 1930, priests have been in Greenland, which is part of the Copenhagen diocese.

Grenada*

Dioc., 1; bp., 1; parishes, 20; priests, 23 (6 dioc., 17 rel.); p.d., 3; sem., 1; bros., 3; srs., 35; catechists, 125; bap., 855; Caths., 54,000; tot. pop., 91,000.

Independent island state in the West Indies; capital, St. George's.

Guadeloupe

Dioc., 1; bp., 2; parishes, 43; priests, 68 (51 dioc., 17 rel.); p.d., 3; sem., 7; bros., 2; srs., 293; catechists, 2,735; bap., 3,809; Caths., 391,000 (95%); tot. pop., 408,000 (AD).

French overseas department in the Leeward Islands of the West Indies; capital, Basse-Terre. Catholicism was introduced in the islands in the 16th century.

Guam

Archd., 1; abp., 1; parishes, 23; priests, 43 (24 dioc., 19 rel.); p.d., 18; sem., 9; bro., 1; srs., 120;

bap., 2,656; Caths., 115,000; tot. pop., 136,000.
Outlying area of U.S. in the southwest Pacific; capital, Agana. The first Mass was offered in the Mariana Islands in 1521. The islands were evangelized by the Jesuits, from 1668, and other missionaries. The first native Micronesian bishop was ordained in 1970. The Agana diocese, which had been a suffragan of San Francisco, was made a metropolitan see in 1984.

Guatemala*

Archd., 2; dioc., 10; prel., 1; v.a., 2; abp., 2; bp., 18; parishes, 407; priests, 864 (315 dioc., 549 rel.); p.d., 5; sem., 568; bros., 439; srs., 1,645; catechists, 3,732; bap., 332,342; Caths. 9,045,000 (85%); tot. pop. 10,620,000.
Republic in Central America; capital, Guatemala City. Evangelization dates from the beginning of Spanish occupation in 1524. The first diocese, for all Central American territories administered by the captaincy general of Guatemala, was established in 1534. The country became independent in 1839, following annexation to Mexico in 1821, secession in 1823 and membership in the Central American Federation from 1825. In 1870, a government installed by a liberal revolution repudiated the concordat of 1853 and took active measures against the Church. Separation of Church and state was decreed; religious orders were suppressed and their property seized; priests and religious were exiled; schools were secularized. Full freedom was subsequently granted. In recent years, the bishops have repeatedly condemned political violence and social injustice which have created a crisis in the country.

Guinea*

Archd., 1; dioc., 2; abp., 1; bp., 2; parishes, 35; priests, 77 (55 dioc., 22 rel.); sem., 39; bros., 13; srs., 79; bap., 2,639; Caths., 129,000 (2%); tot. pop., 6,700,000.
Republic on the west coast of Africa; capital, Conakry. Occasional missionary work followed exploration by the Portuguese about the middle of the 15th century; organized effort dates from 1877. The hierarchy was established in 1955. Following independence from France in 1958, Catholic schools were nationalized, youth organizations banned and missionaries restricted. Foreign missionaries were expelled in 1967. Archbishop Tchidimbo of Conakry, sentenced to life imprisonment in 1971 on a charge of conspiring to overthrow the government, was released in August, 1979; he resigned his see. Private schools, suppressed by the government for more than 20 years, were again authorized in 1984.

Guinea-Bissau*

Dioc., 1; bp., 1; parishes, 28; priests, 65 (9 dioc., 56 rel.); sem., 14; bros., 11; srs., 138; bap., 1,500; Caths., 126,000 (11%); tot. pop., 1,070,000.
Formerly Portuguese Guinea. Independent state on the west coast of Africa; capital, Bissau. Catholicism was introduced in the second half of the 15th century but limited missionary work, hampered by the slave trade, had meager results. Missionary work in this century dates from 1933. A prefecture apostolic was established in 1955 (made a diocese in 1977).

Guyana

Dioc., 1; bp., 1; parishes, 30; priests, 56 (6 dioc., 50 rel.); sem., 6; bros., 3; srs., 46; catechists, 569; bap., 1,736; Caths., 88,000 (10.6%); tot. pop., 830,000.
Republic on the northern coast of South America; capital, Georgetown. In 1899 the Catholic Church and other churches were given equal status with the Church of England and the Church of Scotland, which had sole rights up to that time. Most of the Catholics are Portuguese. The Georgetown diocese was established in 1956, 10 years before Guyana became independent of England. The first native bishop was appointed in 1971. Schools were nationalized in 1976. Increased government interference was reported in 1980-81.

Haiti*

Archd., 2; dioc., 7; abp., 2; bp., 10; parishes, 237; priests, 552 (328 dioc., 224 rel.); sem., 236; bros., 301; srs., 1,007; bap., 206,039; Caths., 6,255,000 (87.1%); tot. pop., 7,180,000.
Caribbean republic on the western third of Hispaniola adjacent to the Dominican Republic; capital, Port-au-Prince. Evangelization followed discovery by Columbus in 1492. Capuchins and Jesuits did most of the missionary work in the 18th century. From 1804, when independence was declared, until 1860, the country was in schism. Relations were regularized by a concordat concluded in 1860, when an archdiocese and four dioceses were established. Factors hindering the development of the Church have been a shortage of native clergy, inadequate religious instruction and the prevalence of voodoo. Political upheavals in the 1960s had serious effects on the Church. In 1984, a new concordat was concluded replacing the one in effect since 1860. In October, 1994, Jean Bertrand Aristide, the democratically elected president, returned to his country after more than three years in exile.

Honduras*

Archd., 1; dioc., 6; abp., 2; bp., 7; parishes, 144; priests, 339 (123 dioc., 216 rel.); pd., 1; sem., 103; bros.,108; srs., 533; catechists, 2,109; bap., 75,249; Caths., 5,517,000 (92.7%); tot. pop., 5,950,000.
Republic in Central America; capital, Tegucigalpa. Evangelization preceded establishment of the first diocese in the 16th century. Under Spanish rule and after independence from 1823, the Church held a favored position until 1880 when equal legal status was given to all religions. Harassment of priests and nuns working among peasants and Salvadoran refugees was reported in recent years.

Hong Kong

Dioc., 1; card., 1; bp., 2; parishes, 62; priests, 321 (74 dioc., 247 rel.); p.d., 1; sem., 25; bros., 85; srs., 576; bap., 4,173; Caths., 237,000 (3.8%); tot. pop., 6,190,000.
Former British colony adjacent to the southeast Chinese province of Kwangtung. The territory was returned to China July 1, 1997. A prefecture apostolic was established in 1841. Members of the Pontifical Institute for Foreign Missions began work there in 1858. The Hong Kong diocese was erected in 1946.

Hungary*

Archd., 4; dioc., 9; abb., 1; ap. ex., 1; mil. ord.; card., 1; abp., 5; bp., 21; parishes, 2,175; priests, 2,644 (2,120 dioc., 524 rel.); p.d., 29; sem., 453; bros., 206; srs., 1,971; bap., 57,099; Caths., 6,602,000 (64.6%); tot. pop., 10,220,000.

Republic in east central Europe; capital, Budapest. The early origins of Christianity in the country, whose territory was subject to a great deal of change, is not known. Magyars accepted Christianity about the end of the 10th century. St. Stephen I (d. 1038) promoted its spread and helped to organize some of its historical dioceses. Bishops early became influential in politics as well as in the Church. For centuries the country served as a buffer for the Christian West against barbarians from the East, notably the Mongols in the 13th century. Religious orders, whose foundations started from the 1130s, provided the most effective missionaries, pastors and teachers. Outstanding for years were the Franciscans and Dominicans; the Jesuits were noted for their work in the Counter-Reformation from the second half of the 16th century onwards. Hussites and Waldensians prepared the way for the Reformation which struck at almost the same time as the Turks. The Reformation made considerable progress after 1526, resulting in the conversion of large numbers to Lutheranism and Calvinism by the end of the century. Most of them or their descendants returned to the Church later, but many Magyars remained staunch Calvinists. Turks repressed the churches, Protestant as well as Catholic, during a reign of 150 years but they managed to survive. Domination of the Church was one of the objectives of government policy during the reigns of Maria Theresa and Joseph II in the second half of the 18th century; their Josephinism affected Church-state relations until the first World War. More than 100,000 Eastern-Rite schismatics were reunited with Rome about the turn of the 18th century. Secularization increased in the second half of the 19th century, which also witnessed the birth of many new Catholic organizations and movements to influence life in the nation and the Church. Catholics were involved in the social chaos and anti-religious atmosphere of the years following World War I, struggling with their compatriots for religious as well as political survival. After World War II Communist strength, which had manifested itself with less intensity earlier in the century, was great long before it forced the legally elected president out of office in 1947 and imposed a Soviet type of constitution on the country in 1949. The campaign against the Church started with the disbanding of Catholic organizations in 1946. In 1948, "Caritas," the Catholic charitable organization, was taken over and all Catholic schools, colleges and institutions were suppressed. Interference in church administration and attempts to split the bishops preceded the arrest of Cardinal Mindszenty on Dec. 26, 1948, and his sentence to life imprisonment in 1949. (He was free for a few days during the unsuccessful uprising of 1956. He then took up residence at the U.S. Embassy in Budapest where he remained until September, 1971, when he was permitted to leave the country. He died in 1975 in Vienna.) In 1950, religious orders and congregations were suppressed and 10,000 religious were interned. At least 30 priests and monks were assassinated, jailed or deported. About 4,000 priests and religious were confined in jail or concentration camps. The government sponsored a national "Progressive Catholic" church and captive organizations for priests and "Catholic Action," which attracted only a small minority. Signs were clear in 1965 and 1966 that a 1964 agreement with the Holy See regarding episcopal appointments had settled nothing. Six bishops were appointed by the Holy See and some other posts were filled, but none of the prelates were free from government surveillance and harassment. Four new bishops were appointed by the Holy See in January and ordained in Budapest in February, 1969; three elderly prelates resigned their sees. Shortly thereafter, peace priests complained that the "too Roman" new bishops would not deal with them. Talks between Vatican and Hungarian representatives in the 1970s resulted in the appointment of diocesan bishops to fill long-vacant sees. On Feb. 9, 1990, an accord was signed between the Holy See and Hungary reestablishing diplomatic relations. Pope John Paul II reorganized the ecclesiastical structure of the country in May, 1993. (See Index for papal visst.)

Iceland*

Dioc., 1; bp., 1; parishes, 4; priests, 9 (6 dioc., 3 rel.); sem., 1; srs., 61; bap., 49; Caths., 3,000; tot. pop., 270,000.

Island republic between Norway and Greenland; capital, Reykjavik. Irish hermits were there in the eighth century. Missionaries subsequently evangelized the island and Christianity was officially accepted about 1000. The first bishop was ordained in 1056. The Black Death had dire effects and spiritual decline set in during the 15th century. Lutheranism was introduced from Denmark between 1537 and 1552 and made the official religion. Some Catholic missionary work was done in the 19th century. Religious freedom was granted to the few Catholics in 1874. A vicariate was erected in 1929 (made a diocese in 1968).

India*

Patriarchate, 1 (titular of East Indies); major archbishopric (Syro-Malabar), 1; archd., 23; dioc., 109; card., 3; patr., 1; abp., 26; bp., 118; parishes, 7,247; priests, 16,593 (9,655 dioc., 6,938 rel.); p.d., 23; sem., 9,525; bros., 2,671; srs., 73,030; catechists, 40,673; bap., 331,668; Caths., 16,016,000 (1.7%); tot. pop. 935,740,000.

Republic on the subcontinent of south central Asia; capital, New Delhi. Long-standing tradition credits the Apostle Thomas with the introduction of Christianity in the Kerala area. Evangelization followed the establishment of Portuguese posts and the conquest of Goa in 1510. Jesuits, Franciscans, Dominicans, Augustinians and members of other religious orders figured in the early missionary history. An archdiocese for Goa, with two suffragan sees, was set up in 1558. Five provincial councils were held between 1567 and 1606. The number of Catholics in 1572 was estimated to be 280,000. This figure rose to 800,000 in 1700 and declined to 500,000 in 1800. Missionaries had some difficulties with the British East India Co. which exercised virtual government control from 1757 to 1858. They also had trouble because of a conflict that developed between policies of the Portuguese government, which pressed its rights of patronage in episcopal and clerical appointments, and the Congregation for the Propagation of the Faith, which sought greater freedom of action in the same appointments. This struggle eventuated in the schism of Goa between 1838 and 1857. In 1886, when the number of Catholics was estimated to be one million, the hierarchy for India and Ceylon was restored. Jesuits contributed greatly to the development of Catholic education from the second half of the 19th century. A large percentage of the Catholic population is located around Goa and Kerala and farther south. The country is predominantly Hindu. So-called anticonversion laws in effect in several states have had a restrictive effect on pastoral ministry and social service. (See Index: Mother Teresa of Calcutta.)

Indonesia*

Archd., 8; dioc., 26; mil. ord.; card., 1; abp., 8; bps., 34; parishes, 991; priests, 2,585 (815 dioc., 1,770 rel.); p.d., 19; sem., 2,602; bros., 1,100; srs., 6,705; catechists, 21,487; bap., 194,196; Caths., 5,380,000 (2.7%); tot. pop., 193,750,000.

East Timor (former Portuguese Timor annexed by Indonesia in 1976): Dioc., 2; bp., 2; parishes, 30; priests, 93 (36 dioc., 57 rel.); p.d., 1; sem., 158; bros., 34; srs., 199; catechists, 1,361; bap., 25,170; Caths., 732,000 (85%); tot. pop., 860,000.

Republic southeast of Asia, consisting of some 3,000 islands including Kalimantan (most of Borneo), Sulawesi (Celebes), Java, the Lesser Sundas, Moluccas, Sumatra, Timor and West Irian (Irian Jaya, western part of New Guinea); capital, Jakarta. Evangelization by the Portuguese began about 1511. St. Francis Xavier, greatest of the modern missionaries, spent some 14 months in the area. Christianity was strongly rooted in some parts of the islands by 1600. Islam's rise to dominance began at this time. The Dutch East Indies Co., which gained effective control in the 17th century, banned evangelization by Catholic missionaries for some time but Dutch secular and religious priests managed to resume the work. A vicariate of Batavia for all the Dutch East Indies was set up in 1841. About 90 per cent of the population is Muslim. The hierarchy was established in 1961.

Iran*

Archd., 4; dioc., 2; abp., 4; bp., 2; parishes, 18; priests, 12 (6 dioc., 6 rel.); p.d., 12; sem., 1; bro., 1; srs., 33; bap., 83; Caths., 13,000 (.02%); tot. pop., 67,280,000.

Islamic republic (Persia until 1935) in southwestern Asia, between the Caspian Sea and the Persian Gulf; capital, Teheran. Some of the earliest Christian communities were established in this area outside the (then) Roman Empire. They suffered persecution in the fourth century and were then cut off from the outside world. Nestorianism was generally professed in the late fifth century. Islam became dominant after 640. Some later missionary work was attempted but without success. Religious liberty was granted in 1834, but Catholics were the victims of a massacre in

1918. Islam is the religion of perhaps 98 per cent of the population. In 1964 the country had approximately 120,000 Orthodox Oriental Christians (not in union with Rome). Catholics belong to the Latin, Armenian and Chaldean rites.

Iraq*

Patriarchate, 1; archd., 9; dioc., 6; patriarch, 1; abp., 10; bp., 3; parishes, 92; priests, 134 (110 dioc., 24 rel.); p.d., 6; sem., 49; bros., 7; srs., 333; bap., 4,212; Caths., 621,000 (3%); tot. pop., 20,450,000.

Republic in southwestern Asia, between Iran and Saudi Arabia; capital, Baghdad. Some of the earliest Christian communities were established in the area, whose history resembles that of Iran. Catholics belong to the Armenian, Chaldean, Latin and Syrian rites; Chaldeans are most numerous. Islam is the religion of some 90 per cent of the population.

Ireland*

Archd., 4; dioc., 22; card., 1; abp., 9; bp., 41; parishes, 1,359; priests, 5,888 (3,554 dioc., 2,334 rel.); p.d., 2; sem., 524; bros., 1,120; srs., 10,280; bap., 60,048 (preceding figures include Northern Ireland); Catholics in Ireland were about 95% of the estimated total population of 3,550,000.

Republic in the British Isles; capital, Dublin. St. Patrick, who is venerated as the apostle of Ireland, evangelized parts of the island for some years after the middle of the fifth century. Conversion of the island was not accomplished, however, until the seventh century or later. Celtic monks were the principal missionaries. The Church was organized along monastic lines at first, but a movement developed in the 11th century for the establishment of jurisdiction along episcopal lines. By that time many Roman usages had been adopted. The Church gathered strength during the period from the Norman Conquest of England to the reign of Henry VIII despite a wide variety of rivalries, wars, and other disturbances. Henry introduced an age of repression of the faith which continued for many years under several of his successors. The Irish suffered from proscription of the Catholic faith, economic and social disabilities, subjection to absentee landlords and a plantation system designed to keep them from owning property, and actual persecution which took an uncertain toll of lives up until about 1714. Some penal laws remained in force until emancipation in 1829. Nearly 100 years later Ireland was divided by two enactments which made Northern Ireland, consisting of six counties, part of the United Kingdom (1920) and gave dominion status to the Irish Free State, made up of the other 26 counties (1922). This state (Eire, in Gaelic) was proclaimed the Republic of Ireland in 1949. The Catholic Church predominates but religious freedom is guaranteed for all.

Northern Ireland

Tot. pop., 1,610,000; Catholics comprise more than one third. (Other statistics are included in Ireland).

Part of the United Kingdom, it consists of six of the nine counties of Ulster in the northeast corner of Ireland; capital, Belfast. History is given under Ireland. (See Index for recent events.)

Israel*

Patriarchates, 2 (Jerusalem for Latins; patriarchal vicariate for Greek-Melkites); archd., 2; patriarch, 1; abp., 3; bp., 3; parishes, 74; priests, 397 (79 dioc., 318 rel.); p.d., 5; sem., 118; bros., 158; srs., 1,036; bap., 642; Caths., 90,000; tot. pop., 5,540,000.

Parliamentary democracy in the Middle East, at the eastern end of the Mediterranean; capitals, Jerusalem and Tel Aviv (diplomatic). Israel was the birthplace of Christianity, the site of the first Christian communities. Some persecution was suffered in the early Christian era and again during the several hundred years of Roman control. Muslims conquered the territory in the seventh century and, except for the period of the Kingdom of Jerusalem established by Crusaders, remained in control most of the time up until World War I. The Church survived in the area, sometimes just barely, but it did not prosper greatly or show any notable increase in numbers. The British took over the protectorate of the area after World War I. Partition into Israel for the Jews and Palestine for the Arabs was approved by the United Nations in 1947. War broke out a year later with the proclamation of the Republic of Israel. The Israelis won the war and 50 percent more territory than they had originally been ceded. War broke out again for six days in June, 1967, and in October, 1973, resulting in a Middle East crisis. Judaism is the faith professed by about 85 percent of the inhabitants; approximately one-third of them are considered observants. Most of the Arab minority are Muslims. Israeli-Palestinian relations took a turn for the better in 1994 as Palestinians gained a measure of freedom. Israeli-Holy See relations improved in 1994 with the implementation of full diplomatic relations.

Italy*

Patriarchate, 1; archd. 58 (37 are metropolitan sees); dioc., 158; prel., 3; abb., 7; mil. ord.; card., 34; abp., 160; bps., 275 (hierarchy includes 218 residential, 33 coadjutors or auxiliaries, 96 in Curia offices, remainder in other offices or retired); parishes, 25,769; priests, 56,752 (37,466 dioc., 19,286 rel.); p.d., 1,661; sem., 6,256; bros., 4,650; srs., 117,761; bap., 482,123; Caths., 55,599,000 (97.2%); tot. pop., 57,190,000.

Republic in southern Europe; capital, Rome. A Christian community was formed early at Rome, probably by the middle of the first century. St. Peter established his see there. He and St. Paul suffered death for the faith there in the 60s. The early Christians were persecuted at various times there, as in other parts of the empire, but the Church developed in numbers and influence, gradually spreading out from towns and cities in the center and south to rural areas and the north. Organization, in the process of formation in the second century, developed greatly between the fifth and eighth centuries. By the latter date the Church had already come to grips with serious problems, including doctrinal and disciplinary disputes that threatened the unity of faith, barbarian invasions, and the need for the pope and bishops to take over civil responsibilities because of imperial default. The Church has been at the center of life on the peninsula throughout the centuries. It emerged

from underground in 313, with the Edict of Milan, and rose to a position of prestige and lasting influence. It educated and converted the barbarians, preserved culture through the early Middle Ages and passed it on to later times, suffered periods of decline and gained strength through recurring reforms, engaged in military combat for political reasons and intellectual combat for the preservation and development of doctrine, saw and patronized the development of the arts, experienced all human strengths and weaknesses in its members, knew triumph and the humiliation of failure. For long centuries, from the fourth to the 19th, the Church was a temporal as well as spiritual power. This temporal aspect complicated its history in Italy. Since the 1870s, however, when the Papal States were annexed by the Kingdom of Italy, the history became simpler _ but remained complicated _ as the Church, shorn of temporal power, began to find new freedom for the fulfillment of its spiritual mission. In 1985, a new concordat was ratified between the Vatican and Italy, replacing one in effect since 1929.

Jamaica*

Archd., 1; dioc., 1; v.a., 1; abp., 1; bp., 2; parishes, 78; priests, 86 (35 dioc., 51 rel.); p.d., 24; sem., 20; bros., 19; srs., 187; bap., 1,418; Caths., 107,000 (4.2%); tot. pop., 2,530,000.

Republic in the West Indies; capital, Kingston. Franciscans and Dominicans evangelized the island from about 1512 until 1655. Missionary work was interrupted after the English took possession but was resumed by Jesuits about the turn of the 19th century. A vicariate apostolic was organized in 1837. The hierarchy was established in 1967.

Japan*

Archd., 3; dioc., 13; p.a., 1; card., 1; abp., 4; bp., 20; parishes, 854; priests, 1,882 (555 dioc., 1,327 rel.); p.d., 6; sem., 243; bros., 304; srs., 6,729; bap., 9,466; Caths., 447,000 (.35%); tot. pop., 125,200,000.

Archipelago in the northwest Pacific; capital, Tokyo. Jesuits began evangelization in the middle of the 16th century and about 300,000 converts, most of them in Kyushu, were reported at the end of the century. The Nagasaki Martyrs were victims of persecution in 1597. Another persecution took some 4,000 lives between 1614 and 1651. Missionaries, banned for two centuries, returned about the middle of the 19th century and found Christian communities still surviving in Nagasaki and other places in Kyushu. A vicariate was organized in 1866. Religious freedom was guaranteed in 1889. The hierarchy was established in 1891.

Jordan*

Archd., l; abp., 1; bp., 1; parishes, 62; priests, 71 (55 dioc., 16 rel.); sem., 5; bros., 9; srs., 240; bap., 744; Caths., 66,000 (1.2%); tot. pop., 5,440,000.

Constitutional monarchy in the Middle East; capital, Amman. Christianity there dates from apostolic times. Survival of the faith was threatened many times under the rule of Muslims from 636 and Ottoman Turks from 1517 to 1918, and in the Islamic Emirate of Trans-Jordan from 1918 to 1949. Since the creation of Israel, some 500,000 Palestinian refugees, some of them Christians, have been in Jordan. Islam is the state religion but religious freedom is guaranteed for all. The Greek Melkite-Rite Archdiocese of Petra and Philadelphia is located in Jordan. Latin (Roman)-Rite Catholics are under the jurisdiction of the Latin Patriarchate of Jerusalem. Established diplomatic relations with the Holy See in 1994.

Kazakhstan*
A.a., 1; bp., 1; priests, 67 (32 dioc.,35 rel.); sem., 18; bros., 1; srs., 52; bap., 1,893; Caths., 300,000 (1.8%); tot. pop., 16,590,000.

Independent republic (1991); formerly part of USSR; capital, Almaty (Alma-Ata). Most of the population are Sunni Muslims and about 30% are Russian Orthodox. The Catholic population is mainly of German, Polish and Ukrainian origin who were deported during the Stalin regime. A Latin-rite apostolic administration was established in 1991.

Kenya*
Archd. 4; dioc., 16; v.a., 1; mil. ord.; card., 1; abp. 3; bp. 18; parishes, 548; priests, 1,547 (712 dioc., 835 rel.); sem., 1,496; bros., 592; srs., 3,386; catechists, 8,263; bap., 214,073; Caths., 6,367,000 (20.1%); tot. pop., 30,520,000.

Republic in eastern Africa bordering on the Indian Ocean; capital, Nairobi. Systematic evangelization by the Holy Ghost Missionaries began in 1889, nearly 40 years after the start of work by Protestant missionaries. The hierarchy was established in 1953. Three metropolitan sees were established in 1990.

Kiribati*
Dioc., 1; bp., 1; parishes, 22; priests, 20 (7 dioc., 13 rel.); sem., 11; bros., 17; srs., 73; bap., 2,150; Caths., 39,000 (52,7%); tot. pop., 74,000.

Former British colony (Gilbert Islands) in Oceania; became independent July 12, 1979; capital, Bairiki on Tarawa. French Missionaries of the Sacred Heart began work in the islands in 1888. A vicariate for the islands was organized in 1897. The hierarchy was established in 1966.

Korea
North Korea: Dioc., 2; abb., 1; bp., 1 (exiled); tot. pop.,23,920,000. No recent Catholic statistics available; there were an estimated 100,000 Catholics reported in 1969.

South Korea: Archd.,3; dioc.,11; mil. ord.; card., 1; abp., 3; bp., 18; parishes, 948; priests, 2,164 (1,786 dioc., 378 rel.); sem., 1,835; bros., 487; srs., 6,936; bap., 137,745; Caths., 3,402,000 (7.6%); tot. pop., 44,850,000.*

Peninsula in eastern Asia, east of China, divided into the (Communist) Democratic People's Republic in the North, formed May 1, 1948, with Pyongyang as its capital; and the Republic of Korea in the South, with Seoul as the capital. Some Catholics may have been in Korea before it became a "hermit kingdom" toward the end of the 16th century and closed its borders to foreigners. The real introduction to Catholicism came in 1784 through lay converts. A priest arriving in the country in 1794 found 4,000 Catho-

lics there who had never seen a priest. A vicariate was erected in 1831 but was not manned for several years thereafter. There were 15,000 Catholics by 1857. Four persecutions in the 19th century took a terrible toll; several thousand died in the last one, 1866-69. (One hundred and three martyrs of this period were canonized by Pope John Paul II during his 1984 apostolic visit to South Korea.) Freedom of religion was granted in 1883 when Korea opened its borders. Progress was made thereafter. The hierarchy was established in 1962. Since the war of 1950-53, there have been no signs of Catholic life in the North which has been blanketed by a news blackout. In July 1972, both Koreas agreed to seek peaceful means of reunification. Bishop Tji of Won Ju, South Korea, convicted and sentenced to 15 years' imprisonment in 1974 on a charge of inciting to rebellion, was released in February, 1975. The 44th International Eucharistic Congress was held in Seoul, South Korea, Oct. 5 to 8, 1989.

Kuwait*
V.a., 1; bp., 1; parishes, 5; priests, 10 (6 dioc., 4 rel.); p.d., 1; srs., 12; bap., 554; Caths., 155,000; tot. pop., 1,690,000.

Constitutional monarchy (sultanate or sheikdom) in southwest Asia bordering on the Persian Gulf. Remote Christian origins probably date to apostolic times. Islam is the predominant and official religion.

Kyrgyzstan*
Priests, 5 (1 dioc., 4 rel.); bro., 1; Caths., 26,000; tot. pop., 4,670,000.

Independent republic bordering China; former Soviet republic; capital, Bishkek (former name, Frunze). Most of the people are Sunni Muslim. Established diplomatic relations with the Holy See, August, 1992.

Laos
V.a., 4; bp., 3; parishes, 31; priests, 23 (17 dioc., 6 rel.); p.d., 1; sem., 7; bros., 1; srs., 94; catechists, 133; bap., 475; Caths., 36,000 (.7%); tot. pop., 4,880,000. (AD)

People's republic in southeast Asia, surrounded by China, Vietnam, Cambodia, Thailand and Myanmar (Burma); capital, Vientiane. Systematic evangelization by French missionaries started about 1881; earlier efforts ended in 1688. The first mission was established in 1885 by Father Xavier Guégo. A vicariate apostolic was organized in 1899 when there were 8,000 Catholics and 2,000 catechumens in the country. Most of the foreign missionaries were expelled following the communist take-over in 1975. Buddhism is the state religion.

Latvia*
Archd., 1; dioc., 3; abp., 1; bp., 4; parishes, 175; priests, 108 (86 dioc., 22 rel.); p.d., 1; sem., 74; bros.,11; srs.,104; bap., 6,411; Caths., 500,000 (19.9%); tot. pop., 2,510,000.

Independent (1991) Baltic republic; capital, Riga. (Forcibly absorbed by the U.S.S.R. in 1940; it regained independence in 1991). Catholicism was introduced late in the 12th century. Lutheranism became the dominant religion after 1530. Catholics were free to practice their faith during the long period of Russian control and during independence from

1918 to 1940. The relatively small Catholic community was repressed during the 1940-91 Soviet takeover of Latvia which was not recognized by the Holy See or the United States.

Lebanon*

Archd., 12 (1 Armenian, 4 Maronite, 7 Greek Melkite); dioc., 7 (1 Chaldean, 6 Maronite); v.a., 1 (Latin); card., 1 (patriarch of the Maronites); patriarchs, 3 (patriarchs of Antioch of the Maronites, Antioch of the Syrians and Cilicia of the Armenians who reside in Lebanon); abp. and bp., 39; parishes, 1,032; priests, 1,407 (730 dioc., 677 rel.); p.d., 13; sem., 435; bros., 126; srs., 2,824; bap., 14,978; Caths., 2,026,000; tot. pop., 3,010,000.

Republic in the Middle East, north of Israel; capital, Beirut. Christianity, introduced in apostolic times, was firmly established by the end of the fourth century and has remained so despite heavy Muslim influence since early in the seventh century. The country is the center of the Maronite Rite. In the 1980s, the country was torn by violence and often heavy fighting among rival political-religious factions drawn along Christian-Muslim lines. (See Index for papal visit.)

Lesotho*

Archd., 1; dioc., 3; abp., 1; bp., 3; parishes, 76; priests, 143 (45 dioc., 98 rel.); p.d., 2; sem., 93; bros., 56; srs., 592; catechists, 1,577; bap., 24,562; Caths., 726,000 (35%); tot. pop., 2,050,000.

Constitutional monarchy, an enclave in the southeastern part of the Republic of South Africa; capital, Maseru. Oblates of Mary Immaculate, the first Catholic missionaries in the area, started evangelization in 1862. A prefecture apostolic was organized in 1894. The hierarchy was established in 1951.

Liberia*

Archd., 1; dioc., 2; abp., 1; bp., 2; parishes, 50; priests, 55 (26 dioc., 29 rel.); p.d., 4; sem., 46; bros., 22; srs., 50; bap. 3,592; Caths., 99,000 (3.6%); tot. pop., 2,760,000.

Republic in western Africa, bordering on the Atlantic; capital, Monrovia. Missionary work and influence, dating interruptedly from the 16th century, were slight before the Society of African Missions undertook evangelization in 1906. The hierarchy was established in 1982. In July, 1993, a peace accord was signed ending the civil war which began in 1989. The war had claimed the lives of 150,000 and made refugees of 100,000.

Libya*

V.a., 3; p.a., 1; bp., 1; parishes, 2; priests, 14 (1 dioc., 13 rel.); srs., 77; bap., 157; Caths., 40,000 (.7%); tot. pop., 5,410,000.

Arab state in northern Africa, on the Mediterranean between Egypt and Tunisia; capital, Tripoli. Christianity was probably preached in the area at an early date but was overcome by the spread of Islam from the 630s. Islamization was complete by 1067 and there has been no Christian influence since then. The Catholics in the country belong to the foreign colony. Islam is the state religion. Established diplomatic relations with the Holy See in 1997.

Liechtenstein*

Parishes, 9; priests, 24 (14 dioc., 10 rel); bros., 4; srs., 80; bap., 190; Caths., 22,000; tot. pop., 29,000.

Constitutional monarchy in central Europe, in the Alps and on the Rhine between Switzerland and Austria; capital, Vaduz. Christianity in the country dates from the fourth century; the area has been under the jurisdiction of Chur, Switzerland, since about that time. The Reformation had hardly any influence in the country. Catholicism is the state religion but religious freedom for all is guaranteed by law.

Lithuania*

Archd., 2; dioc.(1997) , 5; card., 1; abp., 2; bp., 8; parishes, 666; priests, 732 (625 dioc., 107 rel.); p.d., 2; sem., 284; bros., 104; srs., 905; bap., 42,406; Caths., 3,119,000 (84%); tot. pop., 3,710,000.

Baltic republic forcibly absorbed and under Soviet domination from 1940; regained independence, 1991; capital, Vilna (Vilnius). Catholicism was introduced in 1251 and a short-lived diocese was established by 1260. Effective evangelization took place between 1387 and 1417, when Catholicism became the state religion. Losses to Lutheranism in the 16th century were overcome. Efforts of czars to "russify" the Church between 1795 and 1918 were strongly resisted. Concordat relations with the Vatican were established in 1927, nine years after independence from Russia and 13 years before the start of another kind of Russian control with the following results, among others: all convents closed; four seminaries shut down; appointment to one seminary (Kaunas) only with government approval; priests restricted in pastoral ministry and subject to appointment by government officials; no religious services outside churches; no religious press; religious instruction banned; parish installations and activities controlled by directives enacted in 1976; two bishops — Vincentas Sladkevicius and Julijonas Steponavicius — forbidden to act as bishops and relegated to remote parishes in 1957 and 1961, respectively; arrest, imprisonment or detention in Siberia for four bishops, 185 priests, 275 lay persons between 1945 and 1955. Despite such developments and conditions, there was a strong and vigorous underground Church in Lithuania, where the Soviet government found its repressive potential limited by the solidarity of popular resistance. In July, 1982, Rev. Antanas Vaicius was ordained apostolic administrator of the Telsiai diocese and Klaipeda prelature. Auxiliary Bishop Vincentas Sladkevicius, of Kaisiadorys, under severe government restrictions since 1957, was allowed to return to his see in 1982 following his appointment as apostolic administrator. (He was made a cardinal in 1988 and appointed archbishop of Kaunas in March, 1989.) In 1983, four of the five bishops were allowed to go to Rome for their ad limina visit. In December, 1988, Bishop Steponavicius was allowed to return to his diocese and was named an archbishop in 1989. (He died in 1991.) The Vatican announcement in March, 1989, of the reorganization of the hierarchy indicated some change of attitude on the part of the government. Three former apostolic administrators (titular bishops) were named ordinaries; three apostolic administrators (two of them new) were appointed. The Soviet 1940-91 take-over of Lithuania was not recognized by the Holy See or the United States.

Luxembourg*

Archd., 1; abp., 1; parishes, 275; priests, 301 (229 dioc., 72 rel.); p.d., 3; sem., 15; bros., 18; srs., 754; bap., 3,599; Caths. 386,000 (94%); tot. pop., 410,000.

Constitutional monarchy in western Europe, between Belgium, Germany and France; capital, Luxembourg. Christianity, introduced in the fifth and sixth centuries, was firmly established by the end of the eighth century. A full-scale parish system was in existence in the ninth century. Monastic influence was strong until the Reformation, which had minimal influence in the country. The Church experienced some adverse influence from the currents of the French Revolution.

Macau (Macao)

Dioc., 1; bp., 1; parishes, 9; priests, 69 (31 dioc., 38 rel.); bros., 9; srs., 158; bap., 401; Caths., 22,000; tot. pop., 420,000.

Portuguese-administered territory in southeast Asia across the Pearl River estuary from Hong Kong; scheduled to revert to China in 1999. Christianity was introduced by the Jesuits in 1557. Diocese was established in 1576. Macau served as a base for missionary work in Japan and China.

Macedonia*

Dioc., 1; bp., 2; parishes, 25; priests, 59 (50 dioc., 9 rel.); sem., 12; bros., 1; srs., 103; bap., 1,439; Caths., 63,000; tot. pop., 4,400,000.

Former Yugoslav Republic of Macedonia; declared independence in 1992; capital, Skopje.

Madagascar*

Archd., 3; dioc., 15; abp., 4; bp., 16; parishes, 279; priests, 852 (307 dioc., 545 rel.); sem., 803; bros., 141; srs., 2,667; catechists, 18,022; bap.,108,178; Caths., 3,134,000 (21%); tot. pop. 14,760,000.

Republic (Malagasy Republic) off the eastern coast of Africa; capital, Antananarivo. Missionary efforts were generally fruitless from early in the 16th century until the Jesuits were permitted to start open evangelization about 1845. A prefecture apostolic was set up in 1850 and a vicariate apostolic in the north was placed in charge of the Holy Ghost Fathers in 1898. There were 100,000 Catholics by 1900. The first native bishop was ordained in 1936. The hierarchy was established in 1955.

Madeira Islands

Portuguese province, an archipelago 340 miles west of the northwestern coast of Africa; capital, Funchal. Catholicism has had a continuous history since the first half of the 15th century. The diocese of Funchal was established in 1514. Statistics are included in Portugal.

Malawi*

Archd., 1; dioc., 6; abp., 1; bp., 7; parishes, 145; priests, 397 (245 dioc., 152 rel.); sem., 289; bros.,

83; srs., 657; catechists, 6,369; bap.,103,672; Caths., 2,350,000 (23%); tot. pop., 9,970,000.

Republic in the interior of eastern Africa; capital, Lilongwe. Missionary work, begun by Jesuits in the late 16th and early 17th centuries, was generally ineffective until the end of the 19th century. The Missionaries of Africa (White Fathers) arrived in 1889 and later were joined by others. A vicariate was set up in 1897. The hierarchy was established in 1959.

Malaysia

Archd., 2; dioc., 6; abp., 2; bp., 7; parishes, 148; priests, 226 (175 dioc., 51 rel.); p.d., 2; sem., 78; bros., 74; srs., 514; catechists, 1,450; bap., 18,732; Caths., 637,000 (3%); tot. pop., 20,140,000. (AD)

Parliamentary democracy in southeastern Asia; federation of former states of Malaya, Sabah (former Br. North Borneo), and Sarawak; capital, Kuala Lumpur. Christianity, introduced by Portuguese colonists about 1511, was confined almost exclusively to Malacca until late in the 18th century. The effectiveness of evangelization increased from then on because of the recruitment and training of native clergy. Singapore (see separate entry), founded in 1819, became a center for missionary work. Seventeen thousand Catholics were in the Malacca diocese in 1888. Effective evangelization in Sabah and Sarawak began in the second half of the 19th century. The hierarchy was established in 1973.

Maldives

Republic, an archipelago 400 miles southwest of India and Ceylon; capital, Male. No serious attempt was ever made to evangelize the area, which is completely Muslim. Population, 250,000.

Mali*

Archd., 1; dioc., 5; abp., 1; bp., 5; parishes, 39; priests, 157 (68 dioc., 89 rel.); sem., 43; bros., 65; srs., 195; catechists, 1,014; bap., 3,307; Caths., 110,000 (.1%); tot. pop., 10,790,000.

Republic, inland in western Africa; capital, Bamako. Catholicism was introduced late in the second half of the 19th century. Missionary work made little progress in the midst of the predominantly Muslim population. A vicariate was set up in 1921. The hierarchy was established in 1955.

Malta*

Archd., 1; dioc., 1; abp., 2; bp., 1; parishes, 80; priests, 976 (511 dioc., 465 rel.); sem., 84; bros., 119; srs., 1,368; bap., 5,173; Caths., 347,000 (91.7%); tot. pop., 378,000.

Republic 58 miles south of Sicily; capital, Valletta. Early catacombs and inscriptions are evidence of the early introduction of Christianity. St. Paul was shipwrecked on Malta in 60. Saracens controlled the island(s) from 870 to 1090, a period of difficulty for the Church. The line of bishops extends from 1090 to the present. Church-state conflict developed in recent years over passage of government-sponsored legislation affecting Catholic schools and church-owned property. An agreement reached in 1985 ended the dispute and established a joint commission to study other church-state problems.

Marshall Islands*

P.a., 1; parishes, 4; priests, 6 (rel.); p.d., 2; sem., 2; bros., 10; srs., 15; bap., 75; Caths., 4,000; tot. pop., 50,000.

Island republic in central Pacific Ocean; capital, Majura. Formerly administered by U.S. as part of UN Trust Territory of the Pacific; independent nation, 1991. A prefecture apostolic was erected May 25, 1993 (formerly part of Carolines-Marshall diocese), with U.S. Jesuit Rev. James Gould as first prefect apostolic.

Martinique

Archd., 1; abp., 1; parishes, 47; priests, 64 (38 dioc., 26 rel.); sem., 11; bros., 12; srs., 207; catechists, 2,007; bap., 4,2007 Caths., 351,000; tot. pop., 397,000.

French overseas department in the West Indies, about 130 miles south of Guadeloupe; capital, Fort-de-France. Catholicism was introduced in the 16th century. The hierarchy was established in 1967.

Mauritania

Dioc., 1; bp., 2; parishes, 6; priests, 8 (2 dioc., 6 rel.); p.d., 1; srs., 32; bap., 57; Caths., 4,000 (.2%); tot. pop., 2,280,000. (AD)

Islamic republic on the northwest coast of Africa; capital, Nouakchott. With few exceptions, the Catholics in the country are members of the foreign colony.

Mauritius*

Dioc., 1; card., 1; bp., 1; parishes, 49; priests, 91 (57 dioc., 34 rel.); sem., 7; bros., 32; srs., 281; bap.,6,068; Caths., 285,000 (26.1%); tot. pop., 1,090,000.

Island republic in the Indian Ocean about 500 miles east of Madagascar; capital, Port Louis. Catholicism was introduced by Vincentians in 1722. Port Louis, made a vicariate in 1819 and a diocese in 1847, was a jumping-off point for missionaries to Australia, Madagascar and South Africa.

Mayotte

French overseas island territory, in Indian Ocean off southeast coast of Africa; formerly part of Comoros. Statistics included in Comoros.

Melilla

Spanish possession in northern Africa. Statistics are included in those for Spain.

Mexico*

Archd., 14; dioc. (1997), 63; prel., 6; card., 3; abp., 19; bp., 91; parishes, 5,260; priests, 12,684 (9,222 dioc., 3,462 rel.); p.d., 410; sem., 6,919; bros., 1,356; srs., 27,187; bap., 1,804,549; Caths., 86,305,000 (95.3%); tot. pop., 90,490,000.

Republic in Middle America (United States of Mexico); capital, Mexico City. Christianity was introduced early in the 16th century. Mexico City, made a diocese in 1530, became the missionary and cultural center of the whole country. Missionary work, started in 1524 and forwarded principally by Franciscans, Dominicans, Augustinians and Jesuits, resulted in the baptism of all persons in the central plateau by the end of the century. Progress there and in the rest of the country continued in the following century but tapered off and went into decline in the 18th century, for a variety of reasons ranging from diminishing government support to relaxations of Church discipline. The wars of independence, 1810-21, in which some Catholics participated, created serious problems of adjustment for the Church. Social problems, political unrest and government opposition climaxed in the constitution of 1917 which practically outlawed the Church. Persecution took serious tolls of life and kept the Church underground, under Calles, 1924-1928, again in 1931, and under Cardenas in 1934. President Camacho, 1940-1946, ended persecution and instituted a more lenient policy. The Church, however, still labors under some legal and practical disabilities. In 1990, the Mexican president and the Holy See agreed to exchange permanent personal representatives; full diplomatic relations were established in 1992. Cardinal Juan Jesus Posadas Ocampo, Archbishop of Guadalajara, was shot to death May 24, 1993.

Micronesia*

Dioc., 1; bp., 2; parishes, 20; priests, 28 (12 dioc., 16 rel.); p.d., 36; sem., 13; bros., 1; srs., 56; bap., 1,932; Caths., 56,000; tot. pop., 107,000.

Federated States of Micronesia (Caroline archipelago) in southwest Pacific; capital, Palikir; former U.N. trust territory under U.S. administration; became independent nation September, 1991. Effective evangelization began in the late 1880s. Established diplomatic relations with the Holy See in 1994.

Moldova*

Dioc., 1; a.a., 1; parishes, 7; priests, 8 (5 dioc., 3 rel.); sem., 5; srs., 15; bap., 112; Caths., 15,000 (.34%); tot. pop., 4,340,000.

Independent republic bordering Romania; former constituent republic of the USSR; capital, Kishinev. The majority of people belong to the Orthodox Church. Catholics are mostly of Polish or German descent.

Monaco*

Archd., 1; abp., 1, parishes, 6; priests, 23 (13 dioc., 10 rel.); p.d., 1; sem., 2; srs., 22; bap., 243; Caths., 27,000; tot. pop., 30,000.

Constitutional monarchy, an enclave on the Mediterranean coast of France near the Italian border; capital, Monaco-Ville. Christianity was introduced before 1000. Catholicism is the official religion but freedom is guaranteed for all.

Mongolia*

Mission, 1; priests, 4 (rel.); sem., 3; bros.,3; srs., 4; bap.,14; Caths., 1,000; tot. pop., 2,410,000.

Republic in north central Asia; formerly under communist control; capital Ulaanbaatar. Christianity was introduced by Oriental Orthodox. Some Franciscans were in the country in the 13th and 14th centuries, en route to China. Limited evangelization efforts from the 18th century had little success among the Mongols in Outer Mongolia, where Buddhism has predominated for hundreds of years. There may be a few Catholics in Inner Mongolia. No foreign missionaries have been in the country since 1953. Freedom of worship is guaranteed under the new constitution which went into effect in 1992. The government established relations with the Holy See in 1992 and indicated that missionaries would be welcome to help rebuild the country.

Montserrat

Parish, 1; priests, 3 (1 dioc., 2 rel.); p.d., 1; srs., 3; bap., 3; Caths., 1,000; tot. pop., 12,000.
British island possession in Caribbean; capital, Plymouth. Under ecclesiastical jurisdiction of St. John's-Basseterre diocese, Antigua.

Morocco*

Archd., 2; abp., 2; parishes, 46; priests, 66 (21 dioc., 45 rel.); bros., 15; srs., 291; bap., 63; Caths., 24,000 (.08%); tot. pop., 27,110,000.
Constitutional monarchy in northwest Africa with Atlantic and Mediterranean coastlines; capital, Rabat. Christianity was known in the area by the end of the third century. Bishops from Morocco attended a council at Carthage in 484. Catholic life survived under Visigoth and, from 700, Arab rule; later it became subject to influence from the Spanish, Portuguese and French. Islam is the state religion. The hierarchy was established in 1955.

Mozambique

Archd., 3; dioc., 9; card., 1; abp. 3; bp., 9; parishes, 279; priests, 360 (59 dioc., 301 rel.); sem., 252; bros., 84; srs., 809; catechists, 29,382; bap., 91,106; Caths., 2,767,000 (15.8%); tot. pop., 17,420,000. (AD)
Republic in southeast Africa, bordering on the Indian Ocean; former Portuguese territory (independent, 1975); capital, Maputo (formerly Lourenco Marques). Christianity was introduced by Portuguese Jesuits about the middle of the 16th century. Evangelization continued from then until the 18th century when it went into decline largely because of the Portuguese government's expulsion of the Jesuits. Conditions worsened in the 1830s, improved after 1881, but deteriorated again during the anticlerical period from 1910 to 1925. Conditions improved in 1940, the year Portugal concluded a new concordat with the Holy See and the hierarchy was established. Outspoken criticism by missionaries of Portuguese policies in Mozambique resulted in Church-state tensions in the years immediately preceding independence. The first two native bishops were ordained March 9, 1975. Two ecclesiastical provinces were established in 1984.

Myanmar

Archd., 2; dioc., 10; abp., 2; bp., 14; parishes, 252; priests, 429 (401 dioc., 28 rel.); sem., 229; bros., 63; srs., 1,049; catechists, 2,321; bap., 28,081; Caths., 538,000 (1.1%); tot. pop., 46,530,000. (AD)
A socialist republic in southeast Asia, on the Bay of Bengal, formerly Burma; name changed to Myanmar in 1989; capital, Yangon (Rangoon). Christianity was introduced about 1500. Small-scale evangelization had limited results from the middle of the 16th century until the 1850s when effective organization of the Church began. The hierarchy was established in 1955. Buddhism was declared the state religion in

1961, but the state is now officially secular. In 1965, church schools and hospitals were nationalized. In 1966, all foreign missionaries who had entered the country after 1948 for the first time were forced to leave when the government refused to renew their work permits. Despite these setbacks, the Church has shown some progress in recent years.

Namibia* (South West Africa)

Archd., 1; dioc., 1; v.a., 1; abp., 1; bp., 2; parishes, 67; priests, 74 (9 dioc., 65 rel.); p.d., 39; sem., 12; bros., 34; srs., 284; bap., 8,623; Caths., 269,000 (17%); tot. pop., 1,540,000. (AD)
Independent (Mar. 21, 1990) state in southern Africa; capital, Windhoek. The area shares the history of South Africa. The hierarchy was established in 1994.

Nauru*

Parish, 1; priest, 1 (rel); p.d., 2; srs., 3; bap., 140; Caths., 3,000; tot. pop., 7,000.
Independent republic in western Pacific; capital, Yaren. Forms part of the Tarawa and Nauru diocese (Kiribati). Established diplomatic relations with the Holy See in 1992.

Nepal*

P.a. (1997), 1; parishes, 20; priests, 38 (5 dioc.; 33 rel.); sem., 21; bros., 3; srs., 80; bap., 136; Caths., 5,000; tot. pop., 21,920,000.
Constitutional monarchy, the only Hindu kingdom in the world, in central Asia south of the Himalayas between India and Tibet; capital, Kathmandu. Little is known of the country before the 15th century. Some Jesuits passed through from 1628 and some sections were evangelized in the 18th century, with minimal results, before the country was closed to foreigners. Conversions from Hinduism, the state religion, are not recognized in law and punishable by imprisonment. Christian missionary work is not allowed.

Netherlands*

Archd., 1; dioc., 6; mil ord.; card., 2; bp., 24; parishes, 1,718; priests 4,521 (1,754 dioc., 2,767 rel.); p.d., 221; sem., 226; bros., 1,798; srs., 14,250; bap., 41,215; Caths., 5,709,000 (36.9%); tot. pop., 15,450,000.
Constitutional monarchy in northwestern Europe; capital, Amsterdam (seat of the government, The Hague). Evangelization, begun about the turn of the sixth century by Irish, Anglo-Saxon and Frankish missionaries, resulted in Christianization of the country by 800 and subsequent strong influence on The Lowlands. Invasion by French Calvinists in 572 brought serious losses to the Catholic Church and made the Reformed Church dominant. Catholics suffered a practical persecution of official repression and social handicap in the 17th century. The schism of Utrecht occurred in 1724. Only one-third of the population was Catholic in 1726. The Church had only a skeleton organization from 1702 to 1853, when the hierarchy was reestablished. Despite this upturn, cultural isolation was the experience of Catholics until about 1914. From then on new vigor came into the life of the Church, and a whole new climate of inter-

faith relations began to develop. Before and for some years following the Second Vatican Council, the thrust and variety of thought and practice in the Dutch Church moved it to the vanguard position of "progressive" renewal. A particular synod of Dutch bishops held at the Vatican in January, 1980, and aimed at internal improvement of the Church in the Netherlands, had disappointing results, according to reports in 1981.

Netherlands Antilles

Dioc., 1; bp., 1; parishes, 29; priests, 43 (22 dioc., 21 rel.); p.d., 1; sem., 2; bros., 12; srs., 66; bap., 2,066; Caths., 152,000; tot. pop., 200,000. (AD)

Autonomous part of The Netherlands. Consists of two groups of islands in the Caribbean, including Curacao and Bonaire, off the northern coast of Venezuela; and St. Eustatius, Saba and the southern part of St. Maarten, southeast of Puerto Rico; capital, Willemstad on Curacao. Christianity was introduced in the 16th century.

New Caledonia

Archd., 1; abp., 1; parishes, 38; priests, 52 (10 dioc., 42 rel.); p.d., 1; sem., 4; bros., 45; srs., 169; bap., 1,980; Caths., 106,000; tot. pop., 165,000.

French territory consisting of several islands in Oceania east of Queensland, Australia; capital, Noumea. Catholicism was introduced in 1843, nine years after Protestant missionaries began evangelization. A vicariate was organized in 1847. The hierarchy was established in 1966.

New Zealand*

Archd., 1; dioc., 5; mil. ord.; card., 1; bp., 11; parishes, 282; priests, 630 (379 dioc., 251 rel.); p.d., 3; sem., 41; bros., 209; srs., 1,261; bap., 7,374; Caths. 501,000 (14.1%); tot. pop., 3,540,000.

Independent nation in Commonwealth, a group of islands in Oceania 1,200 miles southeast of Australia: capital, Wellington. Protestant missionaries were the first evangelizers. On North Island, Catholic missionaries started work before the establishment of two dioceses in 1848; their work among the Maoris was not organized until about 1881. On South Island, whose first resident priest arrived in 1840, a diocese was established in 1869. These three jurisdictions were joined in a province in 1896. The Marists were the outstanding Catholic missionaries in the area.

Nicaragua*

Archd., 1; dioc., 6; v.a., 1; card., 1; bp., 9; parishes, 205; priests, 356 (187 dioc., 169 rel.); p.d., 42; sem., 225; bros., 96; srs., 893; bap., 86,668; Caths., 4,047,000 (89%); tot. pop., 4,540,000.

Republic in Central America: capital, Managua. Evangelization began shortly after the Spanish conquest about 1524 and eight years later the first bishop took over jurisdiction of the Church in the country. Jesuits were leaders in missionary work during the colonial period, which lasted until the 1820s. Evangelization endeavor increased after establishment of the republic in 1838. In this century it was extended to the Atlantic coastal area where Protestant missionaries had begun work about the middle of the 1900s.

Many church leaders, clerical and lay, supported the aims but not necessarily all the methods of the revolution which forced the resignation and flight July 17, 1979, of Anastasio Somoza Debayle, whose family had controlled the government since the early 1930s. Subsequent developments, especially those related to Sandinista hostility to the Church in the 1980s, have had serious adverse effects on the ministry of the Church.

Niger*

Dioc., 1; bp., 1; parishes, 21; priests, 43 (6 dioc., 37 rel.); sem., 7; bros., 8; srs., 84; bap., 480; Caths., 19,000 (.2%); tot. pop., 9,150,000.

Republic in west central Africa; capital, Niamey. The first mission was set up in 1831. A prefecture apostolic was organized in 1942 and the first diocese was established in 1961. The country is predominantly Muslim.

Nigeria*

Archd., 9; dioc., 31; v.a. (1997), 3; p.a., 1; card., 1; abp., 11; bp., 37; parishes, 1,298; priests, 2,998 (2,249 dioc., 749 rel.); p.d., 7; sem., 3,578; bros., 425; srs., 2,992; catechists, 17,236; bap., 527,721; Caths., 12,412,000 (11%); tot. pop., 111,720,000.

Republic in western Africa; capital, Lagos. The Portuguese introduced Catholicism in the coastal region in the 15th century. Capuchins did some evangelization in the 17th century but systematic missionary work did not get under way along the coast until about 1840. A vicariate for this area was organized in 1870. A prefecture was set up in 1911 for missions in the northern part of the country where Islam was strongly entrenched. From 1967, when Biafra seceded, until early in 1970 the country was torn by civil war. The hierarchy was established in 1950. Six dioceses were made metropolitan sees in 1994; four new dioceses were established as in 1995.

Niue

Parish, 1; priests, 1 (dioc.); srs., 2; bap., 4; Caths., 200; tot. pop., 3,000.

New Zealand self-governing territory in South Pacific. Under ecclesiastical jurisdiction of Rarotonga diocese, Cook Islands.

Northern Mariana Islands

Dioc., 1; bp., 1; parishes, 10; priests, 36 (11 dioc., 25 rel.); p.d., 3; sem., 5; bros., 2; srs., 32; bap., 876; Caths., 56,000; tot. pop., 63,000.

Commonwealth of Northern Mariana Islands, under U.S. sovereignty; formerly part of Trust Territory of Pacific Islands assigned to the U.S. in 1947. Under ecclesiastical jurisdiction of Chalan Kanoa diocese established in 1984.

Norway*

Dioc., 1; prel., 2; bp., 3; parishes, 33; priests, 61 (19 dioc., 42 rel.); p.d., 3; sem., 16; bros., 3; srs., 224; bap., 655; Caths., 41,000 (.9%); tot. pop., 4,360,000.

Constitutional monarchy in northern Europe, the western part of the Scandinavian peninsula; capital, Oslo. Evangelization begun in the ninth century by missionaries from England and Ireland put the Church on a firm footing about the turn of the 11th century. The first diocese was set up in 1153 and development of the Church progressed until the Black Death in 1349 inflicted losses from which it never recovered. Lutheranism, introduced from outside in 1537 and furthered cautiously, gained general acceptance by about 1600 and was made the state religion. Legal and other measures crippled the Church, forcing priests to flee the country and completely disrupting normal activity. Changes for the better came in the 19th century, with the granting of religious liberty in 1845 and the repeal of many legal disabilities in 1897. Norway was administered as a single apostolic vicariate from 1892 to 1932, when it was divided into three jurisdictions under the supervision of the Congregation for the Propagation of the Faith.

Oman

Parishes, 4; priests, 7 (rel.); bap., 214; Caths., 50,000; tot. pop., 2,160,000.

Independent monarchy in eastern corner of Arabian Peninsula; capital, Muscat. Under ecclesiastical jurisdiction of Arabia vicariate apostolic.

Pakistan*

Archd., 2; dioc., 4; abp., 3; bp., 5; parishes, 93; priests, 272 (129 dioc., 143 rel.); sem., 192; bros., 50; srs., 702; bap., 21,228; Caths., 1,009,000 (.8%); tot. pop., 129,810,000.

Islamic republic in southwestern Asia; capital, Islamabad. (Formerly included East Pakistan which became the independent nation of Bangladesh in 1971.) Islam, firmly established in the eighth century, is the state religion. Christian evangelization of the native population began about the middle of the 19th century, years after earlier scattered attempts. The hierarchy was established in 1950.

Palou

Parishes, 2; priests 5 (2 dioc., 3 rel.); bro., 1; srs., 6; bap., 132; Caths., 8,000; tot. pop., 16,000.

Independent (1994) nation in western Pacific; capital, Koror; part of Caroline chain of Islands. Under ecclesiastical jurisdiction of diocese of Caroline Islands, Federated States of Micronesia

Panama*

Archd., 1; dioc., 5; prel., 1; v.a., 1; abp., 3; bp., 11; parishes, 172; priests, 415 (173 dioc., 242 rel.); p.d., 48; sem., 197; bros., 55; srs., 546; bap., 31,499; Caths., 2,276,000 (86.5%); tot. pop., 2,630,000.

Republic in Central America; capital, Panama. Catholicism was introduced by Franciscan missionaries and evangelization started in 1514. The Panama diocese, oldest in the Americas was set up at the same time. The Catholic Church has favored status and state aid for missions, charities and parochial schools, but religious freedom is guaranteed to all religions.

Papua New Guinea*

Archd., 4; dioc., 14; abp., 5; bp., 17; parishes, 380; priests, 489 (120 dioc., 369 rel.); p.d., 8; sem., 274; bros., 307; srs., 879; catechists, 2,257; bap., 34,375; Caths., 1,425,000 (35%); tot. pop., 4,070,000.

Independent (Sept. 16, 1975) republic (formerly under Australian administration) in southwest Pacific. Consists of the eastern half of the southwestern Pacific island of New Guinea and the Northern Solomon Islands; capital, Port Moresby. Marists began evangelization about 1844 but were handicapped by many factors, including "spheres of influence" laid out for Catholic and Protestant missionaries. A prefecture apostolic was set up in 1896 and placed in charge of the Divine Word Missionaries. The territory suffered greatly during World War II. Hierarchy was established for New Guinea and adjacent islands in 1966.

Paraguay*

Archd., 1; dioc., 10; v.a., 2; mil. ord.; abp., 1; bp., 17; parishes, 293; priests, 646 (246 dioc., 400 rel.); p.d., 33; sem., 308; bros.,150; srs., 1,190; bap., 100,936; Caths., 4,531,000 (93.8%); tot. pop., 4,830,000.

Republic in central South America; capital, Asuncion. Catholicism was introduced in 1542, evangelization began almost immediately. A diocese erected in 1547 was occupied for the first time in 1556. On many occasions thereafter dioceses in the country were left unoccupied because of political and other reasons. Jesuits who came into the country after 1609 devised the reductions system for evangelizing the Indians, teaching them agriculture, husbandry, trades and other useful arts, and giving them experience in property use and community life. The reductions were communes of Indians only, under the direction of the missionaries. About 50 of them were established in southern Brazil, Uruguay and northeastern Argentina as well as in Paraguay. They had an average population of three to four thousand. At their peak, some 30 reductions had a population of 100,000. Political officials regarded the reductions with disfavor because they did not control them and feared that the Indians trained in them might foment revolt and upset the established colonial system under Spanish control. The reductions lasted until about 1768 when their Jesuit founders and directors were expelled from Latin America. Church-state relations following independence from Spain in 1811 were tense as often as not because of government efforts to control the Church through continued exercise of Spanish patronage rights and by other means. The Church as well as the whole country suffered a great deal during the War of the Triple Alliance from 1865-70. After that time, the Church had the same kind of experience in Paraguay as in the rest of Latin America with forces of liberalism, anticlericalism, massive educational needs, poverty, a shortage of priests and other personnel. Most recently church leaders have been challenging the government to initiate long-needed economic and social reforms.

Peru*

Archd., 7; dioc., 18; prel., 11; v.a., 8; mil. ord.; card., 1; abp., 11; bp., 46; parishes, 1,388; priests, 2,480 (1,225 dioc., 1,255 rel.); p.d., 70; sem., 1,402; bros., 498; srs., 5,360; catechists, 3,695; bap., 305,672; Caths., 21,545,000 (91.5%); tot. pop., 23,530,000.

Republic on the western coast of South America; capital, Lima. An effective diocese became operational in 1537, five years after the Spanish conquest. Evangelization, already under way, developed for some time after 1570 but deteriorated before the end of the colonial period in the 1820s. The first native-born saint of the new world was a Peruvian, Rose of Lima, a Dominican tertiary who died in 1617 and was canonized in 1671. In the new republic founded after the wars of independence the Church experienced problems of adjustment and many of the difficulties that cropped up in other South American countries: government efforts to control it through continuation of the patronage rights of the Spanish crown; suppression of houses of religious and expropriation of church property; religious indifference and outright hostility. The Church has special status but is not an established religion. Repressive measures by the government against labor protests were condemned by Church leaders in the past several years. Violence related to activities of the Maoist Sendero Luminoso in recent years have had adverse effects on church ministry.

Philippines*

Archd., 16; dioc., 50; prel., 6; v.a., 7; mil. ord.; card., 3; abp., 22; bp.,881; parishes, 2,525; priests, 6,657 (4,353 dioc., 2,304 rel.); p.d., 16; sem., 7,203; bros., 635; srs., 9,824; catechists, 2,204; bap., 1,591,483; Caths., 58,735,000 (83.6%); tot. pop., 70,270,000.

Republic, an archipelago of 7,000 islands off the southeast coast of Asia; capital, Quezon City (de facto, Manila). Systematic evangelization was begun in 1564 and resulted in firm establishment of the Church by the 19th century. During the period of Spanish rule, which lasted from the discovery of the islands by Magellan in 1521 to 1898, the Church experienced difficulties with the patronage system under which the Spanish crown tried to control ecclesiastical affairs through episcopal and other appointments. This system ended in 1898 when the United States gained possession of the islands and instituted a policy of separation of Church and state. Anticlericalism flared late in the 19th century. The Aglipayan schism, an attempt to set up a nationalist church, occurred a few years later, in 1902. The government of Ferdinand Marcos, under attack by people of the church for a number of years for violations of human rights, was replaced in 1986. Since then, communist groups have waged campaigns against the Church.

Poland*

Archd., 15; dioc., 26; mil. ord.; ordinariate, 1; cards.,4; abps.,14; bps.,95; parishes,9,514; priests, 25,838 (20,091 dioc., 5,747 rel.); p.d., 26; sem., 7,310; bros., 1,320; srs., 24,964; bap., 438,461; Caths., 36,835,000 (95.4%); tot. pop., 38,590,000.

Republic in eastern Europe; capital, Warsaw. The first traces of Christianity date from the second half of the ninth century. Its spread was accelerated by the union of the Slavs in the 10th century. The first bishopric was set up in 968. The Gniezno archdiocese, with suffragan sees and a mandate to evangelize the borderlands as well as Poland, was established in 1000. Steady growth continued thereafter, with religious orders and their schools playing a major role. Some tensions with the Orthodox were experienced.

The Reformation, supported mainly by city dwellers and the upper classes, peaked from about the middle of the 16th century, resulting in numerous conversions to Lutheranism, the Reformed Church and the Bohemian Brethren. A successful Counter-Reformation, with the Jesuits in a position of leadership, was completed by about 1632. The movement served a nationalist as well as religious purpose; in restoring religious unity to a large degree, it united the country against potential invaders, the Swedes, Russians and Turks. The Counter-Reformation had bad side effects, leading to the repression of Protestants long after it was over and to prejudice against Orthodox who returned to allegiance with Rome in 1596 and later. The Church, in the same manner as the entire country, was adversely affected by the partitions of the 18th and 19th centuries. Russification hurt the Orthodox who had reunited with Rome and the Latins who were in the majority. Germans extended their Kulturkampf to the area they controlled. The Austrians exhibited some degree of tolerance. In the republic established after World War I the Church reorganized itself, continued to serve as a vital force in national life, and enjoyed generally harmonious relations with the state. Progressive growth was strong until 1939 when disaster struck in the form of invasion by German and Russian forces and six years of war. In 1945, seven years before the adoption of a Soviet-type of constitution, the Communist-controlled government initiated a policy that included a constant program of atheistic propaganda; a strong campaign against the hierarchy and clergy; the imprisonment in 1948 of 700 priests and even more religious; rigid limitation of the activities of religious; censorship and curtailment of the Catholic press and Catholic Action; interference with church administration and appointments of the clergy; the "deposition" of Cardinal Wyszynski in 1953 and the imprisonment of other members of the hierarchy; the suppression of "Caritas," the Catholic charitable organization; promotion of "Progressive Catholic" activities and a small minority of "patriotic priests." Establishment of the Gomulka regime, the freeing of Cardinal Wyszynski in October, 1956, and the signing of an agreement two months later by bishops and state officials, led to some improvement of conditions. The underlying fact, however, was that the regime conceded to Catholics only so much as was necessary to secure support of the government as a more tolerable evil than the harsh and real threat of a Russian-imposed puppet government like that in Hungary. This has been the controlling principle in Church-state relations. Auxiliary Bishop Ladislaw Rubin of Gniezno sketched the general state of affairs in March, 1968. He said that there was no sign that the government had any intention of releasing its oppressive grip on the Church. As evidence of the "climate of asphyxiation" in the country he cited: persistent questioning of priests by officials concerning their activities; the prohibition against Catholic schools, hospitals and charitable works; the financial burden of a 60 per cent tax on church income. Cardinal Wyszynski denounced "enforced atheism" in a Lenten pastoral in the same year. In May, 1969, the bishops drafted a list of grievances against the government which, they said, were "only some examples of difficulties which demonstrated the situation of the Church in our homeland." The grievances were: refusal of permits to build new churches and establish new parishes; refusal of permission "for the organization of new religion classes"; pressure on Catholics who attend religious ceremonies; censorship and the lack of an independent Catholic daily newspaper; lack of representation in public life; restriction of "freedom to conduct normal pastoral work" in the western portion of the country. There was a move toward improvement in Church-state relations in 1971-72. In 1973, the Polish bishops issued a pastoral letter urging Catholics to resist the official atheism imposed by the government. In 1974 the bishops expressed approval of renewed Vatican efforts at regularizing Church-state relations but insisted that they (the bishops) be consulted on every step of the negotiations. The bishops have continued their sharp criticism of anti-religious policies and human rights violations of the government. Regular contacts on a working level were initiated by the Vatican and Poland in 1974; regular diplomatic relations were established in 1989. Cardinal Karol Wojtyla of Cracow was elected to the papacy in 1978. Church support was strong for the independent labor movement, Solidarity, which was recognized by the government in August, 1980, but outlawed in December, 1981, when martial law was imposed (martial law was suspended in 1982). In May, 1989, following recognition of Solidarity and a series of political changes, the Catholic Church was given legal status for the first time since the communists took control of the government in 1944. In 1990, a new constitution was adopted declaring Poland a democratic state. In 1992, the Pope restructured the Church in Poland, establishing 8 more provinces and 13 new dioceses. A new concordat between the Polish government and the Holy See was signed in 1993. Since the fall of communism in 1989, the influence of the Church has declined, according to reports from various sources. (See Index for papal visit.)

Portugal*

Patriarchate, 1; archd., 2; dioc., 17; mil. ord.; card., 1; abp., 7; bp., 40; parishes, 4,346; priests, 4,407 (3,362 dioc., 1,045 rel.); p.d., 74; sem., 716; bros., 392; srs., 7,158; bap., 98,687; Caths., 9,948,000 (92%); tot. pop., 10,800,000.

Republic in the western part of the Iberian peninsula; capital, Lisbon. Christianity was introduced before the fourth century. From the fifth century to early in the eighth century the Church experienced difficulties from the physical invasion of barbarians and the intellectual invasion of doctrinal errors in the forms of Arianism, Priscillianism and Pelagianism. The Church survived under the rule of Arabs from about 711 and of the Moors until 1249. Ecclesiastical life was fairly vigorous from 1080 to 1185, and monastic influence became strong. A decline set in about 1450. Several decades later Portugal became the jumping-off place for many missionaries to newly discovered colonies. The Reformation had little effect in the country. Beginning about 1750, Pombal, minister of foreign affairs and prime minister, mounted a frontal attack on the Jesuits whom he succeeded in expelling from Portugal and the colonies. His anti-Jesuit campaign successful Pombal also attempted, and succeeded to some extent, in controlling the Church in Portugal until his fall from power about 1777. Liberal revolutionaries with anti-Church policies made the 19th century a difficult one for the Church. Similar policies prevailed in Church-state relations in this century until the accession of Salazar to power in 1928. In 1940 he concluded a concordat with the Holy See which regularized Church-state relations but still left the Church in a subservient condition. The prevailing spirit of church authorities in Portugal has been conservative. In 1971 several priests were tried for subversion for speaking out against colonialism and for taking part in guerrilla activities in Angola. A military coup of Apr. 25, 1974, triggered a succession of chaotic political developments which led to an attempt by Communists, after receiving only 18 per cent of the votes cast in a national election, to take over the government in the summer of 1975.

Puerto Rico

Archd., 1; dioc., 4; card., 1; bp., 8; parishes, 353; priests, 793 (414 dioc., 379 rel.); p.d., 398; sem., 126; bros., 85; srs., 1,132; bap., 42,282; Caths., 3,034,000 (82.6%); tot. pop., 3,670,000. (AD)

A U.S. commonwealth, the smallest of the Greater Antilles, 885 miles southeast of the southern coast of Florida; capital, San Juan. Following its discovery by Columbus in 1493, the island was evangelized by Spanish missionaries and remained under Spanish ecclesiastical as well as political control until 1898 when it became a possession of the United States. The original diocese, San Juan, was erected in 1511. The present hierarchy was established in 1960.

Qatar

Parish, 1; priest, 1 (dioc.); bap., 83; tot. pop., 550,000.

Independent state in the Persian Gulf; capital, Doha. Under ecclesiastical jurisdiction of Arabia vicariate apostolic.

Reunion

Dioc., 1; bp., 1; parishes, 76; priests, 105 (56 dioc., 49 rel.); p.d., 6; sem., 24; bros., 38; srs., 377; bap., 10,955; Caths., 574,000 (88.3%); tot. pop., 650,000. (AD)

French overseas department, 450 miles east of Madagascar; capital, Saint-Denis. Catholicism was introduced in 1667 and some intermittent missionary work was done through the rest of the century. A prefecture apostolic was organized in 1712. Vincentians began work there in 1817 and were joined later by Holy Ghost Fathers.

Rhodes

Greek island in the Aegean Sea, 112 miles from the southwestern coast of Asia Minor. A diocese was established about the end of the third century. A bishop from Rhodes attended the Council of Nicaea in 325. Most of the Christians followed the Eastern Churches into schism in the 11th century and became Orthodox. Turks controlled the island from 1522 to 1912. The small Catholic population, for whom a diocese existed from 1328 to 1546, lived in crossfire between Turks and Orthodox. After 1719 Franciscans provided pastoral care for the Catholics, for whom an archdiocese was erected in 1928. Statistics are included in Greece.

Romania*

Archd., 3; dioc., 8; ord., 1; card., 1; abp., 4; bp., 9; parishes, 1,799; priests, 1,525 (1,380 dioc., 145 rel.); p.d., 4; sem., 880; bros., 256; srs., 981; bap., 11,879; Caths., 2,654,000 (11.7%); tot. pop., 22,680,000.

Socialist republic in southeastern Europe; capital, Bucharest. Latin Christianity, introduced in the third century, all but disappeared during the barbarian invasions. The Byzantine Rite was introduced by the Bulgars about the beginning of the eighth century and established firm roots. It eventually became Orthodox, but a large number of its adherents returned later to union with Rome. Attempts to reintroduce the Latin Rite on any large scale have been unsuccessful. Communists took over the government following World War II, forced the abdication of Michael I in 1947, and enacted a Soviet type of constitution in 1952. By that time a campaign against religion was already in progress. In 1948 the government denounced a concordat concluded in 1929, nationalized all schools and passed a law on religions which resulted in the disorganization of Church administration. The 1.5 million-member Romanian Byzantine Rite Church, by government decree, was incorporated into the Romanian Orthodox Church, and the Orthodox bishops then seized the cathedrals of Roman Catholic bishops. Five of the six Latin Rite bishops were immediately disposed of by the government, and the last was sentenced to 18 years' imprisonment in 1951, when a great many arrests of priests and laymen were made. Religious orders were suppressed in 1949. Since 1948 more than 50 priests have been executed and 200 have died in prison. One hundred priests were reported in prison at the end of 1958. Some change for the better in Church-state relations was reported after the middle of the summer of 1964, although restrictions were still in effect. About 1,200 priests were engaged in parish work in August, 1965. Conditions improved in 1990 with the change of government. The hierarchy was restored and diplomatic relations with the Holy See were reestablished.

Russia*

Dioc., 1; a.a., 2 (1 for European Russia, 1 for Siberia); ap. ex., 1; abp., 2; bp., 1; priests, 165 (39 dioc., 126 rel.); p.d., 1; sem., 37; bros., 4; srs, 180; bap., 1,916; Caths.,1,306,000; tot. pop., 148,140,000.

Federation in Europe and Asia; capital, Moscow. (See Union of Soviet Socialist Republic for background information.)

Rwanda*

Archd., 1; dioc., 8; abp., 1; bp., 6; parishes, 127; priests, 484 (316 dioc., 168 rel.); sem., 254; bros., 263; srs., 1,109; bap., 141,859; Caths., 3,642,000 (45.8%); tot. pop., 7,950,000.

Republic in east central Africa; capital, Kigali. Catholicism was introduced about the turn of the 20th century. The hierarchy was established in 1959. Intertribal warfare between the ruling Hutus (90 per cent of the population) and the Tutsis (formerly the ruling aristocracy) plagued the country for a number of years. In April, 1994, the deaths of the presidents of Rwanda and Burundi in a suspicious plane crash sparked the outbreak of a ferocious civil war. Among the thousands of victims — mostly Tutsis— were three bishops and about twenty-five percent of the clergy. Many more thousands fled the country mainly to Zaire which became another attleground in late 1996-97.

Saint Christopher and Nevis

Parishes, 4; priests, 4 (1 dioc., 3 rel.); bro., 1; srs., 5; bap., 42; Caths., 5,000; tot. pop., 46,000. (AD)

Independent (Sept. 19, 1983) island states in West Indies; capital, Basseterre, on St. Christopher; Charlestown, on Nevis. Under ecclesiastical jurisdiction of St. John's-Basseterre diocese, Antigua.

Saint Helena

Independent mission, 1; parish, 1; priests, 2 (rel.); Caths., 100; tot. pop., 7,000.

Comprises British Island possessions of St. Helena, Ascension and Tristan da Cunha in the South Atlantic; formerly under ecclesiastical jurisdiction of Cape Town archdiocese (South Africa).

Saint Lucia*

Archd., 1; abp., 1; bp., 1; parishes, 23; priests, 37 (19 dioc., 18 rel.); p.d., 8; bros., 4; srs., 45; bap., 2,505; Caths., 109,000; tot. pop., 140,000.

Independent (Feb. 22, 1979) island state in West Indies; capital, Castries.

Saint Pierre and Miquelon

V.a., 1; bp., 1; parishes, 3; priests, 2 (rel.); srs., 7; bap., 89; Caths., 6,000; tot. pop., 6,000.

French overseas department, two groups of islands near the southwest coast of Newfoundland; capital, St. Pierre. Catholicism was introduced about 1689.

Saint Vincent and the Grenadines*

Dioc., 1; bp., 1; parishes, 6; priests, 8 (4 dioc., 4 rel.); bros., 4; srs., 13; bap., 148; Caths., 10,000; tot. pop., 110,000.

Independent state (1979) in West Indies; capital, Kingstown. The Kingstown diocese (St. Vincent) was established in 1989; it was formerly part of Bridgetown-Kingstown diocese with see in Barbados.

American Samoa

Dioc., 1; bp., 1; parishes, 8; priests, 10 (9 dioc., 1 rel.); p.d., 18; sem., 9; bros., 2; srs., 15; bap., 397; Caths., 9,000; tot. pop., 56,000.

Unincorporated U.S. territory in southwestern Pacific, consisting of six small islands; seat of government, Pago Pago on the Island of Tutuila. Samoa-Pago Pago diocese established in 1982.

Western Samoa*

Archd., 1; card., 1; parishes, 27; priests, 44 (24 dioc., 20 rel.); p.d., 3; sem., 11; bros., 22; srs., 89; bap., 1,527; Caths., 37,000; tot. pop., 166,000.

Independent state in the southwestern Pacific; capital, Apia. Catholic missionary work began in 1845. Most of the missions now in operation were established by 1870 when the Catholic population numbered about 5,000. Additional progress was made in missionary work from 1896. The first Samoan priest was ordained in 1892. A diocese was established in 1966; elevated to a metropolitan see in 1982.

San Marino*
Parishes, 12; priests, 27 (10 dioc., 17 rel.); p.d., 1; bro., 1; srs., 24; bap., 225; Caths., 24,000; tot. pop., 25,000.

Republic, a 24-square-mile enclave in northeastern Italy; capital, San Marino. The date of initial evangelization is not known, but a diocese was established by the end of the third century. Ecclesiastically, it forms part of the diocese of San Marino-Montefeltro in Italy.

Sao Tome and Principe*
Dioc., 1; bp., 1; parishes, 12; priests, 7 (rel.); sem. 8; bros., 5; srs., 39; bap., 2,882; Caths., 101,000 (83%); tot. pop., 121,000.

Independent republic (July 12, 1975), consisting of two islands off the western coast of Africa in the Gulf of Guinea; former Portuguese territory; capital, Sao Tome. Evangelization was begun by the Portuguese who discovered the islands in 1471-72. The Sao Tome diocese was established in 1534.

Saudi Arabia
Monarchy occupying four-fifths of Arabian peninsula; capital, Riyadh. Population is Muslim; all other religions are banned. Christians in the area are workers from other countries. Under ecclesiastical jurisdiction of Arabia vicariate apostolic.

Population, 17,880,000.

Scotland
Archd., 2; dioc., 6; card., 1; abp., 1; bp., 5; parishes, 450; priests, 873 (680 dioc., 193 rel.); p.d. 14; sem., 69; bros., 107; srs., 812; bap., 11,217; Caths., 748,521 (14.3%); tot. pop., 5,213,100. (1997 Annuario Pontificio.)

Part of the United Kingdom, in the northern British Isles; capital, Edinburgh. Christianity was introduced by the early years of the fifth century. The arrival of St. Columba and his monks in 563 inaugurated a new era of evangelization which reached into remote areas by the end of the sixth century. He was extremely influential in determining the character of the Celtic Church, which was tribal, monastic, and in union with Rome. Considerable disruption of church activity resulted from Scandinavian invasions in the late eighth and ninth centuries. By 1153 the Scottish Church took a turn away from its insularity and was drawn into closer contact with the European community. Anglo-Saxon religious and political relations, complicated by rivalries between princes and ecclesiastical superiors, were not always the happiest. Religious orders expanded greatly in the 12th century. From shortly after the Norman Conquest of England to 1560 the Church suffered adverse effects from the Hundred Years' War, the Black Death, the Western Schism and other developments. In 1560 parliament abrogated papal supremacy over the Church in Scotland and committed the country to Protestantism in 1567. The Catholic Church was proscribed, to remain that way for more than 200 years, and the hierarchy was disbanded. Defections made the Church a minority religion from that time on. Presbyterian church government was ratified in 1690. Priests launched the Scottish Mission in 1653, incorporating themselves as a mission body under a prefect apostolic and working underground to serve the faithful in much the same way their confreres did in England. About 100 heather priests, trained in clandestine places in the heather country, were ordained by the early 19th century. Catholics got some relief from legal disabilities in 1793 and more later. Many left the country about that time. Some of their numbers were filled subsequently by immigrants from Ireland. The hierarchy was restored in 1878. Scotland, though predominantly Protestant, has a better record for tolerance than Northern Ireland.

Senegal*
Archd., 1; dioc., 5; card., 1; bp., 6; parishes, 89; priests, 323 (170 dioc., 153 rel.); sem., 175; bros., 147; srs., 530; bap., 17,340; Caths., 396,000 (4.7%); tot. pop., 8,350,000.

Republic in western Africa; capital, Dakar. The country had its first contact with Catholicism through the Portuguese some time after 1460. Some incidental missionary work was done by Jesuits and Capuchins in the 16th and 17th centuries. A vicariate for the area was placed in charge of the Holy Ghost Fathers in 1779. More effective evangelization efforts were accomplished after the Senegambia vicariate was erected in 1863; the hierarchy was established in 1955.

Seychelles*
Dioc., 1; bp., 1; parishes, 17; priests, 14 (10 dioc., 4 rel.); p.d., 1; bros., 6; srs., 61; bap., 1,390; Caths., 69,000; tot. pop., 77,000.

Independent (1976) group of 92 islands in the Indian Ocean 970 miles east of Kenya; capital, Victoria. Catholicism was introduced in the 18th century. A vicariate apostolic was organized in 1852. All education in the islands was conducted under Catholic auspices until 1954.

Sierra Leone*
Archd., 1; dioc., 2; abp., 2; bp., 2; parishes, 37; priests, 110 (44 dioc., 66 rel.); sem., 78; bros., 39; srs., 65; bap., 2,252; Caths., 135,000 (3%); tot. pop., 4,510,000.

Republic on the western coast of Africa; capital, Freetown. Catholicism was introduced in 1858. Members of the African Missions Society, the first Catholic missionaries in the area, were joined by Holy Ghost Fathers in 1864. Protestant missionaries were active in the area before their Catholic counterparts. Educational work had a major part in Catholic endeavor. The hierarchy was established in 1950. Most of the inhabitants are followers of Traditional African Religions.

Singapore*
Archd., 1; abp., 1; parishes, 30; priests, 129 (79 dioc., 50 rel.); sem., 35; bros., 52; srs., 236; bap.,

3,794; Caths., 132,000 (4.4%); tot. pop., 2,990,000.
Independent island republic off the southern tip of the Malay Peninsula; capital, Singapore. Christianity was introduced in the area by Portuguese colonists about 1511. Singapore was founded in 1819; the first parish church was built in 1846.

Slovakia*

Archd., 2; dioc., 5; ap. ex. (1997), 1; card., 2; abp., 2; bp., 13; parishes, 1,415; priests, 1,981 (1,515 dioc., 466 rel.); p.d., 6; sem., 1,027; bros., 153; srs., 2,953; bap., 54,506; Caths., 3,652,000 (68%); tot. pop., 5,360,000.

Independent state (Jan. 1, 1993); formerly part of Czechoslovakia; capital, Bratislava. Christianity was introduced in Slovakia in the 8th century by Irish and German missionaries and the area was under the jurisdiction of German bishops. In 863, at the invitation of the Slovak ruler Rastislav who wanted to preserve the cultural and liturgical heritage of the people, Sts. Cyril and Methodius began pastoral and missionary work in the region, ministering to the people in their own language. The saints introduced Old Slovak (Old Church Slavonic) into the liturgy and did so much to evangelize the territory that they are venerated as the apostles of Slovakia. A diocese established at Nitra in 880 had a continuous history except for a century ending in 1024. The Church in Slovakia was severely tested by the Reformation and political upheavals. After World War I, when it became part of the Republic of Czechoslovakia, it was 75 per cent Catholic. (For the status of the Church during communist domination, see Czechoslovakia.)

Slovenia*

Archd., 1; dioc., 2; abp., 1; bp., 6; parishes, 797; priests, 1,106 (834 dioc., 292 rel.); p.d., 7; sem., 194; bros., 55; srs., 850; bap., 16,609; Caths., 1,654,000 (83.5%); tot. pop., 1,980,000.

Independent republic (1991) in southeastern Europe; formerly part of Yugoslavia; capital, Ljubljana. Established diplomatic relations with the Holy See in 1992.

Solomon Islands*

Archd., 1; dioc., 2; abp., 1; bp., 3; parishes, 28; priests, 48 (14 dioc., 34 rel.); sem., 33; bros., 18; srs., 109; bap., 2,824; Caths., 72,000 (18.9%); tot. pop., 380,000.

Independent (July 7, 1978) island group in Oceania; capital, Honiara, on Guadalcanal. Evangelization of the Southern Solomons, begun earlier but interrupted because of violence against them, was resumed by the Marists in 1898. A vicariate apostolic was organized in 1912. A similar jurisdiction was set up for the Western Solomons in 1959. World War II caused a great deal of damage to mission installations.

Somalia

Dioc., 1; parish, 1; priests, 3 (1 dioc., 2 rel.); bro., 1; srs., 4; Caths., 200; tot. pop., 9,250,000. (AD)

Republic on the eastern coast of Africa; capital, Mogadishu. The country has been Muslim for centuries. Pastoral activity has been confined to immigrants. Schools and hospitals were nationalized in 1972, resulting in the departure of some foreign missionaries.

South Africa*

Archd., 4; dioc., 21; v.a., 1; mil. ord.; abp., 6; bp., 29; parishes, 731; priests, 1,137 (360 dioc., 777 rel.); p.d., 198; sem., 269; bros., 243; srs., 2,880; catechists, 12,029; bap., 60,459; Caths., 3,030,000 (7.3%); tot. pop., 41,240,000.

Republic in the southern part of Africa; capitals, Cape Town (legislative), Pretoria (administrative) and Bloemfontein (judicial). Christianity was introduced by the Portuguese who discovered the Cape of Good Hope in 1488. Boers, who founded Cape Town in 1652, expelled Catholics from the region. There was no Catholic missionary activity from that time until the 19th century. After a period of British opposition, a bishop established residence in 1837 and evangelization got under way thereafter among the Bantus and white immigrants. The hierarchy was established in 1951. The white supremacy policy of apartheid which seriously infringed on the human rights of native blacks and impeded the Church from carrying out its pastoral, educational and social service functions finally ceased to exist in 1994, following the first all-race election.

Spain*

Archd., 14; dioc., 54; mil. ord.; card., 5; abp., 18; bp., 88; parishes, 21,641; priests, 29,019 (19,542 dioc., 9,477 rel.); p.d., 201; sem., 3,191; bros., 5,529; srs., 65,991; bap., 318,594; Caths., 36,956,000 (94.2%); tot. pop., 39,210,000.

Constitutional monarchy on the Iberian peninsula in southwestern Europe; capital, Madrid. Christians were on the peninsula by 200; some of them suffered martyrdom during persecutions of the third century. A council held in Elvira about 304/6 enacted the first legislation on clerical celibacy in the West. Vandals invaded the peninsula in the fifth century, bringing with them an Arian brand of Christianity which they retained until their conversion following the baptism of their king Reccared, in 589. One of the significant developments of the seventh century was the establishment of Toledo as the primatial see. The Visigoth kingdom lasted to the time of the Arab invasion, 711-14. The Church survived under Muslim rule but experienced some doctrinal and disciplinary irregularities as well as harassment. Reconquest of most of the peninsula was accomplished by 1248; unification was achieved during the reign of Ferdinand and Isabella. The discoveries of Columbus and other explorers ushered in an era of colonial expansion in which Spain became one of the greatest mission-sending countries in history. In 1492, in repetition of anti-Semitic actions of 694, the expulsion of unbaptized Jews was decreed, leading to mass baptisms but a questionable number of real conversions in 1502. (The Jewish minority numbered about 165,000.) Activity by the Inquisition followed. Spain was not seriously affected by the Reformation. Ecclesiastical decline set in about 1650. Anti-Church actions authorized by a constitution enacted in 1812 resulted in the suppression of religious and other encroachments on the leaders, people and goods of the Church.

Political, religious and cultural turmoil recurred during the 19th century and into the 20th. A revolutionary republic was proclaimed in 1931, triggering a series of developments which led to civil war from 1936 to 1939. During the conflict, which pitted leftist Loyalists against the forces of Francisco Franco, 6,632 priests and religious and an unknown number of lay persons perished in addition to thousands of victims of combat. One-man, one-party rule, established after the civil war and with rigid control policies with respect to personal liberties and social and economic issues, continued for more than 35 years before giving way after the death of Franco to democratic reforms. The Catholic Church, long the established religion, was disestablished under a new constitution providing guarantees of freedom for other religions as well. Disestablishment was ratified with modifications of a 1976 revision of the earlier concordat of 1953.

Sri Lanka*

Archd., 1; dioc., 10; abp., 2; bp., 13; parishes, 373; priests, 838 (541 dioc., 297 rel.); p.d., 1; sem., 386; bros., 214; srs., 2,309; bap., 26,226; Caths., 1,210,000 (6.6%); tot. pop., 18,350,000.

Independent socialist republic, island southeast of India (formerly Ceylon); capital, Colombo. Effective evangelization began in 1543 and made great progress by the middle of the 17th century. The Church was seriously hampered during the Dutch period from about 1650 to 1795. Anti-Catholic laws were repealed by the British in 1806. The hierarchy was established in 1886. Leftist governments and other factors have worked against the Church since the country became independent in 1948. The high percentage of indigenous clergy and religious has been of great advantage to the Church.

Sudan*

Archd., 2; dioc., 7; abp., 3; bp., 10; parishes, 103; priests, 215 (107 dioc., 108 rel.); p.d., 4; sem., 221; bros., 65; srs., 271; catechists, 3,410; bap., 56,293; Caths., 2,279,000 (8.1%); tot. pop., 28,100,000.

Republic in northeastern Africa, the largest country on the continent; capital Khartoum. Christianity was introduced from Egypt and gained acceptance in the sixth century. Under Arab rule, it was eliminated in the northern region. No Christians were in the country in 1600. Evangelization attempts begun in the 19th century in the south yielded hard-won results. By 1931 there were nearly 40,000 Catholics there, and considerable progress was made by missionaries after that time. In 1957, a year after the republic was established, Catholic schools were nationalized. An act restrictive of religious freedom went into effect in 1962, resulting in the harassment and expulsion of foreign missionaries. By 1964 all but a few Sudanese missionaries had been forced out of the southern region. The northern area, where Islam predominates, is impervious to Christian influence. Late in 1971 some missionaries were allowed to return to work in the South. Southern Sudan was granted regional autonomy within a unified country in March, 1972, thus ending often bitter fighting between the North and South dating back to 1955. The hierarchy was established in 1974. The imposition of Islamic penal codes in 1984 was a cause of concern to all Christian churches. Recent government policies have denied Christians the right to places of worship and authorization to gather for prayer..

Suriname*

Dioc., 1; bp., 1; parishes, 30; priests, 24 (5 dioc., 19 rel.); sem., 3; bros., 9; srs., 36; bap., 1,942; Caths., 91,000 (21%); tot. pop., 420,000.

Independent (Nov. 25, 1975) state in northern South America (formerly Dutch Guiana); capital, Paramaribo, Catholicism was introduced in 1683. Evangelization began in 1817.

Swaziland*

Dioc., 1; bp., 1; parishes, 14; priests, 33 (6 dioc., 27 rel.); sem., 7; bros., 7; srs., 74; bap., 1,353; Caths., 48,000 (5.2%); tot. pop., 910,000.

Monarchy in southern Africa; almost totally surrounded by South Africa; capital, Mbabane. Missionary work was entrusted to the Servites in 1913. A prefecture apostolic was organized in 1923. The hierarchy was established in 1951. Established diplomatic relations with the Holy See in 1992.

Sweden*

Dioc., 1; bp., 2; parishes, 40; priests, 127 (57 dioc., 70 rel.); p.d., 14; sem., 19; bros., 13; srs., 241; bap., 1,402; Caths., 165,000 (1.8%); tot. pop., 8,830,109.

Constitutional monarchy in northwestern Europe; capital, Stockholm. Christianity was introduced by St. Ansgar, a Frankish monk, in 829/30. The Church became well established in the 12th century and was a major influence at the end of the Middle Ages. Political and other factors favored the introduction and spread of the Lutheran Church which became the state religion in 1560. The Augsburg Confession of 1530 was accepted by the government; all relations with Rome were severed; monasteries were suppressed; the very presence of Catholics in the country was forbidden in 1617. A decree of tolerance for foreign Catholics was issued about 1781. Two years later a vicariate apostolic was organized for the country. In 1873 Swedes were given the legal right to leave the Lutheran Church and join another Christian church. (Membership in the Lutheran Church is presumed by law unless notice is given of membership in another church.) In 1923 there were only 11 priests and five churches in the country. Since 1952 Catholics have enjoyed almost complete religious freedom. The hierarchy was reestablished in 1953. Hindrances to growth of the Church are the strongly entrenched established church, limited resources, a clergy shortage and the size of the country.

Switzerland*

Dioc., 6; abb., 2; card., 2; abp., 4; bp., 17; parishes, 1,668; priests, 3,457 (1,987 dioc., 1,470 rel.); p.d., 80; sem., 226; bros., 484; srs., 7,463; bap., 32,429; Caths., 3,266,000 (46.3%); tot. pop., 7,040,000.

Confederation in central Europe; capital, Bern. Christianity was introduced in the fourth century or earlier and was established on a firm footing before the barbarian invasions of the sixth century. Constance, established as a diocese in the seventh century, was a stronghold of the faith against the pagan Alamanni, in particular, who were not converted until some time in the ninth century. During this period of struggle with the barbarians, a number of monasteries of great influence were established. The Reformation in Switzerland was triggered by Zwingli in 1519 and furthered by him at Zurich until his death in battle against the Catholic cantons in 1531. Calvin set in motion the forces that made Geneva the international capital of the Reformation and transformed it into a theocracy. Catholics mobilized a Counter-Reformation in 1570, six years after Calvin's death. Struggle between Protestant and Catholic cantons was a fact of Swiss life for several hundred years. The Helvetic Constitution enacted at the turn of the 19th century embodied anti-Catholic measures and consequences, among them the dissolution of 130 monasteries. The Church was reorganized later in the century to meet the threats of liberalism, radicalism and the Kulturkampf. In the process, the Church, even though on the defensive, gained the strength and cohesion that characterizes it to the present time. The six dioceses in the country are immediately subject to the Holy See. In 1973, constitutional articles banning Jesuits from the country and prohibiting the establishment of convents and monasteries were repealed.

Syria*

Patriarchates, 3 (Antioch of Maronites, Greek Melkites and Syrians; patriarchs of Maronites and Syrians reside in Lebanon); archd., 12 (1 Armenian, 2 Maronite, 5 Greek Melkite, 4 Syrian); dioc., 3 (Armenian, Chaldean, Maronite); v.a., 1 (Latin); patriarch, 1; abp., 16; bp., 4; parishes, 200; priests, 227 (153 dioc., 74 rel.); p.d., 8; sem., 83; bros., 19; srs., 401; bap., 2,569; Caths., 295,000 (2%); tot. pop., 14,190,000.

Arab socialist republic in southwest Asia; capital, Damascus. Christian communities were formed in apostolic times. It is believed that St. Peter established a see at Antioch before going to Rome. Damascus became a center of influence. The area was the place of great men and great events in the early history of the Church. Monasticism developed there in the fourth century. So did the Monophysite and Monothelite heresies to which portion of the Church succumbed. Byzantine Syrians who remained in communion with Rome were given the name Melkites. Christians of various persuasions _ Jacobites, Orthodox and Melkites _ were subject to various degrees of harassment from the Arabs who took over in 638 and from the Ottoman Turks who isolated the country and remained in control from 1516 to the end of World War II.

Taiwan

Archd., 1; dioc., 6; abp., 3; bp., 9; parishes, 446; priests, 708 (208 dioc., 500 rel.); sem., 138; bros., 108; srs., 1,080; bap., 3,935; Caths., 300,000 (1.3%); tot. pop., 22,425,000.

Democratic island state 100 miles off the southern coast of mainland China (also known as Formosa); capital, Taipei. Attempts to introduce Christianity in the 17th century were unsuccessful. Evangelization in the 19th century resulted in some 1,300 converts in 1895. Missionary endeavor was hampered by the Japanese who occupied the island following the Sino-Japanese war of 1894-95. Nine thousand Catholics were reported in 1938. Great progress was made in missionary endeavor among the Chinese who emigrated to the island (seat of the Nationalist Government of the Republic of China) following the Communist take-over of the mainland in 1949. The hierarchy was established in 1952.

Tajikistan*

Priests, 2 (1 dioc., 1 rel.); srs., 4; Caths., 32,000; tot. pop., 5,840,000.

Independent republic (1992) bordering China and Afghanistan; formerly part of the USSR; capital, Dushanbe. The majority of the population is Sunni Muslim.

Tanzania*

Archd., 4; dioc., 25; card., 1; abp., 5; bp., 28; parishes, 771; priests, 1,909 (1,258 dioc., 651 rel.); sem., 836; bros., 544; srs., 6,543; catechists, 11,761; bap., 255,615; Caths., 7,355,000 (24.2%); tot. pop., 30,340,000.

Republic (consisting of former Tanganyika on the eastern coast of Africa and former Zanzibar, an island group off the eastern coast); capital, Dar es Salaam. The first Catholic mission in the former Tanganyikan portion of the republic was manned by Holy Ghost Fathers in 1868. The hierarchy was established there in 1953. Zanzibar was the landing place of Augustinians with the Portuguese in 1499. Some evangelization was attempted between then and 1698 when the Arabs expelled all priests from the territory. There was no Catholic missionary activity from then until the 1860s. The Holy Ghost Fathers arrived in 1863 and were entrusted with the mission in 1872. Zanzibar was important as a point of departure for missionaries to Tanganyika, Kenya and other places in East Africa. A vicariate for Zanzibar was set up in 1906.

Thailand*

Archd., 2; dioc., 8; card., 1; abp., 4; bp., 11; parishes, 312; priests, 581 (343 dioc., 238 rel.); p.d., 2; sem., 281; bros., 154; srs., 1,441; bap., 6,584; Caths., 247,000 (.4%); tot. pop., 59,400,000.

Constitutional monarchy in southeastern Asia (formerly Siam); capital, Bangkok. The first Christians in the region were Portuguese traders who arrived early in the 16th century. A number of missionaries began arriving in 1554 but pastoral care was confined mostly to the Portuguese until the 1660s. Evangelization of the natives got under way from about that time. A seminary was organized in 1665, a vicariate was set up four years later, and a point of departure was established for missionaries to Tonkin, Cochin China and China. Persecution and death for some of the missionaries ended evangelization efforts in 1688. It was resumed, however, and made progress from 1824 onwards. In 1881 missionaries were sent from Siam to neighboring Laos. The hierarchy was established in 1965. Abp. Michai Kitbunchu was named the first Thai cardinal in 1983.

Togo*

Archd., 1; dioc., 6; abp., 1; bp., 5; parishes, 111; priests, 318 (193 dioc., 125 rel.); sem., 216; bros., 180; srs., 559; bap., 33,836; Caths., 956,000 (21.6%); tot. pop., 4,410,000.

Republic on the western coast of Africa; capital, Lome. The first Catholic missionaries in the area, where slave raiders operated for nearly 200 years, were members of the African Missions Society who arrived in 1563. They were followed by Divine Word Missionaries in 1914, when a prefecture apostolic was organized. At that time the Catholic population numbered about 19,000. The African Missionaries returned after their German predecessors were deported following World War I. The first native priest was ordained in 1922. The hierarchy was established in 1955.

Tokelau

Independent Mission, 1; parishes, 2; priest, 1 (dioc.); p.d., 1; sem., 1; srs., 3; bap., 20; Caths., 1,000; tot. pop., 2,000. (AD)

Pacific islands administered by New Zealand. Established as an independent mission in 1992.

Tonga*

Dioc., 1; bp., 1; parishes, 13; priests, 21 (12 dioc., 9 rel.); sem., 21; bros., 10; srs., 52; bap., 541; Caths., 14,000 (14.5%); tot. pop., 96,000.

Polynesian monarchy in the southwestern Pacific, consisting of about 150 islands; capital Nuku'alofa. Marists started missionary work in 1842, some years after Protestants had begun evangelization. By 1880 the Catholic population numbered about 1,700. A vicariate was organized in 1937. The hierarchy was established in 1966. Established diplomatic relations with the Holy See in 1994.

Trinidad and Tobago*

Archd., 1; abp., 1; bp., 1; parishes, 62; priests, 98 (42 dioc., 56 rel.); sem., 21; bros., 17; srs., 182; bap., 5,325; Caths., 395,000 (31.6%); tot. pop., 1,250,000.

Independent nation, consisting of two islands in the Caribbean; capital, Port-of-Spain. The first Catholic church in Trinidad was built in 1591, years after several missionary ventures had been launched and a number of missionaries killed. Capuchins were there from 1618 until about 1802. Missionary work continued after the British gained control early in the 19th century. Cordial relations have existed between the Church and state, both of which have manifested their desire for the development of native clergy.

Tunisia*

Dioc., 1; abp., 1; parishes, 14; priests, 40 (16 dioc., 24 rel.); sem., 1; bros., 8; srs., 181; bap., 13; Caths., 20,000 (.2%); tot. pop., 8,900,000.

Republic on the northern coast of Africa; capital, Tunis. There were few Christians in the territory until the 19th century. A prefecture apostolic was organized in 1843 and the Carthage archdiocese was established in 1884. The Catholic population in 1892 consisted of most of the approximately 50,000 Europeans in the country. When Tunis became a republic in 1956, most of the Europeans left the country. The

Holy See and the Tunisian government concluded an agreement in 1964 which changed the Carthage archdiocese into a prelacy and handed over some ecclesiastical property to the republic. A considerable number of Muslim students are in Catholic schools, but the number of Muslim converts to the Church has been small.

Turkey*

Patriarchate, 1 (Cilicia for the Armenians; the patriarch resides in Lebanon); archd., 3; v.a., 2; ap. ex., 1; abp., 4; bp., 2; parishes, 50; priests, 62 (16 dioc., 46 rel.); p.d., 15; sem., 8; bros., 13; srs., 114; bap., 119; Caths., 30,000; tot. pop., 61,640,000.

Republic in Asia Minor and southeastern Europe, capital, Ankara. Christian communities were established in apostolic times, as attested in the Acts of the Apostles, some of the Letters of St. Paul, and Revelation. The territory was the scene of heresies and ecumenical councils, the place of residence of Fathers of the Church, the area in which ecclesiastical organization reached the dimensions of more than 450 sees in the middle of the seventh century. The region remained generally Byzantine except for the period of the Latin occupation of Constantinople from 1204 to 1261, but was conquered by the Ottoman Turks in 1453 and remained under their domination until establishment of the republic in 1923. Christians, always a minority, numbered more Orthodox than Latins; they were all under some restrictions during the Ottoman period. They suffered persecution in the 19th and 20th centuries, the Armenians being the most numerous victims. Turkey is overwhelmingly Muslim. Catholics are tolerated to a degree.

Turkmenistan*

Priests, 1 (rel.); Caths., 22,000; tot.pop., 4,100,000.

Former constituent republic of USSR; independent, 1991; capital, Ashkabad. Almost all the population is Sunni Muslim. The few Catholics are entrusted to the care of Franciscans living in Ashkabad.

Turks and Caicos Islands

Independent mission, 1; parishes, 2; priests, 1 (rel.); bap., 38; Caths., 1,000; tot. pop., 11,000. (AD, Antilles)

British possession in West Indies; capital, Grand Turk.

Tuvalu

Independent mission, 1; priest, 1 (rel.); bap., 4; Caths., 100; tot. pop., 9,000.

Independent state (1978) in Oceania, consisting of 9 islands (formerly Ellice Islands); capital, Funafuti.

Uganda*

Archd., 1; dioc., 18; mil. ord.; card., 1; abp., 1; bp., 20; parishes, 367; priests, 1,321 (1,001 dioc., 320 rel.); sem., 719; bros., 386; srs., 2,878; catechists, 11,074; bap., 282,953; Caths., 9,143,000 (42.9%); tot. pop., 21,300,000.

Republic in eastern Africa; capital, Kampala. The Missionaries of Africa (White Fathers) were the first Catholic missionaries, starting in 1879. Persecution broke out from 1885 to 1887, taking a toll of 22 Catholic martyrs, who were canonized in 1964, and a number of Anglican victims. (Pope Paul honored all those who died for the faith during a visit to Kampala in 1969.) By 1888, there were more than 8,000 Catholics. Evangelization was resumed in 1894, after being interrupted by war, and proceeded thereafter. The first native African bishop was ordained in 1939. The hierarchy was established in 1953. The Church was suppressed during the erratic regime of Pres. Idi-Amin, who was deposed in the spring of 1979. The country has suffered greatly from tribal rivalry and conflict in recent years.

Ukraine*
Major archbishopric, 1 (Ukrainian); archd., 2 (1 Armenian and 1 Latin rite); dioc., 9 (6 Byzantine rite, 3 Latin); a.a., 1; card., 1 (Ukrainian Major Archbishop Lubachivsky); abp., 3; bp., 17; parishes, 3,323; priests, 1,842 (1,501 dioc., 341 rel.); p.d., 6; sem., 1,552; bros., 368; srs., 1,039; bap., 52,094; Caths., 5,752,000 (11.1%); tot. pop., 51,640,000.

Independent republic bordering on the Black Sea; former USSR republic; capital, Kiev. The baptism of Vladimir and his people in 988 marked the beginning of Christianity in the territory of Kievan Rus which is included in today's Ukraine. The Byzantine-Rite Catholic Church was officially suppressed and underground in the USSR from the late 1940s. (See USSR below for situation during communist control.)

Union of Soviet Socialist Republics
(The Union of Soviet Socialist Republics disbanded Dec. 25, 1991. Background history of the USSR especially during communist domination is given below. See also separate entries: Armenia, Azerbaijan, Belarus, Estonia, Georgia, Kazakhstan, Kyrgyzstan, Latvia, Lithuania, Moldova, Russian Federation, Tajikistan, Turkmenistan, Ukraine, Uzbekistan.) The Orthodox Church has been predominant in Russian history. It developed from the Byzantine Church before 1064. Some of its members subsequently established communion with Rome as the result of reunion movements but most of them remained Orthodox. The government has always retained some kind of general or particular control of this church. Latins, always a minority, had a little more freedom. From the beginning of the Communist government in 1917, all churches of whatever kind — including Jews and Muslims — became the targets of official campaigns designed to negate their influence on society and/or to eliminate them entirely. An accurate assessment of the situation of the Catholic Church in Russia was difficult to make. Its dimensions, however, could be gauged from the findings of a team of research specialists made public by the Judiciary Committee of the U.S. House of Representatives in 1964. It was reported: "The fate of the Catholic Church in the USSR and countries occupied by the Russians from 1917 to 1959 shows the following: (a) the number killed: 55 bishops; 12,800 priests and monks; 2.5 million Catholic believers; (b) imprisoned or deported: 199 bishops; 32,000 priests and 10 million believers; (c) 15,700 priests were forced to abandon their priesthood and accept other jobs; and (d) a large number of seminaries and religious communities were dissolved; 1,600 monasteries were nationalized, 31,779 churches were closed. 400 newspapers were prohibited, and all Catholic organizations were dissolved." Several Latin Rite churches were open; e.g., in Moscow, Leningrad, Odessa and Tiflis. An American chaplain was stationed in Moscow to serve Catholics at the U.S. embassy there. Despite repression and attempts at Sovietization, Lithuania and Ukraine remained strongholds of Catholicism. In 1991, the Pope reconstituted the Byzantine hierarchy in Ukraine. He also established: two Latin rite apostolic administrations in the Russian Republic; one Latin-rite apostolic administration in the Kazakhstan Republic; a metropolitan see and two suffragans in Byelorussia (now Belarus).

United Arab Emirates
V.a, 1; bp., 1; parishes, 5; priests, 14 (3 dioc., 11 rel.); srs., 36; bap., 1,127; Caths., 122,000; tot. pop., 2,310,000.

Independent state along Persian Gulf; capital, Abu Dhabi. The vicariate apostolic of Arabia has its seat in Abu Dhabi. It includes the states of Bahrain, Oman, Qatar, Saudi Arabia and Yemen (see separate entries) as well as United Arab Emirates.

United States*
See Catholic History in the United States, Statistics of the Church in the United States.

Uruguay*
Archd., 1; dioc., 9; abp., 2; bp., 13; parishes, 229; priests, 539 (229 dioc., 310 rel.); p.d., 61; sem., 81; bros., 104; srs., 1,529; bap., 38,949; Caths., 2,473,000 (77.5%); tot. pop., 3,190,000.

Republic (called the Eastern Republic of Uruguay) on the southeast coast of South America; capital, Montevideo. The Spanish established a settlement in 1624 and evangelization followed. Missionaries followed the reduction pattern to reach the Indians, form them in the faith and train them in agriculture, husbandry, other useful arts, and the experience of managing property and living in community. Montevideo was made a diocese in 1878. The constitution of 1830 made Catholicism the religion of the state and subsidized some of its activities, principally the missions to the Indians. Separation of Church and state was provided for in the constitution of 1917.

Uzbekistan*
Former republic of USSR; independent, 1991; capital, Tashkent. The majority of the population is Sunni Muslim. A small number of Catholics live in Tashkent. Tot. Pop., 22,840,000.

Vanuatu*
Dioc., 1; bp., 1; parishes, 18; priests, 26 (8 dioc., 18 rel.); sem., 10; bros., 20; srs., 70; bap., 842; Caths., 26,000 (16%); tot. pop., 159,000.

Independent (July 29, 1980) island group in the southwest Pacific, about 500 miles west of Fiji (formerly New Hebrides); capital, Vila. Effective, though slow, evangelization by Catholic missionaries began about 1887. A vicariate apostolic was set up in 1904. The hierarchy was established in 1966.

Vatican City
See separate entry.

Venezuela*
Archd., 8; dioc., 21; v.a., 4; ap. ex., 1; mil. ord.; card., 2; abp., 8; bp., 38; parishes, 1,101; priests, 2,212 (1,111 dioc., 1,101 rel.); p.d., 66; sem., 1,012; bros., 315; srs., 4,316; bap., 363,025; Caths., 19,922,000 (92%); tot. pop., 21,640,000.

Republic in northern South America; capital, Caracas. Evangelization began in 1513-14 and involved members of a number of religious orders who worked in assigned territories, developing missions into pueblos or towns and villages of Indian converts. Nearly 350 towns originated as missions. Fifty-four missionaries met death by violence from the start of missionary work until 1817. Missionary work was seriously hindered during the wars of independence in the second decade of the 19th century and continued in decline through the rest of the century as dictator followed dictator in a period of political turbulence. Restoration of the missions got under way in 1922. The first diocese was established in 1531. Most of the bishops have been native Venezuelans. The first diocesan synod was held in 1574. Church-state relations are regulated by an agreement concluded with the Holy See in 1964.

Vietnam
Archd., 3; dioc., 22; card., 1; abp., 1; bp., 30; parishes, 2,122; priests, 2,213 (1,888 dioc., 325 rel.); p.d.,17; sem., 1,091; bros., 624; srs., 6,189; bap., 147,949; Caths., 5,921,000 (7.9%); tot. pop., 74,540,000.

Country in southeastern Asia, reunited officially July 2, 1976, as the Socialist Republic of Vietnam; capital, Hanoi. Previously, from 1954, partitioned into the Democratic Peoples' Republic of Vietnam in the North (capital, Hanoi) and the Republic of Vietnam in the South (capital, Saigon). Catholicism was introduced in 1533 but missionary work was intermittent until 1615 when Jesuits arrived to stay. One hundred thousand Catholics were reported in 1639. Two vicariates were organized in 1659. A seminary was set up in 1666 and two native priests were ordained two years later. A congregation of native women religious formed in 1670 is still active. Severe persecution broke out in 1698, three times in the 18th century, and again in the 19th. Between 100,000 and 300,000 persons suffered in some way from persecution during the 50 years before 1883 when the French moved in to secure religious liberty for the Catholics. Most of the 117 beatified Martyrs of Vietnam were killed during this 50-year period. After the French were forced out of Vietnam in 1954, the country was partitioned at the 17th parallel. The North went Communist and the Viet Cong, joined by North Vietnamese regular army troops in 1964, fought to gain control of the South. In 1954 there were approximately 1,114,000 Catholics in the North and 480,000 in the South. More than 650,000 fled to the South to avoid the government repression that silenced the Church in the North. In South Vietnam, the Church continued to develop during the war years. Fragmentary reports about the status of the Church since the end of the war in 1975 have been ominous. Freedom of religious belief, promised by the Revolutionary Government in May, 1975, shortly after its capture of Saigon (Ho Chi Min City), is denied in practice. Late in 1983, the government initiated support for a "patriotic" Catholic church analogous to the communist-sponsored church in China. The hierarchy was established in 1960. The apostolic delegation, formerly in Saigon, was transferred to Hanoi in 1976; it is presently vacant.

Virgin Islands
Dioc., 1 (St. Thomas, suffragan of Washington, D.C.); bp., 1; parishes, 8; priests, 16 (11 dioc., 5 rel.); p.d., 22; sem., 4; bros., 16; srs., 16; bap., 350; Caths., 30,000; tot. pop., 112,000.

Organized unincorporated U.S. territory, about 34 miles east of Puerto Rico; capital, Charlotte Amalie on St. Thomas (one of the three principal islands). The islands were discovered by Columbus in 1493 and named for St. Ursula and her virgin companions. Missionaries began evangelization in the 16th century. A church on St. Croix dates from about 1660; another, on St. Thomas, from 1774. The Baltimore archdiocese had jurisdiction over the islands from 1804 to 1820 when it was passed on to the first of several places in the Caribbean area. Some trouble arose over a pastoral appointment in the 19th century, resulting in a small schism. The Redemptorists took over pastoral care in 1858; normal conditions have prevailed since.

British Virgin Islands
Parishes, 2; priests, 3 (1 dioc., 2 rel.); srs., 1; bap., 32; Caths., 1,000; tot. pop., 11,000.

British possession in Caribbean; capital, Road Town. Under ecclesiastical jurisdiction of St. John's-Basseterre diocese, Antigua.

Wales
Archd., 1; dioc., 2; abp., 1; bp., 3; parishes, 185; priests, 268 (154 dioc., 114 rel.); p.d., 13; sem., 18; bros., 21; srs., 502; bap, 2,587; Caths., 149,067 (5%);; tot. pop., 3,049,438 (1997 Annuario Pontificio).

Part of the United Kingdom, on the western part of the island of Great Britain. Celtic missionaries completed evangelization by the end of the sixth century, the climax of what has been called the age of saints. Welsh Christianity received its distinctive Celtic character at this time. Some conflict developed when attempts were made _ and proved successful later _ to place the Welsh Church under the jurisdiction of Canterbury; the Welsh opted for direct contact with Rome. The Church made progress despite the depredations of Norsemen in the eighth and ninth centuries. Norman infiltration occurred near the middle of the 12th century, resulting in a century-long effort to establish territorial dioceses and parishes to replace the Celtic organizational plan of monastic centers and satellite churches. The Western Schism produced split views and allegiances. Actions of Henry VIII in breaking away from Rome had serious repercussions. Proscription and penal laws crippled the Church, resulted in heavy defections and touched off a 150-year period of repression in which more than 91 persons died for the faith. Methodism prevailed by

1750. Modern Catholicism came to Wales with Irish immigrants in the 19th century, when the number of Welsh Catholics was negligible. Catholic emancipation was granted in 1829. The hierarchy was restored in 1850.

Wallis and Futuna Islands

Dioc., 1; bp., 1; parishes, 5; priests, 7 (4 dioc., 3 rel.); sem., 5; bros., 5; srs., 40; bap., 415; Caths., 15,000; tot. pop., 15,000.

French overseas territory in the southwestern Pacific; capital Mata-Utu. Marists, who began evangelizing the islands in 1836-7, were the first Catholic missionaries. The entire populations of the two islands were baptized by the end of 1842 (Wallis) and 1843 (Futuna). The first missionary to the latter island was killed in 1841. Most of the priests on the islands are native Polynesians. The hierarchy was established in 1966.

Western Sahara

P.a., 1; parishes, 1; priests, 2 (rel.); Caths., 200; tot. pop., 350,000.

Former Spanish overseas province (Spanish Sahara) on the northwestern coast of Africa. Territory is under control of Morocco. Islam is the religion of non-Europeans. A prefecture apostolic was established in 1954 for the European Catholics there.

Yemen

Parishes, 4; priests, 4 (rel.); srs., 28; bap., 3; Caths., 3,000; tot. pop., 14,500,000.

Republic on southern coast of Arabian peninsula; capital, Sanaa. Formerly North Yemen (Arab Republic of Yemen) and South Yemen (People's Republic of Yemen); formally reunited in 1990. Christians perished in· the first quarter of the sixth century. Muslims have been in control since the seventh century. The state religion is Islam. Under ecclesiastical jurisdiction of Arabia vicariate apostolic.

Yugoslavia*

Archd., 2; dioc., 3; abp., 3; bp., 4; parishes, 214; priests, 190 (152 dioc., 38 rel.); p.d., 1; sem., 24; bros., 8; srs., 347; bap., 4,260; Caths., 446,000 (5.6%); tot. pop., 7,931,000.

Republic in southeastern Europe formed in 1992, consisting of Serbia and Montenegro; capital, Belgrade. The four other republics (Croatia, Slovenia, Bosnia and Herzegovina, and Macedonia) which made up the federation of Yugoslavia created after World War II proclaimed their independence in 1991-1992; see separate entries. Background history of the Church in pre-1991 Yugoslavia, especially during communist domination, is given below. (See Index for 1996 events.)

Christianity was introduced from the seventh to ninth centuries in the regions which were combined to form the nation after World War I. Since these regions straddled the original line of demarcation for the Western and Eastern Empires (and churches), and since the Reformation had little lasting effect, the Christians are nearly all either Roman Catholics or Byzantines (some in communion with Rome, the majority Orthodox). Yugoslavia was proclaimed a Socialist republic in 1945, the year in which began

years of the harshest kind of total persecution of the Church. Cardinal Stepinac, one of its major victims, died in 1960. In an agreement signed June 25, 1966, the government recognized the Holy See's spiritual jurisdiction over the Church in the country and guaranteed to bishops the possibility of maintaining contact with Rome in ecclesiastical and religious matters. The Holy See confirmed the principle that the activity of ecclesiastics, in the exercise of priestly functions, must take place within the religious and ecclesiastical sphere, and that abuse of these functions for political ends would be illegal.

Zambia*

Archd., 2; dioc. (1997), 8; abp., 2; bp., 9; parishes, 257; priests, 632 (243 dioc., 389 rel.); p.d., 1; sem., 349; bros., 142; srs., 953; bap., 52,265; Caths., 2,677,000 (28.5%); tot. pop., 9,370,000.

Republic in central Africa; capital, Lusaka. Portuguese priests did some evangelizing in the 16th and 17th centuries but no results of their work remained in the 19th century. Jesuits began work in the south in the 1880s and White Fathers in the north and east in 1895. Evangelization of the western region began for the first time in 1931. The number of Catholics doubled in the 20 years following World War II.

Zimbabwe*

Archd., 2; dioc., 5; abp., 3; bp., 8; parishes, 140; priests, 391 (135 dioc., 256 rel.); p.d., 13; sem., 233; bros., 106; srs., 1,136; bap., 40,507; Caths., 1,022,000 (8.8%); tot. pop., 11,530,000.

Independent republic (Apr. 18, 1980) in south central Africa (formerly Rhodesia); capital, Harare (Salisbury). Earlier unsuccessful missionary ventures preceded the introduction of Catholicism in 1879. Missionaries began to make progress after 1893. The hierarchy was established in 1955; the first black bishop was ordained in 1973. In 1969, four years after the government of Ian Smith made a unilateral declaration of independence from England, a new constitution was enacted for the purpose of assuring continued white supremacy over the black majority. Catholic and Protestant prelates in the country protested vigorously against the constitution and related enactments as opposed to human rights of the blacks and restrictive of the Church's freedom to carry out its pastoral, educational and social service functions. The Smith regime was ousted in 1979 after seven years of civil war in which at least 25,000 people were killed.

MISSION WEB SITE

The United States office of the Society for the Propagation of the Faith announced during 1997 the establishment of a site on the World Wide Web as part of celebrations marking the 175th anniversary of its foundation. One site address is http:/www.propfaith.org. "We can see the World Wide Web as an instrument for us to educate Catholics about the Church's world-wide missionary efforts and about their responsibility, through baptism, to participate in this mission," said Auxiliary Bishop William J. McCormack of New York, national director. The site features mission news and reports as well as other mission-related items.

CATHOLIC WORLD STATISTICS

(Principal sources: *Statistical Yearbook of the Church, 1995,* the latest edition; figures are as of Dec. 31, 1995, unless indicated otherwise.)

	Africa	North America[1]	South America	Asia	Europe	Oceania	WORLD TOTALS
Patriarchates[2]	2	—	—	8	2	—	12
Archdioceses	77	84	93	112	165	18	549
Dioceses	358	350	386	303	498	54	1,949
Prelatures	—	8	33	6	6	—	53
Abbacies	—	1	2	—	11	—	14
Exarchates/Ords.	—	1	4	2	13	—	20
Military Ords.	3	4	9	3	11	2	32
Vicariates Apostolic	14	6	36	18	1	—	75
Prefectures	4	—	7	3	—	1	15
Apostolic Admin.	1	—	—	3	5	—	9
Independent Missions	2	1	—	2	—	2	7
Cardinals[3]	15	21	17	14	77	4	148
Patriarchs[2]	1	—	—	6	1	—	8
Archbishops	103	122	134	149	317	21	846[4]
Bishops	423	654	677	418	1,042	91	3,305[4]
Priests	23,922	80,480	39,349	38,636	217,275	5,088	404,750
Diocesan	13,421	50,908	21,350	22,456	151,499	2,784	262,418
Religious	10,501	29,572	17,999	16,180	65,776	2,304	142,332
Perm.Deacons	336	13,234	1,913	149	6,610	158	22,390
Brothers	6,635	11,962	5,900	7,078	25,788	2,152	59,515
Sisters	47,572	157,053	91,043	124,091	406,065	12,137	838,961
Maj. Seminarians	17,789	15,110	18,433	24,889	29,351	774	106,346
Sec. Inst. Mbrs. (Men)	28	47	81	53	435	1	645
Sec. Inst. Mbrs. (Women)	340	1,598	3,535	1,078	23,934	47	30,532
Lay Missionaries	1,331	160	197	194	—	231	2,113
Catechists	300,735	17,316	16,889	96,818	60	7,316	439,134
Parishes	9,692	33,057	19,065	18,332	137,484	2,447	220,077[5]
Kindergartens	7,436	8,236	6,086	8,941	23,648	553	54,900
Students	646,220	386,667	655,429	1,327,000	1,901,339	33,876	4,950,531
Elem./PrimarySchools	27,688	13,152	9,969	13,271	18,454	2,509	85,043
Students	9,356,360	3,841,781	3,356,528	4,539,571	3,607,573	544,087	25,245,900
Secondary Schools	5,611	3,529	5,597	7,791	10,132	689	33,349
Students	1,701,705	1,444,872	2,158,868	4,134,499	3,459,202	333,288	13,232,434
Students in Higher Insts.[6]	13,150	368,782	101,760	678,392	193,556	5,727	1,361,367
Social Service Facilities	13,367	16,195	24,164	19.697	34,146	1,403	108,972
Hospitals	832	980	902	998	1,625	145	5,482
Dispensaries	3,938	2,239	3,670	3,222	2,998	159	16,226
Leprosariums	374	16	79	354	32	2	857
Homes for Aged/Handic	459	1,566	1,519	1,184	7,105	244	12,077
Orphanages	743	809	1,292	2,492	2,000	218	7,554
Nurseries	984	1,103	3,661	2,227	2,417	72	10,464
Matrimonial Advice Ctrs.	1,073	2,256	1,303	1,203	3,573	207	9,715
Social Educ.Ctrs.	968	2,330	1,863	2,966	2,948	89	11,164
Other Institutions	3,996	4,796	9,875	5,051	11,448	267	35,433
Baptisms	3,218,801	4,231,554	5,003,762	2,688,588	2,759,959	137,299	18,039,963
Under Age 7	2,117,116	3,990,344	4,634,459	2,321,701	2,680,094	123,242	15,866,956
Over Age 7	1,101,685	241,210	369,303	366,887	79,865	14,057	2,173,007
Marriages	280,539	825,676	895,364	501,461	1,099,899	30,750	3,633,689
Between Catholics	244,483	718,208	877,778	446,270	1,017,967	17,696	3,322,402
Mixed Marriages	36,056	107,468	17,586	55,191	81,932	13,054	311,287
Catholic Pop.[7]	107,077,000	208,276,000	276,090,000	101,210,000	288,953,000	7,760,000	989,366,000
World Population	725,850,000	452,193,000	313,354,000	3,456,280,000	711,497,000	28,200,000	5,689,374,000

[1]Includes Middle America. [2]For listing and description, see Index. [3]As of Aug. 30, 1997. [4]Figures for the hierarchy (cardinals, archbishops and bishops) included 2,533 ordinaries, 595 coadjutors or auxiliaries, 212 with offices in the Roman Curia, 28 in other offices, more than 900 retired. [5]159,372 have parish priests; 55,156 are administered by other priests; 479 are entrusted to permanent deacons; 275 to brothers; 1,093 to women Religious; 1,725 to lay people; 1,977 vacant. [6]There are also approximately 177,807 in universities for ecclesiastical studies and 1,809,186 other university students. [7]Percentages of Catholics in world population: Africa, 14.7; North America (Catholics 69,614,000; tot. pop., 292,762,000), 23.7; Middle America (Catholics, 138,662,000; tot. pop., 159,431,000), 86.9; South America, 88.4; Asia, 2.9; Europe, 40.6; Oceania, 27.5; World, 17.4. (Catholic totals do not include those in areas that could not be surveyed, estimated to be 4.6 million.)

EPISCOPAL CONFERENCES

(Principal source: *Annuario Pontificio*.)

Episcopal conferences, organized and operating under general norms and particular statutes approved by the Holy See, are official bodies in and through which the bishops of a given country or territory act together as pastors of the Church.

Listed below according to countries or regions are titles and addresses of conferences and names and sees of presidents.

Africa, Northern: Conference Episcopale Regionale du Nord de l'Afrique (CERNA), 13 rue Khelifa-Boukhalfa, 16000 Algiers, Algeria. Abp. Henri Teissier (Algiers).

Africa, Southern: Southern African Catholic Bishops' Conference (SACBC), 140 Visagie St., P.O. Box 941, Pretoria 0001, S. Africa. Bp. Louis Ncarmiso Ndlovu, O.S.M. (Manzini, Swaziland).

Albania: Conferenza Episcopale dell'Albania, Sheshi Gijon Pali II, Kryeipeshkëvi, Shkodrë, Abp. Rrok Mirdita (Durrës-Tirana).

Angola and Sao Tome: Conferencia Episcopal de Angola e Sao Tome (CEAST), C.P. 87 Luanda, Angola. Card. Alexandre do Nascimento (Luanda).

Antilles: Antilles Episcopal Conference (AEC), P.O. Box 3086, St. James (Trinidad and Tobago), W.I. Abp. Kelvin Edward Felix (Castries, Santa Lucia).

Arab Countries: Conference des Eveques Latins dans les Regions Arabes (CELRA), Latin Patriarchate, P.O. Box 14152, Jerusalem (Old City). Patriarch Michel Sabbah (Jerusalem).

Argentina: Conferencia Episcopal Argentina (CEA), Calle Suipacha 1034, 1008 Buenos Aires. Abp. Estanislao Esteban Karlic (Parana).

Australia: Australian Catholic Bishops' Conference, 63 Currong St., Braddon, A.C.T. 2601. Card. Edward Bede Clancy (Sydney).

Austria: Osterreichische Bischofskonferenz, Wollzeile 2, A-1010 Vienna. Bp. Johann Weber (Graz-Seckau).

Bangladesh: Catholic Bishops' Conference of Bangladesh (CBCB), P.O. Box 3, Dhaka-1000. Abp. Michael Rozario (Dhaka).

Belgium: Bisschoppenconferentie van Belgie _ Conference Episcopale de Belgique, Rue Guimard 1, B-1040 Brussel. Card. Godfried Danneels (Mechelen-Brussel).

Benin: Conference Episcopale du Benin, B.P. 491, Cotonou. Bp. Lucien Monsi-Agboka (Abomey).

Bolivia: Conferencia Episcopal Boliviana (CEB), Casilla 2309, Calle Potosi 814, La Paz. Abp. Edmundo Luis Flavio Abastoflor Montero (La Paz).

Bosnia and Herzegovina: Biskupska Konferencija Bosne i Hercegovine (B.K. B.i.H.), Nadbiskupski Ordinariat, Kaptol 7, 71000 Sarajevo. Card. Vinko Puljic (Vrhbosna, Sarajevo).

Brazil: Conferencia Nacional dos Bispos do Brasil (CNBB), C.P. 02067, SE/Sul Quadra 801, Conjunto "B," 70259-970 Brasilia, D.F. Card. Lucas Moreira Neves, O.P. (Sao Salvador da Bahia).

Bulgaria: Mejduritual Episcopska Konferenzia vav Bulgaria, Ul. Liulin Planina 5, 1606 Sofia. Bp. Christo Proykov (Briula, titular see).

Burkina Faso and Niger: Conference des Eveques de Burkina Faso et du Niger, B.P. 1195, Ouagadougou, Burkina Faso. Bp. Jean-Baptiste Some (Diebougou).

Burma: See Myanmar.

Burundi: Conference des Eveques Catholiques du Burundi (C.E.C.A.B.), B. P. 1390, 5 Blvd. de l'Uprona, Bujumbura. Bp. Bernard Bududira (Bururi).

Cameroon: Conference Episcopale Nationale du Cameroun (CENC), BP 807, Yaoundé. Bp. Andre Wouking (Bafoussam).

Canada: See Canadian Conference of Catholic Bishops.

Central African Republic: Conference Episcopale Centrafricaine (CECA), B.P. 798, Bangui. Abp. Joachim N'Dayen (Bangui).

Chad: Conference Episcopale du Tchad, B.P. 456, N'Djamena. Abp. Charles Vandame, S.J. (N'Djamena).

Chile: Conferencia Episcopal de Chile (CECH), Casilla 517-V, Correo 21, Cienfuegas 47, Santiago. Card. Carlos Oviedo Cavada, O. de M. (Santiago de Chile).

China: Chinese Regional Episcopal Conference, 34 Lane 32, Kuang-Fu South Rd., Taipeh 10552, Taiwan. Bp. Paul Shan Kuo-hsi, S.J. (Kaohsiung).

Colombia: Conferencia Episcopal de Colombia, Apartado 7448, Carrera 8ª 47, N. 84-85, Santafe de Bogota D.E. Abp. Alberto Giraldo Jaramillo, P.S.S. (Popayan).

Congo: Conference Episcopale du Congo, B.P. 200, Brazzaville. Bp. Bernard Nsayi (Nkayi).

Congo, Democratic Republice (formerly Zaire): Conférence Episcopale du Zaïre (CEZ), B.P. 3258, Kinshasa-Gombe. Bp. Faustin Ngabu (Goma).

Costa Rica: Conferencia Episcopal de Costa Rica (CECOR), Apartado 497, 1000 San Jose. Abp. Roman Arrieta Villalobos (San Jose de Costa Rica).

Côte d'Ivoire: Conference Episcopale de la Côte d'Ivoire, B.P. 1287, Abidjan 01. Abp. Auguste Nobou (Korhogo).

Croatia: Hrvatska Biskupska Konferencija, Kaptol 22, HR-41000 Zagreb. Card. Franjo Kuharic (Zagreb).

Cuba: Conferencia de Obispos Catolicos de Cuba (COCC), Apartado 594, Calle 26 n. 314 Miramar, 10100 Havana 1. Card. Jaime Lucas Ortega y Alamino (Havana).

Czech Republic: Ceska Biskupska Konference, Sekretariat, Thakurova 3, 160 00 Praha (Prague) 6. Card. Miloslav Vlk (Prague).

Dominican Republic: Conferencia del Episcopado Dominicano (CED), Apartado 186, Santo Domingo. Card. Nicolas de Jesus Lopez Rodriguez (Santo Domingo).

Ecuador: Conferencia Episcopal Ecuatoriana, Apartado 1081, Avenida America 1805 y Lagasca, Quito. Abp. Jose Mario Ruiz Navas (Portoviejo).

El Salvador: Conferencia Episcopal de El Salvador (CEDES). 15 Av. Norte 1420, Col. Layco, Apartado 1310, San Salvador. Bp. Marco Rene Revelo Contreras (Santa Ana).

Equatorial Guinea: Conferencia Episcopal de Guinea Ecuatorial, Apartado 106, Malabo. Bp. Anacleto Sima Ngua (Bata).

Ethiopia: Ethiopian Episcopal Conference, P.O. Box 2454, Addis Ababa. Card. Paulos Tzadua (Addis Ababa).

France: Conference des Evêques de France, 106 rue

du Bac, 75341 Paris CEDEX 07. Abp. Louis-Marie Billé (Aix).

Gabon: Conference Episcopale du Gabon, B.P. 209, Oyem. Bp. Basile Mvé Engone, S.D.B. (Oyem).

Gambia, Liberia and Sierra Leone: Inter-Territorial Catholic Bishops' Conference of the Gambia, Liberia and Sierra Leone (ITCABIC), Santanno House, P.O. Box 893, Freetown, Sierra Leone. Bp. Benedict Dotu Sekey (Gbarnga, Liberia).

Germany: Deutsche Bischofskonferenz, Postfach 2962, Kaiserstrasse 163, D-53019 Bonn. Bp. Karl Lehmann (Mainz). Statutes approved Nov. 14, 1992.

Ghana: Ghana Bishops' Conference, National Catholic Secretariat, P.O. Box 9712 Airport, Accra. Bp. Francis Anani Kofi Lodonu (Ho).

Great Britain: Bishops' Conference of England and Wales, General Secretariat, 39 Eccleston Square, London, SWIV IBX. Card. George Basil Hume, O.S.B. (Westminster). Bishops' Conference of Scotland, Archbishop's House, 196 Clyde St., Glasgow GI 4JY. Card. Thomas Winning (Glasgow).

Greece: Conferentia Episcopalis Graeciae, Odos Homirou 9, 106 72 Athens. Abp. Nikolaos Foscolos (Athens).

Guatemala: Conferencia Episcopal de Guatemala (CEG), Apartado 1698, 01901 Ciudad de Guatemala. Bp. Jorge Mario Avila del Aguila, C.M. (Jalapa).

Guinea: Conference Episcopale de la Guinee, B.P. 1006 Bis, Conakry. Abp. Robert Sarah (Conakry).

Guinea-Bissau: See Senegal.

Haiti: Conference Episcopale de Haiti (CEH). B.P. 1572, Angle rues Piquant et Lammarre, Port-au-Prince. Abp. Francois Gayot, S.M.M. (Cap Haïtien).

Honduras: Conferencia Episcopal de Honduras (CEH), Apartado 847, Blvd. Suyapa, Tegucigalpa. Abp. Oscar Andres Rodriguez Maradiaga (Tegucigalpa).

Hungary: Magyar Püspöki Kar Konferenciája, PF 121, H-1364 Budapest. Abp. István Seregély (Eger).

India: Catholic Bishops' Conference of India (CBCI), CBCI Centre, Ashok Place, Goldakkhana, New Delhi-110001. Abp. Joseph Powathil (Changanacherry of the Syro-Malabars); Conference of Catholic Bishops of India — Latin Rite (CBCI — L.R.), A-139, Lok Vihar, Pitampura, New Delhi-110034. Abp. Marianus Arokiasamy (Madurai). Statutes approved experimentally Jan. 13, 1994 .

Indian Ocean: Conference Episcopale de l'Ocean Indien (CEDOI) (includes Islands of Mauritius, Seychelles, Comore and La Reunion), 13 rue Msgr. Gonin, Port Louis, Mauritius. Bp. Maurice Piat, S.S.Sp. (Port Louis).

Indonesia: Konperensi Waligereja Indonesia (KWI), Taman Cut Mutiah 10, Tromolpos 3044, Jakarta 10002. Card. Julius Riyadi Darmaatmadja, S.J. (Jakarta).

Ireland: Irish Episcopal Conference, "Ara Coeli," Armagh BT61 7QY. Abp. Sean B. Brady (Armagh).

Italy: Conferenza Episcopale Italiana (CEI), Circonvallazione Aurelia, 50, 00165 Rome. Card. Camillo Ruini (Vicar General, Rome).

Ivory Coast: See Côte d'Ivoire.

Japan: Catholic Bishops' Conference of Japan, Shiomi 2-10-10, Koto-Ku, Tokyo 135. Bp. Stephen Fumio Hamao (Yokohama).

Kenya: Kenya Episcopal Conference (KEC), The Kenya Catholic Secretariat, P.O. Box 13475, Nairobi. Abp. Zacchaeus Okoth (Kisumu).

Korea: Catholic Bishops' Conference of Korea, Box 16, Seoul 100-600. Bp. Nicholas Cheong Jin-suk (Cheong Ju).).

Laos and Cambodia: Conference Episcopale du Laos et du Cambodge, c/o Msgr. Pierre Bach, Paris Foreign Missions, 254 Silom Rd., Bangkok 10500. Bp. Yves-Georges Ramousse, M.E.P. (vicar apostolic, Phnom Penh, Cambodia).

Latvia: Conferentia Episcopalis Lettoniae, Maza Pils, 2, Riga 226050. Vacant.

Lesotho: Lesotho Catholic Bishops' Conference, Catholic Secretariat, P.O. Box 200, Maseru 100. Bp. Evaristus Thatho Bitsoane (Qacha's Nek).

Liberia: See Gambia, Liberia and Sierra Leone.

Lithuania: Conferentia Episcopalis Lituaniae, Sventaragio, 4, 2001 Vilnius. Abp. Audrys Juozas Backis (Vilnius).

Madagascar: Conference Episcopale de Madagascar, 102 bis Av. Marechal Joffre, Antanimena, B. P 667, Antananarivo. Card. Armand Gaetan Razafindratandra (Antananarivo).

Malawi: Episcopal Conference of Malawi, Catholic Secretariat of Malawi, P.O. Box 30384, Lilongwe 3. Bp. Felix Eugenio Mikhori (Chikwawa).

Malaysia-Singapore-Brunei: Catholic Bishops' Conference of Malaysia, Singapore and Brunei (BCMSB), 4000 Shah Alam, Selangor Darul Ehson, Malaysia. Abp. Peter Chung Hoan Ting (Kuching, Malaysia).

Mali: Conference Episcopale du Mali, B.P. 298, Bamako. Vacant.

Malta: Konferenza Episkopali Maltija, Archbishop's Curia, Floriana. Abp. Joseph Mercieca (Malta).

Mexico: Conferencia del Episcopado Mexicano (CEM), Prolongacion Rio Acatlan, Lago de Guadalupe, 54760 Cuautitlan Izcalli, Mex. Abp. Sergio Obeso Rivera (Jalapa).

Mozambique: Conferencia Episcopal de Mocambique (CEM), Av. Armando Tivene 1701, C. P. 286, Maputo. Bp. Francisco Joao Silota, M.Afr. (Chimoio).

Myanmar: Myanmar Catholic Bishops' Conference (MCBC), 292 Pyi Rd., P.O. Box 1080, Yangon. Bp. Matthias U. Shwe (Taunggyi).

Namibia: Namibian Catholic Bishops' Conference (NCBC). P.O. Box 11525, Windhoek 9000. Abp. Bonifatius Haushiku (Windhoek).

Netherlands: Nederlandse Bisschoppenconferentie, Postbus 13049, NL-3507 LA, Utrecht. Card. Adrianus J. Simonis (Utrecht).

New Zealand: New Zealand Episcopal Conference, Private Bag 1937, Wellington 1. Bp. Leonard Anthony Boyle (Dunedin).

Nicaragua: Conferencia Episcopal de Nicaragua (CEN), Apartado Postal 2407, de Ferreteria Lang 1 cuadro al Norte y 1 cuadro al Este, Managua. Card. Miguel Obando Bravo, S.D.B. (Managua).

Niger: See Burkina Faso.

Nigeria: Catholic Bishops Conference of Nigeria, P.O. Box 951, 6 Force Rd., Lagos. Abp. Albert K. Obiefuna (Onitsha).

Pacific: Conferentia Episcopalis Pacifici (CE PAC), P.O. Box 289, Suva (Fiji). Abp. Michel Marie Bernard Calvet, S.M. (Noumea, New Caledonia).

Pakistan: Pakistan Episcopal Conference, P.O. Box 909, Lahore 54000. Abp. Armando Trindade (Lahore).

Panama: Conferencia Episcopal de Panama (CEP), Apartado 870033, Panama 7. Abp. Jose Dimas Cedeño Delgado (Panama).

Papua New Guinea and Solomon Islands: Catholic Bishops' Conference of Papua New Guinea and Solomon Islands, P.O. Box 398, Waigani, N.C.D., Papua New Guinea. Bp. Raymond Philip Kalisz, S.V.D. (Wewak)..

Paraguay: Conferencia Episcopal Paraguaya (CEP), Alberdi 782, Casilla Correo 1436, Asuncion. Bp. Oscar Paez Garcete (Alto Parana).

Peru: Conferencia Episcopal Peruana, Aprtado 310, Rio de Janeiro 488, Lima 100. Card. Augusto Vargas Alzamora, S.J. (Lima).

Philippines: Catholic Bishops' Conference of the Philippines (CBCP), P.O. Box 3601, 470 General Luna St., 1099 Manila. Abp. Oscar V. Cruz (Lingayen-Dagupan).

Poland: Konferencja Episkopatu Polski, Skwer Kardynala Stefana Wyszynskiego 6, 01-015 Warsaw. Card. Jozef Glemp (Warsaw).

Portugal: Conferencia Episcopal Portuguesa, Campo dos Martires da Patria, 43-1 Esq., 1100 Lisbon. Bp. Joao Alves (Coimbra).

Puerto Rico: Conferencia Episcopal Puertorriqueña (CEP), P.O. Box 40682, Estacion Minillas, San Juan 00940-0682. Bp. Iñaki Mallona Txertudi, C.P. (Arecibo).

Romania: Conferinte Episcopala Romania, Via Popa Tatu 58, Bucharest. Abp. Ioan Robu (Bucharest).

Rwanda: Conference Episcopale du Rwanda (C.Ep.R.), B.P. 357, Kigali.

Scandinavia: Conferentia Episcopalis Scandiae, Trollbärsvägen 16, SE-426 55 Västra Frölunda (Sweden). Bp. Paul Verschuren, S.C.I. (Helsinki, Finland).

Senegal, Mauritania, Cape Verde and Guinea Bissau: Conference Episcopale du Senegal, de la Mauritanie, du Cap-Vert et de Guinée-Bissau, B.P. 941, Dakar, Senegal. Bp. Theodore Adrien Sarr (Kaolack, Senegal).

Sierra Leone: See Gambia, Liberia and Sierra Leone.

Slovakia: Biskupská Konferencia Slovenska, Kapitulská 11, 81521 Bratislava. Abp. Rudolf Balaz (Banska Bystrica)

Slovenia: Slovenska Skofovska Konferenca, Ciril-Metodov trg 4, p.p.121/III, 1001 Ljubljana. Abp. Alojzij Sustar (Ljubljana).

Spain: Conferencia Episcopal Española, Apartado 29075, Calle Añastro 1, 28033 Madrid. Abp. Elias Yanes Alvarez (Zaragoza).

Sri Lanka: Catholic Bishops' Conference of Sri Lanka, 19 Balcombe Place, Cotta Rd., Borella, Colombo 8. Bp. Joseph Vianney Fernando (Kandy).

Sudan: Sudan Catholic Bishops' Conference (SCBC), P.O. Box 6011, Khartoum. Abp. Gabriel Zubeir Wako (Khartoum).

Switzerland: Conference des Eveques Suisses, Secretariat, C.P. 22, av. Moleson 21, CH-1706 Fribourg. Bp. Henri Salina (Abbot Ordinary of Saint Maurice; titular bishop of Monte di Mauritania).

Tanzania: Tanzania Episcopal Conference (TEC), P.O. Box 2133, Mansfield St., Dar-es-Salaam. Bp. Justin Tetemu Samba (Musoma).

Thailand: Bishops' Conference of Thailand, 122/ 6-7 Soi Naaksuwan, Nonsi Road, Yannawa, Bangkok 10120. Card. Michael Michai Kitbunchu (Bangkok).

Togo: Conference Episcopale du Togo, B.P. 348, Lomé. Abp. Philippe Fanoko Kossi Kpodzro (Lomé).

Uganda: Uganda Episcopal Conference, P.O. Box 2886, Kampala. Bp. Paul L. Kalanda (Fort Portal).

Ukraine: Ukraine Episcopal Conference, Obrzadku Lacinskiego, pl. Katedralna 1, 290008 Lviv. Abp. Marian Jaworski (Lviv of Latins).

United States: See National Conference of Catholic Bishops.

Uruguay: Conferencia Episcopal Uruguaya (CEU), Avenida Uruguay 1319, 11100 Montevideo. Bp. Orlando Romero Cabrero (Canelones).

Venezuela: Conferencia Episcopal de Venezuela (CEV), Apartado 4897, Torre a Madrices, Edificio Juan XXIII, Piso 4, Caracas 1010-A. Abp. Tulio Manuel Chirivella Varela (Barquisimeto).

Vietnam: Conferenza Episcopale del Viêt Nam, 40 Pho Nha Chung, Ha Noi. Card. Paul Joseph Pham Dinh Tung (Ha Noi).

Yugoslavia: . . . . .

Zambia: Zambia Epscopal Conference, P.O. Box 31965, 10101 Lusaka. Bp. Telesphore George Mpundu (Mbala-Mpika).

Zimbabwe: Zimbabwe Catholic Bishops' Conference (ZCBC), Causeway, P.O. Box 8135, Harare. Bp. Francis Xavier Mugadzi (Gweru).

Regional Conferences

(Sources: Almanac survey; *Annuario Pontificio*.)

Africa: Symposium of Episcopal Conferences of Africa and Madagascar (SECAM) (Symposium des Conferences Episcopales d'Afrique et de Madagascar, SCEAM): Most Rev. Gabriel G. Ganaka, archbishop of Jos, Nigeria, president. Address: Secretariat, P.O. Box 9156 Airport, Accra, Ghana.

Association of Episcopal Conferences of Central Africa (Association des Conferences Episcopales de l'Afrique Centrale, ACEAC): Comprises Burundi, Rwanda and Zaire. Bp. Evariste Ngoyagoye, Bubanza, Burundi, president. Address: B.P. 20511, Kinshasa, Democratic Republic of Congo..

Association of Episcopal Conferences of the Region of Central Africa (Association des Conferences Episcopales de la Region de l'Afrique Central (ACERAC): Comprises Cameroon, Chad, Congo, Equatorial Guinea, Central African Republic and Gabon. Bp. Basile Mve Engone, S.D.B., Oyem, Gabon, president. Address: Secretariat, B.P. 1518, Bangui, Central African Republic.

Association of Episcopal Conferences of Anglophone West Africa (AECAWA): Comprises Gambia, Ghana, Liberia, Nigeria and Sierra Leone. Bp. Peter Kwasi Sarpong, Kumasi, Ghana, president. Address: P.O. Box 10-502, 1000 Monrovia, Liberia.

Association of Member Episcopal Conferences in Eastern Africa (AMECEA): Represents Eritrea, Ethiopia, Kenya, Malawi, Sudan, Tanzania, Uganda and Zambia. Affiliate members: Seychelles (1979), Somalia (1994). Bp. Josaphat L. Lebulu, Same, Tanzania, president. Address: P.O. Box 21191, Nairobi, Kenya.

Regional Episcopal Conference of French-Speaking West Africa (Conference Episcopale Regionale de l'Afrique de l'Ouest Francophone, CERAO): Comprises Benin, Burkina Faso, Cape Verde, Côte d'Ivoire, Guinea, Guinea-Bissau, Mali, Mauritania, Niger, Senegal and Togo. Abp. Isidore De Souza, Cotonou, Benin, president. Address: Secretariat General, 06 B.P. 470, Abidjan 06, Côte d'Ivoire.

Inter-Regional Meeting of Bishops of Southern Africa (IMBISA): Bishops of Angola, Botswana, Lesotho, Mozambique, Namibia, Sao Tome e Principe, South Africa, Swaziland and Zimbabwe. Bp. Francisco Joao Silota, M. Afr. (Chimoio, Mozambique), president. Address: 4 Bayswater Rd., Highlands, Harare, Zimbabwe.

Asia: Federation of Asian Bishops' Conferences (FABC): Represents 14 Asian episcopal conferences and four independent jurisdictions (Hong Kong, Macau, Nepal, Mongolia) as regular members (excluding the Middle East). Established in 1970; statutes approved experimentally Dec. 6, 1972. Abp. Oscar Cruz, Lingayen-Dagupan, Philippines (elected 1993), secretary general. Address: 16 Caine Road, Hong Kong.

Oceania: Federation of Catholic Bishops' Conferences of Oceania (FCBCO). Statutes approved experimentally July 28, 1992. Card. Thomas Stafford Williams, archbishop of Wellington, New Zealand, president. Address: P.O. Box 1937, Wellington, New Zealand.

Europe: Council of European Bishops' Conferences (Consilium Conferentiarum Episcoporum Europae, CCEE): Card. Miloslav Vlk, Prague, Czech Republic, president. Address of secretariat: Gallusstrasse 24, CH-9000 Sankt Gallen, Switzerland. Reorganized in 1993 in accordance with suggestions made during the 1991 Synod of Bishops on Europe.

Commission of the Episcopates of the European Community (Commissio Episcopatuum Communitatis Europaeae, COMECE): Established in 1980; represents episcopates of states which belong to European Community. Bp. Josef Homeyer, Hildesheim, Germany, president. Address of secretariat: 42 Rue Stevin, B-1040 Brussels, Belgium.

Central and South America: Latin American Bishops' Conference (Consejo Episcopal LatinoAmericano, CELAM): Established in 1956; statutes approved Nov. 9, 1974. Represents 22 Latin American national bishops' conferences. Abp. Oscar Andrés Rodriguez Maradiaga, S.D.B., Tegucigalpa, Honduras, president. Address of the secretariat: Carrera 5 No. 118-31, Usaquén, Bogota, Colombia.

Episcopal Secretariat of Central America and Panama (Secretariado Episcopal de America Central y Panama, SEDAC): Statutes approved experimentally Sept. 26, 1970. Bp. Raul Corriveau, P.M.E., Choluteca, Honduras, president. Address of secretary general: Calle 20 y Av Nexuci 124-25, Apartado 6386, Panama 5, Panama.

INTERNATIONAL CATHOLIC ORGANIZATIONS

(Principal sources: Conference of International Catholic Organizations; Pontifical Council for the Laity; Almanac survey.)

Guidelines

International organizations wanting to call themselves "Catholic" are required to meet standards set by the Vatican's Council for the Laity and to register with and get the approval of the Papal Secretariat of State, according to guidelines dated Dec. 3 and published in *Acta Apostolicae Sedis* under date of Dec. 23, 1971.

Among conditions for the right of organizations to "bear the name Catholic" are:

• leaders "will always be Catholics," and candidates for office will be approved by the Secretariat of State;

• adherence by the organization to the Catholic Church, its teaching authority and teachings of the Gospel;

• evidence that the organization is really international with a universal outlook and that it fulfills its mission through its own management, meetings and accomplishments.

The guidelines also stated that leaders of the organizations "will take care to maintain necessary reserve as regards taking a stand or engaging in public activity in the field of politics or trade unionism. Abstention in these fields will normally be the best attitude for them to adopt during their term of office."

The guidelines were in line with a provision stated by the Second Vatican Council in the i "No project may claim the name 'Catholic' unless it has obtained the consent of the lawful church authority."

They made it clear that all organizations are not obliged to apply for recognition, but that the Church "reserves the right to recognize as linked with her mission and her aims those organizations or movements which see fit to ask for such recognition."

Conference

Conference of International Catholic Organizations: A permanent body for collaboration among various organizations which seek to promote the development of international life along the lines of Christian principles. Eleven international Catholic organizations participated in its foundation and first meeting in 1927 at Fribourg, Switzerland. In 1951, the conference established its general secretariat and adopted governing statutes which were approved by the Vatican Secretariat of State in 1953.

The permanent secretariat is located at 37-39 rue de Vermont, CH-1202 Geneva, Switzerland. Other office addresses are: 1 rue Varembe, CH-1211 Geneva 20, Switzerland (International Catholic Center of Geneva); 9, rue Cler, F-75007 Paris, France (International Catholic Center for UNESCO); ICO Information Center, 323 East 47th St., New York, N.Y. 10017; ICO Antenna of Vienna (Vienna Perspectives), c/o Dennis O. Callagy, Gonzagagasse 13/8, A-1010 Vienna, Austria.

International Organizations

International Catholic organizations are listed below. Information includes name, date and place of establishment (when available), address of general secretariat. An asterisk indicates that the organization is a member of the Conference of International Catholic Organizations. Approximately 30 of the organizations have consultative status with other international or regional non-governmental agencies.

Apostleship of Prayer (1849): Borgo Santo Spirito 5, I-00193 Rome, Italy. National secretariat in most countries. (See Index.)

Apostolatus Maris (Apostleship of the Sea) (1922, Glasgow, Scotland): Pontifical Council for Migrants and Itinerant People, Piazza San Calisto 16, 00153 Rome, Italy. (See Index.)

L'Arche Communities: B.P. 35, 60350 Cuise Lamotte, France.

Associationes Juventutis Salesianae (Associations of Salesian Youth) (1847): Via della Pisana, 1111, 00163 Rome, Italy.

Blue Army of Our Lady of Fatima: (See Index.)

Caritas Internationalis* (1951, Rome, Italy): Piazza San Calisto 16, I-00153, Rome, Italy. Coordinates and represents its 131 national member organizations (in 113 countries) operating in the fields of development, emergency aid, social action.

Catholic International Education Office* (1952): 60, rue des Eburons, B-1040 Brussels, Belgium.

Catholic International Federation for Physical and Sports Education (1911; present name, 1957): 5, rue Cernuschi, F-75017 Pari, France.

Catholic International Union for Social Service* (1925, Milan, Italy): rue de la Poste 111, B-1210 Brussels, Belgium (general secretariat).

Christian Fraternity of the Sick and Handicapped: 9, Avenue de la Gare, CH-1630, Bulle, Switzerland.

Christian Life Community (CVX)* (1953): Borgo Santo Spirito 8, C.P. 6139, I-00195 Rome, Italy. First Sodality of Our Lady founded in 1563.

"Communione e Liberazione" Fraternity (1955, Milan, Italy): Via Marcello Malpighi 2, 00161 Rome, Italy. Catholic renewal movement.

"Focolare Movement" or "Work of Mary" (1943, Trent, Italy): Via di Frascati, 304, I-00040 Rocca di Papa (Rome), Italy. (See Index.)

Foi et Lumiere: 8 rue Serret, 75015 Paris, France.

Franciscans International: 323 E. 47th St., New York, NY 10017. A non-governmental organization at the UN.

Inter Cultural Association, formerly International Catholic Auxiliaries (1937, Belgium): 91, rue de la Servette, CH-1202 Geneva, Switzerland.

International Ascent, The: 84, rue Charles Michels, F-93206 Saint Denis Cedex, France. Member of ICO.

International Association of Charities* (1617, Chatillon les Dombes, France): Rue Joseph Brand, 118, B-1030 Brussels, Belgium.

International Association of Children of Mary (1847): 67 rue de Sèvres, F-75006 Paris, France.

International Catholic Child Bureau* (1948, in Paris): 63, rue de Lausanne, CH-1202 Geneva, Switzerland.

International Catholic Committee of Nurses and Medico-Social Assistants (ICCN)* (1933): Square Vergote, 43, B-1040 Brussels, Belgium.

International Catholic Conference of Scouting* (1948): Piazza Pasquale Paoli, 18, I-00186 Rome, Italy.

International Catholic Migration Commission* (1951): 37-39 rue de Vermont, C.P. 96, CH-1211 Geneva 20, Switzerland. Coordinates activities world-wide on behalf of refugees and migrants, both administering programs directly and supporting the efforts of national affiliated agencies.

International Catholic Organization for Cinema and Audiovisual* (1928, The Hague, The Netherlands): Rue du Saphir, 15, B-1040 Brussels, Belgium (general secretariat). Federation of national Catholic film offices.

International Catholic Rural Association (1962, Rome): Piazza San Calisto, 00153 Rome, Italy. International body for agricultural and rural organizations. Invited member of ICO.

International Catholic Society for Girls* (1897): 37-39, rue de Vermont, CH-1202 Geneva, Switzerland.

International Catholic Union of Esperanto: Via Berni 9, 00185 Rome, Italy.

International Catholic Union of the Press*: 37-39 rue de Vermont, Case Postale 197, CH-1211 Geneva 20 CIC, Switzerland. Coordinates and represents at the international level the activities of Catholics and Catholic federations or associations in the field of press and information. Has seven specialized branches: International Federation of Catholic Journalists; International Federation of Dailies; International Federation of Periodicals; International Federation of Catholic News Agencies; International Catholic Federation of Teachers and Researchers in the Science and Techniques of Information; International Federation of Church Press Associations and International Federation of Book Publishers.

International Centre for Studies in Religious Education LUMEN VITAE (1934-35, Louvain, Belgium, under name Catechetical Documentary Centre; present name, 1956): 184, rue Washington, B-1050 Brussels, Belgium. Also referred to as Lumen Vitae Centre; concerned with all aspects of religious formation.

International Christian Union of Business Executives: Place des Barricades 2, B-1000 Brussels, Belgium. Invited member of ICO.

International Conference of Catholic Guiding* (1965): 5031, rang 8, Deauville, Que. J1N 3G1, Canada; c/o Mlle Francoise Parmentier, rue de la Tour 64, 75016 Paris. Founded by member bodies of interdenominational World Association of Guides and Girl Scouts.

International Cooperation for Development and Solidarity (CIDSE) (1965, Rome, Italy): rue Stévin 16, B-1040 Brussels, Belgium. Invited member of ICO.

International Coordination of Young Christian Workers (YCYCW)*: via dei Barbieri 22, I00186 Rome, Italy.

International Council of Catholic Men (ICCM)* (Unum Omnes) (1948): Wahringer Str. 2-4, A.1090 Vienna IX, Austria.

International Federation of Catholic Medical Associations* (1954): Palazzo San Calisto, I-00120 Vatican City.

International Federation of Catholic Parochial Youth Communities* (1962, Rome, Italy): St. Kariliquai 12, 6000 Lucerne 5, Switzerland.

International Federation of Catholic Pharmacists* (1954): Rue Berckmans 92, B-1060 Brussels, Belgium.

International Federation of Rural Adult Catho-

lic Movements* (1964, Lisbon, Portugal): Rue Jaumain 15, B-5330 Assesse, Belgium.

International Federation of Catholic Universities* (1949): 21, rue d'Assas, F-75270 Paris Cedex 06, France.

International Federation of the Catholic Associations of the Blind*: Avenue Dailly 90, B-1030 Brussels, Belgium. Coordinates actions of Catholic groups and associations for the blind and develops their apostolate.

International Independent Christian Youth (IICY)*: 11, rue Martin Bernard, F-75013 Paris, Francis.

International Military Apostolate* (1967): Breite Strasse 25. D-5311 Bonn, Germany. Comprised of organizations of military men.

International Movement of Apostolate of Children* (1929, France): 24, rue Paul Rivet, F-92350 Le Plessis Robinson, France.

International Movement of Apostolate in the Independent Social Milieux (MIAMSI)* (1963): Piazza San Calisto 16, 00153 Rome, Italy.

International Movement of Catholic Agricultural and Rural Youth* (1954, Annevoie, Belgium): 53, rue J. Coosemans, B-1030 Brussels, Belgium (permanent secretariat).

International Young Catholic Students* (1946, Fribourg, Switzerland; present name, 1954): 171 rue de Rennes, F-75006 Paris, France.

International Young Christian Workers (1925, Belgium): 11, rue Plantin, B-1070 Brussels, Belgium. Associate member of ICO.

Legion of Mary (1921, Dublin, Ireland): De Montfort House, North Brunswick St., Dublin, Ireland. (See Index.)

Medicus Mundi Internationalis: (1964. Bensberg, Germany FR): P.O. Box 1547, 6501 BM Nijmegen, Netherlands. Promote health and medico-social services, particularly in developing countries; recruit essential health and medical personnel for developing countries; contribute to training of medical and auxiliary personnel; undertake research in the field of health.

NOVALIS, Marriage Preparation Center: University of St. Paul, 1 rue Stewart, Ottawa 2, Ont. Canada.

Our Lady's Teams (Equipes Notre-Dame) (1937, France): 49, rue de la Glacière, F-75013 Paris, France. Movement for spiritual formation of couples.

Pax Christi International (1950): rue du Vieux Marché aux grains 21, B-1000 Brussels, Belgium. International Catholic peace movement. Originated in Lourdes, France in 1948 by French and German Catholics to reconcile enemies from World War II; spread to Italy and Poland and acquired its international ctitle when it merged with the English organization Pax. Associate member of ICO. (See Index: Pax Christi USA.)

Pax Romana* (1921, Fribourg, Switzerland, divided into two branches, 1947):

Pax Romana — IMCS* (International Movement of Catholic Students) (1921): 171, rue de Rennes, F-75006, Paris, France. For undergraduates.

Pax Romana — ICMICA* (International Catholic Movement for Intellectual and Cultural Affairs) (1947): rue de Alpes 7, C. P. 1062, CH-1701

Fribourg, Switzerland. For Catholic intellectuals and professionals.

Pro Sanctity Movement: Piazza S. Andrea della Valle 3, 00166 Rome, Italy.

St. Joan's International Alliance (1911, in England, as Catholic Women's Suffrage Society): Quai Churchill 19 - Boite 061, B-4020 Liege, Belgium. Associate member of ICO.

Salesian Cooperators (1876): Don Bosco College, Newton, N.J. 07860. Third Salesian family founded by St. John Bosco. Members commit themselves to an apostolate at the service of the Church, giving particular attention to youth in the Salesian spirit and style.

Secular Franciscan Order (1221, first Rule approved): Via Piemonte, 70, 00187, Rome, Italy. (See Index.)

Secular Fraternity of Charles de Foucauld: Katharinenweg 4, B4700 Eupen, Belgium.

Serra International (1953, in U.S.): (See Index.)

Society of St. Vincent de Paul* (1833, Paris): 5, rue du Pré-aux-Clercs, F-75007 Paris, France.

The Grail (1921, Nijmegen, The Netherlands): Duisburgerstrasse 470, D-4330, Mulheim, West Germany. (See Index.)

Third Order of St. Dominic (1285): Convento Santa Sabina, Piazza Pietro d'Illiria, Aventino, I-00153 Rome, Italy. (See Index.)

Unda: International Catholic Association for Radio and Television* (1928, Cologne, Germany): rue de l'Orme, 12, B-1040 Brussels, Belgium. (See Index.)

Unio Internationalis Laicorum in Servitio Ecclesiae (1965, Aachen, Germany): Postfach 990125, Am Kielshof 2, 5000 Cologne, Germany 91. Consists of national and diocesan associations of persons who give professional services to the Church.

Union of Adorers of the Blessed Sacrament (1937): Largo dei Monti Parioli 3, I-00197, Rome, Italy.

World Catholic Federation for the Biblical Apostolate (1969, Rome): Mittelstrasse, 12, P.O. Box 601, D-7000, Stuttgart 1, Germany.

World Movement of Christian Workers* (1961): 90, rue des Palais, 1210 Brussels, Belgium.

World Organization of Former Pupils of Catholic Education* (1967, Rome): 48, rue de Richelieu, F-75001 Paris, France.

World Union of Catholic Philosophical Societies (1948, Amsterdam, The Netherlands): The Catholic University of America, Washington, D.C. 20064.

World Union of Catholic Teachers* (1951): Piazza San Calisto 16, 00153 Rome, Italy.

World Union of Catholic Women's Organizations* (1910): 20, rue Notre Dame des Champs, F-75006 Paris, France.

Regional Organizations

European Federation for Catholic Adult Education (196, Lucerne, Switzerland): Kapuzinestrasse 84, A-4020 Linz, Austria.

European Forum of National Committees of the Laity (1968): 169, Booterstown Av., Blackrock, Co. Dublin, Ireland.

Movimiento Familiar Cristiano (1949-50, Montevideo and Buenos Aires): Carrera 17 n. 4671, Bogota, D.E., Colombia. Christian Family Movement of Latin America.

THE CATHOLIC CHURCH IN CANADA _____

The first date in the remote background of the Catholic history of Canada was July 7, 1534, when a priest in the exploration company of Jacques Cartier celebrated Mass on the Gaspe Peninsula.

Successful colonization and the significant beginnings of the Catholic history of the country date from the foundation of Quebec in 1608 by Samuel de Champlain and French settlers. Montreal was established in 1642.

The earliest missionaries were Franciscan Récollets (Recollects) and Jesuits who arrived in 1615 and 1625, respectively. They provided some pastoral care for the settlers but worked mainly among the 100,000 Indians — Algonquins, Hurons and Iroquois — in the interior and in the Lake Ontario region. Eight of the Jesuit missionaries, killed in the 1640s, were canonized in 1930. (See Index: Jesuit North American Martyrs.) Sulpician Fathers, who arrived in Canada late in the 1640s, played a part in the great missionary period which ended about 1700.

Kateri Tekakwitha, "Lily of the Mohawks," who was baptized in 1676 and died in 1680, was declared "Blessed" June 22, 1980.

The communities of women religious with the longest histories in Canada are the Canonesses of St. Augustine and the Ursulines, since 1639; and the Hospitallers of St. Joseph, since 1642. Communities of Canadian origin are the Congregation of Notre Dame, founded by St. Marguerite Bourgeoys in 1658, and the Grey Nuns, formed by St. Marie Marguerite d'Youville in 1737.

Mother Marie (Guyard) of the Incarnation, an Ursuline nun, was one of the first three women missionaries to New France; called "Mother of the Church in Canada," she was declared "Blessed" June 22, 1980.

Start of Church Organization

Ecclesiastical organization began with the appointment in 1658 of Francois De Montmorency-Laval, "Father of the Church in Canada," as vicar apostolic of New France. He was the first bishop of Quebec from 1674 to 1688, with jurisdiction over all French-claimed territory in North America. He was declared "Blessed" June 22, 1980.

In 1713, the French Canadian population numbered 18,000. In the same year, the Treaty of Utrecht ceded Acadia, Newfoundland and the Hudson Bay Territory to England. The Acadians were scattered among the American Colonies in 1755.

The English acquired possession of Canada and its 70,000 French-speaking inhabitants in virtue of the Treaty of Paris in 1763. Anglo-French and Anglican-Catholic differences and tensions developed. The pro-British government at first refused to recognize the titles of church officials, hindered the clergy in their work and tried to install a non-Catholic educational system. Laws were passed which guaranteed religious liberties to Catholics (Quebec Act of 1774, Constitutional Act of 1791, legislation approved by

Queen Victoria in 1851), but it took some time before actual respect for these liberties matched the legal enactments. The initial moderation of government antipathy toward the Church was caused partly by the loyalty of Catholics to the Crown during the American Revolution and the War of 1812.

Growth

The 15 years following the passage in 1840 of the Act of Union, which joined Upper and Lower Canada, were significant. New communities of men and women religious joined those already in the country. The Oblates of Mary Immaculate, missionaries par excellence in Canada, advanced the penetration of the West which had been started in 1818 by Abbe Provencher. New jurisdictions were established, and Quebec became a metropolitan see in 1844. The first Council of Quebec was held in 1851. The established Catholic school system enjoyed a period of growth.

Laval University was inaugurated in 1854 and canonically established in 1876.

Archbishop Elzear-Alexandre Taschereau of Quebec was named Canada's first cardinal in 1886.

The apostolic delegation to Canada was set up in 1899. It became a nunciature October 16, 1969, with the establishment of diplomatic relations with the Vatican.

Early in this century, Canada had eight ecclesiastical provinces, 23 dioceses, three vicariates apostolic, 3,500 priests, 2 million Catholics, about 30 communities of men religious, and 70 or more communities of women religious. The Church in Canada was phased out of mission status and removed from the jurisdiction of the Congregation for the Propagation of the Faith in 1908.

Diverse Population

The greatest concentration of Catholics is in the eastern portion of the country. In the northern and western portions, outside metropolitan centers, there are some of the most difficult parish and mission areas in the world. Bilingual (English-French) differences in the general population are reflected in the Church; for example, in the parallel structures of the Canadian Conference of Catholic Bishops, which was established in 1943. Quebec is the center of French cultural influence. Many language groups are represented among Catholics, who include more than 257,000 members of Eastern Rites in one metropolitan see, seven eparchies and an apostolic exarchate.

Education, a past source of friction between the Church and the government, is administered by the civil provinces in a variety of arrangements authorized by the Canadian Constitution. Denominational schools have tax support in one way in Quebec and Newfoundland, and in another way in Alberta, Ontario and Saskatchewan. Several provinces provide tax support only for public schools, making private financing necessary for separate church-related schools.

ECCLESIASTICAL JURISDICTIONS OF CANADA

Provinces

Names of ecclesiastical provinces and metropolitan sees in bold face: suffragan sees in parentheses.
Edmonton (Calgary, St. Paul).

Gatineau-Hull (Amos, Mont-Laurier, Rouyn Noranda).

Grouard-McLennan (Mackenzie-Ft. Smith, Prince George, Whitehorse).

Halifax (Antigonish, Charlottetown, Yarmouth).

Keewatin-LePas (Churchill-Hudson Bay, Labrador-Schefferville, Moosonee).

Kingston (Alexandria-Cornwall, Peterborough, Sault Ste. Marie).

Moncton (Bathurst, Edmundston, St. John).

Montreal (Joliette, St. Jean-Longueuil, St. Jerome, Valleyfield).

Ottawa (Hearst, Pembroke, Timmins).

Quebec (Chicoutimi, Ste.-Anne-de-la-Pocatiere, Trois Rivieres).

Regina (Gravelbourg, Prince Albert, Saskatoon, Abbey of St. Peter).

Rimouski (Baie-Comeau, Gaspe).

St. Boniface (no suffragan).

St. John's (Grand Falls, St. George).

Sherbrooke (Nicolet, St. Hyacinthe).

Toronto (Hamilton, London, St. Catharines, Thunder Bay).

Vancouver (Kamloops, Nelson, Victoria).

Winnipeg — Ukrainian (Edmonton, New Westminster, Saskatoon, Toronto).

Jurisdictions immediately subject to the Holy See: Roman-Rite Archdiocese of Winnipeg, Byzantine Eparchy of Sts. Cyril and Methodius for Slovaks, Byzantine Eparchy of St. Sauveur de Montreal for Greek Melkites; Antiochene Eparchy of St. Maron of Montreal for Maronites.

Jurisdictions, Hierarchy

(Principal sources: Information office, Canadian Conference of Catholic Bishops; Catholic Almanac survey; *Annuario Pontificio; L'Osservatore Romano;* Catholic News Service. As of June 1, 1997.)

Information includes names of archdioceses (indicated by asterisk) and dioceses, date of foundation, present ordinaries and auxiliaries; addresses of chancery office/bishop's residence; cathedral; former ordinaries. For biographies of current hierarchy, see Index.

Alexandria-Cornwall, Ont. (1890 as Alexandria; name changed to Alexandria-Cornwall, 1976): Eugene Philippe LaRocque, bishop, 1974.

Diocesan Center: 220, chemin Montreal, C.P. 1388, Cornwall, Ont. K6H 5V4. Cathedral: St. Finnans (Alexandria); Nativity Co-Cathedral (Cornwall).

Former bishops: Alexander Macdonell, 1890-1905; William A. Macdonell, 1906-20; Felix Couturier, O.P., 1921-41; Rosario Brodeur, 1941-66; Adolphe E. Proulx, 1967-74.

Amos, Que. (1938): Gerard Drainville, bishop, 1978.

Bishop's Residence: 450, rue Principale Nord, Amos, Que. J9T 2M1. Cathedral: St. Theresa of Avila.

Former bishops: Joseph Aldee Desmarais, 1939-68; Gaston Hains, 1968-78.

Antigonish, N.S. (Arichat, 1844; transferred, 1886): Colin Campbell, bishop, 1987.

Chancery Office: 155 Main St., P.O. Box 1330, Antigonish, N.S., B2G 2L7. Cathedral: St. Ninian.

Former bishops: William Fraser, 1844-51; Colin Francis MacKinnon, 1852-77; John Cameron, 1877-1910; James Morrison, 1912-50; John Roderick MacDonald, 1950-59; William E. Power, 1960-86.

Baie-Comeau, Que. (p.a., 1882; v.a., 1905; diocese Gulf of St. Lawrence, 1945; name changed, to

Hauterive, 1960; present title, 1986): Pierre Morissette, bishop, 1990.

Bishop's Residence: 639, rue de Bretagne, Baie-Comeau, Que., G5C 1X2. Cathedral: Paroisse St. Jean-Eudes.

Former bishops: Napoleon-Alexandre Labrie, C.J.M., v.a., 1938-45, first bishop, 1945-56; Gerard Couturier, 1957-74; Jean-Guy Couture, 1975-79; Roger Ebacher, 1979-88; Maurice Couture, R.S.V., 1988-90.

Bathurst, N.B. (Chatham, 1860; transferred, 1938): Andre Richard, C.S.C., bishop, 1989.

Bishop's Residence: 645, avenue Murray, C.P. 460, Bathurst, N.-B., E2A 3Z4. Cathedral: Sacred Heart of Jesus.

Former bishops: James Rogers, 1860-1902; Thomas F. Barry, 1902-20; Patrice-Alexandre Chiasson, C.J.M., 1920-42; Camille-Andre Le Blanc, 1942-69; Edgar Godin, 1969-85; Arsene Richard 1986-89.

Calgary, Alta. (1912): Paul J. O'Byrne, bishop, 1968.

Address: Room 290, Catholic Pastoral Center, 120 17 Ave. SW, Calgary, Alta. T2S 2T2. Cathedral: St. Mary.

Former bishops: John Thomas McNally, 1913-24; John T. Kidd, 1925-31; Peter J. Monahan, 1932-35; Francis P. Carroll, 1936-66; Francis J. Klein, 1967-68.

Charlottetown, P.E.I. (1829): Joseph Vernon Fougere, bishop, 1992.

Bishop's Residence: P.O. Box 907, Charlottetown, P.E.I., C1A 7L9. Cathedral: St. Dunstan's.

Former bishops: Bernard Angus McEachern, 1829-35; Bernard Donald McDonald, 1837-59; Peter McIntyre, 1860-91; James Charles McDonald, 1891-1912; Henry Joseph O'Leary, 1913-20; Louis James O'Leary, 1920-30; J.A. Sullivan, 1931-44; James Boyle, 1944-54; Malcolm A. MacEachern, 1955-70; Francis J. Spence, 1970-82; James H. MacDonald, 1982-91.

Chicoutimi, Que. (1878): Jean-Guy Couture, bishop, 1979. Roch Pedneault, auxiliary.

Bishop's Residence: 602, Racine Est, Chicoutimi, Que. G7H 6J6. Cathedral: St. Francois-Xavier.

Former bishops: Dominique Racine, 1878-88; Louis-Nazaire Begin (later cardinal), 1888-92; Michel-Thomas Labrecque, 1892-1927; Charles Lamarche, 1928-40; Georges Melancon, 1940-61; Marius Pare, 1961-79.

Churchill-Hudson Bay, Man. (p.a., 1925; v.a. Hudson Bay, 1931; diocese of Churchill, 1967; present title, 1968): Reynald Rouleau, O.M.I., bishop, 1987.

Diocesan Office: P.O. Box 10, Churchill, Man. ROB OEO. Cathedral: Holy Canadian Martyrs.

Former bishops: Arsene Turquetil, O.M.I., 1931-43; Armand Clabaut, O.M.I., coadjutor, 1937-40; Marc LaCroix, O.M.I., 1943-68; Omer Alfred Robidoux, 1970-86.

Edmonton,* Alta. (St. Albert, 1871; archdiocese, transferred Edmonton, 1912): Joseph N. MacNeil, archbishop, 1973.

Archdiocesan Office: 8421-101 Avenue, Edmonton, Alta. T6A OL1. Cathedral: Basilica of St. Joseph.

Former bishops: Vital-Justin Grandin, O.M.I., 1871-1902; Emile Legal, O.M.I., 1902-20, first archbishop; Henry Joseph O'Leary, 1920-38; John Hugh

MacDonald, 1938-64; Anthony Jordan, O.M.I., 1964-73.

Edmonton, Alta. (Ukrainian Byzantine) (ap. ex. of western Canada, 1948; eparchy, 1956): Lawrence Daniel Huculak, O.S.B.M., eparch, 1997.
Eparch's Residence: 9645 - 108th Ave., Edmonton, Alta. T5H 1A3. Cathedral: St. Josaphat.
Former bishops: Neil Nicholas Savaryn, O.S.B.M., 1948-86; Demetrius Martin Greschuk, 1986-90; Myron Daciuk, O.S.B.M., 1991-96.

Edmundston, N.B. (1944): François Thibodeau, C.J.M., bishop, 1994.
Diocesan Center: Edmundston, N.B. E3V 3K1. Cathedral: Immaculate Conception.
Former bishops: Marie-Antoine Roy, O.F.M., 1945-48; Joseph-Roméo Gagnon, 1949-70; Fernand Lacroix, C.J.M., 1970-83; Gérard Dionne, 1984-93.

Gaspe, Que. (1922): Raymond Dumais, bishop, 1994.
Bishop's House: 172, rue Jacques-Cartier, C.P. 440, Gaspe, Que. GOC 1RO. Cathedral: Christ the King.
Former bishops: Francois-Xavier Ross, 1922-45; Albini LeBlanc, 1945-57; Paul Bernier (personal title of Archbishop), 1957-64; Jean Marie Fortier, 1965-68; Gilles Ouellet, 1968-73; Bertrand Blanchet, 1973-93.

Gatineau-Hull,* Que. (1963, as Hull; name changed, 1982; archdiocese, 1990): Roger Ebacher, bishop, 1988; first archbishop, Oct. 31, 1990.
Diocesan Center: 180 Boul. Mont-Bleu, Hull, Que. J8Z 3J5.
Former bishops: Paul-Emile Charbonneau, 1963-73; Adolph Proulx, 1974-87.

Grand Falls, Nfld. (Harbour Grace, 1856; present title, 1964): Joseph Faber MacDonald, bishop, 1980.
Chancery Office: P.O. Box 397, Grand Falls, Windsor, Nfld. A2A 2J8. Cathedral: Immaculate Conception.
Former bishops: John Dalton, 1856-69; Henry Carfagnini, 1870-80; R. McDonald, 1881-1906; John March, 1906-40; John M. O'Neill, 1940-72; Alphonsus S. Penney, 1973-79.

Gravelbourg, Sask. (1930): Raymond Roussin, S.M., bishop, 1995.
Bishop's Residence: C.P. 690, Gravelbourg, Sask. SOH 1XO. Cathedral: Our Lady of the Assumption.
Former bishops: Jean-Marie Villeneuve, O.M.I., 1930-31; Arthur Melanson, 1932-36; Joseph Guy, O.M.I., 1937-42; M.-Joseph Lemieux, 1944-53; Aime Decosse, 1954-73; Noel Delaquis, 1974-95.

Grouard-McLennan,* Alta. (v.a. Athabaska-Mackenzie, 1862; Grouard, 1927; archdiocese Grouard-McLennan, 1967); Henri Goudreault, O.M.I., archbishop, 1996.
Archbishop's Residence: C.P. 388, McLennan, Alta. TOH 2LO. Cathedral: St. Jean-Baptiste (McLennan).
Former ordinaries: Henri Faraud, O.M.I., 1864-90; Emile Grouard, O.M.I., 1891-1929; Joseph Guy, O.M.I., 1930-38; Ubald Langlois, O.M.I., 1938-53; Henri Routhier, O.M.I., 1953-72, first archbishop; Henri Legare, O.M.I., 1972-96.

Halifax,* N.S. (1842; archdiocese, 1852): Austin E. Burke, archbishop, 1991.
Chancery Office: P.O. Box 1527, Halifax, N.S. B3J 2Y3.
Former ordinaries: Edmund Burke, vicar apostolic,

1818-20; William Fraser, 1842-44; William Walsh, 1844-58, first archbishop; Thomas L. Connolly, 1859-76; Michael Hannan, 1877-82; Cornelius O'Brien, 1883-1906; Edward J. McCarthy, 1906-31; Thomas O'Donnell, 1931-36; John T. McNally, 1937-52; Joseph G. Berry, 1953-67; James Martin Hayes, 1967-90.

Hamilton, Ont. (1856): Anthony Tonnos, bishop, 1984. Matthew Ustrzycki, auxiliary.
Chancery Office: 700 King St. West, Hamilton, Ont. L8P1C7. Cathedral: Christ the King.
Former bishops: John Farrell, 1856-73; Peter F. Crinnon, 1874-82; James Joseph Carbery, 1884-87; Thomas J. Dowling, 1889-1924; J. T. McNally, 1924-37; Joseph F. Ryan, 1937-73; Paul F. Reding, 1973-83.

Hearst, Ont. (p.a., 1918; v.a., 1920; diocese, 1938): André Vallée, P.M.E., bishop, 1996.
Bishop's Residence: 76 7e rue, C.P. 1330, Hearst, Ont. POL INO. Cathedral: Notre Dame of the Assumption.
Former bishops: Joseph Halle, 1919-38; Joseph Charbonneau, 1939-40; A. LeBlanc, 1941-45; Georges Landry, 1946-52; Louis Levesque, 1952-64; Jacques Landriault, 1964-71; Roger Despatie, 1973-93; Pierre Fisette, P.M.E., 1994-95.

Joliette, Que. (1904): Gilles Lussier, bishop, 1991.
Bishop's Residence: C.P. 470, 2 rue Saint-Charles-Borromée Nord, Joliette, Que. J6E 6H6. Cathedral: St. Charles Borromeo.
Former bishops: Joseph Archambault, 1904-13; Guillaume Forbes, 1913-28; Joseph A. Papineau, 1928-68; Rene Audet, 1968-90.

Kamloops, B.C. (1945): Lawrence Sabatini, C.S., bishop, 1982.
Bishop's Residence: 635A Tranquille Rd., Kamloops, B.C. V2B 3H5. Cathedral: Sacred Heart.
Former bishops: Edward Q. Jennings, 1946-52; Michael A. Harrington, 1952-73; Adam Exner, O.M.I., 1974-82.

Keewatin-Le Pas,* Man. (v.a., 1910; archdiocese, 1967): Peter-Alfred Sutton, O.M.I., archbishop, 1986.
Archbishop's Residence: 108, 1st St. West, P.O. Box 270, The Pas, Man. R9A 1K4. Cathedral: Our Lady of the Sacred Heart.
Former bishops: Ovide Charlebois, O.M.I., 1910-33; Martin LaJeunesse, O.M.I., 1933-54; Paul Dumouchel, O.M.I., 1955-86, first archbishop.

Kingston,* Ont. (1826; archdiocese, 1889): Francis J. Spence, archbishop, 1982.
Chancery Office: 390 Palace Rd., Kingston Ont. K7L 4T3. Cathedral: St. Mary of the Immaculate Conception.
Former bishops: Alexander Macdonell, 1826-40; Remigius Gaulin, 1840-57; Patrick Phelan, 1843-57; Edward J. Horan, 1858-75; John O'Brien, 1875-79; J. V. Cleary, 1880-98, first archbishop; C.-H. Gauthier, 1898-1910; Michael Joseph Spratt, 1911-38; Michael-Joseph O'Brien, 1939-43; Joseph A. O'Sullivan, 1944-66; Joseph L. Wilhelm 1966-82.

Labrador City (Nfld.)-Schefferville, Que. (v.a. Labrador, 1946; diocese, 1967): Vacant as of June 1, 1997. Rev. Joseph Baril, O.M.I., administrator.
Bishop's Residence: 318 avenue Elizabeth, C.P. 545, Labrador City, Labaador, Nfld. A2V 2K7. Cathedral: Our Lady of Perpetual Help.

Former bishops: Lionel Scheffer, O.M.I., 1946-66; Henri Legare, O.M.I., 1967-72; Peter A. Sutton, 1974-86.

London, Ont. (1855; transferred Sandwich, 1859; London, 1869): John M. Sherlock, bishop, 1978.
Bishop's Residence: 1070 Waterloo St., London, Ont. N6A 3Y2. Cathedral: St. Peter's Cathedral Basilica.
Former bishops: Pierre Adolphe Pinsoneault, 1856-66; John Walsh, 1867-89; Dennis O'Connor, C.S.B., 1890-99; F.P. McEvay 1899-1908; Michael F. Fallon, 1910-31; J. Thomas Kidd, 1931-50; John C. Cody, 1950-63; Gerald E. Carter, 1964-78.

Mackenzie-Fort Smith, N.W.T. (v.a. Mackenzie, 1902; diocese Mackenzie-Fort Smith, 1967): Denis Croteau, O.M.I., bishop, 1986.
Diocesan Office: 5117-52nd St., Yellowknife, NWT XIA 1T7. Cathedral: St. Joseph (Ft. Smith).
Former bishops: Gabriel Breynat, O.M.I., 1902-43; Joseph Trocellier, O.M.I., 1943-58; Paul Piche, 1959-86.

Moncton,* N.B. (1936): Ernest Léger, archbishop, 1997..
Archbishop's Residence: 452, rue Amirault, Dieppe, N.B. E1A 1G3. Cathedral: Our Lady of the Assumption.
Former bishops: L.J.-Arthur Melanson, 1937-41; Norbert Robichaud, 1942-72; Donat Chiasson, 1972-95.

Mont-Laurier, Que. (1913): Jean Gratton, bishop, 1978.
Bishop's Residence: 435, rue de la Madone, Mont-Laurier, Que. J9L 1S1. Cathedral: Notre Dame de Fourvières.
Former bishops: Francois-Xavier Brunet, 1913-22; Joseph-Eugene Limoges, 1922-63; Joseph Louis Andre Ouellette, apostolic administrator sede plena, 1963-65; bishop, 1965-78.

Montreal,* Que. (1836; archdiocese, 1886): Cardinal Jean-Claude Turcotte, archbishop, 1990. Jude Saint-Antoine, Neil Willard, André Rivest, André Cimichella, auxiliaries.
Archbishop's Residence: 2000, rue Sherbrooke Ouest, Montreal, Que. H3H 1G4. Cathedral: Basilica of Mary Queen of the World and Saint James.
Former bishops: Jean-Jacques Lartigue, P.S.S., 1836-40; Ignace Bourget, 1840-76; Edouard-Charles Fabre, first archbishop, 1876-96; Paul Bruchési, 1897-1939; Georges Gauthier, administrator 1921-39; archbishop, 1939-40; Joseph Charbonneau, 1940-50; Cardinal Paul-Emile Leger, 1950-67; Cardinal Paul Gregoire, 1968-90.

Moosonee, Ont. (v.a. James Bay, 1938; diocese Moosonee, 1967): Vincent Cadieux, O.M.I., bishop, 1992.
Bishop's Residence: C.P. 40, Moosonee, Ont. P0L 1Y0. Cathedral: Christ the King.
Former bishops: Henri Belleau, O.M.I., 1940-64; Jules LeGuerrier, O.M.I., 1964-91.

Nelson, B.C. (1936): Eugene J. Cooney, bishop, 1996.
Bishop's Residence: 813 Ward St., Nelson, B.C. V1L 1T4. Cathedral: Mary Immaculate.
Former bishops: Martin M. Johnson, 1936-54; Thomas J. McCarthy, 1955-58; Wilfrid E. Doyle, 1958-89; Peter Mallon, 1990-95.

New Westminster, B.C. (Ukrainian Byzantine) (1974): Severian Stephen Yakymyshyn, O.S.B.M., eparch, 1995.
Eparch's address: 502 5th Ave., New Westminster, BC V3L 1S2.
Former eparch: Jerome Chimy, O.S.B.M., 1974-92.

Nicolet, Que. (1885): Raymond Saint-Gelais, bishop, 1989.
Bishop's Residence: 49, rue Mgr Brunault, Nicolet, Que. J3T 1X7. Cathedral: St.-Jean-Baptiste.
Former bishops: Elphege Gravel, 1885-1904; Joseph-Simon-Hermann Brunault, 1904-38; Albini Lafortune, 1938-50; Albert Martin, 1950-89.

Ottawa,* Ont. (Bytown, 1847, name changed, 1854; archdiocese, 1886): Marcel Gervais, archbishop, 1989. Paul Marchand, S.M.M., Frederick Colli, auxiliaries.
Archbishop's Residence: 1247 Place Kilborn, Ottawa, Ont. K1H 6K9. Cathedral: Basilica of Notre Dame-of-Ottawa.
Former bishops: Joseph-Eugene-Bruno Guigues, 1848-74; Joseph Tomas Duhamel, first archbishop, 1874-1909; Charles Hughes Gauthier, 1910-22; Joseph-Medard Emard, 1922-27; Joseph Guillaume Forbes, 1928-40; Alexandre Vachon, 1940-53; Marie-Joseph Lemieux, O.P., 1953-66; Joseph Aurele Plourde, 1967-89.

Pembroke, Ont. (v.a. 1882; diocese, 1898): Brendan M. O'Brien, bishop, 1993.
Bishop's Residence: 188 Renfrew St., P.O. Box 7, Pembroke, Ont. K8A 6X1. Cathedral: St. Columbkille.
Former bishops: Narcisse-Zephirin Lorrain, 1882-1915; Patrick T. Ryan, 1916-37; Charles-Leo Nelligan, 1937-45; William J. Smith, 1945-71; Joseph R. Windle, 1971-93.

Peterborough, Ont. (1882): James L. Doyle, bishop, 1976.
Bishop's Residence: 350 Hunter St. West, PO Box 175, Peterborough, Ont. K9J 6Y8. Cathedral: St. Peter-in-Chains.
Former bishops: John Francis Jamot, 1882-86; Thomas J. Dowling, 1887-89; Richard A. O'Connor, 1889-1913; Michael J. O'Brien, 1913-29; Denis O'Connor, 1930-42; John R. McDonald, 1943-45; Joseph G. Berry, 1945-53; Benjamin I. Webster, 1954-68; Francis A. Marrocco, 1968-75.

Prince Albert, Sask. (v.a., 1890; diocese, 1907): Blaise Morand, bishop, 1983.
Address: 1415-4th Ave. West, Prince-Albert, Sask. S6V 5H1. Cathedral: Sacred Heart.
Former bishops: Albert Pascal, O.M.I., 1907-20; Joseph Henri Prud'homme, 1921-37; R. Duprat, O.P., 1938-52; Leo Blais, 1952-59; Laurent Morin, 1959-83.

Prince George, B.C. (p.a., 1908; v.a. Yukon and Prince Rupert, 1944; diocese Prince George, 1967): Gerald Wiesner, O.M.I., bishop, 1993.
Chancery Office: P.O. Box 7000, 2935 Highway 16 West, Prince George, B.C. V2N 3Z2. Cathedral: Sacred Heart.
Former bishops: Emile-Marie Bunoz, O.M.I., 1917-45; John-Louie Coudert, O.M.I., coadjutor, 1936-44; Anthony Jordan, O.M.I., 1945-55; John F. O'Grady, O.M.I. 1955-86; Hubert P. O'Connor, O.M.I., 1986-91.

Quebec,* Que. (v.a., 1658; diocese, 1674; archdiocese, 1819; metropolitan, 1844; primatial see, 1956): Maurice Couture, R.S.V., archbishop, 1990. Marc Leclerc, Jean Pierre Blais, Eugène Tremblay, auxiliaries.
Chancery Office: 1073, boul. René Lévesque Ouest, Quebec, Que. G1S 4R5. Cathedral: Notre-Dame- de-Quebec (Basilica).
Former bishops: Francois de Laval, vicar apostolic, 1658; bishop 1674-88 (beatified 1980); Jean-Baptiste de La Croix de Chevrières de Saint-Vallier, 1688-1727; Louis-Francois Duplessis de Mornay, 1727-33; Pierre-Herman Dosquet, 1733-39; Francois-Louis de Pourroy de Lauberivière, 1739-40; Henri-Marie Dubreil de Pontbriand, 1741-60; Jean-Olivier Briand, 1766-84; Louis-Philippe Mariauchau d'Esgly, 1784-88; Jean-Francois Hubert, 1788-97; Pierre Denaut, 1797-1806; Joseph-Octave Plessis, first archbishop, 1806-25; Bernard-Claude Panet, 1825-33; Joseph Signay, 1833-50; Pierre-Flavien Turgeon, 1850-67; Charles-Francois Baillargeon, 1867-70; Cardinal Elzear-Alexandre Taschereau, 1870-98; Cardinal Louis-Nazaire Begin, 1898-1925; Paul-Eugène Roy, 1925-26; Cardinal Rymond-Marie Rouleau, O.P., 1926-31; Cardinal Jean-Marie-Rodrigue Villeneuve, O.M.I., 1931-47; Cardinal Maurice Roy, 1947-81; Cardinal Louis-Albert Vachon, 1981-90.
Regina,* Sask. (1910; archdiocese, 1915): Peter Mallon, archbishop, 1995.
Chancery Office: 445 Broad St. North, Regina, Sask. S4R 2X8. Cathedral: Our Lady of the Most Holy Rosary.
Former bishops: Olivier-Elzear Mathieu, 1911-29; James Charles McGuigan, 1930-34; Peter Joseph Monahan, 1935-47; Michael C.O'Neill, 1948-73; Charles A. Halpin, 1973-94.
Rimouski,* Que. (1867; archdiocese, 1946): Bertrand Blanchet, archbishop, 1992.
Archbishop's Residence: 34, rue de l'Évêché Ouest, C.P. 730, Rimouski, Que. G5L 7C7.
Former bishops: Jean Langevin, 1867-91; Andre-Albert Blais, 1891-1919; J.-R. Leonard, 1919-26; Georges Courchesne, 1928-50; Charles-Eugene Parent, 1951-67; Louis Lévesque, 1967-73; Gilles Ouellet, P.M.E., 1973-92.
Rouyn-Noranda, Que. (1973): Jean-Guy Hamelin, bishop, 1974.
Bishop's Residence: 515, avenue Cuddihy, C.P. 1060, Rouyn-Noranda, Que. J9X 4C5. Cathedral: St. Michael the Archangel.
Saint-Boniface,* Man. (1847; archdiocese, 1871): Antoine Hacault, archbishop, 1974.
Archbishop's Residence: 151, avenue de la Cathedrale, Saint-Boniface, Man. R2H OH6. Cathedral: Basilica of St. Boniface.
Former bishops: Joseph-Norbert Provencher, 1847-53; Alexandre-Antonin Tache, O.M.I., 1853-94, first archbishop; Vital-Justin Grandin, O.M.I., coadjutor, 1857-71; Louis-Philippe-Adelard Langevin, O.M.I., 1895-1915; Arthur Beliveau, 1915-55; Emile Yelle, P.S.S., coadjutor, 1933-41; Georges Cabana, coadjutor, 1941-52; Maurice Baudoux, coadjutor 1952-55, archbishop, 1955-74.
St. Catharines, Ont. (1958): John A. O'Mara, bishop, 1994.
Bishop's Residence: 122 Riverdale Ave., St.

Catharines, Ont. L2R 4C2. Cathedral: St. Catherine of Alexandria.
Former bishops: Thomas J. McCarthy, 1958-78; Thomas B. Fulton, 1978-94.
St. George's, Nfld. (p.a., 1870; v.a., 1890; diocese, 1904): Raymond J. Lahey, bishop, 1986.
Bishop's Residence: 16 Hammond Dr., Corner Brook, Nfld. A2H 2W2. Cathedral: Most Holy Redeemer and Immaculate Conception.
Former bishops: Neil McNeil, 1904-10; Michael Power, 1911-20; Henry T. Renouf, 1920-41; Michael O'Reilly, 1941-70; Richard T. McGrath, 1970-85.
Saint-Hyacinthe, Que. (1852): Louis-de-Gonzague Langevin, M.Afr., bishop, 1979.
Bishop's Residence: 1900, rue Girouard Ouest, C.P. 190, Saint-Hyacinthe, Que. J2S 7B4. Cathedral. St. Hyacinthe the Confessor.
Former bishops: Jean-Charles Prince, 1852-60; Joseph Larocque, 1860-65; Charles Larocque, 1866-75; Louis-Zéphirin Moreau, 1875-1901 (beatified 1987); Maxime Decelles, 1901-05; Alexis-Xyste Bernard, 1906-23; Fabien-Zoël Decelles, 1924-42; Arthur Doubille, 1942-67; Albert Sanschagrin, O.M.I., 1967-79.
Saint-Jean-Longueuil, Que. (1933 as St.-Jean-de-Quebec; named changed, 1982): Jacques Berthelet, C.S.V., bishop, 1996.
Bishop's Residence: 740, boulevard Sainte-Foy, C.P. 40, Longueuil, Que. J4K 4X8. Cathedral: St. John the Evangelist.
Former bishops: Anastase Forget, 1934-55; Gerard-Marie Coderre, 1955-78; Bernard Hubert, 1978-96.
St. Jerome, Que. (1951): Vacant as of June 1, 1997. Vital Massé, auxiliary.
Bishop's Residence: 355, rue Saint-Georges, C.P. 580, Saint-Jerome, Que. J7Z 5V3. Cathedral: St. Jerome.
Former bishops: Emilien Frenette, 1951-71; Bernard Hubert, 1971-77; Charles Valois,. 1977-97
Saint John, N.B. (1842): J. Edward Troy, bishop, 1986.
Chancery Office: 1 Bayard Dr., Saint John, N.B. E2L 3L5. Cathedral: Immaculate Conception.
Former bishops: William Dollard, 1843-51; Thomas L. Connolly, 1852-59; John Sweeney, 1860-1901; Timothy Casey, 1901-12; Edward A. LeBlanc, 1912-35; Patrick A. Bray, C.J.M., 1936-53; Alfred B. Leverman, 1953-68; Joseph N. MacNeil, 1969-73; Arthur J. Gilbert, 1974-86.
St. John's,* Nfld. (p.a., 1784; v.a., 1796; diocese, 1847; archdiocese, 1904): James H. MacDonald, C.S.C., archbishop, 1991.
Chancery Office: P.O. Box 1363, St. John's, Nfld. A1C 5H5. Cathedral: St. John the Baptist.
Former bishops: James O'Donel, O.S.F., 1784-1807; Patrick Lambert, O.S.F., 1807-17; Patrick Lambert, O.S.F., 1807-17; Thomas Scallan, O.S.F., 1817-30; Michael A. Fleming, O.S.F., 1830-50; John T. Mullock, O.S.F., 1850-69; Thomas J. Power, 1870-93; Michael Howley, first archbishop, 1895-1914; Edward P. Roche, 1915-50; Patrick J. Skinner, C.J.M., 1951-79; Alphonsus L. Penney, 1979-91.
St. Maron of Montreal (Maronites) (1982): Joseph Khoury, eparch, 1996.
Chancery Office: 12475 rue Grenet, Montreal, Que. H4J 2K4. Cathedral: St. Maron.

Former bishops: Elias Shaheen, 1982-90; Georges Abi-Saber, 1991-96.

St. Paul in Alberta (1948): Thomas Christopher Collins, bishop, 1997.
Bishop's Residence: 4410, 51e avenue, Saint Paul, Alta. TOA 3A2. Cathedral: St. Paul.
Former bishops: Maurice Baudoux, 1948-52; Philippe Lussier, C.Ss.R., 1952-68; Edouard Gagnon, P.S.S., 1969-72; Raymond Roy, 1972-97.

St. Sauveur de Montreal (Greek Melkites) (ap. ex. 1980; eparchy, 1984): Archeparch Michel Hakim, 1980.
Address: 34 Maplewood, Montreal, Que. H2V 2MI.

Sts. Cyril and Methodius of Toronto (Slovakian Byzantine) (1980): Vacant as of June 1, 1997..
Eparch's Residence: 223 Carlton Rd., Unionville, Ont. L3R 3M2.
Former eparch: Michael Rusnak, C.Ss.R., 1980-96.

Sainte-Anne-de-la-Pocatiere, Que. (1951): Clement Fecteau, bishop, 1996.
Bishop's Residence: 1200, 4e avenue, C.P. 430, La Pocatière, Que. GOR 1ZO. Cathedral: St. Anne.
Former bishops: Bruno Desrochers, 1951-68; Charles Henri Levesque, 1968-84; Andre Gaumond, 1985-95.

Saskatoon, Sask. (1933): V. James Weisgerber, bishop, 1996.
Chancery Office: 106-5th Avenue North, Saskatoon, Sask. S7K 2N7. Cathedral: St. Paul.
Former bishops: Gerald C. Murray, C.SS.R., 1934-44; Philip F. Pocock, 1944-51; F. Klein, 1951-67; James P. Mahoney, 1967-95.

Saskatoon, Sask. (Ukrainian Byzantine) (ap. ex., 1951; diocese, 1956): Cornelius Pasichny, O.S.B.M., bishop, 1995.
Address: 866 Saskatechewan Crescent East, Saskatoon, Sask. S7N OL4.
Former bishops: Andrew J. Roborecki, 1951-82; Basil (Wasyl) Filevich, 1984-95.

Sault Ste. Marie, Ont. (1904): Jean-Louis Plouffe, bishop, 1990. Bernard F. Pappin, Paul-André Durocher, auxiliaries.
Chancery Office: 387 Algonquin, P.O. Box 510, North Bay, Ont. P1B 8J1. Sudbury Office: 435, Avenue Notre Dame, Sudbury, Ont. B3C-5K6. Cathedral: Pro-Cathedral of the Assumption, North Bay.
Former bishops: David Joseph Scollard, 1905-34; Ralphael Hubert Dignan, 1934-58; Alexander Carter, 1958-85; Marcel Gervais, 1985-89.

Sherbrooke,* Que. (1874; archdiocese, 1951); André Gaumond, archbishop, 1996.
Archbishop's Residence: 130, rue de la Cathedrale, C.P. 430, Sherbrooke, Que. J1H 5K1. Cathedral: St. Michel.
Former ordinaries: Antoine Racine, 1874-93; Paul Larocque, 1893-1926; Alphonse-Osias Gagnon, 1927-41; Philippe Desranleau, first archbishop, 1941-52; Georges Cabana, 1952-68; J.M. Fortier, 1968-1996.

Thunder Bay, Ont. (Ft. William, 1952; transferred, 1970): Frederick Henry, bishop, 1995.
Bishop's Residence: P.O. Box 756, Thunder Bay, Ont. P7C 4W6. Cathedral: St. Patrick.
Former bishops: Edward Q. Jennings, 1952-69; Norman J. Gallagher, 1970-75; John A. O'Mara, 1976-94.

Timmins, Ont. (v.a. Temiskaming, 1908; diocese Haileybury, 1915; present title, 1938): Gilles Cazabon, O.M.I., bishop, 1992.
Address: 65, Ave. Jubilee Est, Timmins, Ont. P4N 5W4. Cathedral: St. Anthony of Padua.
Former bishops: Elie-Anicet Latulippe, 1908-22; Louis Rheaume, O.M.I., 1922-55; Maxime Tessier, 1955-71; Jacques Landriault, 1971-90.

Toronto,* Ont. (1841; archdiocese, 1870): Aloysius M. Ambrozic, archbishop, 1990. John Stephen Knight, Nicola De Angelis, C.F.I.C., Terrence Prendergast, S.J., Robert B. Clune, Anthony Meagher, auxiliaries.
Chancery Office: 1155 Yonge St., Toronto, Ont. M4Y 1W2. Cathedral: St. Michael.
Former ordinaries: Michael Power, 1842-47; Armand-Francois-Marie de Charbonnel, 1850-60; John Joseph Lynch, first archbishop, 1860-88; John Walsh, 1889-98; Denis O'Connor, 1899-1908; Fergus P. McEvay, 1908-11; Neil McNeil, 1912-34; Cardinal James Charles McGuigan, 1934-71; Philip F. Pocock, 1971-78; Cardinal G. Emmett Carter, 1978-90.

Toronto, Ont. (Ukrainian Byzantine) (ap. ex., 1948; eparchy, 1956): Isidore Borecky (exarch 1948-56), first eparch, 1956. Roman Danylak, apostolic administrator, 1993.
Chancery Office: 143 Franklin Ave.., Toronto, Ont. M6P 3Y9. Cathedral: St. Josaphat.

Trois-Rivieres, Que. (1852): Martin Veillette, bishop, 1996.
Bishop's Residence: 362, rue Bonaventure, C.P. 879, Trois-Rivieres, Que. G9A 5J9. Cathedral: The Assumption.
Former bishops: Thomas Cooke, 1852-70; L.-F. Lafleche, 1870-98; F.-X. Cloutier, 1899-1934; A.-O. Comtois, 1935-45; Maurice Roy, 1946-47; Georges-Leon Pelletier, 1947-75; Laurent Noel, 1975-96.

Unionville, Ont.: See Sts. Cyril and Methodius of Toronto, above.

Valleyfield, Que. (1892): Robert Lebel, bishop, 1976.
Bishop's Residence: 11, rue de l'Eglise, Valleyfield, Que. J6T 1J5. Cathedral: St. Cecilia.
Former bishops: Joseph Médard Emard, 1892-1922; Raymond-M. Rouleau, O.P., 1922-26; Joseph Alfred Langlois, 1926-66; Percival Caza, 1966-69; Guy Belanger, 1969-75.

Vancouver,* B. C. (v.a. British Columbia, 1863; diocese New Westminster, 1890; archdiocese Vancouver, 1908): Adam Exner, O.M.I., archbishop, 1991.
Chancery Office: 150 Robson St., Vancouver, B.C. V6B 2A7. Cathedral: Holy Rosary.
Former ordinaries: Louis-Joseph d'Herbomez, O.M.I., 1864-90; Paul Durieu, O.M.I., 1890-99; Augustin Dontenwill, O.M.I., 1899-1908; Neil McNeil, first archbishop, 1910-12; Timothy Casey, 1912-31; William M. Duke, 1931-64; Martin Michael Johnson, 1964-69; James F. Carney, 1969-90.

Victoria, B.C. (diocese Vancouver Is., 1846; archdiocese, 1903; diocese Victoria, 1908): Remi J. De Roo, bishop, 1962.
Chancery Office: Diocesan Pastoral Centre, #1-4044 Nelthorpe St., Victoria, B.C. V8X 2A1. Cathedral: St. Andrew.

Former bishops: Modeste Demers, 1847-71; Charles J. Seghers, 1873-78; Jean Baptiste Brondel, 1879-84; Charles J. Seghers (2nd time), 1885-86; J. N. Lemmens, 1888-97; Alexander Christie, 1898-99; Bertram Orth, 1900-08; Alexander Macdonald, 1909-23; Thomas O'Donnell, 1924-29; Gerald Murray, C.SS.R., 1930-33; John H. MacDonald, 1933-37; John C. Cody, 1937-46; James M. Hill, 1946-62.

Whitehorse, Y.T. (v.a., 1944; diocese 1967): Thomas Lobsinger, O.M.I., bishop, 1987.

Bishop's Residence: 5119-5th Avenue, Whitehorse, Yukon Y1A 1L5. Cathedral: Sacred Heart.

Former bishops: Jean-Louis Coudert, O.M.I., 1944-65(?); James Mulvihill, O.M.I., 1966-71; Hubert P. O'Connor, O.M.I., 1971-86.

Winnipeg,* Man. (1915): Leonard J. Wall, archbishop, 1992.

Chancery Office: 1495 Pembina Highway, Winnipeg, Man., R3T 2C6. Cathedral: St. Mary.

Former bishops: Alfred Sinnott, 1915-52; Gerald Murray, coadjutor, 1944-51; Philip F. Pocock, 1952-61; Cardinal George B. Flahiff, 1961-82; Adam Exner, O.M.I., 1982-91.

Winnipeg,* Man. (Ukrainian Byzantine) (Ordinariate of Canada, 1912; ap. ex. Central Canada, 1948; ap. ex. Manitoba, 1951; archeparchy Winnipeg, 1956): Michael Bzdel, C.Ss.R., archeparch, 1993. Stefan Soroka, auxiliary.

Archeparchy Office: 233 Scotia St., Winnipeg, Man., R2V 1V7. Cathedral: Sts. Vladimir and Olga.

Former ordinaries: Niceta Budka, 1912-28; Basile-Vladimir Ladyka, O.S.B.M., 1929-56; Maxim Hermaniuk, C.Ss.R., first archbishop, 1956-92.

Yarmouth, N.S. (1953): James M. Wingle, bishop, 1993.

Address: C.P. 278, 53 rue Park, Yarmouth, N.S. B5A 4B2. Cathedral: St. Ambrose.

Former bishops: Albert Lemenager, 1953-67; Austin E. Burke, 1968-91.

Military Ordinariate of Canada (1951): Vacant as of June 1, 1997.

Address: Catholic Chaplain General, National Defense Headquarters, Ottawa, Ont. K1A OK2.

Former military ordinaries: Cardinal Maurice Roy, archbishop of Quebec, 1946-82; John S. Spence, Archbishop of Kingston, 1982-87; André Vallée, 1988-96.

Abbacy of St. Peter, Muenster, Sask. (1921): Peter Novecosky, O.S.B., abbatial blessing, 1990.

Abbot's Residence: St. Peter's Abbey, Muenster, Sask. SOK 2YO.

Former abbots: Bruno Doerfler, 1911-19; Michael Ott, 1921-26; Severinus Gertken, 1927-60; Jerome Weber, 1960-90.

An **Apostolic Exarchate for Armenian-Rite Catholics in Canada and the United States** was established in July, 1981, with headquarters in New York City (110 E. 12th St., New York, NY 10003). Hovhannes Tertzakian, exarch, 1995.

The eparchy of **Our Lady of Deliverance of Newark** for Syrian-rite Catholics in the United States and Canada was established Nov. 6, 1995. Address: 502 Palisade Ave., Union City, NJ 07087. Most Rev. Joseph Younan, bishop.

Most Rev. Attila Mikloshazy, S.J., titular bishop of Castel Minore and bishop for **Hungarian Emigrants throughout the world,** resides in Canada. Address: 2661 Kingston Rd., Scarborough, Ont. M1M 1M3.

Dioceses with Interprovincial Lines

The following dioceses, indicated by + in the table, have interprovincial lines.

Churchill-Hudson Bay includes part of Northwest Territories.

Keewatin-LePas includes part of Manitoba and Saskatchewan provinces.

Labrador City-Schefferville includes the Labrador region of Newfoundland and the northern part of Quebec province.

Mackenzie-Fort Smith, Northwest Territories, includes part of Alberta and Saskatchewan provinces.

Moosonee, Ont., includes part of Quebec province.

Pembroke, Ont., includes one county of Quebec province.

Whitehorse, Y.T., includes part of British Columbia.

RESTORATION OF EASTERN LITURGY

Early in 1996, the Vatican urged Eastern Catholic churches to restore ancient practices of their own traditions that may have been abandoned over time because of Latin-rite influence.

"This is almost a revolutionary document," said Maronite Chorbishop John D. Faris, vicar general of the Diocese of St. Maron in Brooklyn, N.Y., "because it is a very clear statement on the part of the Apostolic See that Latinization (of Eastern rites) has been completely abandoned."

One of the more evident reforms envisioned is a return to giving infants first Communion immediately after baptism and chrismation (confirmation) -- and then having young children continue to receive Communion regularly in their preschool years.

The document, entitled "Instruction for the Application of the Liturgical Prescriptions of the Code of Canons of the Eastern Churches," was published in Italian by the Congregation for Eastern-Rite Churches in January, 1996.

It is the first instruction on liturgical renewal of Eastern churches since the Second Vatican Council. It was issued to clarify and expand on the liturgical implementation of the 1990 Code of Canons of the Eastern Churches, a body of general law governing all Eastern-rite Catholic churches.

The instruction testifies to "the inalienable value of the Eastern churches' own, diversified traditions" and the "richness of (their) liturgical heritage."

It urges Eastern Catholic churches to be faithful to their ancient traditions in part because of their special mission to promote Catholic-Orthodox church unity.

"In every effort of liturgical renewal, the practice of our Orthodox brothers will have to be taken into account," the instruction says. "Now is the time for Catholics and Orthodox to make an extra effort to understand each other better and to recognize with the renewed wonder of brotherhood what the Spirit is accomplishing in their respective traditions toward a new Christian springtime," said Pope John Paul Aug. 11, 1996.

STATISTICS OF THE CATHOLIC CHURCH IN CANADA

(Principal source: *1996-1997 Directory of the Canadian Conference of Catholic Bishops* (figures as of October, 1995); Catholic population statistics are those reported in the 1991 Canadian Census. Archdioceses are indicated by an asterisk. For dioceses marked +, see Canadian dioceses with interprovincial lines.)

Canada's 10 civil provinces and two territories are divided into 18 ecclesiastical provinces consisting of 18 metropolitan sees (archdioceses) and 51 suffragan sees (50 dioceses and one territorial abbacy); there are also one archdiocese and three eparchies immediately subject to the Holy See. (See listing of Ecclesiastical Provinces elsewhere in this section.)

This table presents a regional breakdown of Catholic statistics. In some cases, the totals are approximate because diocesan boundaries fall within several civil provinces.

Civil Province Diocese	Cath. Pop.	Dioc. Priests	Rel. Priests	Total Priests	Perm. Deacs.	Bro- thers	Sis- ters	Lay Assts.	Par- ishes
Newfoundland	**213,055**	**100**	**50**	**150**	**1**	**20**	**364**	**22**	**162**
*St. John's	119,260	47	19	66	-	12	276	6	44
Grand Falls	37,940	27	1	28	-	-	30	1	72
Labrador-Schefferville+	13,550	-	8	8	1	4	29	14	25
St. George's	42,305	26	22	48	-	4	29	1	21
Prince Edward Island									
Charlottetown	**60,625**	**62**	**2**	**64**	**1**	**-**	**180**	**2**	**59**
Nova Scotia	**331,010**	**246**	**83**	**329**	**27**	**12**	**869**	**18**	**220**
*Halifax	152,515	66	62	128	26	1	349	13	53
Antigonish	138,990	157	9	166	-	8	483	-	127
Yarmouth	39,505	23	12	35	1	3	37	5	40
New Brunswick	**386,480**	**254**	**62**	**316**	**2**	**35**	**885**	**27**	**254**
*Moncton	105,775	67	30	97	1	23	329	3	63
Bathurst	115,560	65	9	74	-	8	257	16	65
Edmundston	52,435	45	11	56	-	2	153	8	34
St. John	112,710	77	12	89	1	2	146	-	92
Quebec	**6,057,315**	**3,295**	**2,160**	**5,455**	**335**	**2,311**	**18,509**	**1,309**	**1,892**
*Gatineau-Hull	216,725	64	48	112	1	12	264	91	60
*Montreal	1,656,297	657	903	1,560	92	675	6,369	47	282
*Quebec	902,545	591	391	982	73	462	4,172	105	272
*Rimouski	152,565	145	54	199	3	91	801	31	117
*Sherbrooke	235,145	249	121	370	20	108	1,228	21	139
Amos	103,890	60	23	83	1	11	164	21	67
Baie Comeau	93,715	51	19	70	9	14	116	28	49
Chicoutimi	275,580	218	60	278	34	64	748	98	97
Gaspe	94,645	74	19	93	2	6	189	11	66
Joliette	177,138	106	60	166	3	136	402	86	58
Mont Laurier	72,755	46	30	76	-	27	144	53	59
Nicolet	177,620	179	30	209	19	108	736	17	85
Rouyn-Noranda	56,475	28	16	44	-	2	111	28	41
Ste-Anne-de-la-Pocatiere	87,865	145	1	146	5	3	240	61	54
St. Hyacinthe	330,515	192	91	283	28	215	1,138	179	112
St. Jean-Longueuil	524,150	131	61	192	1	97	435	184	93
St. Jerome	353,310	104	112	216	12	114	266	173	69
St. Maron Montreal (Maronites)	80,000	7	5	12	2	-	3	-	10
St. Sauveur Montreal (Greek-Melkites)	38,000	2	9	11	-	-	-	-	9
Trois Riviers	243,085	151	74	225	22	112	788	-	91
Valleyfield	185,295	95	33	128	8	54	195	75	62
Ontario	**3,575,065**	**1,354**	**1,128**	**2,482**	**339**	**203**	**3,947**	**172**	**1,241**
*Kingston	102,650	68	7	75	7	-	201	9	72
*Ottawa	364,285	151	195	346	29	65	951	-	118
*Toronto	1,420,395	262	506	768	116	75	1,016	-	217

Civil Province Diocese	Cath. Pop.	Dioc. Priests	Rel. Priests	Total Priests	Perm. Deacs.	Bro- thers	Sis- ters	Lay Assts.	Par- ishes
Ontario									
Alexandria-Cornwall	56,020	41	1	42	13	4	77	8	34
Hamilton	480,695	143	115	258	2	25	370	46	122
Hearst	34,840	36	1	37	-	3	23	18	35
London	414,285	227	87	314	2	9	495	54	172
Moosonee+	3,905	-	5	5	1	3	11	-	19
Pembroke+	64,925	76	6	82	8	4	232	-	68
Peterborough	83,680	113	4	117	6	-	141	4	74
St. Catharine's	145,850	68	34	102	2	2	59	4	47
Sts. Cyril and Methodius (Toronto-Slovaks)	10,000	4	5	9	-	-	-	-	12
Sault Ste. Marie	218,850	107	36	143	110	4	241	11	96
Thunder Bay	78,480	30	26	56	20	2	48	2	43
Timmins	55,195	28	6	34	8	6	45	16	34
Toronto (Ukrainians)	41,010	-	94	94	15	1	37	-	78
Manitoba	**346,180**	**170**	**151**	**321**	**28**	**65**	**713**	**75**	**455**
*Keewatin-LePas+	35,195	1	20	21	-	5	22	1	52
*St. Boniface	101,920	87	58	145	9	55	427	70	106
*Winnipeg	170,590	50	56	106	-	3	225	-	150
*Winnepeg (Ukrainians)	33,490	32	10	42	19	1	30	2	130
Churchill-Hudson Bay+	4,985	-	7	7	-	1	9	2	17
Saskatchewan	**301,335**	**149**	**117**	**266**	**9**	**24**	**599**	**18**	**494**
*Regina	124,190	68	25	93	-	4	164	-	166
Gravelbourg	14,775	27	2	29	-	-	56	6	39
Prince Albert	57,580	33	16	49	2	2	114	6	87
Saskatoon	75,140	-	37	37	-	2	160	5	51
Saskatoon (Ukrainians)	20,080	21	15	36	7	2	28	1	131
St. Peter Muenster (Abb.)	9,570	-	22	22	-	14	77	-	20
Alberta	**665,870**	**240**	**206**	**446**	**10**	**45**	**785**	**62**	**535**
*Edmonton	294,935	81	108	189	-	25	509	34	166
*Grouard-McLennan	40,715	6	26	32	-	1	31	14	66
Calgary	250,605	94	55	149	2	14	137	-	130
Edmonton (Ukrainians)	26,250	28	14	42	8	4	36	-	93
St. Paul	53,365	31	3	34	-	1	72	14	80
British Columbia	**600,175**	**194**	**145**	**339**	**7**	**41**	**352**	**49**	**332**
*Vancouver	340,775	99	89	188	-	30	184	14	76
Kamloops	47,010	14	8	22	1	3	23	-	70
Nelson	63,570	27	19	46	-	-	35	10	53
New Westminster (Ukrainians)	7,555	15	2	17	3	-	2	-	17
Prince George	51,200	6	13	19	2	5	30	19	60
Victoria	90,065	33	14	47	1	3	78	6	56
Yukon Territory									
Whitehorse+	**8,235**	**2**	**12**	**14**	**-**	**1**	**10**	**13**	**24**
Northwest Territories									
MacKenzie-Ft. Smith+	**19,745**	**1**	**9**	**10**	**2**	**2**	**20**	**1**	**38**
Military Ordinariate	**35,355**	**-**	**8**	**8**	**1**	**-**	**-**	**16**	**33**
TOTALS	**12,600,445[1]**	**6,067**	**4,125**	**10,192**	**761**	**2,755**	**27,233**	**1,784**	**5,706**

[1]Catholics comprise about 44% of the total population.

Varela Stamp: The first U.S. postage stamp featuring a Catholic priest, Father Felix Varela — Cuban patriot, philosopher, defender of immigrants and vicar general of the Archdiocese of New York — was unveiled in August, 1997, in St. Augustine. "In unveiling this stamp, we also honor all the Cubans and Hispanics who have contributed to the development of Florida," said Mayor Len Weeks, a year before the 200th anniversary of Father Varela's birth.

CANADIAN CONFERENCE OF CATHOLIC BISHOPS

The Canadian Conference of Catholic Bishops was established Oct. 12, 1943, as a permanent voluntary association of the bishops of Canada, was given official approval by the Holy See in 1948, and acquired the status of an episcopal conference after the Second Vatican Council.

The CCCB acts in two ways: (1) as a strictly ecclesiastical body through which the bishops act together with pastoral authority and responsibility for the Church throughout the country; (2) as an operational secretariat through which the bishops act on a wider scale for the good of the Church and society.

At the top of the CCCB organizational table are the president, an executive committee, a permanent council and a plenary assembly. The membership consists of all the bishops of Canada.

Departments and Offices

The CCCB's work is planned and co-ordinated by the Programmes and Priorities Committee composed of the six chairmen of the national episcopal commissions and the two general secretaries. It is chaired by the vice-president of the CCCB.

The CCCB's nine episcopal commissions undertake study and projects in special areas of pastoral work. Six serve nationally (social affairs, canon law/inter-rite, ministries, missions, ecumenism, theology); three relate to French and English sectors (social communications, Christian education, liturgy).

The general secretariat consists of a French and an English general secretary and their assistants and directors of public relations.

Administrative services for purchasing, archives and library, accounting, personnel, publications, printing and distribution are supervised by directors who relate to the general secretaries.

Various advisory councils and committees with mixed memberships of lay persons, religious, priests and bishops also serve the CCCB on a variety of topics.

Operations

Meetings for the transaction of business are held at least once a year by the plenary assembly, six times a year by the executive committee, and four times a year by the permanent council.

Archbishop Francis J. Spence of Kingston, Ont., is president of the CCCB and Cardinal Jean-Claude Turcotte of Montreal, Que., is vice president for the 1995-97 term.

Secretariat is located at 90 Parent Ave., Ottawa, K1N 7B1, Canada.

BIOGRAPHIES OF CANADIAN BISHOPS

(Sources: *Information office of Canadian Conference of Catholic Bishops; Annuario Pontificio; L'Osservatore Romano.* Data as of July 10, 1997.)

Abi-Saber, Georges, O.L.M.: b May 12, 1923, Lebanon; ord. priest July 16, 1952; ord. bishop of Lattaquie of the Maronites, Nov. 12, 1977; titular bishop of Arado and auxiliary of patriarchate of Antioch of the Maronites, May 2, 1986; eparch of St. Maron of Montreal, Nov. 23, 1990; retired Feb. 7, 1996.

Ambrozic, Aloysius M.: b. Jan. 27, 1930, Gabrje, Slovenia; ord. priest June 4, 1955; ord. titular bishop of Valabria and auxiliary bishop of Toronto, May 27, 1976; coadjutor archbishop of Toronto, May 28, 1986; archbishop of Toronto, Mar. 17, 1990.

Audet, Rene: b. Jan. 18, 1920, Montreal, Que.; ord. priest May 30, 1948; ord. titular bishop of Chonochora and auxiliary bishop of Ottawa, July 31, 1963; bishop of Joliette, Jan. 3, 1968; retired Oct. 31, 1990.

Berthelet, Jacques, C.S.V.: b. Oct. 24, 1934, Montreal, Que.; ord. priest June 16, 1962; ord. titular bishop of Lamsorti and auxiliary of Saint-Jean-Longueuil, Mar. 21, 1987; bishop of Saint-Jean-Longueuil, Dec. 27, 1996..

Blais, Jean-Pierre: b. May 21, 1949, Saint-Anselme, Que.; ord. priest May 11, 1974; ord. titular bishop of Tino and auxiliary of Quebec, Jan. 6, 1995.

Blanchet, Bertrand: b. Sept. 19, 1932, Saint Thomas de Montmagny, Que.; ord. priest May 20, 1956; ord. bishop of Gaspe, Dec. 8, 1973; archbishop of Rimouski, Oct. 16, 1992.

Borecky, Isidore: b. Oct. 1, 1911, Ostrovec, Ukraine; ord. priest July 17, 1938; ord. titular bishop of Amathus in Cypro and exarch of Toronto, May 27, 1948; eparch of Toronto (Ukrainians), Nov. 3, 1956.

Burke, Austin-Emile: b. Jan. 11, 1922, Sluice Point, N.S.; ord. priest Mar. 25, 1950; ord. bishop of Yarmouth, May 14, 1968; archbishop of Halifax, July 8, 1991.

Bzdel, Michael, C.Ss.R.: b. July 21, 1930, Wishart, Sask.; ord. priest July 7, 1954; ord. archeparch of Winnipeg of the Ukrainians, Mar. 9, 1993.

Cadieux, Vincent, O.M.I.: b. Feb. 16, 1940, Alfred, Ont.; ord. priest Dec. 17, 1966; ord. bishop of Moosonee, Mar. 29, 1992.

Campbell, Colin: b. June 12, 1931, Antigonish, N.S.; ord. priest May 26, 1956; ord. bishop of Antigonish, Mar. 19, 1987.

Carew, William A.: b. Oct. 23, 1922, St. John's, Nfld., ord. priest June 15, 1947; ord. titular archbishop of Telde, Jan. 4, 1970; nuncio to Rwanda and Burundi, 1970-74; apostolic delegate to Jerusalem and Palestine and pro-nuncio to Cyprus, 1974-83; pro-nuncio to Japan, Aug. 30, 1983.

Carter, Alexander: b. Apr. 16, 1909, Montreal, Que.; ord. priest June 6, 1936; ord. titular bishop of Sita and coadjutor bishop of Sault Ste. Marie, Feb. 2, 1957; bishop of Sault Ste. Marie, Nov. 22, 1958; retired May 8, 1985.

Carter, G. Emmett: (See Cardinals, Biographies.)

Cazabon, Gilles, O.M.I.: b. Apr. 5, 1933, Verner, Ont.; ord. priest June 11, 1960; ord. bishop of Timmins, June 29, 1992.

Charbonneau, Paul-Emile: b. May 4, 1922, Ste. Thérèse de Blainville, Que.; ord. priest May 31, 1947; ord. titular bishop of Thapsus and auxiliary bishop of Ottawa, Jan. 18, 1961; first bishop of Hull (now Gatineau-Hull), May 21, 1963; retired Apr. 12, 1973, because of ill health.

Chiasson, Donat: b. Jan. 2, 1930, Paquetville, N.B.; ord. priest May 6, 1956; ord. archbishop of Moncton, June 1, 1972; retired Sept. 21, 1995.

Cimichella, Andre, O.S.M.: b. Feb. 21, 1921, Grotte Santo Stefano, Italy; ord. priest May 26, 1945; ord. titular bishop of Quiza and auxiliary of Montreal, July 16, 1964; retired Apr. 25, 1996.

Clune, Robert B.: b. Sept. 18, 1920, Toronto, Ont.; ord. priest May 26, 1945; ord. titular bishop of Lacubaza and auxiliary bishop of Toronto, June 21, 1979; retired Dec. 27, 1995.

Colli, Frederick: b. June 17, 1949, St. Catharines, Ont.; ord. priest June 21, 1975; ord. titular bishop of Afufenia and auxiliary of Ottawa, Feb. 22, 1995.

Collins, Thomas Christopher: b. Jan. 16, 1947; ord. priest May 5, 1973; ord. coadjutor bishop of Saint Paul Mar. 25, 1997; bishop of St. Paul, June 30, 1997.

Cooney, Eugene J.: b. Dec. 10, 1931, Medicine Hat, Alta.; ord. priest June 4, 1960; ord. Bishop of Nelson June 11, 1996.

Couture, Jean-Guy: b. May 6, 1929, St.-Jean-Baptiste de Quebec, Que.; ord. priest May 30, 1953; ord. bishop of Hauterive (now Baie-Comeau), Que., Aug. 15, 1975; bishop of Chicoutimi, Apr. 5, 1979.

Couture, Maurice, R.S.V.: b. Nov. 3, 1926, Saint-Pierre-de-Broughton, Que.; ord. priest June 17, 1951; ord. titular bishop of Talaptula and auxiliary bishop of Quebec, Oct. 22, 1982; bishop of Baie Comeau, Dec. 1, 1988; archbishop of Quebec and primate of Canada, Mar. 17, 1990.

Couturier, Gerard: b. Jan. 12, 1913, St. Louis du Ha Ha, Que; ord. priest Mar. 25, 1938; ord. bishop of Hauterive (now Baie-Comeau), Feb. 28, 1957; resigned Sept. 7, 1974.

Croteau, Denis, O.M.I: b. Oct. 23, 1932, Thetford Mines, Que., ord. priest Aug. 31, 1958; ord. bishop of MacKenzie-Fort Smith, June 8, 1986.

Crowley, Leonard: b. Dec. 28, 1921, Montreal, Que.; ord. priest May 31, 1947; ord. titular bishop of Mons and auxiliary bishop of Montreal, Mar. 24, 1971; resigned Mar. 26, 1997..

Danylak, Roman: b. Dec. 29, 1930, Toronto, Ont.; ord. priest Oct. 13, 1957; ord. titular bishop of Nissa and apostolic administrator of Toronto Eparchy (Ukrainians), Mar. 25, 1993.

De Angelis, Nicola, C.F.I.C.: b. Jan. 23, 1939, in Pozzaglia Sabino, Italy; ord. priest for the Conceptionists, Dec. 6, 1970; became Canadian citizen, 1975; ord. titular bishop of Remesiana and auxiliary bishop of Toronto, June 24, 1992.

Delaquis, Noel: b. Dec. 25, 1934, Notre-Dame-de-Lourdes, Man.; ord. priest June 5, 1958; ord. bishop of Gravelbourg, Feb. 19, 1974; resigned Apr. 10, 1995.

De Roo, Remi J.: b. Feb. 24, 1924, Swan Lake, Man.; ord. priest June 8, 1950; ord. bishop of Victoria, Dec. 14, 1962.

Dionne, Gerard: b. June 19, 1919, Saint-Basile, N.B.; ord. priest May 1, 1948; ord. titular bishop of Garba and auxiliary bishop of Sault Ste. Marie, Apr. 8, 1975; bishop of Edmundston, Nov. 17, 1983; retired Oct. 20, 1993.

Doyle, James L.: b. June 20, 1929, Chatham, Ont.; ord. priest June 12, 1954; ord. bishop of Peterborough June 28, 1976.

Doyle, W. Emmett: b. Feb. 18, 1913, Calgary, Alta.: ord. priest June 5, 1938; ord. bishop of Nelson, Dec. 3, 1958; retired Nov. 16, 1989.

Drainville, Gerard: b. May 20, 1930, L'Isle-du-Pas, Que.; ord. priest May 30, 1953; ord. bishop of Amos, June 12 1978.

Dumais, Raymond: b. June 4, 1950, Amqui, Que.; ord. priest June 26, 1976; ord. bishop of Gaspé, May 20, 1994.

Dumouchel, Paul, O.M.I.: b. Sept. 19, 1911, St. Boniface, Man.; ord. priest June 24, 1936; ord. titular bishop of Sufes and vicar apostolic of Keewatin, May 24, 1955; archbishop of Keewatin-Le Pas, July 13, 1967; retired 1986.

Durocher, Paul André: b. May 28, 1954; ord. priest July 2, 1982; ord. titular bishop of Ausuaga and auxiliary bishop of Sault Sainte Marie, Mar. 14, 1997

Ebacher, Roger: b. Oct. 6, 1936, Amos, Que.; ord. priest May 27, 1961; ord. bishop of Hauterive, July 31, 1979; title of see changed to Baie-Comeau, 1986; bishop of Gatineau-Hull, May 6, 1988; first archbishop, Oct 31, 1990, when Gatineau-Hull was made a metropolitan see.

Exner, Adam, O.M.I.: b. Dec. 24, 1928, Killaly, Sask.; ord. priest July 7, 1957; ord. bishop of Kamloops, B.C., Mar. 12, 1974; archbishop of Winnipeg, Mar. 31, 1982; archbishop of Vancouver, 1991.

Fecteau, Clement: b. Apr. 20, 1933, Sainte-Marie-de-Beauce, Que.; ord. priest June 16, 1957; ord. titular bishop of Talattula and auxiliary bishop of Quebec, Oct. 20, 1989; app. bishop of Sainte-Anne-de-la-Pocatiere, May 10, 1996.

Filevich, Basil (Wasyl): b. Jan. 13, 1918; ord. priest Apr. 12, 1942; ord. eparch of Ukrainian eparchy of Saskatoon Feb. 27, 1984; retired Nov. 22, 1995.

Fortier, Jean-Marie: b. July 1, 1920, Quebec, Que.; ord. priest June 16, 1944; ord. titular bishop of Pomaria and auxiliary bishop of Ste. Anne-de-la-Pocatiere, Jan. 23, 1961; bishop of Gaspe, Jan. 19, 1965; archbishop of Sherbrooke, Apr. 20, 1968; retired 1996.

Fougere, Joseph Vernon: b. May 20, 1943, Petit Grat, N.S.; ord. priest May 31, 1969; ord. bishop of Charlottetown, Mar. 19, 1992.

Fulton, Thomas B.: b. Jan. 13, 1918, St. Catharines, Ont.; ord. priest June 7, 1941; ord. titular bishop of Cursola and auxiliary bishop of Toronto, Jan. 6, 1969; bishop of St. Catharines, July 7, 1978; retired Feb. 2, 1994.

Gagnon, Edouard, P.S.S.: (See Cardinals, Biographies.)

Gaumond, Andre: b. June 3, 1936, St. Thomas de Montmagny, Que.; ord. priest May 27, 1961; ord. bishop of Ste.Anne-de-la-Pocatiere, Aug. 15, 1985; app. coadjutor archbishop of Sherbrooke, Feb. 16, 1995; archbishop of Sherbrooke, 1996.

Gervais, Marcel A.: b. Sept. 21, 1931, Elie, Man.; ord. priest May 31, 1958; ord. titular bishop of Rosmarkaeum and auxiliary bishop of London, Ont., June 11, 1980; bishop of Sault Ste. Marie, May 8, 1985; coadjutor archbishop of Ottawa, June 21, 1989;

archbishop of Ottawa, Sept. 27, 1989. President of Canadian Conference of Catholic Bishops, 1991-93.

Gilbert, Arthur J.: b. Oct. 26, 1915, Oromocto, N.B.; ord. priest June 3, 1943; ord. bishop of St. John, N.B., June 19, 1974; retired Apr. 2, 1986.

Goudreault, Henri, O.M.I.: b. Apr. 30, 1928, Belle-Vallee, Ont.; ord. priest June 17, 1956; ord. bishop of Labrador City-Schefferville, June 17, 1987; archbishop of Grouard-McLennan, July 16, 1996.

Gratton, Jean: b. Dec. 4, 1924, Wendover, Ont.; ord. priest Apr. 27, 1952; ord. bishop of Mont Laurier, June 29, 1978.

Hacault, Antoine: b. Jan. 17, 1926, Bruxelles, Man.; ord. priest May 20, 1951; ord. titular bishop of Media and coadjutor of St. Boniface, Sept. 8, 1964; archbishop of St. Boniface, Sept. 7, 1974.

Hakim, Michel: b. Apr. 21, 1921, Magdouche, South Lebanon; ord. priest Nov. 10, 1947; ord. archbishop of Saida of Greek Melkites, Sept. 10, 1977; app. titular archbishop of Caesarea in Cappadocia and apostolic exarch of Greek Melkite Catholics in Canada, Oct. 13, 1980; first eparch (with personal title of archbishop), Sept. 1, 1984, when exarchate was raised to eparchy with title St. Sauveur de Montreal.

Hamelin, Jean-Guy: b. Oct. 8, 1925, St. Severin-de-Proulxville, Que.; ord. priest June 11, 1949; ord. first bishop of Rouyn-Noranda, Que., Feb. 9, 1974. President of Canadian Conference of Catholic Bishops, 1993-95.

Hayes, James M.: b. May 27, 1924, Halifax, N.S.; ord. priest June 15, 1947; ord. titular bishop of Reperi and apostolic administrator of Halifax, Apr. 20, 1965; archbishop of Halifax, June 22, 1967; retired Nov. 6, 1990. President of Canadian Conference of Catholic Bishops, 1987-89.

Henry, Frederick: b. Apr. 11, 1943, London, Ont.; ord. priest May 25, 1968; ord. titular bishop of Carinola and auxiliary bishop of London, Ont., June 24, 1986; app. bishop of Thunder Bay, Mar. 24, 1995.

Huculak, Lawrence Daniel, O.S.B.M.: b. Jan. 25, 1951 ord. priest Aug. 28, 1977; ord. eparch of the Ukrainian eparchy of Edmonton Apr. 3, 1997; installed Apr. 6, 1997.

Khoury, Joseph: b. Nov. 1, 1936; ord. priest Dec. 9, 1964; ord. titular bishop of Conocora , Sept 4, 1993; apostolic visitator for Maronites in western and northern Europe, 1993-96; app. bishop of St. Maron of Montreal for the Maronites, Nov. 11, 1996.

Knight, John Stephen: b. Apr. 10, 1942, Binghamton, N. Y.; moved to Ontario as a child; ord. priest June 2, 1967; ord. titular bishop of Taraqua and auxiliary bishop of Toronto, June 24, 1992.

Labrie, Jean-Paul: b. Nov. 4, 1922, Laurieville, Que.; ord. priest May 20, 1951; ord. titular bishop of Urci and auxiliary bishop of Quebec, May 14, 1977; retired Apr. 19, 1995.

Lacey, Michael Pearse: b. Nov. 27, 1916, Toronto, Ont.; ord. priest May 23, 1943; ord. titular bishop of Diana and auxiliary bishop of Toronto, June 21, 1979; retired May 31, 1993.

Lahey, Raymond: b. May 29, 1940, St. John's Nfld.; ord. priest June 13, 1963; ord. bishop of St. George's, Nfld., Aug. 3, 1986.

Landriault, Jacques: b. Sept. 23, 1921, Alfred,

Ont.; ord. priest Feb. 9, 1947; ord. titular bishop of Cadi and auxiliary bishop of Alexandria, July 25, 1962; bishop of Hearst, May 27, 1964; app. bishop of Timmins, Mar. 24, 1971; retired Dec. 13, 1990.

Langevin, Louis-de-Gonzague, M. Afr.: b. Oct. 31, 1921, Oka, Que.; ord. priest Feb. 2, 1950; ord. titular bishop of Rosemarkie and auxiliary of St. Hyacinthe Sept. 23, 1974; bishop of St. Hyacinthe, July 18, 1979.

LaRocque, Eugene-Philippe: b. Mar. 27, 1927, Windsor, Ont.; ord. priest June 7, 1952; ord. bishop of Alexandria, Ont., Sept. 3, 1974; title of see changed to Alexandria-Cornwall, 1976.

Lebel, Robert: b. Nov. 8, 1924, Trois-Pistoles, Que.; ord. priest June 18, 1950; ord. titular bishop of Alinda and auxiliary of St. Jean de Quebec, May 12, 1974; bishop of Valleyfield, Mar. 26, 1976. President of Canadian Conference of Catholic Bishops, 1989-91.

Leclerc, Marc: b. Jan. 9, 1933, Saint-Gregoire de Montmorency, Que.; ord. priest, May 31, 1958; ord. titular bishop of Eguga and auxiliary bishop of Quebec, Oct. 22, 1982.

Légaré, Henri, O.M.I.: b. Feb. 20, 1918, Willow Bunch, Sask.; ord. priest June 29, 1943; ord. first bishop of Labrador-Schefferville, Sept. 9, 1967; archbishop of Grouard-McLennan, Nov. 21, 1972 (retired July 16, 1996). President of Canadian Conference of Catholic Bishops, 1981-83.

Léger, Ernest: b. Feb. 22, 1944, Haute-Aboujegane, N.B.; ord. priest Mar. 11, 1968; ord. archbishop of Moncton, Jan 29, 1997.

Levesque, Louis: b. May 27, 1908, Amqui, Que.; ord. priest June 26, 1932; ord. bishop of Hearst, Aug. 15, 1952; titular archbishop of Egnatia and coadjutor of Rimouski, Apr. 13, 1964; archbishop of Rimouski, Feb. 25, 1967; retired May 14, 1973.

Lobsinger, Thomas J., O.M.I.: b. Nov. 17, 1927, Ayton, Ont.; ord. priest May 29, 1954; ord. bishop of Whitehorse, Y.T., Oct. 1, 1987.

Lussier, Gilles: b. June 5, 1940, Montreal, Que.; ord. priest Dec. 19, 1964; ord. titular bishop of Augurus and auxiliary bishop of Saint Jerome, Feb. 28, 1989; bishop of Joliette, Sept. 7, 1991.

MacDonald, James H., C.S.C.: b. Apr. 28, 1925, Wycogama, N.S.; ord. priest June 29, 1953; ord. titular bishop of Gibba and auxiliary bishop of Hamilton April 17, 1978; app. bishop of Charlottetown, Aug. 12, 1982; archbishop of St. John's, Nfld., 1991.

MacDonald, Joseph Faber: b. Jan. 20, 1932, Little Pond, P.E.I.; ord. priest Mar. 9, 1963; ord. bishop of Grand Falls, Mar. 19, 1980.

MacNeil, Joseph N.: b. Apr. 15, 1924, Sydney, N.S.; ord. priest May 23, 1948; ord. bishop of St. John, N.B., June 24, 1969; archbishop of Edmonton, July 6, 1973. President Canadian Conference of Catholic Bishops, 1979-81.

Mallon, Peter J.: b. Dec. 5, 1929, Prince Rupert, B.C.; ord. priest May 27, 1956; ord. bishop of Nelson, Feb. 2, 1990; app. archbishop of Regina, June 9, 1995.

Marchand, Paul, S.M.M.: b. Apr. 17, 1937; solemnly professed, Montfort Missionaries, 1961; ord. priest Mar. 17,1962; ord. titular bishop of Tamata and auxiliary of Ottawa, Aug. 20, 1993.

Massé, Vital: b. Dec. 16, 1936, Saint-Narthélémy, Que.; ord. priest May 26, 1962; ord. titular bishop of Giru di Marcello and auxiliary of Saint-Jérôme, Dec. 8, 1993.

Meagher, Anthony: b. 1941; ord. priest 1972; app. titular bishop of Dura and auxiliary of Toronto, Apr. 30, 1997.

Mikloshazy, Attila, S.J.: b. Apr. 5, 1931, Diósgyör, Hungary; ord. priest, June 18, 1961; ord. titular bishop of Castel Minore, Nov. 4, 1989. Bishop for Hungarian emigrants (resides in Canada).

Morand, Blaise E.: b. Sept. 12, 1932, Tecumseh, Ont.; ord. priest Mar. 22, 1958; ord. coadjutor bishop of Prince Albert, June 29, 1981; bishop of Prince Albert, Apr. 9, 1983.

Morissette, Pierre: b. Nov. 22, 1944, Thetford-Mines, Que.; ord. priest June 8, 1968; ord. titular bishop of Mesarfelta and auxiliary of Quebec, June 12, 1987; app. bishop of Baie Comeau, Mar. 17, 1990.

Noel, Laurent: b. Mar. 19, 1920, Saint-Just-de-Bretenieres, Que.; ord. priest June 16, 1944; ord. titular bishop of Agathopolis and auxiliary bishop of Quebec, Aug. 29, 1963; bishop of Trois Rivieres, Nov. 5, 1975; retired Nov. 21, 1996.

Novecosky, Peter, O.S.B.: b. Apr. 27, 1945, Humboldt, Saskatchewan; ord. priest July 11, 1970; app. abbot-ordinary of St. Peter Muenster, July 23, 1990; abbatial blessing Nov. 26, 1990.

O'Brien, Brendan M.: b. Sept. 28, 1943, Ottawa, Ont.; ord. priest June 1, 1968; ord. titular bishop of Numana and auxiliary of Ottawa, June 29, 1987; app. bishop of Pembroke, Apr. 5, 1993.

O'Byrne, Paul J.: b. Dec. 12, 1922, Calgary, Alta.; ord. priest Feb. 21, 1948; ord. bishop of Calgary, Aug. 22, 1968.

O'Connor, Hubert P., O.M.I.: b. Feb. 17, 1928, Huntingdon, Que.; ord. priest June 5, 1955; ord. bishop of Whitehorse, Dec. 8, 1971; bishop of Prince George, June 9, 1986; retired 1991.

O'Grady, John Fergus, O.M.I.: b. July 27, 1908, Macton, Ont.; ord. priest June 29, 1934; ord. titular bishop of Aspendus and vicar apostolic of Prince Rupert, Mar. 7, 1956; first bishop of Prince George, July 13, 1967; retired June 9, 1986.

O'Mara, John A.: b. Nov. 17, 1924, Buffalo, N.Y.; ord. priest June 1, 1951; ord. bishop of Thunder Bay, June 29, 1976; bishop of St. Catharines, April 13, 1994.

Ouellet, Gilles, P.M.E.: b. Aug. 14, 1922, Bromptonville, Que.; ord. priest June 30, 1946; ord. bishop of Gaspe, Nov. 23, 1968; app. archbishop of Rimouski, Apr. 27, 1973; retired Oct. 16, 1992. President Canadian Conference of Catholic Bishops, 1977-79.

Ouellette, André: b. Feb. 4, 1913, Salem, Mass.; ord. priest June 11, 1938; ord. titular bishop of Carre and auxiliary bishop of Mont-Laurier, Feb. 25, 1957; bishop of Mont-Laurier, Mar. 27, 1965; retired Feb. 15, 1978.

Pappin, Bernard F.: b. July 10, 1928, Westmeath, Ont.; ord. priest May 27, 1954; ord. titular bishop of Aradi and auxiliary bishop of Sault Ste. Marie, Apr. 11, 1975.

Pare, Marius: b. May 22, 1903, Montmagny, Que.; ord. priest July 3, 1927; ord. titular bishop of Aegae

and auxiliary bishop of Chicoutimi, May 1, 1956; bishop of Chicoutimi, Feb. 18, 1961; retired Apr. 5, 1979.

Pasichny, Cornelius John, O.S.B.M.: b. Mar. 27, 1927, Winnipeg, Man.; ord. priest July 5, 1953; ord. eparch of Saskatoon of the Ukrainians, Jan. 17, 1996.

Pedneault, Roch: b. Apr. 10, 1927, Saint Joseph d'Alma, Que.; ord. priest Feb. 8, 1953; ord. titular bishop of Aggersel and auxiliary of Chicoutimi, Que., June 29, 1974.

Penney, Alphonsus L.: b. Sept. 17, 1924, St. John's, Nfld.; ord. priest June 29, 1949; ord. bishop of Grand Falls, Jan. 18, 1973; archbishop of St. John's, Nfld., Apr. 5, 1979; retired 1991.

Plouffe, Jean-Louis: b. Oct. 29, 1940, Ottawa, Ont.; ord. priest June 12, 1965; ord. titular bishop of Lamzella and auxiliary of Sault Ste. Marie, Feb. 24, 1987; bishop of Sault Ste. Marie, Dec. 2, 1989.

Plourde, Joseph-Aurele: b. Jan. 12, 1915, St. Francois de Madawaska, N.B.; ord. priest May 7, 1944; ord. titular bishop of Lapda and auxiliary bishop of Alexandria, Aug. 26, 1964; archbishop of Ottawa, Jan. 2, 1967; retired Sept. 27, 1989.

Power, William E.: b. Sept. 27, 1915; Montreal, Que.; ord. priest June 7, 1941; ord. bishop of Antigonish, July 20, 1960 (retired Dec. 12, 1986); president Canadian Conference of Catholic Bishops, 1971-73.

Prendergast, Terrence, S.J.: b. Feb. 19, 1944, in Montreal; ord. priest June 10, 1972; ord. titular bishop of Slebte and auxiliary of Toronto, Apr. 25, 1995.

Richard, Andre, C.S.C.: b. June 30, 1937, St. Ignace, N.B.; ord. priest Feb. 17, 1963; ord. bishop of Bathurst, Aug. 9, 1989.

Rivest, Andre: b.Apr. 28, 1942, Repentigny, Que., ord. priest May 14, 1966; ord. titular bishop of Tubursica and auxiliary bishop of Montreal, Aug. 15, 1995.

Rouleau, Reynald, O.M.I.: b. Nov. 30, 1935, Saint-Jean-de-Dieu, Que.; ord. priest Feb. 2, 1963; ord. bishop of Churchill-Hudson Bay, July 29, 1987.

Roussin, Raymond, S.M.: b. June 17, 1939, Saint-Vital, Manitoba; entered Society of Mary (Marianists), 1955; ord. priest Mar. 21, 1970; ord. bishop of Gravelbourg, Sask., June 14, 1995.

Roy, Raymond: b. May 3, 1919, St. Boniface, Man.; ord. priest May 31, 1947; ord. bishop of St. Paul in Alberta, July 18, 1972; retired June 30, 1997..

Rusnak, Michael, C.Ss.R.: b. Aug. 21, 1921, Beaverdale, Pa.; ord. priest July 4, 1949; ord. titular bishop of Tzernicus and auxiliary eparch of Toronto of the Ukrainians and apostolic visitator to Slovak Catholics of Byzantine rite in Canada, Jan. 2, 1965; first eparch of Sts Cyril and Methodius Eparchy for Slovaks of Byzantine Rite, Feb. 28, 1981; retired Nov. 16, 1996.

Sabatini, Lawrence, C.S.: b. May 15, 1930, Chicago, Ill.; ord. priest Mar. 19, 1957; ord. titular bishop of Nasai and auxiliary bishop of Vancouver, Sept. 21, 1978; bishop of Kamloops, Sept. 30, 1982.

Saint-Antoine, Jude: b. Oct. 29, 1930, Montreal, Que.; ord. priest May 31, 1956; ord. titular bishop of Scardona and auxiliary bishop of Montreal, May 22, 1981. Episcopal vicar of west central region.

Saint-Gelais, Raymond: b. Mar. 23, 1936, Baie

St. Paul, Que.; ord. priest June 12, 1960; ord. titular bishop of Diana and auxiliary bishop of St. Jerome, July 31, 1980; coadjutor bishop of Nicolet, Feb. 19, 1988; bishop of Nicolet, Mar. 14, 1989.

Sanschagrin, Albert, O.M.I.: b. Aug. 5, 1911, Saint-Tite, Que.; ord. priest May 24, 1936; ord. titular bishop of Bagi and coadjutor bishop of Amos Sept. 14, 1957; bishop of Saint-Hyacinthe, June 13, 1967; retired July 18, 1979.

Setian, Nerses Mikaäl: Retired Apostolic Exarch of Armenian Catholics in Canada and the U.S. (see Index).

Sherlock, John M.: b. Jan. 20, 1926, Regina, Sask.; ord. priest June 3, 1950; ord. titular bishop of Macriana and auxiliary of London, Ont., Aug. 28, 1974; bishop of London, July 7, 1978. President of the Canadian Conference of Catholic Bishops, 1983-85.

Soroka, Stephen: b. Nov. 13, 1951, Winnipeg, Man.; ord. priest June 13, 1982; app. titular bishop of Acarassus and auxiliary of the archdiocese of Winnipeg for Ukrainians, Apr. 17, 1996.

Spence, Francis J.: b. June 3, 1926, Perth, Ont.; ord. priest Apr. 16, 1950; ord. titular bishop of Nova and auxiliary bishop of the military vicariate, June 15, 1967; bishop of Charlottetown, Aug. 15, 1970; military vicar of Canada, 1982-87; archbishop of Kingston, Apr. 24, 1982. President CCCB, 1995- .

Sutton, Peter Alfred, O.M.I.: b. Oct. 18, 1934, Chandler, Que.; ord. priest Oct. 22, 1960; ord. bishop of Labrador-Schefferville, July 18, 1974; coadjutor archbishop of Keewatin-Le Pas, Jan. 24, 1986; archbishop of Keewatin-LePas, Nov. 7, 1986.

Tertzakian, Hovhannes, C.M.: b Jan. 3, 1924, Aleppo, Syria; entered Mekhitarist Order of Vienna, 1938, final vows Oct. 24, 1945; ord. priest Sept. 8, 1948; ord. titular bishop of Trebizond for Armenians and apostolic exarch for Armenian Catholics in the United States and Canada, Apr. 29, 1995.

Thibodeau, François, C.J.M.: b. July 27, 1939, Saint-Odilon, Que.; ord. priest May 8, 1965; ord. bishop of Edmundston Jan. 9, 1994.

Tonnos, Anthony: b. Aug. 1, 1935, Port Colborne, Ont.; ord. priest May 27, 1961; ord. titular bishop of Naziona and auxiliary bishop of Hamilton, July 12, 1983; bishop of Hamilton, May 2, 1984.

Tremblay, Eugène: b. Feb. 20, 1936, Saint-Hilarion, Que.; ord. priest June 24, 1962; ord. titular bishop of Succuba and auxiliary of Quebec, Jan. 6, 1995.

Tremblay, Gerard, P.S.S.: b. Oct. 27, 1918, Montreal, Que.; ord. priest June 16, 1946; ord. titular bishop of Trisipa and auxiliary bishop of Montreal, May 22, 1981; retired 1991.

Troy, J. Edward: b. Sept. 3, 1931, Chatham,

N.B.; ord. priest May 28, 1959; ord. coadjutor bishop of St. John, N.B., May 22, 1984; bishop of St. John, N.B., Apr. 2, 1986.

Turcotte, Jean-Claude: (See Cardinals, Biographies.)

Ustrzycki, Matthew: b. Mar. 25, 1932, Saint Catharines, Ont.; ord. priest May 30, 1959; ord. titular bishop of Nationa and auxiliary of Hamilton, July 3, 1985.

Vachon, Louis-Albert: (See Cardinals, Biographies.)

Vallée, Andre, P.M.E.: b. July 31, 1930, Sainte-Anne-de-Perade, Que.; ord. priest June 24, 1956; ord. titular bishop of Sufasar and bishop of the Military Ordinariate of Canada, Jan. 28, 1988; bishop of Hearst, 1996.

Valois, Charles: b. Apr. 24, 1924, Montreal, Que.; ord. priest June 3, 1950; ord. bishop of St. Jerome, June 29, 1977; retired Jan. 22, 1997..

Veillette, Martin: b. Nov. 16, 1936, Saint- Zephirin de Courval, Que., ord. priest June 12, 1960; ord. titular bishop of Valabria and auxiliary of Trois-Rivieres, Dec. 13, 1986; bishop of Trois Rivieres, Nov. 21, 1996..

Wall, Leonard J.: b. Sept. 27, 1924, Windsor, Ont.; ord. priest June 11, 1949; ord. titular bishop of Leptiminus and auxiliary bishop of Toronto, June 21, 1979; archbishop of Winnipeg, Feb. 25, 1992.

Weber, Jerome, O.S.B.: b. Sept. 14, 1915, Muenster, Sask., Canada; ord. priest June 8, 1941; app. abbot-ordinary of St. Peter Muenster, Apr. 6, 1960; abbatial blessing, Aug. 24, 1960; retired June, 1990.

Weisgerber, V. James: b. May 1, 1938, Vibank, Sask.; ord. priest June 1, 1963; ord. bishop of Saskatoon, May 3, 1996.

Wiesner, Gerald, O.M.I.: b. June 25, 1937, Danzil, Sask.; ord. priest Feb. 23, 1963; ord. bishop of Prince George, B.C., Feb. 22, 1993.

Willard, Neil E.: b. May 9, 1937, Montreal; ord. priest May 27, 1961; ord. titular bishop of Tisedi and auxiliary bishop of Montreal Aug. 15, 1995.

Windle, Joseph R.: b. Aug. 28, 1917, Ashdad, Ont.; ord. priest May 16, 1943; ord. titular bishop of Uzita and auxiliary bishop of Ottawa, Jan. 18, 1961; coadjutor bishop of Pembroke, 1969; bishop of Pembroke, Feb. 15, 1971; retired Apr. 5, 1993.

Wingle, James Matthew: b. Sept. 23, 1946, Eganville, Ont.; ord. priest Apr. 16, 1977 (Pembroke diocese); ord. bishop of Yarmouth, Aug. 24, 1993.

Yakymyshyn, Severian Stephen, O.S.B.M.: b. Apr. 22, 1930, Plain Lake, Alberta; ord. priest May 19, 1955; ord. bishop of Ukrainian Eparchy of New Westminster, Mar. 25, 1995.

Younan, Joseph: See Index.

CANADIAN SHRINES

Our Lady of the Cape (Cap de la Madeleine), Queen of the Most Holy Rosary: The Three Rivers, Quebec, parish church, built of fieldstone in 1714 and considered the oldest stone church on the North American continent preserved in its original state, was rededicated June 22, 1888, as a shrine of the Queen of the Most Holy Rosary. Thereafter, the site

increased in importance as a pilgrimage and devotional center, and in 1904 St. Pius X decreed the crowning of a statue of the Blessed Virgin which had been donated 50 years earlier to commemorate the dogma of the Immaculate Conception. In 1909, the First Plenary Council of Quebec declared the church a shrine of national pilgrimage. In 1964, the church at the shrine was given the status and title of minor basilica.

St. Anne de Beaupre: The devotional history of this shrine in Quebec, began with the reported cure of a cripple, Louis Guimont, on Mar. 16, 1658, the starting date of construction work on a small chapel of St. Anne. The original building was successively enlarged and replaced by a stone church which was given the rank of minor basilica in 1888. The present structure, a Romanesque-Gothic basilica, houses the shrine proper in its north transept. The centers of attraction are an eight-foot-high oaken statue and the great relic of St. Anne, a portion of her forearm.

St. Joseph's Oratory: The massive oratory basilica standing on the western side of Mount Royal and overlooking the city of Montreal had its origin in a primitive chapel erected there by Blessed Andre Bessette, C.S.C., in 1904. Eleven years later, a large crypt was built to accommodate an increasing number of pilgrims, and in 1924 construction work was begun on the large church. A belfry, housing a 60-bell carillon and standing on the site of the original chapel, was dedicated May 15, 1955, as the first major event of the jubilee year observed after the oratory was given the rank of minor basilica.

Martyrs' Shrine: A shrine commemorating several of the Jesuit Martyrs of North America who were killed between 1642 and 1649 in the Ontario and northern New York area is located on the former site of old Fort Sainte Marie. Before its location was fixed near Midland, Ont., in 1925, a small chapel had been erected in 1907 at old Mission St. Ignace to mark the martyrdom of Fathers Jean de Brebeuf and Gabriel Lalemant. This sanctuary has a U.S. counterpart in the Shrine of the North American Martyrs near Auriesville, N.Y., under the care of the Jesuits.

Others

Other shrines and historic churches in Canada include the following.

In Quebec City: the Basilica of Notre Dame, dating from 1650, once the cathedral of a diocese stretching from Canada to Mexico; Notre Dame des Victoires, on the waterfront, dedicated in 1690; the Ursuline Convent, built in 1720, on du Parloir St.

In Montreal: Notre Dame Basilica, patterned after the famous basilica of the same name in Paris, constructed in 1829; the Shrine of Mary, Queen of All Hearts.

Near Montreal: the Chapel of St. Marie Marguerite d'Youville, foundress of the Grey Nuns; Notre Dame de Lourdes, at Rigaud.

CANADIAN CATHOLIC PUBLICATIONS

(Principal source: 1997 *Catholic Press Directory.*)

Newspapers

B. C. Catholic, The, w; 150 Robson St., Vancouver, B.C. V6B 2A7.

Catholic New Times (national), biweekly; 80 Sackville St., Toronto, Ont. M5A 3E5.

Catholic Register, The (national), w; 1155 Younge St., Suite 401, Toronto, Ont. M4T 1W2. Lay edited.

Catholic Times, The, 10 times a year; 2005 St. Marc St., Montreal, Que. H3H 2G8.

Diocesan Review, The, m; 16 Hammond Dr., Corner Brook, Nfld. A2H 2W2.

L'Informateur Catholique, semimonthly; 6550 Rte 125, Chertsey, Que. J0K 3K0.

Monitor, The, m; P.O. Box 986, St. John's, Nfld. A1C 5M3.

New Freeman, The, w; 1 Bayard Dr., St. John, N.B. E2L 3L5.

Our Diocese, bm; P.O. Box 397, Grand Falls-Windsor, Nfld. A2A 2J8.

Pastoral Reporter, The, 4 times a year; 290 The Iona Building, 120 17th Ave. SW, Calgary. Alta. T2S 2T2.

Prairie Messenger, w; Box 190, Muenster, Sask. S0K 2Y0.

Teviskes, Ziburiai (The Lights of the Homeland) (Lithuanian), w; 2185 Stavebank Rd., Mississauga, Ont. L5C 1T3.

Western Catholic Reporter, w; 8421 101 Avenue, Edmonton, Alberta T6A 0L1. Edmonton archdiocese.

Magazines, Other Periodicals

Annals of St. Anne de Beaupre, m; Box 1000, Ste. Anne de Beaupre, Que. G0A 3C0; Basilica of St. Anne.

Apostolat (French), bm; 8844 Notre-Dame Est, Montreal, Que. H1L 3M4. Oblates of Mary Immaculate.

Bread of Life, The, 6 times a year; 209 MacNab St., P.O. Box 395, Hamilton, Ont. L8N 3H8.

Canadian Catholic Review, 10 times a year; 1437 College Dr., Saskatoon, Saskatchewan S7N 0W6.

Canadian League, The, 4 times a year; 1-160 Murray Park Rd., Winnipeg, Man. R3J 3X5. Catholic Women's League of Canada.

Caravan, 4 times a year; 90 Parent Ave., Ottawa, Ont. K1N 7B1. Canadian Conference of Catholic Bishops.

Casket, The, w; 88 College St., Antigonish, N.S. B2G 2L7.

Catholic Communicator, m; 222 Albert St. East, Sault Ste. Marie, Ont. P6A 2J4

Celebrate (Novalis), 6 times a year; St. Paul University, 223 Main St., Ottawa, Ont. K1S 1C4.

Chesterton Review, q; 1437 College Dr., Saskatoon, Sask. S7N 0W6.

Companion Magazine, m; P. O. Box 535, Sta. F., Toronto, Ont. M4Y 2L8; Conventual Franciscan Fathers.

Compass — A Jesuit Journal, bm (Jan.-Nov.); Box 400, Stn F, 50 Charles St. East, Toronto, Ont. M4Y 2L8.

CRC Bulletin (French-English), q; 324 E. Laurier St., Ottawa, Ont. K1N 6P6 Canadian Religious Conference.

Fatima Crusader, 4 times a year; P.O. Box 602, Fort Erie, Ont. L2A 4M7.

Global Village Voice, q; 3028 Danforth Ave., Toronto, Ont. M4C 4PC. Canadian Organization for Development and Peace.

Grail: An Ecumenical Journal, q; St. Paul's

University, Ottawa, Ont. K1S 1C4.

Kateri (English-French), q; P.O. Box 70, Kahnawake, Que. JOL 1BO.

L'Almanach Populaire Catholique (French), a; P.O. Box 1000, St. Anne de Beaupre, Que. GOA 3CO.

La Revue d'Sainte Anne de Beaupre (French), m; P.O. Box 1000, Ste. Anne de Beaupre, Quebec GOA 3CO.

L'Eglise Canadienne (French), 11 times a year; 6255 rue Hutchison, Bureau 103, Montreal, Que. H2V 4C7.

Martyrs' Shrine Message, 2 times a year; Midland, Ont. L4R 4K5. Newsletter.

Messager de Saint Antoine, Le (French), 10 times a year; Lac-Bouchette, Que. GOW 1VO.

Messenger of the Sacred Heart, m; 661 Greenwood Ave., Toronto, Ont. M4J 4B3. Apostleship of Prayer.

Mission Canada, 4 times a year; 201-1115 Younge St.,, Toronto, Ont. M4T 1W2.

Missions Etrangeres (French),6 times a year; 180 Place Juge-Desnoyers, Laval, Que. H7G 1A4.

Oratory, 6 times a year; 3800 Ch. Queen Mary, Montreal, Que. H3V 1H6.

Our Family, m; P.O. Box 249, Battleford, Sask.; S0M 0E0; Oblates of Mary Immaculate.

Prete et Pasteur (French), m; 4450 St. Hubert St., Montreal, Que. H2J 2W9.

Relations (French), 10 times a year; 25 Rue Jarry Ouest, Montreal, Que. H2P 1S6.

Restoration, 10 times a year; Madonna House, Combemere, Ont. KOJ 1LO.

Scarboro Missions, 9 times a year; 2685 Kingston Rd., Scarboro, Ont. M1M 1M4.

Spiritan Missionary News, 4 times a year; 131 Victoria Park Ave., Toronto, Ont. M4E 3S2.

Unity, q; 308 Young St., Montreal, Que. H3C 2G2.

MISSIONARIES TO THE AMERICAS

An asterisk with a feast date indicates that the saint or blessed is listed in the General Roman Calendar or the proper calendar for U.S. dioceses.

Allouez, Claude Jean (1622-1689): French Jesuit; missionary in Canada and midwestern U.S.; preached to 20 different tribes of Indians and baptized over 10,000; vicar general of Northwest.

Altham, John (1589-1640): English Jesuit; missionary among Indians in Maryland.

Anchieta, Jose de, Bl. (1534-1597): Portuguese Jesuit, b. Canary Islands; missionary in Brazil; writer; beatified 1980; feast, June 9.

Andreis, Felix de (1778-1820): Italian Vincentian; missionary and educator in western U.S.

Aparicio, Sebastian, Bl. (1502-1600): Franciscan brother, born Spain; settled in Mexico, c. 1533; worked as road builder and farmer before becoming Franciscan at about the age of 70; beatified, 1787; feast, Feb. 25.

Badin, Stephen T. (1768-1853): French missioner; came to U.S., 1792, when Sulpician seminary in Paris was closed; ordained, 1793, Baltimore, the first priest ordained in U.S.; missionary in Kentucky, Ohio and Michigan; bought land on which Notre Dame University now stands; buried on its campus.

Baraga, Frederic (1797-1868): Slovenian missionary bishop in U.S.; studied at Ljubljana and Vienna, ordained, 1823; came to U.S., 1830; missionary to Indians of Upper Michigan; first bishop of Marquette, 1857-1868; wrote Chippewa grammar, dictionary, prayer book and other works.

Bertran, Louis, St. (1526-1581): Spanish Dominican; missionary in Colombia and Caribbean, 1562-69; canonized, 1671; feast, Oct. 9.

Betancur, Pedro de San Jose, Bl. (1626-1667): Secular Franciscan, b. Canary Islands; arrived in Guatemala, 1651; established hospital, school and homes for poor; beatified 1980; feast, Apr. 25.

Bourgeoys, Marguerite, St. (1620-1700): French foundress, missionary; settled in Canada, 1653; founded Congregation of Notre Dame, 1658; beatified, 1950; canonized 1982; feast, Jan. 12.

Brebeuf, John de, St. (1593-1649): French Jesuit; missionary among Huron Indians in Canada; martyred by Iroquois, Mar. 16, 1649; canonized, 1930; one of Jesuit North American martyrs; feast, Oct. 19* (U.S.).

Cancer de Barbastro, Louis (1500-1549): Spanish Dominican; began missionary work in Middle America, 1533; killed at Tampa Bay, Fla.

Castillo, John de, St. (1596-1628): Spanish Jesuit; worked in Paraguay Indian mission settlements (reductions); martyred; beatified, 1934; canonized, 1988; feast, Nov. 16.

Catala, Magin (1761-1830): Spanish Franciscan; worked in California mission of Santa Clara for 36 years.

Chabanel, Noel, St. (1613-1649): French Jesuit; missionary among Huron Indians in Canada; murdered by renegade Huron, Dec. 8, 1649; canonized, 1930; one of Jesuit North American martyrs; feast, Oct. 19* (U.S.).

Chaumonot, Pierre Joseph (1611-1693): French Jesuit; missionary among Indians in Canada.

Claver, Peter, St. (1581-1654): Spanish Jesuit; missionary among Negroes of South America and West Indies; canonized, 1888; patron of Catholic missions among black people; feast, Sept. 9*.

Daniel, Anthony, St. (1601-1648): French Jesuit; missionary among Huron Indians in Canada; martyred by Iroquois, July 4, 1648; canonized, 1930; one of Jesuit North American martyrs; feast, Oct. 19* (U.S.).

De Smet, Pierre Jean (1801-1873): Belgian-born Jesuit; missionary among Indians of northwestern U.S.; served as intermediary between Indians and U.S. government; wrote on Indian culture.

Duchesne, Rose Philippine, St. (1769-1852): French nun; educator and missionary in the U.S.; established first convent of the Society of the Sacred Heart in the U.S., at St. Charles, Mo.; founded schools for girls; did missionary work among Indians; beatified, 1940; canonized, 1988; feast, Nov. 18* (U.S.).

Farmer, Ferdinand (family name, Steinmeyer) (1720-1786): German Jesuit; missionary in Philadelphia, where he died; one of the first missionaries in New Jersey.

Flaget, Benedict J. (1763-1850): French Sulpician

bishop; came to U.S., 1792; missionary and educator in U.S.; first bishop of Bardstown, Ky. (now Louisville), 1810-32; 1833-50.

Gallitzin, Demetrius (1770-1840): Russian prince, born The Hague; convert, 1787; ordained priest at Baltimore, 1795; frontier missionary, known as Father Smith; Gallitzin, Pa., named for him.

Garnier, Charles, St. (c. 1606-1649): French Jesuit; missionary among Hurons in Canada; martyred by Iroquois, Dec. 7, 1649; canonized, 1930; one of Jesuit North American martyrs; feast, Oct. 19* (U.S.).

Gibault, Pierre (1737-1804): Canadian missionary in Illinois and Indiana; aided in securing states of Ohio, Indiana, Illinois, Michigan and Wisconsin for the Americans during Revolution.

Gonzalez, Roch, St. (1576-1628): Paraguayan Jesuit; worked in Paraguay Indian mission settlements (reductions); martyred; beatified, 1934; canonized, 1988; feast, Nov. 16.

Goupil, Rene, St. (1607-1642): French lay missionary; had studied surgery at Orleans, France; missionary companion of St. Isaac Jogues among the Hurons; martyred, Sept. 29, 1642; canonized, 1930; one of Jesuit North American martyrs; feast, Oct. 19* (U.S.).

Gravier, Jacques (1651-1708): French Jesuit; missionary among Indians of Canada and midwestern U.S.

Hennepin, Louis (d. c. 1701): Belgian-born Franciscan missionary and explorer of Great Lakes region and Upper Mississippi, 1675-81, when he returned to Europe.

Jesuit North American Martyrs: Isaac Jogues, Anthony Daniel, John de Brebeuf, Gabriel Lalemant, Charles Garnier, Noel Chabanel (Jesuit priests), and Rene Goupil and John Lalande (lay missionaries) who were martyred between Sept. 29, 1642, and Dec. 9, 1649, in the missions of New France; canonized June 29, 1930; feast, Oct. 19* (U.S.). See separate entries.

Jogues, Isaac, St. (1607-1646): French Jesuit; missionary among Indians in Canada; martyred near present site of Auriesville, N.Y., by Mohawks, Oct. 18, 1646; canonized, 1930; one of Jesuit North American martyrs; feast, Oct. 19* (U.S.).

Kino, Eusebio (1645-1711): Italian Jesuit; missionary and explorer in U.S.; arrived Southwest, 1681; established 25 Indian missions, took part in 14 exploring expeditions in northern Mexico, Arizona and southern California; helped develop livestock raising and farming in the area. He was selected in 1965 to represent Arizona in Statuary Hall.

Lalande, John, St. (d. 1646): French lay missionary, companion of Isaac Jogues; martyred by Mohawks at Auriesville, N.Y., Oct. 19, 1646; canonized, 1930; one of Jesuit North American martyrs; feast, Oct. 19* (U.S.).

Lalemant, Gabriel, St. (1610-1649): French Jesuit; missionary among the Hurons in Canada; martyred by the Iroquois, Mar. 17, 1649; canonized, 1930; one of Jesuit North American martyrs; feast, Oct. 19* (U.S.).

Lamy, Jean Baptiste (1814-1888): French prelate; came to U.S., 1839; missionary in Ohio and Kentucky; bishop in Southwest from 1850; first bishop (later archbishop) of Santa Fe, 1850-1885. He was

nominated in 1951 to represent New Mexico in Statuary Hall.

Las Casas, Bartolome (1474-1566): Spanish Dominican; missionary in Haiti, Jamaica and Venezuela; reformer of abuses against Indians and black people; bishop of Chalapas, Mexico, 1544-47; historian.

Laval, Francoise de Montmorency, Bl. (1623-1708): French-born missionary bishop in Canada; named vicar apostolic of Canada, 1658; first bishop of Quebec, 1674; jurisdiction extended over all French-claimed territory in New World; beatified 1980; feast, May 6.

Manogue, Patrick (1831-1895): Missionary bishop in U.S., b. Ireland; migrated to U.S.; miner in California; studied for priesthood at St. Mary's of the Lake, Chicago, and St. Sulpice, Paris; ordained, 1861; missionary among Indians of California and Nevada; coadjutor bishop, 1881-84, and bishop, 1884-86, of Grass Valley; first bishop of Sacramento, 1886-1895, when see was transferred there.

Margil, Antonio (1657-1726): Spanish Franciscan; missionary in Middle America; apostle of Guatemala; established missions in Texas.

Marie of the Incarnation, Bl. (Marie Guyard Martin) (1599-1672): French widow; joined Ursuline Nuns; arrived in Canada, 1639; first superior of Ursulines in Quebec; missionary to Indians; writer; beatified 1980; feast, Apr. 30.

Marquette, Jacques (1637-1675): French Jesuit; missionary and explorer in America; sent to New France, 1666; began missionary work among Ottawa Indians on Lake Superior, 1668; accompanied Joliet down the Mississippi to mouth of the Arkansas, 1673, and returned to Lake Michigan by way of Illinois River; made a second trip over the same route; his diary and map are of historical significance. He was selected in 1895 to represent Wisconsin in Statuary Hall.

Massias (Macias), John de, St. (1585-1645): Dominican brother, a native of Spain; entered Dominican Friary at Lima, Peru, 1622; served as doorkeeper until his death; beatified, 1837; canonized 1975; feast, Sept. 16.

Mazzuchelli, Samuel C. (1806-1864): Italian Dominican; missionary in midwestern U.S.; called builder of the West; writer. A decree advancing his beatification cause was promulgated July 6, 1993.

Membre, Zenobius (1645-1687): French Franciscan; missionary among Indians of Illinois; accompanied LaSalle expedition down the Mississippi (1681-1682) and Louisiana colonizing expedition (1684) which landed in Texas; murdered by Indians.

Nerinckx, Charles (1761-1824): Belgian priest; missionary in Kentucky; founded Sisters of Loretto at the Foot of the Cross.

Nobrega, Manoel (1517-1570): Portuguese Jesuit; leader of first Jesuit missionaries to Brazil, 1549.

Padilla, Juan de (d. 1542): Spanish Franciscan; missionary among Indians of Mexico and southwestern U.S.; killed by Indians in Kansas; protomartyr of the U.S.

Palou, Francisco (c. 1722-1789): Spanish Franciscan; accompanied Junipero Serra to Mexico, 1749; founded Mission Dolores in San

Francisco; wrote history of the Franciscans in California.

Pariseau, Mother Mary Joseph (1833-1902): Canadian Sister of Charity of Providence; missionary in state of Washington from 1856; founded first hospitals in northwest territory; artisan and architect. Represents Washington in National Statuary Hall.

Peter of Ghent (d. 1572): Belgian Franciscan brother; missionary in Mexico for 49 years.

Porres, Martin de, St. (1579-1639): Peruvian Dominican oblate; his father was a Spanish soldier and his mother a black freedwoman from Panama; called wonder worker of Peru; beatified, 1837; canonized, 1962; feast, Nov. 3*.

Quiroga, Vasco de (1470-1565): Spanish missionary in Mexico; founded hospitals; bishop of Michoacan, 1537.

Ravalli, Antonio (1811-1884): Italian Jesuit; missionary in far-western United States, mostly Montana, for 40 years.

Raymbaut, Charles (1602-1643): French Jesuit; missionary among Indians of Canada and northern U.S.

Richard, Gabriel (1767-1832): French Sulpician; missionary in Illinois and Michigan; a founder of University of Michigan; elected delegate to Congress from Michigan, 1823; first priest to hold seat in the House of Representatives.

Rodriguez, Alfonso, St. (1598-1628): Spanish Jesuit; missionary in Paraguay; martyred; beatified, 1934; canonized, 1988; feast, Nov. 16.

Rosati, Joseph (1789-1843): Italian Vincentian; missionary bishop in U.S. (vicar apostolic of Mississippi and Alabama, 1822; coadjutor of Louisiana and the Two Floridas, 1823-26; administrator of New Orleans, 1826-29; first bishop of St. Louis, 1826-1843).

Sahagun, Bernardino de (c. 1500-1590): Spanish Franciscan; missionary in Mexico for over 60 years; expert on Aztec archaeology.

Seelos, Francis X. (1819-1867): Redemptorist missionary, born Bavaria; ordained, 1844, at Baltimore; missionary in Pittsburgh and New Orleans.

Seghers, Charles J. (1839-1886): Belgian missionary bishop in North America; Apostle of Alaska; archbishop of Oregon City (now Portland), 1880-1884; murdered by berserk companion while on missionary journey.

Serra, Junipero, Bl. (1713-1784): Spanish Franciscan, b. Majorca; missionary in America; arrived Mexico, 1749, where he did missionary work for 20 years; began work in Upper California in 1769 and established nine of the 21 Franciscan missions along the Pacific coast; baptized some 6,000 Indians and confirmed almost 5,000; a cultural pioneer of California. Represents California in Statuary Hall. He was declared venerable May 9, 1985, and was beatified Sept. 25, 1988; feast, July 1* (U.S.).

Solanus, Francis, St. (1549-1610): Spanish Franciscan; missionary in Paraguay, Argentina and Peru; wonder worker of the New World; canonized, 1726; feast, July 14.

Sorin, Edward F. (1814-1893): French priest; member of Congregation of Holy Cross; sent to U.S. in 1841; founder and first president of the University of Notre Dame; missionary in Indiana and Michigan.

Todadilla, Anthony de (1704-1746): Spanish Capuchin; missionary to Indians of Venezuela; killed by Motilones.

Turibius de Mogrovejo, St. (1538-1606): Spanish archbishop of Lima, Peru, c. 1580-1606; canonized 1726; feast, Mar. 23*.

Twelve Apostles of Mexico (early 16th century): Franciscan priests; arrived in Mexico, 1524: Fathers Martin de Valencia (leader), Francisco de Soto, Martin de la Coruna, Juan Suares, Antonio de Ciudad Rodrigo, Toribio de Benevente, Garcia de Cisneros, Luis de Fuensalida, Juan de Ribas, Francisco Ximenes; Brothers Andres de Coroboda, Juan de Palos.

Valdivia, Luis de (1561-1641): Spanish Jesuit; defender of Indians in Peru and Chile.

Vasques de Espinosa, Antonio (early 17th century): Spanish Carmelite; missionary and explorer in Mexico, Panama and western coast of South America.

Vieira, Antonio (1608-1687): Portuguese Jesuit; preacher; missionary in Peru and Chile; protector of Indians against exploitation by slave owners and traders; considered foremost prose writer of 17th-century Portugal.

White, Andrew (1579-1656): English Jesuit; missionary among Indians in Maryland.

Wimmer, Boniface (1809-1887): German Benedictine; missionary among German immigrants in the U.S.

Youville, Marie Marguerite d', St. (1701-1771): Canadian widow; foundress of Sisters of Charity (Grey Nuns), 1737, at Montreal: beatified, 1959; canonized 1990, first native Canadian saint; feast, Dec. 23.

Zumarraga, Juan de (1468-1548): Spanish Franciscan; missionary; first bishop of Mexico; introduced first printing press in New World, published first book in America, a catechism for Aztec Indians; extended missions in Mexico and Central America; vigorous opponent of exploitation of Indians; approved of devotions at Guadalupe; leading figure in early church history in Mexico.

FRANCISCAN MISSIONS

The 21 Franciscan missions of Upper California were established during the 54-year period from 1769 to 1822. Located along the old El Camino Real, or King's Highway, they extended from San Diego to San Francisco and were the centers of Indian civilization, Christianity and industry in the early history of the state.

Junipero Serra (beatified 1988) was the great pioneer of the missions of Upper California. He and his successor as superior of the work, Fermin Lasuen, each directed the establishment of nine missions. One hundred and 46 priests of the Order of Friars Minor, most of them Spaniards, labored in the region from 1769 to 1845; 67 of them died at their posts, two as martyrs. The regular time of mission service was 10 years.

The missions were secularized by the Mexican government in the 1830s but were subsequently restored to the Church by the U.S. government. They are now variously used as the sites of parish churches, a university, houses of study and museums.

The names of the missions and the order of their establishment were as follows:

San Diego de Alcala, San Carlos Borromeo (El Carmelo), San Antonio de Padua, San Gabriel Arcangel, San Luis Obispo de Tolosa, San Francisco de Asis (Dolores), San Juan Capistrano; Santa Clara de Asis, San Buenaventura, Santa Barbara, La Purisima Concepcion de Maria Santisima,

Santa Cruz, Nuestra Senora de la Soledad, San Jose de Guadalupe; San Juan Bautista, San Miguel Arcangel, San Fernando Rey de Espana, San Luis Rey de Francia, Santa Ines, San Rafael Arcangel, San Francisco Solano de Sonoma (Sonoma).

SHRINES AND PLACES OF HISTORIC INTEREST IN THE UNITED STATES

(Principal source: *Catholic Almanac* survey.)

Listed below, according to state, are shrines, other centers of devotion and some places of historic interest with special significance for Catholics. The list is necessarily incomplete because of space limitations.

Information includes: name and location of shrine or place of interest, date of foundation, sponsoring agency or group, and address for more information.

Alabama: St. Jude Church of the City of St. Jude, Montgomery (1934; dedicated, 1938); Mobile Archdiocese. Address: 2048 W. Fairview Ave., Montgomery 36108.

• Shrine of the Most Blessed Trinity, Holy Trinity (1924); Missionary Servants of the Most Blessed Trinity. Address: Holy Trinity 36859.

Arizona: Chapel of the Holy Cross, Sedona (1956); Phoenix Diocese: P.O. Box 1043, W. Sedona 86339.

• Mission San Xavier del Bac, near Tucson (1692); National Historic Landmark; Franciscan Friars and Tucson Diocese; Address: 1950 W. San Xavier Rd., Tucson 85746.

• Shrine of St. Joseph of the Mountains, Yarnell (1939); erected by Catholic Action League; currently maintained by Board of Directors. Address: P.O. Box 267, Yarnell 85362.

California: Mission San Diego de Alcala (July 16, 1769); first of the 21 Franciscan missions of Upper California; Minor Basilica; National Historic Landmark; San Diego Diocese. Address: 10818 San Diego Mission Rd., San Diego 92108.

• Carmel Mission Basilica (Mission San Carlos Borromeo del Rio Carmelo), Carmel by the Sea (June 3, 1770); Monterey Diocese. Address: 3080 Rio Rd., Carmel 93923.

• Old Mission San Luis Obispo de Tolosa, San Luis Obispo (Sept. 1, 1772); Monterey Diocese (Parish Church). Address: Old Mission Church, 751 Palm St., San Luis Obispo 93401.

• San Gabriel Mission, San Gabriel (Sept. 8, 1771); Los Angeles Archdiocese (Parish Church, staffed by Claretians). Address: 537 W. Mission, San Gabriel 91776.

• Mission San Francisco de Asis (Oct. 9, 1776) and Mission Dolores Basilica (1860s); San Francisco Archdiocese. Address: 3321 Sixteenth St., San Francisco 94114.

• Old Mission San Juan Capistrano, San Juan Capistrano (Nov. 1, 1776); Orange Diocese. Address: P.O. Box 697, San Juan Capistrano 92693.

• Old Mission Santa Barbara, Santa Barbara (Dec. 4, 1786); National Historic Landmark; Parish Church, staffed by Franciscan Friars. Address: 2201 Laguna St., Santa Barbara 93105.

• Old Mission San Juan Bautista, San Juan Bautista (June 24, 1797); National Historic Landmark;

Monterey Diocese (Parish Church). Address: P.O. Box 400, San Juan Bautista 95045.

• Mission San Miguel, San Miguel (July 25, 1797); Parish Church, Monterey diocese; Franciscan Friars. Address: 775 Mission St., P.O. Box 69, San Miguel 93451.

• Old Mission Santa Ines, Solvang (1804); Historic Landmark; Los Angeles Archdiocese (Parish Church, staffed by Capuchin Franciscan Friars). Address: P.O. Box 408, Solvang 93464.

Franciscan Friars founded 21 missions in California. (See Index: Franciscan Missions.)

• Shrine of Our Lady of Sorrows, Sycamore (1883); Sacramento Diocese. Address: c/o Our Lady of Lourdes Church, 745 Ware Ave., Colusa 95932.

Colorado: Mother Cabrini Shrine, Golden; Missionary Sisters of the Sacred Heart. Address: 20189 Cabrini Blvd., Golden 80401.

Connecticut: Shrine of Our Lady of Lourdes, Litchfield (1958); Montfort Missionaries. Address: P.O. Box 667, Litchfield 06759.

• Shrine of the Infant of Prague, New Haven (1945); Dominican Friars. Address: P.O. Box 1202, 5 Hillhouse Ave., New Haven 06505.

District of Columbia: Mount St. Sepulchre, Franciscan Monastery of the Holy Land (1897; church dedicated, 1899); Order of Friars Minor. Address: 1400 Quincy St. N.E., Washington, D.C. 20017.

• Basilica of the National Shrine of the Immaculate Conception. See Index for separate entry.

Florida: Mary, Queen of the Universe Shrine, Orlando (1986, temporary facilities; new shrine dedicated, 1993); Orlando diocese. Address: 8300 Vineland Ave., Orlando, 32821.

• Our Lady of La Leche Shrine (Patroness of Mothers and Mothers-to-be) and Mission of Nombre de Dios, Saint Augustine (1565); Angelus Crusade Headquarters. St. Augustine Diocese. Address: 30 Ocean Ave., St. Augustine 32084.

Illinois: Holy Family Log Church, Cahokia (1799; original log church erected 1699); Belleville Diocese (Parish Church). Address: 116 Church St., Cahokia 62206.

• Marytown/Shrine of St. Maximilian Kolbe, Libertyville; Our Lady of the Blessed Sacrament Sanctuary of Perpetual Eucharistic Adoration (1930 and Archdiocesan Shrine to St. Maximilian Kolbe (1989), conducted by Conventual Franciscan Friars, 1600 West Park Ave., Libertyville 60048.

• National Shrine of Our Lady of the Snows, Belleville (1958); Missionary Oblates of Mary Immaculate. Address: 442 S. De Mazenod Dr., Belleville 62223.

• National Shrine of St. Jude, Chicago (1929); located in Our Lady of Guadalupe Church, founded and staffed by Claretians. Address: 3200 E. 91st St., Chicago 60617.

• National Shrine of St. Therese and Museum, Darien (1930, at St. Clara's Church, Chicago; new shrine, 1987, after original destroyed by fire); Carmelites of Most Pure Heart of Mary Province. Address: Carmelite Visitor Center, 8501 Bailey Rd., Darien 60561.

· Shrine of St. Jude Thaddeus, Chicago (1929) located in St. Pius V Church, staffed by Dominicans, Central Province. Address: 1909 S. Ashland Ave., Chicago 60608.

Indiana: Our Lady of Monte Cassino Shrine, St. Meinrad (1870); Benedictines. Address: Saint Meinrad Archabbey, State Highway 62, St. Meinrad 47577.

• Old Cathedral (Basilica of St. Francis Xavier), Vincennes (1826, parish records go back to 1749); Evansville Diocese. Minor Basilica, 1970. Address: 205 Church St., Vincennes 47591.

Iowa: Grotto of the Redemption, West Bend (1912); Sioux City Diocese. Life of Christ in stone. Mailing address: P.O. Box 376, West Bend 50597.

Louisiana: National Votive Shrine of Our Lady of Prompt Succor, New Orleans (1810); located in the Chapel of the Ursuline Convent (a National Historic Landmark). Address: 2635 State St., New Orleans 70118.

• Shrine of St. Ann. Mailing address: 4920 Loveland St., Metaire 70006.

• Shrine of St. Roch, New Orleans (1876); located in St. Roch's Campo Santo (Cemetery); New Orleans Archdiocese. Address: 1725 St. Roch Ave., New Orleans 70117.

Maryland: Basilica of the National Shrine of the Assumption of the Blessed Virgin Mary, Baltimore (1806). Mother Church of Roman Catholicism in the U.S. and the first metropolitan cathedral. Designed by Benjamin Henry Latrobe (architect of the Capitol) it is considered one of the finest examples of neoclassical architecture in the world. The church hosted many of the events and personalities central to the growth of Roman Catholicism in the U.S. Address: Cathedral and Mulberry Sts., Baltimore, MD 21201.

• National Shrine Grotto of Our Lady of Lourdes, Emmitsburg (1809, Grotto of Our Lady; 1875, National Shrine Grotto of Lourdes); Public oratory, Archdiocese of Baltimore. Address: Mount St. Mary's College and Seminary, Emmitsburg 21727.

• National Shrine of St. Elizabeth Ann Seton, Emmitsburg. Religious/Historical. Foundation of Sisters of Charity (1809); first parochial school in America (1810); dedicated as Minor Basilica (1991); Address: 333 South Seton Ave., Emmitsburg 21727.

• St. Francis Xavier Shrine, "Old Bohemia", near Warwick (1704), located in Wilmington, Del., Diocese; restoration under aupices of Old Bohemia Historical Society, Inc. Address: P.O. Box 61, Warwick 21912.

Massachusetts: National Shrine of Our Lady of La Salette, Ipswich (1945); Missionaries of Our Lady of La Salette. Address: 251 Topsfield Rd., Ipswich 01938.

• Our Lady of Fatima Shrine, Holliston (1950); Xaverian Missionaries. Address: 101 Summer St., Holliston 01746.

• St. Anthony Shrine, Boston (1947); downtown Service Church with shrine; Boston Archdiocese and Franciscans of Holy Name Province. Address: 100 Arch St., Boston 02107.

• Saint Clement's Eucharistic Shrine, Boston (1945); Boston Archdiocese, staffed by Oblates of the Virgin Mary. Address: 1105 Boylston St., Boston 02215.

• National Shrine of The Divine Mercy, Stockbridge (1960); Congregation of Marians. Address: National Shrine of The Divine Mercy, Eden Hill, Stockbridge 01262.

Michigan: Cross in the Woods, Indian River (1947); Gaylord diocese; staffed by Franciscan Friars of Sacred Heart Province, St. Louis. Address: 7078 M-68, Indian River 49749.

• Shrine of the Little Flower, Royal Oak (c. 1929, by Father Coughlin); Detroit archdiocese. Address: 2123 Roseland, Royal Oak 48073.

Missouri: Memorial Shrine of St. Rose Philippine Duchesne, St. Charles; Religious of the Sacred Heart of Jesus. Address: 619 N. Second St., St. Charles 63301.

• National Shrine of Our Lady of the Miraculous Medal, Perryville; located in St. Mary of the Barrens Church (1837); Vincentians. Address: 1811 W. St. Joseph St., Perryville 63775.

• Old St. Ferdinand's Shrine, Florissant (1819, Sacred Heart Convent; 1821, St. Ferdinand's Church); Friends of Old St. Ferdinand's, Inc. Address: No. 1 Rue St. Francois, Florissant 63031.

• Shrine of Our Lady of Sorrows, Starkenburg (1888; shrine building, 1910); Jefferson City Diocese. Address: c/o Church of the Risen Savior, Rt. 1, Box 17, Rhineland 65069.

Nebraska: The Eucharistic Shrine of Christ the King (1973); Lincoln diocese and Holy Spirit Adoration Sisters. Address: 1040 South Cotner Blvd., Lincoln 68510.

New Hampshire: Shrine of Our Lady of Grace, Colebrook (1948); Missionary Oblates of Mary Immaculate. Address: R.R. 1, Box 521, Colebrook 03576.

• Shrine of Our Lady of La Salette, Enfield (1951); Missionaries of Our Lady of La Salette. Address: Rt. 4A, P.O. Box 420, Enfield 03748.

New Jersey: Blue Army Shrine of the Immaculate Heart of Mary (1978); National Center of the Blue Army of Our Lady of Fatima, USA, Inc. Address: Mountain View Rd. (P.O. Box 976), Washington 07882.

• Shrine of St. Joseph, Stirling (1924); Missionary Servants of the Most Holy Trinity. Address: 1050 Long Hill Rd., Stirling 07980.

New Mexico: St. Augustine Mission, Isleta (1613); Santa Fe Archdiocese. Address: P.O. Box 463, Isleta, Pueblo 87022.

• Santuario de Nuestro Senor de Esquipulas, Chimayo (1816); Santa Fe archdiocese, Sons of the Holy Family; national historic landmark, 1970. Address: Santuario de Chimayo, P.O. Box 235; Chimayo 87522.

New York: National Shrine of Bl. Kateri Tekakwitha, Fonda (1938); Order of Friars Minor Conventual. Address: P.O. Box 627, Fonda 12068.

• Marian Shrine (National Shrine of Mary Help of Christians), West Haverstraw (1953); Salesians of St. John Bosco. Address: Filors Lane, W. Haverstraw 10993.

• National Shrine of St. Frances Xavier Cabrini, New York (1938; new shrine dedicated 1960); Mis-

sionary Sisters of the Sacred Heart. Address: 701 Fort Washington Ave., New York 10040.
• Original Shrine of St. Ann in New York City (1892); located in St. Jean Baptiste Church; Blessed Sacrament Fathers. Address: 184 E. 76th St., New York 10021.
• Our Lady of Fatima National Shrine Basilica, Youngstown (1954); Barnabite Fathers. Address: 1023 Swan Rd., Youngstown 14174. Designated a national shrine in 1994.
• Our Lady of Victory National Shrine, Lackawanna (1926); Minor Basilica. Address: 767 Ridge Rd., Lackawanna 14218.
• Shrine Church of Our Lady of Mt. Carmel, Brooklyn (1887); Brooklyn Diocese (Parish Church). Address: 275 N. 8th St., Brooklyn 11211.
• Shrine of Our Lady of Martyrs, Auriesville (1885); Society of Jesus. Address: Auriesville 12016.
• Shrine of Our Lady of the Island, Eastport (1975); Montfort Missionaries. Address: Box 26, Eastport, L.I., 11941.
• Shrine of St. Elizabeth Ann Seton, New York City (1975); located in Our Lady of the Rosary Church. Address: 7 State St., New York 10004.
Ohio: Basilica and National Shrine of Our Lady of Consolation, Carey (1867); Minor Basilica; Toledo Diocese; staffed by Conventual Franciscan Friars. Address: 315 Clay St., Carey 43316.
• National Shrine of Our Lady of Lebanon, North Jackson (1965); Eparchy of Our Lady of Lebanon of Los Angeles. Address: 2759 N. Lipkey Rd., N. Jackson 44451.
• Our Lady of Czestochowa, Garfield Heights (1939); Sisters of St. Joseph, Third Order of St. Francis. Address: 12215 Granger Rd., Garfield Hts. 44125.
• Our Lady of Fatima, Ironton (1954); Old Rt. 52, Haverhill, Ohio. Mailing address: St. Joseph Church, 905 S. Fifth St., Ironton 45638.
• St. Anthony Shrine, Cincinnati (1888); Franciscan Friars, St. John Baptist Province. Address: 5000 Colerain Ave., Cincinnati 45223.
• Shrine and Oratory of the Weeping Madonna of Mariapoch, Burton (1956); Social Mission Sisters. Parma Diocese (Byzantine). Address: 17486 Mumford Rd., Burton 44021.
• Shrine of the Holy Relics (1892); Sisters of the Precious Blood. Address: 2291 St. John's Rd., Maria Stein 45860.
• Sorrowful Mother Shrine, Bellevue (1850); Society of the Precious Blood. Address: 4106 State Rt. 269, Bellevue 44811.
Oklahoma: National Shrine of the Infant Jesus of

Prague, Prague (1949); Oklahoma City Archdiocese. Address: P.O. Box 488, Prague 74864.
Oregon: The Grotto (National Sanctuary of Our Sorrowful Mother), Portland (1924); Servite Friars. Address: P.O. Box 20008, Portland 97294.
Pennsylvania: Basilica of the Sacred Heart of Jesus, Conewago Township (1741; present church, 1787); Minor Basilica; Harrisburg Diocese. Address: 30 Basilica Dr., Hanover 17331.
• National Shrine Center of Our Lady of Guadalupe, Allentown (1974); located in Immaculate Conception Church; Allentown Diocese. Address: 501 Ridge Ave., Allentown 18102.
• National Shrine of Our Lady of Czestochowa (1955); Order of St. Paul the Hermit (Pauline Fathers). Address: P.O. Box 2049, Doylestown 18901.
• National Shrine of St. John Neumann, Philadelphia (1860); Redemptorist Fathers, St. Peter's Church. Address: 1019 N. 5th St., Philadelphia 19123.
• National Shrine of the Sacred Heart, Harleigh (1975); Scranton Diocese. Address: P.O. Box 500, Harleigh (Hazleton) 18225.
• Old St. Joseph's National Shrine, Philadelphia (1733); Philadelphia Archdiocese (Parish Church). •Address: 321 Willings Alley, Philadelphia 19106.
• St. Ann's Monastery Shrine, Scranton (1902); Passionist Community. Designated a minor basilica Aug. 29, 1996. Address: 1230 St. Ann's St., Scranton 18504.
• St. Anthony's Chapel, Pittsburgh (1883); Pittsburgh Diocese. Address: 1700 Harpster St., Pittsburgh 15212.
• Shrine of St. Walburga, Greensburg (1974); Sisters of St. Benedict. Address: 1001 Harvey Ave., Greensburg 15601.
Texas: Our Lady of San Juan del Valle Shrine, San Juan (1949); Brownsville Diocese; staffed by Oblates of Mary Immaculate. Mailing address: P.O. Box 747, San Juan 78589.
Vermont: St. Anne's Shrine, Isle La Motte (1666); Burlington Diocese, conducted by Edmundites. Address: West Shore Rd., Isle La Motte 05463.
Wisconsin: Holy Hill — National Shrine of Mary, Help of Christians (1857); Discalced Carmelite Friars. Address: 1525 Carmel Rd., Hubertus 53033.
• National Shrine of St. Joseph, De Pere (1889); Norbertine Fathers. Address: 1016 N. Broadway, De Pere 54115.
• Shrine of Mary, Mother Thrice Admirable Queen and Victress of Schoenstatt (1965), Address: W284 N698 Cherry Lane, Waukesha 53188.

KNIGHTS OF COLUMBUS

The Knights of Columbus, a fraternal benefit society of Catholic men, is a family service organization founded by Father Michael J. McGivney and chartered by the General Assembly of Connecticut Mar. 29, 1882.

K. of C. membership currently totals almost 1.6 million in more than 10,800 councils in the U.S., Canada, the Philippines, Mexico, Puerto Rico, Panama, Guatemala, Guam, the Dominican Republic, the Virgin Islands, the Bahamas and Saipan.

In line with their general purpose to be of service to the Church, the Knights and their families are active in many apostolic works and community programs. The Knights cooperate with the U.S. bishops in pro-life activities and are engaged in other apostolic endeavors as well. In 1996, local units of the Knights contributed more than $105,976,102 million to charitable and benevolent causes, and provided almost 49 million hours of community service. Their publication, *Columbia,* has the largest circulation (over 1.5 million) of any Catholic monthly in North America. Supreme Knight: Virgil C. Dechant. International headquarters: One Columbus Plaza, New Haven, CT 06510.

THE CATHOLIC CHURCH IN THE UNITED STATES_____

The starting point of the mainstream of Catholic history in the United States was Baltimore at the end of the Revolutionary War. Long before that time, however, Catholic explorers had traversed much of the country and missionaries had done considerable work among Indians in the Southeast, Northeast and Southwest. (See also Index: Chronology of Church in U.S.)

Spanish and French Missions

Missionaries from Spain evangelized Indians in Florida (which included a large area of the Southeast), New Mexico, Texas and California. Franciscan Juan de Padilla, killed in 1542 in what is now central Kansas, was the first of numerous martyrs among the early missionaries. The city of St. Augustine, settled by the Spanish in 1565, was the first permanent settlement in the United States and also the site of the first parish, established the same year with secular Father Martin Francisco Lopez de Mendoza Grajales as pastor. Italian Jesuit Eusebio Kino (1645-1711) established Spanish missions in lower California and southern Arizona, where he founded San Xavier del Bac mission in 1700. Bl. Junipero Serra (1713-84), who established nine of the famous chain of 21 Franciscan missions in California, was perhaps the most noted of the Spanish missionaries. He was beatified in 1988.

French missionary efforts originated in Canada and extended to parts of Maine, New York and areas around the Great Lakes and along the Mississippi River as far south as Louisiana. Sts. Isaac Jogues, René Goupil and John de Brébeuf, three of eight Jesuit missionaries of New France martyred between 1642 and 1649 (canonized in 1930), met their deaths near Auriesville, New York. Jesuit explorer Jacques Marquette (1637-75), who founded St. Ignace Mission at the Straits of Mackinac in 1671, left maps and a diary of his exploratory trip down the Mississippi River with Louis Joliet in 1673. Claude Allouez (1622-89), another French Jesuit, worked for 32 years among Indians in the Midwest, baptizing an estimated 10,000. French Catholics founded the colony in Louisiana in 1699. In 1727, Ursuline nuns from France founded a convent in New Orleans, the oldest in the United States.

English Settlements

Catholics were excluded by penal law from English settlements along the Atlantic coast.

The only colony established under Catholic leadership was Maryland, granted to George Calvert (Lord Baltimore) as a proprietary colony in 1632; its first settlement at St. Mary's City was established in 1634 by a contingent of Catholic and Protestant colonists who had arrived from England on the Ark and the Dove. Jesuits Andrew White and John Altham, who later evangelized Indians of the area, accompanied the settlers. The principle of religious freedom on which the colony was founded was enacted into law in 1649 as the Act of Toleration. It was the first such measure passed in the colonies and, except for a four-year period of Puritan control, remained in effect until 1688, when Maryland became a royal colony, and the Anglican Church was made the official religion in 1692. Catholics were disenfranchised and persecuted until 1776.

The only other colony where Catholics were assured some degree of freedom was Pennsylvania, founded by the Quaker William Penn in 1681.

One of the earliest permanent Catholic establishments in the English colonies was St. Francis Xavier Mission, Old Bohemia, in northern Maryland, founded by the Jesuits in 1704 to serve Catholics of Delaware, Maryland and southeastern Pennsylvania. Its Bohemia Academy, established in the 1740s, was attended by sons of prominent Catholic families in the area.

Catholics and the Revolution

Despite their small number, which accounted for about one percent of the population, Catholics made significant contributions to the cause for independence from England.

Father John Carroll (1735-1815), who would later become the first bishop of the American hierarchy, and his cousin, Charles Carroll (1737-1832), a signer of the Declaration of Independence, were chosen by the Continental Congress to accompany Benjamin Franklin and Samuel Chase to Canada to try to secure that country's neutrality. Father Pierre Gibault (1737-1804) gave important aid in preserving the Northwest Territory for the revolutionaries. Thomas FitzSimons (1741-1811) of Philadelphia gave financial support to the Continental Army, served in a number of campaigns and later, with Daniel Carroll of Maryland, became one of the two Catholic signers of the Constitution. John Barry (1745-1803), commander of the Lexington, the first ship commissioned by Congress, served valiantly and is considered a founder of the U.S. Navy. There is no record of the number of Catholics who served in Washington's armies, although 38 to 50 percent had Irish surnames. Casimir Pulaski (1748-79) and Thaddeus Kosciusko (1746-1817) of Poland served the cause of the Revolution. Assisting also were the Catholic nations of France, with a military and naval force, and Spain with money and the neutrality of its colonies.

Acknowledgment of Catholic aid in the war and the founding of the Republic was made by General Washington in his reply to a letter from prominent Catholics seeking justice and equal rights: "I presume your fellow citizens of all denominations will not forget the patriotic part which you took in the accomplishment of our Revolution and the establishment of our government or the important assistance which they received from a nation [France] in which the Roman Catholic faith is professed."

In 1789, religious freedom was guaranteed under the First Amendment to the Constitution. Discriminatory laws against Catholics remained in force in many of the states, however, until well into the 19th century.

Beginning of Organization

Father John Carroll's appointment as superior of the American missions on June 9, 1784, was the first step toward organization of the Church in this country. According to a report he made to Rome the following year, there were 24 priests and approximately 25,000 Catholics, mostly in Maryland and Pennsylvania, in a general population of four million. Many of them had been in the Colonies for several generations. For the most part, however, they were an unknown minority laboring under legal and social handicaps.

Establishment of the Hierarchy

Father Carroll was named the first American bishop in 1789 and placed in charge of the Diocese of Baltimore, whose boundaries were coextensive with those of the United States. He was ordained in England Aug. 15, 1790, and installed in his see the following Dec. 12.

Ten years later, Father Leonard Neale became his coadjutor and the first bishop ordained in the United States. Bishop Carroll became an archbishop in 1808 when Baltimore was designated a metropolitan see and the new dioceses of Boston, New York, Philadelphia and Bardstown (now Louisville) were established. These jurisdictions were later subdivided, and by 1840 there were, in addition to Baltimore, 15 dioceses, 500 priests and 663,000 Catholics in the general population of 17 million.

Priests and First Seminaries

The original number of 24 priests noted in Bishop Carroll's 1785 report was gradually augmented with the arrival of others from France and other countries. Among arrivals from France after the Civil Constitution of the Clergy went into effect in 1790, were Jean Louis Lefebvre de Cheverus and Sulpicians Ambrose Maréchal, Benedict Flaget and William Dubourg, who later became bishops.

The first seminary in the country was St. Mary's, established in 1791 in Baltimore, and placed under the direction of the Sulpicians. French seminarian Stephen T. Badin (1768-1853), who fled to the U.S. in 1792 and became a pioneer missionary in Kentucky, Ohio and Michigan, was the first priest ordained (1793) in the U.S. Demetrius Gallitzin (1770-1840), a Russian prince and convert to Catholicism who did pioneer missionary work in western Pennsylvania, was ordained to the priesthood in 1795; he was the first to receive all his orders in the U.S. By 1815, St. Mary's Seminary had 30 ordained alumni.

Two additional seminaries — Mt. St. Mary's at Emmitsburg, Md., and St. Thomas at Bardstown, Ky. — were established in 1809 and 1811, respectively. These and similar institutions founded later played key roles in the development and growth of the American clergy.

Early Schools

Early educational enterprises included the establishment in 1791 of a school at Georgetown which later became the first Catholic university in the U.S.; the opening of a secondary school for girls, conducted by Visitation Nuns, in 1799 at Georgetown; and the start of a similar school in the first decade of the 19th century at Emmitsburg, Md., by Saint Elizabeth Ann Seton.

By the 1840s, which saw the beginnings of the present public school system, more than 200 Catholic elementary schools, half of them west of the Alleghenies, were in operation. From this start, the Church subsequently built the greatest private system of education in the world.

Sisterhoods

Institutes of women Religious were largely responsible for the development of educational and charitable institutions. Among them were Ursuline Nuns in Louisiana from 1727 and Visitation Nuns at Georgetown in the 1790s.

The first contemplative foundation in the country was established in 1790 at Fort Tobacco, Md., by three American-born Carmelites trained at an English convent in Belgium.

The first community of American origin was that of the Sisters of Charity of St. Joseph, founded in 1808 at Emmitsburg, Md., by Mother Elizabeth Ann Bayley Seton (canonized in 1975). Other early American communities were the Sisters of Loretto and the Sisters of Charity of Nazareth, both founded in 1812 in Kentucky, and the Oblate Sisters of Providence, a black community founded in 1829 in Baltimore by Mother Mary Elizabeth Lange.

Among pioneer U.S. foundresses of European communities were Mother Rose Philippine Duchesne (canonized in 1980), who established the Religious of the Sacred Heart in Missouri in 1818, and Mother Theodore Guérin, who founded the Sisters of Providence of St.-Mary-of-the-Woods in Indiana in 1840.

The number of sisters' communities, most of them branches of European institutes, increased apace with needs for their missions in education, charitable service and spiritual life.

Trusteeism

The initial lack of organization in ecclesiastical affairs, nationalistic feeling among Catholics and the independent action of some priests were factors involved in several early crises.

In Philadelphia, some German Catholics, with the reluctant consent of Bishop Carroll, founded Holy Trinity, the first national parish in the U.S. They refused to accept the pastor appointed by the bishop and elected their own. This and other abuses led to formal schism in 1796, a condition which existed until 1802 when they returned to canonical jurisdiction. Philadelphia was also the scene of the Hogan Schism, which developed in the 1820s when Father William Hogan, with the aid of lay trustees, seized control of St. Mary's Cathedral. His movement, for churches and parishes controlled by other than canonical procedures and run in extralegal ways, was nullified by a decision of the Pennsylvania Supreme Court in 1822.

Similar troubles seriously disturbed the peace of the Church in other places, principally New York, Baltimore, Buffalo, Charleston and New Orleans.

Dangers arising from the exploitation of lay control were gradually diminished with the extension and enforcement of canonical procedures and with changes in civil law about the middle of the century.

Bigotry

Bigotry against Catholics waxed and waned during the 19th century and into the 20th. The first major campaign of this kind, which developed in the wake of the panic of 1819 and lasted for about 25 years, was mounted in 1830 when the number of Catholic immigrants began to increase to a noticeable degree. Nativist anti-Catholicism generated a great deal of violence, represented by climaxes in loss of life and property in Charlestown, Mass., in 1834, and in Philadelphia 10 years later. Later bigotry was fomented by the Know-Nothings, in the 1850s; the Ku Klux Klan, from 1866; the American Protective Association, from 1887, and the Guardians of Liberty. Perhaps the last eruption of virulently overt anti-Catholicism occurred during the campaign of Alfred E. Smith for the presidency in 1928. Observers feel the issue was muted to a considerable extent in the political area with the election of John F. Kennedy to the presidency in 1960.

The Catholic periodical press had its beginnings in response to the attacks of bigots. The U.S. Catholic Miscellany (1822-61), the first Catholic newspaper in the U.S., was founded by Bishop John England of Charleston to answer critics of the Church. This remained the character of most of the periodicals of the 19th and into the 20th century

Growth and Immigration

Between 1830 and 1900, the combined factors of natural increase, immigration and conversion raised the Catholic population to 12 million. A large percentage of the growth figure represented immigrants: some 2.7 million, largely from Ireland, Germany and France, between 1830 and 1880; and another 1.25 million during the 1880s when Eastern and Southern Europeans came in increasing numbers. By the 1860s the Catholic Church, with most of its members concentrated in urban areas, was one of the largest religious bodies in the country.

The efforts of progressive bishops to hasten the acculturation of Catholic immigrants occasioned a number of controversies, which generally centered around questions concerning national or foreign-language parishes. One of them, called Cahenslyism, arose from complaints that German Catholic immigrants were not being given adequate pastoral care.

Immigration continued after the turn of the century, but its impact was more easily cushioned through the application of lessons learned earlier in dealing with problems of nationality and language.

Eastern-Rite Catholics

The immigration of the 1890s included large numbers of Eastern-Rite Catholics with their own liturgies and tradition of a married clergy, but without their own bishops. The treatment of their clergy and people by some of the U.S. (Latin-Rite) hierarchy and the prejudices they encountered resulted in the defection of thousands from the Catholic Church.

In 1907, Basilian monk Stephen Ortynsky was ordained the first bishop of Byzantine-Rite Catholics in the U.S. Eventually jurisdictions were established for most Byzantine- and other Eastern-Rite Catholics in the country.

Councils of Baltimore

The bishops of the growing U.S. dioceses met at Baltimore for seven provincial councils between 1829 and 1849.

In 1846, they proclaimed the Blessed Virgin Mary patroness of the United States under the title of the Immaculate Conception, eight years before the dogma was proclaimed.

After the establishment of the Archdiocese of Oregon City in 1846 and the elevation to metropolitan status of St. Louis, New Orleans, Cincinnati and New York, the first of the three plenary councils of Baltimore was held.

The first plenary assembly was convoked on May 9, 1852, with Archbishop Francis P. Kenrick of Baltimore as papal legate. The bishops drew up regulations concerning parochial life, matters of church ritual and ceremonies, the administration of church funds and the teaching of Christian doctrine.

The second plenary council, meeting from Oct. 7 to 21, 1866, under the presidency of Archbishop Martin J. Spalding, formulated a condemnation of several current doctrinal errors and established norms affecting the organization of dioceses, the education and conduct of the clergy, the management of ecclesiastical property, parochial duties and general education.

Archbishop (later Cardinal) James Gibbons called into session the third plenary council which lasted from Nov. 9 to Dec. 7, 1884. Among highly significant results of actions taken by this assembly were the preparation of the line of Baltimore catechisms which became a basic means of religious instruction in this country; legislation which fixed the pattern of Catholic education by requiring the building of elementary schools in all parishes; the establishment of the Catholic University of America in Washington, D.C., in 1889; and the determination of six holy days of obligation for observance in this country.

The enactments of the three plenary councils have had the force of particular law for the Church in the United States.

The Holy See established the Apostolic Delegation in Washington, D.C., on Jan. 24, 1893.

Slavery

In the Civil War period, as before, Catholics reflected attitudes of the general population with respect to the issue of slavery. Some supported it, some opposed it, but none were prominent in the Abolition Movement. Gregory XVI had condemned the slave trade in 1839, but no contemporary pope or American bishop published an official document on slavery itself. The issue did not split Catholics in schism as it did Baptists, Methodists and Presbyterians.

Catholics fought on both sides in the Civil War. Five hundred members of 20 or more sisterhoods served the wounded of both sides.

One hundred thousand of the four million slaves emancipated in 1863 were Catholics; the highest concentrations were in Louisiana, about 60,000, and Maryland, 16,000. Three years later, their pastoral care was one of the subjects covered in nine decrees issued by the Second Plenary Council of Baltimore. The measures had little practical effect with respect to integration of the total Catholic community, predicated as they were on the proposition that individual bishops should handle questions regarding segregation in churches and related matters as best they could in the pattern of local customs.

Long entrenched segregation practices continued in force through the rest of the 19th century and well into the 20th. The first effective efforts to alter them were initiated by Cardinal Joseph Ritter of St. Louis in 1947, Cardinal (then Archbishop) Patrick O'Boyle of Washington in 1948, and Bishop Vincent Waters of Raleigh in 1953.

Friend of Labor

The Church became known during the 19th century as a friend and ally of labor in seeking justice for the working man. Cardinal Gibbons journeyed to Rome in 1887, for example, to defend and prevent a condemnation of the Knights of Labor by Leo XIII. The encyclical *Rerum Novarum* was hailed by many American bishops as a confirmation, if not vindication, of their own theories. Catholics have always formed a large percentage of union membership, and some have served unions in positions of leadership.

The American Heresy

Near the end of the century some controversy developed over what was characterized as Americanism or the phantom heresy. It was alleged that Americans were discounting the importance of contemplative virtues, exalting the practical virtues, and watering down the purity of Catholic doctrine for the sake of facilitating convert work.

The French translation of Father Walter Elliott's Life of Isaac Hecker, which fired the controversy, was one of many factors that led to the issuance of Leo XIII's Testem Benevolentiae in January, 1899, in an attempt to end the matter. It was the first time the orthodoxy of the Church in the U.S. was called into question.

Schism

In the 1890s, serious friction developed between Poles and Irish in Scranton, Buffalo and Chicago, resulting in schism and the establishment of the Polish National Catholic Church. A central figure in the affair was Father Francis Hodur, who was excommunicated by Bishop William O'Hara of Scranton in 1898. Nine years later, his ordination by an Old Catholic Archbishop of Utrecht gave the new church its first bishop.

Another schism of the period led to formation of the American Carpatho-Russian Orthodox Greek Catholic Church.

Coming of Age

In 1900, there were 12 million Catholics in the total U.S. population of 76 million, 82 dioceses in 14 provinces, and 12,000 priests and members of about 40 communities of men Religious. Many sisterhoods, most of them of European origin and some of American foundation, were engaged in Catholic educational and hospital work, two of their traditional apostolates.

The Church in the United States was removed from mission status with promulgation of the apostolic constitution *Sapienti Consilio* by Pope St. Pius X on June 29, 1908.

Before that time, and even into the early 1920s, the Church in this country received financial assistance from mission-aid societies in France, Bavaria and Austria. Already, however, it was making increasing contributions of its own. At the present time, it is one of the major national contributors to the world-wide Society for the Propagation of the Faith.

American foreign missionary personnel increased from 14 or less in 1906 to an all-time high in 1968 of 9,655 priests, brothers, sisters, seminarians, and lay persons. The first missionary seminary in the U.S. was in operation at Techny, Ill., in 1909, under the auspices of the Society of the Divine Word. Maryknoll, the first American missionary society, was established in 1911 and sent its first priests to China in 1918. Despite these contributions, the Church in the U.S. has not matched the missionary commitment of some other nations.

Bishops' Conference

A highly important apparatus for mobilizing the Church's resources was established in 1917 under the title of the National Catholic War Council. Its name was changed to National Catholic Welfare Conference several years later, but its objectives remained the same: to serve as an advisory and coordinating agency of the American bishops for advancing works of the Church in fields of social significance and impact — education, communications, immigration, social action, legislation, youth and lay organizations.

The forward thrust of the bishops' social thinking was evidenced in a program of social reconstruction they recommended in 1919. By 1945, all but one of their twelve points had been enacted into legislation.

The NCWC was renamed the United States Catholic Conference (USCC) in November, 1966, when the hierarchy also organized itself as a territorial conference with pastoral-juridical authority under the title, National Conference of Catholic Bishops. The USCC is carrying on the functions of the former NCWC.

Catholic Press

The establishment of the National Catholic News Service (NC) — now the Catholic News Service (CNS) — in 1920 was an important event in the development of the Catholic press, which had its beginnings about a hundred years earlier. Early in the 20th century there were 63 weekly newspapers. The *1997 Catholic Press Directory* reported 185 newspapers with a circulation in excess of 5.8 million and 250 magazines with a circulation of over 14.5 million.

Lay Organizations

A burst of lay organizational growth occurred from the 1930s onwards with the appearance of Catholic Action types of movements and other groups and associations devoted to special causes, social service and assistance for the poor and needy. Several special apostolates developed under the aegis of the National Catholic Welfare Conference (now the United States Catholic Conference); the outstanding one was the Confraternity of Christian Doctrine.

Nineteenth-century organizations of great influence included: The St. Vincent de Paul Society, whose first U.S. office was set up in 1845 in St. Louis; the Catholic Central Union (Verein), dating from 1855; the Knights of Columbus, founded in 1882; the Holy Name Society, organized in the U.S. in 1870; the Rosary Society (1891) and scores of chapters of the Sodality of the Blessed Virgin Mary.

Pastoral Concerns

The potential for growth of the Church in this country by immigration was sharply reduced but not entirely curtailed after 1921 with the passage of restrictive federal legislation. As a result, the Catholic population became more stabilized and, to a certain extent and for many reasons, began to acquire an identity of its own.

Some increase from outside has taken place in the past 50 years, however; from Canada, from Central and Eastern European countries, and from Puerto Rico and Latin American countries since World War II. This influx, while not as great as that of the 19th century and early 20th, has enriched the Church here with a sizable body of Eastern-Rite Catholics for whom twelve ecclesiastical jurisdictions have been established. It has also created a challenge for pastoral care of millions of Hispanics in urban centers and in agricultural areas where migrant workers are employed.

The Church continues to grapple with serious pastoral problems in rural areas, where about 600 counties are no-priest land. The National Catholic Rural Life Conference was established in 1922 in an attempt to make the Catholic presence felt on the land, and the Glenmary Society since its foundation in 1939 has devoted itself to this single apostolate. Religious communities and diocesan priests are similarly engaged.

Other challenges lie in the cities and suburbs where 75 percent of the Catholic population lives. Conditions peculiar to each segment of the metropolitan area have developed in recent years as the flight to the suburbs has not only altered some traditional aspects of parish life but has also, in combination with many other factors, left behind a complex of special problems in inner city areas.

Contemporary Factors

The Church in the U.S. is in a stage of transition from a relatively stable and long established order of life and action to a new order of things. Some of the phenomena of this period are:

• differences in trends and emphasis in theology, and in interpretation and implementation of directives of the Second Vatican Council, resulting in situations of conflict;

• the changing spiritual formation, professional education, style of life and ministry of priests and Religious (men and women), which are altering influential patterns of pastoral and specialized service;

• vocations to the priesthood and religious life, which are generally in decline;

• departures from the priesthood and religious life which, while small percentage-wise, are numerous enough to be a matter of serious concern;

• decline of traditional devotional practices, along with the emergence of new ones.

· exercise of authority along the lines of collegiality and subsidiarity;

• structure and administration, marked by a trend toward greater participation in the life and work of the Church by its members on all levels, from the parish on up;

• alienation from the Church, leading some persons into the catacombs of an underground church, "anonymous Christianity" and religious indifferentism;

• education, undergoing crisis and change in Catholic schools and seeking new ways of reaching out to the young not in Catholic schools and to adults;

• social witness in ministry to the world, which is being shaped by the form of contemporary needs — e.g., race relations, poverty, the peace movement, the Third World;

• ecumenism, involving the Church in interfaith relations on a wider scale than before.

BACKGROUND DATES IN U.S. CATHOLIC CHRONOLOGY

Dates in this section refer mostly to earlier "firsts" and developments in the background of Catholic history in the United States. For other dates, see various sections of the Almanac.

Alabama

1540: Priests crossed the territory with De Soto's expedition.

1560: Five Dominicans in charge of mission at Santa Cruz des Nanipacna.

1682: La Salle claimed territory for France.

1704: First parish church established at Fort Louis de la Mobile under the care of diocesan priests.

1829: Mobile diocese established (redesignated Mobile-Birmingham, 1954-69).

1830: Spring Hill College, Mobile, established.

1834: Visitation Nuns established an academy at Summerville.

1969: Birmingham diocese established.

1980: Mobile made metropolitan see.

Alaska

1779: Mass celebrated for first time on shore of Port Santa Cruz on lower Bucareli Bay on May 13 by Franciscan Juan Riobo.

1868: Alaska placed under jurisdiction of Vancouver Island.

1879: Father John Althoff became first resident missionary.

1886: Archbishop Charles J. Seghers, "Apostle of Alaska," murdered by a guide; had surveyed southern and northwest Alaska in 1873 and 1877, respectively. Sisters of St. Ann first nuns in Alaska.

1887: Jesuits enter Alaska territory.

1894: Alaska made prefecture apostolic.

1902: Sisters of Providence opened hospital at Nome.

1916: Alaska made vicariate apostolic.

1917: In first ordination in territory, Rev. G. Edgar Gallant raised to priesthood.

1951: Juneau diocese established.

1962: Fairbanks diocese established.

1966: Anchorage archdiocese established.

1996: The Sisters of St. Ann, the first congregation of women religious in Alaska, left after 110 years of service.

Arizona

1539: Franciscan Marcos de Niza explored the state.

1540: Franciscans Juan de Padilla and Marcos de

Niza accompanied Coronado expedition through the territory.

1629: Spanish Franciscans began work among Moqui Indians.

1632: Franciscan Martin de Arvide killed by Indians.

1680: Franciscans Jose de Espeleta, Augustin de Santa Maria, Jose de Figueroa and Jose de Trujillo killed in Pueblo Revolt.

1700: Jesuit Eusebio Kino, who first visited the area in 1692, established mission at San Xavier del Bac, near Tucson. In 1783, under Franciscan administration, construction was begun of the Mission Church of San Xavier del Bac near the site of the original mission; it is still in use as a parish church.

1767: Jesuits expelled; Franciscans took over 10 missions.

1828: Spanish missionaries expelled by Mexican government.

1863: Jesuits returned to San Xavier del Bac briefly.

1869: Sisters of Loretto arrived to conduct schools at Bisbee and Douglas.

1897: Tucson diocese established.

1969: Phoenix diocese established.

Arkansas

1541: Priests accompanied De Soto expedition through the territory.

1673: Marquette visited Indians in east.

1686: Henri de Tonti established trading post, first white settlement in territory.

1700-1702: Fr. Nicholas Foucault working among Indians.

1805: Bishop Carroll of Baltimore appointed Administrator Apostolic of Arkansas.

1838: Sisters of Loretto opened first Catholic school.

1843: Little Rock diocese established. There were about 700 Catholics in state, two churches, one priest.

1851: Sisters of Mercy founded St. Mary's Convent in Little Rock.

California

1542: Cabrillo discovered Upper (Alta) California; name of priest accompanying expedition unknown.

1602: On Nov. 12 Carmelite Anthony of the Ascension offered first recorded Mass in California on shore of San Diego Bay.

1697: Missionary work in Lower and Upper Californias entrusted to Jesuits.

1767: Jesuits expelled from territory. Spanish Crown confiscated their property, including the Pious Fund for Missions. Upper California missions entrusted to Franciscans.

1769: Franciscan Junipero Serra, missionary in Mexico for 20 years, began establishment of Franciscan missions in California, in present San Diego. He was beatified in 1988.

1775: Franciscan Luis Jayme killed by Indians at San Diego Mission.

1779: Diocese of Sonora, Mexico, which included Upper California, established.

1781: On Sept. 4 an expedition from San Gabriel Mission founded present city of Los Angeles _ Pueblo "de Nuestra Senora de los Angeles."

Franciscans Francisco Hermenegildo Garces, Juan

Antonio Barreneche, Juan Marcello Diaz and Jose Matias Moreno killed by Indians.

1812: Franciscan Andres Quintana killed at Santa Cruz Mission.

1822: Dedication on Dec. 8 of Old Plaza Church, "Assistant Mission of Our Lady of the Angels."

1833: Missions secularized, finally confiscated.

1840: Pope Gregory XVI established Diocese of Both Californias.

1846: Peter H. Burnett, who became first governor of California in 1849, received into Catholic Church.

1848: Mexico ceded California to the United States.

1850: Monterey diocese erected; title changed to Monterey-Los Angeles, 1859; and to Los Angeles-San Diego, 1922.

1851: University of Santa Clara chartered.

Sisters of Notre Dame de Namur opened women's College of Notre Dame at San Jose; chartered in 1868; moved to Belmont, 1923.

1852: Baja California detached from Monterey diocese.

1853: San Francisco archdiocese established.

1855: Negotiations inaugurated to restore confiscated California missions to Church.

1868: Grass Valley diocese established; transferred to Sacramento in 1886. (Grass Valley was reestablished as a titular see in 1995.)

1922: Monterey-Fresno diocese established; became separate dioceses, 1967.

1934: Sesquicentennial of Serra's death observed; Serra Year officially declared by Legislature and Aug. 24 observed as Serra Day.

1936: Los Angeles made archdiocese. San Diego diocese established.

1952: Law exempting non-profit, religious-sponsored elementary and secondary schools from taxation upheld in referendum, Nov. 4.

1953: Archbishop James Francis McIntyre of Los Angeles made cardinal by Pius XII.

1962: Oakland, Santa Rosa and Stockton dioceses established.

1973: Archbishop Timothy Manning of Los Angeles made cardinal by Pope Paul VI.

1976: Orange diocese established.

1981: San Jose diocese established.

Byzantine-Rite eparchy of Van Nuys established.

1991: Archbishop Roger Mahony of Los Angeles made cardinal by Pope John Paul II.

1994: Maronite Diocese of Our Lady of Lebanon of Los Angeles established.

Colorado

1858: First parish in Colorado established.

1864: Sisters of Loretto at the Foot of the Cross, first nuns in the state, established academy at Denver.

1868: Vicariate Apostolic of Colorado and Utah established.

1887: Denver diocese established.

1888: Regis College (now University) founded.

1941: Denver made archdiocese.

Pueblo diocese established.

1983: Colorado Springs diocese established.

Connecticut

1651: Probably first priest to enter state was Jesuit Gabriel Druillettes; ambassador of Governor of

Canada, he participated in a New England Colonial Council at New Haven.

1756: Catholic Acadians, expelled from Nova Scotia, settled in the state.

1791: Rev. John Thayer, first native New England priest, offered Mass at the Hartford home of Noah Webster, his Yale classmate.

1808: Connecticut became part of Boston diocese.

1818: Religious freedom established by new constitution, although the Congregational Church remained, in practice, the state church.

1829: Father Bernard O'Cavanaugh became first resident priest in state.

Catholic Press of Hartford established.

1830: First Catholic church in state dedicated at Hartford.

Father James Fitton (1805-81), New England missionary, was assigned to Hartford for six years. He ministered to Catholics throughout the state.

1843: Hartford diocese established

1882: Knights of Columbus founded by Father Michael J. McGivney.

1942: Fairfield University founded.

1953: Norwich and Bridgeport dioceses established. Hartford made archdiocese.

1956: Byzantine Rite Exarchate of Stamford established; made eparchy, 1958.

Delaware

1730: Mount Cuba, New Castle County, the scene of Catholic services.

1750: Jesuit mission at Apoquiniminck administered from Maryland.

1772: First permanent parish established at Coffee Run.

1792: French Catholics from Santo Domingo settled near Wilmington.

1816: St. Peter's Church, later the cathedral of the diocese, erected at Wilmington.

1830: Daughters of Charity opened school and orphanage at Wilmington.

1868: Wilmington diocese established.

1869: Visitation Nuns established residence in Wilmington.

District of Columbia

1641: Jesuit Andrew White evangelized Anacosta Indians.

1774: Father John Carroll ministered to Catholics.

1789: Georgetown, first Catholic college in U.S., established.

1791: Pierre Charles L'Enfant designed the Federal City of Washington. His plans were not fully implemented until the early 1900s.

1792: James Hoban designed the White House.

1794: Father Anthony Caffrey began St. Patrick's Church, first parish church in the new Federal City.

1801: Poor Clares opened school for girls in Georgetown.

1802: First mayor of Washington, appointed by President Jefferson, was Judge Robert Brent.

1889: Catholic University of America founded.

1893: Apostolic Delegation established; became an Apostolic Nunciature in 1984 with the establishment of full diplomatic relations between the U.S. and the Holy See.

1919: National Catholic Welfare Conference (now the United States Catholic Conference) organized by American hierarchy to succeed National Catholic War Council.

1920: Cornerstone of National Shrine of Immaculate Conception laid. The crypt church was completed in 1926. The entire structure was completed in 1959 and dedicated Nov. 20, 1959. In 1990 it was designated a minor basilica.

1939: Washington made archdiocese of equal rank with Baltimore, under direction of same archbishop.

1947: Washington archdiocese received its own archbishop, was separated from Baltimore; became a metropolitan see in 1965.

1967: Archbishop Patrick A. O'Boyle of Washington made cardinal by Pope Paul VI.

1976: Archbishop William Baum of Washington made a cardinal by Pope Paul VI; transferred to Roman Curia in 1980.

1988: Archbishop James A. Hickey of Washington made a cardinal by Pope John Paul II.

Florida

1513: Ponce de Leon discovered Florida.

1521: Missionaries accompanying Ponce de Leon and other explorers probably said first Masses within present limits of U.S.

1528: Franciscans landed on western shore.

1539: Twelve missionaries landed with De Soto at Tampa Bay.

1549: Dominican Luis Cancer de Barbastro and two companions slain by Indians near Tampa Bay.

1565: City of St. Augustine, oldest in U.S., founded by Pedro Menendez de Aviles, who was accompanied by four secular priests.

America's oldest mission, Nombre de Dios, was established.

Father Martin Francisco Lopez de Mendoza Grajales became the first parish priest of St. Augustine, where the first parish in the U.S. was established.

1572: St. Francis Borgia, general of the Society, withdrew Jesuits from Florida.

1606: Bishop Juan de las Cabeyas de Altamirano, O.P., conducted the first episcopal visitation in the U.S.

1620: The chapel of Nombre de Dios was dedicated to Nuestra Senora de la Leche y Buen Parto (Our Nursing Mother of the Happy Delivery); oldest shrine to the Blessed Mother in the U.S.

1704: Destruction of Florida's northern missions by English and Indian troops led by Governor James Moore of South Carolina. Franciscans Juan de Parga, Dominic Criodo, Tiburcio de Osorio, Augustine Ponze de Leon, Marcos Delgado and two Indians, Anthony Enixa and Amador Cuipa Feliciano, were slain by the invaders.

1735: Bishop Francis Martinez de Tejadu Diaz de Velasco, auxiliary of Santiago, was the first bishop to take up residence in U.S., at St. Augustine.

1793: Florida and Louisiana were included in Diocese of New Orleans.

1857: Eastern Florida made a vicariate apostolic.

1870: St. Augustine diocese established.

1917: Convent Inspection Bill passed; repealed 1935.

1958: Miami diocese established.

1968: Miami made metropolitan see; Orlando and St. Petersburg dioceses established.
1976: Pensacola-Tallahassee diocese established.
1984: Palm Beach and Venice dioceses established.

Georgia

1540: First priests to enter were chaplains with De Soto. They celebrated first Mass within territory of 13 original colonies.
1566: Pedro Martinez, first Jesuit martyr of the New World, was slain by Indians on Cumberland Island.
1569: Jesuit mission was opened at Guale Island by Father Antonio Sedeno.
1572: Jesuits withdrawn from area.
1595: Five Franciscans assigned to Province of Guale.
1597: Five Franciscan missionaries (Fathers Pedro de Corpa, Blas de Rodriguez, Miguel de Anon, Francisco de Berascolo and Brother Antonio de Badajoz) killed in coastal missions. Their cause for beatification was formally opened in 1984.
1606: Bishop Altamirano, O.P., conducted visitation of the Georgia area.
1612: First Franciscan province in U.S. erected under title of Santa Elena; it included Georgia, South Carolina and Florida.
1655: Franciscans had nine flourishing missions among Indians.
1742: Spanish missions ended as result of English conquest at Battle of Bloody Marsh.
1796: Augustinian Father Le Mercier was first post-colonial missionary to Georgia.
1798: Catholics granted right of refuge.
1800: First church erected in Savannah on lot given by city council.
1810: First church erected in Augusta on lot given by State Legislature.
1850: Savannah diocese established; became Savannah-Atlanta, 1937; divided into two separate sees, 1956.
1864: Father Emmeran Bliemel, of the Benedictine community of Latrobe, Pa., was killed at the battle of Jonesboro while serving as chaplain of the Confederate 10th Tennessee Artillery.
1962: Atlanta made metropolitan see.

Hawaii

1825: Pope Leo XII entrusted missionary efforts in Islands to Sacred Hearts Fathers.
1827: The first Catholic missionaries arrived _ Fathers Alexis Bachelot, Abraham Armand and Patrick Short, along with three lay brothers. After three years of persecution, the priests were forcibly exiled.
1836: Father Arsenius Walsh, SS. CC., a British subject, was allowed to remain in Islands but was not permitted to proselytize or conduct missions.
1839: Hawaiian government signed treaty with France granting Catholics freedom of worship and same privileges as Protestants.
1844: Vicariate Apostolic of Sandwich Islands (Hawaii) erected.
1873: Father Damien de Veuster of the Sacred Hearts Fathers arrived in Molokai and spent the remainder of his life working among lepers. He was beatified in 1995.

1941: Honolulu diocese established, made a suffragan of San Francisco.

Idaho

1840: Jesuit Pierre de Smet preached to the Flathead and Pend d'Oreille Indians; probably offered first Mass in state.
1842: Jesuit Nicholas Point opened a mission among Coeur d'Alene Indians near St. Maries.
1863: Secular priests sent from Oregon City to administer to incoming miners.
1867: Sisters of Holy Names of Jesus and Mary opened first Catholic school at Idaho City.
1868: Idaho made a vicariate apostolic.
1870: First church in Boise established.
Church lost most of missions among Indians of Northwest Territory when Commission on Indian Affairs appointed Protestant missionaries to take over.
1893: Boise diocese established.

Illinois

1673: Jesuit Jacques Marquette, accompanying Joliet, preached to Indians.
1674: Father Marquette set up a cabin for saying Mass in what later became City of Chicago.
1675: Father Marquette established Mission of the Immaculate Conception among Kaskaskia Indians, near present site of Utica; transferred to Kaskaskia, 1703.
1679: La Salle brought with him Franciscans Louis Hennepin, Gabriel de la Ribourde, and Zenobius Membre.
1680: Father Ribourde was killed by Kickapoo Indians.
1689: Jesuit Claude Allouez died after 32 years of missionary activity among Indians of Midwest; he had evangelized Indians of 20 different tribes. Jesuit Jacques Gravier succeeded Allouez as vicar general of Illinois.
1699: Mission established at Cahokia, first permanent settlement in state.
1730: Father Gaston, a diocesan priest, was killed at the Cahokia Mission.
1763: Jesuits were banished from the territory.
1778: Father Pierre Gibault championed Colonial cause in the Revolution and aided greatly in securing states of Ohio, Indiana, Illinois, Michigan and Wisconsin for Americans.
1827: The present St. Patrick's Parish at Ruma, oldest English-speaking Catholic congregation in state, was founded.
1833: Visitation Nuns established residence in Kaskaskia.
1843: Chicago diocese established.
1853: Quincy diocese established; transferred to Alton, 1857; Springfield, 1923. (Quincy and Alton were reestablished as titular sees in 1995.)
1860: Quincy College founded.
1877: Peoria diocese established.
1880: Chicago made archdiocese.
1887: Belleville diocese established.
1894: Franciscan Sisters of Bl. Kunegunda (now the Franciscan Sisters of Chicago) founded by Mother Marie Therese (Josephine Dudzik).
1908: Rockford diocese established.

First American Missionary Congress held in Chicago.

1924: Archbishop Mundelein of Chicago made cardinal by Pope Pius XI.

1926: The 28th International Eucharistic Congress, first held in U.S., convened in Chicago.

1946: Blessed Frances Xavier Cabrini, former resident of Chicago, was canonized; first U.S. citizen raised to dignity of altar.

Archbishop Samuel A. Stritch of Chicago made cardinal by Pope Pius XII.

1948: Joliet diocese established.

1958: Cardinal Stritch appointed Pro-Prefect of the Sacred Congregation for the Propagation of the Faith — the first U.S.-born prelate to be named to the Roman Curia.

1959: Archbishop Albert G. Meyer of Chicago made cardinal by Pope John XXIII.

1961: Eparchy of St. Nicholas of the Ukrainians established at Chicago.

1967: Archbishop John P. Cody of Chicago made cardinal by Pope Paul VI.

1983: Archbishop Joseph L. Bernardin of Chicago made cardinal by Pope John Paul II.

Indiana

1679: Recollects Louis Hennepin and Gabriel de la Ribourde passed through state.

1686: Land near present Notre Dame University at South Bend given by French government to Jesuits for mission.

1749: Beginning of the records of St. Francis Xavier Church, Vincennes. These records continue with minor interruptions to the present.

1778: Father Gibault aided George Rogers Clark in campaign against British in conquest of Northwest Territory.

1824: Sisters of Charity of Nazareth, Ky., opened St. Clare's Academy in Vincennes.

1825: Laying of cornerstone of third church of St. Francis Xavier, which later (from 1834-98) was the cathedral of the Vincennes diocese. The church was designated a minor basilica in 1970 and is still in use as a parish church.

1834: Vincennes diocese established with Simon Gabriel Brute as bishop; title transferred to Indianapolis, 1898. (Vincennes was reestablished as a titular see in 1995.)

1840: Sisters of Providence founded St. Mary-of-the-Woods College for women.

1842: University of Notre Dame founded by Holy Cross Father Edward Sorin and Brothers of St. Joseph on land given the diocese of Vincennes by Father Stephen Badin.

1853: First Benedictine community established in state at St. Meinrad. It became an abbey in 1870 and an archabbey in 1954.

1857: Fort Wayne diocese established; changed to Fort Wayne-South Bend, 1960.

1944: Indianapolis made archdiocese. Lafayette and Evansville dioceses established.

1957: Gary diocese established.

Iowa

1673: A Peoria village on Mississippi was visited by Father Marquette.

1679: Fathers Louis Hennepin and Gabriel de la Ribourde visited Indian villages.

1836: First permanent church, St. Raphael's, founded at Dubuque by Dominican Samuel Mazzuchelli.

1837: Dubuque diocese established.

1838: St. Joseph's Mission founded at Council Bluffs by Jesuit Father De Smet.

1843: Sisters of Charity of the Blessed Virgin Mary was first sisterhood in state.

Sisters of Charity opened Clarke College, Dubuque.

1850: First Trappist Monastery in state, Our Lady of New Melleray, was begun.

1881: Davenport diocese established.

1882: St. Ambrose College (now University), Davenport, established.

1893: Dubuque made archdiocese.

1902: Sioux City diocese established.

1911: Des Moines diocese established.

Kansas

1542: Franciscan Juan de Padilla, first martyr of the United States, was killed in central Kansas.

1858: St. Benedict's College (now Benedictine College) founded.

1863: Sisters of Charity opened orphanage at Leavenworth, and St. John's Hospital in following year.

1877: Leavenworth diocese established; transferred to Kansas City in 1947. (Leavenworth was reestablished as a titular see in 1995.)

1887: Dioceses of Wichita and Concordia established. Concordia was transferred to Salina in 1944. (Concordia was reestablished as a titular see in 1995.)

1888: Oblate Sisters of Providence opened an orphanage for African-American boys at Leavenworth, first west of Mississippi.

1951: Dodge City diocese established.

1952: Kansas City made archdiocese.

Kentucky

1775: First Catholic settlers came to Kentucky.

1787: Father Charles Maurice Whelan, first resident priest, ministered to settlers in the Bardstown district.

1793: Father Stephen T. Badin began missionary work in Kentucky.

1806: Dominican Fathers built Priory at St. Rose of Lima.

1808: Bardstown diocese established with Benedict Flaget as its first bishop; see transferred to Louisville, 1841. (Bardstown was reestablished as a titular see in 1995.)

1811: Rev. Guy I. Chabrat first priest ordained west of the Allegheny Mountains.

St. Thomas Seminary founded.

1812: Sisters of Loretto founded by Rev. Charles Nerinckx; first religious community in the United States without foreign affiliation.

Sisters of Charity of Nazareth founded, the second native community of women founded in the West.

1814: Nazareth College for women established.

1816: Cornerstone of St. Joseph's Cathedral, Bardstown, laid.

1822: First foundation of Dominican Sisters in the U.S. established near Springfield.

1836: Hon. Benedict J. Webb founded Catholic Advocate, first Catholic weekly newspaper in Kentucky.

1848: Trappist monks took up residence in Gethsemani.

1849: Cornerstone of Cathedral of the Assumption laid at Louisville.

1852: Know-Nothing troubles in state.

1853: Covington diocese established.

1937: Louisville made archdiocese. Owensboro diocese established.

1988: Lexington diocese established.

Louisiana

1682: La Salle's expedition, accompanied by two priests, completed discoveries of De Soto at mouth of Mississippi. LaSalle named territory Louisiana.

1699: French Catholics founded colony of Louisiana.

First recorded Mass offered Mar. 3, by Franciscan Father Anastase Douay.

1706: Father John Francis Buisson de St. Cosme was killed near Donaldsonville.

1717: Franciscan Anthony Margil established first Spanish mission in north central Louisiana.

1718: City of New Orleans founded by Jean Baptiste Le Moyne de Bienville.

1720: First resident priest in New Orleans was the French Recollect Prothais Boyer.

1725: Capuchin Fathers opened school for boys.

1727: Ursuline Nuns founded convent in New Orleans, oldest convent in what is now U.S.; they conducted a school, hospital and orphan asylum.

1793: New Orleans diocese established.

1842: Sisters of Holy Family, a black congregation, founded at New Orleans by Henriette Delille and Juliette Gaudin.

1850: New Orleans made archdiocese.

1853: Natchitoches diocese established; transferred to Alexandria in 1910; became Alexandria-Shreveport in 1977; redesignated Alexandria, 1986. (Natchitoches diocese reestablished as a titular see in 1995.)

1912: Loyola University of South established.

1918: Lafayette diocese established.

1925: Xavier University established in New Orleans.

1961: Baton Rouge diocese established.

1962: Catholic schools on all levels desegregated in New Orleans archdiocese.

1977: Houma-Thibodaux diocese established.

1980: Lake Charles diocese established.

1986: Shreveport diocese established.

Maine

1604: First Mass in territory celebrated by Father Nicholas Aubry, accompanying De Monts' expedition which was authorized by King of France to begin colonizing region.

1605: Colony founded on St. Croix Island; two secular priests served as chaplains.

1613: Four Jesuits attempted to establish permanent French settlement near mouth of Kennebec River.

1619: French Franciscans began work among settlers and Indians; driven out by English in 1628.

1630: New England made a prefecture apostolic in charge of French Capuchins.

1633: Capuchin Fathers founded missions on Penobscot River.

1646: Jesuits established Assumption Mission on Kennebec River.

1688: Church of St. Anne, oldest in New England, built at Oldtown.

1704: English soldiers destroyed French missions.

1724: English forces again attacked French settlements, killed Jesuit Sebastian Rale.

1853: Portland diocese established.

1854: Know-Nothing uprising resulted in burning of church in Bath.

1856: Anti-Catholic feeling continued; church at Ellsworth burned.

1864: Sisters of Congregation of Notre Dame from Montreal opened academy at Portland.

1875: James A. Healy, first bishop of Negro blood consecrated in U.S., became second Bishop of Portland.

Maryland

1634: Maryland established by Lord Calvert. Two Jesuits among first colonists.

First Mass offered on Island of St. Clement in Lower Potomac by Jesuit Father Andrew White. St. Mary's City founded by English and Irish Catholics.

1641: St. Ignatius Parish founded by English Jesuits at Chapel Point, near Port Tobacco.

1649: Religious Toleration Act passed by Maryland Assembly. It was repealed in 1654 by Puritan-controlled government.

1651: Cecil Calvert, second Lord Baltimore, gave Jesuits 10,000 acres for use as Indian mission.

1658: Lord Baltimore restored Toleration Act.

1672: Franciscans came to Maryland under leadership of Father Massius Massey.

1688: Maryland became royal colony as a result of the Revolution in England; Anglican Church became the official religion (1692); Toleration Act repealed; Catholics disenfranchised and persecuted until 1776.

1704: Jesuits founded St. Francis Xavier Mission, Old Bohemia, to serve Catholics of Delaware, Maryland and southeastern Pennsylvania; its Bohemia Academy established in the 1740s was attended by sons of prominent Catholics in the area.

1784: Father John Carroll appointed prefect apostolic for the territory embraced by new Republic.

1789: Baltimore became first diocese established in U.S., with John Carroll as first bishop.

1790: Carmelite Nuns founded convent at Port Tobacco, the first in the English-speaking Colonies.

1791: First Synod of Baltimore held.

St. Mary's Seminary, first seminary in U.S., established.

1793: Rev. Stephen T. Badin first priest ordained by Bishop Carroll.

1800: Jesuit Leonard Neale became first bishop consecrated in present limits of U.S.

1806: Cornerstone of Assumption Cathedral, Baltimore, was laid.

1808: Baltimore made archdiocese.

1809: St. Joseph's College, Emmitsburg, founded (closed in 1973).

Sisters of Charity of St. Joseph founded by St.

Elizabeth Ann Seton; first native American sister-hood.

1821: Assumption Cathedral, Baltimore, formally opened.

1829: Oblate Sisters of Providence, first congregation of black sisters, established at Baltimore by Mother Mary Elizabeth Lange.

First Provincial Council of Baltimore held; six others followed, in 1833, 1837, 1840, 1843, 1846 and 1849.

1836: Roger B. Taney appointed Chief Justice of Supreme Court by President Jackson.

1852: First of the three Plenary Councils of Baltimore convened. Subsequent councils were held in 1866 and 1884.

1855: German Catholic Central Verein founded.

1886: Archbishop James Gibbons of Baltimore made cardinal by Pope Leo XIII.

1965: Archbishop Lawrence Shehan of Baltimore made cardinal by Pope Paul VI.

1994: Archbishop William H. Keeler of Baltimore made cardinal by Pope John Paul II.

Massachusetts

1630: New England made a prefecture apostolic in charge of French Capuchins.

1647: Massachusetts Bay Company enacted an anti-priest law.

1688: Hanging of Ann Glover, an elderly Irish Catholic widow, who refused to renounce her Catholic religion.

1732: Although Catholics were not legally admitted to colony, a few Irish families were in Boston; a priest was reported working among them.

1755-56: Acadians landing in Boston were denied services of a Catholic priest.

1775: General Washington discouraged Guy Fawkes Day procession in which pope was carried in effigy, and expressed surprise that there were men in his army "so void of common sense as to insult the religious feelings of the Canadians with whom friendship and an alliance are being sought."

1780: The Massachusetts State Constitution granted religious liberty, but required a religious test to hold public office and provided for tax to support Protestant teachers of piety, religion and morality.

1788: First public Mass said in Boston on Nov. 2 by Abbe de la Poterie, first resident priest.

1803: Church of Holy Cross erected in Boston with financial aid given by Protestants headed by John Adams.

1808: Boston diocese established.

1831: Irish Catholic immigration increased.

1832: St. Vincent's Orphan Asylum, oldest charitable institution in Boston, opened by Sisters of Mercy.

1834: Ursuline Convent in Charlestown burned by a Nativist mob.

1843: Holy Cross College founded.

1855: Catholic militia companies disbanded; nunneries' inspection bill passed.

1859: St. Mary's, first parochial school in Boston, opened.

1860: Portuguese Catholics from Azores settled in New Bedford.

1870: Springfield diocese established.

1875: Boston made archdiocese.

1904: Fall River diocese established.

1911: Archbishop O'Connell of Boston made cardinal by Pope Pius X.

1950: Worcester diocese established.

1958: Archbishop Richard J. Cushing of Boston made cardinal by Pope John XXIII.

1966: Apostolic Exarchate for Melkites in the U.S. established, with headquarters in Boston; made an eparchy (Newton) in 1976.

1973: Archbishop Humberto S. Medeiros of Boston made cardinal by Pope Paul VI.

1985: Archbishop Bernard F. Law of Boston made a cardinal by Pope John Paul II.

Michigan

1641: Jesuits Isaac Jogues and Charles Raymbaut preached to Chippewas; named the rapids Sault Sainte Marie.

1660: Jesuit Rene Menard opened first regular mission in Lake Superior region.

1668: Father Marquette founded Sainte Marie Mission at Sault Sainte Marie.

1671: Father Marquette founded St. Ignace Mission on north shore of Straits of Mackinac.

1701: Fort Pontchartrain founded on present site of Detroit and placed in command of Antoine de la Mothe Cadillac. The Chapel of Sainte-Anne-de-Detroit founded.

1706: Franciscan Father Delhalle killed by Indians at Detroit.

1823: Father Gabriel Richard elected delegate to Congress from Michigan territory; he was the first priest chosen for the House of Representatives.

1833: Father Frederic Baraga celebrated first Mass in present Grand Rapids.

Detroit diocese established, embracing whole Northwest Territory.

1843: Western Catholic Register founded at Detroit.

1845: St. Vincent's Hospital, Detroit, opened by Sisters of Charity.

1848: Cathedral of Sts. Peter and Paul, Detroit, consecrated.

1853: Vicariate Apostolic of Upper Michigan established.

1857: Sault Ste. Marie diocese established; later transferred to Marquette. (Sault Ste. Marie reestablished as a titular see in 1995.)

1877: University of Detroit founded.

1882: Grand Rapids diocese established.

1897: Nazareth College for women founded.

1937: Detroit made archdiocese. Lansing diocese established.

1938: Saginaw diocese established.

1946: Archbishop Edward Mooney of Detroit created cardinal by Pope Pius XII.

1949: Opening of St. John's Theological (major) Seminary at Plymouth; this was first seminary in U.S. serving an entire ecclesiastical province (Detroit).

1966: Apostolic Exarchate for Maronites in the United States established, with headquarters in Detroit; made an eparchy in 1972; transferred to Brooklyn, 1977.

1969: Archbishop John Dearden of Detroit made cardinal by Pope Paul VI.

1971: Gaylord and Kalamazoo dioceses established.

1982: Apostolic Exarchate for Chaldean-Rite Catholics in United States established. Detroit designated see city; made an eparchy, 1985, under title St. Thomas Apostle of Detroit.

1988: Archbishop Edmund C. Szoka of Detroit made a cardinal by Pope John Paul II; transferred to Roman Curia in 1990.

1994: Archbishop Adam J. Maida of Detroit made cardinal by Pope John Paul II.

Minnesota

1680: Falls of St. Anthony discovered by Franciscan Louis Hennepin.

1727: First chapel, St. Michael the Archangel, erected near town of Frontenac and placed in charge of French Jesuits.

1732: Fort St. Charles built; Jesuits ministered to settlers.

1736: Jesuit Jean Pierre Aulneau killed by Indians.

1839: Swiss Catholics from Canada settled near Fort Snelling; Bishop Loras of Dubuque, accompanied by Father Pellamourgues, visited the Fort and administered sacraments.

1841: Father Lucian Galtier built Church of St. Paul, thus forming nucleus of modern city of same name.

1850: St. Paul diocese established.

1851: Sisters of St. Joseph arrived in state.

1857: St. John's University founded.

1888: St. Paul made archdiocese; name changed to St. Paul and Minneapolis in 1966.

1889: Duluth, St. Cloud and Winona dioceses established.

1909: Crookston diocese established.

1957: New Ulm diocese established.

Mississippi

1540: Chaplains with De Soto expedition entered territory.

1682: Franciscans Zenobius Membre and Anastase Douay preached to Taensa and Natchez Indians. Father Membre offered first recorded Mass in the state on Mar. 29, Easter Sunday.

1698: Priests of Quebec Seminary founded missions near Natchez and Fort Adams.

1702: Father Nicholas Foucault murdered by Indians near Fort Adams.

1721: Missions practically abandoned, with only Father Juif working among Yazoos.

1725: Jesuit Mathurin de Petit carried on mission work in northern Mississippi.

1729: Indians tomahawked Jesuit Paul du Poisson near Fort Rosalie; Father Jean Souel shot by Yazoos.

1736: Jesuit Antoine Senat and seven French officers burned at stake by Chickasaws.

1822: Vicariate Apostolic of Mississippi and Alabama established.

1825: Mississippi made a separate vicariate apostolic.

1837: Natchez diocese established; became Natchez-Jackson in 1956; transferred to Jackson in 1977. (Natchez was established as a titular see.)

1848: Sisters of Charity opened orphan asylum and school in Natchez.

1977: Biloxi diocese established.

Missouri

1700: Jesuit Gabriel Marest established a mission among Kaskaskia Indians near St. Louis.

1734: French Catholic miners and traders settled Old Mines and Sainte Genevieve.

1750: Jesuits visited French settlers.

1762: Mission established at St. Charles.

1767: Carondelet mission established.

1770: First church founded at St. Louis.

1811: Jesuits established Indian mission school at Florissant.

1818: Bishop Dubourg arrived at St. Louis, with Vincentians Joseph Rosati and Felix de Andreis. St. Louis University, the diocesan (Kenrick) seminary and the Vincentian Seminary in Perryville trace their origins to them.
Rose Philippine Duchesne arrived at St. Charles; founded first American convent of the Society of the Sacred Heart; missionary; beatified 1940; canonized 1988.

1826: St. Louis diocese established.

1828: Sisters of Charity opened first hospital west of the Mississippi, at St. Louis.

1832: The Shepherd of the Valley, first Catholic paper west of the Mississippi.

1845: First conference of Society of St. Vincent de Paul in U.S. founded at St. Louis.

1847: St. Louis made archdiocese.

1865: A Test Oath Law passed by State Legislature (called Drake Convention) to crush Catholicism in Missouri. Law declared unconstitutional by Supreme Court in 1866.

1867: College of St. Teresa for women founded at Kansas City.

1868: St. Joseph diocese established.

1880: Kansas City diocese established.

1946: Archbishop John J. Glennon of St. Louis made cardinal by Pope Pius XII.

1956: Kansas City and St. Joseph dioceses combined into one see. Jefferson City and Springfield-Cape Girardeau dioceses established.

1961: Archbishop Joseph E. Ritter of St. Louis made cardinal by Pope John XXIII.

1969: Archbishop John J. Carberry of St. Louis made cardinal by Pope Paul VI.

Montana

1743: Pierre and Francois Verendrye, accompanied by Jesuit Father Coquart, may have explored territory.

1833: Indian missions handed over to care of Jesuits by Second Provincial Council of Baltimore.

1840: Jesuit Pierre De Smet began missionary work among Flathead and Pend d'Oreille Indians.

1841: St. Mary's Mission established by Father De Smet and two companions on the Bitter Root River in present Stevensville.

1845: Jesuit Antonio Ravalli arrived at St. Mary's Mission; Ravalli County named in his honor.

1859: Fathers Point and Hoecken established St. Peter's Mission near the Great Falls.

1869: Sisters of Charity founded a hospital and school in Helena.

1884: Helena diocese established.

1904: Great Falls diocese established; redesignated Great Falls-Billings in 1980.

1909: Carroll College founded.

1935: Rev. Joseph M. Gilmore became first Montana priest elevated to hierarchy.

Nebraska

1541: Coronado expedition, accompanied by Franciscan Juan de Padilla, reached the Platte River.

1673: Father Marquette visited Nebraska Indians.

1720: Franciscan Juan Miguel killed by Indians near Columbus.

1855: Father J. F. Tracy administered to Catholic settlement of St. Patrick and to Catholics in Omaha.

1856: Land was donated by Governor Alfred Cumming for a church in Omaha.

1857: Nebraska vicariate apostolic established.

1878: Creighton University established.

1881: Poor Clares, first contemplative group in state, arrived in Omaha.
Duchesne College established.

1885: Omaha diocese established.

1887: Lincoln diocese established.

1912: Kearney diocese established; transferred to Grand Island, 1917. (Kearney was reestablished as a titular see in 1995.)

1917: Father Edward Flanagan founded Boy's Town for homeless boys, an institution which gained national and international recognition in subsequent years.

1945: Omaha made archdiocese.

Nevada

1774: Franciscan missionaries passed through Nevada on way to California missions.

1860: First parish, serving Genoa, Carson City and Virginia City, established.

1862: Rev. Patrick Manogue appointed pastor of Virginia City. He established a school for boys and girls, an orphanage and hospital.

1871: Church erected at Reno.

1931: Reno diocese established; name changed to Reno-Las Vegas, 1977.

1995: Reno-Las Vegas made two separate dioceses.

New Hampshire

1630: Territory made part of a prefecture apostolic embracing all of New England.

1784: State Constitution included a religious test which barred Catholics from public office; local support was provided for public Protestant teachers of religion.

1818: The Barber family of Claremont was visited by their son Virgil (converted to Catholicism in 1816) accompanied by Father Charles Ffrench, O.P. The visit led to the conversion of the entire Barber family.

1823: Father Virgil Barber, minister who became a Jesuit priest, built first Catholic church and school at Claremont.

1830: Church of St. Aloysius dedicated at Dover.

1853: New Hampshire made part of the Portland diocese.

1858: Sisters of Mercy began to teach school at St. Anne's, Manchester.

1877: Catholics obtained full civil liberty and rights.

1884: Manchester diocese established.

1893: St. Anselm's College opened; St. Anselm's Abbey canonically erected.

1937: Francis P. Murphy became first Catholic governor of New Hampshire.

New Jersey

1668: William Douglass of Bergen was refused a seat in General Assembly because he was a Catholic.

1672: Fathers Harvey and Gage visited Catholics in Woodbridge and Elizabethtown.

1701: Tolerance granted to all but "papists."

1744: Jesuit Theodore Schneider of Pennsylvania visited German Catholics of New Jersey.

1762: Fathers Ferdinand Farmer and Robert Harding working among Catholics in state.

1765: First Catholic community organized in New Jersey at Macopin in Passaic County.

1776: State Constitution tacitly excluded Catholics from office.

1799: Foundation of first Catholic school in state, St. John's at Trenton.

1814: First church in Trenton erected.

1820: Father Richard Bulger, of St. John's, Paterson, first resident pastor in state.

1844: Catholics obtained full civil liberty and rights.

1853: Newark diocese established.

1856: Seton Hall University established.

1878: John P. Holland, teacher at St. John's School, Paterson, invented first workable submarine.

1881: Trenton diocese established.

1937: Newark made archdiocese. Paterson and Camden dioceses established.

1947: U.S. Supreme Court ruled on N.J. bus case, permitting children attending non-public schools to ride on buses and be given other health services provided for those in public schools.

1957: Seton Hall College of Medicine and Dentistry established: the first medical school in state; it was run by Seton Hall until 1965.

1963: Byzantine Eparchy of Passaic established.

1981: Metuchen diocese established.

1995: Eparchy of Our Lady of the Deliverance of Newark for Syrian-rite Catholics of the U.S. and Canada was established.

New Mexico

1539: Territory explored by Franciscan Marcos de Niza.

1581: Franciscans Agustin Rodriguez, Juan de Santa Maria and Francisco Lopez named the region "New Mexico"; they later died at hands of Indians.

1598: Juan de Onate founded a colony at Chamita, where first chapel in state was built.

1609-10: Santa Fe founded.

1631: Franciscan Pedro de Miranda was killed by Indians.

1632: Franciscan Francisco Letrado was killed by Indians.

1672: Franciscan Pedro de Avila y Ayala was killed by Indians.

1675: Franciscan Alonso Gil de Avila was killed by Indians.

1680: Pueblo Indian revolt; 21 Franciscan missionaries massacred; missions destroyed.

1692: Franciscan missions refounded and expanded.

1696: Indians rebelled, five more Franciscan missionaries killed.

1850: Jean Baptiste Lamy appointed head of newly established Vicariate Apostolic of New Mexico.

1852: Sisters of Loretto arrived in Santa Fe.

1853: Santa Fe diocese established.

1859: Christian Brothers arrived, established first school for boys in New Mexico (later St. Michael's College).

1865: Sisters of Charity started first orphanage and hospital in Santa Fe. It was closed in 1966.

1875: Santa Fe made archdiocese.

1939: Gallup diocese established.

1982: Las Cruces diocese established.

New York

1524: Giovanni da Verrazano was first white man to enter New York Bay.

1642: Jesuits Isaac Jogues and Rene Goupil were mutilated by Mohawks; Rene Goupil was killed by them shortly afterwards. Dutch Calvinists rescued Father Jogues.

1646: Jesuit Isaac Jogues and John Lalande were martyred by Iroquois at Ossernenon, now Auriesville.

1654: The Onondagas were visited by Jesuits from Canada.

1655: First permanent mission established near Syracuse.

1656: Church of St. Mary erected on Onondaga Lake, in first French settlement within state. Kateri Tekakwitha, "Lily of the Mohawks," was born at Ossernenon, now Auriesville (d. in Canada, 1680). She was beatified in 1980.

1658: Indian uprisings destroyed missions among Cayugas, Senecas and Oneidas.

1664: English took New Amsterdam. Freedom of conscience allowed by the Duke of York, the new Lord Proprietor.

1667: Missions were restored under protection of Garaconthie, Onondaga chief.

1678: Franciscan Louis Hennepin, first white man to describe Niagara Falls, celebrated Mass there.

1682: Thomas Dongan appointed governor by Duke of York.

1683: English Jesuits came to New York, later opened a school.

1700: Although Assembly enacted a bill calling for religious toleration of all Christians in 1683, other penal laws were now enforced against Catholics; all priests were ordered out of the province.

1709: French Jesuit missionaries obliged to give up their central New York missions.

1741: Because of an alleged popish plot to burn city of New York, four whites were hanged and 11 blacks burned at stake.

1774: Elizabeth Bayley Seton, foundress of the American Sisters of Charity, was born in New York City on Aug. 28. She was canonized in 1975.

1777: State Constitution gave religious liberty, but the naturalization law required an oath to renounce allegiance to any foreign ruler, ecclesiastical as well as civil.

1785: Cornerstone was laid for St. Peter's Church, New York City, first permanent structure of Catholic worship in state.

Trusteeism began to cause trouble at New York.

1806: Anti-Catholic 1777 Test Oath for naturalization repealed.

1808: New York diocese established.

1823: Father Felix Varela of Cuba, educator, theologian and social reformer, arrived in New York; established churches and charitable organizations; published journals and philosophical works.

1828: New York State Legislature enacted a law upholding sanctity of seal of confession.

1834: First native New Yorker to become a secular priest, Rev. John McCloskey, was ordained.

1836: John Nepomucene Neumann arrived from Bohemia and was ordained a priest in Old St. Patrick's Cathedral, New York City. He was canonized in 1977.

1841: Fordham University and Manhattanville College established.

1847: Albany and Buffalo dioceses established.

1850: New York made archdiocese.

1853: Brooklyn diocese established.

1856: Present St. Bonaventure University and Christ the King Seminary founded at Allegany.

1858: Cornerstone was laid of second (present) St. Patrick's Cathedral, New York City. The cathedral was completed in 1879.

1868: Rochester diocese established.

1872: Ogdensburg diocese established.

1875: Archbishop John McCloskey of New York made first American cardinal by Pope Pius IX.

1878: Franciscan Sisters of Allegany were first native American community to send members to foreign missions.

1880: William R. Grace was first Catholic mayor of New York City.

1886: Syracuse diocese established.

1889: Mother Frances Xavier Cabrini arrived in New York City to begin work among Italian immigrants. She was canonized in 1946.

1911: Archbishop John M. Farley of New York made cardinal by Pope Pius X.

Catholic Foreign Mission Society of America (Maryknoll) opened a seminary for foreign missions, the first of its kind in U.S. The Maryknollers were also unique as the first U.S.-established foreign mission society.

1917: Military Ordinariate established with headquarters at New York; renamed Military Archdiocese and transferred to Washington, D.C., in 1985.

1919: Alfred E. Smith became first elected Catholic governor.

1924: Archbishop Patrick Hayes of New York made cardinal by Pope Pius XI.

1930: Jesuit Martyrs of New York and Canada were canonized on June 29.

1946: Archbishop Francis J. Spellman of New York made cardinal by Pope Pius XII.

1957: Rockville Centre diocese established.

1969: Archbishop Terence Cooke of New York made cardinal by Pope Paul VI.

1981: Apostolic Exarchate for Armenian-Rite Catholics in the United States and Canada established. New York designated see city.

1985: Archbishop John J. O'Connor of New York made cardinal by Pope John Paul II.

North Carolina

1526: The Ayllon expedition attempted to establish a settlement on Carolina coast.

1540: De Soto expedition, accompanied by chaplains, entered state.

1776: State Constitution denied office to "those who denied the truths of the Protestant religion."

1805: The few Catholics in state were served by visiting missionaries.

1821: Bishop John England of Charleston celebrated Mass in the ballroom of the home of William Gaston at New Bern, marking the start of organization of the first parish, St. Paul's, in the state.

1835: William Gaston, State Supreme Court Justice, succeeded in having the article denying religious freedom repealed.

1852: First Catholic church erected in Charlotte.

1868: North Carolina vicariate apostolic established. Catholics obtained full civil liberty and rights.

1874: Sisters of Mercy arrived, opened an academy, several schools, hospitals and an orphanage.

1876: Benedictine priory and school (later Belmont Abbey College) founded at Belmont; priory designated an abbey in 1884.

1910: Belmont Abbey established as an abbacy nullius; abbacy nullius status suppressed in 1977.

1924: Raleigh diocese established.

1971: Charlotte diocese established.

North Dakota

1742: Pierre and Francois Verendrye, accompanied by Jesuit Father Coquart, explored territory.

1818: Canadian priests ministered to Catholics in area.

1840: Jesuit Father De Smet made first of several trips among Mandan and Gros Ventre Indians.

1848: Father George Belcourt, first American resident priest in territory, reestablished Pembina Mission.

1874: Grey Nuns arrived at Fort Totten to conduct a school.

1889: Jamestown diocese established; transferred to Fargo in 1897. (Jamestown was reestablished as a titular see in 1995.)

1893: Benedictines founded St. Gall Monastery at Devil's Lake. (It was moved to Richardton in 1899 and became an abbey in 1903.)

1909: Bismarck diocese established.

1959: Archbishop Aloysius J. Muench, bishop of Fargo, made cardinal by Pope John XXIII.

Ohio

1749: Jesuits in expedition of Céleron de Blainville preached to Indians.

First religious services were held within present limits of Ohio. Jesuit Joseph de Bonnecamps celebrated Mass at mouth of Little Miami River and in other places.

1751: First Catholic settlement founded among Huron Indians near Sandusky by Jesuit Father de la Richardie.

1790: Benedictine Pierre Didier ministered to French immigrants.

1812: Bishop Flaget of Bardstown visited and baptized Catholics of Lancaster and Somerset Counties.

1818: Dominican Father Edward Fenwick (later first bishop of Cincinnati) built St. Joseph's Church.

1821: Cincinnati diocese established.

1830: At request of Bishop Fenwick Dominican Sisters from Kentucky established second Dominican

foundation in U.S. at Somerset (transferred to Columbus in 1868).

1831: Xavier University founded.

1843: Members of Congregation of Most Precious Blood arrived in Cincinnati from Switzerland.

1845: Cornerstone laid for St. Peter's Cathedral, Cincinnati.

1847: Cleveland diocese established.

1850: Cincinnati made archdiocese.

Marianists opened St. Mary's Institute, now University of Dayton.

1865: Sisters of Charity opened hospital in Cleveland, first institution of its kind in city.

1868: Columbus diocese established.

1871: Ursuline College for women opened at Cleveland.

1910: Toledo diocese established.

1935: Archbishop John T. McNicholas, O.P., founded the Institutum Divi Thomae in Cincinnati for fundamental research in natural sciences.

1943: Youngstown diocese established.

1944: Steubenville diocese established.

1969: Byzantine Rite Eparchy of Parma (for Ruthenians) established.

1982: Apostolic Exarchate for Romanian Byzantine-Rite Catholics in the United States established. Canton designated see city. Raised to an eparchy (St. George Martyr) 1987.

1983: Byzantine Rite Eparchy of Saint Josaphat in Parma (for Ukrainians) established.

Oklahoma

1540: De Soto expedition, accompanied by chaplains, explored territory.

1541: Coronado expedition, accompanied by Franciscan Juan de Padilla, explored state.

1630: Spanish Franciscan Juan de Salas labored among Indians.

1700: Scattered Catholic families were visited by priests from Kansas and Arkansas.

1874: First Catholic church built by Father Smyth at Atoka.

1876: Prefecture Apostolic of Indian Territory established with Benedictine Isidore Robot as its head.

1886: First Catholic day school for Choctaw and white children opened by Sisters of Mercy at Krebs.

1891: Vicariate Apostolic of Oklahoma and Indian Territory established.

1905: Oklahoma diocese established; title changed to Oklahoma City and Tulsa, 1930.

1917: Benedictine Heights College for women founded.

Carmelite Sisters of St. Theresa of the Infant Jesus founded at Oklahoma City.

1972: Oklahoma City made archdiocese. Tulsa diocese established.

Oregon

1603: Vizcaino explored northern Oregon coast.

1774: Franciscan missionaries accompanied Juan Perez on his expedition to coast, and Heceta a year later.

1811: Catholic Canadian trappers and traders with John J. Astor expedition founded first American settlement — Astoria.

1834: Indian missions in Northwest entrusted to Jesuits by Holy See.

1838: Abbe Blanchet appointed vicar general to Bishop of Quebec with jurisdiction over area which included Oregon Territory.

1839: First Mass celebrated at present site of St. Paul.

1843: Oregon vicariate apostolic established.
St. Joseph's College for boys opened.

1844: Jesuit Pierre de Smet established Mission of St. Francis Xavier near St. Paul.
Sisters of Notre Dame de Namur, first to enter Oregon, opened an academy for girls.

1846: Vicariate made an ecclesiastical province with Bishop Blanchet as first Archbishop of Oregon City (now Portland).

1847: First priest was ordained in Oregon.

1848: First Provincial Council of Oregon.

1857: Death of Dr. John McLoughlin, "Father of Oregon."

1865: Rev. H. H. Spalding, a Protestant missionary, published the Whitman Myth to hinder work of Catholic missionaries.

1874: Catholic Indian Mission Bureau established.

1875: St. Vincent's Hospital, first in state, opened at Portland.

1903: Baker diocese established.

1922: Anti-private school bill sponsored by Scottish Rite Masons was passed by popular vote, 115,506 to 103,685.

1925: U.S. Supreme Court declared Oregon anti-private school bill unconstitutional.

1953: First Trappist monastery on West Coast established in Willamette Valley north of Lafayette.

Pennsylvania

1673: Priests from Maryland ministered to Catholics in the Colony.

1682: Religious toleration was extended to members of all faiths.

1729: Jesuit Joseph Greaton became first resident missionary of Philadelphia.

1734: St. Joseph's Church, first Catholic church in Philadelphia, was opened by Father Greaton.

1741: Jesuit Fathers Schneider and Wappeler ministered to German immigrants.
Conewego Chapel, a combination chapel and dwelling, was built by Father William Wappeler, S.J., a priest sent to minister to the German Catholic immigrants who settled in the area in the 1730s.

1782: St. Mary's Parochial School opened at Philadelphia.

1788: Holy Trinity Church, Philadelphia, was incorporated; first exclusively national church organized in U.S.

1797: Augustinian Matthew Carr founded St. Augustine parish, Philadelphia.

1799: Prince Demetrius Gallitzin (Father Augustine Smith) built church in western Pennsylvania, at Loretto.

1808: Philadelphia diocese established.

1814: St. Joseph's Orphanage was opened at Philadelphia; first Catholic institution for children in U.S.

1842: University of Villanova founded by Augustinians.

1843: Pittsburgh diocese established.

1844: Thirteen persons killed, two churches and a school burned in Know-Nothing riots at Philadelphia.

1846: First Benedictine Abbey in New World founded near Latrobe by Father Boniface Wimmer.

1852: Redemptorist John Nepomucene Neumann became fourth bishop of Philadelphia. He was beatified in 1963 and canonized in 1977.

1853: Erie diocese established.

1868: Scranton and Harrisburg dioceses established.

1871: Chestnut Hill College, first for women in state, founded.

1875: Philadelphia made archdiocese.

1876: Allegheny diocese established by division of Pittsburgh diocese; reunited to Pittsburgh 1877, with resignation of its first and only bishop; suppressed in 1889. (It was later reestablished as a titular see.)

1891: Katharine Drexel founded Sisters of Blessed Sacrament for Indians and Colored Peoples. She was beatified in 1988.

1901: Altoona-Johnstown diocese established.

1913: Byzantine Rite Apostolic Exarchate of Philadelphia established; became metropolitan see, 1958.

1921: Archbishop Dennis Dougherty made cardinal by Pope Benedict XV.

1924: Byzantine Rite Apostolic Exarchate of Pittsburgh established; made an eparchy in 1963; raised to metropolitan status and transferred to Munhall, 1969; transferred back to Pittsburgh in 1977.

1951: Greensburg diocese established.

1958: Archbishop John O'Hara, C.S.C., of Philadelphia made cardinal by Pope John.

1961: Allentown diocese established.

1967: Archbishop John J. Krol of Philadelphia made cardinal by Pope Paul VI.

1969: Bishop John J. Wright of Pittsburgh made cardinal by Pope Paul VI and transferred to Curia post.

1976: The 41st International Eucharistic Congress, the second held in the U.S., convened in Philadelphia, August 1-8.

1985: Major Archbishop Myroslav Lubachivsky of the Major Archbishopric of Lviv of the Ukrainians, former metropolitan of Byzantine Philadelphia archeparchy (1979-80), made cardinal by Pope John Paul II.

1991: Archbishop Anthony J. Bevilacqua of Philadelphia made cardinal by Pope John Paul II.

Rhode Island

1663: Colonial Charter granted freedom of conscience.

1719: Laws denied Catholics the right to hold public office.

1829: St. Mary's Church, Pawtucket, was first Catholic church in state.

1837: Parochial schools inaugurated in state.
First Catholic church in Providence was built.

1851: Sisters of Mercy began work in Rhode Island.

1872: Providence diocese established.

1900: Trappists took up residence in state.

1917: Providence College founded.

South Carolina

1569: Jesuit Juan Rogel was the first resident priest in the territory.

1573: First Franciscans arrived in southeastern section.

1606: Bishop Altamirano conducted visitation of area.
1655: Franciscans had two missions among Indians; later destroyed by English.
1697: Religious liberty granted to all except "papists."
1790: Catholics given right to vote.
1820: Charleston diocese established.
1822: Bishop England founded U.S. Catholic Miscellany, first Catholic paper of a strictly religious nature in U.S.
1830: Sisters of Our Lady of Mercy, first in state, took up residence at Charleston.
1847: Cornerstone of Cathedral of St. John the Baptist, Charleston, was laid.
1861: Cathedral and many institutions destroyed in Charleston fire.

South Dakota

1842: Father Augustine Ravoux began ministrations to French and Indians at Fort Pierre, Vermilion and Prairie du Chien; printed devotional book in Sioux language the following year.
1867: Parish organized among the French at Jefferson.
1878: Benedictines opened school for Sioux children at Fort Yates.
1889: Sioux Falls diocese established.
1902: Lead diocese established; transferred to Rapid City, 1930. (Lead was reestablished as a titular see in 1995.)
1936: Mount Marty College established.
1952: Blue Cloud Abbey, first Benedictine foundation in state, was dedicated.

Tennessee

1541: Cross planted on shore of Mississippi by De Soto; accompanying the expedition were Fathers John de Gallegos and Louis De Soto.
1682: Franciscan Fathers Membre and Douay accompanied La Salle to present site of Memphis; may have offered the first Masses in the territory.
1800: Catholics were served by priests from Bardstown, Ky.
1822: Non-Catholics assisted in building church in Nashville.
1837: Nashville diocese established.
1843: Sisters of Charity opened a school for girls in Nashville.
1860: Sisters of St. Dominic from Somerset, Ohio, arrived in Nashville to open a school for girls.
1871: Christian Brothers opened a school for boys in Memphis; it later became Christian Brothers College (now University).
1921: Sisters of St. Dominic opened Siena College for women at Memphis; closed in 1971.
1970: Memphis diocese established.
1988: Knoxville diocese established.

Texas

1541: Missionaries with Coronado expedition probably entered territory.
1553: Dominicans Diego de la Cruz, Hernando Mendez, Juan Ferrer, Brother Juan de Mina killed by Indians.
1675: Bosque-Larios missionary expedition entered region; Father Juan Larios offered first recorded high Mass.
1682: Mission Corpus Christi de Isleta (Ysleta) founded by Franciscans near El Paso, first mission in present-day Texas.
1690: Mission San Francisco de los Tejas founded in east Texas.
1703: Mission San Francisco de Solano founded on Rio Grande; rebuilt in 1718 as San Antonio de Valero or the Alamo.
1717: Franciscan Antonio Margil founded six missions in northeast.
1720: San Jose y San Miguel de Aguayo Mission founded by Fray Antonio Margil de Jesus.
1721: Franciscan Brother Jose Pita killed by Indians at Carnezeria.
1728: Site of San Antonio settled.
1738: Construction of San Fernando Cathedral at San Antonio.
1744: Mission church of the Alamo built.
1750: Franciscan Francisco Xavier was killed by Indians; so were Jose Ganzabal in 1752, and Alonzo Ferrares and Jose San Esteban in 1758.
1793: Mexico secularized missions.
1825: Governments of Cohuila and Texas secularized all Indian missions.
1838-39: Irish priests ministered to settlements of Refugio and San Patricio.
1841: Vicariate of Texas established.
1847: Ursuline Sisters established their first academy in territory at Galveston.
Galveston diocese established.
1852: Oblate Fathers and Franciscans arrived in Galveston to care for new influx of German Catholics.
St. Mary's College (now University) founded at San Antonio.
1854: Know-Nothing Party began to stir up hatred against Catholics.
Oldest Polish settlement in Texas established Dec. 24; settlers named the area Panna Maria (Virgin Mary in Polish).
1858: Texas Legislature passed law entitling all schools granting free scholarships and meeting state requirements to share in school fund.
1874: San Antonio diocese established.
Vicariate of Brownsville established.
1881: St. Edward's College founded: became first chartered college in state in 1889.
Sisters of Charity founded Incarnate Word College at San Antonio.
1890: Dallas diocese established; changed to Dallas-Ft. Worth, 1953; made two separate dioceses, 1969.
1912: Corpus Christi diocese established.
1914: El Paso diocese established.
1926: San Antonio made archdiocese. Amarillo diocese established.
1947: Austin diocese established.
1959: Galveston diocese redesignated Galveston-Houston.
1961: San Angelo diocese established.
1965: Brownsville diocese established.
1966: Beaumont diocese established.
1982: Victoria diocese established.
1983: Lubbock diocese established.
1986: Tyler diocese established.

Utah

1776: Franciscans Silvestre de Escalante and Atanasio Dominguez reached Utah (Salt) Lake; first white men known to enter the territory.

1858: Jesuit Father De Smet accompanied General Harney as chaplain on expedition sent to settle troubles between Mormons and U.S. Government.

1866: On June 29 Father Edward Kelly offered first Mass in Salt Lake City in Mormon Assembly Hall.

1886: Utah vicariate apostolic established.

1891: Salt Lake City diocese established.

1926: College of St. Mary-of-the-Wasatch for women was founded.

Vermont

1609: Champlain expedition passed through territory.

1666: Captain La Motte built fort and shrine of St. Anne on Isle La Motte; Sulpician Father Dollier de Casson celebrated first Mass.

1668: Bishop Laval of Quebec (beatified in 1980), administered confirmation in region; this was the first area in northeastern U.S. to receive an episcopal visit.

1710: Jesuits ministered to Indians near Lake Champlain.

1793: Discriminatory measures against Catholics were repealed.

1830: Father Jeremiah O'Callaghan became first resident priest in state.

1853: Burlington diocese established.

1854: Sisters of Charity of Providence arrived to conduct St. Joseph's Orphanage at Burlington.

1904: St. Michael's College founded.

1951: First Carthusian foundation in America established at Whitingham.

Virginia

1526: Dominican Antonio de Montesinos offered first Mass on Virginia soil.

1561: Dominicans visited the coast.

1571: Father John Baptist de Segura and seven Jesuit companions killed by Indians.

1642: Priests outlawed and Catholics denied right to vote.

1689: Capuchin Christopher Plunket was captured and exiled to a coastal island where he died in 1697.

1776: Religious freedom granted.

1791: Father Jean Dubois arrived at Richmond with letters from Lafayette. The House of Delegates was placed at his disposal for celebration of Mass.
A church was built in Norfolk (St. Mary of the Immaculate Conception). It was designated a minor basilica in 1991.

1796: A church was built at Alexandria.

1820: Richmond diocese established.

1822: Trusteeism created serious problems in diocese; Bishop Patrick Kelly resigned the see.

1848: Sisters of Charity opened an orphan asylum at Norfolk.

1866: School Sisters of Notre Dame and Sisters of Charity opened academies for girls at Richmond.

1974: Arlington diocese established.

Washington

1774: Spaniards explored the region.

1838: Fathers Blanchet and Demers, "Apostles of the Northwest," were sent to territory by archbishop of Quebec.

1840: Cross erected on Whidby Island, Puget Sound.

1843: Vicariate Apostolic of Oregon, including Washington, was established.

1844: Mission of St. Paul founded at Colville.
Six Sisters of Notre Dame de Namur began work in area.

1846: Walla Walla diocese established; suppressed in 1850 (reestablished later as a titular see).

1850: Nesqually diocese established; transferred to Seattle, 1907. (Nesqually reestablished as a titular see in 1995.)

1856: Providence Academy, the first permanent Catholic school in the Northwest, was built at Fort Vancouver by Mother Joseph Pariseau of the Sisters of Charity of Providence.

1887: Gonzaga University founded.

1913: Spokane diocese established.

1951: Seattle made archdiocese. Yakima diocese established.

West Virginia

1749: Father Joseph de Bonnecamps, accompanying the Bienville expedition, may have offered first Mass in the territory.

1821: First Catholic church in Wheeling.

1838: Sisters of Charity founded school at Martinsburg.

1848: Visitation Nuns established academy for girls in Wheeling.

1850: Wheeling diocese established; name changed to Wheeling-Charleston, 1974.
Wheeling Hospital incorporated, the oldest Catholic charitable institution in territory.

1955: Wheeling College established.

Wisconsin

1661: Jesuit Rene Menard, first known missionary in the territory, was killed or lost in the Black River district.

1665: Jesuit Claude Allouez founded Mission of the Holy Ghost at La Pointe Chegoimegon, now Bayfield; was the first permanent mission in region.

1673: Father Marquette and Louis Joliet traveled from Green Bay down the Wisconsin and Mississippi rivers.

1762: Suppression of Jesuits in French Colonies closed many missions for 30 years.

1843: Milwaukee diocese established.

1853: St. John's Cathedral, Milwaukee, was built.

1864: State charter granted for establishment of Marquette University. First students admitted, 1881.

1868: Green Bay and La Crosse dioceses established.

1875: Milwaukee made archdiocese.

1905: Superior diocese established.

1946: Madison diocese established.

Wyoming

1840: Jesuit Pierre De Smet offered first Mass near Green River.

1851: Father De Smet held peace conference with Indians near Fort Laramie.

1867: Father William Kelly, first resident priest, arrived in Cheyenne and built first church a year later.

1873: Father Eugene Cusson became first resident pastor in Laramie.
1875: Sisters of Charity of Leavenworth opened school and orphanage at Laramie.
1884: Jesuits took over pastoral care of Shoshone and Arapaho Indians.
1887: Cheyenne diocese established.
1949: Weston Memorial Hospital opened near Newcastle.

Puerto Rico

1493: Island discovered by Columbus on his second voyage; he named it San Juan de Borinquen (the Indian name for Puerto Rico).
1509: Juan Ponce de Leon, searching for gold, colonized the island and became its first governor; present population descended mainly from early Spanish settlers.
1511: Diocese of Puerto Rico established as suffragan of Seville, Spain; Bishop Alonso Manso, sailing from Spain in 1512, became first bishop to take up residence in New World.
1645: Synod held in Puerto Rico to regulate frequency of Masses according to distances people had to walk.
1898: Puerto Rico ceded to U.S. (became self-governing Commonwealth in 1952); inhabitants granted U.S. citizenship in 1917.
1924: Diocese of Puerto Rico renamed San Juan de Puerto Rico and made immediately subject to the Holy See; Ponce diocese established.
1948: Catholic University of Puerto Rico founded at Ponce through efforts of Most Rev. James E. McManus, C.SS.R., bishop of Ponce, 1947-63.
1960: San Juan made metropolitan see. Arecibo diocese established.
1964: Caguas diocese established.
1973: Archbishop Luis Aponte Martinez of San Juan made first native Puerto Rican cardinal by Pope Paul VI.
1976: Mayaguez diocese established.
Virgin of Providence officially approved as Patroness of Puerto Rico by Pope Paul VI.

CATHOLICS IN PRESIDENTS' CABINETS

From 1789 to 1940, nine Catholics were appointed to cabinet posts by six of 32 presidents. The first was Roger Brooke Taney (later named first Catholic Supreme Court Justice) who was appointed in 1831 by Pres. Andrew Jackson. Catholics have been appointed to cabinet posts from the time of Pres. Franklin D. Roosevelt to the present.

Listed below in chronological order are presidents, Catholic cabinet officials, posts held, dates.

Andrew Jackson — Roger B. **Taney,** Attorney General, 1831-33, Secretary of Treasury, 1833-34.

Franklin Pierce — James **Campbell,** Postmaster General, 1853-57.

James Buchanan — John B. **Floyd,** Secretary of War, 1857-61.

William McKinley — Joseph **McKenna,** Attorney General, 1897-98.

Theodore Roosevelt — Robert J. **Wynne,** Postmaster General, 1904-05; Charles **Bonaparte,** Secretary of Navy, 1905-06, Attorney General, 1906-09.

Franklin D. Roosevelt — James A. **Farley,** Postmaster General, 1933-40; Frank **Murphy,** Attorney General, 1939-40; Frank C. **Walker,** Postmaster General, 1940-45.

Harry S. Truman — Robert E. **Hannegan,** Postmaster General, 1945-47; J. Howard **McGrath,** Attorney General, 1949-52; Maurice J. **Tobin,** Secretary of Labor, 1948-53; James P. **McGranery,** Attorney General, 1952-53.

Dwight D. Eisenhower — Martin P. **Durkin,** Secretary of Labor, 1953; James P. **Mitchell,** Secretary of Labor, 1953-61.

John F. Kennedy — Robert F. **Kennedy,** Attorney General, 1961-63; Anthony **Celebrezze,** Secretary of Health, Education and Welfare, 1962-63; John S. **Gronouski,** Postmaster General, 1963.

Lyndon B. Johnson — (Robert F. **Kennedy,** 1963-64, Anthony **Celebrezze,** 1963-65, and John S. **Gronouski,** 1963-65, reappointed to posts held in Kennedy Cabinet _ see above.) John T. **Connor,** Secretary of Commerce, 1965-67; Lawrence **O'Brien,** Postmaster General, 1965-68.

Richard M. Nixon — Walter J. **Hickel,** Secretary of Interior, 1969-71; John A. **Volpe,** Secretary of Transportation, 1969-72; Maurice H. **Stans,** Secretary of Commerce, 1969-72; Peter J. **Brennan,** Secretary of Labor, 1973-74; William E. **Simon,** Secretary of Treasury, 1974.

Gerald R. Ford — (Peter J. **Brennan,** 1974-75, and William E. **Simon,** 1974-76, reappointed to posts held above.)

Jimmy Carter — Joseph **Califano,** Jr., Secretary of Health, Education and Welfare, 1977-79; Benjamin **Civiletti,** Attorney General, 1979-81; Moon **Landrieu,** Secretary of Housing and Urban Development, 1979-81; Edmund S. **Muskie,** Secretary of State, 1980-81.

Ronald Reagan — Alexander M. **Haig,** Secretary of State, 1981-82; Raymond J. **Donovan,** Secretary of Labor, 1981-84; Margaret M. **Heckler,** Secretary of Health and Human Services, 1983-85; William J. **Bennett,** Secretary of Education, 1985-88; Ann Dore **McLaughlin,** Secretary of Labor, 1988-89; Lauro F. **Cavazos,** Secretary of Education, 1988-89; Nicholas F. **Brady,** Secretary of Treasury, 1988-89.

George Bush — Lauro F. **Cavazos** (reappointed), Secretary of Education, 1989-90; Nicholas F. **Brady** (reappointed), Secretary of Treasury, 1989-93 ; James D. **Watkins,** Secretary of Energy, 1989-93; Manuel **Lujan,** Jr., Secretary of Interior, 1989-93 ; Edward J. **Derwinski,** Secretary of Veteran Affairs, 1989-92; Lynn **Martin,** Secretary of Labor, 1990-93; Edward **Madigan,** Secretary of Agriculture, 1991-93; William P. **Barr,** Attorney General, 1991-93.

Bill Clinton — Henry G. **Cisneros,** Secretary of Housing and Urban Development, 1993-97; Federico F. **Pena,** Secretary of Transportation, 1993-97 ; Donna **Shalala,** Secretary of Health and Human Services, 1993- ; William M. **Daley,** Secretary of Commerce, 1997- ; Andrew **Cuomo,** Secretary of Housing and Urban Development, 1997- ; Alexis H. **Herman,** Secretary of Labor, 1997- .

Cabinet members who became Catholics after leaving their posts were: Thomas Ewing, Secretary of Treasury under William A. Harrison, and Secretary of Interior under Zachary Taylor; Luke E. Wright, Secretary of War under Theodore Roosevelt; Albert B. Fall, Secretary of Interior under Warren G. Harding.

CATHOLIC SUPREME COURT JUSTICES

Roger B. Taney, Chief Justice 1836-64; app. by Andrew Jackson.

Edward D. White, Associate Justice 1894-1910, app. by Grover Cleveland; Chief Justice 1910-21, app. by William H. Taft.

Joseph McKenna, Associate Justice 1898-1925; app. by William McKinley.

Pierce Butler, Associate Justice 1923-39; app. by Warren G. Harding.

Frank Murphy, Associate Justice 1940-49; app. by Franklin D. Roosevelt.

William Brennan, Associate Justice 1956-90; app. by Dwight D. Eisenhower.

Antonin Scalia, Associate Justice 1986-; app. by Ronald Reagan.

Anthony M. Kennedy, Associate Justice 1988-; app. by Ronald Reagan.

Clarence Thomas, Associate Justice 1991- ; app. by George Bush.

Sherman Minton, Associate Justice from 1949 to 1956, became a Catholic several years before his death in 1965.

CATHOLICS IN STATUARY HALL

Statues of 13 Catholics deemed worthy of national commemoration by the donating states are among those enshrined in National Statuary Hall and other places in the U.S. Capitol. The Hall, formerly the chamber of the House of Representatives, was erected by Act of Congress July 2, 1864.

Donating states, names and years of placement are listed.

Arizona: Rev. Eusebio Kino, S. J., missionary, 1965.

California: Rev. Junipero Serra, O. F. M. missionary, 1931. (Beatified 1988.)

Hawaii: Father Damien, missionary, 1969.(Beatified 1995.)

Illinois: Gen. James Shields, statesman, 1893.

Louisiana: Edward D. White, Justice of the U.S. Supreme Court (1894-1921), 1955.

Maryland: Charles Carroll, statesman, 1901.

Nevada: Patrick A. McCarran, statesman, 1960.

New Mexico: Dennis Chavez, statesman, 1966. (Archbishop Jean B. Lamy, pioneer prelate of Santa Fe, was nominated for Hall honor in 1951.)

North Dakota: John Burke, U.S. treasurer, 1963.

Oregon: Dr. John McLoughlin, pioneer, 1953.

Washington: Mother Mary Joseph Pariseau, pioneer missionary and humanitarian.

West Virginia: John E. Kenna, statesman, 1901.

Wisconsin: Rev. Jacques Marquette, S.J., missionary, explorer, 1895.

CHURCH-STATE DECISIONS OF THE SUPREME COURT

(Among sources of this selected listing of U.S. Supreme Court decisions was *The Supreme Court on Church and State,* Joseph Tussman, editor; Oxford University Press, New York, 1962.)

Watson v. Jones, 13 Wallace 679 (1872): The Court declared that a member of a religious organization may not appeal to secular courts against a decision made by a church tribunal within the area of its competence.

Polygamy: The Mormon practice of polygamy was at issue in three decisions and was declared unconstitutional: Reynolds v. United States, 98 US 145 (1879); Davis v. Beason, 133 US 333 (1890); Church of Latter-Day Saints v. United States, 136 US 1 (1890).

Bradfield v. Roberts, 175 US 291 (1899): The Court denied that an appropriation of government funds for an institution (Providence Hospital, Washington, D.C.) run by Roman Catholic sisters violated the No Establishment Clause of the First Amendment.

Pierce v. Society of Sisters, 268 US 510 (1925): The Court denied that a state can require children to attend public schools only. The Court held that the liberty of the Constitution forbids standardization by such compulsion, and that the parochial schools involved had claims to protection under the Fourteenth Amendment.

Cochran v. Board of Education, 281 US 370 (1930): The Court upheld a Louisiana statute providing textbooks at public expense for children attending public or parochial schools. The Court held that the children and state were beneficiaries of the appropriations, with incidental secondary benefit going to the schools.

United States v. MacIntosh, 283 US 605 (1931): The Court denied that anyone can place allegiance to the will of God above his allegiance to the government since such a person could make his own interpretation of God's will the decisive test as to whether he would or would not obey the nation's law. The Court stated that the nation, which has a duty to survive, can require citizens to bear arms in its defense.

Everson v. Board of Education, 330 US 1 (1947): The Court upheld the constitutionality of a New Jersey statute authorizing free school bus transportation for parochial as well as public school students. The Court expressed the opinion that the benefits of public welfare legislation, included under such bus transportation, do not run contrary to the concept of separation of Church and State.

McCollum v. Board of Education, 333 US 203 (1948): The Court declared unconstitutional a program for releasing children, with parental consent, from public school classes so they could receive religious instruction on public school premises from representatives of their own faiths.

Zorach v. Clauson, 343 US 306 (1952): The Court upheld the constitutionality of a New York statute permitting, on a voluntary basis, the release during school time of students from public school classes for religious instruction given off public school premises.

Torcaso v. Watkins, 367 US 488 (1961): The Court declared unconstitutional a Maryland requirement that one must make a declaration of belief in the existence of God as part of the oath of office for notaries public.

McGowan v. Maryland, 81 Sp Ct 1101; **Two**

Guys from Harrison v. McGinley, 81 Sp Ct 1135; **Gallagher v. Crown Kosher Super Market,** 81 Sp Ct 1128; **Braunfield v. Brown,** 81 Sp Ct 1144 (1961): The Court ruled that Sunday closing laws do not violate the No Establishment of Religion Clause of the First Amendment, even though the laws were religious in their inception and still have some religious overtones. The Court held that, "as presently written and administered, most of them, at least, are of a secular rather than of a religious character, and that presently they bear no relationship to establishment of religion as those words are used in the Constitution of the United States."

Engel v. Vitale, 370 US 42 (1962): The Court declared that the voluntary recitation in public schools of a prayer composed by the New York State Board of Regents is unconstitutional on the ground that it violates the No Establishment of Religion Clause of the First Amendment.

Abington Township School District v. Schempp and Murray v. Curlett, 83 Sp Ct 1560 (1963): The Court ruled that Bible reading and recitation of the Lord's Prayer in public schools, with voluntary participation by students, are unconstitutional on the ground that they violate the No Establishment of Religion Clause of the First Amendment.

Chamberlin v. Dade County, 83 Sp Ct 1864 (1964): The Court reversed a decision of the Florida Supreme Court concerning the constitutionality of prayer and devotional Bible reading in public schools during the school day, as sanctioned by a state statute which specifically related the practices to a sound public purpose.

Board of Education v. Allen, No. 660 (1968): The Court declared constitutional the New York school book loan law which requires local school boards to purchase books with state funds and lend them to parochial and private school students.

Walz v. Tax Commission of New York (1970): The Court upheld the constitutionality of a New York statute exempting church-owned property from taxation.

Earle v. DiCenso, Robinson v. DiCenso, Lemon v. Kurtzman, Tilton v. Richardson (1971): In Earle v. DiCenso and Robinson v. DiCenso, the Court ruled unconstitutional a 1969 Rhode Island statute which provided salary supplements to teachers of secular subjects in parochial schools; in Lemon v. Kurtzman, the Court ruled unconstitutional a 1968 Pennsylvania statute which authorized the state to purchase services for the teaching of secular subjects in nonpublic schools. The principal argument against constitutionality in these cases was that the statutes and programs at issue entailed excessive entanglement of government with religion. In Tilton v. Richardson, the Court held that this argument did not apply to a prohibitive degree with respect to federal grants, under the Higher Education Facilities Act of 1963, for the construction of facilities for nonreligious purposes by four church-related institutions of higher learning, three of which were Catholic, in Connecticut.

Amish Decision (1972): In a case appealed on behalf of Yoder, Miller and Yutzy, the Court ruled that Amish parents were exempt from a Wisconsin statute requiring them to send their children to school until the age of 16. The Court said in its decision that secondary schooling exposed Amish children to attitudes, goals and values contrary to their beliefs, and substantially hindered "the religious development of the Amish child and his integration into the way of life of the Amish faith-community at the crucial adolescent state of development."

Committee for Public Education and Religious Liberty, et al., v. Nyquist, et al., No. 72-694 (1973): The Court ruled that provisions of a 1972 New York statute were unconstitutional on the grounds that they were violative of the No Establishment Clause of the First Amendment and had the "impermissible effect" of advancing the sectarian activities of church-affiliated schools. The programs ruled unconstitutional concerned: (1) maintenance and repair grants, for facilities and equipment, to ensure the health, welfare and safety of students in nonpublic, nonprofit elementary and secondary schools serving a high concentration of students from low income families; (2) tuition reimbursement ($50 per grade school child, $100 per high school student) for parents (with income less than $5,000) of children attending nonpublic elementary or secondary schools; tax deduction from adjusted gross income for parents failing to qualify under the above reimbursement plan, for each child attending a nonpublic school.

Sloan, Treasurer of Pennsylvania, et al., v. Lemon, et al., No. 72-459 (1973): The Court ruled unconstitutional a Pennsylvania Parent Reimbursement Act for Nonpublic Education which provided funds to reimburse parents (to a maximum of $150) for a portion of tuition expenses incurred in sending their children to nonpublic schools. The Court held that there was no significant difference between this and the New York tuition reimbursement program (above), and declared that the Equal Protection Clause of the Fourteenth Amendment cannot be relied upon to sustain a program held to be violative of the No Establishment Clause.

Levitt, et al., v. Committee for Public Education and Religious Liberty, et al., No. 72-269 (1973): The Court ruled unconstitutional the Mandated Services Act of 1970 under which New York provided $28 million ($27 per pupil from first to seventh grade, $45 per pupil from seventh to 12th grade) to reimburse nonpublic schools for testing, recording and reporting services required by the state. The Court declared that the act provided "impermissible aid" to religion in contravention of the No Establishment Clause.

In related decisions handed down June 25, 1973, the Court: (1) affirmed a lower court decision against the constitutionality of an Ohio tax credit law benefiting parents with children in nonpublic schools; (2) reinstated an injunction against a parent reimbursement program in New Jersey; (3) affirmed South Carolina's right to grant construction loans to church-affiliated colleges, and dismissed an appeal contesting its right to provide loans to students attending church-affiliated colleges (**Hunt v. McNair, Durham v. McLeod**).

Wheeler v. Barrera (1974): The Court ruled that nonpublic school students in Missouri must share in federal funds for educationally deprived students on a comparable basis with public school students under

Title I of the Elementary and Secondary Education Act of 1965.

Norwood v. Harrison (93 S. Ct. 2804): The Court ruled that public assistance which avoids the prohibitions of the "effect" and "entanglement" tests (and which therefore does not substantially promote the religious mission of sectarian schools) may be confined to the secular functions of such schools.

Wiest v. Mt. Lebanon School District (1974): The Court upheld a lower court ruling that invocation and benediction prayers at public high school commencement ceremonies do not violate the principle of separation of Church and state.

Meek v. Pittenger (1975): The Court ruled unconstitutional portions of a Pennsylvania law providing auxiliary services for students of nonpublic schools; at the same time, it ruled in favor of provisions of the law permitting textbook loans to students of such schools. In denying the constitutionality of auxiliary services, the Court held that they had the "primary effect of establishing religion" and involved "excessive entanglement" of Church and state officials with respect to supervision; objection was also made against providing such services only on the premises of nonpublic schools and only at the request of such schools.

TWA, Inc., v. Hardison, 75-1126; **International Association of Machinists and Aero Space Workers v. Hardison,** 75-1385 (1977): The Court ruled that federal civil rights legislation does not require employers to make more than minimal efforts to accommodate employees who want a particular working day off as their religion's Sabbath Day, and that an employer cannot accommodate such an employee by violating seniority systems determined by a union collective bargaining agreement. The Court noted that its ruling was not a constitutional judgment but an interpretation of existing law.

Wolman v. Walter (1977): The Court ruled constitutional portions of an Ohio statute providing taxpaid textbook loans and some auxiliary services (standardized and diagnostic testing, therapeutic and remedial services, off school premises) for nonpublic school students. It decided that other portions of the law, providing state funds for nonpublic school field trips and instructional materials (audio-visual equipment, maps, tape recorders), were unconstitutional.

Parochiaid (1979): The Court decided, in Byrne v. Public Funds for Public Schools, against the constitutionality of a 1976 New Jersey law providing state income tax deductions for tuition paid by parents of students attending parochial and other private schools.

Student Bus Transportation (1979): The Court upheld a Pennsylvania law providing bus transportation at public expense for students to non-public schools up to 10 miles away from the boundaries of the public school districts in which they lived.

Reimbursement (1980): The Court upheld the constitutionality of a 1974 New York law providing direct cash payment to non-public schools for the costs of state-mandated testing and record-keeping.

Ten Commandments (1980): The Court struck down a 1978 Kentucky law requiring the posting of the Ten Commandments in public school classrooms in the state.

Campus Worship (1981): The Court ruled, in Widmar v. Vincent, that the University of Missouri at Kansas City could not deny student religious groups the use of campus facilities for worship services. The Court also, in Brandon v. Board of Education of Guilderland Schools, declined without comment to hear an appeal for reversal of lower court decisions denying a group of New York high school students the right to meet for prayer on public school property before the beginning of the school day.

No Meeting on Public School Property (1983): By refusing to hear an appeal in Lubbock v. Lubbock Civil Liberties Union, the Court upheld a lower court ruling against a public policy of permitting student religious groups to meet on public school property before and after school hours.

Tuition Tax Deduction (1983): In Mueller v. Allen, the Court upheld a Minnesota law allowing parents of students in public and non-public (including parochial) schools to take a tax deduction for the expenses of tuition, textbooks and transportation. Maximum allowable deductions were $500 per child in elementary school and $700 per child in grades seven through 12.

Christmas Nativity Scene (1984): The Court ruled 5-to-4 in Lynch v. Donnelly that the First Amendment does not mandate "complete separation of church and state," and that, therefore, the sponsorship of a Christmas nativity scene by the City of Pawtucket, R.I., was not unconstitutional. The case involved a scene included in a display of Christmas symbols sponsored by the city in a park owned by a non-profit group. The majority opinion said "the Constitution (does not) require complete separation of church and state; it affirmatively mandates accommodation, not merely tolerance, of all religions and forbids hostility toward any. Anything less" would entail callous indifference not intended by the Constitution. Moreover, "such hostility would bring us into 'war with our national tradition as embodied in the First Amendment's guaranty of the free exercise of religion.'" (The additional quotation was from the 1948 decision in McCollum v. Board of Education.)

Christmas Nativity Scene (1985): The Court upheld a lower court ruling that the Village of Scarsdale, N.Y., must make public space available for the display of privately sponsored nativity scenes.

Wallace v. Jaffree, No. 83-812 (1985): The Court ruled against the constitutionality of a 1981 Alabama law calling for a public-school moment of silence that specifically included optional prayer.

Grand Rapids v. Ball, No. 83-990, and **Aguilar v. Felton,** No. 84-237 (1985): The Court ruled against the constitutionality of programs in Grand Rapids and New York City allowing public school teachers to teach remedial entitlement subjects (under the Elementary and Secondary Education Act of 1965) in private schools, many of which were Catholic.

Equal Student Access (1986): In Bender v. Williamsport Area School District, the Court let stand a lower federal court decision allowing a public high school Bible study group the same "equal access" to school facilities as that enjoyed by other extracurricular clubs. A similar decision was handed down in 1990 in Board of Education v. Mergens, involving Westside High School in Omaha.

Creche and Menorah: In County of Allegheny v. American Civil Liberties Union, the Court ruled in

1989 (1) The display of a Christmas nativity scene in the Allegheny County Courthouse in Pittsburgh, Pa., violated the principle of separation of church and state because it appeared to be a government-sponsored endorsement of Christian belief. (2) The display of a Hanukkah menorah outside the Pittsburgh-Allegheny city-county building was constitutional because of its "particular physical setting" with secular symbols.

Peyote Ban (1990): The Court ruled in Unemployment Division v. Smith that religious use of the hallucinogenic cactus peyote is not covered by the First Amendment protection of religious freedom.

No Organized Prayer (1992): In Lee v. Weisman the Court banned officially organized prayer at public school graduation ceremonies.

Equal Access (1993): In Lamb's Chapel v. Center Moriches Union School District, the Court reversed a ruling by the 3rd U.S. Circuit Court of Appeals, declaring that the school district was wrong in prohibiting the congregation of Lamb's Chapel from using public school meeting space after hours to show a film series addressing family problems from a religious perspective. In view of the variety of organizations permitted to use school property after school hours, said the Court's opinion: "There would have been no realistic danger that the community would think that the district was endorsing religion or any particular creed, and any benefit to religion or to the church would have been no more than incidental."

Student Prayers (1993): The Court let stand a ruling by the 5th U.S. Circuit Court of Appeals, permitting students in Texas, Mississippi and Louisiana to include student-organized and student-led prayers in graduation exercises.

Church of Lukumi Babalu Aye v. City of Hialeah (1993): The Court ruled that municipal laws that effectively prohibit a single church from performing its religious rituals are unconstitutional. The ordinances at issue singled out one religion, Santeria, for the purpose of restricting its members from the practice of ritual animal sacrifices.

Zobrest v. Catalina Foothills School District (1993): The Court ruled that a public school district may provide a sign-language interpreter for a deaf student attending a Catholic school without violating constitutional separation of church and state. The majority opinion said: "Handicapped children, not sectarian schools are the primary beneficiaries of the Disabilities Education Act; to the extent sectarian schools benefit at all from (the act), they are only incidental beneficiaries."

Equal Rent (1994): The Court upheld lower court rulings against a Fairfax County, Va., school district's practice of charging churches more rent than other entities for the use of school buildings.

Hasidic School Case (1994): In Board of Education of Kiryas Joel Village School District v. Grumet, the Court ruled in 1994 that a school district created to meet the special education needs of an Hasidic Jewish community violated the Establishment Clause of the Constitution. The Court said the New York Legislature effectively endorsed a particular religion when it established a public school district for the Satmar Hasidic Village of Kiryas Joel.

Agostino v. Felton (1997): The court reversed, 5 to 4, its 1985 Aguilar v. Felton ruling, which had declared it unconstitutional for teachers employed by public school districts to hold Title I remedial programs for low-income students on the property of church-related schools. (See separate entry.)

Boerne v. Flores (1997): The court ruled, 6 to 3, that the Religious Freedom Restoration Act (1993) was unconstitutional because Congress overstepped its constitutional authority in enacting the law. Congress "has been given the power to 'enforce,' not the power to determine what constitutes a constitutional violation," said the majority opinion.

RELIGION IN PUBLIC SCHOOLS

(Based on a Catholic News Service article by Carol Zimmermann.)

A diverse group of religious and civil rights organizations issued a joint statement Apr. 13, 1995, in an effort to clarify the confusing issue of prayer and religious observances or discussions in public schools. Their six-page statement outlines what is and what is not currently permissible in expressing religious beliefs in public schools.

The statement says, for example: "Students have the right to pray individually or in groups, or to discuss their religious views with their peers so long as they are not disruptive." But, the statement specifies that such prayers or discussions do not include "the right to have a captive audience listen or to compel other students to participate."

Prayer at Graduations

Regarding prayer at graduation ceremonies, the document says school officials may not mandate or organize prayer, but hardly sets the record straight about student-led prayer at these services.

"The courts have reached conflicting conclusions under the federal Constitution" in this area, says the statement, recommending that schools consult their lawyers for the rules that apply to them, "until the issue is authoritatively resolved."

Since the Supreme Court's 1992 Lee v. Weisman opinion prohibited school authorities from even arranging for a speaker to present a prayer, lower courts in different states have made various rulings about student-led prayer at commencement exercises.

In Virginia, the state's Attorney General and the Board of Education proposed guidelines in mid-April to allow student-led prayer at graduations, despite a 1994 ruling by a U.S. district judge banning all prayer at graduations.

Religion in the Classroom

"It is both permissible and desirable to teach objectively about the role of religion in the history of the United States and other countries," but public school teachers may not specifically teach religion.

The same rules apply to the recurring controversy surrounding theories of evolution. Teachers may discuss explanations of the beginnings of life, but only within the confines of classes on religion or social studies. Public school teachers are required, according to the statement, to teach only scientific explanations of life's beginnings in science classes. And, just as teachers may not advance a religious view, they should not ridicule a student's religious belief.

Constitutional Protection

The statement says that students' expressions of religious beliefs in reports, homework or artwork are constitutionally protected. Likewise, students have the right to speak to and attempt to persuade their peers on religious topics. "But school officials should intercede to stop student religious speech if it turns into religious harassment aimed at a student or a small group of students."

The statement also says:

• Students have the right to distribute religious literature to their schoolmates, subject to reasonable restrictions for any non-school literature.

• Student religious clubs in secondary schools "must be permitted to meet and to have equal access" to school media for announcing their events.

• Religious messages on T-shirts and the like cannot be singled out for suppression.

• Schools can use discretion about dismissing students for off-site religious instruction.

The 35 organizations that endorsed the statement included the National Association of Evangelicals, the American Jewish Congress, the Christian Legal Society, the National Council of Churches, the Baptist Joint Committee on Public Affairs, the American Muslim Council, the Presbyterian Church (USA) and the American Civil Liberties Union.

Purpose of the Statement

"By making this document available," said Phil Baum, executive director of the American Jewish Congress, "the organizations are attempting to clarify what has become one of the most divisive issues of our time: religion in the public schools."

He said the document attempts to "ensure that the rights of all students are respected in the public schools."

Baum noted that the American Jewish Congress, which initiated the effort to draft the statement, had a long-standing commitment to ensuring that public schools are themselves religiously neutral.

"We believe, however, that it is inconsistent with that historic commitment to ask the public schools to root out private expressions of religious faith."

CHURCH TAX EXEMPTION

The exemption of church-owned property was ruled constitutional by the U.S. Supreme Court May 4, 1970, in the case of Walz v. The Tax Commission of New York.

Suit in the case was brought by Frederick Walz, who purchased in June, 1967, a 22-by-29-foot plot of ground on Staten Island valued at $100 and taxable at $5.24 a year. Shortly after making the purchase, Walz instituted a suit in New York State, contending that the exemption of church property from taxation authorized by state law increased his own tax rate and forced him indirectly to support churches in violation of his constitutional right to freedom of religion under the First Amendment. Three New York courts dismissed the suit, which had been instituted by mail. The Supreme Court, judging that it had probable jurisdiction, then took the case.

In a 7-1 decision affecting Church-state relations in every state in the nation, the Court upheld the New York law under challenge.

For and Against

Chief Justice Warren E. Burger, who wrote the majority opinion, said that Congress from its earliest days had viewed the religion clauses of the Constitution as authorizing statutory real estate tax exemption to religious bodies. He declared: "Nothing in this national attitude toward religious tolerance and two centuries of uninterrupted freedom from taxation has given the remotest sign of leading to an established church or religion, and on the contrary it has operated affirmatively to help guarantee the free exercise of all forms of religious beliefs."

Justice William O. Douglas wrote in dissent that the involvement of government in religion as typified in tax exemption may seem inconsequential but: "It is, I fear, a long step down the establishment path. Perhaps I have been misinformed. But, as I read the Constitution and the philosophy, I gathered that independence was the price of liberty."

Burger rejected Douglas' "establishment" fears. If tax exemption is the first step toward establishment, he said, "the second step has been long in coming."

The basic issue centered on the following question: Is there a contradiction between federal constitutional provisions against the establishment of religion, or the use of public funds for religious purposes, and state statutes exempting church property from taxation? In the Walz decision, the Supreme Court ruled that there is no contradiction.

Legal Background

The U.S. Constitution makes no reference to tax exemption. There was no discussion of the issue in the Constitutional Convention nor in debates on the Bill of Rights.

In the Colonial and post-Revolutionary years, some churches had established status and were state-supported. This state of affairs changed with enactment of the First Amendment, which laid down no-establishment as the federal norm. This norm was adopted by the states which, however, exempted churches from tax liabilities.

No establishment, no hindrance, was the early American view of Church-state relationships.

This view, reflected in custom law, was not generally formulated in statute law until the second half of the 19th century, although specific tax exemption was provided for churches in Maryland in 1798, in Virginia in 1800, and in North Carolina in 1806.

The first major challenge to church property exemption was initiated by the Liberal League in the 1870s. It reached the point that President Grant included the recommendation in a State of the Union address in 1875, stating that church property should bear its own proportion of taxes. The plea fell on deaf ears in Congress, but there was some support for the idea at state levels. The exemption, however, continued to survive various challenges.

About 36 state constitutions contain either mandatory or permissive provisions for exemption. Statutes provide for exemption in all other states.

There has been considerable litigation challenging

this special exemption, but most of it focused on whether a particular property satisfied statutory requirements. Few cases before Walz focused on the strictly constitutional question, whether directly under the First Amendment or indirectly under the Fourteenth Amendment.

Objections

Objectors to the tax exempt status of churches feel that churches should share, through taxation, in the cost of the ordinary benefits of public services they enjoy, and/or that the amount of "aid" enjoyed through exemption should be proportionate to the amount of social good they do.

According to one opinion, exemption is said to weaken the independence of churches from the political system which benefits them by exemption.

In another view, exemption is said to involve the government in decisions regarding what is and what is not religion.

THE WALL OF SEPARATION

Thomas Jefferson, in a letter written to the Danbury (Conn.) Baptist Association Jan. 1, 1802, coined the metaphor, "a wall of separation between Church and State," to express a theory concerning interpretation of the religion clauses of the First Amendment: "Congress shall make no law respecting an establishment of religion or prohibiting the free exercise thereof."

The metaphor was cited for the first time in judicial proceedings in 1879, in the opinion by Chief Justice Waite in Reynolds v. United States. It did not, however, figure substantially in the decision.

Accepted as Rule

In 1947 the wall of separation gained acceptance as a constitutional rule, in the decision handed down in Everson v. Board of Education. Associate Justice Black, in describing the principles involved in the No Establishment Clause, wrote:

"Neither a state nor the Federal Government can set up a church. Neither can pass laws which aid one religion, aid all religions, or prefer one religion over another. Neither can force nor influence a person to go to or to remain away from church against his will or force him to profess a belief or disbelief in any religion. No person can be punished for entertaining or professing religious beliefs or disbeliefs, for church attendance or non-attendance. No tax in any amount, large or small, can be levied to support any religious activities or institutions, whatever they may be called, or whatever form they may adopt to teach or practice religion. Neither a state nor the Federal Government can, openly or secretly, participate in the affairs of any religious organizations or groups and vice versa. In the words of Jefferson, the clause against establishment of religion by law was intended to erect 'a wall of separation between Church and State.'"

Mr. Black's associates agreed with his statement of principles, which were framed without reference to the Freedom of Exercise Clause. They disagreed, however, with respect to application of the principles, as the split decision in the case indicated. Five members of the Court held that the benefits of public welfare legislation — in this case, free bus transportation to school for parochial as well as public school students — did not run contrary to the concept of separation of Church and state embodied in the First Amendment.

Different Opinions

Inside and outside the legal profession, opinion is divided concerning the wall of separation and the balance of the religion clauses of the First Amendment.

The view of absolute separationists, carried to the extreme, would make government the adversary of religion. The bishops of the United States, following the McCollum decision in 1948, said that the wall metaphor had become for some persons the "shibboleth of doctrinaire secularism."

Proponents of governmental neutrality toward religion are of the opinion that such neutrality should not be so interpreted as to prohibit incidental aid to religious institutions providing secular services.

In the realm of practice, federal and state legislatures have enacted measures involving incidental benefits to religious bodies. Examples of such measures are the tax exemption of church property; provision of bus rides, book loans and lunch programs to students in church-related as well as public schools; military chaplaincies; loans to church-related hospitals; the financing of studies by military veterans at church-related colleges under GI bills of rights.

NCCB-USCC REGIONS

I. Maine, Vermont, New Hampshire, Massachusetts, Rhode Island, Connecticut. **II.** New York. **III.** New Jersey, Pennsylvania. **IV.** Delaware, District of Columbia, Florida, Georgia, Maryland, North Carolina, South Carolina, Virgin Islands, Virginia, West Virginia **V.** Alabama, Kentucky, Louisiana, Mississippi, Tennessee. **VI.** Michigan, Ohio. **VII.** Illinois, Indiana, Wisconsin. **VIII.** Minnesota, North Dakota, South Dakota. **IX.** Iowa, Kansas, Missouri, Nebraska. **X.** Arkansas, Oklahoma, Texas. **XI.** California, Hawaii, Nevada. **XII.** Idaho, Montana, Alaska, Washington, Oregon. **XIII.** Utah, Arizona, New Mexico, Colorado, Wyoming.

COMMUNICATIONS ACT UNCONSTITUTIONAL

The U. S. Supreme Court ruled June 26, 1997, that a federal law designed to protect children from sexually explicit material on the Internet was unconstitutional.

In a ruling that was unanimous in all but one small part, the court said the 1996 Communications Decency Act "abridges 'the freedom of speech' protected by the First Amendment."

It said the law's prohibitions against "indecent" and "patently offensive" materials were too vague and swept too broadly over adult rights in an effort to protect children.

Possession or exchange of sexually explicit words and images among adults is constitutionally protected if they are deemed indecent but not obscene.

U.S. CATHOLIC JURISDICTIONS, HIERARCHY, STATISTICS

The organizational structure of the Catholic Church in the United States consists of 33 provinces with as many archdioceses (metropolitan sees); 151 suffragan sees (dioceses); five Eastern Church jurisdictions immediately subject to the Holy See — the eparchies of St. Maron and Our Lady of Lebanon of Los Angeles (Maronites), Newton (Melkites), St. Thomas Apostle of Detroit (Chaldeans) and St. George Martyr of Canton, Ohio (Romanians); and the Military Services Archdiocese. The eparchy of Our Lady of Deliverance of Newark for Syrian-rite Catholics in the U.S. and Canada has its seat in Newark, N.J. An Armenian apostolic exarchate for the United States and Canada has its seat in New York. Each of these jurisdictions is under the direction of an archbishop or bishop, called an ordinary, who has apostolic responsibility and authority for the pastoral service of the people in his care.

The structure includes the territorial episcopal conference known as the National Conference of Catholic Bishops. In and through this body, which is strictly ecclesiastical and has defined juridical authority, the bishops exercise their collegiate pastorate over the Church in the entire country (see Index).

Related to the NCCB is the United States Catholic Conference, a civil corporation and operational secretariat through which the bishops, in cooperation with other members of the Church, act on a wider-than-ecclesiastical scale for the good of the Church and society in the United States (see Index).

The representative of the Holy See to the Church in the United States is an Apostolic Pro-Nuncio.

ECCLESIASTICAL PROVINCES

(Sources: *The Official Catholic Directory,* Catholic News Service.)

The 33 ecclesiastical provinces bear the names of archdioceses, i.e., of metropolitan sees.

Anchorage: Archdiocese of Anchorage and suffragan sees of Fairbanks, Juneau. Geographical area: Alaska.

Atlanta: Archdiocese of Atlanta (Ga.) and suffragan sees of Savannah (Ga.); Charlotte and Raleigh (N.C.), Charleston (S.C.). Geographical area: Georgia, North Carolina, South Carolina.

Baltimore: Archdiocese of Baltimore (Md.) and suffragan sees of Wilmington (Del.); Arlington and Richmond (Va.); Wheeling-Charleston (W. Va.). Geographical area: Maryland (except five counties), Delaware, Virginia, West Virginia.

Boston: Archdiocese of Boston (Mass.) and suffragan sees of Fall River, Springfield and Worcester (Mass.); Portland (Me.); Manchester (N.H.); Burlington (Vt.). Geographical area: Massachusetts, Maine, New Hampshire, Vermont.

Chicago: Archdiocese of Chicago and suffragan sees of Belleville, Joliet, Peoria, Rockford, Springfield. Geographical area: Illinois.

Cincinnati: Archdiocese of Cincinnati and suffragan sees of Cleveland, Columbus, Steubenville, Toledo, Youngstown. Geographical area: Ohio.

Denver: Archdiocese of Denver (Colo.) and suffragan sees of Colorado Springs and Pueblo (Colo.); Cheyenne (Wyo.). Geographical area: Colorado, Wyoming.

Detroit: Archdiocese of Detroit and suffragan sees of Gaylord, Grand Rapids, Kalamazoo, Lansing, Marquette, Saginaw. Geographical area: Michigan.

Dubuque: Archdiocese of Dubuque and suffragan sees of Davenport, Des Moines, Sioux City. Geographical area: Iowa.

Hartford: Archdiocese of Hartford (Conn.) and suffragan sees of Bridgeport and Norwich (Conn.); Providence (R.I.). Geographical area: Connecticut, Rhode Island.

Indianapolis: Archdiocese of Indianapolis and suffragan sees of Evansville, Fort Wayne-South Bend, Gary, Lafayette. Geographical area: Indiana.

Kansas City (Kans.): Archdiocese of Kansas City and suffragan sees of Dodge City, Salina, Wichita. Geographical area: Kansas.

Los Angeles: Archdiocese of Los Angeles and suffragan sees of Fresno, Monterey, Orange, San Bernardino, San Diego. Geographical area: Southern and Central California.

Louisville: Archdiocese of Louisville (Ky.) and suffragan sees of Covington, Lexington and Owensboro (Ky.); Knoxville, Memphis and Nashville (Tenn.). Geographical area: Kentucky, Tennessee.

Miami: Archdiocese of Miami and suffragan sees of Orlando, Palm Beach, Pensacola-Tallahassee, St. Augustine, St. Petersburg, Venice. Geographical area: Florida.

Milwaukee: Archdiocese of Milwaukee and suffragan sees of Green Bay, La Crosse, Madison, Superior. Geographical area: Wisconsin.

Mobile: Archdiocese of Mobile, Ala., and suffragan sees of Birmingham (Ala.); Biloxi and Jackson (Miss.). Geographical area: Alabama, Mississippi.

Newark: Archdiocese of Newark and suffragan sees of Camden, Metuchen, Paterson, Trenton. Geographical area: New Jersey.

New Orleans: Archdiocese of New Orleans and suffragan sees of Alexandria, Baton Rouge, Houma-Thibodaux, Lafayette, Lake Charles and Shreveport. Geographical area: Louisiana.

New York: Archdiocese of New York and suffragan sees of Albany, Brooklyn, Buffalo, Ogdensburg, Rochester, Rockville Centre, Syracuse. Geographical area: New York.

Oklahoma City: Archdiocese of Oklahoma City (Okla.) and suffragan sees of Tulsa (Okla.) and Little Rock (Ark.). Geographical area: Oklahoma, Arkansas.

Omaha: Archdiocese of Omaha and suffragan sees of Grand Island, Lincoln. Geographical area: Nebraska.

Philadelphia: Archdiocese of Philadelphia and suffragan sees of Allentown, Altoona-Johnstown, Erie, Greensburg, Harrisburg, Pittsburgh, Scranton. Geographical area: Pennsylvania.

Philadelphia (Byzantine, Ukrainians): Metropolitan See of Philadelphia (Byzantine) and Eparchies of St. Josaphat in Parma (Ohio), St. Nicholas of the Ukrainians in Chicago and Stamford, Conn. The jurisdiction extends to all Ukrainian Catholics in the U.S. from the ecclesiastical province of Galicia in the Ukraine.

Pittsburgh (Byzantine, Ruthenians): Metropolitan See of Pittsburgh, Pa. and Eparchies of Passaic (N.J.), Parma (Ohio), Van Nuys (Calif.).

Portland: Archdiocese of Portland (Ore.) and suffragan sees of Baker (Ore.); Boise (Ida.); Great Falls-Billings and Helena (Mont.). Geographical area: Oregon, Idaho, Montana.

St. Louis: Archdiocese of St. Louis and suffragan sees of Jefferson City, Kansas City-St. Joseph, Springfield-Cape Girardeau. Geographical area: Missouri.

St. Paul and Minneapolis: Archdiocese of St. Paul and Minneapolis (Minn.) and suffragan sees of Crookston, Duluth, New Ulm, St. Cloud and Winona (Minn.); Bismarck and Fargo (N.D.); Rapid City and Sioux Falls (S.D.). Geographical area: Minnesota, North Dakota, South Dakota.

San Antonio: Archdiocese of San Antonio (Tex.) and suffragan sees of Amarillo, Austin, Beaumont, Brownsville, Corpus Christi, Dallas, El Paso, Fort Worth, Galveston-Houston, Lubbock, San Angelo, Tyler and Victoria (Tex.). Geographical area: Texas.

San Francisco: Archdiocese of San Francisco (Calif.) and suffragan sees of Oakland, Sacramento, San Jose, Santa Rosa and Stockton (Calif.); Honolulu (Hawaii); Reno and Las Vegas (Nev.); Salt Lake City (Utah). Geographical area: Northern California, Nevada, Utah, Hawaii.

Santa Fe: Archdiocese of Santa Fe (N.M.) and suffragan sees of Gallup and Las Cruces (N.M.); Phoenix and Tucson (Ariz.). Geographical area: New Mexico, Arizona.

Seattle: Archdiocese of Seattle and suffragan sees of Spokane, Yakima. Geographical area: Washington.

Washington: Archdiocese of Washington, D.C., and suffragan see of St. Thomas (Virgin Islands). Geographical area: District of Columbia, five counties of Maryland, Virgin Islands.

ARCHDIOCESES, DIOCESES, ARCHBISHOPS, BISHOPS

(Sources: *The Official Catholic Directory;* Catholic News Service; *L'Osservatore Romano.* As of Aug. 20, 1997.)

Information includes name of diocese, year of foundation (as it appears on the official document erecting the see), present ordinaries (year of installation), auxiliaries and former ordinaries (for biographies, see Index).

Archdioceses are indicated by an asterisk.

Albany, N.Y. (1847): Howard J. Hubbard, bishop, 1977.

Former bishops: John McCloskey, 1847-64; John J. Conroy, 1865-77; Francis McNeirny, 1877-94; Thomas M. Burke, 1894-1915; Thomas F. Cusack, 1915-18; Edmund F. Gibbons, 1919-54; William A. Scully, 1954-69; Edwin B. Broderick, 1969-76.

Alexandria, La. (1853): Sam G. Jacobs, bishop, 1989.

Established at Natchitoches, transferred to Alexandria 1910; title changed to Alexandria-Shreveport, 1977; redesignated Alexandria, 1986, when Shreveport was made a diocese.

Former bishops: Augustus M. Martin, 1853-75; Francis X. Leray, 1877-79, administrator, 1879-83; Anthony Durier, 1885-1904; Cornelius Van de Ven, 1904-32; Daniel F. Desmond, 1933-45; Charles P. Greco, 1946-73; Lawrence P. Graves, 1973-82; William B. Friend, 1983-86; John C. Favalora, 1986-89.

Allentown, Pa. (1961): Thomas J. Welsh, bishop, 1983.

Former bishop: Joseph McShea, 1961-83.

Altoona-Johnstown, Pa. (1901): Joseph V. Adamec, bishop, 1987.

Established as Altoona, name changed, 1957.

Former bishops: Eugene A. Garvey, 1901-20; John J. McCort, 1920-36; Richard T. Guilfoyle, 1936-57; Howard J. Carroll, 1958-60; J. Carroll McCormick, 1960-66; James J. Hogan, 1966-86.

Amarillo, Tex. (1926): John W. Yanta, bishop, 1997.

Former bishops; Rudolph A. Gerken, 1927-33; Robert E. Lucey, 1934-41; Laurence J. Fitzsimon, 1941-58; John L. Morkovsky, 1958-63; Lawrence

M. De Falco, 1963-79; Leroy T. Matthiesen, 1980-97.

Anchorage,* Alaska (1966): Francis T. Hurley, archbishop, 1976.

Former archbishop: Joseph T. Ryan, 1966-75.

Arlington, Va. (1974): John R. Keating, bishop, 1983.

Former bishop: Thomas J. Welsh, 1974-83.

Atlanta,* Ga. (1956; archdiocese, 1962): John F. Donoghue, archbishop, 1993.

Former ordinaries: Francis E. Hyland, 1956-61; Paul J. Hallinan, first archbishop, 1962-68; Thomas A. Donnellan, 1968-87; Eugene A. Marino, S.S.J., 1988-90; James P. Lyke, 1991-92.

Austin, Tex. (1947): John E. McCarthy, bishop, 1986.

Former bishops: Louis J. Reicher, 1947-71; Vincent M. Harris, 1971-86.

Baker, Ore. (1903): Thomas J. Connolly, bishop, 1971.

Established as Baker City, name changed, 1952.

Former bishops: Charles J. O'Reilly, 1903-18; Joseph F. McGrath, 1919-50; Francis P. Leipzig, 1950-71.

Baltimore,* Md. (1789; archdiocese, 1808): Cardinal William H. Keeler, archbishop, 1989. P. Francis Murphy, William C. Newman, auxiliaries.

Former ordinaries: John Carroll, 1789-1815, first archbishop; Leonard Neale, 1815-17; Ambrose Marechal, S.S., 1817-28; James Whitfield, 1828-34; Samuel Eccleston, S.S., 1834-51; Francis P. Kenrick, 1851-63; Martin J. Spalding, 1864-72; James R. Bayley, 1872-77; Cardinal James Gibbons, 1877-1921; Michael J. Curley, 1921-47; Francis P. Keough, 1947-61; Cardinal Lawrence J. Shehan, 1961-74; William D. Borders, 1974-89.

Baton Rouge, La. (1961): Alfred C. Hughes, bishop, 1993.

Former bishops: Robert E. Tracy, 1961-74; Joseph V. Sullivan, 1974-82; Stanley J. Ott, 1983-93.

Beaumont, Tex. (1966): Joseph A. Galante, bishop, 1994.

Former bishops: Vincent M. Harris, 1966-71; Warren L. Boudreaux, 1971-77; Bernard J. Ganter, 1977-93.

Belleville, Ill. (1887): Wilton D. Gregory, bishop, 1994.

Former bishops: John Janssen, 1888-1913; Henry Althoff, 1914-47; Albert R. Zuroweste, 1948-76; William M. Cosgrove, 1976-81; John N. Wurm, 1981-84; James P. Keleher, 1984-93.

Biloxi, Miss. (1977): Joseph Lawson Howze, bishop, 1977.

Birmingham, Ala. (1969): David E. Foley, bishop, 1994.

Former bishops: Joseph G. Vath, 1969-87; Raymond J. Boland, 1988-93.

Bismarck, N. Dak. (1909): Paul A. Zipfel, bishop, 1996.

Former bishops: Vincent Wehrle, O.S.B., 1910-39; Vincent J. Ryan, 1940-51; Lambert A. Hoch, 1952-56; Hilary B. Hacker, 1957-82; John F. Kinney, 1982-95.

Boise, Ida. (1893): Tod David Brown, bishop, 1989.

Former bishops: Alphonse J. Glorieux, 1893-1917; Daniel M. Gorman, 1918-27; Edward J. Kelly, 1928-56; James J. Byrne, 1956-62; Sylvester Treinen, 1962-88.

Boston,* Mass. (1808; archdiocese, 1875): Cardinal Bernard F. Law, archbishop, 1984. John R. McNamara, John P. Boles, William F. Murphy, John B. McCormack, Francis Xavier Irwin, Emilio Allué, S.D.B., auxiliaries.

Former ordinaries: John L. de Cheverus, 1810-23; Benedict J. Fenwick, S.J., 1825-46; John B. Fitzpatrick, 1846-66; John J. Williams, 1866-1907, first archbishop; Cardinal William O'Connell, 1907-44; Cardinal Richard Cushing, 1944-70; Cardinal Humberto Medeiros, 1970-83.

Bridgeport, Conn. (1953): Edward M. Egan, bishop, 1988.

Former bishops: Lawrence J. Shehan, 1953-61; Walter W. Curtis, 1961-88.

Brooklyn, N.Y. (1853): Thomas V. Daily, bishop, 1990. Joseph M. Sullivan, Rene A. Valero, Ignatius Catanello, Gerald Barbarito, auxiliaries.

Former bishops: John Loughlin, 1853-91; Charles E. McDonnell, 1892-1921; Thomas E. Molloy, 1921-56; Bryan J. McEntegart, 1957-68; Francis J. Mugavero, 1968-90.

Brownsville, Tex. (1965): Raymundo J. Pena, bishop, 1995.

Former bishops: Adolph Marx, 1965; Humberto S. Medeiros, 1966-70; John J. Fitzpatrick, 1971-91; Enrique San Pedro, S.J., 1991-94.

Buffalo, N.Y. (1847): Henry J. Mansell, bishop, 1995. Edward M. Grosz, auxiliary.

Former bishops: John Timon, C.M., 1847-67; Stephen V. Ryan, C.M., 1868-96; James E. Quigley, 1897-1903; Charles H. Colton, 1903-15; Dennis J. Dougherty, 1915-18; William Turner, 1919-36; John A. Duffy, 1937-44; John F. O'Hara, C.S.C., 1945-51; Joseph A. Burke, 1952-62; James McNulty, 1963-72; Edward D. Head, 1973-95.

Burlington, Vt. (1853): Kenneth A. Angell, bishop, 1992.

Former bishops: Louis De Goesbriand, 1853-99; John S. Michaud, 1899-1908; Joseph J. Rice, 1910-

38; Matthew F. Brady, 1938-44; Edward F. Ryan, 1945-56; Robert F. Joyce, 1957-71; John A. Marshall, 1972-91.

Camden, N.J. (1937): James T. McHugh, bishop, 1989.

Former bishops: Bartholomew J. Eustace, 1938-56; Justin J. McCarthy, 1957-59; Celestine J. Damiano, 1960-67; George H. Guilfoyle, 1968-89.

Charleston, S.C. (1820): David B. Thompson, bishop, 1990.

Former bishops: John England, 1820-42; Ignatius W. Reynolds, 1844-55; Patrick N. Lynch, 1858-82; Henry P. Northrop, 1883-1916; William T. Russell, 1917-27; Emmet M. Walsh, 1927-49; John J. Russell, 1950-58; Paul J. Hallinan, 1958-62; Francis F. Reh, 1962-64; Ernest L. Unterkoefler, 1964-90.

Charlotte, N.C. (1971): William G. Curlin, bishop, 1994.

Former bishops: Michael J. Begley, 1972-84; John F. Donoghue, 1984-93.

Cheyenne, Wyo. (1887): Joseph Hart, bishop, 1978.

Former bishops: Maurice F. Burke, 1887-93; Thomas M. Lenihan, 1897-1901; James J. Keane, 1902-11; Patrick A. McGovern, 1912-51; Hubert M. Newell, 1951-78.

Chicago,* Ill. (1843; archdiocese, 1880): Francis E. George, archbishop, 1997. Thad J. Jakubowski, John R. Gorman, Raymond E. Goedert, Edwin M. Conway, Gerald F. Kicanas, George V. Murry, S.J., John R. Manz, auxiliaries.

Former ordinaries: William Quarter, 1844-48; James O. Van de Velde, S.J., 1849-53; Anthony O'Regan, 1854-58; James Duggan, 1859-70; Thomas P. Foley, administrator, 1870-79; Patrick A. Feehan, 1880-1902, first archbishop; James E. Quigley, 1903-15; Cardinal George Mundelein, 1915-39; Cardinal Samuel Stritch, 1939-58; Cardinal Albert Meyer, 1958-65; Cardinal John Cody, 1965-82; Cardinal Joseph L. Bernardin, 1982-96.

Cincinnati,* Ohio (1821; archdiocese, 1850): Daniel E. Pilarczyk, archbishop, 1982. Carl K. Moeddel, auxiliary.

Former ordinaries: Edward D. Fenwick, O.P., 1822-32; John B. Purcell, 1833-83, first archbishop; William H. Elder, 1883-1904; Henry Moeller, 1904-1925; John T. McNicholas, O.P., 1925-50; Karl J. Alter, 1950-69; Paul F. Leibold, 1969-72; Joseph L. Bernardin, 1972-82.

Cleveland, Ohio (1847): Anthony M. Pilla, bishop, 1980. A. Edward Pevec, A. James Quinn, auxiliaries.

Former bishops: L. Amadeus Rappe, 1847-70; Richard Gilmour, 1872-91; Ignatius F. Horstmann, 1892-1908; John P. Farrelly, 1909-21; Joseph Schrembs, 1921-45; Edward F. Hoban, 1945-66; Clarence G. Issenmann, 1966-74; James A. Hickey, 1974-80.

Colorado Springs, Colo. (1983): Richard C. Hanifen, bishop, 1984.

Columbus, Ohio (1868): James A. Griffin, bishop, 1983.

Former bishops: Sylvester H. Rosecrans, 1868-78; John A. Watterson, 1880-99; Henry Moeller, 1900-03; James J. Hartley, 1904-44; Michael J. Ready, 1944-57; Clarence Issenmann, 1957-64; John J. Carberry, 1965-68; Clarence E. Elwell, 1968-73; Edward J. Herrmann, 1973-82.

Corpus Christi,Tex. (1912): Roberto O. Gonzalez, O.F.M., bishop, 1997.

Former bishops: Paul J. Nussbaum, C.P., 1913-20; Emmanuel B. Ledvina, 1921-49; Mariano S. Garriga, 1949-65;Thomas J. Drury, 1965-83; Rene H. Gracida, 1983-97.

Covington, Ky. (1853): Robert W. Muench, bishop, 1996.

Former bishops: George A. Carrell, S.J., 1853-68; Augustus M. Toebbe, 1870-84; Camillus P. Maes, 1885-1914; Ferdinand Brossart, 1916-23; Francis W. Howard, 1923-44; William T. Mulloy, 1945-59; Richard Ackerman, C.S.Sp., 1960-78; William A. Hughes, 1979-95.

Crookston, Minn. (1909): Victor H. Balke, bishop, 1976.

Former bishops: Timothy Corbett, 1910-38; John H. Peschges, 1938-44; Francis J. Schenk, 1945-60; Laurence A. Glenn, 1960-70; Kenneth J. Povish, 1970-75.

Dallas,Tex. (1890): Charles V. Grahmann, bishop, 1990.

Established 1890, as Dallas, title changed to Dallas-Ft. Worth 1953; redesignated Dallas, 1969, when Ft. Worth was made diocese.

Former bishops: Thomas F. Brennan, 1891-92; Edward J. Dunne, 1893-1910; Joseph P. Lynch, 1911-54; Thomas K. Gorman, 1954-69; Thomas Tschoepe, 1969-90.

Davenport, Ia. (1881): William E. Franklin, bishop, 1993.

Former bishops: John McMullen, 1881-83; Henry Cosgrove, 1884-1906; James Davis, 1906-26; Henry P. Rohlman, 1927-44; Ralph L. Hayes, 1944-66; Gerald F. O'Keefe, 1966-93.

Denver,* Colo. (1887; archdiocese, 1941): Charles J. Chaput, O.F.M. Cap., archbishop, 1997.

Former ordinaries: Joseph P. Machebeuf, 1887-89; Nicholas C. Matz, 1889-1917; J. Henry Tihen, 1917-31; Urban J. Vehr, 1931-67, first archbishop; James V. Casey, 1967-86; J. Francis Stafford, 1986-96.

Des Moines, Ia. (1911): Joseph L. Charron, C.PP.S., bishop, 1993.

Former bishops: Austin Dowling, 1912-19; Thomas W. Drumm, 1919-33; Gerald T. Bergan, 1934-48; Edward C. Daly, O.P., 1948-64; George J. Biskup, 1965-67; Maurice J. Dingman, 1968-86; William H. Bullock, 1987-93.

Detroit,* Mich. (1833; archdiocese, 1937): Cardinal Adam J. Maida, archbishop, 1990. Thomas J. Gumbleton, Moses B. Anderson, S.S.E.,Kevin M. Britt, Bernard J. Harrington, John C. Nienstedt, Allen H. Vigneron, auxiliaries.

Former ordinaries: Frederic Rese, 1833-71; Peter P. Lefevere, administrator, 1841-69; Caspar H. Borgess, 1871-88; John S. Foley, 1888-1918; Michael J. Gallagher, 1918-37; Cardinal Edward Mooney, 1937-58, first archbishop; Cardinal John F. Dearden, 1958-80; Cardinal Edmund C. Szoka, 1981-90.

Dodge City, Kans. (1951): Stanley G. Schlarman, bishop, 1983.

Former bishops: John B. Franz, 1951-59; Marion F. Forst, 1960-76; Eugene J. Gerber, 1976-82.

Dubuque,* Iowa (1837; archdiocese, 1893): Jerome Hanus, O.S.B., archbishop, 1995.

Former ordinaries: Mathias Loras, 1837-58; Clem-

ent Smyth, O.C.S.O., 1858-65; John Hennessy, 1866-1900, first archbishop; John J. Keane, 1900-11; James J. Keane, 1911-29; Francis J. Beckman, 1930-46; Henry P. Rohlman, 1946-54; Leo Binz, 1954-61; James J. Byrne, 1962-83; Daniel W. Kucera, O.S.B., 1984-95.

Duluth, Minn. (1889): Roger L. Schwietz, O.M.I., bishop, 1990.

Former bishops: James McGolrick, 1889-1918; John T. McNicholas, O.P., 1918-25; Thomas A. Welch, 1926-59; Francis J. Schenk, 1960-69; Paul F. Anderson, 1969-82; Robert H. Brom, 1983-89.

El Paso, Tex. (1914): Armando X. Ochoa, bishop, 1996.

Former bishops: Anthony J. Schuler, S.J., 1915-42; Sidney M. Metzger, 1942-78. Patrick F. Flores, 1978-79; Raymundo J. Pena, 1980-95.

Erie, Pa. (1853): Donald W. Trautman, bishop, 1990.

Former bishops: Michael O'Connor, 1853-54; Josue M. Young, 1854-66; Tobias Mullen, 1868-99; John E. Fitzmaurice, 1899-1920; John M. Gannon, 1920-66; John F. Whealon, 1966-69; Alfred M. Watson, 1969-82; Michael J. Murphy, 1982-90.

Evansville, Ind. (1944): Gerald A. Gettelfinger, bishop, 1989.

Former bishops: Henry J. Grimmelsman, 1944-65; Paul F. Leibold, 1966-69; Francis R. Shea, 1970-89.

Fairbanks, Alaska (1962): Michael J. Kaniecki, S.J., bishop, 1985.

Former bishops: Francis D. Gleeson, S.J., 1962-68; Robert L. Whelan, S.J., 1968-85.

Fall River, Mass. (1904): Sean O'Malley, O.F.M. Cap., bishop, 1992.

Former bishops: William Stang, 1904-07; Daniel F. Feehan, 1907-34; James E. Cassidy, 1934-51; James L. Connolly, 1951-70; Daniel A. Cronin, 1970-91.

Fargo, N. Dak. (1889): James S. Sullivan, bishop, 1985.

Established at Jamestown, transferred, 1897.

Former bishops: John Shanley, 1889-1909; James O'Reilly, 1910-34; Aloysius J. Muench, 1935-59; Leo F. Dworschak, 1960-70; Justin A. Driscoll, 1970-84.

Fort Wayne-South Bend, Ind. (1857): John M. D'Arcy, bishop, 1985. John R. Sheets, S.J., auxiliary.

Established as Fort Wayne, name changed, 1960.

Former bishops: John H. Luers, 1858-71; Joseph Dwenger, C.Pp. S., 1872-93; Joseph Rademacher, 1893-1900; Herman J. Alerding, 1900-24; John F. Noll, 1925-56; Leo A. Pursley, 1957-76; William E. McManus, 1976-85.

Fort Worth,Tex. (1969): Joseph P. Delaney, bishop, 1981.

Former bishop: John J. Cassata, 1969-80.

Fresno, Calif. (1967): John T. Steinbock, bishop, 1991.

Formerly Monterey-Fresno, 1922.

Former bishops (Monterey-Fresno): John J. Cantwell, administrator, 1922-24; John B. MacGinley, first bishop, 1924-32; Philip G. Sher, 1933-53; Aloysius J. Willinger, 1953-67.

Former bishops (Fresno): Timothy Manning, 1967-69; Hugh A. Donohoe, 1969-80; Joseph J. Madera, M.Pp.S., 1980-91.

Gallup, N. Mex. (1939): Donald Pelotte, S.S.S., bishop, 1990.

Former bishops: Bernard T. Espelage, O.F.M., 1940-69; Jerome J. Hastrich, 1969-90.

Galveston-Houston, Tex. (1847): Joseph A. Fiorenza, bishop, 1985. Curtis J. Guillory, S.V.D.; James A. Tamayo, auxiliaries.

Established as Galveston, name changed, 1959.

Former bishops: John M. Odin, C.M., 1847-61; Claude M. Dubuis, 1862-92; Nicholas A. Gallagher, 1892-1918; Christopher E. Byrne, 1918-50; Wendelin J. Nold, 1950-75; John L. Morkovsky, 1975-84.

Gary, Ind. (1956): Dale J. Melczek, bishop, 1996.

Former bishops: Andrew G. Grutka, 1957-84; Norbert F. Gaughan, 1984-96.

Gaylord, Mich. (1971): Patrick R. Cooney, bishop, 1989, installed 1990.

Former bishops: Edmund C. Szoka, 1971-81; Robert J. Rose, 1981-89.

Grand Island, Neb. (1912): Lawrence J. McNamara, bishop, 1978.

Established at Kearney, transferred, 1917.

Former bishops: James A. Duffy, 1913-31; Stanislaus V. Bona, 1932-44; Edward J. Hunkeler, 1945-51; John L. Paschang, 1951-72; John J. Sullivan, 1972-77.

Grand Rapids, Mich. (1882): Robert J. Rose, bishop, 1989. Joseph C. McKinney, auxiliary.

Former bishops: Henry J. Richter, 1883-1916; Michael J. Gallagher, 1916-18; Edward D. Kelly, 1919-26; Joseph G. Pinten, 1926-40; Joseph C. Plagens, 1941-43; Francis J. Haas, 1943-53; Allen J. Babcock, 1954-69; Joseph M. Breitenbeck, 1969-89.

Great Falls-Billings, Mont. (1904): Anthony M. Milone, bishop, 1988.

Established as Great Falls; name changed, 1980.

Former bishops: Mathias C. Lenihan, 1904-30; Edwin V. O'Hara, 1930-39; William J. Condon, 1939-67; Eldon B. Schuster, 1968-77; Thomas J. Murphy, 1978-87.

Green Bay, Wis. (1868): Robert J. Banks, bishop, 1990. Robert F. Morneau, auxiliary.

Former bishops: Joseph Melcher, 1868-73; Francis X. Krautbauer, 1875-85; Frederick X. Katzer, 1886-91; Sebastian G. Messmer, 1892-1903; Joseph J. Fox, 1904-14; Paul P. Rhode, 1915-45; Stanislaus V. Bona, 1945-67; Aloysius J. Wycislo, 1968-83; Adam J. Maida, 1984-90.

Greensburg, Pa. (1951): Anthony G. Bosco, bishop, 1987.

Former bishops: Hugh L. Lamb, 1951-59; Willam G. Connare, 1960-87.

Harrisburg, Pa. (1868): Nicholas C. Dattilo, bishop, 1990.

Former bishops: Jeremiah F. Shanahan, 1868-86; Thomas McGovern, 1888-98; John W. Shanahan,1899-1916; Philip R. McDevitt, 1916-35; George L. Leech, 1935-71; Joseph T. Daley, 1971-83; William H. Keeler, 1984-89.

Hartford,* Conn. (1843; archdiocese, 1953): Daniel A. Cronin, archbishop, 1991, installed, 1992. Peter A. Rosazza, Christie A. Macaluso, auxiliaries.

Former ordinaries: William Tyler, 1844-49; Bernard O'Reilly, 1850-56; F. P. MacFarland, 1858-74; Thomas Galberry, O.S.A., 1876-78; Lawrence S.

McMahon, 1879-93; Michael Tierney, 1894-1908; John J. Nilan, 1910-34; Maurice F. McAuliffe, 1934-44; Henry J. O'Brien, 1945-68, first archbishop; John F. Whealon, 1969-91.

Helena, Mont. (1884): Alexander J. Brunett, bishop, 1994.

Former bishops: John B. Brondel, 1884-1903; John P. Carroll, 1904-25; George J. Finnigan, C.S.C., 1927-32; Ralph L. Hayes, 1933-35; Joseph M. Gilmore, 1936-62; Raymond Hunthausen, 1962-75; Elden F. Curtiss, 1976-93.

Honolulu, Hawaii (1941): Francis X. DiLorenzo (apostolic administrator, 1993), bishop, 1994.

Former bishops: James J. Sweeney, 1941-68; John J. Scanlan, 1968-81; Joseph A. Ferrario, 1982-93.

Houma-Thibodaux, La. (1977): C. Michael Jarrell, bishop, 1993.

Former bishop: Warren L. Boudreaux, 1977-92.

Indianapolis,* Ind. (1834; archdiocese, 1944): Daniel M. Buechlein, O.S.B., archbishop, 1992.

Established at Vincennes, transferred, 1898.

Former ordinaries: Simon G. Bruté, 1834-39; Celestine de la Hailandiere, 1839-47; John S. Bazin, 1847-48; Maurice de St. Palais, 1849-77; Francis S. Chatard, 1878-1918; Joseph Chartrand, 1918-33; Joseph E. Ritter, 1934-46, first archbishop; Paul C. Schulte, 1946-70; George J. Biskup, 1970-79; Edward T. O'Meara, 1980-92.

Jackson, Miss. (1837): William R. Houck, bishop, 1984.

Established at Natchez; title changed to Natchez-Jackson, 1956; transferred to Jackson, 1977 (Natchez made titular see).

Former bishops: John J. Chanche, S.S., 1841-52; James Van de Velde, S.J., 1853-55; William H. Elder, 1857-80; Francis A. Janssens, 1881-88; Thomas Heslin, 1889-1911; John E. Gunn, S.M., 1911-24; Richard O. Gerow, 1924-67; Joseph B. Brunini, 1968-84.

Jefferson City, Mo. (1956): John R. Gaydos, bishop, 1997.

Former bishops: Joseph Marling, C.Pp.S., 1956-69; Michael F. McAuliffe, 1969-97.

Joliet, Ill. (1948): Joseph L. Imesch, bishop, 1979. Roger L. Kaffer, auxiliary.

Former bishops: Martin D. McNamara, 1949-66; Romeo Blanchette, 1966-79.

Juneau, Alaska (1951): Michael W. Warfel, bishop, 1996.

Former bishops: Dermot O'Flanagan, 1951-68; Joseph T. Ryan, administrator, 1968-71; Francis T. Hurley, 1971-76, administrator, 1976-79; Michael H. Kenny, 1979-95.

Kalamazoo, Mich. (1971): Vacant as of June 1, 1997.

Former bishop: Paul V. Donovan, 1971-94; Alfred J. Markiewicz, 1995-97.

Kansas City,* Kans. (1877; archdiocese, 1952): James P. Keleher, archbishop, 1993.

Established as vicariate apostolic, 1850, became Diocese of Leavenworth, 1877, transferred to Kansas City 1947.

Former ordinaries: J. B. Miege, vicar apostolic, 1851-74; Louis M. Fink, O.S.B., vicar apostolic, 1874-77, first bishop, 1877-1904; Thomas F. Lillis, 1904-10; John Ward, 1910-29; Francis Johannes,

1929-37; Paul C. Schulte, 1937-46; George J. Donnelly, 1946-50; Edward Hunkeler, 1951-69, first archbishop; Ignatius J. Strecker, 1969-93.

Kansas City-St. Joseph, Mo. (Kansas City, 1880; St. Joseph, 1868; united 1956): Raymond J. Boland, bishop, 1993.

Former bishops: John J. Hogan, 1880-1913; Thomas F. Lillis, 1913-38; Edwin V. O'Hara, 1939-56; John P. Cody, 1956-61; Charles H. Helmsing, 1962-77; John J. Sullivan, 1977-93.

Former bishops (St. Joseph): John J. Hogan, 1868-80, administrator, 1880-93; Maurice F. Burke, 1893-1923; Francis Gilfillan, 1923-33; Charles H. Le Blond, 1933-56.

Knoxville, Tenn. (1988): Anthony J. O'Connell, bishop, 1988.

La Crosse, Wis. (1868): Raymond L. Burke, bishop, 1995.

Former bishops: Michael Heiss, 1868-80; Kilian C. Flasch, 1881-91; James Schwebach, 1892-1921; Alexander J. McGavick, 1921-48; John P. Treacy, 1948-64; Frederick W. Freking, 1965-83; John J. Paul, 1983-94.

Lafayette, Ind. (1944): William L. Higi, bishop, 1984.

Former bishops: John G. Bennett, 1944-57; John J. Carberry, 1957-65; Raymond J. Gallagher, 1965-82; George A. Fulcher, 1983-84.

Lafayette, La. (1918): Edward J. O'Donnell, bishop, 1994.

Former bishops: Jules B. Jeanmard, 1918-56; Maurice Schexnayder, 1956-72; Gerard L. Frey, 1973-89; Harry J. Flynn, 1989-94.

Lake Charles, La. (1980): Jude Speyrer, bishop, 1980.

Lansing, Mich. (1937): Carl F. Mengeling, bishop, 1995; installed 1996.

Former bishops: Joseph H. Albers, 1937-65; Alexander Zaleski, 1965-75; Kenneth J. Povish, 1975-95.

Las Cruces, N. Mex. (1982): Ricardo Ramirez, C.S.B., bishop, 1982.

Las Vegas, Nev. (1995): Daniel F. Walsh, bishop, 1995.

Formerly Reno-Las Vegas, 1976; made separate diocese 1995.

Lexington, Ky. (1988): James Kendrick Williams, bishop, 1988.

Lincoln, Neb. (1887): Fabian W. Bruskewitz, bishop, 1992.

Former bishops: Thomas Bonacum, 1887-1911; J. Henry Tihen, 1911-17; Charles J. O'Reilly, 1918-23; Francis J. Beckman, 1924-30; Louis B. Kucera, 1930-57; James V. Casey, 1957-67; Glennon P. Flavin, 1967-92.

Little Rock, Ark. (1843): Andrew J. McDonald, bishop, 1972.

Former bishops: Andrew Byrne, 1844-62; Edward Fitzgerald, 1867-1907; John Morris, 1907-46; Albert L. Fletcher, 1946-72.

Los Angeles,* Calif. (1840; archdiocese, 1936): Cardinal Roger M. Mahony, archbishop, 1985. Stephen E. Blaire, Thomas J. Curry, Joseph M. Sartoris, Gabino Zavala, auxiliaries.

Founded as diocese of Two Californias, 1840; became Monterey diocese, 1850; Baja California de-

tached from Monterey diocese, 1852; title changed to Monterey-Los Angeles, 1859; Los Angeles-San Diego, 1922; became archdiocese under present title, 1936 (San Diego became separate see).

Former ordinaries: Francisco Garcia Diego y Moreno, O.F.M., 1840-46; Joseph S. Alemany, O.P., 1850-53; Thaddeus Amat, C.M., 1854-78; Francis Mora, 1878-96; George T. Montgomery, 1896-1903; Thomas J. Conaty, 1903-15; John J. Cantwell, 1917-47, first archbishop; Cardinal James McIntyre, 1948-70; Cardinal Timothy Manning, 1970-85.

Louisville,* Ky. (1808; archdiocese, 1937): Thomas C. Kelly, O.P., archbishop, 1982.

Established at Bardstown, transferred, 1841.

Former ordinaries: Benedict J. Flaget, S.S., 1810-32; John B. David, S.S., 1832-33; Benedict J. Flaget, S.S., 1833-50; Martin J. Spalding, 1850-64; Peter J. Lavialle, 1865-67; William G. McCloskey, 1868-1909; Denis O'Donaghue, 1910-24; John A. Floersh, 1924-67, first archbishop; Thomas J. McDonough, 1967-81.

Lubbock, Tex. (1983): Placido Rodriguez, C.M.F., bishop, 1994.

Former bishop: Michael J. Sheehan, 1983-93.

Madison, Wis. (1946): William H. Bullock, bishop, 1993. George O. Wirz, auxiliary.

Former bishops: William P. O'Connor, 1946-67; Cletus F. O'Donnell, 1967-92.

Manchester, N.H. (1884): Leo E. O'Neil, bishop, 1990. Francis J. Christian, auxiliary.

Former bishops: Denis M. Bradley, 1884-1903; John B. Delany, 1904-06; George A. Guertin, 1907-32; John B. Peterson, 1932-44; Matthew F. Brady, 1944-59; Ernest J. Primeau, 1960-74; Odore J. Gendron, 1975-90.

Marquette, Mich. (1857): James H. Garland, bishop, 1992.

Founded as Sault Ste. Marie and Marquette; changed to Marquette, 1937.

Former bishops: Frederic Baraga, 1857-68; Ignatius Mrak, 1869-78; John Vertin, 1879-99; Frederick Eis, 1899-1922; Paul J. Nussbaum, C.P., 1922-35; Joseph C. Plagens, 1935-40; Francis Magner, 1941-47; Thomas L. Noa, 1947-68; Charles A. Salatka, 1968-77; Mark F. Schmitt, 1978-92.

Memphis, Tenn. (1970): J. Terry Steib, S.V.D., bishop, 1993.

Former bishops: Carroll T. Dozier, 1971-82; J. Francis Stafford, 1982-86; Daniel M. Buechlein, O.S.B., 1987-92.

Metuchen, N.J. (1981): Vincent DePaul Breen, bishop, 1997.

Former bishops: Theodore E. McCarrick, 1981-86; Edward T. Hughes, 1987-97.

Miami,* Fla. (1958; archdiocese, 1968): John C. Favalora, archbishop, 1994. Agustin A. Roman, Gilberto Fernandez, Thomas G. Wenski, auxiliaries.

Former ordinaries: Coleman F. Carroll, 1958-77, first archbishop; Edward A. McCarthy, 1977-94.

Milwaukee,* Wis. (1843; archdiocese, 1875): Rembert G. Weakland, O.S.B., archbishop, 1977. Richard J. Sklba, auxiliary.

Former ordinaries: John M. Henni, 1844-81, first archbishop; Michael Heiss, 1881-90; Frederick X. Katzer, 1891-1903; Sebastian G. Messmer, 1903-30; Samuel A. Stritch, 1930-39; Moses E. Kiley, 1940-

53; Albert G. Meyer, 1953-58; William E. Cousins, 1959-77.

Mobile,*Ala. (1829; archdiocese, 1980): Oscar H. Lipscomb, first archbishop, 1980.

Founded as Mobile, 1829; title changed to Mobile-Birmingham, 1954; redesignated Mobile, 1969.

Former bishops: Michael Portier, 1829-59; John Quinlan, 1859-83; Dominic Manucy, 1884; Jeremiah O'Sullivan, 1885-96; Edward P. Allen, 1897-1926; Thomas J. Toolen, 1927-69; John L. May, 1969-80.

Monterey in California (1967): Sylvester D. Ryan, bishop, 1992.

Formerly Monterey-Fresno, 1922. (Originally established in 1850, see Los Angeles listing.)

Former bishops (Monterey-Fresno): John J. Cantwell, administrator, 1922-24; John B. MacGinley, first bishop, 1924-32; Philip G. Sher, 1933-53; Aloysius J. Willinger, 1953-67.

Former bishops (Monterey): Harry A. Clinch, 1967-82; Thaddeus A. Shubsda, 1982-91.

Nashville,Tenn. (1837): Edward U. Kmiec, bishop, 1992.

Former bishops: Richard P. Miles, O.P., 1838-60; James Whelan, O.P., 1860-64; Patrick A. Feehan, 1865-80; Joseph Rademacher, 1883-93; Thomas S. Byrne, 1894-1923; Alphonse J. Smith, 1924-35; William L.Adrian, 1936-69; Joseph A. Durick, 1969-75; James D. Niedergeses, 1975-92.

Newark,*N.J. (1853; archdiocese, 1937): Theodore E. McCarrick, archbishop, 1986. Dominic A. Marconi, David Arias, O.A.R., Charles J. McDonnell, Nicholas A. Di Marzio, Paul G. Bootkoski, auxiliaries.

Former ordinaries: James R. Bayley, 1853-72; Michael A. Corrigan, 1873-80; Winand M. Wigger, 1881-1901; John J. O'Connor, 1901-27; Thomas J. Walsh, 1928-52, first archbishop; Thomas A. Boland, 1953-74; Peter L. Gerety, 1974-86.

New Orleans,* La. (1793; archdiocese, 1850): Francis B. Schulte, archbishop, 1988; installed, 1989. Dominic Carmon, S.V.D., Gregory M. Aymond, auxiliaries.

Former ordinaries: Luis Penalver y Cardenas, 1793-1801; John Carroll, administrator, 1805-15; W. Louis Dubourg, S.S., 1815-25; Joseph Rosati, C.M., administrator, 1826-29; Leo De Neckere, C.M., 1829-33; Anthony Blanc, 1835-60, first archbishop; Jean Marie Odin, C.M., 1861-70; Napoleon J. Perche, 1870-83; Francis X. Leray, 1883-87; Francis A. Janssens, 1888-97; Placide L. Chapelle, 1897-1905; James H. Blenk, S.M., 1906-17; John W. Shaw, 1918-34; Joseph F. Rummel, 1935-64; John P. Cody, 1964-65; Philip M. Hannan, 1965-88.

Newton, Mass. (Melkite) (1966; eparchy, 1976): John A. Elya, B.S.O., eparch, 1993; installed, 1994. Nicholas Samra, auxiliary.

Former ordinaries: Justin Najmy, exarch, 1966-68; Joseph Tawil, exarch, 1969-76, first eparch, 1976-89; Ignatius Ghattas, B.S.O., 1990-92.

New Ulm, Minn. (1957): Raymond A. Lucker, bishop, 1975; installed, 1976.

Former bishop: Alphonse J. Schladweiler, 1958-75.

New York,* N.Y. (1808; archdiocese, 1850): Cardinal John J. O'Connor, archbishop, 1984. Anthony F. Mestice, Austin B. Vaughan, Francisco Garmendia, William J. McCormack, Patrick J. Sheridan, Robert A. Brucato, auxiliaries.

Former ordinaries: Richard L. Concanen, O.P., 1808-10; John Connolly, O.P., 1814-25; John Dubois, S.S., 1826-42; John J. Hughes, 1842-64, first archbishop; Cardinal John McCloskey, 1864-85; Michael A. Corrigan, 1885-1902; Cardinal John Farley, 1902-18; Cardinal Patrick Hayes, 1919-38; Cardinal Francis Spellman, 1939-67; Cardinal Terence J. Cooke, 1968-83.

Norwich, Conn. (1953): Daniel A. Hart, bishop, 1995.

Former bishops: Bernard J. Flanagan, 1953-59; Vincent J. Hines, 1960-75; Daniel P. Reilly, 1975-94.

Oakland, Calif. (1962): John S. Cummins, bishop, 1977.

Former bishop: Floyd L. Begin, 1962-77.

Ogdensburg, N.Y. (1872): Paul S. Loverde, bishop, 1993.

Former bishops: Edgar P. Wadhams, 1872-91; Henry Gabriels, 1892-1921; Joseph H. Conroy, 1921-39; Francis J. Monaghan, 1939-42; Bryan J. McEntegart, 1943-53; Walter P. Kellenberg, 1954-57; James J. Navagh, 1957-63; Leo R. Smith, 1963; Thomas A. Donnellan, 1964-68; Stanislaus J. Brzana, 1968-93.

Oklahoma City,* Okla. (1905; archdiocese, 1972): Eusebius J. Beltran, archbishop, 1993.

Former ordinaries: Theophile Meerschaert, 1905-24; Francis C. Kelley, 1924-48; Eugene J. McGuinness, 1948-57; Victor J. Reed, 1958-71; John R. Quinn, 1971-77, first archbishop; Charles A. Salatka, 1977-92.

Omaha,* Nebr. (1885; archdiocese, 1945): Elden F. Curtiss, archbishop, 1993.

Former ordinaries: James O'Gorman, O.C.S.O., 1859-74, vicar apostolic; James O'Connor, vicar apostolic, 1876-85, first bishop, 1885-90; Richard Scannell, 1891-1916; Jeremiah J. Harty, 1916-27; Francis Beckman, administrator, 1926-28; Joseph F. Rummel, 1928-35; James H. Ryan, 1935-47, first archbishop; Gerald T. Bergan, 1948-69; Daniel E. Sheehan, 1969-93.

Orange, Calif. (1976): Norman F. McFarland, bishop, 1986, installed, 1987. Michael P. Driscoll, auxiliary.

Former bishop: William R. Johnson, 1976-86.

Orlando, Fla. (1968): Norbert M. Dorsey, C.P., bishop, 1990.

Former bishops: William Borders, 1968-74; Thomas J. Grady, 1974-89.

Our Lady of Deliverance of Newark (for Syrian-rite Catholics of the U.S. and Canada) (1995): Joseph Younan, bishop, 1996.

Our Lady of Lebanon of Los Angeles, Calif. (Maronite) (1994): John G. Chedid, eparch, 1994.

Owensboro, Ky. (1937): John J. McRaith, bishop, 1982.

Former bishops: Francis R. Cotton, 1938-60, Henry J. Soenneker, 1961-82.

Palm Beach, Fla. (1984): J. Keith Symons, bishop, 1990.

Former bishop: Thomas V. Daily, 1984-90.

Parma, Ohio (Byzantine, Ruthenian) (1969): Basil Schott, O.F.M., bishop, 1996.

Former bishops: Emil Mihalik, 1969-84; Andrew Pataki, 1984-95.

Passaic, N.J. (Byzantine, Ruthenian) (1963): Andrew Pataki, eparch, 1996.

Former bishops: Stephen Kocisko, 1963-68; Michael J. Dudick, 1968-95.

Paterson, N.J. (1937): Frank J. Rodimer, bishop, 1978.

Former bishops: Thomas H. McLaughlin, 1937-47; Thomas A. Boland, 1947-52; James A. McNulty, 1953-63; James J. Navagh, 1963-65; Lawrence B. Casey, 1966-77.

Pensacola-Tallahassee, Fla. (1975): John H.Ricard, S.S.J., bishop, 1997..

Former bishops: Rene H. Gracida, 1975-83; J. Keith Symons, 1983-90; John M. Smith, 1991-95.

Peoria, Ill. (1877): John J. Myers, bishop, 1990.

Former bishops: John L. Spalding, 1877-1908; Edmund M. Dunne, 1909-29; Joseph H. Schlarman, 1930-51; William E. Cousins, 1952-58; John B. Franz, 1959-71; Edward W. O'Rourke, 1971- 90.

Philadelphia,* Pa. (1808; archdiocese, 1875): Cardinal Anthony J. Bevilacqua, archbishop, 1988. Edward P. Cullen, Robert P. Maginnis, Joseph F. Martino, auxiliaries.

Former ordinaries: Michael Egan, O.F.M., 1810-14; Henry Conwell, 1820-42; Francis P. Kenrick, 1842-51; John N. Neumann, C.SS.R., 1852-60; James F. Wood, 1860-83, first archbishop; Patrick J. Ryan, 1884-1911; Edmond F. Prendergast, 1911-18; Cardinal Dennis Dougherty, 1918-51; Cardinal John O'Hara, C.S.C., 1951-60; Cardinal John Krol, 1961-88.

Philadelphia,* Pa. (Byzantine, Ukrainian) (1924; metropolitan, 1958): Stephen Sulyk, archbishop, 1981. Walter Paska, auxiliary.

Former ordinaries: Stephen Ortynsky, O.S.B.M., 1907-16; Constantine Bohachevsky, 1924-61; Ambrose Senyshyn, O.S.B.M., 1961-76; Joseph Schmondiuk, 1977-78; Myroslav J. Lubachivsky, 1979-80, apostolic administrator, 1980-81.

Phoenix, Ariz. (1969): Thomas J. O'Brien, bishop, 1982.

Former bishops: Edward A. McCarthy, 1969-76; James S. Rausch, 1977-81.

Pittsburgh,* Pa. (Byzantine, Ruthenian) (1924; metropolitan, 1969): Judson M. Procyk, archbishop, 1995.

Former ordinaries: Basil Takach 1924-48; Daniel Ivancho, 1948-54; Nicholas T. Elko, 1955-67; Stephen J. Kocisko, 1968-91, first metropolitan; Thomas V. Dolinay, 1991-93.

Pittsburgh, Pa. (1843): Donald W. Wuerl, bishop, 1988. William J. Winter, David A. Zubic, auxiliaries.

Former bishops: Michael O'Connor, 1843-53, 1854-60; Michael Domenec, C.M., 1860-76; J. Tuigg, 1876-89; Richard Phelan, 1889-1904; J.F. Regis Canevin, 1904-20; Hugh C. Boyle, 1921-50; John F. Dearden, 1950-58; John J. Wright, 1959-69; Vincent M. Leonard, 1969-83; Anthony J. Bevilacqua, 1983-88.

Portland, Me. (1853): Joseph J. Gerry, O.S.B., bishop, 1989. Michael R. Cote, auxiliary.

Former bishops: David W. Bacon, 1855-74; James A. Healy, 1875-1900; William H. O'Connell, 1901-06; Louis S. Walsh, 1906-24; John G. Murray, 1925-31; Joseph E. McCarthy, 1932-55; Daniel J. Feeney, 1955-69; Peter L. Gerety, 1969-74; Edward C. O'Leary, 1974-88.

Portland,* Ore. (1846): Vacant as of June 1, 1997. Kenneth D. Steiner, auxiliary.

Established as Oregon City, name changed, 1928.

Former ordinaries: Francis N. Blanchet, 1846-80 vicar apostolic, first archbishop; Charles J. Seghers, 1880-84; William H. Gross, C.SS.R., 1885-98; Alexander Christie, 1899-1925; Edward D. Howard, 1926-66; Robert J. Dwyer, 1966-74; Cornelius M. Power, 1974-86; William J. Levada, 1986-95; Francis E. George, 1996-97.

Providence, R.I. (1872): Robert E. Mulvee, bishop, 1997.

Former bishops: Thomas F. Hendricken, 1872-86; Matthew Harkins, 1887-1921; William A. Hickey, 1921-33; Francis P. Keough, 1934-47; Russell J. McVinney, 1948-71; Louis E. Gelineau, 1972-97.

Pueblo, Colo. (1941): Arthur N. Tafoya, bishop, 1980.

Former bishops: Joseph C. Willging, 1942-59; Charles A. Buswell, 1959-79.

Raleigh, N.C. (1924): F. Joseph Gossman, bishop, 1975.

Former bishops: William J. Hafey, 1925-37; Eugene J. McGuinness, 1937-44; Vincent S. Waters, 1945-75.

Rapid City, S. Dak. (1902): Vacant as of June 1, 1997.

Established at Lead, transferred, 1930.

Former bishops: John Stariha, 1902-09; Joseph F. Busch, 1910-15; John J. Lawler, 1916-48; William T. McCarty, C.SS.R., 1948-69; Harold J. Dimmerling, 1969-87; Charles J. Chaput, O.F.M. Cap., 1988-97.

Reno, Nev. (1931): Phillip F. Straling, bishop, 1995.

Established at Reno, 1931; title changed to Reno-Las Vegas, 1976; redesignated Reno, 1995, when Las Vegas was made a separate diocese.

Former bishops (Reno/Reno-Las Vegas): Thomas K. Gorman, 1931-52; Robert J. Dwyer, 1952-66; Joseph Green, 1967-74; Norman F. McFarland, 1976-86; Daniel F. Walsh, 1987-95.

Richmond, Va. (1820): Walter F. Sullivan, bishop, 1974.

Former bishops: Patrick Kelly, 1820-22; Ambrose Marechal, S.S., administrator, 1822-28; James Whitfield, administrator, 1828-34; Samuel Eccleston, S.S., administrator, 1834-40; Richard V. Whelan, 1841-50; John McGill, 1850-72; James Gibbons, 1872-77; John J. Keane, 1878-88; Augustine Van de Vyver, 1889-1911; Denis J. O'Connell, 1912-26; Andrew J. Brennan, 1926-45; Peter L. Ireton, 1945-58; John J. Russell, 1958-73.

Rochester, N.Y. (1868): Matthew H. Clark, bishop, 1979.

Former bishops: Bernard J. McQuaid, 1868-1909; Thomas F. Hickey, 1909-28; John F. O'Hern, 1929-33; Edward F. Mooney, 1933-37; James E. Kearney, 1937-66; Fulton J. Sheen, 1966-69; Joseph L. Hogan, 1969-78.

Rockford, Ill. (1908): Thomas G. Doran, bishop, 1994.

Former bishops: Peter J. Muldoon, 1908-27; Edward F. Hoban, 1928-42; John J. Boylan, 1943-53; Raymond P. Hillinger, 1953-56; Loras T. Lane, 1956-68; Arthur J. O'Neill, 1968-94.

Rockville Centre, N.Y. (1957): John R. McGann, bishop, 1976. John C. Dunne, Emil A. Wcela, auxiliaries.

Former bishop: Walter P. Kellenberg, 1957-76.

Sacramento, Calif. (1886): William K. Weigand, bishop, 1993; installed, 1994.

Former bishops: Patrick Manogue, 1886-95; Thomas Grace, 1896-1921; Patrick J. Keane, 1922-28; Robert J. Armstrong, 1929-57; Joseph T. McGucken, 1957-62; Alden J. Bell, 1962-79; Francis A. Quinn, 1979-93.

Saginaw, Mich. (1938): Kenneth E. Untener, bishop, 1980.

Former bishops: William F. Murphy, 1938-50; Stephen S. Woznicki, 1950-68; Francis F. Reh, 1969-80.

St. Augustine, Fla. (1870): John J. Snyder, bishop, 1979.

Former bishops: Augustin Verot, S.S., 1870-76; John Moore, 1877-1901; William J. Kenny, 1902-13; Michael J. Curley, 1914-21; Patrick J. Barry, 1922-40; Joseph P. Hurley, 1940-67; Paul F. Tanner, 1968-79.

St. Cloud, Minn. (1889): John F. Kinney, bishop, 1995.

Former bishops: Otto Zardetti, 1889-94; Martin Marty, O.S.B., 1895-96; James Trobec, 1897-1914; Joseph F. Busch, 1915-53; Peter Bartholome, 1953-68; George H. Speltz, 1968-87; Jerome Hanus, O.S.B.,1987-94.

St. George's in Canton, Ohio (Byzantine, Romanian) (1982; eparchy, 1987): John Michael Botean, bishop, 1996.

Former bishop: Vasile Louis Puscas, 1983-93.

St. Josaphat in Parma, Ohio (Byzantine, Ukrainians) (1983): Robert M. Moskal, bishop, 1984.

St. Louis,* Mo. (1826; archdiocese, 1847): Justin F. Rigali, archbishop, 1994. Edward K. Braxton, Joseph F. Naumann, Michael J. Sheridan, auxiliaries.

Former ordinaries: Joseph Rosati, C.M., 1827-43; Peter R. Kenrick, 1843-95, first archbishop; John J. Kain, 1895-1903; Cardinal John Glennon, 1903-46; Cardinal Joseph Ritter, 1946-67; Cardinal John J. Carberry, 1968-79; John L. May, 1980-92.

St. Maron, Brooklyn, N.Y. (Maronite) (1966; diocese, 1971): Hector Y. Doueihi, eparch, 1997.

Established at Detroit; transferred to Brooklyn, 1977.

Former eparch: Francis Zayek, exarch 1966-72, first eparch 1972-97

St. Nicholas in Chicago (Byzantine Eparchy of St. Nicholas of the Ukrainians) (1961): Michael Wiwchar, C.SS.R., bishop, 1993.

Former bishops: Jaroslav Gabro, 1961-80; Innocent H. Lotocky, O.S.B.M., 1981-93.

St. Paul and Minneapolis,* Minn. (1850; archdiocese, 1888):Harry J. Flynn, archbishop, 1995. Lawrence H. Welsh, auxiliary.

Former ordinaries: Joseph Cretin, 1851-57; Thomas L. Grace, O.P., 1859-84; John Ireland, 1884-1918, first archbishop; Austin Dowling, 1919-30; John G. Murray, 1931-56; William O. Brady, 1956-61; Leo Binz, 1962-75; John R. Roach, 1975-95.

St. Petersburg, Fla. (1968): Robert N. Lynch, bishop, 1996.

Former bishops: Charles McLaughlin, 1968-78; W. Thomas Larkin, 1979-88; John C. Favalora, 1989-94.

St. Thomas the Apostle of Detroit (Chaldean) (1982; eparchy, 1985): Ibrahim N. Ibrahim, exarch, 1982; first eparch, 1985.

Salina, Kans. (1887): George K. Fitzsimons, bishop, 1984.

Established at Concordia, transferred, 1944.

Former bishops: Richard Scannell, 1887-91; John J. Hennessy, administrator, 1891-98; John F. Cunningham, 1898-1919; Francis J. Tief, 1921-38; Frank A. Thill, 1938-57; Frederick W. Freking, 1957-64; Cyril J. Vogel, 1965-79; Daniel W. Kucera, O.S.B., 1980-84.

Salt Lake City, Utah (1891): George H. Niederauer, bishop, 1995.

Former bishops: Lawrence Scanlan, 1891-1915; Joseph S. Glass, C.M., 1915-26; John J. Mitty, 1926-32; James E. Kearney, 1932-37; Duane G. Hunt, 1937-60; J. Lennox Federal, 1960-80; William K. Weigand, 1980-93.

San Angelo, Tex. (1961): Michael D. Pfeifer, O.M.I., bishop, 1985.

Former bishops: Thomas J. Drury, 1962-65; Thomas Tschoepe, 1966-69; Stephen A. Leven, 1969-79; Joseph A. Fiorenza, 1979-84.

San Antonio,* Tex. (1874; archdiocese, 1926): Patrick F. Flores, archbishop, 1979.

Former ordinaries: Anthony D. Pellicer, 1874-80; John C. Neraz, 1881-94; John A. Forest, 1895-1911; John W. Shaw, 1911-18; Arthur Jerome Drossaerts, 1918-40, first archbishop; Robert E. Lucey, 1941-69; Francis Furey, 1969-79.

San Bernardino, Calif. (1978): Gerald R. Barnes, bishop, 1995.

Former bishop: Phillip F. Straling, 1978-95.

San Diego, Calif. (1936): Robert H. Brom, bishop, 1990. Gilbert Espinoza Chavez, auxiliary.

Former bishops: Charles F. Buddy, 1936-66; Francis J. Furey, 1966-69; Leo T. Maher, 1969-90.

San Francisco,* Calif. (1853): William J. Levada, archbishop, 1995. Patrick J. McGrath, auxiliary.

Former ordinaries: Joseph S. Alemany, O.P., 1853-84; Patrick W. Riordan, 1884-1914; Edward J. Hanna, 1915-35; John Mitty, 1935-61; Joseph T. McGucken, 1962-77; John R. Quinn, 1977-95.

San Jose, Calif. (1981): R. Pierre DuMaine, first bishop, 1981.

Santa Fe*, N. Mex. (1850; archdiocese, 1875): Michael J. Sheehan, archbishop, 1993.

Former ordinaries: John B. Lamy, 1850-85; first archbishop; John B. Salpointe, 1885-94; Placide L. Chapelle, 1894-97; Peter Bourgade, 1899-1908; John B. Pitaval, 1909-18; Albert T. Daeger, O.F.M., 1919-32; Rudolph A. Gerken, 1933-43; Edwin V. Byrne, 1943-63; James P. Davis, 1964-74; Robert F. Sanchez, 1974-93.

Santa Rosa, Calif. (1962): G. Patrick Ziemann, bishop, 1992.

Former bishops: Leo T. Maher, 1962-69; Mark J. Hurley, 1969-86; John T. Steinbock, 1987-91.

Savannah, Ga. (1850): John Kevin Boland, bishop, 1995.

Former bishops: Francis X. Gartland, 1850-54; John Barry, 1857-59; Augustin Verot, S.S., 1861-70; Ignatius Persico, O.F.M. Cap., 1870-72; William H.

Gross, C.SS.R., 1873-85; Thomas A. Becker, 1886-99; Benjamin J. Keiley, 1900-22; Michael Keyes, S.M., 1922-35; Gerald P. O'Hara, 1935-59; Thomas J. McDonough, 1960-67; Gerard L. Frey, 1967-72; Raymond W. Lessard, 1973-95.

Scranton, Pa. (1868): James C. Timlin, bishop, 1984. John M. Dougherty, auxiliary.

Former bishops: William O'Hara, 1868-99; Michael J. Hoban, 1899-1926; Thomas C. O'Reilly, 1928-38; William J. Hafey, 1938-54; Jerome D. Hannan, 1954-65; J. Carroll McCormick, 1966-83; John J. O'Connor, 1983-84.

Seattle,* Wash. (1850; archdiocese, 1951): Vacant as of July 5, 1997.

Established as Nesqually, name changed, 1907.

Former ordinaries; Augustin M. Blanchet, 1850-79; Aegidius Junger, 1879-95; Edward J. O'Dea, 1896-1932; Gerald Shaughnessy, S.M., 1933-50; Thomas A. Connolly, first archbishop, 1950-75; Raymond G. Hunthausen, 1975-91; Thomas J. Murphy, 1991-97.

Shreveport, La. (1986): William B. Friend, bishop, 1986.

Sioux City, Ia. (1902): Lawrence D. Soens, bishop, 1983. Daniel N. DiNardo, coadjutor, 1997.

Former bishops: Philip J. Garrigan, 1902-19; Edmond Heelan, 1919-48; Joseph M. Mueller, 1948-70; Frank H. Greteman, 1970-83.

Sioux Falls, S. Dak. (1889): Robert J. Carlson, bishop, 1995.

Former bishops: Martin Marty, O.S.B., 1889-94; Thomas O'Gorman, 1896-1921; Bernard J. Mahoney, 1922-39; William O. Brady, 1939-56; Lambert A. Hoch, 1956-78; Paul V. Dudley, 1978-95.

Spokane, Wash. (1913): William S. Skylstad, bishop, 1990.

Former bishops: Augustine F. Schinner, 1914-25; Charles D. White, 1927-55; Bernard J. Topel, 1955-78; Lawrence H. Welsh, 1978-90.

Springfield, Ill. (1853): Daniel L. Ryan, bishop, 1984.

Established at Quincy, transferred to Alton 1857; transferred to Springfield 1923.

Former bishops: Henry D. Juncker, 1857-68; Peter J. Baltes, 1870-86; James Ryan, 1888-1923; James A. Griffin, 1924-48; William A. O'Connor, 1949-75; Joseph A. McNicholas, 1975-83.

Springfield, Mass. (1870): Thomas I. Dupre, bishop, 1995.

Former bishops: Patrick T. O'Reilly, 1870-92; Thomas D. Beaven, 1892-1920; Thomas M. O'Leary, 1921-49; Christopher J. Weldon, 1950-77; Joseph F. Maguire, 1977-91; John A. Marshall, 1991-94.

Springfield-Cape Girardeau, Mo. (1956): John J. Leibrecht, bishop, 1984.

Former bishops: Charles Helmsing, 1956-62; Ignatius J. Strecker, 1962-69; William Baum, 1970-73; Bernard F. Law, 1973-84.

Stamford, Conn. (Byzantine, Ukrainian) (1956): Basil Losten, eparch, 1977.

Former eparchs: Ambrose Senyshyn, O.S.B.M., 1956-61; Joseph Schmondiuk, 1961-77.

Steubenville, Ohio (1944): Gilbert I. Sheldon, bishop, 1992.

Former bishops: John K. Mussio, 1945-77; Albert H. Ottenweller, 1977-92.

Stockton, Calif. (1962): Donald W. Montrose, bishop, 1986.

Former bishops: Hugh A. Donohoe, 1962-69; Merlin J. Guilfoyle, 1969-79; Roger M. Mahony, 1980-85.

Superior, Wis. (1905): Raphael M. Fliss, bishop, 1985.

Former bishops: Augustine F. Schinner, 1905-13; Joseph M. Koudelka, 1913-21; Joseph G. Pinten, 1922-26; Theodore M. Reverman, 1926-41; William P. O'Connor, 1942-46; Albert G. Meyer, 1946-53; Joseph Annabring, 1954-59; George A. Hammes, 1960-85.

Syracuse, N.Y. (1886): James M. Moynihan, bishop, 1995. Thomas J. Costello, auxiliary.

Former bishops: Patrick A. Ludden, 1887-1912; John Grimes, 1912-22; Daniel J. Curley, 1923-32; John A. Duffy, 1933-37; Walter A. Foery, 1937-70; David F. Cunningham, 1970-76; Frank J. Harrison, 1976-87; Joseph T. O'Keefe, 1987-95.

Toledo, Ohio (1910): James R. Hoffman, bishop, 1980. Robert W. Donnelly, auxiliary.

Former bishops: Joseph Schrembs, 1911-21; Samuel A. Stritch, 1921-30; Karl J. Alter, 1931-50; George J. Rehring, 1950-67; John A. Donovan, 1967-80.

Trenton, N.J. (1881): John M. Smith, bishop, 1997.

Former bishops: Michael J. O'Farrell, 1881-94; James A. McFaul, 1894-1917; Thomas J. Walsh, 1918-28; John J. McMahon, 1928-32; Moses E. Kiley, 1934-40; William A. Griffin, 1940-50; George W. Ahr, 1950-79; John C. Reiss, 1980 -97.

Tucson, Ariz. (1897): Manuel D. Moreno, bishop, 1982.

Former bishops: Peter Bourgade, 1897-99; Henry Granjon, 1900-22; Daniel J. Gercke, 1923-60; Francis J. Green, 1960-81.

Tulsa, Okla. (1972): Edward J. Slattery, bishop, 1993.

Former bishops: Bernard J. Ganter, 1973-77; Eusebius J. Beltran, 1978-92.

Tyler, Tex. (1986): Edmond Carmody, bishop, 1992.

Former bishop: Charles E. Herzig, 1987-91.

Van Nuys, Calif. (Byzantine, Ruthenian) (1981): George M. Kuzma, eparch, 1991.

Former bishop: Thomas V. Dolinay, 1982-90.

Venice, Fla. (1984): John J. Nevins, bishop, 1984.

Victoria, Tex. (1982): David E. Fellhauer, bishop, 1990.

Former bishop: Charles V. Grahmann, 1982-89.

Washington,* D.C. (1939): Cardinal James A. Hickey, archbishop, 1980. Alvaro Corrada del Rio, S.J., Leonard Olivier, S.V.D., William E. Lori, auxiliaries.

Former ordinaries: Michael J. Curley, 1939-47; Cardinal Patrick O'Boyle, 1948-73; Cardinal William Baum, 1973-80.

Wheeling-Charleston, W. Va. (1850): Bernard W. Schmitt, bishop, 1989.

Established as Wheeling; name changed, 1974.

Former bishops: Richard V. Whelan, 1850-74; John J. Kain, 1875-93; Patrick J. Donahue, 1894-1922; John J. Swint, 1922-62; Joseph H. Hodges, 1962-85; Francis B. Schulte, 1985-88.

Wichita, Kans. (1887): Eugene J. Gerber, bishop, 1982, installed, 1983.

Former bishops: John J. Hennessy, 1888-1920; Augustus J. Schwertner, 1921-39; Christian H. Winkelmann, 1940-46; Mark K. Carroll, 1947-67; David M. Maloney, 1967-82.

Wilmington, Del. (1868): Michael A. Saltarelli, bishop, 1995.

Former bishops: Thomas A. Becker, 1868-86; Alfred A. Curtis, 1886-96; John J. Monaghan, 1897-1925; Edmond Fitzmaurice, 1925-60; Michael Hyle, 1960-67; Thomas J. Mardaga, 1968-84; Robert E. Mulvee, 1985-95.

Winona, Minn. (1889): John G. Vlazny, bishop, 1987.

Former bishops: Joseph B. Cotter, 1889-1909; Patrick R. Heffron, 1910-27; Francis M. Kelly, 1928-49; Edward A. Fitzgerald, 1949-69; Loras J. Watters, 1969-86.

Worcester, Mass. (1950): Daniel P. Reilly, bishop, 1994. George E. Rueger, auxiliary.

Former bishops: John J. Wright, 1950-59; Bernard J. Flanagan, 1959-83; Timothy J. Harrington, 1983-94.

Yakima, Wash. (1951):Carlos A. Sevilla, S.J., bishop, 1996

Former bishops: Joseph P. Dougherty, 1951-69; Cornelius M. Power, 1969-74; Nicolas E. Walsh, 1974-76; William S. Skylstad, 1977-90; Francis E. George, O.M.I., 1990-96.

Youngstown, Ohio (1943): Thomas J. Tobin, bishop, 1995; installed 1996.Former bishops: James A. McFadden, 1943-52; Emmet M. Walsh, 1952-68; James W. Malone, 1968-95.

Apostolic Exarchate for Armenian Catholics in the United States and Canada, New York, N.Y. (1981): Hovhannes Tertzakian, O.M. Ven., exarch, 1995.

Former exarch: Nerses Mikael Setian, 1981-93.

Archdiocese for the Military Services, U.S.A., Washington, D.C. (1957; restructured, 1985): Archbishop Edwin F. O'Brien, military ordinary, 1997. Francis X. Roque, John G. Nolan, Joseph J. Madera, M.Pp.S., John J. Glynn, auxiliaries.

Military vicar appointed, 1917; canonically established, 1957, as U.S. Military Vicariate under jurisdiction of New York archbishop; name changed, restructured as independent jurisdiction, 1985.

Former military vicars: Cardinal Patrick Hayes, 1917-38; Cardinal Francis Spellman, 1939-67; Cardinal Terence J. Cooke, 1968-83; Cardinal John J. O'Connor, apostolic administrator, 1984-85.

Former military ordinaries: Archbishop Joseph T. Ryan, 1985-91. Joseph T. Dimino, 1991-97.

MISSIONARY BISHOPS

Africa

South Africa: Keimoes-Upington (diocese), John B. Minder, O.S.F.S.

De Aar (diocese), Joseph J. Potocnak, S.C.J.

Zambia: Mongu (diocese), Paul Duffy, O.M.I.

Asia

Indonesia: Agats (diocese), Alphonse A. Sowada, O.S.C.

Iraq: Mossul (Chaldean-rite archdiocese), George Garmo.

Korea: Inchon (diocese), William J. McNaughton, M.M.

Philippines: Cotabato (archdiocese), Philip F. Smith, O.M.I.

Central America, West Indies

Dominica: Roseau (diocese), Edward J. Gilbert, C.SS.R.

Honduras: Comayagua (diocese), Gerald Scarpone Caporale, O.F.M.

Jamaica: Mandeville (vicariate apostolic), Paul M. Boyle, C.P.

Nicaragua: Bluefields (vicariate apostolic), Paul Schmitz Simon, O.F.M. Cap.

Virgin Islands: St. Thomas (diocese), Elliott G. Thomas, bishop, 1993.

North America

Bermuda: Hamilton (diocese), Robert Kurtz, C.R.

Mexico: Nuevo Laredo (diocese), Ricardo Watty Urquidi, M.Sp.S., first bishop.

Oceania

American Samoa: Samoa-Pago Pago (diocese), John Quinn Weitzel, M.M.

Papua New Guinea: Mendi (diocese), Stephen J. Reichert, O.F.M.Cap.

Wewak (diocese), Raymond P. Kalisz, S.V.D.

South America

Bolivia: Pando (vicariate apostolic), Luis Morgan Casey.

Brazil: Cristalandia (prelacy), Herbert Hermes, O.S.B.

Itaituba (prelacy), Capistran Heim, O.F.M.

Jatai (diocese), Benedict D. Coscia, O.F.M., bishop; Miguel P. Mundo, auxiliary.

Miracema do Tocantins (diocese), John J. Burke, O.F.M.

Paranagua (diocese), Alfred Novak, C.Ss.R.

Valenca (diocese), Elias James Manning, O.F.M. Conv.

Peru: Chulucanas (diocese), John C. McNabb, O.S.A.; Daniel Thomas Turley Murphy, O.S.A., coadjutor.

LUMEN CHRISTI AWARD

Sister Mary Felissa Zander, educator of Native Americans in the Diocese of Superior, was named recipient of the 1997 Lumen Christi Award for outstanding missionary work in the United States.

The School Sister of St. Francis was principal of St. Francis Solanus Indian Mission. She arrived there 36 years ago at the Lac Courte Oreilles Reservation to teach at the mission. She learned the ways of the Ojibwe people from another nun who was Native American.

Bishop Raphael M. Fliss of Superior said there would not be a Catholic community today on the Reservation if Sister Mary Felissa had not come.

CATHOLIC POPULATION OF THE UNITED STATES

(Source: *The Official Catholic Directory, 1997;* figures as of Jan. 1, 1997. Archdioceses are indicated by an asterisk; for dioceses marked +, see Dioceses with Interstate Lines.)

State Diocese	Cath. Pop.	Dioc. Priests	Rel. Priests	Total Priests	Perm. Deac.	Bros.	Sisters	Parishes
Alabama	**136,184**	**172**	**93**	**265**	**65**	**46**	**394**	**139**
* Mobile	67,205	107	44	151	41	15	223	77
Birmingham	68,979	65	49	114	24	31	171	62
Alaska	**50,016**	**44**	**38**	**82**	**63**	**5**	**73**	**69**
* Anchorage	27,019	19	12	31	12	1	47	20
Fairbanks	17,181	9	23	32	42	4	19	41
Juneau	5,816	16	3	19	9	—	7	8
Arizona	**678,051**	**255**	**186**	**441**	**301**	**15**	**521**	**151**
Phoenix	386,821	144	110	254	178	7	232	87
Tucson	291,230	111	76	187	123	8	289	64
Arkansas, Little Rock	**85,992**	**87**	**67**	**154**	**65**	**47**	**364**	**90**
California	**8,053,296**	**2,168**	**1,523**	**3,691**	**592**	**529**	**5,160**	**1,058**
* Los Angeles	3,672,763	572	593	1,165	144	220	1,980	285
* San Francisco	420,000	223	207	430	53	47	873	89
Fresno	323,191	114	38	152	6	10	127	84
Monterey	170,321	84	22	106	2	29	114	46
Oakland	431,272	228	78	306	80	16	330	86
Orange	603,589	165	94	259	50	9	407	54
Sacramento	425,000	163	73	236	106	35	208	98
San Bernardino	626,236	143	75	218	—	20	156	97
San Diego	690,783	212	93	305	95	21	355	98
San Jose	391,313	118	211	329	8	76	440	46
Santa Rosa	137,391	82	19	101	21	42	101	43
Stockton	161,437	64	20	84	27	4	69	32
Colorado	**549,654**	**258**	**191**	**449**	**144**	**35**	**671**	**196**
* Denver	358,600	151	133	284	117	19	433	112
Colorado Springs	86,462	31	18	49	21	3	145	30
Pueblo	104,592	76	40	116	6	13	93	54
Connecticut	**1,359,910**	**832**	**311**	**1,143**	**460**	**113**	**1,918**	**388**
* Hartford	778,856	432	146	578	333	78	1,069	222
Bridgeport	359,455	258	82	340	77	2	523	88
Norwich+	221,599	142	83	225	50	33	326	78
Delaware, Wilmington+	**164,973**	**129**	**86**	**215**	**45**	**35**	**297**	**55**
District of Columbia								
* Washington+	**440,000**	**336**	**495**	**831**	**245**	**125**	**885**	**139**
Florida	**1,982,676**	**849**	**459**	**1,308**	**465**	**150**	**1,351**	**445**
* Miami	760,078	253	122	375	113	56	346	108
Orlando	301,958	123	54	177	109	10	142	70
Palm Beach	215,907	93	41	134	37	5	178	46
Pensacola-Tallahassee	62,735	74	10	84	53	7	61	49
St. Augustine	115,975	90	20	110	22	2	119	50
St. Petersburg	353,117	130	147	277	71	50	350	72
Venice	172,906	86	65	151	60	20	155	50
Georgia	**329,902**	**181**	**124**	**305**	**142**	**19**	**271**	**122**
* Atlanta	256,049	117	94	211	105	1	125	69
Savannah	73,853	64	30	94	37	18	146	53
Hawaii, Honolulu	**232,780**	**75**	**77**	**152**	**36**	**45**	**243**	**69**
Idaho, Boise	**116,500**	**95**	**16**	**111**	**30**	**8**	**121**	**73**
Illinois	**3,650,022**	**1,850**	**1,204**	**3,054**	**922**	**590**	**5,840**	**1,057**
* Chicago	2,342,000	958	859	1,817	595	444	3,434	378
Belleville	109,985	148	45	193	25	10	263	128
Joliet	512,609	204	113	317	117	92	757	119
Peoria	234,298	246	57	303	83	10	303	165
Rockford	280,652	145	61	206	100	15	366	101
Springfield	170,478	149	69	218	2	19	717	166
Indiana	**739,084**	**629**	**365**	**994**	**82**	**213**	**2,070**	**440**
* Indianapolis	213,252	168	127	295	—	60	806	138
Evansville	89,203	106	10	116	22	2	318	73
Ft. Wayne-South Bend	159,659	104	159	263	25	129	697	88

State Diocese	Cath. Pop.	Dioc. Priests	Rel. Priests	Total Priests	Perm. Deac.	Bros.	Sisters	Par- ishes
Indiana								
Gary	184,516	131	50	181	30	20	137	79
Lafayette	92,454	120	19	139	5	2	112	62
Iowa	**509,141**	**708**	**46**	**754**	**201**	**34**	**1,524**	**511**
* Dubuque	206,199	268	32	300	63	28	1,054	213
Davenport	106,460	146	7	153	51	2	214	83
Des Moines	97,105	115	7	122	53	4	128	87
Sioux City	99,377	179	—	179	35	—	128	118
Kansas	**383,428**	**346**	**96**	**442**	**8**	**21**	**1,589**	**363**
* Kansas City	181,638	98	66	164	—	20	840	119
Dodge City	44,504	51	3	54	6	—	122	57
Salina	52,114	68	19	87	—	1	213	92
Wichita	105,172	129	8	137	2	—	414	95
Kentucky	**357,155**	**448**	**94**	**542**	**148**	**107**	**1,975**	**304**
* Louisville	181,570	197	62	259	103	94	1,083	113
Covington	82,341	119	1	120	17	7	464	51
Lexington	41,905	50	21	71	28	5	186	61
Owensboro	51,339	82	10	92	—	1	242	79
Louisiana	**1,336,072**	**700**	**377**	**1,077**	**335**	**205**	**1,374**	**493**
* New Orleans	484,263	231	227	458	198	141	873	147
Alexandria	48,050	64	15	79	7	3	69	48
Baton Rouge	218,576	93	47	140	27	15	120	70
Houma-Thibodaux	109,412	73	7	80	25	12	34	40
Lafayette	355,435	146	52	198	52	30	175	121
Lake Charles	81,971	50	18	68	19	4	32	36
Shreveport	38,365	43	11	54	7	—	71	31
Maine, Portland	**220,983**	**194**	**54**	**248**	**11**	**26**	**501**	**139**
Maryland, *Baltimore	**480,152**	**288**	**257**	**545**	**166**	**121**	**1,332**	**154**
Massachusetts	**2,968,041**	**1,649**	**1,039**	**2,688**	**325**	**310**	**4,735**	**771**
* Boston	2,024,039	977	752	1,729	187	183	3,154	394
Fall River	345,940	179	113	292	36	39	387	112
Springfield	294,269	221	58	279	35	10	644	135
Worcester	303,793	272	116	388	67	78	550	130
Michigan	**2,191,854**	**1,126**	**331**	**1,457**	**290**	**92**	**2,968**	**802**
* Detroit	1,424,616	489	230	719	151	71	1,687	306
Gaylord	82,302	73	15	88	11	3	71	82
Grand Rapids	146,205	131	23	154	20	3	321	90
Kalamazoo	99,922	60	14	74	18	4	230	46
Lansing	223,536	141	28	169	59	9	441	93
Marquette	74,066	110	6	116	17	—	72	75
Saginaw	141,207	122	15	137	14	2	146	110
Minnesota	**1,226,202**	**846**	**312**	**1,158**	**230**	**155**	**2,793**	**737**
* St.Paul and Minneapolis	733,961	345	146	491	166	66	1,189	222
Crookston	42,934	49	5	54	8	2	214	76
Duluth	82,175	83	16	99	19	—	178	95
New Ulm	71,272	95	—	95	3	—	99	81
St. Cloud	147,415	145	131	276	32	68	595	141
Winona	148,445	129	14	143	2	19	518	122
Mississippi	**108,896**	**127**	**57**	**184**	**30**	**44**	**345**	**118**
Biloxi	64,556	56	27	83	19	33	59	44
Jackson	44,340	71	30	101	11	11	286	74
Missouri	**857,239**	**803**	**574**	**1,377**	**316**	**300**	**2,905**	**470**
* St. Louis	568,300	481	397	878	196	187	2,340	227
Jefferson City	84,308	114	10	124	61	4	101	95
Kansas City-St. Joseph	150,106	132	103	235	54	35	329	84
Springfield-Cape Girardeau	54,525	76	64	140	5	74	135	64
Montana	**122,884**	**167**	**24**	**191**	**32**	**1**	**148**	**112**
Great Falls-Billings	56,384	78	15	93	3	—	78	54
Helena	66,500	89	9	98	29	1	70	58
Nebraska	**352,019**	**445**	**140**	**585**	**123**	**36**	**588**	**343**
* Omaha	212,137	230	127	357	123	25	376	165
Grand Island	53,841	81	1	82	—	—	94	44
Lincoln	86,041	134	12	146	—	11	118	134

State Diocese	Cath. Pop.	Dioc. Priests	Rel. Priests	Total Priests	Perm. Deac.	Bros.	Sisters	Par-ishes
Nevada	**438,260**	**68**	**32**	**100**	**15**	**9**	**91**	**51**
Las Vegas	335,124	42	20	62	7	6	53	23
Reno	103,136	26	12	38	8	3	38	28
New Hampshire, Manchester	**321,914**	**243**	**84**	**327**	**21**	**41**	**823**	**131**
New Jersey	**3,308,989**	**1,886**	**632**	**2,518**	**778**	**261**	**4,094**	**709**
* Newark	1,346,185	827	250	1,077	225	124	1,757	238
Camden	406,383	331	42	373	96	14	372	126
Metuchen	483,196	212	45	257	104	24	496	108
Paterson	377,650	273	201	474	138	42	960	111
Trenton	695,575	243	94	337	215	57	509	126
New Mexico	**426,803**	**199**	**184**	**383**	**194**	**103**	**530**	**193**
* Santa Fe	260,313	111	106	217	135	91	299	91
Gallup	41,181	58	31	89	33	12	155	58
Las Cruces	125,309	30	47	77	26	—	76	44
New York	**7,309,228**	**3,583**	**1,898**	**5,481**	**1,076**	**937**	**10,986**	**1,674**
* New York	2,327,300	911	1,120	2,031	307	445	4,020	413
Albany	403,403	324	128	452	91	86	980	188
Brooklyn	1,603,110	685	232	917	164	191	1,572	219
Buffalo	753,117	450	194	644	85	47	1,489	266
Ogdensburg	138,865	178	20	198	58	11	193	121
Rochester	363,672	277	65	342	106	35	675	161
Rockville Centre	1,347,096	458	95	553	196	104	1,543	134
Syracuse	372,665	300	44	344	69	18	514	172
North Carolina	**235,954**	**153**	**112**	**265**	**82**	**13**	**274**	**136**
Charlotte	110,302	82	62	144	60	5	192	66
Raleigh	125,652	71	50	121	22	8	82	70
North Dakota	**165,340**	**204**	**38**	**242**	**86**	**38**	**389**	**225**
Bismarck	66,425	68	28	96	51	23	169	65
Fargo	98,915	136	10	146	35	15	220	160
Ohio	**2,228,085**	**1,608**	**590**	**2,198**	**577**	**305**	**4,760**	**932**
* Cincinnati	546,100	358	281	639	128	179	1,471	236
Cleveland	830,130	502	147	649	155	74	1,628	236
Columbus	216,676	203	45	248	48	8	411	108
Steubenville	46,015	125	20	145	5	11	89	74
Toledo	328,623	217	66	283	190	10	877	163
Youngstown	260,541	203	31	234	51	23	284	115
Oklahoma	**144,335**	**166**	**47**	**213**	**94**	**16**	**256**	**153**
* Oklahoma City	92,080	86	30	116	52	11	151	73
Tulsa	52,255	80	17	97	42	5	105	80
Oregon	**314,387**	**194**	**193**	**387**	**21**	**77**	**566**	**160**
* Portland	282,593	156	184	340	16	77	532	125
Baker	31,794	38	9	47	5	—	34	35
Pennsylvania	**3,552,569**	**2,695**	**942**	**3,637**	**358**	**250**	**9,078**	**1,294**
* Philadelphia	1,404,268	828	407	1,235	142	141	3,996	287
Allentown	258,527	250	81	331	84	11	690	153
Altoona-Johnstown	114,914	158	65	223	16	4	155	113
Erie	235,195	251	14	265	2	2	570	127
Greensburg	195,582	154	96	250	1	38	322	107
Harrisburg	230,000	168	44	212	59	1	571	89
Pittsburgh	753,090	520	134	654	22	44	1,909	218
Scranton	360,993	366	101	467	32	9	865	200
Rhode Island, Providence	**637,554**	**317**	**126**	**443**	**83**	**123**	**759**	**159**
South Carolina, Charleston	**109,629**	**95**	**33**	**128**	**62**	**26**	**164**	**86**
South Dakota	**160,916**	**168**	**76**	**244**	**55**	**24**	**543**	**224**
Rapid City	42,320	40	32	72	31	11	82	68
Sioux Falls	118,596	128	44	172	24	13	461	156
Tennessee	**156,523**	**169**	**46**	**215**	**71**	**44**	**312**	**135**
Knoxville	39,714	46	15	61	23	16	53	43
Memphis	56,885	70	11	81	21	36	100	42
Nashville	59,924	53	20	73	27	2	159	50
Texas	**4,317,171**	**1,188**	**895**	**2,083**	**1,136**	**234**	**3,232**	**983**
* San Antonio	652,413	155	230	385	240	96	879	148
Amarillo	52,431	65	8	73	45	1	143	35
Austin	212,182	137	56	193	104	41	122	91

State / Diocese	Cath. Pop.	Dioc. Priests	Rel. Priests	Total Priests	Perm. Deac.	Bros.	Sisters	Par- ishes
Texas								
Beaumont	85,906	55	25	80	30	3	62	43
Brownsville	717,056	57	51	108	82	18	139	63
Corpus Christi	361,500	108	62	170	66	22	565	84
Dallas	324,820	104	84	188	145	4	161	64
El Paso	579,766	92	43	135	17	16	243	58
Fort Worth	192,890	58	53	111	58	14	99	88
Galveston-Houston	854,653	194	223	417	231	17	553	149
Lubbock	50,378	32	9	41	23	—	32	36
San Angelo	81,807	51	17	68	45	—	39	49
Tyler	42,796	25	21	46	29	1	61	30
Victoria	108,573	55	13	68	21	1	134	50
Utah, Salt Lake City	**81,021**	**54**	**32**	**86**	**25**	**12**	**68**	**43**
Vermont, Burlington	**147,190**	**139**	**48**	**187**	**40**	**21**	**263**	**93**
Virginia	**494,655**	**304**	**113**	**417**	**77**	**28**	**487**	**203**
Arlington	311,351	143	74	217	55	17	218	62
Richmond	183,304	161	39	200	22	11	269	141
Washington	**519,130**	**329**	**239**	**568**	**144**	**44**	**1,026**	**257**
* Seattle	369,050	189	132	321	82	31	674	138
Spokane	80,102	84	97	181	37	13	299	78
Yakima	69,978	56	10	66	25	—	53	41
West Virginia								
Wheeling-Charleston	103,678	123	64	187	26	8	311	115
Wisconsin	**1,759,923**	**1,161**	**554**	**1,715**	**297**	**167**	**4,051**	**910**
* Milwaukee	605,232	490	345	835	154	96	2,233	277
Green Bay	582,681	237	143	380	78	49	714	201
La Crosse	227,937	198	27	225	22	11	544	180
Madison	256,527	157	23	180	1	9	427	137
Superior	87,546	79	16	95	42	2	133	115
Wyoming, Cheyenne+	**48,427**	**52**	**11**	**63**	**7**	**1**	**34**	**36**
EASTERN CHURCHES	**477,574**	**575**	**118**	**693**	**102**	**26**	**302**	**570**
* Philadelphia	69,488	58	6	64	5	3	84	77
St. Nicholas	10,000	37	15	52	14	—	—	33
Stamford	32,117	38	18	56	5	3	42	49
St. Josaphat (Parma)	11,629	38	1	39	9	10	10	35
* Pittsburgh	85,740	65	9	74	—	4	108	87
Parma	12,714	41	—	41	—	—	12	39
Passaic	66,965	93	20	113	18	—	13	102
Van Nuys	2,951	18	4	22	3	4	4	16
St. Maron (Maronites)	30,000	62	10	72	10	1	12	33
Our Lady of Lebanon (Maronites)	21,790	33	5	38	6	—	—	25
Newton (Melkites)	27,730	45	19	64	28	1	3	35
St. Thomas Apostle of Detroit (Chaldean)	63,150	18	—	18	—	—	—	12
St. George Martyr (Romanian)	5,300	15	2	17	–	—	—	15
Our Lady of Deliverance (Syrians, U.S.-Canada)	12,000	10	1	11	4	—	—	6
Armenian Ex. (U.S.-Canada)	26,000	4	8	12	—	—	14	6
MILITARY ARCHD.[1]	**1,215,200**	**—**	**—**	**—**	**—**	**—**	**—**	**—**
OUTLYING AREAS								
Puerto Rico	**2,583,360**	**426**	**328**	**754**	**392**	**51**	**1,056**	**323**
Am. Samoa	**6,676**	**10**	**1**	**11**	**19**	**—**	**16**	**8**
Caroline Islands	**64,089**	**12**	**16**	**28**	**42**	**2**	**33**	**21**
Guam, *Agana	**114,906**	**29**	**19**	**48**	**9**	**1**	**120**	**24**
Northern Mariana Islands	**47,322**	**6**	**1**	**7**	**3**	**—**	**35**	**9**
Marshall Islands	**4,000**	**1**	**5**	**6**	**2**	**2**	**15**	**4**
Virgin Islands, St. Thomas	**30,000**	**13**	**7**	**20**	**22**	**2**	**14**	**8**
GRAND TOTALS 1997	**61,207,914**	**31,977**	**16,120**	**48,097**	**11,788**	**6,293**	**87,644**	**19,677**
Grand Totals 1996	**60,280,454**	**32,442**	**16,629**	**49,009**	**11,527**	**6,357**	**89,125**	**19,726**
Grand Totals 1987	**50,893,217**	**34,471**	**18,911**	**53,382**	**7,981**	**7,418**	**112,489**	**19,546**

[1]Priest chaplains are on loan from their dioceses or religious community. The 1997 *Annuario Pontificio* reported 649 diocesan and 230 religious order chaplains.

PERCENTAGE OF CATHOLICS IN TOTAL POPULATION IN U.S.

(Source: *The Official Catholic Directory, 1997;* figures are as of Jan. 1, 1997. Total general population figures at the end of the table are U.S. Census Bureau estimates for Jan. 1 of the respective years. Archdioceses are indicated by an asterisk; for dioceses marked +, see Dioceses with Interstate Lines.)

State Diocese	Catholic Pop.	Total Pop.	Cath. Pct.	State Diocese	Catholic Pop.	Total Pop.	Cath. Pct.
Alabama	136,184	4,135,392	3.3	Ft.Wayne-S.Bend	159,659	1,960,876	8.1
*Mobile	67,205	1,452,506	4.6	Gary	184,516	759,673	24.3
Birmingham	68,979	2,682,886	2.6	Lafayette	92,454	1,101,765	8.4
Alaska	50,016	612,083	8.2	Iowa	509,141	2,773,350	18.3
* Anchorage	27,019	373,019	7.2	* Dubuque	206,199	923,000	22.3
Fairbanks	17,181	152,194	11.3	Davenport	106,460	707,123	15.0
Juneau	5,816	86,870	6.7	Des Moines	97,105	671,091	14.5
Arizona	678,051	4,021,241	17.0	Sioux City	99,377	472,136	21.0
Phoenix	386,821	2,915,165	13.2	Kansas	383,428	2,403,171	16.0
Tucson	291,230	1,106,076	26.3	* Kansas City	181,638	952,000	19.0
Arkansas, Little Rock	85,992	2,483,769	3.5	Dodge City	44,504	212,147	21.0
California	8,053,296	33,280,324	24.2	Salina	52,114	328,480	16.0
* Los Angeles	3,672,763	11,689,801	31.4	Wichita	105,172	910,544	11.6
* San Francisco	420,000	1,700,000	24.7	Kentucky	357,155	3,694,498	9.7
Fresno	323,191	2,171,617	14.8	* Louisville	181,570	1,139,022	16.0
Monterey	170,321	851,604	20.0	Covington	82,341	401,127	20.5
Oakland	431,272	2,195,411	19.6	Lexington	41,905	1,376,114	3.0
Orange	603,589	2,624,300	23.0	Owensboro	51,339	778,235	6.6
Sacramento	425,000	2,854,000	15.0	Louisiana	1,336,072	4,316,324	31.0
San Bernardino	626,236	3,037,303	20.6	* New Orleans	484,263	1,330,855	36.4
San Diego	690,783	2,782,204	24.8	Alexandria	48,050	393,880	12.2
San Jose	391,313	1,565,253	25.0	Baton Rouge	218,576	798,343	27.4
Santa Rosa	137,391	772,859	17.8	Houma-Thibodaux	109,412	208,185	52.6
Stockton	161,437	1,035,972	15.6	Lafayette	355,435	540,001	65.8
Colorado	549,654	3,709,590	14.8	Lake Charles	81,971	259,425	31.6
* Denver	358,600	2,628,800	13.6	Shreveport	38,365	785,635	4.9
Colorado Springs	86,462	593,175	14.6	Maine,Portland	220,983	1,227,927	18.0
Pueblo	104,592	487,615	21.4	Maryland,*Baltimore	480,152	2,862,671	16.8
Connecticut	1,359,910	3,270,788	41.6	Massachusetts	2,968,041	6,020,374	49.3
* Hartford	778,856	1,814,610	42.9	*Boston	2,024,039	3,793,058	53.4
Bridgeport	359,455	830,728	43.2	Fall River	345,940	715,000	48.4
Norwich+	221,599	625,450	35.4	Springfield	294,269	802,611	36.7
Delaware, Wilmington+	164,973	1,049,769	15.7	Worcester	303,793	709,705	42.8
District of Columbia				Michigan	2,191,854	9,455,625	23.2
* Washington+	440,000	2,388,506	18.4	*Detroit	1,424,616	4,266,654	33.4
Florida	1,982,676	14,310,296	13.8	Gaylord	82,302	437,375	18.8
* Miami	760,078	3,525,351	21.6	Grand Rapids	146,205	1,167,900	12.5
Orlando	301,958	2,955,200	10.2	Kalamazoo	99,922	909,236	11.0
Palm Beach	215,907	1,415,520	15.2	Lansing	223,536	1,670,223	13.4
Pensacola-Tallahassee	62,735	1,256,474	5.0	Marquette	74,066	318,705	23.2
St. Augustine	115,975	1,502,699	7.7	Saginaw	141,207	685,532	20.6
St. Petersburg	353,117	2,287,817	15.4	Minnesota	1,226,202	4,539,922	27.0
Venice	172,906	1,367,235	12.6	* St. Paul and			
Georgia	329,902	7,152,122	4.6	Minneapolis	733,961	2,681,324	27.4
* Atlanta	256,049	4,712,254	5.4	Crookston	42,934	236,100	18.1
Savannah	73,853	2,439,868	3.0	Duluth	82,175	378,000	21.7
Hawaii, Honolulu	232,780	1,178,600	19.7	New Ulm	71,272	282,768	25.2
Idaho,Boise	116,500	1,163,000	10.0	St. Cloud	147,415	433,427	34.0
Illinois	3,650,022	11,805,501	31.0	Winona	148,445	528,303	28.0
*Chicago	2,342,000	5,712,000	41.0	Mississippi	108,896	2,685,188	4.0
Belleville	109,985	855,070	13.0	Biloxi	64,556	705,163	9.1
Joliet	512,609	1,494,976	34.3	Jackson	44,340	1,980,025	2.2
Peoria	234,298	1,436,088	16.3	Missouri	857,239	5,165,640	16.6
Rockford	280,652	1,201,303	23.4	* St. Louis	568,300	2,063,163	27.5
Springfield	170,478	1,106,124	15.4	Jefferson City	84,308	752,716	11.2
Indiana	739,084	6,499,770	11.4	Kansas City-St.Joseph	150,106	1,299,555	11.6
* Indianapolis	213,252	2,201,503	9.7	Springfield-			
Evansville	89,203	475,953	18.7	Cape Girardeau	54,525	1,050,206	5.2

State Diocese	Catholic Pop.	Total Pop.	Cath. Pct.	State Diocese	Catholic Pop.	Total Pop.	Cath. Pct.
Montana	122,884	817,272	15.0	Pennsylvania			
Great Falls-Billings	56,384	392,900	14.3	Erie	235,195	874,244	27.0
Helena	66,500	424,372	15.7	Greensburg	195,582	688,501	28.4
Nebraska	352,019	1,615,167	21.8	Harrisburg	230,000	1,940,954	11.8
*Omaha	212,137	808,076	26.2	Pittsburgh	753,090	2,009,092	37.5
Grand Island	53,841	290,429	18.5	Scranton	360,993	1,036,320	34.8
Lincoln	86,041	516,662	16.7	Rhode Island,Providence	637,554	1,003,000	63.6
Nevada	438,260	1,671,019	26.2	South Carolina,Charleston	109,629	3,673,000	3.0
Las Vegas	335,124	1,155,600	29.0	South Dakota	160,916	711,591	22.6
Reno	103,136	515,419	20.0	Rapid City	42,320	211,591	20.0
New Hampshire				Sioux Falls	118,596	500,000	23.7
Manchester	321,914	1,148,000	28.0	Tennessee	156,523	5,069,870	3.0
New Jersey	3,308,989	7,930,813	41.7	Knoxville	39,714	1,860,218	2.1
*Newark	1,346,185	2,656,348	50.7	Memphis	56,885	1,426,923	4.0
Camden	406,383	1,286,240	31.7	Nashville	59,924	1,782,729	3.3
Metuchen	483,196	1,177,058	41.0	Texas	4,317,171	18,669,605	23.1
Paterson	377,650	1,048,018	36.0	*San Antonio	652,413	1,828,740	35.7
Trenton	695,575	1,763,149	39.4	Amarillo	52,431	386,574	13.6
New Mexico	426,803	1,788,882	23.8	Austin	212,182	1,638,245	13.0
*Santa Fe	260,313	979,742	26.6	Beaumont	85,906	561,605	15.3
Gallup	41,181	355,640	11.6	Brownsville	717,056	888,112	80.7
Las Cruces	125,309	453,500	27.6	Corpus Christi	361,500	792,300	45.6
New York	7,309,228	18,496,487	39.5	Dallas	324,820	2,733,974	11.9
*New York	2,327,300	5,351,854	43.5	El Paso+	579,766	776,724	74.6
Albany	403,403	1,315,414	30.7	Fort Worth	192,890	2,263,399	8.5
Brooklyn	1,603,110	4,207,649	38.1	Galveston-Houston	854,653	4,231,599	20.2
Buffalo	753,117	1,613,258	46.7	Lubbock	50,378	451,995	11.1
Ogdensburg	138,865	420,111	33.0	San Angelo	81,807	675,907	12.1
Rochester	363,672	1,484,426	24.5	Tyler	42,796	1,185,155	3.6
Rockville Centre	1,347,096	2,880,184	46.8	Victoria	108,573	255,276	42.5
Syracuse	372,665	1,223,591	30.5	Utah, Salt Lake City	81,021	1,964,000	4.1
North Carolina	235,954	7,264,913	3.2	Vermont, Burlington	147,190	584,771	25.1
Charlotte	110,302	3,715,535	3.0	Virginia	494,655	6,677,180	7.4
Raleigh	125,652	3,549,378	3.5	Arlington	311,351	2,115,700	14.7
North Dakota	165,340	643,952	25.7	Richmond	183,304	4,561,480	4.0
Bismarck	66,425	253,552	26.2	Washington	519,130	5,452,091	9.5
Fargo	98,915	390,400	25.3	*Seattle	369,050	4,282,200	8.6
Ohio	2,228,085	11,087,919	20.1	Spokane	80,102	708,891	11.3
*Cincinnati	546,100	2,892,000	18.9	Yakima	69,978	461,000	15.1
Cleveland	830,130	2,811,515	29.5	West Virginia			
Columbus	216,676	2,170,007	10.0	Wheeling-Charleston	103,678	1,793,477	5.8
Steubenville	46,015	506,136	9.0	Wisconsin	1,759,923	4,982,442	35.3
Toledo	328,623	1,479,041	22.2	*Milwaukee	605,232	2,080,883	29.1
Youngstown	260,541	1,229,220	21.2	Green Bay	582,681	836,600	69.6
Oklahoma	144,335	3,451,439	4.1	La Crosse	227,937	817,382	27.9
*Oklahoma City	92,080	2,003,512	4.6	Madison	256,527	866,227	29.6
Tulsa	52,255	1,447,927	3.6	Superior	87,546	381,350	23.0
Oregon	314,387	3,132,000	10.0	Wyoming, Cheyenne	48,427	480,184	10.0
* Portland	282,593	2,725,200	10.4	Eastern Churches	477,574	—	—
Baker	31,794	406,800	7.8	Military Archdiocese	1,215,200	—	—
Pennsylvania	3,552,569	12,020,844	29.6	**Outlying Areas**	**2,850,353**	**—**	**—**
*Philadelphia	1,404,288	3,737,583	37.6	**Grand Totals '97**	**61,207,914**	**266,490,000**	**23.0**
Allentown	258,527	1,084,189	23.8	**Grand Totals '96**	**60,280,454**	**264,023,000**	**22.8**
Altoona-Johnstown	114,914	649,961	17.7	**Grand Totals '87**	**50,893,217**	**242,085,811**	**21.0**

BASILICA OF THE NATIONAL SHRINE OF THE IMMACULATE CONCEPTION

The Basilica of the National Shrine of the Immaculate Conception is dedicated to the honor of the Blessed Virgin Mary, declared patroness of the United States under this title in 1846, eight years before the proclamation of the dogma of the Immaculate Conception. The church was designated a minor basilica by Pope John Paul II Oct. 12, 1990. The church is the eighth largest religious building in the world and the largest Catholic church in the Western Hemisphere, with numerous special chapels and with normal seating and standing accommodations for 6,000 people. Open daily, it is adjacent to The Catholic University of America, at Michigan Ave. and Fourth St. N.E., Washington, D.C. 20017. Msgr. Michael J. Bransfield is the rector.

RECEPTIONS INTO THE CHURCH IN THE UNITED STATES

(Source: *The Official Catholic Directory, 1997;* figures as of Jan. 1, 1997. Archdioceses are indicated by an asterisk; for dioceses marked +, see Dioceses with Interstate Lines. Information includes infant and adult baptisms and those received into full communion.)

State Diocese	Infant Baptisms	Adult Bapts.	Rec'd into Full Comm.	State Diocese	Infant Baptisms	Adult Bapts.	Rec'd into Full Comm.
Alabama	2,428	371	804	Indiana			
*Mobile	1,218	191	359	Ft.Wayne-S. Bend	2,534	440	455
Birmingham	1,210	180	445	Gary	2,638	181	282
Alaska	1,143	94	152	Lafayette	1,893	252	310
*Anchorage	538	60	97	Iowa	8,692	712	1,650
Fairbanks	519	19	38	*Dubuque	3,564	158	405
Juneau	86	15	17	Davenport	1,543	236	221
Arizona	17,646	882	1,566	Des Moines	1,801	238	544
Phoenix	10,443	506	845	Sioux City	1,784	80	480
Tucson	7,203	376	721	Kansas	8,052	1,092	1,444
Arkansas, Little Rock	1,815	255	460	*Kansas City	3,678	409	588
California	200,359	8,369	8,680	Dodge City	944	219	264
*Los Angeles	95,611	2,023	2,661	Salina	983	111	211
*San Francisco	8,424	447	337	Wichita	2,447	353	381
Fresno	16,818	507	348	Kentucky	6,192	833	1,196
Monterey	5,532	216	750	*Louisville	2,912	313	523
Oakland	9,265	463	768	Covington	1,603	174	153
Orange	17,833	885	803	Lexington	701	143	287
Sacramento	8,401	705	640	Owensboro	976	203	233
San Bernardino	9,001	1,539	678	Louisiana	21,070	1,265	1,629
San Diego	12,435	566	642	*New Orleans	7,353	406	390
San Jose	8,818	498	497	Alexandria	751	97	131
Santa Rosa	3,097	205	118	Baton Rouge	2,985	264	406
Stockton	5,124	315	438	Houma-Thibodaux	1,827	55	113
Colorado	12,773	1,013	1,614	Lafayette	6,084	180	205
*Denver	9,389	735	968	Lake Charles	1,543	145	199
Colorado Springs	1,312	140	269	Shreveport	527	118	185
Pueblo	2,072	138	377	Maine, Portland	3,141	270	513
Connecticut	21,042	719	982	Maryland,*Baltimore	8,435	692	1,261
*Hartford	11,561	373	489	Massachusetts	41,984	3,751	938
Bridgepor	6,090	202	157	*Boston	26,728	3,346	316
Norwich+	3,391	144	336	Fall River	5,695	103	125
Delaware, Wilmington+	2,886	228	311	Springfield	4,465	156	233
District of Columbia,				Worcester	5,096	146	264
*Washington+	6,924	568	662	Michigan	30,742	3,040	3,817
Florida	38,730	3,116	4,015	*Detroit	17,215	1,285	1,642
*Miami	18,644	986	1,256	Gaylord	1,170	126	226
Orlando	5,482	454	779	Grand Rapids	3,006	420	547
Palm Beach	4,450	338	377	Kalamazoo	1,620	246	197
Pensacola-Tallahassee	1,068	164	295	Lansing	4,222	642	851
St. Augustine	2,000	258	462	Marquette	1,209	64	130
St. Petersburg	4,423	712	567	Saginaw	2,300	257	224
Venice	2,663	204	279	Minnesota	19,367	698	2,231
Georgia	6,947	701	1,344	*St. Paul and			
*Atlanta	5,539	494	932	Minneapolis	11,838	439	1,337
Savannah	1,408	207	412	Crookston	776	15	93
Hawaii, Honolulu	3,603	445	488	Duluth	1,195	43	195
Idaho, Boise	2,579	202	261	New Ulm	1,025	60	112
Illinois	64,923	3,720	4,181	St. Cloud	2,529	73	214
*Chicago	39,989	1,804	1,544	Winona	2,004	68	280
Belleville	1,655	280	251	Mississippi	1,522	689	391
Joliet	11,156	383	871	Biloxi	772	586	135
Peoria	3,124	510	596	Jackson	750	103	256
Rockford	6,411	356	457	Missouri	12,083	1,901	1,820
Springfield	2,588	387	462	*St. Louis	7,734	906	731
Indiana	12,767	1,645	1,931	Jefferson City	1,333	247	295
*Indianapolis	4,106	650	741	Kansas City-			
Evansville	1,596	122	143	St. Joseph	2,324	514	365

State / Diocese	Infant Baptisms	Adult Bapts.	Rec'd into Full Comm.
Missouri			
Springfield- Cape Girardeau	692	234	429
Montana	1,839	318	303
Great Falls-Billings	924	115	153
Helena	915	203	150
Nebraska	6,889	466	835
*Omaha	4,500	179	427
Grand Island	1,012	132	189
Lincoln	1,377	155	219
Nevada	5,002	388	447
Las Vegas	3,351	277	279
Reno	1,651	111	168
New Hampshire, Manchester	5,530	167	184
New Jersey	51,979	1,852	2,807
*Newark	17,656	482	753
Camden	7,305	642	540
Metuchen	7,407	154	280
Paterson	8,887	184	372
Trenton	10,724	390	862
New Mexico	9,723	593	515
*Santa Fe	6,404	243	331
Gallup	886	246	69
Las Cruces	2,433	104	115
New York	109,744	4,002	3,391
*New York	35,522	898	546
Albany	6,017	353	205
Brooklyn	23,753	835	1,077
Buffalo	8,094	501	447
Ogdensburg	1,950	167	94
Rochester	6,291	329	518
Rockville Centre	21,957	545	—
Syracuse	6,160	374	504
North Carolina	5,056	776	888
Charlotte	2,484	574	465
Raleigh	2,572	202	423
North Dakota	2,723	181	221
Bismarck	1,153	113	114
Fargo	1,570	68	107
Ohio	32,011	3,906	3,821
*Cincinnati	8,476	1,206	865
Cleveland	11,294	1,053	930
Columbus	3,787	448	702
Steubenville	785	350	—
Toledo	4,292	467	653
Youngstown	3,377	382	671
Oklahoma	2,607	493	709
*Oklahoma City	1,602	294	411
Tulsa	1,005	199	298
Oregon	5,794	818	818
*Portland	4,918	676	703
Baker	876	142	115
Pennsylvania	45,479	2,942	3,416
*Philadelphia	17,559	1,172	714
Allentown	3,960	193	358
Altoona-Johnstown	1,627	127	207
Erie	2,534	275	266
Greensburg	2,273	115	358
Harrisburg	3,312	350	470
Pittsburgh	9,303	454	754
Scranton	4,911	256	289
Rhode Island, Providence	6,648	169	178
South Carolina, Charleston	2,122	239	467
South Dakota	2,653	115	368
Rapid City	728	51	99
Sioux Falls	1,925	64	269
Tennessee	3,200	565	1,052
Knoxville	777	133	269
Memphis	1,071	203	279
Nashville	1,352	229	504
Texas	84,212	5,314	5,531
*San Antonio	13,709	463	735
Amarillo	1,014	84	106
Austin	5,540	692	464
Beaumont	1,380	139	242
Brownsville	9,280	674	448
Corpus Christi	5,989	240	504
Dallas	10,266	769	637
El Paso	8,307	121	250
Fort Worth	4,663	296	650
Galveston-Houston	16,913	1,363	885
Lubbock	1,910	70	58
San Angelo	2,212	179	255
Tyler	1,387	135	170
Victoria	1,642	89	127
Utah, Salt Lake City	2,328	397	314
Vermont, Burlington	2,012	130	157
Virginia	8,439	2,119	982
Arlington	5,194	1,967	—
Richmond	3,245	152	982
Washington	10,407	1,604	903
*Seattle	6,308	1,129	703
Spokane	1,323	321	117
Yakima	2,776	154	83
West Virginia, Wheeling-Charleston	1,291	327	303
Wisconsin	26,312	2,972	1,726
*Milwaukee	9,417	555	537
Green Bay	9,262	432	705
La Crosse	3,239	122	359
Madison	3,211	408	—
Superior	1,183	1,455	125
Wyoming, Cheyenne+	1,071	218	265
Eastern Churches	**4,306**	**201**	**343**
*Philadelphia	345	2	5
St. Nicholas	120	3	—
Stamford	188	18	7
St. Josaphat (Parma)	132	4	1
*Pittsburgh	521	55	75
Parma	140	13	20
Passaic	395	21	109
Van Nuys	65	7	22
St. Maron (Maronites)	330	9	38
Our Lady of Lebanon (Maronites)	376	27	25
Newton (Melkites)	467	21	29
St. Thomas Apostle of Detroit (Chaldeans)	1,052	17	—
St. George Martyr (Romanian)	24	1	12
Our Lady of Deliverance (Syrians, U.S.-Can.)	74	3	—
Armenian Ex. (U.S.-Can.)	77	—	—
Military Archdiocese	**6,389**	**1,118**	**485**
Outlying Areas	**40,613**	**5,990**	**10,321**
GRAND TOTALS '97	**1,044,304**	**75,645**	**85,970**
Grand Totals '96	**1,029,281**	**69,894**	**92,155**
Grand Totals '87	**941,898**	**80,703**	**—**

STATISTICAL SUMMARY OF THE CHURCH IN THE U.S.

(Principal source: *The Official Catholic Directory, 1997.* Comparisons, where given, are with figures reported in the previous edition of the Directory. Totals below do not include statistics for Outlying Areas of U.S. These are given in tables on the preceding pages and elsewhere in the Almanac; see Index.)

Catholic Population: 58,357,561; increase, 913,269. Percent of total population, 22.

Jurisdictions: 34 archdioceses (includes 33 metropolitan sees and the Military Archdiocese), 157 dioceses (includes St. Thomas, Virgin Islands, and the eparchy of Our Lady of Deliverance of Newark for Syrians of the U.S. and Canada), 1 apostolic exarchate (New York-based Armenian exarchate for U.S. and Canada). Vacant jurisdictions (as of July 10, 1997), 4: Kalamazoo, Portland, Ore., Rapid City, Seattle.

Cardinals: 10 (7 head archiepiscopal sees in U.S.; 2 are Roman Curia officials; 1 is retired). As of July 10, 1997.

Archbishops: 62. Diocesan, in U.S., 32 (includes 7 cardinals and military archbishop); retired, 21 (includes 1 cardinal); outside U.S., 9. As of July 10, 1997.

Bishops: 377. Diocesan, in U.S. (and Virgin Islands), 155; auxiliaries, 88; retired, 109; serving outside U.S., 25. As of July 10, 1997.

Priests: 47,223; decrease, 977. Diocesan, 31,480 (decrease, 467); religious order priests (does not include those assigned overseas), 15,743 (decrease, 510). There were 509 newly ordained priests, an increase of 4.

Permanent Deacons: 11,299; increase, 254.

Brothers: 6,235; decrease, 62.

Sisters: 86,355; decrease, 1,478.

Seminarians: 4,539. Diocesan seminarians, 3,084; religious order seminarians, 1,455.

Receptions into Church: 1,149,042. Includes 1,003,611 infant baptisms; 69,661 adult baptisms and 75,770 already baptized persons received into full communion with the Church.

First Communions: 816,821.

Confirmations: 570,252.

Marriages: 292,282.

Deaths: 485,629.

Parishes: 19,280.

Seminaries, Diocesan: 72.

Religious Seminaries: 121.

Colleges and Universities: 236. Students, 666,467.

High Schools: 1,244. Students, 628,114.

Elementary Schools: 7,006. Students 2,000,471.

Non-Residential Schools for Handicapped: 80. Students, 19,198.

Teachers: 161,304 (priests, 2,064; brothers, 1,155; scholastics, 40; sisters, 10,893; laity, 147,152).

Public School students in Religious Instruction Programs: 4,170,196. High school students, 785,743; elementary school students, 3,384,453.

Hospitals: 587; patients treated, 61,357,538.

Health Care Centers: 363; patients treated, 4,860,903.

Specialized Homes: 1,234; patients assisted, 944,032.

Residential Care of Children (Orphanages): 173; total assisted, 74,169.

Day Care and Extended Day Care Centers: 1,068; total assisted, 124,492.

Special Centers for Social Services: 2,008; assisted annually, 18,251,474.

CATHEDRALS IN THE UNITED STATES

A cathedral is the principal church in a diocese, the one in which the bishop has his seat (cathedra). He is the actual pastor, although many functions of the church, which usually serves a parish, are the responsibility of a priest serving as the rector. Because of the dignity of a cathedral, the dates of its dedication and its patronal feast are observed throughout a diocese.

The pope's cathedral, the Basilica of St. John Lateran, is the highest-ranking church in the world.

(Archdioceses are indicated by asterisk.)

Albany, N.Y.: Immaculate Conception.

Alexandria, La.: St. Francis Xavier.

Allentown, Pa.: St. Catherine of Siena.

Altoona-Johnstown, Pa.: Blessed Sacrament (Altoona); St. John Gualbert (Johnstown).

Amarillo, Tex.: St. Laurence.

Anchorage,* Alaska: Holy Family.

Arlington, Va: St. Thomas More.

Atlanta,* Ga.: Christ the King.

Austin, Tex.: St. Mary (Immaculate Conception).

Baker, Ore.: St. Francis de Sales.

Baltimore,* Md.: Mary Our Queen; Basilica of the National Shrine of the Assumption of the Blessed Virgin Mary (Co-Cathedral).

Baton Rouge, La.: St. Joseph.

Beaumont, Tex.: St. Anthony (of Padua).

Belleville, Ill.: St. Peter.

Biloxi, Miss.: Nativity of the Blessed Virgin Mary.

Birmingham, Ala.: St. Paul.

Bismarck, N.D.: Holy Spirit.

Boise, Ida.: St. John the Evangelist.

Boston,* Mass.: Holy Cross.

Bridgeport, Conn.: St. Augustine.

Brooklyn, N.Y.: St. James (Minor Basilica).

Brownsville, Tex.: Immaculate Conception.

Buffalo, N.Y.: St. Joseph.

Burlington, Vt.: Immaculate Conception.

Camden, N.J.: Immaculate Conception.

Charleston, S.C.: St. John the Baptist.

Charlotte, N.C.: St. Patrick.

Cheyenne, Wyo.: St. Mary.

Chicago,* Ill.: Holy Name (of Jesus).

Cincinnati,* Ohio: St. Peter in Chains.

Cleveland, Ohio: St. John the Evangelist.

Colorado Springs, Colo: St. Mary.

Columbus, Ohio: St. Joseph.

Corpus Christi, Tex.: Corpus Christi.

Covington, Ky.: Basilica of the Assumption.

Crookston, Minn.: Immaculate Conception.

Dallas, Tex.: Cathedral-Santuario de Guadalupe.

Davenport, Ia.: Sacred Heart.

Denver,* Colo.: Immaculate Conception (Minor Basilica).

Des Moines, Ia.: St. Ambrose.
Detroit,* Mich.: Most Blessed Sacrament.
Dodge City, Kans.: Sacred Heart.
Dubuque,* Ia.: St. Raphael.
Duluth, Minn.: Our Lady of the Rosary.
El Paso, Tex.: St. Patrick.
Erie, Pa.: St. Peter.
Evansville, Ind.: Most Holy Trinity (Pro-Cathedral).
Fairbanks, Alaska: Sacred Heart.
Fall River, Mass.: St. Mary of the Assumption.
Fargo, N.D.: St. Mary.
Fort Wayne-S. Bend, Ind.: Immaculate Conception (Fort Wayne); St. Matthew (South Bend).
Fort Worth, Tex.: St. Patrick.
Fresno, Calif.: St. John (the Baptist).
Gallup, N.M.: Sacred Heart.
Galveston-Houston, Tex.: St. Mary (Minor Basilica, Galveston); Sacred Heart Co-Cathedral (Houston).
Gary, Ind.: Holy Angels.
Gaylord, Mich.: St. Mary, Our Lady of Mt. Carmel.
Grand Island, Nebr.: Nativity of Blessed Virgin Mary.
Grand Rapids, Mich.: St. Andrew.
Great Falls-Billings, Mont.: St. Ann (Great Falls); St. Patrick Co-Cathedral (Billings).
Green Bay, Wis.: St. Francis Xavier.
Greensburg, Pa.: Blessed Sacrament.
Harrisburg, Pa.: St. Patrick.
Hartford,* Conn.: St. Joseph.
Helena, Mont.: St. Helena.
Honolulu, Hawaii: Our Lady of Peace; St. Theresa of the Child Jesus (Co-Cathedral).
Houma-Thibodaux, La.: St. Francis de Sales (Houma); St. Joseph Co-Cathedral (Thibodaux).
Indianapolis,* Ind.: Sts. Peter and Paul.
Jackson, Miss.: St. Peter.
Jefferson City, Mo.: St. Joseph.
Joliet, Ill.: St. Raymond Nonnatus.
Juneau, Alaska: Nativity of the Blessed Virgin Mary.
Kalamazoo, Mich.: St. Augustine.
Kansas City,* Kans.: St. Peter the Apostle.
Kansas City-St. Joseph, Mo.: Immaculate Conception (Kansas City); St. Joseph Co-Cathedral (St. Joseph).
Knoxville, Tenn.: Sacred Heart of Jesus.
La Crosse, Wis.: St. Joseph the Workman.
Lafayette, Ind.: St. Mary.
Lafayette, La.: St. John the Evangelist.
Lake Charles, La.: Immaculate Conception.
Lansing, Mich.: St. Mary.
Las Cruces, N. Mex.: Immaculate Heart of Mary.
Las Vegas, Nev.: Guardian Angel.
Lexington, Ky.: Christ the King.
Lincoln, Nebr.: Cathedral of the Risen Christ.
Little Rock, Ark.: St. Andrew.
Los Angeles,* Calif.: St. Vibiana (closed May 22, 1995, because of earthquake-related damage). Ground was broken in 1997 for new Cathedral of Our Lady of the Angels of Los Angeles.
Louisville,* Ky.: Assumption.
Lubbock, Tex.: Christ the King.
Madison, Wis.: St. Raphael.
Manchester, N.H.: St. Joseph.
Marquette, Mich.: St. Peter.
Memphis, Tenn.: Immaculate Conception.

Metuchen, N.J.: St. Francis (of Assisi).
Miami,* Fla.: St. Mary (Immaculate Conception).
Milwaukee,* Wis.: St. John.
Mobile,* Ala.: Immaculate Conception (Minor Basilica).
Monterey, Calif.: San Carlos Borromeo.
Nashville, Tenn.: Incarnation.
Newark,* N.J.: Sacred Heart (Minor Basilica).
New Orleans,* La.: St. Louis. (Minor Basilica)
Newton, Mass. (Melkite): Our Lady of the Annunciation (Boston).
New Ulm, Minn.: Holy Trinity.
New York,* N.Y.: St. Patrick.
Norwich, Conn.: St. Patrick.
Oakland, Calif.: St. Francis de Sales.
Ogdensburg, N.Y.: St. Mary (Immaculate Conception).
Oklahoma City,* Okla.: Our Lady of Perpetual Help.
Omaha,* Nebr.: St. Cecilia.
Orange, Calif.: Holy Family.
Orlando, Fla.: St. James.
Our Lady of Deliverance of Newark, New Jersey for Syrian Rite Catholics in the U.S. and Canada: Our Lady of Deliverance.
Our Lady of Lebanon of Los Angeles, Calif. (Maronite): Our Lady of Mt. Lebanon-St. Peter.
Owensboro, Ky.: St. Stephen.
Palm Beach, Fla.: St. Ignatius Loyola, Palm Beach Gardens.
Parma, Ohio (Byzantine): St. John the Baptist.
Passaic, N.J. (Byzantine): St. Michael.
Paterson, N.J.: St. John the Baptist.
Pensacola-Tallahassee, Fla.: Sacred Heart (Pensacola); Co-Cathedral of St. Thomas More (Tallahassee).
Peoria, Ill.: St. Mary.
Philadelphia,* Pa.: Sts. Peter and Paul (Minor Basilica).
Philadelphia,* Pa. (Byzantine): Immaculate Conception of Blessed Virgin Mary.
Phoenix, Ariz.: Sts. Simon and Jude.
Pittsburgh,* Pa. (Byzantine): St. John the Baptist, Munhall.
Pittsburgh, Pa.: St. Paul.
Portland, Me.: Immaculate Conception.
Portland,* Ore.: Immaculate Conception.
Providence, R.I.: Sts. Peter and Paul.
Pueblo, Colo.: Sacred Heart.
Raleigh, N.C.: Sacred Heart.
Rapid City, S.D.: Our Lady of Perpetual Help.
Reno, Nev.: St. Thomas Aquinas.
Richmond, Va.: Sacred Heart.
Rochester, N.Y.: Sacred Heart.
Rockford, Ill.: St. Peter.
Rockville Centre, N.Y.: St. Agnes.
Sacramento, Calif.: Blessed Sacrament.
Saginaw, Mich.: St. Mary.
St. Augustine, Fla.: St. Augustine (Minor Basilica).
St. Cloud, Minn.: St. Mary.
St. George's in Canton, Ohio (Byzantine, Romanian): St. George.
St. Josaphat in Parma, Oh. (Byzantine): St. Josaphat.
St. Louis,* Mo.: St. Louis.
St. Maron, Brooklyn, N.Y. (Maronite): Our Lady of Lebanon.

St. Nicholas in Chicago (Byzantine): St. Nicholas.
St. Paul and Minneapolis,* Minn.: St. Paul (St. Paul); Basilica of St. Mary Co-Cathedral (Minneapolis).
St. Petersburg, Fla.: St. Jude the Apostle.
St. Thomas the Apostle of Detroit (Chaldean): Our Lady of Chaldeans Cathedral (Mother of God Church), Southfield, Mich.
Salina, Kans.: Sacred Heart.
Salt Lake City, Utah: The Madeleine.
San Angelo, Tex.: Sacred Heart.
San Antonio,* Tex.: San Fernando.
San Bernardino, Calif: Our Lady of the Rosary.
San Diego, Calif.: St. Joseph.
San Francisco,* Calif.: St. Mary (Assumption).
San Jose, Calif.: St. Joseph (Minor Basilica); St. Patrick, Proto-Cathedral.
Santa Fe,* N.M.: San Francisco de Asis.
Santa Rosa, Calif.: St. Eugene.
Savannah, Ga.: St. John the Baptist.
Scranton, Pa.: St. Peter.
Seattle,* Wash.: St. James.
Shreveport, La.: St. John Berchmans.
Sioux City, Ia.: Epiphany.
Sioux Falls, S.D.: St. Joseph.
Spokane, Wash.: Our Lady of Lourdes.
Springfield, Ill.: Immaculate Conception.
Springfield, Mass.: St. Michael.
Springfield-Cape Girardeau, Mo.: St. Agnes

(Springfield): St. Mary (Cape Girardeau).
Stamford, Conn. (Byzantine): St. Vladimir.
Steubenville, Ohio: Holy Name.
Stockton, Calif: Annunciation.
Superior, Wis.: Christ the King.
Syracuse, N.Y.: Immaculate Conception.
Toledo, Ohio: Queen of the Most Holy Rosary.
Trenton, N.J.: St. Mary (Assumption).
Tucson, Ariz.: St. Augustine.
Tulsa, Okla.: Holy Family.
Tyler, Tex.: Immaculate Conception.
Van Nuys, Calif. (Byzantine): St. Mary (Patronage of the Mother of God), Van Nuys; St. Stephen's (Pro-Cathedral), Phoenix, Ariz.
Venice, Fla: Epiphany.
Victoria, Tex.: Our Lady of Victory.
Washington,* D.C.: St. Matthew.
Wheeling-Charleston, W. Va.: St. Joseph (Wheeling); Sacred Heart (Charleston).
Wichita, Kans.: Immaculate Conception.
Wilmington, Del.: St. Peter.
Winona, Minn.: Sacred Heart.
Worcester, Mass.: St. Paul.
Yakima, Wash.: St. Paul.
Youngstown, Ohio: St. Columba.
Apostolic Exarchate for Armenian Catholics in the U.S. and Canada: St. Ann (110 E. 12th St., New York, N.Y. 10003).

BASILICAS IN U.S. AND CANADA

Basilica is a title assigned to certain churches because of their antiquity, dignity, historical importance or significance as centers of worship. Major basilicas have the papal altar and holy door, which is opened at the beginning of a Jubilee Year; minor basilicas enjoy certain ceremonial privileges.

Among the major basilicas are the patriarchal basilicas of St. John Lateran, St. Peter, St. Paul Outside the Walls and St. Mary Major in Rome; St. Francis and St. Mary of the Angels in Assisi, Italy.

The patriarchal basilica of St. Lawrence, Rome, is a minor basilica.

The dates in the listings below indicate when the churches were designated as basilicas.

Minor Basilicas in U.S., Puerto Rico, Guam

Alabama: Mobile, Cathedral of the Immaculate Conception (Mar. 10, 1962).
Arizona: Phoenix, St. Mary's (Immaculate Conception) (Sept. 11, 1985).
California: San Francisco, Mission Dolores (Feb. 8, 1952); Carmel, Old Mission of San Carlos (Feb. 5, 1960); Alameda, St. Joseph (Jan. 21, 1972); San Diego, Mission San Diego de Alcala (Nov. 17, 1975); San Jose, St. Joseph (Jan. 28, 1997).
Colorado: Denver, Cathedral of the Immaculate Conception (Nov. 3, 1979).
District of Columbia: National Shrine of the Immaculate Conception (Oct. 12, 1990).
Florida: St. Augustine, Cathedral of St. Augustine (Dec. 4, 1976).
Illinois: Chicago, Our Lady of Sorrows (May 4, 1956), Queen of All Saints (Mar. 26, 1962).

Indiana: Vincennes, Old Cathedral (Mar. 14, 1970). Notre Dame, Parish Church of Most Sacred Heart, Univ. of Notre Dame (Nov. 23, 1991).
Iowa: Dyersville, St. Francis Xavier (May 11, 1956); Des Moines, St. John the Apostle (Oct. 4, 1989).
Kentucky: Trappist, Our Lady of Gethsemani (May 3, 1949); Covington, Cathedral of Assumption (Dec. 8, 1953).
Louisiana: New Orleans, St. Louis King of France (Dec. 9, 1964).
Maryland: Baltimore, Assumption of the Blessed Virgin Mary (Sept. 1, 1937; designated national shrine, 1993); Emmitsburg, Shrine of St. Elizabeth Ann Seton (Feb. 13, 1991).
Massachusetts: Roxbury, Perpetual Help ("Mission Church") (Sept. 8, 1954); Chicopee, St. Stanislaus (June 25, 1991).
Michigan: Grand Rapids, St. Adalbert (Aug. 22, 1979).
Minnesota: Minneapolis. St. Mary (Feb. 1, 1926).
Missouri: Conception, Basilica of Immaculate Conception (Sept. 14, 1940); St. Louis, St. Louis King of France (Jan. 27, 1961).
New Jersey: Newark, Cathedral Basilica of the Sacred Heart (Dec. 22, 1995).
New York: Brooklyn, Our Lady of Perpetual Help (Sept. 5, 1969), Cathedral-Basilica of St. James (June 22, 1982); Lackawanna, Our Lady of Victory (1926); Youngstown, Blessed Virgin Mary of the Rosary of Fatima (Oct. 7, 1975).
North Carolina: Asheville, St. Lawrence (Apr. 6, 1993; ceremonies, Sept. 5, 1993).
North Dakota: Jamestown, St. James (Oct. 26, 1988).
Ohio: Carey, Shrine of Our Lady of Consolation (Oct. 21, 1971).

Pennsylvania: Latrobe, St. Vincent Basilica, Benedictine Archabbey (Aug. 22, 1955); Conewago, Basilica of the Sacred Heart (June 30, 1962); Philadelphia, Sts. Peter and Paul (Sept. 27, 1976); Danville, Sts. Cyril and Methodius (chapel at the motherhouse of the Sisters of Sts. Cyril and Methodius) (June 30, 1989); Scranton, St. Ann's Monastery Shrine (Aug. 29, 1996).

Texas: Galveston, St. Mary Cathedral (Aug. 11, 1979).

Virginia: Norfolk, St. Mary of the Immaculate Conception (July 9, 1991).

Wisconsin: Milwaukee, St. Josaphat (Mar. 10, 1929).

Puerto Rico: San Juan, Cathedral of San Juan (Jan. 25, 1978).

Guam: Agana, Cathedral of Dulce Nombre de Maria (Sweet Name of Mary) (1985).

Minor Basilicas in Canada

Alberta: Edmonton, Cathedral Basilica of St. Joseph (Mar. 15, 1984).

Manitoba: St. Boniface, Cathedral Basilica of St. Boniface (June 10, 1949).

New Brunswick: Chatham, St. Michael the Archangel (Dec. 9, 1988).

Newfoundland: St. John's, Cathedral Basilica of St. John the Baptist.

Nova Scotia: Halifax, St. Mary's Basilica (June 14, 1950).

Ontario: Ottawa, Basilica of Notre Dame; Saint Patrick's Basilica (Mar. 17, 1995). London, St. Peter's Cathedral (Dec. 13, 1961).

Prince Edward Island: Charlottetown, Basilica of St. Dunstan.

Quebec: Sherbrooke, Cathedral Basilica of St. Michael (July 31, 1959). Montreal, Cathedral Basilica of Our Lady Queen of the World; St. Joseph of Mount Royal; Basilica of Notre Dame (Feb. 15, 1982); St. Patrick (Dec. 9, 1988). Cap-de-la-Madeleine, Basilica of Our Lady of the Cape (Aug. 15, 1964). Quebec, Basilica of Notre Dame; St. Anne de Beaupre, Basilica of St. Anne. Valleyfield, Cathedral Basilica of St. Cecilia (Feb. 9, 1991).

CHANCERY OFFICES OF U.S. ARCHDIOCESES AND DIOCESES

A chancery office, under this or another title, is the central administrative office of an archdiocese or diocese.

(Archdioceses are indicated by asterisk.)

Albany, NY: 40 N. Main Ave. 12203.

Alexandria, LA: P.O. Box 7417. 71306.

Allentown, PA: 202 N. 17th St., P.O. Box F. 18105.

Altoona-Johnstown, PA: 126 Logan Blvd., Hollidaysburg. 16648.

Amarillo, TX: 1800 N. Spring St., P.O. Box 5644. 79117.

Anchorage,* AK: 225 Cordova St., Anchorage 99501.

Arlington, VA: Suite 704, 200 N. Glebe Rd. 22203.

Atlanta,* GA: Catholic Center, 680 W. Peachtree St. N.W. 30308.

Austin, TX: 1600 N. Congress Ave., P.O. Box 13327. 78711.

Baker, OR: P.O. Box 5999, Bend 97708.

Baltimore,* MD: 320 Cathedral St. 21201.

Baton Rouge, LA: Catholic Life Center, 1600 S. Acadian Thruway, P.O. Box 2028. 70821.

Beaumont, TX: 703 Archie St., P.O. Box 3948. 77704.

Belleville, IL: 222 S. Third St., 62220.

Biloxi, MS: P.O. Box 1189. 39533.

Birmingham, AL: P.O. Box 12047. 35202.

Bismarck, ND: 420 Raymond St., Box 1575. 58502.

Boise, ID: 303 Federal Way. 83705.

Boston,* MA: 2121 Commonwealth Ave., Brighton. 02135.

Bridgeport, CT: The Catholic Center, 238 Jewett Ave. 06606.

Brooklyn, NY: 75 Greene Ave., P.O. Box C. 11202.

Brownsville, TX: P.O. Box 2279. 78522.

Buffalo, NY: 795 Main St. 14203.

Burlington, VT: 351 North Ave. 05401.

Camden, NJ: 1845 Haddon Ave., P.O. Box 709, 08101.

Charleston, SC: 119 Broad St., P.O. Box 818. 29402.

Charlotte, NC: P.O. Box 36776. 28236.

Cheyenne, WY: Box 426. 82003.

Chicago,* IL: P.O. Box 1979. 60690.

Cincinnati,* OH: 100 E. 8th St. 45202.

Cleveland, OH: Chancery Bldg., 1027 Superior Ave. 44114.

Colorado Springs, CO: 29 W. Kiowa. 80903.

Columbus, OH: 198 E. Broad St. 43215.

Corpus Christi, TX: 620 Lipan St. P.O. Box 2620. 78403.

Covington, KY: P.O. Box 18548, Erlanger 41018.

Crookston, MN: 1200 Memorial Dr., P.O. Box 610. 56716.

Dallas, TX: 3725 Blackburn, P.O. Box 190507. 75219.

Davenport, IA: St. Vincent Center, 2706 N. Gaines St. 52804.

Denver,* CO: 200 Josephine St. 80206.

Des Moines, IA: P.O. Box 1816. 50306.

Detroit,* MI: 1234 Washington Blvd. 48226.

Dodge City, KS: 910 Central Ave., P.O. Box 137. 67801.

Dubuque,* IA: P.O. Box 479. 52004.

Duluth, MN: 2830 E. 4th St. 55812.

El Paso, TX: 499 St. Matthews St. 79907.

Erie, PA: P.O. Box 10397. 16514.

Evansville, IN: P.O. Box 4169. 47724.

Fairbanks, AK: 1316 Peger Rd. 99709.

Fall River, MA: Box 2577. 02722.

Fargo, ND: 1310 Broadway, Box 1750. 58107.

Fort Wayne-South Bend, IN: P.O. Box 390, Fort Wayne. 46801.

Fort Worth, TX: 800 W. Loop 820 South. 76108.

Fresno, CA: 1550 N. Fresno St. 93703.

Gallup, NM: 711 S. Puerco Dr., P.O. Box 1338. 87305.

Galveston-Houston, TX: P.O. Box 907, Houston. 77001.

Gary, IN: 9292 Broadway, Merrillville. 46410.

Gaylord, MI: 1665 W. M-32. 49735.

Grand Island, NE: 311 W. 17th St., P.O. Box 996. 68802.

Grand Rapids, MI: 660 Burton St., S.E. 49507.

Great Falls-Billings, MT: P.O. Box 1399, Great Falls. 59403.

Green Bay, WI: P.O. Box 23066. 54305.

Greensburg, PA: 723 E. Pittsburgh St. 15601.

Harrisburg, PA: P.O. Box 2153. 17105.

Hartford,* CT: 134 Farmington Ave. 06105.

Helena, MT: 515 North Ewing, P.O. Box 1729. 59624.

Honolulu, HI: 1184 Bishop St. 96813.

Houma-Thibodaux, LA: P.O. Box 9077, Houma, La. 70361.

Indianapolis,* IN: 1400 N. Meridian St., P.O. Box 1410. 46206.

Jackson, MS: 237 E. Amite St., P.O. Box 2248. 39225.

Jefferson City, MO: 605 Clark Ave., P.O. Box 417. 65101.

Joliet, IL: 425 Summit St. 60435.

Juneau, AK: 419 6th St., No. 200. 99801.

Kalamazoo, MI: 215 N. Westnedge Ave. 49007.

Kansas City,* KS: 12615 Parallel Pkwy. 66109.

Kansas City-St. Joseph, MO: P.O. Box 419037, Kansas City. 64141.

Knoxville, TN: 805 Northshore Dr., P.O. Box 11127. 37939.

La Crosse, WI: 3710 East Ave. S., Box 4004. 54602.

Lafayette in Indiana: P.O. Box 260. 47902.

Lafayette, LA: 1408 Carmel Ave. 70501.

Lake Charles, LA: P.O. Box 3223. 70602.

Lansing, MI: 300 W. Ottawa St.. 48933.

Las Cruces, NM: 1280 Med Park Dr., 88005.

Las Vegas, NV: P.O. Box 18316. 89114.

Lexington, KY: P.O. Box 12350. 40582.

Lincoln, NE: P.O. Box 80328. 68501.

Little Rock, AR: 2415 N. Tyler St. P.O. Box 7239. 72217.

Los Angeles,* CA: 3424 Wilshire Blvd. 90010.

Louisville,* Ky.: 212 E. College St., P.O. Box 1073. 40201.

Lubbock, TX: P.O. Box 98700. 79499.

Madison, WI: 15 E. Wilson St., P.O. Box 111. 53701.

Manchester, NH: 153 Ash St., P.O. Box 310. 03105.

Marquette, MI: 444 S. Fourth St., P.O. Box 550. 49855.

Memphis, TN: Catholic Center, P.O. Box 341669. 38184.

Metuchen, NJ: P.O. Box 191. 08840.

Miami,* FL: 9401 Biscayne Blvd., Miami Shores. 33138.

Milwaukee,* WI: P.O. Box 07912. 53207.

Mobile,* AL: 400 Government St., P.O. Box 1966. 36633.

Monterey, CA: P.O. Box 2048. 93942.

Nashville, TN: 2400 21st Ave. S. 37212.

Newark,* NJ: P.O. Box 9500. 07104.

New Orleans,* LA: 7887 Walmsley Ave. 70125.

Newton, MA (Melkite): 19 Dartmouth St., W. Newton. 02165.

New Ulm, MN: 1400 Sixth St. N., 56073.

New York,* NY: 1011 First Ave. 10022.

Norwich, CT: 201 Broadway, P.O. Box 587. 06360.

Oakland, CA: 2900 Lakeshore Ave. 94610.

Ogdensburg, NY: 622 Washington St., P.O. Box 369. 13669.

Oklahoma City,* OK: P.O. Box 32180. 73123.

Omaha,* NE: 100 N. 62nd St. 68132.

Orange, CA: 2811 E. Villa Real Dr., P.O. Box 14195. 92613.

Orlando, FL: P.O. Box 1800. 32802.

Our Lady of Deliverance of Newark, for Syrian rite Catholics of the U.S. and Canada: P.O. Box 8366, Union City, NJ 07087.

Our Lady of Lebanon of Los Angeles, CA (Maronite): P.O. Box 16397, Beverly Hills 90209.

Owensboro, KY: 600 Locust St. 42301.

Palm Beach, FL: P.O. Box 109650, Palm Beach Gardens 33410.

Parma, OH (Byzantine): 1900 Carlton Rd. 44134.

Passaic, NJ (Byzantine): 445 Lackawanna Ave., W. Paterson. 07424.

Paterson, NJ: 777 Valley Rd., Clifton. 07013.

Pensacola-Tallahassee, FL: P.O. Drawer 17329, Pensacola. 32522.

Peoria, IL: 607 N.E. Madison Ave., P.O. Box 1406. 61655.

Philadelphia,* PA: 222 N. 17th St. 19103.

Philadelphia,* PA (Byzantine): 827 N. Franklin St. 19123.

Phoenix, AZ: 400 E. Monroe St. 85004.

Pittsburgh,* PA (Byzantine): 66 Riverview Ave. 15214.

Pittsburgh, PA: 111 Blvd. of the Allies. 15222.

Portland, ME: 510 Ocean Ave., P.O. Box 11559. 04104.

Portland in Oregon*: 2838 E. Burnside St., Portland, OR 97214.

Providence, RI: One Cathedral Sq. 02903.

Pueblo, CO: 1001 N. Grand Ave. 81003.

Raleigh, NC: 300 Cardinal Gibbons Dr. 27606.

Rapid City, SD: 606 Cathedral Dr., P.O. Box 678. 57709.

Reno, NV: P.O. Box 1211. 89504.

Richmond, VA: 811 Cathedral Pl., 23220.

Rochester, NY: 1150 Buffalo Rd. 14624.

Rockford, IL: 1245 N. Court St., P.O. Box 7044, 61126.

Rockville Centre, NY: 50 N. Park Ave. 11570.

Sacramento, CA: 2110 Broadway. 95818.

Saginaw, MI: 5800 Weiss St. 48603.

St. Augustine, FL: P.O. Box 24000, Jacksonville, FL 32241.

St. Cloud, MN: P.O. Box 1248. 56302.

St. George's in Canton, OH (Byzantine, Romanian): 1121 44th St. N.E., Canton. 44714.

St. Josaphat in Parma, OH (Byzantine): P.O. Box 347180, Parma. 44134.

St. Louis,* MO: 4445 Lindell Blvd. 63108.

St. Maron of Brooklyn (Maronite): P.O. Box 360, 294 Howard Ave., Staten Island, NY 10301.

St. Nicholas in Chicago (Byzantine): 2245 W. Rice St. 60622.

St. Paul and Minneapolis,* MN: 226 Summit Ave., St. Paul. 55102.

St. Petersburg, FL: P.O. Box 40200. 33743.

St. Thomas the Apostle of Detroit (Chaldean): 25603 Berg Rd., Southfield, MI 48034.

Salina, KS: P.O. Box 980. 67402.

Salt Lake City, UT: 27 C St. 84103.

San Angelo, TX: P.O. Box 1829. 76902.

San Antonio,* TX: P.O. Box 28410. 78228.

San Bernardino, CA: 1201 E. Highland Ave. 92404.

San Diego, CA: P.O. Box 85728. 92186.
San Francisco,* CA: 445 Church St. 94114.
San Jose, CA: 900 Lafayette St., Suite 301, Santa Clara 95050.
Santa Fe,* NM: 4000 St. Joseph's Pl. N.W., Albuquerque. 87120.
Santa Rosa, CA: P.O. Box 1297. 95402.
Savannah, GA: 601 E. Liberty St. 31401.
Scranton, PA: 300 Wyoming Ave. 18503.
Seattle,* WA: 910 Marion St. 98104.
Shreveport, LA: 2500 Line Ave. 71104.
Sioux City, IA: P.O. Box 3379. 51102.
Sioux Falls, SD: 3100 W. 41st St. 57105.
Spokane, WA: W. 1023 Riverside Ave., P.O. Box 1453. 99210.
Springfield, IL: P.O. Box 3187. 62708.
Springfield, MA: P.O. Box 1730. 01101.
Springfield-Cape Girardeau, MO: 601 S. Jefferson, Springfield. 65806.
Stamford, CT (Byzantine): 14 Peveril Rd. 06902.
Steubenville, OH: P.O. Box 969. 43952.
Stockton, CA: P.O. Box 4237. 95204.
Superior, WI: 1201 Hughitt Ave., Box 969. 54880.

Syracuse, NY: P.O. Box 511. 13201.
Toledo, OH: P.O. Box 985. 43697.
Trenton, NJ: P.O. Box 5309. 08638.
Tucson, AZ: 192 S. Stone Ave., Box 31. 85702.
Tulsa, OK: P.O. Box 2009. 74101.
Tyler, TX: 1015 E.S.E. Loop 323. 75701.
Van Nuys, CA (Byzantine): 8131 N. 16th St., Phoenix, AZ 85020.
Venice, FL: P.O. Box 2006. 34284.
Victoria, TX: P.O. Box 4070. 77903.
Washington,* DC: P.O. Box 29260. 20017.
Wheeling-Charleston, WV: 1300 Byron St., P.O. Box 230, Wheeling. 26003.
Wichita, KS: 424 N. Broadway. 67202.
Wilmington, DE: P.O. Box 2030. 19899.
Winona, MN: P.O. Box 588. 55987.
Worcester, MA: 49 Elm St. 01609.
Yakima, WA: 5301-A Tieton Dr. 98908.
Youngstown, OH: 144 W. Wood St. 44503.
Military Archdiocese: 962 Wayne Ave., Silver Spring, MD 20910.
Armenian Apostolic Exarchate for the United States and Canada: 110 E. 12th St., New York, NY 10003.

NATIONAL CATHOLIC CONFERENCES

The two conferences described below are related in membership and directive control but distinct in nature, purpose and function.

The National Conference of Catholic Bishops (NCCB) is a strictly ecclesiastical body in and through which the bishops of the United States act together, officially and with authority as pastors of the Church. It is the sponsoring organization of the United States Catholic Conference.

The United States Catholic Conference (USCC) is a civil corporation and operational secretariat in and through which the bishops, together with other members of the Church, act on a wider scale for the good of the Church and society. It is sponsored by the National Conference of Catholic Bishops.

The principal officers of both conferences are: Bishop Anthony M. Pilla, president; Bishop Joseph A. Fiorenza, vice president; Bishop Robert J. Banks, treasurer; Archbishop Harry J. Flynn, secretary.

The membership of the Administrative Committee of the NCCB and the Administrative Board of the USCC is identical.

Headquarters of both conferences are located at 3211 Fourth St. N.E., Washington, D.C. 20017.

CONFERENCE OF CATHOLIC BISHOPS

The National Conference of Catholic Bishops (NCCB), established by action of the U.S. hierarchy Nov. 14, 1966, is a strictly ecclesiastical body with defined juridical authority over the Church in this country. It was set up with the approval of the Holy See and in line with directives from the Second Vatican Council. Its constitution was formally ratified during the November, 1967, meeting of the U.S. hierarchy.

The NCCB is a development from the Annual Meeting of the Bishops of the United States, whose pastoral character was originally approved by Pope Benedict XV Apr. 10, 1919.

The address of the Conference is 3211 Fourth St. N.E., Washington, D.C. 20017. Rev. Msgr. Dennis M. Schnurr is general secretary.

Pastoral Council

The conference, one of many similar territorial conferences envisioned in the conciliar Decree on the Pastoral Office of Bishops in the Church (No. 38), is "a council in which the bishops of a given nation or territory (in this case, the United States) jointly exercise their pastoral office to promote the greater good which the Church offers mankind, especially through the forms and methods of the apostolate fittingly adapted to the circumstances of the age."

Its decisions, "provided they have been approved legitimately and by the votes of at least two-thirds of the prelates who have a deliberative vote in the conference, and have been recognized by the Apostolic See, are to have juridically binding force only in those cases prescribed by the common law or determined by a special mandate of the Apostolic See, given either spontaneously or in response to a petition of the conference itself."

All bishops who serve the Church in the U.S., its territories and possessions, have membership and voting rights in the NCCB. Retired bishops cannot be elected to conference offices nor can they vote on matters which by law are binding by two-thirds of the membership. Only diocesan bishops can vote on diocesan quotas, assessments or special collections.

Officers, Committees

The conference operates through a number of bishops' committees with functions in specific areas of work and concern. Their basic assignments are to prepare materials on the basis of which the bishops, assembled as a conference, make decisions, and to put suitable action plans into effect.

The principal officers are: Bishop Anthony M. Pilla, president; Bishop Joseph A. Fiorenza, vice president; Bishop Robert J. Banks, treasurer; Archbishop Harry J. Flynn, secretary.

These officers, with several other bishops, hold positions on executive-level committees _ Executive Committee, the Committee on Budget and Finance, the Committee on Personnel, and the Committee on Priorities and Plans. They also, with other bishops, serve on the NCCB Administrative Committee.

The standing committees and their chairmen (Archbishops and Bishops) are as follows.

African American Catholics, George V. Murry, S.J.

American Board of Catholic Missions, Victor H. Balke.

American College, Louvain, Frank J. Rodimer.

Bishops' Welfare Emergency Relief, Anthony M. Pilla.

Boundaries of Dioceses and Provinces, Anthony M. Pilla.

Canonical Affairs, David E. Fellhauer.

Church in Latin America, Raymundo J. Pena

Diaconate, Edward U. Kmiec.

Doctrine, Daniel E. Pilarczyk.

Ecumenical and Interreligious Affairs, Alexander J. Brunett..

Evangelization, Michael J. Sheehan.

Hispanic Affairs, Gerald R. Barnes.

Laity, G. Patrick Ziemann.

Liturgy, Jerome G. Hanus, O.S.B.

Marriage and Family Life, Thomas J. O'Brien.

Migration, John S. Cummins.

Missions, Sean P. O'Malley., O.F.M. Cap.

North American College, Rome, Cardinal James Hickey.

Pastoral Practices, Joseph L. Imesch.

Priestly Formation, John C. Favalora.

Priestly Life and Ministry, Robert F. Morneau.

Pro-Life Activities, Cardinal Bernard F. Law.

Relationship between Eastern and Latin Catholic Churches, Andrew Pataki.

Religious Life and Ministry, Joseph A. Galante.

Science and Human Values, Edward M. Egan.

Selection of Bishops, Anthony M. Pilla.

Vocations, Paul S. Loverde.

Women in Society and in the Church, John C. Dunne.

Ad hoc committees and their chairmen are as follows.

1999 Special Assembly, Robert N. Lynch.

Aid to the Church in Central and Eastern Europe, Cardinal Adam Maida.

Bishops Life and Ministry, William S. Skylstad.

Catechism of the Catholic Church, Daniel M. Buechlein.

Catholic Charismatic Renewal, Sam G. Jacobs.

Economic Concerns of the Holy See, James P. Keleher.

Forum on the Principle of Translation, Jerome G. Hanus, O.S.B.

Health Care Issues and the Church, Donald W. Wuerl.

Liaison Committee with CNS (Catholic News Service), Vacant.

Mission and Structure of the NCCB, Vacant.

Native American Catholics, Donald E. Pelotte, S.S.S.

Nomination of Conference Officers, Dale C. Melczek.

Review of Scripture Translations, Richard J. Sklba.

Sexual Abuse, John F. Kinney.

Shrines, James P. Keleher.

Stewardship, vacant.

UNITED STATES CATHOLIC CONFERENCE

The United States Catholic Conference, Inc. (USCC), is the operational secretariat and service agency of the National Conference of Catholic Bishops for carrying out the civic-religious work of the Church in this country. It is a civil corporation related to the NCCB in membership and directive control but distinct from it in purpose and function.

The address of the Conference is 3211 Fourth St. N.E., Washington, D.C. 20017. Rev. Msgr. Dennis M. Schnurr is general secretary.

Service Secretariat

The USCC, as of Jan. 1, 1967, took over the general organization and operations of the former National Catholic Welfare Conference, Inc., whose origins dated back to the National Catholic War Council of 1917. The council underwent some change after World War I and was established on a permanent basis Sept. 24, 1919, as the National Catholic Welfare Council to serve as a central agency for organizing and coordinating the efforts of U.S. Catholics in carrying out the social mission of the Church in this country. In 1923, its name was changed to National Catholic Welfare Conference, Inc., and clarification was made of its nature as a service agency of the bishops and the Church rather than as a conference of bishops with real juridical authority in ecclesiastical affairs.

The *Official Catholic Directory* states that the USCC assists "the bishops in their service to the Church in this country by uniting the people of God where voluntary collective action on a broad interdiocesan level is needed. The USCC provides an organizational structure and the resources needed to insure coordination, cooperation, and assistance in the public, educational and social concerns of the Church at the national, regional, state and, as appropriate, diocesan levels."

Officers, Departments

The principal officers of the USCC are: Bishop Anthony M. Pilla, president; Bishop Joseph A. Fiorenza, vice president; Bishop Robert J. Banks, treasurer; Archbishop Harry J. Flynn, secretary. These officers, with several other bishops, hold positions on executive-level committees — the Executive Committee; the Committee on Priorities and Plans; the Committee on Budget and Finance; the Committee on Personnel. They also serve on the Administrative Board.

The Executive Committee, organized in 1969, is authorized to handle matters of urgency between meetings of the Administrative Board and the general conference, to coordinate items for the agenda of general meetings, and to speak in the name of the USCC.

The major departments are: Campaign for Human Development; Communications; Education; Social Development and World Peace. A National Advisory Council of bishops, priests, men and women religious, lay men and women advises the Administrative Board on overall plans and operations of the USCC.

The administrative general secretariat, in addition to other duties, supervises staff-service offices of Finance, General Counsel, Government Liaison, Priorities and Plans, Management Information Services, Human Resources, General Services, Research.

Most of the organizations and associations affiliated with the USCC are covered in separate Almanac entries.

MEETINGS OF THE U.S. BISHOPS

NOVEMBER 11 to 14, 1996

Presidential Address: Bishop-priest relationships and various matters of concern to priests were subjects of Bishop Anthony Pilla's presidential address. He said: "My message to our priests today is one of support, of confidence in them, of respect for them in their ministry and of the love that gathers all together." He mentioned three concerns of priests, regarding the shortage of priests, the challenge of priestly leadership and priestly life in general. He said bishops should ask themselves about the extent to which they empower priests in their ministry, adding that "priests, in turn, should ask themselves about the extent to which they truly empower us bishops." Also, "Do we tell them they are our closest collaborators and then place a level of bureaucracy between them and us?" Regarding clerical celibacy, he said: "There is little attempt by the media or others to understand the witness of celibacy, and its special charism often takes second place to a malign pleasure at instances of its violation."

Pro-Nuncio's Address: Archbishop Agostino Cacciavilllan addressed the bishops Nov. 11, calling their attention to a number of Vatican concerns, including use of the Catechism of the Catholic Church, vocations to the priesthood and religious life, preparations for the Jubilee Year 2000 and the forthcoming Special Assembly of the Synod of Bishops for America.

Items of Business

The bishops acted on the following subjects.

Budget: Ratified a $43.4 million budget for 1997.

Communion Guidelines: Approved the text of guidelines for the reception of the Eucharist, for use in missalettes.

Economic Life: Approved "A Catholic Framework for Economic Life," a 110-point ethical framework for Catholics to use as "principles for reflection, criteria for judgment and directions for action.

Education: Approved a document entitled "Ex Corde Ecclesiae:"An Application to the United States" of higher education norms contained in an apostolic constitution of the same name.

Elections: Elected Bishop Robert J. Banks of Green Bay as conference treasurer, numerous committee heads, and 15 representatives to the future special assembly of the Synod of Bishops for the Americas.

Funerals: Approved proposed adaptations in funeral rites when cremated remains are present.

Liturgy: Approved the final two segments of the general Sacramentary as proposed for use in English-speaking countries, if ratified by the Vatican.

Mass on TV: Approved norms for televised Masses, with preference for "live" celebration over taped broadcasts.

Millennium: Approved funding in the amount of $1 million for the National Office for the Third Millennium from 1997 to 2000.

Reports: Received numerous reports, especially regarding efforts against partial-birth abortions and assisted suicide; authorized a statement by Bishop Pilla affirming the bishops' solidarity with all who might be threatened by assisted suicide; received a report on three-and-a-half years of work by their Ad Hoc Committee on Sexual Abuse.

Taped Confession: Expressed outrage, through a statement by Bishop Pilla, at the taping of a prisoner's sacramental confession in Oregon.

Young Adults: Approved "Sons and Daughters of the Light: A Pastoral Plan for Ministry with Young Adults."

Other Actions: The bishops paid tribute to Cardinal Joseph L. Bernardin, who died on the last day of the meeting. They discussed but did not vote on a series of proposals to restructure the National Conference of Catholic Bishops and the United States Catholic Conference.

JUNE 19 to 21, 1997

More than 230 bishops attended the meeting in Kansas City, Mo. Action was taken on the following, as well as additional, subjects.

Communications: Adopted unanimously a "Pastoral Plan for Church Communications, setting key goals and directions for church engagement with the media.

Conference Restructuring: Took the first real steps toward restructuring the National Conference of Catholic Bishops and the United States Catholic Conference into a single conference, and decided that in the single conference only bishops would be allowed to be committee members. (Non-bishops would be permitted consultative or similar status.)

Home Missions: A proposal for a new collection for home missions on the last Sunday of April each year was debated; adoption was approved on completion of voting by mail.

Liturgy: Approved of all but one of some 3,000 prayers for a new Sacramentary, and debated on acceptance of a compromise text of a new English-language Lectionary for the United States. Approval was voted by mail.

McGivney: Consented unanimously to the plan of the Archdiocese of Hartford to initiate the cause for the canonization of Father Michael McGivney, parish priest and founder of the Knights of Columbus.

Youth Ministry: Approved unanimously a statement entitled "Renewing the Vision -- A Framework for Catholic Youth Ministry," on the essential elements and goals of youth ministry.

The bishops also heard oral reports on (1) a review of catechetical texts in use in the U.S. since publication of the *Catechism of the Catholic Church* and

(2) a survey of the views of active Catholic youths regarding vocations to the priesthood and religious life.

Archbishop Agostino Cacciavillan, papal pro-nuncio to the U.S., during comment June 19, spoke briefly about the sensitive subject of differences between Vatican norms and academic standards in Catholic colleges and universities.

STATE CATHOLIC CONFERENCES

These conferences are agencies of bishops and dioceses in the various states. Their general purposes are to develop and sponsor cooperative programs designed to cope with pastoral and common-welfare needs, and to represent the dioceses before governmental bodies, the public, and in private sectors. Their membership consists of representatives from the dioceses in the states— bishops, clergy and lay persons in various capacities.

The National Association of State Catholic Conference Directors maintains liaison with the general secretariat of the United States Catholic Conference. President: Robert J. Castagna, executive director of Oregon Catholic Conference.

Arizona Catholic Conference, 400 E. Monroe St., Phoenix, AZ 85004; exec. dir., Rev. Msgr. Edward J. Ryle.

California Catholic Conference, 1010 11th St., Suite 200, Sacramento, CA 95814; exec. dir., Edward Dolejsi..

Colorado Catholic Conference, 200 Josephine St., Denver, CO 80206; exec. dir., James P. Tatten.

Connecticut Catholic Conference, 134 Farmington Ave., Hartford, CT 06105; exec. dir., Marie T. Hilliard.

District of Columbia Catholic Conference, 1221 Massachusetts Ave. NW, Washington, DC 20005; exec. dir., Ronald G. Jackson.

Florida Catholic Conference, P.O. Box 1638, Tallahassee, FL 32302; exec. dir., D. Michael McCarron.

Georgia Catholic Conference, Office Bldg., 3200 Deans Bridge Rd., Augusta, GA 30906; exec. dir., Cheatham E. Hodges, Jr.

Hawaii Catholic Conference, St. Stephen Diocesan Center, 6301 Pali Hwy., Kaneohe, Hawaii 96744; exec. dir., Rev. Marc R. Alexander.

Illinois, Catholic Conference of, 500 North Clark St., Chicago, IL 60610; 200 Broadway, Springfield, Ill. 62701; exec. dir., Doug Delaney.

Indiana Catholic Conference, 1400 N. Meridian St., P.O. Box 1410, Indianapolis, IN 46206; exec. dir., M. Desmond Ryan.

Iowa Catholic Conference, 505 Fifth Ave., Suite No. 818, Des Moines, IA 50309; exec. dir., Timothy McCarthy.

Kansas Catholic Conference, 6301 Antioch, Merriam, KS 66202; exec. dir., Robert Runnels, Jr.

Kentucky, Catholic Conference of, 1042 Burlington Lane, Frankfort, KY 40601; exec. dir., Jane J. Chiles.

Louisiana Catholic Conference, 3423 Hundred Oaks, Baton Rouge, LA 70808; exec. dir., Kirby J. Ducote.

Maryland Catholic Conference, 188 Duke of Gloucester St., Annapolis, MD 21401; exec. dir., Richard J. Dowling.

Massachusetts Catholic Conference, 55 Franklin St., Boston, MA 02110; exec. dir., Gerald D. D'Avolio, Esq.

Michigan Catholic Conference, 505 N. Capitol Ave., Lansing, MI 48933; president and CEO, Sr. Monica Kostielney, R.S.M.

Minnesota Catholic Conference, 475 University Ave. W., St. Paul, MN 55103; exec. dir., Rev. David F. McCauley.

Missouri Catholic Conference, P.O. Box 1022, 600 Clark Ave., Jefferson City, MO 65102; exec. dir., Louis C. DeFeo, Jr.

Montana Catholic Conference, P.O. Box 1708, Helena, MT 59624; exec. dir., Sharon Hoff.

Nebraska Catholic Conference, 215 Centennial Mall South, Suite 410, Lincoln, NE 68508; exec. dir., James R. Cunningham.

New Jersey Catholic Conference, 211 N. Warren St., Trenton, NJ 08618; exec. dir., William F. Bolan, Jr., J.D.

New Mexico Catholic Conference, 514 Marble Ave. N.W., Albuquerque, NM 87107; dir., Juan B. Montoya.

New York State Catholic Conference, 465 State St., Albany, NY 12203; exec. dir., John M. Kerry.

North Dakota Catholic Conference, 227 West Broadway Suite No. 2, Bismarck, ND 58501; exec. dir., Christopher T. Dodson.

Ohio, Catholic Conference of, 35 E. Long St., Suite 201, Columbus, OH 43215; exec. dir., Timothy V. Luckhaupt.

Oregon Catholic Conference, 2838 E. Burnside, Portland, OR 97214; exec. dir., Robert J. Castagna.

Pennsylvania Catholic Conference, 223 North St., Box 2835, Harrisburg, PA 17105.; exec. Dir., Robert J. O'Hara, Jr.

Texas Catholic Conference, 1625 Rutherford Lane, Bldg. D, Austin, TX 78754; exec. dir., Bro. Richard Daly, C.S.C.

Washington State Catholic Conference, 419 Occidental Ave. S, Suite 608, Seattle, WA 98104; exec. dir., vacant.

West Virginia State Catholic Conference, P.O. Box 230, Wheeling, WV 26003; dir., Rev. John R. Gallagher.

Wisconsin Catholic Conference, 30 W. Mifflin St., Suite 302, Madison, WI 53703; exec. dir., John A. Huebscher.

Dioceses with Interstate Lines

Diocesan lines usually fall within a single state and in some cases include a whole state.

The following dioceses, with their statistics as reported in tables throughout the Almanac, are exceptions.

Norwich, Conn., includes Fisher's Island, N.Y.

Wilmington, Del., includes all of Delaware and nine counties of Maryland.

Washington, D.C., includes five counties of Maryland.

Gallup, N.M., has jurisdiction over several counties of Arizona.

Cheyenne, Wyo., includes all of Yellowstone National Park.

BIOGRAPHIES OF AMERICAN BISHOPS _____

(Sources: Almanac survey, *The Official Catholic Directory, Annuario Pontificio*, Catholic News Service. As of Aug. 20, 1997. For former bishops of the U.S., see "American Bishops of the Past," elsewhere in this section.)

Information includes: date and place of birth; educational institutions attended; date of ordination to the priesthood with, where applicable, name of archdiocese (*) or diocese in parentheses; date of episcopal ordination; episcopal appointments; date of resignation/retirement.

A

Abramowicz, Alfred L.: b. Jan. 27, 1919, Chicago, Ill.; educ. St. Mary of the Lake Seminary (Mundelein, Ill.), Gregorian Univ. (Rome); ord. priest (Chicago*) May 1, 1943; ord. titular bishop of Paestum and auxiliary bishop of Chicago, June 13, 1968; retired Jan. 24, 1995.

Adamec, Joseph V.: b. Aug. 13, 1935, Bannister, Mich.; educ. Michigan State Univ. (East Lansing), Nepomucene College and Lateran Univ. (Rome); ord. priest (for Nitra diocese, Slovakia), July 3, 1960; incardinated in Saginaw diocese; ord. bishop of Altoona-Johnstown, May 20, 1987.

Adams, Edward J.: b. Aug. 24, 1944. Philadelphia, Pa.; educ. St. Charles Borromeo Seminary (Philadelphia), Pontifical Ecclesiastical Academy (Rome); ord. priest (Philadelphia*), May 16, 1970; in Vatican diplomatic service from 1976; ord. titular archbishop of Scala Oct. 23, 1996; papal nuncio to Bangladesh

Ahern, Patrick V.: b. Mar. 8, 1919, New York, N.Y.; educ. Manhattan College and Cathedral College (New York City), St. Joseph's Seminary (Yonkers, N.Y.), St. Louis Univ. (St. Louis, Mo.), Notre Dame Univ. (Notre Dame, Ind.); ord. priest (New York*) Jan. 27, 1945; ord. titular bishop of Naiera and auxiliary bishop of New York, Mar. 19, 1970; retired Apr. 26, 1994.

Allué, Emilio S., S.D.B.: b. Feb. 18, 1935, Huesca, Spain; educ. Salesain schools (Huesca, Spain) Don Bosco College/Seminary (Newton, N.J.); Salesian Pontifical Univ. (Rome), Fordham Univ. (New York); ord. priest Dec. 22, 1966, in Rome; ord. titular bishop of Croe and auxiliary bishop of Boston, Sept. 17, 1996.

Anderson, Moses B., S.S.E.: b. Sept. 9, 1928, Selma, Ala.; educ. St. Michael's College (Winooski, Vt.), St. Edmund Seminary (Burlington, Vt.), Univ. of Legon (Ghana); ord. priest May 30, 1958; ord. titular bishop of Vatarba and auxiliary bishop of Detroit, Jan. 27, 1983.

Angell, Kenneth A.: b. Aug. 3, 1930, Providence, R.I.; educ. St. Mary's Seminary (Baltimore, Md.); ord. priest (Providence) May 26, 1956; ord. titular bishop of Septimunicia and auxiliary bishop of Providence, R.I., Oct. 7, 1974; bishop of Burlington, Oct. 6, 1992; installed Nov. 9, 1992.

Apuron, Anthony Sablan, O.F.M. Cap.: b. Nov. 1, 1945, Agana, Guam; educ. St. Anthony College and Capuchin Seminary (Hudson, N.H.), Capuchin Seminary (Garrison, N.Y.), Maryknoll Seminary (New York), Notre Dame Univ. (Notre Dame, Ind.); ord. priest Aug. 26, 1972, in Guam; ord. titular bishop of Muzuca in Proconsulari and auxiliary bishop of Agana, Guam (unicorporated U.S. territory), Feb. 19, 1984; archbishop of Agana, Mar. 10, 1986.

Arias, David, O.A.R.: b. July 22, 1929, Leon, Spain; educ. St. Rita's College (San Sebastian, Spain), Our Lady of Good Counsel Theologate (Granada, Spain), Teresianum Institute (Rome, Italy); ord. priest May 31, 1952; ord. titular bishop of Badie and auxiliary bishop of Newark, Apr. 7, 1983; episcopal vicar for Hispanic affairs.

Arkfeld, Leo, S.V.D.: b. Feb. 4, 1912, Butte, Nebr.; educ. Divine Word Seminary (Techny, Ill.), Sacred Heart College (Girard, Pa.); ord. priest Aug. 15, 1943; ord. titular bishop of Bucellus and vicar apostolic of Central New Guinea, Nov. 30, 1948; name of vicariate changed to Wewak, May 15, 1952; first bishop of Wewak, Nov. 15, 1966; app. archbishop of Madang, Papua New Guinea, Dec. 19, 1975; resigned Dec. 31, 1987.

Arzube, Juan A.: b. June 1, 1918, Guayaquil, Ecuador; educ. Rensselaer Polytechnic Institute (Troy, N.Y.), St. John's Seminary (Camarillo, Calif.); ord. priest (Los Angeles*) May 5, 1954; ord. titular bishop of Civitate and auxiliary bishop of Los Angeles, Mar. 25, 1971; retired Sept 7, 1993.

Aymond, Gregory M.: b. Nov. 12, 1949, New Orleans, La.; educ. St. Joseph Seminary College, Notre Dame Seminary (New Orleans, La.); ord. priest (New Orleans*) May 10, 1975; ord. titular bishop of Acolla and auxiliary bishop of New Orleans, Jan. 10, 1997.

B

Balke, Victor H.: b. Sept. 29, 1931, Meppen, Ill.; educ. St. Mary of the Lake Seminary (Mundelein, Ill.), St. Louis Univ. (St. Louis, Mo.); ord. priest (Springfield, Ill.) May 24, 1958; ord. bishop of Crookston, Sept. 2, 1976.

Baltakis, Paul Antanas, O.F.M.: b. Jan. 1, 1925, Troskunai, Lithuania; educ. seminaries of the Franciscan Province of St. Joseph (Belgium); ord. priest Aug. 24, 1952, in Belgium; served in U.S. as director of Lithuanian Cultural Center, New York, and among Lithuanian youth; head of U.S. Lithuanian Franciscan Vicariate, Kennebunkport, Maine, from 1979; ord. titular bishop of Egara, Sept. 24, 1984; assigned to pastoral assistance to Lithuanian Catholics living outside Lithuania (resides in Brooklyn).

Banks, Robert J.: b. Feb. 26, 1928, Winthrop, Mass.; educ. St. John's Seminary (Brighton, Mass.), Gregorian Univ., Lateran Univ. (Rome); ord. priest (Boston*) Dec. 20, 1952, in Rome; rector of St. John's Seminary, Brighton, Mass., 1971-81; vicar general of Boston archdiocese, 1984; ord. titular bishop of Taraqua and auxiliary bishop of Boston, Sept. 19, 1985; bishop of Green Bay, Oct. 16, 1990, installed Dec. 5, 1990.

Barbarito, Gerald M.: b. Jan. 4, 1950, Brooklyn, N.Y.; educ. Cathedral College (Douglaston, N.Y.), Immaculate Conception Seminary (Huntington, N.Y.), Catholic University (Washington, D.C.); ord. priest (Brooklyn) Jan. 31, 1976; ord. titular bishop of Gisipa and auxiliary bishop of Brooklyn, Aug. 22, 1994.

Barnes, Gerald R.: b. June 22, 1945, Phoenix, Ariz., of Mexican descent; educ. St. Leonard Seminary (Dayton, O.), Assumption-St. John's Seminary (San Antonio, Tex.); ord. priest (San Antonio*) Dec.

20, 1975; ord. titular bishop of Montefiascone and auxiliary bishop of San Bernardino, Mar. 18, 1992; bishop of San Bernardino, Dec. 28, 1995.

Baum, William W.: (See Cardinals, Biographies.)

Begley, Michael J.: b. Mar. 12, 1909, Mattineague, Mass.; educ. Mt. St. Mary Seminary (Emmitsburg, Md.); ord. priest (Raleigh) May 26, 1934; ord. first bishop of Charlotte, N.C., Jan. 12, 1972; retired May 29, 1984.

Beltran, Eusebius J.: b. Aug. 31, 1934, Ashley, Pa.; educ. St. Charles Seminary (Philadelphia, Pa.); ord. priest (Atlanta*) May 14, 1960; ord. bishop of Tulsa, Apr. 20, 1978; app. archbishop of Oklahoma City, Nov. 24, 1992; installed Jan 22, 1993.

Bevilacqua, Anthony J.: (See Cardinals, Biographies.)

Blaire, Stephen E.: b. Dec. 22, 1942, Los Angeles, Calif; educ. St. John's Seminary (Camarillo, Calif.); ord. priest (Los Angeles*) Apr. 29, 1967; ord. titular bishop of Lamzella and auxiliary of Los Angeles, May 31, 1990.

Boland, Ernest B., O.P.: b. July 10, 1925, Providence, R.I.; educ. Providence College (Rhode Island), Dominican Houses of Study (Somerset, Ohio; Washington, D.C.); ord. priest June 9, 1955; ord. bishop of Multan, Pakistan, July 25, 1966; resigned Oct. 20, 1984.

Boland, J.(John) Kevin: b. Apr. 25, 1935, Cork, Ireland (brother of Bp. Raymond J. Boland); educ. Christian Brothers School (Cork, Ire.), All Hallows Seminary (Dublin); ord. priest (Savannah), June 14, 1959; ord. bishop of Savannah, Apr. 18, 1995.

Boland, Raymond J.: b. Feb. 8, 1932, Tipperary, Ireland; educ. National Univ. of Ireland and All Hallows Seminary (Dublin); ord. priest (Washington*) June 16, 1957, in Dublin; vicar general and chancellor of Washington archdiocese; ord. bishop of Birmingham, Ala., Mar. 25, 1988; app. bishop of Kansas City-St. Joseph, Mo., June 22, 1993.

Boles, John P.: b. Jan. 21, 1930, Boston, Mass.; educ. St. John Seminary, Boston College (Boston, Mass.); ord. priest (Boston*) Feb. 2, 1955; ord. titular bishop of Nova Sparsa and auxiliary bishop of Boston, May 21, 1992.

Bootkoski, Paul G.: b. July 4, 1940, Newark, N.J.; educ. Seton Hall Univ. (South Orange, N.J.), Immaculate Conception Seminary (Darlington, N.J.); ord. priest (Newark*) May 29, 1966; ord. titular bishop of Zarna and auxiliary bishop of Newark, Sept. 5, 1997.

Borders, William D.: b. Oct. 9, 1913, Washington, Ind.; educ. St. Meinrad Seminary (St. Meinrad, Ind.), Notre Dame Seminary (New Orleans, La.), Notre Dame Univ. (Notre Dame, Ind.); ord. priest (New Orleans*) May 18, 1940; ord. first bishop of Orlando, June 14, 1968; app. archbishop of Baltimore, Apr. 2, 1974, installed June 26, 1974; retired Apr. 11, 1989.

Bosco, Anthony G.: b. Aug. 1, 1927, New Castle, Pa.; educ. St. Vincent Seminary (Latrobe, Pa.), Lateran Univ. (Rome); ord. priest (Pittsburgh) June 7, 1952; ord. titular bishop of Labicum and auxiliary of Pittsburgh, June 30, 1970; app. bishop of Greensburg, Apr. 14, 1987, installed June 30, 1987.

Botean, John Michael: b. July 9, 1955, Canton, Ohio; educ. St. Fidelis Seminary (Herman, Pa.),

Catholic University of America (Washington, DC), St. Gregory Melkite Seminary (Newton Centre, Mass), Catholic Theological Union (Chicago, Ill.); ord. priest (Romanian rite St. George's in Canton), May 18, 1986; ord. bishop of Saint George's in Canton for Romanians Aug. 24, 1996.

Boudreaux, Warren L.: b. Jan. 25, 1918, Berwick, La.; educ. St. Joseph's Seminary (St. Benedict, La.), St. Sulpice Seminary (Paris, France), Notre Dame Seminary (New Orleans, La.), Catholic Univ. (Washington, D.C.); ord. priest (Lafayette, La.) May 30, 1942; ord. titular bishop of Calynda and auxiliary bishop of Lafayette, La., July 25, 1962; app. bishop of Beaumont, June 5, 1971; app. first bishop of Houma-Thibodaux, installed June 5, 1977; retired Dec. 29, 1992.

Boyle, Paul M., C.P.: b. May 28, 1926, Detroit, Mich.; educ. Passionist houses of study, Lateran Univ. (Rome); professed in Congregation of the Passion July 9, 1946; ord. priest May 30, 1953; president of Conference of Major Superiors of Men, 1969-74; superior general of Passionists, 1976-88; ord. titular bishop of Canapium and first vicar apostolic of Mandeville, Jamaica, July 9, 1991.

Braxton, Edward K.: b. June 28, 1944, Chicago, Ill.; educ. Loyola Univ. of Chicago, Univ. of St. Mary of the Lake and Mundelein Seminary (Chicago), Louvain Univ. (Belgium); ord. priest (Chicago*) May 13, 1970; ord. titular bishop of Macomades rusticiana and auxiliary bishop of St. Louis, May 17, 1995.

Breen, Vincent DePaul: b. Dec. 24, 1936, Brooklyn, N.Y.; educ. Cathedral College of Immaculate Conception (Brooklyn, N.Y.), North American College, Gregorian Univ. (Rome); ord. priest (Brooklyn) July 15, 1962, in Rome; vicar of education for diocese of Brooklyn; app. bishop of Metuchen, July 8, 1997.

Breitenbeck, Joseph M.: b. Aug. 3, 1914, Detroit, Mich.; educ. University of Detroit, Sacred Heart Seminary (Detroit, Mich.), North American College and Lateran Univ. (Rome), Catholic Univ. (Washington, D.C.); ord. priest (Detroit*) May 30, 1942; ord. titular bishop of Tepelta and auxiliary bishop of Detroit, Dec. 20, 1965; app. bishop of Grand Rapids, Oct. 15, 1969, installed Dec. 2, 1969; retired July 11, 1989.

Britt, Kevin Michael: b. Nov. 19, 1944, Detroit, Mich.; educ. Sacred Heart Seminary, St. John Provincial Seminary, Universtiy of Detroit Mercy (Detroit, Mich.), Lateran Univ. (Rome); ord. priest (Detroit*) June 28, 1970; ord. titular bishop of Esco and auxiliary of Detroit, Jan. 6, 1994.

Broderick, Edwin B.: b. Jan. 16, 1917, New York, N.Y.; educ. Cathedral College (New York City), St. Joseph's Seminary (Yonkers, N.Y.), Fordham Univ. (New York City); ord. priest (New York*) May 30, 1942; ord. titular bishop of Tizica and auxiliary of New York, Apr. 21, 1967; bishop of Albany, 1969-76; executive director of Catholic Relief Services, 1976-82. Bishop emeritus of Albany.

Brom, Robert H.: b. Sept. 18, 1938, Arcadia, Wis.; educ. St. Mary's College (Winona, Minn.), Gregorian Univ. (Rome); ord. priest (Winona) Dec. 18, 1963, in Rome; ord. bishop of Duluth, May 23, 1983; coadjutor bishop of San Diego, May, 1989; bishop of San Diego, July 10, 1990.

Brown, Tod D.: b. Nov. 15, 1936, San Francisco, Calif.; educ. St. John's Seminary (Camarillo, Calif.), North American College (Rome); ord. priest (Monterey-Fresno) May 1, 1963; ord. bishop of Boise, Apr. 3, 1989.

Brucato, Robert A.: b. Aug. 14, 1931, New York, N.Y. educ. Cathedral College (New York), St. Joseph's Seminary (Dunwoodie, N.Y.), Univ. of Our Lady of the Lake (San Antonio, Tex.); ord. priest (New York*) June 1, 1957; air force chaplain for 22 years; ord. titular bishop of Temuniana and auxiliary of New York, Aug. 25, 1997.

Brunett, Alexander J.: b. Jan. 17, 1934, Detroit, Mich; educ. Gregorian Univ. (Rome), Sacred Heart Seminary, University of Detroit (Detroit, Mich.), Marquette Univ. (Milwaukee, Wis.); ord. priest (Detroit*), July 13, 1958; ord. bishop of Helena, July 6, 1994.

Bruskewitz, Fabian W.: b. Sept. 6, 1935, Milwaukee, Wis.; educ. North American College, Gregorian Univ. (Rome); ord. priest (Milwaukee*) July 17, 1960; ord. bishop of Lincoln, May 13, 1992.

Buechlein, Daniel M., O.S.B.: b. Apr. 20, 1938; educ. St. Meinrad College and Seminary (St. Meinrad, Ind.), St. Anselm Univ. (Rome); solemn profession as Benedictine monk, Aug. 15, 1963; ord. priest (St. Meinrad Archabbey) May 3, 1964; ord. bishop of Memphis, Mar. 2, 1987; app. archbishop of Indianapolis, July 14, 1992; installed Sept. 9, 1992.

Bukovsky, John, S.V.D.: b. Jan. 18, 1924, Cerova, Slovakia; educ. Slovakia, Divine Word Seminary (Techny, Ill.), Catholic Univ. (Washington, D.C.), Univ. of Chicago, Gregorian Univ. (Rome); ord. priest Dec. 3, 1950; became U.S. citizen 1958; worked at East European desk of Secretariat of State; ord. titular archbishop of Tabalta, Oct. 13, 1990; nuncio to Romania, 1990-94; app. papal representative to Russia, Dec. 20, 1994.

Bullock, William H.: b. Apr. 13, 1927, Maple Lake, Minn.; educ. St. Thomas College and St. Paul Seminary (St. Paul, Minn.), Notre Dame Univ. (Notre Dame, Ind.); ord. priest (St. Paul-Minneapolis*) June 7, 1952; ord. titular bishop of Natchez and auxiliary bishop of St. Paul and Minneapolis, Aug. 12, 1980; app. bishop of Des Moines, Feb. 10, 1987; app. bishop of Madison, Wis., Apr. 13, 1993.

Burke, John J., O.F.M.: b. Mar. 16, 1935, River Edge, N.J.; educ. St. Joseph Seminary (Callicoon, N.Y.), St. Bonaventure Univ. (St. Bonaventure, N.Y.), Holy Name College (Washington, D.C.); solemnly professed in Franciscan Order, Aug. 20, 1958; ord. priest Feb. 25, 1961; missionary in Brazil from 1964; ord. coadjutor bishop of Miracema do Tocantins, Brazil, Mar. 25, 1995; bishop of Miracema do Tocantins, Feb. 14, 1996.

Burke, Raymond L.: b. June 30, 1948, Richland Center, Wis.; educ. Holy Cross Seminary (La Crosse, Wis.), Catholic Univ. (Washington, D.C.), North American College and Gregorian Univ. (Rome); ord. priest (La Crosse) June 29, 1975; ord. bishop of La Crosse Jan. 6, 1995, installed Feb. 22, 1995.

Buswell, Charles A.: b. Oct. 15, 1913, Homestead, Okla.; educ. St. Louis Preparatory Seminary (St. Louis, Mo.), Kenrick Seminary (Webster Groves, Mo.), American College, Univ. of Louvain (Belgium); ord. priest (Oklahoma City*) July 9, 1939; ord. bishop of Pueblo, Sept. 30, 1959; resigned Sept. 18, 1979.

C

Camacho, Tomas Aguon: b. Sept. 18, 1933, Chalon Kanoa, Saipan; educ. St. Patrick's Seminary (Menlo Park, Calif.); ord. priest June 14, 1961; ord. first bishop of Chalan Kanoa, Northern Marianas (U.S. Commonwealth), Jan. 13, 1985.

Carberry, John J.: (See Cardinals, Biographies.)

Carlson, Robert J.: b. June 30, 1944, Minneapolis, Minn.; educ. Nazareth Hall and St. Paul Seminary (St. Paul, Minn.), Catholic Univ. (Washington, D.C.): ord. priest (St. Paul-Minneapolis*) May 23, 1970; ord. titular bishop of Avioccala and auxiliary bishop of St. Paul and Minneapolis, Jan. 11, 1984; app. coadjutor bishop of Sioux Falls, Jan. 13, 1994; succeeded as bishop of Sioux Falls, Mar. 21, 1995.

Carmody, Edmond: b. Jan. 12, 1934, Ahalena, Kerry, Ireland; educ. St. Brendan's College (Killarney), St. Patrick Seminary (Carlow, Ire.); ord. priest (San Antonio*) June 8, 1957; missionary in Peru 1984-89; ord. titular bishop of Mortlach and auxiliary bishop of San Antonio, Dec. 15, 1988; app. bishop of Tyler, Mar. 24, 1992.

Carmon, Dominic, S.V.D.: b. Dec. 13, 1930, Opelousas, La.; entered Society of Divine Word, 1946; ord. priest Feb. 2, 1960; missionary in Papua-New Guinea, 1961-68; ord. titular bishop of Rusicade and auxiliary bishop of New Orleans, Feb. 11, 1993.

Casey, Luis Morgan: b. June 23, 1935, Portageville, Mo.; ord. priest (St. Louis*) Apr. 7, 1962; missionary in Bolivia from 1965; ord. titular bishop of Mibiarca and auxiliary of La Paz, Jan. 28, 1984; vicar apostolic of Pando, Bolivia, Jan. 18, 1988 and apostolic administrator (1995) of La Paz.

Catanello, Ignatius A.: b. July 23, 1938, Brooklyn, N.Y.; educ. Cathedral Preparatory Seminary and St. Francis College (Brooklyn, N.Y.), Catholic Univ. (Washington, D.C.); St. John's University (Jamaica, N.Y.), New York University; ord. priest (Brooklyn) May 28, 1966; ord. titular bishop of Deulto and auxiliary bishop of Brooklyn, Aug. 22, 1994.

Chaput, Charles J., O.F.M. Cap.: b. Sept. 26, 1944, Concordia, Kans.; educ. St. Fidelis College (Herman, Pa.), Capuchin College and Catholic Univ. (Washington, D.C.), Univ. of San Francisco; solemn vows as Capuchin, July 14, 1968; ord. priest Aug. 29, 1970; ord. bishop of Rapid City, S.D., July 26, 1988, the second priest of Native American ancestry (member of Prairie Band Potawatomi Tribe) ordained a bishop in the U.S.; app archbishop of Denver, installed Apr. 7, 1997.

Charron, Joseph L., C.PP.S.: b. Dec. 30, 1939, Redfield, S.D.; educ. St. John's Seminary (Collegeville, Minn.); ord. priest June 3, 1967; ord. titular bishop of Bencenna and auxiliary bishop of St. Paul and Minneapolis, Jan. 25, 1990; app. bishop of Des Moines, Nov. 12, 1993.

Chavez, Gilbert Espinoza: b. May 9, 1932, Ontario, Calif.; educ. St. Francis Seminary (El Cajon, Calif.), Immaculate Heart Seminary (San Diego), Univ. of California; ord. priest (San Diego) Mar. 19, 1960; ord. titular bishop of Magarmel and auxiliary of San Diego, June 21, 1974.

Chedid, John: b. July 4, 1923, Eddid, Lebanon; educ.

seminaries in Lebanon and Pontifical Urban College (Rome); ord. priest Dec. 21, 1951, in Rome; ord. titular bishop of Callinico and auxiliary bishop of St. Maron of Brooklyn for the Maronites, Jan. 25, 1981; app. first bishop of Eparchy of Our Lady of Lebanon of Los Angeles for the Maronites, Mar. 1, 1994.

Christian, Francis J.: b. Oct. 8, 1942, Peterborough, N.H.; educ. St. Anselm College (Manchester, N.H.), St. Paul Seminary (Ottawa), American College in Louvain (Belgium); ord. priest (Manchester) June 29, 1968; ord titular bishop of Quincy and auxiliary of Manchester May 14, 1996.

Clark, Matthew H.: b. July 15, 1937, Troy, N.Y.; educ. St. Bernard's Seminary (Rochester, N.Y.), Gregorian Univ. (Rome); ord. priest (Albany) Dec. 19, 1962; ord. bishop of Rochester, May 27, 1979; installed June 26, 1979.

Clinch, Harry A.: b. Oct. 27, 1908, San Anselmo, Calif.; educ. St. Joseph's College (Mountain View, Calif.), St. Patrick's Seminary (Menlo Park, Calif.); ord. priest (Monterey-Fresno) June 6, 1936; ord. titular bishop of Badiae and auxiliary bishop of Monterey-Fresno, Feb. 27, 1957; app. first bishop of Monterey in California, Oct. 16, 1967; resigned Jan. 19, 1982.

Coggin, Walter A., O.S.B.: b. Feb. 10, 1916, Richmond, Va.; ord. priest June 19, 1943; app. abbot ordinary of abbacy nullius of Mary Help of Christians, Belmont N.C., 1959; blessed Mar. 28, 1960; resigned 1970.

Comber, John W., M.M.: b. Mar. 12, 1906, Lawrence, Mass.; educ. St. John's Preparatory College (Danvers, Mass.), Boston College (Boston, Mass.), Maryknoll Seminary (Maryknoll, N.Y.); ord. priest Feb. 1, 1931; superior general of Maryknoll, 1956-66; ord. titular bishop of Foratiana, Apr. 9, 1959.

Connolly, Thomas J.: b. July 18, 1922, Tonopah, Nev.; educ. St. Patrick's Seminary (Menlo Park, Calif.), Catholic Univ. (Washington, D.C.), Lateran Univ. (Rome); ord. priest (Reno-Las Vegas) Apr. 8, 1947; ord. bishop of Baker, June 30, 1971.

Connors, Ronald G., C.SS.R.: b. Nov. 1, 1915, Brooklyn, N.Y.; ord. priest June 22, 1941; ord. titular bishop of Equizetum and coadjutor bishop of San Juan de la Maguana, Dominican Republic, July 20, 1976; succeeded as bishop of San Juan de la Maguana, July 20, 1977; retired Feb. 20, 1991.

Conway, Edwin M.: b. Mar. 6, 1934, Chicago, Ill.; educ. St. Mary of the Lake Seminary (Chicago), Loyola in Chicago; ord. priest (Chicago*) May 3, 1960; ord. titular bishop of Auguro and auxiliary of Chicago, Mar. 20, 1995.

Cooney, Patrick R.: b. Mar. 10, 1934, Detroit, Mich.; educ. Sacred Heart Seminary (Detroit), Gregorian Univ. (Rome), Notre Dame Univ. (Notre Dame, Ind.); ord. priest (Detroit*) Dec. 20, 1959; ord. titular bishop of Hodelm and auxiliary bishop of Detroit, Jan. 27, 1983; app. bishop of Gaylord, Nov. 6, 1989; installed Jan. 28, 1990.

Corrada del Rio, Alvaro, S.J.: b. May 13, 1942, Santurce, Puerto Rico; entered Society of Jesus, 1960, at novitiate of St. Andrew-on-Hudson (Poughkeepsie, N.Y.); educ. Jesuit seminaries, Fordham Univ. (New York), Institut Catholique (Paris); ord. priest July 6, 1974, in Puerto Rico; pastoral coordinator of Northeast Catholic Hispanic Center, New York, 1982-85; ord. titular bishop of Rusticiana and auxiliary bishop

of Washington, D.C., Aug. 4, 1985; app. apostolic administrator of Caguas, Puerto Rico, Aug. 5, 1997 (retains his title as auxiliary bishop of Washington.)

Coscia, Benedict Dominic, O.F.M.: b. Aug. 10, 1922, Brooklyn, N.Y.; educ. St. Francis College (Brooklyn, N.Y.), Holy Name College (Washington, D.C.); ord. priest June 11, 1949; ord. bishop of Jatai, Brazil, Sept. 21, 1961.

Costello, Thomas J.: b. Feb. 23, 1929, Camden, N.Y.; educ. Niagara Univ. (Niagara Falls, N.Y.), St. Bernard's Seminary (Rochester, N.Y.), Catholic Univ. (Washington, D.C.); ord. priest (Syracuse) June 5, 1954; ord. titular bishop of Perdices and auxiliary bishop of Syracuse Mar. 13, 1978.

Cote, Michael R.: b. June 19, 1949, Sanford, Me.; educ. Our Lady of Lourdes Seminary (Cassadaga, N.Y.), St. Mary's Seminary College (Baltimore, Md.); Gregorian Univ. (Rome), Catholic Univ. (Washington, D.C.); ord. priest (Portland, Me.) June 29, 1975 by Pope Paul VI in Rome; secretary, 1989-94 at apostolic nunciature, Washington; ord. titular bishop of Cebarades and auxiliary of Portland, Me., July 27, 1995.

Cotey, Arnold R., S.D.S.: b. June 15, 1921, Milwaukee, Wis.; educ. Divine Savior Seminary (Lanham, Md.), Marquette Univ. (Milwaukee, Wis.); ord. priest June 7, 1949; ord. first bishop of Nachingwea (now Lindi), Tanzania, Oct. 20, 1963; retired Nov. 11, 1983.

Cronin, Daniel A.: b. Nov. 14, 1927, Newton, Mass.; educ. St. John's Seminary (Boston, Mass.), North American College and Gregorian Univ. (Rome); ord. priest (Boston*) Dec. 20, 1952; attaché apostolic nunciature (Addis Ababa), 1957-61; served in papal Secretariat of State, 1961-68; ord. titular bishop of Egnatia and auxiliary bishop of Boston, Sept. 12, 1968; bishop of Fall River, Dec. 16, 1970; archbishop of Hartford, Dec. 10, 1991.

Crowley, Joseph R.: b. Jan. 12, 1915, Fort Wayne, Ind.; educ. St. Mary's College (St. Mary, Ky.), St. Meinrad Seminary (St. Meinrad, Ind.); served in US Air Force, 1942-46; ord. priest (Ft. Wayne-S. Bend) May 1, 1953; editor of Our Sunday Visitor 1958-67; ord. titular bishop of Maraguis and auxiliary bshop of Fort Wayne-South Bend, Aug. 24, 1971; retired May 8, 1990.

Cullen, Edward P.: b. Mar. 15, 1933, Philadelphia, Pa.; educ. St. Charles Borromeo Seminary (Overbrook, Pa.), Univ. of Pennsylvania and LaSalle Univ. (Philadelphia), Harvard Graduate School of Business; ord. priest (Philadelphia*) May 19, 1962; ord. titular bishop of Paria in Proconsolare and auxiliary of Philadelphia, Apr. 14, 1994.

Cummins, John S.: b. Mar. 3, 1928, Oakland, Calif.; educ. St. Patrick's Seminary (Menlo Park, Calif.), Catholic Univ. (Washington, D.C.), Univ. of California; ord. priest (San Francisco*) Jan. 24, 1953; executive director of the California Catholic Conference 1971-76; ord. titular bishop of Lambaesis and auxiliary bishop of Sacramento, May 16, 1974; app. bishop of Oakland, installed June 30, 1977.

Curlin, William G.: b. Aug. 30, 1927, Portsmouth, Va.; educ. Georgetown Univ. (Washington, D.C.), St. Mary's Seminary (Baltimore, Md.); ord. priest (Washington*), May 25, 1957; ord. titular bishop of Rosemarkie and auxiliary bishop of Washington, Dec. 20, 1988; app. bishop of Charlotte, Feb. 22, 1994.

Curry, Thomas J.: b. Jan. 17, 1943, Drumgoon, Ireland; educ. Patrician College (Ballyfin, Ire.), All Hallows Seminary (Dublin, Ire.); ord. priest (Los Angeles*) June 17, 1967; ord. titular bishop of Ceanannus Mór and auxiliary of Los Angeles, Mar. 19, 1994.

Curtis, Walter W.: b. May 3, 1913, Jersey City, N.J.; educ. Fordham Univ. (New York City), Seton Hall Univ. (South Orange, N.J.), Immaculate Conception Seminary (Darlington, N.J.), North American College and Gregorian Univ. (Rome), Catholic Univ. (Washington, D.C.); ord. priest (Newark*) Dec. 8, 1937; ord. titular bishop of Bisica and auxiliary bishop of Newark, Sept. 24, 1957; app. bishop of Bridgeport, 1961, installed Nov. 21, 1961; retired June 28, 1988.

Curtiss, Elden F.: b. June 16, 1932, Baker, Ore.; educ. St. Edward Seminary College and St. Thomas Seminary (Kenmore, Wash.); ord. priest (Baker) May 24, 1958; ord. bishop of Helena, Mont., Apr. 28, 1976; app. archbishop of Omaha, Nebr., May 4, 1993.

D

Daily, Thomas V.: b. Sept. 23, 1927, Belmont, Mass.; educ. Boston College, St. John's Seminary (Brighton, Mass.); ord. priest (Boston*) Jan. 10, 1952; missionary in Peru for five years as a member of the Society of St. James the Apostle; ord. titular bishop of Bladia and auxiliary bishop of Boston, Feb. 11, 1975; app. first bishop of Palm Beach, Fla., July 17, 1984; app. bishop of Brooklyn, Feb. 20, 1990; installed Apr. 18, 1990.

Daly, James: b. Aug. 14, 1921, New York, N.Y.; educ. Cathedral College (Brooklyn, N.Y.), Immaculate Conception Seminary (Huntington, L.I.); ord. priest (Brooklyn) May 22, 1948; ord. titular bishop of Castra Nova and auxiliary bishop of Rockville Centre, May 9, 1977; retired July 1, 1996.

D'Antonio, Nicholas, O.F.M.: b. July 10, 1916, Rochester, N.Y.; educ. St. Anthony's Friary (Catskill, N.Y.); ord. priest June 7, 1942; ord. titular bishop of Giufi Salaria and prelate of Olancho, Honduras, July 25, 1966; resigned 1977; vicar general of New Orleans archdiocese and episcopal vicar for Spanish Speaking, 1977-91.

D'Arcy, John M.: b. Aug. 18, 1932, Brighton, Mass.; educ. St. John's Seminary (Brighton, Mass.), Angelicum Univ. (Rome); ord. priest (Boston*) Feb. 2, 1957; spiritual director of St. John's Seminary; ord. titular bishop of Mediana and auxiliary bishop of Boston, Feb. 11, 1975; app. bishop of Fort Wayne-South Bend, Feb. 26, 1985, installed May 1, 1985.

Dattilo, Nicholas C.: b. Mar. 8, 1932, Mahoningtown, Pa.; educ. St. Vincent Seminary (Latrobe, Pa.), St. Charles Borromeo Seminary (Philadelphia, Pa.); ord. priest (Pittsburgh) May 31, 1958; ord. bishop of Harrisburg, Jan. 26, 1990.

Delaney, Joseph P.: b. Aug. 29, 1934, Fall River, Mass.; educ. Cardinal O'Connell Seminary (Boston, Mass.), Theological College (Washington, D.C.), North American College (Rome), Rhode Island College (Providence, R.I.); ord. priest (Fall River) Dec. 18, 1960; ord. bishop of Fort Worth, Tex., Sept. 13, 1981.

De Palma, Joseph A., S.C.J.: b. Sept. 4, 1913, Walton, N.Y.; ord. priest May 20, 1944; superior general of Congregation of Priests of the Sacred Heart, 1959-67; ord. first bishop of De Aar, South Africa, July 19, 1967; retired Nov. 18, 1987.

De Paoli, Ambrose: b. Aug. 19, 1934, Jeannette, Pa., moved to Miami at age of nine; educ. St. Joseph Seminary (Bloomfield, Conn.), St. Mary of the West Seminary (Cincinnati, O.), North American College and Lateran Univ. (Rome); ord. priest (Miami*) Dec. 18, 1960, in Rome; served in diplomatic posts in Canada, Turkey, Africa and Venezuela; ord. titular archbishop of Lares, Nov. 20, 1983, in Miami; apostolic pro-nuncio to Sri Lanka, 1983-88; apostolic delegate in southern Africa and pro-nuncio to Lesotho, 1988; first apostolic nuncio to South Africa, 1994.

De Simone, Louis A.: b. Feb. 21, 1922, Philadelphia, Pa.; educ. Villanova Univ. (Villanova, Pa.), St. Charles Borromeo Seminary (Overbrook, Pa.); ord. priest (Philadelphia*) May 10, 1952; ord. titular bishop of Cillium and auxiliary bishop of Philadelphia, Aug. 12, 1981; retired Apr. 5, 1997.

Di Lorenzo, Francis X.: b. Apr. 15, 1942, Philadelphia, Pa.; educ. St. Charles Borromeo Seminary (Philadelphia), Univ. of St. Thomas (Rome); ord. priest (Philadelphia*) May 18, 1968; ord. titular bishop of Tigia and auxiliary bishop of Scranton, Mar. 8, 1988; app. apostolic administrator of Honolulu, Oct. 12, 1993; bishop of Honolulu, Nov. 29, 1994.

DiMarzio, Nicholas: b. June 16, 1944, Newark, N.J.; educ. Seton Hall University (South Orange, N.J.), Immaculate Conception Seminary (Darlington, N.J.), Catholic Univ. (Washington, D.C.), Fordham Univ. (New York), Rutgers Univ. (New Brunswick, N.J.); ord. priest (Newark*) May 30, 1970; ord. titular bishop of Mauriana and auxiliary bishop of Newark, Oct. 31, 1996.

Dimino, Joseph T.: b. Jan. 7, 1923, New York, N.Y.; educ. Cathedral College (New York, N.Y.), St. Joseph's Seminary (Yonkers, N.Y.), Catholic Univ. (Washington, D.C.); ord. priest (New York*) June 4, 1949; ord. titular bishop of Carini and auxiliary bishop of the Military Services archdiocese, May 10, 1983; app. ordinary of Military Services archdiocese, May 14, 1991; retired Aug. 12, 1997.

Dion, George E., O.M.I.: b. Sept. 25, 1911, Central Falls, R.I.; educ. Holy Cross College (Worcester, Mass.), Oblate Juniorate (Colebrook, N.H.), Oblate Scholasticates (Natick, Mass., and Ottawa, Ont.); ord. priest June 24, 1936; ord. titular bishop of Arpaia and vicar apostolic of Jolo, Philippines Apr. 23, 1980; retired Oct. 11, 1991; titular bishop of Arpaia.

Donnelly, Robert William: b. Mar. 22, 1931, Toledo, O.; educ. St. Meinrad Seminary College (St. Meinrad, Ind.), Mount St. Mary's in the West Seminary (Norwood, O.); ord. priest (Toledo) May 25, 1957; ord. titular bishop of Garba and auxiliary bishop of Toledo, May 3, 1984.

Donoghue, John F.: b. Aug. 9, 1928, Washington, D.C.; educ. St. Mary's Seminary (Baltimore, Md.), Catholic Univ. (Washington, D.C.); ord. priest (Washington*) June 4, 1955; chancellor and vicar general of Washington archdiocese, 1973-84; ord. bishop of Charlotte, N.C., Dec. 18, 1984; app. archbishop of Atlanta, June 22, 1993; installed Aug. 19, 1993.

Donovan, Paul V.: b. Sept. 1, 1924, Bernard, Iowa; educ. St. Gregory's Seminary (Cincinnati, Ohio), Mt. St. Mary's Seminary (Norwood, Ohio), Lateran Univ. (Rome); ord. priest (Lansing) May 20, 1950; ord. first bishop of Kalamazoo, Mich., July 21, 1971; retired Nov. 22, 1994.

Doran, Thomas George: b. Feb. 20, 1936, Rockford, Ill.; educ. Loras College (Dubuque, Ia.), Gregorian Univ. (Rome), Rockford College (Rockford, Ill.); ord. priest (Rockford) Dec. 20, 1961; ord. bishop of Rockford, June 24, 1994.

Dorsey, Norbert M., C.P.: b. Dec. 14, 1929, Springfield, Mass.; educ. Passionist seminaries (eastern U.S. province), Pontifical Institute of Sacred Music and Gregorian Univ. (Rome, Italy); professed in Passionists, Aug. 15, 1949; ord. priest Apr. 28, 1956; assistant general of Passionists, 1976-86; ord. titular bishop of Mactaris and auxiliary bishop of Miami, Mar. 19, 1986; app. bishop of Orlando, Mar. 20, 1990, installed May 25, 1990.

Doueihi, Stephen Hector: b. June 25, 1927, Zghorta, Lebanon; educ. University of St. Joseph (Beirut, Lebanon), Propaganda Fide, Gregorian Univ. and Institute of Oriental Study (Rome); ord. priest Aug. 14, 1955; came to U.S. in 1973; ord. eparch of Eparchy of St. Maron of Brooklyn, Jan 11, 1997

Dougherty, John Martin: b. Apr. 29, 1932, Scranton, Pa.; educ. St. Charles College (Catonsville, Md.), St. Mary's Seminary (Baltimore), Univ. of Notre Dame (South Bend); ord. priest (Scranton) June 15, 1957; ord. titular bishop of Sufetula and auxiliary bishop of Scranton, Mar. 7, 1995.

Driscoll, Michael P.: b. Aug. 8, 1939, Long Beach, Calif.; educ. St. John Seminary (Camarillo, Calif, Univ. of Southern Calif.; ord. priest (Los Angeles*) May 1, 1965; ord. titular bishop of Massita and auxiliary bishop of Orange, Mar. 6, 1990.

Dudick, Michael J.: b. Feb. 24, 1916, St. Clair, Pa.; educ. St. Procopius College and Seminary (Lisle, Ill.); ord. priest (Passaic, Byzantine Rite) Nov. 13, 1945; ord. bishop of Byzantine Eparchy of Passaic, Oct. 24, 1968; retired Nov. 6, 1995.

Dudley, Paul V.: b. Nov. 27, 1926, Northfield, Minn.; educ. Nazareth College and St. Paul Seminary (St. Paul, Minn.); ord. priest (St. Paul-Minneapolis*) June 2, 1951; ord. titular bishop of Ursona and auxiliary bishop of St. Paul and Minneapolis, Jan. 25, 1977; app. bishop of Sioux Falls, installed Dec. 13, 1978; retired Mar. 21, 1995.

Duffy, Paul, O.M.I.: b. July 25, 1932, Norwood, Mass; educ Oblate houses of study in Canada and Washington, D.C.; ord. priest 1962; missionary in Zambia from 1984; app. first bishop of Mongu, Zambia, July 1, 1997.

Duhart, Clarence James, C.SS.R.: b. Mar. 23, 1912, New Orleans, La.; ord. priest June 29, 1937; ord. bishop of Udon Thani, Thailand, Apr. 21, 1966; resigned Oct. 2, 1975.

DuMaine, (Roland) Pierre: b. Aug. 2, 1931, Paducah, Ky.; educ. St. Joseph's College (Mountain View, Calif.), St. Patrick's College and Seminary (Menlo Park, Calif.), Univ. of California (Berkeley), Catholic Univ. (Washington, D.C.); ord. priest (San Francisco) June 15, 1957; ord. titular bishop of Sarda and auxiliary bishop of San Francisco, June 29, 1978;

app. first bishop of San Jose, Jan. 27, 1981; installed Mar. 18, 1981.

Dunne, John C.: b. Oct. 30, 1937, Brooklyn, N.Y.; educ. Cathedral College (Brooklyn, N.Y.), Immaculate Conception Seminary (Huntington, N.Y.), Manhattan College (New York); ord. priest (Rockville Centre) June 1, 1963; ord. titular bishop of Abercorn and auxiliary bishop of Rockville Centre, Dec. 13, 1988. Vicar for Central Vicariate.

Dupre, Thomas L.: b. Nov. 10, 1933, South Hadley Falls, Mass.; educ. College de Montreal, Assumption College (Worcester, Mass.), Catholic Univ. (Washington, D.C.), ord. priest (Springfield, Mass.) May 23, 1959; ord. titular bishop of Hodelm and auxiliary bishop of Springfield, Mass. May 31, 1990; bishop of Springfield, Mar. 14, 1995.

Durning, Dennis V., C.S.Sp.: b. May 18, 1923, Germantown, Pa.; educ. St. Mary's Seminary (Ferndale, Conn.); ord. priest June 3, 1949; ord. first bishop of Arusha, Tanzania, May 28, 1963; resigned Mar. 6, 1989.

E

Egan, Edward M.: b. Apr. 2, 1932, Oak Park, Ill.; educ. Quigley Preparatory Seminary (Chicago, Ill.), St. Mary of the Lake Seminary (Mundelein, Ill.), Gregorian Univ. (Rome); ord. priest (Chicago*) Dec. 15, 1957, in Rome; judge of Roman Rota, 1972-85; ord. titular bishop of Allegheny and auxiliary bishop of New York, May 22, 1985; bishop of Bridgeport, Nov. 5, 1988.

Elya, John A., B.S.O.: b. Sept. 16, 1928, Maghdouche, Lebanon; educ. diocesan monastery (Sidon, Lebanon), Gregorian Univ. (Rome, Italy); professed as member of Basilian Salvatorian Order, 1949; ord. priest Feb. 17, 1952, in Rome; came to U.S., 1958; ord. titular bishop of Abilene of Syria and auxiliary bishop of Melkite diocese of Newton, Mass., June 29, 1986; app. bishop of Newton (Melkites), Nov. 25, 1993.

F

Favalora, John C.: b. Dec. 5, 1935, New Orleans, La.; educ. St. Joseph Seminary (St. Benedict, La.), Notre Dame Seminary (New Orleans, La.), Gregorian Univ. (Rome), Catholic Univ. of America (Washington, D.C.), Xavier Univ. and Tulane Univ. (New Orleans); ord. priest (New Orleans*) Dec. 20, 1961; ord. bishop of Alexandria, La., July 29, 1986; bishop of St. Petersburg, Mar. 14, 1989; app. archbishop of Miami, installed Dec. 20, 1994.

Federal, Joseph Lennox: b. Jan. 13, 1910, Greensboro, N.C.; educ. Belmont Abbey College (Belmont Abbey, N.C.), Niagara Univ. (Niagara Falls, N.Y.), Univ. of Fribourg (Switzerland), North American College and Gregorian Univ. (Rome); ord. priest (Raleigh) Dec. 8, 1934; ord. titular bishop of Appiaria and auxiliary bishop of Salt Lake City, Apr. 11, 1951; app. coadjutor with right of succession, May, 1958; bishop of Salt Lake City, Mar. 31, 1960; retired Apr. 22, 1980.

Fellhauer, David E.: b. Aug. 19, 1939, Kansas City, Mo.; educ. Pontifical College Josephinum (Worthington, O.), St. Paul Univ. (Ottawa, Ont.); ord. priest (Dallas), May 29, 1965; ord. bishop of Victoria, May 28, 1990.

Fernandez, Gilberto: b. Feb. 13, 1935, Havana, Cuba; educ. El Buen Pastor Seminary (Havana); ord. priest (Havana*), May 15, 1959; came to U.S. 1967; app. titular bishop of Irina and auxiliary of Miami, June 24, 1997.

Ferrario, Joseph A.: b. Mar. 3, 1926, Scranton, Pa.; educ. St. Charles College (Catonsville, Md.), St. Mary's Seminary (Baltimore, Md.), Catholic Univ. (Washington, D.C.); Univ. of Scranton; ord. priest (Honolulu) May 19, 1951; ord. titular bishop of Cuse and auxiliary bishop of Honolulu, Jan. 13, 1978; bishop of Honolulu, May 13, 1982; retired Oct. 12, 1993.

Fiorenza, Joseph A.: b. Jan. 25, 1931, Beaumont, Tex.; educ. St. Mary's Seminary (LaPorte, Tex.); ord. priest (Galveston-Houston) May 29, 1954; ord. bishop of San Angelo, Oct. 25, 1979; app. bishop of Galveston-Houston, Dec. 18, 1984, installed Feb. 18, 1985.

Fitzpatrick, John J.: b. Oct. 12, 1918, Trenton, Ont., Canada; educ. Urban Univ. (Rome), Our Lady of the Angels Seminary (Niagara Falls, N.Y.); ord. priest (Buffalo) Dec. 13, 1942; ord. titular bishop of Cenae and auxiliary bishop of Miami, Aug. 28, 1968; bishop of Brownsville, Tex., May 28, 1971; retired Nov. 30, 1991.

Fitzsimons, George K.: b. Sept. 4, 1928, Kansas City, Mo.; educ. Rockhurst College (Kansas City, Mo.), Immaculate Conception Seminary (Conception, Mo.); ord. priest (Kansas City-St. Joseph) Mar. 18, 1961; ord. titular bishop of Pertusa and auxiliary bishop of Kansas City-St. Joseph, July 3, 1975; app. bishop of Salina, Mar. 28, 1984, installed May 29, 1984.

Flanagan, Bernard Joseph: b. Mar. 31, 1908, Proctor, Vt.; educ. Holy Cross College (Worcester, Mass.), North American College (Rome), Catholic Univ. (Washington, D.C.); ord. priest (Burlington) Dec. 8, 1931; ord. first bishop of Norwich, Nov. 30, 1953; app. bishop of Worcester, installed, Sept. 24, 1959; retired Mar. 31, 1983.

Fliss, Raphael M.: b. Oct. 25, 1930, Milwaukee, Wis.; educ. St. Francis Seminary (Milwaukee, Wis.), Catholic University (Washington, D.C.), Pontifical Lateran Univ. (Rome); ord. priest (Milwaukee*) May 26, 1956; ord. coadjutor bishop of Superior with right of succession, Dec. 20, 1979; bishop of Superior, June 27, 1985.

Flores, Patrick F.: b. July 26, 1929, Ganado, Tex.; educ. St. Mary's Seminary (Houston, Tex.); ord. priest (Galveston-Houston) May 26, 1956; ord. titular bishop of Itolica and auxiliary bishop of San Antonio, May 5, 1970 (first Mexican-American bishop); app. bishop of El Paso, Apr. 4, 1978, installed May 29, 1978; app. archbishop of San Antonio 1979; installed Oct. 13, 1979.

Flynn, Harry J.: b. May 2, 1933, Schenectady, N.Y.; educ. Siena College (Loudonville, N.Y.), Mt. St. Mary's College (Emmitsburg, Md.); ord. priest (Albany) May 28, 1960; ord. coadjutor bishop of Lafayette, La., June 24, 1986; bishop of Lafayette, La., May 15, 1989; app. coadjutor archbishop of St. Paul and Minneapolis, Feb. 24, 1994, installed Apr. 27, 1994; archbishop of St. Paul and Minneapolis, Sept. 8, 1995.

Foley, David E.: b. Feb. 3, 1930, Worcester, Mass.; educ. St. Charles College (Catonsville, Md.), St. Mary's Seminary (Baltimore, Md.); ord. priest (Washington*) May 26, 1952; ord. titular bishop of Octaba and auxiliary bishop of Richmond, June 27, 1986; app. bishop of Birmingham, Mar. 22, 1994.

Foley, John Patrick: b. Nov. 11, 1935, Sharon Hill, Pa.; educ. St. Joseph's Preparatory School (Philadelphia, Pa.), St. Joseph's College (now University) (Philadelphia, Pa.), St. Charles Borromeo Seminary (Overbrook, Pa.), St. Thomas Univ. (Rome), Columbia School of Journalism (New York); ord. priest (Philadelphia*) May 19, 1962; assistant editor (1967-70) and editor (1970-84) of The Catholic Standard and Times, Philadelphia archdiocesan paper; ord. titular archbishop of Neapolis in Proconsulari, May 8, 1984, in Philadelphia; app. president of the Pontifical Council for Social Communications, Apr. 5, 1984.

Forst, Marion F.: b. Sept. 3, 1910, St. Louis, Mo.; educ. St. Louis Preparatory Seminary (St. Louis, Mo.), Kenrick Seminary (Webster Groves, Mo.); ord. priest (St. Louis*) June 10, 1934; ord. bishop of Dodge City, Mar. 24, 1960; app. titular bishop of Scala and auxiliary bishop of Kansas City, Kans., Oct. 16, 1976; retired Dec. 23, 1986. Titular bishop of Leavenworth.

Francis, Joseph A., S.V.D.: b. Sept. 30, 1923, Lafayette, La.; educ. St. Augustine Seminary (Bay St. Louis, Miss.), St. Mary Seminary (Techny, Ill.), Catholic Univ. (Washington, D.C.); ord. priest Oct. 7, 1950; president Conference of Major Superiors of Men, 1974-76, and the National Black Catholic Clergy Caucus; ord. titular bishop of Valliposita and auxiliary bishop of Newark, June 25, 1976; retired June 30, 1995. (Died Sept. 1, 1997.)

Franklin, William Edwin: b. May 3, 1930, Parnell, Iowa; educ. Loras College and Mt. St. Bernard Seminry (Dubuque, Iowa); ord. priest (Dubuque*) Feb. 4, 1956; ord. titular bishop of Surista and auxiliary bishop of Dubuque, Apr. 1, 1987; app. bishop of Davenport, Nov. 12, 1993, installed Jan. 20, 1994.

Franzetta, Benedict C.: b. Aug. 1, 1921, East Liverpool, O.; educ. St. Charles College (Catonsville, Md.), St. Mary Seminary (Cleveland, O.); ord. priest (Youngstown) Apr. 29, 1950; ord. titular bishop of Oderzo and auxiliary bishop of Youngstown, Sept. 4, 1980; retired Sept. 4, 1996.

Freking, Frederick W.: b. Aug. 11, 1913, Heron Lake, Minn.; educ. St. Mary's College (Winona, Minn.), North American College and Gregorian Univ. (Rome), Catholic Univ. (Washington, D.C.); ord. priest (Winona) July 31, 1938; ord. bishop of Salina, Nov. 30, 1957; app. bishop of La Crosse, Dec. 30, 1964, installed Feb. 24, 1965; resigned May 10, 1983.

Frey, Gerard L.: b. May 10, 1914, New Orleans, La.; educ. Notre Dame Seminary (New Orleans, La.); ord. priest (New Orleans*) Apr. 2, 1938; ord. bishop of Savannah, Aug. 8, 1967; app. bishop of Lafayette, La., Nov. 7, 1972, installed Jan, 7, 1973; retired May 15, 1989.

Friend, William B.: b. Oct. 22, 1931, Miami, Fla.; educ. St. Mary's College (St. Mary, Ky.), Mt. St. Mary Seminary (Emmitsburg, Md.), Catholic Univ. (Washington, D.C.), Notre Dame Univ. (Notre Dame, Ind.); ord. priest (Mobile*) May 7, 1959; ord.

titular bishop of Pomaria and auxiliary bishop of Alexandria-Shreveport, La., Oct. 30, 1979; app. bishop of Alexandria-Shreveport, Nov. 17, 1982, installed Jan 11, 1983; app. first bishop of Shreveport, June, 1986; installed July 30, 1986.

G

Galante, Joseph A.: b. July 2, 1938, Philadelphia, Pa.; educ. St. Joseph Preparatory School, St. Charles Seminary (Philadelphia, Pa.); Lateran Univ., Angelicum, North American College (Rome); ord. priest (Philadelphia*) May 16, 1964; on loan to diocese of Brownsville, Tex., 1968-72, where he served in various diocesan posts; returned to Philadelphia, 1972; assistant vicar (1972-79) and vicar (1979-87) for religious; undersecretary of Congregation for Institutes of Consecrated Life and Societies of Apostolic Life (Rome), 1987-92; ord. titular bishop of Equilium and auxiliary bishop of San Antonio, Dec. 11, 1992; app. bishop of Beaumont, Apr. 5, 1994.

Garland, James H.: b. Dec. 13, 1931, Wilmington, Ohio; educ. Wilmington College (Ohio), Ohio State Univ. (Columbus, O.); Mt. St. Mary's Seminary (Cincinnati, O.), Catholic Univ. (Washington, D.C.); ord. priest (Cincinnati*) Aug. 15, 1959; ord. titular bishop of Garriana and auxiliary bishop of Cincinnati, July 25, 1984; app. bishop of Marquette, Oct. 6, 1992; installed Nov. 11, 1992.

Garmendia, Francisco: b. Nov. 6, 1924, Lozcano, Spain; ord. priest June 29, 1947, in Spain; came to New York in 1964; became naturalized citizen; ord. titular bishop of Limisa and auxiliary bishop of New York, June 29, 1977. Vicar for Spanish pastoral development in New York archdiocese.

Garmo, George: b. Dec. 8, 1921, Telkaif, Iraq; educ. St. Peter Chaldean Patriarchal Seminary (Mossul, Iraq), Pontifical Urban Univ. (Rome); ord. priest Dec. 8, 1945; pastor of Chaldean parish in Detroit archdiocese, 1960-64, 1966-80; ord. archbishop of Chaldean archdiocese of Mossul Iraq, Sept. 14, 1980.

Garner, Robert F.: b. Apr. 27, 1920, Jersey City, N.J.; educ. Seton Hall Univ. (S. Orange, N.J.), Immaculate Conception Seminary (Darlington, N.J.); ord. priest (Newark*) June 15, 1946; ord. titular bishop of Blera and auxiliary bishop of Newark, June 25, 1976. Retired July 11, 1995.

Gaughan, Norbert F.: b. May 30, 1921, Pittsburgh, Pa.; educ. St. Vincent College (Latrobe, Pa.), Univ. of Pittsburgh; ord. priest (Pittsburgh) Nov. 4, 1945; ord. titular bishop of Taraqua and auxiliary bishop of Greensburg, June 26, 1975; app. bishop of Gary, July 24, 1984, installed Oct. 2, 1984. Retired June 1, 1996.

Gaydos, John R.: b. Aug. 14, 1943, St. Louis, Mo.; educ Cardinal Glennon College (St. Louis, Mo.), North Americsan College, Gregorian Univ. (Rome); ord. priest (St. Louis*) Dec. 20, 1968; ord. bishop of Jefferson City, Aug. 27, 1997.

Gelineau, Louis E.: b. May 3, 1928, Burlington, Vt.; educ. St. Michael's College (Winooski, Vt.), St. Paul's Univ. Seminary (Ottawa, Ont.), Catholic Univ. (Washington, D.C.); ord. priest (Burlington) June 5, 1954; ord. bishop of Providence, R.I., Jan. 26, 1972; retired June 11, 1997.

Gendron, Odore J.: b. Sept. 13, 1921, Manchester, N.H.; educ. St. Charles Borromeo Seminary (Sherbrooke, Que., Canada), Univ. of Ottawa, St. Paul Univ. Seminary (Ottawa, Ont., Canada); ord. priest (Manchester) May 31, 1947; ord. bishop of Manchester, Feb. 3, 1975; resigned June 12, 1990.

George, Francis E., O.M.I.: b. Jan. 16, 1937, Chicago, Ill.; educ. Univ. of Ottawa (Canada); Catholic Univ. (Washington, D.C.), Tulane Univ. (New Orleans), Urban Univ. (Rome); ord. priest Dec. 21, 1963; provincial of central region of Oblates of Mary Immaculate, 1973-74, vicar general, 1974-86; ord. bishop of Yakima, Sept. 21, 1990; app. archbishop of Portland, Ore., Apr. 30, 1996, installed May 27, 1996; app. archbishop of Chicago, Apr. 8, 1997, installed May 7, 1997.

Gerber, Eugene J.: b. Apr. 30, 1931, Kingman, Kans.; educ. St. Thomas Seminary (Denver, Colo.), Wichita State Univ.; Catholic Univ. (Washington, D.C.), Angelicum (Rome); ord. priest (Wichita) May 19, 1959; ord. bishop of Dodge City, Dec. 14, 1976; app. bishop of Wichita, Nov. 17, 1982, installed Feb. 9, 1983.

Gerety, Peter L.: b. July 19, 1912, Shelton, Conn.; educ. Sulpician Seminary (Paris, France); ord. priest (Hartford*) June 29, 1939; ord. titular bishop of Crepedula and coadjutor bishop of Portland, Me., with right of succession, June 1, 1966; app. apostolic administrator of Portland, 1967; bishop of Portland, Me., Sept. 15, 1969; app. archbishop of Newark, Apr. 2, 1974; installed June 28, 1974; retired June 3, 1986.

Gerry, Joseph J., O.S.B.: b. Sept. 12, 1928, Millnocket, Me.; educ. St. Anselm Abbey Seminary (Manchester, N.H.), Univ. of Toronto (Canada), Fordham Univ. (New York); ord. priest June 12, 1954; abbot of St. Anselm Abbey, Manchester, N.H., 1972; ord. titular bishop of Praecausa and auxiliary of Manchester, Apr. 21, 1986; bishop of Portland, Me., Dec. 27, 1988, installed Feb. 21, 1989.

Gettelfinger, Gerald A.: b. Oct. 20, 1935, Ramsey, Ind.; educ. St. Meinrad Seminary (St. Meinrad, Ind.), Butler Univ. (Indianapolis, Ind.); ord. priest (Indianapolis*) May 7, 1961; ord. bishop of Evansville, Apr. 11, 1989.

Gilbert, Edward J., C.SS.R.: b. Dec. 26, 1936, Brooklyn, N.Y.; educ. Mt. St. Alphonsus Seminary (Esopus, New York), Catholic Univ. (Washington, D.C.); ord. priest (Redemptorists, Baltimore Province) June 21, 1964; ord. bishop of Roseau, Dominica, Sept. 7, 1994.

Glynn, John J.: b. Aug. 6, 1926, Boston, Mass.,; educ. St. John's Seminary (Brighton, Mass.); ord. priest (Boston*), Apr. 11, 1951; Navy chaplain, 1960-85; ord. titular bishop of Monteverde and auxiliary bishop of Military Services archdiocese, Jan. 6, 1992.

Goedert, Raymond E.: b. Oct. 15, 1927, Oak Park, Ill.; educ. Quigley Preparatory Seminary (Chicago, Ill.), St. Mary of the Lake Seminary and Loyola Univ. (Chicago, Ill.), Gregorian Univ. (Rome); ord. priest (Chicago*), May 1, 1952; ord. titular bishop of Tamazeni and auxiliary bishop of Chicago, Aug. 29, 1991.

Gonzalez, Roberto O., O.F.M.: b. June 2, 1950, Elizabeth, N.J.; educ. St. Joseph Seraphic Seminary (Callicoon, N.Y.), Siena College (Loudonville, N.Y.), Washington Theological Union (Silver Spring, Md.),

Fordham Univ. (New York, N.Y.); solemnly professed in Franciscan Order, 1976; ord. priest May 8, 1977; ord. titular bishop of Ursona and auxiliary bishop of Boston, Oct. 3, 1988; app. coadjutor bishop of Corpus Christi, May 16, 1995; bishop of Corpus Christi, Apr. 1, 1997.

Gorman, John R.: b. Dec. 11, 1925, Chicago, Ill.; educ, St. Mary of the Lake Seminary (Mundelein, Ill.), Loyola Univ. (Chicago, Ill.); ord. priest (Chicago*) May 1, 1956; ord. titular bishop of Catula and auxiliary bishop of Chicago, Apr. 11, 1988.

Gossman, F. Joseph: b. Apr. 1, 1930, Baltimore, Md.; educ. St. Charles College (Catonsville, Md.), St. Mary's Seminary (Baltimore, Md.), North American College (Rome), Catholic Univ. (Washington, D.C.); ord. priest (Baltimore*) Dec. 17, 1955; ord. titular bishop of Agunto and auxiliary bishop of Baltimore, Sept. 11, 1968; app. bishop of Raleigh Apr. 8, 1975.

Gottwald, George J.: b. May 12, 1914, St. Louis, Mo.; educ. Kenrick Seminary (Webster Groves, Mo.); ord. priest (St. Louis*) June 9, 1940; ord. titular bishop of Cedamusa and auxiliary bishop of St. Louis, Aug. 8, 1961; resigned Aug. 2, 1988.

Gracida, Rene H.: b. June 9, 1923, New Orleans, La.; educ. Rice Univ. and Univ. of Houston (Houston, Tex.), Univ. of Fribourg (Switzerland); ord. priest (Miami*) May 23, 1959; ord. titular bishop of Masuccaba and auxiliary bishop of Miami, Jan. 25, 1972; app. first bishop of Pensacola-Tallahassee, Oct. 1, 1975, installed Nov. 6, 1975; app. bishop of Corpus Christi, May 24, 1983, installed July 11, 1983; retired Apr. 1, 1997.

Grady, Thomas J.: b. Oct. 9, 1914, Chicago, Ill.; educ. St. Mary of the Lake Seminary (Mundelein, Ill.), Gregorian Univ. (Rome), Loyola Univ. (Chicago, Ill.); ord. priest (Chicago*) Apr. 23, 1938; ord. titular bishop of Vamalla and auxiliary bishop of Chicago, Aug. 24, 1967; app. bishop of Orlando, Fla., Nov. 11, 1974, installed Dec. 16, 1974; resigned Dec. 12, 1989.

Graham, John J.: b. Sept. 11, 1913, Philadelphia, Pa.; educ. St. Charles Borromeo Seminary (Philadelphia, Pa.), Pontifical Roman Seminary (Rome, Italy); ord. priest (Philadelphia*) Feb. 26, 1938; ord. titular bishop of Sabrata and auxiliary bishop of Philadelphia, Jan. 7, 1964; retired Nov. 8, 1988.

Grahmann, Charles V.: b. July 15, 1931, Halletsville, Tex.; educ. The Assumption-St. John's Seminary (San Antonio, Tex.); ord. priest (San Antonio*) Mar. 17, 1956; ord. titular bishop of Equilium and auxiliary bishop of San Antonio, Aug. 20, 1981; app. first bishop of Victoria, Tex., Apr. 13, 1982; app. coadjutor bishop of Dallas, Dec. 9, 1989; bishop of Dallas, July 14, 1990.

Gregory, Wilton D.: b. Dec. 7, 1947, Chicago, Ill.; educ. Quigley Preparatory Seminary South, Niles College of Loyola Univ. (Chicago, Ill.), St. Mary of the Lake Seminary (Mundelein, Ill.), Pontifical Liturgical Institute, Sant'Anselmo (Rome); ord. priest (Chicago*) May 9, 1973; ord. titular bishop of Oliva and auxiliary bishop of Chicago, Dec. 13, 1983; app. bishop of Belleville, Dec. 29, 1993; installed Feb. 10, 1994.

Griffin, James A.: b. June 13, 1934, Fairview

Park, O.; educ. St. Charles College (Baltimore, Md.), Borromeo College (Wicklife, O.); St Mary Seminary (Cleveland, O.); Lateran Univ. (Rome); Cleveland State Univ.; ord. priest (Cleveland) May 28, 1960; ord. titular bishop of Holar and auxiliary bishop of Cleveland, Aug. 1, 1979; app. bishop of Columbus, Feb. 8, 1983.

Grosz, Edward M.: b. Feb. 16, 1945, Buffalo, N.Y.; educ. St. John Vianney Seminary (East Aurora, N.Y.), Notre Dame Univ. (Notre Dame, Ind.); ord. priest (Buffalo) May 29, 1971; ord. titular bishop of Morosbisdus and auxiliary bishop of Buffalo, Feb. 2, 1990.

Guillory, Curtis J., S.V.D.: b. Sept. 1, 1943, Mallet, La.; educ. Divine Word College (Epworth, Iowa), Chicago Theological Union (Chicago), Creighton Univ. (Omaha, Neb.); ord. priest Dec. 16, 1972; ord. titular bishop of Stagno and auxiliary bishop of Galveston-Houston, Feb. 19, 1988.

Gumbleton, Thomas J.: b. Jan. 26, 1930, Detroit, Mich.; educ. St. John Provincial Seminary (Detroit, Mich.), Pontifical Lateran Univ. (Rome); ord. priest (Detroit*) June 2, 1956; ord. titular bishop of Ululi and auxiliary bishop of Detroit, May 1, 1968.

H

Ham, J. Richard, M.M.: b. July 11, 1921, Chicago, Ill.; educ. Maryknoll Seminary (New York); ord. priest June 12, 1948; missionary to Guatemala, 1958; ord. titular bishop of Puzia di Numidia and auxiliary bishop of Guatemala, Jan. 6, 1968; resigned see 1979; auxiliary bishop of St. Paul and Minneapolis, October, 1980; retired Oct. 29, 1990.

Hanifen, Richard C.: b. June 15, 1931, Denver, Colo,; educ. Regis College and St. Thomas Seminary (Denver, Colo.), Catholic Univ. (Washington, D.C.), Lateran Univ. (Rome); ord. priest (Denver*) June 6, 1959; ord. titular bishop of Abercorn and auxiliary bishop of Denver, Sept. 20, 1974; app. first bishop of Colorado Springs, Nov. 10, 1983; installed Jan. 30, 1984.

Hannan, Philip M.: b. May 20, 1913, Washington, D.C.; educ. St. Charles College (Catonsville, Md.), Catholic Univ. (Washington, D.C.), North American College (Rome); ord. priest (Washington*) Dec. 8, 1939; ord. titular bishop of Hieropolis and auxiliary bishop of Washington, D.C., Aug. 28, 1956; app. archbishop of New Orleans, installed Oct. 13, 1965; retired Dec. 6, 1988.

Hanus, Jerome George, O.S.B.: b. May 25, 1940, Brainard, Nebr.; educ. Conception Seminary (Conception, Mo.), St. Anselm Univ. (Rome), Princeton Theological Seminary (Princeton, N.J.); ord. priest (Conception Abbey, Mo.) July 30, 1966; abbot of Conception Abbey, 1977-87; president of Swiss American Benedictine Congregation, 1984-87; ord. bishop of St. Cloud, Aug. 24, 1987; app. coadjutor archbishop of Dubuque, Aug. 23, 1994; archbishop of Dubuque, Oct. 16, 1995.

Harrington, Bernard J.: b. Sept. 6, 1933, Detroit, Mich.; educ. Sacred Heart Seminary (Detroit, Mich.), St. John's Provincial Seminary (Plymouth, Mich.), Univ. of Detroit; ord. priest (Detroit*) June 6, 1959; ord. titular bishop of Uzali and auxiliary of Detroit, Jan. 6, 1994.

Harrison, Frank J.: b. Aug. 12, 1912; Syracuse, N.Y.; educ. Notre Dame Univ. (Notre Dame, Ind.), St. Bernard's Seminary (Rochester, N.Y.), ord. priest (Syracuse) June 4, 1937; ord. titular bishop of Aquae in Numidia and auxiliary of Syracuse, Apr. 22, 1971; app. bishop of Syracuse, Nov. 9, 1976, installed Feb. 6, 1977; retired June 16, 1987.

Hart, Daniel A.: b. Aug. 24, 1927, Lawrence, Mass.; educ. St. John's Seminary (Brighton, Mass.); ord. priest (Boston*) Feb. 2, 1953; ord. titular bishop of Tepelta and auxiliary bishop of Boston, Oct. 18, 1976; bishop of Norwich Sept. 12, 1995.

Hart, Joseph: b. Sept. 26, 1931, Kansas City, Missouri; educ. St. John Seminary (Kansas City, Mo.), St. Meinrad Seminary (Indianapolis, Ind.); ord. priest (Kansas City-St. Joseph) May 1, 1956; ord. titular bishop of Thimida Regia and auxiliary bishop of Cheyenne, Wyo., Aug. 31, 1976; app. bishop of Cheyenne, installed June 12, 1978.

Head, Edward D.: b. Aug. 5, 1919, White Plains, N.Y.; educ. Cathedral College, St. Joseph's Seminary (New York City); ord. priest (New York*) Jan. 27, 1945; director of New York Catholic Charities; ord. titular bishop of Ardsratha and auxiliary bishop of New York, Mar. 19, 1970; app. bishop of Buffalo, Jan. 23, 1973, installed Mar. 19, 1973; retired Apr. 18, 1995.

Heim, Capistran F., O.F.M.: b. Jan. 21, 1934, Catskill, N.Y.; educ. Franciscan Houses of Study; ord. priest Dec. 18, 1965; missionary in Brazil; ord. first bishop of prelature of Itaituba, Brazil, Sept. 17, 1988; installed Oct. 2, 1988.

Hermes, Herbert, O.S.B.: b. May 25, 1933, Scott City, Kans.; ord. priest (St. Benedict Abbey, Atchison, Kans.), May 26, 1960; missionary in Brazil; ord. bishop of territorial prelature of Cristalandia, Brazil, Sept. 2, 1990.

Herrmann, Edward J.: b. Nov. 6, 1913, Baltimore, Md.; educ. Mt. St. Mary's Seminary (Emmitsburg, Md.), Catholic Univ. (Washington, D.C.); ord. priest (Washington*) June 12, 1947; ord. titular bishop of Lamzella and auxiliary bishop of Washington, D.C., Apr. 26, 1966; app. bishop of Columbus, June 26, 1973; resigned Sept. 18, 1982.

Hickey, Dennis W.: b. Oct. 28, 1914, Dansville, N.Y.; educ. Colgate Univ. and St. Bernard's Seminary (Rochester, N.Y.); ord. priest (Rochester) June 7, 1941; ord. titular bishop of Rusuccuru and auxiliary bishop of Rochester, N.Y., Mar. 14, 1968; retired Jan. 16, 1990.

Hickey, James A.: (See Cardinals, Biographies.)

Higi, William L.: b. Aug. 29, 1933, Anderson, Ind.; educ. Our Lady of the Lakes Preparatory Seminary (Wawasee, Ind.), Mt. St. Mary of the West Seminary and Xavier Univ. (Cincinnati, O.); ord. priest (Lafayette, Ind.) May 30, 1959; ord. bishop of Lafayette, Ind., June 6, 1984.

Hoffman, James R.: b. June 12, 1932, Fremont, O.; educ. Our Lady of the Lake Minor Seminary (Wawasee, Ind.), St. Meinrad College (St. Meinrad, Ind.), Mt. St. Mary Seminary (Norwood, O.), Catholic Univ. (Washington, D.C.); ord. priest (Toledo) July 28, 1957; ord. titular bishop of Italica and auxiliary bishop of Toledo, June 23, 1978; bishop of Toledo, Dec. 16, 1980.

Hogan, James J.: b. Oct. 17, 1911, Philadelphia,

Pa.; educ. St. Charles College (Catonsville, Md.), St. Mary's Seminary (Baltimore), Gregorian Univ. (Rome), Catholic Univ. (Washington, D.C.); ord. priest (Trenton) Dec. 8, 1937; ord. titular bishop of Philomelium and auxiliary bishop of Trenton, Feb. 25, 1960; app. bishop of Altoona-Johnstown, installed July 6, 1966; retired Nov. 4, 1986.

Hogan, Joseph L.: b. Mar. 11, 1916, Lima, N.Y.; educ. St. Bernard's Seminary (Rochester, N.Y.), Canisius College (Buffalo, N.Y.), Angelicum (Rome); ord. priest (Rochester) June 6, 1942; ord. bishop of Rochester, Nov. 28, 1969; resigned Nov. 28, 1978.

Houck, William Russell: b. June 26, 1926, Mobile, Ala.; educ. St. Bernard Junior College (Cullman, Ala.), St. Mary's Seminary College and St. Mary's Seminary (Baltimore, Md.), Catholic Univ. (Washington, D.C.); ord. priest (Mobile*) May 19, 1951; ord. titular bishop of Alessano and auxiliary bishop of Jackson, Miss., May 27, 1979, by Pope John Paul II; app. bishop of Jackson, Apr. 11, 1984, installed June 5, 1984.

Howze, Joseph Lawson: b. Aug. 30, 1923, Daphne, Ala.; convert to Catholicism, 1948; educ. St. Bonaventure Univ. (St. Bonaventure, N.Y.); ord. priest (Raleigh) May 7, 1959; ord. titular bishop of Massita and auxiliary bishop of Natchez-Jackson, Jan. 28, 1973; app. first bishop of Biloxi, Miss., Mar. 8, 1977; installed June 6, 1977.

Hubbard, Howard J.: b. Oct. 31, 1938, Troy, N.Y.; educ. St. Joseph's Seminary (Dunwoodie, N.Y.); North American College and Gregorian Univ. (Rome), Catholic Univ. (Washington, D.C.); ord. priest (Albany) Dec. 18, 1963; ord. bishop of Albany, Mar. 27, 1977.

Hughes, Alfred C.: b. Dec. 2, 1932, Boston, Mass.; educ. St. John Seminary (Brighton, Mass.), Gregorian Univ. (Rome); ord. priest (Boston*) Dec. 15, 1957, in Rome; ord. titular bishop of Maximiana in Byzacena and auxiliary bishop of Boston, Sept. 14, 1981; app. bishop of Baton Rouge, Sept. 7, 1993.

Hughes, Edward T.: b. Nov. 13, 1920, Lansdowne, Pa.; educ. St. Charles Seminary, Univ. of Pennsylvania (Philadelphia); ord. priest (Philadelphia*) May 31, 1947; ord. titular bishop of Segia and auxiliary bishop of Philadelphia, July 21, 1976; app. bishop of Metuchen, Dec. 11, 1986, installed Feb. 5, 1987; retired July 8, 1997.

Hughes, William A.: b. Sept. 23, 1921, Youngstown, O.; educ. St. Charles College (Catonsville, Md.), St. Mary's Seminary (Cleveland, O.), Notre Dame Univ. (Notre Dame, Ind.); ord. priest (Youngstown) Apr. 6, 1946; ord. titular bishop of Inis Cathaig and auxiliary bishop of Youngstown, Sept. 12, 1974; app. bishop of Covington, installed May 8, 1979. Retired July 4, 1995.

Hunthausen, Raymond G.: b. Aug. 21, 1921, Anaconda, Mont.; educ. Carroll College (Helena, Mont.), St. Edward's Seminary (Kenmore, Wash.), St. Louis Univ. (St. Louis, Mo.), Catholic Univ. (Washington, D.C.), Fordham Univ. (New York City), Notre Dame Univ. (Notre Dame, Ind.); ord. priest (Helena) June 1, 1946; ord. bishop of Helena, Aug. 30, 1962; app. archbishop of Seattle, Feb. 25, 1975; retired Aug. 21, 1991.

Hurley, Francis T.: b. Jan. 12, 1927, San Francisco, Calif.; educ. St. Patrick's Seminary (Menlo

Park, Calif.), Catholic Univ. (Washington, D.C.); ord. priest (San Francisco*) June 16, 1951; assigned to NCWC in Washington, D.C., 1957; assistant (1958) and later (1968) associate secretary of NCCB and USCC; ord. titular bishop of Daimlaig and auxiliary bishop of Juneau, Alaska, Mar. 19, 1970; app. bishop of Juneau, July 20, 1971, installed Sept. 8, 1971; app. archbishop of Anchorage, May 4, 1976, installed July 8, 1976.

Hurley, Mark J.: b. Dec. 13, 1919, San Francisco, Calif.; educ. St. Patrick's Seminary (Menlo Park, Calif.), Univ. of California (Berkeley), Catholic Univ. (Washington, D.C.), Lateran Univ. (Rome), Univ. of Portland (Portland, Ore.); ord. priest (San Francisco*) Sept. 23, 1944; ord. titular bishop of Thunusuda and auxiliary bishop of San Francisco, Jan. 4, 1968; app. bishop of Santa Rosa, Nov. 19, 1969; resigned Apr. 15, 1986.

I-J

Ibrahim, Ibrahim N.: b. Oct. 1, 1937, Telkaif, Mosul, Iraq.; educ. Patriarchal Seminary (Mosul, Iraq), St. Sulpice Seminary (Paris, France); ord. priest Dec. 30, 1962, in Baghdad, Iraq; ord. titular bishop of Anbar and apostolic exarch for Chaldean Catholics in the United States, Mar. 8, 1982, in Baghdad; installed in Detroit, Apr. 18, 1982; app. first eparch, Aug. 3, 1985, when exarchate was raised to eparchy of St. Thomas Apostle of Detroit.

Imesch, Joseph L.: b. June 21, 1931, Detroit, Mich.; educ. Sacred Heart Seminary (Detroit, Mich.), North American College, Gregorian Univ. (Rome); ord. priest (Detroit*) Dec. 16, 1956; ord. titular bishop of Pomaria and auxiliary bishop of Detroit, Apr. 3, 1973; app. bishop of Joliet, June 30, 1979.

Irwin, Francis X.: b. Jan 9, 1934, Medford, Mass.; educ. Boston College High School, Boston College, St. John's Seminary (Brighton, Mass.), Boston College School of Social Service; ord. priest (Boston*) Feb. 2, 1960; ord. titular bishop of Ubaza and auxiliary bishop of Boston, Sept. 17, 1996.

Jacobs, Sam Galip: b. Mar. 4, 1938, Greenwood, Miss.; educ. Immaculata Seminary (Lafayette, La.), Catholic Univ. (Washington, D.C.); ord. priest (Lafayette) June 6, 1964; became priest of Lake Charles diocese, 1980, when that see was established; ord. bishop of Alexandria, La., Aug. 24, 1989.

Jakubowski, Thad J.: b. Apr. 5, 1924, Chicago, Ill.; educ. Mundelein Seminary, St. Mary of the Lake Univ., Loyola Univ. (Chicago); ord priest (Chicago*) May 3, 1950; ord. titular bishop of Plestia and auxiliary bishop of Chicago, Apr. 11, 1988.

Jarrell, C. Michael: b. May 15, 1940, Opelousas, La.; educ. Immaculata Minor Seminary (Lafayette, La.); Catholic Univ. (Washington, D.C.); ord. priest (Lafayette, La.) June 3, 1967; ord. bishop of Houma-Thibodaux, Mar. 4, 1993.

K

Kaffer, Roger L.: b. Aug. 14, 1927, Joliet, Ill.; educ. Quigley Preparatory Seminary (Chicago, Ill.), St. Mary of the Lake Seminary (Mundelein, Ill.), Gregorian Univ. (Rome); ord. priest (Joliet) May 1, 1954; ord. titular bishop of Dusa and auxiliary bishop of Joliet, June 26, 1985.

Kalisz, Raymond P., S.V.D.: b. Sept. 25, 1927,

Melvindale, Mich.; educ. St. Mary's Seminary (Techny, Ill.); ord. priest Aug. 15, 1954; ord. bishop of Wewak, Papua New Guinea, August 15, 1980.

Kaniecki, Michael Joseph, S.J.: b. Apr. 13, 1935, Detroit Mich.; joined Jesuits 1953; educ. Xavier Univ. (Milford, O.), Mt. St. Michael's Seminary (Spokane, Wash.), Regis College (Willowdale, Ont.); ord. priest June 5, 1965; ord. coadjutor bishop of Fairbanks, May 1, 1984; bishop of Fairbanks, June 1, 1985.

Keating, John Richard: b. July 20, 1934, Chicago, Ill.; educ. Quigley Preparatory Seminary (Chicago, Ill.), St. Mary of the Lake Seminary (Mundelein, Ill.), Gregorian Univ. (Rome); ord. priest (Chicago*) Dec. 20, 1958; ord. bishop of Arlington, Aug. 4, 1983.

Keeler, William Henry: (See Cardinals, Biographies.)

Keleher, James P.: b. July 31, 1931, Chicago, Ill.; educ. Quigley Preparatory Seminary (Chicago, Ill.), St. Mary of the Lake Seminary (Mundelein, Ill.); ord. priest (Chicago*) Apr. 12, 1958; ord. bishop of Belleville, Dec. 11, 1984; app. archbishop of Kansas City, Kans., June 28, 1993.

Kelly, Thomas C., O.P.: b. July 14, 1931, Rochester, N.Y.; educ. Providence College (Providence, R.I.), Immaculate Conception College (Washington, D.C.), Angelicum (Rome); professed in Dominicans, Aug. 26, 1952; secretary, apostolic delegation, Washington, D.C., 1965-71; associate general secretary, 1971-77, and general secretary, 1977-81, NCCB/ USCC; ord. titular bishop of Tusurus and auxiliary bishop of Washington, D.C., Aug. 15, 1977; app. archbishop of Louisville, Dec. 28, 1981, installed Feb. 18, 1982.

Kicanas, Gerald F.: b. Aug. 18, 1941, Chicago, Ill.; educ. Quigley Preparatory Seminary, St. Mary of the Lake Seminary and Loyola University in Chicago; ord. priest (Chicago*) Apr. 27, 1967; ord. titular bishop of Bela and auxiliary of Chicago, Mar. 20, 1995.

Kinney, John F.: b. June 11, 1937, Oelwein, Iowa; educ. Nazareth Hall and St. Paul Seminaries (St. Paul, Minn.); Pontifical Lateran University (Rome); ord. priest (St. Paul-Minneapolis*) Feb. 2, 1963; ord. titular bishop of Caorle and auxiliary bishop of St. Paul and Minneapolis, Jan. 25, 1977; app. bishop of Bismarck June 30, 1982; app. bishop of St. Cloud, May 9, 1995.

Kmiec, Edward U.: b. June 4, 1936, Trenton, N.J.; educ. St. Charles College (Catonsville, Md.), St. Mary's Seminary (Baltimore, Md.), Gregorian Univ. (Rome); ord. priest (Trenton) Dec. 20, 1961; ord. titular bishop of Simidicca and auxiliary bishop of Trenton, Nov. 3, 1982; app. bishop of Nashville, Oct. 13, 1992; installed Dec. 3, 1992.

Koester, Charles R.: b. Sept. 16, 1915, Jefferson City, Mo.; educ. Conception Academy (Conception, Mo.), St. Louis Preparatory Seminary and Kenrick Seminary (St. Louis, Mo.), North American College (Rome); ord. priest (St. Louis*) Dec. 20, 1941; ord. titular bishop of Suacia and auxiliary bishop of St. Louis, Feb. 11, 1971; retired Sept. 10, 1991.

Krawczak, Arthur H.: b. Feb. 2, 1913, Detroit, Mich.; educ. Sacred Heart Seminary, Sts. Cyril and Methodius Seminary (Orchard Lake, Mich.), Catholic Univ. (Washington, D.C.); ord. priest (Detroit*)

May 18, 1940; ord. titular bishop of Subbar and auxiliary bishop of Detroit, Apr. 3, 1973; retired Aug. 17, 1982.

Kucera, Daniel W., O.S.B.: b. May 7, 1923, Chicago, Ill.; educ. St. Procopius College (Lisle, Ill.), Catholic Univ. (Washington, D.C.); professed in Order of St. Benedict, June 16, 1944; ord. priest May 26, 1949; abbot, St. Procopius Abbey, 1964-71; pres. Illinois Benedictine College, 1959-65 and 1971-76; ord. titular bishop of Natchez and auxiliary bishop of Joliet, July 21, 1977; app. bishop of Salina, Mar. 5, 1980; app. archbishop of Dubuque, installed Feb. 23, 1984; retired Oct. 16, 1995.

Kuchmiak, Michael, C.SsR.: b. Feb. 5, 1923, Obertyn, Horodenka, Western Ukraine; left during World War II; educ. St. Josaphat Ukrainian Seminary (Rome, Italy), St. Mary's Seminary (Meadowvale, Ont., Canada); ord. priest May 13, 1956; in the U.S. from 1967; ord. titular bishop of Agathopolis and auxiliary bishop of Ukrainian metropolitan of Philadelphia, Apr. 27, 1988; exarch of apostolic exarchate for Ukrainian Catholics in Great Britain, June 24, 1989.

Kupfer, William F., M.M.: b. Jan. 28, 1909, Brooklyn, N.Y.; educ. Cathedral College (Brooklyn, N.Y.), Maryknoll Seminary (Maryknoll, N.Y.); ord. priest June 11, 1933; missionary in China; app. prefect apostolic of Taichung, Taiwan, 1951; ord. first bishop of Taichung, July 25, 1962; retired Sept. 3, 1986.

Kurtz, Robert, C.R.: b. July 25, 1939, Chicago, Ill.; ord. priest Mar. 11, 1967; ord. bishop of Hamilton, Bermuda, Sept. 15, 1995.

Kuzma, George M.: b. July 24, 1925, Windber, Pa.; educ. St. Francis Seminary (Loretto, Pa.), St. Procopius College (Lisle, Ill.), Sts. Cyril and Methodius Byzantine Catholic Seminary, Duquesne Univ. (Pittsburgh, Pa.); ord. priest (Pittsburgh*, Byzantine Rite), May 5, 1955; ord. titular bishop of Telmisso and auxiliary bishop of Byzantine eparchy of Passaic, 1987; app. bishop of Byzantine diocese of Van Nuys, Calif., Oct. 23, 1990, installed Jan. 15, 1991.

L

Lambert, Francis, S.M.: b. Feb. 7, 1921, Lawrence, Mass.; educ. Marist Seminary (Framingham, Mass.); ord. priest, June 29, 1946; served in Marist missions in Oceania; provincial of Marist Oceania province, 1971; ord. bishop of Port Vila, Vanuatu (New Hebrides), Mar. 20, 1977; retired Nov. 30, 1996..

Larkin, W. Thomas: b. Mar. 31, 1923, Mt. Morris, N.Y.; educ. St. Andrew Seminary and St. Bernard Seminary (Rochester, N.Y.); Angelicum Univ. (Rome); ord. priest (St. Augustine) May 15, 1947; ord. bishop of St. Petersburg, May 27, 1979; retired Nov. 29, 1988.

Law, Bernard F.: (See Cardinals, Biographies.)

Leibrecht, John J.: b. Aug. 30, 1930, Overland, Mo.; educ. Catholic Univ. (Washington, D.C.); ord. priest (St. Louis*) Mar. 17, 1956; superintendent of schools of St. Louis archdiocese, 1962-1981; ord. bishop of Springfield-Cape Girardeau, Mo., Dec. 12, 1984.

Lessard, Raymond W.: b. Dec. 21, 1930, Grafton,

N.D.; educ. St. Paul Seminary (St. Paul, Minn.), North American College (Rome); ord. priest (Fargo) Dec. 16, 1956; served on staff of the Congregation for Bishops in the Roman Curia, 1964-73; ord. bishop of Savannah, Apr. 27, 1973; retired Feb. 7, 1995.

Levada, William J.: b. June 15, 1936, Long Beach, Calif.; educ. St. John's College (Camarillo, Calif.), Gregorian Univ. (Rome); ord. priest (Los Angeles*) Dec. 20, 1961; ord. titular bishop of Capri and auxiliary bishop of Los Angeles, May 12, 1983; app. archbishop of Portland, Ore., July 3, 1986; coadjutor archbishop of San Francisco, Aug. 17, 1995; archbishop of San Francisco Dec. 27, 1995.

Lipscomb, Oscar H.: b. Sept. 21, 1931, Mobile, Ala.; educ. McGill Institute, St. Bernard College (Cullman, Ala.), North American College and Gregorian Univ. (Rome), Catholic Univ. (Washington, D.C.); ord. priest (Mobile*) July 15, 1956; ord. first archbishop of Mobile, Nov. 16, 1980.

Lohmuller, Martin N.: b. Aug. 21, 1919, Philadelphia, Pa.; educ. St. Charles Borromeo Seminary (Philadelphia, Pa.), Catholic Univ. (Washington, D.C.); ord. priest (Philadelphia*) June 3, 1944; ord. titular bishop of Ramsbury and auxiliary bishop of Philadelphia, Apr. 2, 1970; retired Oct. 11, 1994.

Lori, William E.: b. May 6, 1951, Louisville, Ky.; educ. St. Pius X College (Covington, Ky.), Mount St. Mary's Seminary (Emmitsburg, Md.), Catholic Univ. (Washington, D.C.); ord. priest (Washington*) May 14, 1977; ord. titular bishop of Bulla and auxiliary bishop of Washington, D.C., Apr. 20, 1995.

Losten, Basil: b. May 11, 1930, Chesapeake City, Md.; educ. St. Basil's College (Stamford, Conn.), Catholic University (Washington, D.C.); ord. priest (Philadelphia*, Ukrainian Byzantine) June 10, 1957; ord. titular bishop of Arcadiopolis in Asia and auxiliary bishop of Ukrainian archeparchy of Philadelphia, May 25, 1971; app. apostolic administrator of archeparchy, 1976; app. bishop of Ukrainian eparchy of Stamford, Sept. 20, 1977.

Lotocky, Innocent Hilarius, O.S.B.M.: b. Nov. 3, 1915, Petlykiwci, Ukraine; educ. seminaries in Ukraine, Czechoslovakia and Austria; ord. priest Nov. 24, 1940; ord. bishop of St. Nicholas of Chicago for the Ukrainians, Mar. 1, 1981; retired July 15, 1993.

Loverde, Paul S.: b. Sept. 3, 1940, Framingham, Mass.; educ. St. Thomas Seminary (Bloomfield, Conn.), St. Bernard Seminary (Rochester, N.Y.), Gregorian Univ. (Rome), Catholic Univ. (Washington, D.C.); ord. priest (Norwich), Dec. 18, 1965; ord. titular bishop of Ottabia and auxiliary bishop of Hartford, Apr. 12, 1988; app. bishop of Ogdensburg, Nov. 11, 1993; installed Jan. 17, 1994.

Lubachivsky, Myroslav I.: (See Cardinals, Biographies.)

Lucker, Raymond A.: b. Feb. 24, 1927, St. Paul, Minn.; educ. St. Paul Seminary (St. Paul, Minn.); University of Minnesota (Minneapolis), Angelicum (Rome); ord. priest (St. Paul and Minneapolis*) June 7, 1952; director of USCC department of education, 1968-71; ord. titular bishop of Meta and auxiliary bishop of St. Paul and Minneapolis, Sept. 8, 1971; app. bishop of New Ulm, Dec. 23, 1975, installed Feb. 19, 1976.

Lynch, George E.: b. Mar. 4, 1917, New York,

N.Y.; educ. Fordham Univ. (New York), Mt. St. Mary's Seminary (Emmitsburg, Md.), Catholic Univ. (Washington, D.C.); ord. priest (Raleigh) May 29, 1943; ord. titular bishop of Satafi and auxiliary of Raleigh Jan. 6, 1970; retired Apr. 16, 1985.

Lynch, Robert N.: b. May 27, 1941, Charleston, W. Va.; educ. Pontifical College Josephinism (Columbus, Ohio); John XXIII National Seminary (Weston, Mass.); ord. priest (Miami*) May 13, 1978; associate general secretary (1984-89) and general secretary (1989-95) of the NCCB/USCC; app. bishop of St. Petersburg, Dec. 5, 1995; ord. and installed Jan. 26, 1996.

Lyne, Timothy J.: b. Mar. 21, 1919, Chicago, Ill.; educ. Quigley Preparatory Seminary, St. Mary of the Lake Seminary (Mundelein, Ill.); ord. priest (Chicago*) May 1, 1943; ord. titular bishop of Vamalla and auxiliary bishop of Chicago, Dec. 13, 1983; retired Jan. 24, 1995.

M

Macaluso, Christie Albert: b. June 12, 1945, Hartford, Conn.; educ. St. Thomas Seminary (Bloomfield, Conn.), St. Mary's Seminary (Baltimore, Md), Trinity College (Hartford, Conn.), New York University; ord. priest (Hartford*) May 21, 1971; ord. titular bishop of Grass Valley and auxiliary bishop of Hartford, June 10, 1997.

McAuliffe, Michael F.: b. Nov. 22, 1920, Kansas City, Mo.; educ. St. Louis Preparatory Seminary (St. Louis, Mo.), Catholic Univ. (Washington, D.C.); ord. priest (Kansas City-St. Joseph) May 31, 1945; ord. bishop of Jefferson City, Aug. 18, 1969; retired .June, 1997.

McCarrick, Theodore E.: b. July 7, 1930, New York, N.Y.; educ. Fordham Univ. (Bronx, N.Y.), St. Joseph's Seminary (Dunwoodie, N.Y.), Catholic Univ. (Washington, D.C.); ord. priest (New York*) May 31, 1958; dean of students Catholic Univ. of America, 1961-63; pres., Catholic Univ. of Puerto Rico, 1965-69; secretary to Cardinal Cooke, 1970; ord. titular bishop of Rusubisir and auxiliary bishop of New York, June 29, 1977; app. first bishop of Metuchen, N.J., Nov. 19, 1981, installed Jan. 31, 1982; app. archbishop of Newark, June 3, 1986, installed July 25, 1986.

McCarthy, Edward A.: b. Apr. 10, 1918, Cincinnati, O.; educ. Mt. St. Mary Seminary (Norwood, O.), Catholic Univ. (Washington, D.C.), Lateran and Angelicum (Rome); ord. priest (Cincinnati*) May 29, 1943; ord. titular bishop of Tamascani and auxiliary bishop of Cincinnati, June 15, 1965; first bishop of Phoenix, Ariz., Dec. 2, 1969; app. coadjutor archbishop of Miami, Fla., July 7, 1976; succeeded as archbishop of Miami, July 26, 1977; retired Nov. 3, 1994.

McCarthy, John E.: b. June 21, 1930, Houston, Tex.; educ. Univ. of St. Thomas (Houston, Tex.); ord. priest (Galveston-Houston) May 26, 1956; assistant director Social Action Dept. USCC, 1967-69; executive director Texas Catholic Conference; ord. titular bishop of Pedena and auxiliary bishop of Galveston-Houston, Mar. 14, 1979; app. bishop of Austin, Dec. 19, 1985, installed Feb. 25, 1986.

McCormack, John B.: b Aug. 12, 1935, Winthrop, Mass; educ. St. John Seminary College and St. John Seminary Theologate (Boston, Mass.); ord. priest (Boston*) Feb. 2, 1960; ord. titular bishop of Cerbali and auxiliary bishop of Boston, Dec. 27, 1995.

McCormack, William J.: b. Jan. 24, 1924, New York, N.Y.; educ. Christ the King Seminary, St. Bonaventure Univ. (St. Bonaventure, N.Y.); ord. priest (New York*) Feb. 21, 1959; national director of Society for the Propagation of the Faith, 1980; ord. titular bishop of Nicives and auxiliary bishop of New York, Jan. 6, 1987.

McDonald, Andrew J.: b. Oct. 24, 1923, Savannah, Ga.; educ. St. Mary's Seminary (Baltimore, Md.), Catholic Univ. (Washington, D.C.), Lateran Univ. (Rome); ord. priest (Savannah) May 8, 1948; ord. bishop of Little Rock, Sept. 5, 1972.

McDonnell, Charles J.: b. July 7, 1928, Brooklyn, N.Y.; educ. Seton Hall Univ. (South Orange, N.J.), Immaculate Conception Seminary (Darlington, N.J.), Long Island Univ. (Brooklyn, N.Y.); ord. priest (Newark*) May 29, 1954; U.S. Army Chaplain, 1965-89; retired from active duty with rank of Brigadier General; ord. titular bishop of Pocofelto and auxiliary bishop of Newark, May 12, 1994.

McDonough, Thomas J.: b. Dec. 5, 1911, Philadelphia, Pa.; educ. St. Charles Seminary (Overbrook, Pa.), Catholic Univ. (Washington, D.C.); ord. priest (Philadelphia*) May 26, 1938; ord. titular bishop of Thenae and auxiliary bishop of St. Augustine, Apr. 30, 1947; app. auxiliary bishop of Savannah, Jan. 2, 1957; named bishop of Savannah, installed Apr. 27, 1960; app. archbishop of Louisville, installed May 2, 1967; resigned Sept. 29, 1981.

McDowell, John B.: b. July 17, 1921, New Castle, Pa.; educ. St. Vincent College, St. Vincent Theological Seminary (Latrobe, Pa.), Catholic Univ. (Washington, D.C.); ord. priest (Pittsburgh) Nov. 4, 1945; superintendent of schools, Pittsburgh diocese, 1955-70; ord. titular bishop of Tamazuca, and auxiliary bishop of Pittsburgh, Sept. 8, 1966; retired Sept. 9, 1996.

McFarland, Norman F.: b. Feb. 21, 1922, Martinez, Calif.; educ. St. Patrick's Seminary (Menlo Park, Calif.), Catholic Univ. (Washington, D.C.); ord. priest (San Francisco*) June 15, 1946; ord. titular bishop of Bida and auxiliary bishop of San Francisco, Sept. 8, 1970; apostolic adminstrator of Reno, 1974; app. bishop of Reno, Feb. 10, 1976, installed Mar. 31, 1976; title of see changed to Reno-Las Vegas; app. bishop of Orange, Calif., Dec. 29, 1986; installed Feb. 24, 1987.

McGann, John R.: b. Dec. 2, 1924, Brooklyn, N.Y.; educ. Cathedral College (Brooklyn, N.Y.), Immaculate Conception Seminary (Huntington, L.I.); ord. priest (Rockville Centre) June 3, 1950; ord. titular bishop of Morosbisdus and auxiliary bishop of Rockville Centre, Jan. 7, 1971; vicar general and episcopal vicar; app. bishop of Rockville Centre May 3, 1976, installed June 24, 1976.

McGarry, Urban, T.O.R.: b. Nov. 11, 1911, Warren, Pa.; ord. priest Oct. 3, 1942, in India; prefect apostolic of Bhagalpur, Aug. 7, 1956; ord. first bishop of Bhagalpur, India, May 10, 1965; resigned Nov. 30, 1987.

McGrath, Patrick J.: b. July 11, 1945, Dublin, Ire.; educ. St. John's College Seminary (Waterford, Ire.), Lateran Univ. (Rome, Italy); ord. priest in Ireland June 7, 1970; came to U.S. same year and became San Francisco archdiocesan priest; ord. titular bishop of Allegheny and auxiliary bishop of San Francisco, Jan. 25, 1989.

McHugh, James T.: b. Jan. 3, 1932, Orange, N.J. educ. Seton Hall Univ. (S. Orange, N.J.), Immaculate Conception Seminary (Darlington, N.J.), Fordham Univ. (New York, N.Y.), Catholic Univ. (Washington, D.C.), Angelicum (Rome, Italy); ord. priest (Newark*) May 25, 1957; assistant director, 1965-67, and director, 1967-75, of Family Life Division, USCC; director, 1972-78, of NCCB Office for Pro-Life Activities; special advisor to Mission of Permanent Observer of Holy See to UN; ord. titular bishop of Morosbisdo and auxiliary of Newark, Jan. 25, 1988; bishop of Camden, May 22, 1989.

McKinney, Joseph C.: b. Sept. 10, 1928, Grand Rapids, Mich.: educ. St. Joseph's Seminary (Grand Rapids, Mich.), Seminaire de Philosophie (Montreal, Canada), Urban Univ. (Rome, Italy); ord. priest (Grand Rapids) Dec. 20, 1953; ord. titular bishop of Lentini and auxiliary bishop of Grand Rapids, Sept. 26, 1968.

McLaughlin, Bernard J.: b. Nov. 19, 1912, Buffalo, N.Y.; educ. Urban Univ. (Rome, Italy); ord. priest (Buffalo) Dec. 21, 1935, at Rome; ord. titular bishop of Mottola and auxiliary bishop of Buffalo, Jan. 6, 1969; resigned Jan. 5, 1988.

McNabb, John C., O.S.A.: b. Dec. 11, 1925, Beloit, Wis.; educ. Villanova Univ. (Villanova, Pa.), Augustinian College and Catholic Univ. (Washington, D.C.), De Paul Univ. (Chicago, Ill.); ord. priest May 24, 1952; ord. titular bishop of Saia Maggiore, June 17, 1967 (resigned titular see, Dec. 27, 1977); prelate of Chulucanas, Peru, 1967; first bishop of Chulucanas, Dec. 12, 1988.

McNamara, John R.: b. Sept. 4, 1927, Worcester, Mass.; educ. Holy Cross College (Worcester, Mass.), St. John's Seminary (Boston, Mass.); ord. priest (Boston*) Jan. 10, 1952; served as chaplain in the U.S. Navy 1962-88; attained the rank of Rear Admiral and was Chief of Naval Chaplains; ord. titular bishop of Risinium and auxiliary bishop of Boston, May 21, 1992.

McNamara, Lawrence J.: b. Aug. 5, 1928, Chicago, Ill.; educ. St. Paul Seminary (St. Paul, Minn.), Catholic Univ. (Washington, D.C.); ord. priest (Kansas City-St. Joseph) May 30, 1953; executive director of Campaign for Human Development 1973-77; ord. bishop of Grand Island, Nebr., Mar. 28, 1978.

McNaughton, William J., M.M.: b. Dec. 7, 1926, Lawrence, Mass.; educ. Maryknoll Seminary (Maryknoll, N.Y.); ord. priest June 13, 1953; ord. titular bishop of Thuburbo Minus and vicar apostolic of Inchon, Korea, Aug. 24, 1961; first bishop of Inchon, Mar. 10, 1962, when vicariate was raised to diocese.

McRaith, John Jeremiah: b. Dec. 6, 1934, Hutchinson, Minn.; educ. St. John Preparatory School (Collegeville, Minn.), Loras College, St. Bernard Seminary (Dubuque, Ia); ord. priest (New Ulm) Feb. 21, 1960; exec. dir. of Catholic Rural Life Conference, 1971-78; ord. bishop of Owensboro, Ky., Dec. 15, 1982.

Madera, Joseph J., M.Sp.S.: b. Nov. 27, 1927, San Francisco, Calif.; educ. Domus Studiorum of the Missionaries of the Holy Spirit (Coyoacan, D.F.

Mexico); ord. priest June 15, 1957; ord. coadjutor bishop of Fresno, Mar. 4, 1980; bishop of Fresno, July 1, 1980; app. titular bishop of Orte and auxiliary of Military Services archdiocese, June 30, 1991.

Maginnis, Robert P.: b. Dec. 22, 1933, Philadelphia, Pa.; educ. St. Charles Borromeo Seminary (Overbrook, Pa.); ord. priest (Philadelphia*) May 13, 1961; ord. titular bishop of Siminina and auxiliary bishop of Philadelphia, Mar. 11, 1996.

Maguire, Joseph F.: b. Sept. 4, 1919, Boston, Mass.; educ. Boston College, St. John's Seminary (Boston, Mass.); ord. priest (Boston*) June 29, 1945; ord. titular bishop of Macteris and auxiliary bishop of Boston, Feb. 2, 1972; app. coadjutor bishop of Springfield, Mass., Apr. 13, 1976; succeeded as bishop of Springfield, Mass., Oct. 15, 1977; retired Dec. 27, 1991.

Mahoney, James P.: b. Aug. 16, 1925, Kingston, N.Y.; educ. St. Joseph's Seminary (Dunwoodie, N.Y.); ord. priest (New York*) May 19, 1951; ord. titular bishop of Ipagro and auxiliary bishop of New York, Sept. 15, 1972; retired May 10, 1997.

Mahony, Roger M.: (See Cardinals, Biographies.)

Maida, Adam J.: (See Cardinals, Biographies.)

Malone, James W.: b. Mar. 8, 1920, Youngstown, O.; educ. St. Charles Preparatory Seminary (Catonsville, Md.), St. Mary's Seminary (Cleveland, O.), Catholic Univ. (Washington, D.C.); ord. priest (Youngstown) May 26, 1945; ord. titular bishop of Alabanda and auxiliary bishop of Youngstown, Mar. 24, 1960; apostolic administrator, 1966; bishop of Youngstown, installed June 20, 1968; president of NCCB/USCC, 1983-86; retired Dec. 5, 1995.

Maloney, Charles G.: b. Sept. 9, 1912, Louisville, Ky.; educ. St. Joseph's College (Rensselaer, Ind.), North American College (Rome); ord. priest (Louisville*) Dec. 8, 1937; ord. titular bishop of Capsa and auxiliary bishop of Louisville, Feb. 2, 1955; resigned Jan. 8, 1988; transferred to Bardstown, 1995, when it was reestablished as a titular see.

Manning, Elias (James), O.F.M. Conv.: b. Apr. 14, 1938, Troy, N.Y.; educ. Sao José Seminary (Rio de Janeiro, Brazil); ord. priest Oct. 30, 1965, in New York; ord. bishop of Valenca, Brazil, May 13, 1990.

Manning, Thomas R., O.F.M.: b. Aug. 29, 1922, Baltimore, Md.; educ. Duns Scotus College (Southfield, Mich.), Holy Name College (Washington, D.C.); ord. priest June 5, 1948; ord. titular bishop of Arsamosata, July 14, 1959 (resigned titular see Dec. 30, 1977); prelate of Coroico, Bolivia, July 14, 1959; became first bishop, 1983, when prelature was raised to diocese; retired Oct. 9, 1996.

Mansell, Henry J.: b. Oct. 10, 1937, New York, N.Y.; educ. Cathedral College, St. Joseph's Seminary and College (New York); North American College, Gregorian Univ. (Rome); ord. priest (New York*) Dec. 19, 1962; ord. titular bishop of Marazane and auxiliary bishop of New York, Jan. 6, 1993, by John Paul II in Vatican City; app. bishop of Buffalo, Apr. 18, 1995; installed June 12, 1995.

Manz, John R.: b. Nov. 14, 1945, Chicago, Ill; educ. Niles College Seminary (Niles, Ill), Univ. of St. Mary of the Lake-Mundelein Seminary (Chicago); ord. priest (Chicago*) May 12, 1971; ord. titular bishop of Mulia and auxiliary bishop of Chicago, Mar. 5, 1996.

Marcinkus, Paul C.: b. Jan. 15, 1922, Cicero, Ill.; ord. priest (Chicago*) May 3, 1947; served in Vatican secretariat from 1952; ord. titular bishop of Orta, Jan. 6, 1969; secretary (1968-71) and president (1971-89) of Institute for Works of Religion (Vatican Bank); titular archbishop, Sept. 26, 1981; former pro-president of Pontifical Commission for the State of Vatican City (resigned in 1990).

Marconi, Dominic A.: b. Mar. 13, 1927, Newark, N.J.; educ. Seton Hall Univ. (S. Orange, N.J.), Immaculate Conception Seminary (Darlington, N.J.), Catholic Univ. (Washington, D.C.); ord. priest (Newark*) May 30, 1953; ord. titular bishop of Bure and auxiliary bishop of Newark, June 25, 1976.

Marino, Eugene A., S.S.J.: b. May 29, 1934, Biloxi, Miss.; educ. Epiphany Apostolic College and Mary Immaculate Novitiate (Newburgh, N.Y.), St. Joseph's Seminary (Washington, D.C.), Catholic Univ. (Washington, D.C.), Loyola Univ. (New Orleans, La.), Fordham Univ. (New York City); ord. priest June 9, 1962; ord. titular bishop of Walla Walla and auxiliary bishop of Washington, D.C., Sept. 12, 1974; archbishop of Atlanta, installed May 5, 1988; resigned July 10, 1990.

Martino, Joseph F.: b. May 1, 1946, Philadelphia, Pa.; educ. St. Charles Borromeo Seminary (Overbrook, Pa.), Gregorian Univ. (Rome); ord. priest (Philadelphia*) Dec. 18, 1970; ord. titular bishop of Cellae in Mauretania and auxiliary bishop of Philadelphia, Mar. 11, 1996.

Matthiesen, Leroy Theodore: b. June 11, 1921, Olfen, Tex.; educ. Josephinum College (Columbus, O.), Catholic Univ. (Washington, D.C.), Register School of Journalism; ord. priest (Amarillo) Mar. 10, 1946; ord. bishop of Amarillo, May 30, 1980; retired Jan. 21, 1997.

Melczek, Dale J.: b. Nov. 9, 1938, Detroit, Mich.; educ. St. Mary's College (Orchard Lake, Mich.), St. John's Provincial Seminary (Plymouth, Mich.), Univ. of Detroit; ord. priest (Detroit*) June 6, 1964; ord. titular bishop of Trau and auxiliary bishop of Detroit, Jan. 27, 1983; apostolic administrator of Gary, Aug. 19, 1992; coadjutor bishop of Gary, Oct. 28, 1995; bishop of Gary, June 1, 1996.

Mengeling, Carl F.: b. Oct. 22, 1930, Hammond, Ind.; educ. St. Meinrad College and Seminary (St. Meinrad, Ind.), Alphonsianum Univ. (Rome); ord. priest (Gary) May 25, 1957; ord. bishop of Lansing Jan. 25, 1996.

Mestice, Anthony F.: b. Dec. 6, 1923, New York, N.Y.; educ. St. Joseph Seminary (Yonkers, N.Y.); ord. priest (New York*) June 4, 1949; ord. titular bishop of Villa Nova and auxiliary bishop of New York, Apr. 27, 1973.

Michaels, James E., S.S.C.: b. May 30, 1926, Chicago, Ill.; educ. Columban Seminary (St. Columban, Neb.), Gregorian Univ. (Rome); ord. priest Dec. 21, 1951; ord. titular bishop of Verbe and auxiliary bishop of Kwang Ju, Korea, Apr. 14, 1966; app. auxiliary bishop of Wheeling, Apr. 3, 1973 (title of see changed to Wheeling-Charleston, 1974); resigned Sept. 22, 1987.

Milone, Anthony M.: b. Sept. 24, 1932, Omaha, Nebr.; educ. North American College (Rome); ord. priest (Omaha*) Dec. 15, 1957, in Rome; ord. titular bishop of Plestia and auxiliary bishop of Omaha, Jan. 6, 1982; app. bishop of Great Falls-Billings, Dec. 14, 1987, installed Feb. 23, 1988.

Minder, John, O.S.F.S.: b. Nov. 1, 1923, Philadelphia, Pa.; educ. Catholic Univ. (Washington, D.C.); ord. priest June 3, 1950; ord. bishop of Keimos (renamed Keimos-Upington, 1985), South Africa, Jan. 10, 1968.

Moeddel, Carl K.: b. Dec. 28, 1937, Cincinnati, Ohio; educ. Athenaeum of Ohio, Mt. St. Mary's Seminary (Cincinnati); ord. priest (Cincinnati*) Aug. 15, 1962; ord. titular bishop of Bistue and auxiliary bishop of Cincinnati, Aug. 24, 1993.

Montrose, Donald W.: b. May 13, 1923, Denver, Colo.; educ. St. John's Seminary (Camarillo, Calif.); ord. priest (Los Angeles*) May 7, 1949; ord. titular bishop of Forum Novum and auxiliary bishop of Los Angeles, May 12, 1983; app. bishop of Stockton, Dec. 17, 1985, installed Feb. 20, 1986.

Moreno, Manuel D.: b. Nov. 27, 1930, Placentia, Calif.; educ. Univ. of California (Los Angeles), Our Lady Queen of Angels (San Fernando, Calif.), St. John's Seminary (Camarillo, Calif.); ord. priest (Los Angeles*) Apr. 25, 1961; ord. titular bishop of Tanagra and auxiliary bishop of Los Angeles, Feb. 19, 1977; bishop of Tucson, Jan. 12, 1982, installed Mar. 11, 1982.

Morneau, Robert F.: b. Sept. 10, 1938, New London, Wis.; educ. St. Norbert's College (De Pere, Wis.), Sacred Heart Seminary (Oneida, Wis.), Catholic Univ. (Washington, D.C.); ord. priest (Green Bay) May 28, 1966; ord. titular bishop of Massa Lubrense and auxiliary bishop of Green Bay, Feb. 22, 1979.

Moskal, Robert M.: b. Oct. 24, 1937, Carnegie, Pa.; educ. St. Basil Minor Seminary (Stamford, Conn.), St. Josaphat Seminary and Catholic Univ. (Washington, D.C.); ord. priest (Philadelphia*, Byzantine Ukrainian) Mar. 25, 1963; ord. titular bishop of Agatopoli and auxiliary bishop of the Ukrainian archeparchy of Philadelphia, Oct. 13, 1981; app. first bishop of St. Josaphat in Parma, Dec. 5, 1983.

Moynihan, James M.: b. July 16, 1932, Rochester, N.Y.; educ. St. Bernard's Seminary (Rochester, N.Y.), North American College and Gregorian Univ. (Rome); ord. priest (Rochester) Dec. 15, 1957, in Rome; ord. bishop of Syracuse May 29, 1995.

Muench Robert W.: b. Dec. 28, 1942, Louisville, Ky.; educ. St. Joseph Seminary and Notre Dame Seminary (New Orleans, La.), Catholic Univ. (Washington, D.C.); ord. priest (New Orleans*) June 18, 1968; ord. titular bishop of Mactaris and auxiliary bishop of New Orleans, June 29, 1990; app. bishop of Covington Jan., 1996; installed Mar. 19, 1996.

Mulvee, Robert E.: b. Feb. 15, 1930, Boston, Mass.; educ. St. Thomas Seminary (Bloomfield, Conn.), University Seminary (Ottawa, Ont., Canada), American College (Louvain, Belgium), Lateran Univ. (Rome); ord. priest (Manchester) June 30, 1957; ord. titular bishop of Summa and auxiliary bishop of Manchester, N.H., Apr. 14, 1977; app. bishop of Wilmington, Del., Feb. 19, 1985; app. coadjutor bishop of Providence, Feb. 9, 1995; bishop of Providence, June 11, 1997.

Mundo, Miguel P.: b. July 25, 1937, New York, N.Y.; educ. Fordham Univ. (Bronx, N.Y.), St. Jerome's College (Kitchener, Ont., Canada), St

Francis Seminary (Loretto, Pa.); ord. priest (Camden) May 19, 1962; missionary in Brazil from 1963; ord. titular bishop of Blanda Julia and auxiliary bishop of Jatai, Brazil, June 2, 1978.

Murphy, Michael J.: b. July 1, 1915, Cleveland, O.; educ. Niagara Univ. (Niagara Falls, N.Y.); North American College (Rome), Catholic Univ. (Washington, D.C.); ord. priest (Cleveland) Feb. 28, 1942; ord. titular bishop of Ariendela and auxiliary bishop of Cleveland, June 11, 1976; app. coadjutor bishop of Erie, Nov. 20, 1978; bishop of Erie, July 16, 1982; retired June 12, 1990.

Murphy, Philip Francis: b. Mar. 25, 1933, Cumberland, Md.; educ. St. Mary Seminary (Baltimore, Md.), North American College (Rome); ord. priest (Baltimore*) Dec. 20, 1958; ord. titular bishop of Tacarata and auxiliary bishop of Baltimore, Feb. 29, 1976.

Murphy, William F.: b. May 14, 1940, Boston Mass.; educ. Boston Latin School (Boston), Harvard College, St. John's Seminary (Boston), Gregorian Univ. (Rome); ord. priest (Boston*) Dec. 16, 1964; ord. titular bishop of Saia Maggiore and auxiliary bishop of Boston, Dec. 27, 1995.

Murry, George V., S.J.: b. Dec. 28, 1948, Camden, N.J.; educ. St. Joseph's College (Philadelphia, Pa.), St. Thomas Seminary (Bloomfield, Conn.), St. Mary Seminary (Baltimore, Md.), Jesuit School of Theology (Berkeley, Calif), George Washington Univ. (Washington, D.C.); entered Jesuits 1972; ord. priest June 9, 1979; ord. titular bishop of Fuerteventura and auxiliary bishop of Chicago, Mar. 20, 1995.

Myers, John Joseph: b. July 26, 1941, Ottawa, Ill.; educ. Loras College (Dubuque, Ia.), North American College and Gregorian Univ. (Rome), Catholic Univ. of America (Washington, D.C.); ord. priest (Peoria) Dec. 17, 1966, in Rome; ord. coadjutor bishop of Peoria, Sept. 3, 1987; bishop of Peoria, Jan. 23, 1990.

N

Naumann, Joseph F.: b. June 4, 1949, St. Louis, Mo.; educ. Cardinal Glennon Seminary College and Kenrick Seminary (St. Louis, Mo.); ord. priest (St. Louis*) 1975; app. titular bishop of Caput Cilla and auxiliary bishop of St. Louis, July 9, 1997.

Nevins, John J.: b. Jan. 19, 1932, New Rochelle, N.Y.; educ. Iona College (New Rochelle, N.Y.), Catholic Univ. (Washington, D.C.); ord. priest (Miami*) June 6, 1959; ord. titular bishop of Rusticana and auxiliary bishop of Miami, Mar. 24, 1979; app. first bishop of Venice, Fla., July 17, 1984; installed Oct. 25, 1984.

Newman, William C.: b. Aug. 16, 1928, Baltimore, Md.; educ. St. Mary Seminary (Baltimore, Md.), Catholic Univ. (Washington, D.C.), Loyola College (Baltimore, Md.); ord. priest (Baltimore*) May 29, 1954; ord. titular bishop of Numluli and auxiliary bishop of Baltimore, July 2, 1984.

Neylon, Martin J., S.J.: b. Feb. 13, 1920, Buffalo, N.Y.; ord. priest June 18, 1950; ord. titular bishop of Libertina and coadjutor vicar apostolic of the Caroline and Marshall Islands, Feb. 2, 1970; vicar apostolic of Caroline and Marshall Is., Sept. 20, 1971; first bishop of Carolines-Marshalls when vicariate apostolic was raised to diocese, 1979; title

of see changed to Caroline Islands, Apr. 23, 1993; retired Mar. 25, 1995.

Niederauer, George H.: b. June 14, 1936, Los Angeles, Calif.; educ. St. John's Seminary (Camarillo, Calif.), Catholic Univ. (Washington, D.C.), Loyola Univ. of Los Angeles, Univ. of Southern California, Loretta Heights College (Denver, Colo.); ord. priest (Los Angeles*) Apr. 30, 1962; app. bishop of Salt Lake City, Nov. 3, 1994, ord. Jan. 25, 1995.

Niedergeses, James D.: b. Feb. 2, 1917, Lawrenceburg, Tenn.; educ. St. Bernard College (St. Bernard, Ala.), St. Ambrose College (Davenport, Ia.), Mt. St. Mary Seminary of the West and Athenaeum (Cincinnati, Ohio); ord. priest (Nashville) May 20, 1944; ord. bishop of Nashville, May 20, 1975; retired Oct. 13, 1992.

Nienstedt, John C.: b. Mar. 18, 1947, Detroit, Mich.; educ. Sacred Heart Seminary (Detroit), North American College, Gregorian Univ., Alphonsianum (Rome); ord. priest (Detroit*) July 27, 1974; served in Vatican Secretariat of State, 1980-86; rector of Sacred Heart Seminary (Detroit), 1988-94; pastor of the Shrine of the Little Flower (Royal Oak, Mich.), 1994; ord. titular bishop of Alton and auxiliary bishop of Detroit, July 9, 1996.

Nolan, John G.: b. Mar. 15, 1924, Mechanicville, N.Y.; educ. Siena College (Loudonville, N.Y.), St. Charles College (Catonsville, Md.), St. Mary's Seminary (Baltimore, Md.); Catholic Univ. (Washington, D.C.), Fordham Univ. (New York, N.Y.); ord. priest (Albany) June 11, 1949; ord. titular bishop of Natchez and auxiliary bishop of Military Services archdiocese Jan. 6, 1988.

Nolker, Bernard, C.SS.R.: b. Sept. 25, 1912, Baltimore, Md.; educ. St. Mary's College (North East, Pa.), St. Mary's College (Ilchester, Md.), Mt. St. Alphonsus Seminary (Esopus, N.Y.); ord. priest June 18, 1939; ord. first bishop of Paranagua, Brazil, Apr. 25, 1963; retired Mar. 14, 1989.

Novak, Alfred, C.SS.R.: b. June 2, 1930, Dwight, Nebr.; educ. Immaculate Conception Seminary (Oconomowoc, Wis.); ord. priest July 2, 1956; ord. titular bishop of Vardimissa and auxiliary bishop of Sao Paulo, Brazil, May 25, 1979; bishop of Paranagua, Brazil, Mar. 14, 1989.

O

O'Brien, Edwin F.: b. Apr. 8, 1939, Bronx, N.Y.; educ. St. Joseph's Seminary (Yonkers, N.Y.), Angelicum (Rome); ord. priest (New York*) May 29, 1965; ord. titular bishop of Tizica and auxiliary bishop of New York, Mar. 25, 1996; app. coadjutor archbishop for Military Services Archdiocese, Apr. 8, 1997; archbishop of Military Services Archdiocese, Aug. 12, 1997.

O'Brien, Thomas Joseph: b. Nov. 29, 1935, Indianapolis, Ind.; educ. St. Meinrad High School Seminary, St. Meinrad College Seminary (St. Meinrad, Ind.); ord. priest (Tucson) May 7, 1961; ord. bishop of Phoenix, Jan. 6, 1982.

Ochoa, Armando: b. Apr. 3, 1943, Oxnard, Calif.; educ. Ventura College (Ventura, Calif.), St. John's College and St. John's Seminary (Camarillo, Calif.); ord. priest (Los Angeles*) May 23, 1970; ord. titular bishop of Sitifi and auxiliary bishop of Los Angeles, Feb. 23, 1987; app. bishop of El Paso, Apr. 1, 1996; installed June 26, 1996.

O'Connell, Anthony J.: b. May 10, 1938, Lisheen, Co. Clare, Ireland; came to U.S. at the age of 20; educ. Mt. St. Joseph College (Cork, Ire.), Mungret College (Limerick, Ire.), Kenrick Seminary (St. Louis, Mo.); ord. priest (Jefferson City) Mar. 30, 1963; ord. first bishop of Knoxville, Tenn., Sept. 8, 1988.

O'Connor, John J.: (See Cardinals, Biographies.)

O'Donnell, Edward J.: b. July 4, 1931, St. Louis, Mo.; educ. St. Louis Preparatory Seminary and Kenrick Seminary (St. Louis, Mo.); ord. priest (St. Louis*) Apr. 6, 1957; ord. titular bishop of Britania and auxiliary bishop of St. Louis Feb. 10, 1984; app. bishop of Lafayette, La., installed Dec. 16, 1994.

O'Keefe, Gerald F.: b. Mar. 30, 1918, St. Paul, Minn.; educ. College of St. Thomas, St. Paul Seminary (St. Paul, Minn.); ord. priest (St. Paul-Minneapolis*) Jan. 29, 1944; ord. titular bishop of Candyba and auxiliary bishop of St. Paul, July 2, 1961; bishop of Davenport, Oct. 20, 1966, installed Jan. 4, 1967; retired Nov. 12, 1993.

O'Keefe, Joseph Thomas: b. Mar. 12, 1919, New York, N.Y.; educ. Cathedral College (New York City), St. Joseph's Seminary (Yonkers, N.Y.), Catholic Univ. (Washington, DC.); ord. priest (New York*) Apr. 17, 1948; ord. titular bishop of Tre Taverne and auxiliary bishop of New York, Sept. 8, 1982; app. bishop of Syracuse, June 16, 1987, installed Aug. 3, 1987; retired Apr. 4, 1995. (Died Sept. 2, 1997.)

O'Leary, Edward C.: b. Aug. 21, 1920, Bangor, Me.; educ. Holy Cross College (Worcester, Mass.), St. Paul's Seminary (Ottawa, Canada); ord. priest (Portland, Me.) June 15, 1946; ord. titular bishop of Moglena and auxiliary bishop of Portland, Me., Jan. 25, 1971; app. bishop of Portland, installed Dec. 18, 1974; retired Sept. 27, 1988.

Olivier, Leonard J., S.V.D.: b. Oct. 12, 1923, Lake Charles, La.; educ. St. Augustine Major Seminary (Bay St. Louis, Miss.), Catholic Univ. (Washington, D.C.), Loyola Univ. (New Orleans, La.); ord. priest June 29, 1951; ord. titular bishop of Leges in Numidia and auxiliary bishop of Washington, Dec. 20, 1988.

O'Malley, Sean, O.F.M.Cap.: b. June 29, 1944, Lakewood, O.; educ. St. Fidelis Seminary (Herman, Pa.), Capuchin College and Catholic Univ. (Washington, D.C.); ord. priest Aug. 29, 1970; episcopal vicar of priests serving Spanish speaking in Washington archdiocese, 1974-84; executive director of Spanish Catholic Center, Washington, from 1973; ord. coadjutor bishop of St. Thomas, Virgin Islands, Aug. 2, 1984; bishop of St. Thomas, Oct. 16, 1985; app. bishop of Fall River, June 16, 1992.

O'Neil, Leo E.: b. Jan. 31, 1928, Holyoke, Mass.; educ. Maryknoll Seminary (Maryknoll, N.Y.), St. Anselm's College (Manchester, N.H.), Grand Seminary (Montreal, Canada); ord. priest (Springfield, Mass.) June 4, 1955; ord. titular bishop of Bencenna and auxiliary bishop of Springfield, Mass., Aug. 22, 1980; app. coadjutor bishop of Manchester, Oct. 17, 1989; bishop of Manchester, June 12, 1990.

O'Neill, Arthur J.: b. Dec. 14, 1917, East Dubuque, Ill.; educ. Loras Collge (Dubuque, Ia.), St. Mary's Seminary (Baltimore, Md.); ord. priest (Rockford) Mar. 27, 1943; ord. bishop of Rockford, Oct. 11, 1968; retired Apr. 19, 1994.

O'Rourke, Edward W.: b. Oct. 31, 1917, Downs,

Ill.; educ. St. Mary's Seminary (Mundelein, Ill.), Aquinas Institute of Philosophy and Theology (River Forest, Ill.); ord. priest (Peoria) May 28, 1944; executive director of National Catholic Rural Life Conference, 1960-71; ord. bishop of Peoria, July 15, 1971; retired Jan. 22, 1990.

Ottenweller, Albert H.: b. Apr. 5, 1916, Stanford, Mont.; educ. St. Joseph's Seminary (Rensselaer, Ind.), Catholic Univ. (Washington, D.C.); ord. priest (Toledo) June 19, 1943; ord. titular bishop of Perdices and auxiliary bishop of Toledo, May 29, 1974; app. bishop of Steubenville, Oct. 11, 1977, installed Nov. 22, 1977; retired Jan. 28, 1992.

P

Paschang, John L.: b. Oct. 5, 1895, Hemingford, Nebr.; educ. Conception College (Conception, Mo.), St. John Seminary (Collegeville, Minn.), Catholic Univ. (Washington, D.C.); ord. priest (Omaha*) June 12, 1921; ord. bishop of Grand Island, Oct. 9, 1951; resigned July 25, 1972.

Paska, Walter: b. Nov. 29, 1923, Elizabeth, N.J.; educ. St. Charles Seminary (Catonsville, Md.), Catholic Univ. (Washington, D.C.), Fordham Univ. (New York); ord. priest (Philadelphia of Ukrainians*) June 2, 1947; ord. titular bishop of Tigilava and auxiliary of Ukrainian archdiocese of Philadelphia, Mar. 19, 1992.

Pataki, Andrew: b. Aug. 30, 1927, Palmerton,Pa.; educ. St. Vincent College (Latrobe, Pa.), St. Procopius College, St. Procopius Seminary (Lisle, Ill.), Sts. Cyril and Methodius Byzantine Catholic Seminary (Pittsburgh, Pa.), Gregorian Univ. and Oriental Pontifical Institute (Rome, Italy); ord. priest (Pittsburgh,* Ruthenian Byzantine) Feb. 24, 1952; ord. titular bishop of Telmisso and auxiliary bishop of Byzantine diocese of Passaic, Aug. 23, 1983; app. bishop of Ruthenian Byzantine diocese of Parma, July 3, 1984; app. bishop of Ruthenian Byzantine diocese of Passaic, Nov. 6, 1995; installed Feb. 8, 1996.

Paul, John J.: b. Aug. 17, 1918, La Crosse, Wis.; educ. Loras College (Dubuque, Iowa), St. Mary's Seminary (Baltimore, Md.), Marquette Univ. (Milwaukee, Wis.), ord. priest (Lincoln) Jan. 24, 1943; ord. titular bishop of Lambaesis and auxiliary bishop of La Crosse, Aug. 4, 1977; app. bishop of La Crosse, Oct. 18, 1983, installed Dec. 5, 1983; retired Dec. 10, 1994.

Pearce, George H., S.M.: b. Jan. 9, 1921, Brighton, Mass.; educ. Marist College and Seminary (Framington, Mass.); ord. priest Feb. 2, 1947; ord. titular bishop of Attalea in Pamphylia and vicar apostolic of the Samoa and Tokelau Islands, June 29, 1956; title changed to bishop of Apia, June 21, 1966; app. archbishop of Suva, Fiji Islands, June 22, 1967; resigned Apr. 10, 1976.

Pelotte, Donald E., S.S.S.: b. Apr. 13, 1945, Waterville, Me.; educ. Eymard Seminary and Junior College (Hyde Park, N.Y.), John Carroll Univ. (Cleveland, O.), Fordham Univ. (Bronx, N.Y.); ord. priest Sept. 2, 1972; ord. coadjutor bishop of Gallup, May 6, 1986 (first priest of Native American ancestry to be named U.S. bishop); bishop of Gallup, Mar. 20, 1990.

Pena, Raymundo J.: b. Feb. 19, 1934, Robstown,

Tex.; educ. Assumption Seminary (San Antonio, Tex.); ord. priest (Corpus Christi) May 25, 1957; ord. titular bishop of Trisipa and auxiliary bishop of San Antonio, Dec. 13, 1976; app. bishop of El Paso, Apr. 29, 1980; app. bishop of Brownsville, May 23, 1995.

Pevec, A. Edward: b. Apr. 16, 1925, Cleveland, O.; educ. St. Mary's Seminary, John Carroll Univ. (Cleveland, O.); ord. priest (Cleveland) Apr. 29, 1950; ord. titular bishop of Mercia and auxiliary bishop of Cleveland, July 2, 1982.

Pfeifer, Michael, O.M.I.: b. May 18, 1937, Alamo, Tex.; educ. Oblate school of theology (San Antonio, Tex.); ord. priest Dec. 21, 1964; provincial of southern province of Oblates of Mary Immaculate, 1981; ord. bishop of San Angelo, July 26, 1985.

Pilarczyk, Daniel E.: b. Aug. 12, 1934, Dayton, Ohio; educ. St. Gregory's Seminary (Cincinnati, O.), Urban Univ. (Rome), Xavier Univ. and Univ. of Cincinnati (Cincinnati, O.); ord. priest (Cincinnati*) Dec. 20, 1959; ord. titular bishop of Hodelm and auxiliary bishop of Cincinnati, Dec. 20, 1974; app. archbishop of Cincinnati, Oct. 30, 1982; installed Dec. 20, 1982. President of NCCB/USCC, 1989-92.

Pilla, Anthony M.: b. Nov. 12, 1932, Cleveland, O.; educ. St. Gregory College Seminary (Cincinnati, O.), Borromeo College Seminary (Wickliffe, O.), St. Mary Seminary and John Carroll Univ. (Cleveland, O.); ord. priest (Cleveland) May 23, 1959; ord. titular bishop of Scardona and auxiliary bishop of Cleveland, Aug. 1, 1979; app. apostolic administrator of Cleveland, 1980; bishop of Cleveland, Nov. 13, 1980. President of NCCB/USCC, 1995- .

Popp, Bernard F.: b. Dec. 6, 1917, Nada, Tex.; educ. St. John's Seminary and St. Mary's Univ. (San Antonio, Tex.); ord. priest (San Antonio*) Feb. 24, 1943; ord. titular bishop of Capsus and auxiliary bishop of San Antonio, July 25, 1983; retired Mar. 23, 1993.

Potocnak, Joseph J., S.C.J.: b. May 13, 1933, Berwick, Pa.; educ. Dehon Seminary (Great Barrington, Mass.), Kilroe Seminary (Honesdale, Pa.), Sacred Heart (Hales Corners, Wis.); ord. priest Sept 21, 1966; missionary in South Africa from 1973; ord. bishop of De Aar, South Africa, May 1, 1992.

Povish, Kenneth J.: b. Apr. 19, 1924, Alpena, Mich.; educ. St. Joseph's Seminary (Grand Rapids, Mich.), Sacred Heart Seminary (Detroit, Mich.), Cathoic Univ. (Washington, D.C.); ord. priest (Saginaw) June 3, 1950; ord. bishop of Crookston, Sept. 29, 1970; app. bishop of Lansing, Oct. 8, 1975, installed Dec. 11, 1975; retired Nov. 7, 1995.

Procyk, Judson M.: b. Apr. 9, 1931, Greensburg, Pa.; educ. St. Procopius College (Lisle, Ill.), Duquesne University and Byzantine Seminary of Sts. Cyril and Methodius (Pittsburgh, Pa.), Casa Santa Maria (Rome); ord. priest (Pittsburgh*, Byzantine Ruthenian) May 19, 1957; ord. metropolitan archbishop of Byzantine archdiocese of Pittsburgh, Feb. 7, 1995.

Pursley, Leo A.: b. Mar. 12, 1902, Hartford City, Ind.; educ. Mt. St. Mary's Seminary (Cincinnati, O.); ord. priest (Ft. Wayne-S. Bend) June 11, 1927; ord. titular bishop of Hadrianapolis in Pisidia and auxiliary bishop of Fort Wayne, Sept. 19, 1950; app. apostolic administrator of Fort Wayne, Mar. 9, 1955; installed as bishop of Fort Wayne, Feb. 26, 1957;

title of see changed to Fort Wayne-South Bend, 1960; resigned Aug. 31, 1976.

Puscas, Vasile Louis: b. Sept. 13, 1915, Aurora, Ill.; educ. Quigley Preparatory Seminary (Chicago, Ill.), seminary in Oradea-Mare (Romania), Propaganda Fide Seminary (Rome), Illinois Benedictine College (Lisle, Ill.); ord. priest (Erie) May 14, 1942; ord. titular bishop of Leuce and first exarch of apostolic exarchate for Byzantine Romanians in the U.S., June 26, 1983 (seat of the exarchate, Canton, Ohio); app. first eparch, Apr. 11, 1987, when exarchate was raised to eparchy of St. George's in Canton; retired July 15, 1993.

Q

Quinn, Alexander James: b. Apr. 8, 1932, Cleveland, O.; educ. St. Charles College (Catonsville, Md.), St. Mary Seminary (Cleveland, O.), Lateran Univ. (Rome), Cleveland State Univ.; ord. priest (Cleveland) May 24, 1958; ord. titular bishop of Socia and auxiliary bishop of Cleveland, Dec. 5, 1983.

Quinn, Francis A.: b. Sept. 11, 1921, Los Angeles, Calif.; educ. St. Joseph's College (Mountain View, Calif.), St. Patrick's Seminary (Menlo Park, Calif.), Catholic Univ. (Washington, D.C.); Univ. of California (Berkeley); ord. priest (San Francisco*) June 15, 1946; ord. titular bishop of Numana and auxiliary bishop of San Francisco, June 29, 1978; app. bishop of Sacramento Dec. 18, 1979; retired Nov. 30, 1993.

Quinn, John R.: b. Mar. 28, 1929, Riverside, Calif.; educ. St. Francis Seminary (El Cajon, Calif.), North American College (Rome); ord. priest (San Diego) July 19, 1953; ord. titular bishop of Thisiduo and auxiliary bishop of San Diego, Dec. 12, 1967; bishop of Oklahoma City and Tulsa, Nov. 30, 1971; first archbishop of Oklahoma City, Dec. 19, 1972; app. archbishop of San Francisco Feb. 22, 1977, installed Apr. 26, 1977; president NCCB/USCC, 1977-80; resigned see Dec. 27, 1995.

R

Ramirez, Ricardo, C.S.B.: b. Sept. 12, 1936, Bay City, Tex.; educ. Univ. of St. Thomas (Houston, Tex.), Univ. of Detroit (Detroit, Mich.), St. Basil's Seminary (Toronto, Ont.), Seminario Concilium (Mexico City, Mexico), East Asian Pastoral Institute (Manila, Philippines); ord. priest Dec. 10, 1966, ord titular bishop of Vatarba and auxiliary of San Antonio, Dec. 6, 1981; app. first bishop of Las Cruces, N. Mex., Aug. 17, 1982; installed Oct. 18, 1982.

Raya, Joseph M.: b. July 20, 1917, Zahle, Lebanon; educ. St. Louis College (Paris, France), St. Anne's Seminary (Jerusalem); ord. priest July 20, 1941; came to U.S., 1949, became U.S. citizen; ord. archbishop of Acre, Israel, of the Melkites, Oct. 20, 1968; resigned Aug. 20, 1974; assigned titular metropolitan see of Scytopolis (resides in Canada).

Reichert, Stephen J., O.F.M. Cap.: b. May 14, 1943,, Leoville, Kans.; educ. Capuchin minor seminary (Victoria, Kans.), St. Fidelis College (Hermann, Pa.), Capuchin College (Washington, D.C.); ord. priest Sept. 27, 1969; missionary in Papua New Guinea since 1970; ord. bishop of Mendi, Papua New Guinea, May 7, 1995.

Reilly, Daniel P.: b. May 12, 1928, Providence, R.I.;

educ. Our Lady of Providence Seminary (Warwick, R.I.), St. Brieuc Major Seminary (Cotes du Nord, France); ord. priest (Providence) May 30, 1953; ord. bishop of Norwich, Aug. 6, 1975; app. bishop of Worcester, Oct. 27, 1994, installed Nov. 8, 1994.

Reiss, John C.: b. May 13, 1922, Red Bank, N.J.; educ. Catholic Univ. (Washington, D.C.), Immaculate Conception Seminary (Darlington, N.J.); ord. priest (Trenton) May 31, 1947; ord. titular bishop of Simidicca and auxiliary bishop of Trenton, Dec. 12, 1967; app. bishop of Trenton, Mar. 11, 1980; retired July 1, 1997.

Riashi, Georges, B.C.O.: b. Nov. 25, 1933, Kaa-el-Rim, Lebanon; ord. priest Apr. 4, 1965; parish priest of Our Lady of Redemption Parish, Warren, Mich. (Newton Greek-Catholic Melkite eparchy); U.S. citizen; ord. first bishop of eparchy of St. Michael's of Sydney (Australia) for Greek-Catholic Melkites, July 19, 1987; app. archbishop of archeparchy of Tripoli of Lebanon for Greek-Melkites, Aug. 5, 1995.

Ricard, John H., S.S.J.: b. Feb. 29, 1940, Baton Rouge, La.; educ. St. Joseph's Seminary (Washington, D.C.), Tulane Univ. (New Orleans, La.); ord. priest May 25, 1968; ord. titular bishop of Rucuma and auxiliary of Baltimore, July 2, 1984; urban vicar, Baltimore; app. bishop of Pensacola-Tallahassee, Jan 21, 1997.

Rigali, Justin F.: b. Apr. 19, 1935, Los Angeles, Calif.; educ. St. John's Seminary (Camarillo, Calif.); ord. priest (Los Angeles*) Apr. 25, 1961; in Vatican diplomatic service from 1964; ord. titular archbishop of Bolsena, Sept. 14, 1985, by Pope John Paul II; president of the Pontifical Ecclesiastical Academy, 1985-89; secretary of Congregation for Bishops, 1989-94, and the College of Cardinals, 1990-94; app. archbishop of St. Louis, Jan. 25, 1994, installed Mar. 16, 1994.

Riley, Lawrence J.: b. Sept. 6, 1914; Boston, Mass.; educ. Boston College and St. John's Seminary (Boston, Mass.), North American College and Gregorian Univ. (Rome), Catholic Univ. (Washington, D.C.); ord. priest (Boston*) Sept. 21, 1940; ord. titular bishop of Daimlaig and auxiliary bishop of Boston, Feb. 2, 1972; retired Jan. 22, 1990.

Roach, John R.: b. July 31, 1921, Prior Lake, Minn.; educ. St. Paul Seminary (St. Paul, Minn.), Univ. of Minnesota (Minneapolis); ord. priest (St. Paul and Minneapolis*) June 18, 1946; ord. titular bishop of Cenae and auxiliary bishop of St. Paul and Minneapolis, Sept. 8, 1971; app. archbishop of St. Paul and Minneapolis, May 28, 1975; president of NCCB/USCC, 1980-83; retired Sept 8, 1995.

Rodimer, Frank J.: b. Oct. 25, 1927, Rockaway, N.J.; educ. Seton Hall Prep (South Orange, N.J.), St. Charles College (Catonsville, Md.), St. Mary's Seminary (Baltimore, Md.), Immaculate Conception Seminary (Darlington, N.J.), Catholic Univ. (Washington, D.C.); ord. priest (Paterson) May 19, 1951; ord. bishop of Paterson, Feb. 28, 1978.

Rodriguez, Migúel, C.SS.R.: b. Apr. 18, 1931, Mayaguez, P.R.; educ. St. Mary's Minor Seminary (North East, Pa.), Mt. St. Alphonsus Major Seminary (Esopus, N.Y.); ord. priest June 22, 1958; ord. bishop of Arecibo, P.R., Mar. 23, 1974; resigned Mar. 20, 1990.

Rodriguez, Placido, C.M.F.: b. Oct. 11, 1940, Celaya, Guanajuato, Mexico; educ. Claretian Novitate (Los Angeles, Calif.), Claretville Seminary College (Calabasas, Calif.), Catholic Univ. (Washington, D.C.), Loyola Univ. (Chicago, Ill.); ord. priest May 23, 1968; ord. titular bishop of Fuerteventura and auxiliary bishop of Chicago, Dec. 13, 1983; app. bishop of Lubbock, Tex., Apr. 5, 1994.

Roman, Agustin A.: b. May 5, 1928, San Antonio de los Banos, Havana, Cuba; educ. San Alberto Magno Seminary (Matanzas, Cuba), Missions Etrangeres (Montreal, Canada), Barry College (Miami, Fla.); ord. priest July 5, 1959, Cuba; vicar for Spanish speaking in Miami archdiocese, 1976; ord. titular bishop of Sertei and auxiliary bishop of Miami, Mar. 24, 1979.

Roque, Francis X.: b. Oct. 9, 1928, Providence R.I.; educ. St. John's Seminary (Brighton, Mass.); ord. priest (Providence) Sept. 19, 1953; became chaplain in U.S. Army 1961; ord. titular bishop of Bagai and auxiliary bishop of Military Services archdiocese, May 10, 1983.

Rosazza, Peter Anthony: b. Feb. 13, 1935, New Haven, Conn.; educ. St. Thomas Seminary (Bloomfield, Conn.), Dartmouth College (Hanover, N.H.), St. Bernard's Seminary (Rochester, N.Y.), St. Sulpice (Issy, France); ord. priest (Hartford*) June 29, 1961; ord. titular bishop of Oppido Nuovo and auxiliary bishop of Hartford, June 24, 1978.

Rose, Robert John: b. Feb. 28, 1930, Grand Rapids, Mich.; educ. St. Joseph's Seminary (Grand Rapids, Mich.), Seminaire de Philosophie (Montreal, Canada), Urban University (Rome), Univ. of Michigan (Ann Arbor); ord. priest (Grand Rapids) Dec. 21, 1955; ord. bishop of Gaylord, Dec. 6, 1981; app. bishop of Grand Rapids, installed Aug. 30, 1989.

Rueger, George E.: b. Sept. 3, 1933, Framingham, Mass; educ. Holy Cross College (Worcester, Mass.), St. John's Seminary (Brighton), Harvard University (Cambridge, Mass.); ord. priest (Worcester), Jan. 6, 1958; ord. titular bishop of Maronana and auxiliary bishop of Worcester, Feb. 25, 1987.

Ryan, Daniel L.: b. Sept. 28, 1930, Mankato, Minn.; educ. St. Procopius Seminary (Lisle, Ill.), Lateran Univ. (Rome); ord. priest (Joliet) May 3, 1956; ord. titular bishop of Surista and auxiliary bishop of Joliet, Sept. 30, 1981; app. bishop of Springfield, Ill., Nov. 22, 1983, installed Jan. 18, 1984.

Ryan, James C., O.F.M.: b. Nov. 17, 1912, Chicago, Ill.; educ. St. Joseph's Seraphic Seminary (Westmont, Ill.), Our Lady of the Angels Seminary (Cleveland, O.); ord. priest June 24, 1938; ord. titular bishop of Margo and prelate of Santarem, Brazil, April 9, 1958; first bishop of Santarem, Dec. 4, 1979; retired Nov. 27, 1985.

Ryan, Joseph T.: b. Nov. 1, 1913, Albany, N.Y.; educ. Manhattan College (New York City); ord. priest (Albany) June 3, 1939; national secretary of Catholic Near East Welfare Assn. 1960-65; ord. first archbishop of Anchorage, Alaska, Mar. 25, 1966; app. titular archbishop of Gabi and coadjutor archbishop of the military ordinariate, Oct. 24, 1975; app. military vicar of U.S. military archdiocese, Mar. 16, 1985; resigned May 14, 1991.

Ryan, Sylvester D.: b. Mar. 3, 1930, Catalina Is. Calif.; educ. St. John's Seminary (Camarillo, Calif.); ord. priest (Los Angeles*) May 3, 1957; ord. titular bishop of Remesiana and auxiliary bishop of Los Angeles, May 31, 1990; app. bishop of Monterey, Jan. 28, 1992.

S

Salatka, Charles A.: b. Feb. 26, 1918, Grand Rapids, Mich.; educ. St. Joseph's Seminary (Grand Rapids, Mich.), Catholic Univ. (Washington, D.C.), Lateran Univ. (Rome); ord. priest (Grand Rapids) Feb. 24, 1945; ord. titular bishop of Cariana and auxiliary bishop of Grand Rapids, Mich., Mar. 6, 1962; app. bishop of Marquette, installed Mar. 25, 1968; app. archbishop of Oklahoma City, Sept. 27, 1977; retired Nov. 24, 1992.

Saltarelli, Michael A.: b. Jan. 17, 1932, Jersey City, N.J.; educ. Seton Hall College and Immaculate Conception Seminary (S. Orange, N.J.); ord. priest (Newark*), May 28, 1960; ord. titular bishop of Mesarfelta and auxiliary bishop of Newark, July 30, 1990; app. Bishop of Wilmington, Nov. 21, 1995; installed Jan. 23, 1996.

Samra, Nicholas J.: b. Aug. 15, 1944, Paterson, N.J.; educ. St. Anselm College (Manchester, N.H.), St. Basil Seminary (Methuen, Mass.), St. John Seminary (Brighton, Mass.); ord. priest (Newton) May 10, 1970; ord. titular bishop of Gerasa and auxiliary bishop of Melkite diocese of Newton, July 6, 1989.

Sanchez, Robert F.: b. Mar. 20, 1934, Socorro, N.M.; educ. Immaculate Heart Seminary (Santa Fe, N.M.), Gregorian Univ. (Rome), Catholic Univ. (Washington, D.C.); ord. priest (Santa Fe*) Dec. 20, 1959; ord. archbishop of Santa Fe, N.M., July 25, 1974; resigned Apr. 6, 1993.

Sartoris, Joseph M.: b. July 1, 1927, Los Angeles, Calif.; educ. St. John's Seminary (Camarillo, Calif.); ord. priest (Los Angeles*) May 30, 1953; ord. titular bishop of Oliva and auxiliary bishop of Los Angeles, Mar. 19, 1994. San Pedro regional bishop.

Scarpone Caporale, Gerald, O.F.M.: b. Oct. 1, 1928, Watertown, Mass.; ord. priest June 24, 1956; ord. coadjutor bishop of Comayagua, Honduras, Feb. 21, 1979; succeeded as bishop of Comayagua, May 30, 1979.

Schad, James L.: b. July 20, 1917, Philadelphia, Pa.; educ. St. Mary's Seminary (Baltimore, Md.); ord. priest (Camden) Apr. 10, 1943; ord. titular bishop of Panatoria and auxiliary bishop of Camden, Dec. 8, 1966; retired Jan 26, 1993.

Schlarman, Stanley Gerard: b. July 27, 1933, Belleville, Ill.; educ. St. Henry Prep Seminary (Belleville, Ill.), Gregorian Univ. (Rome), St. Louis Univ. (St. Louis, Mo.); ord. priest (Belleville) July 13, 1958, Rome; ord. titular bishop of Capri and auxiliary bishop of Belleville, May 14, 1979; app. bishop of Dodge City, Mar. 1, 1983.

Schleck, Charles A., C.S.C.: b. July 5, 1925, Milwaukee, Wis.; educ. Univ. of Notre Dame (Indiana), Univ. of St. Thomas (Rome); ord. priest Dec. 22, 1951; ord. titular archbishop of Africa (Mehdia), Apr. 1, 1995; adjunct secretary of Congregation for Evangelization of Peoples; president of the superior council of the Pontifical Mission Societies.

Schmidt, Firmin M., O.F.M. Cap.: b. Oct. 12, 1918, Catherine, Kans.; educ. Catholic Univ. (Wash-

ington, D.C.); ord. priest June 2, 1946; app. prefect apostolic of Mendi, Papua New Guinea, Apr. 3, 1959; ord. titular bishop of Conana and first vicar apostolic of Mendi, Dec. 15, 1965; became first bishop of Mendi when vicariate apostolic was raised to a diocese, Nov. 15, 1966; retired Feb. 22, 1995.

Schmitt, Bernard W.: b. Aug. 17, 1928, Wheeling, W. Va.; educ. St. Joseph College (Catonsville, Md.), St. Mary's Seminary (Baltimore), Ohio Univ. (Athens, O.); ord. priest (Wheeling-Charleston) May 28, 1955; ord. titular bishop of Walla Walla and bishop of Wheeling-Charleston, Aug. 1, 1988; bishop of Wheeling-Charleston, Mar. 29, 1989.

Schmitt, Mark F.: b. Feb. 14, 1923, Algoma, Wis.; educ. Salvatorian Seminary (St. Nazianz, Wis.), St. John's Seminary (Collegeville, Minn.); ord. priest (Green Bay) May 22, 1948; ord. titular bishop of Ceanannus Mor and auxiliary bishop of Green Bay, June 24, 1970; app. bishop of Marquette, Mar. 21, 1978, installed May 8, 1978; retired Oct. 6, 1992.

Schmitz Simon, Paul, O.F.M. Cap.: b. Dec. 4, 1943, Fond du Lac, Wis.; ord. priest Sept. 3, 1970; missionary in Nicaragua from 1970; superior of vice province of Capuchins in Central America (headquartered in Managua), 1982-84; ord. titular bishop of Elepla and auxiliary of the vicariate apostolic of Bluefields, Nicaragua, Sept. 17, 1984; app. bishop of vicariate apostolic of Bluefields, Aug. 17, 1994.

Schoenherr, Walter J.: b. Feb. 28, 1920, Detroit, Mich.; educ. Sacred Heart Seminary (Detroit, Mich.), Mt. St. Mary Seminary (Norwood, O.); ord. priest (Detroit*) Oct. 27, 1945; ord. titular bishop of Timidana and auxiliary bishop of Detroit, May 1, 1968; retired Mar. 7, 1995.

Schott, Basil, O.F.M.: b. July 21, 1939, Freeland, Pa.; entered Byzantine Franciscans, professed Aug. 4, 1959; educ. Immaculate Conception College (Troy, N.Y.), St. Mary's Seminary (Norwalk, Conn.) and Post Graduate Center (New York, N.Y.); ord. priest Aug. 29, 1965; ord. bishop of Byzantine eparchy of Parma, July 11, 1996.

Schulte, Francis B.: b. Dec. 23, 1926, Philadelphia, Pa.; educ. St. Charles Borromeo Seminary (Overbrook, Pa.); ord. priest (Philadelphia*) May 10, 1952; ord. titular bishop of Afufenia and auxiliary bishop of Philadelphia, Aug. 12, 1981; app. bishop of Wheeling-Charleston, June 4, 1985; archbishop of New Orleans, Dec. 6, 1988, installed Feb. 14, 1989.

Schuster, Eldon B.: b. Mar. 10, 1911, Calio, N. Dak.; educ. Loras College (Dubuque, Ia.), Catholic Univ. (Washington, D.C.), Oxford Univ. (England), St. Louis Univ. (St. Louis, Mo.); ord. priest (Great Falls) May 27, 1937; ord. titular bishop of Amblada and auxiliary bishop of Great Falls, Mont., Dec. 21, 1961; app. bishop of Great Falls, Dec. 2, 1967, installed Jan. 23, 1968; resigned Dec. 28, 1977.

Schwietz, Roger L., O.M.I.: b. July 3, 1940, St. Paul, Minn.; educ. Univ. of Ottawa (Canada), Gregorian Univ. (Rome); ord. priest Dec. 20, 1967; ord. bishop of Duluth Feb. 2, 1990.

Setian, Nerses Mikail: b. Oct. 18, 1918, Sebaste, Turkey; educ. Armenian Pontifical College and Gregorian Univ. (Rome); ord. priest Apr. 13, 1941, in Rome; ord. titular bishop of Ancira of the Armenians and first exarch of the apostolic exarchate for Armenian Catholics in Canada and the United States (see city New York), Dec. 5, 1981; retired Nov. 24, 1993.

Sevilla, Carlos A., S.J.: b. Aug. 9, 1935, San Francisco, Calif.; entered Jesuits Aug. 14, 1953; educ. Gonzaga Univ. (Spokane, Wash.), Santa Clara Uiv. (Santa Clara, Calif.), Jesuitenkolleg (Innsbruck, Austria), Catholic Institute of Paris (France); ord. priest June 3, 1966; ord. titular bishop of Mina and auxiliary bishop of San Francisco, Jan. 25, 1989; bishop of Yakima, Dec. 31, 1996.

Sheehan, Daniel E.: b. May 14, 1917, Emerson, Nebr.; educ. Creighton Univ. (Omaha, Nebr.), Kenrick Seminary (Webster Groves, Mo.), Catholic Univ. (Washington, D.C.); ord. priest (Omaha*) May 23, 1942; ord. titular bishop of Capsus and auxiliary bishop of Omaha, Mar. 19, 1964; app. archbishop of Omaha, installed Aug. 11, 1969; retired May 4, 1993.

Sheehan, Michael J.: b. July 9, 1939, Wichita, Kans.; educ. Assumption Seminary (San Antonio, Tex.), Gregorian Univ. and Lateran Univ. (Rome); ord. priest (Dallas) July 12, 1964; ord. first bishop of Lubbock, Tex., June 17, 1983; apostolic administrator of Santa Fe, Apr. 6, 1993; app. archbishop of Santa Fe, Aug. 17, 1993.

Sheets, John R., S.J.: b. Sept. 21, 1922, Omaha, Neb.; joined Jesuits, 1940; educ. St. Louis Univ. (St. Louis, Mo.), St. Mary's College (St. Mary's, Kans.), Univ. of Innsbruck (Austria); ord. priest June 17, 1953; final profession of vows as Jesuit, Aug. 15, 1957; ord. titular bishop of Murcona and auxiliary bishop of Fort Wayne-South Bend, Ind., June 25, 1991.

Sheldon, Gilbert I.: b. Sept. 20, 1926, Cleveland, O.; educ. John Carroll Univ. and St. Mary Seminary (Cleveland, O.); ord. priest (Cleveland) Feb. 28, 1953; ord. titular bishop of Taparura and auxiliary bishop of Cleveland, June 11, 1976; app. bishop of Steubenville, Jan. 28, 1992.

Sheridan, Michael J.: b. Mar. 4, 1945, St. Louis, Mo.; educ. Glennon College, Kenrick Seminary (St. Louis, Mo.), Angelicum (Rome); ord. priest (St. Louis*) 1971; app. titular bishop of Thibiuca and auxiliary bishop of St. Louis, July 9, 1997.

Sheridan, Patrick J.: b. Mar. 10, 1922, New York, N.Y.; educ. St. Joseph's Seminary (Yonkers, N.Y.), University of Chicago; ord. priest (New York*) Mar. 1, 1947; ord. titular bishop of Curzola and auxiliary bishop of New York, Dec. 12, 1990.

Sklba, Richard J.: b. Sept. 11, 1935, Racine, Wis.; educ. Old St. Francis Minor Seminary (Milwaukee, Wis.), North American College, Gregorian Univ., Pontifical Biblical Institute, Angelicum (Rome); ord. priest (Milwaukee*) Dec. 20, 1959; ord. titular bishop of Castra and auxiliary bishop of Milwaukee, Dec. 19, 1979.

Skylstad, William S.: b. Mar. 2, 1934, Omak, Wash.; educ. Pontifical College Josephinum (Worthington, Ohio), Washington State Univ. (Pullman, Wash.), Gonzaga Univ. (Spokane, Wash.); ord. priest (Spokane) May 21, 1960; ord. bishop of Yakima, May 12, 1977; app. bishop of Spokane, Apr. 17, 1990.

Slattery, Edward J.: b. Aug. 11, 1940, Chicago, Ill.; educ. Quigley Preparatory, St. Mary of the Lake Seminary (Mundelein, Ill.), Loyola Univ. (Chicago); ord. priest (Chicago*) Apr. 26, 1966; vice president, 1971-76, and president, 1976-94, of the Catholic Church Extension Society; ord. bishop of Tulsa, Jan. 6, 1994.

Smith, John M.: b. June 23, 1935, Orange, N.J.; educ. Immaculate Conception Seminary (Darlington, N.J.), Seton Hall Univ. (South Orange, N.J.), Catholic Univ. (Washington, D.C.); ord. priest (Newark*) May 27, 1961; ord. titular bishop of Tre Taverne and auxiliary bishop of Newark, Jan. 25, 1988; app. bishop of Pensacola-Tallahassee, Fla., June 25, 1991; app. coadjutor bishop of Trenton, Nov. 21, 1995; bishop of Trenton, July 1, 1997.

Smith, Philip F., O.M.I.: b. Oct. 16, 1924, Lowell, Mass.; ord. priest Oct. 29, 1950; ord. titular bishop of Lamfua and vicar apostolic of Jolo, Philippine Islands, Sept. 8, 1972; app. coadjutor archbishop of Cotabato, Philippines, Apr. 11, 1979; archbishop of Cotabato, Mar. 14, 1980.

Snyder, John J.: b. Oct. 25, 1925, New York, N.Y.; educ. Cathedral College (Brooklyn, N.Y.), Immaculate Conception Seminary (Huntington, N.Y.); ord. priest (Brooklyn) June 9, 1951; ord. titular bishop of Forlimpopli and auxiliary bishop of Brooklyn, Feb. 2, 1973; app. bishop of St. Augustine, installed Dec. 5, 1979.

Soens, Lawrence D.: b. Aug. 26, 1926, Iowa City, Ia.; educ. Loras College (Dubuque, Ia.), St. Ambrose College (Davenport, Ia.), Kenrick Seminary (St. Louis, Mo.), Univ. of Iowa; ord. priest (Davenport) May 6, 1950; ord. bishop of Sioux City, Aug. 17, 1983.

Sowada, Alphonse A., O.S.C.: b. June 23, 1933, Avon, Minn.; educ. Holy Cross Scholasticate (Fort Wayne, Ind.), Catholic Univ. (Washington, D.C.), ord. priest May 31, 1958; missionary in Indonesia from 1958; ord. bishop of Agats, Indonesia, Nov. 23, 1969.

Speltz, George H.: b. May 29, 1912, Altura, Minn.; educ. St. Mary's College, St. Paul's Seminary (St. Paul, Minn.), Catholic Univ. (Washington, D.C.); ord. priest (St. Cloud) June 2, 1940; ord. titular bishop of Claneus and auxiliary bishop of Winona, Mar. 25, 1963; app. coadjutor bishop of St. Cloud, Apr. 4, 1966; bishop of St. Cloud, Jan. 31, 1968; retired Jan. 13, 1987.

Speyrer, Jude: b. Apr. 14, 1929, Leonville, La.; educ. St. Joseph Seminary (Covington, La.), Notre Dame Seminary (New Orleans, La.), Gregorian Univ. (Rome), Univ. of Fribourg (Switzerland); ord. priest (Lafayette, La.) July 25, 1953; ord. first bishop of Lake Charles, La., Apr. 25, 1980.

Stafford, James Francis: b. July 26, 1932, Baltimore, Md.; educ. St. Mary's Seminary (Baltimore, Md.), North American College and Gregorian Univ. (Rome); ord. priest (Baltimore*) Dec. 15, 1957; ord. titular bishop of Respecta and auxiliary bishop of Baltimore, Feb. 29, 1976; app. bishop of Memphis, Nov. 17, 1982; app. archbishop of Denver, June 3, 1986, installed July 30, 1986; app. President of Pontifical Council of the Laity, Aug. 20, 1996.

Steib, J. (James) Terry, S.V.D.: b. May 17, 1940, Vacherie, La.; educ. Divine Word seminaries (Bay

St. Louis, Miss., Conesus, N.Y., Techny, Ill.), Xavier Univ. (New Orleans, La.); ord. priest Jan. 6, 1967; ord. titular bishop of Fallaba and auxiliary bishop of St. Louis, Feb. 10, 1984; app. bishop of Memphis, Mar. 24, 1993.

Steinbock, John T.: b. July 16, 1937, Los Angeles, Calif.; educ. Los Angeles archdiocesan seminaries; ord. priest (Los Angeles*) May 1, 1963; ord. titular bishop of Midila and auxiliary bishop of Orange, Calif., July 14, 1984; app. bishop of Santa Rosa, Jan. 27, 1987; app. bishop of Fresno, Oct. 15, 1991.

Steiner, Kenneth Donald: b. Nov. 25, 1936, David City, Nebr.; educ. Mt. Angel Seminary (St. Benedict, Ore.), St. Thomas Seminary (Seattle, Wash); ord. priest (Portland,* Ore.) May 19, 1962; ord. titular bishop of Avensa and auxiliary bishop of Portland, Ore., Mar. 2, 1978.

Straling, Phillip F.: b. Apr. 25, 1933, San Bernardino, Calif.; educ. Immaculate Heart Seminary, St. Francis Seminary, Univ. of San Diego and San Diego State University (San Diego, Calif.), North American College (Rome); ord. priest (San Diego) Mar. 19, 1959; ord. first bishop of San Bernardino, Nov. 6, 1978; app. first bishop of Reno, Mar. 21, 1995, when Reno-Las Vegas diocese was made two separate dioceses.

Strecker, Ignatius J.: b. Nov. 23, 1917, Spearville, Kans.; educ. St. Benedict's College (Atchison, Kans.), Kenrick Seminary (Webster Groves, Mo.), Catholic Univ. (Washington, D.C.); ord. priest (Wichita) Dec. 19, 1942; ord. bishop of Springfield-Cape Girardeau, Mo., June 20, 1962; archbishop of Kansas City, Kans., Oct. 28, 1969; retired June 28, 1993.

Sullivan, James S.: b. July 23, 1929, Kalamazoo, Mich.; educ. Sacred Heart Seminary (Detroit, Mich.), St. John Provincial Seminary (Plymouth, Mich.); ord. priest (Lansing) June 4, 1955; ord. titular bishop of Siccessi and auxiliary bishop of Lansing, Sept. 21, 1972; app. bishop of Fargo, Apr. 2, 1985; installed May 30, 1985.

Sullivan, John J.: b. July 5, 1920, Horton, Kans.; educ. Kenrick Seminary (St. Louis, Mo.); ord. priest (Oklahoma City*) Sept. 23, 1944; vice-president of Catholic Church Extension Society and national director of Extension Lay Volunteers, 1961-68; ord. bishop of Grand Island, Sept. 19, 1972; app. bishop of Kansas City-St. Joseph, June 27, 1977, installed Aug. 17, 1977; retired June 22, 1993.

Sullivan, Joseph M.: b. Mar. 23, 1930, Brooklyn, N.Y.; educ. Immaculate Conception Seminary (Huntington, N.Y.), Fordham Univ. (New York); ord. priest (Brooklyn) June 2, 1956; ord. titular bishop of Suliana and auxiliary bishop of Brooklyn, Nov. 24, 1980.

Sullivan, Walter F.: b. June 10, 1928, Washington, D.C.; educ. St. Mary's Seminary (Baltimore, Md.), Catholic Univ. (Washington, D.C.); ord. priest (Richmond) May 9, 1953; ord. titular bishop of Selsea and auxiliary bishop of Richmond, Va., Dec. 1, 1970; app. bishop of Richmond, June 4, 1974.

Sulyk, Stephen: b. Oct. 2, 1924, Balnycia, Western Ukraine; migrated to U.S. 1948; educ. Ukrainian Catholic Seminary of the Holy Spirit (Hirschberg, Germany), St. Josaphat's Seminary and Catholic Univ. (Washington, D.C.); ord. priest (Philadelphia,* Byz-

antine) June 14, 1952; ord. archbishop of the Ukrainian archeparchy of Philadelphia, Mar. 1, 1981.

Symons, J. Keith: b. Oct. 14, 1932, Champion, Mich.; educ. St. Thomas Seminary (Bloomfield, Conn.), St. Mary Seminary (Baltimore, Md.); ord. priest (St. Augustine) May 18, 1958; ord. titular bishop of Siguitanus and auxiliary bishop of St. Petersburg, Mar. 19, 1981; app. bishop of Pensacola-Tallahassee, Oct. 4, 1983, installed Nov. 8, 1983; app. bishop of Palm Beach, June 12, 1990.

Szoka, Edmund C.: (See Cardinals, Biographies.)

T

Tafoya, Arthur N.: b. Mar. 2, 1933, Alameda, N.M.; educ. St. Thomas Seminary (Denver, Colo.), Conception Seminary (Conception, Mo.); ord. priest (Santa Fe*) May 12, 1962; ord. bishop of Pueblo, Sept. 10, 1980.

Tamayo, James A.: b. Oct. 23, 1949, Brownsville, Tex.; educ. Del Mar College (Corpus Christi, Tex.), Univ. of St. Thomas and Univ. of St. Thomas School of Theology (Houston); ord. priest (Corpus Christi) June 11, 1976; ord. titular bishop of Ita and auxiliary bishop of Galveston-Houston, Mar. 10, 1993. Episcopal vicar for Hispanics.

Tawil, Joseph: b. Dec. 25, 1913, Damascus, Syria; ord. priest July 20, 1936; ord. titular archbishop of Mira and patriarchal vicar for eparchy of Damascus of the Patriarchate of Antioch for the Melkites, Jan. 1, 1960; apostolic exarch for Melkite Catholics in the U.S., Oct. 31, 1969; app. first eparch with personal title of archbishop when exarchate was raised to eparchy, July 15, 1976; title of see changed to Newton, 1977; retired Dec. 2, 1989.

Tertzakian, Hovhannes, O.M.Ven.: b. Jan. 3, 1924, Aleppo, Syria; educ. Mekhitarist Monastery of St. Lazarus (Venice, Italy); Gregorian Univ. (Rome); entered Mekhitarist Order of Venice, 1938, final vows Oct. 24, 1945; ord. priest Sept. 8, 1948; came to U.S., 1984; ord. titular bishop of Trebizond for Armenians and apostolic exarch for Armenian Catholics in the United States and Canada, Apr. 29, 1995.

Thomas, Elliott G.: b. July 15, 1926, Pittsburgh, Pa.; educ. Howard Univ. (Washington, D.C.), Gannon Univ. (Erie, Pa.), St. Vincent de Paul Seminary (Boynton Beach, Fla.); ord. priest (St. Thomas, Virgin Islands) June 6, 1986; ord. bishop of St. Thomas in the Virgin Islands, Dec. 12, 1993.

Thompson, David B.: b. May 29, 1923, Philadelphia, Pa.; educ. St. Charles Seminary (Overbrook, Pa.), Catholic Univ. (Washington, D.C.); ord. priest (Philadelphia*) May 27, 1950; ord. coadjutor bishop of Charleston, May 24, 1989; bishop of Charleston, Feb. 22, 1990.

Timlin, James C.: b. Aug. 5, 1927, Scranton, Pa.; educ. St. Charles College (Catonville, Md.), St. Mary's Seminary (Baltimore, Md.), North American College (Rome); ord. priest (Scranton) July 16, 1951; ord. titular bishop of Gunugo and auxiliary bishop of Scranton, Sept. 21, 1976; app. bishop of Scranton, Apr. 24, 1984.

Tobin, Thomas J.: b. Apr. 1, 1948, Pittsburgh, Pa.; educ. St. Mark Seminary High School, Gannon Univ. (Erie, Pa.), St. Francis College (Loretto, Pa.), North American College (Rome); ord. priest (Pittsburgh) July 21, 1973; ord. titular bishop of Novica and auxiliary bishop of Pittsburgh, Dec. 27, 1992; app. bishop of Youngstown Dec. 5, 1995; installed Feb. 2, 1996.

Trautman, Donald W.: b. June 24, 1936, Buffalo, N.Y.; educ. Our Lady of Angels Seminary (Niagara Falls, N.Y.), Theology Faculty (Innsbruck, Austria), Pontifical Biblical Institute (Rome), Catholic Univ. (Washington, D.C.); ord. priest (Buffalo) Apr. 7, 1962, in Innsbruck; ord. titular bishop of Sassura and auxiliary of Buffalo, Apr. 16, 1985; app. bishop of Erie, June 12, 1990.

Tschoepe, Thomas: b. Dec. 17, 1915, Pilot Point, Tex.; educ. Pontifical College Josephinum (Worthington, O.); ord. priest (Dallas) May 30, 1943; ord. bishop of San Angelo, Tex., Mar. 9, 1966; app. bishop of Dallas, Tex., Aug. 27, 1969; retired July 14, 1990.

Turley Murphy, Daniel T. , O.S.A.: b. Jan. 25, 1943, Chicago, Ill.; ord. priest Dec. 21, 1961; ord. coadjutor bishop of Chulucanas, Peru, Aug. 17, 1996.

U-V

Untener, Kenneth E.: b. Aug. 3, 1937, Detroit, Mich.; educ. Sacred Heart Seminary (Detroit, Mich.), St. John's Provincial Seminary (Plymouth, Mich.), Gregorian Univ. (Rome); ord. priest (Detroit*) June 1, 1963; ord. bishop of Saginaw, Nov. 24, 1980.

Valero, René A.: b. Aug. 15, 1930, New York, N.Y.; educ. Cathedral College, Immaculate Conception Seminary (Huntington, N.Y.), Fordham Univ. (New York); ord. priest (Brooklyn) June 2, 1956; ord. titular bishop of Turris Vicus and auxiliary bishop of Brooklyn, Nov. 24, 1980.

Vaughan, Austin B.: b. Sept. 27, 1927, New York, N.Y.; educ. North American College and Gregorian Univ. (Rome), ord. priest (New York*) Dec. 8, 1951; pres. Catholic Theological Society of America, 1967; rector of St. Joseph's Seminary (Dunwoodie, N.Y.), 1973; ord. titular bishop of Cluain Iraird and auxiliary bishop of New York, June 29, 1977.

Veigle, Adrian J.M., T.O.R.: b. Sept. 15, 1912, Lilly, Pa.; educ. St. Francis College (Loretto, Pa.), Pennsylvania State College; ord. priest May 22, 1937; ord. titular bishop of Gigthi June 9, 1966 (resigned titular see May 26, 1978); prelate of Borba, Brazil, 1966; retired July 6, 1988.

Vigernon, Allen H.: b. Oct. 21, 1948, Detroit, Mich.; educ. Sacred Heart Seminary (Detroit, Mich.), North American College, Gregorian Univ. (Rome) Catholic Univ.(Washington, DC); ord. priest (Detroit*) July 26, 1975; served in Vatican Secretariat of State, 1991-94; rector of Sacred Heart Seminary (Detroit), 1994; ord. titular bishop of Sault Sainte Marie and auxiliary bishop of Detroit, July 9, 1996.

Vlazny, John G.: b. Feb. 22, 1937, Chicago, Ill.; educ. Quigley Preparatory Seminary (Chicago, Ill.), St. Mary of the Lake Seminary (Mundelein, Ill.), Gregorian Univ. (Rome), Univ. of Michigan, Loyola Univ. (Chicago, Ill.); ord. priest (Chicago*) Dec. 20, 1961; ord. titular bishop of Stagno and auxiliary bishop of Chicago, Dec. 13, 1983; app. bishop of Winona, Minn., May 19, 1987.

W

Walsh, Daniel Francis: b. Oct. 2, 1937, San Francisco, Calif.; educ. St. Joseph Seminary (Mountain View, Calif.), St. Patrick Seminary (Menlo Park, Calif.) Catholic Univ. (Washington, D.C.); ord. priest (San Francisco*) Mar. 30, 1963; ord. titular bishop of Tigia and auxiliary bishop of San Francisco, Sept. 24, 1981; app. bishop of Reno-Las Vegas, June 9, 1987; app. first bishop of Las Vegas Mar. 21, 1995, when the Reno-Las Vegas diocese was made two separate dioceses.

Ward, John J.: b. Sept. 28, 1920, Los Angeles, Calif.; educ. St. John's Seminary (Camarillo, Calif.), Catholic Univ. (Washington, D.C.); ord. priest (Los Angeles*) May 4, 1946; ord. titular bishop of Bria and auxiliary of Los Angeles, Dec. 12, 1963; retired May 7, 1996; titular bishop of California.

Warfel, Michael William: b. Sept 16, 1948, Elkhart, Ind.; educ. Indiana Univ, St. Gregory's College Seminary, Mt. St. Mary's Seminary of the West (Cincinnati, Ohio); ord. priest Apr. 26, 1980; ord. bishop of Juneau, Dec. 17, 1996.

Watters, Loras J.: b. Oct. 14, 1915, Dubuque, Ia.; educ. Loras College (Dubuque, Ia.), Gregorian Univ. (Rome), Catholic Univ. (Washington, D.C.); ord. priest (Dubuque*) June 7, 1941; ord. titular bishop of Fidoloma and auxiliary bishop of Dubuque, Aug. 26, 1965; bishop of Winona, installed Mar. 13, 1969; retired Oct. 14, 1986.

Watty Urquidi, Ricardo, M.Sp.S.: b. July 16, 1938, San Diego, Calif.; ord. priest June 8, 1968; ord. titular bishop of Macomedes and auxiliary bishop of Mexico City, July 19, 1980; app. first bishop of Nuevo Laredo, Mexico, Nov. 6, 1989.

Wcela, Emil A.: b. May 1, 1931, Bohemia, N.Y.; educ. St. Francis College (Brooklyn, N.Y.), Immaculate Conception Seminary (Huntington, N.Y.), Catholic Univ. (Washington, D.C.), Pontifical Biblical Institute (Rome, Italy); ord. priest (Brooklyn) June 2, 1956; ord. titular bishop of Filaca and auxiliary bishop of Rockville Centre, Dec. 13, 1988.

Weakland, Rembert G., O.S.B.: b. Apr. 2, 1927, Patton, Pa.; joined Benedictines, 1945; ord. priest June 24, 1951; abbot-primate of Benedictine Confederation, 1967-77; ord. archbishop of Milwaukee, Nov. 8, 1977.

Weigand, William K.: b. May 23, 1937, Bend, Ore.; educ. Mt. Angel Seminary (St. Benedict, Ore.), St. Edward's Seminary and St. Thomas Seminary (Kenmore, Wash.); ord. priest (Boise) May 25, 1963; ord. bishop of Salt Lake City, Nov. 17, 1980; app. bishop of Sacramento, Nov. 30, 1993, installed Jan. 27, 1994.

Weitzel, John Quinn, M.M.: b. May 10, 1928, Chicago, Ill.; educ. Maryknoll Seminary (Maryknoll, N.Y.); ord. priest Nov. 5, 1955; missionary to Samoa, 1979; ord. bishop of Samoa-Pago Pago, American Samoa, Oct. 29, 1986.

Welsh, Lawrence H.: b. Feb. 1, 1935, Winton, Wyo.; educ. Univ. of Wyoming (Laramie, Wyo.), St. John's Seminary (Collegeville, Minn.), Catholic Univ. (Washington, D.C.); ord. priest (Rapid City) May 26, 1962; ord. bishop of Spokane, Dec. 14, 1978; resigned Apr. 17, 1990; app. titular bishop of Aulon and auxiliary bishop of St. Paul and Minneapolis, Nov. 5, 1991.

Welsh, Thomas J.: b. Dec. 20, 1921, Weatherly, Pa.; educ. St. Charles Borromeo Seminary (Philadelphia, Pa.), Catholic Univ. (Washington, D.C.);

ord. priest (Philadelphia*) May 30, 1946; ord. titular bishop of Scattery Island and auxiliary bishop of Philadelphia, Apr. 2, 1970; app. first bishop of Arlington, Va., June 4, 1974; app. bishop of Allentown, Feb. 8, 1983, installed Mar. 21, 1983.

Wenski, Thomas G.: b. Oct. 18, 1950, West Palm Beach, Fla.; educ. St. John Vianney College Seminary, St. Vincent de Paul Regional Seminary, Forham Univ.; ord. priest (Miami*) May 15, 1976; director of Miami Haitian Apostolate; app..titular bishop of Kearney and auxiliary of Miami, June 24, 1997.

Whelan, Robert L., S.J.: b. Apr. 16, 1912, Wallace, Ida.; educ. St. Michael's College (Spokane, Wash.), Alma College (Alma, Calif.); ord. priest June 17, 1944; ord. titular bishop of Sicilibba and coadjutor bishop of Fairbanks, Alaska, with right of succession, Feb. 22, 1968; bishop of Fairbanks, Nov. 30, 1968; retired June 1, 1985.

Williams, James Kendrick: b. Sept. 5, 1936, Athertonville, Ky.; educ. St. Mary's College (St. Mary's, Ky.), St. Maur's School of Theology (South Union, Ky.); ord. priest (Louisville*) May 25, 1963; ord. titular bishop of Catula and auxiliary bishop of Covington, June 19, 1984; first bishop of Lexington, Ky., installed Mar. 2, 1988.

Winter, William J.: b. May 20, 1930, Pittsburgh, Pa.; educ. St. Vincent College and Seminary (Latrobe, Pa.), Gregorian Univ. (Rome, Italy); ord. priest (Pittsburgh), Dec. 17, 1955; ord. titular bishop of Uthina and auxiliary bishop of Pittsburgh, Feb. 13, 1989.

Wirz, George O.: b. Jan. 17, 1929, Monroe, Wis.; educ. St. Francis Seminary and Marquette Univ. (Milwaukee, Wis.); Cath. Univ. (Washington, D.C.); ord. priest (Madison) May 31, 1952; ord. titular bishop of Municipa and auxiliary bishop of Madison, Mar. 9, 1978.

Wiwchar, Michael, C.SS.R.: b. May 9, 1932, Komarno, Manitoba, Canada; educ. Redemptorist Seminary (Windsor, Ontario); made solemn vows as Redemptorist, 1956; ord. priest, June 28, 1959; pastor St. John the Baptist Parish, Newark, N.J., 1990-93; ord. bishop of St. Nicholas of Chicago for the Ukrainians, Sept. 28, 1993.

Wuerl, Donald W.: b. Nov. 12, 1940, Pittsburgh, Pa.; educ. Catholic Univ. (Washington, D.C.), North American College, Angelicum (Rome); ord. priest (Pittsburgh) Dec. 17, 1966, in Rome; ord. titular bishop of Rosemarkie Jan. 6, 1986, in Rome; auxiliary bishop of Seattle, 1986-87; app. bishop of Pittsburgh Feb. 11, 1988, installed Mar. 25, 1988.

Wycislo, Aloysius John: b. June 17, 1908, Chicago, Ill.; educ. St. Mary's Seminary (Mundelein, Ill.), Catholic Univ. (Washington, D.C.); ord. priest (Chicago*) Apr. 4, 1934; ord. titular bishop of Stadia and auxiliary bishop of Chicago, Dec. 21, 1960; app. bishop of Green Bay, installed Apr. 16, 1968; resigned May 10, 1983.

Y-Z

Yanta, John W.: b. Oct. 2, 1931, Runge, Tex.; educ. St. John's Preparatory Seminary and Assumption Seminary (San Antonio); ord. priest (San Antonio*) Mar. 17, 1956; ord. titular bishop of Naratcata and auxiliary bishop of San Antonio Dec. 30, 1994; app. bishop of Amarillo, Jan. 21,1997, installed Mar. 17, 1997..

Younan, Joseph: b. Nov. 15, 1944, Hassakeh, Syria; educ. Our Lady of Deliverance Seminary (Charfet, Lebanon), Pontifical College of the Propagation of the Faith (Rome); ord. priest Sept. 12, 1971; came to U.S., 1986; served Syrian Catholics in U.S.; ord. first bishop Our Lady of Deliverance of Newark for Syrian Catholics in the U.S. and Canada, Jan. 7, 1996, in Kamisly, Syria.

Zavala, Gabino: b. Sept. 7, 1951, Guerrero, Mexico; became U.S. citizen, 1976; educ. St. John's Seminary (Los Angeles), Catholic Univ. (Washington, D.C.); ord. priest (Los Angeles*) May 28, 1977; ord. titular bishop of Tamascani and auxiliary bishop of Los Angeles, Mar. 19, 1994.

Zayek, Francis: b. Oct. 18, 1920, Manzanillo, Cuba; ord. priest Mar. 17, 1946; ord. titular bishop of Callinicum and auxiliary bishop for Maronites in Brazil, Aug. 5, 1962; named apostolic exarch for Maronites in U.S., with headquarters in Detroit; installed June 11. 1966; first eparch of St. Maron of Detroit, Mar. 25, 1972; see transferred to Brooklyn, June 27, 1977; given personal title of archbishop, Dec. 22, 1982; retired Nov. 23, 1996.

Ziemann, G. Patrick: b. Sept. 13, 1941, Pasadena, Calif.; educ. St. John's College Seminary and St. John's Seminary (Camarillo, Calif.), Mt. St. Mary's College (Los Angeles, Calif.); ord. priest (Los Angeles*) Apr. 29, 1967; ord. titular bishop of Obba and auxiliary bishop of Los Angeles, Feb. 23, 1987; app. bishop of Santa Rosa, July 14, 1992.

Zipfel, Paul A.: b. Sept. 22, 1935, St. Louis, Mo.; educ. Cardinal Glennon College, Kenrick Seminary (St. Louis, Mo.), Catholic Univ. (Washington, D.C.), St. Louis Univ. (St. Louis, Mo.); ord. priest (St. Louis*) Mar. 18, 1961; ord. titular bishop of Walla Walla and auxiliary bishop of St. Louis, June 29, 1989; app. bishop of Bismarck, Dec. 31, 1996.

Zubic, David A..: b. Sept. 4, 1949, Sewickley, Pa.; educ. St. Paul Seminary-Duquesne Univ. (Pittsburgh), St. Mary's Seminary (Baltimore), Duquesne Univ. (Pittsburgh); ord. priest (Pittsburgh) May 3, 1975; ord. titular bishop of Jamestown and auxiliary of Pittsburgh, Apr. 6, 1997.

BISHOP-BROTHERS

(The asterisk indicates brothers who were bishops at the same time.)

There have been 10 pairs of brother-bishops in the history of the U.S. hierarchy.

Living: Francis T. Hurley,* archbishop of Anchorage and Mark J. Hurley,* bishop emeritus of Santa Rosa. Raymond J. Boland,* bishop of Kansas City-St. Joseph, Mo. and John Kevin Boland,* bishop of Savannah.

Deceased: Francis Blanchet* of Oregon City (Portland) and Augustin Blanchet* of Walla Walla; John S. Foley of Detroit and Thomas P. Foley of Chicago; Francis P. Kenrick,* apostolic administrator of Philadelphia, bishop of Philadelphia and Baltimore, and Peter R. Kenrick* of St. Louis; Matthias C. Lenihan of Great Falls and Thomas M. Lenihan of Cheyenne; James O'Connor, vicar apostolic of Nebraska and bishop of Omaha, and Michael O'Connor of Pittsburgh and Erie; Jeremiah F. and John W. Shanahan, both of Harrisburg; Sylvester J. Espelage, O.F.M.* of Wuchang, China, who died 10 days after the ordination of his brother, Bernard T. Espelage, O.F.M.* of Gallup; Coleman F. Carroll* of Miami and Howard Carroll* of Altoona-Johnstown.

U.S. BISHOPS OVERSEAS

Cardinal William W. Baum, major penitentiary; Cardinal Edmund C. Szoka, president of Prefecture for Economic Affairs of the Holy See; Archbishop Ambrose de Paoli, first apostolic nuncio to South Africa, pro-nuncio to Lesotho and apostolic delegate to several other countries in southern Africa; Archbishop John P. Foley, president of Pontifical Commission for Social Communications; Archbishop James Francis Stafford, president of the Pontifical Council for the Laity; Archbishop Charles A. Schleck, C.S.C., adjunct secretary of the Congregation for the Evangelization of Peoples; Archbishop Edward Joseph Adams, nuncio in Bangladesh; Most Rev. George Riashi, B.C.O., archbishop of archeparchy of Tripoli of Lebanon (Lebanon) for Greek-Catholic Melkites; Most Rev. Michael R. Kuchmiak, exarch of apostolic exarchate of Great Britain for Ukrainian Catholics; Archbishop John Bukovsky, S.V.D. (naturalized U.S. citizen), papal representative to Russia. Cardinal Myroslav Ivan Lubachivsky, major archbishop of Lviv of the Ukrainians (Ukraine), became a U.S. citizen in 1952 and was archbishop of Philadelphia Ukrainian Archeparchy, 1979-80. (See also Missionary Bishops.)

RETIRED/RESIGNED U.S. PRELATES

Information, as of Aug. 20, 1997, includes name of the prelate and see held at the time of retirement or resignation; archbishops are indicated by an asterisk. Most of the prelates listed below resigned their sees because of age in accordance with church law. See Index: Biographies, U.S. Bishops.

Forms of address of retired residential prelates (unless they have a titular see): Archbishop or Bishop Emeritus of (last see held); Former Archbishop or Bishop of (last see held).

Alfred L. Abramowicz (Chicago, auxiliary), Patrick V. Ahern (New York, auxiliary), Leo Arkfeld, S.V.D.* (Madang, Papua New Guinea), Juan Arzube (Los Angeles, auxiliary), Michael J. Begley (Charlotte), Ernest B. Boland, O.P. (Multan, Pakistan), William D. Borders* (Baltimore), Warren L. Boudreaux (Houma-Thibodaux), Joseph M. Breitenbeck (Grand Rapids), Edwin B. Broderick (Albany), Charles A. Buswell (Pueblo).

Cardinal John Carberry* (St. Louis), Harry A. Clinch (Monterey), John W. Comber, M.M. (Foratiano, titular see), Ronald G. Connors, C.SS.R. (San Juan de la Maguana, Dominican Republic), Arnold R. Cotey, S.D.S. (Nachingwea, now Lindi, Tanzania), Joseph R. Crowley (Ft. Wayne-S. Bend, auxiliary), Walter N. Curtis (Bridgeport), James J. Daly (Rockville Centre, auxiliary), Nicholas D'Antonio, O.F.M. (Olancho, Honduras).

Joseph A. DePalma, S.C.J. (DeAar, South Africa), Louis A. DeSimone (Philadelphia, auxiliary), Joseph T. Dimino* (Military Services archdiocese), George Dion, O.M.I. (titular see, Arpaia), Paul V. Donovan (Kalamazoo), Michael J. Dudick (Passaic, Byzantine rite), Paul V. Dudley (Sioux Falls), Clarence J.

Duhart, C.SS.R. (Udon Thani, Thailand), Dennis V. Durning, C.S.Sp. (Arusha, Tanzania), J. Lennox Federal (Salt Lake City), Joseph A. Ferrario (Honolulu), John J. Fitzpatrick (Brownsville), Bernard J. Flanagan (Worcester), Marion F. Forst (Dodge City), Joseph A. Francis, S.V.D. (Newark, auxiliary), Benedict C. Franzetta (Youngstown, auxiliary), Frederick W. Freking (La Crosse), Gerard L. Frey (Lafayette, La.).

Robert F. Garner (Newark, auxiliary), Norbert F. Gaughan (Gary), Louis E. Gelineau (Providence), Odore Gendron (Manchester), Peter L. Gerety* (Newark), George J. Gottwald (St. Louis, auxiliary), Rene H. Gracida (Corpus Christi), Thomas J. Grady (Orlando), John J. Graham (Philadelphia, auxiliary), J. Richard Ham, M.M. (St. Paul and Minneapolis, auxiliary), Philip M. Hannan* (New Orleans), Frank J. Harrison (Syracuse), Edward D. Head (Buffalo).

Edward J. Herrmann (Columbus), Dennis W. Hickey (Rochester, auxiliary), James J. Hogan (Altoona-Johnstown), Joseph L. Hogan (Rochester), Edward T. Hughes (Metuchen), William A. Hughes (Covington), Raymond G. Hunthausen* (Seattle), Mark J. Hurley (Santa Rosa), Charles R. Koester (St. Louis, auxiliary), Arthur H. Krawczak (Detroit, auxiliary), Daniel W. Kucera, O.S.B.* (Dubuque), William F. Kupfer, M.M. (Taichung, Taiwan), Francis Lambert, S.M. (Port Vila, Vanuatu), W. Thomas Larkin (St. Petersburg) Raymond W. Lessard (Savannah), Martin N. Lohmuller (Philadelphia, auxiliary), Innocent Hilarius Lotocky, O.S.B.M. (St. Nicholas of Chicago for Ukrainians), George E. Lynch (Raleigh, auxiliary), Timothy J. Lyne (Chicago, auxiliary).

Michael F. McAuliffe (Jefferson City), Edward A. McCarthy* (Miami), Thomas J. McDonough* (Louisville), John B. McDowell (Pittsburgh, auxiliary), Urban McGarry, T.O.R. (Bhagalpur, India), Bernard J. McLaughlin (Buffalo, auxiliary), Joseph F. Maguire (Springfield, Mass.), James P. Mahoney (New York, auxiliary), James W. Malone (Youngstown), Charles G. Maloney (Louisville, auxiliary), Thomas R. Manning, O.F.M. (Coroico, Bolivia), Paul C. Marcinkus* (titular see of Orta), Eugene A. Marino, S.S.J.* (Atlanta), Leroy T. Matthiesen (Amarillo), James E. Michaels (Wheeling-Charleston, auxiliary), Michael J. Murphy (Erie), Martin J. Neylon, S.J. (Caroline Islands), James D. Niedergeses (Nashville), Bernard Nolker, C.SS.R. (Parangua, Brazil), Gerald F. O'Keefe (Davenport), Joseph T. O'Keefe (Syracuse), Edward C. O'Leary (Portland, Me.), Arthur J. O'Neill (Rockford).

Edward W. O'Rourke (Peoria), Albert H. Ottenweller (Steubenville), John L. Paschang (Grand Island), John J. Paul (La Crosse), George H. Pearce, S.M.* (Suva, Fiji Islands), Bernard F. Popp (San Antonio, auxiliary), Kenneth J. Povish (Lansing), Leo A. Pursley (Fort Wayne-South Bend), Vasile Louis Puscas (St. George's in Canton of the Romanians), Francis A. Quinn (Sacramento), John R. Quinn* (San Francisco), Joseph M. Raya* (Acre), John C. Reiss (Trenton), Lawrence J. Riley (Boston, auxiliary), John R. Roach* (St. Paul and Minneapolis), Miguel Rodriguez, C.SS.R. (Arecibo, P.R.), James C. Ryan, O.F.M. (Santarem, Brazil), Joseph T. Ryan* (Military Services archdiocese).

Charles A. Salatka* (Oklahoma City), Robert F. Sanchez* (Santa Fe), James L. Schad (Camden, auxiliary), Firmin M. Schmidt, O.F.M. Cap. (Mendi, Papua New Guinea), Mark Schmitt (Marquette), Walter J. Schoenherr (Detroit, auxiliary), Nerses Mikail Setian (Armenian Exarchate), Eldon B. Schuster (Great Falls), Daniel E. Sheehan* (Omaha), George H. Speltz (St. Cloud), Ignatius J. Strecker* (Kansas City, Kans.), John J. Sullivan (Kansas City-St. Joseph, Mo.).

Joseph Tawil* (personal title) (Newton, Greek Melkites), Thomas Tschoepe (Dallas), Adrian Veigle, T.O.R. (Borba, Brazil, Prelate), John J. Ward (Los Angeles, auxiliary), Loras J. Watters (Winona), Robert L. Whelan (Fairbanks), Aloysius J. Wycislo (Green Bay), Francis Zayek (St. Maron of Brroklyn).

AMERICAN BISHOPS OF THE PAST

Information includes: dates; place of birth if outside the U.S.; date of ordination to the priesthood; titular see in parentheses of bishops who were not ordinaries; indication, where applicable, of date of resignation.

Abbreviation code: abp., archbishop; bp., bishop; v.a., vicar apostolic; aux., auxiliary bishop; coad., coadjutor; ord., ordained priest; res., resigned.

A

Acerra, Angelo Thomas, O.S.B. (1925-90): ord. May 20, 1950; aux. Military Services archdiocese (Lete), 1983-90.

Ackerman, Richard H., C.S.Sp. (1903-92): ord. Aug. 28, 1926; aux. San Diego (Lares), 1956-60; bp. Covington 1960-78 (res.).

Adrian, William L. (1883-1972): ord. Apr. 15, 1911; bp. Nashville, 1936-69 (res.).

Ahr, George W. (1904-93): ord. July 29, 1928; bp. Trenton, 1950-79 (res.).

Albers, Joseph (1891-1965): ord. June 17, 1916; aux. Cincinnati (Lunda), 1929-37; first bp. Lansing, 1937-65.

Alemany, Joseph Sadoc, O.P. (1814-88): b. Spain; ord. Mar. 11, 1837; bp. Monterey, 1850-53; first abp. San Francisco, 1853-84 (res.).

Alencastre, Stephen P., SS.CC. (1876-1940): b. Madeira; ord. Apr. 5, 1902; coad. v.a. Sandwich Is. (Arabissus), 1924-36; v.a. Sandwich (Hawaiian) Is., 1936-40.

Alerding, Herman J. (1845-1924): b. Germany; ord. Sept. 22, 1869; bp. Fort Wayne, 1900-24.

Allen, Edward P. (1853-1926): ord. Dec. 17, 1881; bp. Mobile, 1897-1926.

Alter, Karl J. (1885-1977): ord. June 4, 1910; bp. Toledo, 1931-50; abp. Cincinnati, 1950-69 (res.).

Althoff, Henry (1873-1947): ord. July 26, 1902; bp. Belleville, 1914-47.

Amat, Thaddeus, C.M. (1811-78): b. Spain; ord. Dec. 23, 1837; bp. Monterey (title changed to Monterey-Los Angeles, 1859), 1854-78.

Anderson, Joseph (1865-1927): ord. May 20, 1892; aux. Boston (Myrina), 1909-27.

Anderson, Paul F. (1917-87): ord. Jan. 6, 1943; coad. bp. Duluth (Polignana), 1968-69; bp. Duluth, 1969-82 (res.); aux. Sioux Falls, 1983-87.

Anglim, Robert, C.SS.R. (1922-73): ord. Jan. 6, 1948; prelate Coari, Brazil (Gaguari), 1966-73.

Annabring, Joseph (1900-59): b. Hungary; ord. May 3, 1927; bp. Superior, 1954-59.

Arliss, Reginald, C.P. (1906-96): ord. Apr. 28, 1934; prelate Marbel, Philippines (now a diocese), 1970-81 (res.).

Appelhans, Stephen A., S.V.D. (1905-51): ord. May 5, 1932; v.a. East New Guinea (Catula), 1948-51.

Armstrong, Robert J. (1884-1957): ord. Dec. 10, 1910; bp. Sacramento, 1929-57.

Arnold, William R. (1881-1965): ord. June 13, 1908; delegate of U.S. military vicar (Phocaea), 1945-65.

Atkielski, Roman R. (1898-1969): ord. May 30, 1931; aux. Milwaukee (Stobi), 1947-69.

B

Babcock, Allen J. (1898-1969): ord. Mar. 7, 1925; aux. Detroit (Irenopolis), 1947-54; bp. Grand Rapids, 1954-69.

Bacon, David W. (1815-74): ord. Dec. 13, 1838; first bp. Portland, Me., 1855-74.

Baldwin, Vincent J. (1907-79): ord. July 26, 1931; aux. Rockville Centre (Bencenna), 1962-79.

Baltes, Peter J. (1827-86): b. Germany; ord. May 31, 1852; bp. Alton (now Springfield), Ill., 1870-86.

Baraga, Frederic: See Index.

Barron, Edward (1801-54): b. Ireland; ord. 1829; v.a. The Two Guineas (Constantina), 1842-44 (res.) missionary in U.S.

Barry, John (1799-1859): b. Ireland; ord. Sept. 24, 1825; bp. Savannah, 1857-59.

Barry, Patrick J. (1868-1940): b. Ireland; ord. June 9, 1895; bp. St. Augustine, 1922-40.

Bartholome, Peter W. (1893-1982): ord. June 12, 1917; coad. St. Cloud (Lete), 1942-53; bp. St. Cloud, 1953-68 (res.).

Baumgartner, Apollinarls, O.F.M. Cap. (1899-1970): ord. May 30, 1926; v.a. Guam (Joppa), 1945-65; first bp. Agana, Guam, 1965-70.

Bayley, James Roosevelt (1814-77): convert, 1842; ord. Mar. 2, 1843; first bp. Newark, 1853-72; abp. Baltimore, 1872-77.

Bazin, John S. (1796-1848): b. France; ord. July 22, 1822; bp. Vincennes (now Indianapolis), 1847-48.

Beaven, Thomas D. (1851-1920): ord. Dec. 18, 1875; bp. Springfield, Mass., 1892-1920.

Becker Thomas A. (1832-99): ord. June 18, 1859; first bp. Wilmington, 1868-86; bp. Savannah, 1886-99.

Beckman, Francis J. (1875-1948): ord. June 20, 1902; bp. Lincoln, 1924-30; abp. Dubuque, 1930-46 (res.).

Begin, Floyd L. (1902-77): ord. July 31, 1927; aux. Cleveland (Sala), 1947-62; first bp. Oakland, 1962-77.

Bell, Alden J. (1904-82): b. Canada; ord. May 14, 1932; aux. Los Angeles (Rhodopolis), 1956-62; bp. Sacramento, 1962-79 (res.).

Benincasa, Pius A. (1913-86): ord. Mar. 27, 1937; aux. Buffalo (Buruni), 1964-86.

Benjamin, Cletus J. (1909-61): ord. Dec. 8, 1935; aux. Philadelphia (Binda), 1960-61.

Bennett, John G. (1891-1957): ord. June 27, 1914; first bp. Lafayette, Ind. 1944-57.

Bergan, Gerald T. (1892-1972): ord. Oct. 28, 1915; bp. Des Moines, 1934-48; abp. Omaha, 1948-69 (res.).

Bernadin, Joseph L. (1928-96): ord. Apr. 26, 1952; aux. Atlanta (Lugura) 1966-72; abp. Cincinnati, 1972-82; abp. Chicago, 1982-96; cardinal, 1983

Bernarding, George, S.V.D. (1912-87): ord. Aug. 13, 1939; first v.a. Mount Hagen, Papua New Guinea (Belabitene), 1960-66; first bp., 1966-82, and first abp., 1982-87 (res.), Mount Hagen.

Bidawid, Thomas M. (1910-71): b. Iraq; ord. May 15, 1935; U.S. citizen; first abp. Ahwaz, Iran (Chaldean Rite), 1968-70; Chaldean patriarchal vicar for United Arab Republic, 1970-71.

Bilock, John M. (1916-94): ord. Feb. 3, 1946; aux. Byzantine-rite Munhall, now Pittsburgh (Pergamum), 1977-94.

Binz, Leo (1900-79): ord. Mar. 15, 1924; coad. bp. Winona (Pinara) 1942-49; coad. abp. Dubuque (Silyum), 1949-54; abp. Dubuque, 1954-61; abp. St. Paul and Minneapolis, 1962-75 (res.).

Biskup, George J. (1911-79): ord. Mar. 19, 1937; aux. Dubuque (Hemeria), 1957-65; bp. Des Moines, 1965-67; coad. abp. Indianapolis (Tamalluma), 1969-70; abp. Indianapolis, 1970-79 (res.).

Blanc, Anthony (1792-1860): b. France; ord. July 22, 1816; bp. New Orleans, 1835-50; first abp. New Orleans, 1850-60.

Blanchet (brothers): Augustin M. (1797-1887): b. Canada; ord. June 3, 1821; bp. Walla Walla, 1846-50; first bp. Nesqually (now Seattle), 1850-79 (res.). **Francis N.** (1795-1883): b. Canada; ord. July 19, 1819; v.a. Oregon Territory (Philadelphia, Adrasus), 1843-46; first abp. Oregon City (now Portland), 1846-80 (res.).

Blanchette, Romeo R. (1913-82): ord. Apr. 3, 1937; aux. Joliet (Maxita), 1965-66; bp. Joliet, 1966-79 (res.).

Blenk, James H., S.M. (1856-1917): b. Germany; ord. Aug. 16, 1885; bp. San Juan, 1899-1906; abp. New Orleans, 1906-17.

Boardman, John J. (1894-1978): ord. May 21, 1921; aux. Brooklyn (Gunela), 1952-77 (res.).

Boccella, John H., T.O.R. (1912-92): b. Italy, came to U.S. at age of two; ord. Mar. 29, 1941; abp. Izmir, Turkey, 1968-78 (res.); tit. abp. Ephesus.

Boeynaems, Libert H., SS.CC. (1857-1926): b. Belgium; ord. Sept. 11, 1881; v.a. Sandwich (Hawaiian) Is. (Zeugma), 1903-26.

Bohachevsky, Constantine (1884-1961): b. Austria Galicia; ord. Jan. 31, 1909; ap. ex. Ukrainian Byzantine Catholics in U.S. (Amisus), 1924-58; first metropolitan of Byzantine Rite archeparchy of Philadelphia, 1958-61.

Boileau, George, S.J. (1912-65): ord. June 13, 1948; coad. bp. Fairbanks (Ausuccura), 1964-65.

Bokenfohr, John, O.M.I. (1903-82): ord. July 11, 1927; bp. Kimberley, S. Africa, 1953-74 (res,).

Boland, Thomas A. (1896-1979): ord. Dec. 23, 1922; aux. Newark (Irina), 1940-47; bp. Paterson, 1947-52; abp. Newark, 1953-74 (res.).

Bona, Stanislaus (1888-1967): ord. Nov. 1, 1912; bp. Grand Island, 1932-44; coad. bp. Green Bay (Mela), 1944-45; bp. Green Bay, 1945-67.

Bonacum, Thomas (1847-1911): b. Ireland; ord. June 18, 1870; bp. Lincoln, 1887-1911.

Borgess, Caspar H. (1826-90): b. Germany; ord. Dec. 8, 1848; coad. bp. and ap. admin. Detroit (Calydon), 1870-71; bp. Detroit, 1871-87 (res.).

Bourgade, Peter (1845-1908): b. France; ord. Nov. 30, 1869; v.a. Arizona (Thaumacus), 1885-97; first bp. Tucson, 1897-99; abp. Santa Fe, 1899-1908.

Boylan, John J. (1889-1953): ord. July 28, 1915; bp. Rockford, 1943-53.

Boyle, Hugh C. (1873-1950): ord. July 2, 1898; bp. Pittsburgh, 1921-50.

Bradley, Denis (1846-1903): b. Ireland; ord. June 3, 1871; first bp. Manchester, 1884-1903.

Brady, John (1842-1910): b. Ireland; ord. Dec. 4, 1864; aux. Boston (Alabanda), 1891-1910.

Brady, Matthew F. (1893-1959): ord. June 10, 1916; bp. Burlington, 1938-44; bp. Manchester, 1944-59.

Brady, William O. (1899-1961): ord. Dec. 21, 1923; bp. Sioux Falls, 1939-56; coad. abp. St. Paul (Selymbria), June-Oct, 1956; abp. St. Paul, 1956-61.

Brennan, Andrew J. (1877-1956): ord. Dec. 17, 1904; aux. Scranton (Thapsus), 1923-26; bp. Richmond, 1926-45 (res.).

Brennan, Francis J. (1894-1968): ord. Apr. 3, 1920; judge (1940-59) and dean (1959-67) of Roman Rota; ord. bp. 1967; cardinal 1967.

Brennan, Thomas F. (1853-1916): b. Ireland; ord. July 14, 1880; first bp. Dallas, 1881-93; aux. St. John's, Newfoundland (Usula), 1893-1905 (res.).

Brizgys, Vincas (1903-92): b. Lithuania; U.S. citizen, 1958; ord. June 5, 1927; aux. Kaunas, Lithuania (Bosano), 1940; exiled 1944; resided in U.S. (Chicago archdiocese) from 1951.

Broderick, Bonaventure (1868-1943): ord. July 26, 1896; aux. Havana, Cuba (Juliopolis), 1903-05 (res.).

Brondel, John B. (1842-1903): b. Belgium; ord. Dec. 17, 1864; bp. Vancouver Is., 1879-84; first bp. Helena, 1884-1903.

Brossart, Ferdinand (1849-1930): b. Germany; ord. Sept. 1, 1892; bp. Covington, 1916-23 (res.).

Brown, Charles A., M.M. (1919-97): ord. June 9, 1946; aux. Santa Cuz, Bolivia (Vallis), 1957-97

Brunini, Joseph B. (1909-96): ord. Dec. 5, 1933; aux. Natchez-Jackson (Axomis) 1957-66; bp. Natchez-Jackson (now Jackson) 1967-84 (res.).

Brust, Leo J. (1916-95): ord. May 30, 1942; aux. Milwaukee (Suelli) 1969-91 (ret.).

Brute, Simon G. (1779-1839): b. France; ord. June 11, 1808; first bp. Vincennes (now Indianapolis), 1834-39.

Brzana, Stanislaus J. (1917-97): ord. June 7, 1941; aux. Buffalo (Cufruta) 1964-68; bp. Ogdensburg 1968-93 (res.).

Buddy, Charles F. (1887-1966): ord. Sept. 19, 1914; first bp. San Diego, 1936-66.

Burke, James C., O.P. (1926-94): ord. June 8, 1956; prelate of Chimbote, Peru (Lamiggiga), 1967-78 (res.).

Burke, Joseph A. (1886-1962): ord. Aug. 3, 1912; aux. Buffalo (Vita), 1943-52; bp. Buffalo, 1952-62.

Burke, Maurice F. (1845-1923): b. Ireland; ord. May 22, 1875; first bp. Cheyenne, 1887-93; bp. St. Joseph, 1893-1923.

Burke, Thomas M. (1840-1915): b. Ireland; ord. June 30, 1864; bp. Albany, 1894-1915.

Busch, Joseph F. (1866-1953): ord. July 28, 1889; bp. Lead (now Rapid City), 1910-15; bp. St. Cloud, 1915-53.

Byrne, Andrew (1802-62): b. Ireland; ord. Nov. 11, 1827; first bp. Little Rock, 1844-62.

Byrne, Christopher E. (1867-1950): ord. Sept. 23, 1891; bp. Galveston, 1918-50.

Byrne, Edwin V. (1891-1963): ord. May 22, 1915; first bp. Ponce, 1925-29; bp. San Juan, 1929-43; abp. Santa Fe, 1943-63.

Byrne, James J. (1908-96): ord. June 3, 1943; aux. St. Paul (Etenna) 1947-56; bp. Boise, 1956-62; abp. Dubuque, 1962-83 (res.).

Byrne, Leo C. (1908-74): ord. June 10, 1933; aux. St. Louis (Sabadia), 1954-61; coad. bp. Wichita, 1961-67; coad. abp. (Plestra) St. Paul and Minneapolis, 1967-74.

Byrne, Patrick J., M.M. (1888-1950): ord. June 23, 1915; apostolic delegate to Korea (Gazera), 1949-50.

Byrne, Thomas S. (1841-1923): ord. May 22, 1869; bp. Nashville, 1894-1923.

C

Caesar, Raymond R., S.V.D. (1932-87): ord. June 4, 1961; coad. bp. Goroka, Papua New Guinea, 1978-80; bp. Goroka, 1980-87.

Caillouet, L. Abel (1900-84): ord. May 7, 1925; aux. New Orleans (Setea), 1947-76 (res.).

Canevin, J. F. Regis (1853-1927): ord. June 4, 1879; coad. bp. Pittsburgh (Sabrata), 1903-04; bp. Pittsburgh, 1904-21 (res.).

Cantwell, John J. (1874-1947): b. Ireland; ord. June 18, 1899; bp. Monterey-Los Angeles, 1917-22; bp. Los Angeles-San Diego, 1922-36; first abp. Los Angeles, 1936-47.

Carrell, George A., S.J. (1803-68): ord. Dec. 20, 1827; first bp. Covington, 1853-68.

Carroll (brothers) **Coleman F.** (1905-77): ord. June 15, 1930; aux. Pittsburgh (Pitanae), 1953-58; first bp. Miami, 1958-68 and first abp., 1968-77. **Howard J.** (1902-60): ord. Apr. 2, 1927; bp. Altoona-Johnstown, 1958-60.

Carroll, James J. (1862-1913): ord. June 15, 1889; bp. Nueva Segovia, P.I., 1908-12 (res.).

Carroll, John (1735-1815): ord. Feb. 14, 1761; first bishop of the American hierarchy; first bp., 1789-1808, and first abp., 1808-15, of Baltimore.

Carroll, John P. (1864-1925): ord. July 7, 1886; bp. Helena, 1904-25.

Carroll, Mark K. (1896-1985): ord. June 10, 1922; bp. Wichita, 1947-67 (res.).

Cartwright, Hubert J. (1900-58): ord. June 11, 1927; coad. bp. Wilmington (Neve), 1956-58.

Caruana, George (1882-1951): b. Malta; ord. Oct. 28, 1905; bp. Puerto Rico (name changed to San Juan, 1924), 1921-25; ap. del. Mexico (Sebastea in Armenia), 1925-27; internuncio to Haiti, 1927-35; nuncio to Cuba, 1935-47 (res.).

Casey, James V. (1914-86): ord. Dec. 8, 1939; aux. Lincoln (Citium), Apr.-June, 1957; bp. Lincoln, 1957-67; abp. Denver 1967-86.

Casey, Lawrence B. (1905-77): ord. June 7, 1930; aux. Rochester (Cea), 1953-66; bp. Paterson, 1966-77.

Cassata, John J. (1908-89): ord. Dec. 8, 1932; aux. Dallas-Ft. Worth (Bida), 1968-69; bp. Ft. Worth 1969-80 (res.).

Cassidy, James E. (1869-1951): ord. Sept. 8, 1898; aux. Fall River (Ibora), 1930-34; bp. Fall River, 1934-51.

Chabrat, Guy Ignatius, S.S. (1787-1868): b. France; ord. Dec. 21, 1811; coad. bp. Bardstown (Bolina), 1834-47 (res.).

Chanche, John J., S.S. (1795-1852): ord. June 5, 1819; bp. Natchez (now Jackson), 1841-52.

Chapelle, Placide L. (1842-1905): b. France; ord. June 28, 1865; coad. abp. Santa Fe (Arabissus), 1891-94; abp. Santa Fe, 1894-97; abp. New Orleans 1897-1905.

Chartrand, Joseph (1870-1933): ord. Sept. 24, 1892; coad. bp. Indianapolis (Flavias), 1910-18; bp. Indianapolis, 1918-33.

Chatard, Francis S. (1834-1918): ord. June 14, 1862; bp. Vincennes (now Indianapolis _ title changed in 1898), 1878-1918.

Cheverus, John Lefebvre de (1768-1836): b. France; ord. Dec. 18, 1790; bp. Boston, 1810-23 (returned to France, made cardinal 1836).

Christie, Alexander (1848-1925): ord. Dec. 22, 1877; bp. Vancouver Is., 1898-99; abp. Oregon City (now Portland), 1899-1925.

Clancy, William (1802-47): b. Ireland; ord. May 24, 1823; coad. bp. Charleston (Oreus), 1834-37; v.a. British Guiana, 1837-43.

Clavel Mendez, Tomas Alberto (1921-88): b. Panama; ord. Dec. 7, 1947; bp. David, Panama, 1955-64; abp. Panama, 1964-68 (res.); vicar for Hispanics, Orange, Calif., diocese.

Cody, John P. (1907-82): ord. Dec. 8, 1931; aux. St. Louis (Apollonia), 1947-54; coad. bp. St. Joseph, Mo., 1954-55; bp. Kansas City-St. Joseph, 1956-61; coad. abp. 1961-62; ap. admin., 1962-64, and abp., 1964-65, New Orleans; abp. Chicago, 1965-82; cardinal, 1967.

Cohill, John Edward, S.V.D. (1907-94): ord. Mar. 20, 1936; first bp. Goroko, Papua New Guinea, 1967-80 (res.).

Collins, John J., S.J. (1856-1934): ord. Aug. 29, 1891; v.a. Jamaica (Antiphellus), 1907-18 (res.).

Collins, Thomas P., M.M. (1915-73): ord. June 21, 1942; v.a. Pando, Bolivia (Sufetula), 1961-68 (res.).

Colton, Charles H. (1848-1915): ord. June 10, 1876; bp. Buffalo, 1903-15.

Conaty, Thomas J. (1847-1915): b. Ireland; ord. Dec. 21, 1872; rector of Catholic University, 1896-1903; tit. bp. Samos, 1901-03; bp. Monterey- Los Angeles (now Los Angeles), 1903-15.

Concanen, Richard L., O.P. (1747-1810): b. Ireland; ord. Dec. 22, 1770; first bp. New York, 1808-10 (detained in Italy, never reached his see).

Condon, William J. (1895-1967): ord. Oct. 14, 1917; bp. Great Falls, 1939-67.

Connare, William G. (1911-95): ord. June 14, 1936; bp. Greensburg, 1960-87 (ret.).

Connolly, James L. (1894-1986): ord. Dec. 21, 1923; coad bp. Fall River (Mylasa), 1945-51; bp. Fall River, 1951-70 (res.).

Connolly, John, O.P. (1750-1825): b. Ireland; ord. Sept. 24, 1774; bp. New York, 1814-25.

Connolly, Thomas A. (1899-1991): ord. June 11, 1926; aux. San Francisco (Sila), 1939-48; coad. bp. Seattle, 1948-50; bp, 1950-51, and first abp. Seattle, 1951-75 (res.).

Conroy, John J. (1819-95): b. Ireland; ord. May 21, 1842; bp. Albany, 1865-77 (res.).

Conroy, Joseph H. (1858-1939): ord. June 11, 1881; aux. Ogdensburg (Arindela), 1912-21; bp. Ogdensburg, 1921-39.

Conwell, Henry (1748-1842): b. Ireland; ord. 1776; bp. Philadelphia, 1820-42.

Cooke, Terence J. (1921-83): ord. Dec. 1, 1945; aux. New York (Summa), 1965-68; abp. New York, 1968-83; cardinal 1969.

Corbett, Timothy (1858-1939): ord. June 12, 1886; first bp. Crookston, 1910-38 (res.).

Corrigan, Joseph M. (1879-1942): ord. June 6, 1903; rector of Catholic University, 1936-42; tit. bp. Bilta, 1940-42.

Corrigan, Michael A. (1839-1902): ord. Sept. 19, 1863; bp. Newark, 1873-80; coad. abp. New York (Petra), 1880-85; abp. New York, 1885-1902.

Corrigan, Owen (1849-1929): ord. June 7, 1873; aux. Baltimore (Macri), 1908-29.

Cosgrove, Henry (1834-1906): ord. Aug. 27, 1857; bp. Davenport, 1884-1906.

Cosgrove, William M. (1916-92): ord. Dec. 18, 1943; aux. Cleveland (Trisipa), 1968-76; bp. Belleville, 1976-81 (res.).

Costello, Joseph A. (1915-78): ord. June 7, 1941; aux. Newark (Choma), 1963-78.

Cote, Philip, S.J. (1896-1970): ord. Aug. 14, 1927; v.a. Suchow, China (Polystylus), 1935-46; first bp. Suchow, 1946-70 (imprisoned by Chinese Communists, 1951; expelled from China, 1953; ap. admin. Islands of Quemoy and Matsu, 1969-70.)

Cotter, Joseph B. (1844-1909): b. England; ord. May 3, 1871; first bp. Winona, 1889-1909.

Cotton, Francis R. (1895-1960): ord. June 17, 1920; first bp. Owensboro, 1938-60.

Cousins, William E. (1902-88): ord. Apr. 23, 1927, aux. Chicago (Forma), 1949-52; bp. Peoria, 1952-59; abp. Milwaukee 1959-77 (res.).

Cowley, Leonard P. (1913-73): ord. June 4, 1938; aux. St. Paul and Minneapolis (Pertusa), 1958-73.

Crane, Michael J. (1863-1928): ord. June 15, 1889; aux. Philadelphia (Curium), 1921-28.

Cretin, Joseph (1799-1857): b. France; ord. Dec. 20, 1823; bp. St. Paul, 1851-57.

Crimont, Joseph R., S.J. (1858-1945): b. France; ord. Aug. 26, 1888; v.a. Alaska (Ammaedara), 1917-45.

Crowley, Timothy J., C.S.C. (1880-1945): b. Ireland; ord. Aug. 2, 1906; coad. bp. Dacca (Epiphania), 1927-29; bp. Dacca, 1929-45.

Cunningham, David F. (1900-79): ord. June 12, 1926; aux., 1950-67, and coad. bp., 1967-79, Syracuse (Lampsacus); bp. Syracuse, 1970-76 (res.).

Cunningham, John F. (1842-1919): b. Ireland; ord. Aug. 8, 1865; bp. Concordia, 1898-1919.

Curley, Daniel J. (1869-1932): ord. May 19, 1894; bp. Syracuse, 1923-32.

Curley, Michael J. (1879-1947): b. Ireland; ord. Mar. 19, 1904; bp. St. Augustine, 1914-21; abp. Baltimore, 1921-39; title changed to abp. Baltimore and Washington, 1939-47.

Curtis, Alfred A. (1831-1908): convert, 1872; ord. Dec. 19, 1874; bp. Wilmington, 1886-96 (res.).

Cusack, Thomas F. (1862-1918): ord. May 30, 1885; aux. New York (Temiscyra), 1904-15; bp. Albany, 1915-18.

Cushing, Richard J. (1895-1970): ord. May 26, 1921; aux. Boston (Mela), 1939-44; abp. Boston, 1944-70; cardinal 1958.

D

Daeger, Albert T., O.F.M. (1872-1932): ord. July 25, 1896; abp. Santa Fe, 1919-32.

Daley, Joseph T. (1915-83): ord. June 7, 1941; aux. Harrisburg (Barca), 1964-67; coad., 1967-71, and bp., 1971-83, Harrisburg.

Daly, Edward C., O.P. (1894-1964): ord. June 12, 1921; bp. Des Moines, 1948-64.

Damiano, Celestine (1911-67): ord. Dec. 21, 1935; apostolic delegate to South Africa (Nicopolis in Epiro), 1952-60; bp. Camden, 1960-67.

Danehy, Thomas J., M.M. (1914-59): ord. Sept. 17, 1939; ap. admin. v.a. Pando, Bolivia (Bita), 1953-59.

Danglmayr, Augustine (1898-1992): ord. June 10, 1922; aux. Dallas-Ft. Worth (Olba), 1942-69 (res.).

Dargin, Edward V. (1898-1981): ord. Sept. 23, 1922; aux. New York (Amphipolis), 1953-73 (res.).

David, John B., S.S. (1761-1841): b. France; ord. Sept. 24, 1785; coad. bp. Bardstown (Mauricastrum), 1819-32; bp. Bardstown (now Louisville), 1832-33 (res.).

Davis, James (1852-1926): b. Ireland; ord. June 21, 1878; coad. bp. Davenport (Milopotamus), 1904-06; bp. Davenport, 1906-26.

Davis, James P. (1904-88): ord. May 19, 1929; bp. 1943-60, and first abp., 1960-64, San Juan, P.R.; abp. Santa Fe, 1964-74 (res.).

Dearden, John F. (1907-80): ord. Dec. 8, 1932; coad. bp. Pittsburgh (Sarepta), 1948-50; bp. Pittsburgh, 1950-58; abp. Detroit, 1958-80 (res.); cardinal 1969.

De Cheverus, John L.: See Cheverus, John

De Falco, Lawrence M. (1915-79): ord. June 11, 1942; bp. Amarillo, 1963-79 (res.).

De Goesbriand, Louis (1816-99): b. France; ord. July 13, 1840; first bp. Burlington, 1853-99.

De la Hailandiere, Celestine (1798-1882): b. France; ord. May 28, 1825; bp. Vincennes (now Indianapolis), 1839-47 (res.).

Delany, John B. (1864-1906): ord. May 23, 1891; bp. Manchester, 1904-06.

Demers, Modeste (1809-71): b. Canada; ord. Feb. 7, 1836; bp. Vancouver Is., 1846-71.

Dempsey, Michael J., O.P. (1912-96): ord. June 11, 1942; bp. Sokoto, Nigeria, 1967-84 (res.).

Dempsey, Michael R. (1918-74): ord. May 1, 1943; aux. Chicago (Truentum), 1968-74.

De Neckere, Leo, C.M. (1799-1833): b. Belgium; ord. Oct. 13, 1822; bp. New Orleans, 1829-33.

Denning, Joseph P. (1907-90): ord. May 21, 1932; aux. Brooklyn (Mallus), 1959-82 (res.).

De Saint Palais, Maurice (1811-77): b. France; ord. May 28, 1836; bp. Vincennes (now Indianapolis), 1849-77.

Desmond, Daniel F. (1884-1945): ord. June 9, 1911; bp. Alexandria, 1933-45.

Dimmerling, Harold J. (1914-87): ord. May 2, 1940; bp. Rapid City, 1969-87.

Dinand, Joseph N., S.J. (1869-1943): ord. June 25, 1903; v.a. Jamaica (Selinus), 1927-29 (res.).

Dingman, Maurice J. (1914-92): ord. Dec. 8, 1939; bp. Des Moines, 1968-86 (res.).

Dobson, Robert (1867-1942): ord. May 23, 1891; aux. Liverpool, Eng. (Cynopolis), 1922-42.

Dolinay, Thomas V. (1923-93): ord. May 16, 1948; aux. Passaic Byzantine Rite (Tiatira); 1976-81; first bp. Van Nuys Byzantine Rite, 1981-90; coad. abp., 1990-91, and abp., 1991-93, Pittsburgh Byzantine Rite.

Domenec, Michael, C.M. (1816-78): b. Spain; ord. June 30, 1839; bp. Pittsburgh, 1860-76; bp. Allegheny, 1876-77 (res.).

Donaghy, Frederick A., M.M. (1903-88): ord. Jan. 29, 1929; v.a. Wuchow, China (Setea), 1939; first bp. Wuchow, 1946, expelled from China, 1955.

Donahue, Joseph P. (1870-1959): ord. June 8, 1895; aux. New York (Emmaus), 1945-59.

Donahue, Patrick J. (1849-1922): b. England; ord. Dec. 19, 1885; bp. Wheeling, 1894-1922.

Donahue, Stephen J. (1893-1982): ord. May 22, 1918; aux. New York (Medea), 1934-69 (res.).

Donnellan, Thomas A. (1914-87): ord. June 3, 1939; bp. Ogdensburg, 1964-68; abp. Atlanta, 1968-87.

Donnelly, George J. (1889-1950): ord. June 12, 1921; aux. St. Louis (Coela), 1940-46; bp. Leavenworth (now Kansas City _ title changed in 1947), 1946-50.

Donnelly, Henry E. (1904-67): ord. Aug. 17, 1930; aux. Detroit (Tymbrias), 1954-67.

Donnelly, Joseph F. (1909-77): ord. June 29, 1934; aux. Hartford (Nabala), 1965-77.

Donohoe, Hugh A. (1905-87): ord. June 14, 1930; aux. bp. San Francisco (Taium), 1947-62; first bp. Stockton, 1962-69; bp. Fresno, 1969-80 (res.).

Donovan, John A. (1911-91): b. Canada; ord. Dec. 8, 1935; aux. Detroit (Rhasus), 1954-67; bp. Toledo, 1967-80 (res.).

Doran, Thomas F. (1856-1916): ord. July 4, 1880; aux. Providence (Halicarnassus), 1915-16.

Dougherty, Dennis (1865-1951): ord. May 31, 1890; bp. Nueva Segovia, P.I., 1903-08; bp. Jaro, P.I., 1908-15; bp. Buffalo, 1915-18; abp. Philadelphia, 1918-51; cardinal, 1921.

Dougherty, John J. (1907-86): ord. July 23, 1933; aux. Newark (Cotena), 1963-82 (res.).

Dougherty, Joseph P. (1905-70): ord. June 14, 1930; first bp. Yakima, 1951-69; aux. Los Angeles (Altino), 1969-70.

Dowling, Austin (1868-1930): ord. June 24, 1891; first bp. Des Moines, 1912-19; abp. St. Paul, 1919-30.

Dozier, Carroll T. (1911-85): ord. Mar. 19, 1937; first bp. Memphis, 1971-82 (res.).

Driscoll, Justin A. (1920-84): ord. July 28, 1945; bp. Fargo, 1970-84.

Drossaerts, Arthur J. (1862-1940): b. Holland; ord. June 15, 1889; bp. San Antonio 1918-26; first abp. San Antonio, 1926-40.

Drumm, Thomas W. (1871-1933): b. Ireland; ord. Dec. 21, 1901; bp. Des Moines, 1919-33.

Drury, Thomas J. (1908-92): ord. June 2, 1935; first bp. San Angelo, 1962-65; bp. Corpus Christi, 1965-83 (res.).

Dubois, John, S.S. (1764-1842): b. France; ord. Sept. 28, 1787; bp. New York, 1826-42.

Dubourg, Louis William, S.S. (1766-1833): b. Santo Domingo; ord. 1788; bp. Louisiana and the Two Floridas (now New Orleans), 1815-25; returned to France; bp. Montauban, 1826-33; abp. Besancon 1833.

Dubuis, Claude M. (1817-95): b. France; ord. June 1, 1844; bp. Galveston, 1862-92 (res.).

Dufal, Peter, C.S.C. (1822-98): b. France; ord. Sept. 29, 1852; v.a. Eastern Bengal (Delcon), 1860-78; coad. bp. Galveston, 1878-80 (res.).

Duffy, James A. (1873-1968): ord. May 27, 1899; bp. Kearney (see transferred to Grand Island, 1917), 1913-31 (res.).

Duffy, John A. (1884-1944): ord. June 13, 1908; bp. Syracuse, 1933-37; bp. Buffalo, 1937-44.

Duggan, James (1825-99): b. Ireland; ord. May 29, 1847; coad. bp. St. Louis (Gabala), 1857-59; bp. Chicago, 1859-80 (res.). Inactive from 1869 because of illness.

Dunn, Francis J. (1922-89): ord. Jan. 11, 1948; aux. Dubuque (Turris Tamallani), 1969-89.

Dunn, John J. (1869-1933): ord. May 30, 1896; aux. New York (Camuliana), 1921-33.

Dunne, Edmund M. (1864-1929): ord. June 24, 1887; bp. Peoria, 1909-29.

Dunne, Edward (1848-1910): b. Ireland; ord. June 29, 1871; bp. Dallas, 1893-1910.

Durick, Joseph Aloysius (1914-94): ord. May 23, 1940; aux. bp. Mobile-Birmingham (Cerbali), 1955-64; coad. bp. Nashville, 1964-69 (ap. admin. 1966-69); bp. Nashville, 1969-75 (res.).

Durier, Anthony (1832-1904): b. France; ord. Oct. 28, 1856; bp. Natchitoches (now Alexandria), La., 1885-1904.

Dwenger, Joseph, C.Pp.S. (1837-93): ord. Sept. 4, 1859; bp. Fort Wayne, 1872-93.

Dworschak, Leo F. (1900-76): ord. May 29, 1926; coad. bp. Rapid City (Tium), 1946-47; aux. Fargo, 1947-60; bp. Fargo, 1960-70 (res.).

Dwyer, Robert J. (1908-76): ord. June 11, 1932; bp. Reno, 1952-66; abp. Portland, Ore., 1966-74 (res.).

E

Eccleston, Samuel, S.S. (1801-51): ord. Apr. 24, 1825; coad. bp. Baltimore (Thermae), Sept.-Oct., 1834; abp. Baltimore, 1834-51.

Egan, Michael, O.F.M. (1761-1814): b. Ireland; first bp. Philadelphia, 1810-14.

Eis, Frederick (1843-1926): b. Germany; ord. Oct. 30, 1870; bp. Sault Ste. Marie and Marquette (now Marquette), 1899-1922 (res.).

Elder, William (1819-1904): ord. Mar. 29, 1846; bp. Natchez (now Jackson), 1857-80; coad. bp. Cincinnati (Avara), 1880-83; abp. Cincinnati, 1883-1904.

Elko, Nicholas T. (1909-91): ord. Sept. 30, 1934; ap. admin. Byzantine exarchy of Pittsburgh (Apollonias), Mar.-Sept. 1955; exarch, Sept., 1955-63, and first eparch, 1963-67, of Pittsburgh; tit. abp. Dara, 1967, with assignment in Rome; aux. bp. Cincinnati, 1971-85 (res.).

AMERICAN BISHOPS OF THE PAST

Elwell, Clarence E. (1904-73): ord. Mar. 17, 1929; aux. Cleveland (Cone) 1962-68; bp. Columbus, 1968-73.

Emmet, Thomas A., S.J. (1873-1950): ord. July 30, 1909; v.a. Jamaica (Tuscamia), 1930-49 (res.).

England, John (1786-1842): b. Ireland; ord. Oct. 11, 1808; first bp. Charleston, 1820-42.

Escalante, Alonso Manuel, M.M. (1906-67): b. Mexico; ord. Feb. 1, 1931; v.a. Pando, Bolivia (Sora), 1943-60 (res.).

Espelage (brothers): **Bernard T., O.F.M.** (1892-1971): ord. May 16, 1918; bp. Gallup, 1940-69 (res.). **Sylvester J., O.F.M.** (1877-1940): ord. Jan. 18, 1900; v.a. Wuchang, China (Oreus), 1930-40.

Etteldorf, Raymond P. (1911-86): ord. Dec. 8, 1937; apostolic delegate, 1969-73, and nuncio, 1973-74, to New Zealand (Tindari); pro-nuncio to Ethiopia, 1947-82.

Eustace, Bartholomew J. (1887-1956): ord. Nov. 1, 1914; bp. Camden, 1938-56.

Evans, George R. (1922-85): ord. May 31, 1947; aux. Denver (Tubyza), 1969-85.

F

Fahey, Leo F. (1898-1950): ord. May 29, 1926; coad. bp. Baker City (Ipsus), 1948-50.

Falconio, Diomede, O.F.M. (1842-1917): b. Italy; ord. Jan. 3, 1866, Buffalo, N.Y.; missionary in U.S. and Canada; returned to Italy; bp. Lacedonia, 1892-95; abp. Acerenza e Matera, 1895-99; ap. del. Canada (Larissa), 1899-1902, U.S., 1902-11; cardinal 1911.

Farley, John (1842-1918): b. Ireland; ord. June 11, 1870; aux. New York (Zeugma), 1895-1902; abp. New York, 1902-18; cardinal 1911.

Farrelly, John P. (1856-1921): ord. Mar. 22, 1880; bp. Cleveland, 1909-21.

Fearns, John M. (897-1977): ord. Feb. 19, 1922; aux. New York (Geras), 1957-72 (res.).

Fedders, Edward L., M.M. (1913-73): ord. June 11, 1944; prelate Juli, Peru (Antiochia ad Meadrum), 1963-73.

Feehan, Daniel F. (1855-1934): ord. Dec. 29, 1879; bp. Fall River, 1907-34.

Feehan, Patrick A. (1829-1902): b. Ireland; ord. Nov. 1, 1852; bp. Nashville, 1865-80; first abp. Chicago, 1880-1902.

Feeney, Daniel J. (1894-1969): ord. May 21, 1921; aux. Portland, Me. (Sita), 1946-52; coad. bp. Portland, 1952-55; bp. Portland, 1955-69.

Feeney, Thomas J., S.J. (1894-1955): ord. June 23, 1927; v.a. Caroline and Marshall Is. (Agnus), 1951-55.

Fenwick, Benedict J., S.J. (1782-1846): ord. June 11, 1808; bp. Boston, 1825-46.

Fenwick, Edward D., O.P. (1768-1832): ord. Feb. 23, 1793; first bp. Cincinnati, 1822-32.

Fink, Michael, O.S.B. (1834-1904): b. Germany; ord. May 28, 1857; coad. v.a., 1871-74, and v.a., 1874-77, Kansas and Indian Territory (Eucarpia); first bp. Leavenworth (now Kansas City), 1877-1904.

Finnigan, George, C.S.C. (1885-1932): ord. June 13, 1915; bp. Helena, 1927-32.

Fisher, Carl, S.S.J. (1945-93): ord. June 2, 1973; aux. Los Angeles (Tlos), 1987-93.

Fitzgerald, Edward (1833-1907): b. Ireland; ord. Aug. 22, 1857; bp. Little Rock, 1867-1907.

Fitzgerald, Edward A. (1893-1972): ord. July 25, 1916; aux. Dubuque (Cantanus), 1946-49; bp. Winona, 1949-69 (res.).

Fitzgerald, Walter J., S.J. (1883-1947): ord. May 16, 1918; coad. v.a. Alaska (Tymbrias), 1939-45; v.a. Alaska, 1945-47.

Fitzmaurice, Edmond (1881-1962): b. Ireland; ord. May 28, 1904; bp. Wilmington, 1925-60 (res.).

Fitzmaurice, John E. (1837-1920): b. Ireland; ord. Dec. 21, 1862; coad. bp. Erie (Amisus), 1898-99; bp. Erie, 1899-1920.

Fitzpatrick, John B. (1812-66): ord. June 13, 1840; aux. Boston (Callipolis), 1843-46; bp. Boston, 1846-66.

Fitzsimon, Laurence J. (1895-1958): ord. May 17, 1921; bp. Amarillo, 1941-58.

Flaget, Benedict, S.S.: See Index.

Flaherty, J. Louis (1910-75): ord. Dec. 8, 1936; aux. Richmond (Tabudo), 1966-75.

Flannelly, Joseph F. (1894-1973): ord. Sept. 1, 1918; aux. New York (Metelis), 1948-70 (res.).

Flasch, Kilian C. (1831-91): b. Germany; ord. Dec. 16, 1859; bp. La Crosse, 1881-91.

Flavin, Glennon P. (1916-95): ord. Dec. 20. 1941; aux. St. Louis (Joannina) 1957-67; bp. Lincoln, 1967-92 (res.).

Fletcher, Albert L. (1896-1979): ord. June 4, 1920; aux. Little Rock (Samos), 1940-46; bp. Little Rock, 1946-72 (res.).

Floersh, John (1886-1968): ord. June 10, 1911; coad. bp. Louisville (Lycopolis), 1923-24; bp. Louisville, 1924-37; first abp. Louisville, 1937-67 (res.).

Flores, Felixberto C. (1921-85): b. Gaum; ord. Apr. 30, 1949; ap. admin. Agana, Guam (Stonj), 1970-72; bp., 1977-84, and first abp. Agana, 1984-85.

Foery, Walter A. (1890-1978): ord. June 10, 1916; bp. Syracuse, 1937-70 (res.).

Foley (brothers): **John S.** (1833-1918): ord. Dec. 20, 1856; bp. Detroit, 1888-1918. **Thomas** (1822-79): ord. Aug. 16, 1846; coad. bp. and ap. admin. Chicago (Pergamum), 1870-79.

Foley, Maurice P. (1867-1919): ord. July 25, 1891; bp. Tuguegarao, P.I., 1910-16; bp. Jaro, P.I., 1916-19.

Ford, Francis X., M.M. (1892-1952): ord. Dec. 5, 1917; v.a. Kaying, China (Etenna), 1935-46; first bp. Kaying, 1946-52.

Forest, John A. (1838-1911): b. France; ord. Apr. 12, 1863; bp. San Antonio, 1895-1911.

Fox, Joseph J. (1855-1915): ord. June 7, 1879; bp. Green Bay, 1904-14 (res.).

Franz, John B. (1896-1992): ord. June 13, 1920; first bp. Dodge City, 1951-59; bp. Peoria, 1959-71 (res.).

Frosi, Angelo, S.X. (1924-95): b. Italy; U.S. citizen; ord. May 6, 1948; prelate Abaete do Tocantins (Magneta), Brazil, 1970-81; first bp. Abaetetuba, Brazil, 1981-95.

Fulcher, George A. (1922-84): ord. Feb. 28, 1948; aux. Columbus (Morosbisdus), 1976-83; bp. Lafayette, 1983-84.

Furey, Francis J. (1905-79): ord. Mar. 15, 1930; aux. Philadelphia (Temnus), 1960-63; coad bp. San Diego, 1963-66; bp. San Diego, 1966-69; abp. San Antonio, 1969-79.

Furlong, Philip J. (1892-1989): ord. May 18, 1918; aux. Military Vicar (Araxa), 1956-71 (res.).

G

Gabriels, Henry (1838-1921): b. Belgium; ord. Sept. 21, 1861; bp. Ogdensburg, 1892-1921.

Gabro, Jaroslav (1919-80): ord. Sept. 27, 1945; bp. St. Nicholas of Chicago (Byzantine Rite, Ukrainians), 1961-80.

Galberry, Thomas, O.S.A. (1833-78): b. Ireland; ord. Dec. 20, 1856; bp. Hartford, 1876-78.

Gallagher, Michael J. (1866-1937): ord. Mar. 19, 1893; coad. bp. Grand Rapids (Tiposa in Mauretania), 1915-16; bp. Grand Rapids, 1916-18; bp. Detroit, 1918-37.

Gallagher, Nicholas (1846-1918): ord. Dec. 25, 1868; coad. bp. Galveston (Canopus), 1882-92; bp. Galveston, 1892-1918.

Gallagher, Raymond J. (1912-91): ord. Mar. 25, 1939; bp. Lafayette, Ind., 1965-82 (res.).

Gallegos, Alphonse, O.A.R. (1931-91): ord. May 24, 1958; aux. Sacramento (Sassabe), 1981-91.

Gannon, John M. (1877-1968): ord. Dec. 21, 1901; aux. Erie (Nilopolis), 1918-20; bp. Erie, 1920-66 (res.).

Ganter, Bernard J. (1928-93): ord. May 22, 1952; first bp. Tulsa, 1972-77; bp. Beaumont, 1977-93.

Garcia Diego y Moreno, Francisco, O.F.M. (1785-1846): b. Mexico; ord. Nov. 14, 1808; bp. Two Californias (now Los Angeles), 1840-46.

Garriga, Mariano S. (1886-1965): ord. July 2, 1911; coad. bp. Corpus Christi (Syene), 1936-49; bp. Corpus Christi, 1949-65.

Garrigan, Philip (1840-1919): b. Ireland; ord. June 11, 1870; first bp. Sioux City, 1902-19.

Gartland, Francis X. (1808-54): b. Ireland; ord. Aug. 5, 1832; first bp. Savannah, 1850-54.

Garvey, Eugene A. (1845-1920): ord. Sept. 22, 1869; first bp. Altoona (now Altoona-Johnstown), 1901-20.

Gerbermann, Hugo M., M.M. (1918-96): ord. Feb. 7, 1943; prelate (Amathus), 1962-67, and first bp. Huehuetenango, Guatemala, 1967-75; aux. bp. San Antonio (Pinhel), 1975-82 (res.).

Gercke, Daniel J. (1874-1964): ord. June 1, 1901; bp. Tucson, 1923-60 (res.).

Gerken, Rudolph A. (1887-1943): ord. June 10, 1917; first bp. Amarillo, 1927-33; abp. Santa Fe, 1933-43.

Gerow, Richard O. (1885-1976): ord. June 5, 1909; bp. Natchez-Jackson (now Jackson), 1924-67 (res).

Gerrard, James J. (1897-1991): ord. May 26, 1923; aux. Fall River (Forma), 1959-76 (res.).

Ghattas, Ignatius, B.S.O. (1920-92): b. Nazareth, Israel; ord. July 7, 1946; bp. Newton for Greek Melkites, 1990-92.

Gibbons, Edmund F. (1868-1964): ord May 27, 1893; bp. Albany, 1919-54 (res.).

Gibbons, James (1834-1921): ord. June 30, 1861; v.a. North Carolina (Adramyttium), 1868-72; bp. Richmond, 1872-77; coad. Baltimore (Jonopolis), May-Oct., 1877; abp. Baltimore, 1877-1921; cardinal 1886.

Gilfillan, Francis (1872-1933): b. Ireland; ord. June 24, 1895; coad. bp. St. Joseph (Spiga), 1922-23; bp. St. Joseph, 1923-33.

Gill, Thomas E. (1908-73): ord. June 10, 1933; aux. Seattle (Lambesis) 1956-73.

Gilmore, Joseph M. (1893-1962): ord. July 25, 1915; bp. Helena, 1936-62.

Gilmour, Richard (1824-91): b. Scotland; ord. Aug. 30, 1852; bp. Cleveland, 1872-91.

Girouard, Paul J., M.S. (1898-1964): ord. July 26, 1927; first bp. Morondava, Madagascar, 1956-64.

Glass, Joseph S., C.M. (1874-1926): ord. Aug. 15, 1897; bp. Salt Lake City, 1915-26.

Gleeson, Francis D., S.J. (1895-1983): ord. July 29, 1926; v.a. Alaska (Cotenna), 1948-62; first bp. Fairbanks, 1962-68 (res.).

Glenn, Lawrence A. (1900-85): ord. June 11, 1927; aux. Duluth (Tuscamia), 1956-60; bp. Crookston, 1960-70 (res.).

Glennie, Ignatius T., S.J. (1907-93): ord. Nov. 21, 1938; bp. Trincomalee (now Trincomalee-Batticaloa), Sri Lanka, 1947-74 (res.).

Glennon, John J. (1862-1946): b. Ireland; ord. Dec. 20, 1884; coad. bp. Kansas City, Mo. (Pinara), 1896-1903; coad. St. Louis, April-Oct., 1903; abp. St. Louis, 1903-46; cardinal 1946.

Glorieux, Alphonse J. (1844-1917): b. Belgium; ord. Aug. 17, 1867; v.a. Idaho (Apollonia), 1885-93; bp. Boise, 1893-1917.

Gorman, Daniel (1861-1927): ord. June 24, 1893; bp. Boise, 1918-27.

Gorman, Thomas K. (1892-1980): ord. June 23, 1917; first bp. Reno, 1931-52; coad. bp. Dallas-Ft. Worth (Rhasus), 1952-54; bp. Dallas-Fort Worth (now Dallas), 1954-69 (res.).

Grace, Thomas (1841-1921): b. Ireland; ord. June 24, 1876; bp. Sacramento, 1896-1921.

Grace, Thomas L., O.P. (1814-97): ord. Dec. 21, 1839; bp. St. Paul, 1859-84 (res.).

Graner, Lawrence L., C.S.C. (1901-82): ord. June 24, 1928; bp. Dacca, 1947-50, and first abp., 1950-67 (res.).

Granjon, Henry (1863-1922): b. France; ord. Dec. 17, 1887; bp. Tucson, 1900-22.

Graves, Lawrence P. (1916-94): ord. June 11, 1942; aux. Little Rock (Vina), 1969-73; bp. Alexandria (now Alexandria-Shreveport), 1973-82 (res.).

Graziano, Lawrence, O.F.M. (1921-90): ord. Jan. 26, 1947; aux. Santa Ana, El Salvador (Limata), 1961-65; coad. San Miguel, El Salvador, 1965-68; bp. San Miguel, 1968-69 (res.).

Greco, Charles P. (1894-1987): ord. July 25, 1918; bp. Alexandria, La., 1946-73 (res.).

Green, Francis J. (1906-95): ord. May 15, 1932; aux. Tucson (Serra), 1953-60, coad. May-Oct., 1960, and bp. Tucson, Oct. 26, 1960-1981 (ret.).

Green, Joseph J. (1917-82): ord. July 14, 1946; aux. Lansing (Trisipa), 1962-67; bp. Reno 1967-74 (res.).

Grellinger, John B. (1899-1984): ord. priest July 14, 1929; aux. Green Bay (Syene), 1949-74 (res.).

Greteman, Frank H. (1907-87): ord. Dec. 8, 1932; aux. Sioux City (Vissala), 1965-70; bp. Sioux City, 1970-83 (res.).

Griffin, James A. (1883-1948): ord. July 4, 1909; bp. Springfield, Ill., 1924-48.

Griffin, William A. (1885-1950): ord. Aug. 15, 1910; aux. Newark (Sanavus), 1938-40; bp. Trenton, 1940-50.

Griffin, William R. (1883-1944): ord. May 25, 1907; aux. La Crosse (Lydda), 1935-44.

Griffiths, James H. (1903-64): ord. Mar. 12, 1927; aux. New York and delegate of U.S. military vicar (Gaza), 1950-64.

Grimes, John (1852-1922): b. Ireland; ord. Feb. 19, 1882; coad. bp. Syracuse (Hemeria), 1909-12; bp. Syracuse, 1912-22.

Grimmelsman, Henry J. (1890-1972); ord.Aug. 15, 1915; first bp. Evansville, 1945-65 (res.).

Gross, William H., C.SS.R. (1837-98): ord. Mar. 21, 1863; bp. Savannah, 1873-85; abp. Oregon City (now Portland), 1885-98.

Grovas Felix, Rafael (1905-91): b. San Juan, Puerto Rico; ord. Apr. 7, 1928; bp. Caguas, P.R., 1965-81 (res.).

Grutka, Andrew G. (1908-93): ord. Dec. 5, 1933; first bp. Gary, 1957-84 (res.).

Guertin, George A. (1869-1932): ord. Dec. 17, 1892; bp. Manchester, 1907-32.

Guilfoyle, George H. (1913-91): ord. Mar. 25, 1944; aux. New York (Marazane), 1964-68; bp. Camden 1968-89 (res.).

Guilfoyle, Richard T. (1892-1957): ord. June 2, 1917; bp. Altoona (now Altoona-Johnstown), 1936-57.

Guilfoyle, Merlin J. (1908-81): ord. June 10, 1933; aux. San Francisco (Bulla), 1950-69; bp. Stockton, 1969-79 (res.).

Gunn, John E., S.M. (1863-1924): b. Ireland; ord. Feb. 2, 1890; bp. Natchez (now Jackson), 1911-24.

H

Haas, Francis J. (1889-1953): ord. June 11, 1913; bp. Grand Rapids, 1943-53.

Hacker, Hilary B. (1913-90): ord. June 4, 1938; bp. Bismarck, 1957-82 (res.).

Hackett, John F. (1911-90): ord. June 29, 1936; aux. Hartford (Helenopolis in Palaestina),1953-86 (res.).

Hafey, William (1888-1954): ord. June 16, 1914; first bp. Raleigh, 1925-37; coad. bp. Scranton (Appia), 1937-38; bp. Scranton, 1938-54.

Hagan, John R. (1890-1946): ord. Mar. 7, 1914; aux. Cleveland (Limata), 1946.

Hagarty, Paul L., O.S.B. (1909-84): ord. June 6, 1936; v.a. Bahamas (Arba), 1950-60; first bp. Nassau, Bahamas, 1960-81 (res.).

Haid, Leo M., O.S.B. (1849-1924): ord. Dec. 21, 1872; v.a. N. Carolina (Messene), 1888-1910; abbot Mary Help of Christians abbacy, 1910-24.

Hallinan, Paul J. (1911-68): ord. Feb. 20, 1937; bp. Charleston, 1958-62; first abp. Atlanta, 1962-68.

Hammes, George A. (1911-93): ord. May 22, 1937; bp. Superior 1960-85 (res.).

Hanna, Edward J. (1860-1944): ord. May 30, 1885; aux. San Francisco (Titiopolis). 1912-15; abp. San Francisco, 1915-35 (res.).

Hannan, Jerome D. (1896-1965): ord. May 22, 1921; bp. Scranton, 1954-65.

Harkins, Matthew (1845-1921): ord. May 22, 1869; bp. Providence, 1887-1921.

Harper, Edward, C.SS.R. (1910-90): ord. June 18, 1939; first prelate Virgin Islands (Heraclea Pontica), 1960-77, and first bishop (prelacy made diocese of St. Thomas), 1977-85 (res.).

Harrington, Timothy J. (1918-97): ord. Jan. 19, 1946; aux. Worcester (Rusuca) 1968-83; bp. Worcester, 1983-94 (res.).

Harris, Vincent M. (1913-88): ord. Mar. 19, 1938; first bp. Beaumont, 1966-71; coad. bp. Austin (Rotaria), Apr. 27-Nov. 16, 1971; bp. Austin, 1971-85 (res.).

Hartley, James J. (1858-1944): ord. July 10, 1882; bp. Columbus, 1904-44.

Harty, Jeremiah J. (1853-1927): ord. Apr. 28, 1878; abp. Manila, 1903-16; abp. Omaha, 1916- 27.

Hastrich, Jerome J. (1914-95): ord. Feb. 9, 1941; aux. Madison (Gurza), 1963-69; bp. Gallup, 1969-90 (ret.).

Hayes, James T., S.J. (1889-1980): ord. June 29, 1921; bp. of Cagayan, Philippines, 1933-51; first abp. Cagayan, 1951-70 (res.).

Hayes, Nevin W., O. Carm. (1922-88): ord. June 8, 1946; prelate Sicuani, Peru (Nova Sinna), 1965-70; aux. abp. Chicago, 1971-88.

Hayes, Patrick J. (1867-1938): ord. Sept. 8, 1892; aux. New York (Thagaste), 1914-19; abp. New York, 1919-38; cardinal 1924.

Hayes, Ralph L. (1884-1970): ord. Sept. 19, 1909; bp. Helena 1933-35; rector North American College (Hieropolis) 1935-44; bp. Davenport, 1944-66 (res.).

Healy, James A. (1830-1900): ord. June 10, 1854; bp. Portland 1875-1900.

Heelan, Edmond (1868-1948): b. Ireland; ord. June 24, 1890; aux. Sioux City (Gerasa), 1919-20; bp. Sioux City, 1920-48.

Heffron, Patrick (1860-1927): ord. Dec. 22, 1884; bp. Winona, 1910-27.

Heiss, Michael (1818-90): b. Germany; ord. Oct. 18, 1840; bp. La Crosse, 1868-80; coad. abp. Milwaukee (Hadrianopolis), 1880-81; abp. Milwaukee, 1881-90.

Helmsing, Charles H. (1908-93): ord. June 10, 1933; aux. bp. St. Louis (Axomis), 1949-56; first bp. Springfield-Cape Girardeau, 1956-62; bp. Kansas City-St. Joseph, 1962-77 (res.).

Hendrick, Thomas A. (1849-1909): ord. June 7, 1873; bp. Cebu, P.I., 1904-09.

Hendricken, Thomas F. (1827-86): b. Ireland; ord. Apr. 25, 1853; bp. Providence, 1872-86.

Hennessy, John (1825-1900): b. Ireland; ord. Nov. 1, 1850; bp. Dubuque, 1866-93; first abp. Dubuque, 1893-1900.

Hennessy, John J. (1847-1920): b. Ireland; ord. Nov. 28, 1869; first bp. Wichita, 1888-1920; ap. admin. Concordia (now Salina), 1891-98.

Henni, John M. (1805-81): b. Switzerland; ord. Feb. 2, 1829; first bp. Milwaukee, 1844-75; first abp. Milwaukee, 1875-81.

Henry, Harold W., S.S.C. (1909-76): ord. Dec. 21, 1932; v.a. Kwang Ju, Korea (Coridala), 1957-62; first abp. Kwang Ju, 1962-71; ap. admin. p.a. Cheju-Do, Korea (Thubunae), 1971-76.

Herzig, Charles E. (1929-91): ord. May 31, 1955; first bp. Tyler, 1987-91.

Heslin, Thomas (1845-1911): b. Ireland; ord. Sept. 8, 1869; bp. Natchez (now Jackson), 1889-1911.

Heston, Edward L. (1907-73): ord. Dec. 22, 1934; sec. Sacred Congregation for Religious and Secular

Institutes, 1969-71; pres. Pontifical Commission for Social Communications, 1971-73; tit. abp. Numidea, 1972.

Hettinger, Edward G. (1902-96): ord. June 2, 1968; aux. Columbus (Teos), 1942-77 (res.).

Hickey, David F., S.J. (1882-1973): ord. June 27, 1917; v.a. Belize, Br. Honduras (Bonitza), 1948-56; first bp. Belize, 1956-57 (res.); tit. abp. Cabasa, 1957-73.

Hickey, Thomas F. (1861-1940): ord. Mar. 25, 1884; coad. bp. Rochester (Berenice), 1905-09; bp. Rochester, 1909-28 (res.).

Hickey, William A. (1869-1933): ord. Dec. 22, 1893; coad. bp. Providence (Claudiopolis), 1919-21; bp. Providence, 1921-33.

Hillinger, Raymond P. (1904-71): ord. Apr. 2, 1932; bp. Rockford, 1953-56; aux. Chicago (Derbe), 1956-71.

Hines, Vincent J. (1912-90): ord. May 2, 1937; bp. Norwich, 1960-75 (res.).

Hoban, Edward F. (1878-1966): ord. July 11, 1903; aux. Chicago (Colonia), 1921-28; bp. Rockford, 1928-42; coad. Cleveland (Lystra), 1942-45; bp. Cleveland, 1945-66.

Hoban, Michael J. (1853-1926): ord. May 22, 1880; coad. bp. Scranton (Halius), 1896-99; bp. Scranton, 1899-1926.

Hoch, Lambert A. (1903-90): ord. May 30, 1928; bp. Bismarck, 1952-56; bp. Sioux Falls, 1956-78 (res.).

Hodapp, Robert L., S.J. (1910-89): ord. June 18, 1941; bp. Belize (now Belize-Belmopan), 1958-83 (res.).

Hodges, Joseph H. (1911-85): ord. Dec. 8, 1935; aux. Richmond (Rusadus), 1952-61; coad. Wheeling, 1961-62; bp. Wheeling (now Wheeling-Charleston), 1962-85.

Hogan, John J. (1829-1913): b. Ireland; ord. Apr. 10, 1852; first bp. St. Joseph, 1868-80; first bp. Kansas City, 1880-1913.

Horstmann, Ignatius (1840-1908): ord. June 10, 1865; bp. Cleveland, 1892-1908.

Howard, Edward D. (1877-1983): ord. June 12, 1906; aux. Davenport (Isauropolis), 1924-26; abp. Oregon City (title changed to Portland, 1928), 1926-66 (res.).

Howard, Francis W. (1867-1944): ord. June 16, 1891; bp. Covington, 1923-44.

Hughes, John J. (1797-1864): b. Ireland; ord. Oct. 15, 1826; coad. bp. New York (Basilinopolis), 1837-42; bp. New York, 1842-50, and first abp., 1850-64.

Hunkeler, Edward J. (1894-1970): ord. June 14, 1919; bp. Grand Island, 1945-51; bp. Kansas City, Kans. 1951-52; first abp. Kansas City, 1952-69 (res.).

Hunt, Duane G. (1884-1960): ord. June 27, 1920; bp. Salt Lake City, 1937-60.

Hurley, Joseph P. (1894-1967): ord. May 29, 1919; bp. St. Augustine, 1940-67.

Hyland, Francis E. (1901-68): ord. June 11, 1927; aux. Savannah-Atlanta (Gomphi), 1949-56; bp. Atlanta, 1956-61 (res.).

Hyle, Michael W. (1901-67): ord. Mar. 12, 1927; coad. bp. Wilmington, 1958-60; bp. Wilmington, 1960-67.

I

Iranyi, Ladislaus A., Sch. P. (1923-87): ord. Mar. 13, 1948; U.S. citizen, 1958; ord. bp. (Castel Mediano), July 27, 1983, for spiritual care of Hungarian Catholics living outside Hungary.

Ireland, John (1838-1918): b. Ireland; ord. Dec. 21, 1861; coad. bp. St. Paul (Marobea), 1875-84; bp. St. Paul, 1884-88, and first abp. St. Paul, 1888-1918.

Ireton, Peter L. (1882-1958): ord. June 20, 1906; coad. bp. Richmond (Cyme), 1935-45; bp. Richmond, 1945-58.

Issenmann, Clarence G. (1907-82): ord. June 29, 1932; aux. Cincinnati (Phytea), 1954-57; bp. Columbus, 1957-64; coad. bp. Cleveland (Filaca), 1964-66; bp. Cleveland, 1966-74 (res.).

Ivancho, Daniel (1908-72): b. Austria-Hungary; ord. Sept. 30, 1934; coad. bp. Pittsburgh Ruthenian Rite (Europus), 1946-48; bp. Pittsburgh Ruthenian Rite, 1948-54 (res.).

J

Janssen, John (1835-1913): b. Germany; ord. Nov. 19, 1858; first bp. Belleville, 1888-1913.

Janssens, Francis A. (1843-97): b. Holland; ord. Dec. 21, 1867; bp. Natchez (now Jackson) 1881-88; abp. New Orleans, 1888-97.

Jeanmard, Jules B. (1879-1957): ord. June 10, 1903; first bp. Lafayette, La., 1918-56 (res.).

Johannes, Francis (1874-1937): b. Germany; ord. Jan. 3, 1897; coad. bp. Leavenworth (Thasus), 1928-29; bp. Leavenworth (now Kansas City), 1929-37.

Johnson, William R. (1918-86): ord. May 28, 1944; aux. Los Angeles (Blera), 1971-76; first bp. Orange, 1976-86.

Jolson, Alfred, S.J. (1928-94): ord. June 14, 1958; bp. Reykjavik, Iceland, 1988-94.

Jones, William A., O.S.A. (1865-1921): ord. Mar. 15, 1890; bp. San Juan, 1907-21.

Joyce, Robert F. (1896-1990): ord. May 26, 1923; aux. Burlington (Citium), 1954-57; bp. Burlington 1957-71 (res.).

Juncker, Henry D. (1809-68): b. Lorraine (France); ord. Mar. 16, 1834; first bp. Alton (now Springfield), Ill., 1857-68.

Junger, Aegidius (1833-95): b. Germany; ord. June 27, 1862; bp. Nesqually (now Seattle), 1879-95.

K

Kain, John J. (1841-1903): ord. July 2, 1866; bp. Wheeling, 1875-93; coad. abp. St. Louis (Oxyrynchus), 1893-95; abp. St. Louis, 1895-1903.

Katzer, Frederick X. (1844-1903): b. Austria; ord. Dec. 21, 1866; bp. Green Bay, 1886-91; abp. Milwaukee, 1891-1903.

Keane, James J. (1856-1929): ord. Dec. 23, 1882; bp. Cheyenne, 1902-11; abp. Dubuque, 1911-29.

Keane, John J. (1839-1918): b. Ireland; ord. July 2, 1866; bp. Richmond, 1878-88; rector of Catholic University, 1888-97; consultor of Congregation for Propagation of the Faith, 1897-1900; abp. Dubuque, 1900-11 (res.).

Keane, Patrick J. (1872-1928): b. Ireland; ord. June 20, 1895; aux. Sacramento (Samaria), 1920-22; bp. Sacramento, 1922-28.

Kearney, James E. (1884-1977): ord. Sept. 19,

1908; bp. Salt Lake City, 1932-37; bp. Rochester, 1937-66 (res.).

Kearney, Raymond A. (1902-56): ord. Mar. 12, 1927; aux. Brooklyn (Lysinia), 1935-56.

Keiley, Benjamin J. (1847-1925): ord. Dec. 31, 1873; bp. Savannah, 1900-22 (res.).

Kelleher, Louis F. (1889-1946): ord. Apr. 3, 1915; aux. Boston (Thenae), 1945-46.

Kellenberg, Walter P. (1901-86): ord. June 2, 1928; aux. New York (Joannina), 1953-54; bp. Ogdensburg, 1954-57; first bp. Rockville Centre, 1957-76 (res.).

Kelley, Francis C. (1870-1948): b. Canada; ord. Aug. 23, 1893; bp. Oklahoma, 1924-48.

Kelly, Edward D. (1860-1926): ord. June 16, 1886; aux. Detroit (Cestrus), 1911-19; bp. Grand Rapids, 1919-26.

Kelly, Edward J. (1890-1956): ord. June 2, 1917; bp. Boise, 1928-56.

Kelly, Francis M. (1886-1950): ord. Nov. 1, 1912; aux. Winona (Mylasa), 1926-28; bp. Winona, 1928-49 (res.).

Kelly, Patrick (1779-1829): b. Ireland; ord. July 18, 1802; first bp. Richmond, 1820-22 (returned to Ireland; bp. Waterford and Lismore, 1822-29).

Kennally, Vincent, S.J. (1895-1977): ord. June 20, 1928; v.a. Caroline and Marshall Islands (Sassura), 1957-71 (res.).

Kennedy, Thomas F. (1858-1917): ord. July 24, 1887; rector North American College, 1901-17; tit. bp. Hadrianapolis, 1907-15; tit. abp. Seleucia, 1915-17.

Kenney, Lawrence J. (1930-90): ord. June 2, 1956; aux. Military Services archdiocese (Holar),1983-90.

Kenny, Michael H. (1937-95): ord. Mar. 30, 1963; bp. Juneau, 1979-95.

Kenny, William J. (1853-1913): ord. Jan. 15, 1879; bp. St. Augustine, 1902-13.

Kenrick (brothers): **Francis P.** (1796-1863): b. Ireland; ord. Apr. 7, 1821; coad. bp. Philadelphia (Aratha), 1830-42; bp. Philadelphia, 1842-51; abp. Baltimore, 1851-63. **Peter** (1806-96): b. Ireland; ord. Mar. 6, 1832; coad. bp. St. Louis (Adrasus), 1841-43; bp. 1843-47, and first abp. 1847-95, St. Louis (res.).

Keough, Francis P. (1890-1961): ord. June 10, 1916; bp. Providence, 1943-47; abp. Baltimore, 1947-61.

Kevenhoerster, John B., O.S.B. (1869-1949): b. Germany; ord. June 24, 1896, Collegeville, Minn.; ord. tit. bp. Camuliana, 1933; p.a., 1933-41, and v.a., 1941-49, of Bahamas.

Keyes, Michael, S.M. (1876-1959): b. Ireland; ord. June 21, 1907; bp. Savannah, 1922-35 (res.).

Kiley, Moses E. (1876-1953): b. Nova Scotia; ord. June 10, 1911; bp. Trenton, 1934-40; abp. Milwaukee, 1940-53.

Killeen, James (1917-78): ord. May 30, 1942; aux. Military Vicariate (Valmalla), 1975-78.

Klonowski, Henry T. (1898-1977): ord. Aug. 8, 1920; aux. Scranton (Daldis), 1947-73 (res.).

Kocisko, Stephen (1915-95): ord. Mar. 30, 1941; aux. Byzantine ap. ex. Pittsburgh (Teveste), 1956-63; first eparch Passaic, 1963-68; eparch, 1968-69, and first metropolitan of Pittsburgh, 1969-91 (ret.).

Kogy, Lorenz S., O.M. (1895-1963): b. Georgia, Russia; ord. Nov. 15, 1917; U.S. citizen, 1944; patriarchal vicar for Armenian diocese of Beirut (Comana), 1951-63.

Koudelka, Joseph (1852-1921): b. Austria; ord. Oct. 8, 1875; aux. Cleveland (Germanicopolis), 1908-11; aux. Milwaukee, 1911-13; bp. Superior, 1913-21.

Kowalski, Rembert, O.F.M. (1884-1970): ord. June 22, 1911; v.a. Wuchang, China (Ipsus), 1942-46; first bp. Wuchang, 1946-70 (in exile from 1953).

Kozlowski, Edward (1860-1915): b. Poland; ord. June 29, 1887; aux. Milwaukee (Germia), 1914-15.

Krautbauer, Francix X. (1824-85): b. Germany; ord. July 16, 1850; bp. Green Bay, 1875-85.

Krol, John Joseph (1910-96): ord. Feb. 20, 1937; aux. Cleveland (Cadi), 1953-61; archbishop Philadelphia 1961-88 (res.); cardinal 1967.

Kucera, Louis B. (1888-1957): ord. June 8, 1915; bp. Lincoln, 1930-57.

L

Lamb, Hugh (1890-1959): ord. May 29, 1915; aux. Philadelphia (Helos), 1936-51; first bp. Greensburg, 1951-59.

Lamy, Jean B.: See Index.

Lane, Loras (1910-68): ord. Mar. 19, 1937; aux. Dubuque (Bencenna), 1951-56; bp. Rockford, 1956-68.

Lane, Raymond A., M.M. (1894-1974): ord. Feb. 8, 1920; v.a. Fushun, Manchukuo (Hypaepa), 1940-46; sup. gen. Maryknoll, 1946-56.

Lardone, Francesco (1887-1980): b. Italy; ord. June 29, 1910; U.S. citizen 1937; nuncio to various countries (tit. abp. Rhizaeum), 1949-66 (res.).

Laval, John M. (1854-1937): b. France; ord. Nov. 10, 1877; aux. New Orleans (Hierocaesarea), 1911-37.

Lavialle, Peter J. (1819-67): b. France; ord. Feb. 12, 1844; b. Louisville, 1865-67.

Lawler, John J. (1862-1948): ord. Dec. 19, 1885; aux. St. Paul (Hermopolis), 1910-16; bp. Lead (now Rapid City), 1916-48.

Le Blond, Charles H. (1883-1958): ord. June 29, 1909; bp. St. Joseph, 1933-56 (res.).

Ledvina, Emmanuel (1868-1952): ord. Mar. 18, 1893; bp. Corpus Christi, 1921-49 (res.).

Leech, George L. (1890-1985): ord. May 29, 1920; aux. Harrisburg (Mela), Oct.-Dec., 1935; bp. Harrisburg, 1935-71 (res.).

Lefevere, Peter P. (1804-69): b. Belgium; ord. Nov. 30, 1831; coad. bp. and admin. Detroit (Zela), 1841-69.

Leibold, Paul F. (1914-72): ord. May 18, 1940; aux. Cincinnati (Trebenna), 1958-66; bp. Evansville, 1966-69; abp. Cincinnati, 1969-72.

Leipzig, Francis P. (1895-1981): ord. Apr. 17, 1920; bp. Baker, 1950-71 (res.).

Lemay, Leo, S.M. (1909-83): ord. Apr. 15, 1933; v.a. North Solomon Is. (Agbia), 1961-66; first bp. Bougainville, 1966-74 (res.).

Lenihan (brothers): **Mathias C.** (1854-1943): ord. Dec. 20, 1879; first bp. Great Falls, 1904-30 (res.). **Thomas M.** (1844-1901): b. Ireland; ord. Nov. 19, 1868; bp. Cheyenne, 1897-1901.

Leonard, Vincent M. (1908-94): ord. June 16, 1935; aux. Pittsburgh (Arsacal), 1964-69; bp. Pittsburgh, 1969-83 (ret.).

Leray, Francis X. (1825-87): b. France; ord. Mar. 19, 1852; bp. Natchitoches (now Alexandria, La.),

1877-79; coad. bp. New Orleans and admin. of Natchitoches (Jonopolis), 1879-83; abp. New Orleans, 1883-87.

Leven, Stephen A. (1905-83): ord. June 10, 1928; aux. San Antonio (Bure), 1956-69; bp. San Angelo, 1969-79 (res.).

Ley, Felix, O.F.M. Cap. (1909-72): ord. June 14, 1936; ap. admin. Ryukyu Is. (Caporilla), 1968-72.

Lillis, Thomas F. (1861-1938): ord. Aug. 15, 1885; bp. Leavenworth (now Kansas City, Kans.), 1904-10; coad. bp. Kansas City, Mo. (Cibyra), 1910-13; bp. Kansas City, Mo., 1913-38.

Lootens, Louis (1827-98): b. Belgium; ord. June 14, 1851; v.a. Idaho and Montana (Castabala), 1868-75 (res.).

Loras, Mathias (1792-1858): b. France; ord. Nov. 12, 1815; first bp. Dubuque, 1837-58.

Loughlin, John (1817-91): b. Ireland; ord. Oct. 18, 1840; first bp. Brooklyn, 1853-91.

Lowney, Denis M. (1863-1918): b. Ireland; ord. Dec. 17, 1887; aux. Providence (Hadrianopolis), 1917-18.

Lucey, Robert E. (1891-1977): ord. May 14, 1916; bp. Amarillo, 1934-41; abp. San Antonio, 1941-69 (res.).

Ludden, Patrick A. (1838-1912): b. Ireland; ord. May 21, 1865; first bp. Syracuse, 1887-1912.

Luers, John (1819-71): b. Germany; ord. Nov. 11, 1846; first bp. Fort Wayne, 1858-71.

Lyke, James P., O.F.M. (1939-92): ord. June 24, 1966; aux. Cleveland (Furnes Maior) 1979-90; ap. admin. Atlanta, 1990-91; abp. Atlanta, 1991-92.

Lynch, Joseph P. (1872-1954): ord. June 9, 1900; bp. Dallas, 1911-54.

Lynch, Patrick N. (1817-82): b. Ireland; ord. Apr. 5, 1840; bp. Charleston, 1858-82.

Lyons, Thomas W. (1923-88): ord. May 22, 1948; aux. bp. Washington, D.C. (Mortlach), 1974-88.

M

McAuliffe, Maurice F. (1875-1944): ord. July 29, 1900; aux. Hartford (Dercos), 1923-34; bp. Hartford, 1934-44.

McCafferty, John E. (1920-80): ord. Mar. 17, 1945; aux. Rochester (Tanudaia), 1968-80.

McCarthy, Joseph E. (1876-1955): ord. July 4, 1903; bp. Portland, Me., 1932-55.

McCarthy, Justin J. (1900-59): ord. Apr. 16, 1927; aux. Newark (Doberus), 1954-57; bp. Camden, 1957-59.

McCarty, William T., C.SS.R. (1889-1972): ord. June 10, 1915; military delegate (Anea), 1943-47; coad. bp. Rapid City, 1947-48; bp. Rapid City, 1948-69 (res.).

McCauley, Vincent J., C.S.C. (1906-82): ord. June 24, 1943; first bp. Fort Portal, Uganda, 1961-72 (res.).

McCloskey, James P. (1870-1945): ord. Dec. 17, 1898; bp. Zamboanga, P.I., 1917-20; bp. Jaro, P.I., 1920-45.

McCloskey, John (1810-85): ord. Jan. 12, 1834; coad. bp. New York (Axiere), 1843-47; first bp. Albany, 1847-64; abp. New York, 1864-85; first U.S. cardinal 1875.

McCloskey, William G. (1823-1909): ord. Oct. 6, 1852; bp. Louisville, 1868-1909.

McCormick, J. Carroll (1907-96): ord. July 10, 1932; aux. Philadelphia (Ruspae), 1947-60; bp. Altoona-Johnstown, 1960-66; bp. Scranton, 1966-83 (res.).

McCormick, Patrick J. (1880-1953): ord. July 6, 1904; aux. Washington (Atenia), 1950-53.

McCort, John J. (1860-1936): ord. Oct. 14, 1883; aux. Philadelphia (Azotus), 1912-20; bp. Altoona, 1920-36.

McDevitt, Gerald V. (1917-80): ord. May 30, 1942; aux. Philadelphia (Tigias), 1962-80.

McDevitt, Philip R. (1858-1935): ord. July 14, 1885; bp. Harrisburg, 1916-35.

McDonald, William J. (1904-89): b. Ireland; ord. June 10, 1928; aux. Washington (Aquae Regiae), 1964-67; aux. San Francisco, 1967-79 (res.).

McDonnell, Charles E. (1854-1921): ord. May 19, 1878; bp. Brooklyn, 1892-1921.

McDonnell, Thomas J. (1894-1961): ord. Sept. 20, 1919; aux. New York (Sela), 1947-51; coad. bp. Wheeling, 1951-61.

McEleney, John J., S.J. (1895-1986): ord. June 18, 1930; v.a. Jamaica (Zeugma), 1950-56; bp. Kingston, 1956-67; abp. Kingston 1967-70 (res.)

McEntegart, Bryan (1893-1968): ord. Sept. 8, 1917; bp. Ogdensburg, 1943-53; rector Catholic University (Aradi), 1953-57; bp. Brooklyn, 1957-68.

McFadden, James A. (1880-1952): ord. June 17, 1905; aux. Cleveland (Bida), 1932-43; first bp. Youngstown, 1943-52.

MacFarland, Francis P. (1819-74): ord. May 1, 1845; bp. Hartford, 1858-74.

McFaul, James A. (1850-1917): b. Ireland; ord. May 26, 1877; bp. Trenton, 1894-1917.

McGavick, Alexander J. (1863-1948): ord. June 11, 1887; aux. Chicago (Marcopolis), 1899-1921; bp. La Crosse, 1921-48.

McGeough, Joseph F. (1903-70): ord. Dec. 20, 1930; internuncio Ethiopia, 1957-60; apostolic delegate (Hemesa) S. Africa, 1960-67; nuncio Ireland, 1967-69.

McGill, John (1809-72): ord. June 13, 1835; bp. Richmond, 1850-72.

MacGinley, John B. (1871-1969): b. Ireland; ord. June 8, 1895; bp. Nueva Caceres, 1910-24; first bp. Monterey-Fresno, 1924-32 (res.).

McGolrick, James (1841-1918): b. Ireland; ord. June 11, 1867; first bp. Duluth, 1889-1918.

McGovern, Patrick A. (1872-1951): ord. Aug. 18, 1895; bp. Cheyenne, 1912-51.

McGovern, Thomas (1832-98): b. Ireland; ord. Dec. 27, 1861; bp. Harrisburg, 1888-98.

McGrath, Joseph F. (1871-1950): b. Ireland; ord. Dec. 21, 1895; bp. Baker City (now Baker), 1919-50.

McGucken, Joseph T. (1902-84): ord. Jan. 15, 1928; aux. Los Angeles (Sanavus), 1940-55; coad. bp. Sacramento, 1957-62; abp. San Francisco, 1962-77 (res.).

McGuinness, Eugene (1889-1957): ord. May 22, 1915; bp. Raleigh, 1937-44; coad. bp. Oklahoma City and Tulsa (Ilium), 1944-48; bp. Oklahoma City and Tulsa, 1948-57.

McGurkin, Edward A., M.M. (1905-83): ord. Sept. 14, 1930; bp. Shinyanga, Tanzania, 1956-75 (res.).

McIntyre, James F. (1886-1979): ord. May 21, 1921; aux. New York (Cirene), 1941-46; coad. abp. New York (Palto), 1946-48; abp. Los Angeles, 1948-70 (res.); cardinal, 1953.

MacKenzie, Eric F. (1893-1969): ord. Oct. 20, 1918; aux. Boston (Alba), 1950-69.

McLaughlin, Charles B. (1913-78): ord. June 6, 1941; aux. Raleigh (Risinium), 1964-68; first bp. St. Petersburg, 1968-78.

McLaughlin, Thomas H. (1881-1947): ord. July 26, 1904; aux. Newark (Nisa), 1935-37; first bp. Paterson, 1937-47.

McMahon, John J. (1875-1932): ord. May 20, 1900; bp. Trenton, 1928-32.

McMahon, Lawrence S. (1835-93): ord. Mar. 24, 1860; bp. Hartford, 1879-93.

McManaman, Edward P. (1900-64): ord. Mar. 12, 1927; aux. Erie (Floriana), 1948-64.

McManus, James E., C.SS.R. (1900-76): ord. June 19, 1927; bp. Ponce, P.R., 1947-63; aux. New York (Banda), 1963-70 (res.).

McManus, Wlliam E. (1914-97): ord. Apr. 15, 1939; aux. Chicago (Mesarfelta),1967-76; bp. Fort Wayne-South Bend, 1976-85 (res.).

McMullen, John (1832-83): b. Ireland; ord. June 20, 1858; first bp. Davenport, 1881-83.

McNamara, John M. (1878-1960): ord. June 21, 1902; aux. Baltimore (Eumenia), 1928-47; aux. Washington, 1947-60.

McNamara, Martin D. (1898-1966): ord. Dec. 23, 1922; first bp. Joliet, 1949-66.

McNeirny, Francis (1828-94): ord. Aug. 17, 18554; coad. bp. Albany (Rhesaina), 1872-77; bp. Albany, 1877-94.

McNicholas, John T., O.P. (1877-1950); b. Ireland; ord. Oct. 10, 1901; bp. Duluth, 1918-25; abp. Cincinnati, 1925-50.

McNicholas, Joseph A. (1923-83): ord. June 7, 1949; aux. St. Louis (Scala), 1969-75; bp. Springfield, Ill., 1975-83.

McNulty, James A. (1900-72): ord. July 12, 1925; aux. Newark (Methone), 1947-53; bp. Paterson, 1953-63; bp. Buffalo, 1963-72.

McQuaid, Bernard J. (1823-1909): ord. Jan. 16, 1848; first bp. Rochester, 1868-1909.

McShea, Joseph M. (1907-91): ord. Dec. 6, 1931; aux. Philadelphia (Mina), 1952-61; first bp. Allentown, 1961-83 (res.).

McSorley, Francis J., O.M.I. (1913-71): ord. May 30, 1939; v.a. Jolo, P.I. (Sozusa), 1958-71.

McVinney, Russell J. (1898-1971): ord. July 13, 1924; bp. Providence, 1948-71.

Machebeuf, Joseph P. (1812-89): b. France; ord. Dec. 17, 1836; v.a. Colorado and Utah (Epiphania), 1868-87; first bp. Denver, 1887-89.

Maes, Camillus P. (1846-1915): b. Belgium; ord. Dec. 19, 1868; bp. Covington, 1885-1915.

Maginn, Edward J. (1897-1984): b. Scotland; ord. June 10, 1922; aux. Albany (Curium), 1957-72 (res.).

Magner, Francis (1887-1947): ord. May 17, 1913; bp. Marquette, 1941-47.

Maguire, John J. (1904-89): ord. Dec. 22, 1928; aux. New York (Antiphrae), 1959-65; coad. abp. New York (Tabalta), 1965-80 (res.).

Maher, Leo T. (1915-91): ord. Dec. 18, 1943; first bp. Santa Rosa, 1962-69; bp. San Diego, 1969-90(res.).

Mahoney, Bernard (1875-1939): ord. Feb. 27, 1904; bp. Sioux Falls, 1922-39.

Maloney, David M. (1912-95): ord. Dec. 8, 1936; aux. Denver (Ruspe), 1961-67; bp. Wichita, 1967-82 (ret.).

Maloney, Thomas F. (1903-62): ord. July 13, 1930; aux. Providence (Andropolis), 1960-62.

Manning, Timothy (1909-89): b. Ireland; ord. June 16, 1934 (Los Angeles archd.); American citizen, 1944; aux. Los Angeles (Lesvi), 1946-67; first bp. Fresno, 1967-69; coad. abp. Los Angeles (Capri), 1969-70; abp. Los Angeles, 1970-85 (res.); cardinal 1973.

Manogue, Patrick: See Index.

Manucy, Dominic (1823-85): ord. Aug. 15, 1850; v.a. Brownsville (Dulma), 1874-84; bp. Mobile, Mar.-Sept., 1884 (res.); reappointed v.a. Brownsville (Maronea) (now diocese of Corpus Christi), 1884-85.

Mardaga, Thomas J. (1913-84): ord. May 14, 1940; aux. Baltimore (Mutugenna), 1967-68; bp. Wilmington, 1968-84.

Marechal, Ambrose, S.S. (1766-1828): b. France; ord. June 2, 1792; abp. Baltimore, 1817-28.

Markham, Thomas F. (1891-1952): ord. June 2, 1917; aux. Boston (Acalissus), 1950-52.

Markiewicz, Alfred (1928-97): ord. June 6, 1953; sux. Rockville Centre (Afufenia), 1986-94; bp. Kalamazoo, 1994-97.

Marling, Joseph M., C.Pp.S. (1904-79): ord. Feb. 21, 1929; aux. Kansas City, Mo. (Thasus), 1947-56; first bp. Jefferson City, 1956-69 (res.).

Marshall, John A. (1928-94): ord. Dec. 19, 1953; bp. Burlington, 1972-91; bp. Springfield, Mass, 1991-94.

Martin, Augustus M. (1803-75): b. France; ord. May 31, 1828; first bp. Natchitoches (now Alexandria), 1853-75.

Marty, Martin, O.S.B. (1834-96): b. Switzerland; ord. Sept. 14, 1856; v.a. Dakota (Tiberias), 1880-89; first bp. Sioux Falls, 1889-95; bp. St. Cloud, 1895-96.

Marx, Adolph (1915-65): b. Germany; ord. May 2, 1940; aux. Corpus Christi (Citrus), 1956-65; first bp. Brownsville, 1965.

Matz, Nicholas C. (1850-1917): b. France; ord. May 31, 1874; coad. bp. Denver (Telmissus), 1887-89; bp. Denver, 1889-1917.

May, John L. (1922-94): ord. May 3, 1947; aux. bp. Chicago (Tagarbala), 1967-69; bp. Mobile, 1969-80; abp. St. Louis, 1980-92 (res.).

Mazzarella, Bernardino N., O.F.M. (1904-79): ord. June 5, 1931; prelate Olancho, Honduras (Hadrianopolis in Pisidia), 1957-63; first bp. Comayagua, Honduras, 1963-79.

Medeiros, Humberto S. (1915-83): b. Azores; U.S. citizen, 1940; ord. June 15, 1946; bp. Brownsville, 1966-70; abp. Boston, 1970-83; cardinal 1973.

Meerschaert, Theophile (1847-1924): b. Belgium; ord. Dec. 23, 1871; v.a. Oklahoma and Indian Territory (Sidyma), 1891-1905; first bp. Oklahoma, 1905-24.

Melcher, Joseph (1806-73): b. Austria; ord. Mar. 27, 1830; first bp. Green Bay, 1868-73.

Mendez, Alfred, C.S.C. (1907-95): ord. June 24, 1935; first bp. Arecibo, P.R., 1960-74 (res.).

Messmer, Sebastian (1847-1930): b. Switzerland; ord. July 23, 1871; bp. Green Bay, 1892-1903; abp. Milwaukee, 1903-30.

Metzger, Sidney M. (1902-86): ord. Apr. 3, 1926; aux. Santa Fe (Birtha), 1940-41; coad. bp. El Paso, 1941-42; bp. El Paso, 1942-78 (res.).

Meyer, Albert (1903-65): ord. July 11, 1926; bp. Superior, 1946-53; abp. Milwaukee, 1953-58; abp. Chicago, 1958-65; cardinal, 1959.

Michaud, John S. (1843-1908): ord. June 7, 1873; coad. bp. Burlington (Modra), 1892-99; bp. Burlington, 1899-1908.

Miege, John B., S.J. (1815-84): b. France; ord. Sept. 12, 1844; v.a. Kansas and Indian Territory (now Kansas City) (Messene), 1851-74 (res.).

Mihalik, Emil J. (1920-84): ord. Sept. 21, 1945; first bp. Parma (Byzantine Rite, Ruthenians), 1969-84.

Miles, Richard P., O.P. (1791-1860): ord. Sept. 21, 1816; first bp. Nashville, 1838-60.

Minihan, Jeremiah F. (1903-73): ord. Dec. 21, 1929; aux. Boston (Paphus), 1954-73.

Misner, Paul B., C.M. (1891-1938): ord. Feb. 23, 1919; v.a. Yukiang, China (Myrica), 1935-38.

Mitty, John J. (1884-1961): ord. Dec. 22, 1906; bp. Salt Lake, 1926-32; coad. abp. San Francisco (Aegina), 1932-35; abp. San Francisco, 1935-61.

Moeller, Henry (1849-1925): ord. June 10, 1876; bp. Columbus, 1900-03; coad. abp. Cincinnati (Areopolis), 1903-04; abp. Cincinnati, 1904-25.

Molloy, Thomas E. (1884-1956): ord. Sept. 19, 1908; aux. Brooklyn (Lorea), 1920-21; bp. Brooklyn, 1921-56.

Monaghan, Francis J. (1890-1942): ord. May 29, 1915; coad. bp. Ogdensburg (Mela), 1936-39; bp. Ogdensburg, 1939-42.

Monaghan, John J. (1856-1935): ord. Dec. 18, 1880; bp. Wilmington, 1897-1925 (res.).

Montgomery, George T. (1847-1907): ord. Dec. 20, 1879; coad. bp. Monterey-Los Angeles (Thmuis), 1894-96; bp. Monterey-Los Angeles (now Los Angeles), 1896-1903; coad. abp. San Francisco (Auxum), 1903-07.

Mooney, Edward (1882-1958): ord. Apr. 10, 1909; ap. del. India (Irenopolis), 1926-31; ap. del. Japan, 1931-33; bp. Rochester, 1933-37; first abp. Detroit, 1937-58; cardinal, 1946.

Moore, Emerson J. (1938-95): ord. May 30, 1964; aux. New York (Curubi) 1984-95.

Moore, John (1835-1901): b. Ireland; ord. Apr. 9, 1860; bp. St. Augustine, 1877-1901.

Mora, Francis (1827-1905): b. Spain; ord. Mar. 19, 1856; coad. bp. Monterey-Los Angeles (Mosynopolis), 1873-78; bp. Monterey-Los Angeles (now Los Angeles), 1878-96 (res.).

Moran, William J. (1906-96): ord. June 20, 1931; aux. Military Vicariate (Centuria) 1965-81 (res.).

Morkovsky, John L. (1909-90): ord. Dec. 5, 1933; aux. Amarillo (Hieron), 1956-58; bp. Amarillo, 1958-63; coad. bp. Galveston-Houston (Tigava), 1963-75; bp. Galveston, 1975-84 (res.).

Morris, John (1866-1946): ord. June 11, 1892; coad. bp. Little Rock (Acmonia), 1906-07; bp. Little Rock, 1907-46.

Morrow, Louis La Ravoire, S.D.B. (1892-1987): ord. May 21, 1921; bp. Krishnagar, India, 1939-69 (res.).

Mrak, Ignatius (1810-1901): b. Austria; ord. July 31, 1837; bp. Sault Ste. Marie and Marquette (now Marquette), 1869-78 (res.).

Mueller, Joseph M. (1894-1981): ord. June 14, 1919; coad. bp. Sioux City (Sinda), 1947-48; bp. Sioux City, 1948-70 (res.).

Muench, Aloysius (1889-1962): ord. June 8, 1913; bp. Fargo, 1935-59 (res.); apostolic visitator to Germany, 1946; nuncio to Germany 1951-59; cardinal 1959.

Mugavero, Francis J. (1914-91): ord. May 18, 1940; bp. Brooklyn, 1968-90 (res.).

Mulcahy, John J. (1922-94): ord. May 1, 1947; aux. bp. Boston (Penafiel), 1975-92 (res.).

Muldoon, Peter J. (1862-1927): ord. Dec. 18, 1886; aux. Chicago (Tamasus), 1901-08; first bp. Rockford, 1908-27.

Mullen, Tobias (1818-1900): b. Ireland; ord. Sept. 1, 1844; bp. Erie, 1868-99 (res.).

Mulloy, William T. (1892-1959): ord. June 7, 1916; bp. Covington, 1945-59.

Mulrooney, Charles R. (1906-89): ord. June 10, 1930; aux. Brooklyn (Valentiniana), 1959-81 (res.).

Mundelein, George (1872-1939): ord. June 8, 1895; aux. Brooklyn (Loryma), 1909-15; abp. Chicago, 1915-39; cardinal, 1924.

Murphy, Joseph A., S.J. (1857-1939): b. Ireland; ord. Aug. 26, 1888; v.a. Belize, Br. Honduras (Birtha), 1923-39.

Murphy, T.(Thomas) Austin (1911-91): ord. June 10, 1937; aux. Baltimore (Appiaria), 1962-84 (res.).

Murphy, Thomas J. (1932-97): ord. Apr. 12, 1958; bp. Great Falls (renamed Great Falls-Billings) 1978-87; coad. abp. Seattle, 1987-91; abp. Seattle, 1991-97.

Murphy, Thomas W., C.SS.R. (1917-95): ord. June 29, 1943; first bp. Juazeiro, Brazil 1963-73 (res.); aux. Sao Salvador da Bahia, Brazil (Sululos), 1974-95.

Murphy, Willim F. (1885-1950): ord. June 13, 1908; first bp. Saginaw, 1938-50.

Murray, John G. (1877-1956): ord. Apr. 14, 1900; aux. Hartford (Flavias), 1920-25; bp. Portland, 1925-31; abp. St. Paul, 1931-56.

Mussio, John K. (1902-78): ord. Aug. 15, 1935; bp. Steubenville, 1945-77 (res.).

N

Najmy, Justin, O.S.B.M. (1898-1968): b. Syria; ord. Dec. 25, 1926; ap. ex. Melkites (Augustopolis in Phrygia), 1966-68.

Navagh, James J. (1901-65): ord. Dec. 21, 1929; aux. Raleigh (Ombi), 1952-57; bp. Ogdensburg, 1957-63; bp. Paterson, 1963-65.

Neale, Leonard (1746-1817): ord. June 5, 1773; coad. bp. Baltimore (Gortyna), 1800-15; abp. Baltimore, 1815-17.

Nelson, Knute Ansgar, O.S.B. (1906-90): b. Denmark; ord. May 22, 1937; U.S. citizen, 1941; coad. bp. Stockholm, Sweden (Bilta), 1947-57; bp. Stockholm, 1957-62 (res.)

Neraz, John C. (1828-94): b. France; ord. Mar. 19, 1853; bp. San Antonio, 1881-1894.

Neumann, John, St.: See Index.

Newell, Hubert M. (1904-87): ord. June 15, 1930; coad. bp. Cheyenne (Zapara), 1947-51; bp. Cheyenne, 1951-78 (res.).

Newman, Thomas A., M.S. (1903-78): ord. June 29, 1929; first bp. Prome, Burma, 1961-75 (res.).

Niedhammer, Matthew A., O.F.M. Cap. (1901-70): ord. June 8, 1927; v.a. Bluefields, Nicaragua (Caloe), 1943-70.

Nilan, John J. (1855-1934): ord. Dec. 2, 1878; bp. Hartford, 1910-34.

Noa, Thomas L. (1892-1977): ord. Dec. 23, 1916; coad. bp. Sioux City (Salona), 1946-47; bp. Marquette, 1947-68 (res.).

Nold, Wendelin J. (1900-81): ord. Apr. 11, 1925; coad. bp. Galveston (Sasima), 1948-50; bp. Galveston-Houston, 1950-75 (res.).

Noll, John F. (1875-1956): ord. June 4, 1898; bp. Fort Wayne, 1925-56 (pers. tit. abp., 1953).

Northrop, Henry P. (1842-1916): ord. June 25, 1865; v.a. North Carolina (Rosalia), 1881-83; bp. Charleston, 1883-1916.

Noser, Adolph, S.V.D. (1900-81): ord. Sept. 27, 1925; v.a. Accra, British W. Africa (now Ghana) (Capitolias), 1947-50; bp. Accra, 1950-53; v.a. Alexishafen, New Guinea (Hierpiniana), 1953-66; abp. Madang, Papua New Guinea, 1966-75 (res.).

Nussbaum, Paul J., C.P. (1870-1935): ord. May 20, 1894; first bp. Corpus Christi, 1913-20 (res.); bp. Sault Ste. Marie and Marquette (now Marquette), 1922-35.

O

O'Boyle, Patrick A. (1896-1987): ord. May 21, 1921; abp. Washington, D.C., 1948-73 (res.); cardinal 1967.

O'Brien, Henry J. (1896-1976): ord. July 8, 1923 aux. Hartford (Sita), 1940-45; bp. Hartford, 1945-53, and first abp. Hartford, 1953-68 (res.).

O'Brien, William D. (1878-1962): ord. July 11, 1903; aux. Chicago (Calynda), 1934-62.

O'Connell, Denis J. (1849-1927): b. Ireland; ord. May 26, 1877; aux. San Francisco (Sebaste), 1908-12; bp. Richmond, 1912-26 (res.).

O'Connell, Eugene (1815-91): b. Ireland; ord. May 21, 1842; v.a. Marysville (Flaviopolis), 1861-68; first bp. Grass Valley, 1868-84 (res.).

O'Connell, William H. (1859-1944): ord. June 7, 1884; bp. Portland, 1901-06; coad. bp. Boston (Constantia), 1906-07; abp. Boston, 1907-44; cardinal, 1911.

O'Connor (brothers), **James** (1823-90): b. Ireland; ord. Mar. 25, 1848; v.a. Nebraska (Dibon), 1876-85; first bp. Omaha, 1885-90. **Michael, S.J.** (1810-72): b. Ireland; ord. June 1, 1833; first bp. Pittsburgh, 1843-53; first bp. Erie, 1853-54; bp. Pittsburgh, 1854-60 (resigned, joined Jesuits).

O'Connor, John J. (1855-1927): ord. Dec. 22, 1877; bp. Newark, 1901-27.

O'Connor, Martin J. (1900-86): ord. Mar. 15, 1924; aux. Scranton (Thespia), 1943-46; rector North American College, Rome, 1946-64; abp., 1959 (Laodicea); nuncio to Malta, 1965-69; pres. Pontifical Commission for Social Communications, 1964-71.

O'Connor, William A. (1903-83): ord. Sept. 24, 1927; bp. Springfield, Ill., 1949-75 (res.).

O'Connor, William P. (1886-1973): ord. Mar. 10, 1912; bp. Superior, 1942-46; first bp. Madison, 1946-67 (res.).

O'Dea, Edward J. (1856-1932): ord. Dec. 23, 1882; bp. Nesqually (now Seattle _ title changed in 1907), 1896-1932.

Odin, John M., C.M. (1800-70): b. France; ord. May 4, 1823; v.a. Texas (Claudiopolis), 1842-47; first bp. Galveston, 1847-61; abp. New Orleans, 1861-70.

O'Donaghue, Denis (1848-1925): ord. Sept. 6, 1874; aux. Indianapolis (Pomaria), 1900-10; bp. Louisville, 1910-24 (res.).

O'Donnell, Cletus F. (1917-92): ord. May 3, 1941; aux. Chicago (Abritto), 1960-67; bp. Madison, 1967-92 (res.).

O'Dowd, James T. (1907-50): ord. June 4, 1932; aux. San Francisco (Cea), 1948-50.

O'Farrell, Michael J. (1832-94): b. Ireland; ord. Aug. 18, 1855; first bp. Trenton, 1881-94.

O'Flanagan, Dermot (1901-73): b. Ireland; ord. Aug. 27, 1929; first bp. Juneau, 1951-68 (res.).

O'Gara, Cuthbert, C.P. (1886-1968): b. Canada; ord. May 26, 1915; v.a. Yuanling, China (Elis), 1934-46; first bp. Yuanling, 1946-68 (imprisoned, 1951, and then expelled, 1953, by Chinese Communists).

O'Gorman, James, O.C.S.O. (1804-74): b. Ireland; ord. Dec. 23, 1843; v.a. Nebraska (now Omaha) (Raphanea), 1859-74.

O'Gorman, Thomas (1843-1921): ord. Nov. 5, 1865; bp. Sioux Falls, 1896-1921.

O'Hara, Edwin V. (1881-1956): ord. June 9, 1905; bp. Great Falls, 1930-39; bp. Kansas City, Mo., 1939-56 (title changed to Kansas City-St. Joseph, 1956).

O'Hara, Gerald P. (1895-1963): ord. Apr. 3, 1920; aux. Philadelphia (Heliopolis), 1929-35; bp. Savannah (title changed to Savannah-Atlanta in 1937), 1935-59 (res.); regent of Romania nunciature, 1946-50 (expelled); nuncio to Ireland, 1951-54; ap. del. to Great Britain, 1954-63; tit. abp. Pessinus, 1959-63.

O'Hara, John F., C.S.C. (1888-1960): ord. Sept. 9, 1916; delegate of U.S. military vicar (Mylasa), 1940-45; bp. Buffalo, 1945-51; abp. Philadelphia, 1951-60; cardinal, 1958.

O'Hara, William (1816-99): b. Ireland; ord. Dec. 21, 1842; first bp. Scranton, 1868-99.

O'Hare, William F, S.J. (1870-1926): ord. June 25, 1903; v.a. Jamaica (Maximianopolis), 1920-26.

O'Hern, John F. (1874-1933): ord. Feb. 17, 1901; bp. Rochester, 1929-33.

O'Leary, Thomas (1875-1949): ord. Dec. 18, 1897; bp. Springfield, Mass., 1921-49.

Olwell, Quentin, C.P. (1898-1972): ord. Feb. 4, 1923; prelate Marbel, P.I. (Thabraca), 1961-69 (res.).

O'Meara, Edward T. (1921-92): ord. Dec. 21, 1946; aux. St. Louis (Thisiduo), 1972-80; abp. Indianapolis, 1980-92.

O'Regan, Anthony (1809-66): b. Ireland; ord. Nov. 29, 1834; bp. Chicago, 1854-58 (res.).

O'Reilly, Bernard (1803-56): b. Ireland; ord. Oct. 16, 1831; bp. Hartford, 1850-56.

O'Reilly, Charles J. (1860-1923): b. Canada; ord. June 29, 1890; first bp. Baker City (now Baker), 1903-18; bp. Lincoln, 1918-23.

O'Reilly, James (1855-1934): b. Ireland; ord. June 24, 1880; bp. Fargo, 1910-34.

O'Reilly, Patrick T. (1833-92): b. Ireland; ord. Aug. 15, 1857; first bp. Springfield, Mass., 1870-92.

O'Reilly, Peter J. (1850-1924): b. Ireland; ord. June 24, 1877; aux. Peoria (Lebedus), 1900-24.

O'Reilly, Thomas C. (1873-1938): ord. June 4, 1898; bp. Scranton, 1928-38.

Ortynsky, Stephen, O.S.B.M. (1866-1916): b. Poland; ord. July 18, 1891; first Ukrainian Byzantine Rite bishop in U.S. (Daulia), 1907-16.

O'Shea, John A., C.M. (1887-1969): ord. May 30, 1914; v.a. Kanchow, China (Midila), 1928-46; first bp. Kanchow, 1949-69 (expelled by Chinese Communists, 1953).

O'Shea, William F., M.M. (1884-1945): ord. Dec. 5, 1917; v.a. Heijon, Japan (Naissusz), 1939-45; prisoner of Japanese 1941-42.

O'Sullivan, Jeremiah (1842-96): b. Ireland; ord. June 30, 1868; bp. Mobile, 1885-96.

Ott, Stanley J. (1927-92) ord. Dec. 8, 1951; aux. New Orleans (Nicives), 1976-83; bp. Baton Rouge, 1983-92.

Oves Fernandez, Francisco Ricardo (1928-90) b. Cuba; ord. Apr. 13, 1952; aux. Cienfuegas, Cuba (Montecorvino), 1969-70; abp. Havana, 1970-81 (res.); resided in El Paso, Tex., diocese from 1982.

P

Pardy, James V., M.M. (1898-1983): ord. Jan. 26, 1930; v.a. Cheong-Ju, Korea (Irenopolis), 1958-62; first bp. Cheong-Ju, 1962-69 (res.).

Paschang, Adolph J., M.M. (1895-1968): ord. May 21, 1921; v.a. Kong Moon, China (Sasima), 1937-46; first bp. Kong Moon, 1946-68 (expelled by Communists, 1951).

Pechillo, Jerome, T.O.R. (1919-91): ord. June 10, 1947; prelate Coronel Oviedo, Paraguay (Novasparsa), 1966-76; aux. Newark, 1976-91.

Pellicer, Anthony (1824-80): ord. Aug. 15, 1850; first bp. San Antonio, 1874-80.

Penalver y Cardenas, Luis (1749-1810): b. Cuba; ord. Apr. 4, 1772; first bp. Louisiana and the Two Floridas (now New Orleans), 1793-1801; abp. Guatemala, 1801-06 (res.).

Perche, Napoleon J. (1805-83): b. France; ord. Sept. 19, 1829; abp. New Orleans, 1870-83.

Pernicone, Joseph M. (1903-85): b. Sicily; ord. Dec. 18, 1926; aux. New York (Hadrianapolis) 1954-78 (res.).

Perry, Harold R., S.V.D. (1916-91), ord. Jan. 6, 1944; aux. New Orleans (Mons in Mauretania), 1966-91.

Persico, Ignatius, O.F.M. Cap. (1823-95): b. Italy; ord. Jan. 24, 1846; bishop from 1854; bp. Savannah, 1870-72; cardinal, 1893.

Peschges, John H. (1881-1944): ord. Apr. 15, 1905; bp. Crookston, 1938-44.

Peterson, John B. (1871-1944): ord. Sept. 15, 1899; aux. Boston (Hippos), 1927-32; bp. Manchester, 1932-44.

Phelan, Richard (1828-1904): b. Ireland; ord. May 4, 1854; coad. bp. Pittsburgh (Cibyra), 1885-89; bp. Pittsburgh, 1889-1904.

Pinger, Henry A., O.F.M. (1897-1988): ord. June 27, 1927; v.a. Chowtsun, China (Capitolias), 1937-46; first bp. Chowtsun, 1946 (imprisoned, 1951 then released, 1956 and expelled by Chinese Communists).

Pinten, Joseph G. (1867-1945): ord. Nov. 1, 1890; bp. Superior, 1922-26; bp. Grand Rapids, 1926-40 (res.).

Pitaval, John B. (1858-1928): b. France; ord. Dec. 24, 1881; aux. Santa Fe (Sora), 1902-09; abp. Santa Fe, 1909-18 (res.).

Plagens, Joseph C. (1880-1943): b. Poland; ord. July 5, 1903; aux. Detroit (Rhodiapolis), 1924-35; bp. Sault Ste. Marie and Marquette (title changed to Marquette, 1937), 1935-40; bp. Grand Rapids, 1941-43.

Portier, Michael (1795-1859): b. France; ord. May 16, 1818; v.a. Two Floridas and Alabama (Olena), 1826-29; first bp. Mobile, 1829-59.

Power, Cornelius M. (1913-97): ord. June 3, 1939; bp Yakima, 1969-74; abp. Portland, Ore., 1974-86 (res.).

Prendergast, Edmond (1843-1918): b. Ireland; ord. Nov. 17, 1865; aux. Philadelphia (Scilium), 1897-1911; abp. Philadelphia, 1911-18.

Primeau, Ernest J. (1909-89): ord. Apr. 7, 1934; bp. Manchester, 1960-74 (res.); director Villa Stritch, Rome, 1974-79 (ret.).

Prost, Jude, O.F.M. (1915-94): ord. June 24, 1942; aux. Belem do Para, Brazil (Fronta), 1962-92 (res.).

Proulx, Amedee W. (1932-93): ord. May 31, 1958; aux. bp. Portland, Me. (Clipia), 1975-93.

Purcell, John B. (1800-83): b. Ireland; ord. May 20, 1826; bp., 1833-50, and first abp., 1850-83, Cincinnati.

Q

Quarter, William (1806-48): b. Ireland; ord. Sept. 19, 1829; first bp. Chicago, 1844-48.

Quigley, James E. (1855-1915): b. Canada; ord. Apr. 13, 1879; bp. Buffalo, 1897-1903; abp. Chicago, 1903-15.

Quinlan, John (1826-83): b. Ireland; ord. Aug. 30, 1852; bp. Mobile, 1859-83.

Quinn, William Charles, C.M. (1905-60): ord. Oct. 11, 1931; v.a. Yukiang, China (Halicarnassus), 1940-46; first bp. Yukiang, 1946-60 (expelled by Chinese Communists, 1951).

R

Rademacher, Joseph (1840-1900): ord. Aug. 2, 1863; bp. Nashville, 1883-93; bp. Ft. Wayne, 1893-1900.

Rappe, Louis Amadeus (1801-77): b. France; ord. Mar. 14, 1829; first bp. Cleveland, 1847-70 (res.).

Rausch, James S. (1928-81): ord. June 2, 1956; aux. St. Cloud (Summa), 1973-77; bp. Phoenix, 1977-81.

Ready, Michael J. (1893-1957): ord. Sept. 14, 1918; bp. Columbus, 1944-57.

Reed, Victor J. (1905-71): ord. Dec. 21, 1929; aux. Oklahoma City and Tulsa (Limasa), 1957-58; bp. Oklahoma City and Tulsa, 1958-71.

Regan, Joseph W., M.M. (1905-94): ord. Jan. 27, 1929; prelate Tagum, Philippines (Isinda), 1962-80 (ret.).

Reh, Francis F. (1911-94): ord. Dec. 8, 1935; bp. Charleston 1962-64; bp. Saginaw, 1969-80 (ret.).

Rehring, George J. (1890-1976): ord. Mar. 28,

1914; aux. Cincinnati (Lunda), 1937-50; bp. Toledo, 1950-67 (res.).

Reicher, Louis J. (1890-1984): ord. Dec. 6, 1918; first bp. Austin, 1948-71 (res.).

Reilly, Edmond J. (1897-1958): ord. Apr. 1, 1922; aux. Brooklyn (Nepte), 1955-58.

Reilly, Thomas F., C.SS.R. (1908-92): ord. June 10, 1933; prelate San Juan de la Maguana, Dominican Republic (Themisonium), 1956-69; first bp. San Juan de la Maguana, 1969-77 (res.).

Rese, Frederic (1791-1871): b. Germany; ord. Mar. 15, 1823; first bp. Detroit, 1833-71. Inactive from 1841 because of ill health.

Reverman, Theodore (1877-1941): ord. July 26, 1901; bp. Superior, 1926-41.

Reynolds, Ignatius A. (1798-1855): ord. Oct. 24, 1823; bp. Charleston, 1844-55.

Rhode, Paul P. (1871-1945): b. Poland; ord. June 17, 1894; aux. Chicago (Barca), 1908-15; bp. Green Bay, 1915-45.

Rice, Joseph J. (1871-1938): ord. Sept. 29, 1894; bp. Burlington, 1910-38.

Rice, William A., S.J. (1891-1946): ord. Aug. 27, 1925; v.a. Belize, Br. Honduras (Rusicade), 1939-46.

Richter, Henry J. (1838-1916): b. Germany; ord. June 10, 1865; first bp. Grand Rapids, 1883-1916.

Riley, Thomas J. (1900-1977): ord. May 20, 1927; aux. Boston (Regiae), 1956-76 (res.).

Riordan, Patrick W. (1841-1914): b. Canada; ord. June 10, 1865; coad. abp. San Francisco (Cabasa), 1883-84; abp. San Francisco, 1884-1914.

Ritter, Joseph E. (1892-1967): ord. May 30, 1917; aux. Indianapolis (Hippos), 1933-34; bp., 1934-44, and first abp. Indianapolis, 1944-46; abp. St. Louis, 1946-67; cardinal 1961.

Robinson, Pascal C., O.F.M. (1870-1948): b. Ireland; ord. Dec. 21, 1901; ap. visitor to Palestine, Egypt, Syria and Cyprus (Tyana), 1927-29; ap. nuncio to Ireland, 1929-48.

Rooker, Fraderick Z. (1861-1907): ord. July 25, 1888; bp. Jaro, P.I., 1903-07.

Ropert, Gulstan F., SS.CC. (1839-1903): b. France; ord. May 26, 1866; v.a. Sandwich (now Hawaiian) Is. (Panopolis), 1892-1903.

Rosati, Joseph, C.M.: See Index.

Rosecrans, Sylvester (1827-78): ord. June 5, 1853; aux. Cincinnati (Pompeiopolis), 1862-68; first bp. Columbus, 1868-78.

Rouxel, Gustave A. (1840-1908): b. France; ord. Nov. 4, 1863; aux. New Orleans (Curium), 1899-1908.

Rudin, John, M.M. (1916-95): ord. June 11, 1944; first bp. Musoma, Tanzania, 1957-79 (res.).

Rummel, Joseph (1876-1964): b. Germany; ord. May 24, 1902; bp. Omaha, 1928-35; abp. New Orleans, 1935-64.

Ruocco, Joseph J. (1922-80): ord. May 6, 1948; aux. Boston (Polignano), 1975-80.

Russell, John J. (1897-1993): ord. July 8, 1923; bp. Charleston, 1950-58; bp. Richmond, 1958-73 (res.).

Russell, William T. (1863-1927): ord. June 21, 1889; bp. Charleston, 1917-27.

Ryan, Edward F. (1879-1956): ord. Aug. 10, 1905; bp. Burlington, 1945-56.

Ryan, Gerald J. (1923-85): ord. June 3, 1950; aux. Rockville Centre (Munatiana), 1977-85.

Ryan, James (1848-1923): b. Ireland; ord. Dec. 24, 1871; bp. Alton (now Springfield), Ill., 1888-1923.

Ryan, James H. (1886-1947): ord. June 5, 1909; rector Catholic University, 1928-35; tit. bp. Modra, 1933-35; bp., 1935-45, and first abp. Omaha, 1945-47.

Ryan, Patrick J. (1831-1911): b. Ireland; ord. Sept. 8, 1853; coad. bp. St. Louis (Tricomia), 1872-84; abp. Philadelphia, 1884-1911.

Ryan, Stephen, C.M. (1826-96): b. Canada; ord. June 24, 1849; bp. Buffalo, 1868-96.

Ryan, Vincent J. (1884-1951): ord. June 7, 1912; bp. Bismarck, 1940-41.

S

Salpointe, John B. (1825-98): b. France; ord. Dec. 20, 1851; v.a. Arizona (Dorylaeum), 1869-84; coad. abp. Santa Fe (Anazarbus), 1884-85; abp. Santa Fe, 1885-94 (res.).

San Pedro, Enrique, S.J. (1926-94): b. Cuba; ord. May 18, 1957; aux. bp. Galveston-Houston (Siccesi), 1986-81; coad. bp. Brownsville, Aug.-Nov., 1991; bp. Brownsville, 1991-94.

Scanlan, John J. (1906-97): ord. June 22, 1930; aux. Honolulu (Cenae), 1954-68; bp. Honolulu, 1968-81 (res.).

Scanlan, Lawrence (1843-1915): b. Ireland; ord. June 28, 1868; v.a. Utah (Laranda), 1887-91; bp. Salt Lake (now Salt Lake City), 1891-1915.

Scannell, Richard (1845-1916): b. Ireland; ord. Feb. 26, 1871; first bp. Concordia (now Salina), 1887-91; bp. Omaha, 1891-1916.

Scheerer, Louis A., O.P. (1909-66): ord. June 13, 1935; bp. Multan, Pakistan, 1960-66.

Schenk, Francis J. (1901-69): ord. June 13, 1926; bp. Crookston, 1945-60; bp. Duluth, 1960-69.

Scher, Philip G. (1880-1953): ord. June 6, 1904; bp. Monterey-Fresno, 1933-53.

Schexnayder, Maurice (1895-1981): ord. Apr. 11, 1925; aux. Lafayette (Tuscamia), 1951-56; bp. Lafayette, La., 1956-72 (res.).

Schierhoff, Andrew B. (1922-87): ord. Apr. 14, 1948; aux. La Paz, Bolivia (Gerenza), 1969-82; v.a. Pando, Bolivia, 1982-87.

Schinner, Augustine (1863-1937): ord. Mar. 7, 1886; first bp. Superior, 1905-13; first bp. Spokane, 1914-25 (res.).

Schladweiler, Alphonse (1902-96): ord. June 9, 1929; first bp. New Ulm, 1958-75 (res.).

Schlaefer Berg, Salvator, O.F.M. Cap. (1920-93): ord. June 5, 1946; v.a. Bluefields, Nicaragua (Fiumepiscense), 1970-93.

Schlarman, Joseph H. (1879-1951): ord. June 29, 1904; bp. Peoria, 1930-51.

Schlotterback, Edward F. O.S.F.S. (1912-94): ord. Dec. 17, 1938; v.a. Keetmanshoop, Namibia (Balanea) 1956-89 (ret.).

Schmidt, Matthias W., O.S.B. (1931-92): ord. May 30, 1957; aux. Jatai, Brazil (Mutugenna), 1972-76; bp. Ruy Barbosa, Brazil, 1976-92.

Schmitt, Adolph G., C.M.M. (1905-76): b. Bavaria; U.S. citizen 1945; v.a. Bulawayo (Nasai), Rhodesia (now Zimbabwe), 1951-55; first bp. Bulawayo, 1955-74 (res.). Murdered by terrorists.

Schmondiuk, Joseph (1912-1978): ord. Mar. 29, 1936; aux. Philadelphia exarchate (Zeugma in Syria), 1956-61; eparch Stamford, 1961-77; abp. Philadelphia, 1977-78.

Schott, Lawrence F. (1907-63): ord. July 15, 1935; aux. Harrisburg (Eluza), 1956-63.

Schrembs, Joseph (1866-1945): b. Germany; ord. June 29, 1889; aux. Grand Rapids (Sophene), 1911; first bp. Toledo, 1911-21; bp. Cleveland, 1921-45.

Schuck, James A., O.F.M. (1913-93): ord. June 11, 1940; prelate Cristalandia, Brazil (Avissa, 1959-78), 1959-88 (res.).

Schuler, Anthony J., S.J. (1869-1944): ord. June 27, 1901; first bp. El Paso, 1915-42 (res.).

Schulte, Paul (1890-1984): ord. June 11, 1915; bp. Leavenworth, 1937-46; abp. Indianapolis, 1946-70 (res.).

Schwebach, James (1847-1921): b. Luxembourg; ord. June 16, 1870; bp. La Crosse, 1892-1921.

Schwertner, August J. (1870-1939): ord. June 12, 1897; bp. Wichita, 1921-39.

Scully, William (1894-1969): ord. Sept. 20, 1919; coad. bp. Albany (Pharsalus), 1945-54; bp. Albany, 1954-69.

Sebastian, Jerome D. (1895-1960): ord. May 25, 1922; aux. Baltimore (Baris in Hellesponto), 1954-60.

Seghers, Charles J.: See Index.

Seidenbusch, Rupert, O.S.B. (1830-95): b. Germany; ord. June 22, 1853; v.a. Northern Minnesota (Halia), 1875-88 (res.).

Senyshyn, Ambrose, O.S.B.M. (1903-76): b. Galicia; ord. Aug. 23, 1931; aux. Ukrainian Catholic Diocese of U.S. (Maina), 1942-56; first bp. Stamford (Byzantine Rite), 1958-61; abp. Philadelphia (Byzantine Rite), 1961-76.

Seton, Robert J. (1839-1927): b. Italy, ord. Apr. 15, 1865; tit. abp. Heliopolis, 1903-27. Grandson of St. Elizabeth Seton.

Shahan, Thomas J. (1857-1932): ord. June 3, 1882; rector, Catholic University of America, 1909-27; tit. bp. Germanicopolis, 1914-32.

Shanahan (brothers): **Jeremiah F.** (1834-86): ord. July 3, 1859; first bp. Harrisburg, 1868-86. **John W.** (1846-1916): ord. Jan. 2, 1869; bp. Harrisburg, 1899-1916.

Shanley, John (1852-1909): ord. May 30, 1874; first bp. Jamestown (see transferred to Fargo in 1897), 1889-1909.

Shanley, Patrick H., O.C.D. (1896-1970): b. Ireland; ord. Dec. 21, 1930; U.S. citizen; prelate Infanta, P.I. (Sophene), 1953-60 (res.).

Shaughnessy, Gerald, S.M. (1887-1950): ord. June 20, 1920; bp. Seattle, 1933-50.

Shaw, John W. (1861-1934): ord. May 26, 1888; coad. bp. San Antonio (Castabala), 1910-11; bp. San Antonio, 1911-18; abp. New Orleans, 1918-34.

Shea, Francis R. (1913-94): ord. Mar. 19, 1939; bp. Evansville, 1970-89 (ret.).

Sheehan, Edward T., C.M. (1888-1933): ord. June 7, 1916; v.a. Yukiang, China (Calydon), 1929-33.

Sheen, Fulton J. (1895-1979): ord. Sept. 20, 1919; aux. New York (Caesarina), 1951-66; bp. Rochester, 1966-69 (res.); tit. abp. Newport.

Shehan, Lawrence J. (1898-1984): ord. Dec. 23, 1922; aux. Baltimore and Washington (Lidda), 1945-

53; bp. Bridgeport, 1953-61; coad. abp. Baltimore (Nicopolis ad Nestum), Sept.-Dec., 1961; abp. Baltimore, 1961-74 (res.); cardinal 1965.

Sheil, Bernard J. (1886-1969); ord. May 21, 1910; aux. bp. Chicago (Pegae), 1928-69; tit. abp. Selge, 1959-69.

Shubsda, Thaddeus A. (1925-91): ord. Apr. 26, 1950; aux. Los Angeles (Trau), 1977-82; bp. Monterey, 1982-91.

Smith, Alphonse (1883-1935): ord. Apr. 18, 1908; bp. Nashville, 1924-35.

Smith, Eustace, O.F.M. (1908-75): ord. June 12, 1934; v.a. Beirut, Lebanon (Apamea Cibotus), 1958-73 (res.).

Smith, Leo R. (1905-63): ord. Dec. 21, 1929; aux. Buffalo (Marida), 1952-63; bp. Ogdensburg, 1963.

Smyth, Clement, O.C.S.O. (1810-65): b. Ireland; ord. May 29, 1841; coad. bp. Dubuque (Thennesus), 1857-58; bp. Dubuque, 1858-65.

Soenneker, Henry J. (1907-87): ord. May 26, 1934; bp. Owensboro, 1961-82 (res.).

Spalding, John L. (1840-1916): ord. Dec. 19, 1863, first bp. Peoria, 1876-1908 (res.).

Spalding, Martin J. (1810-72): ord. Aug. 13, 1834; aux. Louisville (Lengone), 1848-50; bp. Louisville, 1850-64; abp. Baltimore, 1864-72.

Spellman, Francis J. (1889-1967): ord. May 14, 1916; aux. Boston (Sila), 1932-39; abp. New York, 1939-67; cardinal 1946.

Spence, John S. (1909-73): ord. Dec. 5, 1933; aux. Washington (Aggersel), 1964-73.

Stang, William (1854-1907): b. Germany; ord. June 15, 1878; first bp. Fall River, 1904-07.

Stanton, Martin W. (1897-1977): ord. June 14, 1924; aux. Newark (Citium) 1957-72 (res.).

Stariha, John (1845-1915): b. Austria; ord. Sept. 19, 1869; first bp. Lead (now Rapid City), 1902-09 (res.).

Steck, Leo J. (1898-1950): ord. June 8, 1924; aux. Salt Lake City (Ilium), 1948-50.

Stemper, Alfred M., M.S.C. (1913-84): ord. June 26, 1940; v.a. Kavieng (Eleutheropolis), 1957-66; first bp. Kavieng, 1966-80 (res.).

Stock, John (1918-72): ord. Dec. 4, 1943; aux. Philadelphia (Ukrainian Rite) (Pergamum), 1971-72.

Stritch, Samuel (1887-1958): ord. May 21, 1909; bp. Toledo, 1921-30; abp. Milwaukee, 1930-39; abp. Chicago, 1939 58; cardinal 1946.

Sullivan, Bernard, S.J. (1889-1970): ord. June 26, 1921; bp. Patna, India, 1929-46 (res.).

Sullivan, Joseph V. (1919-82): ord. June 1, 1946; aux. Kansas City-St. Joseph (Tagamuta), 1964-74; bp. Baton Rouge, 1974-82.

Swanstrom, Edward E. (1903-85): ord. June 2, 1928; aux. New York (Arba), 1960-78 (res.).

Sweeney, James J. (1898-1968): ord. June 20, 1925; first bp. Honolulu, 1941-68.

Swint, John J. (1879-1962): ord. June 23, 1904; aux. Wheeling (Sura), 1922; bp. Wheeling, 1922-62.

T

Takach, Basil (1879-1948): b. Austria-Hungary; ord. Dec. 12, 1902; first ap. ex. Pittsburgh Byzantine Rite (Zela), 1924-48.

Tanner, Paul F. (1905-94): ord. May 30, 1931; gen. sec. NCWC (now USCC), 1958-68; tit. bp.

Lamasba, 1965; bp. St. Augustine, 1968-79 (res.).

Tarasevitch, Vladimir L., O.S.B. (1921-86): b. Byelorussia (White Russia); ord. May 26, 1949; ap. visitator (with residence in Chicago) for Byelorussians outside Soviet Union (Mariamme), 1983-86.

Taylor, John E., O.M.I. (1914-76): ord. May 25, 1940; bp. Stockholm, Sweden, 1962-76.

Thill, Francis A. (1893-1957): ord. Feb. 28, 1920; bp. Concordia (title changed to Salina in 1944), 1938-57.

Tief, Francis J. (1881-1965): ord. June 11, 1908; bp. Concordia (now Salina), 1921-38 (res.).

Tierney, Michael (1839-1908): b. Ireland; ord. May 26,1866; bp. Hartford, 1894-1908.

Tihen, J. Henry (1861-1940): ord. Apr. 26, 1886; bp. Lincoln, 1911-17; bp. Denver, 1917-31 (res.).

Timon, John, C.M. (1797-1867): ord. Sept. 23, 1826; first bp. Buffalo, 1847-67.

Toebbe, Augustus M. (1829-84): b. Germany; ord. Sept. 14, 1854; bp. Covington, 1870-84.

Toolen, Thomas J. (1886-1976): ord. Sept. 27, 1910; bp. (pers. tit. abp., 1954), Mobile, 1927-69 (res.).

Topel, Bernard J. (1903-86): ord. June 7, 1927; coad. bp. Spokane (Binda), Sept. 21-25, 1955; bp. Spokane, 1955-78 (res.).

Tracy, Robert E. (1909-80): ord. June 12, 1932; aux. Lafayette, La. (Sergentiza), 1959-61; first bp. Baton Rouge, 1961-74 (res.).

Treacy, John P. (1890-1964): ord. Dec. 8, 1918; coad. bp. La Crosse (Metelis), 1945-48; bp. La Crosse, 1948-64.

Treinen, Sylvester (1917-96): ord. June 11, 1946; bp. Boise, 1962-88 (res.).

Trobec, James (1838-1921): b. Austria; ord. Sept. 8, 1865; bp. St. Cloud, 1897-1914 (res.).

Tuigg, John (1820-89): b. Ireland; ord. May 14, 1850; bp. Pittsburgh, 1876-89.

Turner, William (1871-1936): b. Ireland; ord. Aug. 13, 1893; bp. Buffalo, 1919-36.

Tyler, William (1806-49): ord. June 3, 1829; first bp. Hartford, 1844-49.

U-V

Unterkoefler, Ernest L. (1917-93): ord. May 18, 1944; aux. Richmond (Latopolis) 1962-64; bp. Charleston, 1964-90 (res.).

Van de Velde, James O., S.J. (1795-1855): b. Belgium; ord. Sept. 16, 1827; bp. Chicago, 1849-53; bp. Natchez (now Jackson), 1953-55.

Van de Ven, Cornelius (1865-1932): b. Holland; ord. May 31, 1890; bp. Natchitoches (title changed to Alexandria, 1910), 1904-32.

Van de Vyver, Augustine (1844-1911): b. Belgium; ord. July 24, 1870; bp. Richmond, 1889-1911.

Vath, Joseph G. (1918-87): ord. June 7, 1941; aux. Mobile-Birmingham (Novaliciana), 1966-69; first bp. Birmingham, 1969-87.

Vehr, Urban J. (1891-1973): ord. May 29, 1915; bp. 1931-41, and first abp. Denver, 1941-67 (res.).

Verdaguer, Peter (1835-1911): b. Spain; ord. Dec. 12, 1862; v.a. Brownsville (Aulon), 1890-1911.

Verot, Augustin, S.S. (1805-76): b. France; ord. Sept. 20, 1828; v.a. Florida (Danaba), 1856-61; bp. Savannah, 1861-70; bp. St. Augustine, 1870-76.

Vertin, John (1844-99): b. Austria; ord. Aug. 31, 1866; bp. Sault Ste. Marie and Marquette (now Marquette), 1879-99.

Vogel, Cyril J. (1905-79): ord. June 7, 1931; bp. Salina, 1965-79.

Vonesh, Raymond J. (1916-91): ord. May 3, 1941; aux. Joliet (Vanariona), 1968-1991 (res. May; d. Aug.).

W

Wade, Thomas, S.M. (1893-1969): ord. June 15, 1922; v.a. Northern Solomons (Barbalissus), 1930-69.

Wadhams, Edgar (1817-91): convert, 1846; ord. Jan. 15, 1850; first bp. Ogdensburg, 1872-91.

Waldschmidt, Paul E., C.S.C. (1920-94): ord. June 24, 1946; aux. Portland, Ore. (Citium) 1978-90 (ret.).

Walsh, Emmet (1892-1968): ord. Jan. 15, 1916; bp. Charleston, 1927-49; coad. bp. Youngstown (Rhaedestus), 1949-52; bp. Youngstown, 1952-68.

Walsh, James A., M.M. (1867-1936): ord. May 20, 1892; co-founder (with Thomas F. Price) of Maryknoll, first U.S. established foreign mission society and first sponsor of a U.S. foreign mission seminary; superior of Maryknoll, 1911-36; tit. bp. Syene, 1933-36.

Walsh, James E., M.M. (1891-1981): ord. Dec. 7, 1915; v.a. Kongmoon, China (Sata), 1927-36; superior of Maryknoll, 1936-46; general secretary, Catholic Central Bureau, Shanghai, China, 1948; imprisoned by Chinese communists, 1958-70.

Walsh, Louis S. (1858-1924): ord. Dec. 23, 1882; bp. Portland, Me., 1906-24.

Walsh, Nicolas (1916-97): ord. June 6, 1942; bp. Yakima, 1974-76; aux. Seattle (Bosena), 1976-83 (res.).

Walsh, Thomas J. (1873-1952): ord. Jan. 27, 1900; bp. Trenton, 1918-28; bp., 1928-37, and first abp. 1937-52, Newark.

Ward, John (1857-1929): ord. July 17, 1884; bp. Leavenworth (now Kansas City), 1910-29.

Waters, Vincent S. (1904-74): ord. Dec. 8, 1931; bp. Raleigh, 1945-74.

Watson, Alfred M. (1907-90): ord. May 10, 1934; aux. Erie (Nationa), 1965-69; bp. Erie 1969-82 (res.).

Watterson, John A. (1844-99): ord. Aug. 9, 1868; bp. Columbus, 1880-99.

Wehrle, Vincent, O.S.B. (1855-1941): b. Switzerland; ord. Apr. 23, 1882; first bp. Bismarck, 1910-39 (res.).

Welch, Thomas A. (1884-1959): ord. June 11, 1909; bp. Duluth, 1926-59.

Weldon, Christopher J. (1905-82): ord. Sept. 21, 1939; bp. Springfield, Mass., 1950-77 (res.).

Whealon, John F. (1921-91): ord. May 26, 1945; aux. Cleveland (Andrapa), 1961-66; bp. Erie, 1966-69; abp. Hartford, 1969-91.

Whelan, James O.P. (1822-78): b. Ireland; ord. Aug. 2, 1846; coad. bp. Nashville (Marcopolis), 1859-60; bp. Nashville, 1860-64 (res.).

Whelan, Richard V. (1809-74): ord. May 1, 1831; bp. Richmond, 1841-50; bp. Wheeling, 1850-74.

White, Charles (1879-1955): ord. Sept. 24, 1910; bp. Spokane, 1927-55.

Whitfield, James (1770-1834): b. England; ord. July 24, 1809; coad. bp. Baltimore (Apollonia), 1828; abp. Baltimore, 1828-34.

Wigger, Winand (1841-1901): ord. June 10, 1865; bp. Newark, 1881-1901.

Wildermuth, Augustine F., S.J. (1904-93): ord. July 25, 1935; bp. Patna, India, 1947-80 (res.).

Willging, Joseph C. (1884-1959): ord. June 20, 1908; first bp. Pueblo, 1942-59.

Williams, John J. (1822-1907): ord. May 17, 1845; bp., 1866-75, and first abp., 1875-1907, Boston.

Willinger, Aloysius J., C.SS.R. (1886-1973): ord. July 2, 1911; bp. Ponce, P.R., 1929-46; coad. bp. Monterey-Fresno, 1946-53; bp. Monterey-Fresno, 1953-67 (res.).

Winkelmann, Christian H. (1883-1946): ord. June 11, 1907; aux. St. Louis (Sita), 1933-39; bp. Wichita, 1939-46.

Wood, James F. (1813-83): convert, 1836; ord. Mar. 25, 1844; coad. bp. Philadelphia (Antigonea), 1857-60; bp., 1860-75, and first abp., 1875-83, Philadelphia.

Woznicki, Stephen (1894-1968): ord. Dec. 22, 1917; aux. Detroit (Peltae), 1938-50; bp. Saginaw, 1950-68.

Wright, John J. (1909-79): ord. Dec. 8, 1935; aux. Boston (Egee), 1947-50; bp. Worcester, 1950-59; bp. Pittsburgh, 1959-69; cardinal, 1969; prefect Congregation of the Clergy, 1969-79.

Wurm, John N. (1927-84): ord. Apr. 3, 1954; aux. St. Louis (Plestia), 1976-81; bp. Belleville, 1981-84.

Y-Z

Young, Josue (1808-66): ord. Apr. 1, 1838; bp. Erie, 1854-66.

Zaleski, Alexander, M. (1906-75): ord. July 12, 1931; aux. Detroit (Lybe), 1950-64; coad. bp. Lansing, 1964-65; bp. Lansing 1966-75.

Zardetti, Otto (1847-1902): b. Switzerland; ord. Aug. 21, 1870; first bp. St. Cloud, 1889-94; abp. Bucharest, Rumania, 1894-95 (res.).

Zuroweste, Albert R. (1901-87): ord. June 8, 1924; bp. Belleville, 1948-76 (res.).

HISPANICS

The nation's Hispanic population totaled 22.4 million, according to figures reported by the U.S. Census Bureau in 1990. It was estimated that 80 percent of the Hispanics were baptized Catholics.

Pastoral Patterns

Pastoral ministry to Hispanics varies, depending on differences among the people and the availability of personnel to carry it out.

The pattern in cities with large numbers of Spanish-speaking is built around special and bilingual churches, centers or other agencies where pastoral and additional forms of service are provided in a manner suited to the needs, language and culture of the people. Services in some places are extensive and include legal advice, job placement, language instruction, recreational and social assistance, specialized counseling, replacement services. In many places, however, even where there are special ministries, the needs are generally greater than the means required to meet them.

Some urban dwellers have been absorbed into established parishes and routines of church life and activity. Many Spanish-speaking communities remain in need of special ministries. An itinerant form of ministry best meets the needs of the thousands of migrant workers who follow the crops.

Demographic and ministerial data were the subjects of a national survey commissioned by the Bishops' Committee for Hispanic Affairs and carried out by its secretariat. It was reported in November, 1990, that responses were received from 152 archdioceses and dioceses. Twelve or more dioceses and archdioceses had Hispanic populations of more than 50 percent; 27 others were a quarter or more Hispanic. Fifty-five percent of the reporting jurisdictions had Hispanic apostolates. Overall, ministerial emphasis was reported in six areas: youth, small Christian communities, the Cursillo movement, Catholic Charities and social ministry, lay leadership formation, and charismatic renewal. Other sources reported that well over 80 percent of Hispanics were located in urban areas,

and that 54 percent were 25 years of age or younger. It was estimated that perhaps 100,000 Catholic Hispanics a year were being lost, principally to fundamentalist and pentecostal sects.

Pastoral ministry to Hispanics was the central concern of three national meetings, *Encuentros,* held in 1972, 1977 and 1985.

The third National *Encuentro* in 1985 produced a master pastoral plan for ministry which the National Conference of Catholic Bishops approved in 1987. Its four keys are collaborative ministry; evangelization; a missionary option regarding the poor, the marginalized, the family, women and youth; the formation of lay leadership.

The U.S. bishops, at their annual meeting in November, 1983, approved and subsequently published a pastoral letter on Hispanic Ministry under the title, "The Hispanic Presence: Challenge and Commitment." (For text, see pp. 46-49 of the 1985 *Catholic Almanac.*)

Bishops

As of August 1, 1997, there were 24 (21 active) bishops of Hispanic origin in the United States; all were named since 1970 (for biographies, see Index). Ten were heads of archdioceses or dioceses: Archbishop Patrick F. Flores (San Antonio); Bishops Raymundo J. Pena (Brownsville), Ricardo Ramirez, C.S.B. (Las Cruces), Arthur N. Tafoya (Pueblo), Manuel D. Moreno (Tucson), Placido Rodriguez, C.M.F. (Lubbock), Gerald R. Barnes (San Bernardino), Armando Ochoa (El Paso), Roberto O. Gonzalez, O.F.M. (Corpus Christi) and Carlos A. Sevilla, S.J. (Yakima). Eleven were auxiliary bishops: Gabino Zavala (Los Angeles), Gilbert Espinoza Chavez (San Diego), Joseph J. Madera (Military Services), Francisco Garmendia (New York), Agustin Roman (Miami), Rene Valero (Brooklyn), David Arias, O.A.R. (Newark), Alvaro Corrada del Rio, S.J. (Washington, D.C.), James A. Tamayo (Galveston-Houston), Emilio Simeon Allué (Boston) and Gilberto Fernandez (Miami). Resigned/retired prelates: Archbishop Robert F. Sanchez (Santa Fe), Bishop Juan Arzube (Los Angeles, auxiliary), Bishop Rene H. Gracida (Corpus Christi).

Hispanic priests and nuns in the U.S. number about 1,600 and 2,000, respectively, according to an estimate made in June, 1988, by Father Gary Riebe Estrella, S.V.D., director of a Hispanic vocational recruitment program.

Secretariat for Hispanic Affairs

The national secretariat was established by the U.S. Catholic Conference for service in promoting and coordinating pastoral ministry to the Spanish-speaking. Its basic orientation is toward integral evangelization, combining religious ministry with development efforts in programs geared to the culture and needs of Hispanics. Its concerns are urban and migrant Spanish-speaking people; communications and publications in line with secretariat purposes and the service of people; bilingual and bicultural religious and general education; liaison for and representation of Hispanics with church, civic and governmental agencies.

The secretariat publishes a newsletter, En Marcha, available to interested parties.

Ronaldo M. Cruz is executive director of the national office at 3211 Fourth St. N.E., Washington, D.C. 20017.

The secretariat works in collaboration with regional and diocesan offices and pastoral institutes throughout the country.

The Northeast Regional Office, officially the **Northeast Hispanic Catholic Center,** was established in 1976 under the auspices of the bishops in 12 states from Maine to Virginia. It has established the Conference of Diocesan Directors of the Hispanic Apostolate, the Association of Hispanic Deacons, a Regional Youth Task Force and a Regional Committee of Diocesan Coordinators of Religious Educators for the Hispanics. The office is the official publishing house for the Hispanic Lectionary approved by the National Conference of Catholic Bishops for the United States. The center has liturgical, evangelization and youth ministry departments and an office of cultural affairs. Mario J. Paredes is executive director. The center is located at 1011 First Ave., New York, NY 10022.

The Southeast Regional Office serves 26 dioceses in Tennessee, North and South Carolina, Florida, Georgia, Mississippi, Alabama and Louisiana. Father Mario Vizcaino, Sch. P., is director of the region and institute. The office is located at 7700 S.W. 56 St., Miami, FL 33155. **The Southeast Pastoral Institute** serves as the educational arm of the regional office by providing formation programs for the development of leadership skills focused on ministry among Hispanics, at the Miami site and in the various dioceses of the region.

In the **Southwest,** the Mexican American Cultural Center serves as convener of diocesan directors and representatives of Hispanic ministry in Arkansas, Oklahoma and Texas.

A regional office serving the **Mountain States** (Arizona, New Mexico, Utah, Colorado and Wyoming) is under the coordination of Deacon Germán Toro, 27 C St., Salt Lake City, UT 84103.

The **Northwest Regional Office for Hispanic Affairs** serves 11 dioceses in Alaska, Montana, Washington, Oregon and Idaho. Father Heliodoro Lucatero is president. The office is located at 2838 Burnside, Portland, OR 97214. It serves as convener for regional workshops, retreats, formation programs and social advocacy.

National Hispanic Priests Association

The National Association of Hispanic Priests of the USA (ANSH — *La Asociación Nacional de Sacerdotes Hispanos,* EE. UU.) was established in September, 1989, with a representation of about 2,400 Hispanic priests residing and ministering in the United States. The association is a product of a long process. In 1970, a group of priests formally organized under the name of PADRES, an acronym for the Spanish title, "Padres Asociados para Derechos Religiosos, Educativos y Sociales." They advocated for and organized the first National Hispanic Encounters with important support and leadership of *Las Hermanas.* Among the early issues was the naming of the first Hispanic bishops. In 1985 some members of PADRES and the Asociacion de Sacerdotes Hispanos (ASH) from the eastern United States took the first steps which led four years later to the establishment of ANSH as a national organization. The association collaborates with the laity and bishops in implementing the National Plan for Hispanic Ministry and in developing approaches for a more meaningful ministry. The president is Rev. Juan Carlos Castro, O.M.I., 555 West St. Francis St., Brownsville, TX 78520.

National Catholic Council for Hispanic Ministry (NCCHM)

The council is a volunteer federation of Roman Catholic organizations, agencies and movements committed to the development of Hispanics/Latinos in Church and society. It was established June 17, 1990, at a gathering at Mundelein College, Chicago; its by-laws were adopted in January, 1991, at Mercy Center, Burlingame, Calif. The council convokes a national gathering every three years called *Raices y Alas* (Roots and Wings). With funding from foundations NCCHM has designed and piloted a leadership development program that links contemporary understandings of leadership with experiences and insights from faith and Hispanic cultures. NCCHM has 53 member organizations. It publishes Puentes, a newsletter. The president is Dr. Carmen Maria Cervantes; the executive director is Rev. Allan Figueroa Deck, S.J., 8601 Lincoln Blvd., Rm. 430, Los Angeles, CA 90045.

Mexican American Cultural Center

This national center, specializing in pastoral studies and language education, was founded in 1972 to provide programs focused on ministry among Hispanics and personnel working with Hispanics in the U.S. Courses — developed according to the see-judge-act methodology — include culture, faith development, Scripture, theology, and praxis; some are offered in Spanish, others in English. Intensive language classes are offered in Spanish, with emphasis on pastoral usage.

The center also conducts workshops for the development of leadership skills and for a better understanding of Hispanic communities. Faculty members serve as resource personnel for pastoral centers, dioceses and parishes throughout the U.S. The center offers master-degree programs in pastoral ministry in cooperation with Incarnate Word College, Boston College, the Oblate School of Theology, St. Mary's University and Loyola University, New Orleans and other educational institutions.

The center is a distribution agency for the circulation of bilingual pastoral materials in the U.S. and Latin America. Sister Maria Elena Gonzalez, R.S.M., is president of the center which is located at 3019 W. French Place, San Antonio, TX 78228.

Institute of Hispanic Liturgy

Spanish-speaking communities in the U.S. are served by the Institute of Hispanic Liturgy, a national organization of liturgists, musicians, artists and pastoral agents, funded in part by the U.S. Bishops. The institute promotes the study of liturgical texts, art, music and popular religiosity in an effort to develop liturgical spirituality among Hispanics. It works closely with the U.S. Bishops' Committee on the Liturgy, and has published liturgical materials. Rev. Raúl Gómez, S.D.S., is the president; Sr. Doris Mary Turek, S.S.N.D., is executive director. Address: P.O. Box 29387, Washington, D.C. 20017.

BLACK CATHOLICS IN THE UNITED STATES

National Office

The National Office for Black Catholics, organized in July, 1970, is a central agency with the general purposes of promoting active and full participation by black Catholics in the Church and of making more effective the presence and ministry of the Church in the black community.

Its operations are in support of the aspirations and calls of black Catholics for a number of objectives, including the following:

· representation and voice for blacks among bishops and others with leadership and decision-making positions in the Church;

· promoting vocations to the priesthood and religious life;

· sponsoring programs of evangelization, pastoral ministry, education and liturgy on a national level;

· recognition of the black heritage in liturgy, community life, theology and education.

Walter T. Hubbard is executive director of the NOBC. The NOBC office is located at 3025 Fourth St. N.E., Washington, D.C. 20017.

Clergy Caucus

The National Black Catholic Clergy Caucus, founded in 1968 in Detroit, is a fraternity of several hundred black priests, permanent deacons and brothers pledged to mutual support in their vocations and ministries.

The Caucus develops programs of spiritual, theological, educational and ministerial growth for its members, to counteract the effects of institutionalized racism within the Church and American society. A bimonthly newsletter is published.

The NBCCC office is located at 343 N. Walnut St., P.O. Box 1088, Opelousas, La. 70571.

Other peer and support groups are the National Black Sisters' Conference and the National Black Catholic Seminarians Association.

National Black Catholic Congress

The National Black Catholic Congress, Inc., was formed in 1985 exclusively to assist in the development of the Roman Catholic Church in the African American community and to devise effective means of evangelization of African American peoples in the United States. Its fundamental purpose is the formation and development of concrete approaches toward the evangelization of African Americans through revitalization of African American Catholic life.

The Congress is under the sponsorship of the African American Roman Catholic bishops of the United States, the National Black Catholic Clergy Caucus, the National Black Sisters' Conference, the National Association of Black Catholic Administrators and the Knights of Peter Claver and the Ladies Auxiliary Knights of Peter Claver. The Congress is also in consultation with African American clergy and vowed religious women communities. The Congress sponsors *Pastoring in African American Parishes*, an annual workshop first held in 1988 and *An African American Catholic Ministries Program*, a week-long curriculum presented twice a year, usually in January and June.

The National Black Catholic Congress sponsored the seventh assembly of African-American Catholics and those serving in African American communities, July 9 to 12, 1992, in New Orleans. The most recent National Congress convened in Baltimore, Aug. 27 to 31, 1997.

The Congress is sponsoring construction of "Our Mother of Africa Chapel" at the Basilica of the National Shrine of the Immaculate Conception in Washington, D.C.

The office of the Congress is located at The Archdiocese of Baltimore Catholic Center, 320 Cathedral St., Room 712, Baltimore, MD 21201. The executive director is Dr. Hilbert D. Stanley.

Committee and Secretariat

The **Committee on African American Catholics,** established by the National Conference of Catholic Bishops in 1987, is chaired by Bishop George V. Murry, S.J., auxiliary of Chicago.. The purpose of the committee is to assist the bishops in their evangelization efforts to the African American community by initiating, encouraging and supporting programs which recognize and respect African American genius and values. Priorities of the Committee include implementation of the National Black Catholic Pastoral Plan of 1987, inculturation of liturgy and ministry, and increasing lay leadership and vocations.

Also established as a service agency to the committee was a **Secretariat for African American Catholics** under the executive direction of Beverly Carroll. The secretariat is the officially recognized voice of the African American community as it articulates its gifts and aspirations regarding ministry, evangelization and worship. It also serves as a liaison to the National Black Catholic Clergy Caucus, the National Black Catholic Seminarians Association, the National Black Sisters' Conference, National Black Catholic Administrators, Knights of St. Peter Claver and Ladies Auxiliary, the National Black Catholic Congress, and the National Black Catholic Theological Society.

The committee and secretariat have offices at 3211 Fourth St. N.E., Washington, D.C. 20017.

Bishops

There were 12 (11 active) black bishops, as of Sept. 1, 1997: Five were heads of dioceses: Bishops Joseph L. Howze (Biloxi), J. Terry Steib, S.V.D. (Memphis), Wilton D. Gregory (Belleville), Elliott G. Thomas (St. Thomas, Virgin Islands) and John H. Ricard, S.S.J. (Pensacola-Tallahassee).. Six were auxiliary bishops: Moses Anderson, S.S.E. (Detroit), Curtis J. Guillory, S.V.D. (Galveston-Houston), Leonard J. Olivier, S.V.D. (Washington), Dominic Carmon, S.V.D. (New Orleans), George V, Murry, S.J. (Chicago) and Edward K. Braxton (St. Louis). Archbishop Eugene A. Marino, S.S.J., of Atlanta, resigned in July, 1990. Retired auxiliary bishop Joseph A. Francis, S.V.D., of Newark, died Sept. 1, 1997.

Josephite Pastoral Center

The Josephite Pastoral Center was established in September, 1968, as an educational and pastoral service agency for the Josephites in their mission work, specifically in the black community, subsequently to all those who minister in the African-American community. St. Joseph's Society of the Sacred Heart, the sponsoring body has about 134 priests and 11 brothers in 64 mostly southern parishes in 17 dioceses. The staff of the center includes Father John G.

Harfmann, S.S.J., director, and Maria M. Lannon, administrator. Address: St. Joseph Seminary 1200 Varnum St. N.E., Washington, D.C. 20017

African-American Evangelization

The National Black Catholic Pastoral Plan adopted by the National Black Catholic Congress in May, 1987, was approved and recommended for implementation by the National Conference of Catholic Bishops in November, 1989.

Following is an account of several points in the bishops' statement, based on coverage by the CNS Documentary Service, Origins, Dec. 28, 1989 (Vol. 19, No. 30).

"Evangelization," wrote the bishops, "would not be complete if it did not take account of the unceasing interplay of the Gospel and of man's concrete life, both personal and social. Evangelization involves an explicit message, adapted to the different situations constantly being realized, about the rights and duties of every human being, about family life, without which personal growth and development are hardly possible, about life in society, about international life, peace, justice and development — a message especially energetic today about liberation."

Three Areas

The pastoral plan "embraces three broad areas: 1) the Catholic identity of African-American Catholics; 2) ministry and leadership within the African-American community; and 3) the responsibility of this community to reach out to the broader society. Within these areas are such issues as culture, family, youth, spirituality, liturgy, ministry, lay leadership, parishes, education, social action and community development."

Reflecting a recommendation of the pastoral plan, the bishops encourage African-American Catholics to "discover their past" since "the possession of one's history is the first step in an appreciation of one's culture."

Native American Tekakwitha Conference

The Kateri Tekakwitha Conference is so named in honor of Blessed Kateri Tekakwitha, "Lily of the Mohawks," who was born in 1656 at Ossernenon (Auriesville), N.Y. in 1656, was baptized in 1676, lived near Montreal, died in 1680 and was beatified in 1980 by Pope John Paul.

The conference was established in 1939 as a missionary-priest advisory group in the Diocese of Fargo. It was a missionary-priest support group from 1946 to 1977. Since 1977 it has been a gathering of Catholic Native peoples together with men and women — clerical, religious and lay persons — who minister with Native Catholic communities.

The primary focus of conference concern and activity is evangelization, with specific emphasis on development of Native ministry and leadership.

Other priorities include catechesis, liturgy, family life, social justice ministry, chemical dependency, youth ministry, spirituality and native Catholic dialogue. Annual conferences, regional conferences and local Kateri Circles serve as occasions for the exchange of ideas, approaches, prayer and mutual support. Since 1980, the national center has promoted and registered 111 Kateri Circles in the U.S. and Canada. Publications include a quarterly newsletter.

The conference has a board of 12 directors, the majority of whom are Native people. Archbishop Charles Chaput, O.F.M. Cap. , is the episcopal moderator. Address: Tekakwitha Conference National Center, P.O. Box 6768, Great Falls, Mont. 59406.

The annual conference was held Aug. 6 to 10, 1997, at Marquette University, Milwaukee, Wis.

National Black Catholic Congress

The eighth National Black Catholic Congress was held Aug. 28 to 31, 1997, in Baltimore, with proceedings oriented to the theme, "What We Have Seen and Heard We Proclaim and Celebrate: The Call to Evangelization."

Auxiliary Bishop George V. Murry of Chicago, addressing 3,600 people at a Mass marking the feast day of St. Augustine, called for efforts to evangelize in the African-American community and then extend their efforts beyond it.

RELIGIOUS

Institutes of Consecrated Life

Religious institutes and congregations are special societies in the Church — institutes of consecrated life — whose members, called Religious, commit themselves, by public vows to observance of the evangelical counsels of poverty, chastity and obedience in a community kind of life in accordance with rules and constitutions approved by church authority. Secular institutes (covered in its own Almanac entry) are also institutes of consecrated life.

The particular goal of each institute and the means of realizing it in practice are stated in the rule and constitutions proper to the institute. Local bishops can give approval for rules and constitutions of institutes of diocesan rank. Pontifical rank belongs to institutes approved by the Holy See. General jurisdiction over all Religious is exercised by the Congregation for Institutes of Consecrated Life and Societies of Apostolic Life. General legislation concerning Religious is contained in Canons 573 to 709 in Book II, Part III, of the Code of Canon Law.

All institutes of consecrated life are commonly called religious orders, despite the fact that there are differences between orders and congregations. The best known orders include the Benedictines, Trappists, Franciscans, Dominicans, Carmelites and Augustinians, for men; and the Carmelites, Benedictines, Poor Clares, Dominicans of the Second Order and Visitation Nuns, for women. The orders are older than the congregations, which did not appear until the 16th century.

Contemplative institutes are oriented to divine worship and service within the confines of their communities, by prayer, penitential practices, other spiritual activities and self-supporting work. Examples are the Trappists and Carthusians, the Carmelite and Poor Clare nuns. Active institutes are geared for pastoral ministry and various kinds of apostolic work. Mixed institutes combine elements of the contemplative and active ways of life. While most institutes of men and women can be classified as active, all of them have contemplative aspects.

Clerical communities of men are those whose membership is predominantly composed of priests.

Non-clerical or lay institutes of men are the various brotherhoods.

"The Consecrated Life and Its Role in the Church and in the World," was the topic of the ninth general assembly of the Synod of Bishops held Oct. 2 to 29, 1994.

Societies of Apostolic Life

Some of the institutes listed below have a special kind of status because their members, while living a common life like that which is characteristic of Religious, do not profess the vows of Religious. Examples are the Maryknoll Fathers, the Oratorians of St. Philip Neri, the Paulists and Sulpicians. They are called societies of apostolic life and are the subject of Canons 731 to 746 in the Code of Canon Law.

RELIGIOUS INSTITUTES OF MEN IN THE UNITED STATES

(Sources: *Official Catholic Directory; Catholic Almanac* survey.)

Africa, Missionaries of (M. Afr.): Founded 1868 at Algiers by Cardinal Charles M. Lavigerie; known as White Fathers until 1984. Generalate, Rome Italy; U.S. headquarters, 1624 21st St. N.W., Washington, DC 20009. Missionary work in Africa.

African Missions, Society of, S.M.A.: Founded 1856, at Lyons, France, by Bishop Melchior de Marion Brésillac. Generalate, Rome, Italy; American province (1941), 23 Bliss Ave., Tenafly, NJ 07670. Missionary work.

Alexian Brothers, C.F.A.: Founded 14th century in western Germany and Belgium during the Black Plague. Motherhouse, Aachen, Germany; generalate, Signal Mountain, TN 37377. Hospital and general health work.

Assumptionists (Augustinians of the Assumption), A.A.: Founded 1845, at Nimes, France, by Rev. Emmanuel d'Alzon; in U.S., 1946. General house, Rome, Italy; U.S. province, 330 Market St., Brighton, MA 02135. Educational, parochial, ecumenical, retreat, foreign mission work.

Atonement, Franciscan Friars of the, S.A.: Founded as an Anglican Franciscan community in 1898 at Garrison, N.Y., by Rev. Paul Wattson. Community corporately received into the Catholic Church in 1909. Generalate, St. James Friary, P.O. Box 5, Graymoor, Garrison NY 10524. Ecumenical, mission, retreat and charitable works.

Augustinian Recollects, O.A.R.: Founded 1588: in U.S., 1944. General motherhouse, Rome, Italy. Missionary, parochial, education work.

St. Augustine Province (1944), 29 Ridgeway Ave., W. Orange, NJ 07052.

St. Nicholas Province: U.S. Delegates, 2800 Schurz Ave., Bronx, NY 10465 (New York); P.O. Box 310, Mesilla, NM 88044 (South).

Augustinians (Order of St. Augustine), O.S.A.: Established canonically in 1256 by Pope Alexander IV; in U.S., 1796. General motherhouse, Rome, Italy.

St. Thomas of Villanova Province (1796), P.O. Box 338, Villanova, PA 19085.

Our Mother of Good Counsel Province (1941), Tolentine Center, 20300 Governors Hwy., Olympia Fields, IL 60461.

St. Augustine Province (1969), 1605 28th St., San Diego, CA 92102.

U.S. Address of King City, Ont., Canada, Province: Mother of Consolation Monastery, 3103 Arlington Ave., Bronx, NY 10463.

U.S. Regioon of Castile, Spain, Province (1963), Vicar, 3648 61st St., Port Arthur, TX 77642.

Barnabites (Clerics Regular of St. Paul), C.R.S.P.: Founded 1530, in Milan, Italy, by St. Anthony M. Zaccaria; approved 1533; in U.S., 1952. Historical motherhouse, Church of St. Barnabas (Milan). Generalate, Rome, Italy; North American province, 1023 Swann Rd., Youngstown, NY 14174. Parochial, educational, mission work.

Basil the Great, Order of St. (Basilian Order of St. Josaphat), O.S.B.M.: General motherhouse, Rome, Italy; U.S. province, 31-12 30th St., Long

Island City, NY 11106. Parochial work among Byzantine Ukrainian Rite Catholics.

Basilian Fathers (Congregation of the Priests of St. Basil), C.S.B.: Founded 1822, at Annonay, France. General motherhouse, Toronto, Ont., Canada. U.S. addresses: 445 King's Hwy., Rochester, NY 14617 (East); 4500 Memorial Dr., Houston, TX 77007 (West). Educational, parochial work.

Basilian Salvatorian Fathers, B.S.O.: Founded 1684, at Saida, Lebanon, by Eftimios Saifi; in U.S., 1953. General motherhouse, Saida, Lebanon; American headquarters, 30 East St., Methuen, MA 01844. Educational, parochial work among Eastern Rite peoples.

Benedictine Monks (Order of St. Benedict), O.S.B.: Founded 529, in Italy, by St. Benedict of Nursia; in U.S., 1846.

• American Cassinese Congregation (1855). Pres., Rt. Rev. Melvin J. Valvano, O.S.B., Newark Abbey, 528 Dr. Martin Luther King Blvd., Newark, NJ 07102. Abbeys and Priories belonging to the congregation: St. Vincent Archabbey, 300 Fraser Purchase Rd., Latrobe, PA 15650; St. John's Abbey, P.O. Box 2015, Collegeville, MN 56321; St. Benedict's Abbey, Atchison, KS 66002; St. Mary's Abbey, Delbarton, Morristown, NJ 07960; Newark Abbey, 528 Dr. Martin Luther King, Jr., Blvd., Newark, NJ 07102; Belmont Abbey, 100 Belmont - Mt. Holly Rd., Belmont, NC 28012; St. Bernard Abbey, Cullman, AL 35055; St. Procopius Abbey, 5601 College Rd., Lisle, IL 60532; St. Gregory's Abbey, Shawnee, OK 74801; St. Leo Abbey, St. Leo, FL 33574; Assumption Abbey, P.O. Box A, Richardton, ND 58652; St. Bede Abbey, Peru, IL 61354; St. Martin's Abbey, 5300 Pacific Ave. S.E., Lacey, WA 98503; Holy Cross Abbey, P.O. Box 1510, Canon City, CO 81215; St. Anselm's Abbey, 100 St. Anselm Dr., Manchester, NH 03102; St. Andrew Abbey, 10510 Buckeye Rd., Cleveland, OH 44104; Holy Trinity Priory, P.O. Box 990, Butler, PA 16003; St. Maur Priory, 4615 N. Michigan Rd., Indianapolis, IN 46208; Benedictine Priory, 6502 Seawright Dr., Savannah, GA 31406; Woodside Priory, 302 Portola Rd., Portola Valley, CA 94028; Mary Mother of the Church Abbey, 12617 River Rd., Richmond, VA 23233; Abadia de San Antonio Abad, P.O. Box 729, Humacao, PR 00661.

• Swiss-American Congregation (1870). Abbeys and priory belonging to the congregation: St. Meinrad Archabbey, St. Meinrad, IN 47577; Conception Abbey, Conception, MO 64433; Mt. Michael Abbey, 22520 Mt. Michael Rd., Elkhorn, NE 68022; Subiaco Abbey, Subiaco, AR 72865; St. Joseph's Abbey, St. Benedict, LA 70457; Mt. Angel Abbey, St. Benedict, OR 97373; Marmion Abbey, Butterfield Rd., Aurora, IL 60504; St. Benedict's Abbey, Benet Lake, WI 53102; Glastonbury Abbey, 16 Hull St., Hingham, MA 02043; Blue Cloud Abbey, Marvin, SD 57251; Corpus Christi Abbey, HCR2, Box 6300, Sandia, TX 78383; Prince of Peace Abbey, 650 Benet Hill Rd., Oceanside, CA 92054; St. Benedict Abbey, 252 Still River Rd., PO Box 67, Still River (Harvard), MA 01467.

• Congregation of St. Ottilien for Foreign Missions: St. Paul's Abbey, Newton, NJ 07860; Christ the King Priory, Schuyler, NE 68661.

• Congregation of the Annunciation, St. Andrew Abbey, Valyermo, CA 93563.

• English Benedictine Congregation: St. Anselm's Abbey, 4501 S. Dakota Ave. N.E., Washington, DC 20017; Abbey of St. Gregory, Cory's Lane, Portsmouth, RI 02871; Abbey of St. Mary and St. Louis, 500 S. Mason Rd., St. Louis, MO 63141.

• Houses not in Congregations: Mount Saviour Monastery, Pine City, NY 14871; Conventual Priory of St. Gabriel the Archangel, Weston, VT 05161.

Benedictines, Camaldolese Congregation, O.S.B. Cam.: Founded 1012, at Camaldoli, near Arezzo, Italy, by St. Romuald; in U.S. 1958. General motherhouse, Arezzo, Italy; U.S. foundation, New Camaldoli Hermitage, Big Sur, CA 93920.

Benedictines, Olivetan, O.S.B.: General motherhouse, Siena, Italy. U.S. monasteries, Our Lady of Guadalupe Abbey, Pecos, NM 87552; Holy Trinity Monastery, P.O. Box 298, St. David, AZ 85630; Monastery of the Risen Christ, P.O. Box 3931, San Luis Obispo, CA 93403; Benedictine Monastery of Hawaii, P.O. Box 490, Waialua, Hawaii 96791.

Benedictines, Subiaco Congregation, O.S.B.: Independent priory, 1983. Monastery of Christ in the Desert, Abiquiu, NM 87510; St, Mary's Monastery, P.O. Box 345, Petersham, MA 01366.

Benedictines, Sylvestrine, O.S.B.: Founded 1231, in Italy by Sylvester Gozzolini. General motherhouse, Rome, Italy; U.S. foundations; 17320 Rosemont Rd., Detroit, MI 48219; 2711 E. Drahner Rd., Oxford, MI 48051; 1697 State Highway 3, Clifton, NJ 07012.

Blessed Sacrament, Congregation of the, S.S.S.: Founded 1856, at Paris, France, by St. Pierre Julien Eymard; in U.S., 1900. General motherhouse, Rome, Italy; U.S. province, 5384 Wilson Mills Rd., Cleveland, OH 44143. Eucharistic apostolate.

Brigittine Monks (Order of the Most Holy Savior), O.Ss.S.: Monastery of Our Lady of Consolation, 23300 Walker Lane, Amity, OR 97101.

Camaldolese Hermits of the Congregation of Monte Corona, Er. Cam.: Founded 1520, from Camaldoli, Italy, by Bl. Paul Giustiniani. General motherhouse, Frascati (Rome), Italy; U.S. foundation, Holy Family Hermitage, Rt. 2, Box 36, Bloomington, OH 43910.

Camillian Fathers and Brothers (Order of St. Camillus; Order of Servants of the Sick), O.S.Cam.: Founded 1582, at Rome, by St. Camillus de Lellis; in U.S., 1923. General motherhouse, Rome, Italy; North American province, 10101 W. Wisconsin Ave., Wauwatosa, WI 53226.

Carmelites (Order of Our Lady of Mt. Carmel), O. Carm.: General motherhouse, Rome, Italy. Educational, charitable work.

Most Pure Heart of Mary Province (1864), 1317 Frontage Rd., Darien, IL 60559.

St. Elias Province (1931), P.O. Box 3079, Middletown, NY 10940.

Mt. Carmel Hermitage, Pineland, R.D. 3, Box 36, New Florence, PA 15944.

Carmelites, Order of Discalced, O.C.D.: Established 1562, a Reform Order of Our Lady of Mt. Carmel; in U.S., 1924. Generalate, Rome, Italy. Spiritual direction, retreat, parochial work.

California-Arizona Province, Central Office (1983), 926 E. Highland Ave., P.O. Box 2178, Redlands, CA 92373.

St. Therese of Oklahoma Province (1935), 515 Marylake Dr., Little Rock AR 72206.

Immaculate Heart of Mary Province (1947), 1233 S. 45th St., Milwaukee, WI 53214.

Polish Province of the Holy Spirit (1949), 1628 Ridge Rd., Munster, IN 46321.

Carmelites of Mary Immaculate, C.M.I.: Founded 1831, in India, by Bl. Kuriakose Elias Chavara and two other Syro-Malabar priests; canonically established, 1855. Generalate, Kerala, India; North American headquarters, Holy Family Church, 21 Nassau Ave., Brooklyn, NY 11222.

Carthusians, Order of, O. Cart.: Founded 1084, in France, by St. Bruno; in U.S., 1951. General motherhouse, St. Pierre de Chartreuse, France; U.S. charterhouse of the Transfiguration, R.R. 2, Box 2411, Arlington, VT 05250. Cloistered contemplatives; semi-eremitic.

Charity, Brothers of, F.C.: Founded 1807, in Belgium, by Canon Peter J. Triest. General motherhouse, Rome, Italy: American District (1963), 7720 Doe Lane, Laverock, PA 19038.

Charity, Servants of (Guanellians), S.C.: Founded 1908, in Italy, by Bl. Luigi Guanella. General motherhouse, Rome, Italy; U.S. headquarters, St. Louis School, 16195 Old U.S. 12, Chelsea, MI 48118.

Christ, Society of, S.Ch.: Founded 1932, General Motherhouse, Poznan, Poland; U.S.-Canadian Province, 3000 Eighteen Mile Rd., Sterling Heights, MI 48311.

Christian Brothers, Congregation of, C.F.C. (formerly Christian Brothers of Ireland): Founded 1802 at Waterford, Ireland, by Bl. Edmund Ignatius Rice; in U.S., 1906. General motherhouse, Rome, Italy. Educational work.

American Province, Eastern U.S. (1916), 21 Pryer Terr., New Rochelle, NY 10804.

Brother Rice Province, Western U.S. (1966), 958 Western Ave., Joliet, IL 60435.

Christian Instruction, Brothers of (La Mennais Brothers), F.I.C.: Founded 1817, at Ploermel, France, by Abbe Jean Marie de la Mennais and Abbe Gabriel Deshayes. General motherhouse, Rome, Italy; American province, Notre Dame Institute, P.O. Box 159, Alfred, ME 04002.

Christian Schools, Brothers of the (Christian Brothers), F.S.C.: Founded 1680, at Reims, France, by St. Jean Baptiste de la Salle. General motherhouse, Rome, Italy; U.S. Conference, 4351 Garden City Dr., Suite 200, Landover, MD 20785. Educational, charitable work.

Baltimore Province (1845), Box 29, Adamstown, MD 21710.

Brothers of the Christian Schools (Midwest Province) (1995), 200 S. Frontage Rd., Suite 300, Burr Ridge, IL 60521.

New York Province (1848), 800 Newman Springs Rd., Lincroft, NJ 07738.

Long Island-New England Province (1957), Christian Brothers Center, 635 Ocean Rd., Narragansett, RI 02882.

San Francisco Province (1868), P.O. Box 3720, Napa, CA 94558.

New Orleans-Santa Fe Province (1921), De La Salle Christian Brothers, 1522 Carmel Dr., Lafayette, LA 70501.

Cistercians, Order of, O.Cist.: Founded 1098, by St. Robert. Headquarters, Rome, Italy.

Our Lady of Spring Bank Abbey, Rt. 3, Box 211, Sparta, WI 54656.

Our Lady of Dallas Monastery, 1 Cistercian Rd., Irving, TX 75039.

Cistercian Monastery, 564 Walton Ave., Mt. Laurel, NJ 08054.

Cistercian Conventual Priory, St. Mary's Priory, R.D. 1, Box 206, New Ringgold, PA 17960.

Cistercians of the Strict Observance, Order of (Trappists), O.C.S.O.: Founded 1098, in France, by St. Robert; in U.S., 1848. Generalate, Rome, Italy.

Our Lady of Gethsemani Abbey (1848), Trappist, KY 40051.

Our Lady of New Melleray Abbey (1849), 6500 Melleray Circle, Peosta, IA 52068.

St. Joseph's Abbey (1825), Spencer, MA 01562.

Holy Spirit Monastery (1944), 2625 Hwy. 212 S.W., Conyers, GA 30208.

Our Lady of Guadalupe Abbey (1947), Lafayette, OR 97127.

Our Lady of the Holy Trinity Abbey (1947), Huntsville, Utah 84317.

Abbey of the Genesee (1951), P.O. Box 900, Piffard, NY 14533.

Mepkin Abbey (1949), 1098 Mepkin Abbey Rd., Moncks Corner, SC 29461.

Our Lady of the Holy Cross Abbey (1950), Rt. 2, Box 3870, Berryville, VA 22611.

Assumption Abbey (1950), Rt. 5, Box 1056, Ava, MO 65608.

Abbey of New Clairvaux (1955), Vina, CA 96092.

St. Benedict's Monastery (1956), 1012 Monastery Rd., Snowmass, CO 81654.

Claretians (Missionary Sons of the Immaculate Heart of Mary), C.M.F.: Founded 1849, at Vich, Spain, by St. Anthony Mary Claret. General headquarters, Rome, Italy. Missionary, parochial, educational, retreat work.

Western Province, 1119 Westchester Pl., Los Angeles, CA 90019.

Eastern Province, 400 N. Euclid Ave. Oak Park, IL 60302.

Clerics Regular Minor (Adorno Fathers) C.R.M.: Founded 1588, at Naples, Italy, by Ven. Augustine Adorno and St. Francis Caracciolo. General motherhouse, Rome, Italy; U.S. address, 575 Darlington Ave., Ramsey, NJ 07446.

Columban, Society of St. (St. Columban Foreign Mission Society), S.S.C.: Founded 1918. General headquarters, Dublin, Ireland. U.S. headquarters, P.O. Box 10, St. Columbans, NE 68056. Foreign mission work.

Comboni Missionaries of the Heart of Jesus (Verona Fathers), M.C.C.J.: Founded 1867, in Italy by Bl. Daniel Comboni; in U.S., 1939. General motherhouse, Rome, Italy; North American headquarters, Comboni Mission Center, 8108 Beechmont Ave., Cincinnati, OH 45255. Mission work in Africa and the Americas.

Consolata Missionaries, I.M.C.: Founded 1901, at Turin, Italy, by Bl. Joseph Allamano. General motherhouse, Rome, Italy; U.S. headquarters, P.O. Box 5550, 2301 Rt. 27, Somerset, NJ 08875.

Crosier Fathers (Canons Regular of the Order of the Holy Cross), O.S.C.: Founded 1210, in Belgium by Bl. Theodore De Celles. Generalate, Rome, Italy; U.S. Province of St. Odilia, 3510 Vivian Ave., Shoreview, MN 55126. Mission, retreat, educational work.

Cross, Brothers of the Congregation of Holy, C.S.C.: Founded 1837, in France, by Rev. Basil Moreau; U.S. province, 1841. Generalate, Rome, Italy. Educational, social work; missions.

Midwest Province (1841), Box 460, Notre Dame, IN 46556.

Southwest Province (1956), St. Edward's University, Austin, TX 78704.

Eastern Province (1956), 85 Overlook Circle, New Rochelle, NY 10804.

Cross, Priests of the Congregation of Holy, C.S.C.: Founded 1837, in France; in U.S., 1841. Generalate, Rome, Italy. Educational and pastoral work; home missions and retreats; foreign missions; social services and apostolate of the press.

Indiana Province (1841), 1304 E. Jefferson Blvd., South Bend, IN 46617.

Eastern Province (1952), 835 Clinton Ave., Bridgeport, CT 06604.

Southern Province (1968), 2111 Brackenridge St., Austin, TX 78704.

Divine Word, Society of the, S.V.D.: Founded 1875, in Holland, by Bl. Arnold Janssen. North American Province founded 1897 with headquarters in Techny, IL General motherhouse, Rome, Italy.

Province of Bl. Joseph Freinademetz (Chicago Province) (1985, from merger of Eastern and Northern provinces), 1985 Waukegan Rd., Techny, IL 60082.

St. Augustine (Southern Province) (1940), 201 Ruella Ave., Bay St. Louis, MS 39520.

St. Therese of the Child Jesus (Western Province) (1964), 2737 Pleasant St., Riverside, CA 92507.

Dominicans (Order of Friars Preachers), O.P.: Founded early 13th century by St. Dominic de Guzman. General headquarters, Santa Sabina, Rome, Italy. Preaching, teaching, missions, research, parishes.

St. Joseph Eastern Province (1805), 869 Lexington Ave., New York, NY 10021.

Most Holy Name of Jesus (Western) Province (1912), 5877 Birch Ct., Oakland, CA 94618.

St. Albert the Great (Central) Province (1939), 1909 S. Ashland Ave., Chicago, IL 60608.

Southern Dominican Province (1979), 1421 N. Causeway Blvd., Suite 200, Metairie, LA 70001.

Spanish Province, U.S. foundation (1926), P.O. Box 279, San Diego, TX 78384.

Edmund, Society of St., S.S.E.: Founded 1843, in France, by Fr. Jean Baptiste Muard. General motherhouse, Edmundite Generalate, 270 Winooski Park, Colchester, VT 05439. Educational, missionary work.

Eudists (Congregation of Jesus and Mary), C.J.M.: Founded 1643, in France, by St. John Eudes. General motherhouse, Rome, Italy; North American province, 6125 Premiere Ave., Charlesbourg, Quebec G1H 2V9, Canada; U.S. community, 36 Flohr Ave., W. Seneca, N.Y. 14224. Parochial, educational, pastoral, missionary work.

Francis, Brothers of Poor of St., C.F.P.: Founded

1857. Motherhouse, Aachen, Germany; U.S. province, P.O. Box 187, Burlington, IA 52601. Educational work, especially with poor and neglected youth.

Francis, Third Order Regular of St., T.O.R.: Founded 1221, in Italy; in U.S., 1910. General motherhouse, Rome, Italy. Educational, parochial, missionary work.

Most Sacred Heart of Jesus Province (1910), 215 57th St., Pittsburgh, PA 15201.

Immaculate Conception Province (1925), 2400 Dike Rd., Winter Park, FL 32792.

Commissariat of the Spanish Province (1924), 301 Jefferson Ave., Waco, TX 76702.

Francis de Sales, Oblates of St., O.S.F.S.: Founded 1871, by Fr. Louis Brisson. General motherhouse, Rome, Italy. Educational, missionary, parochial work.

Wilmington-Philadelphia Province (1906), 2200 Kentmere Parkway, Box 1452, Wilmington, DE 19899.

Toledo-Detroit Province (1966), 2056 Parkwood Ave., Toledo, Ohio 43620.

Francis Xavier, Brothers of St. (Xaverian Brothers), C.F.X.: Founded 1839, in Belgium, by Theodore J. Ryken. Generalate, Twickenham, Middlesex, England. Educational work.

Sacred Heart Province, 10318-B Baltimore National Pike, Ellicott City, MD 21043.

St. Joseph Province, 704 Brush Hill Rd., Milton, MA 02186.

Franciscan Brothers of Brooklyn, O.S.F.: Founded in Ireland; established at Brooklyn, 1858. Generalate, 135 Remsen St., Brooklyn, NY 11201. Educational work.

Franciscan Brothers of Christ the King, O.S.F.: Founded 1961. General motherhouse, 3737 N. Marybelle Ave., Peoria, IL 61615.

Franciscan Brothers of the Holy Cross, F.F.S.C.: Founded 1862, in Germany. Generalate, Hausen, Linz Rhein, Germany; U.S. region, 2500 St. James Rd., Springfield, IL 62707. Educational work.

Franciscan Brothers of the Third Order Regular, O.S.F.: Generalate, Mountbellew, Ireland; U.S. region, 2117 Spyglass Trail W., Oxnard, CA 93030. (Mailing address: 4522 Gainsborough Ave., Los Angeles, CA 90029.)

Franciscan Friars of the Immaculate, F.F.I: Founded 1990, Italy. General motherhouse, Benevento, Italy. U.S. addresses, 600 Pleasant St., New Bedford, MA. 02740; 22 School Hill Rd., Baltic, CT 06330.

Franciscan Friars of the Renewal, C.F.R.: Community established under jurisdiction of the archbishop of New York. Central House, St. Crispin Friary, 420 E. 156th St., Bronx, NY 10455.

Franciscan Missionary Brothers of the Sacred Heart of Jesus, O.S.F.: Founded 1927, in the St. Louis archdiocese. Motherhouse, St. Joseph Rd., Eureka, MO 63025. Care of aged, infirm, homeless men and boys.

Franciscans (Order of Friars Minor), O.F.M.: A family of the First Order of St. Francis (of Assisi) founded in 1209 and established as a separate jurisdiction in 1517; in U.S., 1844. General headquarters, Rome, Italy. English-speaking conference: 3140 Meramec St., St. Louis, MO 63118. Preaching, missionary, educational, parochial, charitable work.

St. John the Baptist Province (1844), 1615 Vine St., Cincinnati, Ohio 45210.

Immaculate Conception Province (1855), 147 Thompson St., New York, NY 10012.

Sacred Heart Province (1858), 3140 Meramec St., St. Louis, MO 63118.

Assumption of the Blessed Virgin Mary Province (1887), Pulaski, WI 54162.

Most Holy Name of Jesus Province (1901), 126 W. 32nd St., New York, NY 10001.

St. Barbara Province (1915), 1500 34th Ave., Oakland, CA 94601.

Our Lady of Guadalupe Province (1985), 1350 Lakeview Rd. S.W., Albuquerque, NM 87105.

Holy Cross Custody (1912), 14246 Main St., P.O. Box 608, Lemont, IL 60439.

Most Holy Savior Vice-Province, 232 S. Home Ave., Pittsburgh, PA 15202.

Mt. Alverna Friary, 517 S. Belle Vista Ave., Youngstown, Ohio 44509.

Holy Family Croatian Custody (1926), 4848 S. Ellis Ave., Chicago, IL 60615.

St. Casimir Lithuanian Vice-Province, P.O. Box 980, Kennebunkport, ME 04046.

Holy Gospel Province (Mexico), U.S. foundation, 2400 Marr St., El Paso, TX 79903.

Commissariat of the Holy Land, Mt. St. Sepulchre, 1400 Quincy St. N.E., Washington, DC 20017.

St. Mary of the Angels Custody, Byzantine Slavonic Rite, P.O. Box 270, Sybertsville, PA 18251.

Academy of American Franciscan History, 1712 Euclid Ave., Berkeley, CA 94709.

Franciscans (Order of Friars Minor Capuchin), O.F.M. Cap.: A family of the First Order of St. Francis (of Assisi) founded in 1209 and established as a separate jurisdiction in 1528. General motherhouse, Rome, Italy. Missionary, parochial work, chaplaincies.

St. Joseph Province (1857), 1740 Mt. Elliott Ave., Detroit, MI 48207.

St. Augustine Province (1873), 220 37th St., Pittsburgh, PA 15201.

St. Mary Province (1952), 30 Gedney Park Dr., White Plains, NY 10605.

Province of the Stigmata (1918), P.O. Box 809, Union City, NJ 07087.

Western American Capuchin Province, Our Lady of the Angels, 1345 Cortez Ave., Burlingame, CA 94010.

Sts. Adalbert and Stanislaus Province (1948), 2 Manor Dr., Oak Ridge, NJ 07438.

Province of Mid-America (1977), 3553 Wyandot St., Denver, CO 80211.

Vice-Province of Texas, 2601 Singleton Blvd., Dallas, TX 75212.

St. John the Baptist Vice-Province, 216 Arzuaga St., P.O. Box 21350, Rio Piedras, Puerto Rico 00928.

Franciscans (Order of Friars Minor Conventual), O.F.M. Conv.: A family of the First Order of St. Francis (of Assisi) founded in 1209 and established as a separate jurisdiction in 1517; first U.S. foundation, 1852. General curia, Rome, Italy. Missionary, educational, parochial work.

Immaculate Conception Province (1852), Immaculate Conception Friary, Rensselaer, NY 12144.

St. Anthony of Padua Province (1906), 12300 Folly Quarter Rd., Ellicott City, MD 21043.

St. Bonaventure Province (1939), 6107 Kenmore Ave., Chicago, IL 60660.

Our Lady of Consolation Province (1926), 101 Anthony Dr., Mt. St. Francis, IN 47146.

St. Joseph of Cupertino Province (1981), P.O. Box 820, Arroyo Grande, CA 93421.

Glenmary Missioners (The Home Missioners of America): Founded 1939, in U.S. General headquarters, P.O. Box 465618, Cincinnati, Ohio 45246. Home mission work.

Good Shepherd, Little Brothers of the, B.G.S.: Founded 1951, by Bro. Mathias Barrett. Foundation House, P.O. Box 389, Albuquerque, NM 87102. General headquarters, Hamilton, Ont., Canada. Operate shelters and refuges for aged and homeless; homes for handicapped men and boys, alcoholic rehabilitation center.

Holy Eucharist, Brothers of the, F.S.E.: Founded in U.S., 1957. Generalate, P.O. Box 25, Plaucheville, LA 71362. Teaching, social, clerical, nursing work.

Holy Family, Congregation of the Missionaries of the, M.S.F.: Founded 1895, in Holland, by Rev. John P. Berthier. General motherhouse, Rome, Italy; U.S. provincialate, 10415 Midland Blvd., St. Louis, MO 63114. Belated vocations for the missions.

Holy Family, Sons of the, S.F.: Founded 1864, at Barcelona, Spain, by Bl. Jose Mañanet y Vives; in U.S., 1920. General motherhouse, Barcelona, Spain; U.S. address, 401 Randolph Rd., P.O. Box 4138, Silver Spring, MD 20904.

Holy Ghost Fathers, C.S.Sp.: Founded 1703, in Paris, by Claude Francois Poullart des Places; in U.S., 1872. Generalate, Rome, Italy. Missions, education.

Eastern Province (1872), 6230 Brush Run Rd., Bethel Park, PA 15102. Western Province (1964), 1700 W. Alabama St., Houston, TX 77098.

Holy Ghost Fathers of Ireland (1971), U.S. delegates: 4849 37th St., Long Island City, NY 11101 (East); St. Dunstan's Church, 1133 Broadway, Mill Brae, CA 94030 (West); St. John Baptist Church, 1139 Dryades St., New Orleans, LA 70113.

Holy Spirit, Missionaries of the, M.Sp.S.: Founded 1914, at Mexico City, Mexico, by Felix Rougier. General motherhouse, Mexico City; U.S. headquarters, Our Lady of Guadalupe, 500 N. Juanita Ave., P.O. Box 1091, Oxnard, CA 93030. Missionary work.

Immaculate Heart of Mary, Brothers of the, I.H.M.: Founded 1948, at Steubenville, Ohio, by Bishop John K. Mussio. Motherhouse, 609 N. 7th St., Steubenville, Ohio 43952. Educational, charitable work.

Jesuits (Society of Jesus), S.J.: Founded 1534, in France, by St. Ignatius of Loyola; received papal approval, 1540; first U.S. province, 1833. Generalate, Rome, Italy; U.S. national office, Jesuit Conference, 1616 P Street, Suite 400, Washington, DC 20036. Missionary, educational, literary work.

Maryland Province (1833), 5704 Roland Ave., Baltimore, MD 21210.

New York Province (1943), 39 East 83rd St., New York, NY 10028.

Missouri Province (1863), 4511 W. Pine Blvd., St. Louis, MO 63108.

New Orleans Province (1907), 500 S. Jefferson Davis Pkwy., New Orleans, LA 70119.

California Province (1909), 300 College Ave.,P.O. Box 519, Los Gatos, CA 95031.

New England Province (1926), 771 Harrison Ave., Boston, MA 02118.

Chicago Province (1928), 2050 N. Clark St., Chicago, IL 60614.

Oregon Province (1932), 2222 N.W. Hoyt, Portland, OR 97210.

Detroit Province (1955), 7303 W. Seven Mile Rd., Detroit, MI 48221.

Wisconsin Province (1955), PO Box 08277, Milwaukee, WI 53208.

Province of the Antilles (1947), U.S. address, 13339 S.W. 9 Terrace, Miami, FL 33184.

John of God, Brothers of the Hospitaller Order of St., O.H.: Founded 1537, in Spain. General motherhouse, Rome, Italy; American province, 2425 S. Western Ave., Los Angeles, CA 90018. Nursing work and related fields.

Joseph, Congregation of St., C.S.J.: General motherhouse, Rome, Italy; U.S. vice province, 338 Grand Ave., San Pedro, CA 90731. Parochial, missionary, educational work.

Joseph, Oblates of St., O.S.J.: Founded 1878, in Italy, by Bl. Joseph Marello; in U.S., 1929. General motherhouse, Rome, Italy. Parochial, educational work.

Eastern Province, Route 315, R.R. 4, Box 14, Pittston, PA 18640.

California Province, 544 W. Cliff Dr., Santa Cruz, CA 95060.

Josephite Fathers, C.J.: General motherhouse, Ghent, Belgium; U.S. foundation, 180 Patterson Rd., Santa Maria, CA 93455.

Josephites (St. Joseph's Society of the Sacred Heart), S.S.J.: Established 1893, in U.S. as American congregation (originally established in U.S. in 1871 by Mill Hill Josephites from England). General motherhouse, 1130 N. Calvert St., Baltimore, MD 21202. Evangelization in African American community.

LaSalette, Missionaries of Our Lady of, M.S.: Founded 1852, by Msgr. de Bruillard; in U.S., 1892. Motherhouse, Rome, Italy.

Our Lady of Seven Dolors Province (1934), 915 Maple Ave., Hartford, CT 06114.

Immaculate Heart of Mary Province (1945), 947 Park St., Attleboro, MA 02703.

Mary Queen Province (1958), 4650 S. Broadway, St. Louis, MO 63111.

Mary Queen of Peace Province (1967), P.O. Box 250, Twin Lakes, WI 53181.

Lateran, Canons Regular of the, C.R.L.: General house, Rome, Italy; U.S. address: 2317 Washington Ave., Bronx, NY 10458.

Legionaries of Christ, L.C.: Founded 1941, in Mexico, by Rev. Marcial Maciel; in U.S., 1965. General headquarters, Rome, Italy; U.S. headquarters, 393 Derby Ave., Orange, CT 06477; novitiate, 475 Oak Ave., Cheshire, CT 06410.

Little Brothers of St. Francis, L.B.S.F.: Founded 1970 in Archdiocese of Boston by Bro. James Curran. General fraternity, 785-789 Parker St., Roxbury (Boston), MA 02120. Combine contemplative life with evangelical street ministry.

Marianist Fathers and Brothers (Society of Mary; Brothers of Mary), S.M.: Founded 1817, at Bordeaux, France, by Rev. William-Joseph Chaminade; in U.S., 1849. General motherhouse, Rome, Italy. Educational work.

Cincinnati Province (1849), 4435 E. Patterson Rd., Dayton, Ohio 45430.

St. Louis Province (1908), PO Box 23130, St. Louis, MO 63156.

Pacific Province (1948), PO Box 1775, Cupertino, CA 95015.

New York Province (1961), 4301 Roland Ave., Baltimore, MD 21210.

Province of Meribah (1976), 240 Emory Rd., Mineola, NY 11501.

Mariannhill, Congregation of the Missionaries of, C.M.M.: Trappist monastery, begun in 1882 by Abbot Francis Pfanner in Natal, South Africa, became an independent modern congregation in 1909; in U.S., 1920. Generalate,Rome, Italy; U.S.-Canadian province (1938), Our Lady of Grace Monastery, 23715 Ann Arbor Trail, Dearborn Hts., MI 48127. Foreign mission work.

Marians of the Immaculate Conception, Congregation of, M.I.C.: Founded 1673; U.S. foundation, 1913. General motherhouse, Rome, Italy. Educational, parochial, mission, publication work.

St. Casimir Province (1913), 6336 S. Kilbourn Ave., Chicago, IL 60629.

St. Stanislaus Kostka Province (1948), Eden Hill, Stockbridge, MA 01262.

Marist Brothers, F.M.S.: Founded 1817, in France, by Bl. Marcellin Champagnat. General motherhouse, Rome, Italy. Educational, social, catechetical work.

Esopus Province, 1241 Kennedy Blvd., Bayonne, NJ 07002 (office).

Poughkeepsie Province, 26 First Ave., Pelham, NY 10803.

Marist Fathers (Society of Mary), S.M.: Founded 1816, at Lyons, France, by Jean Claude Colin; in U.S., 1863. General motherhouse, Rome, Italy. Educational, foreign mission, pastoral work.

Washington Province (1924), 815 Varnum St., N.E., Washington, DC 20017.

Boston Province (1924), 27 Isabella St., Boston, MA 02116.

San Francisco Western Province (1962), 625 Pine St., San Francisco, CA 94108.

Maronite Monks, Congregation of (Cloistered Penitents of St. Francis), O. Mar.: Most Holy Trinity Monastery, 67 Dugway Rd., Petersham, MA 01366; Holy Nativity Monastery, Bethlehem, S.D. 57708.

Maronite Lebanese Missionaries, Congregation of, C.M.L.M.: Founded in Lebanon 1865; established in the U.S., 1991. U.S. foundation, St. George Maronite Church, 6070 Babcock Rd., San Antonio, TX 78240.

Mary Immaculate, Oblates of, O.M.I.: Founded 1816, in France, by Bl. Charles Joseph Eugene de Mazenod; in U.S., 1849. General house, Rome, Italy. U.S. consulate, 290 Lenox Ave., Oakland, CA 94610. Parochial, foreign mission, educational work; ministry to marginal.

Southern U.S. Province (1904), 7711 Madonna Dr., San Antonio, TX 78216.

Our Lady of Hope, Eastern Province (1883), 391 Michigan Ave. N.E., Washington, DC 20017.

St. John the Baptist, Northern Province (1921), 61 Burns Hill Rd., Hudson, NH 03051.

Central Province (1924), 267 E. 8th St., St. Paul, MN 55101.

Western Province (1953), 290 Lenox Ave.., Oakland, CA 94610.

Maryknoll (Catholic Foreign Mission Society of America), M.M.: Founded 1911, in U.S., by Frs. Thomas F. Price and James A. Walsh. General Center, Maryknoll, NY 10545.

Mekhitarist Order of Venice, O.M.Ven.: Founded 1701; transferred to Venice, 1717. U.S. address: 110 E. 12th, New York, N.Y. 10003. Promote ecclesial community among Armenians.

Mekhitarist Order of Vienna, C.M.Vd.: Established 1773. General headquarters, Vienna, Austria. U.S. address, 4900 Maryland Ave., La Crescenta, CA 91214. Work among Armenians in U.S.

Mercedarians (Order of Our Lady of Mercy), O. de M.: Founded 1218, in Spain, by St. Peter Nolasco. General motherhouse, Rome, Italy; U.S. headquarters, 3205 Fulton Rd., Cleveland, OH 44109.

Mercy, Brothers of, F.M.M.: Founded 1856, in Germany. General motherhouse, Montabaur, Germany. American headquarters, 4520 Ransom Rd., Clarence, NY 14031. Hospital work.

Mercy, Brothers of Our Lady, Mother of, C.F.M.M.: Founded 1844, in The Netherlands by Abp. Jan Zwijsen. Generalate, Tilburg, The Netherlands; U.S. region, 2336 S. C St., Oxnard, CA 93033.

Mercy, Congregation of Priests of (Fathers of Mercy), C.P.M.: Founded 1808, in France, by Rev. Jean Baptiste Rauzan; in U.S., 1839. General mission house, South Union, KY 42283. Mission work.

Mill Hill Missionaries (St. Joseph's Society for Foreign Missions), M.H.M.: Founded 1866, in England, by Cardinal Vaughan; in U.S., 1951. International headquarters, London, England; American headquarters, 222 W. Hartsdale Ave., Hartsdakem N.Y. 10530.

Minim Fathers, O.M.: General motherhouse, Rome, Italy. North American delegation (1970), 3431 Portola Ave., Los Angeles, CA 90032.

Missionaries of St. Charles, Congregation of the (Scalabrinians), C.S.: Founded 1887, at Piacenza, Italy, by Bl. John Baptist Scalabrini. General motherhouse, Rome, Italy.

St. Charles Borromeo Province (1888), 27 Carmine St., New York, NY 10014.

St. John Baptist Province (1903), 546 N. East Ave., Oak Park, IL 60302.

Missionaries of the Blessed Sacrament, M.S.S.: Regional headquarters, PO Box 4337, Corpus Christi, TX 78469. Promotion of Perpetual Eucharistic adoration.

Missionaries of the Holy Apostles, M.Ss.A.: Founded 1962, Washington, D.C., by Very Rev. Eusebe M. Menard. North American headquarters, 33 Prospect Hill Rd., Cromwell, CT 06416.

Missionary Fraternity of Mary, F.M.M.: General headquarters, Guatemala; U.S. foundation 340 Pine St., Seaford, DE 19973.

Missionary Servants of Christ, M.S.C.: Founded 1979 in U.S. by Bro. Edwin Baker. Headquarters, St.

Anthony in the Hills, 6730 Limestone Rd., Avendale, PA 19311.

Missionary Society of St. Paul of Nigeria: Generalate Abuja, Nigeria; U.S. Region, 12686 Crosby-Lynchburg Rd., P.O. Box 3200, Barrette Station, TX 77532.

Missionhurst — CICM (Congregation of the Immaculate Heart of Mary): Founded 1862, at Scheut, Brussels, Belgium, by Very Rev. Theophile Verbist. General motherhouse, Rome, Italy; U.S. province, 4651 N. 25th St., Arlington, VA 22207. Home and foreign mission work.

Montfort Missionaries (Missionaries of the Company of Mary), S.M.M.: Founded 1715, by St. Louis Marie Grignon de Montfort; in U.S., 1948. General motherhouse, Rome, Italy; U.S. province, 101-18 104th St., Ozone Park, NY 11416. Mission work.

Mother Co-Redemptrix, Congregation of, C.M.C.: Founded 1953 at Lein-Thuy, Vietnam (North), by Fr. Dominic Mary Tran Dinh Thu; in U.S., 1975. General house, Hochiminhville, Vietnam; U.S. provincial house, 1900 Grand Ave., Carthage, MO 64836. Work among Vietnamese Catholics in U.S.

Oblates of the Virgin Mary, O.M.V.: Founded 1815, in Italy; in U.S., 1976; Generalate, Rome, Italy; U.S. provincialate: Two Ipswich St., Boston, MA 02215.

Oratorians (Congregation of the Oratory of St. Philip Neri), C.O.: Founded 1575, at Rome, by St. Philip Neri. A confederation of autonomous houses. U.S. addresses: P.O. Box 11586, Rock Hill, SC 29731; P.O. Box 1688, Monterey, CA 93940; 4450 Bayard St., Pittsburgh, PA 15213; P.O. Drawer II, Pharr, TX 78577; 109 Willoughby St., Brooklyn, NY 11201.

Pallottines (Society of the Catholic Apostolate), S.A.C.: Founded 1835, at Rome, by St. Vincent Pallotti. Generalate, Rome, Italy. Charitable, educational, parochial, mission work.

Immaculate Conception Province (1953), P.O. Box 979, South Orange, NJ 07079.

Mother of God Province (1946), 5424 W. Blue Mound Rd., Milwaukee, WI 53208.

Irish Province (1909), U.S. address: 3352 4th St., P.O. Box 249, Wyandotte, MI 48192.

Queen of Apostles Province (1909), 448 E. 116th St., New York, NY 10029.

Christ the King Province, 3452 Niagara Falls, Blvd., N. Tonawanda, NY 14120.

Paraclete, Servants of the, s.P.: Founded 1947, Santa Fe, N.M., archdiocese. Generalate and U.S. motherhouse, Jemez Springs, NM 87025. Devoted to care of priests.

Paris Foreign Missions Society, M.E.P.: Founded 1662, at Paris, France. Headquarters, Paris, France; U.S. establishment, 930 Ashbury St., San Francisco, CA 94117. Mission work and training of native clergy.

Passionists (Congregation of the Passion), C.P.: Founded 1720, in Italy, by St. Paul of the Cross. General motherhouse, Rome, Italy.

St. Paul of the Cross Province (Eastern Province) (1852), 80 David St., South River, NJ 08882.

Holy Cross Province (Western Province), 5700 N. Harlem Ave., Chicago, IL 60631.

Patrician Brothers (Brothers of St. Patrick), F.S.P.: Founded 1808, in Ireland, by Bishop Daniel Delaney; U.S. novitiate, 7820 Bolsa Ave., Midway City, CA 92655. Educational work.

Patrick's Missionary Society, St., S.P.S.: Founded 1932, at Wicklow, Ireland, by Msgr. Patrick Whitney; in U.S., 1953. International headquarters, Kiltegan Co., Wicklow, Ireland. U.S. foundations: 70 Edgewater Rd., Cliffside Park, NJ 07010; 19536 Eric Dr., Saratoga, CA 95070; 1347 W. Granville Ave., Chicago, IL 60660.

Pauline Fathers (Order of St. Paul the First Hermit), O.S.P.P.E.: Founded 1215; established in U.S., 1955. General motherhouse, Czestochowa, Jasna Gora, Poland; U.S. province, P.O. Box 2049, Doylestown, PA 18901.

Pauline Fathers and Brothers (Society of St. Paul for the Apostolate of Communications), S.S.P.: Founded 1914, by Very Rev. James Alberione; in U.S., 1932. Motherhouse, Rome, Italy; New York province (1932), 6746 Lake Shore Rd., Derby, NY 14047; Los Angeles province, 112 S. Herbert Ave., Los Angeles, CA 90063. Social communications work.

Paulists (Missionary Society of St. Paul the Apostle), C.S.P.: Founded 1858, in New York, by Fr. Isaac Thomas Hecker. Motherhouse: 86-11 Midland Pkwy, Jamaica Estates, N.Y. 11432.. Missionary, ecumenical, pastoral work.

Piarists (Order of the Pious Schools), Sch.P.: Founded 1617, at Rome, Italy, by St. Joseph Calasanctius. General motherhouse, Rome, Italy. U.S. province, 363 Valley Forge Rd., Devon, PA 19333. New York-Puerto Rico vice-province (Calasanzian Fathers), P.O. Box 118, Playa Sta., Ponce, PR 00734. California vicariate, 3951 Rogers St., Los Angeles, CA 90063. Educational work.

Pius X, Brothers of St.: Founded 1952, at La Crosse, Wis., by Bishop John P. Treacy. Motherhouse, P.O. Box 217, De Soto, WI 54624. Education.

Pontifical Institute for Foreign Missions, P.I.M.E.: Founded 1850, in Italy, at request of Pope Pius IX. General motherhouse, Rome, Italy; U.S. province, 17330 Quincy Ave., Detroit, MI 48221. Foreign mission work.

Precious Blood, Society of, C.Pp.S.: Founded 1815, in Italy, by St. Gaspar del Bufalo. General motherhouse, Rome, Italy.

Cincinnati Province, 431 E. Second St., Dayton, OH 45402.

Kansas City Province, P.O. Box 339, Liberty, MO 64068.

Pacific Province, 2337 134th Ave. W., San Leandro, CA 94577.

Atlantic Province, 540 St. Clair Ave. West, Toronto M6C 14A, Canada.

Premonstratensians (Order of the Canons Regular of Premontre; Norbertines), O. Praem.: Founded 1120, at Premontre, France, by St. Norbert; in U.S., 1893. Generalate, Rome, Italy. Educational, parish work.

St. Norbert Abbey, 1016 N. Broadway, DePere, WI 54115.

Daylesford Abbey, 220 S. Valley Rd., Paoli, PA 19301.

St. Michael's Abbey, 19292 El Toro Rd., Silverado, CA 92676.

Priestly Fraternity of St. Peter, F.S.S.P.: Founded and approved Oct. 18, 1988; first foundation in U.S., 1991. U.S. headquarters, Our Lady of Guadalupe Seminary, Griffin Rd., P.O. Box 196, Elmhurst, PA 18416.

Providence, Sons of Divine, F.D.P.: Founded 1893, at Tortona, Italy, by Bl. Luigi Orione; in U.S., 1933. General motherhouse, Rome, Italy; U.S. address, 111 Orient Ave., E. Boston, MA 02128.

Redemptorists (Congregation of the Most Holy Redeemer), C.SS.R.: Founded 1732, in Italy, by St. Alphonsus Mary Liguori. Generalate, Rome, Italy. Mission work.

Baltimore Province (1850), 7509 Shore Rd., Brooklyn, NY 11209.

Redemptorist-Denver Province (1875), 2130 E. 14th Ave., Box 300399, Denver, CO 80203.

New Orleans Vice-Province, 5354 Plank Rd.., P.O. Box 53900, Baton Rouge, LA 70892.

Richmond Vice-Province (1942), 313 Hillman St., P.O. Box 1529, New Smyrna Beach, FL 32170.

Resurrectionists (Congregation of the Resurrection), C.R.: Founded 1836, in France, under direction of Bogdan Janski. Motherhouse, Rome, Italy.

U.S. Province, 2250 N. Latrobe Ave., Chicago, IL 60639.

Ontario Kentucky Province, U.S. address, 338 N. 25th St., Louisville, KY 40212.

Rogationist Fathers, R.C.J.: Founded by Bl. Annibale (Hannibal) di Francia, 1887. General motherhouse, Rome, Italy. U.S. delegation: 2688 S. Newmark Ave., Sanger, CA 91343. Charitable work.

Rosary, Brothers of Our Lady of the Holy, F.S.R.: Founded 1956, in U.S., Motherhouse and novitiate, 1725 S. McCarran Blvd., Reno, NV 89502.

Rosminians (Institute of Charity), I.C.: Founded 1828, in Italy, by Antonio Rosmini-Serbati. General motherhouse, Rome, Italy; U.S. address, 2327 W. Heading Ave., Peoria, IL 61604. Charitable work.

Sacred Heart, Brothers of the, S.C.: Founded 1821, in France, by Rev. Andre Coindre. General motherhouse, Rome, Italy, Educational work.

New Orleans Province (1847), 4540 Elysian Fields Ave., New Orleans, LA 70122.

New England Province (1945), 685 Steere Farm Rd., Pascoag, RI 02859.

New York Province (1960), P.O. Box 68, Belvidere, NJ 07823.

Sacred Heart, Missionaries of the, M.S.C.: Founded 1854, by Rev. Jules Chevelier. General motherhouse, Rome, Italy; U.S. province, 305 S. Lake St., Aurora, IL 60507.

Sacred Heart of Jesus, Congregation of the (Sacred Heart Fathers and Brothers), S.C.J.: Founded 1877, in France. General motherhouse, Rome, Italy; U.S. provincial office: P.O. Box 289, Hales Corners, WI 53130. Educational, preaching, mission work.

Sacred Hearts of Jesus and Mary, Congregation of (Picpus Fathers), SS.CC.: Founded 1805, in France, by Fr. Coudrin. General motherhouse, Rome, Italy. Mission, educational work.

Eastern Province (1946), 77 Adams St. (Box 111), Fairhaven, MA 02719.

Western Province (1970), 724 E. Bonita Ave., San Dimas, CA 91773.

Hawaii Province, Box 797, Kaneohe, Oahu, Hawaii 96744.

Sacred Hearts of Jesus and Mary, Missionaries of the, M.SS.CC.: Founded 1833, in Naples, Italy, by Cajetan Errico. General motherhouse, Rome, Italy; U.S. headquarters, 2249 Shore Rd., Linwood, NJ 08221.

Salesians of St. John Bosco (Society of St. Francis de Sales), S.D.B.: Founded 1859, by St. John (Don) Bosco. Generalate, Rome, Italy. St. Philip the Apostle Province (1902), 148 Main St., New Rochelle, NY 10802.

San Francisco Province (1926), 1100 Franklin St., San Francisco, CA 94109.

Salvatorians (Society of the Divine Savior), S.D.S.: Founded 1881, in Rome, by Fr. Francis Jordan; in U.S., 1896. General headquarters, Rome, Italy; U.S. province, 1735 Hi-Mount Blvd., Milwaukee, WI 53208. Educational, parochial, mission work; campus ministries, chaplaincies.

Scalabrinians: See Missionaries of St. Charles.

Servites (Order of Friar Servants of Mary), O.S.M.: Founded 1233, at Florence, Italy, by Seven Holy Founders. Generalate, Rome, Italy. General apostolic ministry.

Eastern Province (1967), 3121 W. Jackson Blvd., Chicago, IL 60612.

Western Province (1967), 5210 Somerset St., Buena Park, CA 90621.

Somascan Fathers, C.R.S.: Founded 1534, at Somasca, Italy, by St. Jerome Emiliani. General motherhouse, Rome, Italy; U.S. address, Pine Haven Boys Center, River Rd., P.O. Box 162, Suncook, NH 03275.

Society of Our Lady of the Most Holy Trinity, S.O.L.T.: Headquarters, Casa San Jose, 109 W. Avenue F, PO Box 152, Robstown, TX 78380.

Sons of Mary Missionary Society (Sons of Mary, Health of the Sick), F.M.S.I.: Founded 1952, in the Boston archdiocese, by Rev. Edward F. Garesche, S.J. Headquarters, 567 Salem End Rd., Framingham, MA 01701.

Stigmatine Fathers and Brothers (Congregation of the Sacred Stigmata), C.S.S.: Founded 1816, by St. Gaspar Bertoni. General motherhouse, Rome, Italy; North American Province, 554 Lexington St., Waltham, MA 02154. Parish work.

Sulpicians (Society of Priests of St. Sulpice), S.S.: Founded 1641, at Paris, by Rev. Jean Jacques Olier. General motherhouse, Paris, France; U.S. province, 5408 Roland Ave., Baltimore, MD 21210. Education of seminarians and priests.

Theatines (Congregation of Clerics Regular), C.R.: Founded 1524, at Rome, by St. Cajetan. General motherhouse, Rome, Italy; U.S. headquarters, 1050 S. Birch St., Denver, CO 80222.

Trappists: See Cistercians of the Strict Observance.

Trinitarians (Order of the Most Holy Trinity), O.SS.T.: Founded 1198, by St. John of Matha; in U.S., 1911. General motherhouse, Rome, Italy; U.S. headquarters, P.O. Box 5719, Baltimore, MD 21208.

Trinity Missions (Missionary Servants of the Most Holy Trinity), S.T.: Founded 1929, by Fr. Thomas Augustine Judge. Generalate, 1215 N. Scott St., Arlington, VA 22209. Home mission work.

Viatorian Fathers (Clerics of St. Viator), C.S.V.: Founded 1831, in France, by Fr. Louis Joseph Querbes. General motherhouse, Rome, Italy. Province of Chicago (1882), 1212 E. Euclid St., Arlington Hts., IL 60004. Educational work.

Vincentians (Congregation of the Mission; Lazarists), C.M.: Founded 1625, in Paris, by St. Vincent de Paul; in U.S., 1818. General motherhouse, Rome, Italy. Educational work.

Eastern Province (1867), 500 E. Chelten Ave., Philadelphia, PA 19144.

Midwest Province (1888), 13663 Rider Trail North, Earth City, MO 63045.

New England Province (1975), 234 Keeney St., Manchester, CT 06040.

American Italian Branch, Our Lady of Pompei Church, 3600 Claremont St., Baltimore, MD 21224.

American Spanish Branch (Barcelona, Spain), 234 Congress St., Brooklyn, NY 11201.

American Spanish Branch (Zaragoza, Spain), Holy Agony Church, 1834 3rd Ave., New York, NY 10029.

Western Province (1975), 650 W. 23rd St., Los Angeles, CA 90007.

Southern Province (1975), 3826 Gilbert Ave., Dallas, TX 75219.

Vocationist Fathers (Society of Divine Vocations), S.D.V.: Founded 1920, in Italy; in U.S., 1962. Generalate, Rome, Italy; U.S. headquarters, 90 Brooklake Rd., Florham Park, NJ 07932.

Xaverian Missionary Fathers, S.X.: Founded 1895, by Bl. Guido Conforti, at Parma, Italy. General motherhouse, Rome, Italy; U.S. province, 12 Helene Ct., Wayne, NJ 07470. Foreign mission work.

50TH ANNIVERSARY OF SCHOOL INTEGRATION

The opening of the 1997 school year coincided with the 50th anniversary of the integration of Catholic schools in the Archdiocese of St. Louis.

Seven years before the Supreme Court ruled that the "separate but equal" school policies then in place in much of the country were unconstitutional, many people in St. Louis were shaken by then-Archbbishop John E. Ritter's directive that all archdiocesan schools should be open to any child who met the scholastic requirements.

Shortly before the start of the school year in 1947, a memo was sent to all pastors from Auxiliary Bishop John P. Cody. It read: Archbishop Ritter "has instructed me to advise you ... there should be no discrimination and that the same principles for admission are to be followed in admitting colored children as for others. This is in keeping with our Catholic teachng and the best principles of our American form of democratic government."

At issue, according to Jesuit historian Father William B. Faherty, "was the whole area of racial justice — not just integration of schools, but the whole question of integration of parishes, of treating our black Catholics as fellow full Catholics and black citizens as fellow full citizens."

Integrating the schools did not come easily, however. Parents who objected appealed to the apostolic delegate, but he supported Archbishop Ritter.

JULY							SUN	MON	TUE	WED	THU	FRI	SAT	SEPTEMBER						
S	M	T	W	T	F	S	.....	.....	.....	1	2	3	4	S	M	T	W	T	F	S
1	2	3	4	5	6	7	5	6	7	8	9	10	11	.....	.....	.....	.....	.....	.....	1
8	9	10	11	12	13	14	12	13	14	15	16	17	18	2	3	4	5	6	7	8
15	16	17	18	19	20	21	19	20	21	22	23	24	25	9	10	11	12	13	14	15
22	23	24	25	26	27	28	26	27	28	29	30	31	.....	16	17	18	19	20	21	22
29	30	31												23	24	25	26	27	28	29
.....	.....	.....	.....	.....	.....	.....								30	.....	.....	.....	.....	.....	.....

AUGUST
15

WEDNESDAY   1973

8:00	_____
8:30	_____
9:00	_____
9:30	_____
10:00	_____
10:30	_____
11:00	_____
11:30	_____
12:00	_____
12:30	_____
1:00	_____
1:30	_____
2:00	_____
2:30	_____
3:00	_____
3:30	_____
4:00	_____
4:30	_____
5:00	_____

JULIAN 3227

MEMBERSHIP OF RELIGIOUS INSTITUTES OF MEN

(Principal source: *1997 Annuario Pontificio*. Statistics as of Jan. 1, 1996, unless indicated otherwise.)

Listed below are world membership statistics of institutes of men of pontifical right with 500 or more members; the number of priests is in parentheses. Also listed are institutes with less than 500 members with houses in the United States.

Jesuits (15,837) 22,580
Franciscans (Friars Minor) (12,062) 17,981
Salesians (11,150) 17,566
Franciscans (Capuchins) (7,489) 11,405
Benedictines (4,987) 8,601
Brothers of Christian Schools 7,400
Dominicans (4,913) 6,618
Redemptorists (4,380) 5,900
Society of the Divine Word (3,634) 5,780
Marist Brothers 5,356
Oblates of Mary Immaculate (3,720) 5,061
Franciscans (Conventuals) (2,715) 4,510
Vincentians (3,224) 4,005
Discalced Carmelites (O.C.D.) (2,422) 3,809
Holy Spirit (Holy Ghost),
Congregation (2,499) 3,157
Claretians (1,996) 2,926
Augustinians (2,258) 2,911
Trappists (1,143) 2,543
Passionists (1,859) 2,536
Priests of the Sacred Heart (1,705) 2,394
Missionaries of the Sacred Heart
of Jesus (1,605) 2,367
Missionaries of Africa (1,940) 2,304
Combonian Missionaries of the Heart of Jesus
(1,316) 2,298
Pallottines (1,537) 2,283
Carmelites (O.Carm.) (1,434) 2,197
Christian Brothers 1,892
Carmelites of BVM (1,113) 1,861
Holy Cross, Congregation (812) 1,773
Marianists (537) 1,722
Hospitallers of St. John of God (143) 1,493
Marists (1,222) 1,485
Brothers of the Sacred Heart (51) 1,464
Legionaries of Christ (344) 1,460
Piarists (1,134) 1,458
Congregation of the Immaculate Heart of Mary
(Missionhurst; Scheut Missionaries)
(1,017) 1,387
Premonstratensians (968) 1,333
Augustinians (Recollects) (1,016) 1,303
Cistercians (Common Observance) (762) 1,294
Brothers of Christian Instruction
of Ploermel (6) 1,254
Sacred Hearts, Congregation (Picpus) (920) .. 1,254
Brothers of Christian Instruction of St. Gabriel
(33) 1,240
Salvatorians (795) 1,213
Society of St. Paul (579) 1,170
Montfort Missionaries (812) 1,095
Little Workers of Divine Providence (734) 1,066
Society of African Missions (922) 1,037
Consolata Missionaries (754) 1,015
Ministers of Sick (Camillians) (649) 1,015
Blessed Sacrament, Congregation of (695) 1,006
Servants of Mary (761) 1,006

Assumptionists (692) 989
Missionaries of Holy Family (688) 941
Xaverian Missionaries (697) 912
LaSalette Missionaries (670) 899
Franciscans (Third Order Regular) (565) 842
Maryknollers (603) 840
Missionaries of St. Francis de Sales
of Annecy (433) 829
Canons Regular of St. Augustine (663) 828
Viatorians (347) 823
Mill Hill Missionaries (588) 756
Scalabrinians (623) 749
Oblates of St. Francis de Sales (566) 741
Mercedarians (525) 739
Columbans (661) 718
Missionaries of the Most Precious Blood (477) 700
Congregation of St. Joseph (530) 680
Pontifical Institute for Foreign Missions (528) 667
Brothers of Charity (Ghent) 642
Trinitarians (382) 616
Eudists (415) 606
Order of St. Basil the Great (Basilians of St.
Josaphat) (304) 565
Oratorians (382) 548
Marian Fathers and Brothers (350) 532
Brothers of the Immaculate Conception (5) 511
Somascans (328) 499
Society of Christ (384) 494
Crosiers (Order of Holy Cross) (322) 492
Servants of Charity (344) 473
Brothers of Our Lady Mother of Mercy 472
Oblates of St. Joseph (317) 465
Resurrection, Congregation of (345) 430
Order of St. Paul the First Hermit (248) 427
Paris Foreign Mission Society (407) 407
Stigmatine Fathers and Brothers (317) 407
Missionaries of the Holy Spirit (246) 402
Barnabites (319) 398
Sulpicians (384) 384
St. Patrick's Mission Society (363) 381
Mariannhill Missionaries (209) 380
Carthusians (180) 365
Congr. of St. Basil (Canada) (343) 362
Rosminians (263) 360
Rogationists (199) 355
Xaverian Brothers 291
Little Brothers of Jesus (73) 257
Bethlehem Missionaries (180) 238
Paulists (208) 226
Oblates of the Virgin Mary *(1992)* (170) 213
Brothers of St. Patrick 189
Vocationist Fathers (150) 188
Sons of the Holy Family (129) 185
Priestly Fraternity of St. Peter (59) 172
Theatines (111) 170
Franciscan Friars of the Atonement (102) 156
Presentation Brothers *(1991)* 156
Missionary Servants of the Most Holy Trinity
(1994) (101) 145
Josephites (St. Joseph's Society of the Sacred Heart
—S.S.J.) (129) 143
Josephites (C.J.) (99) 121
Alexian Brothers (1) 113
Franciscan Brothers of Brooklyn 113

Basilian Salvatorian Fathers (91) 109
Glenmary Missioners (63) 86
Camaldolese Hermits of Monte Corona (34) 85
Brothers of Mercy 74
Society of St. Edmund (54) 66
Congr. of Sacerdotal Fraternity (32) 64

Franciscan Bros. of Holy Cross (2) 49
Little Brothers of the Good Shepherd (2) 41
Clerics Regular Minor (Adorno Fathers) (30) 41
Fathers of Mercy (12) 25
Servants of Holy Paraclete (16) 22
Mekhitarist Order of Vienna (14) 15

RELIGIOUS INSTITUTES OF WOMEN IN THE UNITED STATES

(Sources: *Official Catholic Directory; Catholic Almanac* survey.)

Adorers of the Blood of Christ, A.S.C.: Founded 1834, in Italy; in U.S., 1870. General motherhouse, Rome, Italy U.S. provinces: 2 Pioneer Lane, Red Bud, IL 62278; 1400 South Sheridan, Wichita, KS 67213; 3950 Columbia Ave., Columbia, PA 17512. Education, retreats, social services, pastoral ministry.

Africa, Missionary Sisters of Our Lady of (Sisters of Africa), M.S.O.L.A.: Founded 1869, at Algiers, Algeria, by Cardinal Lavigerie; in U.S., 1929. General motherhouse, Rome, Italy; U.S. headquarters, 49 W. Spring St., Winooski, VT 05404. Medical, educational, catechetical and social work in Africa.

Agnes, Sisters of St., C.S.A.: Founded 1858, in U.S., by Rev. Caspar Rehrl. General motherhouse, 475 Gillett St., Fond du Lac, WI 54935. Education, health care, social services.

Ann, Sisters of St., S.S.A.: Founded 1834, in Italy; in U.S., 1952. General motherhouse, Rome, Italy; U.S. headquarters, Mount St. Ann, Ebensburg, PA 15931.

Anne, Sisters of St., S.S.A.: Founded 1850, at Vaudreuil, Que., Canada; in U.S., 1866. General motherhouse, Lachine, Que., Canada; U.S. address, 720 Boston Post Rd., Marlboro, MA 01752. Retreat work, pastoral ministry, religious education.

Anthony, Missionary Servants of St., M.S.S.A.: Founded 1929, in U.S., by Rev. Peter Baque. General motherhouse, 100 Peter Baque Rd., San Antonio, TX 78209. Social work.

Antonine Maronite Sisters: Established in U.S., 1966. U.S. address, 2691 N. Lipkey Rd., North Jackson, Ohio 44451.

Apostolate, Sisters Auxiliaries of the, S.A.A.: Founded 1903, in Canada; in U.S., 1911. General motherhouse, 689 Maple Terr., Monongah, WV 26555. Education, nursing.

Armenian Sisters of the Immaculate Conception: U.S. address, 6 Eliot Rd., Lexington, MA 02173.

Assumption, Little Sisters of the, L.S.A.: Founded 1865, in France; in U.S., 1891. General motherhouse, Paris, France; U.S. provincialate, 214 E. 30th St., New York, NY 10016. Social work, nursing, family life education.

Assumption, Religious of the, R.A.: Founded 1839, in France; in U.S., 1919. Generalate, Paris, France; North American province, 227 N. Bowman Ave., Merion Sta., PA 19066.

Assumption of the Blessed Virgin, Sisters of the, S.A.S.V.: Founded 1853, in Canada; in U.S., 1891. General motherhouse, Nicolet, Que., Canada; U.S. province, 316 Lincoln St., Worcester, MA 01605. Education, mission, pastoral ministry.

Augustinian Nuns of Contemplative Life, O.S.A.: Established in Spain in 13th century; U.S. foundation, Convent of Our Mother of Good Counsel, 4328 W. Westminster Pl., St. Louis, MO 63108.

Augustinian Sisters, Servants of Jesus and Mary, Congregation of, O.S.A.: Generalate, Rome, Italy; U.S. foundation, St. John School, 513 E. Broadway, Brandenburg, KY 40108.

Basil the Great, Sisters of the Order of St. (Byzantine Rite), O.S.B.M.: Founded fourth century, in Cappadocia, by St. Basil the Great and his sister St. Macrina; in U.S., 1911. Generalate, Rome, Italy; U.S. motherhouses: Philadelphia Ukrainian Byzantine Rite, 710 Fox Chase Rd., Philadelphia, PA 19111; Pittsburgh Ruthenian Byzantine Rite, Mount St. Macrina P.O. Box 878, Uniontown, PA 15401. Education, health care.

Benedict, Sisters of the Order of St., O.S.B.: Our Lady of Mount Caritas Monastery (founded 1979, Ashford, Conn.), Seckar Rd., Ashford, CT 06278. Contemplative.

Benedictine Nuns, O.S.B.: St. Scholastica Priory, Box 606, Petersham, MA 01366. Cloistered.

Benedictine Nuns of the Congregation of Solesmes, O.S.B.: U.S. establishment, 1981, in Burlington diocese. Monastery of the Immaculate Heart of Mary, H.C.R. #13, Box 11, Westfield, VT 05874. Cloistered, papal enclosure.

Benedictine Nuns of the Primitive Observance, O.S.B.: Founded c. 529, in Italy; in U.S., 1948. Abbey of Regina Laudis, Flanders Rd., Bethlehem, CT 06751. Cloistered.

Benedictine Sisters, O.S.B.: Founded c. 529, in Italy; in U.S., 1852. General motherhouse, Eichstatt, Bavaria, Germany. U.S. addresses: St. Emma's Monastery, Motherhouse and Novitiate, 1001 Harvey Ave., Greensburg, PA 15601; Abbey of St. Walburga, 6717 S. Boulder Rd., Boulder, CO 80303.

Benedictine Sisters (Regina Pacis), O.S.B.: Founded 1627, in Lithuania as cloistered community; reformed 1918 as active community; established in U.S. 1957, by Mother M. Raphaela Simonis. Regina Pacis, 333 Wallace Rd., Bedford, NH 03102.

Benedictine Sisters, Missionary, O.S.B.: Founded 1885. Generalate, Rome, Italy; U.S. motherhouse, 300 N. 18th St., Norfolk, NE 68701.

Benedictine Sisters, Olivetan, O.S.B.: Founded 1887, in U.S. General motherhouse, Holy Angels Convent, P.O. Drawer 130, Jonesboro, AR 72403. Educational, hospital work.

Benedictine Sisters of Perpetual Adoration of Pontifical Jurisdiction, Congregation of the, O.S.B.: Founded in U.S., 1874, from Maria Rickenbach, Switzerland. General motherhouse, 8300 Morganford Rd., St. Louis, MO 63123.

Benedictine Sisters of Pontifical Jurisdiction,

O.S.B.: Founded c. 529, in Italy. No general motherhouse in U.S. Three federations:

• Federation of St. Scholastica (1922). Pres., Sister Regina Crowley, O.S.B., 5807 N. Kolmar Ave., Chicago, IL 60646. Motherhouses belonging to the federation:

Mt. St. Scholastica, 801 S. 8th St., Atchison, Kans. 66002; Benedictine Sisters of Elk Co., St. Joseph's Monastery, St. Mary's, PA 15857; Benedictine Sisters of Erie, 6101 E. Lake Rd., Erie, PA 16511; Benedictine Sisters of Chicago, St. Scholastica Priory, 7430 Ridge Blvd., Chicago, IL 60645; Benedictine Sisters of the Sacred Heart, 1910 Maple Ave., Lisle, IL 60532; Benedictine Sisters of Elizabeth, St. Walburga Monastery, 851 N. Broad St., Elizabeth, NJ 07208; Benedictine Sisters of Pittsburgh, 4530 Perrysville Ave., Pittsburgh, PA 15229;

Red Plains Monastery, 728 Richland Rd. S.W., Piedmont, OK 73078., St. Joseph's Monastery, 2200 S. Lewis, Tulsa, OK 74114; St. Gertrude's Monastery, Ridgely, MD 21660; St. Walburga Monastery, 2500 Amsterdam Rd., Covington, KY 41016; Sacred Heart Monastery, Cullman, AL 35056; Benedictine Sisters of Virginia, Bristow, VA 22013; St. Scholastica Convent, 416 W. Highland Dr., Boerne, TX 78006; St. Lucy's Priory, 19045 E. Sierra Madre Ave., Glendora, CA 91741; Benedictine Sisters of Florida, Drawer H, St. Leo, FL 33574; Benet Hill Monastery, 2555 N. Chelton Rd., Colorado Springs, CO 80909; Queen of Heaven Convent (Byzantine Rite), 8640 Squires Lane N.E., Warren, OH 44484; Benedictine Sisters of Baltimore, Emmanuel Monastery, 2229 W. Joppa Rd., Lutherville, MD 21093; Queen of Angels Monastery, 717 King's Hwy, Liberty, MO 64068.

• Federation of St. Gertrude the Great (1937). Office: Sacred Heart Monastery, P.O. Box 364, Richardton, ND 58652. Pres., Sister Ruth Fox, O.S.B. Motherhouses belonging to the federation:

Mother of God Monastery, 120 SE 28th Ave., Watertown, SD 57201; Sacred Heart Monastery, 1005 W. 8th St., Yankton, SD 57078; Mt. St. Benedict Monastery, 620 E. Summit Ave., Crookston, MN 56716; Sacred Heart Monastery, P.O. Box 364, Richardton, ND 58652; Convent of St. Martin, 2110-C St. Martin's Dr., Rapid City, SD 57702; Monastery of Immaculate Conception, 802 E. 10th St., Ferdinand, IN 47532; Monastery of St. Gertrude, HC3, Box 121, Cottonwood, ID 83522;

Monastery of St. Benedict Center, Box 5070, Madison, WI 53705; Queen of Angels Monastery, 840 S. Main St., Mt. Angel, OR 97362; St. Scholastica Monastery, P.O. Box 3489, Fort Smith, AR 72913; Our Lady of Peace Monastery, 3710 W. Broadway, Columbia, MO 65203; Queen of Peace Monastery, Box 370, Belcourt, ND 58316; Our Lady of Grace Monastery, 1402 Southern Ave., Beech Grove, IN 46107; Holy Spirit Monastery, 22791 Pico St., Grand Terrace, CA 92324; Spirit of Life Monastery, 10760 W. Glennon Dr., Lakewood, CO 80226. St. Benedict's Monastery 225 Masters Ave., RR #1b, Winnipeg, Man. R3C 4A3, Canada; The Dwelling Place Monastery, 150 Mt. Tabor Rd., Martin, KY 41649.

• Federation of St. Benedict (1947). Pres., Sister Colleen Haggerty, O.S.B., St. Benedict Convent, 104 Chapel Lane, St. Joseph, MN 56374.

Motherhouses in U.S. belonging to the federation:
St. Benedict's Convent, St. Joseph, MN 56374; St. Scholastica Monasstery, 1200 Kenwood Ave., Duluth, MN 55811; St. Bede Priory, 1190 Priory Rd., Eau Claire, WI 54702; St. Mary Monastery, Nauvoo, IL 62354; Annunciation Priory, 7520 University Dr., Bismarck, ND 58504; St. Paul's Priory, 2675 Larpenteur Ave., E., St. Paul, MN 55109; St. Placid Priory, 500 College St. N.E., Lacey, WA 98516; Mt. Benedict Priory, 309 E. 5450 South, Ogden, UT 84405.

Bethany, Sisters of, C.V.D.: Founded 1928, in El Salvador; in U.S. 1949. General motherhouse, Santa Tecla, El Salvador. U.S. address: 850 N. Hobart Blvd., Los Angeles, CA 90029.

Bethlemita Sisters, Daughters of the Sacred Heart of Jesus: Founded 1861, in Guatemala. Motherhouse, Bogota, Colombia; U.S. address, St. Joseph Residence, 330 W. Pembroke St., Dallas, TX 75208.

Blessed Virgin Mary, Institute of the (Loreto Sisters), I.B.V.M.: Founded 17th century in Belgium; in U.S., 1954. Motherhouse, Rathfarnham, Dublin, Ireland; U.S. address: 2521 W. Maryland Ave., Phoenix, AZ 85017.

Blessed Virgin Mary, Institute of the (Loretto Sisters), I.B.V.M.: Founded 1609, in Belgium; in U.S., 1880. U.S. address, Loretto Convent, Box 508, Wheaton, IL 60189. Educational work.

Bon Secours, Congregation of, C.B.S.: Founded 1824, in France; in U.S., 1881. Generalate, Rome, Italy; U.S. provincial house, 1525 Marriottsville Rd., Marriottsville, MD 21104. Hospital work.

Brigid, Congregation of St., C.S.B.: Founded 1807, in Ireland; in U.S., 1953. U.S. regional house, 5118 Loma Linda Dr., San Antonio, TX 78201.

Brigittine Sisters (Order of the Most Holy Savior), O.SS.S.: Founded 1344, at Vadstena, Sweden, by St. Bridget; in U.S., 1957. General motherhouse, Rome, Italy; U.S. address, Vikingsborg, 4 Runkenhage Rd., Darien, CT 06820.

Canossian Daughters of Charity (Canossian Sisters): Founded 1808 in Verona, Italy, by St. Magdalen of Canossa. General motherhouse, Rome, Italy; U.S. provincial house, 5625 Isleta Blvd. S.W., Albuquerque, NM 87105.

Carmel, Congregation of Our Lady of Mount, O. Carm.: Founded 1825, in France; in U.S., 1833. Generalate, P.O. Box 476, Lacombe, LA 70445. Education, social services, pastoral ministry, retreat work.

Carmel, Institute of Our Lady of Mount, O. Carm.: Founded 1854, in Italy; in U.S., 1947. General motherhouse, Rome, Italy; U.S. novitiate, 5 Wheatland St., Peabody, MA 01960. Apostolic work.

Carmelite Community of the Word, C.C.W.: Motherhouse and Novitiate, 1304 13th Ave., Altoona, PA 16601.

Carmelite Nuns, Discalced, O.C.D.: Founded 1562, Spain. First foundation in U.S. in 1790, at Charles County, Md.; this monastery was moved to Baltimore. Monasteries in U.S. are listed below, according to states.

Alabama: 716 Dauphin Island Pkwy., Mobile 36606.
Arkansas: 7201 W. 32nd St., Little Rock 72204.
California: 215 E. Alhambra Rd., Alhambra 91801;

27601 Highway 1, Carmel 93923; 68 Rincon Rd., Kensington 94707; 1883 Ringsted Dr., P.O. Box 379, Solvang 93463; 6981 Teresian Way, Georgetown 95634; 5158 Hawley Blvd., San Diego 92116; 721 Parker Ave., San Francisco 94118; 530 Blackstone Dr., San Rafael 94903; 1000 Lincoln St., Santa Clara 9550.
Colorado: 6138 S. Gallup St., Littleton 80120. *Georgia:* Coffee Bluff, 11 W. Back St., Savannah 31419. *Hawaii:* 6301 Pali Hwy., Kaneohe, HI 96744; *Illinois:* River Rd. and Central, Des Plaines 60016. *Indiana:* 2500 Cold Spring Rd., Indianapolis 46222; 59 Allendale Pl., Terre Haute 47802. *Iowa:* 17937 250th St., Eldridge 52748; 2901 S. Cecilia St., Sioux City 51106. *Kentucky:* 1740 Newburg Rd., Louisville 40205. *Louisiana:* 1250 Carmel Ave., Lafayette 70507; 73530 River Rd., Covington 70430.
Maryland: 1318 Dulaney Valley Rd., Towson, Baltimore 21204; 4035-A Mt. Carmel Rd., Port Tobacco 20646. *Massachusetts:* 61 Mt. Pleasant Ave., Roxbury, Boston 02119; 15 Mt. Carmel Rd., Danvers 01923. *Michigan:* 4300 Mt. Carmel Dr. NE, Ada 49301; 35750 Moravian Dr., Clinton Township 48035; U.S. 2 Highway, P.O. Box 397, Iron Mountain 49801; 3501 Silver Lake Rd., Traverse City 49684. *Minnesota:* 8251 De Montreville Trail N., Lake Elmo 55042. *Mississippi:* 2155 Terry Rd., Jackson 39204.
Missouri: 2201 W. Main St., Jefferson City 65101; 9150 Clayton Rd., Ladue, St. Louis Co. 63124; 424 E. Monastery Rd., Springfield 65807. *Nevada:* 1950 La Fond Dr., Reno 89509. *New Hampshire:* 275 Pleasant St., Concord, 03301. *New Jersey:* P.O. Box 785, Flemington 08822; 189 Madison Ave., Morristown 07960. *New Mexico:* Mt. Carmel Rd., Santa Fe 87501. *New York:* 745 St. John's Pl., Brooklyn 11216; 139 De Puyster Ave., Beacon 12508; 75 Carmel Rd., Buffalo 14214; 1931 W. Jefferson Rd., Pittsford 14534; 68 Franklin Ave., Saranac Lake 12983; 428 Duane Ave., Schenectady 12304.
Ohio: 3176 Fairmount Blvd., Cleveland Heights 44118. *Oklahoma:* 20,000 N. County Line Rd., Piedmont 73078. Oregon: 87609 Green Hill Rd., Eugene 97402. *Pennsylvania:* 70 Monastery Rd., Elysburg 17824; 510 E. Gore Rd., Erie 16509; R.D. 6, Box 28, Center Dr., Latrobe 15650; P.O. Box 57, Loretto 15940; Byzantine Rite, R.R. No. 1, Box 1336, Sugarloaf 18249; 66th and Old York Rd., Philadelphia 19126. *Rhode Island:* Watson Ave. at Nayatt Rd., Barrington 02806.
Texas: 600 Flowers Ave., Dallas 75211; 5801 Mt. Carmel Dr., Arlington 76017; 1100 Parthenon Pl., Roman Forest, New Caney 77357; 6301 Culebra and St. Joseph Way, San Antonio 78238. *Utah:* 5714 Holladay Blvd., Salt Lake City 84121. *Vermont:* RR 2, Box 4784, Barre, 05641. *Washington:* 2215 N.E. 147th St., Shoreline 98155. *Wisconsin:* W267 N2517 Meadowbrook Rd., Pewaukee 53072.
Carmelite Nuns of the Ancient Observance (Calced Carmelites), O. Carm.: Founded 1452, in The Netherlands; in U.S., 1930, from Naples, Italy, convent (founded 1856). U.S. monasteries: Carmelite Monastery of St. Therese, 3551 Lanark Rd., Lanark, PA 18036; Carmel of Mary, Wahpeton, ND 58075; Our Lady of Grace Monastery, 1 St. Joseph Pl., San Angelo, TX 76905; Carmel of the Sacred Heart, 430

Laurel Ave., Hudson, WI 54016. Papal enclosure.
Carmelite Sisters (Corpus Christi), O. Carm.: Founded 1908, in England; in U.S., 1920. General motherhouse, Tunapuna, Trinidad, W.I. U.S. address: Mt. Carmel Home, 412 W. 18th St., Kearney, NE 68847. Home and foreign mission work.
Carmelite Sisters for the Aged and Infirm, O. Carm.: Founded 1929, at New York, by Mother M. Angeline Teresa, O. Carm. Motherhouse, 600 Woods Rd., Avila-on-Hudson, Germantown, NY 12526. Social work, nursing and educating in the field of gerontology.
Carmelite Sisters of Charity, C.a.Ch.: Founded 1826 at Vich, Spain, by St. Joaquina de Vedruna. Generalate, Rome, Italy; U.S. address, 701 Beacon Rd., Silver Spring, MD 20903.
Carmelite Sisters of St. Therese of the Infant Jesus, C.S.T.: Founded 1917, in U.S. General motherhouse, 1300 Classen Dr., Oklahoma City, OK 73103. Educational work.
Carmelite Sisters of the Divine Heart of Jesus, Carmel D.C.J.: Founded 1891, in Germany; in U.S., 1912. General motherhouse, Sittard Netherlands. U.S. provincial houses: 1230 Kavanaugh Pl., Milwaukee, WI 52313 (Northern Province); 10341 Manchester Rd., St. Louis, MO 63122 (Central Province); 8585 La Mesa Blvd., La Mesa, CA 92041 (South Western Province). Social services, mission work.
Carmelite Sisters of the Most Sacred Heart of Los Angeles, O.C.D.: Founded 1904, in Mexico. General motherhouse and novitiate, 920 E. Alhambra Rd., Alhambra, CA 91801. Social services, retreat and educational work.
Carmelites, Calced (O. Carm.): Founded 1856 in Naples, Italy. U.S. address: Carmelite Monastery of St Therese, 3551 Lanark Rd., Coopersburg, PA 18036.
Carmelites of St. Theresa, Congregation of Missionary, C.M.S.T.: Founded 1903, in Mexico. General motherhouse, Mexico City, Mexico; U.S. foundation, 9548 Deer Trail Dr., Houston, TX 77038.
Casimir, Sisters of St., S.S.C.: Founded 1907, in U.S. by Mother Maria Kaupas. General motherhouse, 2601 W. Marquette Rd., Chicago, IL 60629. Education, missions, social services.
Cenacle, Congregation of Our Lady of the Retreat in the, R.C.: Founded 1826, in France; in U.S., 1892. Generalate, Rome, Italy. Eastern Province: Cenacle Rd., Lake Ronkonkoma, L.I., NY 11779; Midwestern Province, 513 Fullerton Pkwy., Chicago, IL 60614.
Charity, Daughters of Divine, F.D.C.: Founded 1868, at Vienna, Austria; in U.S., 1913. General motherhouse, Rome, Italy. U.S. province: 205 Major Ave., Staten Island, NY 10305. Education, social services.
Charity, Little Missionary Sisters of, L.M.S.C.: Founded 1915, in Italy by Bl. Luigi Orione; in U.S., 1949. General motherhouse, Rome, Italy; U.S. address, 120 Orient Ave., East Boston, MA 02128.
Charity, Missionaries of, M.C.: Founded 1950, in Calcutta, India, by Mother Teresa; first U.S. foundation 1971. General motherhouse, 54A Lower Circular Road, Calcutta 700016, India. U.S. address, 335 E. 145th St., Bronx, NY 10451. Service of the poor.

Charity, Religious Sisters of, R.S.C.: Founded 1815, in Ireland; in U.S., 1953. Motherhouse, Dublin, Ireland; U.S. headquarters, 206 N. Edgemont St., Los Angeses, CA 90029.

Charity, Sisters of (of Seton Hill), S.C.: Founded 1870, at Altoona, Penn., from Cincinnati foundation. Generalate, Mt. Thor Rd., Greensburg, PA 15601. Educational, hospital, social, foreign mission work.

Charity, Sisters of (Grey Nuns of Montreal), S.G.M.: Founded 1737, in Canada by St. Marie Marguerite d'Youville; in U.S., 1855. General administration, Montreal, Que. H2Y 2L7, Canada; U.S. provincial house, 10 Pelham Rd., Lexington, MA 02173.

Charity, Sisters of (of Leavenworth), S.C.L.: Founded 1858, in U.S. Motherhouse, 4200 S. 4th St., Leavenworth, KS 66048.

Charity, Sisters of (of Nazareth), S.C.N.: Founded 1812, in U.S. General motherhouse, SCN Center, P.O. Box 172, Nazareth, KY 40048. Education, health services.

Charity, Sisters of (of St. Augustine), C.S.A.: Founded 1851, at Cleveland, Ohio. Motherhouse, 5232 Broadview Rd., Richfield, OH 44286.

Charity, Sisters of Christian, S.C.C.: Founded 1849, in Paderborn, Germany, by Bl. Pauline von Mallinckrodt; in U.S., 1873. Generalate, Rome, Italy. U.S. provinces: Mallinckrodt Convent, Mendham, NJ 07945; 1041 Ridge Rd., Wilmette, IL 60091, Education, health services, other apostolic work.

Charity, Vincentian Sisters of, V.S.C.: Founded 1835, in Austria; in U.S., 1902. General motherhouse, 8200 McKnight Rd., Pittsburgh, PA 15237.

Charity, Vincentian Sisters of, V.S.C.: Founded 1928, at Bedford, Ohio. General motherhouse, 1160 Broadway, Bedford, OH 44146.

Charity of Cincinnati, Ohio, Sisters of, S.C.: Founded 1809; became independent community, 1852. General motherhouse, Mt. St. Joseph, Ohio 45051. Educational, hospital, social work.

Charity of Ottawa, Sisters of (Grey Nuns of the Cross), S.C.O.: Founded 1845, at Ottawa, Canada; in U.S., 1857. General motherhouse, Ottawa, Canada; U.S. provincial house, 975 Varnum Ave., Lowell, MA 01854. Educational, hospital work, extended health care.

Charity of Our Lady, Mother of Mercy, Sisters of, S.C.M.M.: Founded 1832, in Holland; in U.S., 1874. General motherhouse, Den Bosch, Netherlands; U.S. provincialate, 520 Thompson Ave., East Haven, CT 06512.

Charity of Our Lady, Mother of the Church, S.C.M.C: U.S. foundation, 1970. General motherhouse, Baltic, CT 06330.

Charity of Our Lady of Mercy, Sisters of, O.L.M.: Founded 1829, in Charleston, S.C. Generalate and motherhouse, 424 Fort Johnson Rd., P. O. Box 12410, Charleston, SC 29422. Education, campus ministry, social services.

Charity of Quebec, Sisters of (Grey Nuns), S.C.Q.: Founded 1849, at Quebec; in U.S., 1890. General motherhouse, 2655 Le Pelletier St., Beauport, Quebec GIC 3X7, Canada; U.S. address, 359 Summer St., New Bedford, MA 02740. Social work.

Charity of St. Elizabeth, Sisters of (Convent Station, N.J.), S.C.: Founded 1859, at Newark, N. J. General motherhouse, P.O. Box 476, Convent Station, NJ 07961. Education, pastoral ministry, social services.

Charity of St. Hyacinthe, Sisters of (Grey Nuns), S.C.S.H.: Founded 1840, at St. Hyacinthe, Canada; in U.S., 1878. General motherhouse, 16470 Avenue Bourdages, SUD, St. Hyacinthe, Quebec J2T 4J8, Canada; U.S. regional house, 98 Campus Ave., Lewiston, ME 04240.

Charity of St. Joan Antida, Sisters of, S.C.S.J.A.: Founded 1799, in France; in U.S., 1932. General motherhouse, Rome, Italy; U.S. provincial house, 8560 N. 76th Pl., Milwaukee, WI 53223.

Charity of St. Louis, Sisters of, S.C.S.L.: Founded 1803, in France; in U.S., 1910. Generalate, Rome, Italy; U.S. provincialate, 4907 S. Catherine St., Plattsburgh, NY 12901.

Charity of St. Vincent de Paul, Daughters of, D.C.: Founded 1633, in France; in U.S. 1809, at Emmitsburg, Md., by St. Elizabeth Ann Seton. General motherhouse, Paris, France. U.S. provinces: Emmitsburg, MD 21727; 7800 Natural Bridge Rd., St. Louis, MO 63121; 9400 New Harmony Rd., Evansville, IN 47712; 96 Menands Rd., Albany, NY 12204; 26000 Altamont Rd., Los Altos Hills, CA 94022.

Charity of St. Vincent de Paul, Sisters of, V.Z.: Founded 1845, in Croatia; in U.S., 1955. General motherhouse, Zagreb, Croatia; U.S. foundation, 171 Knox Ave., West Seneca, NY 14224.

Charity of St. Vincent de Paul, Sisters of, Halifax, S.C.: Founded 1856, at Halifax, N. S., from Emmitsburg foundation. Generalate, Mt. St. Vincent, Halifax, N. S., Canada. U.S. addresses: Commonwealth of Massachusetts, 125 Oakland St., Wellesley Hills, MA 02181; Boston Province, 26 Phipps St., Quincy, MA 02169; New York Province, 84-32 63rd Ave., Middle Village, NY 11379. Educational, hospital, social work.

Charity of St. Vincent de Paul, Sisters of, New York, S.C.: Founded 1817, from Emmitsburg foundation. General motherhouse, Mt. St. Vincent on Hudson, 6301 Riverdale Ave., Bronx, NY 10471. Educational, hospital work.

Charity of the Blessed Virgin Mary, Sisters of, B.V.M.: Founded 1833, in U.S. by Mary Frances Clarke. General motherhouse, Mt. Carmel, 1100 Carmel Dr., Dubuque, IA 52001. Education, pastoral ministry, social services.

Charity of the Immaculate Conception of Ivrea, Sisters of, S.C.I.C.: Founded 18th century, in Italy; in U.S., 1961. General motherhouse, Rome, Italy; U.S. address, Immaculate Virgin of Miracles Convent, R.D. 2, Box 348, Mt. Pleasant, PA 15666.

Charity of the Incarnate Word, Congregation of the Sisters of, C.C.V.I.: Founded 1869, at San Antonio, Tex., by Bishop C. M. Dubuis. Generalate, 4709 Broadway, San Antonio, TX 78209.

Charity of the Incarnate Word, Congregation of the Sisters of (Houston, Tex.), C.C.V.I.: Founded 1866, in U.S., by Bishop C. M. Dubuis. General motherhouse, P.O. Box 230969, Houston, TX 77223. Educational, hospital, social work.

Charity of the Sacred Heart, Daughters of, F.C.S.C.J.: Founded 1823, at La Salle de Vihiers,

France; in U.S., 1905. General motherhouse, La Salle de Vihiers, France; U.S. address, Sacred Heart Province, Grove St., P.O. Box 642, Littleton, NH 03561.

Charles Borromeo, Missionary Sisters of St. (Scalabrini Srs.): Founded 1895, in Italy; in U.S., 1941. American novitiate, 1414 N. 37th Ave., Melrose Park, IL 60601.

Child Jesus, Sisters of the Poor, P.C.J.: Founded 1844, at Aix-la-Chapelle, Germany; in U.S., 1924. General motherhouse, Simpelveld, Netherlands, American provincialate, 4567 Olentangy River Rd., Columbus, OH 43214.

Chretienne, sisters of Ste., S.S.CH.: Founded 1807, in France; in U.S., 1903. General motherhouse, Metz, France; U.S. provincial house, 297 Arnold St., Wrentham, MA 02093. Educational, hospital, mission work.

Christ the King, Missionary Sisters of, M.S.C.K.: Founded 1959 in Poland; in U.S., 1978. General motherhouse, Poznan, Poland; U.S. address, 3030 18 Mile Rd., Sterling Heights, MI 48314.

Christ the King, Sister Servants of, S.S.C.K.: Founded 1936, in U.S. General motherhouse, Loretto Convent, Mt. Calvary, WI 53057. Social services.

Christ the King, Sisters of, S.C.K.: Hermitage of Christ the King, 6501 Orchard Station Rd., Sebastopol, CA 95472.

Christian Doctrine, Sisters of Our Lady of, R.C.D.: Founded 1910, in New York. Central office, 23 Haskell Ave., Suffern, NY 10901.

Christian Education, Religious of, R.C.E.: Founded 1817, in France; in U.S., 1905. General motherhouse, France; U.S. provincial residence, 14 Bailey Rd., Arlington, MA 02174.

Cistercian Nuns, O. Cist.: Headquarters, Rome, Italy; U.S. address, Valley of Our Lady Monastery, E. 11096 Yanke Dr., Prairie du Sac, WI 53578.

Cistercian Nuns of the Strict Observance, Order of, O.C.S.O.: Founded 1125, in France, by St. Stephen Harding; in U.S., 1949. U.S. addresses: Mt. St. Mary's Abbey, 300 Arnold St., Wrentham, MA 02093; Santa Rita Abbey, HC1, Box 929, Sonoita, AZ 85637; Our Lady of the Redwoods Abbey, Whitethorn, CA 95589. Our Lady of the Mississippi Abbey, 8400 Abbey Hill Rd., Dubuque, IA 52001; Our Lady of the Angels Monastery, 3365 Monastery Dr., Crozet, VA 22932.

Clare, Sisters of St., O.S.C.: General motherhouse, Dublin, Ireland; U.S. foundation, St. Francis Convent, 226 Santa Clara Dr.,Vista, CA 92083.

Claretian Missionary Sisters (Religious of Mary Immaculate), R.M.I.: Founded 1855, in Cuba; in U.S., 1956. Generalate, Rome, Italy; U.S. address, 9600 W. Atlantic Ave., Delray Beach, FL 33446.

Clergy, Congregation of Our Lady, Help of the, C.L.H.C.: Founded 1961, in U.S. Motherhouse, Maryvale Convent, 2522 June Bug Rd.,Vale, NC 28168.

Clergy, Servants of Our Lady Queen of the, S.R.C.: Founded 1929, in Canada; in U.S., 1934. General motherhouse, 57 Jules A. Brillant, Rimouski, Que. G5L 1X1 Canada. Domestic work.

Colettines: See Franciscan Poor Clare Nuns.

Columban, Missionary Sisters of St., S.S.C.: Founded 1922, in Ireland; in U.S., 1930. General motherhouse, Wicklow, Ireland; U.S. region, 73 Mapleton St., Brighton, MA 02135.

Comboni Missionary Sisters (Missionary Sisters of Verona), C.M.S.: Founded 1872, in Italy; in U.S., 1950. U.S. address, 1307 Lakeside Ave., Richmond, VA 23228.

Consolata Missionary Sisters, M.C.: Founded 1910, in Italy, by Bl. Giuseppe Allamano; in U.S., 1954. General motherhouse, Turin, Italy; U.S. headquarters, 6801 Belmont Rd., Belmont, MI 49306.

Cordi-Marian Missionary Sisters, M.C.M.: Founded 1921, Mexico City; U.S. foundation, 1926. General motherhouse, Mexico. U.S. address, 11624 FM 471, Apt. 402, San Antonio, TX 78253.

Cross, Daughters of the, D.C.: Founded 1640, in France; in U.S., 1855. General motherhouse, 1000 Fairview St., Shreveport, LA 71104. Educational work.

Cross, Daughters of, of Liege, F.C.: Founded 1833, in Liege, Belgium; in U.S., 1958. U.S. address, 165 W. Eaton Ave., Tracy, CA 95376.

Cross, Sisters of the Holy, C.S.C.: Founded 1841, at Le Mans, France, established 1847, in Canada; in U.S., 1881. General motherhouse, St. Laurent, Montreal, Que., Canada; U.S. regional office, 377 Island Pond Rd., Manchester, NH 03109. Educational work.

Cross, Sisters of the Holy, Congregation of, C.S.C.: Founded 1841, at Le Mans, France; in U.S., 1843. General motherhouse, Saint Mary's, Notre Dame, IN 46556. Education, health care, social services, pastoral ministry.

Cross and Passion, Sisters of the (Passionist Sisters), C.P.: Founded 1852; in U.S., 1924. Generalate, Northampton, England; U.S. address: Holy Family Convent, One Wright Lane, N. Kingstown, RI 02852.

Cyril and Methodius, Sisters of Sts., SS.C.M.: Founded 1909, in U.S., by Rev. Matthew Jankola. General motherhouse, Villa Sacred Heart, Danville, PA 17821. Education, care of aged.

Disciples of the Lord Jesus Christ, D.L.J.C.: Founded 1972; canonically erected 1991. Address, P.O. Box 17, Channing, TX 79018.

Divine Compassion, Sisters of, R.D.C.: Founded 1886, in U.S. General motherhouse, 52 N. Broadway, White Plains, NY 10603. Education, other ministries.

Divine Love, Daughters of, D.D.L.: Founded 1969, in Nigeria; in U.S., 1990. General house, Enugu, Nigeria; U.S. regional house, 140 North Ave., Highwood, IL 60040.

Divine Spirit, Congregation of the, C.D.S.: Founded 1956, in U.S., by Archbishop John M. Gannon. Motherhouse, 409 W. 6th St., Erie, PA 16507. Education, social services.

Divine Zeal, Daughters of, F.D.Z.: Founded 1887 in Italy by Bl. Hannibal Maria DiFrancia; in U.S., 1951. Generalate, Rome; U.S. headquarters, Hannibal House Spiritual Center, 1526 Hill Rd., Reading, PA 19602.

Dominicans

Nuns of the Order of Preachers (Dominican Nuns), O.P.: Founded 1206 by St. Dominic at Prouille, France. Cloistered, contemplative. Two branches in the United States:

•Dominican Nuns having perpetual adoration. First

monastery established 1880, in Newark, N.J., from Oullins, France, foundation (1868). Autonomous monasteries:

St. Dominic, 375 13th Ave., Newark, NJ 07103; Corpus Christi, 1230 Lafayette Ave., Bronx, NY 10474; Blessed Sacrament, 29575 Middlebelt Rd., Farmington Hills, MI 48334; Monastery of the Angels, 1977 Carmen Ave., Los Angeles, CA 90068; Corpus Christi, 215 Oak Grove Ave., Menlo Park, CA 94025; Infant Jesus, 1501 Lotus Lane, Lufkin, TX 75901.

• Dominican Nuns devoted to the perpetual Rosary. First monastery established 1891, in Union City, N.J., from Calais, France, foundation (1880). Autonomous monasteries (some also observe perpetual adoration):

Dominican Nuns of Perpetual Rosary, 14th and West Sts., Union City, NJ 07087; 217 N. 68th St., Milwaukee, WI 53213; Perpetual Rosary, 1500 Haddon Ave., Camden, NJ 08103; Our Lady of the Rosary, 335 Doat St., Buffalo, NY 14211; Our Lady of the Rosary, 543 Spingfield Ave., Summit, NJ 07901; Mother of God, 1430 Riverdale St., W. Springfield, MA 01089; Perpetual Rosary, 802 Court St., Syracuse, NY 13208; Immaculate Heart of Mary, 1834 Lititz Pike, Lancaster, PA 17601; Mary the Queen, 1310 W. Church St., Elmira, NY 14905; St. Jude, Marbury, AL 36051; Our Lady of Grace, North Guilford, CT 06437; St. Dominic, 4901 16th St. N.W., Washington, DC 20011.

Dominican Sisters of Charity of the Presentation, O.P.: Founded 1696, in France; in U.S., 1906. General motherhouse, Tours, France; U.S. headquarters, 3012 Elm St., Dighton, MA 02715. Hospital work.

Dominican Sisters of Hope (O.P.): Formed 1995 through merger of Dominican Sisters of the Most Holy Rosary, Newburgh, NY; Dominican Sisters of the Sick Poor, Ossining, NY and Dominican Sisters of St. Catherine of Siena, Fall River, MA. General Offices: 229 N. Highland Ave., Ossining, NY 10562.

Dominican Sisters of Our Lady of the Rosary and of St. Catherine of Siena (Cabra): Founded 1644 in Ireland. General motherhouse, Cabra, Dublin, Ireland. U.S. regional house, 1930 Robert E. Lee Rd., New Orleans, LA 70122.

Dominican Sisters of the Perpetual Rosary (O.P.): 217 N. 68th St., Milwaukee, WI 53213. Cloistered, contemplative.

Dominican Sisters of the Roman Congregation of St. Dominic, O.P.: Founded 1621, in France; in U.S., 1904. General motherhouse, Rome, Italy; U.S. province, 305 Oberlin St., Iowa City, IA 52245. Educational work.

Eucharistic Missionaries of St. Dominic, O.P.: Founded 1927, in Louisiana. General motherhouse, 3801 Canal St., Suite 400, New Orleans, LA 70119. Parish work, social services.

Religious Missionaries of St. Dominic, O.P.: General motherhouse, Rome, Italy. U.S. address (Spanish province), 2237 Waldron Rd., Corpus Christi, TX 78418.

Sisters of St. Dominic, O.P.: Names of congregations are given below, followed by the date of foundation, and location of motherhouse.

St. Catharine of Siena, 1822. 2645 Bardstown Rd., St. Catharine, KY 40061.

St. Mary of the Springs, 1830. 2320 Airport Dr., Columbus, Ohio 43219.

Most Holy Rosary, 1847. Sinsinawa, WI 53824.

Most Holy Name of Jesus, 1850. 1520 Grand Ave., San Rafael, CA 94901.

Holy Cross, 1853. Albany Ave., Amityville, NY 11701.

St. Cecilia, 1860. 801 Dominican Dr., Nashville, TN 37228.

St. Mary, 1860. 580 Broadway, New Orleans, LA 70118.

St. Catherine of Siena, 1862. 5635 Erie St., Racine, WI 53402.

Our Lady of the Sacred Heart, 1873. 1237 W. Monroe St., Springfield, IL 62704.

Our Lady of the Rosary, 1876. Sparkill, NY 10976.

Queen of the Holy Rosary, 1876. P.O. Box 3908, Mission San Jose, CA 94539.

Most Holy Rosary, 1892. 1257 Siena Heights Dr., Adrian, MI 49221.

Our Lady of the Sacred Heart, 1877. 2025 E. Fulton St., Grand Rapids, MI 49503.

St. Dominic, 1878. Blauvelt, NY 10913.

St. Catherine de Ricci, 1880. 750 Ashbourne Rd., Elkins Park, PA 19117.

Sacred Heart of Jesus, 1881. 1 Ryerson Ave., Caldwell, NJ 07006.

Sacred Heart, 1882. 6501 Almeda Rd., Houston, TX 77021.

St. Thomas Aquinas, 1888. 935 Fawcett Ave., Tacoma, WA 98402.

Holy Cross, 1890. P.O. Box 280, Edmonds, WA 98020.

St. Rose of Lima (Servants of Relief for Incurable Cancer) 1896. Hawthorne, NY 10532.

Dominican Sisters of Great Bend, 1902. 3600 Broadway, Great Bend, KS 67530.

St. Catherine of Siena, 1911. Box 1288, Kenosha, WI 53141.

St. Rose of Lima, 1923. 775 Drahner Rd., Box 167, Oxford, MI 48371.

Immaculate Conception, 1929. 9000 W. 81st St., Justice, IL 60458.

Immaculate Heart of Mary, 1929. 1230 W. Market St., Akron, Ohio 44313.

Dominican Sisters of Oakford (St. Catherine of Siena), 1889. Motherhouse, Oakford, Natal, South Africa. U.S. regional house, 1965. 1855 Miramonte Ave., Mountain View, CA 94040.

(End, Listing of Dominicans)

Dorothy, Institute of the Sisters of St., S.S.D.: Founded 1834, in Italy; by St. Paola Frassinetti; in U.S., 1911. General motherhouse, Rome, Italy; U.S. provincialate, Mt. St. Joseph, 13 Monkeywrench Lane, Bristol, RI 02809.

Eucharist, Religious of the, R.E.: Founded 1857, in Belgium; in U.S., 1900. General motherhouse, Belgium; U.S. foundation, 2907 Ellicott Terr., N.W., Washington, DC 20008.

Family, Congregation of the Sisters of the Holy, S.S.F.: Founded 1842, in Louisiana, by Henriette Delille and Juliette Gaudin. General motherhouse, 6901 Chef Menteur Hway., New Orleans, LA 70126. Educational, hospital work.

Family, Little Sisters of the Holy, P.S.S.F.:

Founded 1880, in Canada; in U.S., 1900. General motherhouse, Sherbrooke, Que., Canada. U.S. novitiate, 285 Andover St., Lowell, MA 01852.

Family, Sisters of the Holy, S.H.F.: Founded 1872, in U.S. General motherhouse, P.O. Box 3248, Mission San Jose, CA 94539. Educational, social work.

Family of Nazareth, Sisters of the Holy, C.S.F.N.: Founded 1875, in Italy; in U.S., 1885. General motherhouse, Rome, Italy. U.S. provinces: Sacred Heart, 310 N. River Rd., Des Plaines, IL 60016; Immaculate Conception BVM, 4001 Grant Ave., Torresdale, Philadelphia, PA 19114; St. Joseph, 285 Bellevue Rd., Pittsburgh, PA 15229; Immaculate Heart of Mary, Marian Heights, 1428 Monroe Turnpike, Monroe, CT 06468; Bl. Frances Siedliska Provincialate, 1814 Egyptian Way, Box 530959, Grand Prairie, TX 75053.

Filippini, Religious Teachers, M.P.F.: Founded 1692, in Italy; in U.S., 1910. General motherhouse, Rome, Italy; U.S. provinces: St. Lucy Filippini Province, Villa Walsh, Morristown, NJ 07960; Queen of Apostles Province, 474 East Rd., Bristol, CT 06010. Educational work.

Francis de Sales, Oblate Sisters of St., O.S.F.S.: Founded 1866, in France; in U.S., 1951. General motherhouse, Troyes, France; U.S. headquarters, Villa Aviat Convent, Childs, MD 21916. Educational, social work.

Franciscans

Bernardine Sisters of the Third Order of St. Francis, O.S.F.: Founded 1457, at Cracow, Poland; in U.S., 1894. Generalate, 403 Allendale Rd., King of Prussia, PA 19406. Educational, hospital, social work.

Capuchin Poor Clares (Madres Clarisas Capuchinas): U.S. establishment, 1981, Amarillo diocese. Convent of the Blessed Sacrament and Our Lady of Guadalupe, 4201 N.E. 18th St., Amarillo, TX 79107. Cloistered.

Congregation of the Servants of the Holy Child Jesus of the Third Order Regular of St. Francis, O.S.F.: Founded 1855, in Germany; in U.S., 1929. General motherhouse, Wuerzburg, Germany; American motherhouse, Villa Maria, P.O. Box 708, North Plainfield, NJ 07061.

Congregation of the Third Order of St. Francis of Mary Immaculate, O.S.F.: Founded 1865, in U.S., by Fr. Pamphilus da Magliano, O.F.M. General motherhouse, 520 Plainfield Ave., Joliet, IL 60435. Educational and pastoral work.

Daughters of St. Francis of Assisi, D.S.F.: Founded 1894, in Hungary; in U.S., 1946. Provincial motherhouse, 507 N. Prairie St., Lacon, IL 61540. Nursing, CCD work.

Eucharistic Franciscan Missionary Sisters, E.F.M.S.: Founded 1943, in Mexico. Motherhouse, 943 S. Soto St., Los Angeles, CA 90023.

Felician Sisters (Congregation of the Sisters of St. Felix), C.S.S.F.: Founded 1855, in Poland by Bl. Mary Angela Truszkowska; in U.S., 1874. General motherhouse, Rome, Italy. U.S. provinces: 36800 Schoolcraft Rd., Livonia, MI 48150; 600 Doat St., Buffalo, NY 14211; 3800 W. Peterson Ave., Chicago, IL 60659; 260 South Main St., Lodi, NJ 07644; 1500 Woodcrest Ave., Coraopolis, PA 15108; 1315

Enfield St., Enfield, CT 06082; 4210 Meadowlark Lane, S.E., Rio Rancho, NM 87124.

Franciscan Handmaids of the Most Pure Heart of Mary, F.H.M.: Founded 1916, in U.S. General motherhouse, 15 W. 124th St., New York, NY 10027. Educational, social work.

Franciscan Hospitaller Sisters of the Immaculate Conception, F.H.I.C.: Founded 1876, in Portugal; in U.S., 1960. General motherhouse, Lisbon, Portugal; U.S. novitiate, 300 S. 17th St., San Jose, CA 95112.

Franciscan Missionaries of Mary, F.M.M.: Founded 1877, in India; in U.S., 1904. General motherhouse, Rome, Italy; U.S. provincialate, 3305 Wallace Ave., Bronx, NY 10467. Mission work.

Franciscan Missionaries of Our Lady, O.S.F.: Founded 1854, at Calais, France; in U.S., 1913. General motherhouse, Desvres, France; U.S. provincial house, 4200 Essen Lane, Baton Rouge, LA 70809. Hospital work.

Franciscan Missionaries of St. Joseph (Mill Hill Sisters), F.M.S.J.: Founded 1883, at Rochdale, Lancashire, England; in U.S., 1952. Generalate, Manchester, England; U.S. headquarters, Franciscan House, 1006 Madison Ave., Albany, NY 12208.

Franciscan Missionary Sisters for Africa, O.S.F.: American foundation, 1953. Generalate, Ireland; U.S. headquarters, 172 Foster St., Brighton, MA 02135.

Franciscan Missionary Sisters of Assisi, F.M.S.A.: First foundation in U.S., 1961. General motherhouse, Assisi, Italy; U.S. address, St. Francis Convent, 1039 Northampton St., Holyoke, MA 01040.

Franciscan Missionary Sisters of Our Lady of Sorrows, O.S.F.: Founded 1939, in China, by Bishop Rafael Palazzi, O.F.M.; in U.S., 1949. U.S. address, 3600 S.W. 170th Ave., Beaverton, OR 97006. Educational, social, domestic, retreat and foreign mission work.

Franciscan Missionary Sisters of the Divine Child, F.M.D.C.: Founded 1927, at Buffalo, NY, by Bishop William Turner. General motherhouse, 6380 Main St., Williamsville, NY 14221. Educational, social work.

Franciscan Missionary Sisters of the Infant Jesus, F.M.I.J.: Founded 1879, in Italy; in U.S., 1961. Generalate, Rome, Italy. U.S. provincialate, 1215 Kresson Rd., Cherry Hill, NJ 08003.

Franciscan Missionary Sisters of the Sacred Heart, F.M.S.C.: Founded 1860, in Italy; in U.S., 1865. Generalate, Rome, Italy; U.S. provincialate, 250 South St., Peekskill, NY 10566. Educational and social welfare apostolates.

Franciscan Poor Clare Nuns (Poor Clares, Order of St. Clare, Poor Clares of St. Colette), P.C., O.S.C., P.C.C.: Founded 1212, at Assisi, Italy, by St. Francis of Assisi; in U.S., 1875. Proto-monastery, Assisi, Italy. Addresses of autonomous motherhouses in U.S. are listed below.

3626 N. 65th Ave., Omaha, NE 68104; 720 Henry Clay Ave., New Orleans, LA 70118; 6825 Nurrenbern Rd., Evansville, IN 47712; 1310 Dellwood Ave., Memphis, TN 38127; 920 Centre St., Jamaica Plain, MA 02130; 201 Crosswicks St., Bordentown, NJ 08505; 1271 Langhorne-Newtown Rd., Langhorne, PA 19047; 4419 N. Hawthorne St., Spokane, WA

99205; 142 Hollywood Ave., Bronx, NY 10465; 421 S. 4th St., Sauk Rapids, MN 56379; 8650 Russell Ave. S., Minneapolis, MN 55431; 3501 Rocky River Dr., Cleveland, OH 44111; 1671 Pleasant Valley Rd., Aptos, CA 95001; 2111 S. Main St., Rockford, IL 61102; 215 E. Los Olivos St., Santa Barbara, CA 93105; 460 River Rd., W. Andover, MA 01810; 809 E. 19th St., Roswell, NM 88201; 28210 Natoma Rd., Los Altos Hills, CA 94022; 1916 N. Pleasantville Dr., Greenville, SC 29609; 28 Harpersville Rd., Newport News, VA 23601; 1175 N. County Rd. 300 W., Kokomo, IN 46901; 3900 Sherwood Blvd., Delray Beach, FL 33445; 200 Marycrest Dr., St. Louis, MO 63129; 6029 Estero Blvd., Fort Myers Beach, FL 33931; 9300 Hwy 105, Brenham, TX 77833.

Franciscan Sisters, Daughters of the Sacred Hearts of Jesus and Mary, O.S.F.: Founded 1860, in Germany; in U.S., 1872. Generalate, Rome, Italy; U.S. motherhouse, P.O. Box 667, Wheaton, IL 60189. Educational, hospital, foreign mission, social work.

Franciscan Sisters Daughters of Mercy, F.H.M.: Founded 1856, in Spain; in U.S., 1962. General motherhouse, Palma de Mallorca, Spain; U.S. address, 612 N. 3rd St., Waco, TX 76701.

Franciscan Sisters of Allegany, O.S.F.: Founded 1859, at Allegany, N.Y., by Fr. Pamphilus da Magliano, O.F.M. General motherhouse Allegany, NY 14706. Educational, hospital, foreign mission work.

Franciscan Sisters of Baltimore, O.S.F.: Founded 1868, in England; in U.S., 1881. General motherhouse, 3725 Ellerslie Ave., Baltimore, MD 21218. Educational work; social services.

Franciscan Sisters of Chicago, O.S.F.: Founded 1894, in U.S., by Mother Mary Therese (Josephine Dudzik). General motherhouse, 14700 Main St., Lemont, IL 60439. Educational work, social services.

Franciscan Sisters of Christian Charity, O.S.F.: Founded 1869, in U.S. Motherhouse, Holy Family Convent, 2409 S. Alverno Rd., Manitowoc, WI 54220. Educational, hospital work.

Franciscan Sisters of Little Falls, Minn., O.S.F.: Founded 1891, in U.S. General motherhouse, Little Falls, MN 56345. Health, education, social services, pastoral ministry, mission work.

Franciscan Sisters of Mary, F.S.M.: Established, 1987, through unification of the Sisters of St. Mary of the Third Order of St. Francis (founded 1872, St. Louis) and the Sisters of St. Francis of Maryville, Mo. (founded 1894). Address of general superior: 1100 Bellevue Ave., St. Louis, MO 63117. Health care, social services.

Franciscan Sisters of Mary Immaculate of the Third Order of St. Francis of Assisi, F.M.I.: Founded 16th century, in Switzerland; in U.S., 1932. General motherhouse, Bogota, Colombia; U.S. provincial house, 4301 N.E. 18th Ave., Amarillo, TX 79107. Education.

Franciscan Sisters of Our Lady of Perpetual Help, O.S.F.: Founded 1901, in U.S., from Joliet, Ill., foundation. General motherhouse, 201 Brotherton Lane, St. Louis, MO 63135. Educational, hospital work.

Franciscan Sisters of Peace, F.S.P.: Established 1986, in U.S., as archdiocesan community, from

Franciscan Missionary Sisters of the Sacred Heart. Congregation center, 20 Ridge St., Haverstraw, NY 10927.

Franciscan Sisters of Ringwood, F.S.R.: Founded 1927, at Passaic, New Jersey. General motherhouse, Mt. St. Francis, Ringwood, NJ 07456. Educational work.

Franciscan Sisters of St. Elizabeth, F.S.S.E.: Founded 1866, at Naples, Italy, by Bl. Ludovico of Casorio; in U.S., 1919. General motherhouse, Rome; U.S. delegate house, 499 Park Rd., Parsippany, NJ 07054. Educational work, social services.

Franciscan Sisters of St. Joseph, F.S.S.J.: Founded 1897, in U.S. General motherhouse, 5286 S. Park Ave., Hamburg, NY 14075. Educational, hospital work.

Franciscan Sisters of St. Joseph (of Mexico): U.S. foundation, St. Paul College, 3015 4th St. N.E., Washington, DC 20017.

Franciscan Sisters of the Atonement, Third Order Regular of St. Francis (Graymoor Sisters), S.A.: Founded 1898, in U.S., as Anglican community; entered Church, 1909. General motherhouse, Graymoor, Garrison P.O., NY 10524. Mission work.

Franciscan Sisters of St. Paul, Minn., O.S.F.: Founded 1863, at Neuwied, Germany (Franciscan Sisters of the Blessed Virgin Mary of the Holy Angels); in U.S., 1923. General motherhouse, Rhine, Germany; U.S. motherhouse, 1388 Prior Ave. S., St. Paul, MN 55116. Educational, hospital, social work.

Franciscan Sisters of the Immaculate Conception, O.S.F.: Founded in Germany; in U.S., 1928. General motherhouse, Kloster, Bonlanden, Germany; U.S. province, 291 W. North St., Buffalo, NY 14201.

Franciscan Sisters of the Immaculate Conception, O.S.F.: Founded 1874, in Mexico; in U.S., 1926. U.S. provincial house, 11306 Laurel Canyon Blvd., San Fernando, CA 91340.

Franciscan Sisters of the Immaculate Conception, Missionary, M.F.I.C.: Founded 1873, in U.S. General motherhouse, Rome, Italy; U.S. address, 790 Centre St., Newton, MA 02158. Educational work.

Franciscan Sisters of the Immaculate Conception and St. Joseph for the Dying, O.S.F.: Founded 1919, in U.S. General motherhouse, 1249 Joselyn Canyon Rd., Monterey, CA 93940.

Franciscan Sisters of the Poor, S.F.P.: Founded 1845, at Aachen, Germany, by Bl. Frances Schervier; in U.S., 1858. Congregational office, 133 Remsen St., Brooklyn, NY 11201. Hospital, social work and foreign missions.

Franciscan Sisters of the Sacred Heart, O.S.F.: Founded 1866, in Germany; in U.S., 1876. General motherhouse, St. Francis Woods, 9201 W. St. Francis Rd., Frankfort, IL 60423. Education, health care, other service ministries.

Hospital Sisters of the Third Order of St. Francis, O.S.F.: Founded 1844, in Germany; in U.S., 1875. General motherhouse, Muenster, Germany; U.S. motherhouse, Box 19431, Springfield, IL 62794. Hospital work.

Institute of the Franciscan Sisters of the Eucharist, F.S.E.: Founded 1973. Motherhouse, 405 Allen Ave., Meriden, CT 06450.

Little Franciscans of Mary, P.F.M.: Founded 1889, in U.S. General motherhouse, Baie St. Paul, Que.,

Canada. U.S. region, 2 Dupont St., Worcester, MA 01604. Educational, hospital, social work.

Missionary Sisters of the Immaculate Conception of the Mother of God, S.M.I.C.: Founded 1910, in Brazil; in U.S., 1922, U.S. provincialate, P.O. Box 3026, Paterson, NJ 07509. Mission, educational, health work, social services.

Mothers of the Helpless, M.D.: Founded 1873, in Spain; in U.S., 1916. General motherhouse, Valencia, Spain; U.S. address, Sacred Heart Residence, 432 W. 20th St., New York, NY 10011.

Poor Clares of Perpetual Adoration, P.C.P.A.: Founded 1854, at Paris, France; in U.S., 1921, at Cleveland, Ohio. U.S. monasteries: 4200 N. Market Ave., Canton, OH 44714; 2311 Stockham Lane, Portsmouth, OH 45662; 4108 Euclid Ave., Cleveland, OH 44103; 3900 13th St. N.E., Washington, DC 20017; 5817 Old Leeds Rd., Birmingham, AL 35210. Contemplative, cloistered, perpetual adoration.

St. Francis Mission Community, O.S.F.: Autonomous province of Franciscan Sisters of Mary Immaculate. Address: 4305 54th St., Lubbock, TX 79413.

School Sisters of St. Francis, O.S.F.: Founded 1874, in U.S. General motherhouse, 1501 S. Layton Blvd., Milwaukee, WI 53215.

School Sisters of St. Francis, (Pittsburgh, Pa.), O.S.F.: Established 1913, in U.S. Motherhouse, Mt. Assisi Convent, 934 Forest Ave., Pittsburgh, PA 15202. Education, health care services and related ministries.

School Sisters of the Third Order of St. Francis (Bethlehem, Pa.), O.S.F.: Founded in Austria, 1843; in U.S., 1913. General motherhouse, Rome, Italy; U.S. province, 395 Bridle Path Rd., Bethlehem, PA 18017. Educational, mission work.

School Sisters of the Third Order of St. Francis (Panhandle, Tex.), O.S.F.: Established 1931, in U.S., from Vienna, Austria, foundation (1845). General motherhouse, Vienna, Austria; U.S. center and novitiate, P.O. Box 906, Panhandle, TX 79068. Educational, social work.

Sisters of Mercy of the Holy Cross, S.C.S.C.: Founded 1856, in Switzerland; in U.S. 1912. General motherhouse, Ingenbohl, Switzerland; U.S. provincial residence, 700 E. Riverside Ave., Merrill, WI 54452.

Sisters of Our Lady of Mercy (Mercedarians), S.O.L.M.: General motherhouse, Rome, Italy; U.S. addresses: Most Precious Blood, 133 27th Ave., Brooklyn, NY 11214; St. Edward School, Pine Hill, NJ 08021.

Sisters of St. Elizabeth, S.S.E.: Founded 1931, at Milwaukee, Wis. Address, 2005 Division St., Manitowoc, WI 53005.

Sisters of St. Francis (Clinton, Iowa), O.S.F.: Founded 1868, in U.S. General motherhouse, 400 N. Bluff Blvd., Clinton, IA 57232. Educational, hospital, social work.

Sisters of St. Francis (Millvale, Pa.), O.S.F.: Founded 1865, Pittsburgh. General motherhouse, 146 Hawthorne Rd., Millvale P.O., Pittsburgh, PA 15209. Educational, hospital work.

Sisters of St. Francis (Hastings-on-Hudson), O.S.F.: Founded 1893, in New York. General motherhouse, 49 Jackson Ave., Hastings-on-Hudson, NY 10706. Education, parish ministry, social services.

Sisters of St. Francis of Assisi, O.S.F.: Founded 1849, in U.S. General motherhouse, 3221 S. Lake Dr., Milwaukee, WI 53207. Education, other ministries.

Sisters of St. Francis of Christ the King, O.S.F.: Founded 1864, in Austria; in U.S., 1909. General motherhouse, Rome, Italy; U.S. provincial house, 13900 Main St., Lemont, IL 60439. Educational work, home for aged.

Sisters of St. Francis of Penance and Christian Charity, O.S.F.: Founded 1835, in Holland; in U.S., 1874. General motherhouse, Rome, Italy. U.S. provinces: 4421 Lower River Rd., Stella Niagara, NY 14144; 2851 W. 52nd Ave., Denver, CO 80221; 3910 Bret Harte Dr., P.O. Box 1028, Redwood City, CA 94064.

Sisters of St. Francis of Philadelphia, O.S.F.: Founded 1855, at Philadelphia, by Mother Mary Francis Bachmann and St. John N. Neumann. General motherhouse, Convent of Our Lady of the Angels, Aston, PA 19014. Education, health care, social services.

Sisters of St. Francis of Savannah, Mo., O.S.F.: Founded 1850, in Austria; in U.S., 1922. Provincial house, La Verna Heights, Box 488, 104 E. Park, Savannah, MO 64485. Educational, hospital work.

Sisters of St. Francis of the Congregation of Our Lady of Lourdes, O.S.F.: Founded 1916, in U.S. General motherhouse, 6832 Convent Blvd., Sylvania, OH 43560. Education, health care, social services, pastoral ministry.

Sisters of St. Francis of the Holy Cross, O.S.F.: Founded 1881, in U.S., by Rev. Edward Daems, O.S.C. General motherhouse, 3025 Bay Settlement Rd., Green Bay, WI 54301. Educational, nursing work, pastoral ministry, foreign missions.

Sisters of St. Francis of the Holy Eucharist, O.S.F.: Founded 1378, in Switzerland; in U.S., 1893. General motherhouse, 2100 N. Noland Rd., Independence, MO 64050. Education, health care, social services, foreign missions.

Sisters of St. Francis of the Holy Family, O.S.F.: U.S. foundation, 1875. Motherhouse, Mt. St. Francis, 3390 Windsor Ave., Dubuque, IA 52001. Varied apostolates.

Sisters of St. Francis of the Immaculate Conception, O.S.F.: Founded 1890, in U.S. General motherhouse, 2408 W. Heading Ave., Peoria, IL 61604. Education, care of aging, pastoral ministry.

Sisters of St. Francis of the Immaculate Heart of Mary, O.S.F.: Founded 1241, in Bavaria; in U.S., 1913. General motherhouse, Rome, Italy; U.S. motherhouse, Hankinson, ND 58041. Education, social services.

Sisters of St. Francis of the Martyr St. George, O.S.F.: Founded 1859, in Germany; in U.S., 1923. General motherhouse, Thuine, Germany; U.S. provincial house, St. Francis Convent, 2120 Central Ave., Alton, IL 62002. Education, social services, foreign mission work.

Sisters of St. Francis of the Perpetual Adoration, O.S.F.: Founded 1863, in Germany; in U.S., 1875. General motherhouse, Olpe, Germany. U.S.

provinces: Box 766, Mishawaka, IN 46544; 7665 Assisi Heights, Colorado Springs, CO 80919.

Sisters of St. Francis of the Providence of God, O.S.F.: Founded 1922, in U.S., by Msgr. M. L. Krusas. General motherhouse, 3603 McRoberts Rd., Pittsburgh, PA 15234. Education, varied apostolates.

Sisters of St. Francis of the Third Order Regular, O.S.F.: Founded 1861, at Buffalo, N.Y., from Philadelphia foundation. General motherhouse, 400 Mill St., Williamsville, NY 14221. Educational, hospital work.

Sisters of St. Joseph of the Third Order of St. Francis, S.S.J.: Founded 1901, in U.S. Administrative office, 1300 Maria Dr., Stevens Pt., WI 54481. Education, health care, social services.

Sisters of the Infant Jesus, I.J.: Founded 1662, at Rouen, France; in U.S., 1950. Motherhouse, Paris, France. Generalate, Rome, Italy. U.S. address: 20 Reiner St., Colma, CA 94014.

Sisters of the Sorrowful Mother (Third Order of St. Francis), S.S.M.: Founded 1883, in Italy; in U.S., 1889. General motherhouse, Rome, Italy. U.S. address: 17600 E. 51st St. S., Broken Arrow, OK 74012. Educational, hospital work.

Sisters of the Third Franciscan Order, O.S.F.: Founded 1860, at Syracuse, N.Y. Generalate offices, 2500 Grant Blvd., Syracuse, NY 13208.

Sisters of the Third Order of St. Francis, O.S.F.: Founded 1877, in U.S., by Bishop John L. Spalding. Motherhouse, St. Francis Lane, E. Peoria, IL 61611. Hospital work.

Sisters of the Third Order of St. Francis (Oldenburg, Ind.), O.S.F.: Founded 1851, in U.S. General motherhouse, Convent of the Immaculate Conception, Oldenburg, IN 47036. Education, social services, pastoral ministry, foreign missions.

Sisters of the Third Order of St. Francis of Penance and Charity, O.S.F.: Founded 1869, in U.S., by Rev. Joseph Bihn. Motherhouse, St. Francis Ave., Tiffin, OH 44883. Education, social services.

Sisters of the Third Order of St. Francis of the Perpetual Adoration, F.S.P.A.: Founded 1849, in U.S. Generalate, 912 Market St., La Crosse, WI 54601. Education, health care.

Sisters of the Third Order Regular of St. Francis of the Congregation of Our Lady of Lourdes, O.S.F.: Founded 1877, in U.S. General motherhouse, Assisi Heights, Rochester, MN 55901. Education, health care, social services.

(End, Listing of Franciscans)

Good Shepherd Sisters (Servants of the Immaculate Heart of Mary), S.C.I.M.: Founded 1850, in Canada; in U.S., 1882. General motherhouse, Quebec, Canada; Provincial House, Bay View, 313 Seaside Ave., Saco, Maine 04072. Educational, social work.

Good Shepherd, Sisters of Our Lady of Charity of the, R.G.S.: Founded 1835, in France by St. Mary Euphrasia Pelletier; in U.S., 1843. Generalate, Rome, Italy. U.S. provinces: 2849 Fischer Pl., Cincinnati, OH 45211; 82-31 Doncaster Pl., Jamaica, NY 11432; 504 Hexton Hill Rd., Silver Spring, MD 20904; 7654 Natural Bridge Rd., St. Louis, MO 63121; 5100 Hodgson Rd., St. Paul, MN 55112. Active and contemplative (Contemplative Sisters of the Good Shepherd, C.G.S.).

Graymoor Sisters: See Franciscan Sisters of the Atonement.

Grey Nuns of the Sacred Heart, G.N.S.H.: Founded 1921, in U.S. General motherhouse, 1750 Quarry Rd., Yardley, PA 19067.

Guadalupan Missionaries of the Holy Spirit, M.G.Sp.S.: Founded 1930 in Mexico by Rev. Felix de Jesus Rougier, M.Sp.S. General motherhouse, Mexico; U.S. delegation: 2483 S.W. 4th St. Miami, FL 33135.

Guardian Angel, Sisters of the, S.A.C.: Founded 1839, in France. General motherhouse, Madrid, Spain; U.S. foundation, 4529 New York St., Los Angeles, CA 90022.

Handmaids of Mary Immaculate, A.M.I.: Founded 1952 in Helena, Mont. Address: Mountain View Rd., Washington, NJ 07882.

Handmaids of the Holy Child Jesus, Congregation of, H.H.C.J.: Founded 1931 in Nigeria. General motherhouse, Nigeria. U.S. headquarters, 1707 Bryant Ave. N., Minneapolis, MN 55411.

Handmaids of the Precious Blood, Congregation of, H.P.B.: Founded 1947, at Jemez Springs, N. Mex. Motherhouse and novitiate, Cor Jesu Monastery, P.O. Box 90, Jemez Springs, NM 87025.

Helpers, Society of, H.H.S.: Founded 1856, in France; in U.S., 1892. General motherhouse, Paris, France; American province, 303 W. Barry Ave., Chicago, IL 60657.

Hermanas Catequistas Guadalupanas, H.C.G.: Founded 1923, in Mexico; in U.S., 1950. General motherhouse, Mexico; U.S. addresses: 4110 S. Flores, San Antonio, TX 78214; 115 Arlington Ct., San Antonio, TX 78210.

Hermanas Josefinas, H.J.: General motherhouse, Mexico; U.S. foundation, Assumption Seminary, 2600 W. Woodlawn Ave., P.O. Box 28240, San Antonio, TX 78284. Domestic work.

Holy Child Jesus, Society of the, S.H.C.J.: Founded 1846, in England; in U.S., 1862. General motherhouse, Rome, Italy. U.S. province: 460 Shadeland Ave., Drexel Hill, PA 19026.

Holy Faith, Congregation of the Sisters of the, C.H.F.: Founded 1856, in Ireland; in U.S., 1953. General motherhouse, Dublin, Ireland; U.S. province, 12322 S. Paramount Blvd., P.O. Box 2085, Downey, CA 90242.

Holy Heart of Mary, Servants of the, S.S.C.M.: Founded 1860, in France; in U.S., 1889. General motherhouse, Montreal, Que., Canada; U.S. province, 145 S. 4th Ave., Kankakee, IL 60901. Educational, hospital, social work.

Holy Names of Jesus and Mary, Sisters of the, S.N.J.M.: Founded 1843, in Canada by Bl. Marie Rose Durocher; in U.S., 1859. Generalate, Longueuil Que., Canada. U.S. addresses: Oregon Province, Box 25, Marylhurst, OR 97036; California Province, P.O. Box 907, Los Gatos, CA 9503; New York Province, 1061 New Scotland Rd., Albany, NY 12208; Washington Province, 2911 W. Ft. Wright Dr., Spokane, WA 99204.

Holy Spirit, Community of the, C.H.S.: Founded 1970 in San Diego, Calif. Address: 6151 Rancho Mission Rd., No. 205, San Diego, CA 95108.

Holy Spirit, Daughters of the, D.H.S.: Founded 1706, in France; in U.S., 1902. Generalate, Bretagne,

France; U.S. motherhouse, 72 Church St., Putnam, CT 06260. Educational work, district nursing; pastoral ministry.

Holy Spirit, Mission Sisters of the, M.S.Sp.: Founded 1932, at Cleveland, Ohio. Motherhouse, 1030 N. River Rd., Saginaw, MI 48603.

Holy Spirit, Missionary Sisters, Servants of the: Founded 1889, in Holland; in U.S., 1901. Generalate, Rome, Italy; U.S. motherhouse, Convent of the Holy Spirit, Techny, IL 60082.

Holy Spirit, Sisters of the, C.S.Sp.: Founded 1890, in Rome, Italy; in U.S. as independent diocesan community, 1929. General motherhouse, 10102 Granger Rd., Garfield Hts., OH 44125. Educational, social, nursing work.

Holy Spirit, Sisters of the, S.H.S.: Founded 1913, in U.S., by Most Rev. J. F. Regis Canevin. General motherhouse, 5246 Clarwin Ave., Ross Township, Pittsburgh, PA 15229. Educational, nursing work; care of aged.

Holy Spirit and Mary Immaculate, Sisters of, S.H.Sp.: Founded 1893, in U.S. Motherhouse, 301 Yucca St., San Antonio, TX 78203. Education, hospital work.

Holy Spirit of Perpetual Adoration, Sister Servants of the: Founded 1896, in Holland; in U.S., 1915. Generalate, Bad Driburg, Germany; U.S. novitiate, 2212 Green St., Philadelphia, PA 19130.

Home Mission Sisters of America (Glenmary Sisters): Founded 1952, in U.S. Glenmary Center, P.O. Box 22264, Owensboro, KY 42302.

Home Visitors of Mary, Sisters, H.V.M.: Founded 1949, in Detroit, Mich. Motherhouse, 356 Arden Park, Detroit, MI 48202.

Humility of Mary, Congregation of, C.H.M.: Founded 1854, in France; in U.S., 1864. U.S. address, Humility of Mary Center, Davenport, IA 52804.

Humility of Mary, Sisters of the, H.M.: Founded 1854, in France; in U.S., 1864. U.S. address, Villa Maria Community Center, Villa Maria, PA 16155.

Immaculate Conception, Little Servant Sisters of the: Founded 1850, in Poland; in U.S., 1926. General motherhouse, Poland; U.S. provincial house, 1000 Cropwell Rd., Cherry Hill, NJ 08003. Education, social services, African missions.

Immaculate Conception, Sisters of the, R.C.M.: Founded 1892, in Spain; in U.S., 1962. General motherhouse, Madrid, Spain; U.S. address, 2230 Franklin, San Francisco, CA 94109.

Immaculate Conception, Sisters of the, C.I.C.: Founded 1874, in U.S. General motherhouse, P.O. Box 50426, New Orleans, LA 70185.

Immaculate Conception of the Blessed Virgin Mary, Sisters of the (Lithuanian): Founded 1918, at Mariampole, Lithuania; in U.S., 1936. U.S. headquarters, Immaculate Conception Convent, 600 Liberty Hwy., Putnam, CT 06260.

Immaculate Heart of Mary, Missionary Sisters, I.C.M.: Founded 1897, in India; in U.S., 1919. Generalate, Rome, Italy; U.S. province, 283 E. 15th St., New York, NY 10003. Educational social, foreign mission work.

Immaculate Heart of Mary, Sisters of the: Founded 1848, in Spain; in U.S., 1878. General motherhouse, Rome, Italy. U.S. province, 4100 Sabino Canyon Rd., Tucson, AZ 85715. Educational work.

Immaculate Heart of Mary, Sisters of the (California Institute of the Most Holy and Immaculate Heart of the B.V.M.), I.H.M.: Founded 1848, in Spain; in U.S., 1871. Generalate, 3431 Waverly Dr., Los Angeles, CA 90027.

Immaculate Heart of Mary, Sisters, Servants of the, I.H.M.: Founded 1845, at Monroe, Mich., by Rev. Louis Florent Gillet. Generalate, 610 W. Elm St., Monroe, MI 48161.

Immaculate Heart of Mary, Sisters, Servants of the, I.H.M.: Founded 1845; established in Scranton, Penn., 1871. General motherhouse, 2300 Adams Ave., Scranton, PA 18509.

Immaculate Heart of Mary, Sisters Servants of the, I.H.M.: Founded 1845; established in West Chester, Penn., 1872. General motherhouse, Villa Maria, Immaculata, PA 19345.

Immaculate Heart of Mary of Wichita, Sisters of, I.H.M.: Established at Wichita, 1979. Address: 605 N. Woodchuck, Wichita, KS 67212.

Incarnate Word, Religious of, C.V.I.: General motherhouse, Mexico City, Mexico. U.S. address, 153 Rainier Ct., Chula Vista, CA 92011.

Incarnate Word and Blessed Sacrament, Congregation of, C.V.I.: Founded 1625, in France; in U.S., 1853. Incarnate Word Convent, 3400 Bradford Pl., Houston, TX 77028.

Incarnate Word and Blessed Sacrament, Congregation of the, I.W.B.S.: Motherhouse, 1101 Northeast Water St., Victoria, TX 77901.

Incarnate Word and Blessed Sacrament, Congregation of the, I.W.B.S.: Motherhouse, 2930 S. Alameda, Corpus Christi, TX 78404.

Incarnate Word and Blessed Sacrament, Sisters of the, S.I.W.: Founded 1625, in France; in U.S. 1853. Motherhouse, 6618 Pearl Rd., Parma Heights, Cleveland, OH 44130.

Infant Jesus, Congregation of the (Nursing Sisters of the Sick Poor), C.I.J.: Founded 1835, in France; in U.S., 1905. General motherhouse, 310 Prospect Park W., Brooklyn, NY 11215.

Jesus, Daughters of, F.I.: Founded 1871, in Spain; in U.S., 1950. General motherhouse, Rome, Italy; U.S. address, 2021 Stuart Ave., Baton Rouge, LA 70808.

Jesus, Daughters of (Filles de Jesus), F.J.: Founded 1834, in France; in U.S., 1904. General motherhouse, Kermaria, Locmine, France; U.S. address, 4209 3rd Ave. S., Great Falls, Mont. 59405. Educational, hospital, parish and social work.

Jesus, Little Sisters of: Founded 1939, in Sahara; in U.S., 1952. General motherhouse, Rome, Italy; U.S. headquarters, 400 N. Streeper St., Baltimore, MD 21224.

Jesus, Servants of, S.J.: Founded 1974, in U.S. Central Office, 9075 Big Lake Rd., P.O. Box 128, Clarkston, MI 48016.

Jesus, Society of the Sisters, Faithful Companions of, F.C.J.: Founded 1820, in France; in U.S., 1896. General motherhouse, Kent, England. U.S. province: St. Philomena Convent, Cory's Lane, Portsmouth, RI 02871.

Jesus and Mary, Little Sisters of, L.S.J.M.: Founded 1974 in U.S. Address: Joseph House, P.O. Box 1755, Salisbury, MD 21801.

Jesus and Mary, Religious of, R.J.M.: Founded

1818, at Lyons, France; in U.S., 1877. General motherhouse, Rome, Italy; U.S. province, 3706 Rhode Island Ave., Mt. Ranier, MD 20712. Educational work.

Jesus Crucified, Congregation of: Founded 1930, in France; in U.S., 1955. General motherhouse, Brou, France; U.S. foundations: Regina Mundi Priory, Devon, PA 19333; St. Paul's Priory, 61 Narragansett, Newport, RI 02840.

Jesus Crucified and the Sorrowful Mother, Poor Sisters of, C.J.C.: Founded 1924, in U.S., by Rev. Alphonsus Maria, C.P. Motherhouse, 261 Thatcher St., Brockton, MA 02402. Education, nursing homes, catechetical centers.

Jesus, Mary and Joseph, Missionaries of, M.J.M.J.: Founded 1942, in Spain; in U.S., 1956. General motherhouse, Madrid, Spain; U.S. regional house, 12940 Up River Rd., Corpus Christi, TX 78410.

Joan of Arc, Sisters of St., S.J.A.: Founded 1914, in U.S., by Rev. Marie Clement Staub, A.A. General motherhouse, 1505, rue de l'Assomption Sillery, Que. G1S 4T3, Canada. U.S. novitiate, 529 Eastern Ave., Fall River, MA 02723. Spiritual and temporal service of priests.

John the Baptist, Sisters of St., C.S.J.B.: Founded 1878, in Italy; in U.S., 1906. General motherhouse, Rome, Italy; U.S. provincialate, 3308 Campbell Dr., Bronx, N.Y. 10465. Education, parish and retreat work; social services.

Joseph, Poor Sisters of St.: Founded 1880, in Argentina. General motherhouse, Muniz, Buenos Aires, Argentina; U.S. addresses, Casa Belen, 305 E. 4th St., Bethlehem, PA 78015; Casa Nazareth, 5321 Spruce St., Reading, PA 19602; St. Gabriel Convent, 4319 Sano St., Alexandria, VA 22312.

Joseph, Religious Daughters of St., F.S.J.: Founded 1875, in Spain. General motherhouse, Spain; U.S. foundation, 319 N. Humphreys Ave., Los Angeles, CA 90022.

Joseph, Religious Hospitallers of St., R.H.S.J.: Founded 1636, in France; in U.S., 1894. Generalate, Montreal, Que., Canada; U.S. address, Holy Family Convent, 100 Mansfield Ave., PO Box 176, Burlington, VT 05401. Hospital work.

Joseph, Servants of St., S.S.J.: Founded 1874, in Spain; in U.S., 1957. General motherhouse, Salamanca, Spain; U.S. address, 203 N. Spring St., Falls Church, VA 22046.

Joseph, Sisters of St., C.S.J. or S.S.J.: Founded 1650, in France; in U.S., 1836, at St. Louis. Independent motherhouses in U.S.:

637 Cambridge St., Brighton, MA 02135; 1515 W. Ogden Ave., La Grange Park, IL, 60525; 480 S. Batavia St., Orange, CA 92668.

St. Joseph Convent, Brentwood, NY 11717; 23 Agassiz Circle, Buffalo, NY 14214; 129 Convent Ave., Rutland, VT 05701; 3430 Rocky River Dr., Cleveland, OH 44111; 1440 W. Division Rd., Tipton, IN 46072; Motherhouse and Novitiate, Nazareth, MI 49074; 1425 Washington St., Watertown, NY 13601; Mt. Gallitzin Academy and Motherhouse, Baden, PA 15005; 5031 W. Ridge Rd., Erie, PA 16502.

4095 East Ave., Rochester, NY 14610; 215 Court St., Concordia, KS 66901; Mont Marie, Holyoke, MA 01040; Pogue Run Rd., Wheeling, WV 26003; 3700 E. Lincoln St., Wichita, KS 67218.

Joseph, Sisters of St. (Lyons, France), C.S.J.: Founded 1650, in France; in U.S., 1906. General motherhouse, Lyons, France; U.S. provincialate, 93 Halifax St., Winslow, ME 04901. Educational, hospital work.

Joseph, Sisters of St., of Peace, C.S.J.P.: Founded 1884, in England; in U.S. 1885. Generalate, 1225 Newton St. N.E., Washington, DC 20017. Educational, hospital, social service work.

Joseph of Carondelet, Sisters of St., C.S.J.: Founded 1650, in France; in U.S., 1836, at St. Louis, Mo. U.S. headquarters, 2307 S. Lindbergh Blvd., St. Louis, MO 63131.

Joseph of Chambery, Sisters of St.: Founded 1650, in France; in U.S., 1885. Generalate, Rome, Italy; U.S. provincial house, 27 Park Rd., West Hartford, CT 06119. Educational, hospital, social work.

Joseph of Chestnut Hill, Sisters of St., S.S.J.: Founded 1650; Philadelphia foundation, 1847. Motherhouse, Mt. St. Joseph Convent, Chestnut Hill, PA 19118.

Joseph of Cluny, Sisters of St., S.J.C.: Founded 1807, in France. Generalate, Paris, France; U.S. provincial house, Brenton Rd., Newport, RI 02840.

Joseph of Medaille, Sisters of, C.S.J.: Founded 1650, in France; in U.S., 1855. Became an American congregation Nov. 30, 1977. Central office, 1821 Summit Rd., Cincinnati, Ohio 45237.

Joseph of St. Augustine, Florida, Sisters of St., S.S.J.: General motherhouse, 241 St. George St., P.O. Box 3506, St. Augustine, FL 32085. Educational, hospital, pastoral, social work.

Joseph of St. Mark, Sisters of St., S.J.S.M.: Founded 1845, in France; in U.S., 1937. General motherhouse, 21800 Chardon Rd., Euclid, Cleveland, OH 44117. Nursing homes.

Joseph the Worker, Sisters of St., S.J.W.: General motherhouse, St. William Convent, 1 St. Joseph Lane, Walton, KY 41094.

Lamb of God, Sisters of the, A.D.: Founded 1945, in France; in U.S., 1958. General motherhouse, France; U.S. address, 2068 Wyandotte Ave., Owensboro KY 42301.

Life, Sisters of, S.V. (Sorer Vitae): Founded by Cardinal John J. O'Connor, 1991, to protect life. Address: St. Frances de Chantal Convent, 198 Hollywood Ave., Bronx, NY 10465.

Little Sisters of the Gospel, L.S.G.: Founded 1963 in France by Rev. Rene Voillaume; in U.S., 1972. U.S. address, Box 305, Mott Haven Sta., Bronx, NY 10454.

Little Workers of the Sacred Hearts, P.O.S.C.: Founded 1892, in Italy; in U.S., 1948. General house, Rome, Italy; U.S. address, Our Lady of Grace Convent, 635 Glenbrook Rd., Stamford, CT 06906.

Living Word, Sisters of the, S.L.W.: Founded 1975, in U.S. Motherhouse, The Center, 800 N. Fernandez Ave., Arlington Heights, IL 60004. Education, hospital, parish ministry work.

Loretto at the Foot of the Cross, Sisters of, S.L.: Founded 1812 in U.S., by Rev. Charles Nerinckx. General motherhouse, Nerinx, KY 40049. Educational work.

Louis, Congregation of Sisters of St., S.S.L.: Founded 1842, in France; in U.S., 1949. General motherhouse, Monaghan, Ireland; U.S. regional house, 22300 Mulholland Dr., Woodland Hills, CA 91364. Educational, medical, parish, foreign mission work.

Lovers of the Holy Cross Sisters (Phat Diem): Founded 1670, in Vietnam; in U.S. 1976. U.S. address, Holy Cross Convent, 14700 South Van Ness Ave., Garden, CA 90249.

Mantellate Sisters, Servants of Mary, of Blue Island, O.S.M.: Founded 1861, in Italy; in U.S., 1916. Generalate, Rome, Italy; U.S. motherhouse, 13811 S. Western Ave., Blue Island, IL 60406. Educational work.

Mantellate Sisters, Servants of Mary, of Plainfield, O.S.M.: Founded 1861 in Italy; in U.S., 1916. Address:16949 S. Drauden Rd., Plainfield, IL 60544.

Marian Sisters of the Diocese of Lincoln: Founded 1954. Motherhouse, Marian Center, R.R. 1, Box 108, Waverly, NE 68462.

Marianites of Holy Cross, Congregation of the Sisters, M.S.C.: Founded 1841, in France; in U.S., 1843. Motherhouse, Le Mans, Sarthe, France. North American headquarters, 1011 Gallier St., New Orleans, LA 70117.

Marist Sisters, Congregation of Mary, S.M.: Founded 1824, in France. General motherhouse, Rome, Italy; U.S. convents: St. Albert the Great, 4855 Parker, Dearborn Hts., MI 48125; St. Barnabas, 24262 Johnston, E. Detroit, MI 48021; Our Lady of the Snows, 4810 S. Leamington, Chicago, IL 60638; Marie, Madre de la Iglesia, 4419 St. James, Detroit, MI 48210.

Mary, Company of, O.D.N.: Founded 1607, in France; in U.S., 1926. General motherhouse, Rome, Italy; U.S. motherhouse, 16791 E. Main St., Tustin, CA 92680.

Mary, Daughters of the Heart of, D.H.M.: Founded 1790, in France; in U.S., 1851. Generalate, Paris, France; U.S. provincialate, 1339 Northampton St., Holyoke, MA 01040. Education, retreat work.

Mary, Missionary Sisters of the Society of (Marist Sisters), S.M.S.M.: Founded 1845, at St. Brieuc, France; in U.S., 1922. General motherhouse, Rome, Italy; U.S. provincial house, 349 Grove St., Waltham, MA 02154. Foreign missions.

Mary, Servants of, O.S.M.: Founded 13th century, in Italy; in U.S., 1893. General motherhouse, England; U.S. provincial motherhouse, 7400 Military Ave., Omaha, NE 68134.

Mary, Servants of (Servite Sisters), O.S.M.: Founded 13th century, in Italy; in U.S., 1912. General motherhouse, Our Lady of Sorrows Convent, 1000 College Ave., Ladysmith, WI 54848.

Mary, Sisters of St., of Oregon, S.S.M.O.: Founded 1886, in Oregon, by Bishop William H. Gross, C.Ss.R. General motherhouse, 4440 S.W. 148thAve., Beaverton, OR 97007. Educational, nursing work.

Mary, Sisters of the Little Company of, L.C.M.: Founded 1877, in England; in U.S., 1893. Generalate, London, England; U.S. provincial house, 9350 S. California Ave., Evergreen Park, IL 60642.

Mary, Sisters Servants of (Trained Nurses), S.M.: Founded 1851, at Madrid, Spain; in U.S., 1914.General motherhouse, Rome, Italy; U.S. motherhouse,

800 N. 18th St., Kansas City, KS 66102. Home nursing.

Mary and Joseph, Daughters of, D.M.J.: Founded 1817, in Belgium; in U.S., 1926. Generalate, Rome, Italy; American provincialate, 5300 Crest Rd., Rancho Palos Verdes, CA 90274.

Mary Help of Christians, Daughters of (Salesian Sisters of St. John Bosco), F.M.A.: Founded 1872, in Italy, by St. John Bosco and St. Mary Dominic Mazzarello; in U.S., 1908. General motherhouse, Rome, Italy; U.S. provinces, 655 Belmont Ave., Haledon, NJ 07508; 6019 Buena Vista St., San Antonio, TX 78237. Education, youth work.

Mary Immaculate, Daughters of (Marianist Sisters), F.M.I.: Founded 1816, in France, by Very Rev. William-Joseph Chaminade. General motherhouse, Rome, Italy; U.S. foundation, 251 W. Ligustrum Dr., San Antonio, TX 78228. Educational work.

Mary Immaculate, Religious of, R.M.I.: Founded 1876, in Spain; in U.S., 1954. Generalate, Rome, Italy: U.S. foundation, 719 Augusta St., San Antonio, TX 78215.

Mary Immaculate, Sisters Minor of, S.M.M.I.: Established in U.S., 1989. Address: 138 Brushy Hill Rd., Danbury, CT 06818.

Mary Immaculate, Sisters of, S.M.I.: Founded 1948, in India, by Bishop Louis LaRavoire Morrow; in U.S., 1981. General motherhouse, Bengal, India; U.S. address, R.D. 5, Box 1231, Leechburg, PA 15656.

Mary Immaculate, Sisters Servants of, S.S.M.I.: Founded 1878 in Poland. General motherhouse, Mariowka-Opoczynska, Poland; American provincialate, 1220 Tugwell Dr., Catonsville, MD 21228.

Mary Immaculate, Sisters Servants of, S.S.M.I: Founded 1892, in Ukraine; in U.S., 1935. General motherhouse, Rome, Italy; U.S. address, 9 Emmanuel Dr., P.O. Box 6, Sloatsburg, NY 10974. Educational, hospital work.

Mary of Namur, Sisters of St., S.S.M.N.: Founded 1819, at Namur, Belgium; in U.S., 1863. General motherhouse, Namur, Belgium. U.S. provinces: 250 Bryant, Buffalo, NY 14222; 909 West Shaw St., Ft. Worth, TX 76110.

Mary of Providence, Daughters of St., D.S.M.P.: Founded 1872, at Como, Italy; in U.S., 1913. General motherhouse, Rome, Italy; U.S. provincial house, 4200 N. Austin Ave., Chicago, IL 60634. Special education for mentally handicapped.

Mary of the Immaculate Conception, Daughters of, D.M.: Founded 1904, in U.S., by Msgr. Lucian Bojnowski. General motherhouse, 314 Osgood Ave., New Britain, CT 06053. Educational, hospital work.

Mary Queen, Congregation of, C.M.R.: Founded in Vietnam; established in U.S., 1979. U.S. region, 535 S. Jefferson, Springfield, MO 65806.

Mary Reparatrix, Society of, S.M.R.: Founded 1857, in France; in U.S., 1908. Generalate, Rome, Italy. U.S. province, 225 E. 234th St., Bronx, NY 10470.

Medical Mission Sisters (Society of Catholic Medical Missionaries, Inc.), M.M.S.: Founded 1925, in U.S., by Mother Anna Dengel. Generalate, London, Eng.; U.S. headquarters, 8400 Pine Rd.,

Philadelphia, PA 19111. Medical work, health education, especially in mission areas.

Medical Missionaries of Mary, M.M.M.: Founded 1937, in Ireland, by Mother Mary Martin; in U.S., 1950. General motherhouse, Dublin, Ireland; U.S. headquarters, 563 Minneford Ave., City Island, Bronx, NY 10464. Medical aid in missions.

Medical Sisters of St. Joseph, M.S.J.: Founded 1946, in India; first U.S. foundation, 1985. General motherhouse, Kerala, S. India; U.S. address, 3435 E. Funston, Wichita, KS 67218. Health care apostolate.

Mercedarian Missionaries of Berriz, M.M.B.: Founded 1930, in Spain; in U.S., 1946. General motherhouse, Rome, Italy. U.S. headquarters, 1400 N.E. 42nd Terr., Kansas City, MO 64106.

Mercy, Daughters of Our Lady of, D.M.: Founded 1837, in Italy, by St. Mary Joseph Rossello; in U.S., 1919. General motherhouse, Savona, Italy; U.S. motherhouse, Villa Rossello, 1009 Main Rd., Newfield, NJ 08344. Educational, hospital work.

Mercy, Missionary Sisters of Our Lady of, M.O.M.: Founded 1938, in Brazil; in U.S., 1955. General motherhouse, Brazil; U.S. address, 388 Franklin St., Buffalo, NY 14202.

Mercy, Religious Sisters of, R.S.M.: Founded 1973 in U.S. Motherhouse, 1835 Michigan Ave., Alma, MI 48801.

Mercy, Sisters of, Daughters of Christian Charity of St. Vincent de Paul, S.M.D.C.: Founded 1842, in Hungary; U.S. foundation, Rt. 1, Box 353A, 240 Longhouse Dr., Hewitt, NJ 07421.

Mercy, Sisters of, of the Americas: Formed in July, 1991, through union of 25 regional communities of Sisters of Mercy which previously were independent motherhouses or houses which formed the Sisters of Mercy of the Union. Mother Mary Catherine McAuley founded the Sisters of Mercy in Dublin, Ireland, in 1831; the first establishment in the U.S., 1843, in Pittsburgh. Address of administrative office: 8300 Colesville Rd., No. 300, Silver Spring, MD 20910. Pres., Sr. Doris Gottemoeller. Total in congregation 6,367.

Mercy of the Blessed Sacrament, Sisters of, H.M.S.S.: Founded 1910 in Mexico; in U.S., 1926. General motherhouse, Mexico. U.S. regional house, 222 W. Cevallos St., San Antonio, TX 78204.

Mill Hill Sisters: See Franciscan Missionaries of St. Joseph.

Minim Daughters of Mary Immaculate, C.F.M.M.: Founded 1886, in Mexico; in U.S., 1926. General motherhouse, Leon, Guanajuato, Mexico; U.S. address, Our Lady of Lourdes High School, Box 1865, Nogales, AZ 85621.

Misericordia Sisters, S.M.: Founded 1848, in Canada; in U.S., 1887. General motherhouse, 12435 Ave. Misericorde, Montreal H4J 2G3, Canada; U.S. address, 820 Jungles Ave., Aurora, IL 60505. Social work with unwed mothers and their children; hospital work.

Mission Helpers of the Sacred Heart, M.H.S.H.: Founded 1890, in U.S. General motherhouse, 1001 W. Joppa Rd., Baltimore, MD 21204. Religious education, evangelization.

Missionary Catechists of the Sacred Hearts of Jesus and Mary (Violetas), M.C.: Founded 1918, in Mexico; in U.S., 1943. Motherhouse, Tlalpan,

Mexico; U.S. address, 805 Liberty St., Victoria, TX 77901.

Missionary Daughters of the Most Pure Virgin Mary, M.D.P.V.M.: Founded in Mexico; in U.S., 1916. Address: 919 N. 9th St., Kingsville, TX 78363.

Mother of God, Missionary Sisters of the, M.S.M.G.: Byzantine, Ukrainian Rite, Stamford. Motherhouse, 711 N. Franklin St., Philadelphia, PA 19123.

Mother of God, Sisters Poor Servants of the, S.M.G.: Founded 1869, in London, England; in U.S., 1947. General motherhouse, Maryfield, Roehampton, London. U.S. address: Maryfield Nursing Home, Greensboro Rd., High Point, NC 27260. Hospital, educational work.

Nazareth, Poor Sisters of: Founded in England; U.S. foundation, 1924. General motherhouse, Hammersmith, London, England; U.S. novitiate, 3333 Manning Ave., Los Angeles, CA 90064. Social services, education.

Notre Dame, School Sisters of, S.S.N.D.: Founded 1833, in Germany; in U.S., 1847. General motherhouse, Rome, Italy. U.S. provinces: 13105 Watertown Plank Rd., Elm Grove, WI 53122; 6401 N. Charles St., Baltimore, MD 21212; 320 E. Ripa Ave., St. Louis, MO 63125; 170 Good Counsel Dr., Mankato, MN 56001; Wilton, CT 06897; P.O. Box 227275, Dallas, TX 75222; 1431 Euclid Ave., Berwyn, IL 60402.

Notre Dame, Sisters of, S.N.D.: Founded 1850, at Coesfeld, Germany; in U.S., 1874. General motherhouse, Rome, Italy. U.S. provinces: 13000 Auburn Rd., Chardon, OH 44024; 1601 Dixie Highway, Covington, KY 41011; 3837 Secor Rd., Toledo, OH 43623; 1776 Hendrix Ave., Thousand Oaks, CA 91360.

Notre Dame, Sisters of the Congregation of, C.N.D.: Founded 1658, in Canada by St. Marguerite Bourgeoys; in U.S., 1860. General motherhouse, Montreal, Que., Canada; U.S. province, 223 West Mountain Rd., Ridgefield, CT 06877. Education.

Notre Dame de Namur, Sisters of, S.N.D.: Founded 1803, in France; in U.S., 1840. General motherhouse, Rome, Italy. U.S. provinces: 351 Broadway, Everett, MA 02149; 30 Jeffrey's Neck Rd., Ipswich, MA 01938; 468 Poquonock Ave., Windsor, CT 06095; 1531 Greenspring Valley Rd., Stevenson, MD 21153; 305 Cable St., Baltimore, MD 21210; 701 E. Columbia Ave., Cincinnati, OH 45215; 14800 Bohlman Rd., Saratoga, CA 95070; Base Communities Province, 3037 Fourth St. N.E., Washington, DC 20017. Educational work.

Notre Dame de Sion, Congregation of, N.D.S.: Founded 1843, in France; in U.S., 1892. Generalate, Rome, Italy; U.S. province, 349 Westminster Rd., Brooklyn, NY 11218. Creation of better understanding and relations between Christians and Jews.

Notre Dame Sisters: Founded 1853, in Czechoslovakia; in U.S., 1910. General motherhouse, Javornik, Czech Republic; U.S. motherhouse, 3501 State St., Omaha, NE 68112. Educational work.

Oblates of the Mother of Orphans, O.M.O: Founded 1945, in Italy. General motherhouse, Milan, Italy. U.S. address, 20 E. 72nd St., New York, NY 10021.

Our Lady of Charity, North American Union of Sisters of, Eudist Sisters (Sisters of Our Lady of Charity of the Refuge), N.A.U.-O.L.C.: Founded 1641, in Caen, France, by St. John Eudes; in U.S., 1855. Autonomous houses were federated in 1944 and in May, 1978, the North American Union of the Sisters of Our Lady of Charity was established. General motherhouse and administrative center, Box 327, Wisconsin Dells, WI 53965. Primarily devoted to re-education and rehabilitation of women and girls in residential and non-residential settings.
Independent houses: 1125 Malvern Ave., Hot Springs, AR 71901; 620 Roswell Rd. N.W., Carrollton, OH 44615; 4500 W. Davis St., Dallas, TX 75211.

Our Lady of Sorrows, Sisters of, O.L.S.: Founded 1839, in Italy; in U.S., 1947. General motherhouse, Rome, Italy; U.S. headquarters, 9894 Norris Ferry Rd., Shreveport, LA 71106.

Our Lady of the Garden, Sisters of, O.L.G.: Founded 1829, in Italy, by St. Anthony Mary Gianelli. Motherhouse, Rome, Italy; U.S. address, 67 Round Hill Rd., Middletown, CT 06457.

Our Lady of Victory Missionary Sisters, O.L.V.M.: Founded 1922, in U.S. Motherhouse, Victory Noll, Box 109, Huntington, IN 46750. Educational, social work.

Pallottine Missionary Sisters (Missionary Sisters of the Catholic Apostolate), S.A.C.: Founded in Rome, 1838; in U.S., 1912. Generalate, Rome, Italy; U.S. provincialate, 15270 Old Halls Ferry Rd., Florissant, MO 63034.

Pallottine Sisters of the Catholic Apostolate, C.S.A.C.: Founded 1843, at Rome, Italy; in U.S., 1889. General motherhouse, Rome; U.S. motherhouse, St. Patrick's Villa, Harriman Heights, Harriman, NY 10926. Educational work.

Parish Visitors of Mary Immaculate, P.V.M.I.: Founded 1920, in New York. General motherhouse, Box 658, Monroe, NY 10950. Mission work.

Passion of Jesus Christ, Religious of (Passionist Nuns), C.P.: Founded 1771, in Italy, by St. Paul of the Cross; in U.S., 1910. U.S. convents: 2715 Churchview Ave., Pittsburgh, PA 15227; 631 Griffin Pond Rd., Clarks Summit, PA 18411; 8564 Crisp Rd., Whitesville, KY 42378; 1151 Donaldson Hwy., Erlanger, KY 41018; 15700 Clayton Rd., Ellisville, MO 63011. Contemplatives.

Passionist Sisters: See Cross and Passion, Sisters of the.

Paul, Daughters of St. (Missionary Sisters of the Media of Communication), D.S.P.: Founded 1915, at Alba, Piedmont, Italy; in U.S., 1932. General motherhouse, Rome, Italy; U.S. provincial house, 50 St. Paul's Ave., Boston, MA 02130. Apostolate of the communications arts.

Paul of Chartres, Sisters of St., S.P.C.: Founded 1696, in France. General house, Rome, Italy; U.S. address, 1300 County Rd. 492, Marquette, MI 49855.

Perpetual Adoration of Guadalupe, Sisters of, A.P.G.: U.S. foundation, 2403 W. Travis, San Antonio, TX 78207.

Peter Claver, Missionary Sisters of St., S.S.P.C.: Founded 1894 in Austria by Bl. Maria Teresa Ledochowska; in U.S., 1914. General motherhouse, Rome, Italy; U.S. address, 667 Woods Mill Rd. S., Chesterfield, MO 63017.

Pious Disciples of the Divine Master, P.D.D.M.: Founded 1924 in Italy; in U.S., 1948. General motherhouse, Rome, Italy; U.S. headquarters, 60 Sunset Ave., Staten Island, NY 10314.

Pious Schools, Sisters of, Sch. P.: Founded 1829 in Spain; in U.S., 1954. General motherhouse, Rome, Italy; U.S. headquarters, 17601 Nordhoff St., Northridge, CA 91325.

Poor, Little Sisters of the, L.S.P.: Founded 1839, in France by Bl. Jeanne Jugan; in U.S., 1868. General motherhouse, St. Pern, France. U.S. provinces: 110-30 221st St., Queens Village, NY 11429; 601 Maiden Choice Lane, Baltimore, MD 21228; 80 W. Northwest Hwy., Palatine, IL 60067. Care of aged.

Poor Clare Missionary Sisters (Misioneras Clarisas), M.C.: Founded Mexico. General motherhouse, Rome, Italy; U.S. novitiate, 1019 N. Newhope, Santa Ana, CA 92703.

Poor Clare Nuns: See Franciscan Poor Clare Nuns.

Poor Handmaids of Jesus Christ (Ancilla Domini Sisters), P.H.J.C.: Founded 1851, in Germany by Bl. Mary Kasper; in U.S., 1868. General motherhouse, Dernbach, Westerwald, Germany; U.S. motherhouse, Ancilla Domini Convent, Donaldson, IN 46513. Educational, hospital work, social services.

Precious Blood, Daughters of Charity of the Most: Founded 1872, at Pagani, Italy; in U.S., 1908. General motherhouse, Rome, Italy; U.S. convent, 1482 North Ave., Bridgeport, CT 06604.

Precious Blood, Missionary Sisters of the, C.P.S.: Founded 1885, at Mariannhill, South Africa; in U.S., 1925. Generalate, Rome, Italy: U.S. novitiate, P.O. Box 97, Reading, PA 19607. Home and foreign mission work.

Precious Blood, Sisters Adorers of the, A.P.B.: Founded 1861, in Canada; in U.S., 1890. General motherhouse, Canada. U.S. autonomous monasteries: 54th St. and Fort Hamilton Pkwy., Brooklyn, NY 11219; 700 Bridge St., Manchester, NH 03104; 7408 S.E. Alder St., Portland, OR 97215; 166 State St., Portland, ME 04101; 1106 State St., Lafayette, IN 47905; 400 Pratt St., Watertown, NY 13601. Cloistered, contemplative.

Precious Blood, Sisters of the, C.Pp.S.: Founded 1834, in Switzerland; in U.S., 1844. Generalate, 4000 Denlinger Rd., Dayton, Ohio 45426. Education, health care, other ministries.

Precious Blood, Sisters of the Most, C.Pp.S.: Founded 1845, in Steinerberg, Switzerland; in U.S., 1870. General motherhouse, 204 N. Main St., O'Fallon, MO 63366. Education, other ministries.

Presentation, Sisters of Mary of the, S.M.P.: Founded 1829, in France; in U.S., 1903. General motherhouse, Broons, Cotes-du-Nord, France. U.S. address, Maryvale Novitiate, 11550 River Rd., Valley City, ND 58072. Educational, hospital work.

Presentation of Mary, Sisters of the, P.M.: Founded 1796, in France by Bl. Marie Rivier; in U.S., 1873. General motherhouse, Castel Gandolfo, Italy. U.S. provincial houses: 495 Mammoth Rd., Manchester, NH 03104; 209 Lawrence St., Methuen, MA 01844.

Presentation of the B.V.M., Sisters of the, P.B.V.M.: Founded 1775, in Ireland; in U.S., 1854, in San Francisco. U.S. motherhouses: 2360 Carter Rd., Dubuque, IA 52001; 880 Jackson Ave., New

Windsor, NY 12553; 2340 Turk Blvd., San Francisco, CA 94118; St. Colman's Convent, Watervliet, NY 12189;
1101 32nd Ave., S., Fargo ND 58103; Presentation Convent, Aberdeen, SD 57401; 99 Church St., Leominster, MA 01453; 419 Woodrow Rd., Staten Island, NY 10312.

Presentation of the Blessed Virgin Mary, Sisters of, of Union: Founded in Ireland, 1775; union established in Ireland, 1976; first U.S. vice province, 1979. Generalate, Kildare, Ireland. U.S. provincialate, 729 W. Wilshire Dr., Phoenix, AZ 85007.

Providence, Daughters of Divine, F.D.P.: Founded 1832, Italy; in U.S., 1964. General motherhouse, Rome, Italy; U.S. address, 3100 Mumphrey Rd., Chalmette, LA 70043.

Providence, Missionary Catechists of Divine, M.C.D.P.: Administrative house, 2318 Castroville Rd., San Antonio, TX 78237.

Providence, Oblate Sisters of, O.S.P.: Founded 1829, in U.S., by Mother Mary Elizabeth Lange and Father James Joubert, S.S. First order of black nuns in U.S. General motherhouse, 701 Gun Rd., Baltimore, MD 21227. Educational work.

Providence, Sisters of, S.P.: Founded 1861, in Canada; in U.S., 1873. General motherhouse, Our Lady of Victory Convent, Gamelin St., Holyoke, MA 01040.

Providence, Sisters of, S.P.: Founded 1843, in Canada; in U.S., 1854. General motherhouse, Montreal, Canada. U.S. provinces: P.O. Box 11038, Seattle, WA 98111; 9 E. 9th Ave., Spokane, WA 99202; 353 N. River Rd., Des Plaines, IL 60616.

Providence, Sisters of (of St. Mary-of-the-Woods), S.P.: Founded 1806, in France; in U.S., 1840. Generalate, St. Mary-of-the-Woods, IN 47876.

Providence, Sisters of Divine, C.D.P.: Founded 1762, in France; in U.S., 1866. Generalate, Box 197, Helotes, TX 78023. Educational, hospital work.

Providence, Sisters of Divine, C.D.P.: Founded 1851, in Germany; in U.S., 1876. Generalate, Rome, Italy. U.S. provinces: 9000 Babcock Blvd., Allison Park, PA 15101; 8351 Florissant Rd., St. Louis, MO 63121; 363 Bishops Hwy., Kingston, MA 02364. Educational, hospital work.

Providence, Sisters of Divine (of Kentucky), C.D.P.: Founded 1762, in France; in U.S., 1889. General motherhouse, Fenetrange, France; U.S. province, St. Anne Convent, Melbourne, KY 41059. Education, social services, other ministries.

Redeemer, Oblates of the Most Holy, O.SS.R.: Founded 1864, in Spain. General motherhouse, Spain; U.S. foundation, 60-80 Pond St., Jamaica Plain, MA 02130.

Redeemer, Order of the Most Holy, O.SS.R.: Founded 1731, by St. Alphonsus Liguori; in U.S., 1957. U.S. addresses: Mother of Perpetual Help Monastery, P.O. Box 220, Esopus, NY 12429; St. Alphonsus Monastery, Liguori, MO 63057.

Redeemer, Sisters of the Divine, S.D.R.: Founded 1849, in Niederbronn, France; in U.S., 1912. General motherhouse, Rome, Italy; U.S. province, 999 Rock Run Road, Elizabeth, PA 15037. Educational, hospital work; care of the aged.

Redeemer, Sisters of the Holy, C.S.R.: Founded

1849, in Alsace; in U.S., 1924. General motherhouse, Wuerzburg, Germany; U.S. provincial house, 521 Moredon Rd., Huntingdon Valley, PA 19006. Personalized medical care in hospitals, homes for aged, private homes; retreat work.

Reparation of the Congregation of Mary, Sisters of, S.R.C.M.: Founded 1903, in U.S. Motherhouse, St. Zita's Villa, Monsey, NY 10952.

Reparation of the Sacred Wounds of Jesus, Sisters of, S.R.: Founded 1959 in U.S. General motherhouse, 2120 S.E. 24th Ave., Portland, OR 97214.

Resurrection, Sisters of the, C.R.: Founded 1891, in Italy; in U.S., 1900. General motherhouse, Rome, Italy. U.S. provinces: 7432 Talcott Ave., Chicago, IL 60631; Mt. St. Joseph, Castleton-on-Hudson, NY 12033. Education, nursing.

Rita, Sisters of St., O.S.A.: General motherhouse, Wurzburg, Germany. U.S. foundation, St. Monica's Convent, 3920 Green Bay Rd., Racine, WI 53404.

Rosary, Congregation of Our Lady of the Holy, R.S.R.: Founded 1874, in Canada; in U.S., 1899. General motherhouse, Rimouski, Que., Canada. U.S. regional house, 20 Thomas St., Portland, ME 04102. Educational work.

Rosary, Missionary Sisters of the Holy, M.S.H.R.: Founded 1924, in Ireland; in U.S., 1954. Motherhouse, Dublin, Ireland. U.S. regional 741 Polo Rd., Bryn Mawr, PA 19010. African missions.

Sacrament, Missionary Sisters of the Most Blessed, M.SS.S.: General motherhouse, Madrid, Spain; U.S. foundation: 1111 Wordin Ave., Bridgeport, CT 06605.

Sacrament, Nuns of the Perpetual Adoration of the Blessed, A.P.: Founded 1807 in Rome, Italy; in U.S., 1925. U.S. monasteries: 145 N. Cotton Ave., El Paso, TX 79901; 771 Ashbury St., San Francisco, CA 94117.

Sacrament, Oblate Sisters of the Blessed, O.S.B.S.: Founded 1935, in U.S.; motherhouse, St. Sylvester Convent, P.O. Box 217, Marty, SD 57361. Care of American Indians.

Sacrament, Servants of the Blessed, S.S.S.: Founded 1858, in France, by St. Pierre Julien Eymard; in U.S., 1947. General motherhouse, Rome, Italy; American provincial house, 1818 Coal Pl. SE, Albuquerque, NM 87106. Contemplative.

Sacrament, Sisters of the Blessed, for Indians and Colored People, S.B.S.: Founded 1891, in U.S., by Bl. Katharine Drexel. General motherhouse, St. Elizabeth's Convent, Bensalem, PA 19020.

Sacrament, Sisters of the Most Holy, M.H.S.: Founded 1851, in France; in U.S., 1872. Generalate, 313 Corona Dr. (P.O. Box 30727), Lafayette, LA 70593.

Sacrament, Sisters Servants of the Blessed, S.J.S.: Founded 1904, in Mexico; in U.S., 1926. General motherhouse, Mexico; U.S. address, 215 Lomita St., El Segundo, CA 90245.

Sacramentine Nuns (Religious of the Order of the Blessed Sacrament and Our Lady), O.S.S.: Founded 1639, in France; in U.S., 1912. U.S. monasteries: 235 Bellvale Lakes Rd., Warwick,, NY 10990; US 31, Conway, MI 49722. Perpetual adoration of the Holy Eucharist.

Sacred Heart, Daughters of Our Lady of the:

Founded 1882, in France; in U.S., 1955. General motherhouse, Rome, Italy; U.S. address, 424 E. Browning Rd., Bellmawr, NJ 08031. Educational work.

Sacred Heart, Missionary Sisters of the (Cabrini Sisters), M.S.C.: Founded 1880, in Italy, by St. Frances Xavier Cabrini; in U.S., 1889. General motherhouse, Rome, Italy; U.S. provincial office: 222 E. 19th St., 5B, New York, NY 10003. Educational, health, social and catechetical work.

Sacred Heart, Religious of the Apostolate of the, R.A.: General motherhouse, Madrid, Spain; U.S. address, 1310 W. 42nd Pl., Hialiah, FL 33012.

Sacred Heart, Society Devoted to the, S.D.S.H.: Founded 1940, in Hungary; in U.S., 1956. U.S. motherhouse, 9814 Sylvia Ave., Northridge, CA 91324. Educational work.

Sacred Heart, Society of the, R.S.C.J.: Founded 1800, in France; in U.S., 1818. Generalate, Rome, Italy. U.S. provincial house, 4389 W. Pine Blvd., St. Louis, MO 63108. Educational work.

Sacred Heart of Jesus, Apostles of, A.S.C.J.: Founded 1894, in Italy; in U.S., 1902. General motherhouse, Rome, Italy; U.S. motherhouse, 265 Benham St., Hamden, CT 06514. Educational, social work.

Sacred Heart of Jesus, Handmaids of the, A.C.J.: Founded 1877, in Spain. General motherhouse, Rome, Italy; U.S. province, 616 Coopertown Rd., Haverford, PA 19041. Educational, retreat work.

Sacred Heart of Jesus, Missionary Sisters of the Most (Hiltrup), M.S.C.: Founded 1899, in Germany; in U.S., 1908. General motherhouse, Rome, Italy; U.S. province, 51 Seminary Ave., Reading, PA 19605. Education, health care, pastoral ministry.

Sacred Heart of Jesus, Oblate Sisters of the, O.S.H.J.: Founded 1894; in U.S., 1949. General motherhouse, Rome, Italy; U.S. headquarters, 50 Warner Rd., Hubbard, Ohio 44425. Educational, social work.

Sacred Heart of Jesus, Servants of the Most, S.S.C.J.: Founded 1894, in Poland; in U.S., 1959. General motherhouse, Cracow, Poland; U.S. address, 866 Cambria St., Cresson, PA 16630. Education, health care, social services.

Sacred Heart of Jesus, Sisters of the, S.S.C.J.: Founded 1816, in France; in U.S., 1903. General motherhouse, St. Jacut, Brittany, France; U.S. provincial house, 5922 Blanco Rd., San Antonio, TX 78216. Educational, hospital, domestic work.

Sacred Heart of Jesus and of the Poor, Servants of the (Mexican), S.S.H.J.P.: Founded 1885, in Mexico; in U.S., 1907. General motherhouse, Apartado 92, Puebla, Pue., Mexico; U.S. address, 3310 S. Zapata Hwy, Laredo, TX 78043.

Sacred Heart of Jesus and Our Lady of Guadalupe, Missionaries of the: U.S. address, 1212 E. Euclid Ave., Arlington Heights, IL 60660.

Sacred Heart of Jesus for Reparation, Congregation of the Handmaids of the, A.R.: Founded 1918, in Italy; in U.S., 1958. U.S. address, Sunshine Park, R.D. 3, Steubenville, Ohio 43952.

Sacred Heart of Mary, Religious of the, R.S.H.M.: Founded 1848, in France; in U.S., 1877.

Generalate, Rome, Italy. U.S. provinces; 50 Wilson Park Dr., Tarrytown, NY 10591; 441 N. Garfield Ave., Montebellow, CA 90640.

Sacred Hearts, Sisters of the Holy Union of the, S.U.S.C.: Founded 1826, in France; in U.S., 1886. Generalate, Rome, Italy. U.S. provinces: 550 Rock St., Fall River, MA 02720; Box 993, Main St., Groton, MA 01450. Varied ministries.

Sacred Hearts and of Perpetual Adoration, Sisters of the, SS.CC.: Founded 1797, in France; in U.S., 1908. General motherhouse, Rome, Italy; U.S. provinces: 1120 Fifth Ave., Honolulu, Hawaii 96816 (Pacific); 419 Hood St., Fall River, MA 02720 (East Coast). Varied ministries.

Sacred Hearts of Jesus and Mary, Sisters of the, S.H.J.M.: Established 1953, in U.S. General motherhouse, Essex, England; U.S. address, 844 Don Carlo Dr., El Cerrito, CA 94530.

Savior, Company of the, C.S.: Founded 1952, in Spain; in U.S., 1962. General motherhouse, Madrid, Spain; U.S. foundation, 820 Clinton Ave., Bridgeport, CT 06604.

Savior, Sisters of the Divine, S.D.S.: Founded 1888, in Italy; in U.S., 1895. General motherhouse, Rome, Italy; U.S. province, 4311 N. 100th St., Milwaukee, WI 53222. Educational, hospital work.

Sisters of St. Benedict Center, Slaves of Mary Immaculate, M.I.C.M.: Founded in U.S. Address: 254 Still River Rd., P.O. Box 22, Still River, MA 01467.

Social Service, Sisters of, S.S.S.: Founded in Hungary, 1923, by Sr. Margaret Slachta. U.S. generalate, 440 Linwood Ave.., Buffalo, NY 14209. Social work.

Social Service, Sisters of, of Los Angeles, S.S.S.: Founded 1908, in Hungary; in U.S., 1926. General motherhouse, 2303 S. Figueroa Way, Los Angeles, CA 90007.

Teresa of Jesus, Society of St., S.T.J.: Founded 1876, in Spain; in U.S., 1910. General motherhouse, Rome, Italy; U.S. provincial house, 18080 St. Joseph's Way, Covington, LA 70433.

Thomas of Villanova, Congregation of Sisters of St., S.S.T.V.: Founded 1661, in France; in U.S., 1948. General motherhouse, Neuilly-sur-Seine, France; U.S. foundation W. Rocks Rd., Norwalk, CT 06851.

Trinity, Missionary Servants of the Most Blessed, M.S.B.T.: Founded 1912, in U.S., by Very Rev. Thomas A. Judge. General motherhouse, 3501 Solly Ave., Philadelphia, PA 19136. Educational, social work; health services.

Trinity, Sisters Oblates to the Blessed, O.B.T.: Founded 1923, in Italy. U.S. novitiate, Beekman Rd., P.O. Box 98, Hopewell Junction, NY 12533.

Trinity, Sisters of the Most Holy, O.Ss.T.: Founded 1198, in Rome; in U.S., 1920. General motherhouse, Rome, Italy; U.S. address, Immaculate Conception Province, 21281 Chardon Rd., Euclid, Ohio 44117. Educational work.

Trinity, Society of Our Lady of the Most Holy, S.O.L.T.: Motherhouse, P.O. Box 189 Skidmore, TX 78389.

Ursula of the Blessed Virgin, Society of the Sisters of St., S.U: Founded 1606, in France; in U.S., 1902. General motherhouse, France; U.S. novitiate,

139 S. Mill Rd., Rhinebeck, NY 12572. Educational work.

Ursuline Nuns (Roman Union), O.S.U.: Founded 1535, in Italy; in U.S., 1727. Generalate, Rome, Italy. U.S. provinces: 323 E. 198th St., Bronx, NY 10458; 210 Glennon Heights Rd., Crystal City, MO 63019; 639 Angela Dr., Santa Rosa, CA 95401; 45 Lowder St., Dedham, MA 02026.

Ursuline Nuns of the Congregation of Paris, O.S.U.: Founded 1535, in Italy; in U.S., 1727, in New Orleans. U.S. motherhouses: 20860 St, Rte 251, St. Martin, OH 45118; 901 E. Miami St., Paola, KS 66071; 3115 Lexington Rd., Louisville, KY 40206; 2600 Lander Rd., Cleveland, O. 44124; Maple Mount, KY 42356; 4045 Indian Rd., Toledo, OH 43606; 4250 Shields Rd., Canfield, OH 44406; 1339 E. McMillan St., Cincinnati, OH 45206.

Ursuline Sisters of the Congregation of Tildonk, Belgium, O.S.U.: Founded 1535, in Italy; Tildonk congregation, 1832; in U.S., 1924. Generalate, Brussels, Belgium; U.S. address, 81-15 Utopia Parkway, Jamaica, NY 11432. Educational, foreign mission work.

Ursuline Sisters of Belleville, O.S.U.: Founded 1535, in Italy; in U.S., 1910; established as diocesan community, 1983. Central house, 1026 N. Douglas Ave., Belleville, IL 62221. Educational work.

Ursuline Sisters (Irish Ursuline Union), O.S.U.: Generalate, Dublin, Ireland; U.S. address, 1973 Torch Hill Rd., Columbus, GA 31903.

Venerini Sisters, Religious, M.P.V.: Founded 1685, in Italy; in U.S., 1909. General motherhouse, Rome, Italy; U.S. provincialate; 23 Edward St., Worcester, MA 01605.

Vietnamese Adorers of the Holy Cross, M.T.G.: Founded 1670 in Vietnam; in U.S. 1976. General motherhouse 7408 S.E. Adler, Portland, OR 97215.

Vincent de Paul, Sisters: See Charity of St. Vincent de Paul, Sisters of.

Visitation Nuns, V.H.M.: Founded 1610, in France; in U.S. (Georgetown, DC), 1799. Contemplative, educational work. Two federations in U.S. First Federation of North America. Major pontifical enclosure. Pres., Mother Mary Jozefa Kowalewski, Monastery of the Visitation, Snellville, GA 30278. Addresses of monasteries belonging to the federation: 2300 Springhill Ave., Mobile, AL 36607; Beach Rd., Tyringham, MA 01264; 12221 Bievenue Rd, Rockville, VA 23146; 5820 City Ave., Philadelphia, PA 19131; 1745 Parkside Blvd., Toledo, OH 43607; 2055 Ridgedale Dr., Snellville, GA 30278.

Second Federation of North America. Constitutional enclosure. Pres., Sr. Anne Madeleine Godefroy, Monastery of the Visitation, St. Louis, MO 63101. Addresses of monasteries belonging to the federation: 1500 35th St., Washington, DC 20007; 3020 N. Ballas Rd., St. Louis, MO 63131; 200 E. Second St., Frederick, MD 21701; Mt. St. Chantal Monastery of the Visitation, Wheeling, WV 26003; 8902 Ridge Blvd., Brooklyn, NY 11209; 2936 36th St., Rock Island, IL 61201; 2455 Visitation Dr., Mendota Heights, St. Paul, MN 55120.

Visitation of the Congregation of the Immaculate Heart of Mary, Sisters of the, S.V.M.: Founded 1952, in U.S. Motherhouse, 2950 Kaufmann Ave., Dubuque, IA 52001. Educational work, parish ministry.

Vocationist Sisters (Sisters of the Divine Vocations): Founded 1921, in Italy; in U.S., 1967 General motherhouse, Naples, Italy; U.S. foundation, Perpetual Help Nursery, 172 Broad St., Newark, NJ 07104.

Wisdom, Daughters of, D.W.: Founded 1703, in France, by St. Louis Marie Grignion de Montfort; in U.S., 1904. General motherhouse, Vendee, France; U.S. province, 385 S. Ocean Ave., Islip, NY 11751. Education, health care, parish ministry, social services.

Xaverian Missionary Society of Mary, Inc., X.M.M.: Founded 1945, in Italy; in U.S., 1954. General motherhouse, Parma, Italy; U.S. address, 242 Salisbury St., Worcester, MA 01609.

ORGANIZATIONS OF RELIGIOUS

Conferences

Conferences of major superiors of religious institutes, dating from the 1950s, are encouraged by the Code of Canon Law (Code 708) "so that joining forces they can work toward the achievement of the purpose of their individual institutes more fully, transact common business and foster suitable coordination and cooperation with conferences of bishops and also with individual bishops." Statutes of the conferences must be approved by the Holy See "by which alone they are erected" (Canon 709). Conferences have been established in 24 countries of Europe, 14 in North and Central America, 10 in South America, 35 in Africa and 19 in Asia and Oceania.

Listed below are U.S. and international conferences.

Conference of Major Superiors of Men: Founded in 1956; canonically established Sept. 12, 1957. Membership, 269 major superiors representing institutes with a combined membership of approximately 24,000. President, Bro. Joseph Klein, F.M.S.; executive director, Rev. Stephen Henrich, O.S.C. National office: 8808 Cameron St., Silver Spring, MD 20910.

Leadership Conference of Women Religious: Founded in 1956; canonically established Dec. 12, 1959. Membership, nearly 1,000 (Dec. 31, 1996), representing approximately 400 religious institutes. President, Sister Mary Waskowiak, R.S.M.; executive director, Sister Mary Christine Fellerhoff, S.S.A. National office: 8808 Cameron St., Silver Spring, MD 20910.

Council of Major Superiors of Women Religious: Canonically erected June 13, 1992. Membership, 141 superiors of 103 religious congregations. Chairperson, Mother Mary Nettle, L.S.P. National office: P.O. Box 4467, Washington, D.C. 20017.

International Union of Superiors General (Women): Established Dec. 8, 1965; approved, 1967. General secretary, Sister Marguerite Letourneau, S.G.M. Address: Piazza di Ponte S. Angelo, 28, 00186, Rome, Italy.

Union of Superiors General (Men): Established in 1957. President, Father Camillo Maccise, O.C.D; general secretary, Bro. Lino Da Campo, F.S.F. Address: Via dei Penitenzieri 19, 00193 Rome, Italy.

Latin American Confederation of Religious (Confederacion Latinoamericana de Religiosos — CLAR): Established in 1959; statutes reformed in 1984. President, Sister Elza Ribeiro, H.P.G.; secretary general, Pedro Acevedo, F.S.C. Address: Calle 64 No 10-45, Piso 5to. Apartado Aéreo 56804, Santafé de Bogotá, Colombia.

Union of European Conferences of Major Superiors: Established Dec. 25, 1983. President, Bro. Jacques Scholte; secretary, Sr. Maria Luz Galvan, R.S.C.J., Avenida Alfonso XIII, 97, 28016 Madrid, Spain.

Other Organizations

Institute on Religious Life (1974). To foster more effective understanding and implementation of teachings of the Church on religious life, promote vocations to religious life and the priesthood, and promote growth in sanctity of all the faithful according to their state in life. Executive director, Rev. James Downey. National office, P.O. Box 41007, Chicago, IL 60641.

National Association of Religious Brothers (1972): To publicize the unique vocations of brothers, to further communication among brothers and provide liaison with various organizations of the Church. Executive secretary, Sr. Emily Wollschlager,

S.S.N.D. National office, 1337 West Ohio, Chicago, IL 60622.

National Black Sisters' Conference (1968): Black Catholic women religious and associates networking to provide support through prayer, study, solidarity and programs. President, Sr. Patricia J. Chappell, S.N.D.de N. Address: 3027 4th St. NE, Washington, DC 20017.

National Conference of Vicars for Religious (1967): National organization of diocesan officials concerned with relations between their respective dioceses and religious communities engaged therein. President, Sr. Therese Sullivan, S.P., 9292 Broadway, Merrillville, IN 46410; secretary, Sr. Doris Rauenhorst, O.P., 244 Dayton Ave., St. Paul, MN 55102.

National Religious Vocation Conference (NRVC) (1988, with merger of National Sisters Vocation Conference and National Conference of Religious Vocation Directors): Service organization of men and women committed to the fostering and discernment of vocations. Executive director, Sr. Catherine Bertrand, S.S.N.D. Address: 1603 S. Michigan Ave., No. 400, Chicago, IL 60616.

Religious Formation Conference (1953): Originally the Sister Formation Conference; membership includes women and men Religious and non-canonical groups. Facilitates the ministry of formation, both initial and ongoing, in religious communities. Executive director, Sister Jane Finnerty, O.S.U. National office: 8820 Cameron St., Silver Spring, MD 20910.

SECULAR INSTITUTES

(Sources: Almanac survey; United States Conference of Secular Institutes; *Annuario Pontificio.*

Secular institutes are societies of men and women living in the world who dedicate themselves to observe the evangelical counsels and to carry on apostolic works suitable to their talents and opportunities in the areas of their everyday life.

"Secular institutes are not religious communities but they carry with them in the world a profession of evangelical counsels which is genuine and complete, and recognized as such by the Church. This profession confers a consecration on men and women, laity and clergy, who reside in the world. For this reason they should chiefly strive for total self-dedication to God, one inspired by perfect charity. These institutes should preserve their proper and particular character, a secular one, so that they may everywhere measure up successfully to that apostolate which they were designed to exercise, and which is both in the world and, in a sense, of the world" (Decree on the Appropriate Renewal of Religious Life, No. 11; Second Vatican Council).

Secular institutes are under the jurisdiction of the Congregation for Institutes of Consecrated Life and Societies of Apostolic Life. General legislation concerning them is contained in Canons 710 to 730 of the Code of Canon Law.

A secular institute reaches maturity in several stages. It begins as an association of the faithful, technically called a pious union, with the approval of a local bishop. Once it has proved its viability, he can give

it the status of an institute of diocesan right, in accordance with norms and permission emanating from the Congregation for Institutes of Consecrated Life and Societies of Apostolic Life. On issuance of a separate decree from this congregation, an institute of diocesan right becomes an institute of pontifical right.

Secular institutes, which originated in the latter part of the 18th century, were given full recognition and approval by Pius XII Feb. 2, 1947, in the apostolic constitution *Provida Mater Ecclesia*. On Mar. 25 of the same year a special commission for secular institutes was set up within the Congregation for Religious. Institutes were commended and confirmed by Pius XII in a motu proprio of Mar. 12, 1948, and were the subject of a special instruction issued a week later, Mar. 19, 1948.

The **World Conference of Secular Institutes (CMIS)** was approved by the Vatican May 23, 1974. Address: Via Tullio Levi-Civita 5, 00146 Rome, Italy.

The **United States Conference of Secular Institutes (USCSI)** was established following the organization of the World Conference of Secular Institutes in Rome. Its membership is open to all canonically erected secular institutes with members living in the United States. The conference was organized to offer secular institutes an opportunity to exchange experiences, to do research in order to help the Church carry out its mission, and to search for ways and means to make known the existence of secular institutes in the

U.S. Address: P.O. Box 4556, 12th St. NE, Washington, DC 20017.

Institutes in the U.S.

Apostolic Oblates: Founded in Rome, Italy, 1947; established in the U.S., 1962; for women. Approved as a secular institute of pontifical right Dec. 8, 1994. Addresses: 2125 W. Walnut Ave., Fullerton, CA 92633; 6762 Western Ave., Omaha, NE 68132; 730 E. 87th St., Brooklyn, NY 11236.

Caritas Christi: Originated in Marseilles, 1937; for women. Established as a secular institute of pontifical right Mar. 19, 1955. Address: P.O. Box 5162, River Forest, IL 60305. International membership.

Company of St. Paul: Originated in Milan, Italy, 1920; for lay people and priests. Approved as a secular institute of pontifical right June 30, 1950. Address: Rev. Stuart Sandberg, 52 Davis Ave., White Plains, NY 10605.

Crusaders of St. Mary: Founded 1947 in Madrid, Spain; approved as a secular institute of diocesan right, 1988; for men. Address: 2001 Great Falls St., McLean, VA 22101

Diocesan Laborer Priests: Founded in Spain 1885; approved as a secular institute of pontifical right, 1952. The specific aim of the institute is the promotion, sustenance and cultivation of apostolic, religious and priestly vocations. Address: Rev. Rutilio J. del Riego, 3706 15th St. N.E., Washington, DC 20017.

Don Bosco Volunteers: Founded 1917 by Bl. Philip Rinaldi; for women. Approved as a secular institute of pontifical right Aug. 5, 1978. Follow spirituality and charism of St. John Bosco. Address: Rev. Paul P. Avallone, S.D.B., Don Bosco Volunteers, 202 Union Ave., Paterson, NJ 07502.

Don Bosco Secular Institute (for men): Same address as above.

Fr. Kolbe Missionaries of the Immaculata: Founded in Bologna, Italy, in 1954, by Fr. Luigi Faccenda, O.F.M. Conv.; for women. Approved as a secular institute of pontifical right Mar. 25, 1992. Live the fullness of baptismal consecration, strive for perfect charity and promote the knowledge and veneration of Mary. Address: 531 E. Merced Ave., West Covina, CA 91790.

Handmaids of Divine Mercy: Founded in Bari, Italy, 1951; for women. Approved as an institute of pontifical right 1972. Address: Elisabeth Gagliano, 2943 Philip Ave., Bronx, NY 10465.

Institute of Secular Missionaries: Founded in Vitoria, Spain, 1939; for women. Approved as a secular institute, 1955. Address: 2710 Ruberg Ave., Cincinnati, OH 45211, Att. E. Dilger.

Institute of the Heart of Jesus: Originated in France Feb. 2, 1791; restored Oct. 29, 1918; for diocesan priests and laity. Received final approval from the Holy See as a secular institute of pontifical right Feb. 2, 1952. U.S. address, Rev. Francis X. Mawn, St. Rose Rectory, 601 Broadway, Chelsea, MA 02150.

Lay Missionaries of the Passion: Founded in Catania, Sicily; for women. Approved as a secular institute of diocesan right July 1, 1980. Address: Dorothy Armstrong, 633 Main St., Dicksen City, PA 18519.

Little Franciscan Family: Founded in Italy, 1929,

by Father Ireneo Mazzotti, O.F.M.; for women. Approved as a secular institute of pontifical right, 1983. Address: Julie Curley, 319 Main St., Cromwell, CT 06416.

Mission of Our Lady of Bethany: Founded in France, 1948; for women. Approved as a secular institute of diocesan right, 1965. Address: Estelle Nichols, 7 Locksley St., Jamaica Plain, MA 02130.

Missionaries of the Kingship of Christ the King: Under this title are included three distinct and juridically separate institutes founded by Agostino Gemelli, O.F.M. (1878-1959) and Armida Barelli (1882-1952). Two are active in the U.S.

(1) Women Missionaries of the Kingship of Christ — Founded in 1919, in Italy; definitively approved as an institute of pontifical right 1953. U.S. branch established 1950.

(2) Men Missionaries of the Kingship of Christ — Founded 1928, in Italy, as an institute of diocesan right. U.S. branch established 1962.

Addresses: Rev. Damien Dougherty, O.F.M., P.O. Box 278, Eime Rd., Dittmer, MO 63023 (for Men Missionaries); Rev. Dominic Monti, O.F.M., 10400 Lorain Ave., Silver Spring, MD 20901 (for Women Missionaries).

Nuestra Senora de la Altagracia: Founded in Dominican Republic, 1956; approved as a secular institute of diocesan right, 1964; for women. Address: Ms. Christiana Perez, 129 Van Siclen Ave., Brooklyn, NY 11207.

Oblate Missionaries of Mary Immaculate: Founded, 1952; approved as a secular institute of pontifical right 1984; for women. Address: Oblate Missionaries of Mary Immaculate, P.O. Box 303, Manville, RI 02838. International membership.

Opus Spiritus Sancti: Originated in West Germany, 1952; for diocesan priests and unmarried permanent deacons. Formally acknowledged by Rome as a secular institute of diocesan right, 1977. Address: Rev. James D. McCormick, 421 E. Bluff, Carroll, IA 51401.

St. Francis de Sales Secular Institute: Founded in Vienna, Austria, 1940; for women. Pontifical right, 1964. Addresses: Rev. John J. Conmy, 1120 Blue Bell Rd., Childs, MD 21916; Joan Bereswill, 3503 Jean St., Fairfax, VA 22030.

Schoenstatt Sisters of Mary: Originated in Schoenstatt, Germany, 1926; for women. Established as a secular institute of diocesan right May 20, 1948; of pontifical right Oct. 18, 1948. Addresses: W. 284 N. 404 Cherry Lane, Waukesha, WI 53188; House Schoenstatt, HCO 1, Box 100, Rockport, TX 78382.

Secular Institute of Pius X: Originated in Manchester, N.H., 1940; for priests and laymen. Approved as a secular institute, 1959. Also admits married couples and unmarried men as associate members. Addresses: C.P. 7731, Charlesbourg, Que. G1G 5W6, Canada; Roger Duchesneu, 27 Cove St., Goffstown, NH 03345.

Secular Institute of Schoenstatt Fathers: Founded in Germany by Fr. Joseph Kentenich in 1965; for priests serving the International Schoenstatt Movement in over 20 countries. Approved as a secular institute of pontifical right, June 24, 1988. Address: W. 284 N. 746 Cherry Lane, Waukesha, WI 53188.

Servitium Christi Secular Institute of the Blessed

Sacrament: Founded in Holland, 1952; for women. Approved as a secular institute of diocesan right May 8, 1963. Address: Miss Elaine Kozlowski, 1215 Greenwood Ave., #2, Pueblo, CO 81003.

Society of Our Lady of the Way: Originated, 1936; for women. Approved as a secular institute of pontifical right Jan. 3, 1953. Addresses: 2339 N. Catalina, Los Angeles, CA 90027; 80 Manhattan Ave., Jersey City, NJ 07307.

Voluntas Dei Institute: Originated in Canada, 1958 by Father L. M. Parent; for secular priests and laymen (with married couples as associates). Approved as a secular institute of pontifical right, July 12, 1987. Established in 21 countries. Address: Rev. Michael Craig, 4257 Tazewell Terr., Burtonsville, MD 20866.

The *Annuario Pontificio* lists the following secular institutes of pontifical right which are not established in the U.S.:

For men: Christ the King; Institute of Our Lady of Life; Institute of Prado; Priests of the Sacred Heart of Jesus.

For women: Alliance in Jesus through Mary; Apostles of the Sacred Heart; Catechists of Mary, Virgin and Mother; Catechists of the Sacred Heart of Jesus (Ukrainian); Company of St. Ursula; Cordimarian Filiation; Daughters of the Nativity of Mary; Daughters of the Queen of the Apostles; Daughters of the Sacred Heart; Evangelical Crusade; Faithful Servants of Jesus; Handmaids of Our Mother of Mercy; Institute of Notre Dame du Travail; Institute of Our Lady of Life; Institute of St. Boniface; Little Apostles of Charity; Life and Peace in Christ Jesus; Missionaries of Royal Priesthood; Missionaries of the Sick; Oblates of Christ the King; Oblates of the Sacred Heart of Jesus; Servants of Jesus the Priest; Servite Secular Institute; Union of the Daughters of God; Workers of Divine Love; Workers of the Cross; Handmaids of Holy Church; Augustinian Auxiliary Missionaries; Heart of Jesus; Apostolic Missionaries of Charity; Combonian Secular Missionaries; Missionaries of the Gospel; Secular Servants of Jesus Christ Priest; Women of Schoenstatt; Missionaries of Infinite Love.

Associations

Caritas: Originated in New Orleans, 1950; for women. Follow guidelines of secular institutes. Small self-supporting groups who live and work among the poor and oppressed; work in Louisiana and Guatemala. Address: Box 308, Abita Springs, LA 70420.

Daughters of Our Lady of Fatima: Originated in Lansdowne, Pa., 1949; for women. Received diocesan approval, Jan., 1952. Address: Fatima House, Rolling Hills Rd., Ottsville, PA 18942.

Focolare Movement: Founded in Trent, Italy, in 1943, by Chiara Lubich; for men and women. Approved as an association of the faithful, 1962. It is not a secular institute by statute; however, vows are observed by its totally dedicated core membership of 4,000 who live in small communities called Focolare (Italian word for "hearth") centers. There are 17 resident centers in the U.S. and four in Canada. GEN (New Generation) is the youth organization of the movement. An estimated 75,000 are affiliated with the movement in the U.S. and Canada; 2,000,000, worldwide. Publications include Living City, monthly; GEN II and GEN III for young people and children. Five week-long summer conventions, called "Mariapolis" ("City of Mary"), are held annually. Address for information: P.O. Box 496, New York, NY 10021 (indicate men's or women's branch).

Jesus-Caritas Fraternity of Priests: An international association of diocesan priests who strive to combine an active life with a contemplative calling by their membership in small fraternities. U.S. address for information: Rev. Paul M. Esser, St. Paul the Apostle Parish, 5700 Washington Ave., Racine, WI 53406.

Franciscan Missionaries of Jesus Crucified: Founded in New York in 1987; separate communities for women and men. Approved as an association of the faithful Jan. 7, 1992. To provide an opportunity for persons with disabilities to live a life of total consecration in the pursuit of holiness in the apostolate of service to the Church and to those who suffer in any way. Address: Louise D. Principe, F.M.J.C., 400 Central Ave., Apt. 3D, Albany, NY 12206.

Madonna House Apostolate: Originated in Toronto, Canada, 1930; for priests and lay persons. Public association of the Christian faithful. Address: Madonna House, Combermere, Ontario, Canada KOJ ILO — Jean Fox (women), Albert Osterberger (men), Rev. Robert Pelton (priests). International membership and missions.

Opus Spiritus Sancti: Originated in Germany; for women. An association of the faithful. Address: Theresa Berger, 415 E. Oak St., Algona, IA 50511.

Pax Christi: Lay institute of men and women dedicated to witnessing to Christ, with special emphasis on service to the poor in Mississippi. Addresses: St. Francis Center, 708 Ave. I, Greenwood, MS 38930; LaVerna House, 2108 Altawoods Blvd., Jackson, MS 39204.

Rural Parish Workers of Christ the King: Founded in 1942; for women. A secular institute of the Archdiocese of St. Louis. Dedicated to the glory of God in service of neighbor, especially in rural areas. Address: Rt. 1, Box 1667, Cadet, MO 63630.

Teresian Institute: Founded in Spain 1911 by Pedro Poveda. Approved as an association of the faithful of pontifical right Jan. 11, 1924. Mailing Address: 3400 S. W. 99th Ave., Miami, FL 33165.

Holy Family Institute (aggregated to the Society of St. Paul) was founded by Fr. James Alberione in 1963 for married couples who wish to commit themselves to seeking evangelical perfection in marriage; definitively approved by the Holy See, 1993. First Americans professed, 1988. Address: 9531 Akron-Canfield Rd., Box 498, Canfield, OH 44406.

SECULAR ORDERS

Secular orders (commonly called third orders) are societies of the faithful living in the world who seek to deepen their Christian life and apostolic commitment in association with and according to the spirit of various religious institutes. The orders are called "third" because their foundation usually followed the establishment of the first and second religious orders with which they are associated.

Augustine, Third Order Secular of St.: Founded, 13th century; approved Nov. 7, 1400.

Carmelites, Lay (Third Order of Our Lady of Mt. Carmel): Rule for laity approved by Pope Nicholas V, Oct. 7, 1452; new statutes, January, 1991. Addresses (Lay Carmelite Office): 8501 Bailey Rd., Darien, IL 60561; P.O. Box 613, Williamston, MA 01267; P.O. Box 27, Tappan, NY 10983. Approximately 270 communities and 10,000 members in the U.S. and Canada.

Carmelites, The Secular Order of Discalced (formerly the Third Order Secular of the Blessed Virgin Mary of Mt Carmel and of St. Teresa of Jesus): Rule based on the Carmelite reform established by St. Teresa and St. John of the Cross, 16th century; approved Mar. 23, 1594. Revised rule approved May 10, 1979. Office of National Secretariat, U.S.A.; P.O. Box 3420, San Jose, CA 95156. Approximately 24,445 members throughout the world; 130 groups/ communities and 5,200 members in the U.S. and Canada.

Dominican Laity: Founded in the 13th century. Addresses of provincial coordinators: 487 Michigan Ave. N.E., Washington, DC 20017; 1909 S. Ashland Ave., Chicago, IL 60608; 5877 Birch Ct., Oakland, CA 94618; 1421 N. Causeway Blvd., Suite 200, Metairie, LA 70001.

Franciscan Order, Secular (SFO): Founded, 1209 by St. Francis of Assisi; approved Aug. 30, 1221. National Minister, Richard Morton, SFO, 3191 71st St. E., Inver Grove Heights, MN 55076. Tau USA,

quarterly. Approximately 780,000 throughout the world; 18,000 in U.S.

Mary, Third Order of: Founded, Dec. 8, 1850; rule approved by the Holy See, 1857. Addresses of provincial directors: Marist Provincial House, 815 Varnum St.. N.E., Washington, DC 20017; Marist Fathers, 518 Pleasant St., Framingham, MA 01701; Marist Fathers, 2335 Warring St., Berkeley, CA 94704. Approximately 14,000 in the world, 5,600 in U.S.

Mary, Secular Order of Servants of (Servite): Founded, 1233; approved, 1304. Revised rule approved 1995. Address: National Assistant for the Secular Order, 3121 W. Jackson Blvd., Chicago, IL 60612.

Mercy, Secular Third Order of Our Lady of (Mercedarian): Founded, 1219 by St. Peter Nolasco; approved the same year.

Norbert, Third Order of St.: Founded, 1122 by St. Norbert; approved by Pope Honorius II, 1126.

Trinity, Third Order Secular of the Most: Founded 1198; approved, 1219.

Oblates of St. Benedict are lay persons affiliated with a Benedictine abbey or monastery who strive to direct their lives, as circumstances permit, according to the spirit and Rule of St. Benedict.

In addition to the recognized secular orders, there are other groups of lay persons with strong ties to religious orders. Relationships of this kind serve the spiritual good of the faithful and also enrich the religious orders in a complementary fashion, with the mutual vitality of prayer in the cloister or convent and action in the marketplace.

CATHOLIC RELIEF SERVICES

Catholic Relief Services is the official overseas aid and development agency of U.S. Catholics; it is a separately incorporated organization of the U.S. Catholic Conference.

Long-term Development Projects

CRS was founded in 1943 by the bishops of the United States to help civilians in Europe and North Africa caught in the disruption and devastation of World War II. As conditions in Europe improved in the late 1940s and early 1950s, the works conducted by CRS spread to other continents and areas — Asia, Africa and Latin America.

Although best known for its record of disaster response, compassionate aid to refugees and commitment to reconstruction and rehabilitation, CRS places primary focus on long-term development projects designed to help people to help themselves and to determine their own future. Administrative funding for CRS comes largely from the Catholic Relief Services Annual Appeal. Major support is derived from private, individual donors and through a program of sacrificial giving called Operation Rice Bowl.

Kenneth F. Hackett is executive director. CRS headquarters are located at 209 W. Fayette St., Baltimore, Md. 21201.

Human Development Campaign

The Campaign for Human Development was inaugurated by the U.S. Catholic Conference in November, 1969, to combat injustice, oppression, alienation and poverty in this country by funding self-help programs begun and carried out by the poor or by the poor and non-poor working together, and by seeking a re-evaluation of the priorities of individuals, families, the Church and the civic community with respect to the stewardship of God-given goods. The campaign got underway with a collection taken up

in all parishes throughout the country on Nov. 22, 1970. Seventy-five percent of the money contributed in this and subsequent annual collections was placed in a national fund principally for funding self-help projects and also for educational purposes; 25 percent remained in the dioceses where it was collected. From 1970, the campaign has distributed approximately $200 million to more than 3,000 self-help projects. National office: 3211 Fourth St. N.E., Washington, D.C. 20017.

Magsaysay Award: Filipino Sister Eva Fidela Maamo received Aug. 31, 1997, the Ramon Magsaysay Award ($50,000) for community service, "for her compelling example in bringing humane assistance and the healing arts to the poorest" of her countrymen. Since 1984, the nun-physician organized at least four missions a year.

MISSIONARY ACTIVITY OF THE CHURCH _____

UNITED STATES OVERSEAS MISSIONARIES

From the *U.S. Catholic Mission Handbook: Mission Inventory 1996-1997*, reproduced with permission of the United States Catholic Mission Council, 3029 Fourth St. N.E.,Washington, D.C.

Field Distribution, 1997

Africa: 799 (449 men; 350 women). Largest numbers in Kenya, 194; Tanzania, 102; Uganda, 68; Nigeria, 52; South Africa, 50.

Asia: 892 (612 men; 280 women). Largest numbers in Philippines, 272; Japan, 174; Taiwan, 105; China PRC-Hong Kong SAR, 88; India,72; Korea,64. (Those present in China were there for professional services.)

Caribbean: 360 (209 men; 151 women). Largest numbers in Puerto Rico, 76; Jamaica, 63; Haiti, 55; Dominican Republic and Belize, 47 each.

Eurasia (Kazakhstan, Russia, Siberia): **12** (8 men; 4 women). Largest group 10, Russia.

Europe 172 (85 men; 87 women).Largest numbers in Italy, 50; Ireland, 21; England, 15; Germany, 13.

Latin America: **1,573** (858 men; 715 women). Largest numbers in Brazil, 303; Peru, 282; Mexico, 243; Bolivia, 155; Guatemala, 143.

Middle East: 61 (45 men; 16 women); Largest numbers in Israel, 29; Sudan, 13.

North America (Canada and Greenland): **82** (38 men; 44 women). Largest number in Canada, 81.

Pacific: 213 (149 men; 64 women). Largest numbers in Papua New Guinea,89; Micronesia, 35; Australia, 22; Guam, 16.

TOTAL: 4,164 (2,453 men; 1,711 women).

Missionary Personnel, 1997

Religious Priests: Sixty-five mission-sending groups had 1,736 priests in overseas assignments. Listed below are those with 15 or more members abroad.

Jesuits, 339; Maryknoll Fathers and Brothers, 311; Redemptorists, 111; Oblates of Mary Immaculate, 106; Society of Divine Word , 92; Franciscans (O.F.M.) 89; Franciscans (O.F.M. Cap), 77; Holy Cross Fathers, 48; Dominicans, 40; Columbans, 39; Vincentians, 31; Franciscans (O.F.M. Conv.), 24; Passionists, 23; Marianists, 20; Oblates of St. Francis de Sales, 19; Society of Precious Blood, 18; Xaverian Missionaries, 16; Congregstion of Sacred Heart, 16; Legionaries of Christ, 15; Salesians, 15; Spiritans, 15.

Diocesan Priests: There were 172 priests from 86 dioceses The majority were in Latin American countries.

Religious Brothers: Forty mission-sending groups had 347 brothers in overseas assignments. Those with 15 or more members:

Christian Brothers (Brothers of the Christian Schools), 54; Holy Cross Brothers, 40; Marianists, 36; Maryknoll Priests and Brothers, 35; Franciscans (O.F.M.), 26.

Religious Sisters: Two hundred and sixty-six mission-sending communities of women Religious had 1,513 sisters in overseas missions. Those with 15 or more members:

Maryknoll Mission Sisters, 239; School Sisters of Notre Dame, 71; Dominicans, 48; Sisters of Mercy (various communities), 42; Daughters of Charity, 37; Sisters of Holy Cross (36); Immaculate Heart of Mary Sisters, 31; Sisters of Notre Dame de Namur, 29; Medical Mission Sisters, 27; Marist Missionary Sisters, 25; Franciscan Sisters of Philadelphia, 23; Ursulines, 21; Little Sisters of the Poor, 20; Franciscan Sisters of Allegany, 19; Missionaries of Charity, 20; Sisters of St. Joseph of Carondelet, 18; Society of the Sacred Heart, 16; Medical Missionaries of Mary, Missionary Sisters of Our Lady of Africa and Congregation of Sisters of St. Agnes, 15 each.

Lay Persons: Forty-five mission sending groups had 343 memers in oveseas missions.

Maryknoll Mission Associates, 101; Jesuit Volunteers International, 30; Salesian Lay Missionaries, 21; Religious of the Assumption, 15.

Seminarians: There were 18 from 5 groups.

Legionaries of Christ, 10; Society of Our Lady of the Most Holy Trintiy, 4; Franciscans, 2; Holy Coss Fathers, 1; Jesuits, 1.

U.S. CATHOLIC MISSION ASSOCIATION

This is a voluntary association of individuals and organizations for whom the missionary presence of the universal Church is of central importance. It is a nonprofit religious, educational and charitable organization which exists to promote global missions. Its primary emphasis is on cross-cultural evangelization and the promotion of international justice and peace. The association is also responsible for gathering and publishing annual statistical data on U.S. missionary personnel overseas. President: Rev. Willaim J. Morton,S.S.; Executive Director, Sister Rosanne Rustemeyer, S.S.N.D. Address: 3029 Fourth St. NE, Washington, D.C. 20017.

Mission Statement

In its 1996-97 handbook, the association included the following in a mission statement.

"In the Church, our understanding of the mission of evangelization is evolving to embrace dialogue, community building, struggles for justice, efforts to model justice and faith in our lifestyles, activities and structures, in addition to the teaching/preaching/witnessing role traditionally at the heart of the mission enterprise. Still, the contemporary 'identity-confusion' about 'mission' stands forth as a major challenge for USCMA as we move toward the 21st century.

"The larger context of mission is the Spirit moving in the Signs of our Times: the liberation movements, the women's movements, the economy movements, the rising awareness and celebration of cultural diversity, the search for ways to live peacefully and creatively with great pluralism, rapid technological change, the emergence of the global economy, the steady increase in poverty and injustice, the realigning of the global political order — and the many ripples radiating out from each of these."

U.S. OVERSEAS MISSIONARIES 1960-1996

Year	Diocesan Priests	Rel. Priests	Rel. Bros.	Rel. Sisters	Seminarians	Lay Persons	Total
1960	14	3018	575	2827	170	178	6872
1962	31	3172	720	2764	152	307	7146
1964	80	3438	782	3137	157	532	8126
1966	215	3731	901	3706	201	549	9303
1968	282	3727	869	4150	208	419	9655
1970	373	3117	666	3824	90	303	8373
1972[1]	246	3182	634	3121	97	376	7655
1973	237	3913[2]	—	3012	—	529	7691
1974	220	3048	639	2916	101	458	7418
1975	197	3023	669	2850	65	344	7148
1976	193	2961	691	2840	68	257	7010
1977	182	2882	630	2781	42	243	6760
1978	166	2830	610	2673	43	279	6601
1979	187	2800	592	2568	50	258	6455
1980	188	2750	592	2592	50	221	6393
1981	187	2702	584	2574	43	234	6324
1982	178	2668	578	2560	44	217	6245
1983	174	2668	569	2450	48	247	6346
1984	187	2603	549	2492	40	263	6134
1985	171	2500	558	2505	30	292	6056
1986	203	2473	532	2481	30	317	6037
1987	200	2394	570	2505	53	351	6073
1988	200	2420	504	2495	50	394	6063
1989	209	2364	494	2473	51	410	6001
1990	200	2257	477	2347	42	421	5744
1991	187	2200	468	2264	30	446	5595
1992	181	2183	449	2222	26	406	5467
1994	177	2007	408	1887	22	374	4875[3]
1996	173	1770	347	1513	18	343	4164[4]

[1] Corrected total for 1972 should read 7937. [2] Includes Religious Brothers and Seminarians. [3] Totals estimated due to inconclusive survey results. [4] Does not include Alaska and Hawaii, which had been included in previous surveys.

HOME MISSIONS

The expression "home missions" is applied to places in the U.S. where the local church does not have its own resources, human and otherwise, which are needed to begin or, if begun, to survive and grow. These areas share the name "missions" with their counterparts in foreign lands because they too need outside help to provide the personnel and means for making the Church present and active there in carrying out its mission for the salvation of people.

Dioceses in the Southeast, the Southwest, and the Far West are most urgently in need of outside help to carry on the work of the Church. Millions of persons live in counties in which there are no resident priests. Many others live in rural areas beyond the reach and influence of a Catholic center. According to recent statistics compiled by the Glenmary Research Center, there are more than 500 priestless counties in the United States.

Mission Workers

A number of forces are at work to meet the pastoral needs of these missionary areas and to establish permanent churches and operating institutions where they are required. In many dioceses, one or more missions and stations are attended from established parishes and are gradually growing to independent status. Priests, brothers and sisters belonging to scores of religious institutes are engaged full-time in the home missions. Lay persons, some of them in affiliation with special groups and movements, are also involved.

The Society for the Propagation of the Faith, which conducts an annual collection for mission support in all parishes of the U.S., allocates 40 per cent of this sum for disbursement to home missions through the American Board of Catholic Missions.

Various mission-aid societies frequently undertake projects in behalf of the home missions.

The **Glenmary Home Missioners,** founded by Father W. Howard Bishop in 1939, is the only home mission society established for the sole purpose of carrying out the pastoral ministry in small towns and rural districts of the United States. Glenmary serves in many areas where at least 20 per cent of the people live in poverty and less than one per cent are Catholic. With 62 priests and 19 professed brothers as of January, 1997, the Glenmary Missioners had missions in the archdioceses of Atlanta and Cincinnati, and in the dioceses of Birmingham, Charlotte, Covington, Jackson, Lexington, Little Rock, Nashville, Owensboro, Richmond, Savannah, Tulsa, Tyler and Wheeling-Charleston. National headquarters are located at 4119 Glenmary Trace, Fairfield, Ohio. The mailing address is P.O. Box 465618, Cincinnati, Ohio 45246.

Organizations

Black and Indian Mission Office (The Commission for Catholic Missions among the Colored People and the Indians): Organized officially in 1885 by decree of the Third Plenary Council of Baltimore. Provides financial support for religious works among Blacks and Native Americans in 133 archdioceses and dioceses through funds raised by an annual collection in all parishes of the U.S. on the first Sunday of Lent, the designated Sunday. In 1996, $7,058,599 was raised; disbursements amounted to $4,672,000 for Black missions and $2,328,000 for Native American missions.

Bureau of Catholic Indian Missions: Established in 1874 as the representative of Catholic Indian missions before the federal government and the public; made permanent organization in 1884 by Third Plenary Council of Baltimore. After a remarkable history of rendering important services to the Indian people, the bureau continues to represent the Catholic Church in the U.S. in her apostolate to the American Indian. Concerns are evangelization, catechesis, liturgy, family life, education, advocacy.

Catholic Negro-American Mission Board (1907): Support priests and sisters in southern states and provide monthly support to sisters and lay teachers in the poorest Black schools.

Board of Directors of the three organizations above are: Cardinal John O'Connor, president; Cardinal Anthony Bevilacqua; Cardinal William Keeler; Msgr.

Paul A. Lenz, secretary-treasurer; Patricia L. O'Rourke, assistant secretary-treasurer.

Address: 2021 H Street NW, Washington, DC 20006.

The Catholic Church Extension Society (1905): Established with papal approval for the purpose of preserving and extending the Church in rural and isolated parts of the U.S. and its dependencies through the collection and disbursement of funds for home mission work. Since the time of its founding, more than $275 million have been received and distributed for this purpose. Disbursements, made at the requests of bishops in 75 designated mission dioceses, exceeded $12 million for fiscal year 1997. The 10,500th church project built with the help of the society was dedicated in 1997. The society also distributes parish calendars. Works of the society are supervised by a 14-member board of governors: Archbishop Francis George of Chicago, chancellor; Rev. Msgr. Kenneth Velo, president; three archbishops, three bishops and six lay people. Headquarters: 35 E. Wacker Drive, Chicago, IL 60601.

National Catholic Rural Life Conference: Founded in 1923 through the efforts of Bishop Edwin V. O'Hara. Applies the Gospel message to rural issues through focus on rural parishes and the provision of services including distribution of educational materials development of prayer and worship resources, advocacy for strong rural communities. Bishop Raymond L. Burke of LaCrosse, president; Brother David G. Andrews C.S.C., executive director. National headquarters: 4625 Beaver Ave., Des Moines, IA 50310.

More Deaths

Continued from page 600
Rambusch, Viggio F. E., 96, Dec. 27, 1996, Scarsdale, N.Y.; noted designer of Catholic Church interiors.

Scanlan, Bishop John J., 90, Jan. 31, 1997, San Rafael, Calif; Irish-born retired bishop of Honolulu (1968-82).

Sigur, Msgr. Alexander, 76, Aug. 13, 1997, Crowley, Ind.; editor, college chaplain, seminary rector.

Smith, Rev. Paul B., 64, Nov. 22 or 23, 1996; Chicago, Ill.; principal of Holy Angels School in one of poorest sections of Chicago; murdered.

Sommer, Rev. Paul James, M.M., 79, June 11, 1997, Marknoll, N.Y.; missioner in Central America, 34 years in Guatemala; 19 years in El Salvador.

Stanley, Rev. David, S.J., 82, Dec. 30, 1996, Pickering, Ont., Canada; Canadian biblical scholar.

Treinen, Bishop Sylvester W., 78, Sept. 30, 1996, Missoula, Mont; retired bishop (1962-88) of Boise, Idaho.

Van Ackeren, Maurice E., S.J., 85, May 12, 1997, Kansas City, Mo.; president (1951-77) and chancellor (from 1977) of Rockhurst College

Walsh, Rev. John, M.M., 90, Jan. 24, 1997,

Maryknoll, N.Y.; missionary in Asia; linguist, teacher, musician.

Walsh, Bishop Nicolas E., 80, Apr. 21, 1997, Tucson, Ariz.; missionary, newspaper editor; retired bishop of Yakima (1974-76); auxiliary bishop of Seattle (1976-83).

Wang Hsueh-ming, Abp. Francis, 87, Feb. 10, 1997, China; archbishop of Hohot, Inner Mongolia; one of last two Vatican appointed bishops on mainland China.

White, Norm, Rev., 72, Aug 28, 1996, Dubuque, Iowa; diocesan rural life director from 1974.

Willems, Robert A., 64, May 24, 1971, Huntington, Ind.; retired associate editor of *Our Sunday Visitor.*

Xiao Liren, Bishop Michael, 87, Oct. 26, 1996, Hebi province, China; clandestinely ordained bishop of Yengtoo in late 1980s; could not serve.

Zong, Bishop Huiade, 80, June 28, 1997, Beijing, China; leader of the government sanctioned Chinese Catholic Patriotic Association and president of the Bishops' Conference of the Catholic Church in China. One of first Chinese bishops ordained without Vatican approval.

EVANGELIZATION

Nigerian Cardinal Francis Arinze, head ot the Pontifical Council for Interreligious Dialogue, in an address Aug. 29, 1997, during the eighth National Black

Catholic Congress in Baltimore, said, "The task of evangelizing all people constitutes the central mission of the Church. The Church has no other assignment."

EDUCATION

LEGAL STATUS OF CATHOLIC EDUCATION

The right of private schools to exist and operate in the United States is recognized in law. It was confirmed by the U.S. Supreme Court in 1925 when the tribunal ruled (Pierce v. Society of Sisters, see Church-State Decisions of the Supreme Court) that an Oregon state law requiring all children to attend public schools was unconstitutional.

Private schools are obliged to comply with the education laws in force in the various states regarding such matters as required basic curricula, periods of attendance, and standards for proper accreditation.

The special curricula and standards of private schools are determined by the schools themselves. Thus, in Catholic schools, the curricula include not only the subject matter required by state educational laws but also other fields of study, principally, education in the Catholic faith.

The Supreme Court has ruled that the First Amendment to the U.S. Constitution, in accordance with the No Establishment of Religion Clause of the First Amendment, prohibits direct federal and state aid from public funds to church-affiliated schools. (See several cases in Church-State Decisions of the Supreme Court.)

Public Aid

This prohibition does not extend to all child-benefit and public-purpose programs of aid to students of non-public elementary and secondary schools.

Statutes authorizing such programs have been ruled constitutional on the grounds that they:
- have a "secular legislative purpose";
- neither inhibit nor advance religion as a "principal or primary effect";
- do not foster "excessive government entanglement with religion."

Aid programs considered constitutional have provided bus transportation, textbook loans, school lunches and health services, and "secular, neutral or non-ideological services, facilities and materials provided in common to all school children," public and non-public.

The first major aid to education program in U.S. history containing provisions benefitting nonpublic school students was enacted by the 89th Congress and signed into law by President Lyndon B. Johnson Apr. 11, 1965. The Elementary and Secondary Education Act was designed to avoid the separation of Church and state impasse which had blocked all earlier aid proposals pertaining to nonpublic, and especially church-affiliated, schools. The objective of the program, under public control, is to serve the public

purpose by aiding disadvantaged pupils in nonpublic as well as public schools.

With respect to college and university education in church-affiliated institutions, the Supreme Court has upheld the constitutionality of statutes providing student loans and, under the Federal Higher Education Facilities Act of 1963, construction loans and grants for secular-purpose facilities.

Catholic schools are exempt from real estate taxation in all of the states. Since Jan. 1, 1959, nonprofit parochial and private schools have also been exempt from several federal excise taxes.

Shared and Released Time

In a shared time program of education, students enrolled in Catholic or other church-related schools take some courses (e.g., religion, social studies, fine arts) in their own schools and others (e.g., science, mathematics, industrial arts) in public schools. Such a program has been given serious consideration in recent years by Catholic and other educators. Its constitutionality has not been seriously challenged, but practical problems _ relating to teacher and student schedules, transportation, adjustment to new programs, and other factors _ are knotty.

Several million children of elementary and high school age of all denominations have the opportunity of receiving religious instruction on released time. Under released time programs they are permitted to leave their public schools during school hours to attend religious instruction classes held off the public school premises. They are released at the request of their parents. Public school authorities merely provide for their dismissal, and take no part in the program.

NCEA

The National Catholic Educational Association, founded in 1904, is a voluntary organization of educational institutions and individuals concerned with Catholic education in the U.S. Its objectives are to promote and encourage the principles and ideals of Christian education and formation by suitable service and other activities.

The NCEA serves approximately 200,000 Catholic educators at all levels from pre-K through university. Its official publication is *Momentum*. Numerous service publications are issued to members.

Bishop John J. Leibrecht of Springfield-Cape Girardeau, chairman of the Board of Directors; Leonard F. DeFiore, president. Address: 1077 30th St. N.W., Washington, D.C. 20007.

Norms for Catholic Higher Education

Mutual trust between Catholic colleges or universities and church authorities, "close and consistent cooperation" and "continuing dialogue," were called for in a document approved by the U.S. bishops Nov. 13, 1996.

The document dealt with norms for application in the United States of provisions on Catholic higher education contained in an apostolic constitution issued by Pope John Paul in 1990 under the title *Ex Corde Ecclesiae*.

The bishops' document says that "a need exists for continued attention and commitment to the far-reaching implications — curricular, staffing, programming — of major themes in *Ex Corde Ecclesiae*. These include Catholic identity, 'communio,' relating faith and culture, pastoral outreach, the new evangelization and relationship with the Church."

The document says a Catholic college or university expects faculty members to uphold their institution's Catholic character.

CATHOLIC SCHOOLS AND STUDENTS IN THE UNITED STATES

(Source: *The Official Catholic Directory, 1997;* figures as of Jan. 1, 1997. Archdioceses are indicated by an asterisk.)

State Diocese	Univs. Colleges	Students	High Schools	Students	Elem. Schools	Students
Alabama	1	946	8	2,961	42	12,785
*Mobile	1	946	3	1,618	21	7,688
Birmingham	–	–	5	1,343	21	5,097
Alaska	–	–	2	265	5	880
*Anchorage	–	–	1	40	3	519
Fairbanks	–	–	1	225	1	261
Juneau	–	–	–	–	1	100
Arizona	–	–	8	5,159	43	12,674
Phoenix	–	–	5	3,576	23	7,642
Tucson	–	–	3	1,583	20	5,032
Arkansas, Little Rock	–	–	5	1,776	31	6,758
California	15	39,973	114	69,576	603	182,037
*Los Angeles	6	9,977	51	30,477	230	70,124
*San Francisco	3	10,930	13	7,578	66	21,114
Fresno	–	–	2	1,426	23	5,715
Monterey	–	–	4	1,375	15	3,872
Oakland	3	4,500	9	6,012	51	14,419
Orange	1	100	6	5,635	37	13,736
Sacramento	–	–	7	4,052	48	13,710
San Bernardino	–	–	2	894	31	8,402
San Diego	1	6,603	5	3,132	44	13,287
San Jose	1	7,863	6	5,596	31	11,126
Santa Rosa	–	–	7	2,075	15	3,093
Stockton	–	–	2	1,324	12	3,439
Colorado	1	9,648	7	2,608	46	13,890
*Denver	1	9,648	5	2,283	37	11,428
Colorado Springs	–	–	–	–	4	1,212
Pueblo	–	–	2	325	5	1,250
Connecticut	6	13,701	24	10,324	129	34,318
*Hartford	3	2,833	11	4,867	73	19,571
Bridgeport	3	10,868	8	3,437	34	10,101
Norwich	–	–	5	2,020	22	4,646
Delaware, Wilmington	–	–	8	4,712	30	10,716
District of Columbia, *Washington	3	20,958	17	7,858	88	24,083
Florida	3	17,557	32	20,587	184	65,871
*Miami	2	10,378	12	9,611	52	22,969
Orlando	–	–	4	2,387	32	11,531
Palm Beach	–	–	3	1,897	16	5,746
Pensacola-Tallahassee	–	–	1	570	8	2,610
St. Augustine	–	–	2	1,720	23	6,985
St. Petersburg	1	7,179	7	2,825	44	12,031
Venice	–	–	3	1,577	9	3,999
Georgia	–	–	7	4,671	30	9,321
*Atlanta	–	–	2	2,035	15	4,812
Savannah	–	–	5	2,636	15	4,509
Hawaii, Honolulu	1	2,528	7	3,675	26	6,574
Idaho, Boise	–	–	1	713	13	2,388
Illinois	14	51,231	81	50,256	521	165,630
*Chicago	6	40,599	48	33,425	276	102,024
Belleville	1	632	3	1,641	39	7,574
Joliet	4	8,171	8	5,602	63	19,372
Peoria	1	152	7	2,674	48	12,517
Rockford	–	–	8	4,223	41	11,451
Springfield	2	1,697	7	2,691	54	12,692
Indiana	12	25,100	23	12,619	175	48,088
*Indianapolis	3	2,573	9	5,185	62	18,767
Evansville	–	–	5	1,823	24	5,745
Ft. Wayne-S. Bend	5	13,805	4	3,045	40	11,542
Gary	1	1,022	4	2,198	31	8,021
Lafayette	3	7,700	1	368	18	4,013

State Diocese	Univs. Colleges	Students	High Schools	Students	Elem. Schools	Students
Iowa	**6**	**8,433**	**25**	**8,227**	**142**	**28,287**
*Dubuque	3	4,198	8	3,189	54	12,447
Davenport	2	3,119	7	1,278	45	4,627
Des Moines	—	—	2	1,380	15	4,673
Sioux City	1	1,116	8	2,380	28	6,540
Kansas	**4**	**4,414**	**16**	**6,042**	**95**	**22,926**
*Kansas City	3	2,430	7	3,421	40	12,137
Dodge City	—	—	—	—	10	1,378
Salina	—	—	5	702	12	1,887
Wichita	1	1,984	4	1,919	33	7,524
Kentucky	**5**	**6,126**	**25**	**10,884**	**125**	**34,344**
*Louisville	3	3,940	10	5,944	59	18,280
Covington	1	1,426	9	3,164	32	8,464
Lexington	—	—	3	742	15	3,185
Owensboro	1	760	3	1,034	19	4,415
Louisiana	**4**	**11,165**	**50**	**27,593**	**175**	**69,546**
*New Orleans	3	10,296	23	16,392	80	34,452
Alexandria	—	—	3	514	9	2,635
Baton Rouge	1	869	8	4,014	26	12,562
Houma-Thibodaux	—	—	3	1,866	10	4,162
Lafayette	—	—	10	3,513	31	10,803
Lake Charles	—	—	1	483	8	2,353
Shreveport	—	—	2	811	11	2,579
Maine, Portland	**1**	**4,785**	**3**	**805**	**19**	**4,083**
Maryland, *Baltimore	**3**	**11,365**	**22**	**10,583**	**74**	**24,397**
Massachusetts	**14**	**32,969**	**51**	**23,105**	**208**	**58,331**
*Boston	9	21,657	36	14,958	130	38,360
Fall River	1	2,882	4	2,467	25	6,018
Springfield	1	1,187	4	1,945	30	8,288
Worcester	3	7,243	7	3,735	23	5,665
Michigan	**6**	**20,533**	**54**	**21,001**	**301**	**75,378**
*Detroit	4	16,122	35	14,132	140	41,178
Gaylord	—	—	4	632	18	2,549
Grand Rapids	1	2,385	4	1,839	41	9,404
Kalamazoo	—	—	3	866	21	4,597
Lansing	1	2,026	5	2,518	39	10,370
Marquette	—	—	—	—	10	1,802
Saginaw	—	—	3	1,014	32	5,478
Minnesota	**7**	**27,400**	**21**	**9,401**	**192**	**45,489**
*St.Paul and Minneapolis	3	14,324	11	6,642	89	27,392
Crookston	—	—	1	150	9	1,250
Duluth	1	2,000	—	—	13	1,689
New Ulm	—	—	3	669	19	3,498
St. Cloud	2	3,689	2	712	35	6,149
Winona	1	7,387	4	1,228	27	5,511
Mississippi	**1**	**28**	**9**	**2,618**	**29**	**6,625**
Biloxi	—	—	5	1,803	14	2,245
Jackson	1	28	4	815	15	4,380
Missouri	**4**	**16,312**	**42**	**20,060**	**246**	**64,043**
*St.Louis	2	12,462	29	15,193	154	43,860
Jefferson City	—	—	2	984	35	6,027
Kansas City-St. Joseph	2	3,850	8	3,095	34	10,355
Springfield-Cape Girardeau	—	—	3	788	23	3,801
Montana	**2**	**2,717**	**4**	**943**	**16**	**3,249**
Great Falls-Billings	1	1,299	2	547	12	2,465
Helena	1	1,418	2	396	4	784
Nebraska	**2**	**7,227**	**27**	**7,882**	**94**	**22,290**
*Omaha	2	7,227	17	5,042	62	15,915
Grand Island	—	—	4	959	7	792
Lincoln	—	—	6	1,881	25	5,583
Nevada	**—**	**—**	**2**	**1,478**	**12**	**3,559**
Las Vegas	—	—	1	1,028	8	2,424
Reno	—	—	1	450	4	1,135

State Diocese	Univs. Colleges	Students	High Schools	Students	Elem. Schools	Students
New Hampshire, Manchester	6	6,690	4	2,280	26	7,487
New Jersey	7	20,288	75	37,048	369	113,878
*Newark	4	16,252	37	15,944	148	45,509
Camden	–	–	11	5,837	61	15,662
Metuchen	–	–	6	3,802	43	14,422
Paterson	2	1,614	10	3,987	61	16,728
Trenton	1	2,422	11	7,478	56	21,557
New Mexico	1	1,600	6	2,097	33	7,024
*Santa Fe	1	1,600	3	1,896	18	4,762
Gallup	–	–	3	201	10	1,609
Las Cruces	–	–	–	–	5	653
New York	30	106,820	129	73,518	715	227,472
*New York	12	60,500	55	28,104	238	78,852
Albany	4	4,550	7	3,106	39	9,746
Brooklyn	3	20,739	22	17,855	158	55,576
Buffalo	7	13,298	17	6,029	94	24,659
Ogdensburg	1	335	2	649	24	4,476
Rochester	–	12	7	3,508	56	16,354
Rockville Centre	2	4,586	13	10,923	67	28,785
Syracuse	1	2,800	6	3,344	39	9,024
North Carolina	2	902	3	1,523	32	10,295
Charlotte	2	902	2	1,084	15	5,462
Raleigh	–	–	1	439	17	4,833
North Dakota	2	2,040	5	1,693	28	3,675
Bismarck	1	2,016	3	1,334	16	2,157
Fargo	1	24	2	359	12	1,518
Ohio	12	32,099	79	45,327	451	146,039
*Cincinnati	4	18,805	22	15,384	113	40,521
Cleveland	3	6,190	23	14,447	141	51,950
Columbus	1	1,883	11	4,819	47	15,393
Steubenville	1	1,936	3	728	16	2,899
Toledo	2	1,838	14	6,924	87	23,034
Youngstown	1	1,447	6	3,025	47	12,242
Oklahoma	1	335	4	2,323	29	10,925
*Oklahoma City	1	335	2	903	18	7,525
Tulsa	–	–	2	1,420	11	3,400
Oregon	2	5,149	9	4,643	45	9,836
*Portland	2	5,149	9	4,643	42	9,221
Baker	–	–	–	–	3	615
Pennsylvania	26	73,356	92	51,418	617	183,227
*Philadelphia	11	31,662	40	29,660	242	91,631
Allentown	2	3,001	9	4,129	55	14,301
Altoona-Johnstown	2	6,083	3	1,230	31	5,336
Erie	2	6,027	8	3,189	45	11,181
Greensburg	2	2,144	2	837	30	6,033
Harrisburg	–	–	8	3,730	40	10,751
Pittsburgh	31	3,380	11	4,460	110	30,320
Scranton	41	1,059	11	4,183	64	13,674
Rhode Island, Providence	2	7,731	11	5,031	53	13,097
South Carolina, Charleston	–	–	3	1,416	25	6,449
South Dakota	2	2,350	5	1,556	26	5,258
Rapid City	–	–	2	436	3	906
Sioux Falls	2	2,350	3	1,120	23	4,352
Tennessee	2	2,199	11	4,508	35	10,697
Knoxville	–	–	2	914	7	2,513
Memphis	1	1,784	7	2,404	13	4,012
Nashville	1	415	2	1,190	15	4,172
Texas	7	19,384	45	16,840	243	66,547
*San Antonio	4	11,090	9	3,401	42	13,163
Amarillo	–	–	1	131	8	911
Austin	1	3,050	3	587	16	3,523
Beaumont	–	–	1	685	7	1,610
Brownsville	–	–	1	673	8	2,613

State Diocese	Univs. Colleges	Students	High Schools	Students	Elem. Schools	Students
Texas						
Corpus Christi	–	–	3	1,037	28	5,098
Dallas	1	2,740	7	3,063	32	10,782
El Paso	–	–	3	1,002	12	4,221
Fort Worth	–	–	4	1,930	16	6,325
Galveston-Houston	1	2,504	8	3,515	51	13,295
Lubbock	–	–	1	78	2	331
San Angelo	–	–	–	–	3	908
Tyler	–	–	1	133	5	963
Victoria	–	–	3	605	13	2,804
Utah, Salt Lake City	–	–	2	1,195	10	2,697
Vermont, Burlington	3	4,029	2	695	11	2,433
Virginia	2	3,035	13	5,400	57	17,830
Arlington	2	3,035	4	3,449	33	12,316
Richmond	–	–	9	1,951	24	5,514
Washington	3	11,919	12	6,428	79	21,449
*Seattle	2	7,503	9	5,113	56	16,315
Spokane	1	4,416	2	1,315	16	3,206
Yakima	–	–	1	–	7	1,928
West Virginia, Wheeling-Charleston	1	1,527	8	1,717	29	5,571
Wisconsin	9	29,241	28	12,506	367	62,923
*Milwaukee	5	21,395	13	7,704	146	28,427
Green Bay	2	4,100	6	2,256	80	13,659
La Crosse	1	1,637	7	1,859	78	10,151
Madison	1	2,109	2	687	45	7,617
Superior	–	–	–	–	18	3,069
Wyoming, Cheyenne	–	–	–	–	7	1,322
EASTERN CHURCHES	1	657	3	570	25	5,780
*Philadelphia	1	657	1	350	7	1,636
St. Nicholas (Chicago)	–	–	1	80	2	465
Stamford	–	–	1	140	4	463
St. Josaphat (Parma)	–	–	–	–	2	262
*Pittsburgh	–	–	–	–	3	580
Parma	–	–	–	–	2	342
Passaic	–	–	–	–	1	1,055
Van Nuys	–	–	–	–	–	–
St. Maron (Maronites)	–	–	–	–	–	–
Our Lady of Lebanon (Maronites)	–	–	–	–	–	–
Newton (Melkites)	–	–	–	–	–	–
St. Thomas Apostle of Detroit (Chaldeans)	–	–	–	–	–	–
St. George Martyr (Romanians)	–	–	–	–	–	–
Armenians (Ap. Ex.)	–	–	–	–	4	977
SCHOOLS AND STUDENTS IN OUTLYING AREAS						
American Samoa	–	–	2	320	2	454
Caroline Islands	–	–	5	701	5	1,644
Guam	–	–	3	1,058	7	2,693
Marshall Islands	–	–	2	289	6	1,248
Marianas	–	–	1	192	2	509
Puerto Rico	52	4,359	98	21,703	134	46,152
Virgin Islands	–	–	2	310	3	642
GRAND TOTALS 1997	**241**	**690,826**	**1,357**	**652,687**	**7,165**	**2,053,819**
Grand Totals 1996	**237**	**691,626**	**1,350**	**647,613**	**7,011**	**2,052,193**
Grand Totals, 1987	**238**	**556,337**	**1,408**	**754,714**	**7,772**	**2,030,598**

North American College

The North American College, founded by the U.S. bishops in 1859, is a residence and house of formation for U.S. seminarians and graduate students in Rome. The first ordination of an alumnus took place June 14, 1862. Pontifical status was granted the college by Pope Leo XIII Oct. 25, 1884. Students pursue theological and related studies principally at the Pontifical Gregorian University.

SUMMARY OF SCHOOL STATISTICS

The status of Catholic educational institutions and programs in the United States and outlying areas at the beginning of 1997 was reflected in figures (as of Jan. 1) reported by *The Official Catholic Directory, 1997.*

Colleges and Universities: 241 (U.S., 236; Outlying Areas, 5).

College and University Students: 690,826 (U.S., 666,467; Outlying Areas, 24,359).

High Schools: 1,357 (794 diocesan and parochial; 563 private). U.S., 1,244 (723 diocesan and parochial; 521 private). Outlying Areas, 113 (71 diocesan and parochial; 42 private).

High School Students: 652,687 (369,281 diocesan and parochial; 283,406 private). U.S., 628,114 (355,556 diocesan and parochial; 272,558 private). Outlying Areas, 24,573 (13,725 diocesan and parochial; 10,841 private).

Public High School Students Receiving Religious Instruction: 804,759 (U.S., 785,743; Outlying Areas, 19,016).

Elementary Schools: 7,165 (6,822 diocesan and parochial; 343 private). U.S., 7,006 (6,725 diocesan and parochial; 281 private). Outlying Areas, 159 (97 diocesan and parochial; 62 private).

Elementary School Students: 2,053,819

(1,960,274 diocesan and parochial; 93,545 private). U.S., 2,000,471 (1,928,041 diocesan and parochial; 72,430 private). Outlying Areas, 53,348 (32,233 diocesan and parochial; 21,115 private).

Public Elementary School Students Receiving Religious Instruction: 3,445,153 (U.S., 3,384,453; Outlying Areas, 60,700).

Non-Residential Schools for Handicapped: 80 (U.S.). Students: 19,198 (U.S.).

Teachers —166,798. U.S., 161,304: Lay Persons, 147,152*; Sisters, 10,893; Priests, 2,064; Brothers, 1,155; Scholastics, 40. Outlying Areas, 5,493: Lay Persons, 5,011*; Sisters, 324; Priests, 110; Brothers, 36; scholastics, 11.

Seminaries — 206 (77 diocesan; 129 religious). U.S.: 193 (72 diocesan; 121 religious). Outlying Areas: 13 (5 diocesan; 8 religious).

Seminarians — 4,645 (3,149 diocesan; 1,496 religious). U.S.: 4,539 (3,084 diocesan; 1,455 religious). Outlying Areas: 106 (65 diocesan; 41 religious).

*1997 figures for lay persons. *The Official Catholic Directory* reported revised figures for 1996: U.S., 147,293; outlying areas, 5,411. These had been reported in the 1996 *Directory* as: U.S., 179,974; outlying areas, 4,691.

UNIVERSITIES AND COLLEGES IN THE UNITED STATES

(Sources: Almanac survey; *The Official Catholic Directory.*)

Listed below are institutions of higher learning established under Catholic auspices. Some of them are now independent.

Information includes: name of each institution; indication of male (m), female (w), coeducational (c) student body; name of founding group or group with which the institution is affiliated; year of foundation; total number of students, in parentheses.

Albertus Magnus College (c): 700 Prospect St., New Haven, CT 06511. Dominican Sisters; 1925; independent (1,200).

Allentown College of St. Francis de Sales (c): 2755 Station Ave., Center Valley, PA 18034. Oblates of St. Francis de Sales; 1965 (1,724).

Alvernia College (c): Reading, PA 19607. Bernardine Sisters; 1958 (1,292).

Alverno College (w): 3401 S. 39th St., Milwaukee, WI 53215. School Sisters of St. Francis; 1887; independent (2,191).

Anna Maria College (c): Sunset Lane, Paxton, MA 01612. Sisters of St. Anne;1946; independent (1,927).

Aquinas College (c): 1607 Robinson Rd. S.E., Grand Rapids, MI 49506. Sisters of St. Dominic; 1922; independent (2,385).

Aquinas College (c): 4210 Harding Rd., Nashville, TN 37205. Dominican Sisters; 1961 (415). Offers B.A. in Elementary Teacher Education.

Assumption College (c): 500 Salisbury St., Worcester, MA 01615. Assumptionist Religious; 1904 (2,588).

Avila College (c): 11901 Wornall Rd., Kansas City,

MO 64145. Sisters of St. Joseph of Carondelet; 1916 (1,275).

Barat College (c): 700 Westleigh Rd., Lake Forest, IL 60045. Society of the Sacred Heart; 1919; independent (757).

Barry University (c): 11300 N.E. 2nd Ave., Miami Shores, FL 33161. Dominican Sisters (Adrian, Mich.); 1940 (7,218).

Bellarmine College (c): 2001 Newburg Rd., Louisville, KY 40205; Louisville archdiocese; independent (2,180).

Belmont Abbey College (c): 100 Belmont-Mt. Holly Rd., Belmont, NC 28012. Benedictine Fathers; 1876 (902).

Benedictine College (c): 1020 N. Second St., Atchison, KS 66002. Benedictines; 1859; independent (1,100).

Benedictine University (formerly Illinois Benedictine College) (c): 5700 College Rd., Lisle, IL 60532. Benedictine Monks of St. Procopius Abbey; 1887 (2,619).

Boston College (University Status) (c): Chestnut Hill, MA 02167. Jesuit Fathers; 1863 (14,455).

Brescia College (c): 717 Frederica St., Owensboro, KY 42301. Ursuline Sisters; 1950 (750).

Briar Cliff College (c): 3303 Rebecca St., P.O. Box 2100, Sioux City, IA 51104. Sisters of St. Francis of the Holy Family; 1930 (1,157).

Cabrini College (c): 610 King of Prussia Rd., Radnor, PA 19087. Missionary Srs. of Sacred Heart; 1957; private (2,119).

Caldwell College (c): 9 Ryerson Ave., Caldwell, NJ 07006. Dominican Sisters; 1939 (1,600).

Calumet College of St. Joseph (c): 2400 New York

Ave., Whiting, IN 46394. Society of the Precious Blood, 1951 (1,100).

Canisius College (c): 2001 Main St., Buffalo, NY 14208. Jesuit Fathers; 1870; independent (4,746).

Cardinal Stritch College (c): 6801 N. Yates Rd., Milwaukee, WI 53217. Sisters of St. Francis of Assisi; 1937 (5,176).

Carlow College (w): 3333 5th Ave., Pittsburgh, PA 15213. Sisters of Mercy; 1929 (2,339).

Carroll College (c): Helena, MT 59625. Diocesan; 1909 (1,117).

Catholic University of America, The (c): 620 Michigan Ave. N.E., Washington, DC 20064. Hierarchy of the United States; 1887. Pontifical University (6,147).

Chaminade University of Honolulu (c): 3140 Waialae Ave., Honolulu, Hawaii 96816. Marianists; 1955 (2,300).

Chestnut Hill College (w): Philadelphia, PA 19118. Sisters of St. Joseph; 1924 (1,340).

Christendom College (c): 134 Christendom Dr., Front Royal, VA 22630. Founded 1977 (213).

Christian Brothers University (c): 650 E. Parkway S., Memphis, TN 38104. Brothers of the Christian Schools; 1871 (1,800).

Clarke College (c): 1550 Clarke Dr., Dubuque, Iowa 52001. Sisters of Charity, BVM; 1843; independent (1,082).

Creighton University (c): 2500 California Plaza, Omaha, NE 68178. Jesuit Fathers; 1878; independent (6,424).

Dallas, University of (c): 1845 E. Northgate, Irving, TX 75062. Dallas diocese; 1956; independent (2,995).

Dayton, University of (c): 300 College Park, Dayton, Ohio 45469. Marianists; 1850 (10,320).

DePaul University (c): One E. Jackson Blvd., Chicago, IL 60604. Vincentians; 1898 (16,747).

Detroit Mercy, University of (c): 4001 W. McNichols Rd., Detroit, MI, 48221; 8200 W. Outer Dr., Detroit MI 48219. Society of Jesus and Sisters of Mercy; 1877; independent (7,284).

Dominican College (c): 50 Acacia Ave., San Rafael, CA 94901. Dominican Sisters; 1890; independent (1,380).

Dominican College of Blauvelt (c):Orangeburg, NY 10962. Dominican Sisters; 1952; independent (1,800).

Dominican University (formerly Rosary College) (c): 7900 W. Division St., River Forest, IL 60305. Sinsinawa Dominican Sisters; 1901 (1,855).

Duquesne University (c): 600 Forbes Ave., Pittsburgh, PA 15282. Congregation of the Holy Ghost; 1878 (appox. 9,400).

D'Youville College (c): 320 Porter Ave., Buffalo, NY 14201. Grey Nuns of the Sacred Heart; 1908; independent (1,900).

Edgewood College (c): 855 Woodrow St., Madison, WI 53711. Sinsinawa Dominican Sisters; 1927 (2,000).

Emmanuel College (w): 400 The Fenway, Boston, MA 02115. Sisters of Notre Dame de Namur; 1919; independent (1,200).

Fairfield University (c): 1073 North Benson Rd., Fairfield, CT 06430. Jesuits; 1942 (5,300).

Felician College (c): 262 S. Main St., Lodi, NJ 07644. Felician Sisters; 1942; independent (1,150).

Fontbonne College (c): 6800 Wydown Blvd., St. Louis, MO 63105. Sisters of St. Joseph of Carondelet; 1917; independent (1,882).

Fordham University (c): Fordham Rd. and Third Ave., New York, NY 10458. Society of Jesus (Jesuits); 1841; independent (14,500).

Franciscan University of Steubenville (c): University Blvd., Steubenville, Ohio 43952. Franciscan TOR Friars; 1946 (1,800).

Gannon University (c): 109 University Square, Erie, PA 16541. Diocese of Erie; 1933 (3,341).

Georgetown University (c): 37th and O Sts. N.W., Washington, DC 20057. Jesuit Fathers; 1789 (11,985).

Georgian Court College (w/c): 900 Lakewood Ave., Lakewood, NJ 08701. Sisters of Mercy; 1908 (2,422).

Gonzaga University (c): Spokane, WA 99258. Jesuit Fathers; 1887 (4,479).

Great Falls, University of (c): 1301 20th St. S., Great Falls, MT 59405. Sisters of Providence; 1932; independent (1,361).

Gwynedd-Mercy College (c): Gwynedd Valley, PA 19437. Sisters of Mercy; 1948; independent (1,700).

Hilbert College (c): 5200 S. Park Ave., Hamburg, NY 14075. Franciscan Sisters of St. Joseph; 1957; independent (888).

Holy Cross, College of the (c): Worcester, MA 01610. Jesuits; 1843 (2,720).

Holy Family College (c): Grant and Frankford Aves., Philadelphia, PA 19114 and One Campus Dr., Newtown, PA 18940. Sisters of Holy Family of Nazareth; 1954; independent (2,124).

Holy Names College (c): 3500 Mountain Blvd., Oakland, CA 94619. Sisters of the Holy Names of Jesus and Mary; 1868; independent (922).

Immaculata College (w): Immaculata, PA 19345. Sisters, Servants of the Immaculate Heart of Mary; 1920 (2,100).

Iona College (c): 715 North Ave., New Rochelle, NY 10801. Congregation of Christian Brothers; 1940; independent (5,184).

John Carroll University (c): 20700 North Park Blvd., Cleveland, OH 44118. Jesuits; 1886 (4,300).

Kansas Newman College (c): 3100 McCormick Ave., Wichita, KS 67213. Sisters Adorers of the Blood of Christ; 1933 (2,048).

King's College (c): Wilkes-Barre, PA 18711. Holy Cross Fathers; 1946 (2,263).

La Roche College (c): 9000 Babcock Blvd., Pittsburgh, PA 15237. Sisters of Divine Providence; 1963 (1,641).

La Salle University (c): 1900 W. Olney Ave., Philadelphia, PA 19141. Christian Brothers; 1863 (6,000).

Le Moyne College (c): Syracuse, NY 13214. Jesuit Fathers; 1946; independent (2,757, full-time, part-time, graduate)

Lewis University (c): Romeoville, IL 60446. Christian Brothers; 1932 (4,300).

Loras College (c): 1450 Alta Vista St., Dubuque, IA 52004. Archdiocese of Dubuque; 1839 (1,825).

Lourdes College (c): 6832 Convent Blvd., Sylvania, OH 43560. Sisters of St. Francis; 1958 (1,490).

Loyola College in Maryland (c): 4501 N. Charles St., Baltimore, MD 21210. Jesuits; 1852; combined with Mt. St. Agnes College, 1971 (6,261).

Loyola Marymount University (c): 7101 W. 80th St., Los Angeles, CA 90045. Society of Jesus; Religious of Sacred Heart of Mary, Sisters of St. Joseph of Orange; 1911.

Loyola University (c): 6363 St. Charles Ave., New Orleans, LA 70118. Jesuit Fathers; 1912 (5,203).

Loyola University Chicago (c): 820 N. Michigan Ave., Chicago, IL 60611. Society of Jesus; 1870 (15,000). Mallinckrodt College (Wilmette) and Mundelein College (Chicago) became part of Loyola University Chicago, in January and June, 1991, respectively.

Madonna University (c): 36600 Schoolcraft Rd., Livonia, MI 48150. Felician Sisters; 1947 (4,000).

Magdalen College (c): 511 Kearsarge Mountain Rd., Warner, NH 03278; Magdalen College Corporation; 1973 (70).

Manhattan College (c): 4513 Manhattan College Pkwy., Riverdale, NY 10471. De La Salle Christian Brothers; 1835; independent (3,400). Cooperative program with College of Mt. St. Vincent.

Marian College (c): 45 S. National Ave., Fond du Lac, WI 54935. Sisters of St. Agnes; 1936 (2,510).

Marian College (c): 3200 Cold Spring Rd., Indianapolis, IN 46222. Sisters of St. Francis (Oldenburg, Ind.); 1851; independent (1,250).

Marist College (c): Poughkeepsie, NY 12601. Marist Brothers of the Schools; 1946; independent (4,300).

Marquette University (c): P.O. Box 1881, Milwaukee, WI 53201. Jesuit Fathers; 1881; independent (10,527).

Mary, University of (c): 7500 University Dr., Bismarck, ND 58504. Benedictine Sisters; 1959 (1,950).

Marygrove College (c): 8425 W. McNichols Rd., Detroit, MI 48221. Sisters, Servants of the Immaculate Heart of Mary; 1905; independent (2,510).

Marylhurst College (c): Marylhurst, OR 97036. Srs. of Holy Names of Jesus and Mary; 1893; independent (1,550).

Marymount College (w): Tarrytown, NY 10591. Religious of the Sacred Heart of Mary; 1907; independent (1,138). Coed in weekend degree programs.

Marymount Manhattan College (w): 221 E. 71st St., New York, NY 10021. Religious of the Sacred Heart of Mary; 1936; independent (1,330).

Marymount University (c): 2807 N. Glebe Rd., Arlington, VA 22007. Religious of the Sacred Heart of Mary; 1950; independent (4,167).

Marywood College (c): Scranton, PA 18509. Sisters, Servants of the Immaculate Heart of Mary; 1915; independent (3,068).

Mater Dei College (c): 5428 State Hwy. 37, Ogdensburg, NY 13669. Sisters of St. Joseph; 1960; independent (506).

Mercyhurst College (c): 501 E. 38th St., Erie, PA 16546. Sisters of Mercy; 1926 (2,700).

Merrimack College (c): North Andover, MA 01845. Augustinians;1947 (2,105).

Misericordia (College Misericordia) (c): Dallas, PA 18612. Religious Sisters of Mercy of the Union; 1924 (1,800).

Molloy College (c): 1000 Hempstead Ave., Rockville Centre, NY 11570. Dominican Sisters; 1955; independent (2,300).

Mt. Aloysius College (c): 7373 Admiral Peary

Hwy., Cresson, PA 16630. Sisters of Mercy; 1939.

Mount Marty College (c): Yankton, SD 57078. Benedictine Sisters; 1936 (1,000).

Mount Mary College (w): 2900 N. Menomonee River Pkwy., Milwaukee, WI 53222. School Sisters of Notre Dame; 1913 (1,524).

Mount Mercy College (c): 1330 Elmhurst Dr. N.E., Cedar Rapids, IA 52402. Sisters of Mercy; 1928; independent (1,200).

Mount St. Clare College (c): 400 N. Bluff Blvd., Clinton, IA 52732. Sisters of St. Francis of Clinton, Iowa; 1918 (515).

Mount St. Joseph, College of (c): 5701 Delhi Rd., Cincinnati, OH 45233. Sisters of Charity; 1920 (2,300).

Mt. St. Mary College (c): Newburgh, NY 12550. Dominican Sisters; 1959; independent (1,835).

Mount St. Mary's College (c): Emmitsburg, MD 21727. Founded by Fr. John DuBois, 1808; independent (1,884).

Mount St. Mary's College (w/c): 12001 Chalon Rd., Los Angeles, CA 90049 and 10 Chester Pl., Los Angeles, CA 90007 (Doheny Campus); 1,966. Sisters of St. Joseph of Carondelet; 1925. Coed in music, nursing and graduate programs.

Mount Saint Vincent, College of (c): 6301 Riverdale Ave., Bronx, NY 10471. Sisters of Charity; 1847; independent (1,600). Cooperative program with Manhattan College.

Neumann College (c):One Neumann Dr., Aston, PA 19014. Sisters of St. Francis; 1965; independent (1,335).

New Rochelle, College of (w/c): 29 Castle Pl., New Rochelle, NY 10805 (main campus). Ursuline Order; 1904; independent (6,500). Coed in nursing, graduate, new resources divisions.

Niagara University (c): Niagara Univ., NY 14109. Vincentian Fathers and Brothers; 1856 (2,935).

Notre Dame, College of (c): 1500 Ralston Ave., Belmont, CA 94002. Sisters of Notre Dame de Namur; 1851; independent (1,740).

Notre Dame du Lac, University of (c): Notre Dame, IN 46556. Congregation of Holy Cross; 1842 (10,281).

Notre Dame College (c): 2321 Elm St., Manchester, NH 03104. Sisters of Holy Cross; 1950; independent (1,291).

Notre Dame College of Ohio (w): 4545 College Rd., Cleveland, OH 44121. Sisters of Notre Dame; 1922 (644).

Notre Dame of Maryland, College of (w): 4701 N. Charles St., Baltimore, MD 21210. School Sisters of Notre Dame; 1873 (3,039).

Ohio Dominican College (c): Columbus, OH 43219. Dominican Sisters of St. Mary of the Springs; 1911 (1,900).

Our Lady of Holy Cross College (c): 4123 Woodland Dr., New Orleans, LA 70131. Congregation of Sisters Marianites of Holy Cross; 1916 (1,360).

Our Lady of the Elms, College of (w): Chicopee, MA 01013. Sisters of St. Joseph; 1928 (1,174).

Our Lady of the Lake University of San Antonio (c): 411 S.W. 24th St., San Antonio, TX 78207. Sisters of Divine Providence; 1895 (3,338).

Parks College of Saint Louis University (c): Cahokia, IL 62206. Jesuits; 1927; independent (600).

Pontifical Catholic University of Puerto Rico (c): Ponce, PR 00731. Hierarchy of Puerto Rico; 1948; Pontifical University (11,480).

Portland, University of (c): 5000 N. Willamette Blvd., Portland, OR 97203. Holy Cross Fathers; 1901; independent (2,700).

Presentation College (c): Aberdeen, SD 7401. Sisters of the Presentation; 1951 (384).

Providence College (c): River Ave. and Eaton St., Providence, RI 02918. Dominican Friars; 1917 (5,500).

Quincy University (c): 1800 College Ave., Quincy, IL 62301. Franciscan Friars; 1860 (1,200).

Regis College (w): Weston, MA 02193. Sisters of St. Joseph; 1927; independent (1,400).

Regis University (c): 3333 Regis Blvd. Denver, CO 80221. Jesuits; 1887 (9,091).

Rivier College (c): Nashua, NH 03060. Sisters of the Presentation of Mary; 1933; independent (2,759).

Rockhurst College (c): 1100 Rockhurst Rd., Kansas City, MO 64110. Jesuit Fathers; 1910 (2,656).

Rosemont College (w): 1400 Montgomery Ave., Rosemont, PA 19010. Society of the Holy Child Jesus; 1921 (749).

Sacred Heart University (c): 5151 Park Ave., Fairfield, CT 06432. Diocese of Bridgeport; 1963; independent (5,600).

St. Ambrose University (c): Davenport, IA 52803. Diocese of Davenport; 1882 (2,604).

Saint Anselm College (c): Manchester NH 03102. Benedictines; 1889 (1,950).

Saint Benedict, College of (w): 37 S. College Ave., St. Joseph, MN 56374. Benedictine Sisters; 1913 (1,893). Sister college of St. John's University, Collegeville (see below).

St. Bonaventure University (c): St. Bonaventure, NY 14778. Franciscan Friars; 1858; independent (2,700).

St. Catherine, College of (w): 2004 Randolph Ave., St. Paul, MN 55105. Sisters of St. Joseph of Carondelet; 1905 (3,827).

St. Edward's University (c): 3001 S. Congress Ave., Austin, TX 78704. Holy Cross Brothers; 1885; independent (3,107).

St. Elizabeth, College of (w): 2 Convent Rd., Morristown, NJ 07960. Sisters of Charity; 1899; independent (1,694). Coed in graduate and weekend college programs.

St. Francis, College of (c): 500 N. Wilcox St., Joliet, IL 60435. Sisters of St. Francis of Mary Immaculate; 1920; independent (1,100).

St. Francis College (c): 180 Remsen St., Brooklyn Heights, NY 11201. Franciscan Brothers; 1884; private, independent in the Franciscan tradition (2,092).

St. Francis College (c): 2701 Spring St., Fort Wayne, IN 46808. Sisters of St. Francis; 1890 (948).

St. Francis College (c): Loretto, PA 15940. Franciscan Friars; 1847; independent (2,020).

St. John's University (c): 8000 Utopia Pkwy., Jamaica, NY 11439 (Queens Campus); 300 Howard Ave., Grymes Hill, Staten Island, NY 10301 (Staten Island Campus). Vincentians; 1870 (19,105).

St. John's University (m): Collegeville, MN 56321. Benedictines; 1857 (1,648). All classes and programs are coeducational with College of St. Benedict (see above).

St. Joseph, College of (c): 171 Clement Rd., Rutland, VT 05701. Sisters of St. Joseph; 1950; independent (500).

Saint Joseph College (w/c): 1678 Asylum Ave., West Hartford, CT 06117. Sisters of Mercy; 1932 (1,859). Women's college in undergraduate liberal arts. Coed in graduate school and Weekend College.

Saint Joseph's College (c): Standish, ME 04084. Sisters of Mercy; 1912 (716, campus; also has distance education program with more than 5,000 students nationwide).

Saint Joseph's College (c): Rensselaer, IN 47978. Society of the Precious Blood; 1891 (876).

St. Joseph's College (c): 245 Clinton Ave., Brooklyn, NY 11205 (1,381) and 155 W. Roe Blvd., Patchogue, N.Y. 11772 (2,500). Sisters of St. Joseph; 1916; independent.

St. Joseph's University (c): 5600 City Ave., Philadelphia, PA 19131. Jesuit Fathers; 1851 (7,000).

Saint Leo College (c): Saint Leo, FL 33574. Order of St. Benedict; 1889; independent (7,123).

St. Louis University (c): 221 N. Grand Blvd., St. Louis, MO 63103. Society of Jesus; 1818; independent (11,000).

Saint Martin's College (c): Lacey, WA 98503. Benedictine Monks; 1895 (950 main campus; 494 extension campuses).

Saint Mary, College of (w): 1901 S. 72nd St., Omaha, NE 68124. Sisters of Mercy; 1923; independent (1,048).

Saint Mary College (c): Leavenworth, KS 66048. Sisters of Charity of Leavenworth; 1923 (578).

Saint Mary-of-the-Woods College (w): St. Mary-of-the-Woods, IN 47876. Sisters of Providence; 1840 (1,250).

Saint Mary's College (w): Notre Dame, IN 46556. Sisters of the Holy Cross; 1844 (1,500).

St. Mary's College (c): Orchard Lake, MI 48324. Secular Clergy; 1885 (375).

St. Mary's College (c): Moraga, CA 94575. Brothers of the Christian Schools; 1863 (4,000).

Saint Mary's University of Minnesota (c): Winona, MN 55987. Brothers of the Christian Schools; 1912 (1,387).

St. Mary's University of San Antonio (c): One Camino Santa Maria, San Antonio, TX 78228. Society of Mary (Marianists); 1852 (4,100).

Saint Meinrad College (m): St. Meinrad, IN 47577. Benedictines. Liberal Arts. Scheduled to close at end of 1997-98 school year.

St. Michael's College (c): Colchester, VT 05439. Society of St. Edmund; 1904 (2,092).

St. Norbert College (c): De Pere, WI 54115. Norbertine Fathers; 1898; independent (2,092).

Saint Peter's College (c): 2641 Kennedy Blvd., Jersey City, NJ 07306. Society of Jesus; 1872; independent (3,863).

Saint Rose, College of (c): 432 Western Ave., Albany, NY 12203. Sisters of St. Joseph of Carondelet; 1920; independent (4,001).

St. Scholastica, College of (c): 1200 Kenwood Ave., Duluth, MN 55811. Benedictine Sisters; 1912; independent (2,101).

St. Thomas, University of (c): 2115 Summit Ave., St. Paul, MN 55105. Archdiocese of St. Paul and Minneapolis; 1885 (10,161).

St. Thomas, University of (c): 3800 Montrose Blvd., Houston, TX 77006. Basilian Fathers; 1947 (2,504).

St. Thomas Aquinas College (c): Sparkill, NY 10976. Dominican Sisters of Sparkill; 1952; independent, corporate board of trustees (2,100).

St. Thomas University (c): 16400 N.W. 32nd Ave., Opa Locka, FL 33054. Archdiocese of Miami; 1962 (3,000).

Saint Vincent College (c): Fraser Purchase Rd., Latrobe, PA 15650. Benedictine Fathers; 1846 (1,215).

St. Xavier University (c): 3700 W. 103rd St., Chicago, IL 60655. Sisters of Mercy; chartered 1847 (4,201).

Salve Regina University (c): Ochre Point Ave., Newport, RI 02840. Sisters of Mercy; 1934 (2,036).

San Diego, University of (c): 5998 Alcala Park, San Diego, CA 92110. San Diego diocese and Religious of the Sacred Heart; 1949; independent (6,603).

San Francisco, University of (c): 2130 Fulton St., San Francisco, CA 94117. Jesuit Fathers; 1855 (6,564).

Santa Clara University (c): 500 El Camino Real, Santa Clara, CA 95053. Jesuit Fathers; 1851; independent (7,700).

Santa Fe, College of (c): Santa Fe, NM 87501. Brothers of the Christian Schools; 1947 (1,600).

Scranton, University of (c): Scranton, PA 18510. Society of Jesus; 1888; independent (5,000).

Seattle University (c): 900 Broadway, Seattle, WA 98122. Society of Jesus; 1891 (5,999).

Seton Hall University (c): South Orange Ave., South Orange, NJ 07079. Diocesan Clergy; 1856 (9,688).

Seton Hill College (w): Greensburg, PA 15601. Sisters of Charity of Seton Hill; 1883 (946).

Siena College (c): Loudonville, NY 12211. Franciscan Friars; 1937 (3,350).

Siena Heights College (c): 1247 E. Siena Heights Dr., Adrian, MI 49221. Adrian Dominican Sisters; 1919 (2,002).

Silver Lake College of Holy Family (c): 2406 S. Alverno Rd., Manitowoc, WI 54220. Franciscan Sisters of Christian Charity; 1935 (1,000).

Spalding University (c): 851 S. 4th Ave., Louisville, KY 40203. Sisters of Charity of Nazareth; 1814; independent (1,423).

Spring Hill College (c): 4000 Dauphin St., Mobile, AL 36608. Jesuit Fathers; 1830 (1,117).

Stonehill College (c): 320 Washington St., North Easton, MA 02357. Holy Cross Fathers; 1948; independent (2,776).

Thomas Aquinas College (c): 10000 N. Ojai Rd., Santa Paula, CA 93060. Founded 1971 (223).

Thomas More College (c): Crestview Hills, Covington, KY 41017. Diocese of Covington; 1921 (1,335).

Trinity College of Vermont (w): 208 Colchester Ave., Burlington, VT 05401. Sisters of Mercy; 1925 (973).

Trinity College (w): 125 Michigan Ave. N.E., Washington, DC 20017. Sisters of Notre Dame de Namur; 1897 (1,458). Coed in graduate school.

University of the Incarnate Word (c): 4301 Broadway, San Antonio, TX 78209. Sisters of Charity of the Incarnate Word; 1881 (2,861).

Ursuline College (w): 2550 Lander Rd., Cleveland, OH 44124. Ursuline Nuns; 1871 (1,446).

Villanova University (c): 800 Lancaster Ave., Villanova, PA 19085. Order of St. Augustine; 1842 (10,189).

Viterbo College (c): 815 S. 9th, La Crosse, WI 54601. Franciscan Sisters of Perpetual Adoration; 1890 (1,600).

Walsh University (c): 2020 Easton St. N.W., North Canton, Ohio 44720. Brothers of Christian Instruction; 1958 (1,450).

Wheeling Jesuit College (c): 316 Washington Ave., Wheeling, WV 26003. Jesuit Fathers; 1954 (1,430).

Xavier University (c): 3800 Victory Pkwy., Cincinnati, OH 45207. Jesuit Fathers; 1831 (6,423).

Xavier University of Louisiana (c): 7325 Palmetto St., New Orleans, LA 70125. Sisters of Blessed Sacrament; 1925 (3,490).

Catholic Two-Year Colleges

Ancilla College (c): Donaldson, IN 46513. Ancilla Domini Sisters; 1937.

Assumption College for Sisters: 350 Bernardsville Rd.,, Mendham, NJ 07945. Sisters of Christian Charity; 1953 (25).

Castle College: 21 Searles Rd., Windham, NH 03087. Sisters of Mercy; 1963; independent (326).

Chatfield College (c): St. Martin, OH 45118. Ursulines; 1971 (300).

The College of St. Catherine-Minneapolis (c): 601 25th Ave. S., Minneapolis, MN 55454. Sisters of St. Joseph of Carondelet (1,227).

Donnelly College (c): 608 N. 18th St., Kansas City, KS 66102. Archdiocesan College; 1949 (871).

Don Bosco Technical Institute (m): 1151 San Gabriel Blvd., Rosemead, CA 91770. Salesians; 1969 (105).

Holy Cross College (c): Notre Dame, IN 46556. Brothers of Holy Cross; 1966 (455).

Manor Junior College (c): 700 Fox Chase Road, Jenkintown, PA 19046. Sisters of St. Basil the Great; 1947 (604).

Maria College (c): 700 New Scotland Ave., Albany, NY 12208. Sisters of Mercy; 1963 (950).

Marymount College Palos Verdes (c): Rancho Palos Verdes, CA 90274. Religious of the Sacred Heart of Mary; independent (1,068).

St. Catharine College (c); St. Catharine, KY 40061. Dominican Sisters; 1931 (375).

St. Gregory's College (c): Shawnee, OK 74801. Benedictine Monks; 1876 (300).

Springfield College in Illinois (c): 1500 N. Fifth St., Springfield, IL 62702. Ursuline Sisters; 1929 (455).

Trocaire College (c): 110 Red Jacket Pkwy., Buffalo, NY 14220. Sisters of Mercy; 1958; independent (960).

Villa Maria College of Buffalo (c): 240 Pine Ridge Rd., Buffalo, NY 14225. Felician Sisters 1960; independent (400).

CAMPUS MINISTRY

Campus ministry is an expression of the Church's special desire to be present to all who are involved in higher education and to further dialogue between the Church and the academic community. In the words of the U.S. bishops' 1985 pastoral letter entitled "Empowered by the Spirit," this ministry is "the public presence and service through which properly prepared baptized persons are empowered by the Spirit to use their talents and gifts on behalf of the Church in order to be sign and instrument of the Kingdom in the academic world."

Campus ministry, carried on by lay, Religious and ordained ministers, gathers members of the Church on campus to form the faith community, appropriate the faith, form Christian consciences, educate for justice and facilitate religious development.

The dimensions and challenge of this ministry are evident from, among other things, the numbers involved: approximately 550,000 Catholics on more than 230 Catholic college and university campuses; about four million in several thousand non-Catholic private and public institutions; 1,200 or more campus ministers. In many dioceses, the activities of ministers are coordinated by a local diocesan director. Two professional organizations serve the ministry on the national level:

The National Association of Diocesan Directors of Campus Ministry, Mr. Joseph J. Kiesel-Nield, president, 706 N. Sprague, Ellensburg, WA 98926,.

The Catholic Campus Ministry Association, with a membership of 1,200, 300 College Park Ave., Dayton, OH 45469. Executive director, Donald R. McCrabb.

DIOCESAN AND INTERDIOCESAN SEMINARIES

(Sources: Almanac survey; *Official Catholic Directory;* Catholic News Service.)

Information, according to states, includes names of archdioceses and dioceses, and names and addresses of seminaries. Types of seminaries, when not clear from titles, are indicated in most cases. Interdiocesan seminaries are generally conducted by religious orders for candidates for the priesthood from several dioceses. The list does not include houses of study reserved for members of religious communities. Archdioceses are indicated by an asterisk.

California: Los Angeles* — St. John's Seminary (major), 5012 Seminary Rd., Camarillo 93012; St. John's Seminary College, 5118 Seminary Rd., Camarillo 93012.

San Diego — St. Francis Seminary (college and pre-theology formation program), 1667 Santa Paula Dr., San Diego 92111.

San Francisco* — St. Patrick's Seminary (major), 320 Middlefield Rd., Menlo Park 94025.

Connecticut: Hartford* — St. Thomas Seminary (college formation program), 467 Bloomfield Ave., Bloomfield 06002.

Norwich — Holy Apostles College and Seminary (adult vocations; minor and major), 33 Prospect Hill Rd., Cromwell 06416.

Stamford Byzantine Rite — Ukrainian Catholic Seminary: St. Basil College Seminary (minor), 195 Glenbrook Rd., Stamford 06902.

District of Columbia: Washington* — Theological College (national, major), The Catholic University of America, 401 Michigan Ave., N.E. 20017.

St. Josaphat's Seminary, 201 Taylor St. N.E., Washington 20017. (Major house of formation serving the four Ukrainian Byzantine-rite dioceses in the U.S.)

Florida: Miami* — St. John Vianney College Seminary, 2900 S.W. 87th Ave., Miami 33165.

Palm Beach — St. Vincent de Paul Regional Seminary (major), 10701 S. Military Trail, Boynton Beach 33436.

Illinois: Chicago*— Archbishop Quigley Preparatory Seminary (high school), 103 East Chestnut St., Chicago 60611; St. Joseph Seminary (college), 6551 N. Sheridan Rd., Chicago 60626. University

of St. Mary of the Lake Mundelein Seminary (School of Theology), 1000 E. Maple Ave., Mundelein 60060.

Indiana: Indianapolis* — Saint Meinrad Seminary, College and School of Theology (interdiocesan), St. Meinrad 47577.

Iowa: Davenport — St. Ambrose University Seminary (interdiocesn), 518 W. Locust St., Davenport 52803.

Dubuque* — Seminary of St. Pius X (interdiocesan), Loras College, Dubuque 52001.

Louisiana: New Orleans*— Notre Dame Seminary Graduate School of Theology, 2901 S. Carrollton Ave., New Orleans 70118; St. Joseph Seminary College (interdiocesan), St. Benedict 70457.

Maryland: Baltimore* — St. Mary's Seminary and University, 5400 Roland Ave., Baltimore 21210; Mt. St. Mary's Seminary, Emmitsburg 21727.

Massachusetts: Boston* — St. John's Seminary, School of Theology, 127 Lake St., Brighton 02135; St. John's Seminary, College of Liberal Arts, 197 Foster St., Brighton 02135; Pope John XXIII National Seminary (for ages 30-60), 558 South Ave., Weston 02193.

Newton — Melkite Greek Catholic _ St. Gregory the Theologian Seminary, 233 Grant Ave., Newton 02159.

Michigan: Detroit* — Sacred Heart Major Seminary (college/theologate and institute for ministry), 2701 Chicago Blvd., Detroit 48206; Sts. Cyril and Methodius Seminary, St. Mary's College (theologate and college) independent, primarily serving Polish-American community, 3535 Indian Trail, Orchard Lake 48324.

Grand Rapids — Christopher House, 723 Rosewood Ave., S.E., East Grand Rapids 49506.

Minnesota: St. John's School of Theology and Seminary, St. John's University, P.O. Box 7288, Collegeville 56321.

St. Paul and Minneapolis* — St. Paul Seminary School of Divinity, University of St. Thomas, 2260 Summit Ave., St. Paul 55105; St. John Vianney Seminary (college residence), 2115 Summit Ave., St. Paul 55105.

Winona — Immaculate Heart of Mary Seminary,

St. Mary's University, No. 43, 700 Terrace Heights, Winona 55987.

Missouri: Jefferson City — St. Thomas Aquinas Preparatory Seminary (High School Seminary), 245 N. Levering Ave., P.O. Box 858, Hannibal 63401.

St. Louis* — Kenrick-Glennon Seminary (St. Louis Roman Catholic Theological Seminary). Kenrick School of Theology and Cardinal Glennon College, 5200 Glennon Dr., St. Louis 63119.

Montana: Helena — Pre-Seminary Program, Carroll College, Helena 59625.

New Jersey: Newark* — Immaculate Conception Seminary — college seminary; major seminary; graduate school — Seton Hall University, 400 South Orange Ave., South Orange 07079.

New Mexico: Santa Fe* — Immaculate Heart of Mary Seminary (college level), Mt. Carmel Rd., Santa Fe 87501.

New York: Brooklyn — Cathedral Seminary Residence of the Immaculate Conception (college and pre-theology), 7200 Douglaston Parkway, Douglaston 11362; Cathedral Preparatory Seminary, 56-25 92nd St., Elmhurst 11373.

Buffalo — Christ the King Seminary (interdiocesan theologate), P.O. Box 607, 711 Knox Rd., East Aurora 14052.

New York* — St. Joseph's Seminary (major), 201 Seminary Ave., Dunwoodie, Yonkers 10704; St. John Neumann Residence (college and pre-theology), 5655 Arlington Ave., Riverdale 10471. Cathedral Preparatory Seminary, 946 Boston Post Rd., Rye 10580.

Ogdensburg — Wadhams Hall Seminary College (interdiocesan), 6866 State Hwy. 37, Ogdensburg 13669.

Rockville Centre — Seminary of the Immaculate Conception (major), Lloyd Harbor, Huntington, L.I. 11743.

St. Maron Eparchy, Brooklyn — Our Lady of Lebanon Maronite Seminary, 7164 Alaska Ave. N.W., Washington, DC 20012.

North Dakota: Fargo — Cardinal Muench Seminary (interdiocesan high school, college and pre-theology), 100 35th Ave. N.E., Fargo 58102.

Ohio: Cincinnati* — Mt. St. Mary's Seminary of the West, 6616 Beechmont Ave., Cincinnati 45230 (division of the Athenaeum of Ohio).

Cleveland — St. Mary Seminary and Graduate School of Theology, 28700 Euclid Ave. Wickliffe 44092.

Columbus — Pontifical College Josephinum (national), theologate and college, Columbus 43235.

Oregon: Portland* — Mount Angel Seminary (interdiocesan, college, pre-theology program, graduate school of theology), St. Benedict 97373.

Pennsylvania: Erie — St. Mark Seminary, P.O. Box 10397, Erie 16514.

Greensburg — St. Vincent Seminary (interdiocesan; pre-theology program; theologate; graduate programs in theology; religious education), 300 Fraser Purchase Rd., Latrobe 15650.

Philadelphia* — Theological Seminary of St. Charles Borromeo, 100 East Wynnewood Rd., Wynnewood 19096. (College, pre-theology program, spirituality year pogram, theologate.)

Pittsburgh* (Byzantine-Ruthenian) — Byzantine Catholic Seminary of Sts. Cyril and Methodius (college, pre-theology program, theologate), 3605 Perrysville Ave., Pittsburgh 15214.

Pittsburgh — St. Paul Seminary (interdiocesan, college and pre-theology), 2900 Noblestown Rd., Pittsburgh 15205.

Scranton — St. Pius X Seminary (college and pre-theology formation; interdiocesan), Dalton 18414. Affiliated with the University of Scranton.

Rhode Island: Providence — Seminary of Our Lady of Providence (House of Formation; college students and pre-theology), 485 Mount Pleasant Ave., Providence 02908.

Texas: Dallas — Holy Trinity Seminary (college and pre-theology; English proficiency and academic foundation programs), P.O. Box 140309, Irving 75014.

El Paso — St. Charles Seminary College, P.O. Box 17548, El Paso 79917.

Galveston-Houston — St. Mary's Seminary (theologate), 9845 Memorial Dr., Houston 77024.

San Antonio* — Assumption Seminary (theologate and pre-theology, Hispanic ministry emphasis), 2600 W. Woodlawn Ave., San Antonio 78228.

Washington: Spokane — Bishop White Seminary, College Formation Program, E. 429 Sharp Ave., Spokane 99202.

Wisconsin: Milwaukee* — St. Francis Seminary, 3257 S. Lake Dr., St. Francis 53235; College Program, East Hall, 915 W. Wisconsin Ave., Milwaukee 53233. Sacred Heart School of Theology (interdiocesan seminary for second-career vocations), P.O. Box 429, Hales Corners, Wis. 53130.

WORLD AND U.S. SEMINARY STATISTICS

The *1995 Statistical Yearbook of the Church* reported the following comparative statistics for the years 1990 to 1995 of candidates in Philosophy and Theology (major seminarians). World totals are given first; U.S. statistics are given in parentheses.

Year	Total Major Seminarians	Diocesan	Religious
1990	96,155 (5,552)	64,629 (3,676)	31,526 (1,876)
1991	99,668 (5,487)	66,305 (3,777)	33,363 (1,710)
1992	102,000 (5,380)	67,960 (3,645)	34,040 (1,735)
1993	103,709 (5,123)	68,829 (3,505)	34,880 (1,618)
1994	105,075 (5,100)	69,613 (3,526)	35,462 (1,574)
1995	106,346 (4,831)	69,777 (3,234)	36,569 (1,597)

PONTIFICAL UNIVERSITIES

(Principal source: *Annuario Pontificio*.)

These universities, listed according to country of location, have been canonically erected and authorized by the Congregation for Catholic Education to award degrees in stated fields of study.

New laws and norms governing ecclesiastical universities and faculties were promulgated in the apostolic constitution *Sapientia Christiana,* issued Apr. 15, 1979.

Argentina: Pontifical Catholic University of S. Maria of Buenos Aires (June 16, 1960): Av. Alicia Moreau de Justo 1400, 1107 Buenos Aires.

Belgium: Catholic University of Louvain (founded Dec. 9, 1425; canonically erected, 1834), with autonomous institutions for French- (Louvain) and Flemish- (Leuven) speaking: Place de l'Universite I, B-1348 Louvain-La-Neuve (French); Naamsestraat 22/b, B-3000 Leuven (Flemish).

Brazil: Pontifical Catholic University of Rio de Janeiro (Jan. 20, 1947): Rua Marques de Sao Vicente 225, 22451-000 Rio de Janeiro, RJ.

Pontifical Catholic University of Minas Gerais (June 5, 1983): Av. Dom Jose Gaspar 500, C.P. 2686, 30161 Belo Horizonte MG.

Pontifical Catholic University of Parana (Aug. 6, 1985): Rua Imaculada Conceicao, 1155, Prado Velho, C.P. 670, 80001 Curitiba, PR.

Pontifical Catholic University of Rio Grande do Sul (Nov. 1, 1950): Av. Ipiranga 6681, C.P. 1429, 90001-000 Porto Alegre, RS.

Pontifical Catholic University of Sao Paulo (Jan. 25, 1947): Rua Monte Alegre 984, 05014-000 Sao Paulo.

Pontifical University of Campinas (Sept. 8, 1956): Rua Marechal Deodoro 1099, 13020-000 Campinas, SP.

Canada: Laval University (Mar. 15, 1876): Case Postale 460, Quebec G1K 7P4.

St. Paul University (formerly University of Ottawa) (Feb. 5, 1889): 223, Rue Main, Ottawa, Ont. K1S 1C4.

University of Sherbrooke (Nov. 21, 1957): Chemin Ste.-Catherine, Cité Universitaire, Sherbrooke, Que. J1K 2R1.

Chile: Pontifical Catholic University of Chile (June 21, 1888): Avenida Bernardo O'Higgins, 340, Casilla 114D. Santiago.

Catholic University of Valparaiso (Nov. 1, 1961): Avenida Brasil 2950, Casilla 4059, Valparaiso.

Colombia: Bolivarian Pontifical Catholic University (Aug. 16, 1945): Circular 1a, N.70-01, Apartado 56006, Medellin.

Pontifical Xaverian University (July 31, 1937): Carrera 7, N. 40-62, Apartado 56710, Santafé de Bogota D.C. Apartado 26239, Calle 18, N. 118-250, Cali (Cali campus).

Cuba: Catholic University of St. Thomas of Villanueva (May 4, 1957): Avenida Quenta 16,660, Marianao.

Dominican Republic: Pontifical Catholic University "Mother and Teacher" (Sept. 9, 1987): Apartado 822, Santiago de Los Caballeros.

Ecuador: Pontifical Catholic University of Ecuador (July 16, 1954): Doce de Octubre, N. 1076, Apartado 17-01-2184, Quito.

France: Catholic University of Lille (Nov. 18, 1875): Boulevard Vauban 60, 59046 Lille.

Catholic Faculties of Lyon (Nov. 22, 1875): 25, Rue du Plat, 69288 Lyon.

Catholic Institute of Paris (Aug. 11, 1875): 21, Rue d'Assas, 75270 Paris.

Catholic Institute of Toulouse (Nov. 15, 1877): Rue de la Fonderie 31, 31068 Toulouse.

Catholic University of the West (Sept. 16, 1875): 3, Place Andre Leroy, B.P. 808, 49005 Angers.

Germany: Eichstatt Catholic University (Apr. 1, 1980): Ostenstrasse 26, D-85072, Eichstatt, Federal Republic of Germany.

Guatemala: Rafael Landivar University (Oct. 18, 1961): 17 Calle 8-64, zone 10 Guatemala.

Ireland: St. Patrick's College (Mar. 29, 1896): Maynooth, Co. Kildare.

Italy: Catholic University of the Sacred Heart (Dec. 25, 1920): Largo Gemelli 1, 20123 Milan.

Libera University Mary of the Assumption (Oct. 26, 1939): Via della Traspontina 21, 00193 Rome, Italy.

Japan: Jochi Daigaku (Sophia University) (Mar. 29, 1913): Chiyoda-Ku, Kioi-cho 7, Tokyo 102.

Lebanon: St. Joseph University of Beirut (Mar. 25, 1881): Rue de l'Universite St.-Joseph, Boite Postale 293, Beyrouth (Beirut).

Netherlands: Nijmegen Roman Catholic University (June 29, 1923): P.B. 9102, Comeniuslaan 4, 6500 HC, Nijmegen.

Panama: University of S. Maria La Antigua (May 27, 1965): Apartado 2143, Panama 1.

Paraguay: Catholic University of Our Lady of the Assumption (Feb. 2, 1965): Independencia Nacional y Comuneros, Casilla 1718, Asuncion.

Peru: Pontifical Catholic University of Peru (Sept. 30, 1942): Av. Universitaria, Pueblo Libre, Apartado 1761, Lima 100.

Philippines: Pontifical University of Santo Tomas (Nov. 20, 1645): España Street, 1008 Manila.

Poland: Catholic University of Lublin (July 25, 1920): Aleje Raclawickie 14, Skr. Poczt. 129, 20-950, Lublin.

Catholic Theological Academy (June 29, 1989): Ul. Dewajtis 5, 01-815, Warsaw.

Pontifical Academy of Theology of Krakow (Dec. 8, 1981): Ul. Kanonicza 25, 31-002 Krakow.

Portugal: Portuguese Catholic University (Nov. 1, 1967): Palma de Cima, 1600 Lisbon.

Puerto Rico: Pontifical Catholic University of Puerto Rico (Aug. 15, 1972): Ponce, Puerto Rico 00731.

Spain: Catholic University of Navarra (Aug. 6, 1960): 31080 Pamplona.

Pontifical University "Comillas" (Mar. 29, 1904): Campus de Cantoblanco, 28049 Madrid.

Pontifical University of Salamanca (Sept. 25, 1940): Apartado 541, 37080 Salamanca.

University of Deusto (Aug. 10, 1963): Avenida de las Universidades, 28, 48007 Bilbao.

Taiwan (China): Fu Jen Catholic University (Nov. 15, 1923, at Peking; reconstituted at Taipeh, Sept. 8, 1961): Hsinchuang, Taipeh Hsien 24205.

United States: Catholic University of America (Mar. 7, 1889): 620 Michigan Ave. N.E., Washington, D.C. 20064.

Georgetown University (Mar. 30, 1833): 37th and O Sts. N.W., Washington, D.C. 20057.

Niagara University (June 21, 1956): Niagara University P.O., Niagara Falls, N.Y. 14109.

Uruguay: Catholic University of Uruguay "Damaso Antonio Larranaga" (Jan. 25, 1985): Avda. 8 de Octubre 2738, Montevideo.

Venezuela: Catholic University "Andres Bello"

(Sept. 29, 1963): Esquina Jesuitas, Apartado 29068, Caracas 1021.

ECCLESIASTICAL FACULTIES

(Principal source: *Annuario Pontificio*)
These faculties in Catholic seminaries and universities, listed according to country of location, have been canonically erected and authorized by the Sacred Congregation for Catholic Education to award degrees in stated fields of study. In addition to those listed here, there are other faculties of theology or philosophy in state universities and for members of certain religious orders only.

Argentina: Faculties of Philosophy and Theology, San Miguel (Sept. 8, 1932).

Australia: Catholic Institute of Theology, Sydney (Feb. 2, 1954).

Austria: Theological Faculty, Linz (Dec. 25, 1978). International Theological Institute for Family Studies (Oct. 1, 1996).

Brazil: Ecclesiastical Faculty of Philosophy "John Paul II," Rio de Janeiro Aug. 6, 1981.

Philosophical and Theological Faculties of the Company of Jesus, Belo Horizonte (July 15, 1941 and Mar. 12, 1949).

Cameroon: Catholic Institute of Yaoundé (Nov. 15, 1991).

Canada: Pontifical Institute of Medieval Studies, Toronto (Oct. 18, 1939).

Dominican Faculty of Theology of Canada, Ottawa (1965; Nov. 15, 1975).

Regis College — Toronto Section of the Jesuit Faculty of Theology in Canada, Toronto (Feb. 17, 1956; Dec. 25, 1977).

College of Immaculate Conception _ Montreal Section of Jesuit Faculties in Canada (Sept. 8, 1932). Suspended.

Cote d'Ivoire (Ivory Coast): Catholic Institute of West Africa, Abidjan (Aug. 12, 1975).

Croatia: Philosophical Faculty, Zagreb (July 31, 1989).

France: Centre Sevres _ Faculties of Theology and Philosophy of the Jesuits, Paris (Sept. 8, 1932).

Germany: Theological Faculty, Paderborn (June 11, 1966).

Theological Faculty of the Major Episcopal Seminary, Trier (Sept. 8, 1955).

Philosophical Faculty, Munich (1932; Oct. 25, 1971).

Theological-Philosophical Faculty, Frankfurt (1932; June 7, 1971).

Theological Faculty, Fulda (Dec. 22, 1978).

Philosophical-Theological School of Salesians, Benediktbeurn (May 24, 1992).

Philosphical-Theological School, Vallendar (Oct. 7, 1993).

Great Britain: Heythrop College, University of London, London (Nov. 1, 1964). Theology, philosophy.

Hungary: Faculty of Theology (1605), Institue on Canon Law (Nov. 30, 1996), Budapest,

India: "Jnana Deepa Vidyapeeth" (Pontifical Athenaeum), Institute of Philosophy and Religion, Poona (July 27, 1926).

Pontifical Institute of Theology and Philosophy at the Pontifical Interritual Seminary of St. Joseph, Alwaye, Kerala (Feb. 24, 1972).

"Vidyajyoti," Institute of Religious Studies, Faculty of Theology, Delhi (1932; Dec. 9, 1974).

"Dharmaram Vidya Kshetram" Pontifical Athenaeum of Theology and Philosophy, Bangalore (theology, Jan. 6, 1976; philosophy, Dec. 8, 1983).

Faculty of Theology, Ranchi (Aug. 15, 1982).

Pontifical Oriental Institute of Religious Studies, Kottayam (July 3, 1982).

St. Peter's Pontifical Institute of Theology, Bangalore (Jan. 6, 1985).

"Satya Nilayam," Institute of Philosophy and Culture. Faculty of Philosophy, Madras (Sept. 8, 1932; Dec. 15, 1976).

Indonesia: Wedabhakti Pontifical Faculty of Theology, Yogyakarta (Nov. 1, 1984).

Ireland: The Milltown Institute of Theology and Philosophy, Dublin (1932).

Israel: French Biblical and Archeological School, Jerusalem (founded 1890; approved Sept. 17, 1892; canonically approved to confer Doctorate in Biblical Science, June 29, 1983).

Italy: Interregional Theological Faculty, Milan (Aug. 8, 1935; restructured 1969).

Pontifical Theological Faculty of Sardinia, Cagliari, (Aug. 5, 1927).

Pontifical Ambrosian Institute of Sacred Music, Milan (Mar. 12, 1940).

Theological Faculty of Sicily, Palermo (Dec. 8, 1980).

Theological Faculty of Southern Italy, Naples. Two sections: St. Thomas Aquinas Capodimonte (Oct. 31, 1941) and St. Louis Posillipo (Mar. 16, 1918). Theological Institute Pugliese, Molfetta (June 24, 1992). Theological Institute Calabro, Catanzaro (Jan. 28, 1993).

Faculty of Philosophy "Aloisianum," Gallarate (1937; Mar. 20, 1974).

Japan: Faculty of Theology, Nagoya (May 25, 1984).

Kenya: Catholic Higher Institute of Eastern Africa, Nairobi (May 2, 1984).

Lebanon: Faculty of Theology, University of the Holy Spirit, Kaslik (May 30, 1982).

Madagascar: Superior Institute of Theology and Philosophy, at the Regional Seminary of Antananarivo, Ambatoroka-Antananarivo (Apr. 21, 1960).

Malta: Faculty of Theology, Tal-Virtu (Nov. 22, 1769), with Institute of Philosophy and Human Studies (Sept. 8, 1984).

Mexico: Theological Faculty of Mexico (June 29, 1982) and Philosophy (Jan. 6, 1986) , Institute of Canon Law (Sept. 4, 1995), Mexico City.

Nigeria: Catholic Institute of West Africa, Port Harcourt (May 9, 1994).

Peru: Pontifical and Civil Faculty of Theology, Lima (July 25, 1571).

Poland: Theological Faculty, Poznan (1969; pontifical designation, June 2, 1974).

Philosophical Faculty, Krakow (1932; Sept. 20, 1984).

Pontifical Theological Faculty, Warsaw (May 3, 1988) with St. John Baptist section (1837, 1920, Nov. 8, 1962) at the "Metropolitan Seminary Duchowne" and "St. Andrew Bobola""Bobolanum" section (Sept. 8, 1932).

Spain: Theological Faculty of Catalunya, (Mar. 7, 1968), with the Institutes of Fundamental Theology (Dec. 28, 1984), Liturgy (Aug. 15, 1986) and Philosophy (July 26, 1988), Barcelona.

Theological Faculty, Granada (1940; July 31, 1973).

Theological Faculty of the North, of the Metropolitan Seminary of Burgos and the Diocesan Seminary of Vitoria (Feb. 6, 1967).

Theological Faculty "San Vicente Ferrer" (two sections), Valencia (Jan. 23, 1974).

Theological Faculty of San Esteban, Salamanca (1947; Oct. 4, 1972).

Theological Faculty "San Damaso" (Sept 19, 1996), Madrid.

Switzerland: Theological Faculty, Chur (Jan. 1, 1974).

Theological Faculty, Luzerne (Dec. 25, 1973).

Theological Faculty, Lugano (Nov. 20, 1993).

United States: St. Mary's Seminary and University. School of Theology, Baltimore (May 1, 1822).

St. Mary of the Lake Faculty of Theology, Mundelein, Ill. (Sept. 30, 1929).

Weston School of Theology, Cambridge, Mass. (Oct. 18, 1932).

The Jesuit School of Theology, Berkeley, Calif. (Feb. 2, 1934, as "Alma College," Los Gatos, Calif.).

Faculty of Philosophy and Letters, St. Louis, Mo. (Feb. 2, 1934).

St. Michael's Institute, Jesuit School of Philosophy and Letters, Spokane, Wash. (Feb. 2, 1934).

Pontifical Faculty of Theology of the Immaculate Conception, Dominican House of Studies, Washington, D.C. (Nov. 15, 1941).

The Marian Library/International Marian Research Institute (IMRI), U.S. branch of Pontifical Theological Faculty "Marianum," University of Dayton, Dayton, O. 45469 (affil. 1976, inc. 1983).

John Paul II Institute for Studies on Marriage and the Family, U.S. section of Pontifical John Paul II Institute for Studies on Marriage and Family at the Pontifical Lateran University, 487 Michigan Ave. NE, Washington, DC 20017 (Aug. 22, 1988).

Vietnam: Theological Faculty of the Pontifical National Seminary of St. Pius X, Dalat (July 31, 1965). Activities suppressed.

Zaire (now Congo): Catholic Faculties of Kinshasa, Kinshasa (theology, Apr. 25, 1957; philosophy, Nov. 25, 1987).

Pontifical College Josephinum (Theologate and College) at Columbus, Ohio, is a national pontifical seminary. Established Sept. 1, 1888, it is directly under the auspices of the Vatican through the Apostolic Pro-Nuncio to the U.S., who serves as the seminary's chancellor.

PONTIFICAL UNIVERSITIES AND INSTITUTES IN ROME

(Source: *Annuario Pontificio*.)

Pontifical Gregorian University (1552): Piazza della Pilotta, 4, 00187 Rome. Associated with the university are:

The **Pontifical Biblical Institute** (May 7, 1909): Via della Pilotta, 25, 00187 Rome.

The **Pontifical Institute of Oriental Studies** (Oct. 15, 1917): Piazza S. Maria Maggiore, 7, 00185 Rome.

Pontifical Lateran University (1773). Piazza S. Giovanni in Laterano, 4, 00184 Rome. Annexed to the university is the Pontifical Institute of Studies of Marriage and the Family, erected by Pope John Paul II, Oct 7, 1982; a section of the Institute was established at the Dominican House of Studies, Washington, D.C., by a decree dated Aug. 22, 1988; sections were opened in Mexico in 1992 and Valencia, Spain, in 1994.

Pontifical Urban University (1627): Via Urbano VIII, 16, 00165 Rome.

Pontifical University of St. Thomas Aquinas (Angelicum) (1580), of the Order of Preachers: Largo Angelicum, 1, 00184 Rome.

Pontifical University Salesianum (May 3, 1940; university designation May 24, 1973), of the Salesians of Don Bosco: Piazza dell' Ateneo Salesiano, 1, 00139 Rome. Associated with the university is the **Pontifical Institute of Higher Latin Studies**, known as the **Faculty of Christian and Classical Letters** (June 4, 1971).

Pontifical Athenaeum of St. Anselm (1687), of the Benedictines: Piazza dei Cavalieri di Malta, 5, 00153 Rome.

Pontifical Athenaeum "Antonianum" (of St. Anthony) (May 17, 1933), of the Order of Friars Minor: Via Merulana, 124, 00185 Rome.

Roman Athenaeum of the Holy Cross (Jan. 9, 1985), of Personal Prelature of Opus Dei: Piazza S. Apollinare, 49, 00186 Rome.

Athenaeum "Regina Apostolorum" of the Legionaries of Christ, Via Aurelia Antica, 460, 00165 Rome.

Pontifical Institute of Sacred Music (1911; May 24, 1931): Via di Torre Rossa, 21, 00165 Rome.

Pontifical Institute of Christian Archeology (Dec. 11, 1925): Via Napoleone III, 1, 00185 Rome.

Pontifical Theological Faculty "St. Bonaventure" (Dec. 18, 1587), of the Order of Friars Minor Conventual: Via del Serafico, 1, 00142 Rome.

Pontifical Theological Faculty, Pontifical Institute of Spirituality "Teresianum" (1935), of the Discalced Carmelites: Piazza San Pancrazio, 5-A, 00152 Rome.

Pontifical Theological Faculty "Marianum" (1398), of the Servants of Mary: Viale Trente Aprile, 6, 00153 Rome.

Pontifical Institute of Arabic and Islamic Studies (1926), of the Missionaries of Africa: Viale di Trastevere, 89, 00153 Rome.

Pontifical Faculty of Educational Science "Auxilium" (June 27, 1970), of the Daughters of Mary, Help of Christians: Via Cremolino, 141, 00166 Rome.

Pontifical Institute "Regina Mundi" (1970): Lungotevere Tor di Nona, 7, 00186 Rome.

Jerome Lejeune: Pope John Paul, while in Paris Aug. 22 for the celebration of World Youth Day 1997, visited the grave of Jerome Lejeune, a member of the Pontifical Academy of Sciences, a geneticist, discoverer of the chromosomal deficiency that causes Down's syndrome, and vigorous pro-life advocate. The Pope's visit, criticized by some, was private, a tribute to a personal friend.

PONTIFICAL ACADEMY OF SCIENCES

(Sources: *Annuario Pontificio,* Catholic News Service.)

The Pontifical Academy of Sciences was constituted in its present form by Pius XI Oct. 28, 1936, in virtue of *In Multis Solaciis,* a document issued on his own initiative.

The academy is the only supranational body of its kind in the world with a pope-selected, life-long membership of outstanding mathematicians and experimental scientists regardless of creed from many countries. The normal complement of 70 members was increased to 80 in 1985-86 by John Paul II. There are additional honorary and supernumerary members.

The academy traces its origin to the *Linceorum Academia* (Academy of the Lynxes — its symbol) founded in Rome Aug. 17, 1603. Pius IX reorganized this body and gave it a new name — *Pontificia Accademia dei Nuovi Lincei* — in 1847. It was taken over by the Italian state in 1870 and called the *Accademia Nationale dei Lincei.* Leo XIII reconstituted it with a new charter in 1887. Pius XI designated the Vatican Gardens as the site of academy headquarters in 1922 and gave it its present title and status in 1936. In 1940, Pius XII gave the title of Excellency to its members; John XXIII extended the privilege to honorary members in 1961.

Members in U.S.

Scientists in the U.S. who presently hold membership in the Academy are listed below according to year of appointment. Nobel prizewinners are indicated by an asterisk.

Franco Rasetti, professor emeritus of physics at Johns Hopkins University, Baltimore, Md. (Oct 28, 1936); Christian de Duve*, professor of biochemistry at the International Institute of Cellular and Molecular Pathology at Brussels, Belgium, and Rockefeller University, New York (Apr. 10, 1970); Marshall Warren Nirenberg*, director of Laboratory on genetics and biochemistry at the National Institutes of Health, Bethesda, Md. (June 24, 1974). George Palade*, professor of cellular biology at University of California, San Diego and Victor Weisskopf, professor of physics at the Massachusetts Institute of Technology, Cambridge, Mass. (Dec. 2, 1975); David Baltimore*, professor of biology at the Massachusetts Institute of Technology, Cambridge, Mass.; Har Gobind Khorana*, professor of biochemistry, and Alexander Rich, professor of biophysics _ both at the Massachusetts Institute of Technology, Cambridge, Mass. (Apr. 17, 1978).

Charles Townes*, professor emeritus of physics at the University of California at Berkeley (Jan. 26, 1983). Beatrice Mintz, senior member of the Cancer Research Institute of Philadelphia and Maxine Singer, biochemist, president of Carnegie Institution, Washington, D.C. (June 9, 1986).

Roald Z. Sagdeev, professor of physics at University of Maryland, College Park and Peter Hamilton Raven, professor of biology at the Missouri Botanical Garden of St. Louis, Mo. (Oct 4, 1990); Luis Angel Caffarelli, professor of mathematics at New York University and Luigi Luca Cavalli-Sforza, professor of genetics at Stanford University (Aug. 2, 1994).

Joshua Lederberg, professor of genetics at Rockefeller Univ., New York (Mar. 4, 1996), Joseph Edward Murray, professor of plastic surgery at Harvard Medical School, Cambridge, Mass., Paul Berg, professor of biochemistry at Stanford Univ. and Vera C. Rubin, professor of astronomy at Carnegie Institution of Washington (June 25, 1996); Gary S. Becker,* professor of economics at the University of Chicago and Chen Ning Yang,* professor of physics and director of the Institute of Theoretical Physics at the State University of New York at Stoney Brook (April 18,1997),

There are also two honorary members from the U.S.: Stanley L, Jaki, O.S.B., professor of physics, history and philosophy at Seton Hall University, South Orange (Sept. 5, 1990) and Robert J. White, professor of neurosurgery at Case Western Reserve University, Cleveland (Mar. 29, 1994).

Members in Other Countries

Listing includes place and date of selection. Nobel prizewinners are indicated by an asterisk.

Armenia: Rudolf M. Muradian (Oct. 16, 1994).

Austria: Hans Tuppy (Apr. 10, 1970); Walter Thirring (June 9, 1986).

Belgium: Paul Adriaan Jan Janssen (June 25, 1990).

Brazil: Carlos Chagas, former president of the academy (Aug. 18, 1961); Johanna Dobereiner (Apr. 17, 1978); Crodowaldo Pavan (Apr. 17, 1978).

Canada: Gerhard Herzberg* (Sept. 24, 1964); John Charles Polanyi* (June 9, 1986).

Chile: Hector Rezzio Croxatto (Dec. 2, 1975).

Denmark: Aage Bohr* (Apr. 17, 1978).

France: Louis Leprince-Ringuet (Aug. 18, 1961); Andre Blanc-LaPierre (Apr. 17, 1978), Andre Lichnerowicz (May 12, 1981), Bernard Pullman (May 12, 1981); Paul Germain (June 9, 1986); Jacques Louis Lions (Oct. 4, 1990) Jean-Marie Lehn (May 30, 1996).

Germany: Rudolf L. Mossbauer* (Apr. 10, 1970); Manfred Eigen* (May 12, 1981); Wolf Joachim Singer (Sept. 18, 1992), Paul Joseph Crutzen (June 25, 1996), Yuri Ivanovich Manin (June 26, 1996),.

Ghana: Daniel Adzei Bekoc (Sept. 26, 1983).

Great Britain: Hermann Alexander Bruck (Apr. 5, 1955); George Porter* (June 24, 1974); Max Ferdinand Perutz* (May 12, 1981); Stanley Keith Runcorn (Sept. 12, 1981); Stephen William Hawking (Jan. 9, 1986); Martin John Rees (June 25, 1990); Sir Richard Southwood (Sept. 18, 1992); Alistair Cameron Crombie (Oct. 16, 1994); Raymond Hide (June 25, 1996)..

India: Mambillikalathil Govind Kumar Menon (May 12, 1981); Chintamani N.R. Rao (June 25, 1990).

Ireland: James Robert McConnell (June 25, 1990).

Israel: Michael Sela (Dec. 2, 1975).

Italy: Giovanni Battista Marini-Bettolo Marconi (Apr. 22, 1968); Rita Levi-Montalcino* (June 24, 1974); Giampietro Puppi (Apr. 17, 1978), Ennio De Giorgi (May 12, 1981), Abdus Salam* (May 12, 1981); Nicola Cabibbo (June 9, 1986); Bernardo Maria Colombo (Sept. 18, 1992).

Japan: Kenichi Fukui* (Dec. 14, 1985); Minoru Oda (Sept. 18, 1992).
Kenya: Thomas R. Odhiambo (May 12, 1981).
Mexico: Marcos Moshinsky (June 9, 1986).
Nigeria: Thomas Adeoye Lambo (June 24, 1974).
Poland: Stanislaw Lojasiewicz (Jan. 28, 1983); Czeslaw Olech (June 9, 1986); Michal Heller (Oct. 4, 1990); Andrzej Szezeklik (Oct. 16, 1994).
Russia: Vladimir Isaakovich Keilis-Borok (Oct. 16, 1994).; Sergei Petrovich Novikov (June 25, 1996)
Spain: Manuel Lora-Tamayo (Sept. 24, 1964).
Sweden: Sven Horstadius (Aug. 18, 1961); Sune Bergstrom* (Dec. 14, 1985); Kai Siegbahn* (Dec. 14, 1985).
Switzerland: John Carew Eccles* (Apr. 8, 1961); Werner Arber* (May 12, 1981); Vladimir Prelog* (Dec. 14, 1985); Carlo Rubbia* (Dec. 14, 1985); Albert Eschenmoser (June 9, 1986).
Taiwan: Te-Tzu Chang (April 18, 1997).
Venezuela: Marcel Roche (Apr. 10, 1970).
Zaire (now Congo): Felix wa Kalengo Malu (Sept. 26, 1983).
Ex officio members: Rev. George V. Coyne, S.J., director of Vatican Observatory (Sept. 2, 1978); Very Rev. Leonard E. Boyle, O.P., prefect of the Vatican Library (May 24, 1984); Rev. Giuseppe Pittau, S.J., chancellor of the Pontifical Academy of Sciences (Jan. 30, 1995); Very Rev.Sergio B. Pagano, prefect of the Secret Vatican Archives (Jan. 7, 1997).
President: Nicola Cabibbo, professor of theoretical physics at Univ. of Rome (app. Apr. 6, 1993).

PONTIFICAL ACADEMY OF SOCIAL SCIENCES

Founded by John Paul II, Jan. 1, 1994 (motu proprio *Socialium scientiarum investigationes*) to promote the study and the progress of social sciences, to advise the Vatican on social concerns and to foster research aimed at improving society. The number of members is not less than 20 nor more than 40. Two of the thirty members of the Academy (as of Jan. 1, 1996) were from the United States: Kenneth J. Arrow of Stanford University and Mary Ann Glendon of Harvard University. President, Prof. Edmond Malinvaud of France. Address: Casino Pio IV, Vatican Gardens.

PONTIFICAL ACADEMY FOR LIFE

Established by John Paul II, Feb. 11, 1994 (motu proprio *Vitae Mysterium*) "to fulfill the specific task of study, information and formation on the principal problems of biomedicine and law relative to the promotion and defense of life, especially in the direct relationship they have with Christian morality and the directives of the Church's magisterium." Members, appointed by the Pope without regard to religion or nationality, represent the various branches of "the biomedical sciences and those that are most closely related to problems concerning the promotion and protection of life." Membership as of Jan. 1, 1996, included four from the United States: Mrs. Mercedes Arzu-Wilson, founder and president of the Foundations Family of the Americas and founder and director of the Commission at the World Organization for the Family; Dr. Thomas Hilgers, founder and director of the Institute "Paul VI," Omaha, Nebr.; Prof. Edmund Pellegrino, director of the Center for Advanced Studies in Ethics at Georgetown University, Washington; Mrs. Christine Vollmer, president of the World Organization for the Family; Dr. Denis Cavanaugh, professor of obstetrics and gynecology at the University of South Florida College of Medicine. President, Prof. Juan de Dios Vial Correa, physician and biologist. Address: Via della Conciliazione, 3, 00193 Rome, Italy.

1997 CHRISTOPHER AWARDS

Christopher Awards are given each year to recognize the creative writers, producers and directors who have achieved artistic excellence in films, books and television specials affirming the highest values of the human spirit. The 1997 awards were presented Feb. 27, 1997, in New York.

Television Specials: Producers, directors and writers of "Race for a Miracle: The Brad and Vicki Margus Story" (ABC News Turning Point); The American Experience: "TR, the Story of Theodore Roosevelt (WGBH/PBS); "The Boys Next Door" (CBS); "A Brother's Promise: The Dan Jansen Story" (CBS); "Color Me Perfect" (Lifetime); Nightline "The Gift" (ABC).

Motion Pictures: Producers, directors and writers of: "Fly Away Home" (Columbia); "Marvin's Room" (Miramax); "Mr. Holland's Opus" (Hollywood Pictures); "The Spitfire Grill" (Castle Rock).

Books: *Fighting for Life,* by Gov. Robert P. Casey (Word); *Living Faith,* by Jimmy Carter (Times Books); *My First White friend: Confessions on Race,* *Love and Forgiveness,* by Patricia Raybon (Viking); *Two Voices: A Father and Son Discuss Family and Faith,* by Jim Doyle and Brian Doyle (Liguori); *Undaunted Courage: Meriwether Lewis, Thomas Jefferson and the Opening of the Americsn West,* by Stephen E. Ambrose (Simon and Schuster).

Books for Young People: *The Log Cabin Quilt,* by Ellen Howard, illustrated by Ronald Himler (Ages 4-6, Holiday House); *Minty: A Story of Young Harriet Tubman,* by Alan Schroeder, pictures by Jerry Pinkney (Ages 6-9, Dial); *Frindle,* by Andrew Clements, pictures by Brian Selznick (Ages 10-12, Simon and Schuster); *Glennis, Before and After,* by Patricia Calvert (Ages 12 and up, Atheneum); *Irrepressible Spirit: Conversations with Human Rights Activists,* by Susan Kuklin (Young Adult; Putnam).

The James Keller Youth Award: Craig Kielburger, 14-year-old who started organization "Free the Children" to abolish forced child labor around the world.

Special Christopher Award: "Touched by an Angel" (CBS Television).

Edith Stein: During a meeting with cardinals in late May, 1997, Pope John Paul formally stated that Blessed Edith Stein would be canonized a saint at a date still to be determined. She was born of Jewish parents in 1891 in what is now Wroclaw, Poland, became a Catholic and was put to death in the Auschwitz death camp near Krakow. Blessed Edith Stein is known for her unique spiritual writings.

SOCIAL SERVICES

Catholic Charities USA (formerly National Conference of Catholic Charities): Founded in 1910 by Most Rev. Thomas J. Shahan and Rt. Rev. Msgr. William J. Kerby in cooperation with lay leaders of the Society of St. Vincent de Paul to help advance and promote the charitable programs and activities of Catholic community and social service agencies in the United States. As the central and national organization for this purpose, it services a network of more than 1,400 agencies and institutions by consultation, information and assistance in planning and evaluating social service programs under Catholic auspices.

Diocesan member agencies provide shelter, food, counseling, services to children, teen parents and the elderly, and a variety of other services to people in need — without regard to religion, gender, age or national origin. Each year millions of people receive help from Catholic Charities; in 1995 (latest statistics available), more than 10 million turned to Catholic Charities agencies for help. In addition, Catholic Charities is an advocate for persons and families in need.

Catholic Charities USA serves members through national and regional meetings, training programs, literature and social policy advocacy on the national level. It is charged by the U.S. bishops with responding to disasters in this country. Catholic Charities USA's president represents North America before Caritas Internationalis, the international conference of Catholic Charities, and thus maintains contact with the Catholic Charities movement throughout the world. Publications include *Charities USA*, a quarterly membership magazine, and a directory of U.S. Catholic Charities agencies and institutions.

Rev. Fred Kammer, S.J., is president of Catholic Charities USA. Address: 1731 King St., Suite 200, Alexandria, VA 22314.

Society of St. Vincent de Paul, Council of the United States (originally called the Conference of Charity): An association of Catholic lay men and women devoted to personal service to the poor through the spiritual and corporal works of mercy. The first conference was formed at Paris in 1833 by Bl. Frederic Ozanam and his associates.

The first conference in the U.S. was organized in 1845 at St. Louis. There are now approximately 4,400 units of the society in this country, with a membership of more than 60,000. The society operates world wide in more than 130 countries and has more than 800,000 members.

In the fiscal year 1994-95, members of the society in this country distributed among poor persons financial and other forms of assistance valued at approximately $165,000,000.

Besides person-to-person assistance, increasing emphasis is being given to stores and rehabilitation workshops of the society through which persons with marginal income can purchase refurbished goods at minimal cost. Handicapped persons are employed in renovating goods and store operations. The society also operates food centers, shelters, criminal justice and other programs.

Publications include *The Ozanam News*, a biannual membership magazine, and *The United States Councilor*, a quarterly newsletter.

Address of the National Council: 58 Progress Parkway, St. Louis, MO 63043. Joseph H. Mueller, national president; Rita W. Porter, executive director.

Catholic Health Association of the United States (CHA), representing more than 1,200 Catholic-sponsored facilities and organizations, works with its members to: promote justice and compassion in healthcare, influence public policy, shape a continuum of care through integraated delivery, and strengthen ministry presence and influence in the U.S. healthcare system. CHA supports and strengthens the Catholic health ministry by being a castalyst through research and development (leading edge tools for sustaining a faith-based ministry in price competitive markets), education and facilitation (annual assembly, conferences, and other methods for engaging the ministry), and advocacy (a united ministry voice for public policy). CHA members make up the nation's largest group of not-for-profit healthcare facilities under a single form of sponsorship.

CHA maintains its national headquarters at 4455 Woodson Road, St. Louis, MO 63134, and an office at 1875 Eye Street N.W., Suite 1000, Washington, DC 20006.

National Association of Catholic Chaplains: Founded in 1965. membership is over 3,500. Address: 3501 S. Lake Dr., Milwaukee, WI 53207.

FACILITIES FOR RETIRED AND AGED PERSONS

(Sources: Almanac survey, *The Official Catholic Directory*.)

This list covers residence, health care and other facilities for the retired and aged under Catholic auspices. Information includes name, type of facility if not evident from the title, address, and total capacity (in parentheses); unless noted otherwise, facilities are for both men and women. Many facilities for the aged offer intermediate nursing care.

Alabama: Allen Memorial Home (Skilled Nursing), 735 S. Washington Ave., Mobile 36603 (94).

Cathedral Place Apartments (Retirement Complex), 351 Conti St., Mobile 36602 (192).

Mercy Medical (Acute Rehabilitation Hospital, Skilled and Post-Acute Nursing, Hospice, Home Health and Assisted and Independent Living), P.O. Box 1090, Daphne 36526 (157 beds; 120 assisted units; 32 independent apartments). Not restricted to elderly.

Sacred Heart Residence Little Sisters of the Poor, 1655 McGill Ave., Mobile 36604 (75).

Seton Haven (Retirement Complex), 3721 Wares Ferry Rd., Montgomery 36193 (104).

Arizona: Desert Crest Campus (Retirement Complex), 2101 E. Maryland Ave., Phoenix 85016 (114 apartments and cottages) and 2151 E. Maryland Ave., Phoenix 85016 (66).

California: Alexis Apartments of St. Patrick's Parish, 756 Mission St. 94103; 390 Clementina St., San Francisco 94103 (206).

Casa Manana Inn, 3700 N. Sutter St., Stockton 95204 (162). Non-profit housing for low-income elderly over 62.

Cathedral Plaza, 1551 Third Ave., San Diego 92101 (222 apartments).

Francis of Assisi Community, 145 Guerrero St., San Francisco 94103 (120). Low-income elderly.

Guadalupe Plaza, 4142 42nd St., San Diego 92105 (127 apartments).

Jeanne d'Arc Manor, 85 S. Fifth St., San Jose 95112 (121). For low income elderly and handicapped.

La Paz Villas, P.O. Box 1962, Palm Desert 92261 (24 units).

Little Flower Haven (Residential Care Facility for Retired), 8585 La Mesa Blvd., La Mesa 91941 (85).

Little Sisters of the Poor, St. Anne's Home, 300 Lake St., San Francisco 94118 (103).

Little Sisters of the Poor, Jeanne Jugan Residence, 2100 South Western Ave., San Pedro, Calif. 90732 (104).

Madonna Residence (Housing for low-income women over 60), 1055 Pine St., San Francisco 94109 (57).

Marian Residence (Retirement Home), 124 S. College Dr., Santa Maria 93454 (34).

Mercy McMahon Terrace (Residential Care Facility), 3865 J St., Sacramento 95816 (118 units).

Mercy Retirement and Care Center, 3431 Foothill Blvd., Oakland 94601 (135 residential; 59 skilled nursing).

Mother Gertrude Home for Senior Citizens, 11320 Laurel Canyon Blvd., San Fernando 91340 (114).

Nazareth House (Residential and Skilled Care), 2121 N. 1st St., Fresno 93703 (85 residential; 39 skilled nursing).

Nazareth House (Residential and Skilled Nursing), 3333 Manning Ave., Los Angeles 90064 (127 residential; 33 skilled nursing).

Nazareth House (Retirement Home), 245 Nova Albion Way, San Rafael 94903 (139).

Nazareth House Retirement Home, 6333 Rancho Mission Rd., San Diego 92108 (122).

O'Connor Woods (Retirement Community), 3400 Wagner Heights, Stockton 95209 (235 independent, 48 assisted living).

Our Lady of Fatima Villa (Skilled Nursing Facility), 20400 Saratoga-Los Gatos Rd., Saratoga 95070 (85).

St. Bernardine Plaza (Retirement Home), 550 W. 5th St., San Bernardino 92401 (150 units).

St. Francis Home, 1718 W. 6th St., Santa Ana 92703 (65).

St. John of God (Retirement and Care Center), 2035 W. Adams Blvd., Los Angeles 90018.

St. John's Plaza, 8150 Broadway, Lemon Grove 91945 (100).

Vigil Light Apartments, 1945 Long Dr., Santa Rosa 95405 (48).

Villa Scalabrini (Retirement Center and Skilled Nursing Care), 10631 Vinedale St., Sun Valley 91352 (130 residence; 58 skilled nursing).

Villa Siena (Residence and Skilled Nursing Care), 1855 Miramonte Ave., Mountain View 94040 (50, residence; 20, skilled nursing care).

Colorado: Francis Heights, Inc., 2626 Osceola St., Denver 80212 (384 units; 431 residents).

Gardens at St. Elizabeth (Congregate Housing and Assisted Living), 2835 W. 32nd Ave., Denver 80211 (209 congregate; 81 assisted living).

Little Sisters of the Poor, 3629 W. 29th Ave., Denver 80211 (78).

Connecticut: Augustana Homes (Residence), Simeon Rd., Bethel 06801.

Carmel Ridge, 6454 Main St., Trumbull 06611.

Holy Family Home and Shelter, Inc., 88 Jackson St., P.O. Box 884, Willimantic 06226.

Matulaitis Nursing Home, 10 Thurber Rd., Putnam 06260 (119).

Monsignor Bojnowski Manor, Inc. (Skilled Nursing Facility), 50 Pulaski St., New Britain 06053 (54).

Notre Dame Convalescent Home, 76 West Rocks Rd., Norwalk 06851 (60).

St. Joseph Living Center, 14 Club Rd., Windham 06280 (120).

St. Joseph's Manor (Health Care Facility; Home for Aged), Carmelite Srs. for Aged and Infirm, 6448 Main St., Trumbull 06611 (297).

St. Joseph's Residence, Little Sisters of the Poor, 1365 Enfield St., Enfield, Conn. 06082 (93)

St. Lucian's Home for the Aged, 532 Burritt St., New Britain 06053 (42).

St. Mary's Home (Residence and Health Care Facility) 2021 Albany Ave., W. Hartford 06117.

Delaware: The Antonian, 1701 W. 10th St., Wilmington 19805 (136 apartments).

Jeanne Jugan Residence, Little Sisters of the Poor, 185 Salem Church Rd., Newark 19713 (80).

Marydale Retirement Village, 135 Jeandell Dr., Newark 19713 (108 apartments).

St. Patrick's House, Inc., 115 E. 14th St., Wilmington 19801 (16).

District of Columbia: Jeanne Jugan Residence _ St. Joseph Villa, Little Sisters of the Poor, 4200 Harewood Rd., N.E. Washington 20017 (87).

Florida: All Saints Home, 5888 Blanding Blvd., Jacksonville 32246 (60).

Archbishop McCarthy Residence (Retirement Apartments), 13201 N.W. 28th Avenue, Opa Locka 33054 (113 apartments).

Bon Secour-Maria Manor Nursing Care Center, 10300 4th St. N., St. Petersburg 33716 (274).

Carroll Manor (Retirement Apartments), 3667 S. Miami Ave., Miami 33133 (230 apartments).

Casa Calderon, Inc. (Retirement Apartments), 800 W. Virginia St., Tallahassee 32304.

Haven of Our Lady of Peace (Assisted Living and Nursing Home)), 5203 N. 9th Ave., Pensacola 32504 (89).

Marian Towers, Inc. (Retirement Apartments), 17505 North Bay Rd., Miami Beach 33160.

Noreen McKeen Residence for Geriatric Care (Skilled and Intermediate Care), 315 Flagler Dr. S., W. Palm Beach 33401.

Palmer House, Inc., 1225 S.W. 107th Ave., Miami 33174 (120 apartments).

St. Andrew Towers (Retirement Apartments), 2700 N.W. 99th Ave., Coral Springs 33065 (432).

St. Catherine Laboure (Skilled and Intermediate Care), 1750 Stockton St., Jacksonville 32204 (232).

St. Dominic Gardens (Retirement Apartments), 5849 N.W. 7th St., Miami 33126 (149 apartments).

St. Elizabeth Gardens, Inc. (Retirement Apartments), 801 N.E. 33rd St., Pompano Beach 33064 (150).

St. John's Rehabilitation Hospital and Nursing Center, Inc., 3075 N.W. 35th Ave., Lauderdale Lakes 33311.

Stella Maris House, Inc., 8636 Harding Ave., Miami Beach 33141 (136 apartments).

Illinois: Addolorata Villa (Sheltered Intermediate, Skilled Care Facility; Apartments), 555 McHenry Rd., Wheeling 60090 (135 health care; 100 apartments).

Alvernia Manor (Sheltered Care), 13950 Main St., Lemont 60439 (50).

Carlyle Healthcare Center, 501 Clinton St., Carlyle 62231 (131).

Carmelite Carefree Village, 8419 Bailey Rd., Darien 60561 (105).

Cor Mariae Center (Assisted Living and Nursing Home), 3330 Maria Linden Dr., Rockford 61107 (90).

Cortland Manor Retirement Home, 1900 N. Karlov, Chicago 60639. (56).

Holy Family Health Center, 2380 Dempster, Des Plaines 60016 (362).

Holy Family Villa (Intermediate Care Facility), 12395 McCarthy Rd., Lemont 60439 (99).

Jugan Terrace, Little Sisters of the Poor, 2300 N. Racine, Chicago 60614 (50 apartments).

Little Sisters of the Poor, St. Joseph's Home for the Elderly, 80 W. Northwest Hwy., Palatine 60067 (67).

Little Sisters of the Poor Center for the Aging, 2325 N. Lakewood Ave., Chicago, Ill. 60614 (96).

Maria Care Center (Skilled Intermediary Facility), 350 W. S. First St., Red Bud 62278 (115).

Marian Heights Apartments (Elderly, Handicapped), 20 Marian Heights Dr., Alton 62002 (127).

Marian Park, Inc., 2126 W. Roosevelt Rd., Wheaton 60187 (117 apartments).

Maryhaven, Inc. (Skilled and Intermediate Care Facility), 1700 E. Lake Ave., Glenview 60025 (147).

Mayslake Village (Retirement Apartments), 1801 35th St., Oak Brook 60521 (630 apartments).

Mercy Residence at Tolentine Center, 20300 Governors Hwy., Olympia Fields 60461 (52).

Meredith Memorial Home, 16 S. Illinois St., Belleville 62220 (70).

Merkle-Knipprath (Apartments and Nursing Facility), Rt. 1, Franciscan Brothers. Clifton 60927 (130).

Mother Theresa Home (Skilled, Intermediate and Sheltered Care), 1270 Franciscan Dr., Lemont 60439 (150).

Nazarethville (Intermediate and Sheltered Care), 300 N. River Rd., Des Plaines 60016 (83).

Our Lady of Angels Retirement Home, 1201 Wyoming, Joliet 60435 (96).

Our Lady of the Snows, Apartment Community, 9500 West Illinois Highway 15, Belleville 62223. Retirement community (166 apartments); adjoining skilled-care facility (57 beds).

Our Lady of Victory Nursing Home (Intermediate and Skilled Care), 20 Briarcliff Lane, Bourbonnais 60914 (97).

Pope John Paul I Apartments (Elderly and Handicapped), 1 Pope John Paul Plaza, Springfield 62703 (150).

Queen of Peace Center, 1910 Maple Ave., Lisle 60532.

Resurrection Nursing Pavilion (Skilled Care), 1001 N. Greenwood, Park Ridge 60068 (295).

Resurrection Retirement Community, 7262 W. Peterson Ave., Chicago, 60631 (473 apartments).

Rosary Hill Home (Women), 9000 W. 81st St., Justice 60458 (50).

St. Andrew Home (Retirement Residence), 7000 N. Newark Ave., Niles 60648 (196).

St. Ann's Healthcare Center, 770 State St., Chester 62233 (119).

St. Anne Center (Nursing Home), 4405 Highcrest Rd., Rockford 61107 (179).

St. Anne Place (Retirement Apartments),4444 Brendenwood Rd., Rockford 61107 (106 apartments).

St. Benedict Home, 6930 W. Touhy Ave., Niles 60714 (130).

St. Elizabeth Home (Residence), 704 W. Marion St., Joliet 60436. Group living for Senior women.

St. James Manor, 1251 East Richton Rd., Crete 60417 (110).

St. Joseph's Home (Sheltered and Intermediate Care), 3306 S. 6th St. Rd., Springfield 62703 (112).

St. Joseph's Home (Sheltered and Intermediate Care), 2223 W. Heading Ave., Peoria 61604 (186).

St. Joseph's Home for the Aged, 659 E. Jefferson St., Freeport 61032 (120).

St. Joseph Home of Chicago, Inc. (Skilled Care), 2650 N. Ridgeway Ave., Chicago 60647 (173).

St. Patrick's Residence, 1400 Brookdale Rd., Naperville 60563 (210).

Villa Franciscan (Skilled Care), Franciscan Sisters Health Care Corporation, 210 N. Springfield, Joliet 60435 (176).

Villa Scalabrini (Sheltered, Intermediate and Skilled), 480 N. Wolf Rd., Northlake 60164 (265).

Indiana: Albertine Home, 1501 Hoffman St., Hammond 46327 (33).

Little Company of Mary Health Facility (Comprehensive Nursing), 7520 S. US Hwy 421, San Pierre 46374 (200).

Providence Retirement Home, 703 E. Spring St., New Albany 47150 (95).

Sacred Heart Home (Comprehensive Nursing), 515 N. Main St., Avilla 46710 (133). LaVerna Terrace, same address; independent living for senior citizens, handicapped and disabled (51 units).

St. Anne Home (Residential and Comprehensive Nursing), 1900 Randallia Dr., Ft. Wayne 46805 (205).

St. Anthony Home, Inc., 203 Franciscan Rd., Crown Point 46307 (219).

St. Augustine Home for the Aged, Little Sisters of the Poor, 2345 W. 86th St., Indianapolis 46260 (90).

St. John's Home for the Aged, Little Sisters of the Poor, 1236 Lincoln Ave., Evansville 47714 (71).

St. Mary's Regina Continuing Care Center (Intermediate Care Facility), 3900 Washington Ave., Evansville 47714 (128).

St. Paul Hermitage (Residential and Intermediate Care Nursing), 501 N. 17thAve., Beech Grove 46107 (95).

Iowa: The Alverno Health Care Facility (Nursing Care), 849 13th Ave. N., Clinton 52732 (138).

Bishop Drumm Retirement Center, 5837 Winwood Dr., Johnston 50131 (nursing care, 150). McAuley Terrace Apartments (85 units).

Hallmar-Mercy Hospital, 701 Tenth St. S.E., Cedar Rapids 52403 (62).

Holy Spirit Retirement Home (Intermediate Care), 1701 W. 25th St., Sioux City 51103 (94).

Kahl Home for the Aged and Infirm (Skilled and Intermediate Care Facility), 1101 W. 9th St., Davenport 52804 (135).

The Marian Home, 2400 6th Ave. North, Fort Dodge 50501 (Intermediate Care, 97) and Marian Village (Apartments), 2320 6th Ave. North, Fort Dodge 50501.

Padre Pio Health Care Center, Stonehill Care Center (Residence, Nursing Home), 3485 Windsor, Dubuque 52001 (250). Stonehill Adult Center (Day Care), same address.

St. Anthony Nursing Home (Intermediate Care), 406 E. Anthony St., Carroll 51401 (80). Orchard View, same address (50 apartments).

St. Francis Continuation Care and Nursing Home Center, Burlington 52601 (19 skilled nursing; 69 intermediate care). Orchard City of St. Francis, same address (12 independent living apartment units).

Kansas: Catholic Care Center (Skilled and Intermediate Care Facility), 6700 E. 45th St, Wichita 67226 (178 beds _ includes 16 Alzheimer and 6 AIDS).

Mt. Joseph Senior Community (Intermediate Care Facility), 1110 W. 11, Concordia 66901 (99 nursing and 20 personal care beds; 12 apartments).

St. Elizabeth Home Health Agency, 2225 Canterbury Rd., Hays 67601.

St. John Rest Home (Nursing Facility), 701 Seventh St., Victoria 67671 (90 nursing).

St. John's of Hays (Nursing Facility), 2010 E. 25th, Hays 67601 (60).

St. Joseph Care Center (Intermediate and Skilled Care Facility), 759 Vermont Ave., Kansas City 66101 (201 nursing).

Villa Maria, Inc. (Intermediate Care Facility), 116 S. Central, Mulvane 67110 (66).

Kentucky: Bishop Soenneker Personal Care Home, 9545 Ky. 144, Philpot 42366 (60).

Carmel Home (Residence, Adult Day Care, Respite Care and Nursing Care), 2501 Old Hartford Rd., Owensboro 42303 (115).

Carmel Manor (Skilled, Intermediate and Personal Care Home), 100 Carmel Manor Rd., Ft. Thomas, 41075 (145).

Madonna Manor Nursing Home, 2344 Amsterdam Rd., Villa Hills 41017 (60). Also has 49 senior citizen apartments.

Marian Home, 3105 Lexington Rd., Louisville 40206 (70).

Nazareth Home, 2000 Newburg Rd., Louisville 40205 (168).

St. Charles Care Center and Village, 500 Farrell Dr., Covington 41011 (147). Nursing home; adult day health program. Independent living cottages (35). Assisted living (60). Independent living apartments (12).

Louisiana: Annunciation Inn, 1220 Spain St., New Orleans 70117 (106 residential units).

Bethany M.H.S. Health Care Center (Women), P.O. Box 2308, Lafayette 70502 (42).

Chateau de Notre Dame (Residence and Nursing Home), 2832 Burdette St., New Orleans 70125 (106 residential units, 6 assisted living units, 180 nursing beds).

Christopher Inn Apartments, 2110 Royal St., New Orleans 70116 (144 residential units).

Consolata Home (Nursing Home), 2319 E. Main St., New Iberia 70560 (114).

Haydel Heights Apartments, 4402 Reynes St., New Orleans 70126 (65 units).

Lafon Nursing Home of the Holy Family, 6900 Chef Menteur Hwy., New Orleans 70126 (171).

Mary-Joseph Residence for the Elderly, 4201 Woodland Dr., New Orleans 70131 (122).

Metairie Manor, 4929 York St., Metairie 70001 (287 residential units).

Nazareth Inn, 9630 Haynes Blvd., New Orleans 70127 (270 apartments).

Ollie Steele Burden Manor (Nursing Home), 4250 Essen Lane, Baton Rouge 70809 (184).

Our Lady of Prompt Succor Home, 751 E. Prudhomme Lane, Opelousas 70570 (80).

Our Lady's Manor, Inc., 402 Monroe St., Alexandria 71301 (104 apartments).

Place Dubourg, 201 Rue Dubourg, LaPlace 70068 (115 residential units).

Rouquette Lodge, 4300 Hwy 22, Mandeville 70471 (119 residential units).

St. John Berchmans Manor, 3400 St. Anthony St., New Orleans 70122 (150 residential units).

St. Joseph's Home (Nursing Home), 2301 Sterlington Rd., Monroe 71211 (132).

St. Margaret's Daughters Home (Nursing Home), 6220 Chartres St., New Orleans 70117 (115).

St. Martin Manor, 1501 N. Johnson St., New Orleans 70116 (140 residential units).

Villa St. Maurice and Villa St. Maurice II, 500 St. Maurice Ave., New Orleans 70117 (185 residential units).

Village du Lac, Inc., 1404 Carmel Ave., Lafayette 70501 (200). For handicapped and elderly.

Wynhoven Apartments and Wynhoven II (Residence for Senior Citizens), 4600-10th St., Marrero 70072 (350).

Wynhoven II, 4606-10th St., Marrero 70072 (150).

Maine: Deering Pavilion (Apartments for Senior Citizens), 880 Forest Ave., Portland 04103 (200 units).

Mt. St. Joseph, Highwood St., Waterville 04901 (88).

St. Andre Health Care Facility, Inc. (Nursing Facility), 407 Pool St., Biddeford 04005 (96).

St. Joseph's Manor (Nursing Care Facility), 1133 Washington Ave., Portland 04103 (50 skilled nursing; 150 intermediate nursing). Adult and child day care centers, same address.

St. Marguerite D'Youville Pavilion, 102 Campus Ave., Lewiston 04240 (280). Maison Marcotte (Independent Living Community), 100 Campus Ave., Lewiston 04240 (128 apartments).
St. Xavier's Home (Apartments), 199 Somerset St., Bangor 04401 (19 units).
Seton Village, Inc., 1 Carver St., Waterville 04901 (140 housing units).

Maryland: Cardinal Shehan Center, Inc., 2300 Dulaney Valley Rd., Towson 21204 (438).
Little Sisters of the Poor, St. Martin's Home (for the Aged), 601 Maiden Choice Lane, Baltimore 21228 (106).
Sacred Heart Home, 5805 Queens Chapel Rd., Hyattsville 20782 (102).
St. Joseph Nursing Home, 1222 Tugwell Dr., Baltimore 21228 (40).
Villa Rosa Nursing Home, 3800 Lottsford Vista Rd., Mitchellville 20721 (101).

Massachusetts: Catholic Memorial Home (Nursing Home), 2446 Highland Ave., Fall River 02720 (300). Alzheimer unit (43)
Don Orione Nursing Home, 111 Orient Ave., East Boston 02128 (190). Adult day care center (30).
D'Youville Manor (Nursing Home), 981 Varnum Ave., Lowell 01854 (196). Day care program (20).
Jeanne Jugan Residence, Little Sisters of the Poor (Home for the Elderly), 186 Highland Ave., Somerville 02143 (84). Jeanne Jugan Pavilion, 190 Highland Ave., Somerville 02143 (apartments, 27; residents, 28).
Madonna Manor (Nursing Home), 85 N. Washington St., N. Attleboro 02760 (129).
Marian Manor, for the Aged and Infirm (Nursing Home), 130 Dorchester St., S. Boston, 02127 (363).
Marian Manor of Taunton (Nursing Home), 33 Summer St., Taunton 02780 (116).
Maristhill Nursing Home, 66 Newton St., Waltham 02154 (120).
MI Nursing/Restorative Center, Zero Bennington St., Lawrence 01841 (250). Alzheimer beds (42).
MI Residential Community, 189 Maple St., Lawrence 01841 (304 apartments). Adult Day Health Care Center (52).
Mt. St. Vincent Nursing Home, 35 Holy Family Rd., Holyoke 01040 (125).
Our Lady's Haven (Nursing Home), 71 Center St., Fairhaven 02719 (117).
Sacred Heart Home (Nursing Home), 359 Summer St., New Bedford 02740 (217).
St. Joseph Manor Nursing Home, 215 Thatcher St., Brockton 02402 (120).
St. Joseph's Nursing Care Center, 321 Centre St., Dorchester, Boston 02122 (123).
St. Patrick's Manor (Nursing Home), 863 Central St., Framingham 01701 (332).

Michigan: Bishop Noa Home for Senior Citizens (Nursing Home and Residence), 2900 3rd Ave. S., Escanaba 49829 (109).
Lourdes Nursing Home (Skilled Facility), 2300 Watkins Lake Rd., Waterford 48328 (108).
McFadden Home (Residence), 2150 Watkins Lake Rd., Waterford 48328 (6).

Marian Hall (Residence), 529 M.L. King Ave., Flint 48502 (97).
Marycrest Manor (Skilled Nursing Facility), 15475 Middlebelt Rd., Livonia 48154 (55).
Ryan Senior Residences of the Archdiocese of Detroit. Nine residences:
Casa Maria, 600 Maple Vista, Imlay City 48444 (87).
Kundig Center, 3300 Jeffries Freeway, Detroit 48208 (153).
Madonna Villa 17825 Fifteen Mile Rd., Clinton Twp. 48035 (89).
Marian-Oakland West, 29250 W. Ten Mile Rd., Farmington Hills 48336 (90).
Marian Place, 408 W. Front St., Monroe 48161 (51).
Marydale Center, 3147 Tenth Ave., Port Huron 48060 (57).
Maryhaven, 11350 Reeck Rd., Southgate 48195 (90).
Stapleton Center, 9341 Agnes St., Detroit 48214 (59).
Villa Marie, 15131 Newburgh Rd., Livonia 48154 (89).
St. Ann's Home, (Residence and Nursing Home), 2161 Leonard St. N.W., Grand Rapids 49504 (130).
St. Catherine House, 1641 Webb Ave., Detroit 48206 (12).
St. Elizabeth Briarbank (Women, Residence), 1315 N. Woodward Ave., Bloomfield Hills 48304 (54).
St. Francis Home (Nursing Home), 915 N. River Rd., Saginaw 48609 (100).
St. Joseph's Home, 4800 Cadieux Rd., Detroit 48224 (104).
St. Jude Home, Inc., (Residence), 2270 Marwood, Waterford 48328 (6).
Villa Elizabeth (Nursing Home), 2100 Leonard St. N.E., Grand Rapids 49505 (136). Country Villa (Assisted Living Apartments), 2110 Leonard N.E., Grand Rapids 49505 (48 units).
Villa Francesca (Residence, Women), 565 W. Long Lake Rd., Bloomfield Hills 48302 (18).

Minnesota: Alverna Apartments, 300 8th Ave. S.E., Little Falls 56345 (60). Retirement community.
Assumption Home, 715 North First St., Cold Spring 56320 (Skilled nursing beds, 95). Respite care. Adult day services; home delivered meals.
Benedictine Health Center, 935 Kenwood Ave., Duluth 55811 (Nursing home, 120; day care, 72). Respite care.
Divine Providence Community Home (Skilled Nursing Care), 700 Third Ave. N.W., Sleepy Eye 56085 (58). Lake Villa Maria Senior Housing (21 units).
Franciscan Health Community, 1925 Norfolk Ave., St. Paul 55116 (140).
John Paul Apartments, 200 8th Ave. N., Cold Spring 56320 (61).
Little Sisters of the Poor, Holy Family Residence (Skilled Nursing and Intermediate Care), 330 S. Exchange St., St. Paul 55102 (76). Independent living apartments (32).
Madonna Towers (Retirement Apartments and Nursing Home), 4001 19th Ave. N.W., Rochester 55901 (182).

Mary Rondorf Retirement Home of Sacred Heart Parish, Inc., 222 N.E. 5th St., Staples 56479 (45). Board and lodging with special services.

Mother of Mercy Nursing Home and Retirement Center, 230 Church Ave., Box 676, Albany 56307 (Skilled nursing home, 84; retirement housing, 33).

Regina Nursing Home and Retirement Residence, Hastings 55033. Nursing home (61); retirement home (42); boarding care (32).

Sacred Heart Hospice (Skilled Nursing Home, Adult Day Care, Home Health Care) 1200 Twelfth St. S.W., Austin 55912 (59).

St. Ann's Residence, 330 E. 3rd St., Duluth 55805 (193). Senior housing. Meals and lodging with supportive services.

St. Anne Hospice, Inc. (Skilled Nursing Home), 1347 W. Broadway, Winona 55987 (134). Adult day care.

St. Benedict's Center, 1810 Minnesota Blvd. S.E., St. Cloud 56304 (222 bed skilled nursing care; adult day care, respite care. Benedict Village (Retirement Apartments), 2000 15th Ave. S.E., St. Cloud 56304. Benedict Homes (Alzheimer Residential Care) and Benedict Court (Assisted Living), 1980 15th Ave. S.E., St. Cloud 56304.

St. Elizabeth's Hospital, Nursing Home and Health Care Center, 1200-5th Grant Blvd., Wabasha 55981 (157). Assisted living apartments (23).

St. Francis Home, 501 Oak St., Breckenridge 56520 (124).

St. Mary's Regional Health Center (Hospital and Nursing Center), 1027 Washington Ave., Detroit Lakes 56501 (100).

St. Mary's Villa (Nursing Home), Box 397, Pierz 56364 (101).

St. Otto's Care Center (Nursing Home), 920 S.E. 4th St., Little Falls 56345 (150).

St. William's Nursing Home, Parkers Prairie 56361 (90).

Villa of St. Francis Nursing Home, 1001 Scott Ave., Morris 56267 (140).

Villa St. Vincent (Skilled Nursing Home and Residence), 516 Walsh St., Crookston 56716. Skilled Nursing home (80);special care unit (24); apartments (27); board and care (34).

Mississippi: Notre Dame de la Mer Retirement Apartments, 292 Hwy. 90, Bay St. Louis 39520.

Santa Maria Retirement Apartments, 674 Beach Blvd., Biloxi, 39530.

Villa Maria Retirement Apartments, 921 Porter Ave., Ocean Springs 39564.

Missouri: Cathedral Square Towers, 444 W. 12th St., Kansas City 64105. Apartments for elderly and handicapped (156).

Chariton Apartments (Retirement Apartments), 4249 Michigan Ave., St. Louis 63111 (122 units; 143 residents).

DePaul Health Center — St. Anne's Division (Skilled Nursing), 12303 DePaul Dr., Bridgeton 63044 (96).

LaVerna Heights Retirement Home (Women), 104 E. Park Ave., Savannah 64485 (40). Nursing facility.

LaVerna Village Nursing Home, 904 Hall Ave., Savannah 64485 (120).

Little Sisters of the Poor (Home for Aged), 3225 N. Florissant Ave., St. Louis 63107 (120).

Mary, Queen and Mother Center (Nursing Care), 7601 Watson Rd., St. Louis 63119.

Mother of Good Counsel Home (Skilled Nursing, Women), 6825 Natural Bridge Rd., Northwoods, 63121 (114).

Our Lady of Mercy Country Home, 2205 Hughes Rd., Liberty 64068 (115).

Price Memorial Skilled Nursing Facility, Forby Rd., P.O. Box 476, Eureka 63025 (120).

St. Agnes Home for the Elderly, 10341 Manchester Rd., Kirkwood 63122 (122).

St. Joseph Hill Infirmary, Inc., (Nursing Care Facility, Men), St. Joseph Road, Eureka 63025 (127).

St. Joseph's Home (Residential and Intermediate Care), 723 First Capitol Dr., St. Charles 63301 (100).

St. Joseph's Home (Residential and Intermediate Care Facility), 1306 W. Main St., Jefferson City 65109 (100).

Nebraska: Bergan Mercy Medical Center, Mercy Care Center (Skilled Nursing Facility for Chronic, Complex and Subacute Levels of Care and Rehabilitation), 1870 S. 75th St., Omaha 68124 (250).

Madonna Rehabilitation Hospital, 5401 South St., Lincoln 68506.

Mercy Villa, 1845 S. 72nd St., Omaha 68124 (36).

Mt. Carmel Home, Keens Memorial (Nursing Home), 412 W. 18th St., Kearney 68847 (79).

New Cassel Retirement Center, 900 N. 90th St., Omaha 68114 (156).

St. Joseph's Nursing Home, 401 N. 18th St., Norfolk 68701 (83).

St. Joseph's Retirement Community, 320 E. Decatur St., West Point 68788 (70). Assisted living.

St. Joseph's Villa (Nursing Home), 927 7th St., David City 68632 (65).

New Hampshire: Mount Carmel Nursing Home, 235 Myrtle St., Manchester 03104 (120).

St. Ann Home (Nursing Home), 195 Dover Point Rd., Dover 03820 (54).

St. Francis Home (Nursing Home), 406 Court St., Laconia 03246 (51). Apartments (25).

St. Teresa Manor (Nursing Home), 519 Bridge St., Manchester 03104 (5). Bishop Primeau Apartments, same address (25).

St. Vincent de Paul Nursing Home, 29 Providence Ave., Berlin 03570 (80).

New Jersey: Holy Family Residence, 44 Rifle Camp Rd., P.O. Box 536, W. Paterson 07424 (64).

McCarrick Care Center, 15 Dellwood Lane, Somerset 08873 (120).

Mater Dei Nursing Home, 176 Rt. 40, Newfield 08344 (64).

Morris Hall (St. Joseph Skilled Nursing Center, St. Mary Residence), 2361 Lawrenceville Rd., Lawrenceville 08648 (220).

Mount St. Andrew Villa (Residence), 55 W. Midland Ave., Paramus 07652 (56).

Our Lady's Residence (Nursing Home), 1100 Clematis Ave., Pleasantville 08232 (214).

St. Ann's Home for the Aged (Skilled and Intermediate Nursing Care Home, Women), 198 Old Bergen

Rd., Jersey City 07305 (106). Adult Medical Day Care (50).

St. Francis Health Resort (Residence), Denville 07834 (100), Apartments, 63.

St. Joseph's Home for the Elderly, Little Sisters of the Poor, 140 Shepherd Lane, Totowa 07512 (116; also, 18 independent living units).

St. Joseph's Rest Home for Aged Women, 46 Preakness Ave., Paterson 07522 (25).

St. Joseph's Senior Residence (Sheltered Care), 1 St. Joseph Terr., Woodbridge 07095 (60).

St. Mary's Catholic Home (Skilled Nursing Home), 1730 Kresson Rd., Cherry Hill 08003 (215). The Manor at St. Mary's, 1743 Kresson Rd., Cherry Hill 08003 (82).

St. Vincent's Nursing Home, 45 Elm St., Montclair 07042 (135).

Villa Maria (Residence and Infirmary, Women), 641 Somerset St., N. Plainfield 07061 (84).

New Mexico: Good Shepherd Manor (Residential Care for Aged Persons), Little Brothers of the Good Shepherd, P.O. Box 10248, Albuquerque 87184 (40).

New York: Bernardine Apartments, 417 Churchill Ave., Syracuse 13205.

Brothers of Mercy Sacred Heart Home (Residence) 4520 Ransom Rd., Clarence 14031 (82). Brothers of Mercy Nursing Home, 10570 Bergtold Rd., Clarence 14031 (240). Brothers of Mercy Housing Co., Inc. (Apartments), 10500 Bergtold Rd., Clarence 14031 (100 units).

Carmel Richmond Nursing Home, 88 Old Town Rd., Staten Island 10304 (300). Skilled Nursing, adult day health care.

Ferncliff Nursing Home, 52 River Rd., Rhinebeck 12572 (328).

Frances Schervier Home and Hospital, 2975 Independence Ave., Bronx 10463 (364). Frances Schervier Long Term Health Care Program, same address (310 slots). Frances Schervier Housing Development Fund Corporation, 2995 Independence Ave., Bronx 10463 (154 units).

Good Samaritan Nursing Home (Skilled Nursing), 101 Elm St., Sayville, N.Y. 11782 (100).

The Heritage (Apartments with Skilled Nursing Care), 1450 Portland Ave., Rochester 14621 (237)

Holy Family Home, 1740-84th St., Brooklyn 11214 (200).

Holy Family Home (Adult Home), 410 Mill St., Williamsville 14221 (85).

Kateri Residence (Skilled Nursing), 150 Riverside Dr., New York 10024 (520).

Little Sisters of the Poor, Jeanne Jugan Residence (Skilled Nursing and Health Related; Adult Care), 3200 Baychester Ave., Bronx 10475 (92).

Little Sisters of the Poor, Queen of Peace Residence, 110-30 221st St., Queens Village 11429 (130).

Mary Manning Walsh Home (Nursing Home), 1339 York Ave., New York 10021 (362).

Mercy Healthcare Center (Skilled Nursing Facility), Tupper Lake 12986 (54).

Mt. Loretto Nursing Home, (Skilled Nursing Home), Sisters of the Resurrection, 302 Swart Hill Rd., Amsterdam 12010 (120).

Nazareth Nursing Home (Women), 291 W. North St., Buffalo 14201 (125).

Our Lady of Consolation Geriatric Care Center (Skilled Nursing) 111 Beach Dr., West Islip 11795 (250). Also long term home health care program.

Our Lady of Hope Residence (Home for the Aged), Little Sisters of the Poor, 1 Jeanne Jugan Lane, Latham 12210 (100; also 16 apartments).

Ozanam Hall of Queens Nursing Home, Inc., 42-41 201st St., Bayside 11361 (432).

Providence Rest, 3304 Waterbury Ave., Bronx 10465 (200).

Resurrection Nursing Home (Skilled Nursing Facility), Castleton 12033 (80).

St. Ann's Home (Skilled Nursing Facility), 1500 Portland Ave., Rochester 14621 (354). Home Connection (Adult Day Health Care Program), same address (60)

St. Cabrini Nursing Home, 115 Broadway, Dobbs Ferry 10522 (304).

St. Clare Manor (Nursing Home), 543 Locust St., Lockport 14094 (28).

St. Columban's on the Lake (Retirement Home), 2546 Lake Rd., Silver Creek 14136 (50).

St. Elizabeth Home (Adult Home), 5539 Broadway, Lancaster 14086 (115).

St. Francis Home (Skilled Nursing Facility), 147 Reist St., Williamsville 14221 (142).

St. Joseph Manor (Nursing Home), W. State St., Olean 14760 (22).

St. Joseph Nursing Home, 2535 Genesee St., Utica 13501 (120).

St. Joseph's Guest Home, Missionary Sisters of St. Benedict,, 350 Cuba Hill Rd., Huntington 11743 (48).

St. Joseph's Home (Nursing Home), 420 Lafayette St., Ogdensburg 13669 (82).

St. Joseph's Villa (Adult Home), 38 Prospect Ave., Catskill 12414 (60).

St. Luke Manor, 17 Wiard St., Batavia 14020 (20).

St. Mary's Manor, 515 Sixth St., Niagara Falls 14301 (119).

St. Patrick's Home for the Aged and Infirm, 66 Van Cortlandt Park S., Bronx 10463 (264).

St. Teresa Nursing Home, 120 Highland Ave., Middletown 10940 (92).

St. Vincent's Home for the Aged, 319 Washington Ave., Dunkirk 14048 (40).

Terence Cardinal Cooke Health Care Center (Skilled Nursing), 1249 Fifth Ave., New York 10029.

Teresian House, Washington Ave. Extension, Albany 12203 (300).

Uihlein Mercy Center (Nursing Home), 420 Old Military Rd., Lake Placid 12946 (155).

North Carolina: Maryfield Nursing Home, Greensboro Rd., High Point 27260 (115).

North Dakota: Carrington Health Center (Nursing Home), Carrington 58421 (40).

Manor St. Joseph (Basic Care Facility), Edgeley 58433 (40).

Marillac Manor Retirement Center, 1016 28th St., Bismarck 58501 (78 apartments).

St. Anne's Guest Home, 524 N. 17th St., Grand Forks 58203 (30) Apartments (56). Adult basic care facility.

St. Vincent's Care Center (Nursing Facility), 1021 N. 26th St., Bismarck 58501 (101).

Ohio: Archbishop Leibold Home for the Aged, Little Sisters of the Poor, 476 Riddle Rd., Cincinnati 45220 (115).

The Assumption Village, 9800 Market St., North Lima 44452 (150). Long term nursing facility.

Francesca Residence (Retirement), 39 N. Portage Path, Akron 44303 (40).

House of Loreto (Nursing Home), 2812 Harvard Ave. N.W., Canton 44709 (100).

Jennings Hall, Inc. (Nursing Care), 10204 Granger Rd., Cleveland 4125 (15000).

Little Sisters of the Poor, Sacred Heart Home, 4900 Navarre Ave., Oregon 43616 (126).

Little Sisters of the Poor, Sts. Mary and Joseph Home for Aged, 4291 Richmond Rd., Cleveland 44122 (124).

The Maria-Joseph Living Care Center, 4830 Salem Ave., Dayton 45416 (420).

Mercy St. Theresa Center, 7010 Rowan Hill Dr., Cincinnati 45227 (177).

Mercy Siena Woods (Nursing Home, Skilled and Intermediate Care, Alzheimer Center), 235 W. Orchard Spring Dr., Dayton 45415 (99).

Mount Alverna (Intermediate Care Nursing Facility), 6765 State Rd., Cleveland 44134 (203).

Mt. St. Joseph (Skilled Nursing Facility, Dual Certified), 21800 Chardon Rd., Cleveland 44117 (100).

Nazareth Towers, 300 E. Rich St., Columbus 43215. Hi-rise apartments for independent living for senior citizens (208).

St. Augustine Manor (Skilled Nursing Facility), 7801 Detroit Ave., Cleveland 44102 (248).

St. Clare Retirement Community (Skilled Nursing, Assisted Care, Apartments), Franciscan Sisters of the Poor, 100 Compton Rd., Cincinnati 45215 (171).

St. Francis Health Care Centre, 401 N. Broadway St., Green Springs 44836 (191).

St. Francis Home, Inc. (Residence and Nursing Care), 182 St. Francis Ave., Tiffin 44883 (116).

St. Joseph's Nursing Home and Assisted Living, 2308 Reno Dr., Louisville 44641 (100, nursing home; 40 assisted living).

St. Margaret Hall (Rest Home and Nursing Facility), Carmelite Sisters for the Aged and Infirm, 1960 Madison Rd., Cincinnati 45206 (135).

St. Raphael Home (Nursing Home), 1550 Roxbury Rd., Columbus 43212 (78).

St. Rita's Home (Skilled Nursing Home), 880 Greenlawn Ave., Columbus 43223 (100).

Schroder Manor Retirement Community (Residential Care, Skilled Nursing Care and Independent Living Units), Franciscan Sisters of the Poor, 1302 Millville Ave., Hamilton 45013 (173).

The Villa Sancta Anna Home for the Aged, Inc., 25000 Chagrin Blvd., Beachwood 44122 (68).

The Village at St. Edward (Apartments, Nursing Care and Assisted Living), 3131 Smith Rd., Fairlawn 44333 (290).

Oklahoma: Franciscan Villa, 17110 E. 51st St., Broken Arrow 74012. Intermediate nursing care (60); apartments (40 independent; 22 assisted living).

St. Ann's Home, 9400 St. Ann's Dr., Oklahoma City 73162 (102).

Westminster Village, Inc. (Residence), 1601 Academy, Ponca City 74604 (108).

Oregon: Benedictine Nursing Center, 540 S. Main St., Mt. Angel 97362 (130). Home Health Agency, Outpatient Therapies. Benedictine Institute for Long Term Care. Child Development Center.

Evergreen Court Retirement Apartments, 451 O'Connell St., North Bend 97459 (80).

Maryville Nursing Home, 14645 S.W. Farmington, Beaverton 97007 (147).

Mt. St. Joseph Residence and Extended Care Center, 3060 S.E. Stark St., Portland 97214 (298).

St. Catherine's Residence and Nursing Center, 3959 Sheridan Ave., North Bend 97459 (153).

St. Elizabeth Hospital and Health Care Center, 3985 Midway Lane, Baker City 97814 (120).

Pennsylvania: Antonian Towers, 2405 Hillside Ave., Easton 18042 (50 apartments).

Ascension Manor I (Senior Citizen Housing), 911 N. Franklin St., Philadelphia 19123 (140 units).

Ascension Manor II (Senior Citizen Housing), 970 N. 7th St., Philadelphia 19123 (140 units).

Benetwood Apartments, Benedictine Sisters of Erie, 641 Troupe Rd., Harborcreek 16421 (75). Subsidized housing for low income elderly and handicapped persons.

Bethlehem Retirement Village, 100 W. Wissahickon Ave., Flourtown 19031. Apartments for well elderly (100).

Christ the King Manor, 1100 W. Long Ave., Du Bois 15801 (160).

D'Youville Manor (Residential Care Facility), 1750 Quarry Rd., Yardley 19067 (50).

Garvey Manor (Nursing Home), Logan Blvd., Hollidaysburg 16648 (150).

Grace Mansion (Personal Care Facility), Holy Family Residential Services , 1200 Spring St., Bethlehem (28).

Holy Family Apartments (Low Income), Clay and Valley Sts., New Philadelphia 17959 (11).

Holy Family Apartments, 330-338 13th Ave., Bethlehem 18018 (50 apartments).

Holy Family Home, Little Sisters of the Poor, 5300 Chester Ave., Philadelphia 19143 (106).

Holy Family Manor (Skilled and Intermediate Nursing Facility), 1200 Spring St., Bethlehem 18018 (208).

Holy Family Residence (Personal Care Facility), 900 W. Market St., Orwigsburg 17961 (50).

Holy Redeemer Health System, Inc., Sisters of the Holy Redeemer: St. Joseph's Manor, 1616 Huntingdon Pike, Meadowbrook 19046 (262 bed personal assisted living; 24 bed cognitive impairment); Lafayette-Redeemer, 8580 Verree Rd., Philadelphia 19111 (295 independent-living apartments; 120 bed nursing; 5 bed assisted living; Redeemer Village, 1551 Huntingdon Pike, Huntingdon Valley 19006 (200 units low income subsidized housing for aged and disabled). Also sponsor a hospital, homecare, hospice and other related facilities.

Immaculate Mary Home (Nursing Care Facility), 2990 Holme Ave., Philadelphia 19136 (296).

John XXIII Home (Skilled, Intermediate and Personal Care), 2250 Shenango Freeway, Hermitage 16148 (142).

Little Flower Manor Nursing Home (Skilled Nursing), 1201 Springfield Rd., Darby 19023 (127).

Little Flower Manor of Diocese of Scranton, (Long-Term Skilled Nursing Care Facility), 200 S. Meade St., Wilkes-Barre 18702 (133).

Little Sisters of the Poor, 1028 Benton Ave., Pittsburgh 15212 (106).

Little Sisters of the Poor, Holy Family Residence, 2500 Adams Ave., Scranton 18509 (58).

Maria Joseph Manor (Skilled Nursing, Personal Care Facility and Independent Living Cottages), 875 Montour Blvd., Danville 17821 (96).

Marian Hall Home for the Aged (Women), 934 Forest Ave., Pittsburgh 15202 (25).

Marian Manor (Intermediate Care), 2695 Winchester Dr., Pittsburgh 15220 (170).

Mount Macrina Manor (Skilled Nursing Facility), 520 W. Main St., Uniontown 15401 (120).

Neumann Apartments (Low Income), 25 N. Nichols St., St. Clair 17970 (25).

Queen of Angels Apartments, 22 Rothermel St., Hyde Park, Reading 19605 (45 units).

Queen of Peace Apartments (Low Income), 777 Water St., Pottsville 17901 (65).

Sacred Heart Manor (Nursing Home and Independent Living), 6445 Germantown Ave., Philadelphia 19119 (171 nursing home; 24 personal care; 72 independent living).

St. Anne's Home and Village, 3952 Columbia Ave., Columbia 17512 (Nursing home, 121; personal care, 18; independent living, 36 cottages).

St. Anne Home (Nursing Facility), 685 Angela Dr., Greensburg 15601 (125).

St. Basil's Home (Personal Care Facility) 530 W. Main St., Box 878, Uniontown 15401 (11).

St. Ignatius Nursing Home, 4401 Haverford Ave., Philadelphia 19104 (176).

St. John Neumann Nursing Home, 10400 Roosevelt Blvd., Philadelphia 19116 (224).

St. Joseph Home for the Aged (Residential and Skilled Nursing Facility), 1182 Holland Rd., Holland 18966 (96).

St. Joseph Nursing and Health Care Center (Skilled Nursing Facility), 5324 Penn Ave., Pittsburgh 15224 (158).

St. Leonard's Home Inc. (Personal Care Facility), 601 N. Montgomery St., Hollidaysburg 16648 (21).

St. Mary of Providence Center, R.D. 2, Box 145, Elverson 19520 (Senior Citizen Housing, 39 units). Center is also a House of Spirituality.

St. Mary's Home of Erie, 607 E. 26th St., Erie 16504. Residential and personal care (131); skilled and intermediate nursing care (228, includes Alzheimer Center, 37); adult day care (49).

Saint Mary's Manor (Residential, Personal Care, Short-Term Rehabilitation and Nursing Care), 701 Lansdale Ave., Lansdale 19446 (160).

St. Mary's Villa Nursing Home, St. Mary's Villa Rd., Elmhurst 18416 (112).

Trexler Pavilion (Personal Care Facility), 1220 Prospect Ave., Bethlehem 18018 (25).

Villa de Marillac Nursing Home, 5300 Stanton Ave., Pittsburgh 15206 (52).

Villa St. Teresa (Residence, Women), 1215 Springfield Rd., Darby 19023 (53).

Villa Teresa (Nursing Home), 1051 Avila Rd., Harrisburg 17109 (184).

Vincentian Home (Nursing Facility), 111 Perrymont Rd., Pittsburgh 15237 (221).

Rhode Island: Jeanne Jugan Residence of the Little Sisters of the Poor, 964 Main St., Pawtucket 02860 (99).

Saint Antoine Residence (Skilled Nursing Facility), 400 Mendon Rd., North Smithfield 02896 (260).

St. Clare Home (Nursing Facility), 309 Spring St., Newport 02840 (46).

St. Francis House, 167 Blackstone St., Woonsocket 02895 (60). Residential, assisted living.

Scalabrini Villa (Convalescent, Rest — Nursing Home). 860 N. Quidnessett Rd., North Kingstown 02852 (70).

South Carolina: Carter-May Home, 1660 Ingram Rd., Charleston 29407 (15). Personal care home for elderly ladies.

South Dakota: Brady Memorial Home (Skilled Nursing Facility), 500 S. Ohlman St., Mitchell 57301 (83). Independent living units (3); congregate apartments (6); adult day care.

Maryhouse, Inc. (Skilled Nursing Facility), 717 E. Dakota, Pierre 57501 (82 skilled nursing, 23 subacute care beds).

Mother Joseph Manor (Skilled Nursing Facility), 1002 North Jay St., Aberdeen 57401 (81). Apartment units (7). Adult day care program. Respite nursing care.

Prince of Peace Retirement Community, 4500 Prince of Peace Pl., Sioux Falls 57103. Skilled nursing home (90 beds); independent living apartments (74); assisted living aprartments (32); Alzheimer Special Care Unit (20).

St. William's Home for the Aged (Intermediate Care, 60), and Angela Hall (Assisted Living Center for Developmentally Handicapped Women, 22), 901 E. Virgil, Box 432, Milbank 57252. Adult day care program (10).

Tekakwitha Nursing Home (Skilled and Intermediate Care), Sisseton 57262 (101). Tekakwitha Housing Corp. (Independent Living), P.O. Box 208, Sisseton 57262 (24 units).

Tennessee: Alexian Village of Tennessee, 100 James Blvd., Signal Mountain 37377 (277 retirement apartments) and Health Care Center (114). Assisted living (33).

St. Mary Manor, 1771 Highway 45 Bypass, Jackson 38305 (149 retirement apartments).

St. Peter Manor (Retirement Community), 108 N. Auburndale, Memphis 38104.

St. Peter Villa (Intermediate and Skilled Care), 141 N. McLean, Memphis 38104 (180).

Villa Maria Manor, 32 White Bridge Rd., Nashville 37205 (214 apartments).

Texas: Casa, Inc., Housing for Elderly and Handicapped, 3201 Sondra Dr., Fort Worth 76107 (200 apartments).

Casa Brendan Housing for the Elderly and Handicapped (56 apartments) and Casa II, Inc. (30 apartments), 1300 Hyman St., Stephenville 76401 (86).

John Paul II Nursing Home (Intermediate Care and Personal Care), 215 Tilden St., Kenedy 78119.

Mother of Perpetual Help Home (Intermediate Care Facility), 519 E. Madison Ave., Brownsville 78520 (33).

Mt. Carmel Home (Personal Care Home), 4130 S. Alameda St., Corpus Christi 78411 (92).

Nuestro Hogar Housing for Elderly and Handicapped, 709 Magnolia St., Arlington 76012 (65 apartments).

The Regis Retirement Home and St. Elizabeth Nursing Home, 400 Austin Ave., Waco 76701 (291).

St. Ann's Nursing Home, P.O. Box 1179, Panhandle 79068 (56).

St. Dominic Nursing Home, 6502 Grand Ave., Houston 77021 (120).

St. Dominic Residence Hall, 2401 E. Holcombe Blvd., Houston 77021 (137).

St. Francis Nursing Home (Intermediate Care Facility), 630 W. Woodlawn, San Antonio 78212 (152).

St. Francis Village, Inc. (Retired and Elderly), 1 Chapel Plaza, Crowley 76036 (450).

St. Joseph Residence (Personal Care Home), 330 W. Pembroke St., Dallas 75208 (49).

San Juan Nursing Home, Inc. (Skilled and Intermediate Care Facility), P.O. Box 1238, San Juan 78589 (127).

Villa Maria (Home for Aged Women-Men), 920 S. Oregon St., El Paso 79901 (24 units).

Villa Maria, Inc. (Apartment Complex), 3146 Saratoga Blvd., Corpus Christi 78415 (48 units). Corpus Christi diocese.

Utah: St. Joseph Villa (Senior Care Complex), 451 Bishop Federal Lane, Salt Lake City 84115 (230).

Vermont: Loretto Home for Aged, 59 Meadow St., Rutland 05701 (57).

Michaud Memorial Manor (Residential Home for Elderly), Derby Line 05830 (24).

St. Joseph's Home for Aged, 243 N. Prospect St., Burlington 05401 (36).

Virginia: Madonna Home (Home for Aged), 814 W. 37th St., Norfolk 23508 (16).

Marian Manor (Assisted Living, Nursing Care), 5345 Marian Lane, Virginia Beach 23462 (100 units; 30 beds nursing care).

Marywood Apartments, 1261 Marywood Lane, Richmond 23229 (112 units).

McGurk House Apartments, 2425 Tate Springs Rd., Lynchburg 24501 (88 units).

Our Lady of the Valley Retirement Community, 650 N. Jefferson St., Roanoke 24016.

Russell House Apartments, 900 First Colonial Rd., Virginia Beach 23454 (127).

St. Francis Home, 2511 Wise St., Richmond 23225 (31).

St. Joseph's Home for the Aged, Little Sisters of the Poor, 1503 Michael Rd., Richmond 23229 (72).

St. Mary's Woods (Independent and Assisted Living Apartments), 1257 Marywood Lane, Richmond 23229 (118 apartments).

Seton Manor (Apartments), 215 Marcella Rd., Hampton 23666 (112).

Washington: Cathedral Plaza Apartments (Retirement Apartments), W. 1120 Sprague Ave., Spokane 99204 (150).

Chancery Place (Retirement Apartments), 910 Marion, Seattle 98104 (84 units; independent living).

The Delaney, W. 242 Riverside Ave., Spokane 99201 (84).

Elbert House, 16000 N.E. 8th St., Bellevue 98008.

Emma McRedmond Manor, 7960-169th N.E., Redmond 98052.

Fahy Garden Apartments, W. 1403-11 Dean Ave., Spokane 99201 (31).

Fahy West Apartments, W. 1523 Dean Ave., Spokane 99201 (55).

The Franciscan (Apartments), 15237-21stAve. S.W., Seattle 98166 (38).

Providence Mt. St. Vincent (Nursing Center and Retirement Apartments), 4831 35th Ave. S.W., Seattle 98126.

St. Brendan Continuing Care Center, E. 17 8th Ave., Spokane 99202.

St. Joseph Care Center, 20 West 9th Ave., Spokane 99204 (103).

Tumwater Apartments, 5701-6th Ave. S.W., Tumwater 98501 (50).

West Virginia: Welty Home for the Aged, 21 Washington Ave., Wheeling 26003 (45).

Wisconsin: Alexian Village of Milwaukee (Retirement Community/Skilled Nursing Home), 7979 W. Glenbrook Rd., Milwaukee 53223 (320 apartments; 87 skilled nursing; 30 assisted living; adult day care).

Bethany-St. Joseph Health Care Center, 2501 Shelby Rd., La Crosse 54601 (226).

Clement Manor (Retirement Community and Skilled Nursing), 3939 S. 92nd St., Greenfield 53228 (164 skilled nursing; 200 units independent and assisted living). Adult day care.

Divine Savior Nursing Home, 715 W. Pleasant St., Portage 53901 (111 skilled nursing; 14 self care).

Felician Village (Independent Living), 1700 S. 18th St., Manitowoc 54020 (134 apartments).

Franciscan Care Center, 2915 North Meade St., Appleton 54911 (235).

Franciscan Skemp Healthcare, Mayo Health System: Arcadia Campus Nursing Home, 464 S. St. Joseph Ave., Arcadia 54612 (75); LaCrosse Campus Nursing Home, 620 S. 11th St., La Crosse 54601 (95).

Franciscan Villa (Skilled Nursing Home), 3601 S. Chicago Ave., S. Milwaukee 53172 (150).

Hope Nursing Home, 438 Ashford Ave., Lomira 53048 (42).

McCormick Memorial Home, 212 Iroquois St., Green Bay 54301 (74).

Marian Catholic Home (Skilled Care Nursing Home), 3333 W. Highland Blvd., Milwaukee 53208 (360).

Marian Franciscan Center, 9632 W. Appleton Ave., Milwaukee 53225 (345).

Marian Housing Center (Independent Living), 4105 Spring St., Racine 53405 (40).

Maryhill Manor Nursing Home (Skilled Nursing Facility), 501 Madison Ave., Niagara 54151 (75).

Milwaukee Catholic Home (Continuing Care Retirement Community), 2462 N. Prospect Ave., Milwaukee 53211 (130 apartments; 56 skilled nursing).

Nazareth House (Skilled Nursing Facility), 814 Jackson St., Stoughton 53589 (99).

St. Ann Rest Home (Intermediate Care Facility, Women), 2020 S. Muskego Ave., Milwaukee 53204 (54).

St. Anne's Home for the Elderly, 3800 N. 92nd St., Milwaukee 53222 (106 skilled nursing beds, 16 independent apartments).

St. Camillus Campus (Continuing Care Retirement Community), 10100 West Blue Mound Road, Wauwatosa 53226 (297 independent apartments; 108 assisted living units; 192 skilled nursing beds). Also adult day care, licensed home health care, support home services; 24-bed subacute care unit.

St. Catherine Infirmary (Nursing Home), 5635 Erie St., Racine 53402 (41).

St. Elizabeth Nursing Home, 502 St. Lawrence Ave., Janesville 53545 (43).

St. Francis Home (Skilled Nursing Facility), 1800 New York Ave., Superior 54880 (192).

St. Francis Home (Skilled Nursing), 365 Gillett St., Fond du Lac 54935 (70).

St. Joan Antida Home (Skilled Nursing), 6700 W. Beloit Rd., W. Allis 53219 (73).

St. Joseph's Home, 705 Clyman St., Watertown 53094 (28).

St. Joseph's Home, 9244 29th Ave., Kenosha 53143 (93). Independent living apartments; skilled nursing home. St. Joseph Adult Day Care, same address.

St. Joseph's Home, 5301 W. Lincoln Ave., W. Allis 53219 (51 assisted living; 74 skilled care; adult day care).

St. Joseph's Nursing Home, 2902 East Ave. S., La Crosse 54601 (80).

St. Joseph's Nursing Home of St. Joseph Memorial Hospital, 400 Water Ave., Hillsboro 54634 (65).

St. Joseph Residence, Inc. (Nursing Home), 107 E. Beckert Rd., New London 54961 (107 skilled nursing; 27 apartments).

St. Mary's Home for the Aged (Skilled Nursing, Alzheimer's Unit, Respite Care), 2005 Division St., Manitowoc 54220 (297).

St. Mary's Nursing Home, 3516 W. Center St., Milwaukee 53210 (130).

St. Monica's Senior Citizens Home, 3920 N. Green Bay Rd., Racine 53404 (125).

St. Paul Home, Inc. (Intermediate and Skilled Nursing Home), 1211 Oakridge Ave., Kaukauna 54130 (129). Assisted living also.

Villa Clement (Health Center), 9047 W. Greenfield Ave., W. Allis 53214 (194).

Villa Loretto Nursing Home, Mount Calvary 53057 (52).

Villa St. Anna (Assisted Living Facility), 5737 Erie St., Racine, 53402 (71 private units).

Villa St. Francis, Inc., 1910 W. Ohio Ave., Milwaukee 53215. Independent and assisted living (142 private units).

FACILITIES FOR CHILDREN AND ADULTS WITH DISABILITIES

Sources: Almanac survey; *The Official Catholic Directory.*

This listing covers facilities and programs with educational and training orientation. Information about other services for the handicapped can generally be obtained from the Catholic Charities Office or its equivalent (c/o Chancery Office) in any diocese. (See Index for listing of addresses of chancery offices in the U.S.)

Abbreviation code: b, boys; c, coeducational; d, day; g, girls; r, residential. Other information includes chronological age for admission. The number in parentheses at the end of an entry indicates total capacity or enrollment.

Deaf and Hearing Impaired

California: St. Joseph's Center for Deaf and Hard of Hearing, 3880 Smith St., Union City 94587.

Louisiana: Chinchuba Institute (d,c; birth through 18 yrs.), 1131 Barataria Blvd., Marrero 70072.

Missouri: St. Joseph Institute for the Deaf (r,d,c; birth to 14 years), 1483 82nd Blvd., University City, St. Louis 63132 (120).

St.Joseph Institute for the Deaf, 1809 Clarkson, Chesterfield, MO 63017.

New York: Cleary School for the Deaf (d,c; infancy through high school), 301 Smithtown Blvd., Nesconset, NY 11767 (105).

St. Francis de Sales School for the Deaf (d,c; infant through elementary grades), 260 Eastern Parkway, Brooklyn 11225 (220).

St. Joseph's School for the Deaf (d,c; parent-infant through 14 yrs.), 100 Hutchinson River Pkwy, Bronx 10465 (160).

Ohio: St. Rita School for the Deaf (r,d,c; birth to 12th grade), 1720 Glendale-Milford Rd., Cincinnati 45215 (162).

Pennsylvania: Archbishop Ryan School for Hearing Impaired Children (d,c; parent-infant programs through 8th grade), 233 Mohawk Ave., Norwood, PA 19024 (49).

De Paul Institute (d,c; birth through 21 yrs.), 2904 Castlegate Ave., Pittsburgh 15226 (115).

Emotionally and/or Socially Maladjusted

This listing includes facilities for abused, abandoned and neglected as well as emotionally disturbed children and youth.

Alabama: St. Mary's Home for Children (r,c; referred from agencies), 4350 Moffat Rd., Mobile 36618 (44).

California: Hanna Boys Center (r,b; 10-15 yrs. at intake; school, 4th to 10th grade), Box 100, Sonoma 95476 (107). Treatment center and therapeutic special school for boys with emotional problems, behavior disorders, learning disabilities.

Rancho San Antonio (r,b; 13-17 yrs.), 21000 Plummer St., Chatsworth 91311 (102).

St. Vincent's (r,d,g; 12-17 yrs.), 4200 Calle Real, P.O. Box 669, Santa Barbara 93102 (14). Rehabilitation programs for girls on probation. Also offers affordable housing and therapy to adult mothers of young children (r,d,w; 18 yrs. and over) (21).

Colorado: Mt. St. Vincent Home (r,c; 5-13 yrs.), 4159 Lowell Blvd., Denver 80211 (45). Day treatment (5-13 yrs.), same address (16).

Connecticut: St. Francis Home for Children (r,d,c;

4-17 yrs.), 651 Prospect St., New Haven 06511 (70).

Mt. St. John (r,b; 11-16 yrs.), 135 Kirtland St., Deep River 06417 (77). Home and school for boys.

Delaware: Our Lady of Grace Home for Children (r,d,c; 6-12 yrs.), 487 E. Chestnut Hill Rd., Newark 19713 (14).

Seton Villa, Siena Hall and Children's Home (r,c; group home; 12-18 yrs,; mothers and their children), c/o 2307 Kentmere Pkwy, Wilmington 19806 (44).

Florida: Boystown of Florida (r,b; 12-16 yrs.; group home), 11400 S.W. 137th Ave., Miami 33186 (43).

Georgia: Village of St. Joseph (r,c; 6-16 yrs.), 2969 Butner Rd. S.W., Atlanta 30331. Residential care center for emotionally disturbed children.

Illinois: Guardian Angel Home (d,c; r,b), 1550 Plainfield Rd., Joliet 60435 (35).

Maryville Academy (r,c; 6-18 yrs.), 1150 North River Rd., Des Plaines 60016.

Mission of Our Lady of Mercy, Mercy Home for Boys and Girls (r,d,c; 15-18 yrs.), 1140 W. Jackson Blvd., Chicago 60607 (100).

St. Joseph's Carondelet Child Center (r,b, 5-21 yrs.; d.c.,5-18 yrs.), 739 E. 35th St., Chicago 60616 (134).

Indiana: Gibault School for Boys (r; 10-18 yrs.), 6301 South U.S. Highway 41, P.O. Box 2316, Terre Haute 47802 (147).

Hoosier Boys Town (r; 10-18 yrs.), 7403 Cline Ave., Schererville 46375 (68).

Kentucky: Boys' Haven (r; 12-18 yrs.), 2301 Goldsmith Lane, Louisville 40218 (67).

Maryhurst School (r,g; 13-17 yrs.), 1015 Dorsey Lane, Louisville 40223 (55).

Louisiana: Hope Haven Center (r,c; 5-18 yrs.), 1101 Barataria Blvd., Marrero 70072 (150). Residential treatment center and school.

Maison Marie Group Home (r,g; 14-18 yrs.), 3020 Independence St., Metairie 70006.

Maryland: Good Shepherd Center (r,g; 13-18 yrs.), 4100 Maple Ave., Baltimore. 21227 (105).

Massachusetts: The Brightside for Families and Children (r,d,c; 6-16 yrs.), 2112 Riverdale St., W. Springfield 01089.

McAuley Nazareth Home for Boys (r; 6-13 yrs.), 77 Mulberry St., Leicester 01524 (16). Residential treatment center.

St. Vincent Home (r,c 5-22 yrs.), 2425 Highland Ave., Fall River 02720 (62). Residential treatment center.

Michigan: Boysville of Michigan, Inc. (r,d,c; 13-17 yrs.), Corporate offices, 8744 Clinton-Macon Rd., Clinton 49236 (650). Facilities located throughout the state and northern Ohio.

Don Bosco Hall (r,b; 13-17 years.), 10001 Petoskey Ave., Detroit 48204 (35).

Vista Maria (r,g; 11-18 yrs.), 20651 W. Warren Ave., Dearborn Heights 48127 (150).

Minnesota: St. Cloud Children's Home (r,c; 8-18 yrs.), 1726 7th Ave. S., St. Cloud 56301 (90). Day Treatment Program (d,c; 7-14 yrs.), same address (12). Intensive Care Unit (r,c; 13-17 yrs.), Box 1006, Fergus Falls 56538 (22).

St. Elizabeth Home (r,c; 18 yrs. and older), 306 15th Ave. N., St. Cloud 56301 (14). Primarily for mentally ill.

Missouri: Child Center of Our Lady (r,d,c; 5-14

yrs.), 7900 Natural Bridge Rd., St. Louis. 63121 (60).

Marygrove (r,d,c; 6-21 yrs.) (97); intense treatment unit (r,b; 13-18 yrs) (13); overnight crises care (r,d,c; birth to 18 yrs.) (8),2705 Mullanphy Lane, Florissant. 63031. Sequoia Group Home (r,g; 17-21 yrs.) (10); Sycamore House, Foster Care (r,c, 6-21 yrs. (3)..

St. Joseph's Home for Boys (r,d,b; 6-14 yrs.), 4753 S. Grand Blvd., St. Louis 63111 (50).

Montana: Big Sky Ranch (r,g; 12-18 yrs.), P.O. Box 1128, Glendive 59330 (8). Moderate level group home.

Nebraska: Father Flanagan's Boys' Home (r,c; 10-16 yrs.), Boys Town 68010 (556). Boys Town National Research Hospital (r,d,c; 1-18 yrs.), 555 N. 30th St., Omaha 68131. Center for Abused Handicapped Children; diagnosis of speech, language and hearing problems in children. Boys Town also has various facilities or programs in Brooklyn, N.Y.; Portsmouth, R.I.; Philadelphia, Pa.; Washington, D.C.; Tallahassee, Orlando and Delray Beach, Fla.; Atlanta, Ga.; New Orleans, La.; San Antonio, Tex., Las Vegas, Nev., and southern California.

New Jersey: Catholic Community Services/Mt. Carmel Guild, 1160 Raymond Blvd., Newark 07102.

Collier Group Home (r,g; 13-18 yrs.), 180 Spring St., Red Bank 07701 (10).

Collier High School (d,c; 13-18 yrs.), 160 Conover Rd., Wickatunk 07765 (140).

Mt. St. Joseph Children's Center (r,d,b; 6-14 yrs.), 124 Shepherd Lane, Totowa 07512 (32).

New York: The Astor Home for Children (r,d,c; 5-12 yrs.), 36 Mill St., P.O. Box 5005, Rhinebeck 12572 (75). Child Guidance Clinics/Day Treatment (Rhinebeck, Poughkeepsie, Beacon, Bronx). Head Start — Day Care (Poughkeepsie, Beacon, Red Hook, Dover, Millerton).

Baker Victory Services, 780 Ridge Rd. Lackawanna 14218.

Good Shepherd Services (r,d,c), 305 Seventh Ave., New York 10001. City-wide residential programs for adolescents (12-21 yrs.), foster care and adoption services (0-21 yrs.); training institute for human services workers; day treatment program (13-18 yrs.); community-based neighborhood family services in South Brooklyn Community (0-adult),

LaSalle School (r,d,b; 12-18 yrs.), 391 Western Ave., Albany. 12203 (145). Fully accredited Jr./Sr. High School with certified special education program. Juvenile sexual victim/offender treatment, drug and alcohol treatment; community services and preventive programs.

Madonna Heights Services (r,d,g; 12-18 yrs.), 151 Burrs Lane, Dix Hills 11746 (110). Also conducts group homes on Long Island and outpatient programs.

Saint Anne Institute (r,d,g; 12-18 yrs.), 160 N. Main Ave., Albany 12206 (124). Critical level, preventive services. Sex abuse prevention and juvenile sex offender programs, substance abuse program. Regents accredited school. Special education pre-school (3-4 yrs.).

St. Catherine's Center for Children (r,d,c; birth through 12 yrs.), 40 N. Main Ave., Albany 12203. Group homes, day treatment, prevention and therapeutic family programs.

St. John's of Rockaway Beach (r,b; 9-21 yrs.), 144 Beach 111th St., Rockaway Park 11694 (100). Programs include Diagnostic centers and independent living programs.

North Dakota: Home on the Range (r,c; 10-18 yrs.), HC1, Box 41, Sentinel Butte. 58654 (79). Residential and emergency shelter therapeutic programs.

Red River Victory Ranch (r,b; 10-18 yrs.), P.O. Box 9615, Fargo 58106 (12). Residential chemical addictions program.

Ohio: Diocesan Child Guidance Center, Inc. (d,c; preschool) Outpatient counseling program (c; 2-18 yrs.), 840 W. State St., Columbus 43222.

Marycrest (r,g; 13-18 yrs.), 7800 Brookside Rd., Independence 44131 (70). Residential treatment and transitional living for adolescent girls and adolescent mothers.

Parmadale Family Services Village (r,c; 12-18 yrs.), 6753 State Rd., Parma 44134.

Rosemont (r,g;d,c; 11-18 yrs.), 2440 Dawnlight Ave., Columbus 43211 (150). Mental health and AOD services; outreach services include baby day care (birth-3 yrs.).

Oregon: St. Mary's Home for Boys (r; 10-18 yrs.), 16535 S.W. Tualatin Valley Highway, Beaverton 97006 (56). Day treatment (20).

Pennsylvania: Auberle (r,c; 7-18 yrs.), 1101 Hartman St., McKeesport 15132 (100). Residential treatment for boys; emergency shelter care, foster care, group home for girls and family preservation program.

De LaSalle in Towne (d,b; 14-17 yrs.), 25 S. Van Pelt St., Philadelphia 19103 (80).

De LaSalle Vocational Day Treatment (b; 15-18 yrs.), P.O. Box 344 — Street Rd. and Bristol Pike, Bensalem 19020 (120).

Gannondale (r,g; 12-17 yrs.), 4635 E. Lake Rd., Erie 16511 (45).

Harborcreek Youth Services (r,d,c; 10-17 yrs.), 5712 Iroquois Ave., Harborcreek 16421 (150). Also conducts group homes.

Holy Family Institute (r,d,c; 0-18 yrs.), 8235 Ohio River Blvd., Emsworth 15202 (125). Also conducts in-home services, foster care and group homes.

Lourdesmont Good Shepherd Youth and Family Services (r,g;d,c; 12-17 yrs.), 537 Venard Rd., Clarks Summit 18411 (100).

St. Gabriel's Hall (r,b; 10-18 yrs.), P.O. Box 7280, Audubon 19407 (220). Also conducts group homes.

St. Michael's School (r,b; d,c; 12-17 yrs.), Box 370, Tuckhannock 18657. Also conducts group homes, day treatment and educational programs.

Tennessee: DeNeuville Heights School for Girls (r; 12-17 yrs.), 3060 Baskin St., Memphis 38127 (52).

St. Peter Home (r,g; 13-18 yrs.), 1805 Poplar, Memphis 38104 (74).

Texas: St. Joseph Adolescent and Family Counseling Center (c; 13-17 yrs.),325 W. 12th St., Dallas 75218 (20).

Washington: Morning Star Boys Ranch (Spokane Boys' Ranch, Inc.), (r,b; 10-18 yrs.), Box 8087 Manito Station, Spokane 99203 (30).

Wisconsin: Our Lady of Charity Center (r,c; 10-17 yrs.), 2640 West Point Rd., P.O. Box 11737, Green Bay 54304.

St. Charles Youth and Family Services (r,d,b; 12-18 yrs.), 151 S. 84th St., Milwaukee 53214 (63).

Wyoming: St. Joseph's Children's Home (r,c; 6-18 yrs.), P.O. Box 1117, Torrington 82240 (50). Also conducts group home. Newell Children's Center (r,c; 6-18 years), same address (12).

Developmentally Disabled

This listing includes facilities for children, youth and adults with learning disabilities.

Alabama: Father Purcell Memorial Exceptional Children's Center (r, c; birth to 10 yrs.), 2048 W. Fairview Ave., Montgomery 36108 (58). Skilled nursing facility.

Father Walter Memorial Child Care Center (r,c; birth-12 yrs.), 2815 Forbes Dr., Montgomery 36110 (44). Skilled nursing facility.

California: Child Study Center of St. John's Hospital (d,c; birth-18 yrs.), 1339 - 20th St., Santa Monica. 90404 (80).

St. Madeleine Sophie's Center (d,c; 18 yrs. and older), 2111 E. Madison Ave., El Cajon 92019 (142).

Tierra del Sol Foundation (d,c; 18 yrs. and older), 9919 Sunland Blvd., Sunland 91040 (200); 14547 Gilmore St., Van Nuys 91411 (50).

Connecticut: Gengras Center (d,c; 3-21 yrs.), St. Joseph College, 1678 Asylum Ave., W. Hartford 06117 (112).

Villa Maria Education Center (d,c; 6-14 yrs.),), 161 Sky Meadow Dr., Stamford 06903 (60). For children with learning disabilities.

District of Columbia: Lt. Joseph P. Kennedy, Jr., Institute (d,c; 6 weeks to 5 yrs. for Kennedy Institute for Child Development Center; 6-21 yrs. for Kennedy School; 18 yrs. and older for training and employment, therapeutic and residential services). Founded in 1959 for people of all ages with developmental disabilities and their families in the Washington archdiocese. Heaquarters: 801 Buchanan St. N.E. Washington 20017. Other locations in District of Columbia and Maryland. No enrollment limit.

Florida: L'Arche Harbor House, (c; 20 yrs. and older; community home), 700 Arlington Rd., Jacksonville 32211.

Marian Center Services for Developmentally Handicapped and Mentally Retarded (r,d,c; 2-21 yrs.), 15701 Northwest 37th Ave., Opa Locka 33054. Pre-school, school, workshop residence services.

Morning Star School (d,c; 4-16 yrs.), 725 Mickler Rd., Jacksonville 32211 (110). For children with learning disabilities.

Morning Star School (d,c; school age), 954 Leigh Ave., Orlando 32804 (55).

Morning Star School (d,c; 6-14 yrs.), 4661-80th Ave. N., Pinellas Park 34665 (60). For children with learning disabilities and other learning handicaps.

Morning Star School (d,c; 6-16 yrs.), 210 E. Linebaugh Ave., Tampa 33612. (87). For children with learning disabilities.

Georgia: St. Mary's Home (r,c), 2170 E. Victory Dr., Savannah 31404.

Illinois: Bartlett Learning Center (r,d,c; 3-21 yrs.), 801 W. Bartlett Rd., Bartlett 60103 (121).

Brother James Court (r, men over 18 yrs.), 2500 St. James Rd., Springfield 62707 (96).

Good Shepherd Manor (men; 18 yrs. and older),

Little Brothers of the Good Shepherd, P.O. Box 260, Momence. 60954 (120). Resident care for developmentally disabled men.

Misericordia Home South (r,c), 2916 W. 47th St., Chicago 60632 (130). For severely and profoundly impaired children.

Misericordia Home - Heart of Mercy Village (r,c; 6-45 yrs.), 6300 North Ridge, Chicago 60660 (400).

Mt. St. Joseph (developmentally disabled women; over age 21), 24955 N. Highway 12, Lake Zurich 60047 (160).

St. Coletta's of Illinois (r,d,; 6 to adult), 123rd and Wolf Rd., Palos Park 60464: St. Coletta's Residential Program (111 in 19 group homes and apartments); Lt. Joseph P. Kennedy, Jr., School (50d, 80r); Kennedy Job Training Center (100d, 40r).

St. Francis School for Exceptional Children (r,c; 6-12 yrs.), 1209 S. Walnut Ave., Freeport 61032 (44).

St. Mary of Providence (r,women; 18 yrs. and older), 4200 N. Austin Ave., Chicago 60634 (96). Day program (c; 6-21 yrs.).

St. Rose Center (d,c; 21 yrs. and older), 4911 S. Hoyne Ave., Chicago 60609 (60). For mentally handicapped adults.

St. Vincent Community Living Facility (r,c; adults, over 18 yrs.) (20), and St. Vincent Supported Living Arrangement (r,c; adults, over 18 yrs.) (20), 659 E. Jefferson St., Freeport 61032.

Springfield Developmental Center (m; 21 yrs. and over), 2500 St. James Rd., Springfield 62707. Vocational training.

Indiana: Marian Day School (d,c; 6-16 yrs.), 700 Herndon Dr., Evansville 47711 (35). For learning disabled and mild mentally retarded.

Kansas: Lakemary Center, Inc. (r,d,c), 100 Lakemary Dr., Paola 66071 (200). Children and adults.

Kentucky: Pitt Academy (d,c), 4605 Poplar Level Rd., Louisville 40213 (75).

Louisiana: Department of Special Education, Archdiocese of New Orleans, St. Michael Special School (d,c; 6-21 yrs.), 1522 Chippewa St., New Orleans 70130.

Holy Angels Residential Facility (r,c; teen-age, 14 yrs. and older), 10450 Ellerbe Rd., Shreveport 71106 (180).

Ocean Avenue Community House, 361 Ocean Ave., Gretna 70053. Group home (6).

Padua Community Services (r,c; birth-25 yrs.), 200 Beta St., Belle Chasse 70037 (32).

St. Jude the Apostle, 1430 Claire Ave., Gretna 70053. Group home, adults (6).

St. Mary's Residential Training School (r,c: 3-22 yrs.), P.O. Drawer 7768, Alexandria 71306 (152).

St. Peter the Fisherman, 62269 Airport Dr., Slidell 70458. Group home (6).

St. Rosalie (r; men 18 and up), 119 Kass St., Gretna 70056. Group home (6).

Sts. Mary and Elizabeth, 720 N. Elm St., Metairie 70003. Group home; men, ages 18-80 (6).

Maryland: The Benedictine School for Exceptional Children (r,c; 6-21 yrs.), Ridgely 21660 (145). Also conducts Habilitation Center (r,c; 17 yrs. and older) (50) and 17 community-based homes (21 yrs. and older).

Francis X. Gallagher Services (r), 2520 Pot Spring Rd., Timonium 21093 (192). Adult vocational program (124); adult medical program (100).

St. Elizabeth School and Habilitation Center (d,c; 11-21 yrs.), 801 Argonne Dr., Baltimore 21218 (120).

Massachusetts: Cardinal Cushing School and Training Center (r,d,c; 16-22 yrs.), Hanover 02339 (116 r; 28d).

Mercy Centre (d,c; 3-22 yrs. and over), 25 West Chester St., Worcester 01605 (176).

St. Coletta Day School (d,c; 3-22 yrs.), 85 Washington St., Braintree 02184 (70).

Michigan: Our Lady of Providence Center (r,g; 11-30 yrs., d,c; 26 yrs. and older), 16115 Beck Rd., Northville. 48167 (100).

St. Louis Center and School (r,d,b; 6-18 yrs. child care; 18-36 yrs. adult foster care), 16195 Old U.S. 12, Chelsea 48118 (68).

Minnesota: Mother Teresa Home (r,c; 18 yrs. and older), 101-10th Ave. N., Cold Spring 56320 (14).

St. Francis Home (r,c; 18 yrs. and older), 25-2nd St. N., Waite Park 56387 (4).

St. Luke's Home (r,; 18 yrs. and older), 411 8th Ave. N., Cold Springs 56320.

Missouri: Department of Special Education, Archdiocese of St. Louis, 4472 Lindell Blvd., St. Louis. 63108. Serves children with developmental disabilities, mental retardation or learning disabilities; services include special ungraded day classes in 8 parish schools (280).

Good Shepherd Homes (residential for developmentally disabled men; 18 yrs. and up), The Community of the Good Shepherd, 10101 James A. Reed Rd., Kansas City 64134 (30).

St.Mary's Special School (r,c; 5-21 yrs.), 1724 Redman, St. Louis 63138 (24). St. Mary's Supported Living (r,c) (24); suprvised homes for adolescents or adults. St. Mary's Early Intervention (d,c) (30); early intervention for toddlers.

Nebraska: Madonna School for Exceptional Children (d,c; 5-21 yrs.), 2537 N. 62nd St., Omaha 68104 (65). Children with learning problems.

Villa Marie School and Home for Exceptional Children (r,d,c; 6-18 yrs.), P.O. Box 80328, Lincoln 68501 (18).

New Jersey: Archbishop Damiano School (d,c; 3-21 yrs.), 1145 Delsea Dr., Westville Grove 08093.

Catholic Community Services, Archdiocese of Newark, 1160 Raymond Blvd., Newark 07102. Services include: Mt. Carmel Guild, St. Anthony's and St. Patrick's Special Education Schools (see separate entries).

Department of Special Education, Diocese of Camden, 1845 Haddon Ave., Camden 08101. Services include: Archbishop Damiano School (above), and full time programs (d,c; 6-21 yrs.) at 4 elementary (96) and 2 high schools (60) and some religious education programs.

Department for Persons with Disabilities, Diocese of Paterson, 1049 Weldon Rd., Oak Ridge, N.J. 07438. Services include 8 residential programs for adults, one adult training center, family support services.

Felician School for Exceptional Children (d,c; 5-21 yrs.), 260 S. Main St., Lodi 07644 (145).

McAuley School for Exceptional Children (d,c; 5-21 yrs.), 1633 Rt. 22 at Terrill Rd., Watchung 07060 (48).

Mt. Carmel Guild Special Education School (d,c ; 6-21 yrs.), 60 Kingsland Ave., Kearny 07032.

St. Anthony's Special Education School (d,c), 25 N. 7th St., Belleville 07104.

Sister Georgine School (d,c; 6-17 yrs.), 544 Chestnut Ave., Trenton 08611 (30).

St. Patrick's Special Education School (d,c), 72 Central Ave., Newark 07102.

New York: Baker Victory Services (r), 790 Ridge Rd., Lackawanna, N.Y. 14218. Residential care for handicapped and retarded children; nursery school program for emotionally disturbed pre-school children.

Cantalician Center for Learning (d,c; birth-21 yrs.), 3233 Main St., Buffalo 14214. Infant and pre-school; elementary and secondary; workshop (500). Three group homes. Rehabilitation, day treatment and senior rehabilitation programs.

Catholic Charities Residential Services, Rockville Center Diocese, 269 W. Main St., Bay Shore 11706. Conducts residences for developmentally disabled adults (88).

Cobb Memorial School (r,d,c; 5-21 yrs.), Altamont 12009 (32).

L'Arche (r, adults), 1232 Teall Ave., Syracuse 13206 (12). Homes where assistants and persons with developmental disabilities share life, following the philosophy of Jean Vanier. Member of International L'Arche Federation.

Maryhaven Center of Hope (r,d,c; school age to adult), Myrtle Ave., Port Jefferson 11777. Offers variety of services.

Mercy Home for Children (r,c), 310 Prospect Park West, Brooklyn 11215. Conducts six residences for adolescents and young adults who are developmentally disabled: Visitation, Warren, Vincent Haire, Santulli and Littlejohn residences (Brooklyn), Kevin Keating Residence (Queens) (72).

Office for Disabled Persons, Catholic Charities, Diocese of Brooklyn, 191 Joralemon St., Brooklyn 11201. Services include: adult day treatment center; community residences for mentally retarded adults; special events for disabled children (from age3) and adults.

Office for Disabled Persons, Archdiocese of New York, 1011 First Ave., New York 10022. Services include consultation and referral, variety of services for deaf, blind, mentally retarded, mentally ill.

School of the Holy Childhood (d,c; 5-21 yrs.), 100 Groton Parkway, Rochester 14623 (115). Adult program, 18-50 yrs (80).

Seton Foundation for Learning (d,c; 5-15 yrs.), 109 Gordon St., Staten Is. 10304.

North Carolina: Holy Angels (r,c; birth to adult), 6600 Wilkinson Blvd., P.O. Box 710, Belmont 28012 (65).

North Dakota: Friendship, Inc. (r,d,c; all ages), 3004 11th St. South, Fargo 58103 (305).

Ohio: Julie Billiart School (d,c; 6-12 yrs.), 4982 Clubside Rd., Cleveland 44124 (125). Non-graded school for children with learning problems.

Mary Immaculate School (d,c; 6-14 yrs.), 3837 Secor Rd., Toledo 43623 (80). For children with learning disabilities.

OLA/St. Joseph Center (d,c; 6-16 yrs.), 2346 W. 14th St., Cleveland 44113 (80).

Rose Mary, The Johanna Graselli Rehabilitation and Education Center (r,c; 5 yrs. and older), 19350 Euclid Ave., Cleveland 44117 (84).

St. John's Villa (r,c; continued care and training, 15 yrs. and over), P.O. Box 457, Carrollton 44615 (143).

Oregon: Providence Montessori School Early Intervention Program (d,c; 3-5 yrs.), 830 N.E. 47th Ave., Portland 97213 (12).

Pennsylvania: Clelian Heights School for Exceptional Children (r,d,c; 5-21 yrs.), R.D. 9, Box 607, Greensburg 15601 (95). Also conducts re-socialization program (r,d,c; young adults).

Divine Providence Village (adults), 686 Old Marple Rd., Springfield 19064 (96).

Don Guanella Village: Don Guanella School (r,d,b; 6-21 yrs.) and C.K. Center (r; adults, post-school age), 1797-1799 S. Sproul Rd., Springfield 19064.

John Paul II, Center for Special Learning (d,c; 3-21 yrs.), 450 S. 6th St., Reading 19602 (65).

McGuire Memorial (r,d,c; 18 mos. to adult.), 2119 Mercer Rd., New Brighton 15066 (99). Also provides respite cre and adult training day program

Mercy Special Learning Center (d,c; 3-21 yrs. and early intervention), 830 S. Woodward St., Allentown 18103 (90).

Our Lady of Confidence Day School (d,c; 4½-21 yrs.), 10th and Lycoming Sts., Philadelphia 19140 (140).

Queen of the Universe Day Center (d,c; 4½-16 yrs.), 2443 Trenton Rd., Levittown 19056 (48).

St. Anthony School Programs (d,c; 5-21 yrs.), 2718 Custer Ave., Pittsburgh 15227 (100). Inclusive education at 9 sites throughout Allegheny County.

St. Joseph Center for Special Learning (d,c; 4-21 yrs.), 2075 W. Norwegian St., Pottsville 17901 (50).

St. Joseph's Center (r,d,c; birth-10 yrs.), 2010 Adams Ave., Scranton 18509 (90).

St. Katherine Day School (d,c; 4½-21 yrs.), 930 Bowman Ave., Wynnewood 19096 (135).

Tennessee: Madonna Learning Center, Inc., for Retarded Children (d,c; 5-16 yrs.), 7007 Poplar Ave., Germantown 38138 (52).

Texas: Notre Dame of Dallas Special School and Vocational Center (d,c; 3-21 yrs.), 2018 Allen St., Dallas, Tex. 75204. Academic and vocational training for developmentally handicapped.

Virginia: St. Coletta School (d,c; 5-22 yrs.), 3130 Lee Highway, Arlington 22201 (25). For developmentally disabled. Services include: occupational, physical and language therapy; vocational program with job search, placement, training and follow-up services.

St. Mary's Infant Home (r,c; birth to 14 yrs.), 317 Chapel St., Norfolk 23504 (88). For multiple handicapped.

Wisconsin: St Coletta School, W495 Hwy 18, Jefferson 53549. Year round special education programs for adolescents and adults; pre-vocational and vocational skills training; residential living alternatives. Young adult population. Employment opportunities for those who qualify (500).

St. Coletta Day School (c; 8-17 yrs.), 1740 N. 55th St., Milwaukee. 53208 (12).

Orthopedically/Physically Handicapped

Pennsylvania: St. Edmond's Home for Children (r,c; 1-21 yrs.)., 320 S. Roberts Rd., Rosemont 19010 (40).

Virginia: St. Joseph Villa Housing Corp. (adults), 8000 Brook Rd., Richmond 23227 (60 apartments).

Visually Handicapped

Maine: Educational Services for Blind and Visually Impaired Children (Catholic Charities, Maine), 1066 Kenduskeag Ave., Bangor 04401; 66 Western Ave., Fairfield 04937; 15 Westminster St., Lewiston 04240; 562 Congress St., Portland 04101. Itinerant teachers, instructional materials center.

New Jersey: St. Joseph's School for the Blind (r,d,c; 3-21 yrs.), 253 Baldwin Ave., Jersey City 07306 (60). For visually impaired, multiple handicapped.

New York: Lavelle School for the Blind (d,c; 3-21 yrs.), East 221st St. and Paulding Ave., Bronx 10469 (100). For visually impaired, multiple handicapped.

Pennsylvania: St. Lucy Day School (d,c; pre-K to 8th grade), 130 Hampden Rd., Upper Darby 19082. For children with visual impairments.

OTHER SOCIAL SERVICES

Cancer Hospitals or Homes: The following homes or hospitals specialize in the care of cancer patients. They are listed according to state.

Our Lady of Perpetual Help Home, Servants of Relief for Incurable Cancer, 760 Washington St., S.W., Atlanta, GA 30315 (48).

Rose Hawthorne Lathrop Home, Servants of Relief for Incurable Cancer, 1600 Bay St., Fall River, MA 02724 (35).

Our Lady of Good Counsel Home, Servants of Relief for Incurable Cancer, 2076 St. Anthony Ave., St. Paul, MN 55104 (40).

Calvary Hospital, Inc., 1740 Eastchester Rd., Bronx, NY 10461 (200). Operated in connection with Catholic Charities, Department of Health and Hospitals, Archdiocese of New York.

St. Rose's Home, Servants of Relief for Incurable Cancer), 71 Jackson St., New York, NY 10002 (60).

Rosary Hill Home, Servants of Relief for Incurable Cancer, 600 Linda Ave., Hawthorne, NY 10532 (72).

Holy Family Home, Servants of Relief for Incurable Cancer, 6707 State Rd., Parma, OH 44134 (50).

Sacred Heart Free Home for Incurable Cancer, Servants of Relief for Incurable Cancer, 1315 W. Hunting Park Ave., Philadelphia, PA 19140 (45).

Substance Abuse: Facilities for substance abuse (alcohol and other drugs) include:

Daytop Village, Inc., 54 W. 40th St., New York, NY 10018. Msgr. William B. O'Brien, president. Twenty-eight residential and ambulatory sites in New York, New Jersey, Pennsylvania, Florida, Texas and California.

Good Shepherd Gracenter, Convent of the Good Shepherd, 1310 Bacon St., San Francisco, CA 94134. Residential program for chemically dependent women.

New Hope Manor, 35 Hillside Rd., Barryville, NY 12719. Residential substance abuse treatment center for teen-age girls and women ages 13-40. Residential; half-way house and aftercare program totaling 6 months or more.

St. Joseph's Hospital, L.E. Phillips Libertas Center for the Chemically Dependent, 2661 County Road I, Chippewa Falls, WI 54729 (46). Residential and outpatient. Adult and adolescent programs. Hospital Sisters of the Third Order of St. Francis.

St. Joseph's Hospital (Chippewa Falls, WI) Libertas Center for the Treatment of Chemical Dependency, 1701 Dousman St., Green Bay, WI 54302 (23). Residental and outpatient adolescent programs. Hospital Sisters of the Third Order of St. Francis.

St. Luke's Addiction Recovery Services, 7707 NW 2nd Ave., Miami, FL 33150. A program of Catholic Community Services, Miami. Adult residential and family outpatient recovery services for drug, alcohol addiction and DUI.

Miami Substance Abuse Prevention Programs, 7707 N.W. Second Ave., Miami, FL 33150. Trains parents, youth, priests and teachers as prevention volunteers in the area of substance abuse.

Transitus House, 1830 Wheaton St., Chippewa Falls, WI 54729. Two programs for chenically dependent: adult intensive residential (15 beds, women); adolescent intensive residential (5 beds; girls 15-18 yrs.). Hospital Sisters of the Third Order of St. Francis.

Matt Talbot Inn, 2270 Professor Ave., Cleveland, OH 44113. Two programs: Chemical dependency Residential Treatment/Halfway House (capacity 27) and outpatient treatment/aftercare. Serves male clients 18 years and over.

Sacred Heart Rehabilitation Center, Inc., 2203 St. Antoine, Detroit, MI 48201 (admissions/assessment, outpatient); 400 Stoddard Rd., P.O. Box 41038, Memphis, MI 48041 (12 beds, detoxification; 70 beds residential treatment) ; 28573 Schoenherr, Warren, MI 48093 (outpatient).. All facilities serve male and female clients 18 and over.

Straight and Narrow, Inc., 396 Straight St., Paterson, NJ 07501. Facilities and services include (at various locations): Straight and Narrow Hospital (Mount Carmel Guild), substance abuse, detoxification (20 beds); Alpha House for Drug and Alcohol Rehabilitation (women; 30 beds — 25 adults, 5 children), Dismas House for Drug and Alcohol Rehabilitation (men; 78 beds); The Guild for Drug and Alcohol Rehabilitation (men, 56 beds); juvenile residential units; outpatient services and facility; three halfway houses; counseling services; employment assistance; intoxicated driver's resource center; medical day care center (available to HIV infected persons and persons diagnosed with AIDS); methadone clinic.

The National Catholic Council on Alcoholism and Related Drug Problems, Inc., 1550 Hendrickson St., Brooklyn, NY 11234, offers educational material to those involved in pastoral ministry on ways of dealing with problems related to alcoholism and medication dependency.

Convicts: Priests serve as full- or part-time chaplains in penal and correctional institutions throughout the country. Limited efforts have been made to assist in the rehabilitation of released prisoners in Halfway House establishments.

Dining Rooms: Facilities for Homeless: Representative of places where meals are provided, and in some cases lodging and other services as well, are:

St. Anthony Foundation, 121 Golden Gate Ave., San Francisco, CA 94102. Founded in 1950 by the Franciscan Friars. Multi-program social service agency serving people who are poor and homeless. Dining room serves up to 2,100 meals daily; more than 25 million since its founding. Other services include free clothing and furniture; free medical clinic; residential drug and alcohol rehabilitation programs; employment program; emergency shelter, housing and daytime facility for homeless women; residence for low-income senior women; free hygiene services; case management for seniors; social services.

St. Vincent de Paul Free Dining Room, 675 23rd St., Oakland, CA 94612. Administered by Daughters of Charity of St. Vincent de Paul, under sponsorship of St. Vincent de Paul Society. Hot meals served at lunch time 7 days a week. Also provides counseling, referral/information services.

St. Vincent's Dining Room, 505 W. 3rd St., Reno, NV 89503.

St. Vincent Dining Room, 1501 Las Vegas Blvd., Las Vegas, NV 89101. Structured program for 275 men in which job development office works with homeless to enable them to find employment. For non-residents, there is a hot meal every day at noon. Emergency overnight shelter facility for families, women and men.

Good Shepherd Center, Little Brothers of the Good Shepherd, 218 Iron St. S.W., P.O. Box 749, Albuquerque, NM 87103.

Holy Name Centre for Homeless Men, Inc., 18 Bleeker St., New York, NY 10012. A shelter for alcoholic, homeless men. Provides social services and aid to transients and those in need. Affiliated with New York Catholic Charities.

St. Francis Inn, 2441 Kensington Ave., Philadelphia, PA 19125. Serves hot meals. Temporary shelter for men. Day center for women. Thrift shop.

St. John's Hospice for Men, staffed by Little Brothers of the Good Shepherd, 1221 Race St., Philadelphia, PA 19107. Hot meals served daily; 36-bed shelter; clothing distribution, showers, mail distribution, drug/alcohol rehabilitation and work programs. Good Shepherd Program of St. John's Hospice, 1225 Race St., Philadelphia, PA 19107. Ten-bed facility for homeless men with AIDS.

Camillus House, Little Brothers of the Good Shepherd, 726 N.E. First Ave., Miami, FL 33132. Free comprehensive services for the poor and homeless including daily dinner; night lodging for 70; clothing distribution; showers; mail distribution; drug/ alcohol rehabilitation program. Forty-eight units of single-room occupancy housing for employed formerly homeless women and men who have completed drug and alcohol rehabilitation programs.

Camillus Health Concern, Little Brothers of the Good Shepherd, 708 N.E. First Ave., Miami, FL 33132. Free comprehensive medical and social services for the homeless.

Shelters: Facilities for runaways, the abused, exploited and homeless include:

Anthony House, supported by St. Anthony's Guild (see Index). Three locations: 38 E. Roosevelt Ave., Roosevelt, NY 11575 (with St. Vincent de Paul Society _ for homeless men); 128 W. 112th St., New York, NY 10026 (emergency food and clothing); 6215 Holly St., P.O. Box 880, Zellwood, FL 32798 (for migrant workers and their families).

Good Shepherd Shelter-Convent of the Good Shepherd. Office, 2561 W. Venice Blvd., Los Angeles, CA 90019. Non-emergency long-term shelter for battered women and their children.

Covenant House, 346 W. 17th St., New York, NY 10011. President, Sister Mary Rose McGeady, D.C. Provides crisis care — food, shelter, clothing, medical treatment, job placement and counseling — for homeless youth without regard to race, creed, color and national origin. Locations: New York, New Jersey (Newark, Atlantic City), Houston, Ft. Lauderdale, New Orleans, Anchorage, Los Angeles, Detroit, Orlando, Washington, D.C.; Toronto (Canada), Tegucigalpa (Honduras), Guatemala City (Guatemala), Mexico City (Mexico).

Crescent House, 1000 Howard Ave., Suite 1200, New Orleans, LA 70113. Provides temporary shelter, counseling and advocacy for battered women and their children.

The Dwelling Place, 409 W. 40th St., New York, NY 10018. For homeless women 30 years of age and over.

Gift of Hope, Missionaries of Charity, 724 N.W. 17th St., Miami, FL 33136. Shelter for women and children; soup kitchen for men.

House of the Good Shepherd, 1114 W. Grace St., Chicago, IL 60613. For abused women with children.

Mercy Hospice, Sisters of Mercy, 334 S. 13th St., Philadelphia, PA 19107. Temporary shelter and relocation assistance for homeless women and children.

Mt. Carmel House, Carmelite Sisters, 471 G Pl., N.W., Washington, DC 20001. For homeless women.

Ozanam Inn, 843 Camp St., New Orleans, LA 70130. Under sponsorship of the St. Vincent de Paul Society. Hospice for homeless men.

St. Christopher Inn, P.O. Box 150, Graymoor, Garrison, NY 10524. Temporary shelter (21 days) for alcohol- and drug-free homeless and needy men.

Siena-Francis House, Inc., P.O. Box 217 D.T.S., Omaha, NE 68102. Two units, both at 1702 Nicholas St., Omaha, NE 68101: Siena House (for homeless and abused women or women with children; provides 24-hour assistance and advocacy services); Francis House (temporary shelter for homeless men). Also at this location: a 50-bed residential substance abuse program.

Unwed Mothers: Residential and care services for unwed mothers are available in many dioceses.

The American College, Louvain

The American College, founded by the U.S. Bishops in 1857, is a seminary for U.S. students. It also serves as a community for English-speaking graduate-student priests and religious pursuing courses at the Catholic University of Louvain (dating from 1425) in Belgium. The college is administered by an American rector and faculty, and operates under the auspices of a committee of the National Conference of Catholic Bishops. Rector: The Very Rev. David Windsor. Address: The American College, Catholic University of Louvain, Naamsestraat 100, B-3000 Leuven, Belgium.

RETREATS, SPIRITUAL RENEWAL PROGRAMS

There is great variety in retreat and renewal programs, with orientations ranging from the traditional to teen encounters. Central to all of them are celebration of the liturgy and deepening of a person's commitment to faith and witness in life.

Features of many of the forms are as follows.

Traditional Retreats: Centered around conferences and the direction of a retreat master; oriented to the personal needs of the retreatants; including such standard practices as participation in Mass, reception of the sacraments, private and group prayer, silence and meditation, discussions.

Team Retreat: Conducted by a team of several leaders or directors (priests, religious, lay persons) with division of subject matter and activities according to their special skills and the nature and needs of the group.

Closed Retreat: Involving withdrawal for a period of time _ overnight, several days, a weekend _ from everyday occupations and activities.

Open Retreat: Made without total disengagement from everyday involvements, on a part-time basis.

Private Retreat: By one person, on a kind of do-it-yourself basis with the one-to-one assistance of a director.

Special Groups: With formats and activities geared to particular groups; e.g., members of Alcoholics Anonymous, vocational groups and apostolic groups.

Marriage Encounters: Usually weekend periods of husband-wife reflection and dialogue; introduced into the U.S. from Spain in 1967.

Charismatic Renewal: Featuring elements of the movement of the same name; "Spirit-oriented," communitarian and flexible, with spontaneous and shared prayer, personal testimonies of faith and witness.

Christian Community: Characterized by strong community thrust.

Teens Encounter Christ (TEC), SEARCH: Formats adapted to the mentality and needs of youth, involving experience of Christian faith and commitment in a community setting.

Christian Maturity Seminars: Similar to teen encounters in basic concept but different to suit persons of greater maturity.

Renew International: Spiritual renewal process involving the entire parish. Office, 1232 George St., Plainfield, NJ 07062. Director, Msgr. Thomas A. Kleissler.

Cursillo: see separate entry.

Conference

Retreats International Inc.: The first organization for promoting retreats in the U.S. was started in 1904 in New York. Its initial efforts and the gradual growth of the movement led to the formation in 1927 of the National Catholic Laymen's Retreat Conference, the forerunner of the men's division of Retreats International. The women's division developed from the National Laywomen's Retreat Movement which was founded in Chicago in 1936. The men's and women's divisions merged July 9, 1977. The services of the organization include an annual summer institute for retreat and pastoral ministry, regional conferences for retreat center leadership and area meetings of directors and key leadership in the retreat movement. The officers are: Auxiliary Bishop Robert Morneau of Green Bay, episcopal advisor; Larry Novakowski, president; Rev. Thomas W. Gedeon, S.J., executive director. National office: Box 1067, Notre Dame, IN 46556.

HOUSES OF RETREAT AND RENEWAL

(Principal sources: Almanac survey; *The Official Catholic Directory.*)

Abbreviation code: m, men; w, women; mc, married couples; y, youth. Houses and centers without code generally offer facilities to most groups. An asterisk after an abbreviation indicates that the facility is primarily for the group designated but that special groups are also accommodated. Houses furnish information concerning the types of programs they offer.

Alabama: Blessed Trinity Shrine Retreat, 107 Holy Trinity Rd., Holy Trinity 36859.

Visitation Sacred Heart Retreat House, 2300 Spring Hill Ave., Mobile 36607.

Alaska: Holy Spirit Retreat House, 10980 Hillside Dr., Anchorage 99516.

Arizona: Franciscan Renewal Center, 5802 E. Lincoln Dr., Box 220, Scottsdale 85252.

Holy Trinity Monastery, P.O. Box 298, St. David 85630. Benedictine community. Self-directed/Spirit-directed monastic retreat.

Mount Claret Retreat Center, 4633 N. 54th St., Phoenix 85018.

Our Lady of Solitude House of Prayer, P.O. Box 1140, Black Canyon City 85324.

Redemptorist Picture Rocks Retreat House, 7101 W. Picture Rocks Rd., Tucson 85743.

Arkansas: Brothers and Sisters of Charity, Little Portion Hermitage, Rt. 3, Box 608, Eureka Springs 72632.

Little Portion Retreat and Training Center, Rt. 4, Box 430, Eureka Springs 72632.

St. Scholastica Retreat Center, P.O. Box 3489, Ft. Smith 72913.

California: Angela Center, 535 Angela Dr., Santa Rosa 95401.

Christ the King Retreat Center, 6520 Van Maren Lane, Citrus Heights 95621.

Claretian Retreat Center, 1119 Westchester Pl., Los Angeles 90019.

De Paul Center, 1105 Bluff Rd., Montebello 90640.

El Carmelo Retreat House, P.O. Box 446, Redlands 92373.

Heart of Jesus Retreat Center, 2927 S. Greenville St., Santa Ana 92704.

Holy Spirit Retreat Center, 4316 Lanai Rd., Encino 91436.

Holy Transfiguration Monastery (m*), Monks of Mt. Tabor (Byzantine Ukrainian), 17001 Tomki Rd., P.O. Box 217, Redwood Valley, Calif. 95470.

Jesuit Retreat House, 300 Manresa Way, Los Altos 94022.

Madonna of Peace Renewal Center (y), P.O. Box 71, Copperopolis 95228.

Mary and Joseph Retreat Center, 5300 Crest Rd., Rancho Palos Verdes 90275.

Marywood Retreat Center, 2811 E. Villa Real Dr., Orange 92667.

Mater Dolorosa Retreat Center, 700 N. Sunnyside Ave., Sierra Madre 91024.

Mercy Center, 2300 Adeline Dr., Burlingame 94010.

Mission San Luis Rey Retreat, P.O. Box 409, San Luis Rey 92068.

Mount Alverno Retreat and Conference Center, 3910 Bret Harte Dr., Redwood City 94061.

New Camaldoli Hermitage, Big Sur 93920.

Poverello of Assisi Retreat House, 1519 Woodworth St., San Fernando 91340.

Presentation Education and Retreat Center, 19480 Bear Creek Rd., Los Gatos 95030.

Prince of Peace Abbey, 650 Benet Hill Rd., Oceanside 92054.

Pro Sanctity Spirituality Center, 205 S. Pine St., Fullerton 92633. For day use.

Sacred Heart Retreat House (w*), 920 E. Alhambra Rd., Alhambra 91801.

St. Andrew's Abbey Retreat House, Valyermo 93563.

St. Anthony's Retreat House, P.O. Box 249, Three Rivers 93271.

St. Clare's Retreat, 2381 Laurel Glen Rd., Soquel 95073.

St. Francis Retreat, P.O. Box 970, San Juan Bautista 95045.

St. Francis Salesian Retreat (Camp St. Francis) (y), 2400 E. Lake Ave., Watsonville 95076.

St. Joseph's Salesian Youth Center, P.O. Box 1639, 8301 Arroyo Dr., Rosemead 91770.

St. Mary's Seminary and Retreat House, 1964 Las Canoas Rd., Santa Barbara 93105.

San Damiano Retreat, P.O. Box 767, Danville 94526.

San Miguel Retreat House, P.O. Box 69, San Miguel 93451.

Santa Sabina Center, 25 Magnolia Ave., San Rafael 94901.

Serra Retreat, 3401 S. Serra Rd., Box 127, Malibu 90265.

Starcross Community, 34500 Annapolis Rd., Annapolis 95412.

Villa Maria del Mar, Santa Cruz. Mailing address, 2-1918 E. Cliff Dr., Santa Cruz 95062.

Villa Maria — House of Prayer (w), 1252 N. Citrus Dr., La Habra 90631.

Colorado: Benet Hill Monastery, 2555 N. Chelton Rd., Colorado Springs 80909.

Benet Pines Retreat Center, 15780 Highway 83, Colorado Springs 80921.

Sacred Heart Retreat House, Box 185, Sedalia 80135.

Spiritual Life Institute (individuals only), Nada Hermitage, P.O. Box 219, Crestone 81131. Private desert retreats with minimal direction.

Connecticut: Archdiocesan Spiritual Life Center, 467 Bloomfield Ave., Bloomfield 06002.

Edmundite Apostolate and Conference Center, Enders Island, Mystic 06355.

Emmaus Spiritual Life Center, 24 Maple Ave., Uncasville 06382.

Holy Family Retreat, 303 Tunxis Rd., West Hartford 06107.

Immaculata Retreat House, P.O. Box 55, Willimantic 06226.

Mercy Center, P.O. Box 191, 167 Neck Rd., Madison 06443.

My Father's House, Box 22, North Moodus Rd., Moodus 06469.

Our Lady of Calvary Retreat (w*), 31 Colton St., Farmington 06032.

Trinita Retreat Center, 595 Town Hill Rd., Rt. 219, New Hartford 06057.

Villa Maria Retreat House, 159 Sky Meadow Dr., Stamford 06903.

Delaware: St. Francis Renewal Center, 1901 Prior Rd., Wilmington 19809.

District of Columbia: Washington Retreat House, 4000 Harewood Rd. N.E., Washington 20017.

Florida: Cenacle Retreat House, 1400 S. Dixie Highway, Lantana 33462.

Dominican Retreat House, Inc., 7275 S.W. 124th St., Miami 33156.

Franciscan Center, 3010 Perry Ave., Tampa 33603.

John Paul II Retreat House, 720 N.E. 27th St., Miami 33137.

Our Lady of Perpetual Help Retreat and Spirituality Center, 3989 S. Moon Dr., Venice 34292.

Saint John Neumann Renewal Center, 685 Miccosukee Rd., Tallahassee 32308.

St. Leo Abbey Retreat Center, P.O. Box 2350, St. Leo 33574.

Georgia: Ignatius House, 6700 Riverside Dr. N.W., Atlanta 30328.

Idaho: Nazareth Retreat Center, 4450 N. Five Mile Rd., Boise 83704.

Illinois: Bellarmine Hall (ma), Box 268, Barrington 60010.

Bishop Lane Retreat House, 7708 E. McGregor Rd., Rockford 61102.

Cabrini Retreat Center, 9430 Golf Rd., Des Plaines 60016.

Carmelite Spiritual Center, 8433 Bailey Rd., Darien 60561.

Cenacle Retreat House, 513 Fullerton Parkway, Chicago 60614.

Cenacle Retreat House, P.O. Box 797, Warrenville 60555.

King's House of Retreats, Henry 61537.

La Salle Manor, Christian Brothers Retreat House, 12480 Galena Rd., Plano 60545.

Retreat and Renewal Center, 700 N. 66th St., Belleville 62223.

St. Mary's Retreat House, P.O. Box 608, 14230 Main St., Lemont 60439.

Tolentine Center, 20300 Governors Highway, Olympia Fields 60461.

Villa Redeemer Retreat Center, 1111 N. Milwaukee Ave., P.O. Box 6, Glenview 60025.

Indiana: Archabbey Guest House, St. Meinrad Archabeey, St. Meinrad 47577

Benedict Inn Retreat and Conference Center, 1402 Southern Ave., Beech Grove 46107.

Fatima Retreat House, 5353 E. 56th St., Indianapolis 46226.

John XXIII Center, 407 W. McDonald St., Hartford City 47348.

Kordes Enrichment Center, 841 E. 14th St., Ferdinand 47532.

Lindenwood, PHJC Ministry Center, P.O. Box 1, Donaldson 46513.

Mary's Solitude, St.Mary's, Notre Dame 46556.

Mount Saint Francis Retreat Center, 101 St. Anthony Dr.,Mount Saint Francis 47146.

Our Lady of Fatima Retreat Center, P.O. Box 929, Notre Dame 46556.

Sarto Retreat House, 4200 N. Kentucky Ave., Evansville 47711.

Iowa: American Martyrs Retreat House, 2209 N. Union Rd., P.O. Box 605, Cedar Falls 50613.

Emmanuel House of Prayer Country Retreat and Solitude Center, 4427 Kotts Rd. N.E., Iowa City 52240.

New Melleray Guest House, 6500 Melleray Circle, Peosta 52068.

Shalom Retreat Center, 1001 Davis Ave., Dubuque 52001.

Kansas: Manna House of Prayer, 323 East 5th St., Box 675, Concordia 66901.

Spiritual Life Center, 7100 E. 45th St., N. Wichita 67226.

Kentucky: Catherine Spalding Center, P.O. Box 24, Nazareth 40048.

Flaget Center, 1935 Lewiston Dr., Louisville 40216.

Marydale Retreat Center, 945 Donaldson Hwy., Erlanger 41018.

Mt. St. Joseph Retreat Center, 8001 Cummings Rd., Maple Mount 42356.

Our Lady of Gethsemani (m, w, private), The Guestmaster, Abbey of Gethsemani, Trappist 40051.

Louisiana: Abbey Christian Life Center, St. Joseph's Abbey, St. Benedict 70457.

Ave Maria Retreat House, HC 62, Box 368 AB, Marrero 70072.

Cenacle Retreat House (w*), 5500 St. Mary St., P.O. Box 8115, Metairie 70011.

Jesuit Spirituality Center (m,w; directed), P.O. Box C, Grand Coteau 70541.

Lumen Christi Retreat Center, 100 Lumen Christi Lane, Hwy. 311, Schriever 70395.

Manresa House of Retreats (m), P.O. Box 89, Convent 70723.

Maryhill Renewal Center, 600 Maryhill Rd., Pineville 71360.

Our Lady of the Oaks Retreat House, P.O. Box D, Grand Coteau 70541.

Regina Coeli Retreat Center, 17225 Regina Coeli Rd., Covington 70433.

Maine: Marie Joseph Spiritual Center, RFD 2, Biddeford 04005.

St. Paul Retreat and Cursillo Center, 136 State St., Augusta 04330.

Maryland: Bon Secours Spiritual Center, Marriottsville 21104.

Christian Brothers Spiritual Center (m,w,y), P.O. Box 29, 2535 Buckeyestown Pike, Adamstown 21710.

Loyola on the Potomac Retreat House, Faulkner 20632.

Msgr. Clare J. O'Dwyer Retreat House (y*), 15523 York Rd., P.O. Box 310, Sparks 21152.

Our Lady of Mattaponi Youth Retreat and Conference Center, 11000 Mattaponi Rd., Upper Marlboro 20772.

Massachusetts: Boston Cenacle Society, 25 Avery St., Dedham 02026.

Calvary Retreat Center, 59 South St., P.O. Box 219, Shrewsbury 01545.

Campion Renewal Center, 319 Concord Rd., Weston 02193.

Don Orione Center, P.O. Box 205, Old Groveland Rd., Bradford 01835.

Eastern Point Retreat House, Gonzaga Hall, 37 Niles Pond Rd., Gloucester 01930.

Espousal Center, 554 Lexington St., Waltham 02154.

Esther House of Spiritual Renewal, Sisters of St. Anne, 1015 Pleasant St., Worcester 01602.

Genesis Spiritual Life Center, 53 Mill St., Westfield 01085.

Glastonbury Abbey (Benedictine Monks), 16 Hull St.,Hingham 02043.

Holy Cross Fathers Retreat House, 490 Washington St., N. Easton 02356.

La Salette Center for Christian Living, 947 Park St., Attleboro 02703.

LaSalette Retreat House, 251 Topsfield Rd., Ipswich 01938.

Marian Center, 1365 Northampton St., Holyoke 01040. Day and evening programs.

Miramar Retreat Center, P.O. Box M, Duxbury, 02331.

Mt. Carmel Christian Life Center, Oblong Rd., Box 613, Williamstown 01267.

Sacred Heart Retreat Center, Salesians of St. John Bosco, P.O. Box 567, Ipswich 01938.

St. Benedict Abbey (Benedictine Monks), 252 Still River Rd., P.O. Box 67, Still River 01467.

St. Joseph Villa Retreat Center, Sisters of St. Joseph, 339 Jerusalem Rd., Cohasset 02025.

St. Joseph's Abbey Retreat House (m) (Trappist Monks), North Spencer Rd., Spencer 01562.

St. Stephen Priory Spiritual Life Center (Dominican), 20 Glen St., Box 370, Dover 02030.

Michigan: Augustine Center, 2798 U.S. 31 North, Box 84, Conway 49722.

Capuchin Retreat, 62460 Mt. Vernon, Box 188, Washington 48094.

Colombiere Conference Center, Box 139, 9075 Big Lake Rd., Clarkston 48347.

Manresa Jesuit Retreat House, 1390 Quarton Rd., Bloomfield Hills 48304.

Queen of Angels Retreat, 3400 S. Washington Rd., P.O. Box 2026, Saginaw 48605.

St. Francis Retreat Center, Diocese of Lansing, 703 E. Main St., De Witt 48820.

St. Lazare Retreat House, 18600 W. Spring Lake Rd., Spring Lake 49456.

St. Mary's Retreat House (w*), 775 W. Drahner Rd., Oxford 48371.

St. Paul of the Cross Retreat Center (m*), 23333 Schoolcraft, Detroit 48223.

Minnesota: Benedictine Center, St. Paul's Monastery, 2675 E. Larpenteur Ave., St. Paul 55109.

Catholic Youth Ministry Services (y*), 328 W. Kellog, St. Paul 55102.

The Cenacle, 1221 Wayzata Blvd., Wayzata 55391.

Center for Spiritual Development, 211 Tenth St. S., P.O. Box 538, Bird Island 55310.

Christ the King Retreat Center, 621 First Ave. S., Buffalo 55313.

Christian Brothers Retreat Center, 15525 St. Croix Trail North, Marine-on-St. Croix 55047.

Franciscan Retreats, Conventual Franciscan Friars, 16385 St. Francis Lane, Prior Lake 55372.

Jesuit Retreat House (m), 8243 DeMontreville Trail North, Lake Elmo 55042.

Maryhill (m,w*), 1988 Summit Ave., St. Paul 55105.

Villa Maria Center, Ursuline Sisters, 29847 County 2 Blvd., Frontenac 55026.

Missouri: The Cenacle, 7654 Natural Bridge Rd., St. Louis 63121.

Il Ritiro - The Little Retreat, P.O. Box 38, Eime Rd., Dittmer 63023.

Maria Fonte Solitude (private; individual hermitages), P.O. Box 322, High Ridge 63049.

Marianist Retreat and Conference Center, P.O. Box 718, Eureka 63025.

Mercy Center, 2039 N. Geyer Rd., St. Louis 63131.

Our Lady of Assumption Abbey (m,w), Trappists, Rt. 5, Box 1056, Ava 65608.

Pallottine Renewal Center, 15270 Old Halls Ferry Rd., Florissant 63034.

Queen of Heaven Solitude (private, individual hermitages), Rt. 1, Box 107A, Marionville 65705.

White House Retreat, 7400 Christopher Dr., St. Louis 63129.

Windridge Solitude, 1932 W. Linda Lane, Lonedell 63060.

Montana: Sacred Heart Retreat Center, 26 Wyoming Ave., P.O. Box 153, Billings 59103.

Ursuline Retreat Centre, 2300 Central Ave., Great Falls 59401.

Nebraska: Crosier Renewal Center, 223 E. 14th St., P.O. Box 789, Hastings 68902.

Our Lady of Good Counsel, R.R. 1, Box 110, Waverly 68462.

Nevada: Monastery of Christ in the Mountains, P.O. Box 708, Caliente 89008.

New Hampshire: Epiphany Monastery, 96 Scobie Rd., P.O. Box 60, New Boston 03070.

La Salette Shrine (private and small groups), Route 4A,, Enfield 03748.

Oblate Retreat House, Oblates of Mary Immaculate, 200 Lowell Rd., Hudson 03051.

New Jersey: Bethlehem Hermitage, 82 Pleasant Hill Rd., P.O. Box 315, Chester 07930.

Carmel Retreat House, 1071 Ramapo Valley Rd., Mahwah 07430.

Cenacle Retreat House, 411 River Rd., Highland Park 08904.

Father Judge Apostolic Center (young adults), 1292 Long Hill Rd., Stirling 07980.

Felician Retreat House, 35 Windemere Ave., Mt. Arlington 07856.

Loyola House of Retreats, 161 James St., Morristown 07960.

Marianist Family Retreat Center (families*), 417 Yale Ave., Box 502, Cape May Point 08212.

Maris Stella (Vacation Home for Sisters*), 7201 Long Beach Blvd., Harvey Cedars 08008.

Mt. St. Francis Retreat House, 474 Sloatsburg Rd., Ringwood 07456.

Queen of Peace Retreat House, St. Paul's Abbey, P.O. Box 7, Newton 07860.

Sacred Heart Retreat Center (y*, m,w), 20 Old Swartswood Rd., Newton 07860.

St. Joseph by the Sea Retreat House, 400 Rte. 35 N., South Mantoloking 08738.

St. Pius X Spioritual Life Center, P.O. Box 216, Blackwood 08012.

San Alfonso Retreat House, P.O. Box 3098, 755 Ocean Ave., Long Branch 07740.

Sanctuary of Mary, Pilgrimage Place, Branchville 07826.

Stella Maris Retreat House, 981 Ocean Ave., Elberon 07740.

Villa Pauline Retreat House, 350 Bernardsville Rd., Mendham 07945.

Xavier Retreat and Conference Center, P.O. Box 211, Convent Station 07961.

New Mexico: Dominican Retreat House, 2348 Pajarito Rd.. S.W., Albuquerque 87105.

Holy Cross Retreat, Conventual Franciscan Friars, P.O. Box 158, Mesilla Park 88047.

Pecos Benedictine Abbey, Pecos 87552.

Sacred Heart Retreat, P.O. Box 1989, Gallup 87301.

New York: Bethany Retreat House, County Road 105, Box 1003, Highland Mills 10930.

Bethlehem Retreat House, Abbey of the Genesee, Piffard 14533.

Bishop Molloy Retreat House, 86-45 Edgerton Blvd., Jamaica, L.I. 11432.

Blessed Kateri Retreat House, National Kateri Shrine, P.O. Box 627, Fonda, N.Y. 12068.

Cardinal Spellman Retreat House, Passionist Community, 5801 Palisade Ave., Bronx (Riverdale) 10471.

Cenacle Center for Spiritual Renewal, 310 Cenacle Rd., Lake Ronkonkoma 11779.

Cenacle Retreat House, State Rd., P.O. Box 467, Bedford Village 10506.

Christ the King Retreat and Conference Center, 500 Brookford Rd., Syracuse 13224.

Cormaria Retreat House, Sag Harbor, L.I. 11963.

Dominican Spiritual Life Center, 1945 Union St., Niskayuma 12309.

Don Bosco Retreat Center, Box 9000, Filor's Lane, West Haverstraw 10993.

Graymoor Christian Unity Center, Graymoor, Garrison 10524.

Jesuit Retreat House, North American Martyrs Shrine, Auriesville 12016.

Monastery of the Precious Blood (w), Ft. Hamilton Parkway and 54th St., Brooklyn 11219. Single day retreats.

Mount Alvernia Retreat House, Box 858, Wappingers Falls 12590.

Mount Irenaeus Franciscan Mountain Retreat, Holy Peace Friary, P.O. Box 100, West Clarksville, NY 14786.

Mount Manresa Retreat House, 239 Fingerboard Rd., Staten Island 10305.

Mt. St. Alphonsus Redemptorist Community, P.O. Box 219, Esopus 12429.

Notre Dame Retreat House, Box 342, 5151 Foster Rd., Canandaigua 14424.

Our Lady of Hope Center, 434 River Rd., Newburgh 12550.

Regina Maria Retreat House, 77 Brinkerhoff St., Plattsburgh 12901.

St. Andrew's House, 257 St. Andrew's Rd., Walden 12586.

St. Columban Center, Diocese of Buffalo, 6892 Lake Shore Rd., P.O. Box 816, Derby 14047.

St. Gabriel Retreat House (y, mc), 64 Burns Rd., P.O. Box P, Shelter Island 11965.

St. Ignatius Retreat House, Searingtown Rd., Manhasset, L.I. 11030.

St. Josaphat's Retreat House, Basilian Monastery, East Beach Rd., Glen Cove 11542.

St. Joseph Center (Spanish Center), 275 W. 230th St., Bronx 10463.

St. Mary's Villa, 150 Sisters Servants Lane, Sloatsburg 10974.

St. Paul Center, 21-35 Crescent St., Astoria 11105.

St. Ursula Center, P.O. Box 86, Middle Rd. and Blue Point Ave., Blue Point 11715.

Stella Maris Retreat Center, 130 E. Genesee St., Skaneateles 13152.

Stella Niagara Center of Renewal, 4421 Lower River Rd., Stella Niagara 14144.

Tagaste Monastery, 220 Lafayette Ave.,, Suffern 10901.

Trinity Retreat, 1 Pryer Manor Rd., Larchmont 10538.

North Carolina: Avila Retreat Center, 711 Mason Rd., Durham 27712.

Living Waters Catholic Reflection Center,103 Living Waters Lane, Maggie Valley 28751.

North Dakota: Presentation Prayer Center, 1101 32nd Ave. S., Fargo 58103.

Queen of Peace Retreat, 1310 Broadway, Fargo 58102.

Ohio: Bergamo, 4400 Shakertown Rd., Dayton 45430.

Franciscan Renewal Center, Pilgrim House, 321 Clay St., Carey 43316.

Friarhurst Retreat House, 8136 Wooster Pike, Cincinnati 45227.

Jesuit Retreat House, 5629 State Rd., Cleveland 44134.

Loyola of the Lakes, 700 Killinger Rd., Clinton 44216.

Maria Stein Center, 2365 St. Johns Rd., Maria Stein 45860.

Milford Spiritual Center, 5361 Milford Rd., Milford 45150.

Our Lady of the Pines, 1250 Tiffin St., Fremont 43420.

Sacred Heart Retreat and Renewal Center, 3128 Logan Ave., P.O. Box 6074, Youngstown 44501.

St. Joseph Christian Life Center, 18485 Lake Shore Blvd., Cleveland 44119.

St. Joseph Renewal Center, 200 St. Francis Ave., Tiffin 44883.

St. Therese Retreat Center, Diocese of Columbus, 5277 E. Broad St., Columbus 43213.

Oklahoma: St. Gregory's Abbey, Shawnee 74801.

Oregon: Franciscan Renewal Center, 0858 S.W. Palatine Hill Rd., Portland 97219.

Loyola Renewal Center, 3220 S.E. 43rd St., Portland 97206.

Mount Angel Abbey Retreat House, St. Benedict 97373.

Our Lady of Peace Retreat, 3600 S. W. 170th Ave., Beaverton 97006.

St. Rita Retreat Center, P.O. Box 310, Gold Hill 97525.

Shalom Prayer Center, Benedictine Sisters, Mt. Angel 97362.

Trappist Abbey Retreat (m,w), P.O. Box 97, Lafayette 97127.

Pennsylvania: Dominican Retreat House, 750 Ashbourne Rd., Elkins Park 19027.

Doran Hall Retreat and Renewal Center, 443 Mt. Thor Rd., Greensburg 15601.

Fatima House, 601 Rolling Hills Rd., Ottsville 18942.

Fatima Renewal Center, 1000 Seminary Rd., Dalton 18414.

Gilmary Diocesan Center, 601 Flaugherty Run Rd., Coraopolis 15108.

Jesuit Center for Spiritual Growth, Box 223, Church Rd., Wernersville 19565.

Kearns Spirituality Center, 9000 Babcock Blvd., Allison Park 15101.

Mariawald Rnewal Center, P.O. Box 97 (Welch Rd.), Reading 19607.

Mount St. Macrina Retreat Center, 510 W. Main St., Box 878, Uniontown 15401.

St. Emma Retreat House, 1001 Harvey Ave., Greensburg 15601.

St. Francis Retreat Center (y*), c/o Dept. of Youth Ministry, 900 W. Market St., Orwigsburg 17961.

St. Francis Center for Renewal, Monocacy Manor, 395 Bridle Path Rd., Bethlehem 18017.

St. Francis Retreat House, 3918 Chipman Rd., Easton 18042.

St. Gabriel's Retreat House, 631 Griffin Pond Rd., Clarks Summit 18411.

St. Joseph's in the Hills, 313 S. Warren Ave., Malvern 19355.

St. Paul of the Cross Retreat Center, 148 Monastery Ave., Pittsburgh 15203.

Saint Raphaela Center, 616 Coopertown Rd., Haverford 19041.

St. Vincent Retreat Program (m,w,mc; summers only), Latrobe 15650.

Villa of Our Lady Retreat Center (w, mc, y), HCR No. 1, Box 41, Mt. Pocono 18344.

Rhode Island: Bethany Renewal Center, 397 Fruit Hill Ave., N. Providence 02911.

Father Marot CYO Center (y), 53 Federal St., Woonsocket 02895.

Our Lady of Peace Spiritual Life Center, 333 Ocean Rd., Box 507, Narragansett 02882.

St. Dominic Savio Youth Center (y*), Broad Rock Rd., Box 67, Peace Dale 02883.

South Carolina: Springbank Retreat Center, Rt. 2, Box 180, Kingstree 29556.

South Dakota: St. Martin's Community Center, 2110C St. Martin's Dr., Rapd City 57702.

Sioux Spiritual Center (for Native Americans), Diocese of Rapid City, HC 77, Box 271, Howes 57748.

Tennessee: Carmelites of Mary Immaculate Center of Spirituality, 610 Bluff Rd., Liberty 37095.

Texas: Bishop DeFalco Retreat Center, 2100 N. Spring, Amarillo 79107.

Bishop Rene H. Gracida Retreat Center, Diocese of Corpus Christi, 3036 Saratoga Blvd., Corpus Christi 78415

Bishop Thomas J. Drury Retreat Center, 1200 Lantana St., Corpus Christi 78407.

Catholic Renewal Center of North Texas, 4503 Bridge St., Ft. Worth 76103.

Cenacle Retreat House, 420 N. Kirkwood, Houston 77079.

Christian Renewal Center (Centro de Renovacion Cristiana), Oblates of Mary Immaculate, P.O. Box 635, Dickinson 77539.

Holy Family Retreat Center, 9920 N. Major Dr., Beaumont 77713.

Holy Name Retreat Center, 430 Bunker Hill Rd., Houston 77024.

Holy Spirit Retreat and Conference Center, 501 Century Dr. S., Laredo 78040.

Montserrat Retreat House, Lake Dallas 75065.

Moye Center, 600 London, Castroville 78009.

Oblate Renewal Center, 285 Oblate Dr., San Antonio 78216 (mailing address) 275 Blanco (physical location).

San Juan Retreat House (Nuestra Señora de San Juan Retreat Center), P.O. Box 747, San Juan 78589.

Utah: Abbey of Our Lady of the Holy Trinity (m), Huntsville 84317.

Our Lady of the Mountains, 1794 Lake St., Ogden 84401.

Virginia: Dominican Retreat, 7103 Old Dominion Dr., McLean 22101.

Holy Family Retreat House, The Redemptorists, P.O. 3151, 1414 N. Mallory St., Hampton 23663.

Missionhurst Mission Center, 4651 N. 25th St., Arlington 22207.

Retreat House, Holy Cross Abbey, Rt. 2, Box 3870, Berryville 22611.

Washington: Immaculate Heart Retreat Center, 6910 S. Ben Burr Rd., Spokane 99223.

Palisades Retreat House, P.O. Box 3739, Federal Way 98063.

St. Peter the Apostle Retreat Center, 15880 Summitview Rd., Cowiche 98923.

West Virginia: Bishop Hodges Pastoral Center, Rt. 1, Box 90,, Huttonsville, 26273.

Cenacle Retreat House, 1114 Virginia St. E., Charleston 25301.

Good Counsel Friary, Rt. 7, Box 183, Morgantown 26505.

John XXIII Pastoral Center, 100 Hodges Rd., Charleston, W. Va. 25314.

Paul VI Pastoral Center, 667 Stone and Shannon Rd., Wheeling 26003.

Priest Field Pastoral Center, Rt. 51, Box 133, Kearneysville 25430.

Wisconsin: Archdiocesan Retreat Center, 3501 S. Lake Dr., P.O. Box 07912, Milwaukee 53207.

Cardoner Retreat Center, 1501 S. Layton Blvd., Milwaukee 53215.

Holy Name Retreat House, Chambers Island; mailing address, 1825 Riverside Drive, P.O. Box 23825, Green Bay 54305.

Jesuit Retreat House, 4800 Fahrnwald Rd., Oshkosh 54901.

Monte Alverno Retreat Center, 1000 N. Ballard Rd., Appleton 54911.

Perpetual Help Retreat Center, 1800 N. Timber Trail Lane, Oconomowoc 53066.

St. Anthony Retreat Center, 300 E. 4h St., Marathon 54448.

St. Bede Retreat and Conference Center, 1190 Priory Rd., P.O. Box 66, Eau Claire 54702.

Saint Benedict Center (monastery and ecumenical retreat and conference center), P.O. Box 5070, Madison 53705.

St. Francis Retreat Center, 503 S. Browns Lake Dr., P.O. Box 368, Burlington 53105.

St. Joseph's Retreat Center, 3035 O'Brien Rd., Bailey's Harbor 54202.

St. Vincent Pallotti Center, N6409 Bowers Rd., Elkhorn 53121.

Schoenstatt Center, W. 284 N. 698 Cherry Lane, Waukesha 53188.

Mary Ann Glendon: Mary Ann Glendon, Harvard professor of law who headed the Vatican delegation to the U.N.-sponsored women's conference in Beijing in 1975, received the 1997 U.S. Catholic Award for her work "as an advocate for women and the family," giving "a fresh and compelling voice" to challenges facing woman.

LAY PERSONS AND THEIR APOSTOLATE

RIGHTS AND OBLIGATIONS OF ALL THE FAITHFUL

The following rights are listed in Canons 208-223 of the revised Code of Canon Law; additional rights are specified in other canons.

They are all equal in dignity because of their baptism and regeneration in Christ.

They are bound always to preserve communion with the Church.

According to their condition and circumstances, they should strive to lead a holy life and promote the growth and holiness of the Church.

They have the right and duty to work for the spread of the divine message of salvation to all peoples of all times and places.

They are bound to obey declarations and orders given by their pastors in their capacity as representatives of Christ, teachers of the faith and rectors of the Church.

They have the right to make known their needs, especially their spiritual needs, to pastors of the Church.

They have the right, and sometimes the duty, of making known to pastors and others of the faithful their opinions about things pertaining to the good of the Church.

They have the right to receive help from their pastors, from the spiritual goods of the Church and especially from the word of God and the sacraments.

They have the right to divine worship performed according to prescribed rules of their rite, and to follow their own form of spiritual life in line with the doctrine of the Church.

They have the right to freely establish and control associations for good and charitable purposes, to foster the Christian vocation in the world, and to hold meetings related to the accomplishment of these purposes.

They have the right to promote and support apostolic action but may not call it "Catholic" unless they have the consent of competent authority.

They have a right to a Christian education.

They have a right to freedom of inquiry in sacred studies, in accordance with the teaching authority of the Church.

They have a right to freedom in the choice of their state of life.

No one has the right to harm the good name of another person or to violate his or her right to maintain personal privacy.

They have the right to vindicate the rights they enjoy in the Church, and to defend themselves in a competent ecclesiastical forum.

They have the obligation to provide for the needs of the Church, with respect to things pertaining to divine worship, apostolic and charitable works, and the reasonable support of ministers of the Church.

They have the obligation to promote social justice and to help the poor from their own resources.

In exercising their rights, the faithful should have regard for the common good of the Church and for the rights and duties of others.

Church authority has the right to monitor the exercise of rights proper to the faithful, with the common good in view.

RIGHTS AND OBLIGATIONS OF LAY PERSONS

In addition to rights and obligations common to all the faithful and those stated in other canons, lay persons are bound by the obligations and enjoy the rights specified in these canons (224-231).

Lay persons, like all the faithful, are called by God to the apostolate in virtue of their baptism and confirmation. They have the obligation and right, individually or together in associations, to work for the spread and acceptance of the divine message of salvation among people everywhere; this obligation is more urgent in those circumstances in which people can hear the Gospel and get to know Christ only through them (lay persons).

They are bound to bring an evangelical spirit to bear on the order of temporal things and to give Christian witness in carrying out their secular pursuits.

Married couples are obliged to work for the building up of the people of God through their marital and family life.

Parents have the most serious obligation to provide for the Christian education of their children according to the doctrine handed down by the Church.

Lay persons have the same civil liberty as other citizens. In the use of this liberty, they should take care that their actions be imbued with an evangelical spirit. They should attend to the doctrine proposed by the magisterium of the Church but should take care that, in questions of opinion, they do not propose their own opinion as the doctrine of the Church.

Qualified lay persons are eligible to hold and perform the duties of ecclesiastical offices open to them in accord with the provisions of law.

Properly qualified lay persons can assist pastors of the Church as experts and counselors.

Lay persons have the obligation and enjoy the right to acquire knowledge of doctrine commensurate with their capacity and condition.

They have the right to pursue studies in the sacred sciences in pontifical universities or facilities and in institutes of religious sciences, and to obtain academic degrees.

If qualified, they are eligible to receive from ecclesiastical authority a mandate to teach sacred sciences.

Laymen can be invested by liturgical rite and in a stable manner in the ministries of lector and acolyte.

Lay persons, by temporary assignment, can fulfill the office of lector in liturgical actions; likewise, all lay persons can perform the duties of commentator or cantor.

In cases of necessity and in the absence of the usual ministers, lay persons — even if not lectors or acolytes — can exercise the ministry of the word, lead liturgical prayers, confer baptism and distribute Communion, according to the prescripts of law.

Lay persons who devote themselves permanently or temporarily to the service of the Church are obliged to acquire the formation necessary for carrying out their duties in a proper manner. They have a right to remuneration for their service which is just and adequate to provide for their own needs and those of their families; they also have a right to insurance, social security and health insurance.

SPECIAL APOSTOLATES AND GROUPS

Apostleship of the Sea (1920, Glasgow, Scotland; 1947 in U.S.): 3211 Fourth St. NE, Washington, DC 20017 (national office). An international Catholic organization for the moral, social and spiritual welfare of seafarers and those involved in the maritime industry. Formally instituted by the Holy See in 1952 (apostolic constitution *Exul Familia*), it is a sector of the Pontifical Council for Migrants and Itinerant Peoples. Its norms were updated by Pope John Paul II in a motu proprio dated Jan. 31, 1997. The U.S. unit, an affiliate of the NCCB-USCC, serves port chaplains in 63 U.S. ports. Nat. Dir., Robert Mario Balderas, a permanent deacon.

Auxiliaries of Our Lady of the Cenacle (1878, France): An association of consecrated Catholic laywomen, under the direction of the Congregation of Our Lady of the Cenacle. They profess annually the evangelical counsels of celibacy, poverty and obedience and serve God through their own professions and life styles and pursue individual apostolates. U.S. address: Dr. Carolyn Jacobs, 22 Bedford Court, Amherst, MA 01002.

Catholic Central Union of America (1855): 3835 Westminster Pl., St. Louis, MO 63108; membership, 2,000; Social Justice Review, bimonthly. One of the oldest Catholic lay organizations in the U.S. and the first given an official mandate for Catholic Action by a committee of the American bishops (1936).

Catholic Medical Mission Board (1928): 10 W. 17th Street, New York, NY 10011. A charitable, non-profit organization dedicated to providing health care supplies and support for the medically disadvantaged in developing and transitional countries. CMMB depends upon the financial generosity of over 25,000 individual donors and through product contributions by major pharmaceutical corporations. In 1996, CMMB provided medical assistance totaling $49,712,669 to Central America (13 countries); Eastern Europe (12 countries); Asia (5 countries); South America (5 countries) and Africa (6 countries). For each single dollar CMMB received in fiscal year 1996, it was able to provide thirteen and a half dollars worth of actual benefit to the missions it serves. CMMB's medical program includes a placement service for health care specialists who volunteer at Catholic medical facilities in developing countries. President, Terry Kirch.

Catholic Movement for Intellectual and Cultural Affairs of Pax Romana: The U.S. affiliate of Pax Romana — ICMICA (see International Catholic Organizations); *The Notebook*, quarterly. Address: 31 Chesterfield Rd., Stamford, CT 06902.

Catholic Network of Volunteer Service (1963; formerly, International Liaison of Lay Volunteers in Mission): 4121 Harewood Rd. N.E., Washington, DC 20017. Network for lay mission programs, coordinating and facilitating efforts of volunteer mission organizations. *The Response*, annual directory. Executive director, Jim Lindsay.

Catholic Volunteers in Florida (1983): P.O. Box 702, Goldenrod, FL 32733. Co-sponsored by the bishops of Florida to promote values of social justice by direct service to farm workers, homeless, hungry, low-income people, single mothers and others in need. Volunteers, 20 years of age and older, serve for a one-year period in urban and rural settings.

Center for Applied Research in the Apostolate (CARA): Georgetown University, Washington, DC 20057. A non-profit research center serving the planning needs of the Catholic Church. CARA gathers empirical data for use by bishops, diocesan agencies, parishes, congregations of men and women religious and Catholic organizations. *The CARA Report,* quarterly ; *CARA Catholic Ministry Formation Directory,* annually.

Christian Family Movement (CFM) (1947): Originated in Chicago to Christianize family life and create communities conducive to Christian family life. Since 1968, CFM in the U.S. has included couples from all Christian churches. National office, Box 272, Ames, IA 50010.

Christian Life Communities (1971, promulgation of revised norms by Pope Paul VI; originated, 1563, as Sodalities of Our Lady, at the Jesuit College in Rome): 3601 Lindell Blvd., Room 202, St. Louis, MO 63108 (national office); the world CLC office is in Rome. Small communities of primarily lay persons who come together to form committed individuals for service to the world and the Church.

Cursillo Movement (1949, in Spain; in U.S., 1957): National Cursillo Center, P.O. Box 210226, Dallas, TX 75211. An instrument of Christian renewal designed to form and stimulate persons to engage in evangelizing their everyday environments.

Franciscan Mission Service of North America, an Overseas Lay Ministry Program (1990): P.O. Box 29034, Washington, DC 20017. Lay missioners work with Franciscan sisters, brothers and priests for a minimum of three years in underdeveloped countries. Exec. Dir. Joseph Nangle, O.F.M.

Grail, The (1921, in The Netherlands, by Rev. Jacques van Ginneken, S.J.; 1940, in U.S.): Grailville, 932 O'Bannonville Rd., Loveland, Ohio 45140 (U. S. headquarters); Duisburger Strasse 442, 45478 Mulheim, Germany (international secretariat). An international movement of women concerned about the full development of all peoples, working in education, religious, social, cultural and ecological areas.

Jesuit Volunteer Corps (1956): 18th and Thompson Sts., Philadelphia, PA 19121 (address for information). Sponsored by the Society of Jesus in the U.S. Men and women volunteers work throughout the U.S. serving the poor directly and working for structural change.

LAMP Ministries (Lay Apostolic Ministries with the Poor): 2704 Schurz Ave., Bronx, NY 10465. Missionary service of evangelization with the materially poor and homeless in the larger metropolitan New York-New Jersey area. Newsletter, two times a year. Directors, Drs. Tom and Lyn Scheuring.

Lay Mission-Helpers Association (1955): 3424 Wilshire Blvd., Los Angeles, CA 90010. Trains and assigns men and women for work in overseas apostolates for periods of two to three years. Approximately 700 members of the association have served in overseas assignments since its founding. Director, Rev. Michael Meyers. The **Mission Doctors Association** (same address) recruits, trains and sends Catholic physicians and their families to mission hospitals and clinics throughout the world for tours of two to three years. Additionally, MDA has a short-tterm program for volunteer physicians with a term of service of 1-2 months. President, Dr. Timothy Lefevre.

Legion of Mary (1921, in Dublin, Ireland, by Frank Duff): P.O. Box 1313, St. Louis, MO 63188 (U.S. address); De Montfort House, Dublin 7, Ireland (headquarters). Membership: active Catholics of all ages, under the direction of local bishops and priests, for the work of conversion, conservation and consolation.

Movimiento Familiar Cristiano — USA (MFC) (1969): Movement of Catholic Hispanic families united in their efforts to promote the human and Christian virtues of the family so that it may become a force that forms persons, transmits the faith and contributes to the total development of the community. Rev. Clemente Barron, C.P., national spiritual director. Address: 700 Waverly, San Antonio, TX 78201.

National Catholic Conference for Seafarers, affiliated with the Apostleship of the Sea in the U.S. Pres., Mrs. Karen Lai, Seaman's Center, 221-20th St., Galveston, TX 77550.

Pax Christi USA (1972): 532 W. 8th St., Erie, PA 16503. U.S. section of Pax Christi (see International Catholic Organizations). Founded to establish peacemaking as a priority for the American Catholic Church. Pax Christi USA, quarterly; membership, 11,500.

Volunteer Missionary Movement (1969): 5980 W. Loomis Rd., Milwaukee, WI 53129. Independent lay international mission organization with origins in the Catholic tradition but ecumenical and open to all Christian denominations. *Bridges*, quarterly.

Volunteers for Educational and Social Services (VESS), 1625 Rutherford Lane, Bldg. D, Austin, TX. 78754. A program of the Texas Catholic Conference. Volunteers offer their services for a year at mission-sites throughout Texas as teachers, social workers, counselors, ESL instructors, immigration and refugee assistants, parish, youth and campus ministers, health care workers and nurses. The experience offers individuals the opportunity to acquire professional experience by ministering to the needs of parishes, agencies and schools that are economically disadvataged..

CATHOLIC YOUTH ORGANIZATIONS

Boy Scouts in the Catholic Church: The National Catholic Committee on Scouting (Eleanore Starr, Admin. Sec., NCCS-BSA, P.O. Box 152079, Irving, TX 75015) works with the Boy Scouts of America in developing the character and spiritual life of members in units chartered to Catholic and non-Catholic organizations. National Committee Chairman, Robert Runnels of Leawood, Kans.

Camp Fire: The National Catholic Committee for Girl Scouts and Camp Fire, a standing committee of the National Federation for Catholic Youth Ministry, cooperates with Camp Fire Boys and Girls (4601 Madison Ave., Kansas City, MO 64112).

Catholic Forester Youth Program, Catholic Order of Foresters: 355 Shuman Blvd., P.O. Box 3012, Naperville, IL 60566. To develop Christian leadership and promote the moral, intellectual, social and physical growth of its youth members. Catholic Forester. Membership: youth up to 16 years of age — over 19,046 in 610 local courts in U.S. High Chief Ranger, Robert Ciesla..

Catholic Youth Organization (CYO): Name of parish-centered diocesan Catholic youth programs throughout the country. CYO promotes a program of spiritual, social and physical activities. The original CYO was organized in 1930 by Archbishop Bernard Sheil, auxiliary bishop of Chicago.

Columbian Squires (1925): 1 Columbus Plaza, New Haven, CT 06510. The official youth organization of the Knights of Columbus. To train and develop leadership through active participation in a well-organized program of spiritual, service, social, cultural and athletic activities. Membership: Catholic young men, 12-18 years old. More than 25,000 in over 1,000 circles (local units) active in the U.S., Canada, Puerto Rico, Philippines, Mexico, the Bahamas, Virgin Islands and Guam. *Squires Newsletter*, monthly.

Girl Scouts: Girls from archdioceses and dioceses in the U.S. and its possessions participate in Girl Scouting through the collaboration of Girl Scouts of the U.S.A. (830 Third Ave., New York, NY 10022) with the National Catholic Committee for Girl Scouts and Camp Fire, a standing committee of the National Federation for Catholic Youth Ministry.

Holy Childhood Association (Pontifical Association of the Holy Childhood) (1843): 1720 Massachusetts Ave. N.W., Washington, DC 20036. The official children's mission-awareness society of the Church. Provides mission awareness for elementary-grade students in parochial schools and religious education programs and financial assistance to children in more than 100 developing countries. Publishes *It's Our World*, three times a year, in two grade levels. National Director, Rev. Francis W. Wright, C.S.Sp.

National Catholic Forensic League (1952): To develop articulate Catholic leaders through an interdiocesan program of speech and debate activities. Newsletter, quarterly. Membership: 925 schools; membership open to Catholic, private and public schools through the local diocesan league. Secretary-Treasurer, Richard Gaudette, 21 Nancy Rd., Milford, MA 01757.

National Catholic Young Adult Ministry Association (1982): 3700-A Oakview Terr. N.E., Washington, DC 20017. A response to the needs of young adults, an invitation to share their gifts with the larger community and a challenge to live gospel values in the world. A national network for single and married young adults. President, James J. Breen.

National Federation for Catholic Youth Ministry, Inc. (1981): 3700-A Oakview Terr. NE, Washington, DC 20017. To foster the development of youth ministry in the United States. Executive Director, Robert McCarty.

Young Christian Students: 7436 W. Harrison, Forest Park, IL 60130. A student movement for Christian personal and social change.

COLLEGE SOCIETIES

Alpha Sigma Nu (1915): Marquette Univ., Brooks 201, P.O. Box 1881, Milwaukee, WI 53201 (national headquarters). National honor society of the 30 Jesuit institutions of higher education in the U.S. and a chapter at Sogany University in Korea; members chosen on the basis of scholarship, loyalty and service; 1,575 student and 38,000 alumni members. Member, Association of College Honor Societies. Gamma Pi Epsilon (1925) merged with Alpha Sigma Nu in 1973 to form society for men and women. Executive Director, Peg Fennig.

Delta Epsilon Sigma (1939): Barry University, Miami Shores, FL 33161. National scholastic honor society for students, faculty and alumni of colleges and universities with a Catholic tradition. *Delta Epsilon Sigma Journal,* three times a year. Membership: 60,000 in 116 chapters. Secretary, Dr. J. Patrick Lee.

Kappa Gamma Pi (1926): A national Catholic college honor society for graduates who, in addition to academic excellence, have shown outstanding leadership in extra-curricular activities. *Kappa Gamma Pi News,* five times a year. Membership: more than 37,000 in 139 colleges; 20 alumnae chapters in metropolitan areas. Executive Secretary, Marjorie Durbin, 2415 Hillcrest Dr., Stow, Ohio 44224.

Phi Kappa Theta: 3901 W. 86th St., Suite 425, Indianapolis, IN 46268. National social fraternity with a Catholic heritage. Merger (1959) of Phi Kappa Fraternity, founded at Brown Univ. in 1889, and Theta Kappa Phi Fraternity, founded at Lehigh Univ. in 1919. *The Temple Magazine,* semi-annually, and newsletters. Membership: 2,800 undergraduate and 50,500 alumni in 63 collegiate and 40 alumni chapters. Executive Director, Mark T. McSweeney.

National Catholic Student Coalition (1982): National coalition of Catholic campus ministry groups at public and private institutions of higher education. Formed after National Newman Club Federation and the National Federation of Catholic College Students dissolved in the 1960s. The U.S. affiliate of Pax Romana — IMCS (see International Catholic Organizations). Publishes *The Catholic Collegian,* four times a year. Membership: 200 campus groups. Executive director, Jamie Williams, 300 College Park Ave., Dayton, Ohio 45469.

ASSOCIATIONS, MOVEMENTS, SOCIETIES IN THE U.S.

(Principal source: Almanac survey.)
See Index for other associations, movements and societies covered elsewhere.

Academy of American Franciscan History (1944), 1712 Euclid Ave., Berkeley, CA 94709. To encourage the study of the Franciscan Order in the New World. Dir., Dr. John F. Schwaller.

Aid to the Church in Need (1947), U.S. office, P.O. Box 576, Deer Park, NY 11729. Assists the pastoral activities of the church in Third World countries, Eastern Europe and the former Soviet Union. *Mirror* (newsletter), 9 times a year.

Albanian Catholic Institute "Daniel Dajani, S.J." (1992), University of San Francisco, Xavier Hall, San Francisco, CA 94117. To assist the rebuilding of the Catholic Church in Albania and to promote the dissemination of knowledge of Albania's national, religious and cultural heritage. Founder, Gjon Sinishta (1930-95). Director, Paul Bernadicou, S.J.

American Benedictine Academy (1947). To promote Benedictine values in contemporary culture. Pres., Mary Forman, O.S.B., Sacred Heart Monastery, Richardton, ND 58652.

American Catholic Correctional Chaplains Association (1952), 220 in 300 institutions. Pres., Bro. Peter Donohue, C.F.X., Office of Detention Ministry, 933 Grattan St., Los Angeles, CA 90015.

American Catholic Historical Association (1919), Catholic University of America, Washington, DC 20064. *The Catholic Historical Review,* quarterly. Sec.-Treas., Rev. Msgr. Robert Trisco.

American Catholic Philosophical Association (1926), The Catholic University of America, Washington, DC 20064. American Catholic Philosophical Quarterly; Proceedings, annually.

American Committee on Italian Migration (1952), 352 W. 44th St., New York, NY 10036; 6,000. *ACIM Newsletter* and *ACIM Nuova Via,* 6 times a year.

American Friends of the Vatican Library (1981), 157 Lakeshore Rd., Grosse Point Farms, MI 48236. Sponsored by the Catholic Library Association. To assist in supporting the Vatican Library: *AMICI,* newsletter.

Ancient Order of Hibernians in America, Inc. (1836); 120,000. *National Hibernian Digest,* bimonthly. Nat. Sec., Thomas McNabb, 31 Logan St., Auburn, NY 13021.

Apostleship of Prayer (1844-France; 1861-U.S.): 3 Stephen Ave., New Hyde Park, NY 11040. Promotes Daily Offering and Sacred Heart devotion. Nat. Dir., Rev. John H. Rainaldo, S.J.

Apostolate for Family Consecration (1975), Pope John Paul II Holy Family Center, known as **Catholic Familyland,** 3375 County Rd. 36, Bloomingdale, OH 43910. Pres., Jerome F. Coniker.

Archconfraternity of Christian Mothers (Christian Mothers) (1881), 220 37th St., Pittsburgh, PA 15201; over 3,500 branches. Dir., Rev. Bertin Roll, O.F.M. Cap.

Archconfraternity of the Holy Ghost (1912), Holy Ghost Fathers, 2401 Bristol Pike, Bensalem, PA 19020 (U.S. headquarters).

Archdiocese for the Military Services Seminary Education Fund (1988), 3311 Toledo Terrace, Hyattsville, MD 20782.

Association for Spiritual, Ethical, and Religious Values in Counseling (ASERVIC), division of the American Counseling Association. *Counseling and Values,* 3 times a year. Address, Dept. of Educational Psychology and Special Education, Southern Illinois Univ. at Carbondale, Carbondale, IL 62901.

Association for Social Economics (formerly the Catholic Economic Association) (1941), Marquette University, Milwaukee, WI 53233; 1,300. *Review of Social Economy,* quarterly.

Association of Catholic Diocesan Archivists (1979): To work for establishment of an archival program in every American diocese. *ACDA Bulletin,* quarterly. Pres. (1995-96), Msgr. Francis Weber, 15151 San Fernando Mission Blvd., Mission Hills, CA 91345.

Association of Marian Helpers (1944), Stockbridge, MA 01263; 900,000, mostly in U.S. *Marian Helpers Bulletin,* quarterly. To promote vocations to Church service and support worldwide apostolates of Marians of the Immaculate Conception.

Beginning Experience (1974), 1209 Washington Blvd., Detroit, MI 48226; 150 teams throughout the world. Adult and youth programs to help divorced, widowed and separated start a new beginning in their lives. Exec. Dir., Emilia Alberico..

The Blue Army USA (A Fatima Apostolate) (1952), Mountain View Rd. (P.O. Box 976), Washington, NJ 07882. Promote Fatima message, Marian devotion. *Soul,* bimonthly; *Hearts Aflame,* quarterly. Natl. Pres., Most Rev. James S. Sullivan.

Calix Society (1947), 7601 Wayzata Blvd., Minneapolis, MN 55426; Association of Catholic alcoholics maintaining their sobriety through 12-step program. Sec.-Treas., Bill Fox.

Canon Law Society of America (1939), Catholic University, Washington, DC 20064. To further research and study in canon law; 1,600. Exec. Coord., Rev. Patrick Cogan, S.A.

Cardinal Mindszenty Foundation (CMF) (1958), P.O. Box 11321, St. Louis, MO 63105. To uphold and defend the Catholic Church, family life and freedom for all under God. Pres., Eleanor Schlafly.

Catholic Aid Association (1878), 3499 N. Lexington Ave., St. Paul, MN 55126; 80,000. *Catholic Aid News,* monthly. Fraternal life insurance society. Pres. F. L. Spanier.

Catholic Alumni Clubs International (1957): To advance social, cultural and spiritual well-being of members. Membership limited to single Catholics with professional education; 7,500 in 48 clubs in U.S. Pres., Guy A. DiMarino, 215 W. Wood St., Lowellville, OH 44436.

Catholic Answers (1982), P.O. Box 17490, San Diego, CA 92177. *This Rock,* monthly. Apologetics and evangelization organization. Founder and dir., Karl Keating.

Catholic Biblical Association of America (1936), Catholic University of America, Washington, DC 20064; 1,350. *The Catholic Biblical Quarterly; Old Testament Abstracts, CBQ* monograph series.

Catholic Book Publishers Association, Inc. (1987), 2 Park Ave., Manhasset, NY 11030. Sec., Charles A. Roth.

Catholic Coalition on Preaching, Madonna Univ., Livonia, MI 48150. Pres., Rev. Francis Tebbe, O.F.M.

Catholic Commission on Intellectual and Cultural Affairs (CCICA) (1946), LaSalle University, Philadelphia, PA 19141; 350; Exec. Dir., Bro. Daniel Burke, F.S.C.

Catholic Committee of Appalachia (1970), 111 Main St., P.O. Box 953, Whitesburg, KY 41858. Exec. Coord., Todd Garland.

Catholic Daughters of the Americas (1903), 10 W. 71st St., New York, NY 10023; 125,000. *Share Magazine.* Nat. Regent, Grace M. Rinaldi.

Catholic Golden Age (1975): P.O. Box 3658, Scranton, PA 18505; CGA World, quarterly. For Catholics over 50 years of age.

Catholic Guardian Society (1913), 1011 First Ave., New York, NY 10022. Exec. Dir., John J. Frein.

Catholic Home Bureau (1899), 1011 First Ave., New York, NY 10022. Exec. Dir., Sr. Una McCormack, O.P.

Catholic Home Study Service (1936), P.O. Box 363, Perryville, MO 63775. Provides instruction in the Catholic faith by mail free of charge. Director, Rev. Oscar Lukefahr, C.M.

Catholic Interracial Council of New York, Inc. (1934), 899 Tenth Ave., New York, NY 10019. To promote racial and social justice.

Catholic Knights of America (1877), 1850 Dalton St., Cincinnati, OH 45214; 7,800. *C K of A Journal,* monthly. Fraternal insurance society.

Catholic Knights of Ohio (1891): 22005 Mastick Rd., Fairview Park, OH 44126; 8,000 in Ohio and Kentucky. *The Messenger,* monthly. Fraternal insurance society. Pres., Victor D. Huss.

Catholic Kolping Society of America (1923), P.O. Box 46252, Chicago, IL 60646. *Kolping Banner,* monthly. International society concerned with spiritual and educational development of members.

Catholic Lawyers' Guild. Organization usually on a diocesan basis, under different titles.

Catholic League (1943), 1200 N. Ashland Ave., Chicago, IL 60622. Exec. Dir., Most Rev. Thad Jakubowski.

Catholic League for Religious and Civil Rights (1973), 1011 First Ave., New York, NY 10022; local chapters throughout U.S. *Catalyst,* League journal. Serves Catholic community as an anti-defamation and civil rights agency. Pres., William A. Donohue.

Catholic Library Association (1921), 100 North St., Suite 224, Pittsfield, MA 01201. *Catholic Library World, Catholic Periodical and Literature Index,* quarterlies. Exec.Dir., Jean R. Bostley, S.S.J.

Catholic Marketing Network (1955), 6000 Campus Circle Dr. #110, Irving, TX 75063. A trade associaiton founded to encourage the most effective production and distribution of Catholic goods and provide a common forum for mutual interchange of ideas .*Catholic Marketing Network,* quarterly.

Catholic Medical Association (formerly National Federation of Catholic Physicians' Guilds) (1927), 850 Elm Grove Rd., Elm Grove, WI 53122; *Linacre Quarterly.* Exec. Dir., Robert H. Herzog.

Catholic Near East Welfare Association (1926),

1011 First Ave., New York, NY 10022. A papal agency for humanitarian and pastoral support serving the churches and peoples of the Middle East, Northeast Africa, India and Eastern Europe, with offices in New York, Vatican City, Addis Ababa, Amman, Jordan, Jerusalem and Beirut, Lebanon. Pres., Cardinal John O'Connor; sec. gen., Msgr. Robert L. Stern.

Catholic Order of Foresters (1883), 355 Shuman Blvd., P.O. Box 3012, Naperville, IL 60566; 136,685. *The Catholic Forester,* bimonthly. Fraternal insurance society. High Chief Ranger, Robert Ciesla.

Catholic Press Association of the U.S. and Canada, Inc. (1911), 3555 Veterans Memorial Highway, Unit O, Ronkonkoma, NY 11779. *The Catholic Journalist,* monthly; *Catholic Press Directory,* annually. Pres., Christopher J. Gunty; exec. dir., Owen P. McGovern.

Catholic Theological Society of America (1946), Ursuline College, 2550 Lander Rd., Pepper Pike, OH 44124. *Proceedings,* annually.

Catholic Union of Texas, The K.J.T. (1889), 214 E. Colorado St., La Grange, TX 78945; 18,226. *Nasinec,* weekly, and *K. J. T. News,* monthly. Fraternal and insurance society. Pres., Elo J. Goerig.

Catholic War Veterans (1935), 441 N. Lee St., Alexandria, VA 22314; 500 posts, *Catholic War Veteran,* bimonthly.

Catholic Worker Movement (1933), 36 E. First St., New York, NY 10003. *The Catholic Worker,* 8 times a year. Lay apostolate founded by Peter Maurin and Dorothy Day; has Houses of Hospitality in over 60 U.S. cities and several communal farms in various parts of the country. Promotes the practice of the works of mercy, nonviolence, personalism, voluntary poverty.

Catholic Workman (Katolicky Delnik) (1891), P.O. Box 47, New Prague, MN 56071; 16,405. *Catholic Workman,* monthly. Fraternal and insurance society.

Catholics against Capital Punishment (1992), P.O. Box 3125, Arlington, VA 22203. Promoes greater awareness of papal and episcopal statements against the death penalty. *CACP News Notes,* bimonthly. Nat. coordinator, Frank McNeirney.

Catholics United for Spiritual Action, Inc. (CUSA) (1947), 63 Wall St., New York, NY 10005. A group-correspondence apostolate for the disabled.

Catholics United for the Faith (1968), 827 N. Fourth St., Steubenville, OH 43952; 23,000 worldwide, *Lay Witness,* monthly. Lay apostolic group concerned with spiritual and doctrinal formation of members. Pres., Curtis Martin.

Center of Concern (1971): 3700 13th St., N.E., Washington, DC 20017.

Central Association of the Miraculous Medal (1915), 475 E. Chelten Ave., Philadelphia, PA 19144. *Miraculous Medal,* quarterly. Dir., Rev. William J. O'Brien, C.M.

Chaplains' Aid Association, Inc. (1917), 3311 Toledo Terrace, Hyattsville, MD 20780. To receive and administer funds toward education of seminarians to become priest-chaplains in military services. Pres., Most Rev. Joseph T. Dimino.

Christian Foundation for Children and Aging, One Elmwood Ave., Kansas City, KS 66103.

Grassroots movement dedicated to improving through sponsorship the lives of children and aging at Catholic mission sites around the world. Exec. Dir., Bernard A. Hentzen.

Christophers, Inc., The (1945), 12 E. 48th St., New York, NY 10017. Founded by Rev. James Keller, M.M. The Christophers stimulate personal initiative and responsible action in line with Judeo-Christian principles through broadcast of Christopher radio and TV programs; free distribution of *Christopher News Notes,* ten times a year; publication of a weekly Christopher column in over 200 newspapers; Spanish literature; annual media awards; youth outreach. Dir., Rev. Thomas J. McSweeney.

Citizens for Educational Freedom (1959): Nonsectarian group concerned with parents' right to educational choice by means of tuition tax credits and vouchers. Exec. dir., Patrick J. Reilly, 921 S. Walter Reed Dr., Suite 1, Arlington, VA 22204.

Confraternity of Bl. Junipero Serra (1989): P.O. Box 7125, Mission Hills, CA 91346; 3,500 in U.S. and foreign countries. Founded in Monterey (Calif.) diocese to help promote process of canonization of Bl. Junipero Serra and increase spiritual development of members. Dir., Rev. Thomas L. Davis, Jr.; Spiritual Dir., Rev. Noel F. Moholy, O.F.M.

Confraternity of Catholic Clergy (1976): Association of priests pledged to pursuit of personal holiness, loyalty to the Pope, theological study and adherence to authentic teachings of the Catholic faith. Sec., Rev. L. Dudley Day, O.S.A., 4445 W. 64th St., Chicago, IL 60629.

Confraternity of Christian Doctrine, Inc., 3211 Fourth St., N.E., Washington, DC 20017. A distinct entity, separately incorporated and directed by a Board of Trustees from the United States Catholic Conference of Bishops. Its purpose is to foster and promote the teaching of Christ as understood and handed down by the Roman Catholic Church. To this end it licenses use of the *Lectionary for Mass* and the *New American Bible (NAB),* the *Revised Psalms of the NAB* and the *Revised New Testament of the NAB,* translations made from the original languages in accordance with the papal encyclical *Divino Afflante Spiritu* of Pope Pius XII.

Confraternity of the Immaculate Conception of Our Lady of Lourdes (1874), Box 561, Notre Dame, IN 46556. Distributors of Lourdes water.

Confraternity of the Most Holy Rosary: See Dominican Rosary Apostolate.

Couple to Couple League (1971), P.O. Box 111184, Cincinnati, OH 45211. Founded to teach and promote marital chastity through Natural Family Planning.

Courage (1980), c/o St. Michael's Rectory, 424 W. 34th St., New York, NY 10001. To live chaste lives in accordance with the Church's teaching on homosexuality. Newsletter, 4 times a year. Nat. Dir., Rev. John F. Harvey, O.S.F.S.

Damien-Dutton Society for Leprosy Aid, Inc. (1944), 616 Bedford Ave., Bellmore, NY 11710; 25,000. *Damien Dutton Call,* quarterly. Provides medicine, rehabilitation and research for conquest of leprosy. Pres., Howard E. Crouch; Vice Pres., Elizabeth Campbell.

Daughters of Isabella (1897), P.O. Box 9585, New Haven, CT 06535; 100,000. To unite Catholic women into a fraternal order for spiritual benefits and to promote higher ideals within society.

Disaster Response Office (1990), Catholic Charities USA, 1731 King St., Suite 200, Alexandria, VA 22314. Promotes and facilitates Catholic disaster response in the U.S. Dir., Jane A. Gallagher.

Dominican Rosary Apostolate (1806), 141 E. 65th St., New York, NY 10021. Dir., Rev. Edward L. Martin, O.P.

Edith Stein Guild, Inc. (1955), Church of St. John the Baptist, 210 W. 31st St., New York, NY 10001. Assists and encourages Jewish Catholics; fosters among Catholics a better understanding of their Jewish heritage; promotes spread of knowledge of life and writings of Bl. Edith Stein; fosters better understanding between Jews and Christians and supports the Church's spirit of ecumenism. Pres., Mrs. Cabiria Nardiello; Liaison,. Rev. Philip F. Romano, O.F.M. Cap..

Enthronement of the Sacred Heart in the Home (1907), P.O. Box 111, Fairhaven, MA 02719.

Family Rosary, Inc., The (1942), 4 Pine West Plaza, Albany, NY 12205. Founded by Father Patrick Peyton, C.S.C. Encourages family prayer, especially the Rosary. Pres., Rev. John Phalen, C.S.C.

Federation of Diocesan Liturgical Commissions (FDLC) (1969), P.O. Box 29039, Washington, DC 20017. Voluntary association of personnel from diocesan liturgical commissions and worship offices. The main purpose is promotion of the liturgy as the heart of Christian life, especially in the parish community. Exec. Dir., Rev. Michael J. Spillane.

Federation of Seminary Spiritual Directors (1972). Pres., Rev. Thomas Krenik, St.Paul Seminary School of Divinity of the University of St. Thomas, 2260 Summit Ave., St. Paul, MN 55105. Responsible for priestly spiritual formation in high school and college seminaries, novitiates, theologates and houses of formation in the U.S.

Fellowship of Catholic Scholars (1977), Prof. Gerard V. Bradley, president, 21 Law School, Notre Dame, IN 46556; 1,000 members. Interdisciplinary research and publications of Catholic scholars in accord with the magisterium of the Catholic Church.

First Catholic Slovak Ladies' Association, USA (1892), 24950 Chagrin Blvd., Beachwood, OH 44122; 102,000. *Fraternally Yours,* monthly. Fraternal insurance society. Pres., Mary Ann Johanek.

First Catholic Slovak Union (Jednota) (1890), FCSU Corporate Center, 6611 Rockside Rd., Independence, OH 44131; 96,206. *Jednota,* biweekly. Nat. Sec., Kenneth A. Arendt.

Foundation for the Family (1986), P.O. Box 111184, Cincinnati, OH 45211. Established by Couple to Couple League (see entry above) to provide materials for family not relating to Natural Family Planning.

Foundations and Donors Interested in Catholic Activities, Inc. (FADICA), 1350 Connecticut Ave. N.W., Suite 303, Washington, DC 20036. A consortium of private foundations providing continuing education and research to members to make church-related philanthropy more effective. Pres., Francis J. Butler.

Franciscan Apostolate of the Way of the Cross (1949), P.O. Box 23, Boston, MA 02112. Distributes religious materials to the sick and shut-in. Dir., Rev. Robert Lynch, O.F.M.

Franciscan Canticle, Inc. (1983), 370 W. Arenas Rd., Palm Springs, CA 92262. Community of men and women artists who use their gifts and talents to promote the work of God.

Free The Fathers (1983), 845 Oak St. Chattanooga, TN 37403. To work for the freedom of bishops and priests imprisoned in China. Pres., John M. Davies.

Friends of the Holy Land, Inc. (1974), 347 Mile Square Rd., Yonkers, NY 10701; 300 members. To provide spiritual and material support for the Christian communities in the Holy Land; *Friends of the Holy Land Newsletter.* Gen. Dir., Ernest F. Russo.

Gabriel Richard Institute (1949), 2820 West Maple Rd., Suite No. 101, Troy, MI 48084. Conducts Christopher Leadership Course. Dir., Rev. Thomas J. Bresnahan; nat. mgr., Dolores Ammar.

Guard of Honor of the Immaculate Heart of Mary (1932), 135 West 31st St., New York, NY 10001. An archconfraternity approved by the Holy See whose members cultivate devotion to the Blessed Virgin Mary, particularly through a daily Guard Hour of Prayer.

Holy Name Society: Founded in 1274 by Blessed John Vercelli, master general of the Dominicans, to promote reverence for the Holy Name of Jesus; this is still the principal purpose of the society, which also develops lay apostolic programs in line with directives of the Second Vatican Council. Introduced in the U.S. by Dominican Father Charles H. McKenna in 1870-71, the society has about 5 million members on diocesan and parochial levels. With approval of the local bishop and pastor, women as well as men may be members.

Holy Name Society, National Association (NAHNS) (1970), P.O. Box 26038, Baltimore, MD 21224. *Holy Name Newsletter,* monthly. Association of diocesan and parochial Holy Name Societies.

Hungarian Catholic League of America, Inc. (1945), Rev. Msgr. William I. Varsanyi, chairman, One Cathedral Sq., Providence, RI 02903.

International Institute of the Heart of Jesus (1972), 7236 Wellauer Rd., Milwaukee, WI 53213; Rev. Walter O. Kern, 5337 Genesee St., Bowmansville, NY 14026; Delegacion Latino-americana, IIHJ, Casilla 118, Correo 35, Las Condes, Santiago, Chile (president's office). Promote awareness and appreciation of the mystery of the Heart of Christ.

Italian Catholic Federation, Central Council (1924), 675 Hegenberger Rd., #110, Oakland, CA 94621; 19,000. Fraternal organization of Italian-American Catholics.

John Carroll Society, The (1951), P.O. Box

29260, Washington, DC 20017. Chaplain, Rev. Peter Vaghi.

Judean Society, Inc., The (1966), 1075 Space Park Way No. 336, Mt. View, CA 94043.

Knights of Peter Claver (1909), and Knights of Peter Claver, Ladies Auxiliary (1926), 1825 Orleans Ave., New Orleans, LA 70116. 35,000. *The Claverite,* biannually. Fraternal and aid society. National Chaplain, Most Rev. Curtis J. Guillory, S.V.D.

Knights of St. John, International Supreme Commandery (1886), 89 So. Pine Ave., Albany, N.Y. 12208.

Ladies of Charity of the United States of America (1960), P.O. Box 31697, St. Louis, MO 63131; 25,000 in U.S.; 250,000 worldwide. International Association founded by St. Vincent de Paul in 1617.

Latin Liturgy Association (1975), Office of Chairman, Dr. Robert J. Edgeworth, 740 Carriage Way, Baton Rouge, LA 70808; 850. To promote the use of the Latin language and music in the approved rites of the Church. Quarterly journal.

Legatus (1987), 30 Frank Lloyd Wright Dr., P.O. Box 997, Ann Arbor, MI 48106. To apply Church's moral teaching in business and personal lives of members. *Legatus Newsletter,* monthly.

Lithuanian Groups: Ateitininkai, members of Lithuanian Catholic Federation Ateitis (1910), 1209 Country Lane, Lemont, IL 60439; *Ateitis,* bimonthly; Pres., Juozas Polikaitis. Knights of Lithuania (1913), Roman Catholic educational-fraternal organization; *Vytis,* monthly; Pres., Evelyn Ozelis, 2533 W. 45th St., Chicago, IL 60632. Lithuanian Catholic Alliance (1886), 71-73 S. Washington St., Wilkes-Barre, PA 18701; fraternal insurance organization; Pres., Thomas E. Mack. Lithuanian Roman Catholic Federation of America (1906), umbrella organization for Lithuanian parishes and organizations; *The Observer,* bimonthly; Pres., Saulius Kuprys, 4545 W. 63rd St., Chicago, IL 60629. Lithuanian Roman Catholic Priests' League (1909): religious-professional association, Pres., Rev. Albert Contons, 50 Orton-Marotta Way, Boston, MA 02127. Lithuanian Catholic Religious Aid, Inc. (1961), 351 Highland Blvd., Brooklyn, NY 11207; to assist Catholics in Lithuania; Chairman and Pres., Most Rev. Paul Baltakis.

Little Flower Mission League (1957), P.O. Box 25, Plaucheville, LA 71362. Sponsored by the Brothers of the Holy Eucharist. Dir., Bro. André M. Lucia, F.S.E.

Little Flower Society (1923), 1313 Frontage Rd.; Darien, IL 60561; 200,000 Nat. Dir., Rev. Robert E. Colaresi, O. Carm.

Liturgical Conference, The, 8750 Georgia Ave., Suite 123, Silver Spring, MD 20910. *Liturgy, Homily Service.* Education, research and publication programs for renewing and enriching Christian liturgical life. Ecumenical.

Loyal Christian Benefit Association (1890), P.O. Box 13005, Erie, PA 16514. Fraternal benefit and insurance society. *The Fraternal Leader,* quarterly.

Marian Movement of Priests (1972), P.O. Box 8, St. Francis, ME 04774 (U.S.); Via Mercalli, 23, 20122 Milan, Italy (internatl. headquarters); 4,000 clergy;

53,000 religious and laity (U.S.). Spiritual renewal through consecration to the Immaculate Heart of Mary. Pres. Rev. Albert G. Roux.

Mariological Society of America (1949), Sec., Rev. Thomas A. Thompson, S.M., Marian Library, Box 1390, University of Dayton, Dayton, OH 45469. *Marian Studies,* annually. Founded by Rev. Juniper B. Carol, O.F.M., to promote greater appreciation of and scientific research in Marian theology.

Maryheart Crusaders, The (1964), 22 Button St., Meriden, CT 06450. Pres., Louise D'Angelo.

Men of the Sacred Heart (1964), Shrine of the Sacred Heart, P.O. Box 500, Harleigh, PA 18225. Promote enthronement of Sacred Heart.

Militia Immaculata National Center — Marytown (1917), 1600 W. Park Ave., Libertyville, IL 60048; canonically established with international headquarters in Rome. A pious association for evangelization and catechesis beginning with members' own total consecration to the Immaculate Virgin Mary.

Missionary Association of Catholic Women (1916), 3501 S. Lake Dr., P.O. Box 07912, Milwaukee, WI 53207.

Missionary Vehicle Association, Inc. (MIVA America) (1971), 1400 Michigan Ave., N.E., Washington, DC 20017. To raise funds and distribute them annually as vehicle grants to missionaries working with the poor in Third World countries. Nat. Dir., Rev. Philip De Rea, M.S.C.; Exec. Dir., Rev. Anthony F. Krisak.

Morality in Media, Inc. (1962), 475 Riverside Dr., New York, NY 10115. Interfaith national organization. Newsletter, bimonthly. Works by constitutional means to curb the explosive growth of hard-core pornography and to turn back the tide of grossly offensive, indecent media. A major project is the National Obscenity Law Center which provides legal information for prosecutors and other attorneys. Pres., Robert W. Peters.

National Assembly of Religious Women (NARW): Founded as the National Assembly of Women Religious, 1970; title changed, 1980. A movement of feminist women committed to prophetic tasks of giving witness, raising awareness and engaging in public action and advocacy for justice in church and society. Address: 529 S. Wabash Ave., Suite 404, Chicago, IL 60605.

National Association for Lay Ministry (1977), 5420 S. Cornell Ave., Chicago, IL 60615. Acts as advocate and support for lay people who respond to a call to ministry in the Church.

National Association of Catholic Family Life Ministers, Univ. of Dayton, 300 College Park, Dayton, OH 45469. Strives to be a voice and advocate for families and family ministry in Church and society. Pres., Kay Ryan, C.S.J..

National Association of Catholic Home Educators (1993), P.O. Box 420225, San Diego, CA 92142. Promotion of homeschooling. *The Catholic Home Educator,* quarterly.

National Association of Church Personnel Administrators (1971), 100 E. 8th St., Cincinnati, OH 45202. Exec. Dir., Sr. Ann White, S.L. Association for human resource and personnel directors dedicated to promotion and development of just personnel practices for all church employees.

National Association of Diocesan Ecumenical Officers, Network of Catholics involved in ecumenical and interreligious work. Pes., Rev. Vincent A. Heier, 462 N. Taylor St., St. Louis, MO 63108.

National Association of Pastoral Musicians (1976), 225 Sheridan St., N.W., Washington, DC 20011; 9,000. Dedicated to fostering the art of musical liturgy. *Pastoral Music,* six times a year. Exec. Dir., Rev. Virgil C. Funk.

National Association of Priest Pilots (1964), Pres., Rev. John Hemann, 660 Bush Ave., Garner, IA 50438.

National Catholic AIDS Network, P.O. Box 422984, San Francisco, CA 94142. Exec. dir., Rev. Rodney DeMartini, S.M.

National Catholic Band Association (1953), Box 1023, Notre Dame University, Notre Dame, IN 46556.

National Catholic Cemetery Conference (1949), 710 N. River Rd., Des Plaines, IL 60016. Exec. Dir., Leo A. Droste.

National Catholic Conference for Interracial Justice (NCCIJ) (1960), 11200 Varnum St.. N.E., Washington, DC 20017.

National Catholic Conference of Airport Chaplains (1986), Chicago O'Hare International Airport, P.O. Box 66353, Chicago, IL 60666. Provides support and communication for Catholics performing pastoral ministry to airport and airline workers and Catholic travelers; affiliated with Bishops' Committee on Migration, NCCB. Episcopal liaison, Most Rev. James C. Timlin. Pres., Rev. John A. Jamnicky.

National Catholic Council on Alcoholism and Related Drug Problems, Inc. 1550 Hendrickson St., Brooklyn, NY 11234. An affiliate of the NCCB/USCC. Committed to assisting members in a greater awareness of alcoholism, other chemical addictions and prevention issues.

National Catholic Development Conference (1968), 86 Front St., Hempstead, NY 11550. Professional association of organizations and individuals engaged in raising funds for Catholic charitable activities. Pres., Rev. Charles F. Shelby, C.M.; Exec. Dir., George T. Holloway.

National Catholic Ministry to the Bereaved (NCMB) (1990), 606 Middle Ave. Elyria, OH 44035. Offers ongoing education, resources and assistance to dioceses, parishes and caregivers in their ministry to the bereaved. Pres., Sr. Mauryeen O'Brien, O.P.

National Catholic Pharmacists Guild of the United States (1962): *The Catholic Pharmacist.* Co-Pres. and Exec. Dir., John P. Winkelmann, 1012 Surrey Hills Dr., St. Louis, MO 63117.

National Catholic Society of Foresters (1891), 320 S. School St., Mt.. Prospect, IL 60056 52,000; *National Catholic Forester,* quarterly. A fraternal insurance society. Pres., Sue Koleczek.

National Catholic Stewardship Council (1962), 1275 K St. N.W., Suite 980, Washington, DC 20005. A professional association which fosters an environment in which stewardship is understood, accepted and practiced throughout the church. Nat. Dir., Matthew R. Paratore.

National Catholic Women's Union (1916), 3835 Westminster Pl., St. Louis, MO 63108; 7,000.

National Center for the Laity (1977), 10 E. Pearson St., No. 101, Chicago, IL 60611. *Initiatives,* six times a year. To promote and implement the vision of Vatican II: That the laity are the Church in the modern world as they attend to their occupational, family and neighborhood responsibilities.

National Center for Urban Ethnic Affairs (1971): P.O. Box 20, Cardinal Station, Washington, DC 20064. Research and action related to the Church's concern for cultural pluralism and urban neighborhoods. An affiliate of the USCC. Pres., Dr. John A. Kromkowski.

National Christ Child Society Inc. (1887): 5101 Wisconsin Ave. N.W., Suite 304, Washington, DC 20016. Founder, Mary V. Merrick. A non-profit Catholic association of volunteers of all denominations dedicated to the service of needy children and youth regardless of race or creed. Membership: approximately 8,000 adult members in 37 chapters in U.S. President, Mrs. Kathleen Gibbons.

National Committee of Catholic Laymen, The (1977), 150 E. 35th St., Room 840, New York, NY 10016. Lobbying and publishing organization representing "orthodox" Catholics who strongly support Pope John Paul II; *catholic eye,* monthly. Pres., J.P. McFadden.

National Conference of Catechetical Leadership (formerly, National Conference of Diocesan Directors of Religious Education) (1936): 3021 4th St. N.E., Washington, DC 20017; 1,300. To promote catechetical ministry at the national diocesan and parish levels. Exec. Dir., Neil A. Parent.

National Conference of Diocesan Vocation Directors (NCDVD) (1961), P.O. Box 1570, Little River, SC 29566. Professional organization for diocesan vocation personnel providing resources and on-going education in their promoting, assessing and forming of candidates for the diocesan priesthood.

National Council for Catholic Evangelization (1983), 905 E. 166th St., P.O. Box 1260, S. Holland, IL 60473. To promote evangelization as the "primary and essential mission of the Church," in accordance with Evangelii Nuntiandi, the 1975 apostolic exhortation of Pope Paul VI. Pres., Rev. Carl Tenhundfeld; exec. dir., John Simon.

National Council of Catholic Men, 4712 Randolph Dr., Annandale, VA 22003. A federation of Catholic organizations through which Catholic men may be heard nationally on matters of common interest. NCCM is a constituent of the National Council of Catholic Laity.

National Council of Catholic Women (1920), 1275 K St. N.W., Suite 975, Washington, DC 20005. A federation of some 7,000 organizations of Catholic women in the U.S. *Catholic Woman,* bimonthly. NCCW unites Catholic organizations and individual Catholic women of the U.S., develops their leadership potential, assists them to act upon current issues in the Church and society, provides a medium through which Catholic women may speak and act upon matters of common interest, and relates to other national and international organizations in the solution of present-day problems. It is an affiliate of the World Union of Catholic Women's Organizations. Exec. Dir., Annette P. Kane.

National Evangelization Teams (NET), 110 Crusader Ave., West St. Paul, MN 55118. Trains Catholic young adults to be evangelists to peers and high school/junior high youth through traveling retreat teams.

National Federation of Priests' Councils (1968), 1337 West Ohio, Chicago, IL 60622. To give priests' councils a representative voice in matters of presbyteral, pastoral and ministerial concern to the U.S. and the universal Church. Pres., Rev. Donald Wolf; exec. dir., Bro. Bernard Stratman, S.M.

National Institute for the Word of God (1972), 487 Michigan Ave. N.E., Washington, DC 20017. For renewed biblical preaching, Bible sharing and evangelization. Dir., Rev. John Burke, O.P.

National Life Center, Inc., 686 N. Broad St., Woodbury, NJ 08096. Interdenominational guidance and referral service organization offering pregnant women alternatives to abortion. Pres., Denise F. Cocciolone,

National Organization for Continuing Education of Roman Catholic Clergy, Inc. (1973), 1337 W. Ohio St., Chicago, IL 60622. Membership: 152 dioceses, 66 religious provinces, 46 institutions, 49 individuals in U.S., 18 associates outside U.S. Pres., Rev. Francis S. Tebbe, O.F.M.; Exec. Dir., Bro. Paul J. Murray, C.F.X.

National Pastoral Life Center, 18 Bleeker St., New York, NY 10012. Services for parishes. Church, quarterly. Director, Rev. Philip Murnion.

NETWORK (1971), 801 Pennsylvania Ave. S.E., Suite 460, Washington, DC 20003. *NETWORK Connection,* bimonthly. A national Catholic social justice lobby. Nat. Coord., Kathy Thornton, R.S.M.

Nocturnal Adoration Society of the United States (1882), 184 E. 76th St., New York, NY 10021. Nat. Dir., Rev. Bernard J. Camire, S.S.S.

North American Academy of Liturgy, c/o CSSR Executive Office, Valparaiso Univ., Valparaiso, IN 46383. *Proceedings,* annually. Foster ecumenical and interreligious liturgical research, publication and dialogue on a scholarly level. Pres., Edward. Foley, O.F.M. Cap.

North American Conference of Separated and Divorced Catholics (1972), President, Kathy Brewer, P.O. Box 1301, LaGrande, OR 97850.

North American Forum on the Catechumenate, 3033 Fourth St. NE, Washington, DC 20017. An international network committed to the implementation of the Order of Christian Initiation of Adults. Exec. Dir., Thomas H. Morris.; Asst. Dir., Maureen A. Kelly.

Order of the Alhambra (1904), 4200 Leeds Ave., Baltimore, MD 21229. 7,000 in U.S. and Canada. Fraternal society dedicated to assisting developmentally disabled and handicapped children. Supreme Commander, Thomas G. Kelly.

Our Lady's Rosary Makers (1949), 4611 Poplar Level Rd., P.O. Box 37080, Louisville, KY 40233; 23,000 members. To supply missionaries with free rosaries for distribution throughout the world. News Bulletin, monthly. Pres., Harry Prestwood, Deacon.

Paulist National Catholic Evangelization Association (1977), 3031 Fourth St., N.E., Washington, DC 20017. *Share the Word,* bimonthly magazine; *Evangelization Update,* bimonthly newsletter. To work with unchurched and alienated Catholics; to develop, test and document contemporary ways in which Catholic parishes and dioceses can evangelize the unchurched and inactive Catholics. Dir., Rev. Kenneth Boyack, C.S.P.

Perpetual Eucharistic Adoration, 660 Club View Dr., Los Angeles, CA 90024. Promote programs of Perpetual Eucharistic adoration/exposition in parishes throughout the world.

Philangeli (Friends of the Angels) (1949 in England; 1956 in U.S.), Viatorian Fathers, 1115 E. Euclid St., Arlington Heights, IL 60004.

Pious Union of Prayer (1898), St. Joseph's Home, 541 Pavonia Ave., Jersey City, NJ 07306; 20,000. *St. Joseph's Messenger and Advocate of the Blind,* quarterly.

Polish Roman Catholic Union of America (1887): 984 N. Milwaukee Ave., Chicago, IL 60622. Narod Polski, bimonthly. Fraternal benefit society.

Pontifical Mission for Palestine (1949), 1011 First Ave., New York, NY 10022. A papal relief and development agency of the Holy See for the Middle East, with offices in New York, Vatican City, Amman, Beirut and Jerusalem.

Pontifical Missionary Union (1916), 366 Fifth Ave., New York, NY 10001. To promote mission awareness among clergy, religious, candidates to priestly and religious life, and others engaged in pastoral ministry of the Church. Nat. Dir., Most Rev. William J. McCormack; Nat. Sec., Rev. Eugene LaVerdiere, S.S.S.

Priests' Eucharistic League (1887), 5384 Wilson Mills Rd., Cleveland, OH 44143; 5,000. *Emmanuel,* 10 issues a year. Nat. Dir., Rev. Anthony Schueller, S.S.S.

Pro Ecclesia Foundation (1970), 350 5th Ave., Room 3304, New York, NY 10118. Pres., Dr. Timothy A. Mitchell.

Pro Maria Committee (1952), 22 Second Ave., Lowell, MA 01854. Promote devotion to Our Lady of Beauraing (See Index).

Pro Sanctity Movement. A worldwide force of laity organized to spread God's call of all persons to holiness. Addresses: 205 S. Pine Dr., Fullerton, CA 92633; 730 E. 87th St., Brooklyn, NY 11236; 6762 Western Ave., Omaha, NE 68132; 1102 N. 204 St. Elkhorn, NE 68022.

Project Children (1975), P.O. Box 933, Greenwood Lake, NY 10925. Nonsectarian volunteer group; provide children of Northern Ireland with a six-week summer vacation with host families in the U.S.

The Providence Association of the Ukrainian Catholics in America (Ukrainian Catholic Fraternal Benefit Society) (1912), 817 N. Franklin St., Philadelphia, PA 19123.

Queen of the Americas Guild, Inc. (1979), P.O. Box 851, 345 Kautz Rd., St. Charles, IL 60174; 7,000 members. To build English information center and retreat center near Basilica in Mexico City and spread the message of Guadalupe. Pres., Frank E. Smoczynski.

Raskob Foundation for Catholic Activities, Inc. (1945), Kennett Pike and Montchanin Rd., P.O. Box 4019, Wilmington, DE 19807. Pres., Gerard S. Garey.

Reparation Society of the Immaculate Heart of Mary, Inc. (1946), 100 E. 20th St., Baltimore, MD 21218. *Fatima Findings,* monthly.

Sacred Heart League, 6050 Hwy 61 N, P.O. Box 190, Walls, MS 38680. Pres., Rev. Robert Hess, S.C.J.

St. Ansgar's Scandinavian Catholic League (1910), 40 W. 13th St., New York, NY 10011; 1,000. *St. Ansgar's Bulletin,* annually. Prayers and financial support for Church in Scandinavia. Pres., Astrid M. O'Brien.

St. Anthony's Guild (1924), Paterson, NJ 07509; 100,000. Promotes devotion to St. Anthony of Padua and support for formation programs, infirm friars and ministries of the Franciscans of Holy Name Province. *The Anthonian,* quarterly. Dir., Rev. Joseph Hertel, O.F.M.

St. Bernadette Institute of Sacred Art (1993), P.O. Box 8249, Albuquerque, NM 87198. To promote, initiate, encourage interest and sustain projects and persons engaged in sacred art.

St. Gregory Foundation for Latin Liturgy (1989); To promote within the Church in the U.S. the use of the Latin language in the Mass in accordance with the teachings of Vatican II. Founder and Pres., Rev. Peter M.J. Stravinskas, Newman House, 21 Fairview Ave., Mount Pocono, PA 18344..

St. Jude League (1929), 205 W. Monroe St., Chicago, IL 60606. Promotes devotion to St. Jude; supports work of Claretian Missionaries throughout the world. Dir., Rev. Mark J. Brummel, C.M.F.

St. Margaret of Scotland Guild, Inc. (1938), Graymoor, Garrison, NY 10524; 500. Moderator, Bro. Nicholas De Gruccio, S.A.

St. Martin de Porres Guild (1935), 141 E. 65th St., New York, NY 10021. Dir., Rev. Edward L. Martin, O.P.

Serra International (1934), 65 E. Wacker Pl., suite 1210, Chicago, IL 60601; 21,000 members in 673 clubs in 35 countries. Serran, bimonthly. Fosters vocations to the priesthood, and religious life, trains Catholic lay leadership. Formally aggregated to the Pontifical Society for Priestly Vocations, 1951.

Slovak Catholic Federation (1911): Founded by Rev. Joseph Murgas to promote and coordinate religious activities among Slovak Catholic fraternal societies, religious communities and Slovak ethnic parishes in their effort to address themselves to the special needs of Slovak Catholics in the U.S. and Canada. Pres., Rev. Msgr. Thomas V. Banick, 134 S. Washington St., P.O. Box 348, Wilkes-Barre, PA 18703.

Slovak Catholic Sokol (1905), 205 Madison St., Passaic, NJ 07055; 38,000. Slovak Catholic Falcon, weekly. Fraternal benefit society.

Society for the Propagation of the Faith (1822), 366 Fifth Ave., New York, NY 10001; established in all dioceses. Church's principal instrument for promoting mission awareness and generating financial support for the missions. General fund for ordinary and extraordinary subsidies for all mission dioceses. *Mission,* 4 times a year; *Director's Newsletter,* monthly. Is subject to Congregation for the Evange-lization of Peoples. Nat. Dir., Most Rev. William J. McCormack.

Society of St. Monica (1986): 215 Falls Ave., Cuyahoga Falls, OH 44221; more than 10,000 members worldwide. Confident, daily prayer for the return of inactive Catholics and Catholics who have left the Church. Founder and spiritual director, Rev. Dennis M. McNeil.

Society of St. Peter Apostle (1889), 366 Fifth Ave., New York, NY 10001; all dioceses. Church's central fund for support of seminaries, seminarians and novices in all mission dioceses. Nat. Dir., Most Rev. William J. McCormack.

Society of the Divine Attributes (1974). Contemplative prayer society; 3,000 members worldwide (lay, clerical and religious). Spir. Dir. Rev. Ronald D. Lawler, O.F.M. Cap., 2905 Castlegate Ave., Pittsburgh, PA 15226.

Spiritual Life Institute of America (1960), Box 219, Crestone, CO 81131. Forefront, seasonal. An eremetical movement to foster the contemplative spirit in America. Founder, Rev. William McNamara, O.C.D. Second foundation: Nova Nada, Primitive Wilderness Hermitage, Kemptville, Nova Scotia, Canada B0W 1Y0. Third foundation, Holy Hill Hermitage, Skreen, Co. Sligo, Ireland.

Support Our Aging Religious (SOAR) (1986), 1400 Spring St., Suite 320, Silver Spring, MD 20910. Laity-led campaign to raise funds for retired religious.

Theresians of the United States (1961), 2577 N. Chelton Rd., Suite 207, Colorado Springs, CO 80909. Spiritual, educational and ministerial organization of Christian women. Exec. Dir., Sr. Rose Ann Barmann, O.S.B. International division: *Theresian World Ministry* (1971), same address.

United Societies of U.S.A. (1903), 613 Sinclair St., McKeesport, PA 15132; 3,755 members. Prosvita-Enlightenment, bimonthly newspaper.

United States Catholic Historical Society (1884), The Catholic Center, 1011 First Ave., New York, NY 10022. Chairman, Brian Butler. Exec Dir., Charles J. Eames.

Western Catholic Union (1877), 510 Maine St., Quincy, IL 62301; 19,000 members. *Western Catholic Union Record,* quarterly. A fraternal benefit society. Pres., Mark A. Wiewel.

Women for Faith and Family (1984), P.O. Box 8326, St. Louis, MO 63132. *Voices,* quarterly. An international movement to promote Catholic teachings especially on all issues involving the family and roles for women. Members sign an 8-point statement of fidelity to the Church; 60,000 signers worldwide. Dir., Helen Hull Hitchcock.

Young Ladies' Institute (1887), P.O. Box 640687, San Francisco, CA 94164; 13,000. *Voice of YLI,* bimonthly. Grand Sec., Claire Skidmore.

Young Men's Institute (1883), 50 Oak St., San Francisco, CA 94102; 4,500. *Institute Journal,* bimonthly. Grand Sec., S. J. Welch.

Mass Times: Mass Times (800 Masstim) is a free computerized search service developed by Robert Hummel of Key Largo, Fla., to help traveling Catholics find out where and when they can attend Mass in more than 20,000 churches in the United States. Hummel said about 6,000 inquiries were received a year.

COMMUNICATIONS

CATHOLIC PRESS STATISTICS

The *1997 Catholic Press Directory*, published by the Catholic Press Association, reported a total of 644 periodicals in North America with a circulation of 25,076,680. The figures included 199 newspapers with a circulation of 6,067,304; 272 magazines with a circulation of 14,639,749; 136 newsletters with a circulation of 3,800,394, and 37 other-language periodicals (newspapers and magazines) with a circulation of 569,228.

Newspapers in the U.S.

There were 185 newspapers in the United States, with a circulation 5,869,509. Five of these had national circulation; 167 were diocesan newspapers; 13 were Eastern Catholic Church publications.

National newspapers included: *National Catholic Register*, founded 1900; *Our Sunday Visitor*, founded 1912; *National Catholic Reporter*, founded 1964; *Catholic Twin Circle*, founded 1967 and *The Wanderer*.

The oldest Catholic newspaper in the United States is *The Pilot* of Boston, established in 1829 (under a different title).

Other Diocesan Newspapers: There were four other diocesan newspapers located outside continental North America (Puerto Rico, Samoa, U.S. Virgin Islands, West Indies), with a circulation of 81,700.

Magazines in U.S.

The *Catholic Press Directory* reported 250 magazines in the U.S. with a circulation of 13,778,138. In addition, there were 135 newsletters; circulation, 3,788,394.

America and *Commonweal* are the only weekly and biweekly magazines, respectively, of general interest.

The monthly magazines with the largest circulation are *Columbia* (1,454,282), the official organ of the Knights of Columbus, *Catholic Digest* (500,000) and *St. Anthony's Messenger* (341,673).

Other-Language Publications: There were an additional 25 publications (newspapers and magazines) in the U.S. in languages other than English with a circulation of 392,128.

Canadian Statistics

There were 10 newspapers in Canada with a circulation of 116,100. These included two national newspapers (*The Catholic Register*, founded 1893; *Catholic New Times*, founded 1976) and 8 diocesan.

There were 22 magazines with a circulation of 861,611; one newsletter with a circulation of 12,000; and 12 publications in languages other than English, circulation, 177,100.

CATHOLIC NEWSPAPERS AND MAGAZINES IN THE U.S.

(Sources: *Catholic Press Directory; The Catholic Journalist;* Almanac survey; Catholic News Service.)

Abbreviation code: a, annual; bm, bimonthly; m, monthly; q, quarterly; w, weekly.

Newspapers

Acadiana Catholic, m; 1408 Carmel Ave., Lafayette, LA 70501; Lafayette diocese.

A.D. Times, biweekly; 2141 Downyflake Lane, Allentown, PA 18103. Allentown diocese.

Agua Viva, m; 1280 Med Park Dr., Las Cruces, NM 88005; Las Cruces diocese.

Alaskan Shepherd, 6 times a year; 1312 Peger Rd., Fairbanks, AK 99709; Fairbanks diocese.

America (Ukrainian-English), 2 times a week; 817 N. Franklin St., Philadelphia, PA 19123. Providence Association of Ukrainian Catholics in America.

Anchor, The, w; P.O. Box 7, Fall River, MA 02722; Fall River diocese.

Arkansas Catholic, w; P.O. Box 7417, Little Rock, AR 72217; Little Rock diocese.

Arlington Catholic Herald, w; 200 N. Glebe Rd., Suite 607, Arlington, VA 22203; Arlington diocese.

Bayou Catholic, The, w; P.O. Box 9077, Houma, LA 70361; Houma-Thibodaux diocese.

Beacon, The, w; P.O. Box 1887, Clifton, NJ 07015. Paterson diocese.

Bishop's Bulletin, m; P.O. Box 665, Yankton, SD 57078. Sioux Falls diocese.

Byzantine Catholic World, biweekly; 925 Liberty Ave., P.O. Box 1215, Pittsburgh, PA 15230; Pittsburgh Byzantine archdiocese.

Catholic Accent, 40 times a year; P.O. Box 850, Greensburg, PA 15601; Greensburg diocese.

Catholic Advance, The, w; 424 N. Broadway, Wichita, KS 67202; Wichita diocese.

Catholic Advocate, The, w; 171 Clifton Ave., Newark, NJ 07104; Newark archdiocese.

Catholic Calendar, semi-monthly; 4029 Avenue G, Lake Charles, LA 70615; one page in local newspaper twice a month; Lake Charles diocese.

Catholic Chronicle, biweekly; P.O. Box 1866, Toledo, OH 43603; Toledo diocese.

Catholic Commentator, The, biweekly; P.O. Box 14746, Baton Rouge, LA 70898; Baton Rouge diocese.

Catholic Connector, The, m; 660 Burton, SE, Grand Rapids, MI 49507; Grand Rapids diocese.

Catholic Courier, w; 1150 Buffalo Rd., Rochester, NY 14624. Rochester diocese.

Catholic East Texas, biweekly; 1015 ESE Loop 323, Tyler, TX 75701. Tyler diocese.

Catholic Exponent, biweekly; P.O. Box 6787, Youngstown, OH 44501; Youngstown diocese.

Catholic Free Press, w; 47 Elm St., Worcester, MA 01609; Worcester diocese.

Catholic Herald, The, m; 29 W. Kiowa St., Colorado Springs, CO 80903; Colorado Springs diocese.

Catholic Herald, w; P.O. Box 07913, Milwaukee, WI 53207; Milwaukee archdiocese. Also publishes editions for Madison and Superior dioceses.

Catholic Herald — Madison Edition, w; P.O. Box 5913, Madison, WI 53705.

Catholic Herald — Superior Edition, w; P.O. Box 969, Superior, WI 54880.

Catholic Herald, biweekly; 5890 Newman Ct., Sacramento, CA 95819; Sacramento diocese.

Catholic Key, 44 times a year; P.O. Box 419037, Kansas City, MO 64141; Kansas City-St. Joseph diocese.

Catholic Lantern, m; P.O. Box 4237, Stockton, CA 95204; Stockton diocese.

Catholic Light, biweekly; P.O. Box 708, Scranton, PA 18501; Scranton diocese.

Catholic Lighthouse, m; P.O. Box 4070, Victoria, TX 77903; Victoria diocese.

Catholic Messenger, w; P.O. Box 460, Davenport, IA 52805; Davenport diocese.

Catholic Mirror The, m; P.O. Box 10372, Des Moines, IA 50306. Des Moines diocese.

Catholic Missourian, w; P.O. Box 1107, Jefferson City, MO 65102; Jefferson City diocese.

Catholic Moment, The, w; P.O. Box 1603, Lafayette, IN 47902; Lafayette diocese.

Catholic New York, w; P.O. Box 5133, New York, NY 10150; New York archdiocese.

Catholic News and Herald, The, w; 1524 E. Morehead St., Charlotte, NC 28207. Charlotte diocese.

Catholic Northwest Progress,The, w; 910 Marion St., Seattle, WA 98104; Seattle archdiocese.

Catholic Observer, biweekly; Box 1570, Springfield, MA 01101; Springfield diocese.

Catholic Post, The, w; P.O. Box 1722, Peoria, IL 61656; Peoria diocese.

Catholic Register, biweekly; 126C Logan Blvd., Hollidaysburg, PA 16648; Altoona-Johnstown diocese.

Catholic Review, w; P.O. Box 777, Baltimore, MD 21203; Baltimore archdiocese.

Catholic Sentinel, w; P.O. Box 18030, Portland, OR 97218; Portland archdiocese, Baker diocese.

Catholic Spirit, The, w; 244 Dayton Ave., St. Paul, MN 55102; St. Paul and Minneapolis archdiocese.

Catholic Spirit, The, w; P.O. Box 5247, Kendall Park, NJ 08824; Metuchen diocese.

Catholic Spirit, The, m; P.O. Box 13327, Capitol Sta., Austin, TX 78711; Austin diocese.

Catholic Spirit, The, m; P.O. Box 951, Wheeling, WV 26003; Wheeling-Charleston diocese.

Catholic Standard, w; P.O. Box 4464, Washington, DC 20017; Washington archdiocese.

Catholic Standard and Times, w; 222 N. 17th St., Philadelphia, PA 19103; Philadelphia archdiocese.

Catholic Star Herald, w; 1845 Haddon Ave., Camden, NJ 08101; Camden diocese.

Catholic Sun, The, semimonthly; 400 E. Monroe, Phoenix, AZ 85004; Phoenix diocese.

Catholic Sun, The, w; 421 S. Warren St., Syracuse, NY 13202; Syracuse diocese.

Catholic Telegraph, w; 100 E. 8th St., Cincinnati, OH 45202; Cincinnati archdiocese.

Catholic Times, w; 197 E. Gay St., Columbus, OH 43215; Columbus diocese.

Catholic Times, w; P.O. Box 4248, Flint, MI 48504. Lansing diocese.

Catholic Times, w; 1615 W. Washington St., P.O. Box 3187, Springfield, IL 62708; Springfield diocese.

Catholic Today, m; P.O. Box 31,Tucson,AZ 85702; Tucson diocese.

Catholic Transcript, w; 785 Asylum Ave., Hartford, CT 06105; Hartford archdiocese; Bridgeport and Norwich dioceses.

Catholic Twin Circle, w; 33 Rosotto Dr., Hamden, CT 06514; national.

Catholic Universe Bulletin, biweekly; 1027 Superior Ave. N.E., Cleveland, OH 44114; Cleveland diocese.

Catholic Virginian, biweekly; Box 26843, Richmond, VA 23261; Richmond diocese.

Catholic Voice, The, biweekly; 3014 Lakeshore Ave., Oakland, CA 94610; Oakland diocese.

Catholic Voice, The, biweekly; P.O. Box 4010, Omaha, NE 68104; Omaha archdiocese.

Catholic Week, w; P.O. Box 349, Mobile, AL 36601; Mobile archdiocese.

Catholic Weekly,The, w; 1520 Court St., Saginaw, MI 48602; Saginaw diocese.

Catholic Weekly,The, w; P.O. Box 1405, Saginaw, MI 48605. Gaylord diocese.

Catholic Witness, The, biweekly; P.O. Box 2555, Harrisburg, PA 17105; Harrisburg diocese.

Catolico de Texas, El (Spanish), m; P.O. Box 190347, Dallas, TX 75219; Dallas diocese.

Centinela, El (Spanish), m; P.O.Box 18030, Portland, OR 97216.

Central Washington Catholic, 6 times a year; 5301-A Tieton Dr., Yakima, WA 98908. Yakima diocese.

Challenge,The, semimonthly; 2530 Victory Pkwy., Cincinnati, OH 45206. St. Maron diocese.

Chicago Catolico (Spanish), m; 1144 W. Jackson Blvd., Chicago, IL 60607; Chicago archdiocese.

Chronicle of Catholic Life, bm; 1001 N. Grand Ave., Colorado Springs, CO 81003; Pueblo diocese.

Church Today, twice a month; P.O. Box 7417, Alexandria, LA 71306; Alexandria diocese.

Church World, w; Industry Rd., P.O. Box 698, Brunswick, ME 04011; Portland diocese.

Clarion Herald, biweekly; P.O. Box 53247, New Orleans, LA 70153; New Orleans archdiocese.

Common Sense, w; P. O. Box 341669, Memphis, TN 38184; Memphis diocese.

Community, w; P.O. Box 24000, Jacksonville, FL 32241; half-page weekly in Sunday editions of two daily newspapers; St. Augustine diocese.

Compass,The, w; P.O. Box 23825, Green Bay, WI 54305; Green Bay diocese.

Courier, The, m; P.O. Box 949, Winona, MN 55987; Winona diocese.

Criterion, The, w; P.O. Box 1717, Indianapolis, IN 46206; Indianapolis archdiocese.

Cross Roads, 26 times a year; 1310 Leestown Rd., Lexington, KY 40508. Lexington diocese.

Dakota Catholic Action, m (exc. May and Aug.); P.O. Box 1137, Bismarck, ND 58502; Bismarck diocese.

Darbininkas (The Worker) (Lithuanian), w; 341 Highland Blvd., Brooklyn, NY 11207; Lithuanian Franciscans.

Denver Catholic Register, w; 200 Josephine St., Denver, CO 80206; Denver archdiocese.

Dialog, The, w; P.O. Box 2208, Wilmington, DE 19899; Wilmington diocese.

Diocese of Orange Bulletin, m; P.O. Box 14195, Orange, CA 92613.

East Tennessee Catholic, The, biweekly; P.O. Box 11127, Knoxville, TN 37939; Knoxville diocese.
East Texas Catholic, semimonthly; P.O. Box 3948, Beaumont, TX 77704; Beaumont diocese.
Eastern Catholic Life, biweekly; 445 Lackawanna Ave., W. Paterson, NJ 07424; Passaic Byzantine eparchy.
Eastern Oklahoma Catholic, biweekly; Box 520, Tulsa, OK 74101; Tulsa diocese.
Evangelist, The, w; 40 N. Main Ave., Albany, NY 12203; Albany diocese.

Fairfield County Catholic, m; 238 Jewett Ave., Bridgeport, CT 06606; Bridgeport diocese.
Florida Catholic, The, w; P.O. Box 609512, Orlando, FL 32860; Orlando diocese. Publishes editions for Miami archdiocese and Palm Beach, Pensacola-Tallahassee, St. Petersburg and Venice dioceses.
Florida Catholic — Miami Edition, w; 9401 Biscayne Blvd., Miami, FL 33138.
Florida Catholic — Palm Beach Edition, w; 9995 N. Military Trail, Palm Beach Gardens, FL 33410.
Florida Catholic — Pensacola-Tallahassee Edition, w; 11 North B St., Pensacola, FL 32501.
Florida Catholic — St. Petersburg Edition, w; P.O. Box 43022, St. Petersburg, FL 33743.
Florida Catholic — Venice Edition, w; 1000 Pinebrook Rd., Venice, FL 34292.
Four County Catholic, m; 1595 Norwich New London Turnpike, Uncasville, CT 06382. Norwich diocese.

Georgia Bulletin, w; 680 W. Peachtree St. N.W., Atlanta, GA 30308; Atlanta archdiocese.
Glasilo KSKJH Amerikanski Slovenec (Slovenian), biweekly; 708 E. 159th, Cleveland, OH 44110; American Slovenian Catholic Union.
Globe, The, w; 1825 Jackson St., Sioux City, IA 51105; Sioux City diocese.
Gulf Pine Catholic, w; P.O. Box 1189, Biloxi, MS 39533; Biloxi diocese.

Hawaii Catholic Herald, biweekly; 1184 Bishop St., Honolulu, HI 96813; Honolulu diocese.
Heraldo Catolico, El (Spanish), biweekly; 5890 Newman Ct., Sacramento, CA 95819; Sacramento diocese.
Hlas Naroda (Voice of the Nation) (Czech-English), biweekly; 2340 61st Ave., Cicero, IL 60650.
Horizons, twice a month; 1900 Carlton Rd., Parma, OH 44134; Parma Byzantine eparchy.

Idaho Catholic Register, twice a month; 303 Federal Way, Boise, ID 83705; Boise diocese.
Inland Catholic, m; 1201 E. Highland Ave., San Bernardino, CA 92404. San Bernardino diocese.
Inland Register, every 3 weeks; P.O. Box 48, Spokane, WA 99210; Spokane diocese.
Inside Passage, biweekly; 419 6th St., Juneau, AK 99801; Juneau diocese.
Intermountain Catholic, w; P.O. Box 2489, Salt Lake City, UT 84110; Salt Lake City diocese.

Jednota (Slovak-Eng.), w; 6611 Rockside Rd., Independence, OH 44131; First Catholic Slovak Union.

Lake Shore Visitor, w; P.O. Box 10668, Erie, PA 16514; Erie diocese.
Leaven, The, w; 12615 Parallel Parkway, Kansas City, KS 66109; Kansas City archdiocese.
Long Island Catholic, The, w; P.O. Box 9009, Rockville Centre, NY 11571; Rockville Centre diocese.

Maronites Today, m; P.O. Box 1891, Austin, TX 78767; Maronite Epachy of Our lady of Lebanon of Los Angeles.
Message, The, w; P.O. Box 4169, Evansville, IN 47724; Evansville diocese.
Messenger, The, w; 2620 Lebanon Ave., Belleville, IL 62221; Belleville diocese.
Messenger, The, 45 times a year; P.O. Box 18068, Covington, KY 41018; Covington diocese.
Michigan Catholic, The, w; 305 Michigan Ave., Detroit, MI 48226; Detroit archdiocese.
Mirror, The, w; 601 S. Jefferson Ave., Springfield, MO 65806; Springfield-Cape Girardeau diocese.
Mississippi Today, w; P.O. Box 2130, Jackson, MS 39225; Jackson diocese.
Monitor, The , w; P.O. Box 3095, Trenton, NJ 08619; Trenton diocese.
Montana Catholic, The, 16 times a year; P.O. Box 1729, Helena, MT 59624; Helena diocese.

Narod Polski (Polish Nation) (Polish-Eng.) semimonthly; 984 Milwaukee Ave., Chicago, IL 60622.
National Catholic Register, w; 33 Rosotto Dr., Hamden, CT 06514; national.
National Catholic Reporter, w; P.O. Box 419281, Kansas City, MO 64141 ; national.
New Catholic Explorer, w (biweekly July, Aug.); 402 S. Independence Blvd., Romeoville, IL 60446; Joliet diocese.
New Catholic Miscellany, The, w; 119 Broad St., Charleston, SC 29401; Charleston diocese.
New Earth, The, m; 244 Dayton Ave., St. Paul, MN 55102. Fargo diocese.
New Star, The, every 3 weeks; 2208 W. Chicago Ave., Chicago, IL 60622; St. Nicholas of Chicago Ukrainian diocese.
New World, The, w; 1144 W. Jackson Blvd., Chicago, IL 60607; Chicago archdiocese.
Newsletter, The, 9 times a year; 215 N. Westnedge, Kalamazoo, MI 49007; Kalamazoo diocese.
NC Catholic, 26 times a year; 300 Cardinal Gibbons Dr., Raleigh, NC 27606. Raleigh diocese.
North Country Catholic, w; P.O. Box 326, Ogdensburg, NY 13669; Ogdensburg diocese.
North Texas Catholic, w; 800 West Loop 820 South, Fort Worth, TX 76108; Fort Worth diocese.
Northwest Indiana Catholic, w; 9292 Broadway, Merrillville, IN 46410; Gary diocese.
Northwestern Kansas Register, w; P.O. Box 1038, Salina, KS 67402; Salina diocese.

Observer, The, m; P.O. Box 2079, Monterey, CA 93942; Monterey diocese.
Observer, The, twice a month; 921 W. State St., Rockford, IL 61102; Rockford diocese.

One Voice, w; P.O. Box 10822, Birmingham, AL 35202; Birmingham diocese.
Our Northland Diocese, semi-monthly; P.O. Box 610, Crookston, MN 56716; Crookston diocese.
Our Sunday Visitor, w; 200 Noll Plaza, Huntington, IN 46750; national.

People of God, m; 4000 St. Joseph Pl. N.W., Albuquerque, NM 87120; Santa Fe archdiocese.
Pilot, The, w; 49 Franklin St., Boston, MA 02110; Boston archdiocese.
Pittsburgh Catholic, w; 135 First Ave., Suite 200, Pittsburgh, PA 15222; Pittsburgh diocese.
Prairie Catholic, m; 1400 6th St. North, New Ulm, MN 56073. New Ulm diocese.
Pregonero, El (Spanish), w; P.O. Box 4464, Washington, DC 20017; Washington archdiocese.
Providence Visitor, The, w; 184 Broad St., Providence, RI 02903. Providence diocese.

Record, The, w; 1200 S. Shelby St., Louisville, KY 40203; Louisville archdiocese.
Redwood Crozier, The, m; P.O. Box 1297, Santa Rosa, CA 95402; Santa Rosa diocese.
Rio Grande Catholic, The, 12 times a year; 499 St. Matthews St., El Paso, TX 79907; El Paso diocese.

St. Cloud Visitor, w; P. O. Box 1068, St. Cloud, MN 56302; St. Cloud diocese.
St. Louis Review, w; 462 N. Taylor Ave., St. Louis, MO 63108; St. Louis archdiocese.
Seasons, q; 5800 Weiss St., Saginaw, MI 48603.
Slovak Catholic Falcon (Slovak-English), w; 205 Madison St., P.O.Box 899, Passaic, NJ 07055; Slovak Catholic Sokol.
Sooner Catholic, The, biweekly; P.O. Box 32180, Oklahoma City, OK 73123; Oklahoma City archdiocese.
Sophia, q; 11245 Rye St., North Hollywood, CA 91602; Newton Melkite eparchy.
South Plains Catholic, twice a month; P.O. Box 98700, Lubbock, TX 79499; Lubbock diocese.
South Texas Catholic, biweekly; 1200 Lantana St., Corpus Christi, TX 78407; Corpus Christi diocese.
Southern Cross, semimonthly; P.O. Box 81869, San Diego, CA 92138; San Diego diocese.
Southern Cross, The, w; 601 E. Liberty Street, Savannah, GA 31401; Savannah diocese.
Southern Nebraska Register, w; P.O. Box 80329, Lincoln, NE 68501; Lincoln diocese.
Southwest Catholic, m; 4029 Avenue G, Lake Charles, LA 70615 Lake Charles diocese.
Southwest Kansas Register, biweekly; P.O. Box 137, Dodge City, KS 67801; Dodge City diocese.
Sower (Ukrainian and English), biweekly; 14 Peveril Rd., Stamford, CT 06902. Stamford Ukrainian diocese.
Star of Chaldeans (Arabic and English), bm; 25585 Berg Rd., Southfield, MI 48034. St. Thomas the Apostle Chaldean diocese.
Steubenville Register, biweekly; P.O. Box 160, Steubenville, OH 43952; Steubenville diocese.

Tablet, The, w; 653 Hicks St., Brooklyn, NY 11231; Brooklyn diocese.

Tennessee Register, The, biweekly; 2400 21st Ave. S., Nashville, TN 37212; Nashville diocese.
Texas Catholic, biweekly; P.O. Box 190347, Dallas, TX 75219; Dallas diocese.
Texas Catholic Herald, The, twice a month; 1700 San Jacinto St., Houston, TX 77002; Galveston-Houston diocese.
Tidings, 11 times a year; 153 Ash St., Manchester, NH 03105.
Tidings, The, w; 3424 Wilshire Blvd, Los Angeles, CA 90010; Los Angeles archdiocese.
Times Review, The, w; P.O. Box 4004, La Crosse, WI 54602; La Crosse diocese.
Today's Catholic, w; P.O. Box 11169, Fort Wayne, IN 46856; Fort Wayne-S. Bend diocese.
Today's Catholic, biweekly; P.O. Box 28410, San Antonio, TX 78228; San Antonio archdiocese.

UNIREA (The Union) (Romanian) (10 times a year), 1121 44th St. N.E., Canton, OH 44714; Romanian diocese of Canton.
U. P. Catholic, The, semi-monthly; P.O. Box 548, Marquette, MI 49855; Marquette diocese.

Valley Catholic, m; 900 Lafayette St., Suite 301, Santa Clara, CA 95050; San Jose diocese.
Vermont Catholic Tribune, biweekly; 351 North Ave., Burlington, VT 05401; Burlington diocese.
Vida Nueva (Spanish), w; 3424 Wilshire Blvd., Los Angeles, CA 90010; Los Angeles archdiocese.
Visitante de Puerto Rico, El (Spanish), w; Apartado 41305, Est Minillas, San Juan, PR 00940. Puerto Rican Catholic Conference.
Voice of the Southwest, m; 414 N. Allen, Farmington, NM 87401; Gallup diocese.
Voz Catolica, La (Spanish); m; 9401 Biscayne Blvd., Miami, FL 33138; Miami archdiocese.

Wanderer, The, w; 201 Ohio St., St. Paul, MN 55107; national.
The Way (Ukrainian-Eng.), biweekly; 827 N. Franklin St., Philadelphia, PA 19123; Philadelphia archeparchy.
West Nebraska Register, w; P.O. Box 608, Grand Island, NE 68802; Grand Island diocese.
West River Catholic, m; P.O. Box 678, Rapid City, SD 57709; Rapid City diocese.
West Texas Angelus, m; P.O. Box 1829, San Angelo, TX 76902; San Angelo diocese.
West Texas Catholic, biweekly; P.O. Box 5644, Amarillo, TX 79117; Amarillo diocese.
Western Kentucky Catholic, m; 600 Locust St., Owensboro, KY 42301; Owensboro diocese.
Western New York Catholic, m; 795 Main St., Buffalo, NY 14203; Buffalo diocese.
Witness, The, w; P.O. Box 917, Dubuque, IA 52004; Dubuque archdiocese.
Wyoming Catholic Register, m; P.O. Box 1308, Cheyenne, WY 82003; Cheyenne diocese.

Magazines
Action News, q; 6160 North Cicero Ave., Chicago, IL 60646; Pro-Life Action League.
AIM: Liturgy Resources, q; P.O. Box 2703, Schiller Park, IL 60176.

America, w; 106 W. 56th St., New York, NY 10019. Jesuits of U.S. and Canada.

American Benedictine Review, q; Assumption Abbey, Box A, Richardton, ND 58652.

American Catholic Philosophical Quarterly (formerly The New Scholasticism), Institute of Philosophical Studies, Univ. of Dallas, Irving, TX 75062. American Catholic Philosophical Assn.

American Midland Naturalist, q; Notre Dame, IN 46556.

Anthonian, The, q; Paterson, NJ 07509; St. Anthony's Guild.

Anthropological Quarterly; 620 Michigan Ave. N.E., Washington, DC 20064.

Apostolate of the Little Flower, bm; P.O. Box 5280, San Antonio, TX 78201; Discalced Carmelite Fathers.

Association of Marian Helpers Bulletin, q; Eden Hill Stockbridge, MA 01263. Congregation of Marians.

Atchison Benedictines, q; Mount St. Scholastica Convent, 801 S. 8th St., Atchison, KS 66002.

Augustinian Journey, m; 101 Barry Rd., Worcester, MA 01609.

Barry Magazine, 2 times a year; 11300 NE 2nd Ave., Miami Shores, FL 33161; Barry Univ.

Bible Today, The, bm; Liturgical Press, Collegeville, MN 56321.

Biblical Theology Bulletin, q; P.O. Box 1038, South Orange, NJ 07079.

BLUEPRINT for Social Justice, 10 times a year; Twomey Center for Peace through Justice, Loyola University, Box 12, New Orleans, LA 70118.

Bolletino, m; 1801 Van Ness Ave., Suite 330, San Francisco, CA 94109; Italian Catholic Federation.

Brothers Voice, 5 times a year; 1337 W. Ohio St. Chicago, IL 60622; National Association of Religious Brothers.

Caelum et Terra, q; P.O. Box 1494, Wooster, OH 44691. Journal of Catholic Culture.

Carmelite Digest, q; P.O. Box 3180, San Jose, CA 95156.

Carmelite Review, The, m; 8433 Bailey Rd., Darien, IL 60561. Canadian-American Province of Carmelite Order.

Catechist, The, 7 times a year; 330 Pogress Rd., Dayton, OH 45449.

Catechumenate: A Journal of Christian Initiation, 6 times a year; 1800 N. Hermitage Ave., Chicago, IL 60622.

Catholic Aid News, m; 3499 N. Lexington Ave., St. Paul, MN 55126.

Catholic Answer, The, bm; 200 Noll Plaza, Huntington, IN 46750; Our Sunday Visitor.

Catholic Biblical Quarterly; Catholic University of America, Washington, DC 20064; Catholic Biblical Assn.

Catholic Cemetery, The, m; 710 N. River Rd., Des Plaines, IL 60016; National Catholic Cemetery Conference.

Catholic Digest, m; P.O. Box 64090, St. Paul, MN 55164.

Catholic Digest Reader, q; P.O. Box 64090, St. Paul, MN 55164. Large print magazine.

Catholic Dossier, bm; P.O. Box 591120, San Francisco, CA 94159.

Catholic Faith, The, bm; P.O. Box 591120, San Francisco, CA 94159.

Catholic Forester Magazine, bm; 355 Shuman Blvd., P.O. Box 3012, Naperville, IL 60566; Catholic Order of Foresters.

CGA World, q; P.O. Box 3658, Scranton, PA 18505. Catholic Golden Age.

Catholic Health World, semimonthly; 4455 Woodson Rd., St. Louis, MO 63134. Catholic Health Association.

Catholic Heritage, bm; 200 Noll Plaza, Huntington, IN 46750. Our Sunday Visitor.

Catholic Historical Review, q; 620 Michigan Ave. N.E., Washington, DC 20064.

Catholic International, m; Cathedral Foundation, P.O. Box 777, Baltimore, MD 21203.

Catholic Journalist, The, m; 3555 Veterans Highway, Unit O, Ronkonkoma, NY 11779; Catholic Press Association.

C.K. of A. Journal, m; 1850 Dalton St., Cincinnati, OH 45214; Catholic Knights of America.

Catholic Lawyer, q; St. John's University, Jamaica, NY 11439; St. Thomas More Institute for Legal Research.

Catholic Library World, 4 times a year; 9009 Carter Ave., Allen Park, MI 48101; Catholic Library Association.

Catholic Near East Magazine, bm; 1011 First Ave., New York, NY 10022; Catholic Near East Welfare Assn.

Catholic Outlook, m; 2830 E. 4th St., Duluth, MN 55812; Duluth diocese.

Catholic Parent, bm; 200 Noll Plaza, Huntington, IN 46750; Our Sunday Visitor.

Catholic Peace Voice, q; 348 E. 10th St., Erie, PA 16503; Pax Christi USA.

Catholic Pharmacist, q; 1012 Surrey Hills Dr., St. Louis, MO 63117; National Catholic Pharmacists Guild.

Catholic Press Directory, a; 3555 Veterans Highway, Unit O, Ronkonkoma, NY 11779; Catholic Press Assn.

Catholic Quote, m; Valparaiso, NE 68065.

Catholic Review (Braille, tape, large print), bm; 154 E. 23rd St., New York, NY 10010; Xavier Society for the Blind.

Catholic Rural Life, twice a year; 4625 Beaver Ave., Des Moines, IA 50310.

Catholic Singles Magazine, two times a year; 8408 S. Muskegon, Chicago, IL 60617.

Catholic Telephone Guide, a; 210 North Ave., New Rochelle, NY 10801.

Catholic University of America Law Review, q; Washington, DC 20064.

Catholic War Veteran, bm; 441 N. Lee St., Alexandria, VA 22314.

Catholic Woman, bm; 1275 K St. N.W., Suite 975, Washington, DC 20005. National Council of Catholic Women.

Catholic Women's Network, bm; 877 Spinosa Dr., Sunnyvale, CA 94087.

Catholic Worker, 7 times a year; 36 E. First St., New York, NY 10003. Catholic Worker Movement.

Catholic Workman, m; 111 W. Main, P.O. Box 47, New Prague, MN 56071.

Catholic World Report, The, 11 times a year; P.O. Box 1328, Dedham, MA 02027 (editorial office). Ignatius Press.

Celebration, m; 207 Hillsboro Dr., Silver Spring, MD 20902; National Catholic Reporter Publishing Co.

Charities USA, q; 1731 King St., Suite 200, Alexandria, VA 22314.

Chicago Studies, 3 times a year; 1800 N. Hermitage Ave., Chicago, IL 60622.

Christian Renewal News, 4 times a year; 411 First St., Flllmore, CA 93016. Apostolate of Christian Renewal.

Church, q; 18 Bleeker St., St., New York, NY 10012; National Pastoral Life Center.

Cistercian Studies Quarterly; Santa Rita Abbey, HC 1, Box 929, Sonoita, AZ 85637; international review of monastic and contemplative spirituality, history and theology.

Columban Mission, 8 times a year; St. Columbans, NE 68056; Columban Fathers.

Columbia, m; One Columbus Plaza, New Haven, CT 06510; Knights of Columbus.

Commonweal, biweekly; 475 Riverside Dr., Room 405, New York, NY 10115.

Communio — International Catholic Review, q; P.O. Box 4557, Washington, D.C. 20017.

Company, q; 3441 N. Ashland Ave., Chicago, IL 60657. Jesuit Magazine.

Concilium, 5 times a year; Orbis Books, Walsh Bldg., Box 308, Maryknoll, NY 10545.

Consecrated Life, semi-annually; P.O. Box 41007, Chicago, IL 60641; Institute on Religious Life. English edition of Informationes, official publication of Congregation for Institutes of Consecrated Life and Societies of Apostolic Life.

Consolata Missionaries, bm; P.O. Box 5550, Somerset, NJ 08875.

Cord, The, m; P.O. Drawer F, St. Bonaventure, NY 14778; Franciscan Institute.

Counseling and Values, 3 times a year; Dept. of Educational Psychology and Special Education, Southern Illinois Univ., Carbondale, IL 62901.

Crescat, 3 times a year; Belmont Abbey, Belmont, NC 28012; Benedictine Monks.

Crisis, 11 times a year; 1511 K Street NW, Suite 525, Washington, DC; Journal of lay Catholic opinion.

Critic, The, q; 205 W. Monroe St., 6th floor, Chicago, IL 60606. Thomas More Assn.

Cross Currents, q; College of New Rochelle, New Rochelle, NY 10805; interreligious; Association for Religion and Intellectual Life.

CUA Magazine, 3 times a year; 620 Michigan Ave. N.E., Washington, DC 20064.

Deaf Blind Weekly, The (Braille), w; 154 E. 23rd St., New York, NY 10010; Xavier Society for the Blind.

DeSales World, The, twice a year; P.O. Box 1452, Wilmington, DE 19899.

Diakonia, 3 times a year; Univ. of Scranton, Scranton, PA 18510; Center for Eastern Christian Studies.

Divine Word Missionaries, q; Techny, IL 60082.

Ecumenical Trends, m (exc. Aug.); Graymoor, Route 9, P.O. Box 306, Garrison, NY 10524; Graymoor Ecumenical Institute.

Eglute (The Little Fir Tree) (Lithuanian), m; 13648 Keckapoo Trail, Lockport, IL 60441; children ages 5-10.

Emmanuel, 10 times a year; 5384 Wilson Mills Rd., Cleveland, OH 44143; Congregation of Blessed Sacrament.

Envoy, bm; P.O. Box 65, Drexel Hill, PA 19026. Journal of Catholic apolgetics and evangelization.

Eternal Flame (Armenian-Engish), 110 E. 12th St., New York, NY 10003; Armenian exarchate.

Explorations, q; 321 Chestnut St., Philadelphia, PA 19106; American Interfaith Institute.

Extension, 12 times a year; 35 E. Wacker Dr., Suite 400, Chicago, IL 60601; Catholic Church Extension Society.

Faith and Reason, q; 134 Christendom Dr., Front Royal, VA 22630.

Family Digest, The, bm; P.O. Box 40137, Fort Wayne, IN 46804 (editorial address).

Family Friend, q; P.O. Box 11563, Milwaukee, WI 53211; Catholic Family Life Insurance.

Fidelity, m; 206 Marquette Ave., South Bend, IN 46617.

Flame, The, 2 times a year; Barry Univ., 11300 N.E. 2nd Ave., Miami Shores, FL 33161.

Forefront, q; Box 219, Crestone, CO 81131; Spiritual Life Institute of America.

F.M.A. Focus, q; P.O. Box 598, Mt. Vernon, NY 10551; Franciscan Mission Associates.

Franciscan Studies, a; St. Bonaventure, NY 14778; Franciscan Institute.

Franciscan Way, q; University Blvd., Steubenville, OH 43952.

Fraternal Leader, q; P.O. Box 13005; Erie, PA 16514; Loyal Christian Benefit Association.

Fraternally Yours (Eng.-Slovak), m; 24950 Chagrin Blvd., Beachwood, OH 44122; First Catholic Slovak Ladies Assn.

Glenmary Challenge, The, q; P.O. Box 465618, Cincinnati, OH 45246; Glenmary Home Missioners.

God's Word Today, m; P. O. Box 64088, St. Paul, MN 55164. Univ. of St. Thomas.

Good News, m; P.O. Box 432, Milwaukee, WI 53201. Liturgical Publications.

Good News for Children, 32 times during school year; 330 Progress Rd., Dayton, OH 45449.

Good Shepherd (Dobry Pastier) (Slovak-English), a; 8200 McKnight Rd., Pittsburgh, PA 15237.

Greyfriars Review, 3 times a year; St. Bonventure Univ., St. Bonaventure, NY 14778; Franciscan Institute.

Guide to Religious Ministries, A, a; 210 North Ave., New Rochelle, NY 10801.

Health Progress, bm; 4455 Woodson Rd., St. Louis, MO 63134; Catholic Health Association.

Hearts Aflame, q; P.O. Box 976, Washington, NJ 07882. For youth (13-23).

HNP, bm; 127 W. 31st St., New York, NY 10001 Holy Name Province, OFM.

Homiletic and Pastoral Review, m; 86 Riverside Dr., New York, NY 10024.

Horizon, 4 times a year; 1603 S. Michigan Ave. No. 400, Chicago, IL 60616.

Horizons, 2 times a year; Villanova University, Villanova, PA 19085. College Theology Society.

Human Development, q; c/o St. John's Seminary, 127 Lake St., Brighton, MA 02135.

Immaculata, 6 times a year; 1600 W. Park Ave., Libertyville, IL 60048.

Immaculate Heart Messenger, q; P.O. Box 158, Alexandria, SD 57311.

In a Word, m; 199 Seminary Dr., Bay Saint Louis, MS 39520; Society of the Divine Word.

Jesuit Bulletin, 3 times a year; 4511 W. Pine Blvd., St. Louis, MO 63108; Jesuit Seminary Aid Association.

Jesuit Journeys, 3 times a year; 3400 W. Wisconsin Ave., Milwaukee, WI 53208.

Josephite Harvest, The, q; 1130 N. Calvert St., Baltimore, MD 21202; Josephite Missionaries.

Journal of Texas Catholic History and Culture, a; 3001 S. Congress Ave., Austin, TX 78704.

Jurist, The, semiannually; Catholic University of America, Washington, DC 20064; Department of Canon Law.

Kinship, q; P.O. Box 22264, Owensboro, KY 42304; Glenmary Sisters.

Knights of St. John International, q; 89 South Pine Ave., Albany, NY 12208.

Kolping Banner, m; P.O. Box 46252, Chicago, IL 60646; Catholic Kolping Society.

Latin Mass, The, q; 1331 Red Cedar Circle, Ft. Collins, CO 80524.

Law Briefs, 12 times a year; 3211 Fourth St. N.E. Washington, DC 20017; Office of General Counsel, USCC.

Leaflet Missal, 16565 South State St., S. Holland, IL 60473.

Leaves, bm; 23715 Ann Arbor Trail, Dearborn Heights, MI 48127; Mariannhill Mission Society.

Liguorian, m; 1 Liguori Dr., Liguori, MO 63057; Redemptorists.

Linacre Quarterly; 850 Elm Grove Rd., Elm Grove, WI 53122; Catholic Medical Association (National Federation of Catholic Physicians Guilds).

Liturgia y Cancion (Spanish and English), q; 5536 NE Hassalo, Portland, OR 97213. Oregon Catholic Press.

Liturgy, q; 8750 Georgia Ave., Suite 123, Silver Spring, MD 20910. Liturgical Conference.

Liturgy 90, 8 times a year; 1800 N. Hermitage Ave., Chicago, IL 60622; Liturgy Training Publications.

Liturgy Planner, The, semi-annual; . P.O. Box 13071, Portland, OR 97213.

Living City, m; P.O. Box 837, Bronx, NY 10465; Focolare Movement.

Living Faith, q; 10300 Watson Rd., St. Louis, MO 63127.

Living Light, The, q; 3211 Fourth St. N.E., Washington, DC 20017; Department of Education, USCC.

Living Prayer, bm; Beckley Hill, R.R. 2, Box 4784, Barre, Vt. 05641.

Living Pulpit, The, q; 5000 Independence Ave., Riverdale, NY 10471.

Marian Library Studies, a; Marian Library, Dayton, OH 45469.

Marian Studies, a; Marian Library, Dayton, OH 45469; Mariological Society of America (proceedings).

Marriage, 6 times a year; 955 Lake Dr., St. Paul, MN 55120; International Marriage Encounter.

Maryknoll, m; Maryknoll, NY 10545; Catholic Foreign Mission Society.

Mary's Shrine, 2 times a year; Michigan Ave. and 4th St. N.E., Washington, DC 20017. Basilica of National Shrine of the Immaculate Conception.

Matrimony, q; 215 Santa Rosa Pl., Santa Barbara, CA 93109. Worldwide Marriage Encounter.

Medical Mission News, q; 10 W. 17th St., New York, NY 10011; Catholic Medical Mission Board, Inc.

Medjugorje Magazine, q; P.O. Box 99, Bloomingdale, IL 60108.

Merciful Love, q; 5654 E. Westover, No. 103, P.O. Box 24, Fresno, CA 93727.

Mid-America: An Historical Review, 3 times a year; Loyola University, Chicago, IL 60626.

Migration World, 5 times a year; 209 Flagg Pl., Staten Island, NY 10304; Center for Migration Studies.

Miraculous Medal, q; 475 E. Chelten Ave., Philadelphia, PA 19144; Central Association of the Miraculous Medal.

Mission, q; 1663 Bristol Pike, Bensalem, PA 19020; Sisters of the Blessed Sacrament.

Mission Magazine, 4 times a year; 366 Fifth Ave., Ne York, NY 10001; Society for Propagation of the Faith.

Mission Helper, The, q; 1001 W. Joppa Rd., Baltimore, MD 21204; Mission Helpers of the Sacred Heart.

Missionhurst, 6 times a year; 4651 N. 25th St., Arlington, VA 22207.

Mission of the Immaculata, The, 10 times a year; 1600 W. Park Ave., Libertyville, IL 60048; Conventual Franciscan Friars.

Modern Liturgy, 10 times a year; 160 E. Virginia St., No. 290, San Jose, CA 95112.

Modern Schoolman, The, q; 221 N. Grand Blvd., St. Louis, MO 63103; St. Louis University Philosophy Department.

Momentum, 4 times a year; Suite 100, 1077 30th St., N.W., Washington, DC 20007; National Catholic Educational Association.

Mountain Spirit, The, 6 times a year; 322 Crab Orchard Rd., Lancaster, KY 40446; Christian Appalachian Project.

My Daily Visitor, bm; 200 Noll Plaza, Huntington, IN 46750; Our Sunday Visitor, Inc.

My Friend, 10 times a year; 50 St. Paul's Ave., Jamaica Plain, Boston, MA 02130; for children, ages 6-12.

National Apostolate with People with Mental Retardation, q; 4516 30th St., NW, Washington, DC 20008.

National Catholic Forester, q; 320 S. School St., Mt. Prospect,IL 60056.

National Jesuit News, m; 1616 P St. N.W., Suite 400, Washington, D.C. 20036.

Network, bm; 801 Pennsylvania Ave. S.E., Washington, DC 20003; Network.

New Covenant, m; Our Sunday Visitor, Inc., 200 Noll Plaza, Huntington, IN 46750.

New Oxford Review, 10 issues a year; 1069 Kains Ave., Berkeley, CA 94706.

Notebook, The, q; 31 Chesterfield Rd., Stamford, CT 06902. Catholic Movement for Intellectual and Cultural Affairs.

Notre Dame Magazine, q; Notre Dame Univ., Notre Dame, IN 46556.

Nova-Voice of Ministry, bm; P.O. Box 432, Milwaukee, WI 53201. Liturgical Publications.

Oblate World and Voice of Hope, bm; 486 Chandler St., P.O. Box 680, Tewksbury, MA 01876; Oblates of Mary Immaculate.

Observer, The, m; 4545 W. 63rd St., Chicago, IL 60629; Lithuanian Roman Catholic Federation of America.

Old Testament Abstracts, 3 times a year; Catholic University of America, Washington, DC 20064.

Onward (a) ; 448 Decatur St., Toledo, OH 43609; Barry Publishing Services.

Origins, 48 times a year; 3211 Fourth St. N.E., Washington, DC 20017; Catholic News Service.

Padres' Trail, 4 times a year; Box 645, St. Michael, AZ 86511; Franciscan Friars.

ParishArts Magazine, biannually, P.O. Boc 13071, Portland, OR 97213.

Parish Liturgy, q; 16565 S. State St., S. Holland, IL 60473.

Passage, q; 90 Cherry Lane, Hicksville, NY 11801.

Passionists' Compassion, The, q; 526 Monastery Pl., Union City, NJ 07087.

Pastoral Life, m; Box 595, Canfield, OH 44406; Society of St. Paul.

Pastoral Music, bm; 225 Sheridan St., N.W. Washington, DC 20011; National Association of Pastoral Musicians.

Philosophy Today, q; De Paul University, 1150 W. Fullerton Ave., Chicago, IL 60614; Philosophy Department.

PIME World, m (exc. July-Aug.); 17330 Quincy St., Detroit, MI 48221; PIME Missionaries.

Plenty Good Room, 6 times a year; 1800 N. Hermitage Ave., Chicago, IL 60622.

Pope Speaks, The: Church Documents Bimonthly; Our Sunday Visitor, Inc., 200 Noll Plaza, Huntington, IN 46750.

Portland, 4 issues a year; 5000 N. Willamette Blvd., Portland, OR 97203; Univ. of Portland.

Poverello, The, 10 times a year; 6832 Convent Blvd., Sylvania, OH 43560. Sisters of St. Francis of Sylvania.

Praxis Press, 10 times a year; P.O. Box 508, San Jose, CA 95103.

Prayers for Worship, q; P.O. Box 432, Milwaukee, WI 53201.

Praying, 6 times a year; 115 E. Armour Blvd., Kansas City, MO 64111.

Priest, The, m; 200 Noll Plaza, Huntington, IN 46750; Our Sunday Visitor, Inc.

Probe, q; 529 S. Wabash Ave., Room 404, Chicago, IL 60605; National Assembly of Religious Women.

Proceedings of the American Catholic Philosophical Association, a; Catholic Univ. of America, Washington, DC 20064.

Queen of All Hearts, bm; 26 S. Saxon Ave., Bay Shore, NY 11706; Montfort Missionaries.

Reign of the Sacred Heart, q; 6889 S. Lovers Lane, Hales Corners, WI 53130.

Religion Teacher's Journal, m (Sept.-May); P.O. Box 180, Mystic, CT 06355.

Renascence, q; Marquette University, Milwaukee, WI 53233.

Report on U.S. Catholic Overseas Mission, biannually; 3029 Fourth St. N.E., Washington, DC 20017. United States Catholic Mission Association.

Response: Volunteer Opportunities Directory, a; 4121 Harewood Rd. N.E., Washington, DC 20017; Catholic Network of Volunteer Service.

Review for Religious, bm; Room 428, 3601 Lindell Blvd., St. Louis, MO 63108.

Review of Politics, q; Box B, Notre Dame, IN 46556.

Review of Social Economy, 4 times a year; Marquette University, Milwaukee, WI 53233. Association for Social Economics.

Revista Maryknoll (Spanish-English), m; Maryknoll, NY 10545; Catholic Foreign Mission Society of America.

Roze Maryi (Polish), m; Eden Hill, Stockbridge, MA 01263; Marian Helpers Center.

Sacred Music, q; 548 Lafond Ave., St. Paul, MN 55103.

St. Anthony Messenger, m; 1615 Republic St., Cincinnati, OH 45210; Franciscan Friars.

St. Augustine Catholic, bm (Sept-May), P.O. Box 24000, Jacksonville, FL. St. Augustine diocese.

St. Joseph's Messenger and Advocate of the Blind, biannual; St. Joseph Home, 541 PavoniaAve., Jersey City, NJ 07303.

St. Paul's Family Magazine, q; 14780 W. 159th St., Olathe, KS 66062.

Salesian Bulletin (q); **Salesian Directory** (a); Salesian Missions of St. John Bosco, 4 times a year; 148 Main St., New Rochelle, NY 10802.

Salt of the Earth, bm; 205 W. Monroe St., Chicago, IL 60606; Claretians.

Salt/Sisters of Charity, BVM, q; 1100 Carmel Dr., Dubuque, IA 52001.

Scalabrinians, 4 times a year; 209 Flagg Pl., Staten Island, NY 10304.

SC News, q; P.O. Box 172, Nazareth, KY 40048; Sisters of Charity of Nazareth.

School Guide, a; 210 North Ave., New Rochelle, NY 10801.

SCRC Spirit, The, bm; 2810 Artesia Blvd., Redondo Beach, CA 90278; Southern California Renewal Communities.

Serenity, q; 601 Maiden Choice Lane, Baltimore, MD 21228; Little Sisters of the Poor.

Serran, The, bm; 65 E. Wacker Pl., Suite 1210, Chicago, IL 60601; Serra International.

Share Magazine, q times a year; 10 W. 71st St., New York, NY 10023; Catholic Duaghters of the Americas.

Share the Word, bm; 3031 Fourth St. N.E., Washington, DC 20017; Paulist Catholic Evangelization Association.

SilentAdvocate, q; St. Rita School for the Deaf, 1720 Glendale-Milford Rd., Cincinnati, OH 45215.

Sister Miriam Teresa League of Prayer Bulletin, q; League Headquarters, Convent Station, NJ 07961.

Sisters Today, bm; Liturgical Press, Collegeville, MN 56321.

Social Justice Review, bm; 3835 Westminster Pl., St. Louis, MO 63108; Catholic Central Union of America.

Soul Magazine, bm; P.O. Box 976, Washington, NJ 07882; World Apostolate of Our Lady of Fatima.

Spinnaker, 5 times a year; 610 W. Elm, Monroe, MI 48161; IHM Sisters.

Spirit, biannually; Seton Hall University, South Orange, NJ 07079.

Spirit, w; 1884 Randolph Ave., St. Paul, MN 55105. For teens.

Spirit and Life, 6 times a year; 800 N. Country Club Rd., Tucson, AZ 85716; Benedictine Srs. of Perpetual Adoration.

Spiritual Life, q; 2131 Lincoln Rd. N.E., Washington, DC 20002; Discalced Carmelite Friars.

Star, 10 times a year; 22 W. Kiowa, Colorado Springs, CO 80903.

Studies in the Spirituality of Jesuits, 5 times a year; 3700 W. Pine Blvd., St. Louis, MO 63108.

Sunday by Sunday, w; 1884 Randolph Ave., St. Paul, MN 55105.

Sword Magazine, 2 times a year; 120 Monroe Ave., Cresskill, NJ 07626; Carmelite Fathers.

Theological Studies, q; 37th and O Sts. NW, Washington, DC 20057.

Theology Digest, q; 3634 Lindell Blvd., St. Louis, MO 63108; St. Louis Univesity.

This Rock, m; P.O. Box 17181, San Diego, CA 92177.

Thomist, The, q; 487 Michigan Ave. N.E., Washington, DC 20017; Dominican Fathers.

Today's Catholic Teacher, m (Sept.-April); 330 Progress Rd., Dayton, OH 45449.

Today's Liturgy, q; 5536 NE Hassalo, Portland, OR 97213.

Today's Parish, m (Sept.-May); P.O. Box 180, Mystic, CT 06355.

Together in the Word, biannual; Box 577, Techny, IL 60082; Chicago province Society of Divine Word.

Tracings, q; Gamelin St., Holyoke, MA 01040; Sisters of Providence.

Trinity Missions Magazine, q; 9001 New Hampshire Ave., Silver Spring, MD 20903.

TV Prayer Guide; 19 Second Ave., P.O. Box 440, Pelham, NY 10803.

Ultreya Magazine, 6 times a year; 4500 W. Davis St., P.O. Box 210226, Dallas, TX 75211. Cursillo Movement.

L'Union (French and English), q; P.O. Box F, Woonsocket, RI 02895.

Universitas, q; 221 N. Grand, Room 39, St. Louis, MO 63103; St. Louis University.

U.S. Catholic, m; 205 W. Monroe St., Chicago, IL 60606; Claretians.

U.S. Catholic Historian, q; 200 Noll Plaza, Huntington, IN 46750.

Venture, 32 times during school year; 330 Progress Rd., Dayton, OH 45449, Intermediate grades.

Verelk (Armenian-English), bimonthly; 1327 Pleasant Ave., Los Angeles, CA 90033.

Vincentian Heritage, twice a year; 2233 N. Kenmore Ave., Chicago, IL 60614.

Vision, annually, 448 Decatur St., Toledo, OH 43609. Berry Publishing Services in conjunction with National Religious Vocation Conference.

Vision, 3 times a year; 7202 Buchanan St., Landover Hills, MD 20784. National Catholic Office for the Deaf.

Vision (Spanish-English), P.O. Box 28185, San Antonio, TX 78228. Mexican American Cultural Center.

Visions, 32 times during school year; 330 Progress Rd., Dayton, OH 45449. For students in grades 7 to 9.

Vocations and Prayer, q; 9815 Columbus Ave., North Hills, CA 91343. Rogationist Fathers.

Waif's Messenger, q; 1140 W. Jackson Blvd., Chicago, IL 60607; Mission of Our Lady of Mercy.

Way of St. Francis, bm; 1500 34th Ave., Oakland, CA 94601; Franciscan Friars of California, Inc.

Wheeling Jesuit University Chronicle, 3 times a year; 316 Washington Ave., Wheeling, WV 26003.

Word Among Us, The, m; 9639 Dr. Perry Rd., No. 126, Ijamsville, MD 21754.

World Lithuanian Catholic Directory, 50 Orton Marotta Way, S. Boston, MA 02127.

Worship, 6 times a year; St. John's Abbey, Collegeville, MN 56321.

You! Magazine, 10 times a year; 31194 La Baya Dr., Suite 200, Westlake Village, CA 91362. Catholic youth magazine.

Newsletters

Act, 10 times a year; Box 272, Ames, IA 60010; Christian Family Movement.

ADRIS Newsletter, q; Department of Theological Studies, St. Louis University, St. Louis, MO 63103.

Angel Guardian Herald, 4 times a year; 6301 12th Ave., Brooklyn, NY 11219.

Annual Report, 2021 H St. N.W., Washington, DC 20006. Black and Indian Mission Office.

Archdiocesan Bulletin, bm; 827 N. Franklin St., Philadelphia, PA 19123; Philadelphia archeparchy.

Aylesford Carmelite Newsletter, q. 8501 Bailey Rd., Darien, IL 60561.

Baraga Bulletin, The, q; 444 S. 4th St., P.O. Box 550, Marquette, MI 49855.

Benedictine Orient, twice a year; 2400 Maple Ave., Lisle, IL 60532.

Bringing Religion Home, 10 times a year; 205 W. Monroe St., Chicago, IL 60606.

Call Board, The, 12 times a year; 1501 Broadway, Suite 518, New York, NY 10036; Catholic Actors' Guild.

Campaign Update, bm; 16011st St. NW, Washington, DC 20006. Catholic Campaign for America.

CHD News, q; 3211 Fourth St. N.E. Washington, DC 20017; Campaign for Human Development.

Caring Community, The, m; 115 E. Armour Blvd., Kansas City, MO 64111.

Catalyst, 10 times a year; 6324 W. North Ave., Milwaukee, WI 53213 (publications office). Catholic League for Civil and Religious Rights.

Catechist's Connection, The, 10 times a year; 115 E. Armour Blvd., Kansas City, MO 64111.

Catholic Communicator, The, q; 781 Catoctin Ridge, Paeonian Springs, VA 21229; Catholic Home Study Institute.

Catholic Connection, The, m (Aug.-May); 2500 Line Ave., Shreveport, LA 71104. Shreveport diocese.

Catholic Trends, biweekly; 3211 Fourth St. N.E., Washington, DC 20017; Catholic News Service.

Catholic Update, m; 1615 Republic St., Cincinnati, OH 45210.

CARA Report, The, q; Georgetown Univ., Washington, DC 20057; Center for Applied Research in the Apostolate.

C.F.C. Newsletter, 5 times a year; 33 Pryer Terr., New Rochelle, NY 10804. Christian Brothers.

Chariscenter USA Newsletter, 5 times a year; P.O. Box 628, Locust Grove, VA 22508.

Christ the King Seminary Newsletter, 3 times a year; 711 Knox Rd., Box 607, E. Aurora, NY 14052.

Christian Beginnings, 5 times a year; 200 Noll Plaza, Huntington, IN 46750. Our Sunday Visitor.

Christian Foundation for Children and Aging (Newsletter), 3 times a year; 1 Elmwood Ave., Kansas City, KS 66103.

Christian Response Newsletter, P.O. Box 125, Staples, MN 56479.

Christopher News Notes, 10 times a year; 12 E. 48th St., New York, NY 10017; The Christophers.

Clarion, The, 5 times a year; Box 159, Alfred, ME 04002; Brothers of Christian Instruction.

Comboni Mission Newsletter, q; 8108 Beechmont Ave., Cincinnati, OH 45255.

Commentary, 6 times a year; 1010 11th St., Suite 200, Sacramento, CA 95814.

Context, 22 issues a year; 205 W. Monroe St., Chicago, IL 60606.

Crossroads, 8 times a year; 300 College Park Ave., Dayton, OH 45469. Catholic Campus Ministry Association.

CRUX of the News, w; 24 Wade Rd., Latham, NY 12210.

Cycles of Faith, P.O. Box 432, Milwaukee, WI 53201.

Damien-Dutton Call, q; 616 Bedford Ave., Bellmore, NY 11710.

Dimensions, m; 86 Front St., Hempstead, NY 11550; National Catholic Development Conference.

Diocesan Newsletter, The, m; P.O. Box 2147, Harlingen, TX 78551; Brownsville diocese.

Environment and Art Letter, m; 1800 N. Hermitage Ave., Chicago, IL 60622.

Envisioning, 55 5 Albany Ave., Amityville, NY 11701. Sisters of St. Dominic.

Ethics and Medics, m; 186 Forbes Rd., Braintree, MA 02184.

Eucharistic Minister, m; 115 E. Armour, P.O. Box 419493, Kansas City, MO 64141.

Evangelization Update, 6 times a year; 3031 Fourth St. NE, Washington, DC 20017.

Family Connection, The, 6 times a year; 3753 MacBeth Dr., San Jose, CA 95127.

Father Flood, q; P.O. Box 432, Milwaukee, WI 53201.

Fatima Findings, m; 8600 Calivurn Ct.; Pasadena, MD 21122. Reparation Society of the Immaculate Heart of Mary.

Fellowship of Catholic Scholars Newsletter Quarterly; Jacques Maritain Center, 215 Hesburgh Library, Notre Dame, IN 46556.

Fonda Tekakwitha News, P.O. Box 627, Fonda, NY 12068.

Food for the Poor, 3 times a year; 550 SW 12th Ave., Deerfield Beach, FL 33442.

Franciscan Reporter, annually; 3140 Meramec St., St. Louis, MO 63118; Franciscan Friars of Sacred Heart Province.

Franciscan World Care, 4 times a year; P.O. Box 29034, Washington, D.C. 20017. Franciscan Mission Service.

Frontline Report, bm; 23 Bliss Ave., Tenafly, NJ 07670. Society of African Missions.

Graymoor Today, m; Graymoor, Garrison, NY 10524.

Guadalupe Missioners Newsletter, m; 4714 W. 8th St., Los Angeles, CA 90005.

Happiness, q; 567 Salem End Rd., Framingham, MA 01701; Sons of Mary, Health of the Sick.

Harmony, 3 times a year; 800 N. Country Club Rd., Tucson, AZ 85716. Benedictine Srs. of Perpetual Adoration.

Holy Name National Newsletter, 6 times a year; 1169 Market St., No. 304, San Francisco, CA 94103.

HNP Today, w; 127 W. 31st St., New York, NY 10001. Franciscans of Holy Name Province.

HLI Reports, m; 4 Family Life, Front Royal, VA 22630.Human Life International.

Immaculate Heart of Mary Shrine Bulletin, 3 times a year; Mountain View Road, P.O. Box 976, Washington, NJ 07882.

In Between, q; 1257 E. Siena Hts. Dr., Adrian, MI 49221; Adrian Dominican Sisters.

Initiatives, 6 times a year; 205 W. Monroe St., No. 300, Chicago, IL 60606; National Center for the Laity.

Interchange, P.O. Box 4900, Rochester, MN 55903. Rochester Franciscan Sisters,

It's Our World, 4 times during school year; 1720 Massachusetts Ave. N.W., Washington, DC 20036. Young Catholics in Mission.

Journey, The, 4 times a year; 210 W. 31st St., New

York, NY 10001; Province of St. Mary of Capuchin Order.

Joyful Noiseletter, The, m; P.O. Box 895, Portage, MI 49081; Fellowship of Merry Christians.

Land of Cotton, q; 2048 W. Fairview Ave., Montgomery, AL 39196; City of St. Jude.

Law Reports, q; 4455 Woodson Rd., St. Louis, MO 63134; Catholic Health Association.

Lay Witness, m; 827 N. Fourth St., Steubenville, OH 43952. Catholics United for the Faith.

LCWR Update, m; 8808 Cameron St., Silver Spring, MD 20910; Leadership Conference of Women Religious.

League of St. Michael the Archangel Newsletter, 545 Colonial Dr., Suite C, Baton Rouge, LA 70806.

Legatus, m; 30 Frank Lloyd Wright Dr., Ann Arbor, MI 48105.

Let's Talk! (English edition), **Hablemos!** (Spanish edition), 6 times a year; 3031 Fourth St. N.E., Washington, DC 20017; prison ministries of Paulist National Catholic Evangelization Assn.

Life at Risk, 10 times a year; 3211 Fourth St. N.E., Washington, DC 20017. Pro-Life Activities Committee, NCCB.

Life Insight, m; 3211 Fourth St. N.E., Washington, DC 20017; Committee for Pro-Life Activities, NCCB.

Liturgical Images, m; P.O. Box 2225, Hickory, NC 28603.

Markings, m; 205 W. Monroe St., Chicago, IL 60606.

Medical Mission Sisters News, 4 times a year; 8400 Pine Road, Philadelphia, PA 19111.

Messenger of St. Joseph's Union, The, 3 times a year; 108 Bedell St., Staten Island, NY 10309.

Men of Malvern, q; Malvern, PA 19355.

Missionaries of Africa Report, q; 1624 21st St. N.W., Washington, DC 20009; Society of Missionaries of Africa (White Fathers).

Mission Messenger, The, q; P.O. Box 610, Thoreau, NM 87323; St. Bonaventure Indian Mission and School.

NCCB/USCC Currents, 10 times a year; 3211 Fourth St., N.E., Washington, DC 20017.

NCPD National Update, q; P.O. Box 29113, Washington, DC 20017; National Catholic Office for Persons with Disabilities.

NCSC Commitment, biannually; 1275 K St. N.W., Suite 980, Washington, DC 20005. National Catholic Stewardship Council.

News and Views, q; 3900 Westminster Pl.; St. Louis, MO 63108; Sacred Heart Program.

Newsletter of the Bureau of Catholic Indian Missions, 10 times a year; 2021 H St. N.W., Washington, DC 20006.

Northern Nevada Catholic Newsletter, m; P.O. Box 1211, Reno, NV 89504; Reno diocese.

Nuestra Parroquia (Spanish-English), m; 205 W. Monroe St., Chicago, IL 60606. Claretians.

Oblates, bm; 9480 North De Mazenod Dr., Belleville, IL 62223; Missionary Oblates of Mary Immaculate.

Overview, m; 205 W. Monroe St., Chicago, IL 60606; Thomas More Assn.

Palabra Entre Nosotros, La, bm; P.O. Box 826, Gaithersburg, MD 20884.

Paulist, The, q; 997 Macarthur Blvd., Mahwah, NJ 07656.

Perpetual Eucharistic Adoration Newsletter, 3 times a year; P.O. Box 84595, Los Angeles, CA 90073.

Perspectives, q; 912 Market St., La Crosse, WI 54601.

Pilgrim, q; Jesuit Fathers, Auriesville, NY 12016; Shrine of North American Martyrs.

Priestly Heart Newsletter, 5337 Genessee St., Bowmansville, NY 14026. Apostleship of Prayer.

Priests for Life, bm; P.O. Box 307, Port Chester, NY 10573.

Program Supplement, 18 times a year; 1 Columbus Plaza, New Haven, CT 06510; Knights of Columbus.

Religious Life, m (bm, May-Aug.); P.O. Box 41007, Chicago, IL 60641; Institute on Religious Life.

RSCJ Newsletter, m; 54 Robin Dr., Skillman, NJ 08558. Religious of Sacred Heart.

SCJ News, 9 times a year; P.O. Box 289, Hales Corners, WI 53130; Sacred Heart Fathers and Brothers.

St. Anthony's Newsletter, 12 times a year; Mt. St. Francis, IN 47146; Conventual Franciscans.

Spiritual Book Associates, 8 times a year; Notre Dame, IN 46556.

Squires Newsletter, m; One Columbus Plaza, New Haven, CT 06510; Columbian Squires.

SSPS Mission, q; P.O. Box 6026, Techny, IL 60082; Holy Spirit Missionary Sisters.

Tekakwitha Conference Newsletter (Cross and Feather News), q; P.O. Box 6768, Great Falls, MT 59406.

Touchstone, 4 times a year; 1337 W. Ohio St., Chicago, IL 60622; National Federation of Priests' Councils.

Trinity Review, m; P.O. Box 1666, Hobbs, NM 88240.

Unda USA Newsletter, 4 times a year; 901 Irving Ave., Dayton, OH 45409.

Vision — National Association of Catholic Chaplains, 10 times a year; 3501 S. Lake Dr., Milwaukee, WI 53207.

Visions, 2 times a year; Victory Noll, P.O. Box 109, Huntington, IN 46750; Our Lady of Victory Missionary Sisters.

Voices, q; P.O. Box 8326, St. Louis, MO 63132; Women for Faith and Family.

Voices, 2 times a year; 1625 Rutherford Lane, Bldg. D, Austin, TX 78754. Volunteers for Educational and Social Services.

Washington Theological Union Report, 3 times a year; Washington Theological Union, 9001 New Hampshire Ave., Silver Spring, MD 20903.

Wooden Bell, The, 5 times a year; 209 W. Fayette St., Baltimore, MD 21201. Catholic Relief Services.

Woodstock Report, q; Georgetown Univ., Washington, DC 20057. Woodstock Theological Center.

Word One, 5 times a year; 205 W. Monroe St., Chicago, IL 60606; Claretians.

World Parish, 6 times a year; Maryknoll Fathers; Maryknoll, NY 10545.

Xaverian Missions Newsletter, six times a year; 101 Summer St., Holliston, MA 01746; Xaverian Missionary Fathers.

Your Edmundite Missions Newsletter, bm; 1428 Broad St., Selma, AL 36701; Southern Missions of Society of St. Edmund.

Youth Update, m; 1615 Republic St., Cincinnati, OH 45210.

Zeal Newsletter, 3 times a year; P.O. Box 86, Allegany, NY 14706; Franciscan Sisters of Allegany.

BOOKS

The Official Catholic Directory, annual; P.J. Kenedy & Sons in association with R.R. Bowker, a Reed Reference Publishing Company, 121 Chanlon Rd., New Providence, NJ 07974. First edition, 1817.

The Catholic Almanac, annual; Our Sunday Visitor, Inc., 200 Noll Plaza, Huntington, IN, 46750, publisher; editorial offices, P.O. Box 3765, Wallington, NJ 07057. First edition, 1904.

BOOK CLUBS

Catholic Book Club (1928), 106 W. 56th St., New York, NY 10019. Sponsors the Campion Award.

Catholic Digest Book Club (1954), 475 Riverside Dr., Suite 1268, New York, NY 10115.

Spiritual Book Associates (1934), Notre Dame, IN 46556.

Thomas More Book Club (1939), Thomas More Association, 205 W. Monroe St., Sixth Floor, Chicago, IL 60606.

FOREIGN CATHOLIC PERIODICALS

Principal source: Catholic Almanac survey. Included are English-language Catholic periodicals published outside the U.S.

African Ecclesial Review (AFER), bm; Gaba Publications, P.O. Box 4002, Eldoret, Kenya.

Australasian Catholic Record, q; 99 Albert Rd., Strathfield 2135, New South Wales, Australia.

Christ to the World, 5 times a year; Via di Propaganda 1- C, 00187, Rome, Italy.

Christian Orient, q; P.B. 1 Vadavathoor, Kottayam 686010, Kerala, India.

Doctrine and Life, m; Dominican Publications, 42 Parnell Sq., Dublin 1, Ireland.

Downside Review, q; Downside Abbey, Stratton on Fosse, Bath, BA3 4RH, England.

East Asian Pastoral Review, q; East Asian Pastoral Institute, P.O. Box 221 U.P. Campus, 1101 Quezon City, Philippines.

Furrow, The, m; St. Patrick's College, Maynooth, Ireland.

Heythrop Journal, q; Heythrop College,

Kensington Sq., London W8 5HQ, England (Editorial Office). Published by Blackwell Publishers, 108 Cowley Rd., Oxford, OX4 1JF, U.K.

Holy Land Magazine, q; P.O. Box 186, 91001 Jerusalem, Israel. Illustrated.

Irish Biblical Studies, The, q; Union Theological College, Belfast BT7 1JT, N. Ireland.

Irish Journal of Sociology, The, a; St. Patrick's College, Maynooth, Ireland.

Irish Theological Quarterly, q; St. Patrick's College, Maynooth, Ireland.

L'Osservatore Romano, w; Vatican City. (See Index.)

Louvain Studies, q; Peeters Publishers, Bondgenotenlaan 153, B-3000, Leuven, Belgium.

Lumen Vitae (French, with English summaries), q; International Center for Studies in Religious Education, 186, rue Washington, B-1050 Brussels, Belgium.

Mediaeval Studies, annual; Pontifical Institute of Mediaeval Studies, 59 Queen's Park Crescent East, Toronto, Ont., Canada M5S 2C4.

Month, m; 114 Mount St., London, WIY 6AH, England.

Music and Liturgy, 6 times a year; The Editor, 33 Brockenhurst Rd., Addiscombe Croydan, Surrey CRO 7DR, England.

New Blackfriars, m; edited by English Dominicans, Blackfriars, Oxford, OX1 3LY, England.

Omnis Terra (English Edition), m; Pontifical Missionary Union, Congregation for the Evangelization of Peoples, Via di Propaganda 1/c, 00187 Rome, Italy.

One in Christ, q; Edited at: Turvey Abbey, Turvey, Beds. MK43 8DE, England.

Priests & People (formerly The Clergy Review), 11 times a year; Blackfriars, Buckingham Rd., Cambridge CB3 0DD, England.

Recusant History, biannual; Catholic Record Society, 12 Melbourne Pl., Wolsingham, Durham DL13 3EH, England.

Religious Life Review, bm; Dominican Publications, 42 Parnell Sq., Dublin 1, Ireland.

Scripture in Church, q; Dominican Publications, 42 Parnell Sq., Dublin 1, Ireland.

Southwark Liturgy Bulletin, q; The Editor, 10 Claremont Rd., Maidstone, Kent ME14 5L2, England.

Spearhead, 5 times a year; Gaba Publications, P.O. Box 4002, Eldoret, Kenya.

Spirituality, bm; Dominican Publications, 42 Parnell Sq., Dublin 1, Ireland.

Tablet, The, w; 1 King Street Cloisters, Clifton Walk, London W6 0QZ, England.

Way, The, q; 114 Mount St., London W1Y 6AN, England.

CATHOLIC NEWS AGENCIES

(Sources: International Catholic Union of the Press, Geneva; Catholic Press Association, U.S.)

Argentina: Agencia Informativa Catolica Argentina (AICA), av. Rivadavia, 413, 40 Casilla de Correo Central 2886, 1020 Buenos Aires.

Austria: Katholische Presse-Agentur (Kathpress), Singerstrasse 7/6/2, 1010 Vienna 1.

Belgium: Centre d'Information de Presse (CIP), 35 Chausée de Haecht, 1030 Brussels.

Bolivia: Agencia Noticias Fides, ANF, Casilla 5782, La Paz.

ERBOL, Casilla 5946, La Paz.

Chile: Agencia informativa y de comunicaciones (AIC Chile), Brasil 94, Santiago.

Croatia: Christian Information Service, Marulicev 14, PP 434, 410001 Zagreb.

Germany: Katholische Nachrichten Agentur (KNA), Adenauer Allee 134, 5300 Bonn 1.

Greece: Agence TYPOS Rue Acharnon 246, Athens 815.

Hong Kong: UCA-News, P.O. Box 69626, Kwun Tong (Hong Kong).

Hungary: Magyar Kurir, Milkszath ter 1, 1088, Budapest.

India: South Asian Religious News (SAR-News), PB 6236, Mazagaon, Bombay 400 010.

Italy: Servizio Informazioni Religiosa (SIR), Via di Porta Cavalleggeri 143, I-00165 Roma.

Centrum Informationis Catolicae (CIC-Roma), via Delmonte de la Farina, 30/4, 00186 Roma.

Peru: ACI-PRENSA, A.P. 040062, Lima.

Switzerland: Katholische Internationale Presse-Agentur (KIPA), Case Postale 1054 CH 1701, Fribourg.

Centre International de Reportages et d'Information Culturelle (CIRIC), Chemin Clochetons 8, P.O. Box 1000, Lausanne.

United States of America: Catholic News Service (CNS), 3211 Fourth St. N.E., Washington, DC 20017.

Zaire (now Congo): Documentation et Information Africaine (DIA), B.P. 2598, Kinshasa I.

Missions: Agenzia Internationale Fides (AIF), Palazzo di Propagande Fide, Via di Propaganda I-c, 00187 Rome, Italy.

U.S. PRESS SERVICES

Catholic News Service (CNS), established in 1920 (NC News Service), provides a worldwide daily news report by satellite throughout the U.S. and Canada and by wire and computer links into several foreign countries, and by mail to other clients, serving Catholic periodicals and broadcasters including Vatican Radio in about 40 countries. CNS also provides feature and photo services and a weekly religious education package, "FaithAlive!" It publishes "Origins," a weekly documentary service, and "Catholic Trends," a fortnightly newsletter, the weekly TV and Movie Guide and Movie Guide Monthly. CNS maintains a full-time bureau in Rome. It is a division of the United States Catholic Conference, with offices at 3211 Fourth St. N.E., Washington, DC 20017. The director and editor-in-chief is Thomas N. Lorsung.

Spanish-Language Service: A weekly news summary provided by Catholic News Service is used by a number of Catholic newspapers. Some papers carry features of their own in Spanish.

Religion News Service (RNS) provides coverage of all religions as well as ethics, spirituality and moral issues. Founded in 1934 (as the Religious News Service) by the National Conference of Christian and Jews as an independent agency, RNS became an editorially independent subsidiary of the United Methodist Reporter, an interfaith publishing company, in 1983. It was acquired by Newhouse News Service in 1994. Address: 1101 Connecticut Ave. NW, Suite 350, Washington, DC 20036.

RADIO, TELEVISION, THEATRE

Christopher Radio Program: 14-minute interview series, "Christopher Closeup," weekly and "Christopher Minutes," daily, on 400 stations. Address: 12 E. 48th St., New York, NY 10017.

Christopher TV Series, "Christopher Closeup": Originated in 1952. Half-hour interviews, weekly, on commecial TV and numerous cable outlets. Address: 12 E. 48th St., New York, NY 10017.

Journeys Thru Rock (Radio): Produced in cooperation with the Department of Communication, NCCB/USCC. A 15-minute weekly program currently employing a youth-oriented music and commentary format (ABC).

Religious Specials (TV): The NCCB/USCC Catholic Communication Campaign produces two one-hour Catholic specials a year and additional seasonal liturgical services. The specials cover a variety of topics and are broadcast on the ABC and NBC television networks.

Catholic Actors' Guild of America, Inc.: Established in 1914 to provide material and spiritual assistance to people in the theatre. Has more than 500 members; publishes The Call Board. Address: 1501 Broadway, Suite 510, New York, NY 10036.

Communications Services

Black Catholic Televangelization Network: Consists of production organizations that promote the evangelization of the Black community and share the gifts of Black Catholics. The member production groups are: Black and Catholic (TV); This Far by Faith (Radio); Search; and Catholic African World Network, Rev. Clarence Williams, C.Pp.S., is president. Address: P.O. Box 13220, Detroit, MI 48213.

Catholic Views Broadcasts, Inc., 10 Audrey Place, Fairfield, NJ 07004. Produces weekly 15-minute radio program Views of the News. Also operates Catholic community TV stations in Chicago and Minneapolis.

Clemons Productions, Inc.: Produces "That's the Spirit," a family show for television; "Thoughts for the Week," on the ABC Satellite Network and "Spirituality for Today" on the internet. Available to dioceses, organizations or channels. Address: P.O. Box 7466, Greenwich, CT 06830.

Eternal Word Television Network (EWTN), 5817 Old Leeds Rd., Birmingham, AL 35210. America's largest religious cable network; features 24 hours of spiritual-growth programming for the entire family. Offers documentaries, weekly teaching series and talk shows, including the award-winning "Mother Angelica Live." Also features live Church events from around the world and devotional programs such as "The Holy Rosary." Mother M. Angelica, P.C.P.A., foundress.

Father Justin Rosary Hour: P.O. Box 454, Athol Springs, NY 14010. Founded in 1931. Polish Catechetical Radio Network. Rev. Marion M. Tolczyk, O.F.M. Conv., director.

Family Theater Productions: Founded by Father Peyton. Video cassettes, films for TV. Address: 7201 Sunset Blvd., Hollywood, CA 90046. Pres., Rev. John P. Phalen, C.S.C.

Franciscan Communications: Producer of video and print resources for pastoral ministry. Address: St. Anthony Messenger Press, 1615 Republic St., Cincinnati, OH 45210.

Hispanic Telecommunications Network, Inc. (HTN): Produces Nuestra Familia, a national weekly Spanish-language TV series. Address: 1405 N. Main, Suite 240, San Antonio, TX 78212.

Jesuit Productions/Sacred Heart Program, Inc.: Produces and distributes free of charge the weekly "CONTACT" program in 30-, 15-, and 5-minute formats to more than 400 stations in North America. Address: 3900 Westminster Pl., St. Louis, MO 63108.

Mary Productions: Originated in 1950. Offers royalty-free scripts for stage, film, radio and tape production. Audio and video tapes of lives of the saints and historical characters. Traveling theatre company. Address: Mary Productions, 212 Oakdale Dr., Tomaso Plaza, Middletown, NJ 07748.

Oblate Media and Communication Corporation: Producers, Broadcast syndicators and distributors of Catholic and value-centered video programming. Address:7315 Manchester Rd., St. Louis, MO 63143.

Passionist Communications, Inc.: Present Sunday Mass on TV seen in U.S. and available to dioceses and channels; publish "TV Prayer Guide," semi-annually. Address: 19 Second Ave., P.O. Box 440, Pelham, NY 10803.

Paulist Communications: Full service audio production in syndication to dioceses, religious communities and church groups. Address: 3055 4th St. NE, Wasington, DC 20017.Rev. John Geaney, C.S.P., president.

Paulist Productions: Producers and distributors of the INSIGHT Film Series (available for TV) and educational film series. Address: 17575 Pacific Coast Hwy., Pacific Palisades, CA 90272.

Radio Maria (Italian): Italian Catholic radio station founded in 1992, 352 W. 44th St., New York, NY 10036. Rev. Mariano Cisco, C.S., executive director.

Odyssey— Interfaith Cable Television Channel: Policies shaped by consortium of 28 members representing 64 faith groups from Roman Catholic, Jewish, Protestant and Eastern Orthodox traditions. Address: National Interfaith Cable Coalition, 9th Floor, 74 Trinity Place, New York, NY 10006.

Catholic Television Network (CTN): Instructional TV operations have been established in the following archdioceses and dioceses. Archdioceses are indicated by an asterisk.

Boston,* Mass.: Rev. Francis McFarland, Director, P.O. Box 9109, Newton, MA 02160.

Brooklyn, NY: Rev. Msgr. Michael J. Dempsey, Director, 1712 10th Ave. 11215.

Chicago, *IL: Mr. Joseph Loughlin, Director, 155 E. Superior. 60611.

Corpus Christi,TX: Mr. Martin L. Wind, 1200 Lantana St., Corpus Christi, TX 78407.

Dallas, TX: Mr. Michael McGee, 3725 Blackburn, P.O.Box 190507. 75219.

Detroit,* MI: Mr. Ned McGrath, Director, 305 Michigan Ave., Detroit, Mich. 48226.

Los Angeles,* CA: Mr. David Moore, 3424 Willshire Ave. 90010.

New York,* NY: Mr. Michael Lavery, Director, 215 Seminary Ave., Yonkers, NY 10704.

Oakland, San Jose, San Francisco,* CA: Shirley Connolly, Director, 324 Middlefield Rd., Menlo Park, CA 94025.

Orlando, FL: Rev. Robert Hoeffner. Director, P.O. Box 1800, Orlando, FL 32802.

Rockville Centre, NY: Rev. Msgr. Thomas Hartman, Director, 1200 Glen Curtiss Blvd., Uniondale, NY 11553.

San Bernardino, CA: Caritas Telecommunications, Clare Colella, Director, 1201 E. Highland Ave. 92404.

Youngstown, OH: Rev. James Korda, P.O. Box 430, Canfield, OH 44406.

Unda-USA: A national professional Catholic association for broadcasters and other allied communicators in church ministry; organized in 1972. It succeeded the Catholic Broadcasters Association of America which in 1948 had replaced the Catholic Forum of the Air organized in 1938. It is a member of Unda-International, the international Catholic association for radio and television (Unda is the Latin word for "wave," symbolic of air waves of communication). In addition to providing support and network opportunities in church communications the organization works to encourage the secular media to produce value-oriented programs and stories. Unda-USA sponsors an annual general assembly and presents the Gabriel Awards annually for excellence in broadcasting. It publishes six newsletters for its membership. President, Frank Morock. Address: Unda-USA, 901 Irving Ave., Dayton, OH 45409.

The Catholic Communications Foundation (CCF) was established by the Catholic Fraternal Benefit Societies in 1966 to lend support and assistance to development of the communications apostolate of the Church. The CCF promotes the development of diocesan communications capabilities and funds a scholarship program at the Annual Institute for Religious Communications. CCF officers include Bishop Anthony G. Bosco, chairman of the board. Address: P.O. Box 374, Pawling, NY 12564.

Federal Religious Freedom Guidelines

Federal employees in their workplaces may wear religious emblems, discuss religion and invite fellow workers to join their faith under new religious freedom guidelines President Clinton sent out Aug. 14, 1997, to heads of all federal agencies. The guidelines say that, if employees can get together in a cafeteria at lunch to discuss politics or sports, they cannot be barred from using the same time and space to discuss the Bible or the Koran. White House Counsel William P. Marshall told reporters at a press conference that the aim of the guidelines is to clarify existing law and policy in areas where "there has always been confusion," such as the permissibility of having religious books at one's desk.

HONORS AND AWARDS

PONTIFICAL ORDERS

The Pontifical Orders of Knighthood are secular orders of merit whose membership depends directly on the pope.

Supreme Order of Christ (Militia of Our Lord Jesus Christ): The highest of the five pontifical orders of knighthood, the Supreme Order of Christ was approved Mar. 14, 1319, by John XXII as a continuation in Portugal of the suppressed Order of Templars. Members were religious with vows and a rule of life until the order lost its religious character toward the end of the 15th century. Since that time it has existed as an order of merit. Paul VI, in 1966, restricted awards of the order to Christian heads of state.

Order of the Golden Spur (Golden Militia): Although the original founder is not certainly known, this order is one of the oldest knighthoods. Indiscriminate bestowal and inheritance diminished its prestige, however, and in 1841 Gregory XVI replaced it with the Order of St. Sylvester and gave it the title of Golden Militia. In 1905 St. Pius X restored the Order of the Golden Spur in its own right, separating it from the Order of St. Sylvester. Paul VI, in 1966, restricted awards of the order to Christian heads of state.

Order of Pius IX: Founded by Pius IX June 17, 1847, the order is awarded for outstanding services for the Church and society, and may be given to non-Catholics as well as Catholics. The title to nobility formerly attached to membership was abolished by Pius XII in 1939. In 1957 Pius XII instituted the Class of the Grand Collar as the highest category of the order; in 1966, Paul VI restricted this award to heads of state "in solemn circumstances." The other three classes are of Knights of the Grand Cross, Knight Commanders with and without emblem, and Knights. The new class was created to avoid difficulties in presenting papal honors to Christian or non-Christian leaders of high merit.

Order of St. Gregory the Great: First established by Gregory XVI in 1831 to honor citizens of the Papal States, the order is conferred on persons who are distinguished for personal character and reputation, and for notable accomplishment. The order has civil and military divisions, and three classes of knights.

Order of St. Sylvester: Instituted Oct. 31, 1841, by Gregory XVI to absorb the Order of the Golden Spur, this order was divided into two by St. Pius X in 1905, one retaining the name of St. Sylvester and the other assuming the title of Golden Militia. Membership consists of three degrees: Knights of the Grand Cross, Knight Commanders with and without emblem, and Knights.

PAPAL MEDALS

Pro Ecclesia et Pontifice: This decoration ("For the Church and the Pontiff") had its origin in 1888 as a token of the golden sacerdotal jubilee of Leo XIII; he bestowed it on those who had assisted in the observance of his jubilee and on persons responsible for the success of the Vatican Exposition. The medal, cruciform in shape, bears the likenesses of Sts. Peter and Paul, the tiara and the papal keys, the words Pro Ecclesia et Pontifice, and the name of the present pontiff, all on the same side; it is attached to a ribbon of yellow and white, the papal colors. Originally, the medal was issued in gold, silver or bronze. It is awarded in recognition of service to the Church and the papacy.

Benemerenti: Several medals ("To a well-deserving person") have been conferred by popes for exceptional accomplishment and service. The medals, which are made of gold, silver or bronze, bear the likeness and name of the reigning pope on one side; on the other, a laurel crown and the letter "B."

These two medals may be given by the pope to both men and women. Their bestowal does not convey any title or honor of knighthood.

ECCLESIASTICAL ORDER

Equestrian Order of the Holy Sepulchre of Jerusalem: The order traces its origin to Godfrey of Bouillon who instituted it in 1099. It took its name from the Basilica of the Holy Sepulchre where its members were knighted. After the fall of the Latin Kingdom of Jerusalem and the consequent departure of the knights from the Holy Land, national divisions were established in various countries.

The order was reorganized by Pius IX in 1847 when he reestablished the Latin Patriarchate of Jerusalem and placed the order under the jurisdiction of its patriarch. In 1888, Leo XIII confirmed permission to admit women _ Ladies of the Holy Sepulchre _ to all degrees of rank. Pius X reserved the office of grand master to himself in 1907; Pius XII gave the order a cardinal patron in 1940 and, in 1949, transferred the office of grand master from the pope to the cardinal patron. Pope John XXIII approved updated constitutions in 1962; the latest statutes were approved by Paul VI in 1977.

The purposes of the order are strictly religious and charitable. Members are committed to sustain and aid the charitable, cultural and social works of the Catholic Church in the Holy Land, particularly in the Latin Patriarchate of Jerusalem.

The order is composed of knights and ladies grouped in three classes: class of Knights of the Collar and Ladies of the Collar; Class of Knights (in four grades); Class of Ladies (in four grades). Members are appointed by the cardinal grand master according to procedures outlined in the constitution.

Under the present constitution the order is divided into national lieutenancies, largely autonomous, with international headquarters in Rome. Cardinal Carlo Furno is the grand master of the order.

There are nine lieutenancies of the order in the United States and one in Puerto Rico. Address of Vice Governor General: F. Russell Kendall, 309 Knipp Rd., Houston, TX 77024.

ORDER OF MALTA

The Sovereign Military Hospitaller Order of St. John of Jerusalem of Rhodes and of Malta traces its origin to a group of men who maintained a Christian hospital in the Holy Land in the 11th century. The group was approved as a religious order — the Hospitallers of St. John — by Paschal II in 1113.

The order, while continuing its service to the poor, principally in hospital work, assumed military duties in the twelfth century and included knights, chaplains and sergeants-at-arms among its members. All the knights were professed monks with the vows of poverty, chastity and obedience. Headquarters were located in the Holy Land until the last decade of the 13th century and on Rhodes after 1308 (whence the title, Knights of Rhodes).

After establishing itself on Rhodes, the order became a sovereign power like the sea republics of Italy and the Hanseatic cities of Germany, flying its own flag, coining its own money, floating its own navy, and maintaining diplomatic relations with many nations.

The order was forced to abandon Rhodes in 1522 after the third siege of the island by the Turks under Sultan Suliman I. Eight years later, the Knights were given the island of Malta, where they remained as a bastion of Christianity until near the end of the 18th century. Headquarters have been located in Rome since 1834.

The title of Grand Master of the Order, in abeyance for some time, was restored by Leo XIII in 1879. A more precise definition of both the religious and the sovereign status of the order was embodied in a new constitution of 1961 and a code issued in 1966.

The four main classifications of members are: Knights of Justice, who are religious with the vows of poverty, chastity and obedience; Knights of Obedience, who make a solemn promise to strive for Christian perfection; Knights of Honor and Devotion and of Grace and Devotion — all of noble lineage; and Knights of Magistral Grace. There are also chaplains, Dames and Donats of the order.

The order, with six grand priories, three sub-priories and 40 national associations, is devoted to hospital and charitable works of all kinds in some 100 countries.

Under the provisions of international law, the order maintains full diplomatic relations with the Holy See — on which, in its double nature, it depends as a religious Order, but of which, as a sovereign Order of Knighthood, it is independent — and 68 countries throughout the world.

The Grand Master, who is the head of the order, has the title of Most Eminent Highness with the rank of Cardinal. He must be of noble lineage and under solemn vows for a minimum period of 10 years, if under 50.

The present Grand Master is Fra' Andrew Willoughby Ninian Bertie, member of the British aristocracy, who was elected for life Apr. 8, 1988, by the Council of State. His election was approved by the Pope.

The address of headquarters of the order is Via Condotti, 68, Palazzo Malta, 00187 Rome, Italy. U.S. addresses: American Association, 1011 First Ave., New York, NY 10022; Western Association of U.S.A., 465 California St., Suite 524, San Francisco, CA 94104; Federal Association of U.S.A., 1730 M St. N.W., Suite 403, Washington, DC 20036.

Order of St. George

The Sacred Military Constantinian Order of St. George was established by Pope Clement XI in 1718. The purposes of the order are to work for the preaching and defense of the Catholic faith and to promote the spiritual and physical welfare of sick, disabled, homeless and other unfortunate persons. The principal officer is Prince Carlo of Bourbon-Two Sicilies, Duke of Calabria. Addresses: Via Sistina 121, 00187 Rome, Italy; Via Duomo 149, 80138 Naples, Italy; Address of United States Delegation, 3731 Olympia Dr., Houston, TX 77019.

AMERICAN CATHOLIC AWARDS

Most of the awards listed below are presented annually. Recipients for 1996/1997 are given where available; an asterisk indicates that the award has not been presented recently. See earlier editions of the Almanac for award winners of previous years. See also Index for other awards.

Aquinas Medal (1956), by the American Catholic Philosophical Association for outstanding contributions to the field of Catholic philosophy. Luis Dupré (1997).

Bellarmine Medal (1955), by Bellarmine College (Louisville, Ky.), to persons in national or international affairs who, in controversial matters, exemplify the characteristics of St. Robert Bellarmine in charity, integrity, sensitivity, justice and temperateness. Arthur Ashe (1993).

Berakah Award (1976), by the North American Academy of the Liturgy, to recognize distinguished contribution to the professional work of liturgy by a liturgist or person of an allied vocation. Frank Henderson (1997).

Bishop John England Award (1994), by the Catholic Press Association for outstanding performance by a publisher in the Catholic press. Bishop David B. Thompson (1997).

Borromeo Award (1960), by Carroll College (Hel-

ena, Mont.), for zeal, courage and devotion in the spirit of St. Charles Borromeo. The Hunthausen Family (1997).

Brent Award (1976), by the Diocese of Arlington, Va., for distinguished service to others. William Donohue (1997).

Campion Award (1955), by the Catholic Book Club for distinguished service in Catholic letters. Chinua Achebe (1996).

Cardinal Gibbons Medal (1949) by the Alumni Association of The Catholic University of America for distinguished and meritorious service to the Church, the United States or The Catholic University of America. Cardinal James Hickey (1996).

Cardinal Wright Award (1980), by the Fellowship of Catholic Scholars to a Catholic adjudged to have done an outstanding service for the Church. Ralph McInerney (1996). The organization also presents the **Cardinal O'Boyle Award** intermittently to a Catholic for his or her defense of the faith.

Cardinal Wright Mariological Award (1950; as the Marian Award) by the Mariological Society of America to recognize and encourage significant writing on the Virgin Mary. Nicholas Ayo, C.S.C. (1995).

Caritas Medal (1992), by St. John's University (Jamaica, N.Y.) for humanitarian service to the people of New York City. Little Sisters of the Poor (1995).

Christian Culture Award (1941), by Assumption University (Canada) to outstanding exponents of Christian ideals. Josephine B. Magno, M.D. (1997).

College of New Rochelle Pope John XXIII Award* (1963), by College of New Rochelle (N.Y.) to those whose lives are witness "to the centrality of human dignity in the creation of peace."

Damien-Dutton Award (1953), by the Damien-Dutton Society for service toward conquest of leprosy or for the promotion of better understanding of social problems connected with the disease. Richard Marks of Molokai (1996).

Edith Stein Award (1955), by the Edith Stein Guild for service toward better understanding between Christians and Jews. Rev. John Sullivan, O.C.D. (1995).

Emmanuel D'Alzon Medal (1954), by Assumptionists to persons exemplifying the ideals of their founder. Joseph Hagan, Dr. Francis X. Dufault, Fr. Arnold Grol, M.Afr., and Sr. Clare Teresa Tjader, R.A. (1995).

Father McKenna Award (1950), by the National Association of the Holy Name Society. Awarded biennially to recognize a member of the clergy for service to the society.

Fidelitas Medal (1949), by Orchard Lake Schools (SS Cyril and Methodius Seminary, St. Mary's College, St. Mary's Preparatory), to an outstanding American Catholic of Polish descent for fidelity in serving God and country. Rev. Msgr. John R. Gabalski, P.A. (1997).

Franciscan International Award (1958), by the Conventual Franciscan Friars of the Franciscan Retreat House (Prior Lake, Minn.) to an individual or group committed to serving the ideals of Christ, especially as proclaimed by St. Francis of Assisi. Marty Haugen (1997).

Gaudium Medal, The* (1982, as The Compostela Award), by the Oratory of St. Philip Neri in the Diocese of Brooklyn to men and women whose lives represent the noblest ideals of the human tradition of fidelity to justice, truth, beauty and peace.

George M. Cohan Award (1970), by the Catholic Actors Guild of America, Inc., Jean Stapleton (1994). Other awards presented by the organization include: **St. Genesius Award**, Michael Learned, Hal Linden (1993); **Fred Allen Humanitarian Award**, Celeste Holm (1994).

Good Samaritan Award (1968), by the National Catholic Development Conference to recognize the concern for one's fellowman exemplified by the parable of the Good Samaritan. Sr. Peter Claver Fahy, M.S.B.T. (1995).

Hoey Awards* (1942), by the Catholic Interracial Council of New York, to persons who have worked to combat racism and have promoted social and interracial justice.

Honor et Veritas Award (1959), by the Catholic War Veterans to outstanding Americans. Tom Foerester (1994).

Howard R. Marraro Prize (1973), by the American Catholic Historical Association for a book on Italian history or Italo-American history or relations. Frederick J. McGuiness (1996).

Insignis Medal (1951), by Fordham University for extraordinary distinction in the service of God and humanity. Rev. George J. McMahon (1994).

John Courtney Murray Award (1972), by the Catholic Theological Society for distinguished achievement in theology. Originated in 1947 as the Cardinal Spellman Award. Rev. David N. Power, O.M.I. (1996).

John Gilmary Shea Prize (1944), by the American Catholic Historical Association for scholarly works on the history of the Catholic Church broadly considered. John T. McGreevy (1996).

Laetare Medal (1883), by Notre Dame University for distinguished accomplishment for Church or nation by an American Catholic. Rev. Virgilio Elizondo (1997).

Lumen Christi Award (1978), by the Catholic Church Extension Society to persons making outstanding contributions in service to the American home missions. Sr. Maria Sarto Moreau, O.P. (1996); Sr. Mary Felissa Zander, S.S.S.F. (1997).

The Manhattan College De La Salle Medal, by Manhattan College, to corporate and civic leaders for excellence and service. Mayor Rudolph W. Giuliani (1997).

Marianist Award (1949), by the University of Dayton for outstanding service in America to the Mother of God (until 1966); for outstanding contributions to mankind (from 1967); for outstanding scholarship by a Roman Catholic (from 1986). Gustavo Gutierrez (1997).

Marian Library Medal (1953), by the Marian Library of the University of Dayton. Awarded annually (until 1967) to encourage books in English on the Blessed Virgin Mary. Awarded every four years (from 1971) to a scholar for Mariological studies. Paul Melada, O.F.M. (1992).

Mendel Medal (1928), by Villanova University. Named in honor of Gregor Mendel, Augustinian priest and discoverer of laws of genetics. Awarded to outstanding scientists who, by their standing before the world as scientists, have demonstrated that there is no intrinsic conflict between true science and true religion. Peter H. Raven, Ph.D. (1997).

The Patronal Medal (1974), by the Catholic University of America in cooperation with the National Shrine of the Immaculate Conception for outstanding contributions to the Catholic Church and in promoting interest and devotion to Mary, patroness of the University. Rev. Frederick M. Jelly, O.P. (1993).

Pax Christi Award (1963), by St. John's University (Collegeville, Minn.), to honor persons of strong faith whose lives exemplify the importance of spiritual values and concern for the welfare of others. Cardinal Joseph Bernardin (1996).

Peter Guilday Prize* (1972), by the American Catholic Historical Association for articles accepted by the editors of the Catholic Historical Review which are the first scholarly publications of their authors.

Poverello Medal (1949), by Franciscan University of Steubenville (Ohio), "in recognition of great benefactions to humanity, exemplifying in our age the Christ-like spirit of charity which filled the life of St. Francis of Assisi." L'Arche (1997)

Regina Medal (1959), by the Catholic Library Association for outstanding contributions to children's literature. Eve Bunting (1997).

Role of Law Award (1973), by the Canon Law Society of America, to recognize a canon lawyer who embodies a pastoral attitude and is committed to research and study. Msgr. William Varvaro (1996).

St. Elizabeth Ann Seton Medal (1976), by St. John's University (Jamaica, N.Y.), to an American Catholic laywoman who exemplifies the qualities and virtues of America's first native-born saint. Lucy Ann Bartilucci (1995).

St. Francis de Sales Award (1958), by the Catholic Press Association for distinguished contribution to Catholic journalism. Rev. Norman Perry, O.F.M. (1997).

St. Vincent de Paul Medal (1948), by St. John's University (Jamaica, N.Y.), for outstanding service to Catholic charities. Andrew J. Bartilucci (1995).

Signum Fidei Medal (1942), by the Alumni Association of La Salle University (Phila.) for noteworthy contributions to the advancement of humanitarian principles in keeping with the Christian Judeo tradition. Rev. David I Hagan, O.S.F.S. (1997).

Sword of Loyola (1964), by Loyola University, Chicago, to person or persons exemplifying Ignatius of Loyola's courage, dedication and service in a field other than medicine. Sister Helen Prejean, C.S.J. (1996).

U.S. Catholic Award (1978), by the editors of U.S. Catholic magazine for furthering the cause of women in the Church. Mary Ann Glendon (1997).

SOCIAL SERVICE ORGANIZATIONS

(See separate article for a listing of facilities for the handicapped.)

The Carroll Center for the Blind (formerly the Catholic Guild for All the Blind): Located at 770 Centre St., Newton, MA 02158, the center conducts diagnostic evaluation and rehabilitation programs for blind people over 16 years of age, and provides computer training and other services. The president is Rachel Rosenbaum.

Xavier Society for the Blind: The Society is located at 154 E. 23rd St., New York, NY 10010. Founded in 1900 by Rev. Joseph Stadelman, S.J., it is a center for publications for the blind and partially sighted. The director is Rev. Alfred E. Caruana, S.J.

International Catholic Deaf Association: Established by deaf adults in Toronto, Canada, in 1949, the association has more than 8,000 members in 130 chapters, mostly in the U.S. It is the only international lay association founded and controlled by deaf Catholic adults. The ICDA publishes *The Deaf Catholic*, bimonthly, sponsors regional conferences, workshops and an annual convention. The ICDA-US president is Kathleen Kush, 8002 S. Sawyer Rd., Darien, IL 60561.

National Catholic Office for the Deaf: Formally established in 1971, at Washington, D.C., to provide pastoral service to those who teach deaf children and adults, to the parents of deaf children, to pastors of deaf persons, and to organizations of the deaf. Executive director: Nora Letourneau, 7202 Buchanan St., Landover Hills, MD 20784.

National Apostolate with People with Mental Retardation: Established in 1968 to promote the full participation by persons with mental retardation in the life of the Church. It publishes the *NAPMR Quarterly* and a newsletter (four times a year). Provides consultation, information and referral services on Church-related questions about mental retardation. The executive director is Dr. Michela M. Perrone, 4516 30th St. N.W., Washington, DC 20008.

National Catholic Office for Persons with Disabilities (NCPD): NCPD's mission is to provide resources and consultation to a national network of diocesan directors who oversee access and inclusion at the parish level; to collaborate with other national Catholic organizations, advocating for inclusion within all their programs and initiatives and to work with Catholic organizations addressing the concerns and needs of those with various disabilities. Established in 1982 as a result of the 1978 Pastoral Statement of the U.S. Catholic Bishops on People with Disabilities., the office continues to press for words and actions which promote meaningful participation and inclusion at all levels of the Church. Address: P.O. Box 29113, Washington, D.C. 20017.

DEATHS SEPTEMBER 1996 TO AUGUST 1997

Badiali, Rev. Daniele, 35, March 1997, Peru; Italian missionary kidnapped and murdered by bandits.

Bergwell, Rev. John E., M.M., 69, Nov. 14, 1996, Ossining, N. Y.; physician; missionary work in Africa (1959-62) cut short by Multiple Sclerosis.

Bernardin, Cardinal Joeph, 68, Nov. 14, 1996, Chicago, Ill.; archbishop of Chicago; cardinal from 1983..

Bodin, Bro. Raphael, 72, June, 1997, Nigeria; U.S. Christian Brother; murdered during apparent robbery at his rectory; missionary in Nigeria for 10 years.

Bozell, L. Brent, 71, Apr. 15, 1997, Washington, D.C.; writer; founded *Triumph* in the 60s to counter "left wing" elements in the church.

Brennan, William J., 91, July 24, 1997, Washing-ton, D.C.; Supreme Court Justice 1956 to 1990, when he retired; wrote about 1,200 opinions; considered a primary influence on the Court's 1973 Roe v. Wade decision legalizing abortion.

Brown, Bishop Charles A., M.M.,77, May 14, 1997, Sleepy Hollow, N.Y.; missionary in Bolivia for 51 years; auxiliary bishop of Santa Cruz, Bolivia, from 1956 to 1995 when he retired.

Brown, Rev. Francis F., 80, Nov. 9, 1996, Steubenville, Ohio; served for 28 years on staff of Steubenville diocesan paper .

Bruns, Rev. J. Edgar, 73, May 29, 1997, New Orleans, La.; author, scripture scholar; historian of New Orleans archdiocese.

Brzana, Bishop Stanislaus, 79, Mar. 1, 1997, Buffalo, N.Y.; retired bishop (1968-93) of Ogdensburg.

Cafferty, Sister Margaret, P.B.V.M., 61, Apr. 20, 1997, San Francisco, Calif.; educator, social justice leader; executive director of Leadership Conference of Women Religious 1992 to March, 1997, when advancing bone cancer forced her to resign.

Cooke, Msgr. Vincent W., 91, May 20, 1997, Niles, Ill.; headed Chicago Catholic Charities for more than 20 years..

Cunningham, Rev. Willliam T., 67, May 26, 1997, Detroit, Mich.; executive director of *Focus:Faith,* a food program he founded with Eleanor Josaitis in 1968, which is now a very successful work training program for inner city residents.

De Jesus, Bishop Benjamin, 56, Feb. 4, 1997, Jolo, Philippines; shot to death outside his cathedral.

Devlin, Bro. Majella (Francis), C.SS.R., 99, Jan. 18, 1997, Liguori, Mo.; oldest US Redemptorist.

Dossetti, Rev. Giuseppe, 83, Dec. 14, 1996, Rome, Italy; postwar political leader in Italy; among group who formed Christian Democratic Party; left politics in 1952 to found monastic order; ordained priest 1959.

Endo, Shusako, 73, Sept. 29, 1996, Tokyo, Japan; novelist; popularized religious themes in his work.

Eno, Rev. Robert, S.S., 60, Feb. 13, 1997, Washington, D.C.; patristic scholar at Catholic University; ecumenist.

Farina, Rev. Edward, 78, Mar. 19, 1997, Pittsburgh, Pa.; last of five priest-brothers who served the Pittsburgh diocese over a 60-year period.

Ferigle, Father Salvador, 73, Jan. 9, 1997, Cambridge, Mass.; Spanish-born priest who, as a layman, helped bring Opus Dei to the U.S.

Gerbermann, Bishop Hugo M., M.M., 83, Oct. 19. 1996, Hillje, Texas; missionary in Guatemala; retired auxiliary bishop (1975-82) of San Antonio.

Graham, Rev. Robert, S.J., 84, Feb. 11, 1997, Los Gatos, Calif.; Church historian; staunch defender of Pius XII against charges that he did nothing about nazi atrocities against Jews.

Hamer, Cardinal Jean, 80, Dec. 2, 1996, Rome, Italy; headed Congregation for Institutes of Consecrated Life and Societies of Apostolic Life, 1985-92; cardinal from 1985.

Harrington, Bishop Timothy J., 78., March 23, 1997, Worcester, Mass.; retired bishop of Worcester (1983-94).

Hettinger, Bishop Edward G., 94, Dec. 28, 1996, Columbus, Ohio; retired auxiliary bishop of Columbus (1942-77).

Hill, Garry E., 46, June 23, 1997, New York, N.Y.; president and CEO of Odyssey, the interfaith cable channel outlet.

Hollings, Rev. Michael, 75, Feb. 21, 1997, London, England; well known parish priest in inner city London.

Houle, Rev. John, S.J., 82, Aug. 9, 1997, Duarte, Calif; missionary in China; jailed 1953-57; his miraculous cure from a terminal illness in 1990 after he was blessed with a relic of Bl. Claude Colombiere, was one of the miracles accepted for the canonization of Bl. Claude in 1992.

Jenks, Barbara C., May, 1997, Providence, R.I.; Catholic journalist; with *Providence Visitor* for 49 years.

Kelley, Rev. Dean M., 70, May 11, 1997, West Swanzey, N.H.; United Methodist minister regarded as a leading church-state expert and advocate of religious liberty.

Kerr, Walter, 83, Oct. 9, 1996, Dobbs Ferry, NY; noted drama critic.

Koliqi, Cardinal Mikel, 94, Jan. 28, 1997, Shkoder, Albania; first cardinal from Albania; imprisoned for 37 of his 65 years in the priesthood.

Lewers, Rev. William, C.S.C., 69, Apr. 19, 1997, Notre Dame, Ind.; human rights leader; head of U.S. Bishops Office of International Justice and Peace, 1983-88.

McCarthy, Rev. William R., M.M., 99, July 21, 1997, Maryknoll, N.Y.; oldest Maryknoll priest; missionary in Peru 1946-74.

McCormick, Bishop J. Carroll, 88, Nov. 2, 1996, Scranton, Pa; retired bishop of Scranton (1966-83).

McManus, Bishop William E., 83, Mar. 3, 1997, Des Plaines, Ill.; retired bishop of Fort Wayne-South Bend (1976-85); educator.

McNeill, Charles, 84, May 16, 1997, Bronx, N.Y.; publisher, consultant, founder of Catholic Lists; former president of Catholic Press Association and recipient of its St. Francis de Sales Award.

Markiewicz, Bishop Alfred, 68, Jan 8, 1997, Huntington, N.Y.; bishop of Kalamazoo, Mich,, from 1995.

Martinez, Rev. Armando, 62, May 3, 1997, near Albuquerque, N.M.; murdered during robbery.

Moran, Bishop William J., 90, Aug. 23, 1996, San Francisco, Calif.; retired auxiliary of Military Archdiocese (1965-86).

Morin, Bishop Laurent, 88, Dec. 31, 1996, Canada; retired bishop of Prince Albert, Sask.

Munzihirwa Mwene Ngabo, Abp. Christophe, S.J., 70, Oct. 29, 1996, Bukavu, Zaire; killed during military activity there; archbishop of Bukavu.

Nasser, Msgr. Louis, M. Afr., 71, Jan. 31, 1997, Tenafly, N.J.; served Coptic communities in Jersey City and Brooklyn; helped establish Coptic parish in Brooklyn.

Nouwen, Rev. Henri J.M., 66, Sept. 21, 1996, Netherlands; Dutch theologian; author of more than 30 books on spiritual themes; pastor of L'Arche Community, Toronto, from 1986.

O'Donnell, Rev. Thomas J., S.J., 79, March 13, 1997, Philadelphia, Pa.; prominent in medical ethics field.

Peters, Msgr. Robert G., 79, Sept. 7, 1996, Peoria, IL; involved in Catholic press for almost six decades; president of. Catholic Press Association.,1962-64; winner St. Francis de Sales Medal, 1970; editor of Peoria diocesan paper, 1944-82.

Peloquin, C. Alexander, 78, Feb. 27, 1997, Providence, R.I.; renowned Catholic music composer.

Poletti, Cardinal Ugo, 82, Feb. 25, 1997, Rome, Italy; papal vicar of Rome, 1973-81 ; cardinal from 1973.

Power, Abp. Cornelius M., 83, May 22, 1997, Portland, Ore.; retired archbishop of Portland (1974-86).

Quinlan, Joseph T., 71, Dec. 7, 1996, Wantage, N.J.; father of Karen Ann Quinlan who was the focus of a legal battle and national debate in the 70s on when to remove artificial life supports.

See "More Deaths" on page 530